TREATIES AND ALLIANCES
OF THE WORLD

TREATIES AND ALLIANCES
OF THE WORLD

4th edition

Compiled and written by

Henry W. Degenhardt

General editor: Alan J. Day

A KEESING'S REFERENCE PUBLICATION

Longman

TREATIES AND ALLIANCES OF THE WORLD

1st edition 1968
2nd edition 1974
3rd edition 1981
4th edition 1986

Published by Longman Group UK Limited, Longman House,
Burnt Mill, Harlow, Essex, CM20 2JE, United Kingdom

Distributed exclusively in the United States and Canada
by Gale Research Company, Book Tower, Detroit,
Michigan 48226, United States of America

ISBN 0-582-90277-0 (Longman)
      0-8103-2347-8 (Gale)

Library of Congress Catalog Card Number: 86-21009

British Library in Cataloguing in Publication Data
Degenhardt, Henry W.
   Treaties and alliances of the world.——
   4th ed. —— (A Keesing's reference
   publication).
   1. Treaties —— History —— 19th century
   2. Treaties —— History —— 20th century
   I. Title   II. Series
   341.3'7'09034   JX2441

   ISBN 0-582-90277-0

Library of Congress Cataloging-in-Publication Data
Treaties and alliances of the world.
   (A Keesing's reference publication)
   Includes index.
   1. Alliances. 2. Treaties. I. Degenhardt, Henry W.
II. Day, Alan J. (Alan John) III. Series.
JX4005.T72   1986   341.2   86-21009

   ISBN 0-8103-2347-8

Printed and bound in the United Kingdom by
The Eastern Press, London and Reading

Contents

List of Maps

List of Tables and Diagrams

Introduction

Following the third edition of *Treaties and Alliances of the World* (published in 1981), this fourth edition includes new treaties and agreements concluded up to September 1986 and also describes a number of organizations reflecting international co-operation but not recorded in the third edition. In addition, the number of multilateral and bilateral agreements on co-operation in the economic, scientific, technical and cultural fields recorded here is more comprehensive.

Salient points in developments during the past five years can be briefly summarized as follows. East-West relations deteriorated owing to the Soviet intervention in Afghanistan in December 1979, the proclamation of martial law in Poland in December 1981 and the failure of the great powers to find a basis for agreement on arms control and disarmament negotiations. A return to more normal relations between the United States and the Soviet Union, however, became apparent towards the end of 1985. The North Atlantic Treaty alliance remained intact and the deployment of cruise missiles and Pershing II launchers in Europe, as decided in December 1979, was carried out in subsequent years.

Elsewhere, efforts were made to create nuclear-free zones but were successful only in the case of the Pacific, where the member states of the South Pacific Forum adopted, in August 1985, the South Pacific Nuclear Free Zone Treaty. Concurrently, serious strains developed within the Australia-New Zealand-United States (ANZUS) alliance, as the New Zealand (Labour) Government insisted on the exclusion of (US) nuclear weapons from its territory and thus effectively excluded itself from the alliance.

Following the disaster at the nuclear power station at Chernobyl (Soviet Union) on April 26, 1986, and growing concern about the safety of nuclear power stations, two nuclear accident conventions were adopted on Sept. 26, 1986, under the auspices of the International Atomic Energy Agency (IAEA).

In the areas of continuing open conflict, efforts made by international organizations to reach peaceful settlements remained fruitless. This was the case in particular with efforts made by the Organization of the Islamic Conference and the Gulf Co-operation Council to find a basis for ending the Iran-Iraq war, and with those of the Contadora Group of American states proposing measures to end the conflict between the Sandinista Government of Nicaragua and anti-Sandinista forces backed by the United States. Plans of the Arab League for a comprehensive and lasting settlement of the Arab-Israeli conflict also remained ineffectual, although the Egyptian-Israeli peace treaty of 1979 continued to be observed.

In the context of the growing isolation of the South African Government, the Organization of African Unity, the Non-Aligned Movement and a majority of the Commonwealth member states expressed support for the African National Congress (ANC) and the South West Africa People's Organization (SWAPO) in their long drawn-out struggle against the South Africa regime. International support for the Black "front-line" states was organized in the Southern African Development Co-operation Conference, within which (and elsewhere) pressure mounted for the imposition of comprehensive economic sanctions against South Africa.

In preparing this volume, the author has again made extensive use of the information resources of *Keesing's Contemporary Archives*, whose editorial team have provided assistance of various kinds. Particular thanks are due to Jean Wilkins, keeper of the *Keesing's* information depositaries, for her unfailing diligence in responding to requests for material therefrom.

Bath, October 1986   *HWD*

ABOUT THE AUTHOR. Henry W. Degenhardt, a former managing editor of *Keesing's Contemporary Archives,* has compiled or edited several of the Keesing's Reference Publications (KRP) series of books, notably *Political Dissent: An International Guide to Dissident, Extra-Parliamentary, Guerrilla and Illegal Political Movements* (1983), *Political Parties of the World* (2nd edition, 1984, jointly with Alan J. Day) and *Maritime Affairs—A World Handbook* (1985). Other titles available in the KRP series are:

Border and Territorial Disputes, edited by Alan J. Day (1982)

State Economic Agencies of the World, edited by Alan J. Day (1985)

Latin American Political Movements, edited by Ciarán Ó Maoláin (1985)

Communist and Marxist Parties of the World, compiled by Charles Hobday (1986)

Peace Movements of the World, edited by Alan J. Day (1986)

OPEC, Its Member States and the World Energy Market, compiled by John Evans (1986)

1. Early International Agreements and their Later Expansion

Early international agreements and their later expansion dealt with in this section comprise (i) the various 19th and 20th century agreements on the conduct of war, notably the Geneva and Hague Conventions; (ii) various conventions safeguarding intellectual property by means of copyright and patent arrangements; (iii) Concordats and other agreements entered into by the Roman Catholic Church; (iv) certain treaties and agreements concluded after World War I which are still in force; and (v) early conventions regulating the Suez Canal and the Bosphorus/Dardanelles Straits.

Agreements on the Conduct of War

The Declaration of Paris of 1856

The Congress of Paris, attended by representatives of the leading European powers, in 1856 adopted the Declaration of Paris designed to assimilate the provisions of the maritime law of individual states in the event of war. After being signed by Austria, Britain, France, Prussia, Russia, Sardinia and Turkey, the declaration was eventually adhered to by all civilized states except Bolivia, the United States, Uruguay and Venezuela.

The declaration provided for:

(*a*) The continued prohibition of privateering (i.e. warfare by privately armed vessels under a commission from the state);

(*b*) acceptance of the principle that a neutral flag covers enemy goods except contraband of war, and that neutral goods—again except contraband of war—are not liable to confiscation under an enemy flag; and

(*c*) the principle that blockades, in order to be binding, must be effective—i.e. maintained "by forces sufficient to prevent access to the enemy coast line". (This provision on blockades was repeated in the Declaration of London of February 1909, which was, however, never ratified.)

The Geneva Conventions of the International Red Cross

EARLY CONVENTIONS

First Geneva Convention. The first Geneva Convention, signed by delegates from 16 European countries in Geneva in 1864, established the principle that sick and wounded combatants in war should be respected and cared for irrespective of their nationality; that the personnel caring for them, as well as buildings, equipment and transport used for their care, should be protected, and that a distinctive emblem—the Red Cross (to which the Red Crescent for Moslem countries and the Red Lion and Sun in Persia (Iran) were added later)—should be the symbol of their immunity. This protection was to be claimed only in respect of medical personnel, buildings, equipment and transport operating as part of the medical services of the armed forces of the belligerents.

Second Geneva Convention. The second Geneva Convention of 1906 extended the above principles to maritime warfare and included shipwrecked persons among those to be protected.

Third Geneva Convention. The third Geneva Convention of 1929 contained amendments to the earlier conventions arising out of experiences during World War I and incorporated provisions from a Prisoners of War Convention of the same year. This provided for information bureaux in the belligerent countries to circulate information on prisoners of war, and to safeguard their interests through a neutral power, whose representatives were allowed to visit prisoner of war camps and to question prisoners.

At the outbreak of World War II the Geneva Conventions had not been signed by a number of states, including Japan and the Soviet Union.

1948 CONVENTIONS

Further conventions were drafted at an International Red Cross conference in Stockholm held on Aug. 23–30, 1948. These included:

Convention on the Protection of Civilians in Wartime. This convention was to apply not only in circumstances of war declared between states but also in interstate conflicts where one of the belligerents did not recognize the existence of a formal state of war, including civil, colonial and religious wars.

The convention (*a*) recommends the immediate designation in peacetime of "security zones" (which will be recognized by signatory belligerents in wartime) for the wounded, children under 15, pregnant mothers and mothers with children under 7, and persons over 65, without discrimination on racial, national, religious or political grounds;

(*b*) provides, in addition, for the setting up of "neutral zones" in actual fighting areas to which the sick and injured, as well as all non-combatant civilians, may be removed;

(*c*) grants special protection from attack to civilian hospitals marked with the Red Cross sign, as well as to transports of sick and injured;

(*d*) prohibits the sending of "protected persons" (i.e. all those who in the case of war or occupation come under the rule of a power whose nationality they do not possess, or those who in the case of civil war do not take part in hostilities) to, or their retention in, areas subject to warlike actions; their misuse for the safeguarding of certain areas or military operations; physical or mental torture and similar practices to obtain information; collective punishment, reprisals, and the destruction of property if not necessitated by military operations; and the taking of hostages;

(*e*) prohibits also, in the case of occupation, deportations, evacuations not required for military reasons, and conscription of "protected persons" for combatant units or auxiliary forces, or their voluntary recruitment, and allows conscription for work only to safeguard public services, as well as laying down specific rules concerning labour conditions, hygiene and sanitary measures, the prevention of epidemics etc., in occupied countries;

(*f*) makes the occupying power in wartime responsible for feeding the civilian population, prohibits the removal of food if there is any shortage, and likewise prohibits the transfer of part of the occupying power's own civilian nationals to occupied territory;

(*g*) grants analogous protection to aliens in belligerent countries, who are given the right to return to their home country unless a special court set up to examine these cases orders their retention for cogent security reasons, the court having also to make a decision as to whether the alien concerned is to be placed under supervision or to be detained, all proceedings being subject to the ordinary guarantees of law;

(*h*) provides, as far as civilian internment camps are concerned, that internees must be grouped according to nationality, language and habits, that family members should not be separated and parents be entitled to have their children with them, that internment and P.O.W. camps must be separated, and that internees must not be forced to work unless they choose; detailed provisions also deal with housing and sanitary conditions in such camps, protection against air attack and war operations, feeding, postal communications, receipt of gift parcels, censorship, etc.;

(*i*) empowers the representatives of the Protecting Power to visit any place where there are "protected persons" and to talk to them personally without observers;

(*j*) lays down that the free passage of medical supplies and, in the case of children and pregnant mothers, of food and clothing, must be allowed by belligerents even if destined for civilians of an enemy country.

Convention on the Treatment of Prisoners of War.

This amends the 1929 convention to enable prisoners of war to receive collective relief assignments; pledges signatories to give them adequate rations to keep them in good health (instead of "rations equal to those of their captors", as previously); and extends the application of the 1929 convention to include not only members of the armed forces and civilians openly bearing arms in defence against enemy forces, but also members of military organizations or resistance movements fighting an occupying power, provided they wear armlets or other visible signs and carry arms openly (the existing requirement of a uniform being dropped).

Convention on Relief of the Wounded and Sick in Armies of the Field.

Convention adapting the principles of the Geneva Convention of 1906 to maritime warfare.

These conventions were approved in Geneva on Aug. 12, 1949, by the representatives of 58 countries—although only a minority of these signed all of them.

By Dec. 31, 1985, a total of 156 states were parties to these four conventions.

1977 ADDITIONAL PROTOCOLS

An international Diplomatic Conference on Humanitarian Law Applicable in Armed Conflicts adopted, on June 10, 1977, two protocols additional to the 1949 Geneva Conventions.

Protocol I. Article I of this protocol contained a statement to the effect that "the people's struggle against colonial domination, against occupation by a foreign power and against racist regimes in accordance with their right of self-determination and the Charter of the United Nations" should be regarded as an "armed international conflict". In Article 42, dealing with conflicts involving national liberation movements recognized by the Organization of African Unity or the Arab League, it was laid down that armed combatants should be given protection equivalent to that accorded to prisoners of war even if such combatants did not comply with the conditions of wearing armlets or other visible signs and carrying arms openly.

In other articles mercenaries were declared not to be entitled to the status of combatants or prisoners of war; "war crimes" were listed as including attacks on the civilian population by target area (or "carpet") bombing, the destruction of nuclear power stations, dams, food supplies and water installations indispensable to the survival of civilians, and also "inhuman and degrading practices . . . based on racial discrimination".

Protocol II. This set out a "humanitarian minimum" of provisions relating to internal conflicts, in particular for the protection of the sick, the wounded and medical personnel; the obligation to protect objects and installations essential to the survival of the civilian population; the prohibition of forcible deportation; the privileged treatment of children; and the prohibition of starvation of the civilian population as a method of combat.

These two protocols were signed on Dec. 12, 1977, by ambassadors of 42 countries, including almost all Western states (except France), those of Eastern Europe and several Latin American states, but almost none in Africa or Asia.

By May 28, 1986, a total of 56 states were parties to Protocol I and 49 to Protocol II.

The Hague Conventions of 1899 and 1907

1899 Conventions. At an international conference held at The Hague in 1899 on the initiative of Czar Nicholas II of Russia and attended by representatives of 26 nations (which included the USA and Mexico), a number of conventions were adopted, and declarations issued, limiting methods of warfare and providing for peaceful settlement of disputes.

The first of the conventions adopted concerned the laws and customs of war. In this connexion the conference issued three declarations prohibiting (*a*) the discharge of projectiles from balloons; (*b*) the use of asphyxiating gases; and (*c*) the use of expanding bullets.

Further a *Convention for the Pacific Settlement of International Disputes* established the Hague Permanent Court of Arbitration, the forerunner of the International Court of Justice.

1907 Conventions. A second international conference, held at The Hague from June 15 to Oct. 18, 1907, and attended by representatives of 44 countries, revised and renewed the 1899 conventions (though without renewing the declarations on asphyxiating gases and expanding bullets).

In a *Convention on Prisoners of War* it laid down rules, largely already in practice, on their treatment.

In accordance with this convention, prisoners of war must be humanely treated, protected from violence, not subjected to reprisals, and supplied with reasonable nourishment as well as medical and sanitary facilities. They are regarded as being in the power of the government of the captors, and not in that of the captors themselves; their personal belongings (other than arms and military papers) remain their own; they may not be detained in a convict prison; the captor state may utilize their labour, except in the case of officers, with payment according to rank and ability, but they may not be engaged in excessive work or any task relating to military operations.

Prisoners of war need not give any other information than their true name and rank, but these they must give under penalty of losing normal prisoner of war advantages. The convention also provides for exchange procedure.

The conference also adopted 10 new conventions, notably a *Convention respecting the Limitation of Force for the Recovery of Contract Debts.* The nine others dealt with:

(*a*) the need for a declaration of war, i.e. "previous and explicit warning, in the form either of a reasoned declaration of war or of an ultimatum with a conditional declaration"; (*b*) the rights and duties of neutrals in war on land; (*c*) the status of enemy merchant vessels at the outbreak of war; (*d*) the conversion of merchant vessels into warships; (*e*) the laying of automatic submarine contact mines; (*f*) bombardment by naval forces; (*g*) the right of capture in maritime war; (*h*) the setting-up of an international prize court; and (*i*) the rights and duties of neutral powers in maritime war.

The Geneva Protocol

A protocol prohibiting the use in war of asphyxiating, poisonous and other gases, and of bacteriological methods of warfare, was signed at Geneva on June 17, 1925. Twenty-nine countries signed the protocol originally, the Soviet Union adhering in 1928. Although the United States had adhered to the protocol in 1925, the US Senate did not ratify it until December 1974, whereafter President Ford signed the instrument of ratification on Jan. 22, 1975. By Dec. 31, 1985, the protocol was adhered to by 105 countries.

Other Agreements on the Conduct of War

Briand-Kellogg Treaty or Paris Pact. A General Treaty for Renunciation of War as an Instrument of National Policy was signed in Paris on Aug. 27, 1928, by the governments of nine states (Belgium, Czechoslovakia, France, Germany, Italy, Japan, Poland, the United Kingdom and the United States), which ratified it by July 25, 1929, when it came into force. It was acceded to by another 43 of the world's then 67 independent states.

Its two material articles were as follows:

"**Art. 1.** The high contracting parties solemnly declare in the name of their peoples that they condemn recourse to war for the solution of international controversies, and renounce it as an instrument of national policy in their relations with one another.

"**Art. 2.** The high contracting parties agree that the settlement or solution of all disputes or conflicts of whatever nature or of whatever origin they may be, which may arise among them, shall never be sought except by pacific means."

The Pact was binding only upon the parties to it.

Submarine Warfare. A protocol (to a London naval treaty of 1930) on rules of submarine warfare was signed on Nov. 6, 1936, by France, India, Italy, Japan, the United Kingdom and Dominions, and the United States; it required submarines to conform to the law of prize, which forbade the sinking of merchant ships before passengers and crews had been saved. By Dec. 31, 1985, it was adhered to by 46 countries.

Convention on the Protection of Cultural Property in the Event of Armed Conflict. Under this convention, signed in The Hague on May 14, 1954, and in force from Aug. 7, 1976, parties were obliged to safeguard property of cultural importance in their own or other states' territories in the event of armed conflict. The convention thus supplemented the Hague conventions of 1907. By Dec. 31, 1985, the convention was adhered to by 71 states.

Conventions for Protection of Intellectual Property*

The Convention of the Union of Paris for the Protection of Industrial Property

This convention, approved in Paris on March 20, 1883, and revised in Brussels (on Dec. 14, 1900), in Washington (on June 2, 1911), in the Hague (on Nov. 6, 1925), in London (on June 2, 1934), in Lisbon (on Oct. 31, 1958), and in Stockholm (on July 14, 1967), came into force on April 26 or May 19, 1970, when the World Intellectual Property Organization (WIPO) was established [see page 41].

This convention gave inventors' patents protection in foreign countries by providing that patent applications in the other member countries should apply from the same date as the patent application in the inventor's home country. By Dec. 31, 1985 a total of 96 countries were parties to these conventions.

European Patent Conventions

European Patent Convention. A *Convention on the Grant of European Patents*, which had been approved by representatives of 21 European countries and signed by 14 of them in Munich on Oct. 5, 1973, provided for 20-year "European patents" to be valid in all acceding states (but in most cases subject to the patent laws of each state), with these patents being available from a European Patent Office (which was opened in Munich on Nov. 2, 1977). The agreement first became effective on Oct. 7, 1977, for Belgium, France, the Federal Republic of Germany, the Netherlands, Luxembourg, Switzerland and the United Kingdom; by Dec. 31, 1979, it was also in force for Austria, Italy and Sweden, and from April 1, 1980, in Liechtenstein. It was repeatedly amended between 1977 and 1985.

A European Patent Organization, headed by an Administrative Council, was constituted on Oct. 19, 1977, to implement the 1973 Munich convention.

European Community Patent Convention. A Community patents convention, signed in Luxembourg on Dec. 15, 1975, by the nine member states of the European Communities, provided for the harmonization of patent laws within the European Communities, with the latter becoming a uniform bloc within the framework of the broader 1973 Convention on the Grant of European Patents.

Copyright Conventions

1866 Berne Convention. The Berne Copyright Convention of 1886 was adhered to by 41 countries (mostly European, with only Brazil and Canada from the western hemisphere), and was revised in Paris in 1896, in Berlin in 1908, in Berne in 1914, in Rome in 1928 and 1941, and in Brussels in 1948.

* See also World Intellectual Property Organization, page 41.

The Brussels revision of 1948 extended the protection previously given to authors of works of literature, art, and music to the spheres of film, radio, television and allied arts, and laid down that disputes between countries on the interpretation or application of the convention were to be submitted to the International Court of Justice.

The convention was further amended at the 1967 Stockholm Conference on Intellectual Property by a protocol (proposed by Sweden) giving preferential rights to those developing countries which are members of the Berne Copyright Convention.

This protocol authorized these countries; (a) To translate into their own language and publish, without permission by its author and immediately after publication of the original, "any book to be used for teaching, study and research in all fields of education"; (b) to translate and publish literary and artistic works similarly three years or more after their original publication (though reprinting of such books in the original language remained subject to the existing copyright regulations); and (c) to pay, in all these cases, royalties to authors in accordance with the developing countries' own rates.

The protocol was applicable only against a country of origin which had agreed to its provisions. Of the developing countries, India is the most prominent member of the Berne Convention, while most other developing countries are not members.

The protocol was adopted without dissent, but with Britain abstaining, and the British Government did not sign it.

Pan-American Conventions. Several Pan-American conventions have also been signed between western hemisphere countries, the most important being the Buenos Aires Convention of Aug. 11, 1910, with 15 adherents, including the USA.

Universal Copyright Convention. Under the auspices of UNESCO, a conference held in Geneva from Aug. 25 to Sept. 7, 1952, resulted in the signing by representatives of 35 countries of a *Universal Copyright Convention*, the principal provisions of which were:

(1) Each signatory country undertakes to give to foreign works the same copyright protection as that given to works of its own nationals. The terms of protection will be not less than the life of the author and 25 years after his death.

(2) All existing formalities of registration and legal deposit will be eliminated, and will be replaced by a simple system under which the letter "C" will be imprinted within a circle on each copy of the works protected, accompanied by the author's name and the date of the first publication.

(3) Translation rights will also be covered, and during a minimum period of seven years authors will have the exclusive right to publish translations of their works, or to authorize the making and publication of such translations.

The convention came into force (with three protocols) on Sept. 16, 1955. By Dec. 31, 1978, it had been ratified by 72 countries. The Soviet Union acceded on May 27, 1973. The convention does not supersede the Berne Convention, which remains binding upon its members.

A Rome **Convention for the Protection of Performers, Producers of Phonograms and Broadcasting Organizations** of Oct. 26, 1961, was adhered to by 27 states (as at May 15, 1985). It is open to states parties to the Berne Convention or the Universal Copyright Convention.

1971 Revision of Universal and Berne Copyright Conventions. The Universal Copyright Convention was revised at a conference of 46 countries—the contracting parties to the convention—in Paris on July 5–24, 1971, by the addition of three new articles:

(1) Defining "non-industrialized countries" and the period of preferential treatment to be granted to them for their needs in teaching, scholarship and research;

(2) reducing the seven-year period for authors' exclusive rights to translation of their work [see (3) above] in the case of editions to be used for teaching, scholarship or research to three years for works published in a widely-used language, and to one year in the case of a little-used language—subject to a ban on exports of such translations; and

(3) enabling any national of a contracting country to obtain a licence, under certain conditions, for reproduction, for the purpose of "systematic instructional activities", of a work of which the first issue had not been distributed within a specified period.

At the same time the Berne Convention of 1886 was modified so as to give non-industrialized countries the same advantages as they had under the Universal Convention.

A Geneva **Convention for the Protection of Producers of Phonograms against Unauthorized Duplication of their Phonograms**, of Oct. 29, 1971, was adhered to by 38 states (as at May 15, 1985). It is open to all member states of the United Nations Organization or any of its agencies.

A **Brussels Convention relating to the Distribution of Programme-Carrying Signals Transmitted by Satellite**, of May 21, 1974, was adhered to by nine states (as at May 15, 1985). It is open to any member state of the United Nations Organization or any of its agencies.

Agreements entered into by the Roman Catholic Church

Concordats

Concordats are treaties concluded between the Pope, as head of the Roman Catholic Church, and secular governments on matters concerning the interests of Roman Catholic citizens, especially in education, and property of the Catholic Church.

Concordats recognizing Roman Catholicism as the state religion have been concluded by Bolivia, Colombia, Costa Rica, the Dominican Republic, Ecuador, Guatemala, Haiti, Ireland, Paraguay and Peru.

Other Concordats signed since the end of World War I were the following:

Germany. The Concordat concluded with Nazi Germany on July 20, 1933, was ruled by the German Federal Constitutional Court in 1957 to be still in force though not binding on *Länder* (i.e. federal units of the Federal Republic of Germany) in regard to school legislation. A Concordat concluded with Bavaria in 1924 was expressly reaffirmed in the 1946 Constitution of the *Land* (state) of Bavaria. A new Concordat was subsequently concluded between the Vatican and the *Land* of Lower Saxony on Feb. 26, 1965, covering provisions for the establishment and maintenance of Roman Catholic schools, a grant-in-aid towards salaries of ministers of religion, and the setting up of a Roman Catholic Theological Faculty at the *Land*'s university in Göttingen.

Italy. Three Lateran treaties, signed by the Cardinal Secretary of State of the Vatican and Benito Mussolini, then head of the Italian Government, on Feb.11, 1929, embodied recognition by the Government of Italy of the sovereignty of the Vatican City State, and provided for compensation by the Italian state for Church property seized in 1870.

A promise to recognize the Roman Catholic religion as Italy's state religion, contained in the Lateran treaties, was rescinded in a new Concordat signed on Feb. 18, 1984. This Concordat made religious instruction in state schools optional, and it made the annulment of marriages by the Vatican subject to review by an Italian court if one of the parties requested it. On the other hand it continued to give automatic recognition to church marriages and full freedom to Catholic schools, while all priests remained exempt from military service. Ratification documents concerning this Concordat were exchanged on June 3, 1985.

Portugal. The Concordat with Portugal, signed on May 7, 1940, included an acknowledgment by the state of the intangible character of church marriage, as well as provisions confirming the Church's possession of property and the appointment of bishops by the Pope with their formal nomination by the head of the state.

The validity of the 1940 Concordat was confirmed in a protocol which was signed on Feb. 15, 1975, but which recognized the legal right of couples married in church (and not only, as hitherto, of those Catholics who had contracted civil marriages, and of non-Catholics) to obtain a civil divorce, while reaffirming the doctrine of the Church on the indissolubility of marriage.

Other Agreements

Other agreements concluded by the Catholic Church and a secular government have included the following:

Hungary. An agreement was concluded between Archbishop Grosz of Kalocsa and the Hungarian state on Aug. 30, 1950, by which the bishops undertook to "recognize and support the Constitution and state order of the Hungarian People's Republic".

Spain. Under an agreement signed in Rome on July 28, 1976, the King of Spain renounced the right—as granted to him in a Concordat signed on Aug. 27, 1953—of proposing bishops and archbishops for appointment, and the Vatican renounced the right of priests and nuns not to be tried by civil courts without authorization by their Church superiors. Instruments of ratification of these agreements were exchanged on Aug. 20, 1976.

The 1953 Concordat with Spain was replaced by four agreements signed on Jan. 3, 1979, specifying that (i) the Spanish Government recognized the Roman Catholic Church and its activities, the inviolability of its places of worship and the full civil effects of marriage under canon law, while rulings of the ecclesiastical court (on nullity) would be subject ultimately to state law in the case of civil marriages; (ii) the state would phase out its annual direct subsidy to the Roman Catholic Church and instead raise a "religious levy" so that the Church would receive a percentage of the state's income and wealth tax revenue; (iii) religious instruction would be a non-compulsory part of the school syllabus; and (iv) guidelines were laid down for clerics carrying out military service. These agreements came into force on Jan. 4, 1980. (Under a decree issued at the same time civil rather than ecclesiastical courts were invested with the authority to grant legal separation to married couples.)

Treaties and Agreements concluded in the Wake of World War I

Among treaties concluded in the aftermath of World War I and still in force are the following:

The Svalbard Treaty (or Treaty of Spitsbergen)

As a result of work by a commission under the auspices of the Versailles peace conference, this treaty was concluded on Feb. 9, 1920, and was eventually adhered to by 41 countries (including Norway as well as China, France, Germany, the Soviet Union, the United Kingdom and the United States). It entered into force on June 14, 1925.

The treaty granted Norway "full and absolute sovereignty" over the Svalbard archipelago (of which Spitsbergen is the main island) while economic activities such as fishing, hunting and mining were open to nationals of all the contracting states on a footing of absolute equality. At the same time Svalbard was made a demilitarized area not to be used for war purposes. (The only countries economically active in Svalbard have been Norway and the Soviet Union.)

Under an agreement signed in Oslo on March 7, 1974, the Soviet Union was granted landing rights and other rights for civil aircraft at an all-year airport to be built on West Spitsbergen.

The Aaland Islands Convention

A convention on the demilitarization and neutralization of the (Finnish) Aaland Islands, signed on Oct. 20, 1921, entered into force on April 6, 1922, for Denmark, Germany, Finland, France, Sweden and the United Kingdom, on May 11, 1922, for Italy and on June 29, 1922, for Poland.

The convention, based on a decision by the Council of the League of Nations, provided also that the Aalanders, who had in two plebiscites voted overwhelmingly in favour of Swedish sovereignty over the islands, should have far-reaching internal autonomy and be exempt from Finnish military service and that the islands should be demilitarized.

Soviet Treaties with Iran

1921 Soviet-Iranian Treaty. This treaty, signed between Iran and the Russian Socialist Federative Soviet Republic (RSFSR) on Feb. 26, 1921, consists of a preamble, 26 articles and an exchange of notes.

The provisions of the treaty included:

Russian renunciation of all privileges which Iran had allowed Czarist Russia; the annulling of all treaties concerning Iran made by the former Russian regime with third powers; the opening of the Caspian Sea to Iran, in return for which Iran conceded fishing rights to the RSFSR; the restoration to validity of Iran's frontiers of 1881; and the cancellation of debts arising out of Czarist loans.

The most significant articles of the treaty were Articles 5 and 6. In Article 5 the two Governments agreed: (i) not to permit the creation or presence on their territory of any organization or group hostile to the RSFSR, Iran or their allies; (ii) not to permit any third party to import into, or convey through the territory of either of the partners to the treaty any materials which could be used against the other partner; and (iii) to prevent, with all the means at their command, the presence of any military forces of a third power on their territory, in case the presence of such forces could be interpreted as a threat to the borders, the interests or the security of the other partner to the treaty.

Article 6 read as follows:

"If a third party should attempt to carry out a policy of usurpation by means of armed intervention in Iran, or if such power should desire to use Iran's territory as a base of operations against Russia, or if a foreign power should threaten the frontiers of Federal Russia (i.e. the RSFSR) or those of its allies, and if the Iranian Government should not be able to put a stop to such menace after having been called upon to do so by Russia, Russia shall have the right to advance her troops into the interior of Iran for the purpose of carrying out the military operations necessary for its defence."

In the exchange of notes Iran asked for clarification of Articles 5 and 6. The clarification given by the RSFSR read as follows:

"Articles 5 and 6 are intended to apply only to cases in which preparations have been made for a considerable armed attack upon Russia, or the Soviet Republics allied to her, by the partisans of the regime which has been overthrown (i.e., the Czarist regime), or by its supporters among the foreign powers which are in a position to assist the enemies of the Workers' and Peasants' Republics and at the same time to possess themselves, by force or by underhand methods, of part of Iran's territory."

1927 Amended Soviet-Iranian Treaty. This new treaty, signed on Oct. 1, 1927, embodied the clarification of Articles 5 and 6 of the 1921 treaty, and also included a new article providing for the neutrality of either party should the other be involved in conflict with one or several powers.

During Soviet-Iranian negotiations for a non-aggression treaty from Jan. 29 to Feb. 11, 1959, Iran requested the annulment of Articles 5 and 6 of the 1921 treaty, as being no longer applicable to the situation. The Iranian request was, however, refused by the USSR, and on this point—and others—the negotiations broke down.

On Nov. 5, 1979, however, the Government of the Islamic Republic of Iran announced its abrogation of the above Articles 5 and 6.

International Disaster Relief

Under an agreement which came into force on Dec. 12, 1932, for Albania, Belgium, Bulgaria, Ecuador, Finland, Germany, Iran, Italy, Morocco, Poland, San Marino, the Sudan, Sweden, Switzerland, Turkey and Venezuela (and on Aug. 27, 1935, for China), the International Relief Union (IRU) was founded with the objective of co-ordinating international disaster relief.

Suez Canal and Bosphorus/Dardanelles Conventions

The Constantinople Convention on Free Navigation of the Suez Canal

On Oct. 29, 1888, Austria-Hungary, Britain, France, Germany, Italy, the Netherlands, Russia, Spain and Turkey signed the Convention respecting the Free Navigation of the Suez Maritime Canal.

The fundamental provisions of this convention are contained in Articles 1 and 4 as follows:

"The Suez Maritime Canal shall always be free and open, in time of war as in time of peace, to every vessel of commerce or of war, without distinction of flag. . . . The canal shall never be subject to the exercise of the right of blockade."

"The maritime canal remaining open in time of war as a free passage, even to ships of war of belligerents . . . , the high contracting parties agree that no right of war, no act of hostility, nor any act having for its object to obstruct the free navigation of the canal, shall be committed in the canal and its ports of access . . . though the Ottoman Empire should be one of the belligerent powers." (In the terms of the convention the legal successor to the Ottoman Empire is Egypt).

The convention also confirmed and completed the system of international operation embodied by the Universal Suez Canal Company, set up in 1863.

Egypt nationalized the Suez Canal Company in July 1956, an act which was regarded by many users of the canal as a contravention of the 1888 convention.

In April 1957, when the canal was re-opened to navigation, after it had been obstructed for several months, the Egyptian government issued a declaration in which it stated its intention to respect "the terms and spirit of the Constantinople Convention and the rights and obligations arising therefrom. . .".

The canal was again closed by Egyptian action in the June 1967 Arab-Israeli war and was not re-opened until June 1975. Under the March 1979 Egyptian-Israeli peace treaty [see Section 15], Israeli ships and cargoes were granted the same right of passage in the Suez Canal and its approaches as the vessels of other countries (whereas under the second Egyptian-Israeli disengagement agreement of September 1975 Israel's access to the canal had been confined to non-military cargoes carried by non-Israeli ships).

The Montreux Convention

A conference held in Montreux (Switzerland) from June 22 to July 20, 1936, by delegates from Bulgaria, France, Greece, Italy, Japan, Romania, the Soviet Union, Turkey, the United Kingdom and Yugoslavia agreed to replace the 1923 Straits Convention (part of the peace treaty signed with Turkey at Lausanne on July 24, 1923) by a new convention.

The 1923 convention had provided for freedom of transit and navigation by sea and air in the Bosphorus and the Dardanelles; for the demilitarization of both shores of the straits, the Sea of Marmara and certain islands in the Aegean Sea; and for the establishment in Constantinople (now Istanbul) of an international commission to supervise the implementation of the convention. The 1936 convention essentially restored Turkish sovereignty over the straits area by ending their demilitarization and transferring the duties of the international commission to the Turkish government. Its principal provisions are as follows:

If Turkey considers itself menaced by a danger of war the straits shall remain open to merchant vessels except that entry must be made by day and the route indicated by the Turkish authorities must be followed (Art. 2). (Traffic schemes have been in force since May 1, 1982). In time of peace light surface craft (whether those of a Black Sea power or not) have complete freedom of passage through the straits (Art. 10).

Black Sea powers may send their vessels through the straits even if their tonnage is in excess of 15,000 tons, provided the vessels make the passage singly and are escorted by no more than two torpedo boats (Art. 11). The Black Sea powers have the right to send through the straits submarines constructed or purchased at some port not on the Black Sea provided satisfactory notice is given to the Turkish government. Submarines must pass by day and on the surface.

At least eight days' notice, and for non-Black Sea powers preferably 15 days' notice, must be given to the Turkish government prior to the passage of warships through the straits. The maximum tonnage for all non-Turkish naval forces in transit must not exceed 15,000 tons (except under the conditions laid down in Art. 11—see above). Courtesy visits of non-Turkish warships made by invitation of the Turkish government are exempt from the provisions of the convention. Limitations on the tonnage of warships of non-Black Sea powers within the Black Sea in times of peace are: (1) a total of 30,000 tons and (ii) 45,000 tons if the strongest Black Sea fleet should at any time exceed by at least 10,000 tons the strength of the strongest fleet present in the Black Sea on the date of signature of the convention.

If, however, "for humanitarian reasons", several non-Black Sea powers should desire to despatch naval forces, they may be admitted to the Black Sea, but their tonnage is in no case to exceed 8,000. The permission will be extended by the Turkish government as expeditiously as possible after consultation with the other Black Sea powers.

In time of war, Turkey not being a belligerent, warships will have complete liberty of passage and of navigation in the straits under the limitations above mentioned (limit of 30,000 tons, prior authority and passage by day).

Nevertheless, warships of any belligerent power shall be accorded passage through the straits only if acting under obligations devolving from the League of Nations Covenant or "in the event of assistance being given to a State which is the victim of aggression in virtue of a mutual assistance pact to which Turkey is a party and concluded within the framework of the League of Nations Covenant". (For the purposes of the convention, the League of Nations Covenant has been superseded by the UN Charter.)

Belligerent warships may not have rights of search or capture or perform hostile acts within the straits.

In time of war, Turkey being a belligerent, the passage of warships through the straits is left entirely to the discretion of the Turkish government.

If Turkey considers herself menaced by "an imminent danger of war" she may use her discretion regarding permitting the passage of warships, that is to say, she may close the straits as in time of war.

Civil aircraft have the right of passage from the Mediterranean to the Black Sea along a route outside the prohibited zones and prescribed by the Turkish government. Warning, but no prior authority, is necessary. Unmolested passage of civil aircraft from Europe to Asia is, notwithstanding remilitarization of the straits, accorded by Turkey. This air passage is effected through a prescribed corridor, but prior authority is necessary from the Turkish government.

Although the convention provided, in paragraph 3 of Article 28, that it would remain in force for 20 years, it was also laid down in that article that it would continue to be in force only until two years after a contracting party had given notice of denunciation of the convention "two years prior to the expiry of the said period of 20 years". No such notice has been given, and the convention is therefore still in force, the parties to it being Australia, Belgium, France, Greece, Japan, Romania, the Soviet Union, Turkey, the United Kingdom and Yugoslavia.

2. World War II: Treaties and Agreements on Territorial Changes, Frontiers and Other Matters arising out of the War

During and after World War II the Allied Powers, in a series of treaties and agreements, determined their proposed treatment of the countries of the Axis Powers after the conclusion of hostilities. The most important conferences at which such agreements were reached were the Yalta Conference and the Potsdam Conference of 1945. Also dealt with in this section are the Allied agreements regulating the post-war status of Germany and the post-1945 peace treaties between Allied Powers and Siam (Thailand), Bulgaria, Finland, Italy (including the later Italian-Yugoslav agreement on the status of Trieste), Hungary, Romania and Japan, as well as the 1955 Austrian State Treaty and the 1956 Franco-German Treaty on the Saar. (No peace treaty has been concluded between the World War II Allies and Germany.)

Inter-Allied Agreements on Shape of Post-War World

The Yalta Conference

At this conference, held in Yalta (Crimea) on Feb. 4–11, 1945, the US, UK and Soviet leaders (Franklin D. Roosevelt, Winston Churchill and Joseph Stalin) confirmed previous agreements on the occupation of Germany.

These agreements included:

Acceptance of a proposal made by the European Advisory Commission of the Allied Powers at the Second Quebec Conference of September 1944; France, as a fourth occupying power, now associated herself with this proposal. It involved (a) Allied administration of Germany in British, French, Soviet and United States occupation zones; and (b) the control of Berlin by the four Allied Powers.

Further decisions reached at Yalta were:

(1) Britain and the USA would support membership in the United Nations General Assembly for the Soviet republics of the Ukraine and Byelorussia, in addition to the Soviet Union itself.

(2) Under the terms of a secret protocol, the Soviet Union would enter the war against Japan "within two or three months" after the surrender of Germany, and the Western Powers would in return (a) recognize the independence of Outer Mongolia and (b) agree to the transfer to the Soviet Union of Southern Sakhalin, adjacent islands, and the Kurile Islands, as well as to her recovery of certain rights in the Far East which Russia had lost in the war against Japan in 1904–05.

The Potsdam Conference

At the Potsdam Conference, held on July 17–Aug. 2, 1945, President Truman of the United States, Clement Attlee (British Prime Minister) and Joseph Stalin agreed inter alia on the following points:

(1) Germany was not to be partitioned, but to be treated as a single economic unit with certain central administrative departments though with a programme of decentralization to be carried out.

(2) Britain and the USA would support, at the eventual peace settlement, the Soviet annexation of the northern half of East Prussia (including Königsberg).

(3) "Pending the final delimitation of Poland's western frontier", the "former German territories" east of the Oder and Neisse Rivers and the former free city of Danzig were to be left under Polish administration and should not be considered as part of the Soviet zone of occupation in Germany.

(4) Peace treaties should be concluded with Bulgaria, Finland, Hungary, Italy and Romania.

(5) The remaining German population in Poland, Czechoslovakia and Hungary was to be transferred to Germany.

The Potsdam Agreement included inter alia the following specific provisions:

I. On the political principles which were to govern the treatment of Germany in an initial control period:

"(1) In accordance with the agreement on control machinery in Germany, supreme authority in Germany is exercised, on instructions from their respective Governments, by the commanders-in-chief of the armed forces of the United States of America, the United Kingdom, the Union of Soviet Socialist Republics, and the French Republic, each in his own zone of occupation, and also jointly, in matters affecting Germany, as a whole, in their capacity as members of the Control Council.

"(2) So far as is practicable, there shall be uniformity of treatment of the German population throughout Germany.

"(3) The purposes of the occupation of Germany by which the Control Council shall be guided are:

(i) The complete disarmament and demilitarization of Germany and the elimination or control of all German industry that could be used for military production. . . .

"(4) All Nazi laws which provided the basis of the Hitler regime or established discrimination on grounds of race, creed, or political opinion shall be abolished. No such discriminations, whether legal, administrative, or otherwise, shall be tolerated.

"(5) War criminals and those who have participated in planning or carrying out Nazi enterprises involving or resulting in atrocities or war crimes shall be arrested and brought to judgment. Nazi leaders, influential Nazi supporters and high officials of Nazi organizations and institutions, and any other persons dangerous to the occupation or its objectives, shall be arrested and interned.

"(6) All members of the Nazi party who have been more than nominal participants in its activities, and all other persons hostile to allied purposes, shall be removed from public and semi-public office and from positions of responsibility in important private undertakings. Such persons shall be replaced by persons who, by their political and moral qualities, are deemed capable of assisting in developing genuine democratic institutions in Germany.

"(7) German education shall be so controlled as completely to eliminate Nazi and militarist doctrines and to make possible the successful development of democratic ideas.

"(8) The judicial system will be reorganized in accordance with the principles of democracy, of justice under law, and of equal rights for all citizens without distinction of race, nationality, or religion."

II. On the western frontier of Poland:

"In conformity with the agreement on Poland reached at the Crimea conference, the three heads of Government have sought the opinion of the Polish Provisional Government of National Unity in regard to the accession of territory in the north and west which Poland should receive. The President of the National Council of Poland and members of the Polish Provisional Government of National Unity have been received at the conference and have fully presented their views. The three heads of Government reaffirm their opinion that the final delimitation of the western frontier of Poland should await the peace settlement.

"The three heads of Government agree that, pending the final determination of Poland's western frontier, the former German territories east of a line running from the Baltic Sea immediately west of Swinemünde, and thence along the Oder River to the confluence of the western Neisse River and along the western Neisse to the Czechoslovak frontier, including that portion of East Prussia not placed under the administration of the Union of Soviet Socialist Republics in accordance with the understanding reached at this conference and including the area of the former free city of Danzig, shall be under the administration of the Polish State and for such purposes should not be considered as part of the Soviet zone of occupation in Germany."

Between 1945 and 1947 the British and US Governments repeatedly stated that they had only reluctantly agreed to the frontier changes insisted upon by the Soviet Union and that they were not committed to supporting the "provisional" arrangements concerning Poland's western borders at a peace conference. The Soviet Union, however, appeared to depart from the position which it had taken at the Potsdam conference (when it had agreed that the transfer of former German territories to Poland was made "pending final determination"). On Sept. 17, 1946, the Soviet Foreign Minister (V. M. Molotov) declared that the Potsdam "decision to shift the western Polish frontier to the Oder and western Neisse" had been taken after prolonged discussion, including also the Polish Provisional Government, and that the three Allied powers "never envisaged any revision of this decision in the future"; at the same time, he admitted that it

was correct that the conference had "believed it necessary to postpone a final definition of the Polish western frontier until the peace conference".

The Polish Government has always regarded the Potsdam decision on Poland's western frontiers as quite unambiguous on the following grounds: (i) that it refers, in an introductory section, to "the western frontier of Poland" and not to any provisional line of demarcation; (ii) that it uses the term "former German territories", thereby indicating that they are no longer regarded as belonging to Germany; (iii) that, as these territories were "not part of the Soviet zone of occupation", they were not part of Germany (the whole of which was placed under Allied occupation), and the "administration" referred to in the agreement had nothing in common with the Allied occupation but meant that the parties to the agreement consented to Polish administration in these territories; and (iv) that the transfer of the German population from the territories confirmed that the words "final delimitation" meant only the formal tracing of the border on the ground, which was also, in the Polish view, confirmed by the statement that the "final delimitation" would await a "peaceful settlement"—not a peace treaty. The Polish Government has also regarded the former German territories as part of Poland on historical grounds going back to the existence of a Polish state embracing these areas 1,000 years ago.

Decisions by the Allied Control Council

Allied policy on Germany was implemented by the Allied Control Council, consisting of the Supreme Commanders of the British, French, Soviet and US Armed Forces.

On June 5, 1945, the Allied Control Council declared that the four Allied Governments would "hereafter determine the boundaries of Germany or any part thereof and the status of Germany or of any area at present being part of Germany". It also established the occupation of Berlin by all four Powers and its government by an inter-Allied Kommandatura. (The Kommandatura was, however, reduced to its three Western members when the Soviet commandant withdrew from it on July 1, 1948, an event from which dates the division of the city into East Berlin and West Berlin.)

On March 1, 1947, the Allied Control Council decreed that "the Prussian State, which from its early days has been a promoter of militarism and reaction in Germany, has de facto ceased to exist".

Establishment of Federal Republic of Germany

The Western Powers subsequently reached agreements which led to the establishment of the Federal Republic of Germany (often referred to as West Germany), without a peace settlement having been reached with Germany as a whole.

(1) A six-power conference agreed in London on June 2, 1948, on the structure of a German Federal Government for the British, French and US occupation zones; an Allied occupation statute; an economic merger of the French zone with the US and British zones (which had already been merged in a "bi-zone" on Jan. 1, 1947); and the establishment of an international coal and steel authority (later set up as the European Coal and Steel Community).

(2) The Paris Agreements of Oct. 23, 1954, gave full sovereign status to the Federal Republic of Germany as from May 5, 1955, and also gave it membership in the North Atlantic Treaty Organization and the Western European Union.

Peace Treaties between Allied Nations and Ex-Enemy Countries

Siam (Thailand)

The first peace treaty concluded by the Allied nations with an ex-enemy country was signed by Britain and India on the one hand and the Kingdom of Siam (now Thailand) on the other on Jan. 1, 1946.

The preamble stated inter alia that the British and Indian Governments had taken note of the fact that the Siamese Government had already repudiated the declaration of war against the British Empire made in 1942. The treaty nullified all Siamese acquisitions of British territories (in Malaya and Burma) made during the war; provided for Siamese collaboration in all international security arrangements approved by the United Nations, especially those relating to South-East Asia; and provided for the restoration of diplomatic, economic and commercial links between the parties. Siam also undertook not to construct a canal across the Kra Isthmus (linking the Indian Ocean and the Gulf of Siam) without British consent.

Countries in Europe

Peace treaties between the Allied and Associated Powers on the one hand and Bulgaria, Finland, Hungary, Italy and Romania were signed in Paris on Feb. 10, 1947. All these treaties contained provisions for reparations and imposed limitations on the armed forces of the countries concerned and in particular prohibited their possession or construction of atomic weapons. The five peace treaties came into force on Sept. 16, 1947, after the instruments of ratification had been deposited as required in the treaties.

BULGARIA

The Bulgarian peace treaty confirmed Bulgaria's frontiers as those of Jan. 1, 1941, i.e. as including the Southern Dobruja ceded by Romania in August 1940. It further stipulated inter alia: "Navigation on the Danube shall be free and open for the nationals, commercial vessels and goods of all states."

FINLAND

Under the Finnish peace treaty Finland confirmed the cession to the Soviet Union of the province of Petsamo (which meant that Finland no longer had direct access to the Arctic Ocean and the Soviet Union obtained a common frontier with Norway). The peace treaty also confirmed the frontier changes of the Moscow Peace Treaty of 1940, whereby the Soviet Union acquired the Karelian Isthmus, Viborg and other territories west of Lake Ladoga. Renouncing her right (under the terms of the 1940 treaty) of leasing the Hangö peninsula, the Soviet Union obtained a 50-year lease of the Porkkala-Udd area (SW of Helsinki) for the establishment of a Soviet naval base. (The Porkkala base, however, was evacuated by the Soviet Union in 1955 after a 20-year extension of the Soviet-Finnish treaty of friendship and mutual assistance of 1948—see page 257.)

ITALY

The Italian peace treaty provided for the demarcation of Italy's frontiers with her neighbours, including the Free Territory of Trieste set up by the treaty, and involving cessions: (a) to France, of several areas in the Alps, among them the Little St Bernard Pass and the Mont Cenis plateau; (b) to Yugoslavia, of Zara and islands off the Dalmatian coast; and (c) to Greece, of the Dodecanese Islands (in the Eastern Mediterranean). Italy also renounced all rights to Libya, Eritrea and Italian Somaliland, and recognized the independence of Albania and of Ethiopia.

South Tirol. The treaty also incorporated an agreement on South Tirol reached by the Austrian and Italian Governments on Sept. 5, 1946, providing full equality of rights with Italian-speaking inhabitants to German-speaking inhabitants of Bolzano Province and of bilingual townships in Trento Province.

A new treaty, giving extended rights to the German-speaking inhabitants of South Tirol, was concluded between Austria and Italy and initialled in Vienna on Dec. 2, 1969.

Status of Trieste. The status of the Free Territory of Trieste was ended under the terms of an agreement initialled in London on Oct. 5, 1954, whereby Italy provisionally obtained most of its northern part (known as Zone A) including the city and port of Trieste, and Yugoslavia its southern part (Zone B), together with about five square miles of Zone A. The agreement was implemented on Oct. 25–29, 1954.

The London agreement was, however, superseded by a treaty concluded by Italy and Yugoslavia in 1975 (known as the *Treaty of Osimo*), formally signed on Nov. 10, 1975, and duly ratified by the parliaments of both countries between Dec. 17, 1976, and March 1, 1977.

Under this treaty both Italy and Yugoslavia accepted the provisions of the London agreement as permanent, though with slight alterations to the frontier in favour of Italy, while guarantees were given relating to free access for shipping to Trieste and arrangements for free port facilities. National minorities were to be protected, with new citizenship regulations providing opportunities for members of such minorities to return to their respective country of origin and for citizenship to be regulated by Italian or Yugoslav law according to a person's place of residence at the time when the treaty came into force.

Under a simultaneous agreement co-operation was to be developed among the northern Adriatic ports, on the construction of natural gas terminals both in Italy and in Yugoslavia, and in industry and water resources management and transport, and a free industrial zone was to be set up on both sides of the frontier (this provision being subsequently approved by the European Communities).

HUNGARY

The Hungarian peace treaty re-established Hungary's frontiers as those of Jan. 1, 1938. This meant the reversion of Transylvania to Romania and of Eastern Slovakia to Czechoslovakia and confirmation of the transfer of Ruthenia to the Soviet Union—which had obtained this territory from Czechoslovakia under the terms of a treaty of June 29, 1945. Hungary also ceded several villages near Bratislava to Czechoslovakia. The treaty contained the same provisions for navigation on the Danube as the Bulgarian peace treaty.

An agreement between the USA and Hungary on the settlement of claims for war-damaged and nationalized American property in Hungary was signed on March 6, 1973.

ROMANIA

The Romanian peace treaty defined Romania's frontiers as those of Jan. 1, 1941 (i.e. including Transylvania) but with the cession of Bessarabia and the Bukovina to the Soviet Union and of the Southern Dobruja to Bulgaria. It also contained the clause on freedom of navigation on the Danube.

Peace Treaties of Japan

1951 Allied-Japan Peace Treaty. A peace treaty with Japan was signed in San Francisco on Sept. 8, 1951, by all Allied Powers represented at a 52-nation conference except Czechoslovakia, Poland and the Soviet Union. The conference was not attended by Burma, India and Yugoslavia.

The treaty came into force on April 28, 1952, after the instruments of ratification had been deposited in Washington by the USA and Japan and by nine out of 13 other countries specified in the treaty.

Under the terms of this treaty Japan recognized the independence of Korea; renounced all claims to Korea, Formosa (Taiwan) and the Pescadores, the Kurile Islands and South Sakhalin, and the Pacific Islands formerly mandated to Japan by the League of Nations. Japan also agreed to the proposal to place under the UN trusteeship system, with the USA as the sole administering authority, the Ryukyu Islands (south of 29° N.), the Bonin Islands, the Volcano Islands, Marcus Island and some smaller islands.

The treaty contained no specific definition of reparations to be made by Japan.

The Governments of both Communist China and Nationalist China took no part in the conclusion of the Japanese peace treaty.

1968 US-Japan Agreement. Under an agreement signed on April 5, 1968, by the USA and Japan, the Bonin and Volcano Islands, together with the Rosario, Parece and Marcus Islands, were returned to Japan.

The agreement also provided that the US-Japanese Security Treaty [see page 448] would apply to the islands after their return to Japan; that the USA would continue to use two radio stations on Iwo Jima (the largest of the Bonin Islands) and Marcus Island under a US-Japanese Status of Forces Agreement; but that all other installations and sites on the islands would be transferred to Japan.

Return of Ryukyu Islands. An agreement on the transfer of sovereignty over the Ryukyu Islands (including Okinawa) to Japan was signed on June 17, 1971, and after ratification of the agreement both in Japan and in the USA the reversion of the islands to Japanese jurisdiction took place on May 15, 1972.

The agreement accordingly amended the relevant article of the San Francisco Peace Treaty, but at the same time laid down that Japan would grant the United States, as from the date of entry into force of the agreement, the use of "facilities and areas" in the Ryukyu Islands in accordance with the 1960 Treaty of Mutual Co-operation and Security [see page 448]. These included the Kadena Air Force base on Okinawa, though the Japanese Government's approval was required for air or ground military operations to be launched by the USA.

1978 China-Japan Peace Treaty. Following many years of negotiations a treaty of peace and friendship was signed in Peking (Beijing) on Aug. 17, 1978, between Japan and the People's Republic of China (which had taken no part in the conclusion of the peace treaty signed by Japan and the majority of the Allied Powers in 1951).

This treaty contains the following operative articles:

"**Art. 1.** (1) The contracting parties shall develop durable relations of peace and friendship between the two countries on the basis of the principles of mutual respect for sovereignty and territorial integrity, mutual non-aggression, non-interference in each other's internal affairs, equality and mutual benefit and peaceful coexistence.

"(2) In keeping with the foregoing principles and the principles of the United Nations Charter, the contracting parties affirm that in their mutual relations all disputes shall be settled by peaceful means without resorting to the use or threat of force.

"**Art. 2.** The contracting parties declare that neither of them should seek hegemony in the Asia-Pacific region or in any other region and that each is opposed to efforts by any other country or group of countries to establish such hegemony.

"**Art. 3.** The contracting parties shall, in a good-neighbourly and friendly spirit and in conformity with the principles of equality and mutual benefit and non-interference in each other's internal affairs, endeavour to further develop economic and cultural relations between the two countries and to promote exchanges between the peoples of the two countries.

"**Art. 4.** The present treaty shall not affect the position of either contracting party regarding its relations with third countries."

The treaty was concluded for a 10-year period and was to continue in force until terminated by one year's notice given by either party at any time after the initial 10-year period.

The treaty was ratified by the Standing Committee of the National People's Congress in Peking on Aug. 16, 1978, and by the Japanese Diet on Oct. 16–18, coming into force on Oct. 23, 1978, after instruments of ratification had been signed and exchanged in Tokyo.

The Soviet Union, which had concluded no peace treaty with Japan, repeatedly warned the Japanese Government that the Soviet side regarded the conclusion of such a treaty with China as a hostile act by Japan.

Other Agreements arising from World War II

The Austrian State Treaty

The Austrian State Treaty, which ended more than 10 years of Allied occupation of Austria, preceded by seven years of German occupation, was signed at the Belvedere Palace in Vienna on May 15, 1955, by the Foreign Ministers and ambassadors in Vienna of the four occupying powers (Soviet Union, Britain, USA and France) and by the Austrian Foreign Minister.

Its main operative clauses are as follows:

"**Art. 1. Re-establishment of Austria as a Free and Independent State.** The Allied and Associated Powers recognize that Austria is re-established as a sovereign, independent and democratic state.

"**Art. 2. Maintenance of Austria's Independence.** The Allied and Associated Powers declare that they will respect the independence and territorial integrity of Austria as established under the present treaty.

"**Art. 3. Recognition by Germany of Austrian Independence.** The Allied and Associated Powers will incorporate in the German peace treaty provisions for securing from Germany the recognition of Austria's sovereignty and independence and the renunciation by Germany of all territorial and political claims in respect of Austria and Austrian territory.

"**Art. 4. Prohibition of Anschluss.** (1) The Allied and Associated Powers declare that political or economic union between Austria and Germany is prohibited. Austria fully recognizes its responsibilities in this matter and shall not enter into political or economic union with Germany in any form whatsoever. . . .

"**Art. 5. Frontiers of Austria.** The frontiers of Austria shall be those existing on January 1, 1938. . . .

"**Art. 8. Democratic Institutions.** Austria shall have a democratic government based on elections by secret ballot and shall guarantee to all citizens free, equal and universal suffrage, as well as the right to be elected to public office without discrimination as to race, sex, language, religion or political opinion. . . .

"**Art. 13. Prohibition of Special Weapons.** (1) Austria shall not possess, construct, or experiment with (a) any atomic weapons, (b) any other major weapon adaptable now or in the future to mass destruction and defined as such by the appropriate organ of the United Nations, (c) any self-propelled or guided missiles or torpedoes, or apparatus connected with their discharge or control, (d) sea mines, (e) torpedoes capable of being manned, (f) submarines or other submersible craft, (g) motor torpedo-boats, (h) specialized types of assault craft, (i) guns with a range of more than 30 kilometres, (j) asphyxiating, vesicant or poisonous materials or biological substances in quantities greater than, or of types other than, are required for legitimate civil purposes. . . .''

Other articles deal with the rights of minority groups and the security of human rights. Most clauses, however, were of only transitional significance, dealing with matters immediately arising from the war.

Following the signature of the treaty, the Austrian Foreign Ministry published the text of a resolution on Austria's permanent neutrality, which was passed as a constitutional law by the *Nationalrat* (Austrian Lower House) on Oct. 26, 1955, and came into force on Nov. 5, 1955.

Its significant paragraphs were as follows:

(1) With the object of the lasting and perpetual maintenance of her independence from without and the inviolability of her territory, as well as in the interest of maintaining internal law and order, Austria declares of her own free will her perpetual neutrality, and is resolved to maintain and defend it with all means at her disposal.

(2) Austria, in order to secure these objectives, will join no military alliances and will not permit the establishment of military bases of foreign states on her territory.

The Franco-German Treaty on the Saar

The importance of the Saar region, the status of which was in dispute for decades, rests on its deposits of coal. After World War I the Saar came under the administration of the League of Nations. From 1920 to 1935 France possessed the rights to exploit the Saar coal fields, but in 1935, after a plebiscite, the region reverted to Germany. After World War II the Saar was first a *Land* within the French zone of Germany, and later, under a new Constitution ratified in November 1947, an autonomous state having an economic union with France. An agreement between France and the Federal Republic of Germany on the future status of the Saar, of October 1954, was rejected in a referendum a year later. A final treaty settling the future of the Saar region was signed by France and West Germany in Luxembourg on Oct. 27, 1956. The treaty provided for the political incorporation of the Saar into the Federal Republic of Germany on Jan. 1, 1957, and full economic re-integration with Germany by Dec. 31, 1959. Until that date the Franco-Saar customs union would remain in force and the Saar would retain French currency. For 25 years France would purchase from the Saar a total of 90,000,000 tons of coal; a special Franco-German organization would be set up to handle Saar coal supplies.

The Saar territory duly became part of the Federal Republic of Germany at midnight of Dec. 31, 1956. On June 25, 1959, the French and the German Federal Governments agreed that the Saar should be fully incorporated economically in the Federal Republic of Germany by July 6, 1959.

3. The United Nations

Address. United Nations Plaza, New York, NY 10017, USA. Geneva Office: Palais des Nations, 1211 Geneva 10, Switzerland. Vienna Office: P.O. Box 500, 1400 Vienna, Austria.

Officer. Javier Pérez de Cuéllar (sec. gen.).

This section traces the origins of the United Nations and deals with the subsequent development of the organization from the signature of the UN Charter in June 1945 until the present day, with particular reference to the creation and role of the large number of specialized, associated and subsidiary bodies which form part of the UN organization as a whole. Also covered are the major UN declarations and conventions, while a table of membership of the UN and its related organizations is given on pages 60–68.

Historical Origins and Basic Principles

The United Nations Organization came into being during World War II as a collaboration of the Allied nations against the Axis powers (Germany, Italy and Japan).

The Atlantic Charter

The first steps toward the working out of a programme of principles and policy—later to take shape as the Charter of the United Nations—were taken by President Roosevelt of the United States and the British Prime Minister, Winston Churchill, in August 1941. After a meeting between the two, on board ship in the Atlantic, a joint declaration of principles was issued on Aug. 14, 1941. This declaration, generally referred to as the *Atlantic Charter*, ran as follows:

"The President of the United States and the Prime Minister, Mr Churchill, representing HM Government in the United Kingdom, being met together, deem it right to make known certain common principles in the national policies of their respective countries on which they base their hopes for a better future for the world.

"(1) Their countries seek no aggrandisement, territorial or other.

"(2) They desire to see no territorial changes that do not accord with the freely expressed wishes of the peoples concerned.

"(3) They respect the right of all peoples to choose the form of government under which they will live; and they wish to see sovereign rights and self-government restored to those who have been forcibly deprived of them.

"(4) They will endeavour, with due respect for their existing obligations, to further enjoyment by all states, great or small, victor or vanquished, of access, on equal terms, to the trade and to the raw materials of the world which are needed for their economic prosperity.

"(5) They desire to bring about the fullest collaboration between all nations in the economic field, with the object of securing for all improved labour standards, economic advancement and social security.

"(6) After the final destruction of Nazi tyranny, they hope to see established a peace which will afford to all nations the means of dwelling in safety within their own boundaries, and which will afford assurance that all the men in all the lands may live out their lives in freedom from fear and want.

"(7) Such a peace should enable all men to traverse the high seas and oceans without hindrance.

"(8) They believe all of the nations of the world, for realistic as well as spiritual reasons, must come to the abandonment of the use of force. Since no future peace can be maintained if land, sea or air armaments continue to be employed by nations which threaten, or may threaten, aggression outside of their frontiers, they believe, pending the establishment of a wider and permanent system of general security, that the disarmament of such nations is essential. They will likewise aid and encourage all other practicable measures which will lighten for peace-loving peoples the crushing burden of armament."

The Atlantic Charter was referred to in a joint declaration of the 26 Allied nations at war with Germany, Italy and Japan, signed on Jan. 1, 1942. The declaration stated that the Governments of the Allies, "having subscribed to a common programme of purposes and principles embodied in the joint declaration . . . known as the Atlantic Charter, being convinced that complete victory over their enemies is essential to defend life, liberty, independence and religious freedom, and to preserve human rights and justice in their own lands as well as in other lands", pledged themselves to employ their full resources against the enemy and to make no separate armistice or peace.

Dumbarton Oaks Conference

A four-power conference was held at Dumbarton Oaks, near Washington, on Aug. 21–Oct. 7, 1944, to establish the framework of a post-war international security organization. The participants in the talks were the United States, Britain, the Soviet Union and China.

At the close of the conference it was stated that 90 per cent agreement had been reached by the four powers. The proposals contained in their draft for a post-war international security organization were largely embodied in the later Charter of the United Nations. They dealt with the maintenance of international peace and security and established most of the main organs of the United Nations, namely the General Assembly, the Security Council, the International Court of Justice and the Economic and Social Council.

The Yalta Conference

At the tripartite summit conference held at Yalta in the Crimea on Feb. 4–11, 1945 [see page 8], the participants—the United Kingdom, the United States and the Soviet Union—agreed, inter alia, that a conference of the United Nations should be called to meet at San Francisco on April 25, 1945. The question of voting procedure within the new organization, which had not been settled at Dumbarton Oaks, was resolved at the Yalta Conference.

The San Francisco Conference

The United Nations Conference on International Organization (UNCIO) was held at San Francisco from April 25 to June 25, 1945. it was sponsored by the United Kingdom, the USA, the Soviet Union and China. France, although she refused an invitation to become a sponsor, participated in all meetings of the sponsoring powers on a basis of full equality, forming one of the so-called "Big Five".

The three most controversial issues discussed at the conference were: (1) The question of the veto power of the "Big Five" and voting procedure in the Security Council; (2) the question of the integration of regional pacts and arrangements into the general framework of world security; (3) the question of trusteeship over dependent areas and backward peoples. All three questions were finally settled, although the solution of the first took several weeks.

The United Nations Charter

The Charter of the United Nations was signed on June 26, 1945, at the end of the San Francisco Conference. It entered into force on Oct. 24, 1945.

The contents of the Charter are described, with extracts, below.

Preamble

"We, the peoples of the United Nations,

"determined to save succeeding generations from the scourge of war, which twice in our lifetime has brought untold sorrow to mankind;

"to reaffirm faith in fundamental human rights, in the dignity and worth of the human person, and in the equal rights of men and women and of nations large and small;

"to establish conditions under which justice and respect for obligations arising from treaties and other sources of international law can be maintained;

"to promote social progress and better standards of life in larger freedom;

"to practise tolerance and live together in peace with one another as good neighbours;

"to unite our strength to maintain international peace and security;

"to ensure, by the acceptance of principles and the institution of methods, that armed force shall not be used, save in the common interest;

"to employ international machinery for the promotion of the economic and social advancement of all peoples;

"have resolved to combine our efforts to accomplish these aims, have agreed to the present Charter of the United Nations, and do hereby establish an international organization to be known as the United Nations.

Chapter 1

Purposes

"Art. 1. The purposes of the United Nations are:

"(1) To maintain international peace and security, and to that end: To take effective collective measures for the prevention and removal of threats to the peace and for the suppression of acts of aggression or other breaches of the peace, and to bring about by peaceful means, and in conformity with the principles of justice and international law, adjustment or settlement of international disputes or situations which might lead to a breach of the peace;

"(2) to develop friendly relations among nations based on respect for the principle of equal rights and self-determination of peoples, and to take other appropriate measures to strengthen universal peace;

"(3) to achieve international co-operation in solving international problems of an economic, social, cultural or humanitarian character, and in promoting and encouraging respect for human rights and for the fundamental freedoms for all without distinction of race, sex, language or religion; and

"(4) to be a centre for harmonizing the actions of nations in the attainment of these common ends.

Principles

"Art. 2. The organization and its members, in pursuit of the purposes stated in Art. 1, shall act in accordance with the following principles:

"(1) The organization is based on the principle of the sovereign equality of all its members.

"(2) All members shall fulfil in good faith the obligations assumed by them in accordance with the Charter.

"(3) All members shall settle their international disputes by peaceful means in such a manner that international peace, security and justice are not endangered.

"(4) All members shall refrain in their international relations from the threat or use of force against the territorial integrity or political independence of any member or state or in any other manner inconsistent with the purposes of the United Nations.

"(5) All members shall give the United Nations every assistance in any action it takes in accordance with the provisions of the Charter, and shall refrain from giving assistance to any state against which the United Nations is taking preventive or enforcement action.

"(6) The organizations shall ensure that states not members act in accordance with these principles so far as may be necessary for the maintenance of international peace and security.

"(7) Nothing in the Charter shall authorize the United Nations to intervene in matters which are essentially within the domestic jurisdiction of any state, or shall require the members to submit such matters to settlement under the present Charter; but this principle shall not prejudice the application of enforcement measures under Chapter 7."

Chapter 2 deals with the conditions of membership and provides for the suspension or expulsion from the organization of erring members.

Chapter 3 enumerates the main organs and provides for universal eligibility to serve on them.

Chapter 4 gives details of the composition, functions and powers of, and procedure, in the General Assembly. Important provisions on voting are:

"**Art. 18.** Decisions of the General Assembly on important questions shall be made by a two-thirds majority of those present and voting. These questions shall include: Recommendations with respect to the maintenance of international peace and security; the election of non-permanent members of the Security Council; the election of members of the Economic and Social Council; the election of members of the United Nations which are to designate the members on the Trusteeship Council . . .; the admission of new members to the United Nations; the expulsion of members; the suspension of the rights and privileges of members; questions relating to the operations of the trusteeship system; and budgetary questions. . . .

"**Art. 19.** A member in arrears in the payment of its financial contributions to the organization shall have no vote if the amount of arrears equals or exceeds the amount of the contributions due from it for the preceding two full years. The General Assembly may, nevertheless, permit such a member to vote if it is satisfied that the failure to pay is due to conditions beyond the member's control."

Chapter 5 gives details of the composition and responsibility of the Security Council and of its procedure. Amendments to the Charter, which came into force on Aug. 31, 1965, affected Articles 23 and 27 of this chapter, raising the membership of the Council from 11 to 15, and the number of affirmative votes to carry decisions from seven to nine.

Chapter 6

Pacific Settlement of Disputes

"**Art. 33.** (1) The parties to any dispute whose continuance is likely to endanger the maintenance of international peace and security shall, first of all, seek a solution by negotiation, inquiry, mediation, conciliation, arbitration, judicial settlement, resort to regional agencies or arrangements, or other peaceful means of their own choice.

"(2) The Security Council shall, when it deems necessary, call upon the parties to settle their dispute by such means.

"**Art. 34.** The Security Council may investigate any dispute, or any situation which might lead to international friction or give rise to a dispute, in order to determine whether its continuance is likely to endanger the maintenance of international peace and security.

"**Art. 35.** (1) Any member of the United Nations may bring any dispute or situation of the nature referred to in Art. 34 to the attention of the Security Council or the General Assembly.

"(2) A state which is not a member of the United Nations may bring to the attention of the Security Council or the General Assembly any dispute to which it is a party, if it accepts in advance, for the purposes of the dispute, the obligations of pacific settlement provided in the Charter. . . .

Chapter 7

Action with Respect to Threats to the Peace, Breaches of the Peace and Acts of Aggression

"**Art. 39.** The Security Council shall determine the existence of any threat to the peace, breach of the peace or act of aggression, and shall make recommendations, or decide what measures shall be taken in accordance with Art. 41 and 42, to maintain or restore international peace and security.

"**Art. 40.** In order to prevent an aggravation of the situation, the Security Council may, before making the recommendations or deciding upon the measures provided for in Art. 41, call upon the parties concerned to comply with such provisional measures as it deems necessary or desirable. Such provisional measures shall be without prejudice to the rights, claims or position of the parties concerned. The Security Council shall duly take account of failure to comply with such provisional measures.

"**Art. 41.** The Security Council may decide what measures not involving the use of armed force are to be employed to give effect to its decisions, and may call upon members of the United Nations to apply such measures. These may include complete or partial interruption of economic relations and of rail, sea, air, postal, telegraphic, radio and other means of communication, and the severance of diplomatic relations.

"**Art. 42.** Should the Security Council consider that measures provided for in Art. 41 would be inadequate, or have proved to be inadequate, it may take such action by air, sea or land forces as may be necessary to maintain or restore international peace and security. Such action may include demonstrations, blockade, and other operations by air, sea or land forces of members of the United Nations.

"**Art. 43.** (1) All members of the United Nations, in order to contribute to the maintenance of international peace and security, undertake to make available to the Security Council, on its call and in accordance with a special agreement or agreements, armed forces, assistance and facilities, including rights of passage, necessary for the purpose of maintaining international peace and security.

"(2) Such agreement or agreements shall govern the numbers and type of forces, their degree of readiness and general location, and the nature of the facilities and assistance to be provided.

"(3) The agreement or agreements shall be negotiated as soon as possible on the initiative of the Security Council. They shall be concluded between the Security Council and member states or between the Security Council and groups of member states, and shall be subject to ratification by the signatory states.

"**Art. 45.** In order to enable the United Nations to take urgent military measures, members shall hold immediately available national air force contingents for combined international enforcement action. The strength and degree of readiness of these contingents, and plans for their combined action, shall be determined, within the limits laid down in the special agreement or agreements referred to in Art. 43, by the Security Council with the assistance of the Military Staff Committee.

"**Art. 48.** (1) The action required to carry out the decisions of the Security Council for the maintenance of international peace and security shall be taken by all the members of the United Nations, or by some of them, as the Security Council may determine.

"(2) Such decisions shall be carried out by the members of the United Nations directly and through their action in the appropriate international agencies of which they are members.

"**Art. 50.** If preventive or enforcement measures against any state are taken by the Security Council, any other state, whether a member of the United Nations or not, which finds itself confronted with special economic problems arising from the carrying out of those measures, shall have the right to consult the Security Council with regard to a solution of those problems.

"**Art. 51.** Nothing in the present Charter shall impair the inherent right of individual or collective self-defence, if an armed attack occurs against a member of the organization, until the Security Council has taken the measures necessary to maintain international peace and security. Measures taken by members in the exercise of this right of self-defence shall be immediately reported to the Security Council and shall not in any way affect the authority and responsibility of the Security Council to take at any time such action as it may deem necessary in order to maintain or restore international peace and security.

Chapter 8
Regional Arrangements

"**Art. 52.** (1) Nothing in the present Charter precludes the existence of regional arrangements or agencies for dealing with such matters relating to the maintenance of international peace and security as are appropriate for regional action, provided that such arrangements or agencies and their activities are consistent with the purposes and principles of the organization.

"(2) The members of the United Nations entering into such arrangements or constituting such agencies shall make every effort to achieve peaceful settlement of local disputes through such regional arrangements or agencies before referring them to the Security Council.

"(3) The Security Council should encourage the development of peaceful settlement of local disputes through such regional arrangements or agencies either on the initiative of the states concerned or by reference from the Security Council.

"(4) This article in no way impairs the application of Arts. 34 and 35.

"**Art. 53.** (1) The Security Council shall, where appropriate, utilize such arrangements or agencies for enforcement action under its authority. But no enforcement action shall be taken under regional arrangements or by regional agencies without the authorization of the Security Council, with the exception of measures against any enemy state, as described below, or in regional arrangements directed against renewal of aggressive policy on the part of any such state, until such time as the organization may, on request of the governments concerned, be charged with the responsibility for preventing further aggression by such a state.

"(2) The term 'enemy state' applies to any state which during the Second World War has been an enemy of any signatory of the Charter.

Chapter 9
International Economic and Social Co-operation

"**Art. 55.** With a view to the creation of conditions of stability and well-being which are necessary for peaceful and friendly relations among nations, based on respect for the principle of equal rights and self-determination of peoples, the United Nations shall promote:

"(*a*) Higher standards of living, full employment and conditions of economic and social progress and development;

"(*b*) solutions of international economic, social, health and related problems and international cultural and educational co-operation; and

"(*c*) universal respect for, and observance of, human rights and fundamental freedoms for all without distinction as to race, sex, language or religion."

Chapter 10 gives details of the composition, functions and powers of, and procedure in the Economic and Social Council.

Chapter 11
Declaration Regarding Non-Self-Governing Territories

"**Art. 73.** Members of the United Nations which have or assume responsibilities for the administration of territories whose peoples have not yet attained a full measure of self-government recognize the principle that the interests of the inhabitants of these territories are paramount, and accept as a sacred trust the obligation to promote to the utmost the well-being of the inhabitants of these territories, and to this end:

"(*a*) To ensure, with due respect for the culture of the peoples concerned, their political, economic, social and educational advancement, their just treatment, and their protection against abuses;

"(*b*) to develop self-government, to take due account of the political aspirations of the peoples, and to assist them in the progressive development of their free political institutions, according to the particular circumstances of each territory and its peoples and their varying stages of advancement;

"(*c*) to further international peace and security;

"(*d*) to promote constructive measures of development, to encourage research, and to co-operate with one another and with appropriate international bodies with a view to the practical achievement of the social, economic and scientific purpose set forth in this paragraph; and

"(*e*) to transmit regularly to the Secretary-General for information purposes, subject to such limitations as security and constitutional considerations may require, statistical and other information of a technical nature relating to economic, social and educational conditions in the territories for which they are respectively responsible, other than those territories to which Chapters 12 and 13 apply.

Chapter 12
International Trusteeship System

"**Art. 75.** The United Nations shall establish under its authority an international trusteeship system for the administration and supervision of such territories as may be placed thereunder by subsequent individual agreements. These territories are hereafter referred to as 'trust territories'.

"**Art. 76.** The basic objectives of the trusteeship system shall be:

"(*a*) To further international peace and security;

"(*b*) to promote the political, economic, social and educational advancement of the inhabitants of the trust territories, and their progressive development towards self-government or independence as may be appropriate to the particular circumstances of each territory and its peoples and the freely expressed wishes of the peoples concerned, and as may be provided by the terms of each trusteeship agreement;

"(*c*) to encourage respect for human rights and for fundamental freedoms for all without distinction as to race, sex, language or religion, and to encourage recognition of the interdependence of the peoples of the world; and

"(*d*) to ensure equal treatment in social, economic and commercial matters for all members of the United Nations and their nationals, and also equal treatment for the latter in the administration of justice, without prejudice to the attainment of the foregoing objectives. . . .

"**Art. 77.** (1) The trusteeship system shall apply to such territories in the following categories as may be placed thereunder by means of trusteeship agreements:

"(*a*) Territories now held under mandate;

"(*b*) territories which may be detached from enemy states as a result of the Second World War; and

"(*c*) territories voluntarily placed under the system by states responsible for their administration.

"(2) It will be a matter for subsequent agreement as to which territories in the foregoing categories will be brought under the trusteeship system and upon what terms.

"**Art. 78.** The trusteeship system shall not apply to territories which have become members of the United Nations, relationship among which should be based on respect for the principle of sovereign equality.

"**Art. 79.** The terms of trusteeship for each territory to be placed under the trusteeship system, including any alteration or amendment, shall be agreed upon by the states directly concerned, including the mandatory power in the case of territories held under mandate by a member of the United Nations. . . ."

Chapter 13 deals with the compositions, functions and powers of, and procedure in, the Trusteeship Council.

Chapter 14 deals with the International Court of Justice.

Chapter 15 deals with the Secretariat and includes details of the functions of the Secretary-General.

Chapter 16 contains miscellaneous provisions, including:

"**Art. 103.** In the event of a conflict between the obligations of the members of the United Nations under the Charter and any other international obligations to which they are subject, their obligations under the Charter shall prevail.

"**Art. 105.** (1) The organization shall enjoy in the territory of each of its members such privileges and immunities as are necessary for the fulfilment of its purposes.

"(2) Representatives of the members of the United Nations and officials of the organization shall similarly enjoy such privileges and immunities as are necessary for the independent exercise of their functions in connexion with the organization."

Chapter 17 provides for certain transitional security arrangements.

Chapter 18 gives the procedure for the adoption of amendments to the Charter and provides for the convening of a conference for the purpose of reviewing the Charter.

Chapter 19 contains provisions on the ratification and signature of the Charter.

The principles of the UN Charter incorporated those of the Briand-Kellogg Treaty signed in Paris on Aug. 27, 1928 [see page 3].

The Universal Declaration of Human Rights and the Covenants on Human Rights

The UN General Assembly on Dec. 10, 1948, adopted, by 48 votes to none (with eight abstentions by the Communist member states, South Africa and Saudi Arabia), the Universal Declaration of Human Rights, the first international Bill of Rights in human history.

The declaration is worded as follows:

Preamble

"Whereas recognition of the inherent dignity and of the equal and inalienable rights of all members of the human family is the foundation of freedom, justice and peace in the world;

"whereas disregard and contempt for human rights have resulted in barbarous acts which have outraged the conscience of mankind, and the advent of a world in which human beings shall enjoy freedom of speech and belief and freedom from fear and want has been proclaimed as the highest aspiration of the common people;

"whereas it is essential, if man is not to be compelled to have recourse, as a last resort, to rebellion against tyranny and oppression, that human rights should be protected by the rule of the law;

"whereas it is essential to promote the development of friendly relations between nations;

"whereas the people of the United Nations have in the Charter reaffirmed their faith in fundamental human rights, in the dignity and worth of the human person and in the equal rights of men and women, and have determined to promote social progress and better standards of life in larger freedom;

"whereas member states have pledged themselves to achieve, in co-operation with the United Nations, the promotion of universal respect for and observance of human rights and fundamental freedoms;

"whereas a common understanding of these rights and freedoms is of the greatest importance for the full realization of this pledge;

"the General Assembly proclaims this Universal Declaration of Human Rights as a common standard of achievement for all peoples and nations, to the end that every individual and every organ of society, keeping this declaration constantly in mind, shall strive by teaching and education to promote respect for these rights and freedoms, and by progressive measures, national and international, to secure their universal and effective recognition and observance, both among the peoples of member

states themselves and among the peoples of territories under their jurisdiction.

Articles

"**Art. 1.** All human beings are born free and equal in dignity and rights. They are endowed with reason and conscience, and should act towards one another in a spirit of brotherhood.

"**Art. 2.** Everyone is entitled to all the rights and freedoms set forth in this declaration, without distinction of any kind, such as race, colour, sex, language, religion, political or other opinion, national or social origin, property, birth or other status.

"Furthermore, no distinction shall be made on the basis of the political, jurisdictional or international status of the country or territory to which a person belongs, whether it be independent, trust, non-self-governing or under any other limitation of sovereignty.

"**Art. 3.** Everyone has the right to life, liberty and security of person.

"**Art. 4.** No one shall be held in slavery or servitude; slavery and the slave trade shall be prohibited in all their forms.

"**Art. 5.** No one shall be subjected to torture or to cruel, inhuman or degrading treatment or punishment.

"**Art. 6.** Everyone has the right to recognition everywhere as a person before the law.

"**Art. 7.** All are equal before the law and are entitled without any discrimination to equal protection of the law. All are entitled to equal protection against any discrimination in violation of this declaration and against any incitement to such discrimination.

"**Art. 8.** Everyone has the right to an effective remedy by the competent national tribunals for acts violating the fundamental rights granted him by the Constitution or by law.

"**Art. 9.** No one shall be subjected to arbitrary arrest, detention or exile.

"**Art. 10.** Everyone is entitled in full equality to a fair and public hearing by an independent and impartial tribunal, in the determination of his rights and obligations and of any criminal charge against him.

"**Art. 11.** (1) Everyone charged with a penal offence has the right to be presumed innocent until proved guilty according to law in a public trial at which he has had all the guarantees necessary for his defence.

"(2) No one shall be held guilty of any penal offence on account of any act or omission which did not constitute a penal offence, under national or international law, at the time when it was committed. Nor shall a heavier penalty be imposed than the one that was applicable at the time the penal offence was committed.

"**Art. 12.** No one shall be subjected to arbitrary interference with his privacy, family, home or correspondence, nor to attacks upon his honour and reputation. Everyone has the right to the protection of the law against such interference or attacks.

"**Art. 13.** (1) Everyone has the right to freedom of movement and residence within the borders of each state.

"(2) Everyone has the right to leave any country, including his own, and to return to his country.

"**Art. 14.** (1) Everyone has the right to seek and enjoy in other countries asylum from persecution.

"(2) This right may not be invoked in the case of prosecutions genuinely arising from non-political crimes or from acts contrary to the purposes and principles of the United Nations.

"**Art. 15.** (1) Everyone has the right to a nationality.

"(2) No one shall be arbitrarily deprived of his nationality nor denied the right to change his nationality.

"**Art. 16.** (1) Men and women of full age, without any limitation due to race, nationality or religion, have the right to marry and to found a family. They are entitled to equal rights as to marriage, during marriage, and at its dissolution.

"(2) Marriage shall be entered into only with the free and full consent of the intending spouses.

"(3) The family is the natural and fundamental group unit of society and is entitled to protection by society and the state.

"**Art. 17.** (1) Everyone has the right to own property alone as well as in association with others.

"(2) No one shall be arbitrarily deprived of his property.

"**Art. 18.** Everyone has the right to freedom of thought, conscience and religion. This right includes freedom to change his religion or belief, and freedom, either alone or in community with others, and in public or private, to manifest his religion or belief in teaching, practice, worship and observance.

"**Art. 19.** Everyone has the right to freedom of opinion and expression. This right includes freedom to hold opinions without interference and to seek, receive and impart information and ideas through any media and regardless of frontiers.

"**Art. 20.** (1) Everyone has the right to freedom of peaceful assembly and association.

"(2) No one may be compelled to belong to an association.

"**Art. 21.** (1) Everyone has the right to take part in the government of his country, directly or through freely chosen representatives.

"(2) Everyone has the right of equal access to public service in his country.

"(3) The will of the people shall be the basis of the authority of government; this will shall be expressed in periodic and genuine elections which shall be by universal and equal suffrage, and shall be held by secret vote or by equivalent free voting procedures.

"**Art. 22.** Everyone, as a member of society, has the right to social security and is entitled to the realization, through national effort and international co-operation and in accordance with the organization and resources of each state, of the economic, social and cultural rights indispensable for his dignity and the free development of his personality.

"**Art. 23.** (1) Everyone has the right to work, to free choice of employment, to just and favourable conditions of work and to protection against unemployment.

"(2) Everyone, without any discrimination, has the right to equal pay for equal work.

"(3) Everyone who works has the right to just and favourable remuneration, ensuring for himself and his family an existence worthy of human dignity and supplemented, if necessary, by other means of social protection.

"(4) Everyone has the right to form and to join trade unions for the protection of his interests.

"**Art. 24.** Everyone has the right to rest and leisure, including reasonable limitation of working hours and periodic holidays with pay.

"**Art. 25.** Everyone has the right to a standard of living adequate for the health and well-being of himself and his family, including food, clothing, housing, and medical care and necessary social services, and the right to security in the event of unemployment, sickness, disability, widowhood, old age or other lack of livelihood in circumstances beyond his control.

"(2) Motherhood and childhood are entitled to special care and assistance. All children, whether born in or out of wedlock, shall enjoy the same social protection.

"**Art. 26.** (1) Everyone has the right to education. Education shall be free, at least in the elementary and fundamental stages. Elementary education shall be compulsory. Technical and professional education shall be made generally available, and higher education shall be equally accessible to all on the basis of merit.

"(2) Education shall be directed to the full development of the human personality and to the strengthening of respect for human rights and fundamental freedoms. It shall promote understanding, tolerance and friendship among all nations, racial or religious groups, and shall further the activities of the United Nations for the maintenance of peace.

"(3) Parents have a prior right to choose the kind of education that shall be given to their children.

"**Art. 27.** (1) Everyone has the right freely to participate in the cultural life of the community, to enjoy the arts and to share in scientific advancement and its benefits.

"(2) Everyone has the right to the protection of the moral and material interests resulting from any scientific, literary or artistic production of which he is the author.

"**Art. 28.** Everyone is entitled to a social and international order in which the rights and freedoms set forth in this declaration can be fully realized.

"**Art. 29.** (1) Everyone has duties to the community in which alone the free and full development of his personality is possible.

"(2) In the exercise of his rights and freedoms, everyone shall be subject only to such limitations as are determined by law solely for the purpose of securing due recognition and respect for the rights and freedoms of others, and of meeting the just requirements of morality, public order and the general welfare in a democratic society.

"(3) These rights and freedoms may in no case be exercised contrary to the purposes and freedoms set forth herein.

"**Art. 30.** Nothing in this declaration may be interpreted as implying for any state, group or person any right to engage in any activity or to perform any act aimed at the destruction of any of the rights and freedoms set forth herein."

In implementation of the declaration, the UN General Assembly unanimously adopted, on Dec. 16, 1966, (*a*) an International Covenant on Economic, Social and Cultural Rights; (*b*) an International Covenant on Civil and Political Rights, and (*c*) an Optional Protocol to the latter.

The covenant under (*a*), consisting of 31 articles, recognizes, inter alia, the right to work, to social security, to adequate standards of living, to freedom from hunger, and to health and education. It provides that states parties to the covenant would report to the UN Economic and Social Council on the measures adopted and progress made towards the realization of these rights.

The covenant under (*b*), consisting of 53 articles, provides, inter alia, for the right to life, liberty, security and privacy; for the right to a fair trial and to freedom from arbitrary arrest; for freedom of thought, conscience and religion; and for freedom of association. Other articles provide for freedom of consent to marriage, the protection of children and the preservation of the cultural, religious and linguistic heritage of minorities. It is laid down that the implementation of this covenant will be supervised by a Human Rights Committee consisting of 18 persons elected by the states acceding to the covenant.

The optional protocol empowers the Human Rights Committee to receive and consider communications from individuals claiming to be victims of a violation by a state party to the covenant of any of the rights set forth in the covenant.

The covenant under (*b*) came into force on Jan. 3, 1976—three months after ratification by 35 governments; by Dec. 31, 1985, it had been acceded to by 78 countries (while those which had not signed the text included the United States).

The covenant under (*a*) similarly came into force on March 23, 1976. By Dec. 31, 1985, it had been ratified by 82 states.

Principal Organs of the United Nations

The General Assembly

The General Assembly, the main deliberative organ of the United Nations, is composed of delegations representing all the member countries of the United Nations. Each delegation comprises not more than five full representatives with their five deputies and any number of advisers and experts.

The General Assembly meets regularly once a year in ordinary session, but a special session may be convened at the request of the Security Council or of a majority of Assembly members.

The Assembly has power to make recommendations only, and not decisions binding on member states. Each member has one vote. Decisions on important questions are adopted by a two-thirds majority; other questions are decided by a simple majority.

The General Assembly is empowered to discuss and make recommendations on all questions which fall within the scope of the UN Charter. Under Article 12 of the Charter, however, "while the Security Council is exercising in respect of any dispute or situation the functions assigned to it in the present Charter, the General Assembly shall not make any recommendations with regard to that dispute or situation unless the Security Council so requests". On Nov. 3, 1950, the plenary session of the General Assembly adopted a plan of the US Government (the "United Action for Peace" Resolution), by which, at the request of any seven members of the Security Council, the General Assembly can be called in emergency session if the Security Council is prevented, through exercise of the veto, from taking action in any case "where there appears to be a threat to the peace, breach of the peace or act of aggression".

The General Assembly is led by a President, who is elected for each session, and a number of Vice-Presidents.

ASSEMBLY COMMITTEES

The seven main committees of the General Assembly, on which all UN members have the right of representation, are as follows:

(1) Political and Security Committee.
(2) Economic and Financial Committee.
(3) Social, Humanitarian and Cultural Committee.
(4) Decolonization Committee.
(5) Administrative and Budgetary Committee.
(6) Legal Committee.

(7) Special Political Committee (set up to aid the first Committee).

These committees consider questions referred to them by the General Assembly, and prepare draft resolutions for submission to the Assembly.

There are two procedural committees, the 25-man General (Steering) Committee and the nine-man Credentials Committee, and two principal standing committees, these being a 13-man Advisory Committee on Administrative and Budgetary Questions and an 18-man Committee on Contributions.

A permanent subsidiary committee is the 25-member **International Law Commission**, which meets annually to discuss the development and codification of international law. The General Assembly also sets up ad hoc committees from time to time in accordance with the world situation.

Special Committee on Decolonization. In connexion with Trust Territories and colonial questions the UN General Assembly has set up a Special Committee on the situation with regard to the implementation of the declaration on the granting of independence to colonial countries and peoples (adopted by the UN General Assembly on Dec. 14, 1960, establishing the right of all peoples to self-determination and to "freely determine their political status"). This committee, formed in 1961 and for many years known as the "Committee of 24", at present has 25 members as follows: Afghanistan, Austria, Bulgaria, Chile, China, the Congo, Côte d'Ivoire, Cuba, Czechoslovakia, Denmark, Ethiopa, Fiji, India, Indonesia, Iran, Iraq, Mali, Sierra Leone, the Soviet Union, Syria, Tanzania, Trinidad and Tobago, Tunisia, Venezuela and Yugoslavia.

Council for Namibia. In the same connexion the UN Council for Namibia (originally the UN Council for South West Africa) was formed in 1967 for the purpose of taking over the administration of that territory from the Government of South Africa. The council has 31 members as follows: Algeria, Angola, Australia, Bangladesh, Belgium, Botswana, Bulgaria, Burundi, Cameroon, Chile, China, Colombia, Cyprus, Egypt, Finland, Guyana, Haiti, India, Indonesia, Liberia, Mexico, Nigeria, Pakistan, Poland, Romania, Senegal, the Soviet Union, Turkey, Venezuela, Yugoslavia and Zambia.

Under the aegis of the Council a UN Institute for Namibia was established in Lusaka (Zambia) on Dec. 29, 1979, for the training of public service personnel for a future independent Namibia.

Other Bodies Responsible to the General Assembly

United Nations Conference on Trade and Development (UNCTAD)

Address. Palais des Nations, CH-1211 Geneva 10, Switzerland.

Officer. Kenneth K. S. Dadzie (sec. gen.).

Founded. 1964.

Object. To accelerate the economic development of the developing countries.

Structure. The Conference, which meets every four years, has as its executive organ a Trade and Development Board which has six main committees on commodities, manufactures, invisibles and financing related to trade, shipping, transfer of technology, and economic co-operation among developing countries, to implement the work of the Board.

Activities. The 77 developing countries represented at the first UNCTAD meeting became known as the "Group of 77", and this group later expanded to 120 members.

At a meeting of ministers from 71 developing countries held in Algiers on Oct. 10–24, 1967, 63 of these ministers signed the "Algiers Charter of the Economic Rights of the Third World", which was to be presented to the developed nations. The Charter stated that between 1953 and 1966 the share of the developing countries in total world exports had fallen from 27 per cent to 19.3, and the purchasing power of their export earnings by one-tenth, while their debt service payments were equalling the entire amount of loans granted. The Charter therefore urged the implementation of a comprehensive programme of action.

(Later UNCTAD conferences are dealt with in Section 6 on International Economic Co-operation, page 126.)

Finance. The appropriation for UNCTAD for the 1986–87 biennium was US$60,135,300.

United Nations Relief and Works Agency for Palestine Refugees in the Near East (UNRWA)

Address. P.O.B. 700, 1400, Vienna, Austria; and P.O.B. 484, Amman, Jordan.

Officer. Giorgio Giacomelli (commissioner-general).

Founded. 1950.

History. The UNRWA was founded as a temporary body to bring immediate assistance to Palestinian Arab refugees and to help them become self-supporting. It has a 10-member Advisory Commission.

Its mandate has repeatedly been renewed (most recently, on Dec. 15, 1983, until June 30, 1987), and its work has been extended to cover relief, health, education and welfare services to Palestinian refugees. The Israeli invasion of Lebanon in June 1982, had, according to the UNRWA's commissioner-general, the effect that it "largely undid the Agency's work of 30 years in Lebanon and transformed the environment in which the UNRWA carries out its mandate in ways which had repercussions well beyond that field".

As at June 30, 1984, there were 2,034,314 refugees registered with the UNRWA, of whom 716,701 were in camps. The total of pupils attending 653 UNRWA schools during 1983–84 was 342,252, of whom 134,527 were in Jordan.

Finance. The UNRWA's total expenditure for the year 1984 was US$235,100,000 (against $207,493,000 in 1983).

UN Commission on Human Settlements

Address. P.O. Box 30030, Nairobi, Kenya.

Officer. Dr Arcot Ramachandran (exec. dir.).

Founded. October 1978.

Activities. This 58-member commission meets once a year and has set up a UN Centre for Human Settlements (HABITAT) in Nairobi to co-ordinate activities in the field of human settlements, in particular planning for settlements in disaster-prone areas and transport for low-income urban and rural areas.

Finance. For the centre the sum of US$8,610,400 was appropriated for the 1986–87 biennium.

The Security Council

The Security Council functions continuously, and its decisions are binding on all members of the United Nations. The Council is composed of 15 members, five of whom—China, France, the Soviet Union, the United Kingdom and the United States—are permanent. The remaining 10 members are elected by the General Assembly, normally to serve a term of two years. Each member state of the Council holds the Presidency for one month, the rotation following the English alphabetical order.

Each member has one vote. Decisions on important (non-procedural) questions must be carried by nine affirmative votes, but any one of the permanent members, exercising the right of veto, can prevent the adoption of a decision. Procedural matters may be decided by the affirmative votes of any nine members.

The Security Council has "primary responsibility for the maintenance of international peace and security", and to this end it acts for all UN members (Article 24 of the UN Charter). The tasks of the Security Council include the pacific settlement of international disputes (Articles 33–38), determination of the existence of any threat to the peace, breach of the peace or act of aggression, and, where necessary, the carrying out of preventive or enforcement measures of a political, economic or military nature through some or all UN members (Articles 39–45). Under Article 26 of the Charter the Security Council is also "responsible for formulating plans . . . for the establishment of a system for the regulation of armaments".

In all questions of a military nature the Council is aided by a Military Staff Committee, consisting of the Chiefs of Staff of the five permanent members of the Security Council.

Peace-Keeping Bodies Responsible to the Security Council

United Nations Truce Supervision Organization (UNTSO). Originally formed to maintain the 1949 Armistice Agreements between Israel on the one hand and the Arab nations of Egypt, Lebanon, Jordan and Syria on the other, the United Nations Truce Supervision Organization later had the task of supervising the ceasefire line established at the end of the six-day Arab–Israeli war of June 1967. In 1973 it was ordered to supervise a ceasefire in the Suez Canal area, and in July 1979 the UN Security Council charged it with monitoring compliance with the military provisions of the 1979 Egyptian–Israeli peace treaty and thus replacing a UN Emergency Force (UNEF) which had been established after the 1973 Arab–Israeli war. Its headquarters are in Jerusalem.

United Nations Military Observer Group for India and Pakistan (UNMOGIP). Established in 1949, UNMOGIP is responsible for supervising the Indian–Pakistani ceasefire line along the Kashmir border. The group consists of about 60 military observers and civilian specialists.

United Nations Command in Korea. The United Nations Command in Korea was set up in July 1950 to assist the Republic of Korea (South Korea) in defending itself against attack. The UN Force originally consisted of troops from 16 nations under the command of the United States. The force was later reduced to US troops only (about 30,000 men since mid-1977).

A military armistice agreement (ending the Korean War of 1950–53), signed at Panmunjon on July 27, 1953, established a military demarcation line and a demilitarized zone. Inconclusive peace negotiations have since taken place at Panmunjon (since 1979 between the Red Cross Societies of the two countries).

United Nations Peace-Keeping Force in Cyprus (UNFICYP). The UN Force in Cyprus was set up in March 1964, initially for three months, for the purpose of keeping the peace between the Greek and Turkish communities in Cyprus. Following the invasion of Cyprus by Turkish troops in July 1974 the UN Security Council authorized a strengthening of UNFICYP's forces and charged it with supervising a ceasefire between Turkish and Greek or Greek Cypriot forces and also with protecting Turkish enclaves after these were evacuated by Greek or Greek Cypriot troops. UNFICYP's mandate has since then been regularly renewed for a further six months each time.

United Nations Disengagement Observer Force (UNDOF). UNDOF was established on May 31, 1974, to secure the implementation of a disengagement agreement between Syrian and Israeli forces, and its mandate has repeatedly been extended for six months at a time.

United Nations Interim Force in Lebanon (UNIFIL). UNIFIL was set up by the UN Security Council in March 1978 "for the purpose of confirming the withdrawal of Israeli forces, restoring international peace and security and assisting the Government of Lebanon in ensuring the return of its effective authority in the area". In May 1978 the strength of UNIFIL was increased to 6,000 men, and its mandate has since then repeatedly been extended for six-monthly periods.

The Trusteeship Council

The task of the UN Trusteeship Council, with headquarters in New York, has been the supervision of the administration of UN Trust Territories, i.e. territories which had been dependencies of powers defeated in World War II and were subsequently placed under UN trusteeship with the object of leading these territories, through political, economic, social and educational development, to self-government and independence.

By the end of 1980 only one territory remained under UN trusteeship—the Trust Territory of the Pacific Islands, administered by the United States and placed, as a strategic area, under supervision by the Trusteeship Council under the authority of the UN Security Council. (The Trust Territory consists of the Republic of Belau, the Federated States of Micronesia, the Marshall Islands and the Northern Marianas.)

The members of the Trusteeship Council are the United States (as the administering country) and the four other permanent members of the UN Security Council.

The Economic and Social Council (ECOSOC)

The Economic and Social Council is responsible for co-ordinating the United Nations' policy in the economic, social, cultural and humanitarian fields.

Its functions are:

(1) To make studies of, and reports and recommendations on, world co-operation in these fields;
(2) to promote the observation and pursuit of human rights and fundamental freedoms for all;
(3) to convene international conferences;
(4) to consult with the Specialized Agencies (see below) and co-ordinate their activities;
(5) to consult with non-governmental organizations which are concerned with ECOSOC matters.

The UN General Assembly decided (i) on Dec. 17, 1963, to increase the membership of the Council from 18 to 27 (this decision coming into force on Aug. 31, 1965), and (ii) on Dec. 20, 1971, by 105 votes to 2 (France and Great Britain) and with 15 abstentions, to enlarge the Council from 27 to 54 members and to amend Article 61 of the Charter accordingly.

Under the second amendment, the General Assembly each year elects 18 members to the Council for a term of three years. Of the Council's 54 members, 14 were to be from African states; 11 from Asian states; 10 from Latin American states; 13 from Western European and other states; and six from socialist states of Eastern Europe.

Most of the work of ECOSOC is carried out through functional and regional commissions. The following are the functional commissions:

(1) Statistical Commission.
(2) Population Commission.
(3) Commission for Social Development.
(4) Commission on Human Rights.
(5) Commission on the Status of Women.
(6) Commission on Narcotic Drugs.

The regional commissions (see below for details) are the following:

(1) Economic Commission for Europe (ECE).
(2) Economic and Social Commission for Asia and the Pacific (ESCAP).
(3) Economic Commission for Latin America (ECLA).
(4) Economic Commission for Africa (ECA).
(5) Economic Commission for Western Asia (ECWA), which was established on Jan. 1, 1974 (and does not include Israel).

ECOSOC also has the following committees and subsidiary bodies:

(1) Committee on Non-Governmental Organizations.
(2) Committee on Negotiations with Inter-governmental Organizations.
(3) Committee for Programme and Co-ordination (CPC).
(4) Committee for Development Planning.
(5) Committee on Natural Resources.
(6) Committee on Science and Technology for Development.
(7) Committee on Review and Appraisal.
(8) Committee on Crime Prevention and Control.
(9) Commission on Transnational Corporations.
(10) Commission on Human Settlements [see below].

Economic Commission for Europe (ECE)

Address. Palais des Nations, 1211 Geneva 10, Switzerland.

Officer. Klaus Aksel Sahlgren (exec. sec.).

Founded. 1947.

Membership. All European member countries of the United Nations, and also Canada and the United States.

Structure. The ECE has numerous subsidiary bodies, including committees on agricultural problems; timber; coal; electric power; housing, building and planning; inland transport; steel;

development of trade; water; and the chemical industry.

Finance. For the 1967–68 biennium the sum of US$ 26,767,900 was appropriated for the ECE.

Economic and Social Commission for Asia and the Pacific (ESCAP)

Address. United Nations Bldg., Rajadamnern Avenue, Bangkok, 10200, Thailand.

Officer. Shah A. M. S. Kibria (exec. sec.).

Founded. 1947.

Membership. 36 full and eight associated members.

History. The ESCAP was founded as the Economic Commission for Asia and the Far East (ECAFE) to promote the economic and social development of the region, and in 1974 it became the ESCAP.

Activities. The ESCAP has launched a number of regional projects and set up research and development centres as well as specialized organizations, such as an Asian Free Trade Zone (in 1975), an Asia-Pacific Telecommunity (in 1974), two commodity organizations (an Asian and Pacific Coconut Community and an International Pepper Community—see Section 7), as well as, in co-operation with the World Meteorological Organization, a typhoon committee and a panel on tropical cyclones.

In 1966 the ECAFE had set up a committee for co-ordination of joint prospecting for mineral resources in Asian offshore areas, and at a meeting of this committee in Tokyo on Aug. 22, 1975, agreement was reached between Indonesia, Japan, the Republic of Korea, Malaysia, the Philippines, Singapore and Thailand on extending their offshore oil and mineral survey activities beyond the continental shelf.

Finance. The appropriation for the ESCAP for the 1986–87 biennium was US$34,818,400.

Economic Commission for Latin America (ECLA)

Address. United Nations Bldg., Casilla 179 D, Santiago, Chile.

Officer. Enrique V. Iglesias (exec. sec.).

Founded. 1948.

Membership. 43 full members, including Canada, France, the Netherlands, Portugal, Spain, the United Kingdom and the United States; two associate members (the Netherlands Antilles and the US Virgin Islands).

Recent activities. At a ministerial meeting held in Lima (Peru) on April 4–6, 1984, the ECLA called for the renegotiation of Latin America's foreign debt of US$350,000 million (in a resolution on which Canada, France, the Netherlands, Spain, the United Kingdom and the United States abstained from voting). The ECLA executive secretary said that the effect of debt repayments was "to make Latin America a net exporter of capital resources . . . in flagrant contradiction to the nature of developing countries as net importers of capital".

Finance. The sum appropriated for the ECLA for the 1986–87 biennium was US$45,293,700.

Economic Commission for Africa (ECA)

Address. P.O.B. 3001, Addis Ababa, Ethiopia.

Officer. Dr Adebayo Adedeji (exec. sec.).

Founded. 1958.

Membership. All African member states of the United Nations, among which South Africa's membership was suspended in 1963.

Activities. The ECA secretariat inter alia prepared in 1977 a revised framework of principles for the implementation of the new international economic order for 1976–81–86, and in 1979 a development strategy for Africa for the Third Development Decade, aimed at an African common market to be established by the year 2000.

Finance. The sum appropriated for the ECA for the 1986–87 biennium was US$48,166,300.

Economic Commission for Western Asia (ECWA)

Address. P.O.B. 27, Baghdad, Iraq.

Officer. Mohamed Said al-Attar (exec. sec.).

Founded. Jan. 1, 1974.

Membership. All Arab states of Western Asia, and also the Palestine Liberation Organization (PLO).

Activities. The ECWA co-operates with other UN bodies such as the FAO, UNIDO, UNEP and UNCTAD.

Finance. The sum appropriated for the 1986–87 biennium for the ECWA was US$33,707,500.

United Nations Social Defence Research Institute

Address. Via Giulia 52, 00186 Rome, Italy.

Officer. Tolani Asuni (dir.).

Founded. 1968.

Objects. To promote, under ECOSOC auspices, international action in prevention and control of juvenile delinquency and adult criminality as well as research on crime problems, to be related to the needs of policy makers and law enforcement officers.

World Tourism Organization (WTO)

Address. Apdo. de Correos 28020, Madrid, Spain.

Officer. Robert C. Lonati (sec. gen.).

Founded. 1974.

Membership. 105 countries, three associated members, one observer and 155 affiliated members.

Objects. To link national tourism organizations, study general problems and facilitate travel between and within member countries.

History. In 1974 the WTO's activities were co-ordinated in the ECOSOC.

Special Bodies functioning under the Authority of ECOSOC and the General Assembly

Office of the United Nations High Commissioner for Refugees (UNHCR)

Address. Palais des Nations, 1211 Geneva 10, Switzerland.

Officer. Jean-Pierre Hocké (high commissioner).

Founded. 1951.

Structure of Office. The high commissioner is elected by the General Assembly on the recommendation of the Secretary-General. He is assisted by a deputy high commissioner. A 40-member Executive Committee of the High Commissioner's Office directs the policy of the programme at its twice-yearly meetings.

The High Commissioner's Office in Geneva has four divisions—external affairs, protection, assistance, and administration and management. There are 11 regional offices, 30 branch offices and 12 sub-offices, as well as 67 chargés de mission and honorary representatives or correspondents in 125 countries.

Activities. The UNHCR is responsible to ECOSOC and the General Assembly for the "international protection" of refugees. His mandate does not, however, cover refugees who have the same rights and obligations as nationals of their country of residence, or who receive assistance from other UN agencies.

The activities of the High Commissioner include efforts to facilitate the naturalization of refugees and to improve their legal status; repatriation; local integration by helping refugees to become self-supporting; and resettlement through emigration. An important task of the UNHCR is to supervise the application of the 1951 Convention determining the status of refugees, this being the principal relevant legal document.

By September 1982 it had (with a 1967 protocol) been acceded to by 93 nations.

The UNHCR has been faced with the problem of relief for refugees in many parts of the world. Major UNHCR operations have been necessitated by masses of refugees from Vietnam, Afghanistan and numerous African countries.

According to UNHCR sources the number of refugees ("boat people") who fled from Vietnam by sea and succeeded in reaching countries of first asylum was 202,000 in 1979, over 40,000 in 1982 and some 30,000 in 1983.

In an UNHCR report of April 22, 1982, it was claimed that about 2,700,000 Afghan refugees had been registered in Pakistan. With large numbers of unregistered Afghan refugees in Pakistan, and others in Iran, the grand total was assumed to exceed 3,000,000.

A first conference on assistance to refugees in Africa, held under the joint auspices of the United Nations, the Organization of African Unity and the UNHCR in Geneva on April 9–10, 1981, was attended by representatives of some 100 countries; as a result (as announced by the UNHCR on June 16, 1981) $556,900,000 was pledged for humanitarian programmes in Africa (including $285,000,000 from the USA, $68,000,000 from the European Communities, $34,500,000 from the Federal Republic of Germany, $33,000,000 from Japan and $30,000,000 from Saudi Arabia).

A second international conference on assistance to refugees in Africa, held in Geneva on July 9–11, 1984, and attended by delegates and observers from 112 countries and from various international organizations, adopted a declaration and programme of action on a long-term strategy on some of the problems of an estimated 3,000,000 refugees in Africa. The assistance needed was estimated at some US$155,000,000 for 1984. Fourteen African countries submitted for consideration a total of 128 development projects to the value of $367,000,000.

Finance. The UNHCR's programme budget for the 1986–87 biennium was US$34,485,200.

Conventions on statelessness. Three international conventions on the problem of statelessness have been concluded.

A *Convention on the Legal Status of Stateless Persons*, signed on Sept. 28, 1954, was by Dec. 31, 1985, in force for 34 states.

A *Convention on the Reduction of Statelessness*, signed in New York on Aug. 30, 1961 and May 31, 1962, provided for the acquisition of the nationality of the contracting state by children born in its territory of stateless parents. By Dec. 31, 1985, the convention had been ratified by 14 states.

A *Convention on the Reduction of Cases of Statelessness* signed on Sept. 13, 1973, was by Dec. 31, 1985, in force in five countries (the Federal Republic of Germany, Greece, Luxembourg, the Netherlands and Turkey).

United Nations Development Programme (UNDP)

Address. One United Nations Plaza, New York, NY 10017, USA.

Officer. F. Bradford Morse (administrator).

Founded. November 1965.

Membership. The governing council of the UNDP consists of representatives of 27 developing countries and 20 economically more advanced countries.

History. The UNDP was formed by the merger of a UN Special Fund and an Expanded Programme of Technical Assistance.

Activities. Functioning under the joint authority of ECOSOC and the General Assembly, the UNDP supports pre-investment projects in developing countries. The fields of activity of the UNDP include development planning, agricultural and industrial productivity, education, health, and public and social services; the work is carried out through the various specialized agencies of the United Nations and also the UN Office of Technical Co-operation, three regional development banks, the Arab Fund for Economic and Social Development and the International Fund for Agricultural Development (IFAD).

The UNDP has an Inter-Agency Consultative Board, composed of the UN Secretary-General and the Executive Heads of the UNDP's participating and executing agencies.

The UNDP also finances, and its Governing Council administers, a **United Nations Capital Development Fund** which was set up by the UN General Assembly in December 1966, became fully operational in 1974 and had, by 1978, resources exceeding the equivalent of $18,000,000 pledged by 68 countries.

In addition the UNDP Governing Council is the governing body of a **United Nations Fund for Population Activities** (UNFPA), set up in 1967 as the Trust Fund for Population Activities and constituted as a Fund of the UN General Assembly in 1972. It is located at 220 E. 42nd St., New York, NY 10017, USA, and is headed by an Executive Director. Its function is to finance projects in the fields of basic population data, population dynamics and policy, family planning, and communication and education. A World Population Conference held in Bucharest in August 1974 adopted a plan of action which called, inter alia, for a reduction in birth rates by 1985 and the provision of family planning advice and services to all who wanted them. For 1982 the UNFPA received contributions totalling $128,000,000 and approved allocations for expenditure of $120,400,000, of which 40.5 per cent was for family planning, 16.2 per cent for basic data collection, 11.8 per cent for communications and education and the remainder mainly for other activities and special programmes.

At the second such conference, held in Mexico City on Aug. 6–14, 1984, the US Administration declared its intention to terminate US funding of international population programmes and agencies which promoted or called for abortion. (The US Administration advocated a free-market economy for the solution of population problems.) The conference adopted an unopposed "Declaration of Mexico" setting out its main conclusions for population control, especially for countries where population growth was regarded as detrimental to development plans and where "timely action" could avoid the accentuation of problems such as over-population, food shortages and environmental degradation. The declaration, however, also stated the "in no way should abortion be promoted as a method of family planning". (The Holy See nevertheless publicly dissociated itself from the declaration.)

In a report published on June 13, 1984, the UNFPA stated that the world population growth rate was then 1.7 per cent per annum (as against 2 per cent 10 years earlier). It forecast that world population would rise to 6,100 million by the year 2000 and to over 10,500 million by the year 2095, when it was likely to stabilize.

A **United Nations Sudano-Sahelian Office** (UNSO) affiliated to the UNDP has as its object to co-ordinate UN efforts to aid 15 drought-stricken Sudano-Sahelian countries to carry out recovery and development plans. The UNSO has also, in co-operation with the UNDP and the UN Environment Programme (UNEP), taken measures to combat desertification.

World Food Council (WFC)

Address. Via delle Terme di Caracalla, 00100 Rome, Italy.

Officer. Maurice J. Williams (exec. dir.).

Founded. December 1974.

Membership. The WFC has 36 members (nine from Africa, eight from Asia, seven from Latin America, four from the socialist states in Eastern Europe and eight from West European and other countries).

Objects. To provide overall, integrated and continuing attention to the co-ordination of policies on food production, nutrition, food security, food trade and food aid as well as related matters among UN agencies.

Activities. At its third session, held in Manila in June 1977, the WFC adopted a 22-point "programme of action to eradicate malnutrition and hunger" which called for efforts to increase the growth of food production in 43 "food priority" countries from the existing 2.7 per cent to 4 per cent per annum. The programme estimated that the developing countries needed about $8,300 million in annual aid for agricultural development, and it called for the creation of an international emergency food reserve (IEFR) of 500,000 tonnes of grain (or the equivalent) by the end of 1977, and for the rapid conclusion of negotiations for an international grains arrangement and the attainment of a 10,000,000-tonne target for annual food aid to poor countries.

At its fifth session in Ottawa in September 1979 the WFC called for further replenishment of the IEFR, which then stood at 380,000 tonnes, and deplored the failure of the international community to "make the world's food system work for everyone".

In a report published by the WFC in February 1984 it was claimed that earlier forecasts of increasing world food shortages had been wrong and that the threat of a global food crisis seemed remote. Despite the fact that millions of people were suffering chronic hunger, the rising demand for food due to population growth had, according to the report, not outstripped food output.

At a ministerial sesssion of the WFC on June 11–15, 1984, recommendations were made to meet the need for a co-ordinated effort to resolve the food and development crisis in Africa through the provision of increased resources and better utilization of such resources.

International Court of Justice (ICJ)

Address. Peace Palace, 2517 KJ The Hague, Netherlands.

Officer. Santiago Torres Bernárdez (registrar).

Founded. 1945.

Structure. The principal judical organ of the United Nations is the International Court of Justice, which sits at The Hague. It functions in accordance with a statute annexed to the Charter of the United Nations, and is permanently in session.

The 15 judges who constitute the Court are elected for nine years by both the General Assembly and the Security Council. Five new judges are elected every three years. In addition to possessing first-class legal qualifications the judges must be people of high moral character. No two judges may be of the same nationality, and the Court should include representatives of all the main legal systems of the world.

Functions and Powers. The International Court is not authorized to hear cases brought by individuals. Those states which may submit a dispute are all the members of the United Nations with the addition of Liechtenstein, San Marino and Switzerland.

The court has jurisdiction over all cases referred to it by the parties to its Statute, and also over matters specially provided for in the UN Charter and in treaties in force. In addition, 45 states which are parties to the Statute have voluntarily recognized the compulsory jurisdiction of the court in relation to states accepting the same obligation and over certain specified classes of international disputes.

Should a party to a case refuse to comply with the judgment of the court, the other party may have recourse to the Security Council, which may decide upon measures to give effect to the judgment.

The court may give advisory opinions on legal questions to the General Assembly, the Security Council and other organs of the United Nations if requested to do so.

The United States, having on Jan. 18, 1985, withdrawn from court proceedings (in the case of a Nicaraguan complaint), declared on Oct. 7, 1985, that it would no longer accept the court's jurisdiction (after Canada had indicated that it might submit its claim to sovereignty over the North-West Passage to the International Court).

The Secretariat and Secretary-General

The general administration of the United Nations is the responsibility of the Secretariat in New York, headed by the Secretary-General.

The Secretary-General is elected by the General Assembly, on the recommendation of the Security Council, for a period of five years and is re-eligible. The Secretary-General acts as the United Nations' chief administrative officer at all meetings of the General Assembly, the Security Council, the Economic and Social Council and the Trusteeship Council. Among his duties are the preparation of an annual report which he submits to the General Assembly, and general vigilance over the international scene, so that he may bring to the attention of the Security Council any situations which he considers to be a threat to international peace.

Offices of the Secretariat include one each for:
(1) Special Political Questions.
(2) Political and General Assembly Affairs.
(3) Economic and Social Matters.
(4) Legal Affairs.

There are also departments for:
(1) Political and Security Council Affairs.
(2) Political Affairs, Trusteeship and Decolonization.
(3) International Economic and Social Affairs.
(4) Technical Co-operation for Development.
(5) Administration, Finance and Management.
(6) Conference Services.
(7) Special Assignments.
(8) Public Information.

Other bodies attached to the Secretariat are as follows:
(1) Office of the UN Commissioner for Namibia.
(2) Secretariat of the Third UN Conference on the Law of the Sea.

European Office of the United Nations. The European Secretariat of the United Nations has its office at Geneva. It is headed by a Director-General and a Deputy Director, who are responsible to the Secretary-General in New York.

United Nations Commission on International Trade Law (UNCITRAL). The Commission was set up in 1968 to co-ordinate the activities of international organizations in the field of international trade. Its secretariat is the International Trade Law Branch of the UN Secretariat's Office of Legal Affairs, based in Vienna. The Commission has 36 members elected by the UN General Assembly for a period of six years.

It has elaborated a number of conventions subsequently approved by the UN General Assembly.

Budgetary Arrangements

The UN budget appropriation for the 1986–87 biennium, as approved by the General Assembly on Dec. 18, 1985, was US$1,663,341,000 (whereas the final budget appropriation for the 1984–85 biennium was $1,608,954,000), the vote being 127 to 10 (eight communist states in Europe, Israel and the United States) with 11 abstentions (Belgium, France, the Federal Republic of Germany, Italy, Japan, Luxembourg, the Netherlands, Portugal, Romania, Spain and the United Kingdom).

The Assembly also approved a new scale of percentage contributions of member states to the UN budget for the years 1986, 1987 and 1988. The 10 largest assessments were as follows: The United States 25 per cent; the Soviet Union (including Byelorussia and the Ukraine) 11.82 per cent; Japan 10.84 per cent; the Federal Republic of Germany 8.26 per cent; France 6.37 per cent; the United Kingdom 4.67 per cent; Italy 3.79 per cent; Canada 3.06 per cent; Spain 2.03 per cent; and the Netherlands 1.74 per cent. The lowest percentages were 0.01 per cent (for 78 member states); 0.02 per cent (for a further 11 member states); and 0.03 per cent (for five member states).

Other Bodies operating within the UN Framework

United Nations Children's Fund (UNICEF)

Address. 866 United Nations Plaza, New York, NY, 10017, USA.

Officer. James P. Grant (exec. dir.).

Founded. 1946.

Objects. The United Nations Children's Fund is an operating agency of the United Nations, founded in December 1946 to aid mothers and children in need as a result of the devastation of war.

The work of UNICEF is carried out in conjunction with WHO, *FAO, and UNESCO (see below under "Specialized Agencies"), and is now mainly directed towards aiding children and young people in developing countries through health, nutrition and social welfare projects.

Structure. The decision-making organ of UNICEF is its 30-member Executive Board, which meets annually. There is also a Secretariat, headed by an Executive Director.

United Nations Research Institute for Social Development (UNRISD)

Address. Palais des Nations, 1211 Geneva 10, Switzerland.

Officers. P. M. Henry (ch. of Board); E. Oteiza (dir.).

Founded. 1964.

Activities. UNRISD was established as an autonomous UN body with the object of conducting research into problems and policy of social development and relationships between various types of social and economic development during different phases of economic growth, and of thus contributing to the work of other UN bodies and of national institutes. UNRISD's activities are supervised by a Board consisting of representatives of various UN bodies concerned with social and economic development.

United Nations Institute for Training and Research (UNITAR)

Address. 801 United Nations Plaza, New York, NY 10017, USA.

Officer. Michel Doo Kingue (exec. dir.).

Founded. 1965.

Activities. The United Nations Institute for Training and Research was created, as an autonomous body within the framework of the United Nations, to train personnel—particularly from developing countries—for service with member governments and organizations of the United Nations. Another of UNITAR's functions is to study major questions relating to the promotion of economic and social development and the maintenance of international peace and security.

A Board of Trustees, whose members are appointed by the UN Secretary-General to sit for three years, directs the policy of the organization. Meetings of the Board take place once a year and are attended, where appropriate, by representatives of the specialized agencies. The direction and general administration of the Institute are the responsibility of an Executive Director.

United Nations Environment Programme (UNEP)

Address. P.O. Box 30552, Nairobi, Kenya.

Officer. Mostafa K. Tolba (Egypt, exec. dir.).

Founded. 1972.

History. The UN Environment Programme was set up under a resolution passed by the UN General Assembly on Dec. 15, 1972, by 116 votes to none with 10 abstentions in order to implement a recommendation made at a UN Conference on the Human Environment held in Stockholm on June 5–16, 1972.

Activities. UNEP has been responsible for launching a number of action plans for combating marine pollution [see pages 96ff.] and also, in 1984, for a plan for the conservation of whales and other marine mammals, including the creation of whale sanctuaries.

Structure. UNEP has a Governing Council of 58 members (representing 16 African, 13 Asian, 10 Latin American, six Eastern European and 13 Western European and other states) and a Secretariat. The duties of the council were to include the promotion of international co-operation in the environmental field, the recommendation of appropriate polices, and the receiving and reviewing of reports by UNEP's Executive Director (elected for a four-year term) on the implementation of environmental programmes within the UN system.

UNEP also has a Liaison Office in New York (at ALCOA Bldg., Room A3630, 866 United Nations Plaza, New York NY 10163, USA) and four regional offices—for Europe (at the Palais des Nations, 1211 Geneva 10, Switzerland), for Asia and the Pacific (at UN Bldg., 10th floor, Rajadamnern Ave., Bangkok, Thailand), for Latin America (at Presidente Mazaryk 29, Ap. Postal 6-718, México 5, DF, Mexico) and for West Asia (at P.O. Box 4656, Ouiedat Bldg., Bir Hassan, Beirut, Lebanon).

The UN General Assembly also set up a voluntary fund, effective Jan. 1, 1973, for financing inter alia regional and global monitoring, assessment and data-collecting systems—an "Earthwatch" to warn against impending crises—as proposed in an "Action Plan" of recommendations made by the Stockholm Conference.

Finance. The appropriation for the UNEP for the 1986–87 biennium totalled US$10,142,400.

UN Office for Emergency Operations (OEOA)

Officers. Bradford Morse (ch.); Maurice Strong (exec. co-ordinator).

Founded. December 1984.

Activities. In a report submitted to an international conference on the emergency situation in Africa, held in Geneva on March 11–12, 1985, the OEOA claimed that some $1,500 million in short-term emergency aid was required for 20 African countries (with some 150,000,000 people) adversely affected by drought and its consequences. This amount was said to include sums previously appealed for by the UN Disaster Relief Office (UNDRO), UNICEF, the World Food Programme and the FAO.

In a report issued in September 1985 the OEOA declared that at the height of the 1984–85 African drought crisis over 35,000,000 people had been threatened by famine; that over 4,500,000 tonnes of grain had been delivered; that over 1,000,000 lives had been saved; and that during 1986 emergency food aid and other supplies would continue to be required by Angola, Botswana, Burkina Faso, Cape Verde, Chad, Ethiopia, Mali, Mauritania, Mozambique, Niger and the Sudan.

Office of the United Nations Disaster Relief Co-ordinator (UNDRO)

Address. Palais des Nations, 1211 Geneva 10, Switzerland.

Officer. M'Hamed Essaafi (co-ordinator).

Founded. 1972.

Objects. The co-ordination and mobilization of aid furnished by other bodies for international emergency relief to disaster-stricken areas, and the promotion of disaster-preparedness and prevention.

Finance. For the 1986–87 biennium the appropriation for the UNDRO was US$5,708,300.

United Nations University (UNU)

Address. Toho Seimei Bldg., 15–1, Shibuya 2-chome, Shibuya-ku, Tokyo 150, Japan.

Officer. Soedjatmoko (rector).

Founded. September 1975.

Objects. To carry out "action-orientated research into the pressing global problems of human survival, development and welfare that are the concern of the United Nations and its agencies, and . . . the post-graduate training of young scholars and research workers for the benefit of the world community".

History. The UNU was set up under a charter approved by the UN General Assembly in 1973. In 1984 it established a World Institute for Development Economic Research in Helsinki.

University for Peace—Universidad de la Paz

Address. Apdo, postal 199, 1.250 Escazú, Costa Rica.

Officer. Rodrigo Carazo (rector).

Founded. 1985.

History. This university was established in terms of UN General Assembly resolutions

(34/111 of Dec. 14, 1979, and 35/55 of Dec. 5, 1980, both adopted without a vote). It was given its own charter and plans were formulated in line with the intention that it should be financed by voluntary contributions.

Objects. This university was to be "a specialized institution for post-graduate studies, research and dissemination of knowledge specifically aimed at training for peace within the system of the UN University".

UN Specialized Agencies, the IAEA and GATT

The United Nations specialized agencies are independent international organizations, which function in co-operation with the United Nations under agreements made with an ECOSOC Committee. They have responsibilities in a wide variety of fields. Membership of the specialized agencies is not restricted to the members of the United Nations (see table on pages 60–68).

International Labour Organization (ILO)

Address. 4 route des Morillons, CH-1211, Geneva 22, Switzerland.

Officer. Francis Blanchard (France, dir.-gen. of International Labour Office).

Founded. Founded in 1919, the International Labour Organization became the first specialized agency of the United Nations in 1946.

Objects. To formulate international policies and programmes for improving working and living conditions, enhancing employment opportunities and promoting human rights; to set international labour standards to be achieved by national authorities; to provide a programme of international technical co-operation towards the implementation of these policies; and to engage in training, education, research and publishing towards these ends.

The aims and purposes of the ILO were defined in the *Philadelphia Charter*, adopted on May 10, 1944, and reading as follows:

"The general Conference of the ILO, meeting in its 26th session in Philadelphia, hereby adopts the present declaration of the aims and purposes of the ILO and of the principles which should inspire the policy of its members.

"The Conference reaffirms the fundamental principles on which the organization is based and, in particular, that labour is not a commodity; that freedom of expression and association are essential to sustained progress; that poverty anywhere constitutes a danger to prosperity everywhere; and that accordingly the war against want, while it requires to be carried on with unrelenting vigour within each nation, equally requires continuous and concerted international effort in which the representatives of workers and employers, enjoying equal status with those of governments, join with them in free discussion and democratic decision with a view to the promotion of the common welfare.

"The Conference affirms that all human beings, irrespective of race, creed or sex, have the right to pursue both their material well-being and spiritual development in conditions of freedom and dignity, of economic security and equal opportunity, that the attainment of the conditions in which this shall be possible must constitute the central aim of national and international policy, and that all policies and measures, in particular those of an economic and financial character, must be judged in this light and accepted only in so far as they may

be held to promote and not to hinder the achievement of this fundamental objective. The Conference declares that it is accordingly a responsibility of the ILO to examine all international economic and financial policies and measures in the light of this fundamental objective and that in discharging the tasks entrusted to it the ILO may consider all relevant economic and financial factors and include in its decisions and recommendations any provisions which it considers appropriate.

"Among the matters to which urgent attention should be given by the ILO, the Conference attaches special importance to the following: The maintenance of full employment and the raising of standards of living; the employment of workers in occupations in which they can have the satisfaction of giving the fullest measure of their skill and attainments and make their greatest contribution to the common well-being and, as a means to the attainment of this end, the provision under adequate guarantees for all concerned of facilities for training and the transfer of labour, including migration for employment and settlement; the application of policies in regard to wages, earnings, hours and other conditions of work calculated to ensure a just share of the fruits of progress to all, and the assurance of a minimum living wage to all in need of such protection; the effective recognition of the right of collective bargaining, the co-operation of management and labour in the continuous improvement of productive efficiency, and the collaboration of workers and employers in the initiation and application of social and economic measures; the extension to the whole population of social security measures providing a basic income in case of inability to work or to obtain work, and providing comprehensive medical care; the provision of adequate protection for the life and health of workers in all occupations; provision for child welfare and maternity protection, and the provision of adequate nutrition, housing and facilities for recreation and culture; the assurance of equality of educational and vocational opportunity.

"Confident that the fuller and broader utilization of the world's productive resources necessary for the achievement of the objectives set forth in this declaration can be secured by effective international and national action, including, for example, measures to avoid severe economic fluctuations, to maintain consumption at a high level, to ensure the productive investment of all savings, to promote the economic and social advancement of the less developed regions of the world, to assure greater stability in world prices of primary products, and to promote a high and steady volume of international trade, the Conference pledges the full co-operation of the ILO with such international bodies as may be entrusted with a share of the responsibility for this great task and for the promotion of the health, education and well-being of all peoples.

"The Conference affirms that the principles set forth in this declaration are fully applicable to all peoples everywhere and that, while the manner of their application must be determined with due regard to the stage of social and economic development reached by each people, their progressive application to peoples who are still dependent, as well as to those who have already achieved self-government, is a matter of concern to the whole civilized world."

Structure. The principal organ of the ILO is the International Labour Conference, meeting annually and attended by delegations from member countries, and with workers' and employers' representatives having an equal voice with those of governments. The ILO's Governing Body is its executive body, consisting of 28 government, 14 employers' and 14 workers' members and meeting three to four times a year. The International Labour Office is the ILO's secretariat, operational headquarters and publishing house.

Two institutions founded by the ILO are the International Institute for Labour Studies, set up in March 1960 in Geneva as an advanced educational and research institute, and the International Centre for Advanced Technical and Vocational Training, established in March 1963 in Turin, Italy.

Activities. The ILO has approved some 150 conventions and more than 160 recommendations, forming an international labour code intended to serve as a guideline for governments. Member countries are committed to conventions after ratification, and have to submit to the ILO periodical reports on their implementation.

The ILO has also inquired into alleged violations of human rights, e.g. in Chile, about which an ILO commission appointed in June 1974 reported in May 1975 (after a visit paid to Chile) that there was a lack of legal safeguards for trade union officials in that country, and in 1977–78 the ILO inquired into alleged violations of ILO conventions in the Soviet Union and Czechoslovakia.

The United States, on Nov. 5, 1975, gave the required two years' notice of termination of its ILO membership (after 41 years), stating that it objected to "the workers' and employers' groups in the ILO falling under the domination of governments", to the ILO's alleged failure to apply human rights universally, and to the "increasing politicization" of the ILO, i.e. its growing involvement "in political issues quite beyond its competence and mandate" (after the ILO had decided to allow certain liberation movements to address ILO conferences). A US resolution seeking to reform the ILO so as to exclude "political" matters from discussion without having first been "screened" was turned down by the International Labour Conference in June 1977, and the US withdrawal from the ILO became effective on Nov. 5, 1977. (The USA had met about one-quarter of the ILO's budget.) However, on Feb. 13, 1980, the US President announced that his country was rejoining the ILO, seeing that the latter had made efforts to "return to its original purposes".

Food and Agriculture Organization (FAO)

Address. Via delle Terme di Caracalla, 00100 Rome, Italy.

Officer. Edouard Saouma (dir.-gen.).

Founded. October 1945.

Objects. In FAO's constitution (accepted by over 20 countries in Aug. 30, 1945), the organization's aims were listed as follows:

"To raise levels of nutrition and standards of living among the peoples of the world; improve the efficiency of production and distribution of food and agricultural products; better the condition of the rural population; and thus contribute to an expanding world economy." To this end FAO would function principally as an advisory body, collecting, analysing and disseminating information on nutrition, food and agriculture, and promoting and recommending national and international action with respect to research, the improvement of education and administration relating to these subjects, the spread of public knowledge of nutritional and agricultural science and practice, the conservation of natural resources and the adoption of improved agricultural production methods, improved processing, marketing and distribution, and the provision of adequate agricultural credit. FAO was also to furnish technical assistance to governments when requested.

Structure. The supreme organ of FAO is the Conference of all the member nations, which sits every two years. Between sessions of the Conference the work of the organization is carried on by a 49-member Council, meetings of which are normally held twice a year and after each Conference session. There is also a Secretariat headed by a director-general.

FAO has set up numerous commissions and councils with special functions in various areas for matters of agriculture, animal production and health, fisheries, food standards, forestry, horticulture, land and water use, locust control and plant protection.

FAO has four regional offices and 74 offices of country representatives.

Activities. FAO's allocation of resources has been concentrated on the elimination of hunger and poverty. Over three-quarters of its field programme has been dedicated to agriculture, mainly to increasing crop production. Of its professional staff (of about 3,400 persons in 1985) nearly two-thirds have been assigned to field projects.

An Office for Special Relief Operations (OSRO), first set up in 1973 to cope with the Sahel (West Africa) drought of that year, was in 1975 expanded in order to deal with such emergencies on a global scale.

A Technical Co-operation Programme (TCP) was launched in 1976 to enable FAO to meet emergencies created by natural disasters or project difficulties.

Under a major reform approved by the FAO Council in July 1976, substantial savings were made (on salaries, publications and meetings), the proceeds of which were used to set up a $18,500,000 technical co-operation fund to provide aid directly to developing countries for agricultural purposes.

A Global Information and Early Warning System to monitor world food supply and demand, with 42 governments participating in it, came into operation in 1977.

A World Conference on Agrarian Reform and Rural Development, convened by FAO and held in Rome on July 12–20, 1979, adopted a declaration of principles and recommended a programme of national and international action. It called on the international community to participate in the rural development policies defined by each country, with special attention to be given to priority for rural development, increased popular participation and recognition of the essential role of women in development.

Under a five-point plan for increased world food security, announced in March 1979 and approved by the FAO Conference in November of that year, FAO called on all countries to adopt national grain reserve policies, with targets of two months' supply, and on exporting countries to hold additional cereal stocks against national shortages. It also proposed that guidelines for the release of reserve stocks, to be drawn up by a FAO Committee on World Food Security, should cover crop failures, natural disasters and the needs of poor countries for supplies at reasonable prices, and that the 10,000,000-tonne target for annual shipments by food donor countries (see under World Food Council, page 26) should be raised to 13,000,000 tonnes per annum by 1982 and to 16,000,000 tonnes per annum by 1985.

FAO's assessed budget for regular projects for 1984–85 was just over $420,000,000. On its field programme FAO spent $313,000,000 in 1984. The total investment cost of 41 projects approved for financing was, including the assistance given by FAO, $2,306 million in 1984.

The 23rd biennial session of the FAO Conference, held in Rome from Nov. 9 to 28, 1985, approved a budget of $437,000,000 (with 12 industrial countries, including the United Kingdom and the United States, abstaining from the vote on Nov. 20) for the 1986–87 biennium.

The Conference also adopted a World Food Security Compact which, although not legally binding, set out guidelines (for governments, non-governmental organizations and individuals) to ensure the aims of world food security, namely that all peoples should have access at all times to the basic food which they need.

In addition the Conference approved an international code of conduct on the distribution and use of pesticides, this being the first attempt to establish international guidelines for the handling, trade and safe use of pesticides, particularly in developing countries lacking control over their use.

The Conference further adopted a resolution— by 90 votes to one (the United States), with abstentions by European countries—accusing South Africa of carrying out a policy of violence leading to "destabilization" with harmful effects for the peoples of southern Africa and their agricultural production (this being FAO's first political resolution directed against South Africa).

World Food Programme. The World Food Programme (WFP), a joint UN-FAO enterprise established in 1963 to provide aid, in the form of food, to less developed countries, is headed by a Committee on Food Aid Policies and Programmes (CFAPP), appointed under a resolution of the UN General Assembly of Nov. 28, 1975, to replace an earlier Intergovernmental Committee of the WFP. The CFAPP consists of 15 members elected by ECOSOC and 15 others elected by FAO. The WFP's day-to-day activities are carried out by a Joint UN–FAO Administrative Unit headed by an Executive Director.

For the biennium of 1983–84 the WFP received pledges from more than 131 donor countries, totalling $982,000,000. Of this amount $925,000,000 was devoted to development projects ($403,000,000 to agricultural production, $357,000,000 to human resources development, $124 to rural development, and the rest to other projects). $64,000,000 from donor pledges was used for emergency relief, in addition to $180,000,000 supplied by the International Emergency Food Reserve [see page 26], which had received pledges of $317,000,000.

United Nations Educational, Scientific and Cultural Organization (UNESCO)

Address. 7 place de Fontenoy, 75700 Paris, France.

Officer. Amadou Mahtar M'Bow (dir.-gen.).

Founded. November 1945.

Objects. The basic purpose of the organization is to promote international collaboration in the fields of education, science and culture, and through this, to foster and strengthen universal respect for the human rights and fundamental freedoms affirmed in the Charter of the United Nations.

Under UNESCO's Constitution, approved by representatives of 44 nations on Nov. 15, 1945, the main purposes of the organization were (i) to develop and maintain mutual understanding and appreciation of the life, culture, arts, humanities and sciences of the peoples of the world as a basis for effective international organization and world peace; (ii) to co-operate in extending and making available to all peoples for the service of common human needs the world's full body of knowledge and culture, and in assuring its contribution to economic stability, political security and general well-being.

To achieve these purposes UNESCO would (a) facilitate consultation among leaders in the educational and cultural life of all peace-loving countries; (b) assist the free flow of ideas and information among the peoples of the world through schools, universities, other educational and research institutions, libraries, publications, the press, radio, the cinema, international conferences and the exchange of students, teachers, etc., with special attention to exchange of information on major educational, cultural and scientific developments; (c) foster the growth within each country, and in its relations with other countries, of educational and cultural programmes supporting international peace and security; (d) develop and make available educational and cultural plans and materials for consideration and use by each country as it thinks fit; (e) conduct and encourage research and studies on educational and cultural problems related to the maintenance of peace and the advancement of human welfare; and (f) assist countries needing and requesting help in developing their educational and cultural activities.

Activities. The work of UNESCO includes the documentation of information of all kinds; the extension of free and compulsory education;

the improvement of facilities for vocational and technical training and for higher education; the promotion of scientific research; the preservation of the world's cultural heritage in books, works of art, and historical and scientific monuments; and the improvement of all means of communication in order to encourage the free flow of ideas and knowledge.

Structure. The organs of UNESCO are a General Conference of the member nations, meeting every two years; a 45-member Executive Board which meets at least twice a year to prepare the organization's programme; and a Secretariat. National commissions and co-operating bodies within the member countries serve to co-ordinate the work of UNESCO with national efforts in the same fields.

UNESCO's member states are organized in five regional groups—for Europe, Africa, the Arab world, Asia and Latin America.

In 1963 UNESCO established in Paris an International Institute for Educational Planning (IIEP) to assist all UNESCO member states in planning their educational systems and obtaining competent experts in this field.

An International Bureau of Education (IBE), founded in 1925 and based in Geneva, was incorporated in UNESCO in January 1969. Its Council is composed of representatives of 24 member states appointed by UNESCO's General Conference.

In 1978 UNESCO established in Paris an Intergovernmental Committee for Physical Education and Sport (ICPES), consisting of 30 representatives of UNESCO member states elected by the General Conference. The ICPES is to facilitate the adoption and implementation of an International Charter of Physical Education and Sport.

UNESCO CONFERENCES

A conference on cultural policies, organized by UNESCO and held in Mexico City from July 26 to Aug. 6, 1982, issued a Mexico Declaration which inter alia emphasized the need for opening new paths to political democracy, for restoring to their country of origin works of art illicitly removed, for facilitating objective information on cultural events without prejudicing creative freedom and the cultural liberty of nations, and for ensuring that the expansion and interaction of culture, science and education contributed to the consolidation of peace, respect for human rights and the elimination of colonialism, neo-colonialism, racism and all forms of aggression and domination.

At an extraordinary session of UNESCO's General Conference held in Paris on Nov. 23–Dec. 3, 1982, UNESCO's Director-General issued a warning that technological progress had made nations so interdependent that their fate was increasingly being determined by decisions taken in other parts of the world, and it was no longer possible to make neat distinctions between political, economic, social and cultural activities.

UNESCO CONVENTIONS AND DECLARATIONS

Conventions and declarations adopted by UNESCO's General Conference have included the following:

Convention on the Preservation of the World's Cultural and Natural Heritage. This convention, adopted by a UNESCO General Conference on Nov. 16, 1972, by 75 votes to one (Thailand) with 17 abstentions, aimed at providing both emergency and long-term protection for monuments, monumental sculpture and painting, groups of buildings, archaeological sites, natural features and habitats of animals and plants of "outstanding universal value". States ratifying the convention would be required to take all necessary measures to protect their cultural and natural heritage; close international co-operation would be provided through an Intergovernmental Heritage Committee to ensure the protection of this heritage; and there would be an agency ready to provide immediate aid for the repair of monuments and sites damaged by catastrophes and to assist in preventive measures against latent dangers.

Signatory states were called upon to draw up an inventory of property belonging to their cultural and natural heritage, to be included in a "world heritage list" to be updated every two years. A second inventory "list of world heritage in danger" would include those monuments, buildings and sites for which major conservation operations were urgently needed. The convention also called for the establishment of a World Heritage Fund to be financed by compulsory and voluntary contributions by the states parties to the convention as well as by other states, international and other organizations or individuals.

The convention came into force on Dec. 17, 1975 (three months after ratification by 20 countries) and by Dec. 31, 1979, it was ratified by 49 countries (which did not include the Soviet Union, the United Kingdom and various other countries in Europe).

Declaration on Fundamental Principles for the Mass Media. The 20th session of UNESCO's General Conference adopted, in Paris on Nov. 22, 1978, by acclamation a "draft declaration on fundamental principles concerning the contribution of the mass media to strengthening peace and international understanding, the promotion of human rights, and to countering racialism, apartheid and incitement to war".

The declaration called for "a free flow and a wider and better balanced dissemination of information" to which the mass media had "a leading contribution to make". In particular, "access by the public to information should be guaranteed by the diversity of the sources and means of information available to it, thus enabling each individual to check the accuracy of facts and to appraise events objectively" and "it is important that the mass media be responsive to concerns of peoples and individuals, thus promoting the participation of the public in the elaboration of information" (Art. II(2)). The mass media should also give "expression to oppressed peoples who struggle against colonialism, neo-colonialism, foreign occupation and all forms of racial discrimination and oppression and who are unable to make their voices heard within their own territories" (Art. II(3)).

The declaration further stated that it was "necessary that states should facilitate the procurement, by the mass media in the developing countries, of adequate conditions and resources enabling them to gain strength and expand" and that "bilateral and multilateral exchanges of information among all states, and in particular between those which have different economic and social systems, be encouraged and developed" (Art. X).

UNESCO RESOLUTIONS

Resolution on New World Information and Communications Order. The 21st session of UNESCO's General Council, held in Belgrade in October 1980, adopted by consensus a resolution calling for the establishment of a New World

Information and Communications Order (NWICO) based on a report prepared by an International Commission for the Study of Communication Problems and published in August 1980 under the title "Many Voices, One World".

The resolution stated inter alia that the NWICO would be based on:

"(i) Elimination of the imbalances and inequalities which characterize the present situation; (ii) elimination of the negative effects of certain monopolies, public or private, and excessive concentrations; (iii) removal of the internal and external obstacles to a free flow and wider and better balanced dissemination of information and ideas; (iv) plurality of sources and channels of information; (v) freedom of the press and information; (vi) the freedom of journalists and all professionals in the communication media, a freedom inseparable from responsibility; (vii) the capacity of developing countries to achieve improvement of their own situations, notably by providing their own equipment, by training their personnel, by improving their infrastructures and by making their information and communication media suitable to their needs and aspirations; (viii) the sincere will of developed countries to help them attain these objectives; (ix) respect for each people's cultural identity and for the right of each nation to inform the world public about its interests, its aspirations and its social and cultural values; (x) respect for the right of all peoples to participate in international exchanges of information on the basis of equality, justice and mutual benefit; [and] (xi) respect for the right of the public, of ethnic and social groups and of individuals to have access to information sources and to participate actively in the communication process".

It also stated that a NWICO "should be based on the fundamental principles of international law, as laid down in the Charter of the United Nations'; and that "diverse solutions to information and communication problems are required because social, political, cultural and economic problems differ from one country to another and, within a given country, from one group to another".

The United Kingdom delegation supported the resolution "with great reluctance", inter alia because it omitted to state certain fundamental principles, such as "the right to freedom of thought, opinion and expression; the free circulation of information and ideas; the freedom of movement; freedom from censorship and arbitrary governmental control; and access to all sources of information unofficial as well as official".

Resolution on International Programme for the Development of Communications. In another resolution the UNESCO General Assembly invited the UNESCO Director-General to make arrangements for the establishment, development and efficient implementation of an International Programme for the Development of Communications (IPDC) to be co-ordinated by an intergovernmental council. Such a council, whose 35 members were elected on Oct. 28, 1980, held various meetings between June 1981 and December 1982, which approved considerable funds for 33 projects, including the creation of a Pan-African news agency, an Asia-Pacific news network and a feature agency in Latin America.

These decisions were opposed by the United States and most of the Western UNESCO member states and eventually led to the withdrawal from the organization of the United States on Jan. 1,

1985, the United Kingdom as from Jan. 1, 1986, and Singapore by the same date.

The departure of the United States was based on objections to alleged "increased politization" of UNESCO's activities, many of which the United States deemed to lie outside the provisions of UNESCO's Charter. (The United States had contributed 25 per cent of UNESCO's funds, as well as considerable technical and intellectual expertise.)

World Health Organization (WHO)

Address. Avenue Appia, 1211 Geneva 27, Switzerland.

Officer. Dr Halfdan Mahler (dir.-gen.).

Founded. April 1948.

Objects. To raise the standard of health of all peoples to the highest possible level through, inter alia, health education; the promotion of work to eradicate disease; the promotion of maternal and child health welfare; the fostering of mental health activities; and the improvement of environmental hygiene and sanitation. The WHO provides its members with both advisory services and technical assistance.

The constitution of the WHO, as proposed by ECOSOC and signed by 60 nations on July 22, 1946, defined the organization's functions as follows:

The WHO was to be "the directing and co-ordinating authority in all matters concerning international health" and in particular "(1) to assist governments in strengthening their national health services; (2) to furnish technical assistance and, in emergencies, give necessary aid at the request of governments; (3) to assist in developing an informed public opinion among all peoples in matters of health; (4) to stimulate and advance work to eradicate disease, particularly of an epidemic, endemic or social nature; (5) to promote research in the field of health; (6) to promote maternal and child health welfare; (7) to foster mental health activities necessary to improve and harmonize human relations; (8) to foster education through improved standards of teaching and training in the health, medical and related professions by means of fellowships, courses, study tours, etc.; (9) to study administrative and social techniques affecting sanitation and medical care from a curative and preventive point of view as regards both medical and hospital practice; (10) to develop central information services and the interchange of information with respect to health and medical care; (11) to promote, with the co-operation of other specialized agencies, the improvement of nutrition, working conditions, housing and other factors related to environmental hygiene and sanitation; (12) to establish an epidemiological and statistical service for the collection, analysis, interpretation and dissemination of information; (13) to establish and promote international standards with respect to pharmaceutical, biological and related products; (14) to standardize diagnostic procedure as desirable; (15) to establish and revise, as necessary, international nomenclature of diseases, causes of death and public health practice; (16) to promote conventions, regulations and agreements with respect to international health and sanitary matters; (17) to provide, on request of the United Nations, health services and facilities to special groups, including displaced persons and peoples of trust territories; (18) to establish and maintain effective collaboration with the United Nations and its affiliated organizations, with national health administrations and with other appropriate organizations". The WHO was also given authority to adopt regulations which would be binding on all member nations unless they notified the organization to the contrary.

Structure. The supreme organ of the WHO is the World Health Assembly, which meets annually to decide on a programme of world health. Other organs are the 31-man Executive Board which meets at least twice a year, and the Secretariat, headed by a Director-General.

The WHO has regional offices for Africa, the Americas, the Eastern Mediterranean, Europe, South-East Asia and the Western Pacific.

Activities. An International Agency for Research on Cancer was established in Lyons (France) in 1965 as a self-governing body within the framework of the WHO.

The World Health Assembly decided in May 1976 that under "a new world health order" at least 60 per cent of the WHO's budget (of $146,184,000 for 1977) should be devoted to technical co-operation and services to the Third World.

In a report by the WHO's Director-General, approved by the World Health Assembly in May 1979, strategies were recommended to attain the goal of "health for all by the year 2000"; the report also endorsed the conclusions of an International Conference on Primary Health Care, held under the joint auspices of the WHO and the UN Children's Fund (UNICEF) in Alma Ata (Soviet Union) in September 1978, calling on governments to develop national strategies and action plans to implement primary health care and to end "the inadequate and inequitable distribution of health resources between and within countries".

On Oct. 26, 1979, the WHO's Director-General announced the eradication of smallpox throughout the world.

The 35th World Health Assembly, held on May 3–14, 1982, unanimously passed a resolution urging member states "to establish adequate drug procurement, storage and distribution systems in order to make available drugs of adequate quality, at reasonable prices, to the population" and to establish "national drug lists" including "essential drugs selected on the basis of the health needs of countries". (A WHO study group had found that expensive Western drugs consumed health budgets without meeting the real needs of the people and these drugs could be dangerous when sold indiscriminately in poor areas.)

The 36th World Health Assembly, held in Geneva on May 2–16, 1983, inter alia approved (on May 13 by 97 votes to 12 with nine abstentions) a resolution describing nuclear weapons as "the greatest immediate threat to the health and welfare of mankind". The resolution was based on a report by a committee of 10 medical scientists which estimated the likely effect of a nuclear holocaust to be the death of, or injury to, more than 2,200 million people.

International Bank for Reconstruction and Development (IBRD, or World Bank)

Address. 1818 H Street, N.W., Washington D.C. 20433, USA.

Officer. Barber B. Conable, Jr. (pres. & ch. of exec. directors).

Founded. Dec. 27, 1945.

Objects. The International Bank for Reconstruction and Development, or World Bank as it is commonly designated, was set up to assist in the economic development of member nations by making loans to governments and private enterprises for productive purposes. The Bank's main objectives are to facilitate the investment of capital and to promote private foreign investment; to further the balanced growth of international trade; and to maintain equilibrium in the balance of payments of its members.

The Articles of Agreement of the IBRD of Dec. 27, 1945, read as follows:

"**Introductory Article.** The International Bank for Reconstruction and Development is established and shall operate in accordance with the following provisions:

"**Art. 1.** Purposes. The purposes of the Bank are:

"(i) To assist in the reconstruction and development of territories of members by facilitating the investment of capital for productive purposes, including the restoration of economies destroyed or disrupted by war, the reconversion of productive facilities to peacetime needs and the encouragement of the development of productive facilities and resources in less developed countries.

"(ii) To promote private foreign investment by means of guarantees or participations in loans and other investments made by private investors; and, when private capital is not available on reasonable terms, to supplement private investment by providing, on suitable conditions, finance for productive purposes out of its own capital, funds raised by it and its other resources.

"(iii) To promote the long-range balanced growth of international trade and the maintenance of equilibrium in balances of payments by encouraging international investment for the development of the productive resources of members, thereby assisting in raising productivity, the standard of living and conditions of labour in their territories.

"(iv) To arrange the loans made or guaranteed by it in relation to international loans through other channels so that the more useful and urgent projects, large and small alike, will be dealt with first.

"(v) To conduct its operations with due regard to the effect of international investment on business conditions in the territories of members and, in the immediate post-war years, to assist in bringing about a smooth transition from a wartime to a peacetime economy.

"The Bank shall be guided in all its decisions by the purposes set forth above."

The capital of the Bank is derived from the members' subscriptions, the amount of each subscription being based on the country's economic resources. The Bank acquires additional funds by borrowing in world capital markets, and by selling some of its loans to private investors.

The powers of the Bank are vested in the Board of Governors, on which each of the member nations is represented by one Governor. A body of 20 Executive Directors, to which the Board has delegated most of its power, meets monthly. The President of the Bank, who is also the Chairman of Executive Directors, is responsible for conducting the business of the Bank.

In 1955 the IBRD established an Economic Development Institute (EDI) for training government officials with responsibility for development programmes or projects.

The President of the IBRD is ex officio the non-voting chairman of the Administrative Council of an **International Centre for the Settlement of Investment Disputes** (ICSID), created in 1966 under a Convention on the Settlement of Investment Disputes between States and Nationals of Other States.

The IBRD is also chairman of a **Consultative Group for International Agricultural Research** (CGIAR), founded in 1971 under joint sponsorship with the Food and Agriculture Organization (FAO) and the UN Development Programme.

On Jan. 14, 1980, it was announced that the Board of Governors had approved an increase equivalent to $40,000 million in the Bank's authorized capital (as recommended by the Board of Executive Directors on June 28, 1979), this representing roughly a doubling of the Bank's current authorized stock.

A Special Assistance Facility for Sub-Saharan Africa, established by the World Bank in 1984, had by January 1985 received pledges totalling $1,100 million from various donor nations (not including the United States, which had launched its own bilateral aid programme for $500,000,000 over five years for the region).

For the year ended June 30, 1984, the Bank's total income was US$4,654,522,000, and its total expenditure was $4,022,483,000.

On March 13, 1985, the World Bank released details of long-term and short-term debts and use of IMF credits for developing countries (not including high-income oil exporting countries). For 1984 these countries' external liabilities were estimated at $895,000 million (i.e. 6 per cent more than $843,000 million in 1983), and this total was expected to rise in 1985 by 8.4 per cent to $970,000 million. Of these aggregates long-term debts were estimated to have increased from $657,000 million in 1983 to $717,000 million in 1984 (of which about $400,000 million was accounted for by 12 major debtor countries with each having at least $15,000 million in long-term debts at the end of 1983). Short-term debt and use of IMF credit was estimated to have fallen from $185,000 million in 1983 to $178,000 million in 1984, but was expected to rise again to $196,000 million in 1985. The Bank's report also noted that whereas debt rescheduling had initially been conceived as a stopgap response to acute liquidity shortages in the debtor countries, it was now accepted as an important aspect of dealing with interruptions to normal debt servicing and had acquired the longer-term function of improving the debt profile of developing countries.

On April 19, 1985, the World Bank's Interim Committee called for the adoption of measures designed to encourage domestic savings and investment, the promotion of realistic exchange rates and prices, and the encouragement of spontaneous lending by commercial banks and flows from official sources. The committee also urged inter alia that the current trend towards protectionism should be reversed and freer world trade be promoted; that those countries with large fiscal deficits should take action to reduce public-sector reliance on domestic and foreign savings, which might lead to lower interest rates and also foster growth; that measures should be taken to improve the functioning of labour, financial and goods markets through the removal of structural rigidities; and that greater exchange rate stability should be sought.

International Finance Corporation (IFC)

Address. 1818 H Street, N.W., Washington, D.C. 20433, USA.

Officer. Barber B. Conable, Jr. (pres.).

Founded. July 1956.

Objects. Under its Charter the IFC, an affiliate of the World Bank, was to encourage the growth of productive private enterprises, particularly in the less developed areas of the world, by investing in undertakings where sufficient private capital was not available on reasonable terms, by seeking to recruit private capital and to find experienced management, and by generally creating conditions which would stimulate investment. The IFC would be open to all members of the IBRD.

The IFC was to make its investments without governmental guarantee. It was authorized to make both fixed-interest loans and investments of other kinds, but not to invest in capital stock or to assume responsibility for managing the enterprises in which it invested. The IFC was also to serve as a clearing house to bring together investment opportunities, private capital and experienced management. It would seek to revolve its funds by selling its investments to private investors whenever it could appropriately do so on satisfactory terms. It was authorized to raise additional funds by selling its own obligations in the market.

Structure. The share of capital subscribed by the IFC's members is supplemented by a loan provided by the World Bank.

The IFC is served by a President, an Executive Vice-President and three Vice-Presidents. Its Directors are drawn from the Executive Directors of the World Bank.

International Development Association (IDA)

Address. 1818 H Street, Washington, D.C. 20433, USA.

Officer. Ch. of the World Bank (pres. & ch. of exec. directors).

Founded. November 1960.

Objects. In the Charter of the IDA, an affiliate of the World Bank, its aims were defined as being:

"To promote economic development, increase productivity, and thus raise standards of living in the less-developed areas of the world included within the Association's membership, in particular by providing finance to meet their important developmental requirements on terms which are more flexible and bear less heavily on the balance of payments than those of conventional loans, thereby furthering the developmental objectives of the IBRD and supplementing its activities", and the IDA would finance any specific project which would make an important contribution to the development of the area or areas concerned, whether or not the project was revenue-producing or directly productive. In cases where a loan was made other than to a member government the IDA had discretion to decide whether or not a government guarantee was required.

Activities. The greater part of the Association's funds is derived from members' subscriptions, but supplementary resources include transfers from the World Bank. The IDA is operated concurrently with the World Bank by the same officers and staff.

The IDA's resources are periodically replenished by contributions from its affluent member countries. A fifth replenishment, agreed by 26 donor countries in March 1977 for the 1978–81 fiscal years, exceeded $7,637 million. As at June 30, 1979, the IDA's total resources amounted to $19,661 million in current US dollars. A sixth replenishment, agreed to by 33 countries and announced on Jan. 17, 1980, but in force only from Aug. 24, 1981, totalled $12,000 million and provided the IDA with commitment authority for the three years until 1984.

The seventh replenishment, announced on May 24, 1984, totalled $9,000 million over the 1984–87 period. This sum was contributed by 33 donor countries, the largest amounts coming from the USA (27 per cent), Japan (18.7 per cent), the Federal Republic of Germany (11.5 per cent), the United Kingdom (6.7 per cent), France (6.6 per cent), Canada (4.5 per cent), Italy (4.3 per cent), Saudi Arabia (3.5 per cent), the Netherlands (3 per cent), Sweden (2.5 per cent), Australia (1.98 per cent), Belgium (1.68 per cent), Norway (1.27 per cent) and Denmark (1.2 per cent).

International Monetary Fund (IMF)

Address. 700 10th Street, N.W., Washington, D.C. 20431, USA.

Officer. Jacques de Larosière de Champfeu (man. dir.).

Founded. Dec. 27, 1945.

History. The establishment of the IMF and the IBRD [see above] had been agreed upon at a conference held in Bretton Woods (New Hampshire) on July 1–22, 1944, and attended by representatives of 44 countries.

Objects. The Articles of Agreement of the IMF of Dec. 27, 1945, read as follows:

"**Introductory Article.** The International Monetary Fund is established and shall operate in accordance with the following provisions:

"**Art. 1.** Purposes. The purposes of the International Monetary Fund are:

"(i) To promote international monetary co-operation through a permanent institution which provides the machinery for consultation and collaboration on international monetary problems.

"(ii) To facilitate the expansion and balanced growth of international trade, and to contribute thereby to the promotion and maintenance of high levels of employment and real income and to the development of the productive resources of all members as primary objectives of economic policy.

"(iii) To promote exchange stability, to maintain orderly exchange arrangements among members, and to avoid competitive exchange depreciation.

"(iv) To assist in the establishment of a multilateral system of payments in respect of current transactions between members and in the elimination of foreign exchange restrictions which hamper the growth of world trade.

"(v) To give confidence to members by making the Fund's resources available to them under adequate safeguards, thus providing them with opportunity to correct maladjustments in their balance of payments without resorting to measures destructive of national or international prosperity.

"(vi) In accordance with the above, to shorten the duration and lessen the degree of disequilibrium in these international balances of payments of members.

"The Fund shall be guided in all its decisions by the purposes set forth in this article."

Structure. The organs of the Fund are the Board of Governors, on which each member is represented by a Governor and an alternate, and a Board of Executive Directors of 22 members (of whom one each are appointed by the members with the largest quotas—France, the Federal Republic of Germany, Japan, the United Kingdom and the United States, one is appointed by Saudi Arabia, and the remaining 16 are elected, one of these being China). Members may purchase foreign exchange from the Fund to make short-term or medium-term payments. Each member is assigned a quota which determines its subscription, its voting power, and the amount of foreign exchange which it may purchase. In addition to making available foreign exchange the Fund provides financial advice to its members on request.

Under a **General Agreement to Borrow** (GAB), which was agreed to on Jan. 8, 1962, and came into force on Oct. 25, 1962, the "Group of Ten" major industrial countries outside the Communist world (the United States, the Federal Republic of Germany, the United Kingdom, France, Italy, Japan, Canada, the Netherlands, Belgium and Sweden) undertook to "stand ready to lend their currencies to the Fund up to specified amounts when the Fund and these countries consider that supplementary resources are needed to forestall or cope with an impairment of the international monetary system". The Group of Ten was joined by Switzerland, which is not a member of the IMF but became a member of the GAB on Sept. 10, 1984. The GAB was repeatedly renewed, most recently on Dec. 26, 1983 [see below].

The Fund's Articles of Agreement were amended in June 1968 so as to create a new facility of "special drawing rights" (SDRs), which came into force on July 28, 1969. The SDRs would be distributed among participating countries according to their Fund quotas and would entitle the countries concerned to make drawings of currency unconditionally to meet balance-of-payments difficulties. The SDRs would be additional to the Fund's normal stand-by and drawing arrangements, which would continue to be operated subject to certain conditions as before.

The IMF announced on July 28, 1972, the establishment of a Committee of the Board of Governors on Reform of the International Monetary System and Related Issues (the "Committee of Twenty"), representing both developed and developing countries. Its aim would be to "provide a forum in which momentum can be maintained at high policy-making level for all aspects of reform of the international monetary system".

The Committee of Twenty was in June 1974 replaced by an Interim Committee of the Board of Governors, with advisory functions, pending the establishment of a Permanent and Representative Council with decision-making powers on the management and adaptation of the monetary system.

Subsequent to the amendment of the IMF's Articles of Agreement introducing the SDR, a second amendment, which came into force on April 1, 1978, inter alia enabled the IMF to use its holdings of each member country's currency in its operations and transactions and for promoting previously agreed objectives of reducing the role of gold in the international monetary system and making the SDR the principal reserve asset (with the official price of gold being abolished, a free market in gold being created and the IMF selling part of its gold holdings, the profits from such sales being used to set up a Trust Fund for poorer developing countries). Under this amendment the IMF would "exercise firm surveillance over the exchange rate policies" of its members and would "adopt specific principles for the guidance of all its members".

On March 31, 1978, it was decided that the "basket" of currencies, which formed the basis for calculating the value of the SDR, was to be revised every five years.

A new GAB of SDR17,000 million became effective on Dec. 26, 1983.

By March 15, 1984, the total of IMF quotas issued had risen to SDR89,236 million.

On Sept. 23, 1985, it was announced that the list of currencies to be used to calculate the value of the SDR would continue for a further five years from Jan. 1, 1986, consisting of the US dollar (42 per cent), the Deutsche Mark (19 per cent), the Japanese yen (15 per cent, against 13 per cent during the previous five years), the French franc (12 per cent) and the UK pound sterling (12 per cent) (the contribution of the two last-named currencies having stood at 13 per cent in 1981–85).

During 1984–85 the IMF entered into short-term borrowing arrangements with the Bank for International Settlements (BIS), the Saudi Arabian Monetary Agency (SAMA), Japan and the National Bank of Belgium.

IMF FINANCING FACILITIES

In January 1974 the IMF's Board of Governors decided to allow the Bank for International Settlements (BIS, see page 192) to hold IMF SDRs—which would enable IMF members holding SDRs to use them to obtain currency from the BIS, with the assurance that the BIS would use the same amount of SDRs within six months to obtain currency from the participants.

The nature and conditionality of the various financing facilities of the IMF are as follows:

Gold Tranche. Since July 1969, when the Articles of Agreement were amended [see above], gold tranche drawings (i.e. drawings in the first 25 per cent tranche, corresponding to the 25 per cent of quota which must be paid in gold rather than in the member's own currency) have been legally automatic.

First Credit Tranche. All requests for the use of the IMF's resources other than use of the gold tranche are examined by the Fund to determine whether the proposed use would be consistent with the provisions of the Articles of Agreement and with Fund policies. The criteria used by the Fund in determining whether assistance should be given are more liberal when the request is in the first credit tranche than when it is in higher credit tranches. For the first credit tranche, the member's programme is expected to show that it is making reasonable efforts to overcome its difficulties, but "performance criteria" are not set, and the member is not required to make drawings on an instalment basis.

Higher Credit Tranches. Requests for purchases in the higher credit tranches require substantial justification of the member's efforts to overcome its balance-of-payments difficulties, and under current practices purchases are normally made in instalments and under standby arrangements rather than outright. The programme presented for higher credit tranche assistance is usually comprehensive and in a quantified form, and the member's right to draw is made subject to the observance of certain key policy indicators or "performance criteria" described in the programme.

Extended Facility. This facility was set up in 1974 to provide medium-term assistance for up to three years to enable members to overcome structural balance-of-payments adjustments. A detailed statement of policies and measures for the first and subsequent 12-month periods is required, and resources are provided in the form of extended arrangements which include performance criteria and drawing in instalments.

Export Compensatory Facility. This facility, which was created in 1963 and expanded in 1966, is designed to compensate a member for a temporary shortfall in export earnings due to circumstances beyond its control. Use of the facility obliges a member to co-operate with the Fund in an effort to find appropriate solutions for balance-of-payments difficulties arising from the shortfall. The facility was further extended in December 1975.

Buffer Stock Financing Facility. Established in 1969, this facility is designed to assist members in financing contributions to buffer stocks in connexion with international commodity agreements. Members using it are obliged to co-operate with the Fund as under the compensatory facility.

Oil Facility. This facility was introduced in June 1974 and expanded in January 1975 to SDR 5,000 million, being designed to recycle surplus oil and other revenues by assisting members in balance-of-payments difficulties arising from the sharp increase in world oil prices of late 1973 and early 1974. Under the January 1975 arrangements, which also incorporated a special Subsidy Account from which most-seriously-affected (MSA) developing countries might obtain assistance with interest payable under the facility, access was subject to the Fund's assessment of the adequacy of the member's medium-term economic policies and the member's commitment to avoiding restrictive measures, as stipulated in the January 1974 Rome communiqué of the IMF. The final purchases under the 1975 oil facility were approved in March 1976, and the first payments under the Subsidy Account facility were made to 18 MSA countries on July 22, 1976 (SDR 13,800,000, representing a 5 per cent subsidy on qualifying drawings on the 1975 oil facility).

Witteveen Facility. A new "supplementary financing facility" (the "Witteveen facility") came into force on Feb. 23, 1979 (having been approved by the IMF's Executive Board on Aug. 29, 1977). This facility was designed to provide supplementary financing in conjunction with other IMF resources to members facing serious payment imbalances (large in relation to their IMF quota), in particular as a result of the rise of oil prices. The resources made available for this facility totalled SDR 7,754 million (including SDR 1,934 million from the Saudi Arabian Monetary Agency, SDR 1,550 million from the United States, SDR 1,050 million from the Deutsche Bundesbank of the Federal Republic of Germany and SDR 900,000,000 from Japan).

International Civil Aviation Organization (ICAO)

Address. 1000 Sherbrooke St. West, Montreal, P.Q. H3A 2R2, Canada.

Officer. Yves Lambert (sec. gen.).

Founded. April 1947.

History. Agreement on the creation of the ICAO was reached at a conference on civil aviation held in Chicago from Nov. 1 to Dec. 6, 1944. The conference approved a Chicago *Convention on International Civil Aviation* which contains the statutes of the ICAO as well as detailed provisions on the regulation of international civil aviation (with all aircraft involved to be registered by the ICAO). The latter's work covered mainly three areas—air navigation (in particular the safety and regularity of international flights, regulated by ICAO Standards and Recommended Practices adopted in 1949 as an amendment to the Chicago Convention), the economic aspects of air transportation, and international air law.

Structure. The two organs of the ICAO are the Assembly of all the member nations, which meets every three years, and the Council, composed of representatives of the member nations elected by the Assembly, acting as executive organ and in session almost continuously. There are also an Air Navigation Commission, standing committees and regional offices.

Activities. A number of conventions have been adopted within the ICAO framework for dealing with specific problems.

A Warsaw *Convention on the Liability of Air Carriers for Damage caused to Passengers and Cargo*, agreed to in 1929, was repeatedly amended, in particular by the Hague Protocol of 1955, which doubled the maximum amount of compensation payable for such damage. By Dec. 31, 1985, it was in force for 124 countries.

A 1952 Rome *Convention on Damage caused by Aircraft to Third Parties on the Surface*, which set limits on the operator's liability for such damage, replaced an earlier convention and protocol on this subject. By Dec. 31, 1985, it was in force for 28 countries.

A *Convention on Offences and Certain Other Acts Committed on Board Aircraft*, opened for signature in Tokyo on Sept. 14, 1963, came into force on Dec. 4, 1969, after it had been ratified by 12 countries (including the USA, Denmark, Italy, Mexico, Norway, the Philippines, Portugal, Sweden and the United Kingdom). The convention laid down rules on jurisdiction over aircraft, also for extradition purposes, and defined the authority of the aircraft commander. All parties to the convention undertook to take all appropriate measures, in cases of hijacking, to restore control of the aircraft to its lawful commander. By Dec. 31, 1985, it was in force for 121 countries.

A *Convention for the Suppression of Unlawful Seizure of Aircraft*, concluded by a Diplomatic Conference on Air Law under ICAO auspices in The Hague on Dec. 16, 1970, entered into force on Oct. 14, 1971, after it had been ratified by 10 countries (including Bulgaria, Hungary, Israel, Japan, Norway, Sweden, Switzerland and the USA). The convention defined unlawful seizure, or attempt at seizure, of civil aircraft as an offence and committed each contracting state to make the offence punishable by severe penalties. It also defined the jurisdiction of contracting states and laid down procedure against offenders, including their possible extradition to another contracting state. The convention further required offences to be reported to the ICAO; it enjoined the contracting states to submit any disputes to arbitration; and it authorized them to appeal, if necessary, to the International Court of Justice. By Dec. 31, 1985, it was in force for 127 countries.

A *Convention for the Suppression of Unlawful Acts against the Safety of Civil Aviation* was adopted by a Diplomatic Conference on Air Law under ICAO auspices in Montreal on Sept. 23, 1971. The convention defined offences against the safety of civil aircraft and committed contracting states to make such offences punishable by severe penalties; to take all necessary measures to establish its jurisdiction; and to take offenders into custody. Other provisions of the convention were similar to those of the Convention for the Suppression of Unlawful Seizure of Aircraft [see above]. By Dec. 31, 1985, it was in force for 110 countries.

BILATERAL ANTI-HIJACKING AGREEMENTS

USA–Cuba. An agreement between the USA and Cuba on the prevention of aerial and maritime hijacking was signed on Feb. 15, 1973, and entered into force immediately. Its provisions included the following:

(1) Any person who hereafter seizes, removes, appropriates or diverts from its normal route or activities an aircraft or vessel registered under the laws of one of the parties and brings it to the territory of the other party shall be considered to have committed an offence and therefore shall either be returned to the party of registry of the aircraft or vessel, to be tried by the courts of that party in conformity with its laws, or be brought before the courts of the party whose territory he reached for trial in conformity with its laws for the offence punishable by the most severe penalty according to the circumstances and seriousness of the acts to which this article refers.

(2) Each party shall try with a view to severe punishment in accordance with its laws any person who, within its territory, hereafter conspires to promote, or promotes, or prepares, or directs, or forms part of an expedition which from its territory or any other place carries out acts of violence or depredation against aircraft or vessels of any kind or registration coming or going to the territory of the other party or who, within its territory, hereafter conspires to promote, or promotes, or

prepares, or directs, or forms part of an expedition which from its territory or any other place carries out such acts or other similar unlawful acts in the territory of the other party.

Although Dr Castro (then Prime Minister of Cuba) announced in October 1976 that he would abrogate the agreement, its terms have largely continued to be observed by Cuba.

Canada–Cuba. A similar agreement between Canada and Cuba was signed simultaneously with the US–Cuban agreement. This contained undertakings by both governments to prosecute hijackers or to return them to the countries in which the hijackings had been committed.

Cuba–Mexico. An agreement on the prevention of aerial and maritime hijacking was signed by Cuba and Mexico on June 7, 1973. Under its terms the two parties undertook to try or to extradite hijackers other than those acting for political motives.

Cuba–Venezuela. An agreement on the prevention of aerial hijacking was signed by Cuba and Venezuela on July 6, 1973.

Universal Postal Union (UPU)

Address. 3000 Berne 15, Switzerland.

Officer. Advaldo Cardoso Botto de Barros (dir.-gen. of International Bureau).

History. The Universal Postal Union was established in Berne (Switzerland) in 1874, when the first International Postal Convention was signed, creating the General Union of Posts (which changed its name to UPU in 1878). In 1948 it became a UN specialized agency.

The convention was based on five principles:

(1) For the purposes of postal communication all member states formed a single territory. This means that in effect every member state has the full use of postal services throughout the world.
(2) Uniformity of postage rates and units of weight. After World War I this principle of a uniform rate was changed to that of a maximum and a minimum rate.
(3) Classification of mail matter into letters, postcards and "other matter", with detailed rules for their distinction.
(4) The making of definite payments by the country dispatching mail for the use of services of other countries—except the country of destination (it being assumed that the traffic in either direction is approximately equal).
(5) A universal system of registration and compensation.

The organs of the UPU are its Congress, a legislative body meeting every five years; a 40-member Executive Council elected by the Congress and meeting annually; a 35-member Consultative Council for Postal Studies (which in 1969 superseded a Consultative Committee for Postal Studies set up in 1957); and an International Bureau as the UPU's permanent administrative organ, headed by a Director-General.

Postal services other than letter mail are governed by eight special UPU agreements.

Activities. At a congress meeting held between June 18 and July 26, 1984, South Africa was reported to have been expelled from the UPU because of its apartheid policy.

International Telecommunication Union (ITU)

Address. Palais des Nations, 1211 Geneva 10, Switzerland.

Officer. Richard E. Butler (sec. gen.).

Founded. 1865.

History. The International Telecommunication Union originated as the International Telegraph Union, and came into being under its present title in January 1934. The ITU became a UN specialized agency in November 1947.

Objects. The ITU's main functions are to promote international co-operation in telecommunications, and to encourage the development of radio, telegraph and telephone installations with their efficient operation at the lowest possible rates.

Structure. The structure and administrative regulations of the ITU are set out in an International Telecommunications Convention and Optional Protocol concluded on Nov. 6, 1982, and in force since Jan. 1, 1984. (This convention replaced an earlier convention adopted on Oct. 25, 1973.)

The supreme organ of the ITU is the Plenipotentiary Conference of all the members, which meets every five years. Other organs are the 36-member Administrative Council, which meets once a year, and the General Secretariat. Administrative Conferences are held from time to time in accordance with technical requirements.

Other bodies within the framework of the ITU are the International Frequency Registration Board (IFRB); the International Telegraph and Telephone Consultative Committee (CCITT); and the International Radio Consultative Committee (CCIR).

Activities. At a **World Administrative Radio Conference** held by the ITU in Geneva from Sept. 24 to Dec. 6, 1979, agreements were reached on the reallocation of radio frequencies between different types of usage to take effect from Jan. 1, 1982.

World Meteorological Organization (WMO)

Address. Case postale 5, CH–1211, Geneva 20, Switzerland.

Officers. R. L. Kintanar (pres. of exec. committee); Prof. G. O. P. Obasi (sec. gen.).

Founded. April 1951.

History. The World Meteorological Organization became operative as a UN specialized agency in April 1951, although the convention of the organization had been in effect since March 1950.

Objects. The convention defined the purposes of the WMO as being

(i) to facilitate worldwide co-operation in establishing networks of stations for meteorological observations; (ii) to promote the rapid exchange of weather information; (iii) to promote the standardization of meteorological observations and ensure the uniform publication of statistics; (iv) to further the application of meteorology to aviation, shipping, agriculture and other activities; and (v) to encourage research and training in meteorology, and to co-ordinate the international aspects of such training.

Structure. The supreme organ of the WMO is the World Meteorological Congress held every four years and attended by representatives of all the members of the organization. The executive organ is the Executive Committee, whose 29 members include the Presidents of the six Regional Associations. The Executive Committee meets at least once a year. There is also a Secretariat, which is responsible for general administration. The six Regional Associations are for Africa, Asia, South America, North and Central America, the South-West Pacific and Europe.

Activities. The WMO implements a World Weather Watch Programme and has set up a Global Observing System (involving land stations, aircraft, ships and satellites), a Global Data Processing System and a Global Telecommunications System. Special programmes of the WMO include a Tropical Cyclone Programme, a Weather Modification Programme, a Global Atmospheric Research Programme, a Hydrology and Water Resources Programme and a World Climate Programme.

International Maritime Organization (IMO)

Address. 4 Albert Embankment, London SE1 7SR, UK.

Officers. W. A. O'Neill (ch.); C. P. Srivastava (sec. gen.).

Founded. March 17, 1958.

History. The organization was established under the name of Inter-Governmental Maritime Consultative Organization (IMCO) in terms of a Convention which had been approved on March 6, 1948, at an international maritime conference held in Geneva and called by the UN Economic and Social Council (ECOSOC). Following ratification by the required number of 21 governments, the Convention came into force on March 17, 1958, and on Jan. 13, 1959, IMCO became a UN specialized agency. The name International Maritime Organization (IMO) was formally adopted on May 22, 1982.

Objects. The 1948 convention laid down that IMCO was a consultative and advisory body, whose functions were (*a*) to provide machinery for inter-governmental co-operation on regulations and practices affecting shipping engaged in international trade, and to encourage the adoption of the highest practicable standards of safety and efficient navigation; (*b*) to encourage the removal of discriminatory action and unnecessary governmental restrictions on international shipping, though subsidies and other governmental assistance for the development of national shipping and security purposes would not constitute discrimination unless based on measures

(e.g. flag discrimination, arbitrary port charges, etc.) designed to restrict the freedom of shipping of all flags to take part in international trade; (*c*) to consider unfair procedure by shipping concerns which had proved incapable of settlement through the normal processes of international shipping business; (*d*) to consider any matters connected with shipping referred to it by any UN specialized agency; (*e*) to provide for the exchange of information among governments on matters under consideration by the organization.

Structure. IMO's organs are the Assembly, composed of representatives of all the member states as well as various observers, and meeting every two years, and a 16-member Council, as the organization's governing body, meeting about twice a year; the Council has established a Legal Committee, a Facilitation Committee and a Committee on Technical Co-operation (membership of these committees being open to all IMO member states). There are also a Maritime Safety Committee, meeting at least once a year (and open to all IMO members) and a Maritime Environment Committee (set up in 1973), as well as a Secretariat headed by a Secretary-General.

Activities. IMO is the depository for a number of conventions on maritime practices and safety at sea, not all of which have to date entered into force.*

(1) A 1965 *Convention on Facilitation of International Maritime Traffic* came into force in March 1967.

(2) A 1966 *International Convention on Load Lines* came into force in March 1967.

(3) A 1969 *International Convention on Tonnage Measurement of Ships* came into force on July 18, 1982.

(4) A *Convention relating to Civil Liability in the Field of Maritime Carriage of Nuclear Material*, adopted in December 1971, came into force on July 15, 1975 (90 days after the deposit of the fifth instrument of ratification, countries having ratified it being France, Spain, Denmark, Sweden and Norway). By March 1984 the Convention was in force in 11 countries.

(5) A 1972 *Convention on International Regulations for Preventing Collisions at Sea* contained a revised text of 1960 Regulations for Preventing Collisions at Sea and came into force on July 15, 1977. In November 1981 these regulations were revised by the IMCO Assembly, and the resulting amendments came into force on June 1, 1983. By March 1, 1984, there were 87 contracting states.

(6) A 1972 *International Convention for Safe Containers* came into force in September 1977.

(7) An *International Convention for the Safety of Life at Sea* (SOLAS), adopted at an IMCO conference which ended on Nov. 1, 1974, incorporated amendments to a 1960 International Convention on the Safety of Life at Sea, repeatedly amended between 1966 and 1973. The revised convention contained new provisions on fire protection for passenger ships and tankers and on the carriage of grain in bulk. It came into force on May 25, 1980.

The Convention inter alia required ships with 50 or more passengers to be equipped with radio able to transmit messages to at least a radius of 100 miles; ships receiving distress messages to be under obligation to give aid; and ships in distress to be able to demand it; as well as some lifeboats to be radio-equipped. Navigational aids employed under the SOLAS Convention are radio direction finders and radar.

---

* IMCO/IMO conventions relating to maritime pollution are listed in Section 5, see pages 94–95.

A protocol to SOLAS was adopted in February 1978 by a conference on tanker safety and pollution prevention, and it came into force in May 1981.

A first set of amendments (to the 1974 Convention and the 1978 protocol) was adopted by the IMCO Maritime Safety Committee in November 1981 and came into force on Sept. 1, 1984. By March 1 of that year there had been 79 contracting parties to the Convention and 46 to the protocol.

(8) A *Convention on an International Maritime Satellite Organization* (INMARSAT) was signed in London on Sept. 3, 1976, by representatives of 42 states. It provides for the use of satellites for maritime telecommunications, and it came into force in July 1979, when the organization was officially established in London.

(9) A 1972 *International Convention for Safe Containers* (SCS) came into force in September 1977. It had two main objectives: to maintain the existing high level of safety in the handling and transport of containers by providing generally acceptable test procedures and related strength requirements; and to facilitate international transport of containers by providing uniform regulations to all modes of transport (avoiding the proliferation of divergent national standards).

Amendments to the Convention were adopted by the Maritime Safety Committee in July 1983 and came into force on Jan. 1, 1984. These amendments enabled governments to introduce a continuous examination programme, with examinations to take place at least once every 30 months, and with approved containers to be marked ACEP (Approved Continuous Examination Programme) as from Jan. 1, 1987.

By March 1, 1984, the Convention had 38 contracting states.

(10) An *International Convention on Maritime Search and Rescue* (SAR) was adopted at a conference held in Hamburg under IMCO auspices in 1979. It was by June 22, 1984, acceded to by 15 states (the latest being Denmark) and came into force on June 22, 1985.

This Convention was aimed at facilitating co-operation between the various organizations responsible and neighbouring states by establishing a legal international plan for search and rescue. Parties to the Convention undertook to make the necessary arrangements for coast-watching and for rescuing those in distress and for the provision of the necessary maritime safety facilities. Neighbouring states were encouraged to pool services; to use common procedures, co-operation, training and liaison; and to authorize the entry into their territorial waters of search and rescue units from other states.

The Convention also aimed at the establishment of co-ordination centres and sub-centres, and it outlined procedures to be followed in emergency or distress alerts and during search and rescue operations. It regarded ship reporting systems as necessary to shorten the time involved in initiating action and to alert vessels in the vicinity of the incident, to define the search areas and to speed up the provision of medical aid. It called for continued co-operation between IMCO (later IMO) and the International Civil Aviation Organization (ICAO) in search and rescue operations, and for the allocation of search and rescue frequencies (involving the International Telecommunication Union, ITU), the harmonization of weather forecasts and warnings (involving the World Meteorological Organization, WMO), and the promotion of technical co-operation through IMO itself.

The Convention further provided for the establishment of SAR regions, the delimitation of which would not be related to or prejudice the delimitation of any boundary between states.

The Convention came into force on June 22, 1985, having been ratified by 18 countries (Algeria, Argentina, Australia, Barbados, Belgium, Brazil, Canada, Chile, Denmark, France, the German Democratic Republic, the Federal Republic of Germany, the Netherlands, New Zealand, Norway, Sweden, the United Kingdom and the United States).

(11) An *International Treaty on Crew Standards* entered into force in April 1984. It covered nearly two-thirds of the world's fleets.

IMCO, and later the IMO, has issued codes on specific practices relating to both maritime transport and the exploitation of ocean resources.

An *International Maritime Dangerous Goods Code* (IMDG), adopted by IMCO in 1960 and amended annually since then, had by April 1984 been fully adopted by 37 countries, while among the major seafaring nations Japan had adopted it only in part.

New guidelines (replacing a set issued in 1972) for reporting incidents involving dangerous goods in packaged form were issued in 1984.

A *Code for the Construction and Equipment of Mobile Offshore Drilling Units* (MODU), adopted by the IMCO Assembly in 1981, has been applied by Liberia (since Oct. 1, 1980), Japan (since Dec. 25, 1981), China (since Sept. 1, 1982), Yugoslavia (since 1982), Romania (since April 1, 1984) and the United States (since early 1984). Australia, Panama and the United Kingdom were expected to apply it also.

A *Code of Safety for Nuclear Merchant Ships* was adopted by the IMCO Assembly in 1981.

The organization has also issued routeing instructions and designed numerous traffic separation schemes to avoid collisions at sea.

World Intellectual Property Organization (WIPO)

Address. 34 Chemin des Colombettes, 1211 Geneva 20, Switzerland.

Officer. Dr Arpad Bogsch (dir.-gen.).

Founded. 1970.

Membership. 112 states.

History. This organization was established under a convention adopted at a conference held in Stockholm from June 12 to July 14, 1967, by representatives of 132 countries (including the Soviet Union and other Communist states), and it became a UN specialized agency in December 1974.

Structure. WIPO's organs are (i) a General Assembly of representatives of all member states; (ii) a co-ordinating committee with consultative and executive functions; and (iii) a permanent secretariat designated as the International Bureau for Intellectual Property.

Objects. WIPO's tasks include the centralization of the administration of intellectual property— i.e. industrial property (in inventions, trade-marks and designs) and copyright—hitherto carried out by the United International Bureaux for the Protection of Intellectual Property on behalf of the Union of Paris and the Union of the Berne Copyright Convention (see page 4).

Activities. WIPO has since 1973 implemented a Permanent Programme for Development Co-operation related to Industrial Property and since 1976 a Permanent Programme for Development Co-operation related to Copyright and Neighbouring Rights. It has set up a WIPO Permanent Committee on Patent Information and an International Patent Documentation Centre (INPADOC, in Vienna).

It has operated the international registration of trademarks; the international deposit of designs;

the international registration of the appellations of origin; and the recording of international applications for patents received under a *Patent Co-operation Treaty* which was signed in Washington on June 19, 1970, by representatives of 78 countries and which came into force on June 1, 1978. It was amended in 1979 and 1984. Under this treaty an international patent application would be filed at a "receiving office" which would be either a national patent office or the European Patent Office in Munich—see page 41. As at May 15, 1985, this treaty was in force in 39 states (Australia, Austria, Barbados, Belgium, Brazil, Bulgaria, Cameroon, the Central African Republic, Chad, the Congo, Denmark, Finland, France, Gabon, the Federal Republic of Germany, Hungary, Italy, Japan, the Democratic People's Republic of Korea, Liechtenstein, Luxembourg, Madagascar, Malawi, Mali, Mauritania, Monaco, the Netherlands, Norway, Romania, Senegal, the Soviet Union, Sri Lanka, the Sudan, Sweden, Switzerland, Togo, the United Kingdom and the United States).

Other treaties and conventions now under the auspices of WIPO are the following:

Madrid *Agreement for the Repression of False or Deceptive Indications of Source on Goods,* concluded on April 14, 1891; revised in 1911, 1925, 1934, 1958 and 1967. It is open to states parties to the 1883 Paris Convention, and by May 15, 1985, it was accepted by 32 states.

Madrid *Agreement concerning the International Registration of Marks,* also concluded on April 14, 1891; revised in 1900, 1911, 1925, 1934, 1957 and 1967; amended in 1979; adhered to by 27 states (as at May 15, 1985).

Nice *Agreement* of June 15, 1957, *concerning the International Classification of Goods and Services for the Purposes of the Registration of Marks,* revised in 1967 and 1977 and amended in 1979; adhered to by 33 states (as at May 15, 1985).

Lisbon *Agreement* of Oct. 31, 1958, *for the Protection of Appellations of Origin and their International Registration,* revised in 1967 and amended in 1979; adhered to by 16 states (as at May 15, 1985).

Locarno *Agreement* of Oct. 8, 1968, *establishing an International Classification for Industrial Design,* amended in 1979; adhered to by 15 states (as at May 15, 1985).

International Patent Classification Agreement of March 24, 1971, amended in 1979; adhered to by 27 states (as at May 15, 1985).

Trade Mark Registration Treaty of June 12, 1973, amended in 1980; adhered to by five states (as at May 15, 1985).

Budapest *Treaty* of April 28, 1977, *on the International Recognition of the Deposit of Micro-organisms for the Purposes of Patent Procedures,* amended in 1980; adhered to by 15 states (as at May 15, 1985).

The director-general of the WIPO is also secretary-general of the Union for the Protection of New Varieties of Plants set up under an international convention of Dec. 2, 1961, and located at the same address as the WIPO. By May 15, 1985, a total of 17 states were parties to the convention. Its object is to grant protection to the largest number of botanical genera and species in the form of a special title (such as a registration certificate of plant breeders' rights or a plant patent).

International Fund for Agricultural Development (IFAD)

Address. Via del Serafico 107, 00142 Rome, Italy.

Officer. Idriss Jazairy (pres.).

Founded. 1977.

History. This Fund held its constituent meeting on Dec. 13–16, 1977. It was established on a proposal made principally by member states of the Organization of Petroleum Exporting Countries (OPEC) at a World Food Conference in November 1974 and under an agreement which was reached at a Food and Agriculture Organization (FAO) conference held on June 10–13, 1976, and which came into force on Nov. 30, 1977. IFAD was recognized as a UN specialized agency in December 1977 and began its activities on Jan. 2, 1978, with a membership of 114 countries.

Structure. IFAD has a Governing Council on which each member state is represented by a Governor and an Alternative, and an Executive Board of 18 members and 18 alternatives elected by the Government Council in which 600 votes are held by each of three groups of member states—*Group 1:* member states of the Organization for Economic Co-operation and Development (OECD); *Group 2:* OPEC member states; and *Group 3:* recipient developing countries. Within each group the votes are distributed as follows: Group 1—17.5 per cent divided equally among group members and 92.5 per cent divided on the basis of their financial contributions (giving the United States 179 votes, the Federal Republic of Germany and Japan 53 each, the Netherlands 45, and the United Kingdom and Canada 32 each); Group 2—25 per cent divided equally and 75 per cent on the basis of financial contributions; and Group 3—votes distributed equally among member countries. Each group is thus given one-third of the seats on the Board.

Objects. IFAD's objectives are to raise resources for concessional loans or grants for agricultural development projects, principally to the poorest countries with food deficits, in order to increase food production, to provide employment and additional income for poor and landless farmers and to reduce malnutrition. Grants are limited to 12.5 per cent of IFAD's resources committed during any financial year.

Activities. Between 1977 and 1985 the Fund carried out 160 projects in 84 developing countries at a total cost of $8,000 million, of which about $6,000 million was raised by donors other than IFAD or by recipient countries themselves. In January 1986 IFAD finally approved a special programme for Africa south of the Sahara at a cost of $300,000,000.

Finance. The initial capital of the Fund was $1,000 million, contributed by the OECD member states and the OPEC member countries. In

January 1982 the IFAD Council reached agreement on a first replenishment of its resources at about $1,100 million for 1981–83, and this, together with available resources carried over, enabled the Fund to undertake an operational programme costing about $1,350 million in those years. This decision was later carried forward to 1984. After protracted negotiations agreement was reached on Jan. 23, 1986, on a second replenishment (for 1985–87) of at least $460,000,000, of which amount $276,000,000 was to come from OECD member states and $184,000,000 from the OPEC member countries.

United Nations Industrial Development Organization (UNIDO)

Address. P.O. Box 300, 1400 Vienna, Austria.

Officer. Domingo Siazon (dir.-gen.).

Founded. January 1967.

History. UNIDO was established as an organ of the UN General Assembly and subsequently operated principally as an executive agency of the UN Development Programme (UNDP), deriving its finance from that body and other sources within the UN system.

At its second session held in Lima (Peru) in March 1975 a recommendation was adopted to the effect that UNIDO should become a UN specialized agency, and this recommendation was endorsed at a special session of the UN General Assembly in September 1975. A conference of plenipotentiaries of 82 UN member countries held in Vienna from March 19 to April, 8, 1979, adopted by consensus a Constitution and Final Act under which UNIDO would become a UN specialized agency subject to ratification by at least 80 participating states.

Under its new Constitution the objects of UNIDO would be

(i) To encourage and extend, as appropriate, assistance to the developing countries for the development, expansion and modernization of their industries; (ii) to assist the developing countries in the establishment and operation of industries, including agriculture-related as well as basic industries, to achieve the full utilization of locally available natural and human resources and contribute to self-reliance; (iii) to provide a forum and act as an instrument to serve the developing and industrialized countries in their contacts, consultations and negotiations; and (iv) to develop special measures designed to promote co-operation among developing countries and between the developed and developing states.

In 1975 UNIDO had set a target of 25 per cent of world industrial production to be reached by the developing countries by the end of the century. However, at the fourth general conference of UNIDO, held in Vienna on Aug. 2–20, 1984, and attended by delegates from 139 countries, it was found that the rate reached in 1983 was only 11.9 per cent, and that the 25 per cent target for the year 2000 was unlikely to be reached.

UNIDO eventually became a UN specialized agency with effect from Jan. 1, 1986.

Structure. UNIDO's principal organs are, under the new constitution, the General Conference (generally meeting every two years); an Industrial Development Board consisting of 53 members (33 from developing countries, 15 from developed market-economy countries and five from countries with centrally-planned economies); and a Secretariat headed by a Director-General. UNIDO would continue to administer a UN Industrial Development Fund set up under a UN General Assembly resolution of Dec. 22, 1976.

International Atomic Energy Agency (IAEA)

Address. P.O. Box 100, 1400 Vienna, Austria.

Officer. Hans Blix (dir.-gen.).

Founded. July 1957.

Structure. The Agency's principal organs consist of a General Conference of all the member-nations, which meets annually; a 34-member Board of Governors (12 members being designated by the Board itself and 22 elected by the General Conference) meeting about four times a year and acting as the Agency's executive organ; and a Director-General, who heads a secretariat divided into departments for Technical Assistance and Publications, Technical Operations, Research and Isotopes, Safeguards and Inspection, and Administration. There is also a 15-man Scientific Advisory Committee of nuclear experts. A Technical Assistance and Co-operation Fund is financed from voluntary contributions. The Agency submits reports to the General Assembly, to ECOSOC, to the Security Council, and to other UN organs where appropriate, thus differing from the specialized agencies, which report only to ECOSOC.

Membership of the IAEA is open to all members of the United Nations and the specialized agencies.

Objects. In its statute the IAEA was authorized:

(*a*) To encourage and assist research on and the development of atomic energy for peaceful uses throughout the world, and to act as an intermediary between members for the performance of services or the supply of materials, equipment or facilities;

(*b*) to make provision for the materials and services needed for the development of atomic energy for peaceful purposes, with due consideration for the needs of under-developed areas of the world;

(*c*) to foster the exchange of scientific and technical information on the peaceful uses of atomic energy;

(*d*) to encourage the exchange and training of scientists and experts;

(*e*) to establish and administer safeguards designed to ensure that special fissionable and other materials made available by the Agency should not be used in such a way as to further any military purpose;

(*f*) to acquire or establish any facilities, plant and equipment necessary for the execution of its authorized functions.

In carrying out these functions the Agency would:

(1) Conduct its activities in accordance with the purposes and principles of the United Nations to promote peace and international co-operation;

(2) establish control over the use of special fissionable materials received by the Agency to ensure that they would be used only for peaceful purposes;

(3) allocate its resources in such a manner as to secure efficient utilization and the greatest possible general benefit in all areas;

(4) submit reports on its activities annually to the UN General Assembly and, when appropriate, to the Security Council;

(5) submit reports to the Economic and Social Council and other UN organs on matters within their competence;

(6) assist members without any political, economic, military or other conditions incompatible with the provisions of the statute;

(7) show due respect for the sovereign rights of states. (Article 3.)

Activities. The IAEA has established a number of institutions: a laboratory for physics, chemistry and agriculture at Seibersdorf in Austria; a laboratory for medical physics and hydrology in Vienna; a laboratory in Monaco for the study of marine radioactivity and other forms of marine pollution; an International Centre for Theoretical Physics in Trieste; an International Nuclear Information System (INIS); and a Nuclear Data Section.

Safeguards agreements concluded by the IAEA (in addition to those under the 1968 Nuclear Non-Proliferation Treaty—see pages 71–73) include:

(*a*) One signed in Seoul on Oct. 31, 1975, entrusting the IAEA with control over nuclear equipment to be sold to the Republic of Korea by France and Canada so as to guarantee that this equipment would not be used for military purposes;

(*b*) one signed in Vienna on Sept. 6, 1976, with the United Kingdom and Euratom for the submission of UK non-military nuclear installations to IAEA supervision, this agreement coming into force on Aug. 14, 1978;

(*c*) one signed in Vienna on July 27, 1978, with France and Euratom (although France—not a signatory to the Nuclear Non-Proliferation Treaty—reserved the right to decide which of its installations would be open to inspection by the IAEA); and

(*d*) one with Cuba, signed on April 28, 1980.

Under an agreement signed in Vienna on Dec. 1, 1975, and coming into effect immediately, the IAEA and the Commission of the European Communities entered into close co-operation and regular consultation on matters of common interest.

An agreement between the IAEA and France on the application of safeguards to South Africa's first nuclear power plant (at Koeberg) and to materials used for it was signed on Dec. 16, 1976.

In an exchange of letters with France (published in September 1979) Iraq undertook to provide the IAEA with design information of its nuclear facilities and to notify the IAEA of "any unexpected transfer into Iraq of nuclear material required to be subject to safeguards" if the shipment exceeded one effective kilo.

IAEA agreements with Spain are: one on technical assistance by the IAEA to Spain of April 18 and June 10, 1980; another on nuclear control of Feb. 27, 1981; and a third on the application of safeguards relating to four nuclear installations in Spain of April 1, 1981. In addition an agreement on safeguards to be applied in a nuclear co-operation agreement between the Federal Republic of Germany and Spain was concluded on June 9, 1982.

In 1981 a divergence of opinion arose between the industrialized member states, which insisted that the IAEA should continue to concentrate on the promotion and supervision of nuclear safeguards arrangements, and the developing countries, which wished greater emphasis to be placed on the development of nuclear power in the third world.

Under an agreement announced on Feb. 20, 1985, and in force from June 10, 1985, the Soviet Union consented to allowing international inspection of its nuclear reactors. The first such inspections were carried out in August 1985 at a power station and a research reactor.

China announced at the 29th annual IAEA conference held on Sept. 23–27, 1985, that it had "decided to voluntarily offer to place some of its civil nuclear installations under IAEA safeguards at an appropriate time" and would "have consultations with the Agency in this matter". (China had formally become a member of the IAEA with effect from Jan. 1, 1984, and had thereupon obtained a seat on the IAEA Board of Governors.)

The 29th annual conference inter alia reiterated an earlier call on South Africa "to submit immediately all its nuclear installations and facilities to Agency safeguards" and on IAEA member states "to halt all nuclear co-operation with South Africa", in particular "all purchases of uranium from South Africa".

According to figures released by the IAEA in January 1986, there were at the end of 1985 a total of 374 nuclear reactors, with 31 of them having been completed during 1985. During that year, however, construction had begun on only six new reactors. Nuclear power generated in that year was 248,600 megawatts (MW) or 15 per cent of electricity generated worldwide (against 13 per cent in 1984 and 12 per cent in 1983). Detailed figures for 1984 showed the level of reliance on nuclear power in percentages of electricity generated for the leading producer countries as follows:

Country	Number of reactors	Percentage of electricity
France	41 (+23 under construction)	58.7
Belgium	6	50.8
Finland	4	41.0
Sweden	10	40.6
Switzerland	5	36.6
Bulgaria	4	28.6
West Germany	19	23.2
Japan	31	22.9
USA	85	13.5
UK	37 (+5 under construction)	13.5
Soviet Union	46	9.0

The largest producers of nuclear power in absolute terms were the United States (68,867 MW), France (32,993 MW), the Soviet Union (22,997 MW) and Japan (21,751 MW).

Developing countries with nuclear reactors in operation at the end of 1984 were Argentina (two), Brazil (one), India (five), the Republic of Korea (three), Pakistan (one), Taiwan (two) and

Yugoslavia (with plants being under construction in China, Cuba, Mexico and the Philippines).

Nuclear Accident Conventions. A *Convention on Early Notification of a Nuclear Accident*, drawn up under IAEA auspices in the wake of the Soviet nuclear reactor disaster at Chernobyl in April 1986, was signed in Vienna on Sept. 26, 1986, by 51 countries, and entered into force on Oct. 27, 1986, after the required three states (Czechoslovakia, Denmark and Norway) had given immediate notification of their consent to be bound by its provisions. The convention established an early-warning system for all nuclear accidents with potential trans-boundary consequences, requiring governments to report, either directly to affected states or through the IAEA, the accident's time, location, radiation releases and other data essential for assessing the situation. Reporting was mandatory for any nuclear accident involving civilian or military nuclear facilities or materials, with the only exception of nuclear weapons or nuclear weapons testing; however, the five nuclear-weapon states (USA, Soviet Union, France, United Kingdom and China, all of which signed the convention) affirmed their intention of also reporting accidents arising from such activities.

Also on Sept. 26, 1986, the same 51 countries signed a *Convention on Assistance in the Case of a Nuclear Accident or Radiological Emergency*, creating an international framework to facilitate prompt assistance, in particular by requiring states to notify the IAEA of available experts, equipment and other materials, with the IAEA serving as the focal point for such assistance.

Trilateral and Quadrilateral Agreements. Agreements signed between the IAEA, the United States and other countries for the application of safeguards by the IAEA to equipment, devices and materials supplied under the bilateral agreements for co-operation concerning civil uses of atomic energy between the United States and other countries are listed below with the names of these countries and the date of signature (and, in parenthesis, the date of entry into force where different from that of signature).

Argentina, June 13, 1969 (July 25, 1969).
Australia, Sept. 26, 1966; suspended July 10, 1974.
Austria, Aug. 20, 1969 (Jan. 24, 1970); suspended Sept. 21, 1971.
Brazil, March 10, 1967 (Oct. 31, 1968); amended July 27, 1972.
Colombia, Dec. 9, 1970; extended March 28, 1977.
India, Jan. 27, 1971.
Iran, March 4, 1969 (Aug. 20, 1969); suspended June 19, 1973.
Israel, April 4, 1975; extended April 7, 1977.
Japan, July 10, 1968.
Republic of Korea, Jan. 5, 1968; amended Nov. 30, 1972.
Philippines, July 15, 1968 (July 19, 1968); suspended Feb. 21, 1973.
Portugal, July 11, 1969 (July 19, 1969); suspended Sept. 23, 1980.
South Africa, July 26, 1967; amended June 20, 1974.
Spain, Dec. 9, 1966; amended June 28, 1974.
Sweden, March 1, 1972; suspended April 14, 1975.

Switzerland, Feb. 28, 1972; suspended Sept. 23, 1980.
Taiwan, Dec. 6, 1971.
Turkey, Sept. 30, 1968 (June 5, 1969); extended June 30, 1981.
Venezuela, March 27, 1968; extended Feb. 8, 1981; suspended Sept. 27, 1983.

Agreements signed between the IAEA, the United States and other countries for the application of safeguards pursuant to the Nuclear Non-Proliferation Treaty of July 1, 1968, are similarly listed for these countries as follows:—

Australia, July 10, 1974.
Austria, Sept. 21, 1971 (July 23, 1972).
Denmark, March 1, 1972.
Greece, March 1, 1972.
Iran, June 19, 1973 (May 15, 1974).
Norway, Sept. 25, 1973.
Philippines, Feb. 21, 1973 (Oct. 16, 1974).
Portugal, Sept. 23, 1980.
Sweden, April 14, 1975 (May 6, 1975).
Switzerland, Sept. 23, 1980.
Thailand, June 27, 1974.
Venezuela, Sept. 27, 1983.

Agreements between the IAEA, the United States and other countries for the supply of nuclear material or equipment have been concluded with the following countries:

Argentina–Peru, May 9, 1978; with exchanges of notes on March 31, April 7, May 10 and 22, 1978.
Canada–Jamaica, Jan. 25, 1984.
Indonesia, Dec. 7, 1979.
Malaysia, Sept. 22, 1980; amended June 12 and July 22, 1981.
Mexico, Dec. 18, 1963; Oct. 4, 1972; Feb. 12, 1974; June 14, 1974; March 6, 1980.
Morocco, Dec. 2, 1983.
Yugoslavia, June 14, 1974; Jan. 16, 1980 (July 14, 1980); Feb. 26, 1980; Dec. 14, 15 and 20, 1982 (Dec. 20, 1982); Feb. 23, 1983.

Similar supply agreements were concluded in the 1960s and early 1970s with Argentina, Chile, Finland, Greece, India, Iran, Iraq, Norway, Pakistan, Philippines, Romania, Spain, Turkey, Venezuela and Zaïre.

Finance. The IAEA's regular budget for 1986, as approved in September 1985, was US$98,600,000 (against some $95,000,000 for 1985) and the target for the Technical Assistance and Co-operation Fund was fixed at $31,000,000.

General Agreement on Tariffs and Trade (GATT)

Address. Centre William Rappard, Rue de Lausanne 154, CH-1211 Geneva 21, Switzerland.

Officer. Arthur Dunkel (dir.-gen.).

Founded. 1948.

History. The General Agreement on Tariffs and Trade is a multilateral trade agreement concluded in October 1947 at a 23-nation UN Conference on Trade and Employment, held in Geneva from April 10 to Oct. 30, 1947. It co-operates with the United Nations at secretariat and intergovernmental levels but does not have the formal status of a UN specialized agency.

One of the main purposes of the 1947 conference was to draft a charter for a proposed

International Trade Organization (ITO). The provisions of GATT were intended to be superseded by the ITO Charter as soon as the latter should come into force. Although a final text of the ITO Charter was approved at the subsequent Havana Conference on Trade and Employment (Nov. 21, 1947–March 24, 1948), it has never been ratified. Thus, GATT—originally intended as an interim institution—has developed into a permanent international instrument for the regulation of world trading practices.

Objects. The aims of GATT are to raise standards of living, to ensure full employment, to develop resources, to expand the production and exchange of goods, and to promote economic development.

The GATT, published on Nov. 18, 1974, consisted of three parts. In the first part the principle of most-favoured-nation treatment (as set out in the ITO Charter) was specified as requiring that "with respect to customs duties and charges of any kind . . . any advantage, favour, privilege or immunity granted by any member to any product originating in or destined for any other country shall be accorded immediately and unconditionally to the like product originating in or destined for all other member countries respectively". In the second part rules were laid down inter alia for the equal treatment of imported and home-produced goods, the possible imposition of anti-dumping duties by importing countries, conditions for the imposition of import restrictions, the notification to other signatory countries of subsidies granted by any country, and non-discrimination by state enterprises. The third part allowed the formation of customs unions provided that no increase of duties was involved, and the modification of concessions by negotiation.

Tariff concessions negotiated at the same time were listed in 20 schedules to the Agreement.

In a fourth part of the Agreement, which was approved on Feb. 8, 1965, and came into force on June 27 of that year (for those contracting parties which had accepted it), rules were laid down for policies in relation to trade and economic development of developing countries with the object of promoting "rapid and sustained expansion" of these countries' export earnings and ensuring "stable, equitable and remunerative prices" for these exports. At the same time a Trade and Development Committee was established to administer the provisions of the fourth part of the Agreement and to make recommendations in connexion with them.

Structure. The members of GATT (contracting parties and other members) meet in session once a year. Matters arising between sessions are dealt with by a Council of Representatives, and there is also a Secretariat, headed by a Director-General and composed of trade specialists and administrative staff.

Conferences on the reduction and stabilization of tariffs are held at irregular intervals, as a result of which tariffs have been reduced on goods accounting for about half the world's trade.

An International Trade Centre, to provide information and advice to developing countries, was established in Geneva in May 1964.

Activities. The principal achievements of GATT include world-wide tariff reductions agreed upon:

(*a*) In the "Dillon Round" of 1960–62, under which many customs tariffs were reduced by an average of 20 per cent between the USA and the EEC, between the USA and Britain, between Britain and the EEC, and between the USA and

other countries, with all bilateral concessions being granted to all other GATT member countries under the "most-favoured-nation" principle;

(*b*) in the "Kennedy Round" of 1963–67, in which the "linear approach" for tariff reductions "across the board", instead of item-by-item bargaining for different commodities, was applied for the first time; this approach eventually led to a reduction of tariffs for industrial goods, carried out in agreed stages, averaging over 30 per cent on trade between the participating countries, and reaching up to 50 per cent in many cases; and

(*c*) in the "Tokyo Round" of 1973–79, which resulted, in April 1979, in agreements with binding force as from Jan. 1, 1980, for those participants which had accepted them (while others might accept them until June 30, 1980); these agreements covered tariff reductions to be implemented generally in equal annual rate reductions between Jan. 1, 1980, and Jan. 1, 1987, in particular by the industrialized countries, and according to the GATT Secretariat the level of industrial tariffs was on average to be reduced by about one-third more, on which agreements were signed in Geneva on Dec. 17, 1979. (In May 1984 the member governments of the Organization for Economic Co-operation and Development—OECD—decided to advance to early 1985 all tariff cuts scheduled for 1986.)

A ministerial meeting was held in Geneva in November 1982 as a result of a proposal approved by the GATT contracting parties and made in 1981 by a Consultative Group of 18 (consisting of high-level representatives with responsibility for trade policies in their countries, established in 1975 and meeting about three times a year). The Geneva meeting issued a ministerial declaration designed to bridge differences which had arisen, in particular between the United States and the European Community.

While reaffirming the contracting members' commitment to the GATT, the declaration also contained specific undertakings by these members, inter alia

"to abstain from restrictive trade measures, for reasons of a non-economic character not consistent [with the GATT]"; "to ensure special treatment for the least developed countries, in the context of differential and more favourable treatment . . . in order to ameliorate the grave economic situation of these countries"; and "to bring agriculture more fully into the multilateral trading system by improving the effectiveness of GATT rules, provisions and disciplines" by means of a "major two-year work programme".

In a report issued on Sept. 26, 1985, on International Trade 1984–85 the GATT found that the unit volume of world trade, which had grown by 9 per cent in the previous year, was increasing by only about 3 per cent in the current year, and that as a result of the decline of the US dollar the monetary value of world trade was likely to show an overall decline in 1985. The dollar value of exports from non-oil developing countries was stated to have fallen by 13 per cent below levels a year earlier.

The report also stated that market-sharing arrangements, such as those applied to third-world textiles, Japanese automobiles and consumer electronics, were encumbering the international trading system, and that commodity prices (apart from oil) had declined more than anticipated, which had reduced the importing capacities of many producers of primary goods.

The report found that countries were taking more measures which contravened their commitments under the GATT, especially by entering into agreements aimed at restricting competition by sharing markets—measures which were not inducive to curbing inflation and unemployment. The report therefore called for a new round of trade negotiations aiming at opening up markets and restoring the authority of GATT rules.

Moreover, the report found that the distinction between developing and developed countries among leading exporters of manufactures was becoming blurred, as by 1984, for instance, the Republic of Korea and Taiwan had overtaken Sweden and Switzerland; six new countries—China, Hong Kong, the Republic of Korea, Mexico, Singapore and Taiwan—had displaced Australia, Czechoslovakia, Denmark, the German Democratic Republic and Poland in the top 20 exporting countries; and trans-Pacific trade (exports and imports between all the Americas on the one hand and Japan and 12 other Pacific countries on the other hand) surpassed in value trans-Atlantic trade (between the Americas on the one and Western Europe and Africa on the other hand).

Major UN Conventions and Declarations

The UN General Assembly has adopted a number of conventions and declarations, among them those detailed below.

Convention on the Prevention and Punishment of the Crime of Genocide

This convention, adopted on Dec. 9, 1948, provided inter alia as follows:

"**Art. 1.** The Contracting Parties confirm that genocide, whether committed in time of peace or of war, is a crime under international law which they undertake to prevent and punish.

Art. 2. Genocide means any of the following acts committed with intent to destroy, in whole or part, a national, ethnical, racial or religious group:
"(*a*) Killing members of the group;
"(*b*) causing serious bodily or mental harm to members of the group;
"(*c*) deliberately inflicting on the group conditions of life calculated to bring about its physical destruction in whole or part;
"(*d*) imposing measures intended to prevent births within the group;
"(*e*) forcibly transferring children of the group to another group.

"**Art. 3.** The following acts shall be punishable:
"(*a*) Genocide;
"(*b*) conspiracy to commit genocide;
"(*c*) direct and public incitement to commit genocide,
"(*d*) attempt to commit genocide;
"(*e*) complicity in genocide.

"**Art. 4.** Persons committing genocide or any of the other acts enumerated in Art. 3 shall be punished, whether they are constitutionally responsible rulers, public officials or private individuals.

"**Art. 5.** The Contracting Parties undertake to enact, in accordance with their respective constitutions, the necessary legislation to give effect to the provisions of the convention, and, in particular, to provide effective penalties for persons guilty of genocide or any of the other acts enumerated in Art. 3.

"**Art. 6.** Persons charged with genocide or any of the other acts enumerated in Art. 3 shall be tried by a competent tribunal of the state in the territory of which the act was committed, or by such international penal tribunal as may have jurisdiction with respect to such Contracting Parties as shall have accepted the jurisdiction of such tribunal.

"**Art. 7.** Genocide and the other acts enumerated in Art. 3 shall not be considered as political crimes for the purpose of extradition. The Contracting Parties pledge themselves in such cases to grant extradition in accordance with their laws and treaties in force.

"**Art. 8.** Any Contracting Party may call upon the competent organs of the United Nations to take such action under the UN Charter as they consider appropriate for the prevention and suppression of acts of genocide or any of the other acts enumerated in Art. 3.

"**Art. 9.** Disputes between the Contracting Parties relating to the interpretation, application, or fulfilment of the convention, including those relating to the responsibility of a state for genocide or any of the other acts enumerated in Art. 3, shall be submitted to the International Court of Justice at the request of any of the parties to the dispute."

The convention came into force on Jan. 12, 1951. By Dec. 31, 1985, it was in force for 94 states. The United States Senate did not approve it until Feb. 20, 1986 (casting 83 votes in favour to 11 against).

Supplementary Convention on the Abolition of Slavery, the Slave Trade, and Institutions and Practices Similar to Slavery

A United Nations convention on slavery, based on the 1951 report of a four-member committee appointed by the Secretary-General in 1949 at the request of the Economic and Social Council, was designed to supplement a League of Nations convention of 1926. (This convention on the abolition of slavery and the slave trade was amended in 1953 and was by Dec. 31, 1979, in force in 93 countries.) The Supplementary Convention on the Abolition of Slavery, the Slave Trade, and Institutions and Practices Similar to Slavery was adopted and opened for signature on Sept. 9, 1956, and has been in force since April 30, 1957. By the end of December 1985, 111 nations had ratified or acceded to it.

The UN convention differs from the earlier one in dealing with a number of institutions and practices similar to slavery in their effect. The institutions and practices outlawed by the 1956 convention are debt bondage, serfdom, marriage by payment or inheritance, and the exploitation of child labour.

The convention advocates the prescribing of minimum ages of marriage and the registration of marriages. It also provides for the punishment of persons participating in the slave trade and of persons guilty of enslaving another person or of inducing another person to give himself or a dependent into slavery. Provision is made for the co-operation of states parties to the convention to give effect to its provisions, and for the communication to the UN Secretary-General of laws, regulations and administrative measures enacted or put into effect to implement the provisions of the convention. The convention applies to all non-self-governing, trust, colonial and other non-metropolitan territories for the international relations of which any state party is responsible.

International Convention on the Elimination of All Forms of Racial Discrimination

On Dec. 21, 1965, the UN General Assembly adopted by 106 votes to none (with Argentina abstaining) a 25-article convention on the elimination of all forms of racial discrimination. The convention entered into force on Jan. 4, 1969. By Dec. 31, 1985, it was in force for 121 countries.

The convention defined (in Article 1) racial discrimination as "any distinction, exclusion, restriction, or preference based on race, colour, descent, or national or ethnic origin which has the purpose or effect of nullifying or impairing the recognition, enjoyment, or exercise, on an equal footing, of human rights and fundamental freedoms in the political, economic, social, cultural or any other field of public life".

In order to "eradicate all incitement to, or acts of, such discrimination" the states parties to the convention decided (in Article 4) to take the following measures:

(i) Declare as an offence punishable by law "all dissemination of ideas based on racial superiority or hatred, or incitement to racial discrimination, as well as all acts of violence or incitement to such acts against any group of persons of another colour or ethnic origin".

(ii) Declare illegal and prohibit "organizations, and also all propaganda activities, which promote and incite racial discrimination". Participation in such organizations and activities would constitute an offence punishable by law.

(iii) Not permit public authorities or public institutions, national or local, to promote or incite racial discrimination.

States parties to the convention were to guarantee (under Article 5) the following rights:

(i) The right to equal treatment before all organs administering justice.

(ii) The right to security of person and protection by the state against violence or bodily harm, "whether inflicted by government officials or by any individual, group, or institution".

(iii) Political rights, including the right to vote and to stand for election on the basis of universal and equal suffrage; to take part in the government and in the conduct of public affairs at any level; and to have equal access to the public service.

(iv) Other civil rights, including the right to freedom of movement and residence within the borders of the state; to leave the country and return thereto; to nationality; to marriage and choice of spouse; to own property; to inherit; to freedom of thought, conscience and religion; and to freedom of peaceful assembly and association.

(v) Economic, social and cultural rights, including the right to work; to free choice of employment; to just and favourable conditions of work; to protection against unemployment; to equal pay for equal work; to just and favourable remuneration; to form and join trade unions; to housing; to public health, medical care and social security; to education and training; and to equal participation in cultural activities.

(vi) The right of access to any place or service intended for use by the general public, e.g. transport, hotels, restaurants, cafés, theatres, parks.

The convention also provided (in Article 8) for the establishment of a committee on the elimination of racial discrimination "consisting of 18 experts of high moral standing and acknowledged impartiality" who would (as laid down in Article 9) consider reports submitted to the UN Secretary-General by states parties to the convention on measures which they had taken to give effect to the provisions of the convention. The Committee would have powers to deal with complaints by states parties to the convention and to appoint a conciliation commission to try to settle any disputes (Articles 12–13).

Convention on the Non-Applicability of Statutory Limitations to War Crimes and Crimes against Humanity

A *Convention on the Non-Applicability of Statutory Limitations to War Crimes and Crimes against Humanity*, drafted in the Third (Social, Humanitarian and Cultural) Committee of the UN General Assembly, was adopted by the Assembly on Nov. 26, 1968, by 58 votes to seven (Australia, El Salvador, Honduras, Portugal, South Africa, United Kingdom and United States), with 36 abstentions.

In its preamble, the convention affirmed "the principle that there is no period of limitation for war crimes and crimes against humanity", and in one of its articles the states parties to the convention undertook "to ensure that statutory or other limitations shall not apply to the prosecution and punishment" of such crimes.

The convention entered into force on Nov. 11, 1970, after ratification by 10 countries (all of them communist states).

Declaration of Principles of International Law concerning Friendly Relations and Co-operation among States

The General Assembly adopted without a vote, at its 25th regular session on Oct. 24, 1970, a *Declaration of Principles of International Law concerning Friendly Relations and Co-operation among States in Accordance with the Charter of the United Nations*.

In this declaration the Assembly solemnly proclaimed the following principles: (i) The principle that states shall refrain in their international relations from the threat or use of force against the territorial integrity or political independence of any state, or in any other manner inconsistent with the purposes of the United Nations; (ii) the principle that states shall settle their international disputes by peaceful means in such a manner that international peace and security and justice are not endangered; (iii) the principle concerning the duty not to intervene in matters within the domestic jurisdiction of any state, in accordance with the Charter; (iv) the duty of states to co-operate with one another in accordance with the Charter; (v) the principle of equal rights and self-determination of peoples; (vi) the principle of sovereign equality of states; and (vii) the principle that states shall fulfil in good faith the obligations assumed by them in accordance with the Charter (laying down also that where obligations arising out of international agreements are in conflict with the obligations of UN members under the UN Charter, the obligations under the Charter shall prevail).

It was also stated in the declaration that in their interpretation and application the above principles were interrelated and that each principle should be construed in the context of the other principles, and an appeal was made for strict observance of these "basic principles of international law".

Protection and Punishment of Crimes against Internationally Protected Persons

A *Convention on the Protection and Punishment of Crimes against Internationally Protected Persons including Diplomatic Agents* was adopted on Dec. 14, 1973, and entered into force on Feb. 20, 1977. Parties to the convention undertook to make the murder and kidnapping of heads of state, diplomatic agents and other internationally protected persons a crime under their law. By Dec. 31, 1985, a total of 61 countries were parties to the convention.

Charter of Economic Rights and Duties of States

The UN General Assembly also adopted, on Dec. 12, 1974 (against the votes of Belgium, Britain, Denmark, the Federal Republic of Germany and the United States) a *Charter of the Economic Rights and Duties of States* (based on a proposal made by Mexico and approved by the UN Conference on Trade and Development—UNCTAD—in 1972).

This Charter read as follows:

Chapter I

Fundamentals of International Economic Relations

"Economic as well as political and other relations among states shall be governed, inter alia, by the following principles:

"(*a*) Sovereignty, territorial integrity and political independence of states;

"(*b*) sovereign equality of all states;

"(*c*) non-aggression;

"(*d*) non-intervention;

"(*e*) mutual and equitable benefit;

"(*f*) peaceful coexistence;

"(*g*) equal rights and self-determination of peoples;

"(*h*) peaceful settlement of disputes;

"(*i*) remedying of injustices which have been brought about by force and which deprive a nation of the natural means necessary for its normal development;

"(*j*) fulfilment in good faith of international obligations;

"(*k*) respect for human rights and fundamental freedoms;

"(*l*) no attempt to seek hegemony and spheres of influence;

"(*m*) promotion of international social justice;

"(*n*) international co-operation for development;

"(*o*) free access to and from the sea by land-locked countries within the framework of the above principles.

Chapter II

Economic Rights and Duties of States

"**Art. 1.** Every state has the sovereign and inalienable right to choose its economic system as well as its political, social and cultural systems in accordance with the will of its people, without outside interference, coercion or threat in any form whatsoever.

"**Art. 2.** (1) Every state has and shall freely exercise full permanent sovereignty, including possession, use and disposal, over all its wealth, natural resources and economic activities.

"(2) Each state has the right:

"(*a*) To regulate and exercise authority over foreign investment within its national jurisdiction in accordance with its laws and regulations and in conformity with its national objectives and priorities. No state shall be compelled to grant preferential treatment to foreign investment;

"(*b*) to regulate and supervise the activities of transnational corporations within its national jurisdiction and take measures to ensure that such activities comply with its laws, rules and regulations and conform with its economic and social policies.

Transnational corporations shall not intervene in the internal affairs of a host state. Every state should, with full regard for its sovereign rights, co-operate with other states in the exercise of the right set forth in this subparagraph;

"(*c*) to nationalize, expropriate or transfer ownership of foreign property, in which case appropriate compensation should be paid by the state adopting such measures, taking into account its relevant laws and regulations and all circumstances that the state considers pertinent. In any case where the question of compensation gives rise to a controversy, it shall be settled under the domestic law of the nationalizing state and by its tribunals, unless it is freely and mutually agreed by all states concerned that other peaceful means be sought on the basis of the sovereign equality of states and in accordance with the principle of the choice of means.

"**Art. 3.** In the exploitation of natural resources shared by two or more countries, each state must co-operate on the basis of a system of information and prior consultations in order to achieve optimum use of such resources without causing damage to the legitimate interest of others.

"**Art. 4.** Every state has the right to engage in international trade and other forms of economic co-operation irrespective of any differences in political, economic and social systems. No state shall be subjected to discrimination of any kind based solely on such differences. In the pursuit of international trade and other forms of economic co-operation, every state is free to choose the forms of organization of its foreign economic relations and to enter into bilateral and multilateral arrangements consistent with its international obligations and with the needs of international economic co-operation.

"**Art. 5.** All states have the right to associate in organizations of primary commodity producers in order to develop their national economies to achieve stable financing for their development, and in pursuance of their aims assisting in the promotion of sustained growth of the world economy, in particular accelerating the development of developing countries. Correspondingly all states have the duty to respect that right by refraining from applying economic and political measures that would limit it.

"**Art. 6.** It is the duty of states to contribute to the development of international trade of goods particularly by means of arrangements and by the conclusion of long-term multilateral commodity agreements, where appropriate, and taking into account the interests of producers and consumers. All states share the responsibility to promote the regular flow and access of all commercial goods traded at stable, remunerative and equitable prices, thus contributing to the equitable development of the world economy, taking into account, in particular, the interests of developing countries.

"**Art. 7.** Every state has the primary responsibility to promote the economic, social and cultural development of its people. To this end, each state has the right and the responsibility to choose its means and goals of development, fully to mobilize and use its resources, to implement progressive economic and social reforms and to ensure the full participation of its people in the process and benefits of development. All states have the duty, individually and collectively, to co-operate in order to eliminate obstacles that hinder such mobilization and use.

"**Art. 8.** States should co-operate in facilitating more rational and equitable international economic relations and in encouraging structural changes in the context of a balanced world economy in harmony with the needs and interests of all countries, especially developing countries, and should take appropriate measures to this end.

"**Art. 9.** All states have the responsibility to co-operate in the economic, social, cultural, scientific and technological fields for the promotion of economic and social progress throughout the world, especially that of the developing countries.

"**Art. 10.** All states are judicially equal and, as equal members of the international community, have the right to participate fully and effectively in the international decision-making process in the solution of world economic, financial and monetary problems, inter alia, through the appropriate international organizations in accordance with their existing and evolving rules, and to share equitably in the benefits resulting therefrom.

"**Art. 11.** All states should co-operate to strengthen and continuously improve the efficiency of international organizations in implementing measures to stimulate the general economic progress of all countries, particularly of developing countries, and therefore should co-operate to adapt them, when appropriate, to the changing needs of international economic co-operation.

"**Art. 12.** (1) States have the right, in agreement with the parties concerned, to participate in sub-regional, regional and interregional co-operation in the pursuit of their economic and social development. All states engaged in such co-operation have the duty to ensure that the policies of those groupings to which they belong correspond to the provisions of the Charter and are outward-looking, consistent with their international obligations and with the needs of international economic co-operation, and have full regard for the legitimate interests of third countries, especially developing countries.

"(2) In the case of groupings to which the states concerned have transferred or may transfer certain competences as regards matters that come within the scope of this Charter, its provisions shall also apply to those groupings, in regard to such matters, consistent with the responsibilities of such states as members of such groupings. Those states shall co-operate in the observance by the groupings of the provisions of this Charter.

"**Art. 13.** (1) Every state has the right to benefit from the advances and developments in science and technology for the acceleration of its economic and social development.

"(2) All states should promote international scientific and technological co-operation and the transfer of technology with proper regard for all legitimate interests including, inter alia, the rights and duties of holders, suppliers and recipients of technology, In particular, all states should facilitate: the access of developing countries to the achievements of modern science and technology, the transfer of technology and the creation of indigenous technology for the benefit of the developing countries in forms and in accordance with procedures which are suited to their economies and their needs.

"(3) Accordingly, developed countries should co-operate with the developing countries in the establishment, strengthening and development of their scientific and technological infrastructures and their scientific research and technological activities so as to help to expand and transform the economies of developing countries.

"(4) All states should co-operate in exploring with a view to evolving further internationally accepted guidelines or regulations for the transfer of technology taking fully into account the interests of developing countries.

"**Art. 14.** Every state has the duty to co-operate in promoting a steady and increasing expansion and liberalization of world trade and an improvement in the welfare and living standards of all peoples, in particular those of developing countries. Accordingly, all states should co-operate, inter alia, towards the progressive dismantling of obstacles to trade and the improvement of the international framework for the conduct of world trade and, to those ends, co-ordinated efforts shall be made to solve in an equitable way the trade problems of all countries, taking into account the specific trade problems of the developing countries. In this connexion, states shall take measures aimed at securing additional benefits for the international trade of developing countries so as to achieve a substantial increase in their foreign exchange earnings, the diversification of their exports, the acceleration of the rate of growth of their trade, taking into account their development needs, an improvement in the possibilities for these countries to participate in the expansion of world trade and a balance more favourable to developing countries in the sharing of the

advantages resulting from this expansion, through, in the largest possible measure, a substantial improvement in the conditions of access for the products of interest to the developing countries and, wherever appropriate, measures designed to attain stable, equitable and remunerative prices for primary products.

"**Art. 15.** All states have the duty to promote the achievement of general and complete disarmament under effective international control and to utilize the resources freed by effective disarmament measures for the economic and social development of countries, allocating a substantial portion of such resources as additional means for the development needs of developing countries.

"**Art. 16.** (1) It is the right and duty of all states, individually and collectively, to eliminate colonialism, apartheid, racial discrimination, neo-colonialism and all forms of foreign aggression, occupation and domination, and the economic and social consequences thereof, as a prerequisite for development. States which practise such coercive policies are economically responsible to the countries, territories and peoples affected for the restitution and full compensation for the exploitation and depletion of, and damages to, the natural and all other resources of those countries, territories and peoples. It is the duty of all states to extend assistance to them.

"(2) No state has the right to promote or encourage investments that may constitute an obstacle to the liberation of a territory occupied by force.

"**Art. 17.** International co-operation for development is the shared goal and common duty of all states. Every state should co-operate with the efforts of developing countries to accelerate their economic and social development by providing favourable external conditions and by extending active assistance to them, consistent with their development needs and objectives, with strict respect for the sovereign equality of states and free of any conditions derogating from their sovereignty.

"**Art. 18.** Developed countries should extend, improve and enlarge the system of generalized, non-reciprocal and non-discriminatory tariff preferences to the developing countries consistent with the relevant agreed conclusions and relevant decisions as adopted on this subject, in the framework of the competent international organizations. Developed countries should also give serious consideration to the adoption of other differential measures, in areas where this is feasible and appropriate and in ways which will provide special and more favourable treatment, in order to meet trade and development needs of the developing countries. In the conduct of international economic relations the developed countries should endeavour to avoid measures having a negative effect on the development of the national economies of the developing countries, as promoted by generalized tariff preferences and other generally agreed differential measures in their favour.

"**Art. 19.** With a view to accelerating the economic growth of developing countries and bridging the economic gap between developed and developing countries, developed countries should grant generalized preferential, non-reciprocal and non-discriminatory treatment to developing countries in those fields of international economic co-operation where it may be feasible.

"**Art. 20.** Developing countries should, in their efforts to increase their overall trade, give due attention to the possibility of expanding their trade with socialist countries, by granting to these countries conditions for trade not inferior to those granted normally to the developed market economy countries.

"**Art. 21.** Developing countries should endeavour to promote the expansion of their mutual trade and to this end may, in accordance with the existing and evolving provisions and procedures of international agreements where applicable, grant trade preferences to other developing countries without being obliged to extend such preferences to developed countries, provided these arrangements do not constitute an impediment to general trade liberalization and expansion.

"**Art. 22.** (1) All states should respond to the generally recognized or mutually agreed development needs and objectives of developing countries by promoting increased net flows of real resources to the developing countries from all sources, taking into account any obligations and commitments undertaken by the states concerned, in order to reinforce the efforts of developing countries to accelerate their economic and social development.

"(2) In this context, consistent with the aims and objectives mentioned above and taking into account any obligations and commitments undertaken in this regard, it should be their endeavour to increase the net amount of financial flows from official sources to developing countries and to improve the terms and conditions.

"(3) The flow of development assistance resources should include economic and technical assistance.

"**Art. 23.** To enhance the effective mobilization of their own resources, the developing countries should strengthen their economic co-operation and expand their mutual trade so as to accelerate their economic and social development. All countries, especially developed countries, individually as well as through the competent international organizations of which they are members, should provide appropriate and effective support and co-operation.

"**Art. 24.** All states have the duty to conduct their mutual economic relations in a manner which takes into account the interests of other countries. In particular, all states should avoid prejudicing the interests of developing countries.

"**Art. 25.** In furtherance of world economic development, the international community, especially its developed members, shall pay special attention to the particular needs and problems of the least developed among the developing countries, of land-locked developing countries and also island developing countries, with a view to helping them to overcome their particular difficulties and thus contribute to their economic and social development.

"**Art. 26.** All states have the duty to coexist in tolerance and live together in peace, irrespective of differences in political, economic, social and cultural systems, and to facilitate trade between states having different economic and social systems. International trade should be conducted without prejudice to generalized non-discriminatory and non-reciprocal preferences in favour of developing countries, on the basis of mutual advantage, equitable benefits and the exchange of most-favoured-nation treatment.

"**Art. 27.** (1) Every state has the right to fully enjoy the benefits of world invisible trade and to engage in the expansion of such trade.

"(2) World invisible trade, based on efficiency and mutual and equitable benefit, furthering the expansion of the world economy, is the common goal of all states. The role of developing countries in world invisible trade should be enhanced and strengthened consistent with the above objectives, particular attention being paid to the special needs of developing countries.

"(3) All states should co-operate with developing countries in their endeavours to increase their capacity to earn foreign exchange from invisible transactions, in accordance with the potential and needs of each developing country, and consistent with the objectives mentioned above.

"**Art. 28.** All states have the duty to co-operate in achieving adjustments in the prices of exports of developing countries in relation to prices of their imports so as to promote just and equitable terms of trade for them, in a manner which is remunerative for producers and equitable for producers and consumers.

Chapter III
Common Responsibilities towards the International Community

"**Art. 29.** The seabed and ocean floor and the sub-soil thereof, beyond the limits of national jurisdiction, as well as the resources of the area, are the common heritage of mankind. On the basis of the principles adopted by the General Assembly in Resolution 2749 (XXV) of Dec. 17, 1970, all states shall ensure that the exploration of the area and exploitation of its resources are carried out exclusively for peaceful purposes and that the benefits derived therefrom are shared equitably by all states, taking into account the particular interests and needs of developing countries; an international regime applying to the area and its resources and including appropriate international machinery to give effect to its provisions shall be established by an international treaty of a universal character, generally agreed upon.

"**Art. 30.** The protection, preservation and the enhancement of the environment for the present and future generations is the responsibility of all states. All states shall endeavour to establish their own environment and developmental policies in conformity with such responsibility. The environmental politics of all states should enhance [and] not adversely affect the present and future development potential of developing countries. All states have the responsibility to ensure that activities within their jurisdiction or control do not cause damage to the environment of other states or of areas beyond the limits of national jurisdiction. All states should co-operate in evolving international norms and regulations in the fields of the environment.

Chapter IV
Final Provisions

"**Art. 31.** All states have the duty to contribute to the balanced expansion of the world economy, taking duly into account the close interrelationship between the well-being of the developed countries and the growth and development of the developing countries and that the prosperity of the international community as a whole depends upon the prosperity of its constituent parts.

"**Art. 32.** No state may use or encourage the use of economic, political or any other type of measures to coerce another state in order to obtain from it the subordination of the exercise of its sovereign rights.

"**Art. 33.** (1) Nothing in the present Charter shall be constructed as impairing or derogating from the provisions of the Charter of the United Nations or actions taken in pursuance thereof.

(2) In their interpretation and application, the provisions of the present Charter are interrelated and each provision should be construed in the context of the other provisions.

"**Art. 34.** An item on the Charter of Economic Rights and Duties of States shall be inscribed on the agenda of the General Assembly at its thirtieth session, and thereafter on the agenda of every fifth session. In this way a systematic and comprehensive consideration of the implementation of the Charter, covering both progress achieved and any improvements and additions which might become necessary, would be carried out and appropriate measures recommended. Such consideration should take into account the evolution of all the economic, social, legal and other factors related to the principles upon which the present Charter is based and on its purpose."

UN Definition of Aggression

A definition of aggression designed to command general acceptance by the international community was approved without a vote by the UN General Assembly on Dec. 14, 1974.

Such a definition had been unsuccessfully attempted on several previous occasions—at the 1815 Congress at Vienna, at the 1899 peace conference in The Hague, at the 1919 Versailles peace conference, and by the League of Nations between World Wars I and II—while at the 1945 San Francisco conference (which drafted the UN Charter) it was decided not to attempt to define aggression. The definition was approved without a vote on April 12, 1974, by a 35-member special commission which had been drafting it for the previous six years.

The text of the definition read as follows:

"**Art. 1.** Aggression is the use of armed force by a state against the sovereignty, territorial integrity or political independence of another state or in any other manner inconsistent with the Charter of the United Nations, as set out in this definition.

"*Explanatory Notes*. In this definition the term 'state'

"(*a*) is used without prejudice to questions of recognition or to whether a state is a member of the United Nations, and

"(*b*) includes the concept of a 'group of states' where appropriate.

"**Art. 2.** The first use of armed force by a state in contravention of the Charter shall constitute prima facie evidence of an act of aggression, although the Security Council may, in conformity with the Charter, conclude that a determination that an act of aggression has been committed would not be justified in the light of other relevant circumstances, including the fact that the acts concerned or their consequences are not of sufficient gravity.

"**Art. 3.** Any of the following acts, regardless of a declaration of war, shall, subject to and in accordance with the provisions of Article 2, qualify as an act of aggression:

"(*a*) The invasion or attack by the armed forces of a state of the territory of another state, or any military occupation, however temporary, resulting from such invasion or attack, or any annexation by the use of force of the territory of another state or part thereof;

"(*b*) bombardment by the armed forces of a state against the territory of another state or the use of any weapon by a state against the territory of another state;

"(*c*) the blockade of the ports or coasts of a state by the armed forces of another state;

"(*d*) an attack by the armed forces of a state on the land, sea or air forces, marine and air fleets of another state;

"(*e*) the use of armed forces of one state, which are within the territory of another state with the agreement of the receiving state, in contravention of the conditions provided for in the agreement or any extension of their presence in such territory beyond the termination of the agreement;

"(*f*) the action of a state in allowing its territory, which it has placed at the disposal of another state, to be used by that other state for perpetrating an act of aggression against a third state;

"(*g*) the sending by or on behalf of a state of armed bands, groups, irregulars or mercenaries, which carry out acts of armed force against another state of such gravity as to amount to the acts listed above, or its substantial involvement therein.

"**Art. 4.** The acts enumerated above are not exhaustive and the Security Council may determine that other acts constitute aggression under the provisions of the Charter.

"**Art. 5.** No consideration of whatever nature, whether political, economic, military or otherwise, may serve as a justification for aggression.

"A war of aggression is a crime against international peace. Aggression gives rise to international responsibility.

"No territorial acquisition or special advantage resulting from aggression are or shall be recognized as lawful.

"**Art. 6.** Nothing in this definition shall be construed as in any way enlarging or diminishing the scope of the Charter, including its provisions concerning cases in which the use of force is lawful.

"**Art. 7.** Nothing in this definition, and in particular Article 3, could in any way prejudice the right to self-determination, freedom and independence, as derived from the Charter, of peoples forcibly deprived of that right and referred to in the Declaration on Principles of International Law concerning Friendly Relations and Co-operation among States in accordance with the Charter of the United Nations, particularly peoples under colonial and racist regimes or other forms of alien domination; nor the right of these peoples to struggle to that end and to seek and receive support, in accordance with the principles of the Charter and in conformity with the above-mentioned declaration.

"**Art. 8.** In their interpretation and application the above provisions are inter-related and each provision should be construed in the context of the other provisions."

Convention against the Taking of Hostages

An *International Convention against the Taking of Hostages* was adopted by consensus by the UN General Assembly on Dec. 17, 1979.

The convention contained a definition of the offence of hostage-taking; required states to make it a punishable offence; and gave procedures for extradition where relevant. In the last-named context it was stated (in Article 9) that states should not grant requests for extradition if there were "substantial grounds for believing that the alleged offender would be punished on account of his race, religion, nationality, ethnic origin or political opinion" (this article being opposed by the Soviet Union).

The convention came into force on June 3, 1983, for the following states: the Bahamas, Barbados, Bhutan, Chile, Egypt, El Salvador, Finland, the Federal Republic of Germany, Guatemala, Honduras, Iceland, Kenya, the Republic of Korea, Lesotho, Mauritius, Norway, Panama, the Philippines, Suriname, Sweden, Trinidad and Tobago, and the United Kingdom; on April 25, 1984, for Spain; on Aug. 5, 1984, for Portugal; on April 4, 1985, for Switzerland; and on May 19, 1985, for Yugoslavia.

Conventions on the Status of Women

Political Rights of Women. A convention on the political rights of women, adopted by the UN General Assembly on March 31, 1953, came into force for the states parties to it on July 7, 1954, and by Dec. 31, 1985 it had been acceded to by a total of 90 states.

Nationality of Married Women. Based on the provisions of Art. 15 of the UN Declaration on Human Rights, an international convention on the nationality of married women was adopted by the UN General Assembly on Feb. 20, 1957, by 48 votes to two (Egypt and Syria) with 24 abstentions (including the United States). It laid down inter alia that neither the contracting nor the dissolution of a marriage between a national and an alien in the contracting states should automatically affect the nationality of the woman.

By Dec. 31, 1985, the contracting states numbered 55 (though not including the United States).

Elimination of Discrimination against Women.

The UN General Assembly on Nov. 7, 1967, adopted by 111 votes to nil, with 11 countries absent, a *Declaration on the Elimination of Discrimination against Women*.

The declaration proclaimed inter alia that women should have equal rights with men in the political sphere and in the field of civil law, in economic and social life and in education at all levels. It called for the abolition of all laws and customs which had the effect of discriminating against women and of all practices based on the idea of the inferiority of women; for the prohibition of child marriage and of betrothal of girls before puberty; and for measures to combat traffic in women and exploitation of prostitution. Among rights enumerated were those of a wife to retain her nationality if married to an alien; to have free choice of a husband; and to enjoy equality of treatment with men in respect of work of equal value.

Subsequently, a convention on the elimination of all forms of discrimination against women was adopted by the UN General Assembly on Dec. 18, 1979, by 130 votes to none with 10 abstentions (Bangladesh, Brazil, Comoros, Haiti, Mali, Mauritania, Mexico, Morocco, Saudi Arabia and Senegal). All states parties to the convention would commit themselves to measures to eliminate political, social, economic, legal and cultural discrimination against women.

The convention came into force on Sept. 3, 1981, after ratification by the required minimum of 20 states on that date. By May 1, 1986, it had been ratified by a total of 86 countries, including the United Kingdom.

Declaration on Elimination of Intolerance and Discrimination Based on Religion or Belief

The UN General Assembly adopted on Nov. 25, 1981, without a vote, the following "Declaration on the Elimination of All Forms of Intolerance based on Religion or Belief".

"Article I. (1) Everyone shall have the right to freedom of thought, conscience and religion. This right shall include freedom to have a religion or whatever belief of his choice, and freedom, either individually or in community with others and in public or private, to manifest his religion or belief in worship, observance, practice and teaching.

"(2) No one shall be subject to coercion which would impair his freedom to have a religion or belief of his choice.

"(3) Freedom to manifest one's religion or beliefs may be subject only to such limitations as are prescribed by law and are necessary to protect public safety, order, health or morals or the fundamental rights and freedoms of others.

"Article II. (1) No one shall be subject to discrimination by any state, institution, group of persons, or person on grounds of religion or other beliefs.

"(2) For the purposes of the present declaration, the expression 'intolerance and discrimination based on religion or belief' means any distinction, exclusion, restriction or preference based on religion or belief and having as its purpose or as its effect nullification or impairment of the recognition, enjoyment or exercise of human rights and fundamental freedoms on an equal basis.

"Article III. Discrimination between human beings on grounds of religion or belief constitutes an affront to human dignity and a disavowal of the Charter of the United Nations, and shall be condemned as a violation of the human rights and fundamental freedoms proclaimed in the Universal Declaration of Human Rights and enunciated in detail in the International Covenants on Human Rights, and as an obstacle to friendly and peaceful relations between nations.

"Article IV. (1) All states shall take effective measures to prevent and eliminate discrimination on the grounds of religion or belief in the recognition, exercise and enjoyment of human rights and fundamental freedoms in all fields of civil, economic, political, social and cultural life.

"(2) All states shall make all efforts to enact or rescind legislation where necessary to prohibit any such discrimination, and to take all appropriate measures to combat intolerance on the grounds of religion or other beliefs in this matter.

"Article V. (1) The parents or, as the case may be, the legal guardians of the child have the right to organize the life within the family in accordance with their religion or belief and bearing in mind the moral education in which they believe the child should be brought up.

"(2) Every child shall enjoy the right to have access to education in the matter of religion or belief in accordance with the wishes of his parents or, as the case may be, legal guardians, and shall not be compelled to receive teaching on religion or belief against the wishes of his parents or legal guardians, the best interests of the child being the guiding principle.

"(3) The child shall be protected from any form of discrimination on the ground of religion or belief. He shall be brought up in a spirit of understanding, tolerance, friendship among peoples, peace and universal brotherhood, respect for freedom of religion or belief of others, and in full consciousness that his energy and talents should be devoted to the service of his fellow men.

"(4) In the case of a child who is not under the care either of his parents or of legal guardians, due account shall be taken of their expressed wishes or of any other proof of their wishes in the matter of religion or belief, the best interests of the child being the guiding principle.

"(5) Practices of a religion or beliefs in which a child is brought up must not be injurious to his physical or mental health or to his full development, taking into account Article I, paragraph (3) of the present declaration.

"Article VI. In accordance with Article I of the present declaration, and subject to the provisions of Article I, paragraph (3), the right to freedom of thought, conscience, religion or belief shall include, inter alia, the following freedoms: (*a*) to worship or assemble in connexion with a religion or belief, and to establish and maintain places for these purposes; (*b*) to establish and maintain appropriate charitable or humanitarian institutions; (*c*) to make, acquire and use to an adequate extent the necessary articles and materials related to the rites or customs of a religion or belief; (*d*) to write, issue and disseminate relevant publications in these areas; (*e*) to teach a religion or belief in places suitable for these purposes; (*f*) to solicit and receive voluntary financial and other contributions from individuals and institutions; (*g*) to train, appoint, elect or designate by succession appropriate leaders called for by the requirements and standards of any religion or belief; (*h*) to observe days of rest and to celebrate holidays and ceremonies in accordance with the precepts of one's religion or belief; and (*i*) to establish and maintain communications with individuals and communities in matters of religion and belief at the national and international levels.

"Article VII. The rights and freedoms set forth in the present declaration shall be accorded in national legislation in such a manner that everyone shall be able to avail himself of such rights and freedoms in practice.

"**Article VIII.** Nothing in the present declaration shall be construed as restricting or derogating from any right defined in the Universal Declaration of Human Rights and the International Covenants on Human Rights."

Convention against Torture

A *Convention against Torture and Other Cruel, Inhuman or Degrading Treatment or Punishment* (drafted by the UN Commission on Human Rights) was adopted by the UN General Assembly (without a vote) on Dec. 10, 1984.

The convention was based on the principles enshrined in the 1945 UN Charter, the 1948 Universal Declaration of Human Rights and the 1966 International Covenant on Civil and Political Rights [see pages 18ff.]. Its substantive passages contained the following provisions:

Art. 1 contained a definition of the term "Torture".

Art. 2 stated (i) that each state party to the convention "shall take effective legislative, administrative, judicial or other measures to prevent acts of torture in any territory under its jurisdiction"; (ii) that "no exceptional circumstances whatsoever, whether a state of war or a threat of war, internal political instability or any other public emergency, may be invoked as a justification of torture"; and (iii) that "an order from a superior officer or a public authority may not be invoked as a justification of torture".

Art. 3 stipulated that "no state party shall expel, return or extradite a person to another state where there are substantial grounds for believing that he would be in danger of being subjected to torture".

Art. 4 provided (i) that "each state party shall ensure that all acts of torture are offences under its criminal law", with the same applying to "an attempt to commit torture and to an act by any person which constitutes complicity or participation in torture"; and (ii) that "each state party shall make these offences punishable by appropriate penalties which take into account their grave nature".

Art. 5 stated (i) that "each state party shall take such measures as may be necessary to establish its jurisdiction over the offences referred to in Article 4 in the following cases: (*a*) when the offences are committed in any territory under its jurisdiction or on board a ship or aircraft registered in that state; (*b*) when the alleged offender is a national of that state; (*c*) when the victim is a national of that state if that state considers it appropriate"; and (ii) that "each state party shall

likewise take such measures as may be necessary to establish its jurisdiction over such offences in cases where the alleged offender is present in any territory under its jurisdiction and it does not extradite him pursuant to Article 8".

Art. 6 provided that "upon being satisfied after an examination of information available to it that the circumstances so warrant", any state party with a person present in its territory alleged to have committed any offence referred to in Article 4 "shall take him into custody or take other legal measures to ensure his presence" and "shall immediately make a preliminary inquiry into the facts". When such a person had been taken into custody, the state in question should immediately notify the states referred to in Article 5 "of the fact that such person is in custody and of the circumstances which warrant his detention". The state making the preliminary inquiry "shall promptly report its findings to the said states and shall indicate whether it intends to exercise jurisdiction".

Art. 7 specified that "the state party in the territory under whose jurisdiction a person alleged to have committed any offence referred to in Article 4 is found shall in the cases contemplated in Article 5, if it does not extradite him, submit the case to its competent authorities for the purposes of prosecution".

Art. 8 stated (i) that "the offences referred to in Article 4 shall be deemed to be included as extraditable offences in any extradition treaty existing between states parties", the latter undertaking "to include such offences in every extradition treaty to be concluded between them"; and (ii) that "if a state party which makes extradition conditional on the existence of a treaty receives a request for extradition from another state party with which it has no extradition treaty, it may consider this convention as the legal basis for extradition in respect of such offences".

Art. 9 specified that "states parties shall afford one another the greatest measure of assistance in connexion with criminal proceedings brought in respect of any of the offences referred to in Article 4".

Art. 13 enjoined that "each state party shall ensure that any individual who alleges [that] he has been subjected to torture in any territory under its jurisdiction has the right to complain to, and to have his case promptly and impartially examined by, its competent authorities".

Art. 14 specified that "each state party shall ensure in its legal system that the victim of an act of torture obtains redress and has an enforceable right to adequate and fair compensation".

Arts. 17–24 provided for the establishment, once the convention had come into force, of a 10-member UN Committee against Torture, which would seek to monitor and ensure observance of the convention's provisions.

UN Conferences and Conventions on Law of the Sea—Other Legal Conventions

First UN Conference on Law of the Sea

The first UN Conference on the Law of the Sea (UNCLOS) was held in Geneva from Feb. 24 to April 28, 1958, and adopted, after preparation by the International Law Commission, four Conventions and a protocol on compulsory settlement of disputes, but reached no agreement on the maximum width of territorial waters and the maximum limits of exclusive fishing rights.

(1) The *Convention on the Territorial Sea and the Contiguous Zone* defined the "territorial sea" and the "contiguous zone" of the high seas.

Specifically, Articles 1 and 2 of this Convention laid down that the coastal state's sovereignty extended over its territorial

sea and to the airspace and sea-bed and subsoil thereof, subject to the provisions of the Convention and of international law. The coastal state might exclude foreign nationals and vessels from fishing and also from coastal trading (cabotage) in its territorial waters.

The Convention emphasized the right of innocent passage for merchant ships (but not warships) through the territorial sea and the coastal state's duty to publicize any dangers to navigation in these waters. A coastal state might, for security reasons, temporarily suspend innocent passage provided the suspension was published and did not cover international straits.

For the latter the Convention provided in Article 16(4) that "there shall be no suspension of the innocent passage of foreign ships through straits which are used for international navigation". (The question of innocent passage of warships was not dealt with in the Convention.)

Article 3 of the Convention laid down that the width of the territorial sea was to be delimited from the low-water mark around the coasts of the state ("as marked on large-scale charts officially recognized by the coastal state"). Article 4 laid down that in cases of indented coastlines, or a fringe of islands and rocks (*skjaergaard*) running parallel to the coast, the system which could be used was that of a straight baseline linking the outermost parts of land (a system later regarded as a valid principle of international law by the International Court of Justice in an Anglo-Norwegian fisheries case dealt with in 1969).

Article 5(2) of the Convention stated that a right of innocent passage should be deemed to exist in areas enclosed as internal waters as a result of the straight baseline method but previously regarded as part of the territorial or high seas. Article 7 of the Convention declared that "if the distance between the low-water marks of the natural entrance points of a bay does not exceed 24 nautical miles a closing line may be drawn between these two low-water marks, and the water enclosed thereby shall be considered as internal waters". This provision, however, does not apply to "historic bays", i.e. bays the waters of which are treated by the coastal state as internal (e.g. Canada has thus claimed the Hudson Bay, against opposition by the United States, and the case of Fonseca Bay, disputed by El Salvador and Nicaragua, was decided on that principle by the Central American Court of Justice in 1917—see Section 14).*

Article 24 of the Convention declared that "in a zone of the high seas contiguous to its territorial sea, the coastal state may exercise the control necessary to (*a*) prevent infringement of its customs, fiscal, immigration or sanitary regulations within its territory or territorial sea, and (*b*) punish infringement of the above regulations within its territory or territorial sea".

Fishing vessels were obliged to observe the laws of the coastal state and submarines to navigate on the surface and show their flag; the coastal state's civil and criminal laws were (to a limited extent) to be applied to merchant vessels but not to non-commercial government ships.

(2) The *Convention on the High Seas* proclaimed the freedom of the high seas (including the freedom to fly over them, to fish and to lay submarine cables and pipelines, as well as other freedoms "recognized by the general principles of international law").

The Convention also proclaimed the right of land-locked states to have free access to the sea; granted each state the right to determine conditions for the grant of its nationality to ships; gave immunity from the jurisdiction of any state other than the flag state to warships and other non-commercial government vessels on the high seas; and enjoined states to ensure safety at sea, to prevent the slave trade and piracy and to prevent pollution of the sea.

The Convention also reaffirmed (in Article 23) the customary doctrine of hot pursuit, i.e. the right of a state to pursue, for violations of regulations related to its internal waters, territorial sea or contiguous zone, a foreign vessel on the high seas provided the pursuit is commenced while that vessel is still

within those waters; the pursuit can continue on the high seas only if it is not interrupted.

(3) The *Convention on Fishing and Conservation of the Living Resources of the High Seas* provided inter alia for agreement on conservation measures and for arbitration procedure in the event of disputes.

(4) The *Convention on the Continental Shelf* gave coastal states exclusive rights to exploit universal and other non-living resources as well as "sedentary" living organisms (e.g. oysters) of the continental shelf, i.e. "the sea-bed and subsoil of the submarine areas adjacent to the coast, but outside the area of the territorial sea, up to the point where the waters above are 200 metres deep, or beyond that limit if the depth allows exploitation of natural resources". The boundary of the coastal shelf adjacent to any state lying opposite another state on the same shelf was to be determined by mutual agreement or, failing such agreement, would be the median line.

(5) The *Protocol on Settlement of Disputes* provided for compulsory jurisdiction of the International Court of Justice in disputes arising out of the interpretation or application of any Convention on the Law of the Sea (except as covered by the arbitration procedure under (3) above), as well as for arbitration or conciliation where both parties agreed to this procedure instead of resorting to the International Court of Justice.

Second and Third UN Conferences

A second UN Conference on the Law of the Sea, held in Geneva between March 17 and April 26, 1960, and dealing with the width of the territorial sea and the breadth of a "contiguous zone" in which coastal states would exercise exclusive fishing rights, failed to reach agreement on these subjects.

Sessions of a third UN Conference on the Law of the Sea were held in New York on Dec. 3–15, 1973, in Caracas from June 20 to Aug. 29, 1974, and in Geneva from March 17 to May 9, 1975, when provisional agreement was reached (i) on the establishment of an international sea-bed authority which would oversee the exploitation of ocean floor resources beyond national jurisdiction (i.e. in an area described as "the common heritage of mankind" in a "declaration on principles concerning the sea-bed, the ocean floor and the subsoil thereof" adopted by the UN General Assembly in 1970) and (ii) on a territorial limit of 12 nautical miles and a 200-mile economic zone in which coastal states would control both fisheries and mineral resources.

Further sessions of the third conference were held in New York from March 15 to May 7, 1976; from Aug. 2 to Sept. 17, 1976; and from May 23 to July 15, 1977 (whereafter an "informal composite negotiating text" was published, containing provisions for an international regime for the conduct of deep sea-bed mining—which were immediately rejected as "fundamentally

---

* The US Supreme Court took the view (in 1975) that a "historic bay" can be recognized only where there is continuous exercise of authority and acquiescence of foreign states (in the case of Cook Inlet, United States *versus* State of Alaska, where the court ruled that the United States was entitled to the sub-surface lands of Cook Inlet).

Examples of historic bays, where the coastal states have rights approximating to those held in internal waters, are given by Gilbert Gidel in his *Traité de droit international de la mer* of 1934 as being the Rio de la Plata, Chesapeake and Delaware Bays, the Bay of Fundy between Canada and the United States, Cancale or Granville Bay in Normandy, France, the Gulf of Tunis, the Bristol Channel and several Norwegian fjords.

unacceptable" by the United States); in Geneva from March 28 to May 19, 1978; in New York from Aug. 21 to Sept. 15, 1978; in Geneva from March 19 to April 27, 1979; in New York from July 19 to Aug. 24, 1979; in New York from March 3 to April 4, 1980; in Geneva from July 28 to Aug. 29, 1980; in New York from March 9 to April 24, 1981; in Geneva from Aug. 3 to Aug. 28, 1981; and again in New York from March 8 to April 30, 1982.

1982 UN Convention on Law of the Sea

A comprehensive UN Convention on the Law of the Sea was eventually approved in New York on April 30, 1982, when 130 delegations at the third UNCLOS voted in favour of the draft Convention and four against it (Israel, Turkey, the United States and Venezuela); there were 17 abstentions (Belgium, Bulgaria, Byelorussia, Czechoslovakia, the German Democratic Republic, the Federal Republic of Germany, Hungary, Italy, Luxembourg, Mongolia, the Netherlands, Poland, the Soviet Union, Spain, Thailand, the Ukraine and the United Kingdom), 14 other delegations were absent (Antigua and Barbuda, Belize, the Comoros, Dominica, Equatorial Guinea, The Gambia, Kiribati, Liberia, Maldives, Nauru, the Solomon Islands, Tonga, Tuvalu and Vanuatu) and three took no part in the vote (Albania, Ecuador and the Holy See).

The conference also adopted four resolutions:

(i) to establish a Preparatory Commission to set up the Sea-Bed Authority and the Law of the Sea Tribunal provided for in the Convention; (ii) to govern preparatory investments in pioneer activities by states and private consortia relating to polymetallic nodules in the deep sea-bed; (iii) to deal with rights and interests of territories which had not yet attained independence or self-government; and (iv) to grant national liberation movements the right to sign the Final Act of the conference.

In the second of these resolutions four countries (France, India, Japan and the Soviet Union) as well as four multinational consortia—the (US) Kennecott Group (with six mining companies), Ocean Mining Associates (with four companies), Ocean Management Inc. (with four companies) and Ocean Minerals Company (with five companies)—were recognized as "pioneer investors", each of whom was expected to sign the Convention stating that prior to Jan. 1, 1983, the investor had expended no less than $30,000,000 in pioneer activities of deep-sea mineral extraction and no less than 10 per cent of that amount in the location, survey and evaluation of a specific mining site. It was specified that such a site should be large enough to be later divided into two pioneer areas of equal estimated commercial value; the size of one pioneer area should not exceed 150,000 square kilometres.

At the further session held in New York on Sept. 22–24, 1982, the UN conference approved certain changes made in the Convention by its drafting committee and adopted the Final Act recapitulating the history of the third conference.

At the end of the concluding session of the UNCLOS held in Montego Bay (Jamaica) on Dec. 6–10, 1982, the Convention was signed by representatives of 117 sovereign states as well as the UN Council for Namibia and the Cook Islands (a dependent territory of New Zealand). The Convention was to come into force 12 months after instruments of ratification had been deposited by 60 countries, and it was to become binding for each state which had ratified it.

Also on Dec. 10, 1982, the Final Act of the UNCLOS was signed by 150 delegations (including that of the UN Council for Namibia and nine observer delegations). Of these delegations several industrialized market-economy countries (among them Belgium, the Federal Republic of Germany, Italy, Spain, the United Kingdom and the United States) had not signed the Convention itself (whereas Japan signed it on Feb. 7, 1983).

The delegate of Venezuela had earlier explained that, although he would sign the Final Act, he would not sign the Convention because it might affect his country's disputes with Colombia over the Gulf of Venezuela (where large oil deposits were reported to exist) and with Trinidad and Tobago.

Principal Provisions of Convention

The Convention laid down four maritime boundaries as follows:

(1) A boundary of 12 nautical miles (nm) from baselines of a coastal state for that country's territorial sea;
(2) a boundary of up to 24 nm from baselines for a contiguous zone;
(3) a boundary of 200 nm from baselines for an exclusive economic zone (EEZ); and
(4) a continental shelf boundary at 200 nm from the shore baseline, but at up to 350 nm in cases where the true shelf extended further (to be claimed in accordance with a specific formula based on the thickness of the sedimentary rock on the shelf floor) or a further boundary 100 nm outward from a 2,500-metre isobath.

Beyond the continental shelf there would be the "Area", declared to be the "common heritage of mankind", the resources of which would be exploited by the proposed International Sea-Bed Authority headed by a 36-member Council.

In the territorial sea foreign vessels would be allowed "innocent passage" for purposes of peaceful navigation.

In the contiguous zone the coastal state would be able to exercise control of customs, fiscal, immigration and sanitary laws and regulations.

Through straits used for international navigation ships and aircraft would be allowed "transit passage" as long as they proceeded without delay and without threatening the bordering states; states alongside the straits would, however, be able to regulate navigation and other aspects of passage.

Archipelagic states would have sovereignty over a sea enclosed by straight lines drawn between the outermost points of their islands, with ships of all other states having the right of passage through sea lanes designated by the archipelagic state.

In the exclusive economic zone coastal states would have sovereign rights over natural resources and certain economic activities, and jurisdiction over certain types of scientific research and environmental protection. All other states would have freedom of navigation and overflight, as well as freedom to lay submarine cables and pipelines. Landlocked states and "states with special geographical characteristics" would have the right to participate in the exploitation of part of the zone's fisheries when the coastal state could not itself harvest them all. Delimitation of overlapping economic zones was to be effected by agreement. Special protection was to be accorded to highly migratory species of fish and marine mammals.

For the exploration and exploitation of the "Area" (the international sea-bed) a "parallel system" was to be established, with all activities being under the control of the International Sea-Bed Authority which would (i) conduct its own mining operations through its "enterprise" and (ii) contract with private and state ventures by granting them mining rights in the Area. Once mining was authorized, a first generation of sea-bed prospectors, the "pioneer operators", would have guarantees of production. The Convention contained an anti-monopoly clause aimed at ensuring that no single nation obtained too large a share of the sea-bed or a whole or any sizeable area of it.

For the purpose of environmental protection the Convention laid down that states would have to use "the best practical means at their disposal" to prevent and control marine pollution from any source. The Convention determined which category of states (coastal states, port states or flag states) would be responsible for preventing pollution and punishing polluters, and what kind of enforcement actions were allowable. States would be liable for damage caused by violations of their international obligation to combat marine pollution and would be bound to co-operate globally and regionally in formulating rules and standards of environmental protection and to promote technical assistance to developing countries in the area.

All marine scientific research in the exclusive economic zone and on the continental shelf would be subject to the consent of the coastal state, but the latter would be obliged to grant consent to foreign states if the research was to be conducted for peaceful purposes and met certain other criteria laid down in the Convention; a coastal state could deny consent and insist on the cessation of such research only under circumstances defined in the Convention. In the event of a dispute the researching state could require the coastal state to submit to international conciliation.

States would be bound to promote the development and transfer of marine technology "on fair and reasonable conditions", with proper regard to all legitimate interests, including the rights of holders, suppliers and recipients of technology.

States would be obliged to settle by peaceful means their disputes over the interpretation or application of the Convention. When they could not agree on the means of settlement they would have to submit most types of dispute to a compulsory procedure entailing decisions binding on all parties. The dispute could be submitted to (i) an International Tribunal for the Law of the Sea, to be set up under the Convention; (ii) the existing International Court of Justice; (iii) arbitration or (iv) special arbitration procedures. Certain types of dispute would have to be submitted to conciliation, the outcome of which would not be binding on the parties.

International Impact of the Convention

The UNCLOS Convention gave the great naval powers—in particular the United States and the Soviet Union—freedom of navigation (e.g. in straits less than 22 nautical miles wide), enabled them to combat pollution of the sea, and gave each coastal state a vast exclusive fishing area.

France, in particular, benefited greatly from the Convention by obtaining exclusive economic zones not only around metropolitan France but also around its Overseas Departments and Territories where it gained sovereignty over the resources of some 11,000,000 square kilometres,

which made France the third maritime nation after the United Kingdom and the United States.

The Intergovernmental Oceanographic Commission (IOC) had estimated in a report published on Jan. 1, 1980, that the UNCLOS extension of fishery limits to a maximum of 200 nautical miles by all coastal states would mean that over 35 per cent of the world's oceans would be enclosed within national zones of control which would cover over 90 per cent of the living marine resources currently under exploitation. Moreover, the coastal states would face increased responsibilities for conservation and management measures; for promotion of the optimum utilization of their resources; for determining their own capacity to harvest the available catch and giving other states access to any surplus; and for the conservation and development of any stock shared by two or more coastal states (or any other states) fishing beyond their own zones.

In a report by the UN Secretary-General submitted in compliance with UN General Assembly Resolution 38/59 of Dec. 14, 1983, it was stated that, although not yet in force, the Convention was already having "a stabilizing effect" on the law of the sea through the rationalization of different uses of the oceans and the reconciliation of competing interests of states, and that it was also having an impact on the attitudes of states towards marine affairs at national and international levels. In particular, the report referred to a growing number of states which were bringing their maritime boundaries in line with those set by the Convention; it further stated that the International Court of Justice had, in the settlement of maritime disputes, begun to rely (directly or indirectly) on the Convention.

The Convention was not approved by the governments of the United States, the United Kingdom and the Federal Republic of Germany which refused to sign it, mainly because of its provisions on deep sea-bed mining. Israel, Turkey and Venezuela were also opposed to it.

In the absence of any veto by the United Kingdom or the Federal Republic of Germany, the European Communities subsequently signed the Convention, which by Dec. 9, 1984, had obtained the signatures of 159 states and other entities. However, by Aug. 31, 1985, the Convention had been ratified by only 21 states (mainly in Africa and the Caribbean).

Conventions on Diplomatic and Consular Relations

Vienna Convention on Diplomatic Relations. In terms of a resolution adopted by the UN General Assembly on Dec. 7, 1959, a conference was held in Vienna on April 2–14, 1961, leading to the approval of a convention on diplomatic relations, issued on April 18, 1961. The convention first came into force on April 24, 1964, and by Dec. 31, 1985, it was in force for 143 countries.

The convention contained definitions concerning the personnel and buildings of diplomatic missions, the tasks of such missions, procedures for their establishment, the rights and duties of their personnel, the right of the host country to declare any member of such a mission persona non grata without stating any reason, the conditions of immunity, and guaranteed uncontrolled communications for official purposes.

Vienna Convention on Consular Relations. A similar convention on consular relations was adopted at a Vienna conference on April 24, 1963; it first entered into force on March 19, 1967, and by Dec. 31, 1985, it was in force for 110 countries.

Vienna Convention on the Representation of States and their Relations with International Organizations of a Universal Character. This convention was adopted on March 14, 1975.

Law of Treaties Convention and Declarations

On the basis of 75 draft articles prepared by the International Law Commission, a **UN Convention on the Law of Treaties** comprising 85 articles was approved by a UN conference on the law of treaties in Vienna on May 22, 1969, and was opened for signature on the following day.

The convention codified many fundamental principles of the customary international law of treaties concluded between states, including the universally-recognized principle of *pacta sunt servanda*, formulated as follows: "Every treaty in force is binding upon the parties to it and must be performed by them in good faith." (Article 26.)

The convention provided inter alia that, in the interpretation of a treaty, account might be taken of subsequent practice in the application of the treaty, which established agreement of the parties regarding its interpretation (Art. 31).

The convention also laid down the pre-eminence of peremptory rules of international law (*jus cogens*) as follows: "A treaty is void if, at the time of its conclusion, it conflicts with a peremptory norm of general international law. For the purposes of the present convention, a peremptory norm of general international law is a norm accepted and recognized by the international community of states as a norm from which no derogation is permitted and which can be modified only by a subsequent norm of general international law having the same character." (Article 53.)

Procedures were provided for judicial settlement, arbitration and conciliation either by way of application to the International Court of Justice or by setting in motion the procedure specified in an annex. (Article 66.)

The convention was to enter into force on the 30th day after the deposition (with the UN Secretary-General) of the 35th ratification or accession document, while for countries ratifying it or acceding to it afterwards it would come into force on the 30th day after the deposition of their ratification or deposition document. (Article 84.)

The convention was adopted by 79 votes to one (France, which objected to Article 53) with 19 abstentions.

The conference also approved several declarations and resolutions, including a declaration on the prohibition of military, political or economic coercion in the conclusion of treaties in violation of the principles of the sovereign equality of states and freedom of consent.

A further UN conference held in Vienna in August 1978 approved a convention establishing international legal standards regulating the preservation in force or the termination of international treaties in the case of the formation of new states as a result of decolonization or of the unification or division of states, and also asserting the inviolability of existing frontiers.

A **Vienna Convention on Succession of States in Respect of Treaties,** adopted on Aug. 23, 1978, deals inter alia with the succession, as a party to a treaty, of a newly independent state.

Membership of the United Nations and Related Agencies

The table on pages 60–68 lists the members of the United Nations, its specialized agencies and the International Atomic Energy Agency, and also the contracting parties to the General Agreement on Tariffs and Trade, as at September 1986.

The complete names of the organizations included in this table are:

UN	United Nations
ILO	International Labour Organization
FAO	Food and Agriculture Organization of the United Nations
UNESCO	United Nations Educational, Scientific and Cultural Organization
ICAO	International Civil Aviation Organization
WHO	World Health Organization
IBRD	International Bank for Reconstruction and Development (World Bank)
IFC	International Finance Corporation
IDA	International Development Association
IMF	International Monetary Fund
UPU	Universal Postal Union
ITU	International Telecommunication Union
WMO	World Meteorological Organization
IMO	International Maritime Organization
WIPO	World Intellectual Property Organization

IFAD	International Fund for Agricultural Development
UNIDO	United Nations Industrial Development Organization
IAEA	International Atomic Energy Agency
GATT	General Agreement on Tariffs and Trade

Countries which have not applied for UN membership are Andorra, Liechtenstein, Monaco, San Marino, Switzerland and the Vatican. Of these countries, Andorra is, in foreign relations, represented by France, and Liechtenstein by Switzerland (except in its relations with Austria and the Holy See).

Switzerland has refrained from applying for UN membership, for many years mainly on the grounds that the imposition of any sanctions under Chapter VII of the UN Charter would be in conflict with the Swiss neutrality status. In 1977 a Swiss government commission recommended Swiss membership of the United Nations, and this recommendation was approved by the main political parties and by both Houses of Parliament (on March 15 and Dec. 14, 1984, respectively). However, a referendum held on March 16, 1986, resulted in a majority of 75.7

per cent of votes being cast against Swiss UN membership (in a turnout of 52.2 per cent).

The question of UN membership of the People's Republic of China was the subject of a vote at almost every session of the UN General Assembly in the two decades after 1950. The United States announced on Jan. 21, 1951, that it recognized the Nationalist Chinese Government in Taiwan (Formosa) as the only legal representative of China, and until 1960 the USA succeeded in having discussion of the Chinese membership question deferred. From 1961 onwards the question of the admission of the People's Republic was, at the instance of the United States, judged to be an "important" one to be decided upon only by a two-thirds majority in accordance with the UN Charter. It was not until 1970 that an Albanian move to give the People's Republic of China a seat in the United Nations obtained a simple majority in the General Assembly. On Oct. 15, 1971, however, the General Assembly adopted by 76 votes to 35, with 17 abstentions and three delegations absent, an Albanian resolution appointing the People's Republic of China to the Chinese seat in all its functions and to exclude the Taiwan Government, as having usurped these rights, from the organization. (The Government of Taiwan was thus the first to be expelled from the United Nations.) The People's

Republic subsequently took its seat in all UN organs, including that of a permanent member of the Security Council, and in most of the specialized agencies, with the result that Taiwan is no longer represented in the UN system.

Both the Democratic People's Republic of Korea (North Korea) and the Republic of Korea (South Korea) first applied for UN membership in 1949, when the North Korean application was rejected by the UN Security Council and the South Korean application was vetoed by the Soviet Union, as were renewed applications by South Korea in 1955, 1957 and 1958. A Soviet proposal for the simultaneous admission to the United Nations of both Koreas was rejected by the Security Council in 1957 and 1958. On June 23, 1973, South Korea announced that it had abandoned its previous opposition to simultaneous entry of both Koreas, whereas North Korea proposed that the two states should enter the United Nations as a single confederal republic. On July 29, 1975, South Korea made a further application, which North Korea denounced as "aimed at perpetuating the division of the nation" and which failed to obtain the necessary nine votes to enable it to be placed on the Security Council's agenda (with the People's Republic of China, the Soviet Union, Byelorussia, Mauritania, Tanzania and Iraq opposing the proposal and Cameroon and Guyana abstaining from voting).

Members of the United Nations, the Specialized Agencies and IAEA, and Contracting Parties to GATT

Country	UN	ILO	FAO	UNESCO	ICAO	WHO	IBRD	IFC	IDA	IMF	UPU	ITU	WMO	IMO	WIPO	IFAD	UNIDO	IAEA	GATT
Afghanistan	☆	☆	☆	☆	☆	☆	☆	☆	☆	☆	☆	☆	☆	—	—	—	☆	☆	—
Albania	☆	—	☆	☆	—	☆	—	—	—	—	☆	☆	☆	—	—	—	—	☆	—
Algeria	☆	☆	☆	☆	☆	☆	☆	—	☆	☆	☆	☆	☆	☆	☆	☆	☆	☆	—
Angola	☆	☆	☆	☆	☆	☆	—	—	—	—	☆	☆	☆	☆	☆	☆	☆	—	—
Antigua and Barbuda	☆	☆	☆	☆	☆	☆	☆	—	—	☆	—	—	—	☆	—	—	—	—	—
Argentina	☆	☆	☆	☆	☆	☆	☆	☆	☆	☆	☆	☆	☆	☆	☆	☆	☆	☆	☆
Australia	☆	☆	☆	☆	☆	☆	☆	☆	☆	☆	☆	☆	☆	☆	☆	☆	☆	☆	☆
Austria	☆	☆	☆	☆	☆	☆	☆	☆	☆	☆	☆	☆	☆	☆	☆	☆	☆	☆	☆
Bahamas	☆	☆	☆	☆	☆	☆	☆	—	—	☆	☆	☆	☆	☆	☆	—	—	—	—
Bahrain	☆	☆	☆	☆	☆	☆	☆	—	—	☆	☆	☆	☆	☆	—	—	☆	—	—
Bangladesh	☆	☆	☆	☆	☆	☆	☆	☆	☆	☆	☆	☆	☆	☆	☆	☆	☆	☆	☆
Barbados	☆	☆	☆	☆	☆	☆	☆	☆	—	☆	☆	☆	☆	☆	☆	☆	☆	—	☆
Belgium	☆	☆	☆	☆	☆	☆	☆	☆	☆	☆	☆	☆	☆	☆	☆	☆	☆	☆	☆
Belize	☆	☆	☆	☆	—	—	☆	☆	☆	☆	☆	☆	☆	—	—	—	—	—	☆
Benin	☆	☆	☆	☆	☆	☆	☆	☆	☆	☆	☆	☆	☆	☆	☆	☆	☆	—	☆
Bhutan	☆	—	☆	☆	—	☆	☆	☆	☆	☆	☆	—	—	—	—	☆	☆	—	—
Bolivia	☆	☆	☆	☆	☆	☆	☆	☆	☆	☆	☆	☆	☆	—	—	☆	☆	☆	—
Botswana	☆	☆	☆	☆	☆	☆	☆	☆	☆	☆	☆	☆	☆	—	—	☆	☆	—	—
Brazil	☆	☆	☆	☆	☆	☆	☆	☆	☆	☆	☆	☆	☆	☆	☆	☆	☆	☆	☆

Country	UN	ILO	FAO	UNESCO	ICAO	WHO	IBRD	IFC	IDA	IMF	UPU	ITU	WMO	IMO	WIPO	IFAD	UNIDO	IAEA	GATT
Brunei	☆	—	—	—	☆	☆	—	—	—	—	—	☆	☆	☆	—	—	—	—	—
Bulgaria	☆	☆	☆	☆	☆	☆	—	—	—	—	☆	☆	☆	☆	☆	—	☆	☆	—
Burkina Faso	☆	☆	☆	☆	☆	☆	☆	☆	☆	☆	☆	☆	—	☆	☆	☆	☆	—	☆
Burma	☆	☆	☆	☆	☆	☆	☆	☆	☆	☆	☆	☆	☆	☆	—	—	☆	☆	☆
Burundi	☆	☆	☆	☆	☆	☆	☆	☆	☆	☆	☆	☆	—	—	☆	☆	☆	—	☆
Byelorussia	☆	☆	—	☆	—	☆	—	—	—	—	☆	☆	☆	—	☆	—	☆	☆	—
Cameroon	☆	☆	☆	☆	☆	☆	☆	☆	☆	☆	☆	☆	☆	—	☆	☆	☆	☆	☆
Canada	☆	☆	☆	☆	☆	☆	☆	☆	☆	☆	☆	☆	☆	☆	☆	☆	☆	☆	☆
Cape Verde	☆	☆	☆	☆	☆	☆	☆	—	☆	☆	☆	☆	☆	☆	—	☆	☆	—	—
Central African Republic	☆	☆	☆	☆	☆	☆	☆	—	☆	☆	☆	☆	—	—	☆	☆	☆	—	☆
Chad	☆	☆	☆	☆	☆	☆	☆	—	☆	☆	☆	☆	☆	—	☆	☆	—	—	☆
Chile	☆	☆	☆	☆	☆	☆	☆	☆	☆	☆	☆	☆	☆	☆	☆	☆	☆	☆	☆
China	☆	☆	☆	☆	☆	☆	☆	☆	☆	☆	☆	☆	☆	☆	☆	☆	☆	☆	—
Colombia	☆	☆	☆	☆	☆	☆	☆	☆	☆	☆	☆	☆	☆	☆	☆	☆	☆	☆	☆
Comoros	☆	☆	☆	☆	☆	☆	☆	—	☆	☆	☆	☆	—	—	—	☆	☆	—	—
Congo	☆	☆	☆	☆	☆	☆	☆	☆	☆	☆	☆	☆	☆	☆	☆	☆	☆	—	☆
Costa Rica	☆	☆	☆	☆	☆	☆	☆	☆	☆	☆	☆	☆	☆	☆	☆	☆	—	☆	—
Côte d'Ivoire	☆	☆	☆	☆	☆	☆	☆	☆	☆	☆	☆	☆	☆	☆	☆	☆	☆	☆	☆
Cuba	☆	☆	☆	☆	☆	☆	—	—	—	—	☆	☆	☆	☆	☆	☆	☆	☆	☆
Cyprus	☆	☆	☆	☆	☆	☆	☆	☆	☆	☆	☆	☆	☆	☆	☆	☆	☆	☆	☆
Czechoslovakia	☆	☆	☆	☆	☆	☆	—	—	—	—	☆	☆	☆	☆	☆	—	☆	☆	☆

Country	UN	ILO	FAO	UNESCO	ICAO	WHO	IBRD	IFC	IDA	IMF	UPU	ITU	WMO	IMO	WIPO	IFAD	UNIDO	IAEA	GATT
Denmark	☆	☆	☆	☆	☆	☆	☆	☆	☆	☆	☆	☆	☆	☆	☆	☆	☆	☆	☆
Djibouti	☆	☆	☆	—	☆	☆	☆	☆	☆	☆	☆	☆	☆	☆	—	☆	—	—	—
Dominica	☆	☆	☆	☆	—	☆	☆	☆	☆	☆	☆	—	☆	☆	☆	☆	☆	—	—
Dominican Republic	☆	☆	☆	☆	☆	☆	☆	☆	☆	☆	☆	☆	☆	☆	—	☆	☆	☆	☆
Ecuador	☆	☆	☆	☆	☆	☆	☆	☆	☆	☆	☆	☆	☆	☆	—	☆	☆	☆	—
Egypt	☆	☆	☆	☆	☆	☆	☆	☆	☆	☆	☆	☆	☆	☆	☆	☆	☆	☆	☆
El Salvador	☆	☆	☆	☆	☆	☆	☆	☆	☆	☆	☆	☆	☆	☆	☆	☆	—	☆	—
Equatorial Guinea	☆	☆	☆	☆	☆	☆	☆	—	☆	☆	☆	☆	—	☆	—	☆	☆	—	—
Ethiopia	☆	☆	☆	☆	☆	☆	☆	☆	☆	☆	☆	☆	☆	☆	—	☆	☆	☆	—
Fiji	☆	☆	☆	☆	☆	☆	☆	☆	☆	☆	☆	☆	☆	☆	☆	☆	☆	—	—
Finland	☆	☆	☆	☆	☆	☆	☆	☆	☆	☆	☆	☆	☆	☆	☆	☆	☆	☆	☆
France	☆	☆	☆	☆	☆	☆	☆	☆	☆	☆	☆	☆	☆	☆	☆	☆	☆	☆	☆
Gabon	☆	☆	☆	☆	☆	☆	☆	☆	☆	☆	☆	☆	☆	☆	☆	☆	☆	—	☆
Gambia	☆	—	—	☆	☆	☆	☆	☆	☆	☆	☆	☆	☆	☆	☆	☆	☆	—	—
German Democratic Republic	☆	☆	—	☆	—	☆	—	—	—	—	☆	☆	☆	☆	☆	—	☆	☆	—
Germany, Federal Republic of	☆	☆	☆	☆	☆	☆	☆	☆	☆	☆	☆	☆	☆	☆	☆	☆	☆	☆	☆
Ghana	☆	☆	☆	☆	☆	☆	☆	☆	☆	☆	☆	☆	☆	☆	☆	☆	☆	☆	☆
Greece	☆	☆	☆	☆	☆	☆	☆	☆	☆	☆	☆	☆	☆	☆	☆	☆	☆	☆	☆
Grenada	☆	☆	☆	☆	☆	☆	☆	☆	☆	☆	☆	☆	—	—	—	☆	☆	—	—
Guatemala	☆	☆	☆	☆	☆	☆	☆	☆	☆	☆	☆	☆	☆	☆	☆	☆	☆	☆	—

Country	UN	ILO	FAO	UNESCO	ICAO	WHO	IBRD	IFC	IDA	IMF	UPU	ITU	WMO	IMO	WIPO	IFAD	UNIDO	IAEA	GATT
Guinea	☆	☆	☆	☆	☆	☆	☆	☆	☆	☆	☆	☆	☆	☆	☆	☆	☆	—	—
Guinea-Bissau	☆	☆	☆	☆	☆	☆	☆	☆	☆	☆	☆	☆	☆	☆	—	☆	☆	—	—
Guyana	☆	☆	☆	☆	☆	☆	☆	☆	☆	☆	☆	☆	☆	☆	—	☆	☆	—	☆
Haiti	☆	☆	☆	☆	☆	☆	☆	☆	☆	☆	☆	☆	☆	☆	☆	☆	☆	☆	☆
Holy See	—	—	—	—	—	—	—	—	—	—	☆	☆	—	☆	☆	—	☆	☆	—
Honduras	☆	☆	☆	☆	☆	☆	☆	☆	☆	☆	☆	☆	☆	—	☆	☆	☆	—	—
Hungary	☆	☆	☆	☆	☆	☆	☆	☆	☆	☆	☆	☆	☆	☆	☆	—	☆	☆	☆
Iceland	☆	☆	☆	☆	☆	☆	☆	☆	☆	☆	☆	☆	☆	☆	☆	—	—	☆	☆
India	☆	☆	☆	☆	☆	☆	☆	☆	☆	☆	☆	☆	☆	☆	☆	☆	☆	☆	☆
Indonesia	☆	☆	☆	☆	☆	☆	☆	☆	☆	☆	☆	☆	☆	☆	☆	☆	☆	☆	☆
Iran	☆	☆	☆	☆	☆	☆	☆	☆	☆	☆	☆	☆	☆	☆	—	☆	☆	☆	—
Iraq	☆	☆	☆	☆	☆	☆	☆	☆	—	☆	☆	☆	☆	☆	☆	☆	☆	☆	—
Ireland	☆	☆	☆	☆	☆	☆	☆	☆	☆	☆	☆	☆	☆	☆	☆	☆	☆	☆	☆
Israel	☆	☆	☆	☆	☆	☆	☆	—	☆	☆	☆	☆	☆	☆	☆	☆	☆	☆	☆
Italy	☆	☆	☆	☆	☆	☆	☆	☆	☆	☆	☆	☆	☆	☆	☆	☆	☆	☆	☆
Jamaica	☆	☆	☆	☆	☆	☆	☆	☆	☆	☆	☆	☆	☆	☆	☆	☆	☆	☆	☆
Japan	☆	☆	☆	☆	☆	☆	☆	☆	☆	☆	☆	☆	☆	☆	☆	☆	☆	☆	☆
Jordan	☆	☆	☆	☆	☆	☆	☆	☆	☆	☆	☆	☆	☆	☆	☆	☆	☆	☆	—
Kampuchea	☆	☆	☆	☆	☆	☆	☆	—	☆	☆	☆	☆	☆	—	—	—	—	☆	—
Kenya	☆	☆	☆	☆	☆	☆	☆	☆	☆	☆	☆	☆	☆	☆	☆	☆	☆	☆	☆
Kiribati	—	—	—	—	☆	☆	—	—	—	☆	☆	—	—	—	—	—	—	—	—

Country	UN	ILO	FAO	UNESCO	ICAO	WHO	IBRD	IFC	IDA	IMF	UPU	ITU	WMO	IMO	WIPO	IFAD	UNIDO	IAEA	GATT
Korea, Democratic People's Republic of	—	—	☆	☆	☆	☆	—	—	—	—	☆	☆	☆	☆	☆	—	☆	☆	—
Korea, Republic of	—	—	☆	☆	☆	☆	☆	☆	☆	☆	☆	☆	☆	☆	☆	☆	☆	☆	☆
Kuwait	☆	☆	☆	☆	☆	☆	☆	☆	☆	☆	☆	☆	☆	—	—	☆	☆	☆	☆
Laos	☆	☆	☆	☆	☆	☆	☆	—	☆	☆	☆	☆	☆	—	—	☆	☆	—	—
Lebanon	☆	☆	☆	☆	☆	☆	☆	☆	☆	☆	☆	☆	☆	☆	—	☆	☆	☆	—
Lesotho	☆	☆	☆	☆	☆	☆	☆	☆	☆	☆	☆	☆	☆	—	—	☆	☆	—	—
Liberia	☆	☆	☆	☆	☆	☆	☆	☆	☆	☆	☆	☆	☆	☆	—	☆	☆	☆	—
Libya	☆	☆	☆	☆	☆	☆	☆	☆	☆	☆	☆	☆	☆	☆	☆	☆	☆	☆	—
Liechtenstein	—	—	—	—	—	—	—	—	—	—	☆	☆	—	—	☆	—	—	☆	—
Luxembourg	☆	☆	☆	☆	☆	☆	☆	☆	☆	☆	☆	☆	☆	—	☆	☆	☆	☆	☆
Madagascar	☆	☆	☆	☆	☆	☆	☆	☆	☆	☆	☆	☆	☆	☆	—	☆	☆	☆	☆
Malawi	☆	☆	☆	☆	☆	☆	☆	☆	☆	☆	☆	☆	☆	—	☆	☆	☆	—	☆
Malaysia	☆	☆	☆	☆	☆	☆	☆	☆	☆	☆	☆	☆	☆	☆	—	—	☆	☆	☆
Maldives	☆	—	☆	☆	☆	☆	☆	☆	☆	☆	☆	☆	☆	☆	—	☆	—	—	☆
Mali	☆	☆	☆	☆	☆	☆	☆	☆	☆	☆	☆	☆	☆	—	☆	☆	☆	☆	☆
Malta	☆	☆	☆	☆	☆	☆	☆	—	—	☆	☆	☆	☆	☆	☆	☆	☆	—	☆
Mauritania	☆	☆	☆	☆	☆	☆	☆	☆	☆	☆	☆	☆	☆	☆	☆	☆	☆	—	☆
Mauritius	☆	☆	☆	☆	☆	☆	☆	☆	☆	☆	☆	☆	☆	☆	☆	☆	☆	☆	☆
Mexico	☆	☆	☆	☆	☆	☆	☆	☆	—	☆	☆	☆	☆	☆	☆	☆	☆	☆	☆
Monaco	—	—	—	☆	—	☆	—	—	—	—	☆	☆	—	—	☆	—	—	☆	—
Mongolia	☆	☆	☆	☆	—	☆	—	—	—	—	☆	☆	☆	—	☆	☆	☆	☆	—

Country	UN	ILO	FAO	UNESCO	ICAO	WHO	IBRD	IFC	IDA	IMF	UPU	ITU	WMO	IMO	WIPO	IFAD	UNIDO	IAEA	GATT
Morocco	☆	☆	☆	☆	☆	☆	☆	☆	☆	☆	☆	☆	☆	☆	☆	☆	☆	☆	—
Mozambique	☆	☆	☆	☆	☆	☆	☆	☆	☆	☆	☆	☆	☆	☆	—	☆	☆	—	—
Namibia (UN Council)	—	☆	☆	☆	—	—	—	—	—	—	—	☆	—	—	—	—	☆	☆	—
Nauru	—	—	—	—	—	—	—	—	—	—	☆	☆	—	—	—	—	—	—	—
Nepal	☆	☆	☆	☆	☆	☆	☆	☆	☆	☆	☆	☆	☆	☆	—	☆	☆	—	—
Netherlands	☆	☆	☆	☆	☆	☆	☆	☆	☆	☆	☆	☆	☆	☆	☆	☆	☆	☆	☆
New Zealand	☆	☆	☆	☆	☆	☆	☆	☆	☆	☆	☆	☆	☆	☆	☆	☆	☆	☆	☆
Nicaragua	☆	☆	☆	☆	☆	☆	☆	☆	☆	☆	☆	☆	☆	☆	☆	☆	☆	☆	☆
Niger	☆	☆	☆	☆	☆	☆	☆	☆	☆	☆	☆	☆	☆	—	☆	☆	☆	☆	☆
Nigeria	☆	☆	☆	☆	☆	☆	☆	☆	☆	☆	☆	☆	☆	☆	—	☆	☆	☆	☆
Norway	☆	☆	☆	☆	☆	☆	☆	☆	☆	☆	☆	☆	☆	☆	☆	☆	☆	☆	☆
Oman	☆	—	☆	☆	☆	☆	☆	☆	☆	☆	☆	☆	☆	☆	—	☆	☆	—	—
Pakistan	☆	☆	☆	☆	☆	☆	☆	☆	☆	☆	☆	☆	☆	☆	☆	☆	☆	☆	☆
Panama	☆	☆	☆	☆	☆	☆	☆	☆	☆	☆	☆	☆	☆	☆	☆	☆	☆	☆	—
Papua New Guinea	☆	☆	☆	☆	☆	☆	☆	☆	☆	☆	☆	☆	☆	☆	—	☆	—	—	—
Paraguay	☆	☆	☆	☆	☆	☆	☆	☆	☆	☆	☆	☆	☆	—	—	☆	☆	☆	—
Peru	☆	☆	☆	☆	☆	☆	☆	☆	☆	☆	☆	☆	☆	☆	☆	☆	☆	☆	☆
Philippines	☆	☆	☆	☆	☆	☆	☆	☆	☆	☆	☆	☆	☆	☆	☆	☆	☆	☆	☆
Poland	☆	☆	☆	☆	☆	☆	—	—	—	—	☆	☆	☆	☆	☆	—	☆	☆	☆
Portugal	☆	☆	☆	☆	☆	☆	☆	☆	—	☆	☆	☆	☆	☆	☆	☆	☆	☆	☆
Qatar	☆	☆	☆	☆	☆	☆	☆	—	—	☆	☆	☆	☆	☆	☆	☆	☆	☆	—

Country	UN	ILO	FAO	UNESCO	ICAO	WHO	IBRD	IFC	IDA	IMF	UPU	ITU	WMO	IMO	WIPO	IFAD	UNIDO	IAEA	GATT
Romania	☆	☆	☆	☆	☆	☆	☆			☆	☆	☆	☆	☆	☆	☆	☆	☆	☆
Rwanda	☆	☆	☆	☆	☆	☆	☆	☆	☆	☆	☆	☆	☆		☆	☆	☆		☆
St Christopher and Nevis	☆			☆		☆	☆			☆									
St Lucia	☆	☆	☆	☆	☆	☆	☆	☆	☆	☆	☆	☆	☆	☆	☆	☆	☆		
St Vincent and the Grenadines	☆		☆	☆	☆	☆	☆		☆	☆	☆		☆	☆	☆				
Samoa, Western	☆		☆	☆		☆	☆	☆	☆	☆			☆		☆	☆			
San Marino		☆		☆		☆					☆	☆							
São Tomé and Príncipe	☆	☆	☆	☆	☆	☆	☆		☆	☆	☆	☆	☆		☆	☆	☆		
Saudi Arabia	☆	☆	☆	☆	☆	☆	☆	☆	☆	☆	☆	☆	☆	☆	☆	☆	☆	☆	
Senegal	☆	☆	☆	☆	☆	☆	☆	☆	☆	☆	☆	☆	☆	☆	☆	☆	☆	☆	☆
Seychelles	☆	☆	☆	☆	☆	☆	☆		☆	☆	☆		☆	☆	☆	☆	☆		
Sierra Leone	☆	☆	☆	☆	☆	☆	☆	☆	☆	☆	☆	☆	☆	☆	☆	☆	☆	☆	☆
Singapore	☆	☆			☆	☆	☆	☆		☆	☆	☆	☆	☆					☆
Solomon Islands	☆	☆	☆			☆	☆	☆	☆	☆	☆	☆	☆		☆	☆	☆		
Somalia	☆	☆	☆	☆	☆	☆	☆	☆	☆	☆	☆	☆	☆	☆	☆	☆	☆		
South Africa	☆				☆	☆	☆	☆	☆	☆	☆	☆	☆	☆	☆			☆	☆
Spain	☆	☆	☆	☆	☆	☆	☆	☆	☆	☆	☆	☆	☆	☆	☆	☆	☆	☆	☆
Sri Lanka	☆	☆	☆	☆	☆	☆	☆	☆	☆	☆	☆	☆	☆	☆	☆	☆	☆	☆	☆
Sudan	☆	☆	☆	☆	☆	☆	☆	☆	☆	☆	☆	☆	☆	☆	☆	☆	☆	☆	
Suriname	☆	☆	☆	☆	☆	☆	☆			☆	☆	☆	☆	☆	☆	☆	☆		☆

Country	UN	ILO	FAO	UNESCO	ICAO	WHO	IBRD	IFC	IDA	IMF	UPU	ITU	WMO	IMO	WIPO	IFAD	UNIDO	IAEA	GATT
Swaziland	☆	☆	☆	☆	☆	☆	☆	☆	☆	☆	☆	☆	☆	—	—	☆	☆	—	—
Sweden	☆	☆	☆	☆	☆	☆	☆	☆	☆	☆	☆	☆	☆	☆	☆	☆	☆	☆	☆
Switzerland	—	☆	☆	☆	☆	☆	—	—	—	—	☆	☆	☆	☆	☆	☆	☆	☆	☆
Syria	☆	☆	☆	☆	☆	☆	☆	☆	☆	☆	☆	☆	☆	☆	☆	☆	☆	☆	—
Tanzania	☆	☆	☆	☆	☆	☆	☆	☆	☆	☆	☆	☆	☆	☆	☆	☆	☆	☆	☆
Thailand	☆	☆	☆	☆	☆	☆	☆	☆	☆	☆	☆	☆	☆	☆	—	☆	☆	☆	☆
Togo	☆	☆	☆	☆	☆	☆	☆	☆	☆	☆	☆	☆	☆	☆	☆	☆	☆	—	☆
Tonga	—	—	☆	☆	☆	☆	—	—	—	☆	☆	—	—	☆	—	☆	☆	—	—
Trinidad and Tobago	☆	☆	☆	☆	☆	☆	☆	☆	☆	☆	☆	☆	☆	☆	—	—	☆	—	☆
Tunisia	☆	☆	☆	☆	☆	☆	☆	☆	☆	☆	☆	☆	☆	☆	☆	☆	☆	☆	—
Turkey	☆	☆	☆	☆	☆	☆	☆	☆	☆	☆	☆	☆	☆	☆	☆	☆	☆	☆	☆
Tuvalu	—	—	—	—	—	—	—	—	—	—	☆	—	—	—	—	—	—	—	—
Uganda	☆	☆	☆	☆	☆	☆	☆	☆	☆	☆	☆	☆	☆	☆	☆	☆	☆	☆	☆
Ukraine	☆	☆	—	☆	☆	☆	—	—	—	—	☆	☆	☆	☆	☆	—	☆	☆	—
USSR	☆	☆	—	☆	☆	☆	—	—	—	—	☆	☆	☆	☆	☆	—	☆	☆	—
United Arab Emirates	☆	☆	☆	☆	☆	☆	☆	☆	☆	☆	☆	☆	—	☆	☆	☆	☆	☆	—
United Kingdom	☆	☆	☆	—	☆	☆	☆	☆	☆	☆	☆	☆	☆	☆	☆	☆	☆	☆	☆
United States	☆	☆	☆	—	☆	☆	☆	☆	☆	☆	☆	☆	☆	☆	☆	☆	☆	☆	☆
Uruguay	☆	☆	☆	☆	☆	☆	☆	☆	☆	☆	☆	☆	☆	☆	☆	☆	☆	☆	☆
Vanuatu	☆	—	—	—	—	☆	☆	—	—	☆	☆	—	☆	—	—	—	—	—	—
Venezuela	☆	☆	☆	☆	☆	☆	☆	☆	—	☆	☆	☆	☆	☆	☆	☆	☆	☆	—

Country	UN	ILO	FAO	UNESCO	ICAO	WHO	IBRD	IFC	IDA	IMF	UPU	ITU	WMO	IMO	WIPO	IFAD	UNIDO	IAEA	GATT
Vietnam	☆	—	☆	☆	☆	☆	☆	☆	☆	☆	☆	☆	☆	☆	☆	☆	☆	☆	—
Yemen Arab Republic	☆	☆	☆	☆	☆	☆	☆	☆	☆	☆	☆	☆	☆	☆	☆	☆	☆	—	—
Yemen, People's Democratic Republic of	☆	☆	☆	☆	☆	☆	☆	—	—	☆	☆	☆	☆	☆	—	☆	☆	—	—
Yugoslavia	☆	☆	☆	☆	☆	☆	☆	☆	☆	☆	☆	☆	☆	☆	☆	☆	☆	☆	☆
Zaïre	☆	☆	☆	☆	☆	☆	☆	☆	☆	☆	☆	☆	☆	☆	☆	☆	☆	☆	☆
Zambia	☆	☆	☆	☆	☆	☆	☆	☆	☆	☆	☆	☆	☆	—	☆	☆	☆	☆	☆
Zimbabwe	☆	☆	☆	☆	☆	☆	☆	☆	☆	☆	☆	☆	☆	—	☆	☆	☆	—	☆
Totals	159	150	158[1]	158[2]	156[3]	166[4]	148	127	127	151	168[5]	160	159[6]	129[7]	114	139		112	92[8]

[1] Total includes Cook Islands.
[2] British Virgin Islands and Netherlands Antilles are associate members.
[3] USSR membership covers Byelorussia and Ukraine.
[4] Total includes Cook Islands; Namibia is associate member.
[5] Total includes Netherlands Antilles and UK overseas territories as two additional members.
[6] Total includes British Caribbean Territories, French Polynesia, Hong Kong, Netherlands Antilles and New Caledonia.
[7] Hong Kong is associate member.
[8] Total includes Hong Kong; Tunisia has provisionally acceded to GATT, while 31 former colonial dependencies now independent maintain a de facto application of GATT.

4. Nuclear and Conventional Disarmament

This section deals with the major post-war initiatives and agreements on a multilateral level designed to promote both conventional and nuclear disarmament and safeguards, notably the 1963 nuclear test-ban treaty, the 1967 Tlatelolco treaty and the 1968 nuclear non-proliferation treaty.*

Disarmament Bodies and Arms Limitation Agreements

UN Disarmament Commissions and Committees

Since 1946 the United Nations has created a series of commissions and committees to consider the question of world disarmament.

The first of these, the **Atomic Energy Commission,** was approved by the General Assembly in January 1946. Its creation was followed, a year later, by the setting up of a **Commission for Conventional Armaments** under a resolution of the Security Council passed on Feb. 13, 1947. These two commissions were superseded by a new **Disarmament Commission** approved by a plenary session of the General Assembly in January 1952. Its 12 members were the 11 nations represented in the Security Council together with Canada.

In November 1957 the General Assembly approved the enlargement of the Disarmament Commission from 12 to 25 members, and a year later, in November 1958, the Commission was reconstituted to include all the members of the United Nations. It did not meet again after 1965.

A special session on disarmament of the UN General Assembly, held from May 23 to July 1, 1978, resolved, inter alia, to establish, as successor to the Disarmament Commission, "a Disarmament Commission composed of all states members of the United Nations" and added that it should be "a deliberative body, a subsidiary organ of the General Assembly, the function of which shall be to consider and make recommendations on various problems in the field of disarmament and to follow up the relevant decisions and recommendations of the special session devoted to disarmament".

Geneva Disarmament Committees

A 10-power **Disarmament Committee**, compri-

sing five Eastern and five Western bloc nations, was set up in September 1959. The negotiations of this committee, which was not a UN organ, broke down in June 1960.

A joint resolution of the USA and the Soviet Union on the setting up of a new 18-nation **Disarmament Committee** was adopted by the General Assembly on Dec. 20, 1961. The committee, which was formed by five NATO countries (Britain, Canada, France, Italy and the USA), five Warsaw Pact countries (Bulgaria, Czechoslovakia, Poland, Romania and the Soviet Union) and eight uncommitted countries (Brazil, Burma, Ethiopia, India, Mexico, Nigeria, Egypt and Sweden), was in almost continuous session in Geneva. France, although a member of the committee, boycotted its work from its inception.

Following agreement between the United States and the Soviet Union, the Committee's membership was in 1969 enlarged from 18 to 26 by the addition of Japan, Mongolia, the Netherlands, Hungary, Argentina, Morocco, Pakistan and Yugoslavia, and its name was changed to the Conference of the Committee on Disarmament. As from March 1975 the conference was joined by five other countries—the German Democratic Republic, the Federal Republic of Germany, Iran, Peru and Zaïre.

In June–August 1975 the US and Soviet delegates at the conference reached "basic agreement" on a convention outlawing "weather warfare" by banning artificially induced changes in the elements and climate for the purpose of war and providing that signatories would not engage in "military or other hostile use of environmental techniques". [For convention to this effect see page 75 below.]

Creation of Committee on Disarmament, 1978–79. After agreement had been reached on June 28, 1978, at the special session of the UN General Assembly, by Britain, France, the Soviet Union and the United States on the creation of a new Committee on Disarmament, it was stated in the final document issued by the special session: "The Assembly attaches great importance to the

* Specifically East-West arms limitation and other agreements and negotiations are dealt with in Section 11, pages 284–96; for the 1985 South Pacific Nuclear Free Zone Treaty, see Section 17, pages 456–57.

participation of all the nuclear-weapon states in an appropriately constituted negotiating body, the Committee on Disarmament . . . [which] will be open to the nuclear-weapon states and 32 to 35 other states to be chosen in consultation with the President of the 32nd session of the Assembly; that the membership of the Committee on Disarmament will be reviewed at regular intervals; that [it] will be convened in Geneva not later than January 1979 . . . [and that] it will (i) conduct its work by consensus, (ii) adopt its own rules of procedure, (iii) request the (UN) Secretary-General . . . to appoint [its] secretary, (iv) rotate the chairmanship of the Committee among all its members on a monthly basis; and (v) adopt its own agenda."

The new Committee held its first formal session in January 1979 with the participation of France (which had boycotted the previous committee since 1962) and also of 35 non-nuclear-weapon states, namely Algeria, Argentina, Australia, Belgium, Brazil, Bulgaria, Burma, Canada, Cuba, Czechoslovakia, Egypt, Ethiopia, the German Democratic Republic, the Federal Republic of Germany, Hungary, India, Indonesia, Iran, Italy, Japan, Kenya, Mexico, Mongolia, Morocco, the Netherlands, Nigeria, Pakistan, Peru, Poland, Romania, Sri Lanka, Sweden, Venezuela, Yugoslavia and Zaïre. China took its seat on Feb. 5, 1980, with the result that all five nuclear-weapon states were represented on the Committee.

As from its 1984 session the Committee was renamed the UN Conference on Disarmament.

On April 1, 1986, it was reported that a group of government-appointed experts from 32 states (including the Soviet Union, the United Kingdom and the United States), meeting under the auspices of the UN Disarmament Conference, had produced a report on experiments showing that 50 seismological stations around the globe could ensure reliable identification of underground nuclear tests provided they had modern digital seismographs with standard characteristics. The experts expressed the hope that this might lead to a lowering by at least 50 per cent of the yield set in the 1974 test ban treaty and pave the way towards a comprehensive test ban.

Nuclear Test-Ban Treaty

A treaty banning all nuclear tests except those held underground was signed in Moscow on Aug. 5, 1963, by the Soviet Union, the United Kingdom and the United States.

The operative articles of this treaty read as follows:

"**Art. 1.** (1) Each of the parties to this treaty undertakes to prohibit, to prevent and not to carry out any nuclear weapon test explosion, or any other nuclear explosion, at any place under its jurisdiction or control:

"(*a*) In the atmosphere; beyond its limits, including outer space; or under water, including territorial waters or high seas; or

"(*b*) in any other environment if such explosion causes radioactive debris to be present outside the territorial limits of the state under whose jurisdiction or control such explosion is

conducted. It is understood in this connexion that the provisions of this sub-paragraph are without prejudice to the conclusion of a treaty resulting in the permanent banning of all nuclear test explosions, including all such explosions underground, the conclusion of which, as the parties have stated in the preamble to this treaty, they seek to achieve.

"(2) Each of the parties to this treaty undertakes furthermore to refrain from causing, encouraging or in any way participating in the carrying out of any nuclear weapon test explosion, or any other nuclear explosion, anywhere, which would take place in any of the environments described, or have the effect referred to, in paragraph 1 of this article.

"**Art. 2.** (1) Any party may propose amendments to this treaty. The text of any proposed amendment shall be submitted to the depository governments, which shall circulate it to all parties to this treaty. Thereafter, if requested to do so by one-third or more of the parties, the depository governments shall convene a conference, to which they shall invite all the parties, to consider such amendment.

"(2) Any amendment to this treaty must be approved by a majority of the votes of all the parties to this treaty, including all of the original parties. The amendment shall enter into force for all parties upon the deposit of instruments of ratification by a majority of all the parties, including the instruments of ratification of all of the original parties.

"**Art. 3.** (1) This treaty shall be open to all states for signature. Any state which does not sign this treaty before its entry into force in accordance with paragraph 3 of this article may accede to it at any time.

"(2) This treaty shall be subject to ratification by signatory states. Instruments of ratification and instruments of accession shall be deposited with the governments of the original parties— the USSR, the United Kingdom and the United States—which are hereby designated the depository governments.

"(3) This treaty shall enter into force after its ratification by all the original parties and the deposit of their instruments of ratification.

"(4) For states whose instruments of ratification or accession are deposited subsequent to the entry into force of this treaty, it shall enter into force on the date of the deposit of their instruments of ratification or accession.

"(5) The depository governments shall promptly inform all signatory and acceding states of the date of each signature, the date of deposit of each instrument of ratification of and accession to this treaty, the date of its entry into force, and the date of receipt of any requests for conferences or other notices.

"(6) This treaty shall be registered by the depository governments pursuant to Article 102 of the Charter of the United Nations.

"**Art. 4.** This treaty shall be of unlimited duration. Each party shall, in exercising its national sovereignty, have the right to withdraw from the treaty if it decides that extraordinary events, related to the subject matter of this treaty, have jeopardized the supreme interest of its country. It shall give notice of such withdrawal to all other parties to the treaty three months in advance."

A joint statement issued by the three powers at the time of signature expressed the hope that other states would adhere to the treaty. From Aug. 8, 1963, the treaty was open for signature in all three capitals (Washington, Moscow and London). By the date of the treaty's entry into force (Oct. 10, 1963) 105 nations had signed it, most of them in all three capitals. Of the states which refused to sign, the most important were the People's Republic of China and France; other governments which have not signed the treaty include those of Albania, Cuba, Guinea, Kampuchea, North Korea and Saudi Arabia.

The Treaty of Tlatelolco

A Treaty for the Prohibition of Nuclear Weapons in Latin America was signed at Tlatelolco, Mexico, by representatives of 21 Latin American countries on Feb. 14, 1967.

Under Art. 1 of the treaty the contracting parties undertook "to use exclusively for peaceful purposes the nuclear material and facilities which are under their jurisdiction, and to prohibit and prevent in their respective territories (a) the testing, use, manufacture, production or acquisition . . . of any nuclear weapons, by the parties themselves, directly or indirectly, on behalf of anyone else or in any other way; and (b) the receipt, storage, installation, deployment and any form of possession of any nuclear weapon, directly or indirectly, by the parties themselves, by anyone on their behalf, or in any other way". The parties also undertook "to refrain from engaging in, encouraging or authorizing, directly or indirectly, or in any way participating in the testing, use, manufacture, production, possession or control of any nuclear weapon".

The zone of application of the treaty was precisely defined (in Art. 4) as part of the Western hemisphere south of 35°N except the continental part of the territory of the United States of America and its territorial waters.

Under the treaty the Agency for the Prohibition of Nuclear Weapons was to be set up with headquarters in Mexico City for the purpose of consultation and supervision of compliance with the obligations arising from the treaty (Art. 7). This agency was to have as its supreme organ a General Conference, which would hold general sessions every two years and special sessions as required (Art. 9), and which would elect a five-member Council, to function continuously (Art. 10).

Explosions of nuclear devices for peaceful purposes would be permitted, subject to prior notification of the International Atomic Energy Agency (IAEA) (Art. 18).

Entry into force of the treaty was subject to the following requirements being met:

(i) Deposit of the instruments of ratification by all the sovereign states in the treaty's zone of application; (ii) signature and ratification of Additional Protocols I and II annexed to the treaty by the powers concerned; and (iii) conclusion of bilateral agreements with the IAEA on the application of safeguards on each country's nuclear activities.

Under *Additional Protocol I* Britain, France, the Netherlands and the United States were required to apply the status of denuclearization to the territories for which they were internationally responsible and which were situated within the treaty zone.

Under *Additional Protocol II* the powers possessing nuclear weapons (the United States, the Soviet Union, Britain, France and the People's Republic of China) were requested to respect fully "the status of denuclearization of Latin America" and to undertake "not to use or threaten to use nuclear weapons" against the contracting parties of the treaty.

Additional Protocol II has been ratified by all five nuclear-weapon states, while Additional Protocol I has been ratified by Britain, the Netherlands and the United States but only signed by France. Moreover, Cuba and Guyana have neither signed nor ratified the treaty, which therefore remains in abeyance as a multilateral instrument. On the other hand, the treaty came into force between El Salvador and Mexico on April 22, 1968, after both sides had waived the requirements described above, and has subsequently been regarded as operative for other full adherents in the treaty zone. (For list of parties to the treaty and its protocols see table on pages 77–82.)

OPANAL. The agency provided for in Article 7 of the treaty—the Agency for the Prohibition of Nuclear Weapons in Latin America (*Organismo para la Proscripción de las Armas Nucleares en la América Latina*, OPANAL)—held its inaugural meeting on Sept. 2, 1969. In addition to administering the treaty, the functions of OPANAL included endeavours to provide protection against possible nuclear attacks and to strengthen the movement against the proliferation of nuclear weapons. The Agency's membership consisted of 22 states which had fully ratified the treaty.

Nuclear Non-Proliferation Treaty

The Treaty on the Non-Proliferation of Nuclear Weapons, adopted by the UN General Assembly on June 12, 1968, and signed in London, Moscow and Washington on July 1, 1968, came into force on March 5, 1970, by which date a total of 47 countries had deposited instruments of ratification. The operative articles of the treaty (NPT) read as follows:

"**Art. 1.** Each nuclear-weapon state party to the treaty undertakes not to transfer to any recipient whatsoever nuclear weapons or other nuclear explosive devices or control over such weapons or explosive devices directly, or indirectly; and not in any way to assist, encourage, or induce any non-nuclear-weapon state to manufacture or otherwise acquire nuclear weapons or other nuclear explosive devices, or control over such weapons or explosive devices.

"**Art. 2.** Each non-nuclear-weapon state party to the treaty undertakes not to receive the transfer from any transferor whatsoever of nuclear weapons or other nuclear explosive devices or of control over such weapons of explosive devices directly, or indirectly; not to manufacture or otherwise acquire nuclear weapons or other nuclear explosive devices; and not to seek or receive any assistance in the manufacture of nuclear weapons or other nuclear explosive devices.

"**Art. 3.** (1) Each non-nuclear-weapon state party to the treaty undertakes to accept safeguards, as set forth in an agreement to be negotiated and concluded with the International Atomic Energy Agency in accordance with the Statute of the International Atomic Energy Agency and the Agency's safeguards system, for the exclusive purpose of verification of the fulfilment of its obligations assumed under this treaty with a view to preventing diversion of nuclear energy from peaceful uses to nuclear weapons or other nuclear explosive devices. Procedures for the safeguards required by this article shall be followed with respect to source or special fissionable material whether it is being produced, processed, or used in any principal nuclear facility or is outside any such facility. The safeguards required by this article shall be applied on all source or special fissionable material in all peaceful nuclear activities within the territory of such state, under its jurisdiction, or carried out under its control anywhere.

"(2) Each state party to the treaty undertakes not to provide: (a) source or special fissionable material, or (b) equipment or material especially designed or prepared for the processing, use, or production of special fissionable material, to any non-nuclear-weapon state for peaceful purposes, unless the source or special fissionable material shall be subject to the safeguards required by this article.

"(3) The safeguards required by this article shall be implemented in a manner designed to comply with Article 4 of this treaty, and to avoid hampering the economic or technological development of the parties or international co-operation in the field of peaceful nuclear activities, including the international exchange of nuclear material and equipment for the processing, use, or production of nuclear material for peaceful purposes in accordance with the provisions of this article and the principle of safeguarding set forth in the preamble.

"(4) Non-nuclear-weapon states party to the treaty shall conclude agreements with the International Atomic Energy Agency to meet the requirements of this article either individually, or together with other states in accordance with the Statute of the International Atomic Energy Agency. Negotiation of such agreements shall commence within 180 days from the original entry into force of this treaty. For states depositing their instruments of ratification or accession after the 180-day period, negotiation of such agreements shall commence not later than the date of such deposit. Such agreements shall enter into force not later than eighteen months after the date of initiation of negotiations.

"Art. 4. (1) Nothing in this treaty shall be interpreted as affecting the inalienable right of all the parties to the treaty to develop research, production and use of nuclear energy for peaceful purposes without discrimination and in conformity with Articles 1 and 2 of this treaty.

"(2) All the parties to the treaty undertake to facilitate, and have the right to participate in, the fullest possible exchange of equipment, materials, and scientific and technological information for the peaceful uses of nuclear energy. Parties to the treaty in a position to do so shall also co-operate in contributing alone or together with other states or international organizations to the further development of the applications of nuclear energy for peaceful purposes, especially in the territories of non-nuclear-weapon states party to the treaty, with due consideration for the needs of the developing areas of the world.

"Art. 5. Each party to the treaty undertakes to take appropriate measures to ensure that, in accordance with this treaty, under appropriate international observation and through appropriate international procedures, potential benefits from any peaceful applications of nuclear explosions will be made available to non-nuclear-weapon states party to the treaty on a non-discriminatory basis and that the charge to such parties for the explosive devices used will be as low as possible and exclude any charge for research and development. Non-nuclear-weapon states party to the treaty shall be able to obtain such benefits, pursuant to a special international agreement or agreements, through an appropriate international body with adequate representation of non-nuclear-weapon states. Negotiations on this subject shall commence as soon as possible after the treaty enters into force. Non-nuclear-weapon states party to the treaty so desiring may also obtain such benefits pursuant to bilateral agreements.

"Art. 6. Each of the parties to the treaty undertakes to pursue negotiations in good faith on effective measures relating to cessation of the nuclear arms race at an early date and to nuclear disarmament, and on a treaty on general and complete disarmament under strict and effective international control.

"Art. 7. Nothing in this treaty affects the right of any group of states to conclude regional treaties in order to assure the total absence of nuclear weapons in their respective territories.

"Art. 8. (1) Any party to the treaty may propose amendments to this treaty. The text of any proposed amendment shall be submitted to the depositary governments which shall circulate it to all parties to the treaty. Thereupon, if requested to do so by one-third or more of the parties to the treaty, the depositary governments shall convene a conference, to which they shall invite all the parties to the treaty, to consider such an amendment.

"(2) Any amendment to this treaty must be approved by a majority of the votes of all the parties to the treaty, including the votes of all nuclear-weapon states party to the treaty and all other parties which, on the date the amendment is circulated, are members of the Board of Governors of the International Atomic Energy Agency. The amendment shall enter into force for each party that deposits its instrument of ratification of the amendment upon the deposit of such instruments of ratification by a majority of all the parties, including the instruments of ratification of all nuclear-weapon states party to the treaty and all other parties which, on the date the amendment is circulated, are members of the Board of Governors of the International Atomic Energy Agency. Thereafter, it shall enter into force for any other party upon the deposit of its instrument of ratification of the amendment.

"(3) Five years after the entry into force of this treaty, a conference of parties to the treaty shall be held in Geneva, Switzerland, in order to review the operation of this treaty with a view to assuring that the purposes of the preamble and the provisions of the treaty are being realized. At intervals of five years thereafter, a majority of the parties to the treaty may obtain, by submitting a proposal to this effect to the depositary government, the convening of further conferences with the same objective of reviewing the operation of the treaty.

"Art. 9. (1) This treaty shall be open to all states for signature. Any state which does not sign the treaty before its entry into force in accordance with paragraph 3 of this article may accede to it any time.

"(2) This treaty shall be subject to ratification by signatory states. Instruments of ratification and instruments of accession shall be deposited with the Governments of the Union of Soviet Socialist Republics, the United Kingdom of Great Britain and Northern Ireland and the United States of America, which are hereby designated the depositary governments.

"(3) This treaty shall enter into force after its ratification by the states, the governments of which are designated depositaries of the treaty, and forty other states signatory to this treaty and the deposit of their instruments of ratification. For the purposes of this treaty, a nuclear-weapon state is one which has manufactured and exploded a nuclear weapon or other nuclear explosive device prior to Jan. 1, 1967.

"(4) For states whose instruments of ratification or accession are deposited subsequent to the entry into force of this treaty, it shall enter into force on the date of the deposit of their instruments of ratification or accession.

"(5) The depositary governments shall promptly inform all signatory and acceding states of the date of each signature, the date of deposit of each instrument of ratification or of accession, the date of the entry into force of this treaty, and the date of receipt of any requests for convening a conference or other notices.

"(6) This treaty shall be registered by the depositary governments pursuant to Article 102 of the Charter of the United Nations.

"Art. 10. (1) Each party shall in exercising its national sovereignty have the right to withdraw from the treaty if it decides that extraordinary events, related to the subject-matter of this treaty, have jeopardized the supreme interests of its country. It shall give notice of such withdrawal to all other parties to the treaty and to the United Nations Security Council three months in advance. Such notice shall include a statement of the extraordinary events it regards as having jeopardized its supreme interests.

"(2) Twenty-five years after the entry into force of the treaty, a conference shall be convened to decide whether the treaty shall continue in force indefinitely, or shall be extended for an additional fixed period or periods. This decision shall be taken by a majority of the parties to the treaty. . . ."

Countries which had not signed the treaty by July 31, 1985, included France (which had, however, indicated that it would abide by the treaty's principles), Albania, Argentina, Brazil,

Chile, China, India, Israel, North Korea, Pakistan, Saudi Arabia, South Africa and Spain.

Following the signature of the treaty by five member states of the European Communities—Belgium, West Germany, Italy, Luxembourg and the Netherlands—the European Commission began negotiations with the IAEA on an inspection agreement as stipulated in Article 3, with the objective of reaching agreement on how the Euratom control system, as previously applied, could be adapted and verified by the Agency in accordance with the treaty requirements. The Council of Ministers on Sept. 25, 1972, approved the text of the agreement, which was signed on April 5, 1973. It came into force on Feb. 21, 1977, with Denmark and Ireland as additional parties to it.

STATES PARTIES TO NPT

The treaty was signed on July 1, 1968, by the Soviet Union, the United Kingdom and the United States, 56 other countries signing on the same day.

As of July 31, 1985 a total of 120 states were parties to the treaty. Of these states, 78 non-nuclear-weapon states had negotiated safeguards agreements with the International Atomic Energy Agency (IAEA), and 69 of these agreements were in force, while another nine such agreements, approved by the IAEA Board of Governors, were awaiting entry into force.

(For list of signatories see pages 77ff.)

NPT REVIEW CONFERENCES

First Review Conference. A first review conference (as provided for in Article 8 of the treaty) was held in Geneva on May 5–30, 1975.

Of the non-signatory countries, 10—including Argentina, Brazil, Chile, Israel, Pakistan, Saudi Arabia and Spain—were then considered to have the capability of becoming nuclear-weapon states within the next two years. Of the above seven, only Argentina, Brazil and Israel were represented at the conference as observers, as were also Algeria, Cuba, South Africa, the Arab League and the Agency for the Prohibition of Nuclear Weapons in Latin America (OPANAL). Of the existing nuclear-weapon states, China, France and India (which had conducted its first nuclear test explosion on May 18, 1974) were not represented at the conference. (Among potential nuclear-weapon states, Canada, Iran and Sweden have specifically decided to forgo the production or acquisition of nuclear arms.)

The conference adopted by consensus a declaration calling inter alia for (*a*) International Atomic Energy Agency safeguards against the diversion of fissionable materials imported for peaceful purposes; (*b*) efficient protection against accidents and theft of nuclear materials during their use, storage and transport; (*c*) accelerated negotiations between the Soviet Union and the United States for the conclusion of a further strategic arms limitation agreement [for the first such agreement, see page 284]; (*d*) the seeking of a complete ban on nuclear-weapon tests and, pending such a ban, the restriction of underground tests to a minimum; and (*e*) the creation of internationally-recognized zones free from nuclear weapons, and set up on the initiative and with the approval of the states directly interested in the zone concerned and with the co-operation of the nuclear-weapon powers.

Second Review Conference. A second review conference was held in Geneva from Aug. 11 to Sept. 7, 1980. At this conference the Director-General of the IAEA stated that there were 50,000 nuclear weapons on earth with a total explosive capacity a million times that of the bomb dropped on Hiroshima (Japan) in 1945. He also said that 95 per cent of the nuclear plants in all the non-nuclear-weapon countries—whether parties to the NPT or not—were under IEAE safeguards, and that 69 of the NPT parties had IEAE safeguards in force. The conference, however, did not issue a final document, mainly because of disagreements between the nuclear-weapon powers and the non-nuclear-weapon states.

Delegates of the latter accused the Soviet Union, the United Kingdom and the United States of failure to fulfil their treaty obligations to reduce nuclear arsenals and to ban nuclear tests, and also of protecting their own nuclear monopoly by restricting the supply of peaceful nuclear technology to non-nuclear-weapon countries; these delegates unsuccessfully called for (i) the immediate cessation of all nuclear tests (of which 53 had been carried out in 1979); (ii) negotiation of a comprehensive test-ban treaty to be carried out within the Geneva Committee on Disarmament, rather than by the Soviet Union, the United Kingdom and the United States (as currently); (iii) a commitment by the USA and the USSR to honour the strategic arms limitation treaty (SALT II—see page 291) pending its ratification by the US Senate; (iv) a demand for an end to nuclear co-operation with Israel and South Africa.

The conference was nevertheless reported to have made progress towards agreements on an international plutonium-storage system, incentives for other non-nuclear-weapon states to adhere to the NPT, and drafting measures to protect fissionable materials in transit. It was also said that the participants' support for non-proliferation remained undiminished and that they had agreed to tighten safeguards against the abuse of exported nuclear technology while ensuring that it was shared for peaceful purposes.

Third Review Conference. A third review conference, held in Geneva from Aug. 27 to Sept. 21, 1985, called on (i) the United States, the Soviet Union and the United Kingdom to resume talks on a comprehensive nuclear test-ban treaty and (ii) France and China to participate in the negotiations.

Nuclear Suppliers' Group ("London Club")

Founded. Jan. 27, 1976.

Membership. Belgium, Canada, Czechoslovakia, France, the German Democratic Republic, the Federal Republic of Germany, Italy, Japan, the Netherlands, Poland, the Soviet Union, Sweden, Switzerland, the United Kingdom and the United States.

Object. To harmonize export policy in regard to nuclear materials (fuels, reactors and enrichment or retreatment plants).

History. The agreement establishing the group, as adopted by the founding members (Canada,

France, the Federal Republic of Germany, the Soviet Union, the United Kingdom and the United States), embodied two principles—

(i) that the seven countries agreed to consult each other on any negotiations for foreign sales of fuels and materials and to adopt the same rules of conduct to avoid competition and (ii) that control by the International Atomic Energy Agency (IAEA) would be extended from fuel to nuclear materials in order to avoid that a country buying a nuclear reactor or plant would later be able to reproduce them on its own or even to re-export them.

The Nuclear Suppliers' Group was in June 1976 enlarged by the accession of the German Democratic Republic, Italy, the Netherlands and Sweden, and subsequently by that of Belgium, Czechoslovakia and Poland, and on April 20, 1977, by that of Switzerland.

Activities. At a meeting of the group held in London on April 28–29, 1977, the United States was reported to have informed the other members of the group that it intended to prevent (or severely limit) the spread of nuclear weapons to some 12 to 15 countries said to be capable of producing them and having political reasons for doing so. According to the (US) Ford Foundation these nuclear "threshold countries" were (i) five "insecure states"—Israel, the Republic of Korea, South Africa, Taiwan and Yugoslavia; (ii) four "status-seeking states"—Brazil, India, Iran and Spain; and (iii) four "traditional rivals" of some of the above countries—Argentina, Egypt, the Democratic People's Republic of Korea and Pakistan.

A set of rules for the export of nuclear equipment and fuel, adopted by the group in London on Sept. 21, 1977, was published by the US State Department on Jan. 11, 1978.

Under these rules countries purchasing such equipment and fuel would have to give formal assurances not to use the material or facilities for producing a nuclear explosive device for either military or peaceful purposes; they must accept international inspection by the IAEA; they must give adequate guarantees for the effective physical protection of imported materials and equipment against theft and sabotage; these guidelines would apply also to exports of such material or equipment to a third country, with prior permission of the original exporting country being required for the export of sensitive items; and in the event of a clear or suspected violation of these rules the supplying countries would consult together to decide on any possible sanctions to be taken. (It was said that these rules would not be applied retroactively to transactions already concluded.)

At a meeting held (upon an initiative by the United States) in Luxembourg in July 1984 by the Western members of the group it was agreed to insist on tougher control of nuclear technology exports, including more stringent safeguards on existing plants and pressure on new suppliers to apply similar rules to those of the group on technology sales.

Treaty on Control of Arms on the Seabed

A Treaty on the Prohibition of the Emplacement of Nuclear Weapons and Other Weapons of Mass Destruction on the Seabed and the Ocean Floor and in the Subsoil thereof, which had been submitted to the UN General Assembly by the Conference of the Committee on Disarmament, was signed on Feb. 11, 1971, by the Soviet Union, the United Kingdom and the United States. By the time of its entry into force on May 18, 1972, a total of 34 countries had deposited instruments of ratification, while another five had signed the treaty but not yet ratified it.

The parties to the treaty undertook not to place on the seabed "any nuclear weapons or any other types of weapons of mass destruction as well as structures, launching installations, or any other facilities specifically designed for storing, testing, or using such weapons".

(For list of parties to the treaty see pages 77–82.)

Convention on the Prohibition and Destruction of Bacteriological Weapons

The UN General Assembly adopted on Dec. 16, 1971, by 110 votes to none, with one abstention, a resolution commending for signature a draft *Convention on the Prohibition of the Development, Production and Stockpiling of Bacteriological (Biological) and Toxin Weapons and on their Destruction*, which had been submitted to it by the Conference of the Committee on Disarmament.

The convention provided inter alia:

"Art. 1. Each state party to this convention undertakes never in any circumstances to develop, produce, stockpile or otherwise acquire or retain:

(*a*) microbial or other biological agents or toxins, whatever their origin or method of production, of types and in quantities that have no justification for prophylactic, protective or other peaceful purposes;

(*b*) weapons, equipment or means of delivery designed to use such agents or toxins for hostile purposes or in armed conflict.

"Art. 2. Each state party to this convention undertakes to destroy, or to divert to peaceful purposes, as soon as possible but not later than nine months after the entry into force of the convention, all agents, toxins, weapons, equipment, and means of delivery specified in Article 1 . . ., which are in its possession or under its jurisdiction or control. In implementing the provisions of this article all necessary precautions shall be observed to protect populations and the environment.

"Art. 8. Nothing in this convention shall be interpreted as in any way limiting or detracting from the obligations assumed by any state under the Protocol . . . signed at Geneva on June 17, 1925 [see page 3].

The convention was signed on April 10, 1972, by the Soviet Union, the United Kingdom and the United States, about 70 other countries signing on the same day. It came into force on March 26, 1975, when instruments of ratification were deposited by the Soviet Union, the United Kingdom, and the United States (as the three depository governments), a total of 37 of the more than 100 signatories having ratified it.

(For list of parties to the convention at July 31, 1985, see pages 77–82.)

UN Resolutions on Zones of Peace or Nuclear-Weapon-Free Zones

In a declaration adopted by the UN General Assembly on Dec. 16, 1971, by 61 votes to none with 55 abstentions, the Indian Ocean, together with the airspace above it and the ocean floor below it, was "designated for all time as a zone of peace", from which the great powers were asked to eliminate "all bases, military installations, logistical supply facilities, disposition of nuclear weapons and weapons of mass destruction".

A further resolution, urging all states to accept the above resolution, was adopted by the UN General Assembly on Dec. 6, 1973, by 95 votes to none with 35 abstentions (including four of the five permanent members of the UN Security Council—France, the Soviet Union, the United Kingdom and the United States).

On Dec. 11, 1975, the UN General Assembly adopted by 110 votes to none with 20 abstentions a resolution endorsing the idea of establishing a nuclear-weapon-free zone in the South Pacific.

Later UN General Assembly resolutions (adopted without negative votes on Dec. 12, 1977) called for nuclear-weapon-free zones in Africa, the Middle East and South Asia.

Convention on the Prohibition of Military or Any Other Hostile Use of Environmental Modification Techniques

This convention was adopted by the UN General Assembly on Dec. 10, 1976, by 96 votes to eight with 30 abstentions (being approved by all nuclear powers except France, which abstained, and China, which took no part in the vote). It was signed in Geneva on May 18, 1977. Provisions contained in this convention included the following:

"**Art. I.** (1) Each state party to this Convention undertakes not to engage in military or any other hostile use of environmental modification techniques having widespread, long-lasting or severe effects as the means of destruction, damage or injury to any other state party.

"(2) Each state party to this Convention undertakes not to assist, encourage or induce any other state, group of states or international organization to engage in activities contrary to the provisions of paragraph 1 of this article.

"**Art. II.** As used in Article I, the term 'environmental modification techniques' refers to any technique for changing—through the deliberate manipulation of natural processes—the dynamics, composition or structure of the earth, including its biota, lithosphere, hydrosphere and atmosphere, or of outer space.

"**Art. III.** (1) The provisions of this Convention shall not hinder the use of environmental modification techniques for peaceful purposes and shall be without prejudice to generally recognized principles and applicable rules of international law concerning such use. . . ."

The convention was to be of unlimited duration, but its operation was to be reviewed by a conference of the states parties to the convention to be convened five years after its entry into force—which would take place upon the deposit of instruments of ratification by 20 governments.

The convention came into force on Oct. 5, 1978, the 20 countries which had ratified it by then comprising mainly communist states but also Cyprus, Denmark, Sri Lanka, Tunisia, Finland, Britain, Ghana and Spain.

(For list of parties to this convention at July 31, 1985, see pages 77–82.)

Declaration on the Preparation of Societies for Life in Peace

This declaration, approved by the UN General Assembly on Dec. 15, 1978, by 138 votes to none (with Israel and the United States abstaining and China not voting), contained the following paragraphs:

"(1) Every nation and every human being, regardless of race, conscience, language or sex, has the inherent right to life in peace. Respect for that right, as well as for the other human rights, is in the common interest of all mankind and an indispensable condition of advancement of all nations, large and small, in all fields.

"(2) A war of aggression, its planning, preparation or initiation are crimes against peace and are prohibited by international law.

"(3) In accordance with the purposes and principles of the United Nations, states have the duty to refrain from propaganda for wars of aggression.

"(4) Every state, acting in the spirit of friendship and good-neighbourly relations, has the duty to promote all-round, mutually advantageous and equitable political, economic, social and cultural co-operation with other states, notwithstanding their socio-economic systems, with a view to securing their common existence and co-operation in peace, in conditions of mutual understanding and of respect for the identity and diversity of all peoples, and the duty to take up actions conducive to the furtherance of the ideals of peace, humanism and freedom.

"(5) Every state has the duty to respect the right of all peoples to self-determination, independence, equality, sovereignty, the territorial integrity of states and the inviolability of their frontiers, including the right to determine the road of their development, without interference or intervention in their internal affairs. . . .

"(7) Every state has the duty to discourage all manifestations and practices of colonialism, as well as racism, racial discrimination and apartheid, as contrary to the right of peoples to self-determination and to other human rights and fundamental freedoms."

Convention on the Protection of Nuclear Material

A *Convention on the Physical Protection of Nuclear Material*, drawn up under the auspices of the International Atomic Energy Agency, was opened for signature on March 3, 1980, and was to enter into force 30 days after ratification, acceptance or approval by 21 states.

The convention is designed to achieve international co-operation in order "to avert the potential dangers posed by the unlawful taking and use of nuclear material", to make it possible to ensure the prevention, detection and punishment of such offences, "to facilitate the safe transfer of nuclear material" and to protect it "in domestic use, storage and transport" (while stressing the need for "stringent physical protection" for nuclear material used for military purposes). Under the convention the unlawful taking and use of nuclear material as well as attempts at such action, or to use force or other forms of intimidation in this connexion or to use nuclear material "to cause death or injury to persons or substantial property damage" are made punishable and extraditable offences. In two annexes to the convention detailed levels of protection are given for three different categories of nuclear materials.

The implementation of the convention was to be reviewed five years after its entry into force. It also provided for an optional procedure for the settlement of disputes concerning the interpretation or application of the convention.

Convention on Excessively Injurious Conventional Weapons

A *Convention on Prohibitions or Restrictions of Use of Certain Conventional Weapons which may be deemed to be Excessively Injurious or have Indiscriminate Effects* was endorsed by the UN General Assembly on Oct. 10, 1980, and came into force on Oct. 2, 1983, together with three protocols on (i) non-detectable fragments, (ii) mines, booby-traps and other devices and (iii) incendiary weapons. The convention and its protocols were supplementary to the 1949 Geneva Conventions and their 1977 protocols [see pages 1–2]. (For list of parties to the convention at July 31, 1985, see pages 77–82.)

Signatories of and Parties to Multilateral Disarmament Agreements

A composite table of signatories of and parties to multilateral disarmament agreements, based on information submitted to the UN Secretary-General as at July 31, 1985, is shown below.

The agreements listed are as follows:

Geneva Protocol – of 1925, see page 3
Antarctic Treaty – of 1959, see page 83
Partial Test Ban – the Nuclear Test-Ban Treaty of 1963, see page 70
Outer Space – The Outer Space Treaty of 1966, see page 87
Treaty of Tlatelolco – of 1967, see page 71
Non-Proliferation – the Nuclear Non-Proliferation Treaty of 1968, see pages 71–73
Seabed – the Treaty on Control of Arms on the Seabed, see page 74
BW Convention – the Convention on the Prohibition and Destruction of Bacteriological Weapons of 1971, see page 74
ENMOD – the Convention on the Prohibition of Military or Any Other Hostile Use of Environmental Modification Techniques of 1976, see page 75

Celestial Bodies – the Agreement governing the Activities of States on the Moon and Other Celestial Bodies of 1979, see page 89
Conventional Weapons – the Convention on Prohibition or Restrictions on the Use of Certain Conventional Weapons which may be deemed to be Excessively Injurious or to have Indiscriminate Effects of 1981, see above

Note:
Kampuchea—*see* Democratic Kampuchea
Korea, Democratic People's Republic of—*see* Democratic People's Republic of Korea
Korea, Republic of—*see* Republic of Korea
Tanzania—*see* United Republic of Tanzania
Vatican—*see* Holy See
Yemen Arab Republic—*see* Yemen
Yemen, People's Democratic Republic of—*see* Democratic Yemen

(s) = signed; (r) = ratified (including accessions and successions)

State	Geneva Protocol (s)	(r)	Antarctic Treaty (s)	(r)	Partial Test Ban (s)	(r)	Outer Space (s)	(r)	Treaty of Tlatelolco (s)	(r)	Non-proliferation (s)	(r)	Seabed (s)	(r)	BW Convention (s)	(r)	ENMOD (s)	(r)	Celestial bodies (s)	(r)	Conventional weapons (s)	(r)[1]
Afghanistan		☆			☆	☆	☆				☆	☆	☆	☆	☆	☆					☆	
Albania					☆						☆		☆	☆	☆	☆						
Algeria	☆	☆			☆																	
Angola																						
Antigua and Barbuda									☆	☆		☆										
Argentina	☆		☆	☆	☆		☆		☆		☆		☆		☆	☆					☆	
Australia	☆	☆	☆	☆	☆	☆	☆	☆			☆	☆	☆	☆	☆	☆	☆				☆	☆
Austria	☆	☆			☆	☆	☆	☆			☆	☆	☆	☆	☆	☆	☆	☆	☆	☆	☆	☆
Bahamas						☆		☆	☆	☆		☆	☆		☆							
Bahrain											☆											
Bangladesh												☆						☆				
Barbados	☆						☆		☆	☆	☆		☆		☆	☆						
Belgium	☆	☆	☆	☆	☆	☆	☆	☆			☆	☆	☆	☆	☆	☆	☆	☆			☆	
Belize																						
Benin					☆						☆		☆		☆		☆					
Bhutan						☆						☆			☆	☆						
Bolivia		☆			☆		☆		☆	☆	☆	☆	☆	☆	☆		☆					
Botswana						☆	☆				☆	☆	☆		☆							
Brazil	☆	☆		☆	☆	☆	☆	☆	☆	☆			☆	☆	☆	☆		☆				
Brunei Darussalam							☆					☆										
Bulgaria	☆	☆	☆	☆	☆	☆	☆	☆			☆	☆	☆	☆	☆	☆	☆	☆			☆	☆
Burkina Faso		☆			☆		☆				☆		☆		☆	☆	☆					
Burma					☆		☆				☆		☆		☆							
Burundi					☆		☆								☆							
Byelorussian Soviet Socialist Republic					☆	☆	☆	☆			☆	☆	☆	☆	☆	☆	☆	☆			☆	☆
Cameroon					☆		☆				☆	☆	☆		☆							
Canada	☆	☆	☆	☆	☆	☆	☆	☆			☆	☆	☆	☆	☆	☆	☆	☆			☆	
Cape Verde					☆						☆		☆	☆	☆	☆	☆	☆			☆	
Central African Republic		☆			☆		☆				☆	☆			☆							

State	Geneva Protocol		Antarctic Treaty		Partial Test Ban		Outer Space		Treaty of Tlatelolco		Non-proliferation		Seabed		BW Convention		ENMOD		Celestial bodies		Conventional weapons[1]	
	(s)	(r)	(s)	(r)	(s)	(r)	(s)	(r)	(s)	(r)	(s)	(r)	(s)	(r)	(s)	(r)	(s)	(r)	(s)	(r)	(s)	(r)
Chad					☆	☆					☆	☆										
Chile	☆		☆	☆	☆	☆	☆	☆	☆	☆					☆	☆			☆	☆		☆
China		☆		☆				☆	☆[2]	☆[2]						☆					☆	☆
Colombia					☆		☆		☆		☆		☆		☆	☆						
Comoros																						
Congo											☆	☆	☆	☆	☆	☆						
Costa Rica						☆			☆	☆	☆	☆	☆	☆	☆	☆						
Côte d'Ivoire					☆	☆					☆	☆	☆	☆	☆							
Cuba	☆						☆						☆	☆	☆	☆	☆				☆	
Cyprus	☆			☆	☆	☆	☆	☆			☆	☆	☆	☆	☆	☆	☆	☆				
Czechoslovakia	☆			☆	☆	☆	☆	☆			☆	☆	☆	☆	☆	☆	☆	☆			☆	☆
Democratic Kampuchea	☆										☆		☆									
Democratic People's Republic of Korea*																	☆					
Democratic Yemen	☆					☆		☆			☆	☆	☆	☆	☆	☆		☆			☆	☆
Denmark	☆		☆	☆	☆	☆	☆	☆			☆	☆	☆	☆	☆	☆	☆	☆			☆	☆
Djibouti												☆										
Dominica																						
Dominican Republic	☆				☆	☆	☆	☆	☆	☆	☆	☆	☆	☆	☆	☆					☆	
Ecuador	☆				☆	☆	☆	☆	☆	☆	☆	☆	☆	☆	☆	☆					☆	
Egypt	☆				☆	☆	☆	☆			☆	☆	☆	☆	☆			☆				
El Salvador	☆				☆	☆	☆	☆	☆	☆	☆	☆	☆	☆	☆							
Equatorial Guinea											☆	☆		☆								
Ethiopia	☆						☆				☆	☆	☆	☆	☆	☆		☆				
Fiji	☆				☆	☆		☆			☆	☆	☆	☆	☆	☆						
Finland	☆		☆	☆	☆	☆	☆	☆			☆	☆	☆	☆	☆	☆	☆	☆			☆	☆
France	☆		☆	☆			☆	☆	☆[3]	☆[3]			☆		☆	☆			☆		☆	☆
Gabon					☆		☆						☆		☆							
Gambia	☆				☆	☆	☆				☆		☆		☆							
German Democratic Republic	☆		☆	☆	☆	☆	☆	☆			☆	☆	☆	☆	☆	☆	☆	☆			☆	☆

State	Geneva Protocol (s)	(r)	Antarctic Treaty (s)	(r)	Partial Test Ban (s)	(r)	Outer Space (s)	(r)	Treaty of Tlatelolco (s)	(r)	Non-proliferation (s)	(r)	Seabed (s)	(r)	BW Convention (s)	(r)	ENMOD (s)	(r)	Celestial bodies (s)	(r)	Conventional weapons (s)	(r)[1]
Germany, Federal Republic of		☆		☆	☆	☆	☆	☆			☆	☆	☆	☆	☆	☆	☆	☆			☆	
Ghana		☆			☆	☆	☆				☆	☆	☆	☆	☆	☆	☆	☆				
Greece	☆	☆			☆	☆	☆	☆			☆	☆	☆	☆	☆	☆	☆	☆			☆	
Grenada									☆	☆		☆										
Guatemala		☆			☆	☆	☆		☆	☆	☆	☆	☆		☆	☆			☆			☆
Guinea										☆		☆	☆									
Guinea-Bissau						☆		☆						☆		☆						
Guyana							☆								☆							
Haiti		☆			☆		☆		☆	☆	☆	☆	☆		☆							
Holy See*		☆					☆				☆	☆					☆					
Honduras					☆	☆	☆		☆	☆	☆	☆	☆	☆	☆	☆						
Hungary		☆		☆	☆	☆	☆	☆			☆	☆	☆	☆	☆	☆	☆	☆			☆	☆
Iceland		☆			☆	☆	☆	☆			☆	☆	☆	☆	☆	☆	☆				☆	☆
India	☆	☆		☆	☆	☆	☆	☆				☆	☆	☆	☆	☆	☆	☆	☆	☆	☆	☆
Indonesia		☆			☆	☆					☆	☆	☆		☆							
Iran (Islamic Republic of)		☆			☆	☆	☆				☆	☆	☆	☆	☆	☆	☆					
Iraq		☆			☆	☆	☆				☆	☆	☆	☆	☆		☆	☆				
Ireland		☆			☆	☆	☆	☆			☆	☆	☆	☆	☆	☆	☆				☆	
Israel	☆	☆			☆	☆	☆	☆			☆		☆	☆			☆	☆	☆		☆	
Italy	☆	☆		☆	☆	☆	☆	☆			☆	☆	☆	☆	☆	☆	☆	☆			☆	☆
Jamaica		☆			☆				☆	☆	☆		☆		☆	☆						
Japan	☆	☆	☆	☆	☆	☆	☆	☆			☆	☆	☆	☆	☆	☆	☆		☆		☆	☆
Jordan		☆			☆	☆	☆				☆	☆	☆	☆	☆	☆						
Kenya		☆				☆					☆	☆			☆							
Kiribati**												☆										
Kuwait		☆					☆				☆	☆	☆	☆	☆	☆	☆					
Lao People's Democratic Republic		☆			☆	☆	☆	☆			☆	☆	☆	☆	☆	☆	☆	☆			☆	☆
Lebanon		☆	☆	☆	☆	☆	☆	☆			☆	☆	☆	☆	☆	☆		☆				
Lesotho		☆			☆	☆	☆				☆	☆	☆	☆	☆	☆	☆					
Liberia		☆			☆	☆					☆	☆	☆	☆	☆		☆					

79

State	Geneva Protocol (s)	(r)	Antarctic Treaty (s)	(r)	Partial Test Ban (s)	(r)	Outer Space (s)	(r)	Treaty of Tlatelolco (s)	(r)	Non-proliferation (s)	(r)	Seabed (s)	(r)	BW Convention (s)	(r)	ENMOD (s)	(r)	Celestial bodies (s)	(r)	Conventional weapons (s)	(r)[1]
Libyan Arab Jamahiriya	☆				☆	☆		☆			☆	☆				☆						
Liechtenstein**		☆									☆	☆									☆	
Luxembourg	☆	☆			☆	☆	☆				☆	☆	☆	☆	☆	☆	☆				☆	
Madagascar		☆			☆	☆		☆			☆	☆	☆	☆	☆							
Malawi		☆				☆					☆	☆	☆	☆	☆			☆				
Malaysia		☆			☆	☆	☆				☆	☆	☆	☆	☆							
Maldives		☆						☆			☆	☆	☆	☆								
Mali					☆						☆	☆	☆	☆	☆							
Malta		☆				☆		☆			☆	☆	☆	☆	☆	☆						
Mauritania					☆						☆	☆	☆	☆								
Mauritius		☆				☆		☆			☆	☆	☆	☆	☆	☆						
Mexico		☆			☆	☆	☆	☆	☆	☆	☆	☆	☆	☆	☆	☆			☆		☆	☆
Monaco*		☆											☆	☆	☆							
Mongolia		☆			☆	☆	☆	☆			☆	☆	☆	☆	☆	☆	☆	☆	☆	☆	☆	☆
Morocco		☆			☆	☆	☆	☆			☆	☆	☆	☆	☆				☆		☆	
Mozambique																						
Nauru**												☆										
Nepal		☆			☆	☆		☆			☆	☆	☆	☆	☆							
Netherlands	☆	☆		☆	☆	☆	☆	☆	☆[4]	☆[4]	☆	☆	☆	☆	☆	☆	☆	☆	☆	☆	☆	☆
New Zealand		☆	☆	☆	☆	☆	☆	☆			☆	☆	☆	☆	☆	☆	☆	☆	☆	☆	☆	
Nicaragua					☆	☆		☆	☆	☆	☆	☆	☆	☆	☆		☆				☆	
Niger		☆			☆	☆	☆	☆			☆	☆	☆	☆	☆						☆	
Nigeria		☆			☆	☆	☆	☆			☆	☆	☆	☆	☆						☆	
Norway	☆	☆		☆	☆	☆	☆	☆			☆	☆	☆	☆	☆	☆	☆	☆			☆	☆
Oman																						
Pakistan		☆			☆	☆	☆	☆			☆	☆	☆	☆	☆	☆	☆				☆	
Panama		☆			☆	☆		☆	☆	☆	☆	☆	☆	☆	☆	☆	☆					
Papua New Guinea		☆				☆		☆			☆	☆	☆	☆	☆	☆	☆					
Paraguay		☆			☆	☆		☆	☆	☆	☆	☆	☆	☆	☆	☆						
Peru					☆	☆		☆	☆	☆	☆	☆	☆	☆	☆		☆		☆			
Philippines		☆			☆	☆	☆	☆			☆	☆	☆	☆	☆	☆	☆		☆	☆	☆	☆
Poland	☆	☆		☆	☆	☆	☆	☆			☆	☆	☆	☆	☆	☆	☆	☆			☆	☆

State	Geneva Protocol (s)	(r)	Antarctic Treaty (s)	(r)	Partial Test Ban (s)	(r)	Outer Space (s)	(r)	Treaty of Tlatelolco (s)	(r)	Non-proliferation (s)	(r)	Seabed (s)	(r)	BW Convention (s)	(r)	ENMOD (s)	(r)	Celestial bodies (s)	(r)	Conventional weapons (s)	(r) [1]
Portugal	☆	☆			☆							☆	☆	☆	☆	☆	☆				☆	
Qatar		☆												☆	☆	☆						
Republic of Korea*	☆	☆		☆	☆	☆	☆	☆			☆	☆	☆	☆	☆	☆				☆		
Romania	☆	☆		☆	☆	☆	☆	☆			☆	☆	☆	☆	☆	☆	☆	☆	☆	☆	☆	
Rwanda		☆			☆	☆	☆					☆	☆	☆	☆	☆						
Saint Christopher and Nevis												☆										
Saint Lucia												☆										
Saint Vincent and the Grenadines												☆										
Samoa					☆							☆										
San Marino**					☆	☆	☆	☆			☆	☆		☆	☆	☆		☆				
São Tomé and Príncipe							☆															
Saudi Arabia	☆												☆	☆	☆	☆						
Senegal	☆				☆						☆	☆	☆	☆	☆	☆						
Seychelles							☆				☆	☆	☆	☆	☆	☆						
Sierra Leone	☆				☆		☆	☆			☆	☆	☆	☆	☆	☆	☆	☆		☆		
Singapore					☆	☆	☆	☆			☆	☆	☆	☆	☆	☆						
Solomon Islands	☆											☆	☆	☆	☆	☆		☆				
Somalia					☆		☆				☆	☆			☆							
South Africa	☆	☆	☆	☆	☆	☆	☆	☆			☆	☆	☆	☆	☆	☆	☆	☆		☆		
Spain	☆	☆	☆	☆	☆	☆	☆	☆			☆	☆	☆	☆	☆	☆	☆	☆				
Sri Lanka	☆				☆		☆	☆			☆	☆	☆	☆	☆	☆	☆	☆				
Sudan	☆				☆		☆	☆			☆	☆	☆		☆					☆		
Suriname							☆	☆	☆	☆	☆	☆	☆	☆								
Swaziland	☆				☆		☆	☆			☆	☆	☆	☆	☆	☆						
Sweden	☆	☆			☆	☆	☆	☆			☆	☆	☆	☆	☆	☆	☆	☆		☆	☆	☆
Switzerland*	☆	☆		☆	☆	☆	☆	☆			☆	☆	☆	☆	☆	☆				☆	☆	☆
Syrian Arab Republic	☆				☆		☆				☆	☆			☆		☆					
Thailand	☆	☆			☆	☆	☆	☆			☆	☆	☆	☆	☆	☆						
Togo	☆				☆	☆	☆	☆			☆	☆	☆	☆	☆	☆				☆		
Tonga**	☆				☆		☆				☆	☆			☆							
Trinidad and Tobago	☆				☆	☆	☆		☆	☆	☆					☆						

81

State	Geneva Protocol (s)	(r)	Antarctic Treaty (s)	(r)	Partial Test Ban (s)	(r)	Outer Space (s)	(r)	Treaty of Tlatelolco (s)	(r)	Non-proliferation (s)	(r)	Seabed (s)	(r)	BW Convention (s)	(r)	ENMOD (s)	(r)	Celestial bodies (s)	(r)	Conventional weapons (s)	(r)[1]
Tunisia		☆			☆	☆	☆	☆			☆	☆	☆	☆	☆	☆	☆	☆				
Turkey**	☆	☆	☆	☆	☆	☆	☆	☆			☆	☆	☆	☆	☆	☆	☆	☆			☆	
Tuvalu**												☆										
Uganda		☆			☆			☆				☆			☆		☆					
Ukrainian Soviet Socialist Republic					☆	☆	☆	☆			☆	☆	☆	☆	☆	☆	☆	☆			☆	☆
Union of Soviet Socialist Republics	☆	☆	☆	☆	☆	☆	☆	☆	☆[5]	☆[5]	☆	☆	☆	☆	☆	☆	◆	☆			☆	☆
United Arab Emirates															☆							
United Kingdom of Great Britain and Northern Ireland	☆	☆	☆	☆	☆	☆	☆	☆	☆[6]	☆[6]	☆	☆	☆	☆	☆	☆	☆	☆			☆	
United Republic of Tanzania		☆			☆									☆	☆							
United States of America	☆	☆	☆	☆	☆	☆	☆	☆	☆[7]	☆[7]	☆	☆	☆	☆	☆	☆	☆	☆			☆	
Uruguay	☆	☆	☆	☆	☆	☆	☆	☆	☆	☆	☆	☆	☆	☆	☆	☆			☆	☆		
Vanuatu																						
Venezuela	☆	☆			☆	☆	☆	☆	☆	☆	☆	☆	☆	☆	☆	☆					☆	
Vietnam		☆				☆		☆				☆		☆		☆		☆				
Yemen		☆			☆									☆	☆		☆					
Yugoslavia	☆	☆			☆	☆	☆	☆			☆	☆	☆	☆	☆	☆	☆	☆			☆	☆
Zaire						☆					☆	☆		☆	☆	☆	☆					
Zambia								☆					☆									
Zimbabwe																						

* Non-member states maintaining permanent observer missions to the United Nations.
** Non-member and non-observer states belonging to specialized agencies.
[1] All states ratifying this convention so far have given notification of their acceptance of Protocols I, II and III.
[2] China has signed and ratified Additional Protocol II.
[3] France has signed Additional Protocols I and II but only ratified II.
[4] The Netherlands has signed and ratified Additional Protocol I.
[5] The USSR has signed and ratified Additional Protocol II.
[6] The United Kingdom has signed and ratified Additional Protocols I and II.
[7] The United States has signed and ratified Additional Protocols I and II.

5. Agreements and Organizations concerned with Scientific, Communications, Space and Environmental Co-operation

The following section covers (i) the major international and multilateral agreements entered into by governments in the fields of scientific co-operation as well as organizations concerned with such co-operation; (ii) postal and telecommunications organizations; (iii) international co-operation and agreements on matters of space research and utilization; (iv) major international declarations, conventions and conferences on environmental problems; (v) organizations for the preservation of the living resources of the sea; and (vi) international fisheries organizations for the regulation of fisheries in various regions of the world's oceans and seas.

Agreements and Organizations in the Field of Scientific Co-operation

Antarctic Treaty

On Dec. 1, 1959, a 30-year treaty was signed in Washington at the end of a 12-nation conference on peaceful international scientific co-operation in Antarctica. The 12 original signatories were Argentina, Australia, Belgium, Britain, Chile, France, Japan, New Zealand, Norway, South Africa, the Soviet Union and the United States, all of them members of a Scientific Committee for Antarctic Research founded in September 1958. Other countries subsequently became parties to the treaty as follows: Brazil (on May 16, 1975), Bulgaria (on Sept. 11, 1978), China (on June 8, 1974), Cuba (on Aug. 16, 1984), Czechoslovakia (on June 14, 1962), Denmark (on May 20, 1965), Finland (on May 15, 1984), the German Democratic Republic (on Nov. 19, 1974), the Federal Republic of Germany (on Feb. 5, 1979), Hungary (on Jan. 27, 1984), India (on Aug. 19, 1983), Italy (on March 18, 1981), the Netherlands (on March 30, 1967), Papua New Guinea (on March 16, 1981), Peru (on April 10, 1981), Poland (on June 8, 1981), Romania (on Sept. 15, 1971), Spain (on March 31, 1982), Sweden (on April 25, 1984) and Uruguay (on Jan. 11, 1980).

The main provisions of the treaty, which came into force on June 23, 1961, are summarized below.

Art. 1. Antarctica shall be used for peaceful purposes only. The contracting parties are forbidden to establish military bases in the area, to carry out military manoeuvres, or to test any kind of weapons.

Art. 2. Freedom of scientific investigation and co-operation towards that end should be maintained.

Art. 3. Scientific information and personnel should be exchanged by the contracting parties.

Art. 4. Nothing contained in the treaty may be interpreted as a renunciation, denial or support of a claim to territorial sovereignty in Antarctica. No new claim to territorial sovereignty may be asserted while the treaty is in force.

Art. 5. Any nuclear explosions in Antarctica and the disposal there of radioactive waste shall be prohibited.

Art. 6. The provisions of the treaty apply to the land area south of 60 degrees South latitutde.

Art. 7. Each contracting party has the right to send observers to carry out inspections in Antarctica. Notification must be given of all expeditions and stations in Antarctica.

Art. 8. Observers and scientific personnel in Antarctica are subject to the jurisdiction of their own country.

Art. 9. The contracting parties shall meet at suitable intervals to consult together on measures for the furtherance of the principles and objectives of the treaty.

Later Agreements. On Feb. 11, 1972, the treaty's original signatories concluded an agreement on the protection of seals in the Antarctic, including those in the open sea and on floating ice, and this agreement came into force on March 11, 1978.

At a consultative meeting of the treaty signatories held in Washington from Sept. 17 to Oct. 5, 1979, it was agreed (i) to maintain voluntary restraint in the exploration and exploitation of Antarctic minerals (notably oil and gas), (ii) to move towards adoption of a draft convention for the regulation of fishing, and

(iii) to co-operate in telecommunications, the development of guidelines for tourism and the study of the impact of various measures on the environment.

Living Resources Convention. A convention on the conservation of Antarctic living resources, in particular krill (a protein-rich crustacean), was signed at a meeting held in Canberra (Australia) on May 7–20, 1980, by 15 countries and by observers (including the European Community). Agreement on the convention had been reached by the 12 original signatories of the Antarctic Treaty and also by Poland, the German Democratic Republic and the Federal Republic of Germany. Under the convention an international commission was to be established in Hobart (Tasmania) to supervise the preservation of marine life, to study the food-chain of Antarctic fish and bird life and to recommend measures to protect the species.

The convention came into force on April 7, 1981, and the 18 parties to it are Argentina, Australia, Belgium, Chile, the EEC, France, the German Democratic Republic, the Federal Republic of Germany, Japan, New Zealand, Norway, Poland, South Africa, the Soviet Union, Spain, Sweden, the United Kingdom and the United States.

Organizations

Intergovernmental Oceanographic Commission (ICO)

Address. c/o UNESCO, 7 place de Fontenoy, 75700 Paris, France.

Officers. Prof. I. A. Ronquillo (pres.); Dr Mario Ruivo (sec.).

Founded. 1960.

Membership. 111 Governments.

Object. To promote scientific investigation into the nature and resources of the oceans through concerted action of IOC members.

Activities. The IOC has carried out a Long-term and Expanded Programme of Ocean Exploration and Research (LEPOR), involving an International Decade of Ocean Exploration (1971–80). Its ocean science section embraces a Comprehensive Plan for Global Investigation of Pollution in the Marine Environment (GIPME) and a first regional association for the Caribbean and adjacent regions (IOCARIBE), which has 18 member states (including Brazil and the Soviet Union). Other ocean services of the IOC are an Integrated Global Ocean Station System (IGOSS) for monitoring pollution, and an International Oceanographic Data Exchange (IODE) with working groups for various problems. The IOC has been involved in numerous projects, many of them carried out in co-operation with other international organizations. The IOC is assisted by a Scientific Advisory Board of 15 members and by three non-governmental advisory bodies.

International Association for Earthquake Engineering

Address. Kenchiku Kaikan, 3rd Floor, 5-26-20, Shiba, Minato-ku, Tokyo 108, Japan.

Officer. Donald E. Hudson (pres.).

Founded. 1963.

Membership. 34 countries.

Object. To exchange knowledge and results both of practical experience and of research in earthquake engineering.

International Association for the Physical Sciences of the Ocean (IAPSO)

Address. LaFond Oceanic Consultants, P.O.B. 7325, San Diego, California 92107, USA.

Officers. Prof. Wolfgang Krauss (Federal Republic of Germany, pres.); Dr Eugene C. LaFond (USA, sec. gen.).

Founded. 1919.

Membership. 78 countries and territories.

Objects. To promote the study of scientific problems relating to the ocean and interactions taking place at its boundaries, chiefly in so far as such studies may be carried out by the aid of mathematics, physics and chemistry; to initiate, facilitate and co-ordinate research into and investigations of those problems of the ocean which require international co-operation; and to provide for discussion, comparison and publications.

Activities. Holding of symposia; participation, with the International Association of Meteorology and Atmospheric Physics (IAMAP), in a Scientific Assembly held in Honolulu, Hawaii, on Aug. 5–16, 1985; General Assembly to be held in Vancouver, Canada, in August 1987.

International Bureau for Informatics (IBI)

Address. P.O.B. 10253, 00144 Rome, Italy.

Officer. Prof. F. A. Bernasconi (dir.-gen.).

Founded. Nov. 28, 1961.

Membership. Algeria, Argentina, Benin, Bolivia, Burkina Faso, Cameroon, Chile, the Congo, Côte d'Ivoire, Cuba, Egypt, Ecuador, France, Gabon, Ghana, Haiti, Iraq, Italy, Jordan, Lebanon, Madagascar, Mexico, Morocco, Nicaragua, Niger, Nigeria, Panama, São Tomé and Príncipe, Senegal, Spain, Swaziland, Syria, Togo, Tunisia, Venezuela and Zaïre.

Object. To promote the development and diffusion of informatics.

Structure. The IBI has a general assembly which meets every two years.

International Commission for the Scientific Exploration of the Mediterranean Sea (ICSEM)

Address. 16 blvd. de la Suisse, MC-98030, Monaco.

Officers. Prince Rainier III of Monaco (pres.); Commandant Jacques-Yves Cousteau (sec. gen.).

Founded. 1919.

Membership. 17 countries, 1,200 scientists and 12 scientific committees.

International Hydrographic Organization (IHO)

Address. Directing Committee, International Hydrographic Bureau (Secretariat of IHO), Ave. Président J. F. Kennedy (B.P.345), Monte Carlo, MC 98000, Monaco.

Founded. June 1921.

Directing Committee. Rear-Adml. F. L. Fraser (pres.); Vice-Adml. O. A. A. Afonso and Capt. J. E. Ayres (directors).

History. The IHO was founded as the International Hydrographic Bureau, which name it changed to IHO in 1967 (while retaining its former name for its headquarters in Monaco).

Membership. 52 countries (Argentina, Australia, Belgium, Brazil, Canada, Chile, China, Cuba, Denmark, the Dominican Republic, Ecuador, Egypt, Fiji, Finland, France, the Federal Republic of Germany, Greece, Guatemala, Iceland, India, Indonesia, Iran, Italy, Japan, the Republic of Korea, Malaysia, Monaco, the Netherlands, New Zealand, Nigeria, Norway, Pakistan, Peru, the Philippines, Poland, Portugal, Singapore, South Africa, the Soviet Union, Spain, Sri Lanka, Sweden, Syria, Thailand, Trinidad and Tobago, Turkey, the United Kingdom, the United States, Uruguay, Venezuela, Yugoslavia and Zaïre); membership pending for three others (the German Democratic Republic, Papua New Guinea and Suriname).

Objects. The main purpose of this organization is to make international navigation safer and easier by co-ordinating and expanding hydrographic work and giving relevant assistance to developing countries.

International Institute of Refrigeration
Institut International du Froid

Address. 177 blvd. Malesherbes, 75017 Paris, France.

Officer. A. Gac (dir.).

Founded. 1920.

Membership. 41 countries (Algeria, Australia, Austria, Belgium, Bulgaria, Cameroon, Canada, Chad, Chile, China, Côte d'Ivoire, Cuba, Czechoslovakia, Denmark, Egypt, Finland, France, the German Democratic Republic, the Federal Republic of Germany, Guinea, Hungary, Ireland, Israel, Italy, Jordan, Mali, Morocco, the Netherlands, New Zealand, Niger, Norway, Portugal, Romania, Senegal, South Africa, the Soviet Union, Spain, Sweden, Togo, the United Kingdom and Yugoslavia). (Switzerland has transferred its rights and obligations to the Association Suisse du Froid.)

History. The institute was set up under a convention of June 21, 1920, which was amended on May 31, 1937, and superseded by a new convention of Dec. 1, 1954, in force for 10 years and thereafter for successive four-year periods.

International Institute of Seismology and Earthquake Engineering

Address. Building Research Institute, Ministry of Construction, 1 Tatehara, Oho-machi, Tsukuba-gun, Ibaraki Pref., Japan.

Officer. M. Otsuka (dir.).

Founded. 1962.

Membership. 45 countries.

Objects. To reduce earthquake damage by training seismologists and earthquake engineers from seismic countries and to carry out surveys, research, guidance and analysis of information on earthquakes and related matters.

International Red Locust Control Organization

Address. P.O.B. 37, Mbala, Zambia.

Officers. W. R. Meswele (ch.); Dr M. E. A. Materu (dir.).

Founded. 1971.

Membership. 10 countries.

History. Before the creation of this organization an international convention for the permanent control of the red locust had been signed in London in October 1953 by Belgium, South Africa, Southern Rhodesia (now Zimbabwe) and the United Kingdom.

International Union of Pure and Applied Physics

Address. Chalmers University of Technology, 412 96 Göteborg, Sweden.

Officers. Prof. D. A. Bromley (pres.); Jan S. Nilsson (sec. gen.).

Founded. 1922.

Membership. 42 countries.

Sundry Agreements

Convention on Co-operation in Astrophysics. A convention on co-operation in astrophysics, signed on May 26, 1979, came into force on May 17, 1982, for Denmark, Sweden, Spain and the United Kingdom, and on Feb. 15, 1983, for the Federal Republic of Germany.

Agreements concerning Polymetallic Nodules. An agreement on provisional regulations for the exploitation of polymetallic nodules on the deep sea-bed signed on Sept. 2, 1982, came into force on that date for France, the Federal Republic of Germany, the United Kingdom and the United States. These parties signed, on Aug. 3, 1984, a provisional understanding regarding deep sea-bed matters with Belgium, Italy, Japan and the Netherlands (which came into force on Sept. 2, 1984).

Agreement on Sodium-cooled Breeder Reactors. An agreement on co-operation in the field of sodium-cooled breeder reactors was signed and came into force on Jan. 1, 1984, for France, the Federal Republic of Germany, the United Kingdom and the United States.

Posts and Telecommunications Organizations

African Postal and Telecommunications Union

Address. B.P. 44, Brazzaville, Congo.

Founded. 1935.

Membership. 14 countries.

Asia-Pacific Telecommunity

Address. Office Compound of the Communications Authority of Thailand, Bangkok 10500, Thailand.

Officer. Boonchoo Phienpanij (exec. dir.).

Founded. March 27, 1976.

Membership. Afghanistan, Australia, Bangladesh, Brunei, China, India, Iran, Japan, the Republic of Korea, Malaysia, Maldives, Nauru, Nepal, Pakistan, Papua New Guinea, the Philippines, Singapore, Sri Lanka, Thailand, the United Kingdom and Vietnam.

History. The constitution of this organization came into force on Feb. 25, 1979, and was amended in 1981.

Asian-Pacific Postal Union

Address. Post Office Bldg., Manila, Philippines 2801.

Officer. J. Roilo S. Golez (dir.).

Founded. 1962.

Membership. 18 countries.

International Maritime Satellite Organization (INMARSAT)

Address. 40 Melton St., London NW1 2EQ, UK.

Officers. E. J. Martin (ch. of council); O. Lundberg (dir.-gen.).

Founded. July 16, 1979.

Membership. Ministries and organizations in 37 countries—Algeria, Argentina, Australia, Belgium, Brazil, Bulgaria, Canada, Chile, China, Denmark, Egypt, Finland, France, the Federal Republic of Germany, Greece, India, Iraq, Italy, Japan, Kuwait, Liberia, the Netherlands, New Zealand, Norway, Oman, the Philippines, Poland, Singapore, the Soviet Union, Spain, Sri Lanka, Sweden, Tunisia, the United Arab Emirates, the United Kingdom and the United States.

Objects. Under a Convention on an International Satellite Organization signed in London by representatives of 42 states on Sept. 3, 1976, and in force since July 16, 1979, the purposes of INMARSAT are "to make provision for the space segment necessary for improving maritime communications, thereby assisting in improving distress and safety-of-life-at-sea communications, efficiency and management of ships, maritime public correspondence services and radio determination capabilities".

Activities. On March 1, 1980, a British maritime communications satellite project known as *Marots* was brought under INMARSAT's programme, and on May 1, 1982, a British-built satellite (*Marecs-A*), weighing 1,014 kg and designed for transatlantic communications, was brought into service; it was part of the payload of the European Space Agency's *Ariane* rocket L04 launched on Dec. 19, 1981. By October 1983 INMARSAT operated via three geostationary satellites (above the Atlantic, Indian and Pacific Oceans) with seven coast earth stations and six others under construction, as well as an NCS network co-ordination station in the United States. It provided services to over 1,600 ships from 47 different countries and was directed by both US and Soviet officials.

The principal shareholders of INMARSAT were then the (US) Communications Satellite Corporation (23.3 per cent), the (Soviet) Morsviazsputnik (14 per cent), British Telecom (9.8 per cent) and Norwegian Telecom (7.87 per cent).

Structure. INMARSAT has an Assembly (which meets every two years and in which each member has one vote), a Council (meeting every three months) and a directorate.

International System and Organization for Space Communications (Intersputnik)

Address. P.B. 438, 107 053 Moscow, USSR.

Officer. Jury Ivanovich Krupin (dir.-gen.).

Founded. Nov. 15, 1971.

Membership. Bulgaria, Cuba, Czechoslovakia, the German Democratic Republic, Hungary, Mongolia, Poland, Romania and the Soviet Union.

Objects. As an institution of the Council for Mutual Economic Assistance (CMEA) this organization was to provide CMEA member countries with international telephone, telegraph and phototelegraph communication and an exchange of television programmes, and to develop mutual co-operation in space communication. It was to be open also to non-members of the CMEA, and to co-ordinate its work with the International Telecommunication Union (ITU).

Activities. The Intersputnik has created a complex of communication satellites and ground steering elements, and earth stations in contact through satellites. It has used *Molniya* ("Lightning") satellites, one of which has served to improve direct radio communications between the Soviet Union and the United States under an agreement signed in Washington on Sept. 30, 1971 [see page 282].

International Telecommunications Satellite Organization (INTELSAT)

Address. 490 L'Enfant Plaza, S.W., Washington, D.C. 20024, USA.

Officer. Santiago Astrain (dir.-gen.).

Founded. 1964.

Membership. 110 governments.

History. The INTELSAT was set up under the inter-governmental treaty of Aug. 20, 1964 (see under European Conference of Postal and Telecommunications Administration in Chapter 8) as the International Telecommunications Satellite System, which became the INTELSAT on Feb. 12, 1973, under an agreement concluded on Aug. 20, 1971.

Activities. Eleven INTELSAT satellites placed in synchronous orbit provide a global communications service covering over half the world's overseas traffic, using over 200 Standard A and 47 Standard B earth stations antennae and also eight facilities for specialized services.

Postal Union of the Americas and Spain
Unión Postal de las Américas y España

Address. Casilla de Correos 1242, Montevideo, Uruguay.

Officer. Pedro Miguel Cabero (dir.).

Founded. 1911.

Membership. 23 countries.

History. The constitution of this union was adopted on Nov. 26, 1971, and an additional protocol in 1981.

Convention on Programme-bearing Signals transmitted by Satellites

A convention signed on May 21, 1974, concerning the dissemination of programme-bearing signals transmitted by satellites was by Dec. 31, 1985, in force for 10 countries (Austria, the Federal Republic of Germany, Italy, Kenya, Mexico, Morocco, Nicaragua, Peru, the United States and Yugoslavia). Parties to the convention have undertaken to prevent ground stations in their territories from receiving and redistributing signals from satellites without permission.

Bilateral Agreements
France and the Federal Republic of Germany. An agreement on the construction, launching and use of an experimental telecommunications satellite, signed on June 6, 1967, came into force on Nov. 10, 1967.

An agreement on technical and industrial co-operation on radio satellites, signed on April 29, 1980, came into force on Dec. 1, 1980.

An agreement on the joint export of radio satellites, was signed and came into force on Sept. 22, 1981.

Co-operation in Space Research and Utilization

Outer Space Treaty

It was announced at the United Nations on Dec. 8, 1966, that agreement had been reached on the first international treaty governing space exploration. The treaty, officially designated the *Treaty on the Principles of the Activity of States in the Exploration and Use of Outer Space Including the Moon and Other Celestial Bodies*, was unanimously approved by the UN General Assembly on Dec. 19, 1966. It was signed by the United States, the Soviet Union, and the United Kingdom in their respective capitals on Jan. 27, 1967, and by the date of its entry into force (Oct. 10, 1967), it had been signed in Washington, London or Moscow by a total of 93 nations.

The operative articles of the treaty read as follows:

"**Art. 1.** The exploration and use of outer space, including the moon and other celestial bodies, shall be carried out for the benefit and in the interests of all countries, irrespective of their degree of economic or scientific development, and shall be the province of all mankind.

"Outer space, including the moon and other celestial bodies, shall be free for exploration and use by all states without discrimination of any kind, on a basis of equality and in accordance with international law, and there shall be free access to all areas of celestial bodies.

"There shall be freedom of scientific investigation in outer space, including the moon and other celestial bodies, and states shall facilitate and encourage international co-operation in such investigation.

"**Art. 2.** Outer space, including the moon and other celestial bodies, is not subject to national appropriation by claim of sovereignty, by means of use or occupation or by any other means.

"**Art. 3.** States parties to the treaty shall carry on activities in the exploration and use of outer space, including the moon and other celestial bodies, in accordance with international law, including the Charter of the United Nations, in the interest of maintaining international peace and security and promoting international co-operation and understanding.

"**Art. 4.** States parties to the treaty undertake not to place in orbit around the earth any objects carrying nuclear weapons or any other kinds of weapons of mass destruction, install such weapons on celestial bodies, or station such weapons in outer space in any other manner.

"The moon and other celestial bodies shall be used by all states parties to the treaty exclusively for peaceful purposes. The establishment of military bases, installations and fortifications, the testing of any type of weapons, and the conduct of military manoeuvres on celestial bodies shall be forbidden. The use of military personnel for scientific research or for any other peaceful purposes shall not be prohibited. The use of any equipment or facility necessary for peaceful exploration of the moon and other celestial bodies shall also not be prohibited.

"**Art. 5.** States parties to the treaty shall regard astronauts as envoys of mankind in outer space and shall render to them all possible assistance in the event of accident, distress or emergency landing on the territory of another state party or on the high seas. When astronauts make such a landing, they shall be safely and promptly returned to the state of registry of their space vehicle.

"In carrying on activities in outer space and on celestial bodies, the astronauts of one state party shall render all possible assistance to the astronauts of other states parties.

"States parties to the treaty shall immediately inform the other states parties to the treaty or the Secretary-General of the United Nations of any phenomena they discover in outer space, including the moon and other celestial bodies, which could constitute a danger to the life or health of astronauts.

"**Art. 6.** States parties to the treaty shall bear international responsibility for national activities in outer space, including the moon and other celestial bodies, whether such activities are carried on by governmental agencies or by non-governmental entities, and for assuring that national activities are carried out in conformity with the provisions set forth in the present treaty.

"The activities of non-governmental entities in outer space, including the moon and other celestial bodies, shall require authorization and continuing supervision by the state concerned. When activities are carried on in outer space, including the moon and other celestial bodies, by an international organization, responsibility for compliance with this treaty shall be borne both by the international organization and by the states parties to the treaty participating in such organization.

"**Art. 7.** Each state party to the treaty that launches or procures the launching of an object into outer space, including the moon and other celestial bodies, and each state party from whose territory or facility an object is launched, is internationally liable for damage to another state party to the treaty or to its natural or juridical persons by such object or its component parts on the earth, in airspace, or in outer space, including the moon and other celestial bodies.

"**Art. 8.** A state party to the treaty on whose registry an object launched into outer space is carried shall retain jurisdiction and control over such object, and over any personnel thereof, while in outer space or on a celestial body. Ownership of objects launched into outer space, including objects landed or constructed on a celestial body, and of their component parts, is not affected by their presence in outer space, including the body, or by their return to the earth. Such objects or component parts found beyond the limits of the state party to the treaty on whose registry they are carried shall be returned to that state, which shall, upon request, furnish identifying data prior to their return.

"**Art. 9.** In the exploration and use of outer space, including the moon and other celestial bodies, states parties to the treaty shall be guided by the principle of co-operation and mutual assistance and shall conduct all their activities in outer space, including the moon and other celestial bodies, with due regard to the corresponding interests of all other states parties to the treaty.

"States parties to the treaty shall pursue studies of outer space, including the moon and other celestial bodies, and conduct exploration of them so as to avoid their harmful contamination and also adverse changes in the environment of the earth resulting from the introduction of extra-terrestrial matter, and, where necessary, shall adopt appropriate measures for this purpose.

"If a state party to the treaty has reason to believe that an activity or experiment planned by it or its nationals in outer space, including the moon and other celestial bodies, would cause potentially harmful interference with activities of other states parties in the peaceful exploration and use of outer

space, including the moon and other celestial bodies, it shall undertake appropriate international consultations before proceeding with any such activity or experiment.

"A state party to the treaty which has reason to believe that an activity or experiment planned by another state party in outer space, including the moon and other celestial bodies, would cause potentially harmful interference with activities in the peaceful exploration and use of outer space, including the moon and other celestial bodies, may request consultation concerning the activity or experiment.

"**Art. 10.** In order to promote international co-operation in the exploration and use of outer space, including the moon and other celestial bodies, in conformity with the purposes of this treaty, the states parties to the treaty shall consider on a basis of equality any requests by other states parties to the treaty to be afforded an opportunity to observe the flight of space objects launched by those states. The nature of such an opportunity for observation and the conditions under which it could be afforded shall be determined by agreement between the states concerned.

"**Art. 11.** In order to promote international co-operation in the peaceful exploration and use of outer space, states parties to the treaty conducting activities in outer space, including the moon and other celestial bodies, agree to inform the Secretary-General of the United Nations as well as the public and the international scientific community, to the greatest extent feasible and practicable, of the nature, conduct, locations and results of such activities. On receiving the said information, the UN Secretary-General should be prepared to disseminate it immediately and effectively.

"**Art. 12.** All stations, installations, equipment and space vehicles on the moon and other celestial bodies shall be opened to representatives of other states parties to the treaty, on a basis of reciprocity. Such representatives shall give reasonable advance notice of a projected visit, in order that appropriate consultations may be held and that maximum precautions may be taken to assure safety and to avoid interference with normal operations in the facility to be visited.

"**Art. 13.** The provisions of this treaty shall apply to the activities of states parties to the treaty in the exploration and use of outer space, including the moon and other celestial bodies, whether such activities are carried on by a single state party to the treaty or jointly with other states, including cases where they are carried on within the framework of international inter-governmental organizations.

"Any practical questions arising in connexion with activities carried on by international inter-governmental organizations in the exploration and use of outer space, including the moon and other celestial bodies, shall be resolved by the states parties to the treaty either with the appropriate international organization or with one or more state members of that international organization, which are parties to this treaty.

"**Art. 14.** (1) This treaty shall be open to all states for signature. Any state which does not sign this treaty before its entry into force in accordance with Paragraph 3 of this article may accede to it at any time.

"(2) This treaty shall be subject to ratification by signatory states. Instruments of ratification and of accession shall be deposited with the Governments of the Union of Soviet Socialist Republics, the United Kingdom of Great Britain and Northern Ireland and the United States of America, which are hereby designated the depositary governments.

"(3) This treaty shall enter into force upon the deposit of instruments of ratifications by five governments, including the governments designated as depositary governments.

"(4) For states whose instruments of ratification or accession are deposited subsequent to the entry into force of this treaty, it shall enter into force on the date of the deposit of their instruments of ratification or accession.

"(5) The depositary governments shall promptly inform all signatory and acceding states of the date of each signature, the date of deposit of each instrument of ratification of and accession to this treaty, the date of its entry into force, and other notices.

"(6) This treaty shall be registered by the depositary governments pursuant to Article 102 of the UN Charter.

"Art. 15. Any state party to the treaty may propose amendments to this treaty. Amendments shall enter into force for each state party to the treaty accepting the amendments upon their acceptance by a majority of the states parties to the treaty, and thereafter for each remaining state party to the treaty on the date of acceptance by it.

"Art. 16. Any state party to the treaty may give notice of its withdrawal from the treaty one year after its entry into force by written notification to the depositary governments. Such withdrawal shall take effect one year from the date of receipt of this notification."

A UN Committee on the Peaceful Uses of Outer Space, set up by the General Assembly in 1959, was, by a resolution passed by the Assembly on Dec. 20, 1977, enlarged from 37 to 47 members.

UN conferences on the exploration and peaceful uses of outer space were held in Vienna in 1968 and 1982. The second of these conferences (Unispace 82), held on Aug. 9–21, 1982, and attended by delegates from over 100 countries, approved the following principal recommendations:

(i) That a UN space information system be established; (ii) that agreement should be reached on the principles governing satellite remote sensing and ensuring that states under satellite observation had "timely and non-discriminatory access under reasonable conditions" to the information collected; (iii) that the long-term implications of the use of geostationary orbit should be "both equitable and flexible and take into consideration the economic, technical and legal aspects"; (iv) that where possible direct broadcasting systems should share a space segment or use one already in operation; and (v) that "the testing, stationing and deployment of any weapon in space should be banned" and that there should be legislation to prohibit the placing of weapons in outer space.

Agreement on Rescue and Return of Astronauts

An *Agreement on the Rescue of Astronauts, the Return of Astronauts and the Return of Objects Launched into Outer Space* was approved by the UN General Assembly on Dec. 19, 1967, by 115 votes to none, with no abstentions.

Under this agreement, which had been worked out by the United States and the Soviet Union in co-operation with the Committee on Outer Space of the UN General Assembly, signatories were bound to render "all possible assistance to astronauts in the event of accident, distress, emergency or unintended landing". The agreement also provided for safe and prompt return of astronauts and space objects, and reimbursement of expenses to the launching state, as well as for notification of unplanned landings by space travellers or spacecraft.

The agreement was signed on April 22, 1968, and entered into force on Dec. 3, 1968, after ratification by Britain, the Soviet Union and the United States. It was accepted by the European Space Agency with effect from Dec. 31, 1975.

Convention of International Liability

The UN General Assembly approved on Nov. 29, 1971, by 93 votes to none with four abstentions (Canada, Iran, Japan and Sweden) a *Convention on International Liability for Damage Caused by Space Objects*. The convention was signed in London, Moscow and Washington on March 29, 1972, and by Dec. 31, 1985, it was in force for 69 countries and the European Space Agency.

Convention on Registration of Objects launched into Outer Space

On Nov. 12, 1974, the UN General Assembly unanimously approved a *Convention on Registration of Objects launched into Outer Space* (which in effect was an extension of the provisions of the Treaty on Principles governing the Activities of States in the Exploration and Use of Outer Space—see above).

The convention required each launching state to keep a registry showing details of any space object launched into earth orbit or beyond and this information to be furnished to the UN Secretary-General for entry in a register to be kept by him and offering "full and open access" to its information. The convention was to enter into force for those states which had ratified it upon the deposit of the fifth instrument of ratification with the UN Secretary-General and for other states on the date of the deposit of their instrument of ratification or accession. The convention was subject to review 10 years after its entry into force, or after five years upon request by one-third of the states parties to it.

The convention came into force on Jan. 19, 1976, after being ratified by the United States, Bulgaria, Canada, France and Sweden (with 22 other countries having signed but not ratified it). By Dec. 31, 1985, it was in force for 31 countries and the European Space Agency.

Agreement on Monitoring of the Stratosphere

An agreement between France, the United Kingdom and the United States regarding monitoring of the stratosphere was signed in Paris on May 5, 1976.

Agreement governing the Activities of States on the Moon and Other Celestial Bodies

This agreement was adopted without a vote by the UN General Assembly on Dec. 5, 1979. Its principal provisions were as follows:

All activities on the moon or other celestial bodies (other than the earth) within the solar system, as well as in orbits around or other trajects to or around them, were to be carried out in accordance with international law (Arts. 1 and 2). These bodies were to be used exclusively for peaceful purposes (Art. 3). Their exploration and use should be carried out for the benefit and in the interests of all countries (Art. 4, paragraph 1).

States parties to the agreement were to supply detailed information about their activities to the UN Secretary-General and to the public (Art. 5). Measures were to be taken to prevent the disruption of the existing balance of the environment of the celestial bodies, and the UN Secretary-General was to be informed in advance of any placement of radioactive materials on celestial bodies, and of the purpose of such placements (Art. 7).

The agreement permitted states parties to it to land space objects on, and to launch them from, celestial bodies, as well as to place personnel or equipment on or below the surface of celestial bodies (Art. 9). Details of manned or unmanned stations on celestial bodies were to be supplied to the UN Secretary-General (Art. 9). Celestial bodies were not to be subject to national appropriation (Art. 11, paragraph 2). States parties to the agreement were to undertake to establish an international regime to govern the exploitation of the natural resources of celestial bodies as such exploitation became possible (Art. 11, paragraphs 6 and 7).

The agreement was to be subject to review not later than 10 years after its entry into force (Art. 18), which took place on July 11, 1984.

European Space Agency (ESA)

Address. 8–10 rue Mario Nikis, 15738 Paris Cédex 15, France.

Officers. Prof. H. Curien (ch.); Reimer Luest (dir.-gen.).

Founded. May 30, 1975.

Membership. Belgium, Denmark, France, the Federal Republic of Germany, Ireland, Italy, the Netherlands, Spain, Sweden and the United Kingdom (*associate members:* Austria and Norway; *observer:* Canada).

History. The decision to establish the ESA was made in an agreement signed in Brussels on July 31, 1973, at a meeting of the European Space Conference—set up on Dec. 13, 1966, and consisting of representatives of the European Launcher Development Organization (ELDO), the European Space Research Organization (ESRO) and the European Conference on Satellite Communications (CETS).

ELDO had been formed under a convention which was signed on April 12, 1962 (by Australia, Belgium, France, the Federal Republic of Germany, Italy, the Netherlands and the United Kingdom). The object of ELDO was to develop a European earth-satellite launcher in preparation for the possible use of satellites for various purposes. ELDO's original programme (ELDO-A) covered the development and construction of a three-stage satellite-launching vehicle, with the work being distributed among the ELDO member countries and firings to be made at Woomera (Australia). In 1966 this programme was modified in order to enable a synchronous telecommunications satellite to be placed in orbit; the modified programme—ELDO-PAS—required two additional stages and an equatorial launching site.

In July 1966 it was decided to apply a new scale of contributions to the implementation of the ELDO-PAS programme, with an overall cost ceiling of about $330,000,000 to be divided between the United Kingdom (27 per cent), the Federal Republic of Germany (27 per cent), France (25 per cent), Italy (12 per cent) and Belgium and the Netherlands (4½ per cent each) and to use Kourou (French Guiana) as an operational equatorial launching site. The British Government, however, announced on April 16, 1968, that it would make no further contributions after 1971 because the costs were prohibitive and the potential applications of the programme were "both limited and speculative". In fact, ELDO launcher firings made at Woomera in 1967–70 were failures, and one made at Kourou in November 1971 also failed. The United Kingdom withdrew from ELDO with effect from Jan. 1, 1973, and all further work on ELDO programmes was discontinued in April 1973.

ESRO was set up under a convention which was signed on June 14, 1962, by representatives of 12 countries (Austria, Belgium, Denmark, France, the Federal Republic of Germany, Italy, the Netherlands, Norway, Spain, Sweden, Switzerland and the United Kingdom) and entered into force on March 21, 1964. ESRO's first work programme for an eight-year period included the firing of fully instrumental vertical sounding-rockets, the launching of satellites (at first in near-earth orbits and later in eccentric orbits), of fully instrumental space probes or large satellites, and eventually of several large astronomical satellites. Some 300 research rockets were fired (from Sardinia) from July 1964 onwards. An ESRO spacecraft was first successfully launched on May 17, 1968. Between 1968 and 1972 ESRO conducted a series of satellite launchings using US rocket vehicles fired in the United States.

Under ESRO, installations were established as follows:

(1) A Space Technology Centre (ESTEC) at Noordwijk (Netherlands), responsible for technical research connected with ESRO's launching programme;

(2) a Space Research Laboratory (ESLAB) at Noordwijk, to co-ordinate the various projects;

(3) a Data Centre (ESDAC) at Darmstadt (Federal Republic of Germany);

(4) a Sounding-Rocket Launching Range (ES-RANGE) at Kiruna in Arctic Sweden, operational from 1966 onwards;

(5) a Space Research Institute (ESRIN) at Frascati (Italy) for theoretical research on the physical and chemical phenomena of space;

(6) a Tracking and Telemetry Network (ESTRACK) to track and communicate with satellites, with four stations—at Fairbanks (Alaska), Ny-Alesund (Svalbard), Port Stanley (Falkland Islands) and Redu (Belgium).

For the Svalbard station ESRO concluded two agreements in September 1965: (i) with the Norwegian Government on the construction and conditions of operation of the station; and (ii) with the Norwegian Technical and Scientific Research Council on the operation of the station; both agreements were conditional upon restricting the station's activities to purely scientific and peaceful ends.

The CETS was established in 1963 by member governments of the European Conference of Postal and Telecommunications Administrations (CEPT, see page 193).

An agreement on a programme of co-operation in the development, procurement and use of a space laboratory was concluded on Aug. 14, 1973, between the United States and five member countries of ESRO (Italy, the Netherlands, Spain, Switzerland and the United Kingdom).

The ESA was formally established under a convention signed in Paris on May 30, 1975. The 10 countries signing the convention were Belgium, Denmark, France, the Federal Republic of Germany, Italy, the Netherlands, Spain, Sweden, Switzerland and the United Kingdom. Ireland signed the agreement on Dec. 30, 1975; Austria, Canada and Norway attended the first ministerial-level meeting of the ESA's council in Paris on Feb. 14–15, 1977, as observers. On the basis of an agreement signed in Brussels on Oct. 17, 1979, Austria became an associate member of the ESA on April 1, 1981. As provided in an agreement signed in Paris on April 2, 1981, Norway became an associate member for five years as from Nov. 1, 1981. The Irish Republic became its 11th full member on Dec. 10, 1980. The ESA convention entered into force on Oct. 30, 1980.

The ESA was not to be involved in the International Telecommunications Satellite

Organization (INTELSAT) or the UK Skynet defence satellite system, but it took up three projects, namely (i) a French proposal for developing the L3-S (*Ariane*) satellite launcher; (ii) a 10 per cent share in the US post-Apollo space shuttle programme, for which a European space laboratory was to be created; and (iii) the development of a satellite for marine communications. The first European-built satellites under ESA auspices were put into orbit in August 1975 and April 1977 by US Delta rockets under co-operation agreements with the (US) National Astronautics and Space Administration.

Agreements signed between the ESA and France on May 5, 1976, provided that (i) the space station at Kourou was made available for unrestricted use by the ESA and each of its member states, with administrative control of Kourou being transferred to the ESA from the French *Centre national d'études spatiales* (CNES) and (ii) the ESA and its member states were given full access to the L3-S rocket launcher being developed at the site.

The launching of the first European telecommunications satellite (Orbital Test Satellite, OTS) from Cape Canaveral (USA) on Sept. 13, 1977, was a failure, but a second OTS, successfully launched on May 11, 1978, was on May 24 of that year placed in geo-stationary orbit 36,000 kilometres above the earth and by Oct. 17, 1978, completed its first tests transmitting television programmes beyond continental Europe. [See also below under European Telecommunications Satellite Organization—EUTELSAT.]

A first meteorological satellite was, under an ESA programme, launched into orbit from Cape Canaveral on Nov. 22, 1977, and inter alia carried out two research projects for the World Meteorological Organization (WMO).

The ESA also co-operated in the launching, in the United States in October 1977 and January 1978, of two International Sun-Earth Explorer Satellites. Europe's first geostationary scientific satellite, *Geos-2*, was launched by a Delta rocket on July 14, 1978, with a scientific payload supplied by 11 research institutes in eight of the ESA member countries.

A five-year agreement on co-operation between the ESA and Canada, which came into force on Jan. 1, 1979, was on Jan. 9, 1984, extended for a further five years, with Canada agreeing to increase its contribution to the ESA's budget.

The *Ariane* satellite launcher, under development since 1973, had its first launching at Kourou on Dec. 24, 1979. The second launch (on May 23, 1981) was a failure, but the third and fourth launches (respectively on June 19 and Dec. 19, 1981) were successful and placed into orbit inter alia the ESA satellite *Meteosat 2*, the Indian satellite *Apple* and the British-built *Marecs-A* (originally called *Marots*). *Ariane L06* was successfully launched on June 16, 1983, when its *Sylda* satellite release system placed the payload of two satellites into geostationary orbit. *Ariane L07* and *L08* were launched successfully on May

23, 1984, delivering into geostationary orbit a communications satellite of the US GTE Spacenet Corporation.

After nine consecutive successful launches at Kourou, an *Ariane* rocket carrying two satellites was on Sept. 12, 1985, destroyed by ground control after malfunctioning shortly after lift-off. Two successful launches (each of two satellites) followed on Feb. 21 and March 28, 1986, respectively—the latter from a new launchpad intended to double the programme's launch capacity to some 10 flights a year. However, on May 30 *Ariane V18*, carrying an Intelsat communications satellite, was destroyed by remote control $4\frac{1}{2}$ minutes after launch following the failure of its third stage to ignite. This failure was the *Ariane* programme's fourth out of 18 launches.

A Spacelab complex developed by the ESA and originally planned to be launched in 1980 was carried by the US space shuttle *Columbia* launched in Florida on Nov. 8, 1983.

On July 2, 1985, an *Ariane* rocket launched from Kourou the space probe *Giotto* with the object of passing as closely as possible Halley's comet due to be near the earth in March 1986. *Giotto* in fact passed the comet on March 13, 1986, within 50 kilometres of its nucleus and at about 52 million miles from the earth. The operation was controlled by the European Organizing Centre for Space Research (ESOC) in Darmstadt (Federal Republic of Germany). *Giotto* had been built by an international consortium headed by British Aerospace. The ESA director of the *Giotto* programme was one of several scientists (from Europe, Japan and the United States) who shared information received at the Moscow Space Research Institute from two other probes—*Vega 1* and *Vega 2*—which had passed Halley's comet within 6,250 miles (10,000 kilometres), while a Japanese probe *Sakigeke* (launched on Jan. 8, 1986) also approached close to the comet.

At its 74th meeting held in Paris on June 25–27, 1986, the ESA Council approved the "Europeanization" of the *Hermes* manned spaceplane project (hitherto a French undertaking) by adopting an enabling resolution on the execution within the ESA framework of a preparatory programme for the project.

Convention on the Establishment of a European Organization for the Exploitation of Meteorological Satellites (EUMETSAT)

This convention was approved at the second session of an Intergovernmental Conference on an operational European Meteorological Programme, held in Paris on March 21–23, 1983. At the conference delegations from the 11 ESA member states as well as from Austria, Finland, Greece, Norway, Portugal and Turkey decided on a 12-year programme designed to launch three improved versions of a *Meteosat* spacecraft and to benefit European meteorological organizations in their research and forecasting.

The convention was signed by Belgium, France, the Federal Republic of Germany, Italy, the Netherlands, Norway, Portugal, Spain, Switzerland, Turkey and the United Kingdom in Geneva on May 24, 1983.

Bilateral US-Soviet Space Co-operation

Bilateral co-operation in space matters between the United States and the Soviet Union was first implemented by the link-up in space of a (US) *Apollo* and a (Soviet) *Soyuz* spacecraft on July 17, 1975, as provided for under plans agreed upon in May 1972. This was followed by a meeting of US and Soviet officials in October 1976 to discuss the possible establishment of a network of satellites to search for stranded ships and downed aircraft and to measure air pollution.

An agreement on co-operation between the two states in the exploration and use of outer space for peaceful purposes, signed in Geneva on May 18, 1977, contained the following operative articles:

"**Art. 1.** The parties will continue to develop co-operation in such fields of space science and applications as space meteorology; study of the natural environment; exploration of near-Earth space, the Moon and the planets; space biology and medicine; satellite search and rescue systems; and, in particular, will co-operate to take all appropriate measures to encourage and achieve the fulfilment of the Summary of Results of Discussion on Space Co-operation between the Academy of Sciences of the USSR and the US National Aeronautics and Space Administration [NASA], dated Jan. 21, 1971, periodically renewed.

"**Art. 2.** The parties will carry out such co-operation through their appropriate national agencies by means of mutual exchanges of scientific information and delegations, and meetings of scientists and specialists of both countries, and also in such other ways as may be mutually agreed. Joint working groups may be created for the development and implementation of appropriate programmes of co-operation.

"**Art. 3.** The parties will take all necessary measures for the further development of co-operation in the area of manned space flight for scientific and practical objectives, including the use in joint flights of compatible docking and rendezvous systems derived from those developed during the experimental flight of *Soyuz* and *Apollo* spacecraft in July 1975. Joint work in this direction will be carried out in accordance with the Agreement between the Academy of Sciences of the USSR and the US National Aeronautics and Space Administration on Co-operation in the Area of Manned Space Flight dated May 11, 1977.

"**Art. 4.** The parties will encourage international efforts to resolve problems of international law in the exploration and use of outer space for peaceful purposes with the aim of strengthening the legal order in space and further developing international space law and will co-operate in this field.

"**Art. 5.** The parties may by mutual agreement determine other areas of co-operation in the exploration and use of outer space for peaceful purposes.

"**Art. 6.** This agreement shall enter into force on May 24, 1977, and shall remain in force for five years. It may be modified or extended by mutual agreement of the parties. . . ."

This agreement replaced one signed in 1972 (during a visit to Moscow by President Nixon—see page 285).

There followed a further agreement, concluded in November 1977, on discussion of the operation of an international space station in the 1980s, and the inauguration on Jan. 16, 1978, of a two-channel system of direct space communication between Washington and Moscow.

The agreement was, however, not renewed in May 1982 (as part of the US sanctions imposed against the Soviet Union in connexion with the proclamation of martial law in Poland).

Organizations, Declarations and Conventions concerned with Environmental Problems

International Union for the Conservation of Nature and Natural Resources (IUCN)

Address. 1196 Gland, Switzerland.

Officer. Dr Lee M. Talbot (dir.-gen.).

Founded. 1948.

Membership. Governments of 56 countries and several hundred government agencies and non-governmental organizations (at national and international level).

Objects. To carry out scientific monitoring of the conditions of natural resources; to determine scientific priorities for conservation; to recommend solutions to the most serious conservation problems; to develop programmes for the protection of the most threatened species and ecosystems; and to assist governments to devise and carry out conservation projects.

Activities. The IUCN has a conservation library, a documentation centre and units for monitoring traffic in wildlife.

A new statute of the IUCN, approved on Oct. 4, 1978, was by Jan. 1, 1985, in force for 47 countries.

Declarations issued under Council of Europe Auspices

(1) A *Declaration on the Management of the Natural Environment of Europe* was adopted on Feb. 12, 1970, by a European Conservation Conference convened in Strasbourg by the Council of Europe and attended by the Council's 17 members as well as by representatives of 10 other countries (Canada, Czechoslovakia, Finland, Israel, Liechtenstein, Portugal, Romania, Spain, the United States and Yugoslavia).

The declaration laid down guidelines for the "rational use and management of the environment"; for the harmonization of legislation for safeguarding the environment; and for co-operation between public authorities, industry and conservationists.

(2) A *Declaration on the Problem of Sea Pollution* was issued by the Consultative Assembly of the Council of Europe on Sept. 24, 1970, calling on member governments to "take forthwith drastic measures" to end pollution of the sea which threatened "directly the very life of the sea and . . . put in question the survival of humanity as a whole".

Oslo Commission–Paris Commission

Address. New Court, 48 Carey St., London WC2A 2JE, UK.

Officer. F. A. Hayward (sec.).

Founded. April 6, 1974 (Oslo Commission); May 6, 1978 (Paris Commission).

Activities. Conventions and an agreement administered by the Oslo Commission, set up in London under the first convention listed below, are as follows:

(1) A *Convention against Marine Pollution*, designed to prevent sea pollution by the dumping of waste from ships and aircraft, was signed in Oslo on Feb. 15, 1972, by Belgium, Denmark, Finland, France, the Federal Republic of Germany, Iceland, the Netherlands, Norway, Portugal, Spain, Sweden and the United Kingdom.

The area covered by the convention comprised the high seas and territorial waters of the northeast Atlantic and part of the Arctic area, its western boundary being the longitude of Greenland and its southern boundary the latitude of the Straits of Gibraltar.

This convention came into effect on April 7, 1974, after the required ratification by seven of its 12 signatories, i.e. by Denmark, France, Iceland, Norway, Portugal, Spain and Sweden. In 1982 it was adhered to by Ireland.

(2) A *Convention for the Prevention of Marine Pollution from Land-based Sources* was signed in Paris on June 4, 1974, by Belgium, Denmark, France, the Federal Republic of Germany, Iceland, Ireland, Luxembourg, the Netherlands, Norway, Portugal, Spain, Sweden and the United Kingdom, as well as by the European Communities. It entered into force on May 6, 1978. In 1984 it was adhered to by Belgium and Ireland. (The Paris Commission was established under this convention.)

(3) An *Agreement for Co-operation in Dealing with Pollution of the North Sea by Oil* was concluded in Bonn on June 9, 1969, by representatives of Belgium, Denmark, France, the Federal Republic of Germany, Norway, Sweden and the United Kingdom. It required the signatory governments to request ships and aircraft to report major oil slicks; to circulate reports on the presence, extent and movements of slicks; and on request to use their best endeavours to assist other countries in disposing of oil threatening their coasts. The agreement also established zones of responsibility for each country in the North Sea area.

The agreement entered into force on Aug. 9, 1969, in all signatory states except Norway, where it came into force on Nov. 28, 1970, and it was acceded to by the Netherlands on March 8, 1974.

Conventions on Protection of Wildlife

(1) A *Convention on Nature Protection and Wildlife Preservation in the Western Hemisphere*, concluded between the member states of the Pan-American Union [see page 341] was opened for signature on Oct. 12, 1940, and was ratified by 10 of these states in 1941–42, coming into force on May 1, 1942.

(2) A *Convention on Wetlands of International Importance, especially as Wildfowl Habitat* was adopted at a conference held at Ransar (Iran) on Feb. 2, 1971. It came into force on Dec. 21, 1975. By Dec. 31, 1985, it was adhered to by 38 countries, and its protection applied to sites at 216 localities totalling 6,000,000 hectares. Under this convention Denmark and the Netherlands co-operated in the conservation of the Wadden Zee off their coasts.

(3) A *Convention on International Trade in Endangered Species of Wild Fauna and Flora* was signed in Washington on March 3, 1973. It came into force on July 1, 1975. By Dec. 31, 1985, it was in force for 86 countries.

(4) An *Agreement on the Conservation of Polar Bears* was signed in Oslo on Nov. 15, 1973, and came into force on May 26, 1976, after being adhered to by Canada, Denmark, Norway, the Soviet Union and the United States. The agreement forbade the taking of polar bears (subject to certain exceptions) and required the parties to it to take action to protect the bears' ecosystem.

(5) A *Convention on the Conservation of European Wildlife and Natural Habitats*, signed in Berne on Sept. 19, 1979, provided for strict protection of 119 plant species and 400 species of fauna threatened with extinction, and for lesser protection of other species. It came into force on June 1, 1982. The 15 parties to the convention are Austria, Denmark, the EEC, the Federal Republic of Germany, Greece, Ireland, Italy, Liechtenstein, Luxembourg, the Netherlands, Portugal, Sweden, Switzerland, the United Kingdom and Turkey.

(6) A *Convention on the Conservation of Migratory Species of Wild Animals* was signed in Bonn on June 23, 1979, and came into force on Nov. 1, 1983. The 16 parties to the convention are Cameroon, Chile, Denmark (though not for the Faroes and Greenland), the EEC, Egypt, the Federal Republic of Germany, Hungary, India, Ireland, Israel, Italy, Luxembourg, the Netherlands, Niger, Portugal and Sweden.

IMO Conventions on Marine Pollution

A number of conventions have been concluded under the auspices of the International Maritime Organization (IMO) [see page 40] with the object of preventing pollution of the sea and of dealing with such pollution.

(1) An *International Convention for the Prevention of Pollution of the Sea by Oil* (OILPOL), agreed on May 12, 1954, and banning the discharging into the sea of crude oil, fuel oil, diesel oil and lubricating oil within specified zones, came into force for tankers on July 26, 1958, and for dry cargo ships on July 26, 1961. Amendments to this Convention were signed in 1962, 1969, and 1971. It was to be superseded by the 1973 MARPOL Convention [see below] when the latter came into force.

(2) An *International Convention Relating to Intervention on the High Seas in Cases of Oil Pollution Casualties* was adopted at the end of a conference held from Nov. 10 to 29, 1969. The Convention dealt with the right of a coastal state to protect its own interests when a casualty occurred on the high seas which might damage those interests. This Convention entered into force on May 6, 1975. By Dec. 31, 1985, it had been accepted by 48 contracting states.

A protocol to the Convention extending its provisions to pollution by substances other than oil and adopted on Nov. 2, 1973, came into force on March 30, 1983, and was by March 1, 1984, adhered to by 17 nations.

(3) At the same conference, an *International Convention on Civil Liability for Oil Pollution Damage* (CLC) was adopted, providing that the owner of a ship from which polluting oil escaped would be held liable for any pollution damage caused. This Convention entered into force on June 19, 1975. By Dec. 31, 1985, it had been accepted by 56 countries.

A protocol to the Convention, adopted in 1976, entered into force in 1981 and was by Dec. 31, 1985, adhered to by 19 countries.

Under a further protocol, adopted in May 1984, the scope of the Convention was extended into the territorial sea and the exclusive economic zone of contracting states, and a minimal liability was introduced for owners of small vessels, while the liability of owners of larger vessels was increased (by as much as four to six times).

At a conference held on Nov. 29–Dec. 18, 1971, another agreement resulted, known as the *Convention on the Establishment of an International Fund for Compensation for Oil Pollution Damage*, which came into force on Oct. 16, 1978. The fund was designed to offer compensation in cases of large-scale pollution where the terms of provisions for civil liability were inadequate to cover the damage incurred. By Dec. 31, 1985, it was adhered to by 31 countries.

A 1976 protocol to the Convention—to cover various substances other than oil and to enable states to take preventive action outside their territorial waters when faced with massive pollution or the threat of it—was by March 1, 1984, agreed to by 12 countries, but this fact did not fulfil all conditions for its entry into force, and the protocol is therefore not yet applicable.

Under a further protocol, adopted in May 1984, the scope of this Convention was extended and the upper limit of compensation payable by oil and shipping companies was raised to £150,000,000. However, implementation of this amendment was expected to take five years, since it was dependent on ratification by the United States, which had refused to sign the Convention.

The International Fund for Compensation for Oil Pollution Damage was established in 1978 and is located at IMO's address. Japan has been the major contributor to the fund. By March 1984 the fund had paid compensation and indemnification amounting to about £29,000,000. It then had a membership of 29 states.

(4) A *Convention on the Prevention of Marine Pollution by Dumping* was adopted at an intergovernmental conference held in London on Oct. 30–Nov. 13, 1972, and attended by representatives of 81 Governments and observers from 12 other countries. The Soviet Union participated, but the People's Republic of China was absent.

The main aim of the convention is to prevent indiscriminate disposal at sea of waste chemicals and minerals, on the understanding that the sea's capacity to assimilate waste and to regenerate natural resources is not unlimited. The dumping of certain categories of waste will be prohibited or subject to permit.

At the close of the conference the convention had been initialled by 57 countries. It was finally concluded on Dec. 29, 1972, and it came into force on Aug. 30, 1975. By Dec. 31, 1985, it had been ratified by 54 countries.

Under the convention the dumping of high-level radioactive waste was prohibited, and that of low-level waste was allowed only under certain conditions. A moratorium on such dumping had been introduced by the United States in 1970, and in 1974 France, the Federal Republic of Germany, Italy and Sweden ceased such dumping, whereas Belgium, the Netherlands, Switzerland and the United Kingdom continued it. The observation of a two-year moratorium on such dumping was approved in February 1983, and this was extended indefinitely at a conference held on Sept. 23–27, 1985, when the voting was 25 in favour of the moratorium, six against (Canada, France, South Africa, Switzerland, the United Kingdom and the United States), with seven abstentions (Argentina, Belgium, Greece, Italy, Japan, Portugal and the Soviet Union).

(5) A *Convention for the Prevention of Pollution from Ships* (MARPOL) was adopted at a conference held in London from Oct. 8 to Nov. 2, 1973, and attended by delegates from 79 countries and numerous international organizations.

The Convention contained provisions aimed at eliminating pollution of the sea by both oil and other noxious substances which might be discharged operationally, and at minimizing the amount of oil which would be released accidentally in collisions or strandings by ships of any type whatsoever, including also fixed or floating platforms. The convention did not, however, deal with dumping—which was covered by the Convention listed immediately above—nor with the release of harmful substances directly arising from the exploration, exploitation and associated offshore processing of seabed mineral resources. The Convention incorporated certain amendments made earlier to the OILPOL Convention described above. It also laid down that the Mediterranean, the Black Sea, the Baltic Sea, the Red Sea and the Gulf area (including the Sea of Oman) were designated as special areas in which oil discharge was completely prohibited (except by very small ships). Moreover, the Convention contained special requirements for the control of pollution by over 400 different noxious substances and for sewage and garbage disposal.

The MARPOL Convention was modified by a protocol which was adopted on Feb. 17, 1978, by a conference on tanker safety and the prevention of pollution. The amended Convention requires (i) an initial survey before the ship is put into service or before an International Oil Pollution Prevention (IOPP) Certificate is issued; (ii) periodical surveys at intervals not exceeding five years; (iii) a minimum of one intermediate survey to be carried out during the period of validity of the IOPP certificate; and (iv) unscheduled inspection or mandatory annual surveys to be carried out (with most nations favouring the latter).

After the entry into force of the modified Convention any ship which did not conform to its requirements was unable to operate unless modified to meet these requirements.

Both the Convention and the protocol were to come into force one year after ratification by countries representing over 50 per cent of world merchant shipping and by 15 states. These conditions were fulfilled by the ratification by Greece (on Sept. 23, 1982) and Italy (on Oct. 1, 1982), and both the Convention and the protocol thus entered into force on Oct. 2, 1983. The modified Convention was to supersede the OILPOL Convention which had come into force in 1958–61 [see above] and it was to form part of the UN Law of the Sea. By Dec. 31, 1985, it had been adhered to by 36 contracting states.

Regional Environmental Protection Organizations and Agreements

THE BALTIC SEA

Baltic Marine Environment Protection Commission (Helsinki Commission)

Address. Etaläesplanadi 22 C 43, 00130 Helsinki 13, Finland.

Officers. Dr Peter Ehlers (ch.); Prof. Harald Velner (exec. sec.).

Founded. May 3, 1980.

Membership. Denmark, Finland, the German Democratic Republic, the Federal Republic of Germany, Poland, the Soviet Union and Sweden.

History. Following the UN Conference of the Human Environment held in Stockholm in 1972, experts from the Baltic Sea states held a preparatory meeting in Helsinki early in 1973, which led to a conference at which a *Convention*

on the Protection of the Marine Environment of the Baltic Sea Area was signed on March 22, 1974. This Helsinki convention was the first international convention on the protection of the marine environment against pollution from all sources. The Commission was established to implement the convention.

Objects. The Commission's contracting parties are to take all appropriate legislative, administrative or other relevant measures to prevent and abate pollution and to protect and enhance the marine environment of the Baltic Sea area, and to use their best endeavours to ensure that the implementation of the Helsinki convention shall not cause an increase in the pollution of sea areas outside the Baltic Sea area. The Commission is to prepare proposals and recommendations to the contracting parties for measures to prevent and reduce pollution and to protect and improve the marine environment of the Baltic Sea area.

Activities. The Helsinki convention covers the Baltic Sea area consisting of the Baltic Sea proper, the Gulf of Bothnia, the Gulf of Finland and the entrance to the Baltic Sea bounded by the parallel of the Skaw in the Skagerrak at 57°44.8′N; it does not include the contracting parties' internal waters (on the landward side of the baseline from which the breadth of the territorial sea is measured).

In the convention the contracting parties undertake to counteract the introduction, whether airborne, waterborne or otherwise, into the Baltic Sea area of certain hazardous substances (Article 5), as specified in an annex and including PCBs and DDT. Landbased pollution, caused by direct discharges via sewers or by substances carried in river water discharge or so-called diffuse load originating from agricultural and less densely populated areas—including the pollution load carried by air, is to be controlled and minimized in respect of 16 specified substance groups listed in another annex (Article 6).

The provisions concerning the prevention of pollution from ships (Article 7) follow closely those of the MARPOL 73/78 convention of the International Maritime Organization (IMO) [see pages 94–95], where the Baltic Sea is defined as a "special area" requiring severe discharge restrictions. The provisions of the convention are binding only on the contracting parties, while IMO recommendations apply to ships of other nations. The convention also applies to pleasure craft (Article 8). Dumping in the Baltic Sea area is prohibited, except where human life is at risk or a craft is threatened by complete destruction or loss, or in the case of dredged spoils without substances listed in the annexes, for the dumping of which special permission is required (Article 9).

The convention came into force on May 3, 1980, all Baltic Sea states having ratified it. The Commission has issued 32 recommendations concerning the detailed implementation of the convention.

Structure. The offices of a chairman and vice-chairman of the commission rotate between the member states every two years. The commission has a scientific-technological committee, a maritime committee, an expert group on co-operation in combating matters and ad hoc subsidiary bodies.

Baltic Sea Agreements. Agreements relating to the protection of the whole or parts of the Baltic Sea area were the result of bilateral or multilateral negotiations between riparian states.

(1) Denmark, Finland, Norway and Sweden concluded, on Sept. 16, 1971, an agreement (which came into force on Oct. 16, 1971) on co-operation in taking measures against pollution of the sea by oil.

(2) Denmark and Sweden signed a convention, in April 1974, on the protection of the Öresund (linking the Baltic Sea proper with the Kattegat). It involved the construction, by 1979, of a purification plant to reduce oil pollution by industrial and organic waste.

(3) Finland and the Soviet Union formed, in 1968, a Working Group on the Protection of the Gulf of Finland (in association with a Finnish–USSR Committee for Scientific and Technical Co-operation).

(4) Finland and Sweden have formed a Committee for the Gulf of Bothnia.

(5) The German Democratic Republic and Poland have formed an Odra Haff Committee.

THE ENGLISH CHANNEL AND THE NORTH SEA

Anti-Pollution Agreements. The United Kingdom Government announced on Aug. 9, 1972, that it had concluded agreements with Belgium and France on co-operation in the surveillance of oil slicks in the Channel area.

At a conference held in Bremen (Federal Republic of Germany) on Oct. 30–31, 1984, by ministers concerned with the environment from eight states (Belgium, Denmark, France, the Federal Republic of Germany, the Netherlands, Norway, Sweden and the United Kingdom) it was agreed to reinforce anti-pollution measures in the North Sea, in particular by strengthening existing surveillance measures on ships and their discharges, reducing the sewage discharge from rivers, attempting to reduce the dumping of radioactive waste and intensifying research on the impact of air pollution on the sea.

The conference failed to endorse a proposal by the Federal Republic of Germany to declare the North Sea a "special area" (under the MARPOL convention—see pages 94–95) in which the disposal of chemicals and the dumping of all dangerous waste would be prohibited. (It was estimated that some 22,000 tons of poisonous heavy metals were dumped into the North Sea every year, in addition to oil spills and sewage disposal. On the other hand the water of the North Sea was said to be replaced on average at the rate of once every twelve months— but not in the German Bight, where this process was three times slower, largely as a result of the pollution of continental rivers.)

On Sept. 14, 1983, Norway and the United Kingdom signed an agreement relating to oil spills.

THE MEDITERRANEAN SEA

Barcelona Convention. An Action Plan for the protection of the Mediterranean Sea (from the entrance to the Straits of Gibraltar to the southern end of the Dardanelles Straits) was agreed upon at a conference of representatives of 16 Mediterranean coastal states (i.e. all except Albania and Cyprus), of three observer countries (Britain, the Soviet Union and the United States)

and of several international organizations, held in Barcelona from Jan. 28 to Feb. 4, 1975, under the auspices of UNEP.

The plan provided for "integrated planning of the development and management of the resources of the Mediterranean basin"; "co-ordinated pollution monitoring and research" in the Mediterranean; the drafting of a "framework convention and related protocols with their technical annexes for the protection of the Mediterranean environment"; and "institutional and financial procedures" to be followed in respect of the plan.

At a further conference of the 16 coastal states, held in Barcelona on Feb. 2–16, 1976, under UNEP auspices, a convention and two protocols were signed by 12 of these states. They entered into force on Feb. 12, 1978, after being ratified by 16 states (but not by Albania or Turkey).

The *Barcelona Convention* laid down that its signatories should take all necessary measures to prevent pollution of the sea by dumping from ships and aircraft, by exploitation of the continental shelf and the seabed, or by sources of pollution on land such as rivers or sewage effluent. The first protocol banned the dumping at sea of toxic substances from ships and aircraft and contained a "black list" of prohibited substances and a restricted list of substances for which a special permit was required. The second protocol provided for co-ordinated action in the event of oil spills and for the establishment of regional headquarters (opened in Malta on Dec. 11, 1976) to direct such operations.

A "blue plan", designed to cover the period up to the end of the century and to harmonize activities in order to ensure continuous economic and social development of the ecological environment of the whole Mediterranean region was unanimously adopted at a meeting in Split (Yugoslavia) from Jan. 31 to Feb. 4, 1977, by representatives of 15 nations (i.e. all coastal countries except Albania, Lebanon and Syria). The plan is carried out by a Group Co-ordination and Synthesis (GCS) multi-disciplinary unit co-ordinating all study activities.

A protocol on the protection of the Mediterranean against pollution from land-based sources was signed at a conference organized by UNEP and held in Athens on May 12–17, 1980. An annex to the convention listed prohibited substances (as laid down in the first protocol to the Barcelona Convention— see above) to be eliminated progressively from wastes and also specified common guidelines, criteria or standards for implementing the protocol, which came into force on June 17, 1983.

All Mediterranean coastal states except Albania had in February 1979 agreed to take over the burden of financing the Mediterranean action plan, with UNEP aid to cease by 1981. In May 1980 it was announced that the headquarters of the secretariat for the Mediterranean action plan would be transferred from Geneva to Barcelona.

At a conference held in Cannes (France) on March 2–7, 1981, by representatives of 16 Mediterranean states, it was decided to move the headquarters of the action plan co-ordinating group from Barcelona to Athens and to set up in Tunis a regional centre to monitor a network of specially protected reserves to help preserve plants and animals threatened with extinction throughout the Mediterranean region, including the monk seal and the marine turtle. The conference also found that the rapid depletion of stocks of some 500 species of Mediterranean fish was due to pollution of the posidonic grass beds providing shelter, food and spawning and nursery grounds for these fish.

At a meeting held in Geneva representatives of the European Community and 16 Mediterranean states approved, on April 2, 1982, a fourth protocol to the Barcelona Convention, calling for the establishment of up to 100 protected marine areas in the Mediterranean Sea to conserve endangered species, halt the spread of pollution and enhance tourism. Albania and Syria were not represented at the conference, and Turkey registered a strong protest, objecting to possible Greek establishment of marine parks in the eastern Aegean Sea, which would prejudice the two countries' dispute over maritime boundaries. By June 30, 1984, only the EEC, Egypt and Tunisia had become parties to the protocol, which is not yet in force.

Representatives of 11 European cities agreed at a meeting in La Coruña (Spain) on April 2–3, 1982, on a Charter for the Protection of the Environment, in particular against marine pollution. (According to UNEP sources about 500,000 tonnes of hydrocarbons were dumped in the Mediterranean every year, against 4,000,000 tonnes in the remaining seas of the world.)

Turkey signed the Barcelona Convention and its first two protocols in November 1980. The Convention as amended in Athens in 1980 came into force in August 1983 after it had been ratified by six states (Algeria, Egypt, France, Monaco, Tunisia and Turkey).

Earlier Regional Agreement. Italy and Yugoslavia signed, in 1974, an agreement on co-operation for the protection of the waters of the Adriatic Sea.

THE PERSIAN (ARABIAN) GULF

Regional Organization for the Protection of the Marine Environment (ROPME)

Address. P.O. Box 26388, Safat, Kuwait.

Founded. Jan. 1, 1982.

Membership. Bahrain, Iran, Iraq, Kuwait, Oman, Qatar, Saudi Arabia and the United Arab Emirates.

Objects. Protection of marine environment, implementation of regional action plans, application of the *Kuwait Regional Convention*, co-ordination and co-operation in case of pollution by oil or other harmful substances in the marine environment resulting from marine emergencies.

Activities. The Kuwait Regional Convention, together with a protocol and an action plan, adopted on April 24, 1978, had come into force on June 30, 1979.

In the Convention the signatory states had undertaken to "prevent, abate and combat pollution . . . caused by intentional or accidental discharge from ships . . ., by dumping of waste and other matter from ships and aircraft, . . . by discharges from land reaching the sea, whether waterborne or directly from the coast, including outfalls and pipelines" or "resulting from land reclamation and associated suction dredging and coastal dredging".

The protocol called upon the signatories to "co-operate in protection of the coastline" from "the threats and effects of pollution due to the presence of oil or other harmful substances . . . resulting from marine emergencies".

The action plan stressed the need for applied research and development, for contingency planning for accidents and for the establishment of a permanent pollution monitoring system. Its secretariat co-operated with the Regional Seas Programme Activity Centre of UNEP, and in November 1979 a total of 17 specific projects were approved. A Marine Emergency Mutual Aid Centre (MEMAC) was set up between December 1979 and April 1981. A Task Team on Oceanography and a Task Team on Baseline Studies of Oil and Non-Oil Pollutants held their first meetings in Kuwait on Sept. 5–10, 1981, and decided on the formulation of their programmes.

Structure. The ROPME has a council which has established an executive committee (consisting of the ministers of health of Bahrain, Iraq and Kuwait and the Iranian ambassador in Kuwait) and a scientific advisory committee.

RED SEA AND GULF OF ADEN

The *Jeddah Convention for the Conservation of the Red Sea and Gulf of Aden Environment* was adopted under UNEP auspices on Feb. 14, 1982, together with a *Protocol concerning Regional Co-operation in Combating Marine Pollution by Oil and Other Harmful Substances in Cases of Emergency*. Of the signatories (Jordan, the Palestine Liberation Organization, Saudi Arabia, Somalia, the Sudan, the Yemen Arab Republic and the People's Democratic Republic of Yemen) only the Sudan and the Yemen Arab Republic have become parties to the convention and protocol, which are not yet in force.

WEST AND CENTRAL AFRICA

The *Abidjan Convention for Co-operation in the Protection and Development of the Marine and Coastal Environment of the West and Central African Region* (covering the coastal states from Mauritania to Namibia) was signed on March 23, 1981, together with a *Protocol on Co-operation in Combating Pollution in Cases of Emergency*. They came into force on Aug. 5, 1984. The parties to them are Cameroon, Côte d'Ivoire, The Gambia, Guinea, Nigeria, Senegal and Togo.

The major problems of the region had been identified as oil pollution from ships, landbased pollution from industry, sewage, pesticides and fertilizers, and coastal erosion. The action plan therefore provided for assessment of oil pollution, suspended and dissolved matter in rivers, chemical residues and domestic wastes; training in coastal management and waste control; and the establishment of facilities for the inspection of tankers before they deballasted.

The states also (i) agreed on a protocol committing them to co-operating in pollution emergencies; (ii) pledged $2,500,000 over the period 1982–83 for a special regional trust fund to which Nigeria would contribute $550,000 and UNEP (during 1981–83) £1,400,000; and (iii) approved a resolution giving their naval vessels the "right of hot pursuit" of oil tankers which cleaned their tanks in West African coastal waters. Both the convention and the protocol had earlier been approved at a meeting of legal experts from 13 countries in Togo in 1980.

EAST AFRICA

On June 21, 1985, an agreement reached in Nairobi was signed by representatives of the governments of the Comoros, France (for the French overseas department of Réunion), Kenya, Madagascar, Mauritius, Mozambique, Seychelles, Somalia and Tanzania. The agreement provided for joint action to reduce and prevent pollution in the Indian Ocean and to protect the area from the effects of encroaching urbanization along the African coast. The European Communities were to assist in the financing of a joint organization designed to monitor any threat to the sea in the area, especially that presented by the heavy traffic of oil tankers from the Persian (Arabian) Gulf to Europe.

ASIA AND THE PACIFIC

In a memorandum of understanding signed in Jakarta on Feb. 11, 1981 by representatives of Indonesia, Japan, Malaysia and Singapore it was agreed to set up a fund of 400,000,000 yen for the prevention of pollution in the Malacca Strait, with Japan contributing threequarters of the amount required and the management of the fund rotating every five years between Indonesia, Malaysia and Singapore.

At a meeting held in Manila in April 1981 five South-East Asian nations (Indonesia, Malaysia, the Philippines, Singapore and Thailand) adopted an action plan on the protection and development of the marine environment and coastal areas in the South-East Asian region.

Under a South Pacific Regional Environment Programme (SPREP) of UNEP, the South Pacific Bureau for Economic Co-operation (SPEC), the South Pacific Commission (SPC) and the (UN) Economic and Social Commission for Asia and the Pacific (ESCAP), an action plan was drawn up in June 1981, leading to the adoption, at a conference on the human environment in the South Pacific held in March 1982, of a *South Pacific Declaration on Natural Resources and the Environment* (the *Rarotonga Declaration*).

The documents contained guidelines for the sustainable management of land, sea and air recourses of the region. In the declaration it was also stated that "the storage and release of nuclear wastes in the Pacific regional environment shall be prevented" and that "the testing of nuclear devices against the wishes of the people shall not be permitted".

A *Lima Convention for the Protection of the Marine Environment and Coastal Areas of the South-East Pacific* was adopted under UNEP auspices on Nov. 12, 1981, together with an *Agreement on Regional Co-operation in Combating Pollution of the South-East Pacific by Hydrocarbons and Other Harmful Substances in Cases of Emergency*. Of the five signatories (Chile, Colombia, Ecuador, Panama and Peru) only Ecuador has become a party to the convention and agreement, which have not yet entered into force.

A conference on the protection of the environment in Asia and the Pacific was held in Tokyo on June 5–11, 1984, with the participation of some 60 experts from 15 countries (Australia, China, Fiji, India, Indonesia, Japan, the Republic of Korea, Malaysia, Nepal, New Zealand, Papua New Guinea, the Philippines, Sri Lanka, Thailand and the United States). The conference agreed on a regional action programme intended to harmonize development and environmental protection, in particular to create a system of monitoring residual agricultural chemicals harmful to nature and health.

THE CARIBBEAN SEA

The *Cartagena Convention for the Protection and Development of the Marine Environment of the Wider Caribbean* was signed in Cartagena (Colombia) on March 24, 1983, by representatives of Colombia, Grenada, Honduras, Jamaica, Mexico, Nicaragua, Panama, St Lucia, the United States and Venezuela, as well as of France, the Netherlands and the United Kingdom on behalf of their respective dependent territories in the region. It was supported also by delegates from Costa Rica, Cuba, Guatemala and Trinidad and Tobago.

The convention arose out of an action plan drafted in Managua (Nicaragua) in February 1981 and approved by experts from 23 countries at a conference held on April 6–8, 1981, and sponsored by UNEP and the UN Economic Commission for Latin American (ECLA).

The countries participating were Barbados, Colombia, Costa Rica, Cuba, Dominica, Dominican Republic, Grenada, Guyana, Haiti, Honduras, Jamaica, Mexico, Nicaragua, Panama, St Lucia, Suriname, Trinidad and Tobago, Venezuela and the West Indies Associated States, as well as Britain, France, Netherlands and the USA; a proposal of the Commission of the European Community to participate actively was also accepted. Those countries which did not attend the conference were Bahamas, Guatemala and St Vincent and the Grenadines, although the latter expressed support in a telegram.

The action plan contained 66 specific environmental projects for the combating of oil spills, the protection of coral reefs, mangroves, tropical forests and endangered species such as turtles and parrots, the management of watersheds, and the monitoring of coastal water pollution, as well as for studies on the impact of tourism and on ways of mitigating natural disasters. To finance the plan, a sum of $8,200,000 was initially to be raised over the period 1981–83, including $1,500,000 for a Caribbean trust fund. A nine-country monitoring committee (Colombia, Costa Rica, Cuba, Dominican Republic, France, Grenada, Mexico, St Lucia and Venezuela) was named to carry out the plan in conjunction with UNEP, and Jamaica was chosen as the headquarters of the action plan co-ordinating unit.

RIVER POLLUTION

In Western Europe commissions have been set up by riparian states of the Rhine, the Moselle and the Saar to prevent pollution of these rivers.

Rhine. The **International Commission for the Protection of the Rhine against Pollution** was established on July 1, 1950, and on April 29, 1963, its members, the governments of France, the Federal Republic of Germany, Luxembourg, the Netherlands and Switzerland, signed a convention which came into force on May 1, 1965. The Commission is responsible for all necessary research on the nature, quantity and origin of pollution of the Rhine, and its technical secretariat works out proposals for the protection of the river's waters. In May 1976 the Commission agreed on a long-term plan involving the underground storage of salt from potash mines in

Alsace (previously discharged into the Rhine) and also decided to take precautions against thermal pollution of the Rhine by nuclear power stations.

A convention for the protection of the Rhine against chemical pollution and another convention for the protection of the Rhine against pollution by chloride were both signed on Dec. 3, 1976, and entered into force on Feb. 1, 1979, and July 5, 1985, respectively for France, the Federal Republic of Germany, Luxembourg, the Netherlands and Switzerland.

Moselle. The **International Commission for the Protection of the Moselle against Pollution** was established on Dec. 20, 1961, by France, the Federal Republic of Germany and Luxembourg with the object of recommending to member governments measures to protect the river against further pollution (including the inspection of sewage farms).

Saar. The **International Commission for the Protection of the Saar** against pollution, established by France and the Federal Republic of Germany, holds meetings simultaneously with those of the Commission for the Protection of the Moselle.

Air Pollution

A *Convention and Resolution on Long-Range Transboundary Air Pollution* was adopted, under the auspices of the (UN) Economic Commission for Europe, in Geneva on Nov. 13, 1979, by the United States, Canada and all European states except Albania, Cyprus and Malta. It obliged signatory states to "develop without undue delay policies and strategies which shall serve as a means of combating the discharge of air pollutants" and to engage in full exchange of information on environment protection technology.

The Convention came into force on March 16, 1983, for Austria, Belgium, Bulgaria, Canada, Denmark, the German Democratic Republic, the Federal Republic of Germany, Finland, France, Hungary, Ireland, Italy, Luxembourg, the Netherlands, Norway, Portugal, the Soviet Union, Spain, Sweden, the United Kingdom, the United States and the EEC; on July 7, 1983, for Turkey; on Aug. 3, 1983, for Iceland; on Aug. 4, 1983, for Switzerland; on Nov. 28, 1983, for Greece; on Feb. 2, 1984, for Liechtenstein; on March 22, 1984, for Czechoslovakia; and on Oct. 17, 1985, for Poland.

Under the convention an executive body was set up to carry out a co-operative programme for monitoring and evaluating the long-range transmission of air pollutants in Europe (EMEP).

At a ministerial meeting held in Stockholm eight countries (Austria, Canada, Denmark, Finland, Liechtenstein, Norway, Sweden and Switzerland) agreed on July 5, 1985, on the early introduction of the US-Norm 83 for the reduction of exhaust gases.

A bilateral agreement on monitoring and reducing air pollution was signed between Finland and the Soviet Union early in July 1985.

A protocol on the reduction of sulphur emissions and their transboundary fluxes by at least 30 per cent was signed in Helsinki on July 9, 1985, by 21 countries (including Canada but not Poland, the United Kingdom and the United States).

Agreement was reached by Canada and the United States on March 19, 1986, on a plan to combat the effect of "acid rain" (caused in Canada by wind-borne pollution from power plants and factories in the United States) by means of a five-year project to develop methods of reducing sulphur and nitrogen oxide emissions from coal-burning plants.

Protection of the Ozone Layer

A convention for the protection of the ozone layer was signed in Vienna on March 22, 1985, by 20 states (Argentina, Belgium, Byelorussia, Canada, Chile, Denmark, Egypt, Finland, France, the Federal Republic of Germany, Greece, Italy, the Netherlands, Norway, Peru, the Soviet Union, Sweden, Switzerland, the Ukraine and the United States) and the European Economic Community.

The convention obliged the parties to it to take appropriate measures to protect human health and the environment against the adverse effects of modification of the ozone layer (the belt of rarified gas some 10–50 kilometres above the surface of the earth, shielding it from the sun's fatal ultraviolet-B radiation). The convention was to enter into force 19 days after the deposit of the 20th instrument of ratification.

Environmental Conferences

1972 Stockholm Conference. The Stockholm Conference on the Human Environment held on June 5–16, 1972, and which had recommended the establishment of the UN Environment Programme [see page 28], also issued a *Declaration on the Human Environment* enumerating 26 principles (of which the first 25 were approved by acclamation and the 26th by a separate vote, against opposition by China).

The 26 principles were as follows:

(1) "Man has the fundamental right to freedom, equality and adequate conditions of life, in an environment of a quality which permits a life of dignity and well-being, and bears a solemn responsibility to protect and improve the environment for present and future generations. In this respect, policies promoting or perpetuating apartheid, racial segregation, discrimination, colonial and other forms of oppression and foreign domination stand condemned and must be eliminated.

(2) "The natural resources of the earth including the air, water, land, flora and fauna, and especially representative samples of natural ecosystems, must be safeguarded for the benefit of present and future generations through careful planning or management as appropriate.

(3) "The capacity of the earth to produce vital renewable resources must be maintained and wherever practicable restored or improved.

(4) "Man has a special responsibility to safeguard and wisely manage the heritage of wildlife and its habitat which are now gravely imperilled by a combination of adverse factors. Nature conservation including wildlife must therefore receive importance in planning for economic development.

(5) "The non-renewable resources of the earth must be employed in such a way as to guard against the danger of their future exhaustion and to ensure that benefits from such employment are shared by all mankind.

(6) "The discharge of toxic substances or of other substances and the release of heat, in such quantities or concentrations as to exceed the capacity of the environment to render them harmless, must be halted in order to ensure that serious or irreversible damage is not inflicted upon ecosystems. The just struggle of the peoples of all countries against pollution should be supported.

(7) "States shall take all possible steps to prevent pollution of the seas by substances that are liable to create hazards to human health, to harm living resources and marine life, to damage amenities or to interfere with other legitimate uses of the sea.

(8) "Economic and social development is essential for ensuring a favourable living and working environment for man and for creating conditions on earth that are necessary for the improvement of the quality of life.

(9) "Environmental deficiencies generated by the conditions of under-development and natural disasters pose grave problems and can best be remedied by accelerated development through the transfer of substantial quantities of financial and technological assistance as a supplement to the domestic effort of the developing countries and such timely assistance as may be required.

(10) "For the developing countries, stability of prices and adequate earnings for primary commodities and raw material are essential to environmental management since economic factors as well as ecological processes must be taken into account.

(11) "The environmental policies of all states should enhance, not adversely affect, the present or future development potential of developing countries, nor should they hamper the attainment of better living conditions for all, and appropriate steps should be taken by states and international organizations with a view to reaching agreement on meeting the possible national and international economic consequences resulting from the application of environmental measures.

(12) "Resources should be made available to preserve and improve the environment, taking into account the circumstances and particular requirements of developing countries and any costs which may emanate from their incorporating environmental safeguards into their development planning and the need for making available to them, upon their request, additional international technical and financial assistance for this purpose.

(13) "In order to achieve a more rational management of resources and thus to improve the environment, states should adopt an integrated and co-ordinated approach to their development planning so as to ensure that development is compatible with the need to protect and improve the human environment for the benefit of their population.

(14) "Rational planning constitutes an essential tool for reconciling any conflict between the needs of development and the need to protect and improve the environment.

(15) "Planning must be applied to human settlements and urbanization with a view to avoiding adverse effects on the environment and obtaining maximum social, economic and environmental benefits for all. In this respect projects which are designed for colonialist and racist domination must be abandoned.

(16) "Demographic policies, which are without prejudice to basic human rights and which are deemed appropriate by governments concerned, should be applied in those regions where the rate of population growth or excessive population concentrations are likely to have adverse effects on the environment or development, or where low population density may prevent improvement of the human environment and impede development.

(17) "Appropriate national institutions must be entrusted with the task of planning, managing or controlling the environmental resources of states with the view to enhancing environmental quality.

(18) "Science and technology, as part of their contribution to economic and social development, must be applied to the identification, avoidance and control of environmental risks and the solution of environmental problems and for the common good of mankind.

(19) "Education in environmental matters, for the younger generation as well as adults, giving due consideration to the underprivileged, is essential in order to broaden the basis for an enlightened opinion and responsible conduct by individuals, enterprises and communities in protecting and improving the environment in its full human dimension. It is also essential that mass media of communications avoid contributing to the deterioration of the environment, but, on the contrary, disseminate information of an educational nature on the need to enable man to develop in every respect.

(20) "Scientific research and development in the context of environmental problems, both national and multinational, must be promoted in all countries, especially the developing countries. In this connexion, the free flow of up-to-date scientific information and transfer of experience must be supported and assisted, to facilitate the solution of environmental problems; environmental technologies should be made available to developing countries on terms which would encourage their wide dissemination without constituting an economic burden on the developing countries.

(21) "States have, in accordance with the Charter of the United Nations and the principles of international law, the sovereign right to exploit their own resources pursuant to their own environmental policies, and the responsibility to ensure that activities within their jurisdiction or control do not cause damage to the environment of other states or of areas beyond the limits of national jurisdiction.

(22) "States shall co-operate to develop further the international law regarding liability and compensation for the victims of pollution and other environmental damage caused by activities within the jurisdiction or control of such states to areas beyond their jurisdiction.

(23) "Without prejudice to such criteria as may be agreed upon by the international community, or to the standards which will have to be determined nationally, it will be essential in all cases to consider the systems of values prevailing in each country, and the extent of the applicability of standards which are valid for the most advanced countries but which may be inappropriate and of unwarranted social cost for the developing countries.

(24) "International matters concerning the protection and improvement of the environment should be handled in a co-operative spirit by all countries, big or small, on an equal footing. Co-operation through multilateral or bilateral arrangements or other appropriate means is essential to effectively control, prevent, reduce and eliminate adverse environmental effects resulting from activities conducted in all spheres, in such a way that due account is taken of the sovereignty and interest of all states.

(25) "States shall ensure that international organizations play a co-ordinated, efficient and dynamic role for the protection and improvement of the environment.

(26) "Man and his environment must be spared the effects of nuclear weapons and all other means of mass destruction. States must strive to reach prompt agreement, in the relevant international organs, on the elimination and complete destruction of such weapons."

1976 UN Habitat Conference. A UN Conference on Human Settlements (Habitat) was held in Vancouver (Canada) from May 31 to June 11, 1976.

The Conference adopted a *Vancouver Declaration of Human Settlements* by 89 votes to 15 (of the member states of the European Communities, Australia, Canada, Israel, New Zealand, Norway and the United States) with 10 abstentions.

The declaration embodied a number of principles listed by a preparatory committee as the main objectives of human settlement policies and strategies, as follows:

(1) The rapid and continuous improvement in the quality of life of all people, beginning with the satisfaction of the basic needs and without discrimination of any kind.

(2) According to priority of the needs of the least advantaged people.

(3) Protection of the environmental resources upon which life itself depends.

(4) Reduction of disparities between rural and urban areas, between regions and within the urban areas themselves.

(5) Preservation of diversities reflected in cultural and aesthetic values.

(6) Effective use of all human resources, skilled and unskilled.

(7) Full participation of people in making and implementing decisions affecting their lives.

The conference reinforced these principles by declaring:

"Land, because of its unique nature and the crucial role it plays in human settlement, cannot be treated as an ordinary asset, controlled by individuals and subject to the pressures and inefficiencies of the market. Private land ownership also is a principal instrument of accumulation and concentration of wealth and therefore contributes to social injustice. If unchecked it may become a major obstacle in the planning and implementation of development schemes."

On water the conference recommended the launching of an international programme for the supply of drinking water to the entire population of the world, if possible by 1999.

On urban growth the conference's final recommendation reflected a move away from total urban renewal to small-scale development retaining much of the traditional architecture.

The declaration contained no decisions on new institutional arrangements within the United Nations.

1977 UN Water Conference. A UN Water Conference was held at Mar del Plata (Argentina) on March 14–25, 1977, after being prepared by a 54-member UN Committee on Natural Resources set up in 1970.

The conference made numerous recommendations, including (i) an action plan on community water supply and waste disposal, calling on national governments "to provide all people with water of safe quality and adequate quantity and basic sanitary facilities by 1990, according priority to the poor and less privileged", with activities to be focused on an "International Drinking Water Supply and Sanitation Decade" during 1980–90; (ii) an action programme for agricultural water use (consuming more than 80 per cent of all water used by man), aimed at improving and extending irrigation and rain-fed agriculture and protecting agricultural land from flooding and waterlogging; (iii) conservation and rational exploitation of fisheries; and (iv) the development of economic measures of re-using and recycling water, and economic incentives to use water efficiently and to treat wastes at their source. The conference also called, inter alia, for a national water policy to be formulated by each country and for the strengthening of international water law.

1977 UN Desertification Conference. A UN Desertification Conference was held in Nairobi

from Aug. 29 to Sept. 9, 1977, under UNEP auspices. The conference unanimously adopted a plan of action containing 26 specific recommendations designed to halt the spread of deserts by the year 2000.

Corrective measures proposed were the efficient planning, development and management of water resources, the improvement of degraded rangelands and the introduction of suitable systems of rangeland, livestock and wildlife management; soil conservation and improvement; prevention or control of waterlogging, salinization or alkalinization of irrigated lands; improved irrigation and drainage systems; and improvement of the social and economic conditions of people dependent on irrigation culture—which would include "maintenance of an adequate rural labour force, sedentarization of nomads and resettlement of those migrating from rural to urban areas" as well as "an adequate level of primary health care services, including family planning where necessary".

With regard to energy, the plan recommended that the use of conventional energy sources based on vegetation (e.g. firewood and charcoal burning) should be controlled and improved, and it called for research to be "vigorously pursued on the use of alternative or unconventional energy sources in the drylands that will yield simple, inexpensive, useful and socially acceptable devices to serve the needs of the dryland people".

Among recommendations for international action and co-operation, the first was to enlist the aid of UN organizations, and another was that countries of a region should co-operate in the sound and judicious management of shared water resources as a means of effectively combating desertification.

Immediate initial actions proposed at national level were the setting-up of governmental authorities to combat desertification, the preparation of national plans of action, and the preparation of requests for international support for specific activities. At the regional level such actions included in particular the implementation of transnational regional projects (such as studies on the major regional aquifers—or underground water-bearing strata—of North-East Africa and the Arabian peninsula, a proposed "green belt" in North Africa, and the transnational development of grazing resources in the Sudano-Sahel regions).

1986 Conference on the Protection of Forests. An International Conference on the Protection of Forests (the Silva Conference) was held in Paris on Feb. 5–7, 1986, and was attended by representatives of over 60 countries (including heads of state or government).

The conference discussed two main subjects—the deforestation in Africa (where the increasing use of firewood threatened to reduce forest areas by half within the next 50 years) and the damage caused to forests in Europe and attributed to atmospheric pollution.

At the conference France, the Federal Republic of Germany and the Netherlands announced that they would double their contributions in aid of reafforestation in developing countries over five years. Additional aid was also pledged by the Nordic countries and Japan. These increases were thought to bring the total of such aid to $8,000 million over five years.

For Europe it was decided to set up a research network on the physiology of trees (Eurosilva) and to organize collaboration among Mediterranean countries towards a forest protection charter.

Organizations for the Preservation of the Living Resources of the Sea

Commission for the Conservation of Antarctic Marine Living Resources

Address. 25 Old Wharf, Hobart, Tasmania 7000, Australia.

Officer. Dr Darry L. Powell (exec. sec.).

Founded. 1982.

Membership. Argentina, Australia, Chile, the German Democratic Republic, the Federal Republic of Germany, France, Japan, New Zealand, South Africa, the Soviet Union, the United Kingdom and the United States, as well as the European Economic Community.

Objects. The Commission was founded under a 1982 convention based on an ecosystem-wide approach to the conservation of marine living resources in the waters surrounding Antarctica, and incorporating standards designed to ensure the conservation of not only individual populations and species but also the maintenance of the breadth of the Antarctic marine ecosystem as a whole.

Activities. The Commission has planned a management programme for which baseline information is supplied by international scientific programmes under the Scientific Committee for Antarctic Research (SCAR).

International Whaling Commission (IWC)

Address. The Red House, 135 Station Road, Histon, Cambridge CB4 4NP, UK.

Officer. Dr R. Gambell (sec.).

Founded. Dec. 2, 1946.

Membership. Antigua and Barbuda, Argentina, Australia, Belize, Brazil, Chile, China, Costa Rica, Denmark, Egypt, Finland, France, the Federal Republic of Germany, Iceland, India, Japan, Kenya, the Republic of Korea, Mauritius, Mexico, Monaco, the Netherlands, New Zealand, Norway, Oman, Peru, the Philippines, St Lucia, St Vincent and the Grenadines, Senegal, Seychelles, South Africa, the Soviet Union, Spain, Sweden, Switzerland, the United Kingdom, the United States and Uruguay. (Canada withdrew from the IWC in June 1982.)

History. An international agreement on the protection of whales was first signed in London on June 8, 1937, by representatives of nine governments (Argentina, Australia, Germany, the Irish Free State, New Zealand, Norway, South Africa, the United Kingdom and the United States). This agreement provided for a nine-month closed season for ships attached to floating factories, for the absolute protection of certain species and classes of whales and a six-month closed season for whaling at land stations; it was amended by a protocol adopted in November 1945, which, inter alia, required contracting governments to supply an International Bureau of Whaling Statistics with weekly data of blue whale units caught by each factory ship.

The IWC was set up under an International Convention for the Regulation of Whaling designed to provide for the proper conservation of whale stocks and the orderly development of the whaling industry.

Objects. To keep under review and revise as necessary the measures laid down in the schedule to the above convention, which provide for the complete protection of certain species of whales; to designate specific ocean areas as whale sanctuaries; to set the maximum catches of whales which may be taken in any one season; to prescribe open and closed seasons and areas for whaling; to fix size limits above and below which certain species of whales may not be killed; to prohibit the capture of suckling calves and female whales accompanied by calves; and to require the compilation of catch reports and other statistical and biological records. The IWC is also to encourage, co-ordinate and fund research on whales and related matters (such as the humaneness of the killing operations, the ethics of killing cetaceans and the management of aboriginal subsistence whaling).

Activities. The IWC meets at least once a year and is assisted in its work by a scientific committee, a technical committee, and a finance and administration committee. Information provided by the scientific committee forms the basis on which the technical committee develops the regulations made by the IWC for the control of whaling. The adoption of regulations requires a three-quarters majority of the commissioners voting. (The changes become effective 90 days later unless a member government has lodged an objection, in which case the new regulation is not binding on that country. This procedure, however, is now only used when a member government considers its national interests or sovereignty to be unduly affected.)

In 1974 the IWC incorporated into its management procedure a strategy recommended by the scientific committee and classifying all whale stocks into three categories: (i) initial management stocks which may be reduced in a controlled manner to achieve "maximum sustainable yield" (MSY) levels or optimum levels as these are determined; (ii) sustained management stocks which will be maintained at or near MSY levels and at optimum levels as these are determined; and (iii) protection stocks which are below the level of sustained management stocks and will be fully protected from commercial whaling. This policy was designed to produce the greatest long-term harvests. However, in 1979 the ICW decided to ban factory-ship whaling for 10 years (except for minke whales) and to impose a complete ban on whaling in the Indian Ocean, as well as to determine quotas for certain species of whales in other seas.

Because of uncertainties about the precise status of the various exploited whale stocks, the ICW decided in 1982 that there should be a pause in commercial whaling from 1985/86 and that a comprehensive assessment of the effects of this decision should be undertaken by 1990. This decision was opposed by Brazil, Iceland, Japan, the Republic of Korea, Norway, Peru and the Soviet Union. Of these, Japan, Norway and the Soviet Union, accounting for about 90 per cent of the world's current whaling catch, maintained their formal objections made in 1982. On April 5, 1985, however, the Japanese Foreign Minister announced that Japan agreed to end commercial whaling from April 1, 1988, and that it would comply with a compromise agreement concluded with the United States (an agreement which had included not only Japan's belated acceptance of the IWC's five-year moratorium on whaling from 1985 but also an interim limit on sperm whale catches).

A minke whale quota of 4,224 set by the IWC for the 1984/85 Southern Hemisphere (Antarctic) catches was not accepted by Brazil, the Soviet Union and Japan; the two last-named countries, however, announced in January 1985 that they would voluntarily limit their minke whale catches to the previous year's level (at 3,027 and 3,028 respectively), while Japan stated that it would consult the United States over its actual catch.

During the IWC's 37th annual meeting held in Bournemouth (UK) on July 15–19, 1985, it was announced that the Soviet Union would temporarily end commercial whaling in the Atlantic from the 1987–88 season "for technical reasons". Decisions taken at the meeting included (i) classification of western North Pacific sperm whales as protection stock from 1988 (agreed unanimously), and (ii) classification of North-East Atlantic minke whales as protection stock from the beginning of the 1985–86 season (Iceland voting against and Norway taking no part in the vote).

The Norwegian government announced on July 3, 1986, that it would halt its whaling operations from 1987 (having already scaled down its minke whale quota to 400 for 1986).

All regulations adopted by the IWC are enforced by nationally appointed inspectors and overseen by international observers reporting directly to the IWC. The only whaling for large whales carried on outside IWC control is by Portugal (from the Azores).

North Pacific Fur Seal Commission

Address. c/o Office of International Fisheries Affairs, National Marine Fisheries Service, Washington, DC 20235, USA.

Officer. Jack Gehringer (exec. sec.).

Founded. 1958.

Membership. Canada, Japan, the Soviet Union and the United States.

History. The commission was established under an Interim Convention on the Conservation of North Pacific Fur Seals signed in Washington on Feb. 9, 1957, and in force from Oct. 14, 1957. The convention has repeatedly been extended for four-year periods, most recently in 1984.

Objects. To achieve the maximum sustainable productivity of the fur seal herds through the co-ordination of research programmes carried out by the member governments, and to implement the desire of the parties to prohibit pelagic sealing because of its past detrimental effect on fur seal populations, and to provide for regulated land harvesting of animals by the Soviet Union and the United States.

Activities. The commission does not conduct programmes of its own but co-ordinates those instituted by party governments. Through the operation of its standing scientific committee the commission may recommend to member governments appropriate measures dealing with the commercial harvest, pelagic or land-based research, collection of data on reproduction, morphology, feeding habits, migration routes and any other topic regarded as important for the conservation, protection and management of the fur seal populations. Through public relations and research the commission seeks to stem the entanglement of fur seals in fishing debris discarded at sea. The commission meets annually to report to the parties on current research activities and to consider the estimates of the yearly harvest by the United States and the Soviet Union.

Permanent Commission of the Conference on the Use and Conservation of the Marine Resources of the South Pacific (PCSP)

Address. Traslado A, Lima, Peru.

Founded. Aug. 18, 1952.

Membership. Chile, Ecuador and Peru.

Activities. The PCSP has conducted a Regional Study of the El Niño Phenomenon (Estudio Regional del Fenomeno El Niño, ERFEN).

Structure. The PCSP has a general secretariat, a juridical commission and a scientific research co-ordinating commission.

International Fisheries Organizations and Arrangements

Fishery Committee for the Eastern Central Atlantic (CECAF)
Comité des Pêches pour l'Atlantique Centre-Est

Address. c/o UN Development Programme (UNDP), B.P. 154, Dakar, Senegal, West Africa.

Officer. M. Ansa-Emmim (sec. and technical co-ordinator).

Founded. Sept. 19, 1967.

Membership. Benin, Cameroon, Cape Verde, the Congo, Côte d'Ivoire, Gabon, The Gambia, Ghana, Guinea, Guinea-Bissau, Equatorial Guinea, Liberia, Mauritania, Morocco, Nigeria, São Tomé and Príncipe, Senegal, Sierra Leone, Spain, Togo and Zaïre—as well as Cuba, France, Greece, Italy, Japan, the Republic of Korea, Norway, Poland, Romania and the United States.

Objects. To promote, co-ordinate and assist national and regional programmes of research and development leading to the rational utilization of the marine fishery resources of the area, and to assist in their implementation through sources of international aid; to enable member countries to analyse and monitor the state of their shared stocks and the fisheries fed by these stocks and to exchange their experiences and points of view on fishery development problems and study programmes for co-management for the resources.

Activities. The CECAF had given special attention to improving the regional statistical system and to stock assessment. In 1972 it recommended the fixing of a minimum mesh size for hake and seabream trawl fishing, and in 1979 it decided in addition to impose the utilization of a single mesh with an opening size of at least 60 mm for the exploitation of all demersal resources, and it also agreed that fish handling, processing and marketing activities should be intensified. The CECAF is assisted by a working party on fishery statistics and resources evaluation, which deals with resource management within the limits of national jurisdiction and is open only to coastal member nations (which can, within this framework, discuss problems specific to their exclusive economic zones, such as management of shared stocks). There is also a sub-committee for fishery development.

Indian Ocean Fishery Commission (IOFC)

Address. c/o FAO Regional Office, Maliwan Mansion, Phra Atit Road, Bangkok 2, Thailand.

Founded. 1967.

History. The IOFC was established under a resolution of the Council of the (UN) Food and Agriculture Organization (FAO).

Membership. 40 states.

Objects. To promote national programmes as well as research and development activities, and to examine management problems.

Indo-Pacific Fishery Commission (IPFC)

Address. FAO Regional Officer for Asia and the Pacific, Maliwan Mansion, Phra Atit Road, Bangkok 10200, Thailand.

Officer. V. L. C. Pietersz (regional fisheries officer and sec.).

Founded. Nov. 9, 1948.

Membership. 19 governments (i.e. those of Australia, Bangladesh, Burma, France, India, Indonesia, Japan, Democratic Kampuchea, the Republic of Korea, Malaysia, Nepal, New Zealand, Pakistan, the Philippines, Sri Lanka, Thailand, the United Kingdom, the United States and Vietnam).

Objects. To promote the proper utilization of living aquatic resources by the development and management of fishing and culture operations, and by the development of related processing and marketing activities, and for this purpose to keep under review the state of the resources and of the industries based on them; to formulate and recommend measures and to initiate and carry out projects to create new fisheries and increase the production, efficiency and productivity of existing fisheries, conserve management resources and protect resources from pollution; to keep under review the economic and social aspects of fishing and aquaculture industries and recommend measures aimed at improving the living and working conditions of fishermen and other workers in these industries and at improving the contribution of each fishery to attain social and economic goals; to encourage, co-ordinate and undertake training and extension activities, as well as research and development activities, and to assemble, publish and disseminate information on the living aquatic resources and fisheries based on them.

Activities. The major fields of IPFC activities are training; meetings; publications; fisheries resources assessment, research and development; reduction of post-harvest losses; environmental protection; rural fisheries and community development; planning and technical assistance to member governments; investment; co-operation with other regional and international organizations; and promotion of technical co-operation among developing countries.

Structure. The IPFC holds regular sessions every two years. It has nine subsidiary bodies—an executive committee, a special committee on management of Indo-Pacific tuna, a committee for the development and management of fisheries in the South China Sea (SCSC), a standing committee on resources research and development (SCORRAD), a joint working party (with the Indian Ocean Fishery Commission, IOFC) of experts on Indian Ocean and Western Pacific fishery statistics, working parties of experts on fish technology and marketing, on aquaculture, on inland fisheries and on Central and Western Pacific skipjack. In addition there are three co-operative programmes—on research on aquaculture, on fish product development and on information among fisheries libraries, institutions and scientists in the region.

Inter-American Tropical Tuna Commission (IATTC)

Address. c/o Scripps Institution of Oceanography, La Jolla, California 92093, USA.

Officer. Dr James Joseph (dir. of investigations).

Founded. 1950.

Membership. France, Japan, Nicaragua, Panama and the United States.

History. The IATTC has operated under a convention originally concluded by Costa Rica and the United States and open to adherence by other governments whose nationals fished for tropical tunas in the eastern Pacific Ocean. It was adhered to by Panama in 1953, Ecuador in 1961, Mexico in 1964, Canada in 1968, Japan in 1970 and France and Nicaragua in 1973. However,

Ecuador withdrew from the IATTC in 1968, Mexico in 1978, Costa Rica in 1979 and Canada in 1984.

Objects. To study the biology of the tunas and related species of the eastern Pacific Ocean with a view to determining the effects of fishing and natural factors on their abundance, and to recommend appropriate conservation measures in order to maintain stocks of fish at levels which would afford maximum sustainable catches if and when the IATTC research showed such measures to be necessary. In 1976 the IATTC defined new objectives as being to maintain a high level of tuna production and also to maintain porpoise stocks at or above levels that assured their survival in perpetuity, with every reasonable effort being made to avoid needless or careless killing of porpoises.

Activities. The IATTC has engaged in monitoring population sizes and mortality incidental to fishing, aerial surveys and dolphin tagging, analyses of indices of abundance of dolphins, computer simulation studies, and gear and behavioural research and education.

International Baltic Sea Fishery Commission

Address. ul. Hoza 20, 00-950 Warszawa, Poland.

Officers. Stefan de Maré (ch.); Jan Piotr Jaremczuk (sec.).

Founded. Sept. 13, 1973.

Membership. Six contracting parties (the European Economic Community, Finland, the German Democratic Republic, Poland, the Soviet Union and Sweden).

Objects. To co-ordinate the management of the living resources in the Baltic Sea and the Belts by collecting, aggregating, analysing and disseminating statistical data (concerning catch, fishing effort, etc.) and other information; to promote co-ordination of scientific research and joint programmes and, in particular, to prepare and submit recommendations regarding total allowable catches, the type of fishing gear used, establishing closed seasons or areas, the amount of fishing effort and other measures related to the conservation and rational exploitation of the living resources.

Activities. The Commission has sought to implement a Convention on Fishing and Conservation of the Living Resources in the Baltic Sea and the Belts, signed in Gdansk (Poland) on Sept. 13, 1973, and amended with effect from Feb. 10, 1984. It has issued fishery rules (last revised with effect from Jan. 1, 1984), for the application of which the Baltic Sea and the Belts are divided into 11 areas, each of which is broken down into statistical rectangles as laid down by the International Council for the Exploration of the Sea (ICES).

International Commission for the Conservation of Atlantic Tunas (ICCAT)

Address. Príncipe de Vergara, 17, 28001 Madrid, Spain.

Officers. Olegário Rodríguez Martín (exec. sec.).

Founded. May 14, 1966.

Membership. Angola, Benin, Brazil, Canada, Cape Verde, Côte d'Ivoire, Cuba, France, Gabon, Ghana, Japan, the Republic of Korea, Morocco, Portugal, São Tomé and Príncipe, Senegal, South Africa, the Soviet Union, Spain, the United States, Uruguay and Venezuela.

History. The ICCAT was founded under an International Convention for the Conservation of Atlantic Tunas approved at a conference of 17 countries in Rio de Janeiro on May 2–14, 1966, and in effect since March 1969 (after ratification by seven countries).

Objects. To co-operate in maintaining the population of tunas and tuna-like fishes of the Atlantic Ocean at levels which will permit the maximum sustainable yield for food and other purposes.

Activities. Under the 1966 convention the ICCAT is responsible for research on the abundance, biometry and ecology of the fishes, the oceanography of their environment, and the effects of natural and human factors on their abundance. Activities have included the collecting and analysing of statistical information, the study and appraisal of information concerning measures and methods to ensure maintenance of the populations, the recommendation of studies and investigations to the contracting parties, and the publication and dissemination of reports of findings and other information relating to the tuna fisheries of the convention area. It has carried out an International Skipjack Year Programme (1979–83), culminating in a Skipjack Conference held in Tenerife in 1983 (the skipjack being regarded as the most abundant of the commercial tuna species). It has recently made recommendations concerning the conservation of yellowfin, bigeye and bluefin tunas.

Structure. The ICCAT has a council which normally meets once a year in Spain, and subcommittees and working groups which have held more than 30 meetings at various locations since 1971. Its official languages are English, French and Spanish.

International Commission for the South-East Atlantic Fisheries (ICSEAF)

Address. Paseo de la Habana, 65, 28036 Madrid, Spain.

Officers. P. Kruger (ch.); Dr Bohdan Draganik (asst. exec. sec.).

Founded. Oct. 24, 1971.

Membership. Angola, Bulgaria, Cuba, France, the German Democratic Republic, the Federal

Republic of Germany, Iraq, Israel, Italy, Japan, the Republic of Korea, Poland, Portugal, Romania, South Africa, the Soviet Union and Spain.

History. The ICSEAF was set up by a conference called by the (UN) Food and Agriculture Organization (FAO) and held in Rome in October 1969 with the participation of Belgium, Cuba, France, the Federal Republic of Germany, Italy, Japan, the Republic of Korea, Panama, Portugal, South Africa, Spain and Togo. The conference adopted a convention (concluded on Oct. 23, 1969, and in force from Oct. 24, 1971) which defined the South-East Atlantic area as bordered by the coast of Africa and lying between the latitudes of 6°S and 50°S and the longitudes of 20°W and 40°E, and the objects of the ICSEAF as being to study the living resources in the area and to make recommendations for the regulation of catches which would, under specified conditions, be binding on the contracting parties.

Activities. The ICSEAF has repeatedly imposed quotas for catches, among them one (laid down in December 1976) for an annual quota of 700,000 tonnes of whitefish (hake) in South Africa's 200-mile economic zone (including 149,000 tonnes for South Africa itself).

International Council for the Exploration of the Sea (ICES)

Address. Palaegade 2, DK-1261 Copenhagen K, Denmark.

Officers. Prof. Warren S. Wooster (pres.); Dr B. B. Parrish (gen. sec.).

Founded. 1902.

Membership. Belgium, Canada, Denmark, Finland, France, the German Democratic Republic, the Federal Republic of Germany, Iceland, Ireland, the Netherlands, Norway, Poland, Portugal, the Soviet Union, Spain, Sweden, the United Kingdom and the United States.

Objects. To promote and co-ordinate international investigations of the marine environment and its living resources in the North Atlantic and adjacent seas, and to publish or otherwise disseminate the results of this research, including the provision of scientific information and advice to national governments and regional fishery management and pollution control commissions.

Activities. The founder members of the ICES were Denmark, Finland, Germany, the Netherlands, Norway, Sweden, Russia and the United Kingdom, whose contract establishing the ICES was renewed every five years but was, as from July 22, 1968, replaced by a 1964 Convention for the International Council for the Exploration of the Sea. Under this convention membership of the ICES was open to any state upon approval by three-quarters of its member states.

The work of the ICES is carried out by (i) its finance committee; (ii) its consultative committee in charge of the general oversight of the Council's scientific interests and work; (iii) an advisory committee on fishery management (ACFM) responsible for liaison with the North-East Atlantic Fisheries Commission (NEAFC) and other fisheries commissions and for giving member governments, groups of governments or commissions scientific advice when requested, and comprising a demersal, a pelagic and a Baltic fish committee; (iv) an advisory committee on marine pollution (ACMP), established in 1972, with sub-committees on hydrography, marine environmental quality and biological oceanography; and (v) a publications committee.

Further work is carried out by standing area and subject committees including the following: a fish capture committee concerned with studies of detection and searching techniques, design and operation of fishing gear, and behaviour of fish in relation to fishing; a statistics committee; a mariculture committee concerned with investigations relating to the culture of marine organisms, including transplantation and introduction of new species; a shellfish committee concerned with molluscs and crustacea; an anadromous and catadromous fish (Anacat) committee; and a marine mammals committee. There are also numerous working groups, meeting usually once a year.

Structure. The ICES Council, which holds statutory meetings every year, has a bureau consisting of a president, a first vice-president and five other vice-presidents. The Council's secretariat is responsible for the administrative, hydrographic and statistical services of the ICES.

International North Pacific Fisheries Commission (INPFC)

Address. 6640 N.W. Marine Drive, Vancouver, Canada V6T 1X2.

Officers. C. R. Forrester (exec. dir.); four commissioners from each of Canada, Japan and the United States.

Founded. June 12, 1953.

Membership. Canada, Japan, the Soviet Union and the United States.

History. The INPFC was created by an *International Convention for the High Seas Fisheries of the North Pacific Ocean*, signed by Canada, Japan and the United States on May 9, 1952, ratified in June 1953 and amended on April 25, 1978, by a protocol which came into force in February 1979 and covered new fishing management rights of Canada and the United States in their respective 200-mile exclusive economic zones.

Objects. To ensure the maximum sustainable productivity of the fishery resources of the waters of the North Pacific Ocean and adjacent seas (except territorial waters); to promote and co-ordinate the scientific studies necessary to ascertain the conservation measures required; to provide (under the amending protocol) for scientific studies and the co-ordination of collections, exchange and analysis of scientific data regarding anadromous species; and (also under the protocol) to provide, pending the establishment of an international organization with broader membership dealing with species other than anadromous ones, a forum for co-operation in the study, analysis and exchange of information and views on stocks of non-anadromous species of the convention area.

Activities. The INPFC has reported the results of research conducted on its behalf by the three contracting parties in annual reports; a Statistical Yearbook contains catch and effort data for salmon, herring, halibut, groundfish, shrimp, and king and tanner crab fisheries, and in some years data supplied by the Soviet Union for that country's salmon fishery in the Pacific. In the past few years updated joint comprehensive reports have been published on five species of Pacific salmon, on North Pacific oceanography, and on historical salmon and groundfish statistics.

Structure. The INFPC consists of three national sections each of which is assisted by scientific, technical and legal experts and advisers. The Canadian and US sections have formally organized advisory committees of fishing industry representatives. The INFPC meets annually in Vancouver, Tokyo or Anchorage (Alaska). It has standing committees on finance and administration, and on biology and research; the latter has sub-committees on salmon and on non-anadromous species; the second of these sub-committees has a Bering Sea panel, a Northeast Pacific panel, groundfish working groups as required, and a king and tanner crab panel; and there is also an ad hoc committee on marine mammals, with a scientific sub-committee.

International Pacific Halibut Commission (IPHC)

Address. P.O. Box 95009, Seattle, WA 98145-2009, USA.

Officer. Donald A. McCaughran (dir.).

Founded. 1923.

History. The IPHC was created as the International Fisheries Commission in 1923 by a convention between Canada and the United States, which came into force on Oct. 23, 1924. It was continued under subsequent conventions of 1930, 1937 and 1953 (when the commission adopted its present name) and amended by a protocol in 1979.

Objects. To regulate the fishing of halibut (a large-sized flatfish found on the continental shelf of the North Pacific).

Activities. The IPHC meets annually to review all regulatory proposals, including those made by its scientific staff and a conference board representing vessel owners and fishermen. Regulatory alternatives are discussed with an advisory group composed of fishermen, vessel owners and processors. The measures recommended by the IPHC are submitted to the two governments (of Canada and the United States) for approval, and upon approval the measures are enforced by appropriate agencies of both governments.

Structure. The IPHC consists of three commissioners appointed by the Governor General of Canada and three appointed by the President of the United States. The commissioners appoint a director who supervises the scientific and administrative staff. The scientific staff collects and analyses statistical and biological data needed to manage the halibut industry.

North Atlantic Salmon Conservation Organization

Address. Dept. of Agriculture, Fisheries and Food for Scotland, Chesser House, 500 Gorgie Road, Edinburgh EH11 3AW, Scotland.

Officer. Dr Malcolm Windsor (sec.).

Founded. 1982.

Membership. Canada, Denmark (in respect of the Faroe Islands and Greenland), the European Economic Community, Finland, Iceland, Norway, Sweden and the United States.

Objects. The organization was established under an Atlantic Salmon Convention (concluded on March 2, 1982, and in force from Oct. 1, 1983) to promote (i) the acquisition, analysis and dissemination of scientific information pertaining to salmon stocks in the North Atlantic Ocean and (ii) the conservation, restoration, enchancement and rational management of the stocks through international co-operation.

Activities. The convention applies to the salmon stocks which migrate beyond areas of fisheries jurisdiction of coastal states of the Atlantic Ocean north of 36°N latitude throughout their migratory range. (Within areas of coastal state fisheries jurisdiction salmon fishing is prohibited beyond 12 nautical miles from baselines used to measure the breadth of the territorial sea except off West Greenland, where salmon fishing may take place up to 40 miles from baselines, and off the Faroe Islands, where it may take place within the Faroes area of fisheries jurisdiction.) The organization held its inaugural meeting on Jan. 17–20, 1984, and its first annual meeting on May 22–25, 1974 (both in Edinburgh).

Structure. The organization has a council, three regional commissions—a North American Commission (NAC), a West Greenland Commission (WGC) and a North-East Atlantic Commission (NEAC)—and a secretary.

North-East Atlantic Fisheries Commission (NEAFC)

Address. Room 339, Great Westminster House, Horseferry Road, London SW1P 2AE, UK.

Officers. J. L. Arnalds (pres.); (Mrs) E. A. Blackwell (sec.).

Founded. 1959.

Membership. Bulgaria, Denmark (for the Faroe Islands), the European Economic Community, the German Democratic Republic, Iceland, Norway, Portugal, the Soviet Union, Spain and Sweden.

History. The NEAFC was established under a convention signed on Jan. 24, 1959, by representatives of Belgium, Denmark, France, the Federal Republic of Germany, Iceland, Ireland, the Netherlands, Norway, Poland, Portugal, the Soviet Union, Spain, Sweden and the United Kingdom. This convention came into force on June 27, 1963, and it applied to parts of the Atlantic and Arctic Oceans north of 36°N and between the longitudes of 42°W and 51°E (excluding the Mediterranean and Baltic Seas) and also part of the Atlantic Ocean north of 59°N and between 44°W and 42°W. The NEAFC was reconstituted under a new convention which was signed on Nov. 18, 1980, and came into force on March 17, 1982.

Objects. To ensure, through consultation and exchange of information, the conservation and the rational exploitation of fish stocks in the North-East Atlantic and adjacent waters of concern to members states; to encourage international co-operation with respect to these resources; and to recommend conservation measures in waters outside national jurisdiction.

Activities. In carrying out its objectives the NEAFC co-operates closely with the International Council for the Exploration of the Sea (ICES), to which it makes a financial contribution, and with the FAO Committee on Fisheries. It holds annual meetings in London, and at its 1983 meeting it decided to set up an ad hoc committee on technical conservation measures (which related inter alia to mesh sizes, fish sizes, attachments to nets and by-catches).

North-West Atlantic Fisheries Organization (NAFO)

Address. P.O. Box 638, Dartmouth, Nova Scotia, B2Y 3Y9, Canada.

Officers. Dr V. K. Zilanov (ch. of General Council & pres.); Capt. J. C. Esteves Cardoso (perm. exec. sec.).

Founded. 1979.

Membership. Bulgaria, Canada, Cuba, Denmark (in respect of the Faroe Islands and Greenland), the European Economic Community, the German Democratic Republic, Iceland, Japan, Norway, Poland, Portugal, Romania, the Soviet Union and Spain.

History. The NAFO was preceded by an International Commission for the North-West Atlantic Fisheries (ICNAF), set up in 1949 under a convention signed by 11 nations and responsible for the investigation, protection and conservation of the fishery resources of the North-West Atlantic Ocean. The ICNAF was authorized to recommend measures for the maintenance of a maximum sustained catch from those fisheries which support international fisheries in the area, and (under a 1971 amendment to the convention) to recommend measures to achieve the optimum utilization of those stocks of fish which support such fisheries. On Oct. 24, 1978, Canada and eight other signatories of the ICNAF convention signed a Convention on Future Multilateral Co-operation in the North-West Atlantic Fisheries

which replaced the ICNAF by the NAFO with a more developed structure and safeguards for the sovereign jurisdiction of coastal states over the living resources of the sea within their 200-mile limits. This convention came into force on Jan. 1, 1979.

Objects. The optimum utilization and rational management of the fishery resources of the North-West Atlantic (between the coasts of the United States, Canada and Greenland and the 35°N parallel in the south and the 40°W meridian in the east).

Activities. The collection of basic data relating to the resources, analysis of these data, choice of most suitable conservation measures in light of scientific, economic, social and political factors, and implementation of measures (inspection and enforcement).

Structure. The NAFO's General Council has established a standing committee on finance and administration (STACFAD), and the Scientific Council has set up standing committees on fisheries science (STACFIS), on research co-ordination (STACREC) and on publications (STACPUB). The Fisheries Commission has created a standing committee on international control (STACTIC).

Pacific Salmon Fishery Commission

Address. P.O. Box 30, Dominion Bldg., New Westminster, BC, Canada.

Founded. 1985.

History. This commission, consisting of four members each from Canada and the United States, was established under a treaty signed in Ottawa (Canada) on Jan. 28, 1985, by representatives of the two countries, ending 15 years of negotiations. Previously the two countries had co-operated on the preservation and promotion of salmon fishing within the International Pacific Salmon Fisheries Commission founded in 1937.

A bill designed to implement the new treaty was approved by voice vote in the US House of Representatives on March 5, 1985, and by the US Senate on March 7, when the Senate also approved the treaty by 96 votes to none.

Objects. To attempt to control over-fishing of salmon in the Pacific Ocean and to manage the fishing rights of the two countries.

Regional Fisheries Advisory Commission for the South-West Atlantic
Comisión Asesora Regional de Pesca para el Atlántico Sudoccidental (CARPAS)

Address. c/o International Institution and Liaison Unit, Fishery Policy and Planning Division, FAO, Via delle Terme di Caracalla, 00100 Rome, Italy.

Officer. Dr Elda Fagetti (sec.).

Founded. 1961.

Membership. Argentina, Brazil, Uruguay.

Objects. To promote fuller use of the marine resources in the western South Atlantic in accordance with sound economic and scientific principles, to co-ordinate studies, research and techniques and to determine common needs.

Activities. The CARPAS is open to all nations with coasts on the Western Atlantic south of the equator. It has a working party on fisheries statistics, an ad hoc working party on fishery economic development in the South-West Atlantic, a working party on biological research and evaluation of fishery resources, a joint working party (with the FAO Advisory Committee on Marine Resources Research, ACMRR) on the scientific evaluation of the state of the stocks in the South-West Atlantic, and a number of experts from its member countries.

South East Asian Fisheries Development Centre (SEAFDEC)

Address. P.O. Box 4, Phrapradeng, Samutprakarn, Thailand.

Founded. Dec. 28, 1967.

Membership. Japan, the Philippines, Singapore and Thailand.

South Pacific Forum Fisheries Agency

Address. P.O. Box 629, Honiara, Solomon Islands.

Officer. D. A. P. Müller (dir.).

Founded. August 1977.

Membership. Australia, the Cook Islands, Fiji, Kiribati, the Federated States of Micronesia, Nauru, New Zealand, Niue, Papua New Guinea, the Solomon Islands, Tonga, Tuvalu, Vanuatu and Western Samoa.

Objects. To promote regional co-operation and co-ordination in respect of fisheries policies; to facilitate the collection, analysis, evaluation and dissemination of relevant statistical, scientific and economic information about the living marine resources of the region, and in particular the highly migratory species; to secure the maximum benefits from the marine living resources of the region for the peoples of the region as a whole and in particular of the developing countries; and to police a 200-mile exclusive economic zone of member states.

South Pacific Islands Fisheries Development Agency

Address. c/o South Pacific Commission, Post Box D5, Nouméa Cédex, New Caledonia.

Officer. Francis Bugotu (sec. gen.).

Founded. May 1970.

Membership. American Samoa, the Republic of Belau, the Cook Islands, Fiji, French Polynesia, Guam, Kiribati, the Marshall Islands, the Federated States of Micronesia, Nauru, New Caledonia, Niue, the Northern Mariana Islands, Papua New Guinea, Pitcairn Island, the Solomon Islands, Tokelau, Tonga, Tuvalu, Vanuatu, Wallis and Futuna, and Western Samoa.

Objects. To increase fisheries production in line with national planning objectives through a more accurate assessment of the nature and extent of available fisheries resources, the introduction of improved fishing gear and techniques, and an increased understanding of management and conservation measures necessary to sound development; to upgrade the technical expertise of national fisheries administration through the provision of specialized training opportunities, inter-country study visits etc., and the promotion of interchange of experts, information and experience between countries of the region.

Activities. In the technical assistance given by the South Pacific Commission on request to the countries of its region particular emphasis is laid on the assessment and development of marine resources, and training and provision of expert advice on a wide range of problems associated with subsistence, artisanal, commercial and international fisheries. The Commission also carries out investigation projects, assists applied research, acts as a centre for collection and dissemination of information and produces technical publications.

Western Central Atlantic Fisheries Commission (WECAFC)

Address. Via delle Terme di Caracalla, 00100 Rome, Italy.

Officer. E. Fagetti (fishery liaison officer, sec.).

Founded. 1973.

Membership. Antigua and Barbuda, the Bahamas, Barbados, Brazil, Colombia, Cuba, Dominica, France, Grenada, Guatemala, Guinea, Guyana, Haiti, Italy, Jamaica, Japan, the Republic of Korea, Mexico, the Netherlands, Nicaragua, Panama, St Christopher and Nevis, St Lucia, Spain, Suriname, Trinidad and Tobago, the United Kingdom, the United States and Venezuela.

History. The WECAFC was established, and is administered, by the (UN) Food and Agriculture Organization (FAO).

Objects. To facilitate the co-ordination of research leading to the conservation, development and utilization of the living resources including shrimps, of the Western Central Atlantic Ocean; to encourage education and training; to assist member governments in establishing rational policies; and to promote the rational management of resources which are of interest to two or more countries.

Multilateral Fisheries Conventions

A Fisheries Convention, signed on March 9, 1964, and in force from March 15, 1966, established a 12-mile-wide exclusive fishing zone for the coastal states and has been acceded to by Belgium, Denmark, France, the Federal Republic of Germany, Ireland, Italy, the Netherlands, Poland, Portugal, Spain, Sweden and the United Kingdom.

A Convention on the Conduct of Fishing Operations in the North Atlantic, concluded on June 1, 1967, and in force from Sept. 26, 1976, contained regulations on identification of fishing vessels and gear, marking of nets and lines, signals and the operation of fishing vessels. The parties to it are Belgium, Denmark, France, the German Democratic Republic, the Federal Republic of Germany, Iceland, Italy, the Netherlands, Norway, Portugal, the Soviet Union, Spain, Sweden and the United Kingdom.

6. International Economic Co-operation

The need for international economic co-operation, including that of arresting and eventually reversing the widening gap between the economies of the developed and those of the developing countries, has been the motive for the creation of the Organization for Economic Co-operation and Development (OECD) and the subject of declarations and resolutions adopted by the UN General Assembly and also of consultations leading to agreements between groups of nations as well as between individual governments. Within the developed world, co-operation on international economic questions has been pursued not only within established institutions but also at a series of summit conferences of the major non-communist industrialized states beginning in 1975. Also covered in this section are the Conference on International Economic Co-operation (the "North-South dialogue"), the Independent Commission on International Development Issues (the "Brandt Commission"), recent sessions of the UN Conference on Trade and Development (UNCTAD) on international economic co-operation and the Customs Co-operation Council (CCC).

Organization for Economic Co-operation and Development (OECD)

Address. 2 rue André-Pascal, 75775 Paris Cédex 16, France.

Officer. Jean-Claude Paye (sec. gen.).

Founded. Sept. 30, 1961.

Membership. Australia, Austria, Belgium, Canada, Denmark, Finland, France, the Federal Republic of Germany, Greece, Iceland, Ireland, Italy, Japan, Luxembourg, the Netherlands, New Zealand, Norway, Portugal, Spain, Sweden, Switzerland, Turkey, the United Kingdom and the United States (full members); Yugoslavia (observer, with full member status in the fields of comparison of economic policies, science and technology, agriculture and fisheries, technical assistance, and productivity).

History. The OECD superseded an Organization for European Economic Co-operation (OEEC) which had been established by 16 nations under a convention signed on April 16, 1948, as a permanent body to implement a European Recovery Programme embodying the Marshall Plan (a four-year programme of US economic aid to Europe). With the accession of the Federal Republic of Germany in October 1949 and of Spain in July 1959, the OEEC membership reached 18 countries, with the United States and Canada participating as associate members, Yugoslavia taking part in certain OEEC activities and Finland sending observers to some of its committees.

The formation of the OECD with Canada and the United States as full members was proposed in a report by a four-member group, published on April 20, 1960, and specifying that the new organization should have the aim of promoting "within the framework of free political institutions" policies designed

(i) To facilitate the attainment of the highest sustainable economic growth, while maintaining financial stability and high levels of employment, and thus to contribute to the development of the world economy and the promotion of world trade on a multilateral and non-discriminatory basis; and (ii) to contribute to sound economic growth in areas in the process of economic development, both in member countries and elsewhere, by appropriate means, including the encouragement of the flow of development capital to those areas.

Representatives of the 18 members of the OEEC and of the USA, Canada and the Commission of the EEC met in Paris on May 24–25, 1960, and again on July 22–23, 1960, to discuss a draft covention for the proposed OECD. At the second meeting the broad outlines of the draft convention were agreed upon, and a preparatory committee was then charged with completing the final draft. This meeting also approved the setting up of a trade committee within the OECD, its functions being defined as the confrontation of general trade policies and practices; the examination of specific trade problems affecting members; and the examination of other short-term and long-term trade problems.

The final draft of the *Convention of the Organization for Economic Co-operation and Development* was signed on Dec. 14, 1960, by the 18 full members of the OEEC and by Canada and the USA. It entered into force on Sept. 30, 1961.

A summary of the principal articles of the convention is given below:

"**Art. 1.** The aims of the OECD shall be to promote policies designed:

"(*a*) To achieve the highest sustainable economic growth and employment and a rising standard of living in member countries, while maintaining financial stability, and thus to contribute to the development of the world economy;

"(b) to contribute to sound economic expansion in member as well as non-member countries in the process of economic development; and

"(c) to contribute to the expansion of world trade on a multilateral, non-discriminatory basis, in accordance with international obligations.

"**Art. 2.** In pursuit of these aims, the members agree that they will, both individually and jointly,

"(a) promote the efficient use of their economic resources;

"(b) in the scientific and technological field, promote the development of their resources, encourage research, and promote vocational training;

"(c) pursue policies designed to achieve economic growth and internal and external financial stability and to avoid developments which might endanger their economies or those of other countries;

"(d) pursue their efforts to reduce or abolish obstacles to the exchange of goods and services and current payments, and maintain and extend the liberalization of capital movements; and

"(e) contribute to the economic development of both member and non-member countries in the process of economic development by appropriate means and in particular by the flow of capital to those countries, having regard to the importance to their economies of receiving technical assistance and of securing expanding export markets.

"**Art. 3.** The members therefore agreed that they would

"(a) keep each other informed and furnish the Organization with the information necessary for the accomplishment of its tasks;

"(b) consult together on a continuing basis, carry out studies, and participate in agreed projects; and

"(c) co-operate closely, and where appropriate take co-ordinated action. . . ."

"**Art. 5.** In order to achieve its aims, the OECD might:

"(a) take decisions which, except as otherwise provided, shall be binding on all the members;

"(b) make recommendations to members; and

"(c) enter into agreements with members, non-member states and international organizations."

"**Art. 6.** Unless the organization otherwise agrees unanimously for special cases, decisions shall be taken and recommendations shall be made by mutual agreement of all the members.

Each member shall have one vote. If a member abstains from voting on a decision or recommendation, such abstention shall not invalidate the decision or recommendation, which shall be applicable to the other members but not to the abstaining member.

No decision shall be binding on any member until it has complied with the requirements of its own constitutional procedures. The other members may agree that such a decision shall apply provisionally to them.

"**Art. 7–9.** A council composed of all the members should be set up as the executive body of the organization and might meet in sessions of Ministers or of Permanent Representatives. It would designate each year a Chairman to preside at its ministerial sessions, and two Vice-Chairmen, and might establish an Executive Committee and "such subsidiary bodies as required for the achievement of the aims of the Organization". A Chairman could be relected only for two consecutive terms.

"**Art. 10–11.** A Secretary-General responsible to the Council would be appointed by it for a term of five years, and would be assisted by one or more Deputy or assistant Secretaries-General appointed by the Council on his recommendation. He would serve as Chairman of the Council meeting at sessions of Permanent Representatives; would assist the Council in all appropriate ways; might submit proposals to the Council or to any other body of the organization; and would appoint the staff required in accordance with organizational plans approved by the Council. Staff regulations would be subject to Council approval.

Having regard to the international character of the organization, the Secretary-General, the Deputy or Assistant Secretaries-General and the staff shall neither seek nor receive instructions from any of the members or from any government or authority external to the organization.

"**Art. 12.** Upon such terms and conditions as the Council may determine, the organization may (a) address communications to non-member states or organizations; (b) establish and maintain relations with non-member states or organizations; and (c) invite non-member governments or organizations to participate in activities of the organization.

"**Art. 13** and Supplementary protocol No. 1 provided that representation in the OECD of the European Communities established by the Treaty of Paris of April 18, 1951, and the Treaty of Rome of March 25, 1957, should be determined in accordance with the institutional provisions of those Treaties, and that the Commissions of the EEC and of the European Atomic Energy Community (Euratom), as well as the High Authority of the European Coal and Steel Community, should take part in the work of the OECD.

"**Art. 15.** When this convention comes into force, the reconstitution of the OEEC shall take effect, and its aims, organs, powers and name shall thereupon be as provided herein. The legal personality possessed by the OEEC shall continue in the organization, but decisions, recommendations and resolutions of the OEEC shall require approval of the Council to be effective after the coming into effect of this convention.

"**Art. 19** and Supplementary Protocol No. 2 set out the legal capacity of the organization and the privileges, exemptions and immunities of the organization, its officials and representatives.

In addition to the two Supplementary Protocols [see above], a protocol was signed dealing with the revision of the Convention for European Economic Co-operation of April 16, 1948.

Under this protocol, the members of the OEEC, "desirous that the aims, organs, and powers of the OEEC be re-defined and that the Governments of Canada and the USA be members of that organization as reconstituted", agreed (a) that the convention should be revised and replaced by the Convention on the OECD; (b) that the Protocol should come into force together with the Convention on the OECD, and that the Convention for European Economic Co-operation should cease to have effect as regards any signatory of the Protocol when the Convention on the OECD came into force.

Japan became a full member of the OECD on April 28, 1964; Finland on Jan. 28, 1969; Australia on June 7, 1971; and New Zealand on May 29, 1973, bringing the membership to 24.

Structure. The supreme body of the OECD is its Council, composed of one representative for each member country. The Council meets either at permanent representative level (about once a week) under the chairmanship of the Secretary-General, or at ministerial level (usually once a year) under the chairmanship of a minister elected annually. Decisions and recommendations are adopted by mutual agreement of all members of the Council.

The Council is assisted by an Executive Committee composed of 14 members of the Council designated annually by the latter. The major part of the OECD's work is, however, prepared and carried out by numerous specialized committees and working parties, of which there exist more than 200. The committees are those for:

Economic Policy
Economic and Development Review

Development Assistance (DAC)
Technical Co-operation
Trade
Payments
Capital Movements and Invisible Transactions
Financial Markets
Fiscal Affairs
Restrictive Business Practices
Consumer Policies
Tourism
Maritime Transport
International Investment and Multinational Enterprises
Energy Policy
Industry
Steel

Scientific and Technological Policy
Information, Computer and Communications Policy
Education
Manpower and Social Affairs
Environment
Agriculture
Fisheries

There are also a High-Level Group on Commodities, a Group on North-South Issues, a Steering Committee of the Programme of Co-operation in the Field of Road Research, and a Steering Committee of the Programme of Educational Building.

Iceland
Sweden
Finland
Norway
Denmark
Danish
Soviet Union
Irish Republic
United Kingdom
N
B
Federal Republic of Germany
German Democratic Republic
Poland
Czechoslovakia
France
S
Austria
Hungary
Romania
Italy
Yugoslavia
Bulgaria
Portugal
Spain
A
Greece
Turkey
Malta
Cyprus

A = Albania
B = Belgium
L = Luxembourg
N = Netherlands
S = Switzerland

= European members of OECD (which also includes Australia, Canada, Japan, New Zealand and the United States)

= Country with special status in OECD

Map 1   European members of Organization for Economic Co-operation and Development (OECD)

An International Secretariat, headed by the Secretary-General of the OECD, services the Council, the committees and other bodies. There are two Deputy Secretaries-General, a co-ordinator of energy policies (who is the Executive Director of the International Energy Agency—see below), an economic adviser and two special counsellors to the Secretary-General.

The Secretariat comprises an economics and statistic department and directorates for agriculture; data processing and statistical services; development co-operation; the environment; financial and fiscal affairs; science, technology and industry; social affairs, manpower and education; trade; and the executive; as well as an information service and a technical co-operation service.

Co-operation with Other Organizations. Among intergovernmental organizations, the Commission of the European Communities generally takes part in the work of the OECD (under Supplementary Protocol No. 1 signed at the same time as the OECD Convention); the European Free Trade Association (EFTA) may send representatives to OECD meetings; and most of the UN specialized agencies have official relations with the OECD, as have the European Conference of Ministers of Transport (ECMT), the Organization of American States (OAS), the Intergovernmental Committee for European Migration (ICEM) and the Customs Co-operation Council.

The OECD Council also decided on March 13, 1962, that international non-governmental organizations deemed to be widely representative in general economic matters or in a specific economy sector might be granted consultative status enabling them to discuss subjects of common interest with a liaison committee under the chairmanship of the OECD Secretary-General and to be consulted in a particular field by the relevant OECD committee or its officers.

Financial Support Fund. Under a formal agreement signed in Paris on April 9, 1975, by ministers and representatives of all full member countries of the OECD except Turkey (which signed the agreement in May of that year) and previously approved by the "Group of Ten" (leading member countries of the International Monetary Fund), a two-year Financial Support ("safety net") Fund of $25,000 million, open to all OECD member countries, was set up to enable these countries to finance their external deficits. The agreement fixed quotas according to the member countries' gross national product and foreign trade (and ranging from 27.8 per cent of the total for the United States to 2.3 per cent for Australia and New Zealand). The fund would grant loans for a period not exceeding seven years under strict conditions of approval by member countries other than the prospective borrowing country. The fund was intended to be used only as a last resort in a "severe balance of payments crisis".

Economic Outlook. One of the OECD's important activities has been the publication of a bi-annual Economic Outlook, which surveys economic performance in the OECD member countries and makes forecasts on the rates of growth of their gross national product, of consumer price inflation, of wages and unemployment, and on their balances of current accounts, trends in investment and fiscal and monetary policies of OECD member governments. In these reports the OECD also makes recommendations for dealing with unemployment, inflation and declining real income per head of the population.

Guidelines and Declarations. The OECD has also issued guidelines on various matters from time to time.

In June 1976 all its member governments except that of Turkey adopted a set of guidelines for multinational enterprises (as part of a package of measures aimed at improving the international investment climate).

In May 1980 the OECD adopted a set of guidelines designed to control the testing and marketing of new chemicals, enabling member governments to work to common standards in developing chemicals which would be universally acceptable on both health and environmental grounds.

In June 1980 the OECD issued a declaration on trade policies, emphasizing the need to strengthen trade with developing countries and to pursue, during the 1980s, policies which contribute to their economic prosperity. The declaration stressed the crucial importance of export earnings for developing countries and the favourable effect of high growth in those countries on the world economy, and it contained commitments by the OECD member countries to maintain and improve the open and multilateral trading system; to strengthen the role of the General Agreement on Trade and Tariffs (GATT); to avoid restrictive trade measures which could have an adverse effect on inflation, productivity and growth; and to avoid policies leading to a distortion of export competition, in particular in the field of export financing.

Development Assistance Committee. Of the OECD's committees, the Development Assistance Committee (DAC) has 19 members (the Governments of Australia, Austria, Belgium, Canada, Denmark, Finland, France, the Federal Republic of Germany, Ireland, Italy, Japan, the Netherlands, New Zealand, Norway, Sweden, Switzerland, the United Kingdom and the United States, and the Commission of the European Communities). (Ireland joined the DAC on Nov. 22, 1985.)

A Special Economic Committee which met in Paris on Jan. 12–13, 1960, had adopted a resolution on the formation of a Development Assistance Group to co-ordinate aid to under-developed countries.

The founder-members of the group were Belgium, Canada, France, the Federal Republic of Germany, Italy, Japan, Portugal, the United Kingdom, the USA and the EEC Commission. The Netherlands joined later in 1960.

In a communiqué of Dec. 14, 1960, it was stated that, on the inception of the OECD, the Development Assistance Group would be constituted as an organ of the OECD to be known as the Development Assistance Committee (DAC).

The main objectives of the DAC are to examine ways of increasing the volume of development assistance; to assess the indebtedness of the less-developed countries and the appropriate terms of assistance; and to co-ordinate assistance efforts, both capital and technical.

The DAC works primarily through the Annual Aid Review, a systematic and detailed examination of each member country's programme of aid, taking in the volume, financial terms, geographical distribution, purposes and techniques of the assistance. Meetings of the DAC are also held to discuss specific subjects connected with development aid.

In a report of January 1986 the OECD reviewed the efforts and policies of the DAC over 25 years and gave a table to illustrate trends in aid from major donors to sub-Saharan Africa. The table showed that in 1982–83 such aid totalled (at 1983 prices and exchange rates) US$8,554 million (against 5,185 million in 1970–71), of which bilateral aid by the DAC amounted to $5,146 million (against $2,901 million in 1970–71).

The report also showed the official development assistance from DAC member countries to sub-Saharan Africa as a percentage of their gross national product (GNP) for 1983–84. From the list given it emerged that only five countries had exceeded the target of 0.7 per cent of GNP (Norway 1.04 per cent, the Netherlands 0.96 per cent; Sweden 0.82 per cent; Denmark 0.79 per cent; France 0.75 per cent).

Export Credit Arrangements. Under such arrangements industrialized countries continued to apply an internal consensus agreement on terms and conditions of loans granted to finance purchases of their exports. Such arrangements were made by the OECD in 1976 (for four years), in October 1981 and again on July 22, 1982 (to cover the period up to May 1, 1983). The last-named arrangement was to be made at varying rates of interest for different categories of countries, ranging from "relatively poor" to "intermediate" and "relatively rich", the last category to include, from 1982, the Soviet Union and several East European states.

Autonomous and Semi-Autonomous Bodies of the OECD

OECD Nuclear Energy Agency (NEA)

Membership. All full members of the OECD except New Zealand.

History. The NEA was set up as the European Nuclear Energy Agency (ENEA) with effect from Feb. 1, 1958, after its statutes had been adopted by the OEEC on Dec. 20, 1957, and it was taken over by the OECD on the latter's foundation in September 1961. The ENEA changed its name to NEA in May 1972.

Structure. The NEA is governed by a Steering Committee consisting of a chairman and two vice-chairmen, and it has a Secretariat headed by a Director-General and a Deputy Director-General. It also has a number of committees, in particular for: Technical and economic studies on nuclear energy development and the fuel cycle; safety of nuclear installations; radiation protection and public health; radioactive waste management; nuclear data; and reactor physics. It also has a Group of Governmental Experts on third-party liability in the field of nuclear energy and a co-ordinating group on gas-cooled fast reactor development.

Objects. The main purpose of the NEA is to promote international co-operation within the OECD area for the development and application of nuclear power for peaceful purposes through international research and development projects and exchange of scientific and technical experience and information. The NEA also maintains a continual survey, with the co-operation of other organizations, notably the International Atomic Energy Agency (IAEA), of world uranium resources, production and demand, and of economic and technical aspects of the nuclear fuel cycle. An expanding part of the NEA's work is devoted to safety and regulatory aspects of nuclear energy, including the development of uniform standards governing safety and health protection, and a uniform legislative regime for nuclear liability and insurance.

Activities. The NEA has been involved in various joint projects:

The Halden Reactor. The Experimental Boiling Heavy Water Reactor at Halden in southern Norway was built by the Norwegian *Institutt for Atomenergi*. It became a joint undertaking under the ENEA in June 1958, and a research and development programme was initiated in July 1958. This programme, completed early in 1964, was succeeded by a further programme of specialized research and development work, scheduled for completion at the end of 1969; extensions of the programme provided for its further continuation, and under an extension of the original agreement the project was to be continued until 1984.

Participants in the programme have been atomic energy institutions or authorities in Britain, Denmark, Finland, Italy, Japan, the Netherlands, Norway and Sweden; the Swiss Government; and a West German industrial group working in agreement with the Federal Ministry of Scientific Research. The Austrian Atomic Energy Study Company and the US Atomic Energy Commission have participated as associate members.

Other Projects. An International Project on Food Irradiation was established in Karlsruhe

(Federal Republic of Germany) in 1971 to carry out testing of irradiated food items and to conduct a systematic review of all available data from national institutions. It is jointly sponsored by the NEA, the IAEA and the Food and Agriculture Organization (FAO), with 24 countries participating in its programme.

An NEA Data Bank, set up in 1978 at Saclay (France), replaced an earlier Computer Programme Library (at the Euratom Joint Research Establishment at Ispra, Italy) and a Neutron Data Compilation Centre (at Saclay). It enables the 17 participating countries to share computer programmes used in reactor calculations and also nuclear data applications; it is one of a worldwide network of four nuclear data centres.

Conventions. A convention on security control was signed by the OEEC Council on Dec. 20, 1957.

The basic rules of this security control closely follows those defined in the statute of the International Atomic Energy Agency and the Euratom Treaty. They provide for an examination of all plants subject to control; a system of quantitative control for nuclear fuel; on-the-spot supervision by international inspectors; and, in cases of non-observance, the possibility of imposing penalties by a majority vote. Provision was made for an international tribunal to settle certain disputes to which the exercise of control might give rise.

An important convention providing for uniform rules on third-party liability in the field of nuclear energy was signed in Paris on July 29, 1960, and came into force on April 1, 1968.

The convention is designed to ensure that the effects of a nuclear incident do not stop at political or geographical boundaries, and that claimants may proceed with their claims against any reactor operator in any of the signatory countries. The liability of reactor operators for any damage caused by the escape of radioactive material from nuclear installations is absolute in the sense that there is liability without any need to prove fault or blame on the part of the reactor owner; liability will cover all incidents occurring both in connexion with the installations and in the course of transport of radioactive substances.

A supplementary convention was signed in Brussels in January 1963, extending the maximum limit of compensation.

OECD Development Centre

Membership. All full OECD members except New Zealand.

Activities. The Development Centre was established by a decision of the OECD Council in 1962 with the object of bringing together the knowledge and experience available in member countries of both economic development and the formulation and execution of general policies of economic aid, and of placing such knowledge and experience at the disposal of developing countries as adapted to their needs. Although an integral part of the OECD, the Development Centre enjoys autonomy and thus has scientific independence. Its activities include research on basic development problems, such as employment, technology and industrialization, social development and demography. The centre co-operates with the OECD and with other international organizations dealing with development matters.

Centre for Educational Research and Innovation (CERI)

Membership. All full OECD member countries and Yugoslavia.

Objects. CERI was established in 1968 with the objects of promoting and assisting the development of research activities in the field of education, and of carrying out advanced experiments designed to test innovations in education and to stimulate research and development.

International Energy Agency (IEA)

Membership. Australia, Austria, Belgium, Canada, Denmark, the Federal Republic of Germany, Greece, Ireland, Italy, Japan, Luxembourg, the Netherlands, New Zealand, Norway, Portugal, Spain, Sweden, Switzerland, Turkey, the United Kingdom and the United States. The Commission of the European Communities is also represented on the IEA's Governing Board.

History. The IEA was set up by the Council of the OECD on Nov, 18, 1974, under an agreement approved by 16 oil-consuming countries (Austria, Belgium, Canada, Denmark, the Federal Republic of Germany, Ireland, Italy, Japan, Luxembourg, the Netherlands, Spain, Sweden, Switzerland, Turkey, the United Kingdom and the United States), with Finland, France and Greece abstaining from voting on the Council's decision and Norway taking no part in the agreement.

The agreement, concluded for 10 years but subject to a general review after five years, provided inter alia for an oil-sharing scheme coming automatically into operation in the event of a shortfall of 7 per cent or more affecting any or all of the participating countries. In the event of overall supplies of oil falling short by 12 per cent, each country would have to curb demand by 10 per cent even if not directly affected. The agreement also provided for weighted majority decisions on over 20 subjects relating inter alia to stock-piling, oil-sharing and conservation, under a complex voting system which gave each member a vote approximately in proportion to its oil consumption in 1973 and under which a total of 148 votes was distributed as follows: United States 51, Japan 18, Federal Republic of Germany 11, United Kingdom and Italy 9 each, Canada 8, Belgium, the Netherlands, Spain and Sweden 5 each, Austria, Denmark, Switzerland and Turkey 4 each and Ireland and Luxembourg 3 each. The automatic activation of the oil-sharing scheme could be prevented by 89 (or 60 per cent) of the 148 votes or by the votes of at least 12 countries. The participating countries were also to maintain contingency oil stocks equal to at least 60 day's consumption initially (90 days at a date to be agreed later) and would, if the oil-sharing scheme came into operation, have to make specific cutbacks in consumption and to use existing stocks on an agreed basis.

Structure. The IEA has a Governing Body assisted by four standing groups (on energy questions, long-term co-operation, the oil market and relations with producer and other consumer countries).

Activities. At a ministerial meeting held in Paris on Oct. 5–6, 1977, the IEA's Governing Board adopted a 12-point basic "Principles for Energy Policy", the main object of which was to reduce future oil imports and to expand indigenous energy sources of oil substitutes. The measures proposed included the progressive replacement of oil in electricity generation, district heating industries and other sectors; the application of a strong steam coal utilization strategy and active promotion of a reliable and expanded international trade in steam coal; the "concentration of the use of natural gas on premium users' requirements"; and "steady expansion of nuclear generating capacity". Appendices to the text of the Principles listed (i) suggested energy conservation measures and (ii) the principal research, development and demonstration areas requiring emphasis. (On the principle of expanding nuclear energy capacity, reservations were expressed by the governments of Denmark, the Netherlands, New Zealand, Spain and Sweden.)

At further ministerial meeting, held in Paris on Dec. 10, 1979, the Governing Board agreed on a net oil import ceiling for each IEA member country for 1980 and a net oil import target for 1985, subject to quarterly monitoring by the IEA.

At a ministerial meeting held in Paris on May 22, 1980, it was agreed that member countries should aim at reducing their aggregate net oil imports in 1985 by an extra 4,000,000 barrels per day (bpd) below the ceiling of 26,200,000 bpd agreed in December 1979 and at reducing the share of oil in the total energy demand to about 40 per cent by 1990 (against the existing level of 52 per cent).

A ministerial meeting held in Paris on June 15, 1981, stressed the need for stronger action to realize the full potential for expansion of coal production and use on an economic basis; endorsed the work of a Coal Industry Advisory Board (CIAB) set up in April 1980; and emphasized that nuclear power would have to play a major and increasing role in many countries.

In 1985 the IEA negotiated an agreement on international co-operation in the field of research on nuclear fusion technology, which was signed in Munich on Jan. 15, 1986, by the European Community, Japan and the United States.

The agreement provided for exchanges of information concerning the working of the Tokamak fusion reactors—the Joint European Torus (JET) reactor at Culham (United Kingdom), the TFTR at Princeton (Mass., USA) and the JT60 at Naka-machi (Japan).

UN and Other Initiatives in the Economic Sphere

Special UN General Assembly Sessions

April–May 1974. A special session of the UN General Assembly on the problem of raw materials and development was held in New York from April 9 to May 2, 1974, and ended with the adoption of a *Declaration on the Establishment of a New International Economic Order* and of a *Programme of Action* to carry it out.

The Declaration read as follows:

"We, the members of the United Nations;

"Having convened a special session of the General Assembly to study for the first time the problems of raw materials and development, devoted to the consideration of the most important economic problems facing the world community;

"Bearing in mind the spirit, purposes and principles of the Charter of the United Nations to promote the economic advancement and social progress of all peoples;

"Solemnly proclaim our united determination to work urgently for the Establishment of a New International Economic Order based on equity, sovereign equality, interdependence, common interest and co-operation among all states, irrespective of their economic and social systems, which shall correct inequalities and redress existing injustices, make it possible to eliminate the widening gap between the developed and the developing countries, and ensure steadily accelerating economic and social development in peace and justice for present and future generations.

"The greatest and most significant achievement during the last decades has been the independence from colonial and alien domination of a large number of peoples and nations which has enabled them to become members of the community of free peoples. Technological progress has also been made in all spheres of economic activities in the last three decades, thus providing a solid potential for improving the well-being of all peoples. However, the remaining vestiges of alien and colonial domination, foreign occupation, racial discrimination, apartheid and neo-colonialism in all its forms continue to be among the greatest obstacles to the full emancipation and progress of the developing countries and all the peoples involved. The benefits of technological progress are not shared equitably by all members of the international community. The developing countries, which constitute 70 per cent of the world population, account for only 30 per cent of the world's income. It has proved impossible to achieve an even and balanced development of the international community under the existing international economic order. The gap between the developed and the developing countries continues to widen in a system which was established at a time when most of the developing countries did not even exist as independent states and which perpetuates inequality.

"The present international economic order is in direct conflict with current developments in international political and economic relations. Since 1970 the world economy has experienced a series of grave crises which have had severe repercussions, especially on the developing countries because of their generally greater vulnerability to external economic impulses. The developing world has become a powerful factor that makes its influence felt in all fields of international activity. These irreversible changes in the relationship of forces in the world necessitate the active, full and equal participation of the developing countries in the formulation and application of all decisions that concern the international community.

"All these changes have thrust into prominence the reality of interdependence of all the members of the world community. Current events have brought into sharp focus the realization that the interests of the developed countries and the interests of the developing countries can no longer be isolated from each other; that there is close inter-relationship between the prosperity of the developed countries and the growth and development of the developing countries; and that the prosperity of the international community as a whole depends upon the prosperity of its constituent parts.

"International co-operation for development is the shared goal and common duty of all countries. Thus the political, economic and social well-being of present and future generations depends more than ever on co-operation between all members of the international community on the basis of sovereign equality and the removal of the disequilibrium that exists between them.

"The new international economic order should be founded on full respect for the following principles:

"(a) Sovereign equality of states, self-determination of all peoples, inadmissibility of the acquisition of territories by force, territorial integrity and non-interference in the internal affairs of other states;

"(b) broadest co-operation of all the member states of the international community, based on equity, whereby the prevailing disparities in the world may be banished and prosperity secured for all;

"(c) full and effective participation on the basis of equality of all countries in the solving of world economic problems in the common interest of all countries, bearing in mind the necessity to ensure the accelerated development of all the developing countries, while devoting particular attention to the adoption of special measures in favour of the least developed, land-locked and island developing countries, as well as those developing countries most seriously affected by economic crises and natural calamities, without losing sight of the interests of other developing countries;

"(d) every country has the right to adopt the economic and social system that it deems to be the most appropriate for its own development and not to be subjected to discrimination of any kind as a result;

"(e) full permanent sovereignty of every state over its natural resources and all economic activities. In order to safeguard these resources each state is entitled to exercise effective control over them and their exploitation with means suitable to its own situation, including the right to nationalization or transfer of ownership to its nationals, this right being an expression of the full permanent sovereignty of the state. No state may be subjected to economic, political or any other type of coercion to prevent the free and full exercise of this inalienable right;

"(f) all states, territories and peoples under foreign occupation, alien and colonial domination or apartheid have the right to restitution and full compensation for the exploitation and depletion of, and damages to, the natural and all other resources of those states, territories and peoples;

"(g) regulation and supervision of the activities of transnational corporations by taking measures in the interest of the national economies of the countries where such transnational corporations operate on the basis of the full sovereignty of those countries;

"(h) right of the developing countries and the peoples of territories under colonial and racial domination and foreign occupation to achieve their liberation and to regain effective control over their natural resources and economic activities;

"(i) extending of assistance to developing countries, peoples and territories under colonial and alien domination, foreign occupation, racial discrimination or apartheid or which are subjected to economic, political or any other type of measures to coerce them in order to obtain from them the subordination of the exercise of their sovereign rights and to secure from them advantages of any kind, and to neo-colonialism in all its forms, and which have established or are endeavouring to establish effective control over their natural resources and economic activities that have been or are still under foreign control;

"(j) just and equitable relationship between the prices of raw materials, primary products, manufactured and semi-manufactured goods exported by developing countries, and the prices of raw materials, primary commodities, manufactures, capital goods and equipment imported by them with the aim of bringing about sustained improvement in their unsatisfactory terms of trade and the expansion of the world economy;

"(k) extension of active assistance to developing countries by the whole international community, free of any political or military conditions;

"(l) ensuring that one of the main aims of the reformed international monetary system shall be the promotion of the development of the developing countries and the adequate flow of real resources to them;

"(m) improving the competitiveness of natural materials facing competition from synthetic substitutes;

"(n) preferential and non-reciprocal treatment for developing countries, wherever feasible, in all fields of international economic co-operation;

"(o) securing favourable conditions for the transfer of financial resources to developing countries;

"(p) to give the developing countries access to the achievements of modern science and technology, to promote the transfer of technology and the creation of indigenous technology for the benefit of the developing countries in forms and in accordance with procedures which are suited to their economies;

"(q) necessity for all states to put an end to the waste of natural resources, including food products;

"(r) the need for developing countries to concentrate all their resources for the cause of development;

"(s) strengthening through individual and collective actions of mutual economic, trade, financial and technical co-operation among the developing countries, mainly on a preferential basis;

"(t) facilitating the role which producers' associations may play, within the framework of international co-operation, and in pursuance of their aims, inter alia, assisting in promotion of sustained growth of the world economy and accelerating development of developing countries.

"The unanimous adoption of the International Development Strategy for the Second Development Decade [i.e. the years 1971–80] was an important step in the promotion of international economic co-operation on a just and equitable basis. The accelerated implementation of obligations and commitments assumed by the international community within the framework of the Strategy, particularly those concerning imperative development needs of developing countries, would contribute significantly to the fulfilment of the aims and objectives of the present Declaration.

"The United Nations as a universal organization should be capable of dealing with problems of international economic co-operation in a comprehensive manner and ensuring equally the interests of all countries. It must have an even greater role in the establishment of a new international economic order. The Charter of Economic Rights and Duties of States [see pages 49–51], for the preparation of which this Declaration will provide an additional source of inspiration, will constitute a significant contribution in this respect. All the states members of the UN are therefore called upon to exert maximum efforts with a view to securing the implementation of this Declaration, which is one of the principal guarantees for the creation of better conditions for all peoples to reach a life worthy of human dignity.

"This Declaration on the Establishment of a New International Economic Order shall be one of the most important bases of economic relations between all peoples and all nations."

The Programme of Action contained, inter alia, a 12-month emergency aid programme for those poor countries which were most severely affected by the sharply increased prices of essential imports such as foodstuffs, fertilizers, oil and capital goods. In addition it called for the establishment of a special fund under UN auspices to provide emergency relief and assistance as from Jan. 1, 1975, and for 12 special aid measures for the neediest countries, including "soft" loans and debt renegotiation.

September 1975. A special session of the UN Generaly Assembly, devoted to development and international co-operation, was held on Sept. 1–16, 1975, in order to deal with the possible implementation of the decisions taken at the Assembly's 1974 special session [see above].

The session unanimously adopted a lengthy resolution containing proposals for taking numerous measures in the fields of international trade; the transfer of real resources for financing the development of developing countries and international monetary reform; the use of science and technology for development; industralization; an increase in food production in developing countries; and co-operation among these countries.

The proposals included in particular the creation of an Ad Hoc Committee on the Restructuring of the Economic and Social Sectors of the UN System, which would be a committee of the whole of the General Assembly open to participation of all states.

Summits of Major Non-Communist Industralized States

The original proposal which led to a series of summit conferences of the major non-communist industrialized states was made by President Giscard d'Estaing of France in July 1975, when he proposed that a conference of the "Group of Five" (the United States, Japan, West Germany, France and the United Kingdom) and possibly other industrialized countries should be held to discuss international monetary problems arising from the massive increase in world oil prices dating from 1973–74. The first such conference, attended by the "Group of Five" and Italy, was held in France in November 1975 and further conferences took place in succeeding years as described below. Canada took part from the second such summit in 1976 and the European Community was represented as such from the third in 1977. The agendas of this series of conference have steadily been expanded to cover broader aspects of international economic co-operation and also pressing political questions affecting the international situation.

Rambouillet Summit. The first of this series of summits, involving the heads of government of six major non-communist economic powers (the United States, Japan, the Federal Republic of Germany, France, the Untied Kingdom and Italy), was held as Rambouillet (near Paris) on Nov. 15–17, 1975. Agreement was reached by the participants on the world economic situation, as expressed in a joint declaration.

After affirming their determination to play their full parts and strengthen their "efforts for closer international co-operation and constructive dialogue with all countries" and "to overcome high unemployment, continuing inflation and serious energy problems" by means of "growth that is steady and lasting", the six leaders continued: "Growth and price stability will be fostered by maintenance of an open trading system. . . . There is a responsibility on all countries, especially those with strong balance-of-payments positions and on those with current deficits, to pursue policies which will permit the expansion of world trade to their mutual advantage. . . . Multilateral trade negotiations (within the framework of the General Agreement on Trade and Tariffs—GATT) should be accelerated . . .; they would aim at substantial tariff cuts, even eliminating tariffs in some areas, at significantly expanding agricultural trade and at reducing non-tariff measures. They should aim at achieving the maximum possible level of trade liberalization therefrom. We propose as our goal the completion of the negotiations in 1977. We look to an orderly and fruitful increase in our economic relations with socialist countries as an important element in progress on détente, and on world economic growth. . . .

"A co-operative relationship and improved understanding between the developing nations and the industrial world is fundamental to the prosperity of each. . . . Early practical action is needed to assist the developing countries. . . . We will play our part, through the International Monetary Fund and other appropriate international fora, in making urgent improvements in international arrangements for the stabilization of the export earnings of developing countries and in measures to assist them in financing their deficits. In this context, priority should be given to the poorest developing countries."

The participants of the meeting also agreed that they would continue to co-operate in order to reduce their dependence on imported energy, and they added: "Through these measures, as well as through international co-operation between producer and consumer countries responding to long-term interests of both, we shall spare no effort in order to ensure more balanced conditions and a harmonious and steady development in the world energy market."

Puerto Rico Summit. A further meeting of the six heads of government of the countries represented at Rambouillet in November 1975 and also that of Canada took place in Puerto Rico on June 27–28, 1976.

This meeting adopted a declaration in which it was noted that economic recovery was "well under way". At the same time it was stated that what was needed was "to manage effectively a transition to expansion which will be sustainable, which will reduce the high level of unemployment which persists in many countries and will not jeopardize our common aim of avoiding a new wave of inflation". The meeting welcomed "the steady growth in East–West trade" and stated: "Our efforts for international economic co-operation must be considered as complementary to the policies of the developing countries themselves to achieve sustainable growth and rising standards of living." The declaration continued: "We attach the greatest importance to the dialogue between the developed and developing nations in the expectation that it will achieve concrete results in areas of mutual interest. And we reaffirm our countries' determination to participate in this process in the competent bodies, with a political will to succeed, looking towards negotiations in appropriate cases."

London Summit. A third economic summit conference was held in London on May 7–8, 1977, by the heads of government of the seven major non-communist states. Under a compromise agreement the President of the European Commission was enabled to participate in the deliberations on the second day of the conference (although the European Community had not as such been represented at the previous two conferences).

The conference resulted in the publication of a communiqué and an accompanying appendix in which it was stated that the heads of government had entered into seven main undertakings—to create more jobs; to maintain economic growth; to improve international financial resources; to expand opportunities for trade; to bring the Conference on International Economic Co-operation (CIEC) to a successful conclusion; and to initiate a special study on the supply of nuclear equipment to non-nuclear countries.

Bonn Summit. The fourth economic summit conference of the above seven powers was held in Bonn on July 16–17, 1978, with the European Community being represented "for discussion of matters within the Community's competence" by the President of the European Commission and the President-in-office of the Community's Council of Ministers.

The proceedings of the conference were described in a declaration issued afterwards, listing in *particular specific measures which each of the participating countries had taken or was taking to ensure non-inflationary economic growth; reaffirming the leaders' commitment to reduce their countries' dependence on imported oil and emphasizing the need to reverse "the slippage in the execution of nuclear power programmes"; reaffirming their determination to expand international trade; and stating their undertaking to provide an increased flow of financial assistance and other resources to the developing countries.

In a separate statement the participants in the conference stated their intention to intensify their joint efforts to combat international terrorism through action in cases of hijackings of aircraft.

Tokyo Summit. The fifth economic summit conference of the seven powers was held in Tokyo on June 28–29, 1979, with the European Community being represented by the Presidents of the European Council and of the European Commission.

The conference was mainly concerned with energy policy, and in their final declaration the participants deplored "the very serious economic and social consequences" of the latest oil price increases agreed upon by the Organization of Petroleum Exporting Countries (OPEC); expressed their readiness to discuss with oil-exporting countries "how to define supply and demand prospects on the world oil market"; and give details of agreement on a common strategy to reduce oil consumption and to hasten the development of alternative energy sources, stemming largely from proposals earlier agreed upon by the European Community.

Venice Summit. The sixth summit conference was held in Venice (Italy) on June 22–23, 1980, again with the participation of the seven major non-communist industrial powers and the European Community.

A declaration issued by the heads of government again stressed the adverse effects of further oil price rises, particularly on developing countries, and expressed the belief "that these consequences are increasingly coming to be appreciated by some of the oil-exporting countries". Reiterating that the reduction of inflation "is our immediate top priority", the declaration said that the existing link between economic growth

and oil consumption must be broken in the 1980s, to which end certain oil consumption and conservation targets were laid down and a commitment entered into to develop other energy sources such as coal and nuclear power. The declaration also dealt with relations with developing countries, international monetary problems and trade, it being stressed under this last heading that the participating countries would "resist pressures for protectionist actions, which can only be self-defeating and aggravate inflation".

On political aspects of the international situation, the Venice summit (i) condemned as "unacceptable" the Soviet military intervention in Afghanistan dating from late December 1979; (ii) expressed deep concern "at the plight of the ever-increasing number of refugees throughout the world"; (iii) emphasized that "hijacking remains a threat to international civil aviation" and looked forward to "continuing co-operation with all other governments to combat this threat; and (iv) condemned "the taking of hostages and the seizure of diplomatic and consular premises and personnel in contravention of the basic norms of international law and practice".

Ottawa Summit. The seventh summit conference was held in Ottawa (Canada) on July 19–21, 1981.

In a declaration on economic issues, adopted by the conference, the primary challenge was defined as the need to revitalize the economies of the industrial democracies. In this context it was stated: "The fight to bring down inflation and reduce unemployment must be our highest priority, and these linked problems must be tackled at the same time. . . . We must involve our peoples in a greater appreciation of the need for change; change in expectations about growth and earnings, change in management and labour relations and practices, change in the pattern of industry, change in the direction and scale of investment and change in energy use and supply. We need in most countries urgently to reduce public borrowing. . . . We see low and stable monetary growth as essential to reducing inflation. Interest rates have to play their part in achieving this and are likely to remain high where fears of inflation remain strong. . . . It is also highly desirable to minimize volatility of interest rates and exchange rates."

With regard to developing countries it was stated: "We are committed to maintaining substantial and, in many cases, growing levels of development assistance and will seek to increase public understanding of its importance. We will direct the major portion of our aid to poorer countries. . . . The Soviet Union and its partners, whose contributions are meagre, should make more development assistance available and take a greater share of exports of developing countries, while respecting their independence and non-alignment."

As in previous years the conference adopted a number of statements on international political questions, to which it added a statement on international terrorism in which the heads of government approved continued co-operation in the events of attacks on diplomatic or consular establishments or personnel and added that "any state which directly aids or abets the commission of terrorist acts . . . should face a prompt international response" and that there should be "more effective implementation of anti-terrorist conventions" and "wider adherence to them".

Versailles Summit. The eighth summit conference was held in Versailles (France) on June 4–6, 1982.

It dealt inter alia with the state of the Western economies and the continuing industrial recession, with the situation on the Israel–Lebanon border and with the Falklands conflict between Argentina and the United Kingdom.

In its main summit declaration the meeting confirmed lines of action to be taken by continuing the fight against inflation, which would help to bring down interest rates and bring about more stable exchange rates; by resisting protectionist pressures and trade-distorting practices; by co-operating with the developing countries and expanding trade opportunities, in particular with the newly industrialized countries; and by pursuing a prudent and diversified economic approach to the Soviet Union and Eastern Europe "consistent with our political and security interests".

The meeting also considered a French proposal for examining "the immense opportunities presented by the new technologies, particularly for creating new employment". In a statement on international monetary undertakings the meeting accepted joint responsibility to work for greater stability of the world monetary system and to give full support to the IMF and its efforts to foster stability.

Williamsburg Summit. The ninth economic summit conference was held in Williamsburg (Virginia) on May 28–30, 1983.

It issued a "Williamsburg declaration on economic recovery" and an annex on "strengthening economic co-operation for growth and stability", as well as a statement on arms control.

In the declaration the participants in the conference again committed themselves to the policies agreed at earlier meetings. With regard to the heavy weight of the recession which had fallen on the developing countries, they stated: "Restoring sound economic growth while keeping our markets open is crucial. . . . We reaffirm our commitments to provide agreed funding levels for the International Development Association." They further agreed on "the need to encourage both the development of advanced technology and the public acceptance of its role in promoting growth, employment and trade".

The statement on arms control contained a commitment to US and NATO policies (although France did not participate in NATO's military structure and Japan was not a member of NATO).

London Summit. The 10th summit conference was held in London on June 8–9, 1984, and issued an economic declaration and a statement by the chair expressing concern at the continuing Iran–Iraq war.

In the declaration the participants in the conference agreed to continue and where necessary to strengthen policies to reduce inflation and interest rates, to control monetary growth and where necessary to reduce budgetary deficits, to seek to reduce obstacles to the creation of new jobs, to support and strengthen work in the appropriate international organizations, to continue to implement the strategy on debts and develop it flexibly case by case, and to carry forward procedures previously agreed on promoting lower inflation and higher growth. The declaration also affirmed a commitment to "a rule of law which respects and protects without fear or favour the rights and liberties of every citizen" and "a system of democracy which ensures genuine choice in elections freely held, free expression of opinion and the capacity to respond to change in all its aspects". The declaration further contained proposals for combating international terrorism.

Bonn Summit. The 11th summit conference was held in Bonn on May 2–4, 1985. It concluded with a "declaration towards sustained growth and higher employment".

The declaration specified as important challenges "to strengthen the ability of our economies to respond to new developments; to increase job opportunities; to reduce social inequalities; to correct persistent economic imbalances; to halt protectionism; and to improve the stability of the world monetary system. It listed principles for responding to these challenges as follows: "Unremittingly to pursue, individually in our own countries and co-operatively together, policies conducive to sustained growth and higher employment"; to "continue to work with the developing countries in a spirit of true partnership"; to "urge an early and substantial reduction of barriers to trade"; "to make the functioning of the world monetary system more stable and more effective"; and

to ensure "effective environmental protection". The seven participating governments and also the Commission of the European Communities each stated their specific priorities among these principles.

Tokyo Summit. The 12th summit conference was held in Tokyo on May 4–6, 1986, and issued an economic declaration as well as statements on international terrorism and the Soviet nuclear accident at Chernobyl the previous month. It also decided to create a Group of Seven (G-7) made up of the Finance Ministers of the participating countries with a view to strengthening multilateral surveillance of the world economy.

The statement on international terrorism named Libya as a source of this phenomenon and identified specific measures to be taken, including (i) a refusal to export arms to states which sponsored or supported terrorism; (ii) strict limits on the size of overseas diplomatic and consular missions of states engaged in terrorism; (iii) denial of entry to suspected terrorists; and (iv) stricter immigration and visa requirements and procedures. These measures would be applied by the participating countries within the framework of international law and in their own jurisdictions to any state involved in sponsoring or supporting international terrorism.

Conference on International Economic Co-operation (CIEC)

In October 1974 President Giscard d'Estaing of France proposed, in the context of the transformed international economic situation created by the massive rise in world oil prices from late 1973, that a tripartite conference of industrialized, oil-producing and other development countries should be held to work out an agreement on oil prices and international inflation. The developing countries subsequently pressed for a broadening of the conference's agenda to encompass other raw materials, development and international financial questions, with the result that a first preparatory meeting held in Paris in April 1975 ended in failure. However, after the industrialized countries had made progress within the framework of the International Energy Agency [see page 116] towards co-ordinating their energy supply policies, agreement was reached in mid-1975 to expand the scope of the Paris conference as requested by the developing countries. Accordingly, a second preparatory meeting held in Paris in October 1975 reached broad agreement on the agenda and purposes of a fullscale ministerial conference.

First CIEC Conference. A ministerial level Conference on International Economic Co-operation (CIEC)—also referred to as the "North-South dialogue"—duly took place in Paris on Dec. 16–19, 1975, under the co-chairmanship of Canada and Venezuela; 19 of the 27 seats were occupied by oil-exporting and other developing countries and the remaining eight by industrialized nations (including the European Economic Community as a single participant). The principal outcome of the conference was an agreement to establish four expert-level commissions—on energy, raw materials, development and financial questions—which were instructed to draw up concrete proposals for a further ministerial conference.

The 19 oil-producing and other developing countries participating in CIEC were: Algeria, Argentina, Brazil, Cameroon, Egypt, India, Indonesia, Iran, Iraq, Jamaica, Mexico, Nigeria, Pakistan, Peru, Saudi Arabia, Venezuela, Yugoslavia, Zaïre and Zambia.

The eight industrialized participants were: Australia, Canada, European Economic Community, Japan, Spain, Sweden, Switzerland and the United States.

Second CIEC Conference. A second and final CIEC ministerial session took place in Paris from May 30 to June 2, 1977, with the same participants as at the Paris session of December 1975.

This session reached agreement on (i) increased aid from the industrialized to the developing countries and (ii) the eventual establishment of a common fund to support commodity prices, but not on other items of its agenda, notably future formal consultations on energy questions and on the rescheduling of developing countries' debts.

On aid to developing countries it was agreed, inter alia, that provision should be made "by developed countries of $1,000 million in a special action programme for individual low-income countries facing general problems of transfer of resources", and that assistance should be given to "infrastructure development in developing countries with particular reference to Africa". The establishment of "a common (commodity) fund with purposes, objectives and other constituent elements" was to be further negotiated in the UN Conference on Trade and Development (UNCTAD) [see below].

Later Developments. Although the CIEC initiative itself ended with the mid-1977 conference in Paris, the state of the "North-South dialogue" was further discussed at an informal meeting held in Jamaica on Dec. 28–29, 1978, by the heads of government of Australia, Canada, the Federal Republic of Germany and Norway on the one hand and of Jamaica, Nigeria and Venezuela on the other.

The participants agreed on the need of "speedy conclusion of negotiations on the common fund" and on the desirability of inviting the Soviet Union, China and other communist countries to participate in the common fund and other aspects of the North-South dialogue. Other points of agreement included the recognition that measures to curb population growth and to modernize agriculture in developing countries were important aspects of future progress towards a new international economic order.

Subsequently the focus of the North-South dialogue was provided by the recommendations of the Brandt Commission published in February 1980 [see below].

Independent Commission on International Development Issues (ICIDI)

As proposed in January 1977 by the then President of the World Bank (Mr Robert McNamara) as a measure to "enable the international community to break out of the current impasse" in the North-South dialogue, an Independent Commission on International Development Issues (ICIDI) was set up in November 1977 by Herr Willy Brandt (former Chancellor of the Federal Republic of Germany) with the object of "identifying those ways of restructuring international economic relations which would command the widest possible support".

The Commission, under the chairmanship of Herr Brandt, comprised 17 other members drawn from both developed and developing countries, as well as an honorary treasurer, an executive secretary-general and a director of its secretariat, established in Geneva. The Commission held eight sessions in various parts of the world, and its report was published in February 1980.

Passages from the Commission's summary of recommendations are quoted below.

The Poorest Countries. "An action programme must be launched comprising emergency and longer-term measures, to assist the poverty belts of Africa and Asia and particularly the least developed countries. Measures would include large regional projects of water and soil management; the provision of health care and the eradication of such diseases as river-blindness, malaria, sleeping sickness and bilharzia; afforestation projects; solar energy development; mineral and petroleum exploration; and support for industrialization, transport and other infrastructural investment.

"Such a programme would require additional financial assistance of at least $4,000 million per year for the next two decades, at grant or special concessional terms, assured over long periods and available in flexibly usable forms. New machinery is required on a regional basis to co-ordinate funding and to prepare plans in co-operation with lending and borrowing countries. Greater technical assistance should be provided to assist such countries with the preparation of programmes and projects.

Hunger and Food. "There must be an end to mass hunger and malnutrition. The capacity of food-importing developing countries, particularly the low-income countries, to meet their food requirements should be expanded and their mounting food import bill reduced through their own efforts and through expanded financial flows for agricultural development. Special attention should be given to irrigation, agricultural research, storage and increased use of fertilizer and other inputs, and to fisheries development.

"Agrarian reform is of great importance in many countries both to increase agricultural productivity and to put higher incomes into the hands of the poor.

"International food security should be assured through the early establishment of an International Grains Arrangement, larger international emergency reserves, and the establishment of a food financing facility.

"Food aid should be increased and linked to employment promotion and agricultural programmes and projects without weakening incentives to food production.

"Liberalization of trade in food and other agricultural products within and between North and South would contribute to the stabilization of food supplies.

"Support for international agricultural research institutions should be expanded with greater emphasis given to regional co-operation.

Population: Growth, Movement and the Enrivonment. "In view of the vicious circle between poverty and high birth rates, the rapid population growth in developing countries gives added urgency to the need to fight hunger, disease, malnutrition and illiteracy.

"We also believe that development policies should include national population programmes aiming at a satisfactory balance between population and resources and making family planning freely available. International assistance and support of population programmes must be increased to meet the unmet needs for such aid.

"The many migrant workers in the world should be assured fair treatment, and the interests of their home countries and the countries of immigration must be better reconciled. Governments should seek bilateral and multilateral co-operation to harmonize their policies of emigration and immigration, to protect the rights of migrant workers, to make remittances more stable and to mitigate the hardships of unanticipated return migration.

"The rights of refugees to asylum and legal protection should be strengthened. We also believe that commitments to international co-operation in the resettlement of refugees in the future will be necessary to protect countries of first asylum from unfair burdens. . . .

"Ocean resources outside the 'exclusive economic zones' of 200 miles should be developed under international rules in the balanced interests of the whole world community.

Disarmament and Development. "The mutual distrust which stimulates the arms race between East and West calls for continuing the process of détente through agreements on confidence-building measures. All sides should be prepared for negotiations (including those on the regional level) to get the arms race under control at a time before new weapons systems have been established.

"The world needs a more comprehensive understanding of security which would be less restricted to the purely military aspects.

"Every effort must be made to secure international agreements preventing the proliferation of nuclear weapons.

"A globally respected peace-keeping mechanism should be built up, strengthening the role of the United Nations (UN). In securing the integrity of states such peace-keeping machinery might free resources for development through a sharing of military expenditures, a reduction in areas of conflict and of the arms race which they imply.

"Military expenditure and arms exports might be one element entering into a new principle for international taxation for development purposes. A tax on arms trade should be at a higher rate than that on other trade.

"Increased efforts should be made to reach agreements on the disclosure of arms exports and exports of arms-producing facilities. The international community should become more seriously concerned about the consequences of arms transfers or of exports of arms-producing facilities and reach agreement to restrain such deliveries to areas of conflict or tension.

"More research is necessary on the means of converting arms production to civilian production which could make use of the highly skilled scientific and technical manpower currently employed in arms industries.

The Task of the South. "In countries where essential reforms have not yet taken place, redistribution of productive resources and incomes is necessary. A broader package of policy improvements would include expansion of social services to the poor, agrarian reform, increased development expenditures in rural areas, stimulation of small-scale enterprises and better tax administration. Such measures are important both for satisfying elementary needs and for increasing productivity, particularly in rural areas.

"The full potential of the informal sector to contribute to economic development requires the provision of increased resources in the form of easier access to credit, and expanded training and extension services.

"The strengthening of indigenous technological capacity often requires a more scientific bias in education, the encouragement of a domestic engineering industry, increased emphasis on intermediate technology and the sharing of experience.

"Improved economic management and the increased mobilization of domestic resources are essential to the promotion of development. In many countries there is scope for improvements in such fields as taxation policies, public administration and the operation of the pricing system.

"Wider participation in the development process should be encouraged; measures to achieve this could include decentralized governmental administrative systems and support for relevant voluntary organizations.

"Regional and sub-regional integration, or other forms of close co-operation, still offer a viable strategy for accelerated economic development and structural transformation among developing countries, especially the smaller ones. It supports industrialization and trade expansion and provides opportunities for multi-country ventures.

"Developing countries should take steps to expand preferential trade schemes among themselves. This could be encouraged by such measures as the untying of aid.

"Developing countries should give special attention to the establishment and extension of payments and credit arrangements among themselves to facilitate trade and to ease balance of payments problems.

"The emergence of capital-surplus developing countries provides special scope for the establishment of projects on the basis of tripartite arrangements involving developing countries alone or in partnership with industrialized countries. Such arrangements should be supported by both developed and developing countries. Tripartite projects (including, when appropriate, industrialized countries) should be encouraged by nations with complementary resources such as capital and technology.

"Developing countries should consider what forms of mutual assistance organization might help them to participate more effectively in negotiations and in the work of international organizations and to promote economic co-operation among themselves.

Commodity Trade and Development. "The commodity sector of developing countries should contribute more to economic development through the greater participation of these countries in the processing, marketing and distribution of their commodities. Action for the stabilization of commodity prices at remunerative levels should be undertaken as a matter of urgency.

"Measures to facilitate the participation of developing countries in processing and marketing should include the removal of tariff and other trade barriers against developing countries' processed products, the establishment of fair and equitable international transport rates, the abolition of restrictive business practices, and improved financial arrangements for facilitating processing and marketing.

"Adequate resources should be provided to enable the Common Fund [part of the Integrated Commodity Programme then under negotiation in the United Nations Conference on Trade and Development (UNCTAD)—see pages 126ff.] to encourage and finance effective international commodity agreements (ICAs) which would stabilize prices at remunerative levels; to finance national stocking outside ICAs; and to facilitate the carrying out of 'second window' activities such as storage, processing, marketing, productivity improvement and diversification.

"Greater efforts should be made to bring to a rapid and successful conclusion negotiations on individual commodity agreements wherever these are feasible.

"Compensatory financing facilities should be expanded and improved to provide more adequately for shortfalls in real commodity export earnings.

"The mutual interest of producing and consuming countries in the development of mineral resources requires the creation of new financial arrangements leading to more equitable and stable mineral development agreements, greater assurance of world mineral supplies and increased developing country participation in their resource development. A new financing facility, whose primary function will be to provide concessional finance for mineral exploration, should be established on the basis of a global responsibility for investment in mineral development.

Energy. "An orderly transition is required from high dependence on increasingly scarce non-renewable energy sources.

"Immediate steps towards an international strategy on energy should be taken as part of the emergency programme recommended in the final chapter of the report."

(These recommendations were that (i) all oil-exporting countries should assure levels of production and not reduce supplies arbitrarily or suddenly, with special arrangements being made to ensure supplies to developing countries; (ii) all major energy-consuming countries should agree on targets to hold down their consumption of oil and other energy; (iii) oil prices should be agreed in such a way as to avoid sudden major increases; and (iv) there should be major investment in oil and natural gas development in third-world countries and also in available alternative energy sources and in research and development in new types of energy use.)

"A global energy research centre should be created under UN auspices to co-ordinate information and projections and to support research on new energy resources.

Industrialization and World Trade. "The industrialization of developing countries, as a means of their overall development efforts, will provide increasing opportunities for world trade and need not conflict with long-term interests of developed countries. It should be facilitated as a matter of international policy.

"Protectionism threatens the future of the world economy and is inimical to the long-term interests of developing and developed countries alike. Protectionism by industrialized countries against the exports of developing countries should be rolled back; this should be facilitated by improved institutional machinery and new trading rules and principles.

"Adjustment to new patterns of world industrial production should be accepted as a necessary and desirable process. Industrialized countries should vigorously pursue positive and time-bound adjustment programmes developed through international consultation and subject to international surveillance.

"Safeguard measures must be internationally negotiated and should be taken only on the basis of established need. They should be non-discriminatory, of limited duration and subject to international surveillance.

"The generalized system of preferences (GSP—see page 178) should be eased in respect of its rules of origin, its exceptions and its limits. It should be extended beyond its present expiration and not be liable to unilateral termination.

"Financial support and technical assistance should be given to the poorer countries to facilitate their establishment of improved commercial infrastructure and their participation in international trade negotiations.

"Fair labour standards should be internationally agreed in order to prevent unfair competition and to facilitate trade liberalization.

"An international trade organization incorporating both the General Agreement on Tariffs and Trade (GATT) and UNCTAD is the objective towards which the international community should work. Meanwhile, there is need for improvement in existing arrangements including wider development of trade co-operation in such matters as the establishment and administration of rules, principles and codes covering restrictive business practices and technology transfer.

Transnational Corporations, Investment and the Sharing of Technology. "Effective national laws and international codes of conduct are needed to govern the sharing of technology, to control restrictive business practices, and to provide a framework for the activities of transnational corporations.

"The investment regime we propose would include (i) reciprocal obligations on the part of host and home countries covering foreign investment, transfer of technology, and repatriation of profits, royalties and dividends, (ii) legislation, co-ordinated in home and host countries, to regulate transitional corporation activities in matters such as ethical behaviour, disclosure of information, restrictive business practices and labour standards, (iii) intergovernmental co-operation in regard to tax policies and the monitoring of transfer pricing, and (iv)

harmonization of fiscal and other incentives among host developing countries.

"In addition to improved access to international development finance, the bargaining capacity of developing countries, particularly of the smaller and least developed countries, vis-à-vis the transnational corporations should be strengthened with the technical assistance now increasingly available from the UN and other agencies.

"Permanent sovereignty over natural resources is the right of all countries. It is necessary, however, that nationalization be accompanied by appropriate and effective compensation, under internationally comparable principles which should be embodied in national laws. Increasing use should also be made of international mechanisms for settling disputes.

"Greater international, regional and national efforts are needed to support the development of technology in developing countries and the transfer of appropriate technology to them at reasonable cost.

"These should be increased efforts in both rich and poor countries to develop appropriate technology in the light of changing constraints regarding energy and ecology; the flow of information about such technology should be improved. The international aid agencies should change those of their practices which restrict the recipients' freedom to choose technology, and should make more use of local capacities in preparing projects.

The World Monetary Order. "The reform of the international monetary system should be urgently undertaken by all interested parties building on the large measure of consensus which emerged in the Committee of Twenty [the Committee of the Board of Governors of the International Monetary Fund—IMF—on Reform of the International Monetary System and Related Issues, which held its final meeting in June 1974—see page 37], and taking account of current difficulties and dangers. Reform involves improvements in the exchange rate regime, the reserve system, the balance of payments adjustment process, and the overall management of the system which should permit the participation of the whole international community.

"Mechanisms should be agreed for creating and distributing an international currency to be used for clearing and settling outstanding balances between central banks. Such a currency would replace the use of national currencies as international reserves. It could take the form of an improved special drawing right (SDR), and could be facilitated by an appropriately designed 'substitution account'.

"New SDRs should be created to the extent called for by the need for non-inflationary increases in world liquidity. The distribution of such unconditional liquidity should favour the developing countries who presently bear high adjustment burdens. Such a distribution, often referred to as an SDR link, would also assist the adjustment process of the international monetary system.

"There should be agreement on an adjustment process which will not increase contractionist pressures in the world economy. The adjustment process of developing countries should be placed in the context of maintaining long-term economic and social development. The IMF should avoid inappropriate or excessive regulation of their economies, and should not impose highly deflationary measures as standard adjustment policy. It should also improve and greatly extend the scope of its compensatory financing facility, for example by relaxing quota limits, measuring shortfalls in real terms and making repayment terms more flexible. Surplus countries should accept greater responsibility for payments adjustments, and IMF measures to encourage this should be considered.

"Increased stability of international exchange rates, particularly among key currencies, should be sought through domestic discipline and co-ordination of appropriate national policies.

"The participation of developing countries in the staffing, management and decision-making of the IMF should be enlarged.

"In furthering the demonetization of gold, the bulk of the IMF gold stock should, after the competition of the present sales arrangements, be used as collateral against which the IMF can borrow from the market for onward lending particularly to middle-income developing countries. Staggered sales should also be undertaken and accruing profits of such sales should be used as interest subsidy on loans to low-income developing countries.

A New Approach to Development Finance. "There must be a substantial increase in the transfer of resources to developing countries in order to finance (i) projects and programmes to alleviate poverty and to expand food production, especially in the least developed countries, (ii) exploration and development of energy and mineral resources, and (iii) stabilization of the prices and earnings of commodity exports and expanded domestic processing of commodities.

"The flow of official development finance should be enlarged by (i) an international system of universal revenue mobilization, based on a sliding scale related to national income, in which East European and developing countries (except the poorest countries) would participate, (ii) the adoption of timetables to increase official development assistance (ODA) from industrialized countries to the level of 0.7 per cent of gross national product (GNP) by 1985, and to 1 per cent before the end of the century, and (iii) introduction of automatic revenue transfers through international levies on some of the following: international trade, arms production or exports; international travel; the global commons, especially seabed minerals.

"Lending through international financial institutions should be improved through (i) effective utilization of the increased borrowing capacity of the World Bank resulting from the recent decision to double its capital to $80,000 million [see page 35], (ii) doubling the borrowing-to-capital ratio of the World Bank from its present gearing of 1:1 to 2:1, and similar action by regional development banks, (iii) abstaining from the imposition of political conditions on the operations of multilateral financial institutions, (iv) channelling an increasing share of development finance through regional institutions, (v) a substantial increase in programme lending, (vi) the use of IMF gold reserves either for further sales, whose profits would subsidize interest on development lending, or as collateral to borrow for on-lending to developing countries, and (vii) giving borrowing countries a greater role in decision-making and management.

International Organizations and Negotiations. "Policies, agreements and institutions in the field of international economic, financial and monetary co-operation should be guided by the principle of universality.

"The UN system, which faces ever-expanding tasks, needs to be strengthened and made more efficient. This calls for more co-ordination of budgets, programmes and personnel policies, to avoid duplication of tasks and wasteful overlapping.

"The performance of the various multilateral organizations in the field of international development should be regularly monitored by a high-level advisory body.

"There needs to be a review of the present system of negotiations to see whether more flexible, expeditious and result-oriented procedures can be introduced without detracting from co-operation within established groups.

"Increased attention should be paid to educating public opinion and the younger generation about the importance of international co-operation.

"The occasional use of limited summit meetings should be considered to advance the cause of consensus and change.

"Resource transfer should be made more predictable by long-term commitments to provide ODA, increasing use of automatically mobilized revenues, and the lengthening of the International Development Association (IDA) replenishment period.

"Consideration should be given to the creation of a new international financial institution—a World Development Fund—with universal membership, and in which decision-making is more evenly shared between lenders and borrowers, to supplement existing institutions and diversify lending policies and practices. The World Development Fund would seek to satisfy the unmet needs in the financing structure, in particular that of programme lending. Ultimately, it could serve as a channel for such resources as may be raised on a universal and automatic basis.

"There is need for major additional multilateral finance to support mineral and energy exploration and development in developing countries. Some of this will come from existing institutions, but we believe there is a case for a new facility for this purpose.

"The flow of lending from commercial banks and other private financial bodies to developing countries must be strengthened. Middle-income countries need special measures to lengthen the maturity of their debt structures and poorer developing countries should be enabled to borrow more easily in the market. The World Bank and other international financial institutions should assist this process by co-financing, by the provision of guarantees, and by using concessional funds to improve lending terms and reduce interest rates.

"Measures should be adopted to facilitate the placing of bonds by developing countries in international markets. These should include the removal of restrictions and the provision of guarantees and adequate arrangements for the assessment of risks.

On Feb. 11, 1983, the Commission published a memorandum entitled "Common Crisis—North-South: Co-operation for World Recovery", which called for immediate action on a series of financial measures.

These included a reform of the IMF, with at least a doubling of its quotas; an increase in programme lending by the World Bank and the International Development Association (IDA); a doubling of aid to the poorest countries by 1985 and full implementation of the agreement to waive official debts of the least developed countries; expansion of bridge-finance operations by the Bank for International Settlements (BIS); and, by these and other means, the creation of "a framework of confidence in which private bank lending to developing countries would be able to expand".

Emergency measures were also proposed (i) for improving the world trading environment, involving closer co-operation between GATT, UNCTAD and other international bodies, and (ii) for increasing food production and security, including increased food aid, with an increase in the target for minimum quantities of food aid to 10,000,000 tonnes. In addition the Commission called for the creation of a new energy agency to increase energy production in developing countries.

The official disbandment of the Brandt Commission was reported on Feb. 10, 1983.

UN Conference on New and Renewable Sources of Energy

A first UN Conference on New and Renewable Sources of Energy was held in Nairobi (Kenya) on Aug. 10–21, 1981, and attended by delegates from over 120 countries.

The conference adopted a "programme of action" calling for a peaceful, orderly transition from the existing hydrocarbon-based international economy to one based increasingly on new and renewable sources and recommending that the launching of the programme should be entrusted to an intergovernmental interim committee presided over by the Director-General for Development and International Economic Co-operation at the United Nations, to present its report to the UN General Assembly.

The Cancún Summit Meeting

An International Meeting on Co-operation and Development held in Cancún (Mexico) on Oct. 21–23, 1981, was attended by leaders of 14 developing countries (Algeria, Bangladesh, Brazil, China, Côte d'Ivoire, Guyana, India, Mexico, Nigeria, the Philippines, Saudi Arabia, Tanzania, Venezuela and Yugoslavia) and eight industrialized nations (Austria, Canada, France, the Federal Republic of Germany, Japan, Sweden, the United Kingdom and the United States), and also by the Secretary-General of the United Nations.

A plan for the meeting had been presented by the Independent Commission on International Development Issues (ICIDI, i.e. the Brandt Commission) at a meeting in West Berlin on May 28–31, 1981. This plan called for agreement on steps towards a world food programme, a global energy strategy, increased loans and investment for the poorer countries and a broadening of the bases of international financial institutions.

At the end of the Cancún proceedings it was announced that consensus had been reached on launching global negotiations on restructuring the world economy "on a basis to be mutually agreed and in circumstances offering the prospect of meaningful progress". While 19 of the leaders favoured placing ultimate authority over such negotiations in the United Nations, those of the Federal Republic of Germany, the United Kingdom and the United States maintained that the negotiations should take place in the relevant international agencies.

New Delhi Meeting of Developing Countries

A meeting held (at the invitation of India) in New Delhi on Feb. 22–24, 1982, was attended by representatives of 44 developing countries and discussed the approach to be pursued within the "Group of 77" (of 120 developing countries) in the proposed "North-South" negotiations on international economic co-operation for development.

Although differences emerged over the strategy for bringing about such negotiations, the conference concluded with the unanimous acceptance of the importance of co-operation for collective self-reliance and with a renewed call for efforts to reach agreement on the launching of North-South global negotiations.

1984 Vienna Roundtable

A Vienna Roundtable on World Monetary, Financial and Human Resources was held on Sept. 9–12, 1984, under the joint sponsorship of a North-South Roundtable and a Development Study Programme of the UN Development Programme (UNDP). It was attended by 40 financial and development experts and adopted a Vienna Statement proposing inter alia a cut in real interest rates through a phased reduction in the US budgetary deficit and a relaxation of US monetary policy. It also expressed the view that there was a strong case for the cancellation of all official debts and suggested the setting-up of an IMF refinancing subsidiary.

Sessions of UN Conference on Trade and Development

The problems of international economic co-operation were dealt with at successive sessions of the UN Conference on Trade and Development (UNCTAD).

Second UNCTAD Session. At the second UNCTAD session, held in New Delhi from Feb. 1 to March 29, 1968, the demands of the developing countries for increased aid were supported by the Communist countries (with the Soviet Minister for Foreign Trade calling on the capitalist countries and the international lending institutions to provide more aid as "compensation for damage caused by colonial domination and neo-colonialist policies"). Representatives of the United States and Britain, on the other hand, stressed the difficulties of further increasing their countries' large aid commitments in times of balance-of-payments crises.

Among the numerous resolutions adopted by the conference was one setting a new target for transfers from developed to developing countries at 1 per cent of the gross national product (as against the previously agreed target of 1 per cent of the national income). Newly elected members of UNCTAD's Trade and Development Board comprised representatives of 22 African and Asian countries, 18 developed market-economy countries, nine Latin American nations, and six from socialist countries.

The UNCTAD Trade and Development Board adopted, on Oct. 31, 1971, a system of preferential tariffs for imports from developing countries by developed industrialized countries on the basis of a concept of "generalized tariff preferences" discussed at UNCTAD sessions since 1964 and finally agreed to by a special UNCTAD committee on preferences on Oct. 11, 1970. The agreement was first put into effect by the European Economic Community on July 1, 1971, and by most major industrialized countries on Jan. 1, 1972.

Third UNCTAD Session. At the third UNCTAD session, held in Santiago (Chile) between April 13 and May 21, 1972, some 40 resolutions were adopted, including:

(1) One urging "the widest possible participation of developed and developing countries" in "a more satisfactory system of monetary co-operation", with strong representation of the developing countries in a proposed "Committee of Twenty" to advise the International Monetary Fund (IMF) on a reform of the international monetary system;

(2) one asking for relief, both by donor-countries and by the IMF, for developing countries, which had suffered adverse effects from currency realignments;

(3) one containing recommendations for special treatment of 25 countries regarded as the "least developed" of the "Third World", i.e. mainly those with a per capita gross domestic product of $100 or less; and

(4) others containing suggestions on improvements to existing aid systems and on setting up a special UNCTAD body to investigate the effects of debt-service payments on economic growth in developing countries.

Fourth UNCTAD Session. At the fourth UNCTAD session, held in Nairobi on May 5–31, 1976, a report drawn up by the organization's secretariat described the situation of the developing countries as follows:

In the 20 years ending in 1972 the average per capita income of developing countries had risen from $125 to $300, while that of developed market-economy countries had grown from $2,000 to $4,000; the latter countries, with 20 per cent of the world's population, enjoyed about two-thirds of the world's income, whereas the poorest countries with 30 per cent of the world's population had only 3 per cent of world income.

The real value of official development assistance from the developed market-economy countries—in terms of purchasing power—had declined by about 3 per cent over the past 10 years. The indebtedness of developing countries had risen from $9,000 million at the end of 1956 to $19,000 million (for the non-oil-exporting developing countries) at the end of 1973, and their overall payments deficit had increased from $12,000 million in 1973 to $45,000 million in 1975.

Among resolutions adopted by the session was one on "a programme of global action to improve market structures in international trade in commodities of interest to developing countries".

This "integrated programme" was to achieve "stable conditions in commodity trade" at levels which would "(a) be remunerative and just to producers and equitable to consumers; (b) take account of world inflation and changes in the world economic and monetary situations; and (c) promote equilibrium between supply and demand within expanding commodity trade". The programme was also to improve and sustain real income of developing countries through increased export earnings, improved market access, diversified production and expanded processing of primary products in developing countries, and it would seek to improve the competitiveness of natural products competing with synthetics and substitutes, and to increase developing countries' earnings from marketing, distribution and transport of their products. The programme was to cover "bananas, bauxite, cocoa, coffee, copper, cotton and cotton yarns, hard fibres and products, iron, jute and products, manganese, meat, phosphates, rubber, sugar, tea, tropical timber, tin and vegetable oils (including olive oil and oilseeds)—as proposed by the 'Group of 77' [see page 470]—it being understood that other products could be included".

The programme also provided for steps to be taken towards the negotiation of the common fund to support market prices of raw materials [see below].

With reference to co-operation among developing countries, the conference declared the commitment of "both the developed market-economy countries and the socialist countries of Eastern Europe" to "abstain from adopting any kind of measure which could adversely affect the decisions of the developing countries in favour of the strengthening of their economic co-operation and the diversification of their production structures". Socialist countries of Eastern Europe were asked to provide "technical assistance for setting up state export and import enterprises and to promote links . . . between the transferable rouble system of the International Bank for Co-operation (set up by the Council for Mutual Economic Assistance, CMEA) and regional payments arrangements of developing countries", and also "effectively and substantially to increase economic and technical assistance to developing countries" and to ensure that the flow of mutual trade should not necessarily and always be conducted on the basis of equivalent volumes of exports and imports.

In a resolution adopted by 84 votes to none with 16 abstentions, it was recommended that action should be taken to achieve "a reorientation in the activities of transnational

corporations towards more complete manufacture in developing countries" and towards further processing of raw materials, and that there should be increased participation by national enterprises of developing countries in the activities of transnational corporations, with rules to be developed to control practices of transnational corporations likely to have adverse effects on developing countries' trade in manufactures.

With regard to the target of 0.7 per cent of gross national product (GNP) to be devoted to official development assistance by developed countries, the session recommended that, in order to reach this target, the aid budgets should be increased annually by a fixed percentage (in real terms) and that 1 per cent of the annual growth in the GNP of the developed countries should be earmarked for aid.

The session also launched an action programme for "least developed countries" (as defined by the UN General Assembly), as well as special measures to aid landlocked and island developing countries, which would include: (i) "greatly expanded assistance" in 1979–81 and (ii) a concerted strategy embracing structural change, social needs, transformational investment and emergency support in the forthcoming decade.

The world's "least developed countries" (LDC, i.e. those with an average GDP of less than $350 per annum per head of the population) comprised, by mid-1986, the following 37 countries: Afghanistan, Bangladesh, Benin, Bhutan, Botswana, Burkina Faso (formerly Upper Volta), Burundi, Cape Verde, the Central African Republic, Chad, the Comoros, Djibouti, Equatorial Guinea, Ethiopia, The Gambia, Guinea, Guinea-Bissau, Haiti, Laos, Lesotho, Malawi, Maldives, Mali, Nepal, Niger, Rwanda, São Tomé and Príncipe, Sierra Leone, Somalia, the Sudan, Tanzania, Togo, Uganda, Vanuatu, Western Samoa, the People's Democratic Republic of Yemen (South Yemen) and the Yemen Arab Republic (North Yemen).

The following 45 countries were in mid-1986 listed as the "most seriously affected" (MSA) by increases in prices of essential imports: Afghanistan, Bangladesh, Benin, Burkina Faso, Burma, Burundi, Cambodia, Cameroon, the Cape Verde Islands, the Central African Republic, Chad, Côte d'Ivoire, Egypt, El Salvador, Ethiopia, The Gambia, Ghana, Guatemala, Guinea, Guinea-Bissau, Guyana, Haiti, Honduras, India, Kenya, Laos, Lesotho, Madagascar, Mali, Mauritania, Mozambique, Nepal, Niger, Pakistan, Rwanda, Senegal, Sierra Leone, Somalia, Sri Lanka, the Sudan, Tanzania, Uganda, Western Samoa, North Yemen and South Yemen.

Fifth UNCTAD Session. The fifth UNCTAD session was held in Manila from May 7 to June 3, 1979.

A UN negotiating conference on the proposed common fund had in March 1979 agreed that the fund should have an initial capital of $750,000,000, of which $400,000,000 would be for the "first window" ($150,000,000 contributed in cash by governments, a further $150,000,000 available in case of need, and $100,000,000 in callable capital for use by fund managers as security for raising loans on the open market).

Each commodity agreement linked to the fund would raise one-third of its own requirements for buffer stock operations and would be able to draw a further two-thirds in credits from the fund. A minimum contribution to the fund of $1,000,000 per member country was agreed. Of the $150,000,000 thus raised, $80,000,000 would go to the "first window", with the balance contributed by country groups in a fixed ratio (68 per cent coming from the industrialized countries). The "second window" of $350,000,000 would be funded, in addition to the $70,000,000 from the minimum contributions, by voluntary contributions.

The negotiating conference had also agreed on a voting system, which inter alia provided that the "Group of 77" developing countries would hold 47 per cent of the votes, the industrialized countries 42 per cent, the East European socialist countries 8 per cent and China 3 per cent.

The UNCTAD session itself called for intensified efforts to draft articles of agreement for the common fund and urged governments to announce contributions to the "second window" (with the result that by the end of the session 13 countries had specifically pledged voluntary contributions totalling some $87,000,000).

The session also proposed the establishment of a framework for studies and consultations on expanding the integrated commodity programme agreed upon in Nairobi in 1976 [see above] to cover not only price regulation but also processing, marketing and distribution.

Sixth UNCTAD Session. The sixth UNCTAD session was held in Belgrade (Yugoslavia) from June 6 to July 3, 1983.

During this session the group of developed market-economy countries rejected a demand by the "Group of 77" developing countries for the conversion into straight grants of all bilateral loans made to least developed countries under development aid schemes and not yet repaid. The session was also in disagreement over (i) an Immediate Action Programme (issued by the UNCTAD secretariat on Jan. 25, 1983) designed to raise the commodity export earnings of developing countries over a three-year period by US$20,000 million, (ii) the abolition of protectionist barriers in industrialized countries and (iii) the relief of foreign debt problems for developing countries through the postponement of debt repayments.

The session ended with a statement on the world economic situation in which it stated inter alia that "problems of the magnitude and complexity that the world faces today call for a global approach in which all countries must play their part". It continued: "The reactivation of the growth process in the developing countries will not come about merely as the trickle-down effect of growth in developed countries. What is needed is an integrated set of policies, encompassing short-term measures in areas of critical importance to developing countries and long-term changes relevant to the attainment of a new international economic order."

Code of Conduct for Liner Conferences. Among various codes and conventions adopted by UNCTAD in the field of shipping, a *Convention on a Code of Conduct for Liner Conferences*, adopted in April 1974, finally entered into force on Oct. 6, 1983, but it has not been ratified or acceded to by a number of developed market-economy countries, notably Japan and some members of the European Community.

UNCTAD Common Fund. Articles of agreement for the proposed common fund for commodity stabilization were adopted at a negotiating conference in Geneva on June 27, 1980, and were opened for signature and ratification on Sept. 1, 1980. They would, however, not come into force until ratified by at least 90 states contributing at least two-thirds of the total of $470,000,000 to be directly contributed to the fund, a further condition for the articles' entry into force, relating to the minimum voluntary contribution to the fund's "second window" having already been met. By April 24, 1984, the articles had been ratified by only 72 states and were therefore not yet in force.

Other Bodies

Central Office for International Carriage by Rail

Address. Thunplatz, Berne, Switzerland.
Officer. Peter Trachsel (dir.-gen.).
Founded. 1893.
Membership. 33 states.

Customs Co-operation Council (CCO)

Address. 26–38 rue de l'Industrie, 1040 Brussels, Belgium.
Officers. J. Uitto (ch.); G. R. Dickerson (sec. gen.)
Founded. Nov. 4, 1952.
Membership. 96 countries, including Algeria, Argentina, Australia, Austria, Bahamas, Belgium, Bulgaria, Burkina Faso, Burundi, Cameroon, Canada, Chile, Congo, Côte d'Ivoire, Cyprus, Czechoslovakia, Denmark, Egypt, Ethiopia, Finland, France, Gabon, the Federal Republic of Germany, Ghana, Greece, Guyana, Haiti, Hungary, Iceland, India, Indonesia, Iran, Ireland, Israel, Italy, Jamaica, Japan, Jordan, Kenya, the Republic of Korea, Lebanon, Liberia, Luxembourg, Madagascar, Malawi, Malaysia, Malta, Mauritius, Morocco, Netherlands, New Zealand, Nigeria, Norway, Pakistan, Paraguay, Peru, Poland, Portugal, Romania, Rwanda, Saudi Arabia, Senegal, Sierra Leone, Singapore, South Africa, Spain, Sri Lanka, Sudan, Sweden, Switzerland, Syria, Tanzania, Thailand, Trinidad and Tobago, Tunisia, Turkey, Uganda, the United Kingdom, the United States, Yugoslavia and Zaïre.
History. The CCO was established under a convention concluded on Dec. 15, 1950, by 13 governments which also signed conventions on customs nomenclature and customs valuation.
Objects. To create harmony and uniformity in customs systems, to circulate information on customs regulations and procedures, and to supervise and take conciliatory action in regard to the uniform application of customs conventions prepared by it.

Food Aid Committee

Address. 28 Haymarket, London SW1Y 4SS, UK.
Founded. 1967.

Activities. This committee administers a Food Aid Convention which was concluded in London on March 6, 1980, and entered into force on July 1, 1980. This convention superseded an earlier Food Aid Convention concluded in 1971 as part of an International Wheat Agreement. By a protocol of 1983 the 1980 convention was extended until June 30, 1986.

The parties to this protocol are Argentina, Austria, Belgium, Canada, Denmark, Finland, France, the Federal Republic of Germany, Ireland, Italy, Japan, Luxembourg, the Netherlands, Norway, Spain, Sweden and the United Kingdom. The protocol has also been provisionally accepted by Australia, the EEC, Greece, Switzerland and the United States. The parties to the protocol have undertaken to contribute, at varying levels, towards a target of 10,000,000 tonnes of food aid annually for developing countries in the form of wheat and other grains suitable for human consumption.

OPEC Fund for International Development

Address. P.O. Box 995, 1011 Vienna, Austria.
Officer. Dr Y. Seyyid Abdulai (dir.-gen.).
Founded. Jan 28, 1976.
Membership. All member countries of the Organization of the Petroleum Exporting Countries (OPEC).
Objects. To strengthen financial co-operation between OPEC member countries and other developing countries, mainly by providing concessional loans to such countries and also to international development agencies.
Structure. The Fund is administered by a Ministerial Council and a Governing Committee comprising one member from each of the parties contributing to the Fund.

Activities. The Fund has inter alia contributed to the capitalization of the International Fund for Agricultural Development (IFAD), in which the OPEC countries (except Ecuador) constituted one of three groups with equal voting rights. By Dec. 31, 1983, the Fund's member countries had pledged basic contributions to the Fund of US$2,463,100,000, of which $1,621,200,000 were paid up. The Fund's accumulated loan commitments by that date totalled $1,812 million (47.7 per cent to African countries, 44.3 per cent to Asian countries and 11 per cent to countries in Latin America and the Caribbean).

Permanent International Association of Navigation Congresses (PIANC)

Address. 155, rue de la Loi, B–1040 Brussels, Belgium.
Officers. Ir. R. de Paepe (pres.); Henri Vandervelden (sec. gen.).
Founded. 1885.
Membership. 40 governments; 2,587 other members.
Objects. To promote design, construction, improvement and operation of inland and maritime waterways and coastal areas, and to disseminate related information.
Structure. The PIANC holds congresses every four years; it has a permanent international commission which meets annually and is composed of delegates appointed by member governments; and it has an executive committee and study commissions on force of waves, reception of large ships, sport and pleasure navigation, locks, ship lifts, drydocks, the environment, effects of dredging and disposal of dredged material.

7. Commodity and Raw Material Producers' Organizations and Agreements

This section covers the organizations of producers of commodities and raw materials which have been set up by a number of governments for various products as well as the international agreements which have been concluded in this field. The international agreements, normally drawn up in the context of the 1976 UNCTAD plan for an integrated commodity programme, have been signed by producer and consumer governments with the object of keeping prices stable within a negotiated band acceptable to both sides. This object was to be achieved by regulating supplies through intervention operations by a buffer stock or through export quotas. (In the case of tin both these mechanisms have been used.) These agreements have, however, been under rising pressures in the 1980s caused by increasing output and falling demand, and some of the principal agreements (e.g. those for sugar, rubber and wheat) have lost their powers to regulate supplies and prices.

Bananas

Union of Banana Exporting Countries
Unión de Paises Exportadores de Banano (UPEB)

Address. Apdo. 4273, Panamá 5, Panama.

Officer. Abelardo Carles (exec. dir.).

Founded. Sept. 19, 1974.

Membership. Colombia, Costa Rica, the Dominican Republic, Ecuador, Guatemala, Honduras, Nicaragua, Panama and Venezuela.

History. The UPEB was formed under an agreement concluded in April 1974.

Activities. On March 5, 1977, the member states of the UPEB signed a charter establishing a multinational banana corporation known as **Comercializador Multinacional de Banano** (Comunbana) for the promotion of banana sales, especially in Eastern Europe and the Arab countries.

Bauxite

International Bauxite Association (IBA)

Address. P.O.B. 551, Kingston 5, Jamaica.

Officer. Henry O. Bovell (sec.).

Founded. March 1974.

Membership. *Full members*: Australia, the Dominican Republic, Ghana, Guinea, Guyana, Indonesia, Jamaica, Sierra Leone, Suriname and Yugoslavia; *observers*: Greece, India and Trinidad and Tobago.

History. The IBA was set up by representatives of seven countries (Australia, Guinea, Guyana, Jamaica, Sierra Leone, Suriname and Yugoslavia) then producing about 60 per cent of the world's bauxite.

Objects. Under its charter drafted in 1974, the IBA's aim was to "promote the orderly and rational development of the bauxite industry" and "to secure fair and reasonable profits for member countries in the processing and marketing of bauxite, bearing in mind the interests of the consumer countries". The charter called for bauxite-producing countries to process their bauxite so as to become producers of aluminium and thus to increase their income, and it also stated that multinational companies should not be allowed to operate to the detriment of any one country and that member governments should "secure the maximum national ownership of their natural resources".

Activities. At its fourth annual meeting, held in Kingston in December 1977, the IBA's ministerial council decided to approve an agreed minimum price of $24 per tonne c.i.f. for base-grade bauxite ore exported to the North American market in 1978 (while no announcement was made on any other bauxite pricing).

Cocoa

Cocoa Producers' Alliance (COPAL)

Address. P.O.B. 1718, Lagos, Nigeria.

Officer. Ayotunde Olatunde Oshinibi (sec.gen.).

Founded. May 1962.

Membership. Brazil, Cameroon, Côte d'Ivoire, Ecuador, Gabon, Ghana, Mexico, Nigeria, São Tomé and Príncipe, Togo and Trinidad and Tobago.

Objects. To discuss cocoa producers' problems, to exchange technical and scientific information, and to ensure adequate supplies at remunerative prices.

Activities. In 1977 the COPAL member states agreed that the minimum and maximum prices laid down in the 1975 agreement of the International Cocoa Organization [see next entry] should be increased.

International Cocoa Organization (ICCO)

Address. 22 Berners St., London W1P 4DD, UK.

Officers. Orlando Carbonar (ch.); K. G. Erbynn (exec. dir.).

Founded. 1973.

History. The ICCO was created under an *International Cocoa Agreement* concluded in Geneva on Oct. 21, 1972. The main features of this agreement were an export quota system for producing countries, a fixed price range for cocoa and a buffer stock to support the agreed prices. Following signature by countries representing some 70 per cent of cocoa consumption, the agreement came into provisional effect on June 30 and was formally implemented on Oct. 31, 1973. (Its main provisions, however, remained inoperative as during 1973 the world market price of cocoa rose to twice the maximum envisaged in the agreement.)

A meeting held in Geneva from Sept. 22 to Oct. 20, 1975, negotiated a new agreement laying down new arrangements for a scale of maximum and minimum prices, an export quota system, a mechanism for adjusting quotas and the buffer stock. This agreement, however, was opposed by the United States (the largest cocoa importer), but it came into force provisionally on Oct. 1, 1976.

A new *International Cocoa Agreement*, concluded on Nov. 19, 1980, by delegates from 63 out of 67 countries represented at a UN cocoa conference in Geneva, set minimum and maximum prices (at $1.00 and $1.60 respectively per lb. payable to the producer) with buffer stock operations to stabilize prices within this range. The agreement, to become operative after ratification by countries accounting for 80 per cent of total cocoa exports, was not accepted by Côte d'Ivoire, Gabon, Togo and the United States, but came provisionally into force on Aug. 1, 1981. It was twice extended (in 1984 until Sept. 30, 1985, and subsequently until Sept. 30, 1986), together with the deadline for the deposit of instruments of ratification.

As at Jan. 1, 1986, there were 43 parties to the agreement, as follows: Argentina,* Belgium and Luxembourg, Brazil,* Bulgaria, Cameroon,* Colombia, Czechoslovakia, Denmark,* Dominica, Ecuador, the European Communities, Finland, France, the German Democratic Republic, the Federal Republic of Germany, Ghana,* Greece,* Grenada, Guatemala, Haiti,* Hungary, Ireland,* Italy, Jamaica, Japan, Mexico, the Netherlands, Nigeria,* Norway, Papua New Guinea, Peru, Portugal, São Tomé and Príncipe, Sierra Leone, the Soviet Union, Spain, Sweden, Switzerland,* Trinidad and Tobago, the United Kingdom,* Venezuela, Western Samoa and Yugoslavia (*provisional application).

The agreement was, however, not effective. By 1982 its buffer stock finances were depleted and buffer stock intervention was discontinued. There followed marked fluctuations in cocoa prices.

A new three-year agreement to replace the 1980 agreement was eventually reached on July 16, 1986. It was to come into force on Oct. 1, 1986 (after ratification by five cocoa-producing countries representing at least 80 per cent of world exports and by countries taking at least 65 per cent of total imports).

A price-adjusting mechanism under the agreement centred on a reference price of 103 cents per pound, with the buffer stock manager being obliged to buy cocoa if the price fell to 85 cents and to sell if it reached 121 cents (but being able to buy at 88 cents and sell at 118 cents at his own discretion). Prices were to be expressed in Special Drawing Rights (SDRs) of the IMF instead of US dollars, and the reference price was translated to SDR 1,935 a tonne with intervention levels at SDR 1,600 and SDR 2,2270. Moreover, producers would withhold cocoa from the market if the indicator price fell below the lower intervention level for five consecutive days and the buffer stock at the same time was at 80 per cent of its capacity or had only enough cash left to buy 30,000 tonnes more cocoa. This withholding scheme was limited to a maximum of 120,000 tonnes, with cocoa being withheld in tranches of 30,000 tonnes a time. (World trade in cocoa was said to amount to some 1,400,000 tonnes a year.)

The agreement was accepted by Côte d'Ivoire, which had not been a party to the 1980 agreement but which produced about one-third of the world's cocoa crop. The United States and Malaysia did not take part in the agreement, but the European Community and the Soviet Union did.

Coconuts

Asian and Pacific Coconut Community

Address. P.O.B. 343, Jakarta, Indonesia.

Officer. Godofredo P. Reyes, Jr. (dir.).

Founded. Oct. 16, 1968.

Membership. India, Indonesia, Malaysia, Papua New Guinea, the Philippines, the Solomon Islands, Sri Lanka, Thailand, the (US) Trust Territory of the Pacific Islands, Western Samoa and Vanuatu.

History. The community was established as the Asian Coconut Community under the sponsorship of the then (UN) Economic Commission for Asia and the Far East (ECAFE), which in 1974 became the Economic and Social Commission for Asia and the Pacific (ESCAP). The community assumed its present name in December 1975.

Objects. To promote and co-ordinate the coconut industry's activities by improving production, processing, marketing and research.

Coffee

International Coffee Organization (ICO)

Address. 22 Berners St., London W1P 4DD, UK.

Officers. H. Buchmann (ch. of Council); Alexander F. Beltrão (exec. dir.).

Founded. January 1958.

Activities. The ICO has concluded a number of *International Coffee Agreements* (annually between 1958 and 1962, and for five-year periods from Dec. 27, 1963, and from Dec. 30, 1968). The ICO fixed export quotas, agreed on an "indicator price range" and took other measures to bring supply and demand more into line with one another. The 1968 agreement was approved by 41 coffee-exporting and 20 coffee-importing countries, but it lapsed on Sept. 30, 1973.

It was eventually replaced by a new agreement of Dec. 3, 1975, which became fully effective on Aug. 1, 1977, and which was to remain in force for six years (although it was subject to renegotiation after three years). It provided for the continuation of the **International Coffee Council** first set up under the 1962 agreement, but its export quotas were unrealistic in view of the world coffee shortage which set in during the early 1970s. This agreement was adhered to by 44 exporting countries or territories (representing over 99 per cent of world coffee exports) and 24 importing countries (accounting for about 88 per cent of world imports).

The agreement was revised on Oct. 3, 1980, to the effect that prices should range between 115 and 155 cents per lb (with revision after one year) and that an initial global export quota of 57,370,000 bags would be relaxed in a series of steps if prices moved upwards past a trigger price of 135 cents per lb (and suspended if prices remained above the 155 cent maximum) and be gradually reduced if prices moved downwards from 135 cents per lb.

This agreement was in September 1981 extended until Sept. 30, 1983.

A new agreement was concluded in London on Sept. 16, 1982. It came provisionally into effect on Oct. 1, 1983, for six years until Sept. 30, 1989 (unless extended or terminated). It definitively entered into force on Sept. 11, 1985.

As at Jan. 1, 1986, there were 76 parties to the agreement as follows: *Exporting countries—* Angola, Benin, Bolivia, Brazil, Burundi, Cameroon, the Central African Republic, Colombia, the Congo, Costa Rica, Côte d'Ivoire, Cuba, the Dominican Republic, Ecuador, El Salvador, Equatorial Guinea, Ethiopia, Gabon, Ghana, Guatemala, Guinea, Haiti, Honduras, India, Indonesia, Jamaica, Kenya, Liberia, Madagascar, Malawi, Mexico, Nicaragua, Nigeria, Panama, Papua New Guinea, Paraguay, Peru, the Philippines, Rwanda, Sierra Leone, Sri Lanka, Tanzania, Thailand, Togo, Trinidad and Tobago, Uganda, Venezuela, Zaïre and Zambia; *importing countries*—Australia, Austria, Belgium, Canada, Cyprus, Denmark, the European Communities, Fiji, Finland, France, the Federal Republic of Germany, Greece, Ireland, Italy, Japan, Luxembourg, the Netherlands, New Zealand, Norway, Portugal, Singapore, Spain, Sweden, Switzerland, the United Kingdom, the United States, Yugoslavia and Zambia.

Under the agreement the ICO was empowered to fix export quotas, to be triggered at an average daily price of 134.55 cents per lb. In February 1985 quotas were suspended after a sharp increase in prices resulting from a drought in Brazil.

On Oct. 9, 1985, the ICO established price stabilization measures for the 1985–86 fiscal year (with the United States voting against them and Costa Rica, Honduras, India, Indonesia and Peru abstaining). The agreement fixed an initial global export quota of 58,000,000 bags (of 132 lb or 60 kg each) and an unchanged price range of between 120 and 140 cents per lb.

Associated Coffee Producers
Productores de Cafés Asociados (PANCAFE)

Address. c/o Jorge Canavati, Paseo de la Reforma, México 5, D.F., Mexico.

History. This organization replaced the Cafés Suaves Centrales set up in March 1975 by Costa Rica, El Salvador, Mexico and Venezuela and dissolved in 1978.

Inter-African Coffee Organization (IACO)

Address. B.P. V 210, Abidjan, Côte d'Ivoire.

Officers. Yona Kanyomozi (pres.); Arega Worku (sec. gen.).

Founded. 1960.

Membership. 24 coffee-producing countries in Africa, including Angola, Benin, Burundi, Cameroon, the Central African Republic, the Congo, Côte d'Ivoire, Ethiopia, Kenya, Liberia, Madagascar, Nigeria, Rwanda, Sierra Leone, Tanzania, Togo, Uganda and Zaïre (all of them members of the International Coffee Organization—see above).

Objects. To study common problems and to ensure the smooth disposal of production and the optimum level of selling prices.

African and Malagasy Coffee Organization (OAMCAF)

Membership. Benin, Cameroon, the Central African Republic, the Congo, Côte d'Ivoire, Gabon, Madagascar and Togo.

Pan-American Coffee Bureau

Membership. 12 South and Central American governments (which are also members of the International Coffee Organization—see above).

Objects. To study coffee problems of common interest to Latin American countries and to promote the consumption of coffee in the United States and Canada as well as international co-operation.

Copper

Intergovermental Council of Copper Exporting Countries
Conseil intergouvernemental des pays exportateurs du cuivre (CIPEC)

Address. 39 rue de la Bienfaisance, 75008 Paris, France.

Officer. Dongé Nigu (sec. gen.).
Founded. June 7, 1967.
Membership. Full members: Chile, Indonesia, Peru, Zaïre and Zambia; *associate members*: Australia, Papua New Guinea and Yugoslavia.
Objects. To co-ordinate research and information policies among its member countries.
Activities. To counter a fall in world copper prices CIPEC reduced its member states' copper exports by 10 per cent in November 1974, by another 5 per cent in February 1975 and by a further 5 per cent in April 1975. As these measures proved inadequate to sustain prices, a conference held in March 1976 by CIPEC member states and copper-consuming countries (under UNCTAD auspices) decided to establish a permanent international consultative body on copper, but no agreement has yet been reached on this issue. The position of the CIPEC member countries is weakened by the fact that the United States is not only the world's largest consumer of copper but also its bigger producer (followed by the Soviet Union).

Cotton

International Cotton Advisory Committee

Address. 1225 19th St. N.W., Suite 650, Washington, DC 20036, USA.
Officer. J. C. Santley (exec. dir.).
Founded. 1939.
Membership. 48 states.
Activities. Established as a cotton producers' association, the committee was in 1945 opened to all nations "interested in the production, export and import of cotton". It collects and disseminates statistics on developments in the world's cotton situation and suggests to its member states suitable measures for the joint maintenance and development of a sound cotton economy in the world.

International Institute for Cotton (IIC)

Address. 10 rue du Commerce, 1040 Brussels, Belgium.
Officers. Paul Bomani (pres.); Peter Pereira (exec. dir.); Harpal Luther (sec.).
Founded. Jan. 17, 1966.
Membership. Nine countries (Brazil, Côte d'Ivoire, India, Mexico, Nigeria, Tanzania, Uganda, the United States and Zimbabwe).
History. Argentina was a member from May 6, 1981, to Dec. 31, 1982; Greece from July 28, 1968, to Dec. 31, 1983; Iran from Nov. 8, 1976, to Dec. 31, 1979; Spain from March 31, 1975, to Dec. 31, 1982.
Activities. The institute conducts research in the utilization of and markets for cotton, promotes sales and constitutes a link between exporting countries and the principal importing countries. The IIC has a technical research centre in Manchester (UK) and an office in Washington (DC).

Groundnuts

African Groundnut Council
Conseil africain de l'arachide

Address. P.O.B. 3025, Lagos, Nigeria; 66 ave. de Cortenberg, 1040 Brussels, Belgium.
Officers. Abas Bah (ch.); Mour Mamadou Samb (exec. sec.).
Founded. June 1964.
Membership. The Gambia, Mali, Niger, Nigeria, Senegal and the Sudan.
Objects. To ensure remunerative prices for groundnuts and their by-products, and the promotion of groundnut consumption and also of solidarity among the member states.

Iron Ore

Association of Iron-Ore Exporting Countries (AIOEC)

Address. Le Château, 14 chemin Auguste Vilbert, 1218 Grand Saconnex, Geneva, Switzerland.
Officer. I. Arcaya (sec. gen.).
Founded. Oct. 12, 1975.
Membership. Nine countries.
History. The association was formed under an agreement signed at a meeting held in Geneva on April 2–3, 1975, by ministers from Algeria, Australia, Brazil, Chile, India, Mauritania, Peru, Sierra Leone, Sweden, Tunisia and Venezuela (while other countries represented at the meeting but not signatories to the agreement were Canada, Liberia and the Philippines). The agreement was, however, not ratified by Brazil, Peru, Sierra Leone, Sweden and Tunisia, which therefore did not become members of the AIOEC.
Objects. The association was to play merely a consultative role without powers for concerted governmental action by its member countries, and its aims were to ensure the orderly and healthy growth of the export trade in iron ore, to secure fair and remunerative returns from its exploration, processing and marketing, and to promote close co-operation among member countries.

Jute

International Jute Organization (IJO)

Address. P.O.B. 6073, Gulshan, Dhaka, Bangladesh.
Founded. January 1984.
Membership. Five exporting and 23 importing countries.
History. The IJO, with a Council as its executive organ, was established under an *International Agreement on Jute and Jute Products*, which was signed in Geneva on Oct. 1, 1982, and provisionally entered into force on Jan. 9, 1984. This agreement contained no provision for a buffer stock. While it was supported by exporting countries accounting for 99 per cent of world exports, it was adhered to by consuming countries

representing only 41 per cent of world net imports; moreover, the absence of the Soviet Union, most East European countries and almost all developing nations imposed limitations on the scope of IJO action.

Objects. To improve structural conditions in the jute market, the competitiveness of jute and jute products and the quantity and quality of jute products.

Parties to the agreement. 31 (Australia, Austria, Bangladesh, Belgium, Canada, China, Denmark, Egypt, the European Communities, Finland, France, the Federal Republic of Germany, Greece, India, Indonesia, Italy, Japan, Luxembourg, Nepal, the Netherlands, Norway, Pakistan, Poland, Spain, Sweden, Switzerland, Thailand, Turkey, the United Kingdom, the United States and Yugoslavia).

Lead and Zinc

International Lead and Zinc Study Group

Address. Metro House, 58 St. James's St., London SW1A 1LD, UK.

Officer. B. F. Meere (ch.).

Founded. 1959.

Membership. The governments of 33 countries (including Algeria, Australia, Austria, Belgium, Bulgaria, Canada, Czechoslovakia, Denmark, Finland, France, the Federal Republic of Germany, Hungary, India, Ireland, Italy, Japan, Mexico, Morocco, the Netherlands, Norway, Peru, Poland, South Africa, the Soviet Union, Spain, Sweden, Tunisia, the United Kingdom, the United States, Yugoslavia and Zambia).

Activities. The group, which superseded an earlier Lead and Zinc Study Committee set up in 1958 and held its first meeting in Geneva in 1960, has a standing committee serving as a forum for consultation between producing and consuming countries (inter alia on world trade), as well as an economic and a statistical committee.

Olive Oil

International Olive Oil Council (IOOC)

Address. Juan Bravo 10–2°, 28006 Madrid, Spain.

Officer. Gabriele Luzi (dir.).

Founded. 1959.

History. The IOOC was created to administer an *International Olive Oil Agreement* of 1958 with the object of promoting international co-operation in dealing with olive oil problems; preventing unfair competition in the world's olive oil trade; taking and applying measures to extend the production, consumption and sale of olive oil; and preventing disruption caused by fluctuations in supply. This agreement was amended in 1963, 1967, 1969 and 1973. It was succeeded by a new agreement which was concluded in Madrid on July 1, 1979, and definitively entered into force on Jan. 1, 1981. It was to run until Dec. 31,

1984, but was in fact extended until Dec. 31, 1986.

A new international agreement covering the period 1987–91 was adopted under UNCTAD auspices on July 1, 1986, taking account of the enlargement of the European Economic Community to include Portugal and Spain and also giving the IOOC greater capacity to carry out technical co-operation programmes pursuant to the agreement's main objectives. The new agreement referred to the need to "prevent excessive fluctuations in prices, which must be at levels that are remunerative and just to producers and equitable to consumers", but contained no economic provisions aimed at stabilizing prices or limiting production of olive oil.

Parties to the agreement. Algeria, European Economic Community, Egypt, Libya , Morocco, Tunisia, Turkey and Yugoslavia.

International Olive Oil Federation
Fédération internationale d'oléoculture

Address. Via del Governo Vecchio 3, 00186, Rome, Italy.

Founded. 1934.

Membership. Organizations and government departments in Algeria, Argentina, France, Greece, Israel, Italy, Lebanon, Libya, Morocco, Portugal, Spain, Syria and Tunisia.

Objects. To promote the interests of olive growers, improvements in growing and manufacturing, and the use of olive oil.

Pepper

International Pepper Community

Address. 9th Floor, Sarinah Bldg., 11 Jalan Thamrin, Jakarta, Indonesia.

Officer. Lakshmi Narain Salkani (dir.).

Founded. Sept. 11, 1972.

Membership. Brazil, India, Indonesia, Madagascar and Malaysia.

History. The community was formed under an agreement signed in Bangkok by India, Indonesia and Malaysia on April 16, 1971, and in force from March 29, 1972.

Objects. To co-ordinate action among pepper-producing countries in regard to standard, supplies and marketing of pepper.

Petroleum

Organization of the Petroleum Exporting Countries (OPEC)

Address. Obere Donaustrasse 93, 1020 Vienna, Austria.

Officer. (vacant).

Founded. Sept. 24, 1960.

Membership. Algeria, Ecuador, Gabon, Indonesia, Iran, Iraq, Kuwait, Libya, Nigeria,

Qatar, Saudi Arabia, the United Arab Emirates and Venezuela.

History. OPEC was set up as a result of a conference of representatives from Iraq, Iran, Kuwait, Saudi Arabia and Venezuela held in Baghdad on Sept. 10–14, 1960, with the above five countries as its initial members. Qatar became a member in January 1961, Indonesia and Libya joined it in June 1962, Abu Dhabi in November 1967, Algeria in July 1969, Ecuador in December 1973, Gabon (which had become an associate member in December 1973) in June 1975, and Venezuela in 1981. The membership of Abu Dhabi was transferred to the United Arab Emirates (UAE) in January 1974.

The member countries of OPEC include neither the world's two largest single oil producing countries (the Soviet Union and the United States) nor Mexico, Norway and the United Kingdom.

Object. To increase the share of petroleum revenue of its members.

Structure. OPEC's supreme authority is its Conference, which is responsible for formulating the organization's general policy. OPEC's management is directed by a Board of Governors consisting of one governor from each member country and meeting at least twice a year. OPEC also has an economic commission which is to assist the organization in promoting stability in international oil prices at an equitable level.

Activities. An agreement concluded in Tehran on Feb. 14, 1971, by Abu Dhabi, Iran, Kuwait and Saudi Arabia with 23 international oil companies provided for security of supply and stability in financial arrangements for the five-year period from 1971 to 1975.

Agreements subsequently concluded were (i) the Geneva agreement of Jan. 20, 1972, providing for an immediate rise of 8.49 per cent in the posted price of crude oil in the Persian Gulf and at Eastern Mediterranean terminals and for further adjustments until 1975, based on an index measuring significant changes in the exchange rate of the US dollar, and (ii) the Geneva agreement of June 2, 1973, when eight of OPEC's 11 member states raised posted prices of crude oil by an aggregate of 11.9 per cent and a new mechanism was provided to make monthly adjustments in prices in future.

Following a 10 per cent devaluation of the US dollar in February 1973, further negotiations between OPEC and oil companies broke down and on Oct. 17, 1973, the Gulf states unilaterally declared 70 per cent increases in posted prices (from $3.01 to $5.11 per barrel). At a further conference held in Tehran on Dec. 22–23, 1973, OPEC increased the posted price by almost 130 per cent (from $5.11 to $11.56 per barrel) from Jan. 1, 1974. At an extraordinary OPEC conference in Geneva in January 1974 prices were held at the current level, which was eventually maintained for the remainder of 1974.

At a meeting in Quito (Ecuador) in June 1974 royalties charged on oil companies were increased from 12.5 to 14.1 per cent by all OPEC member states except Saudi Arabia. Further royalty and tax increases were decided at a Vienna meeting in September 1974 (raising royalties on equity crude oil to 16.67 per cent and taxes to 65.65 per cent, again except in Saudi Arabia).

At a first summit conference, held by the heads of state of eight of OPEC's 13 member countries in Algiers on March 4–6, 1975, a "solemn declaration" was issued on OPEC's role in the world economic crisis.

In their declaration the heads of state attributed "the present world economic crisis" to "profound inequalities in the economic and social progress among countries" which had their "decisive causes" in "long-standing and persistent ills which have been allowed to accumulate over the years, such as the general tendency of the developed countries to consume excessively and to waste scarce resources", as well as "inappropriate and shortsighted policies". They therefore rejected any allegation that the price of petroleum was responsible for the existing instability of the world economy and claimed that oil was "the cheapest source of energy available". They reaffirmed the solidarity of OPEC and pointed out that the OPEC member countries had "contributed through multilateral and bilateral channels to the development efforts and balance of payments adjustments of other developing countries as well as industrialized nations". They emphasized that the developed countries "must contribute to the progress and development of the developing countries through concrete action".

At a ministerial meeting held in Vienna in September 1975 OPEC oil prices were raised by a further 10 per cent until June 1976. A meeting of OPEC member countries' Ministers of Finance in Vienna on Nov. 17–18, 1975, agreed to recommend to their governments the establishment of a new facility for providing additional financial support to developing countries. (According to an UNCTAD report of Nov. 25, 1975, the OPEC member countries' contribution to official development aid for the Third World had risen from 10 per cent in 1973 to almost 23 per cent in 1974.) In January 1976 the OPEC Finance Ministers signed an agreement establishing a joint "Special Fund" to "provide interest-free long-term loans to developing countries", with an initial one-year commitment of $800,000,000 to be made to the fund, of which one-half was to be used for agricultural development provided that developed countries also made substantial aid pledges for this purpose. The Special Fund came into operation in August 1976. An agreement signed in New York on Sept. 30, 1977, provided for disbursement of up to $20,000,000 from this fund for projects administered by the UN Development Programme. [See also page 129.]

On prices no unanimous decision was made at an OPEC ministerial conference held in Bali (Indonesia) in May 1976, but Saudi Arabia's prices remained unchanged. At a further such conference, held at Doha (Qatar) on Dec. 15–17, 1976, price increases amounting to about 10.3 per cent on Jan. 1, 1977, and a further 4.7 per cent on July 1, 1977, were made by 11 OPEC member states, but these proposals were not accepted by Saudi Arabia, with the result that the new prices in force from Jan. 1, 1977, were increased by varying percentages (ranging from 3 to 11.5 per cent). In *The Times* of Nov. 30, 1976, it was calculated that the "real" price of OPEC oil had risen by 385 per cent since 1972.

A more or less uniform price level was restored at an OPEC ministerial conference held at Saltsjøbaden (Sweden) in July 1977, when Saudi Arabia and the UAE agreed to raise their prices by 5 per cent and the other member states waived price increases which they had proposed earlier. A second 1977 conference, held in Caracas in December, failed to reach any agreement on prices. An informal ministerial meeting held at At Ta'if (Saudi Arabia) on May 6–7, 1978, concentrated on long-term policies and appointed a committee to study them. At a formal conference held in Geneva on June 17–19, 1978, it was generally accepted that market conditions precluded any rise in the basic "marker" price from the current level of $12.70 per barrel (in force for 11 countries since Jan. 1, 1977, and for Saudi Arabia and the UAE since July 1, 1977) and that, on Saudi Arabia's insistence, the pricing in US dollars should be retained (contrary to a proposal made at a conference in Gabon in June 1974 to quote prices in Special Drawing Rights—SDRs—of the International Monetary Fund).

However, at an OPEC conference held in Abu Dhabi on Dec. 16–17, 1978, it was decided, in view of the "high rate of inflation and dollar depreciation over the last two years", to increase the price of oil by 10 per cent on average over the year 1979 (by means of quarterly adjustments). This decision was changed at an extraordinary session of the OPEC Conference in Geneva on March 26–27, 1979, when the 1979 adjustments were brought forward to April 1 of that year and each OPEC member country was allowed to add to its price market premia deemed justifiable. The average official price for OPEC crude oil thereupon rose to $17.28 per barrel in May 1979, while the unofficial "spot" price reached up to $40.

Even higher minimum prices were agreed at OPEC meetings during 1980. A meeting in Algiers on June 9–10, 1980, decided, against the votes of Saudi Arabia and the United Arab Emirates, to set the theoretical base and ceiling prices at $32 and $37 per barrel respectively. At a conference held in Bali (Indonesia) on Dec. 15–16, 1980, it was decided to fix the official price of the marker crude oil at $32 per barrel, with a ceiling of $36 per barrel for deemed marker crude and a maximum price for OPEC crudes of $41 per barrel.

At a further meeting of the OPEC Conference in Geneva on May 25–26, 1981, it was decided, in view of a surplus of oil supplies in the first quarter of 1981, to maintain the deemed marker crude price at a ceiling of $36 per barrel with a maximum OPEC price of $41 per barrel until the end of the year, while the majority of member countries decided to cut production by a minimum of 10 per cent, effective June 1, 1981.

These decisions, however, failed to reverse the decline in world oil prices. A consultative meeting of the OPEC Conference in Geneva on Aug. 19–21, failed to reach agreement on further price reductions, and Saudi Arabia insisted that it would continue to use a $32 marker price and wanted firm guarantees by other member countries to accept a unified $34 marker price. Following

further price reductions by several OPEC member states, a meeting of oil ministers in Geneva on Oct. 29, 1981, set the official price of marker crude at $34 per barrel, effective not later than Nov. 1, 1981, this price to be abided by until the end of 1982.

During that year, however, the price fell below the $34 mark in some producer countries, and at an OPEC emergency meeting held in March 1982 it was decided (for the first time) to set an overall production ceiling, which in effect was 17,500,000 barrels per day (bpd), while Saudi Arabia announced a reduction in its own production to 7,000,000 bpd.

At an OPEC meeting held in December 1982 a new production ceiling of 18,500,000 bpd was agreed as an annual average for 1983, but no agreement was reached on any national production quotas.

Following a general decline in oil prices in early 1983, a compromise agreement was reached by OPEC member countries on March 14, 1983, reducing the official price of marker crude oil to $29 per barrel (with existing differentials among member countries to be generally maintained), and establishing an agreed production ceiling of 17,500,000 bpd to be observed until the end of 1983, while allowing quotas to each member country except Saudi Arabia. This agreement was reaffirmed at an OPEC Conference meeting held on July 18–19, 1983. By that time OPEC's total production had reached 17,000,000 bpd, but by September 1983 it rose to 18,000,000 bpd.

The official marker price of $29 per barrel of crude oil was reaffirmed at OPEC meetings in July, October and December 1984. However, between July and October of that year there was increasing pressure on that price, in particular by price cuts applied by major producers, both by countries outside OPEC (such as Norway and the United Kingdom) and by Nigeria (an OPEC member). In order to support the $29 price the October OPEC Conference meeting therefore decided to cut, as from Nov. 1, 1984, and on a temporary basis, the global production ceiling of OPEC from 17,500,000 to 16,000,000 bpd (or by 8.6 per cent in OPEC's daily production ceiling).

After the new ceiling had been substantially exceeded, 11 of the 13 member states (but not Algeria and Nigeria) approved, at the December OPEC Conference meeting, slight price reductions for specific crude oils. The meeting also decided to create a "ministerial executive council" to administer "a system of internal control on production, exports and prices in order to ascertain compliance with the organization's decisions".

At an extraordinary OPEC Conference meeting held on Jan. 28–30, 1985, a majority of members agreed on a price reduction from $29 to $28 per barrel for Saudi Arabian marker light crude oil, and also on the introduction of a new differentials structure as from Feb. 1, 1985, with the effect that the overall spread of such differentials was reduced to about $2.40 per barrel—which was said to mean that the weighted average price per barrel of OPEC oil was reduced to $27.96. (Algeria and Libya opposed the new structure, while Gabon abstained from voting for it.)

An OPEC ministerial meeting held on July 22–25, 1985, reduced OPEC prices by a few cents per barrel but left them about $2.00 above those prevailing on the free market. On July 26 Ecuador unilaterally took measures which were to reduce its actual price to about $25.00 per barrel (its output of 280,000 bpd having greatly exceeded its quota of 183,000 bpd), and it also indicated that it might leave OPEC.

Oil prices on the free market subsequently declined to still lower levels. On Jan. 21, 1986, the spot price of North Sea Brent crude oil fell below $20.00 per barrel, and by the end of March 1986 the spot price had fallen to about $10.00 per barrel.

An OPEC meeting held between March 16 and 24, 1986, broke up without reaching any new agreements, in particular on production quotas. However, at a resumed meeting on April 15–21, 1986, 10 of the 13 OPEC member states agreed to restore output discipline within a new ceiling of an estimated 16,300,000 bpd for the third quarter of 1986. (Algeria, Iran and Libya had sought a lower ceiling of 14,000,000 to 14,500,000 bpd.)

By June 1986, however, actual production by OPEC member states was thought to total about 20,000,000 bpd. At a further meeting held from July 30 to Aug. 5, 1986, agreement was reached by 12 member states to reduce the total output (of all 13 members) to some 16,400,000 bpd by fixing the following new quotas: Algeria 663,000 bpd, Ecuador 183,000 bpd, Gabon 137,000 bpd, Indonesia 1,180,000 bpd, Iran 2,300,000 bpd, Kuwait 900,000 bpd, Libya 950,000 bpd, Nigeria 1,300,000 bpd, Qatar 280,000 bpd, Saudi Arabia 4,350,000 bpd, the United Arab Emirates 950,000 bpd, and Venezuela 1,550,000 bpd. Iraq remained outside the agreement with 1,600,000 bpd (against its previous output of 1,200,000 bpd). The declared aim of this agreement was to restore the price to about $19 by the end of 1986.

Organization of Arab Petroleum Exporting Countries (OAPEC)

Address. P.O. Box 20501, Safat, Kuwait City, Kuwait.

Officer. Dr Ali Ahmad Attiga (sec. gen.).

Founded. Jan. 9, 1968.

Membership. Algeria, Bahrain, Egypt, Iraq, Kuwait, Libya, Qatar, Saudi Arabia, Syria, Tunisia and the United Arab Emirates. (Egypt was suspended from membership on April 17, 1979.)

Objects. To represent the special interests of Arab petroleum exporting countries while respecting the charter of the Organization of Petroleum Exporting Countries (OPEC); to protect the interests of its members in relations with the importing countries and with foreign oil companies; and to develop co-operation between the petroleum industries of member states.

History. The possible use of petroleum as a political weapon to force the United States (as the largest importer) to apply an "impartial" policy on the Arab-Israeli conflict was first discussed at a meeting of the Foreign Ministers of the OAPEC member countries on Sept. 4, 1973. On Oct. 17 of that year OAPEC's member states decided to reduce their production by at least 5 per cent progressively each month until Israel had withdrawn its forces completely from Arab territories occupied in the 1967 war and the legal rights of Palestinians had been restored. In addition OAPEC member states imposed total embargoes on oil shipments to the United States and also to the Netherlands. On Nov. 4–5, 1973, it was decided to increase the overall production cutback from Sept. 1, 1973, to 25 per cent, but by the end of 1973 this decision was reversed, and (following a disengagement agreement concluded between Egypt and Israel in January 1974) the embargo against the United States was lifted in March 1974, and that against the Netherlands in July 1974.

At a meeting of ministers from OAPEC member countries and a special commission of the Organization of African Unity held in Cairo on Jan. 22–23, 1974, the OAPEC ministers agreed to accelerate the establishment of an Arab bank for the economic development of Africa (as decided at an Algiers Arab summit meeting) with an increased capital of $500,000,000, and to recommend the creation of a $200,000,000 fund for the granting of credits to African countries (at no or purely nominal interest) for the purchase of Arab oil.

Structure. The organization's supreme authority is its Council of Ministers, normally composed of the member countries' Ministers of Petroleum and meeting at least twice a year. There are also an executive bureau, a secretariat and a judicial board.

Between 1973 and 1981 the OAPEC established the following subsidiary organizations:

(1) The **Arab Maritime Petroleum Transport Company** in Safat (Kuwait) with a subscribed capital of $500,000,000, which was formed in 1973 and by 1978 had six supertankers.

(2) The **Arab Petroleum Investments Corporation** at Dhahran airport, Saudi Arabia, with a subscribed capital of $400,000,000, to assist in the development of oil industry projects in Arab countries, as decided on July 19, 1974.

(3) The **Arab Shipbuilding and Repair Company**, formed at Manama (Bahrain) in 1974 with a subscribed capital of $340,000,000; it opened a drydock in Bahrain in December 1977.

(4) The **Arab Petroleum Services Company**, formed in Tripoli (Libya) in January 1977 with a subscribed capital of 15,000,000 Libyan dinars and with specialized subsidiaries to to provide technical services to Arab state companies. These subsidiaries include the **Arab Drilling and Workover Company** set up in Tripoli in 1977.

(5) The **Arab Petroleum Training Institute**, established in Baghdad in 1979.

(6) The **Arab Engineering and Consulting Company**, established in Abu Dhabi (United Arab Emirates) in 1981, with a subscribed capital of $12,000,000.

Mutual Assistance of the Latin American Government Oil Companies

Asistencia Recíproca Petrolera Estatal Latino-americana (ARPEL)

Address. Javier de Viana 2345, Montevideo, Uruguay.

Officer. Gustavo Jarrín Ampudia (sec. gen.).

Founded. 1965.

Membership. State oil enterprises in Argentina, Bolivia, Brazil, Chile, Colombia, Ecuador, Mexico, Paraguay, Peru, Uruguay and Venezuela.

Objects. To study and carry out implementation of mutually beneficial agreements among members; to promote interchange of technical assistance and information, as well as Latin American intergration; and to plan meetings and lectures concerning the oil industry.

Phosphorites

Organization of Phosphorites Exporting Countries

Address. Algiers, Algeria.

Founded. 1976.

Membership. Algeria, Jordan, Morocco, Senegal, Togo and Tunisia (representing about 34 per cent of the world's phosphorites production).

Activities. An agreement signed in November 1976 provided for common price policies for phosphorites.

Rice

International Rice Commission

Address. c/o FAO, Via delle Terme di Caracalla, 00100 Rome, Italy.

Founded. 1948.

Membership. 53 countries (Australia, Bangladesh, Benin, Brazil, Burkina Faso, Burma, Cameroon, Colombia, Cuba, the Dominican Republic, Ecuador, Egypt, France, The Gambia, Ghana, Guatemala, Guinea, Guyana, Haiti, India, Indonesia, Iran, Italy, Japan, Kampuchea, Kenya, the Republic of Korea, Laos, Liberia, Madagascar, Malaysia, Mali, Mauritania, Mexico, Nepal, the Netherlands, Nicaragua, Nigeria, Pakistan, Panama, Paraguay, the Philippines, Portugal, Senegal, Sierra Leone, Sri Lanka, Suriname, Thailand, the United Kingdom, the United States, Uruguay, Venezuela and Vietnam).

Objects. To deal with all matters concerning the production, conservation, distribution and consumption of rice (but not international trade).

Activities. The commission holds sessions every four years, and its three technical working parties meet every three years.

West African Rice Development Association (WARDA)

Address. P.O. Box 1019, Monrovia, Liberia.

Officer. Alieu M.B. Jagne (acting exec. sec.).

Founded. 1970.

Membership. Benin, Burkina Faso, Chad, Côte d'Ivoire, The Gambia, Ghana, Guinea, Guinea-Bissau, Liberia, Mali, Mauritania, Niger, Nigeria, Senegal, Sierra Leone and Togo.

Object. To obtain, as an international organization, self-sufficiency in rice for West Africa by means of regional research, development and training programmes.

Rubber

Association of Natural Rubber Producing Countries (ANRPC)

Address. Natural Rubber Bldg., 148 Jalan Ampang, Kuala Lumpur, Malaysia.

Officer. Dr Pimol Chitman (sec. gen.).

Founded. October 1970.

Membership. India, Indonesia, Malaysia, Papua New Guinea, Singapore, Sri Lanka and Thailand.

History. The ANRPC was formed as a result of a meeting organized by rubber producing countries in October 1967 with the object of achieving co-operation among its member states as well as fair and stable prices.

At a meeting of the ANRCP in Kuala Lumpur in May 1975 it was agreed in principle to introduce a buffer-stock system and a "supply rationalization scheme" and also to limit member countries' combined exports.

At a further ANRPC meeting (in Jakarta) an *International Rubber Agreement on Price Stabilization* was signed on Nov. 30, 1976, by ministers from Indonesia, Malaysia, Singapore, Sri Lanka and Thailand, establishing an international council to stabilize rubber prices by stockpiling and production controls. This International Natural Rubber Council was to operate the agreement and to determine the proportion of buffer-stock resources to be contributed in rubber and cash by each member state and the price levels governing buffer-stock intervention in the market to limit price fluctuations.

A new *International Natural Rubber Agreement* (INRA) reached under UNCTAD auspices on Oct. 6, 1979, included provisions for price stabilization (between minimum and maximum indicative prices set at 150 and 270 Malaysian/Singapore cents per kilogramme) with semi-automatic procedures for the periodic revision of the agreed price range every 30 months. The sole mechanism for price stabilization was the operation of buffer stocks of 500,000 tonnes in all, the creation of which would begin only after the agreement had definitely entered into force.

The INRA entered provisionally into force on Oct. 24, 1980, after being ratified by countries accounting for 65 per cent of the world's natural rubber production and consumption respectively, and its definitive entry into force would take place only after ratification by countries accounting for 80 per cent of world production and consumption respectively.

The INRA finally came into force on April 15, 1982, for the following countries: Australia,

Austria, Belgium, Brazil, Canada, China, Czechoslovakia, Denmark, France, the Federal Republic of Germany, Indonesia, Iraq, Ireland, Italy, Japan, Luxembourg, Malaysia, Mexico, the Netherlands, Nigeria, Norway, Papua New Guinea, Peru, the Soviet Union, Sri Lanka, Sweden, Thailand, Turkey, the United Kingdom and the United States, and also for the EEC; on July 22, 1982, for Switzerland; on Aug. 24, 1982, for Finland; and on June 5, 1984, for Greece. Turkey withdrew from the agreement on Nov. 26, 1983.

The agreement established the International Natural Rubber Organization [see below] and was to apply for five years, subject to extension for another two years, but could be terminated at any time by the International Natural Rubber Council. On June 12, 1985, it was decided to extend it for two years after its scheduled expiry on Oct. 22, 1985.

The agreement provided for the maintenance of a buffer stock which would buy or sell rubber in support of an original midpoint of 2.10 Malaysian ringgit per kg, with a maximum permitted deviation of 20 per cent from this level. However, a steady decline in prices brought about a reduction of the midpoint to 2.0166 by August 1985 and an increase in the buffer stock, by December 1985, to 375,000 tonnes (well above its nominal maximum of 300,000 tonnes).

International Natural Rubber Organization (INRO)

Address. 12th Floor, MUI Plaza, Jalan P. Ramlee, P.O. Box 10374, Kuala Lumpur 01–02, Malaysia.

Officer. Pang Soeparto (exec. dir.).

Founded. 1980.

Membership. The parties to the International Natural Rubber Agreement [see above].

International Rubber Study Group

Address. Brettenham House, 5–6 Lancaster Place, London WC2E 7ET, UK.

Officer. J. Carr (sec. gen.)

Founded. 1944.

Membership. 27 governments.

Silk

International Sericultural Commission

Address. 25 quai Jean Jacques Rousseau, 69350 La Mulatière, France.

Officer. Dr H. Bouvier (sec. gen.).

Founded. Oct. 12, 1959.

Membership. Algeria, Brazil, the Central African Republic, Egypt, France, India, Iran, Japan, Lebanon, Madagascar, Mauritius, Romania, Spain, Tunisia and Yugoslavia.

History. The commission superseded an earlier Permanent Commission of the International Sericultural Congresses set up in 1948. The new commission was established under a convention concluded in Paris on July 1, 1957.

Objects. To further the development of sericulture, to disseminate information and to carry out research concerning silkworms and other sericigenous insects.

Sugar

International Sugar Organization (ISO)

Address. 28 Haymarket, London SW1 4SP, UK.

Officers. William K. Miller (exec. dir.); C. Politoff (sec.).

Founded. 1968.

Membership. 47 exporting and 13 importing countries.

History. The organization was set up under an *International Sugar Agreement* (ISA), negotiated under UNCTAD auspices, covering fixed prices and export quotas and in force from 1969 to 1973.

This ISA was superseded by a new agreement which was in force from 1974 to 1976 but contained no economic provisions. A new ISA concluded on Oct. 7, 1977, by a UN Sugar Conference came into force provisionally on Jan. 1, 1978 (as the first international commodity agreement negotiated since the fourth UNCTAD session had adopted an "integrated programme for commodities"—see page 127). This ISA was ratified by the United States with effect from Jan. 1, 1980, and definitively came into force on the following day.

The objectives of this ISA, as defined in its Article 1, included the raising of "the level of international trade in sugar, particularly to increase the export earnings of the developing exporting countries"; the achievement of "stable conditions in the international trade in sugar"; provision of "adequate supplies of sugar to meet the requirements of importing countries at fair and reasonable prices"; and "adequate participation in, and growing access to, the markets of the developed countries for sugar from the developing countries". The extensive provisions of the ISA were to be administered by an **International Sugar Council** (ISC). Among arrangements excluded from the ISA's provisions were those for exports of sugar to the European Economic Community (under the 1975 Lomé Convention or under agreements with other states).

Inter alia the ISA laid down "basic export tonnages" (i.e. quotas) totalling 15,905,000 tonnes for 29 major sugar-exporting countries (subject to revision and renegotiation) and also of 70,000 tonnes for each of 22 smaller exporting countries. In addition the ISA contained provisions for a price stabilization mechanism. By Jan. 1, 1978, the ISA had been approved by 25 exporting countries or territories (Argentina, Australia, Barbados, Belize, Brazil, Costa Rica, Cuba, El Salavador, Fiji, Guatemala, Honduras, Hungary, India, Jamaica, Madagascar, Mauritius, Nicaragua, Panama, St Kitts-Nevis-Anguilla, South Africa, Swaziland, Thailand, Trinidad and Tobago, and Venezuela) and also by eight importing countries (including Canada, Japan, the Soviet Union and the United States).

The 1977 ISA expired on Dec. 31, 1984, and was replaced by a new ISA concluded on July 5, 1984, and in force from April 4, 1985. It was to run to the end of the second year after its entry into force but could be extended annually. It was an administrative agreement only, as no consensus was reached on economic clauses to replace those of the 1977 agreement. Its objective was to promote international co-operation in negotiating a new agreement with economic provisions.

Group of Latin American and Caribbean Sugar Exporting Countries (GEPLACEA)

Address. Ejército Nacional 373, Piso 1, Col. Granada ZC 11520, México DF, Mexico.

Officer. Eduardo Latorre (exec. sec.).

Membership. 21 Latin American and Caribbean countries and the Philippines.

Founded. 1974.

Objects. To serve as a forum for consultation on the production and sale of sugar; to take up agreed positions at international meetings on sugar; to exchange scientific and technical knowledge; to co-ordinate the various branches of sugar processing; and to achieve fair and remunerative prices.

Tea

International Tea Promotion Association

Address. P.O. Box 30007, Coolsingel 58, 3011 AE Rotterdam, Netherlands.

Officer. Ngaima wa Mwaura (liaison officer).

Founded. 1979.

Membership. Bangladesh, Indonesia, Kenya, Malawi, Mauritius, Mozambique, Tanzania and Uganda.

Textiles

An **Arrangement regarding International Trade in Textiles,** commonly known as the **Multi-Fibre Arrangement** (MFA), concluded in Geneva on Dec. 30, 1973, by representatives of some 50 countries meeting under the auspices of the General Agreement on Tariffs and Trade (GATT), laid down, for a four-year period, rules for international trade in textile products of wool, cotton and man-made fibres.

This arrangement came into force on Jan. 1, 1974, and provided for the establishment of a permanent **Textiles Surveillance Body** (superseding an earlier arrangement on world trade in cotton textiles agreed upon in February 1962). The basic objects of the arrangement were (i) to expand the trade through progressive liberalization of world trade in textile products while ensuring the orderly and equitable development of the trade and avoidance of disruptive effects in both importing and exporting countries, and (ii) "to further the economic and social development of developing countries and secure substantial increases in their export earnings from textile products and to provide scope for a greater share for them in world trade in these products". The operation of the arrangement was to be reviewed by a Textile Committee of representatives of all participating countries.

The arrangement was signed by the European Communities and 41 governments of countries other than the former's members. It was endorsed by the GATT Council on Jan. 28, 1974, and on Dec. 14, 1977, was extended unchanged for a further four years from Jan. 1, 1978.

Bilateral textile agreements were concluded in 1978–79 by the European Economic Community with a total of 27 low-price textile exporting countries—four from the Eastern block in Europe (Bulgaria, Hungary, Poland and Romania), Yugoslavia, Egypt, eight countries in Latin America and 13 in Asia (including China—in July 1979). An agreement with Malta was concluded on July 8, 1982.

Under a protocol opened for signature on Dec. 22, 1981, the MFA was extended for another four years and seven months, i.e. from Dec. 31, 1981, to July 31, 1986. By March 23, 1983, this protocol had been accepted by 36 signatories representing 45 countries (i.e. the then 10 members of the European Communities and 35 other countries). Bilateral agreements between the European Communities and 26 exporting countries, initialled in 1982, ran for four years from Jan. 1, 1983.

China, the world's largest producer of textiles and clothing, adhered to the MFA on Jan. 18, 1984.

Timber

African Timber Organization

Address. B.P. 67, Libreville, Gabon.

Officer. André Christian Zane-Fe Fouam Bona (sec. gen.).

Founded. May 26, 1975.

Membership. Cameroon, the Central African Republic, the Congo, Côte d'Ivoire, Equatorial Guinea, Gabon, Ghana, Liberia, Madagascar, Tanzania and Zaïre.

History. The organization was formed as the Inter-African Organization for Forestry Economy and Marketing of Timber, established under a decision by the above 11 states taken in order to secure easier access to markets for timber producers, to stabilize prices and to take "a unified stand towards carriers so as to ensure acceptable prices for transport services".

International Tropical Timber Organization (ITTO)

Founded. 1984.

History. This organization was formed under an *International Tropical Timber Agreement* concluded for five years (unless extended) on Nov. 18, 1983, and provisionally in force from Oct. 1, 1984.

Parties to the agreement (as at Jan. 1, 1986): Belgium*, Brazil*, Bolivia*, Cameroon, the Congo, Côte d'Ivoire*, Denmark, Ecuador*, Egypt*, the European Communities*, Finland, France, Gabon*, the German Federal Republic*, Ghana, Greece*, Honduras*, Indonesia, Ireland, Italy, Japan, the Republic of Korea, Liberia, Luxembourg*, Malaysia, the Netherlands*, Norway, Papua New Guinea, Peru*, the Philippines*, the Soviet Union, Spain*, Sweden, Switzerland, Thailand, the United Kingdom and the United States* (*provisional applications).

Objects. To provide an effective framework for co-operation and consultation between producers and consumers and to promote the expansion of international trade in tropical timber. (The ITTO was not to use a buffer stock for influencing market prices.)

Structure. The main organ of the ITTO is the International Tropical Timber Council (the location of which had by mid-1986 not yet been agreed).

South-East Asia Lumber Producers Association (SEALPA)

Founded. December 1974.

History. The association was formed by Indonesia, Malaysia and the Philippines with the object of collecting economic and marketing data from timber-using countries as a guideline for the formulation of joint sales and production measures, maintaining a minimum fair price level and protecting the economic interests of the member countries. For the year 1975 SEALPA imposed export quotas for logs.

Tin

International Tin Council (ITC)

Address. Haymarket House, 1 Oxendon St., London SW1Y 4EQ, UK.

Officers. Peter Lai (exec. ch.); N.L. Phelps (sec.).

Founded. July 1956.

Activities. The ITC operates an *International Tin Agreement* (ITA), renewed from time to time.

The first ITA, drawn up in 1953, had come into force on July 1, 1956; it had established a 25,000-ton buffer stock and fixed floor and ceiling prices per long ton. Similar second, third and fourth agreements were in force between 1962 and 1976. During a period of generally low prices the ITC imposed, in 1968, quotas on exports by the then six producer countries, but in December 1969 the ITC lifted export controls.

Under a fifth ITA, reached on June 21, 1975, and in force provisionally from July 1, 1976, and definitively from June 14, 1977, the buffer stock was increased to 30,000 tons. Among the general objectives of the fifth ITA were "to provide for adjustment between world production and consumption of tin", "to prevent excessive fluctuations in the price of tin and in export earnings from it"; "to increase the export earnings from tin, especially those of the developing producing countries"; and "to improve further the expansion in the use of tin and the indigenous processing of tin, especially in the developing producing countries". Producer countries which approved the fifth ITA were Australia, Bolivia, India, Indonesia, Malaysia, Nigeria, Thailand and Zaïre (but not Burma and China), and consumer countries which did so included the member states of the European Communities, Canada, Denmark, Japan, the United States and also the Communist countries of Europe (except the German Democratic Republic).

The sixth ITA, adopted on June 26, 1981, for a five-year period from June 30, 1982, set the ITC buffer stock at 50,000 tonnes, of which 30,000 were to be financed by governmental contributions and 20,000 by borrowing.

By Jan. 1, 1986, there were 25 parties to the sixth ITA—Australia*, Belgium, Canada, Denmark, the European Communities*, Finland, France, the Federal Republic of Germany†, Greece, India, Indonesia, Ireland, Italy, Japan, Luxembourg, Malaysia, the Netherlands, Nigeria, Norway, Poland*, Sweden, Switzerland, Thailand, the United Kingdom* and Zaïre (*=provisional application; †=provisional application without contribution to buffer stock account).

Under the agreement the ITC was empowered to fix floor and ceiling prices for tin and otherwise to manage the international tin market. For this purpose the ITC could fix quotas to be adjusted upwards or downwards depending on price movements, and maintain a buffer stock whose manager would buy in the market place to guarantee a floor price and sell to ensure that the ceiling of an agreed price range was not breached.

In 1983–85 there was a growing over-supply of tin. Despite tighter export control by ITC producers' members, surplus stocks were accumulated, partly owing to increasing production of tin by non-members of the ITC, notably Brazil and China. In order to prevent the price from falling drastically, the ITC bought up surplus stocks; the funds needed were largely raised by loans, for which stockpiled tin was used as collateral. Interest payments became an increasingly heavy burden on the ITC, which could not be alleviated by sales.

In April 1985 the ITC member governments decided to relieve the buffer stock manager of his obligation under the ITA to defend the agreed floor price for tin (at Malaysian ringgits 29.15 a kg, or £8,500 a tonne). Additional funds of £60,000,000 were pledged to the buffer stock manager's reserve by ITC producer members. However, on Oct. 24, 1985, tin sales were suspended on the London Metal Exchange and in Kuala Lumpur, and the ITC buffer stock manager announced that he had no funds left to support prices, which had fallen to £8,140 a tonne. The buffer stock then stood at more than 62,000 tonnes (worth under £500,000,000 or $760,000,000, funded by an estimated £200,000,000 from ITC members and the rest by borrowings).

Following the failure of negotiations to find a solution to the ITC's debt problem, the London Metal Exchange council decided on March 7, 1986, to bring tin trading to a permanent close. A newly opened tin exchange in Kuala Lumpur remained virtually inactive. Thailand announced on March 31 that it would declare its own tin price and unilaterally lift its export controls. Indonesia announced on April 6, 1986, that it would raise its export volumes from 23,000 to 27,000 tonnes a year. The ITA thus appeared to have become inoperative.

141

Association of Tin Producing Countries

Membership. Australia, Bolivia, Indonesia, Malaysia, Nigeria, Thailand and Zaïre.

History. The ATPC was established under an agreement concluded on March 29, 1983, and was to replace an earlier Tin Producers' Association, which had ceased to exist in 1958.

Object. To obtain remunerative and equitable returns to tin producers and adequate supplies to consumers at fair and stable prices.

South-East Asia Tin Research and Development Centre

Address. 14 Tiger Lane, Ipoh, Malaysia.
Officer. Dr Abdullah Hasbi (dir.).
Founded. April 1977.
Membership. Indonesia, Malaysia and Thailand.
Objects. To develop new methods of locating new primary ore deposits, of efficient mining and of ore processing.

Wheat

International Wheat Council

Address. 28 Haymarket, London SW1Y 4SS, UK.
Officer. J. H. Parotte (exec. sec.)
Founded. July 1, 1949.
Membership. Eight exporting countries and 42 importing countries, as well as the EEC.

Activities. The council was established with a membership of nine wheat exporting countries and 40 importing countries—the exporting countries being Argentina, Australia, Canada, Greece, Kenya, Spain, Sweden, the Soviet Union and the United States (with the European Economic Community being both an exporter and an importer). The council has been responsible for the administration of the *Wheat Trade Convention* of 1971 which was part of an *International Wheat Agreement* concluded on Feb. 20, 1971, and in force from July 1 of that year. The agreement covered arrangements for consultation and exchange of information but contained no provisions for price control mechanisms. It was repeatedly extended, most recently in March 1983 until June 30, 1986. (The other part of the International Wheat Agreement is the Food Aid Convention—see pages 128–29.)

Wine

International Vine and Wine Office
Office international de la vigne et du vin (OIV)

Address. 1 rue Roquépine, 75008, Paris, France.
Officer. Gilbert Constant (dir.).
Founded. 1924.
Membership. 31 countries (including Algeria, Argentina, Austria, Belgium, Chile, Cyprus, Czechoslovakia, France, Greece, Israel, Luxembourg, Morocco, the Netherlands, Portugal, Romania, the Soviet Union, Spain, Switzerland, Tunisia, the Ukraine and Yugoslavia).

Objects. To study all problems connected with the vine and its products, to promote contacts among researchers and to establish international research programmes.

History. The office was set up under a convention of Nov. 29, 1924. An international convention on the harmonization of methods of testing and judging wines was signed on Oct. 13, 1954, and is in force in 14 countries (Argentina, Austria, Chile, France, the Federal Republic of Germany, Greece, Hungary, Italy, Morocco, Portugal, South Africa, Spain, Turkey and Yugoslavia).

Wool

International Wool Study Group

Address. Ashdown House, 123 Victoria St., London SW1E 6RB, UK.
Officer. M. T. Dunn (sec. gen.).
Founded. 1946.
Membership. 17 countries.

Activities. The group collects statistics on world supply of and demand for wool and considers possible solutions to problems. It has introduced the Woolmark as an international wool quality mark.

International Wool Textile Organization
Fédération lainière internationale

Address. 19–21 rue de Luxembourg, 1040 Brussels, Belgium.
Officers. G. J. ten Broeke (pres.); W. H. Lakin (sec.).
Founded. 1929.
Membership. 26 countries.

8. Groupings, Treaties and Agreements in Western Europe

West European groupings, treaties and agreements covered in this section comprise (i) the major international organizations set up in the aftermath of World War II, (ii) the European Communities, (iii) the European Free Trade Association, (iv) West European co-operation in other important spheres and (v) major bilateral treaties and agreements in force. (For bilateral agreements concluded by the United Kingdom, Malta and Cyprus, see Section 12: The Commonwealth.)

Post-War Co-operation in Western Europe

Western European Union (WEU)

Address. 9 Grosvenor Place, London SW1X 7HL, UK.

Officer. Alfred Cahen (sec. gen.).

Founded. May 6, 1955.

Membership. Belgium, France, the Federal Republic of Germany, Italy, Luxembourg, the Netherlands and the United Kingdom.

History. The basis of this alliance was laid in a Treaty of Dunkirk, an Anglo-French treaty of alliance signed on March 4, 1947, when the two signatories agreed to give mutual support to each other in the event of renewed German aggression and to take common action should either party be prejudiced by any failure of Germany to fulfil its economic obligations.

A Brussels Treaty ("Treaty of Economic, Social and Cultural Co-operation and Collective Self-Defence") signed on March 17, 1948, by representatives of Belgium, France, Luxembourg, the Netherlands and the United Kingdom, implemented proposals for a Western European Union made earlier by the UK Foreign Secretary (Ernest Bevin). This treaty, concluded for a period of 50 years, had among its aims the strengthening of economic, social and cultural ties between the signatories, the co-ordination of efforts to create a firm basis for European economic recovery, and mutual assistance in maintaining international peace and security. Article 4 of the treaty provided for mutual automatic military assistance in the event of an armed attack in Europe, and Article 7 created a Consultative Council to discuss matters covered by the treaty.

Following a breakdown of discussions on the creation of a European Defence Council, the Brussels Treaty was amended and expanded by the Paris Agreements which were concluded at a nine-power conference held in London from Sept. 28 to Oct. 3, 1954, and signed in Paris on Oct. 23, 1954, by representatives of Belgium, Canada, France, the Federal Republic of Germany, Italy, Luxembourg, the Netherlands, the United Kingdom and the United States, and which came into force on May 6, 1955. The expanded Brussels Treaty Organization was renamed the Western European Union (WEU).

Those documents of the Paris Agreements which are relevant to the formation of the WEU comprise four protocols and a resolution on the production and standardization of armaments.

Protocol I amended the Brussels Treaty of 1948 to permit the entry of the Federal Republic of Germany and Italy into the Treaty Organization. The system of mutual automatic assistance in case of attack was extended to the two new entrants. The Consultative Council set up under the original treaty was given powers of decision and renamed the Council of Western European Union.

Protocol II laid down the maximum strength of land and air forces to be maintained in Europe at the disposal of the Supreme Allied Commander of NATO by each of the member countries of the WEU in peacetime. The contribution of naval forces to NATO by each of the WEU countries would be determined annually. Regular inspections would be held by the Supreme Allied Commander, Europe, to ensure that the limits were observed. A special article recapitulated an undertaking by Britain not to withdraw or diminish her forces in Europe against the wishes of the majority of her partners. In 1957 Britain was given permission, by the WEU Council, to withdraw some of her forces from the Federal Republic of Germany.

Protocol III embodied resolutions on the control of armaments on the European mainland. The Federal Republic of Germany was forbidden to manufacture atomic, biological or chemical weapons, and stocks of such weapons in other countries of continental Europe were to be strictly controlled. In addition, Germany undertook not to manufacture long-range and guided missiles, influence mines, warships and strategic bombers unless the competent NATO Supreme Commander should recommend any change in the ruling.

Protocol IV set up an Agency for the Control of Armaments and defined its functions, these being mainly to enforce the provisions of Protocol III.

LATER DECISIONS OF THE WEU

The most important decisions taken at subsequent meetings of the WEU have concerned amendments to Protocol III of the revised Brussels Treaty.

The first such decision was taken at a meeting of the Permanent Council on April 23, 1958, when West Germany's request to manufacture short-range, anti-tank, guided missiles with only conventional warheads was approved.

On Oct. 21, 1959, the Council of the WEU removed the restriction on the construction of ground-to-air and air-to-air anti-aircraft missiles by Germany.

Between May 1961 and October 1963, the WEU approved a number of revisions to the permitted limits on West German naval construction. On May 24, 1961, the Council of the WEU raised the tonnage limit for eight West German destroyers to 6,000 tons (double the existing general limit), and permitted the Federal Republic of Germany to build fleet auxiliary vessels of up to 6,000 tons and to manufacture influence mines for port protection.

On Oct. 19, 1962, the WEU announced its agreement to increase from 350 to 450 tons the limit for West German submarines "to fulfil NATO requirements". A year later, on Oct. 9, 1963, the WEU Permanent Council agreed to raise the tonnage limit for West German submarines from 450 to 1,000 tons, and to allow six submarines of the latter size to be built in the Federal Republic of Germany.

These limits were subsequently further relaxed under a series of amendments, so that by 1980 the permitted limits were (i) 3,000 tons for combat vessels except eight destroyers of up to 6,000 tons and one training ship of up to 5,000 tons, (ii) 6,000 tons for permanent auxiliary vessels, and (iii) 1,800 tons for submarines.

On July 21, 1980, the Council of the WEU unanimously agreed to a proposal (approved by the WEU Parliamentary Assembly on June 2 by 55 votes to six) to remove with immediate effect all restrictions on the permitted size of West German warships.

TEMPORARY FRENCH WITHDRAWAL FROM MINISTERIAL COUNCIL

France withdrew from meetings of the WEU Ministerial Council on Feb. 19, 1969, and did not return to them until June 5, 1970.

France's withdrawal followed (i) discussions by the Council on Oct. 21–22, 1968, and Feb. 6–7, 1969, of the "Harmel Plan"—a proposal made by Pierre Harmel, the Belgian Foreign Minister, for co-operation between the European Community and Britain in the fields of foreign, defence, technological and monetary policy, and (ii) a meeting held by the WEU Permanent Council, against France's wishes and without her participation, for discussions on the Middle East situation.

OTHER WEU ACTIVITIES

After the entry of the United Kingdom into the European Communities in 1973 the WEU concentrated its activities on deliberations concerning political questions, including East-West relations, the changes brought about by the institution of democratic regimes in Greece, Portugal and Spain and the Arab-Israeli conflict.

The WEU was reactivated (at the first meeting, since 1973, of the seven member countries' Defence Ministers) in Paris on June 12, 1984, and at an extraordinary meeting of Foreign and Defence Ministers in Rome on Oct. 26–27, 1984, which adopted a "Rome Declaration" expressing their determination to "increase co-operation . . . in the field of security policy and to encourage consensus", with ministerial meetings of the Council to be held twice a year. The ministers also agreed that the last of the post-war controls on West German conventional rearmament should be substantially reduced by Jan. 1, 1985, and entirely lifted by Jan. 1, 1986.

Structure. The Council of the WEU is composed either of the member states' Foreign Ministers or of their ambassadors in London, and its decisions are normally taken unanimously. The Council is served by an international Secretariat-General whose secretary-general is chairman of the Council. The Secretariat-General has a division for political affairs and a division of administration. A committee of directors, including the secretary-general, is responsible for administrative and legal affairs, documentation, security, and linguistic services.

There are three agencies for security questions, each based in Paris. They are Agency I—for the study of arms control and disarmament questions; Agency II—for the study of security and defence questions; Agency III—for the development of co-operation in the field of armaments.

The Assembly of the WEU is composed of the member states' delegates to the Parliamentary Assembly of the Council of Europe [see below]. It normally meets twice a year, usually in Paris, and it has set up six committees—(i) on defence questions and armaments (27 seats), (ii) on general affairs (27 seats), (iii) on scientific, technological and aerospace questions (21 seats), (iv) on budgetary affairs and administration (21 seats), (v) on rules of procedure and privileges (21 seats), and (vi) on parliamentary and public relations (14 seats).

Council of Europe

Address. Avenue de l'Europe, 67006 Strasbourg, France.

Officer. Marcelino Oreja Aguirre (sec. gen.).

Founded. May 5, 1949.

Membership. Austria, Belgium, Cyprus, Denmark, France, the Federal Republic of Germany, Greece, Iceland, Ireland, Italy, Liechtenstein, Luxembourg, Malta, the Netherlands, Norway, Portugal, Spain, Sweden, Switzerland, Turkey and the United Kingdom.

History. The Council of Europe was established under its Statute, signed on May 5, 1949, by the Foreign Ministers of 10 European states—Belgium, Denmark, France, Ireland, Italy, Luxembourg, the Netherlands, Norway, Sweden and the United Kingdom—and effective from Aug. 3, 1949. The Council was subsequently joined by Greece and Turkey (August 1949), Iceland (March 1950), the Federal Republic of Germany (May 1951), Austria (April 1956), Cyprus (April 1961), Switzerland (May 1963), Malta (January 1965), Portugal (September 1976), Spain (November 1977) and Liechtenstein (November 1978), bringing the Council's total membership to 21.

Greece was not a member of the Council between December 1969 and November 1974, having withdrawn from membership after the Council had, on Sept. 26, 1967, released a report describing the regime set up in Greece on April 21, 1967, as "undemocratic, illiberal, authoritarian and repressive", and being readmitted after the restitution of parliamentary democracy in Greece in 1974.

Structure and Activities. In the preamble to the Statute of the Council of Europe the parties to it reaffirmed "their devotion to the spiritual and moral values which are the common heritage of their peoples and the true source of individual freedom, political liberty and the rule of law,

A = Albania
B = Belgium
L = Luxembourg
Li = Liechtenstein
N = Netherlands
S = Switzerland

▨ = Council of Europe members

Map 2   Member states of Council of Europe

principles which form the basis of all genuine democracy".

The principal clauses of the Statute are given below:

Chapter I: Aim of the Council of Europe

"**Art. 1.** (*a*) The aim of the Council of Europe is to achieve a greater unity between its members for the purpose of safeguarding and realizing the ideals and principles which are their common heritage and facilitating their economic and social progress.

"(*b*) This aim shall be pursued through the organs of the Council by discussion of questions of common concern and by agreements and common action in economic, social, cultural, scientific, legal and administrative matters.

"(*c*) Participation in the Council of Europe shall not affect the collaboration of its members in the work of the United Nations and of other international organizations or unions to which they are parties.

"(*d*) Matters relating to national defence do not fall within the scope of the Council of Europe.

Chapter II: Membership

"**Art. 2.** The members of the Council of Europe are the parties to this statute.

"**Art. 3.** Every member of the Council of Europe must accept the principles of the rule of law and of the enjoyment by all persons within its jurisdiction of human rights and fundamental freedoms, and collaborate sincerely and effectively in the realization of the aim of the Council as specified in Chapter I.

"**Art. 4.** Any European state, which is deemed to be able and willing to fulfil the provisions of Art. 3, may be invited to become a member of the Council of Europe by the Committee of Ministers. Any state so invited shall become a member on the deposit on its behalf with the Secretary-General of an instrument of accession to the present statute." (By a later revision of this article the Council's Consultative Assembly must be consulted before the issue of an invitation to join the Council.)

Other articles of the statute deal with the functions and activities of the various organs of the Council, with matters of finance, and with the privileges and immunities to be enjoyed by representatives of members of the Council of Europe in the territories of members of the Council.

ORGANS OF THE COUNCIL OF EUROPE

(1) **The Committee of Ministers.** The Committee of Ministers, consisting of the 21 Foreign Ministers of the member states, meets in Strasbourg twice a year. Its work programme is based on a medium-term (five-year) plan revised every two years according to political developments and results achieved. The Committee decides on recommendations submitted to it by the Parliamentary Assembly and on proposals made by committees of government experts, and its decisions may take the form of resolutions recommending common measures to governments, or of conventions or agreements binding on the states which ratify them. The Committee's decisions are taken by a simple or a two-thirds majority while unanimity is required for major issues.

The Committee's work programme is implemented by 11 (permanent) steering committees, five ad hoc committees of experts (set up for the duration of a specific activity) and 88 committees of experts (dissolved upon completion of their work).

The Foreign Ministers' Deputies, being the permanent representatives of their governments to the Council of Europe, meet every fortnight.

(2) **The Parliamentary Assembly.** This consultative Assembly consists of 170 representatives (and an equal number of substitutes) appointed by the national parliaments as follows: 18 each from France, the Federal Republic of Germany, Italy and the United Kingdom; 12 each from Spain and Turkey; seven each from Belgium, Greece, the Netherlands and Portugal; six each from Austria, Sweden and Switzerland; five each from Denmark and Norway; four from Ireland; three each from Cyprus, Iceland, Luxembourg and Malta; and two from Liechtenstein. The representatives have formed six multinational groups—Socialists, Christian Democrats, Independents (Conservatives), a Joint Group of Democrats (of the French *Rassemblement pour la république*, the Spanish Democratic Centre Union and the Portuguese Social Democrats), Liberals and Communists.

The Assembly holds three public sessions a year (from one week to 10 days each) in Strasbourg, with Israel being admitted as an observer. The Assembly's President is elected for one year but may be re-elected and normally remains in office for three years.

The Assembly has a Standing Committee consisting of the Assembly's President, its Vice-Presidents, the chairman of the specialized committees and a number of parliamentarians per member state. It meets at least three times a year and is empowered to adopt recommendations and resolutions.

There are 12 specialized committees consisting of members of the Assembly for various fields as follows: Political affairs; economic affairs and development; social and health questions; legal affairs; culture and education; science and technology; regional planning and local authorities; agriculture; relations with European non-member countries; the budget and the intergovernmental work programme; migration, refugees and demography; and parliamentary and public relations.

Turkey was, on May 14, 1981, effectively suspended from membership of the Parliamentary Assembly because of alleged violations of human rights in Turkey. On Sept. 30, 1983, the Assembly decided (in a resolution accepted by all except the British Conservative group) to bar any members of the newly to be elected Turkish Grand National Assembly from its own sessions on the grounds that the Turkish general election of Nov. 6, 1983, would be unrepresentative. Turkey continued, however, to be represented on the Council's Committee of Ministers, where it was, on Jan. 27, 1983, requested not to exercise its voting rights.

On May 8, 1984, Turkish delegates were readmitted to the Parliamentary Assembly, and on May 10 of that year the Assembly noted that Turkey was clearly on the way to democratic normalization, but called on the Turkish authorities to continue the removal of all undemocratic conditions which violated human rights.

(3) **The Conference of Local and Regional Authorities.** This Conference (which has no equivalent in any other European intergovernmental organization) is composed of 170 representatives (and an equal number of substitutes) appointed directly or elected by local and regional authorities in the Council of Europe's 21 member states. The Conference meets annually, has consultative powers and provides liaison between the Council of Europe and the European Communities.

At the initiative of the Conference a conference of European island regions was held in Tenerife (Canary Islands) on April 7–9, 1981, by representatives of 16 island regions and delegations from various European islands. This conference approved a Declaration of Tenerife which called for strict policies for island systems in the fields of territorial organization, industrial installations, and protection of the environment and the ecological balances; for the establishment of a European transport fund to extend communications and to make fares comparable to those applicable to mainland travel; for attention to over-exploitation of maritime resources; for special protection to be given by the European Community to the island countries' fisheries; for control of the social impact of tourism; and for a special statute for the development of island regions within the European Community.

(4) **Conferences of Specialist Ministers.** Such conferences are organized periodically to analyse major problems in the fields of justice, education, family affairs, regional planning, the environment, labour, culture, sport, local government and social security, and projects suitable for inclusion in the Council of Europe's work programme are communicated to the Committee of Ministers.

(5) **Specific Bodies.** Certain sections of the Council's work programme are assigned to the following specific bodies: The European Commission of Human Rights; the European Court of Human Rights; the European Youth Centre; and the European Youth Foundation.

(6) **The Secretariat.** The Council of Europe's permanent international secretariat, located in Strasbourg, provides services to the organization's ministerial, governmental and parliamentary committees. Its 800 members are required to undertake (i) not to be influenced by national considerations and (ii) not to accept instructions from any government.

The Secretary-General, Deputy Secretary-General and Clerk of the Parliamentary Assembly are elected for five years by the Assembly from a list of candidates proposed by the Committee of Ministers. The Secretariat has eight directorates, in addition to the Office of the Clerk of the Parliamentary Assembly.

(7) **Committees of Experts.** Among the Council's committees of experts are (i) the European Committee on Legal Co-operation (CDCJ), which drafts conventions and recommendations on questions relating to civil, commercial, administrative and international law and encourages consultation in the preparatory stages of legislation, and (ii) the European Committee on Crime Problems (CDPC) with competence in penal law, criminology and penology, and assisted by a Criminological Scientific Council of seven distinguished criminologists.

The Council for Cultural Co-operation (CCC) (on which all member states and also Finland and the Holy See are represented) implements the Council of Europe's educational and cultural programme.

The Committee for the Development of Sport (with the same membership as the CCC) was formed in 1977 and implements a European Sport for All Charter drawn up in 1975 by European ministers responsible for sport.

(8) **The European Resettlement Fund.** This Fund was set up in 1956 under an agreement by eight of the Council of Europe's member states with a subscribed capital of $7,000,000. By 1979 the Fund had 18 member states (Belgium, Cyprus, Denmark, France, the Federal Republic of Germany, Greece, the Holy See, Iceland, Italy, Liechtenstein, Luxembourg, Malta, the Netherlands, Norway, Portugal, Sweden, Switzerland and Turkey). By 1982 the Fund had made loans totalling $1,793,950,000 for programmes designed to create opportunities for employment of refugees and surplus population and for resettlement overseas.

CONVENTIONS AND AGREEMENTS
Human Rights

The *European Convention for the Protection of Human Rights and Fundamental Freedoms*, signed in Rome on Nov. 4, 1950, and in force since Sept. 3, 1953, differs from the Universal Declaration on Human Rights of 1948 [see page 18] in that it sets up machinery for the examination of complaints of any violation of human rights and fundamental freedoms on the part of signatories to the convention. These decision-taking bodies are the European Commission of Human Rights and the European Court of Human Rights.

All member-countries of the Council of Europe have signed and ratified the convention and are thus bound by its provisions.

The principal provisions relating to specific human rights are given below:

Art. 2. (1) Everyone's right to life shall be protected by law. No one shall be deprived of his life intentionally save in the execution of a sentence of a court following his conviction of a crime for which this penalty is provided by law. . . .

Art. 3. No one shall be subjected to torture or to inhuman or degrading treatment or punishment.

Art. 4. (1) No one shall be held in slavery or servitude.

(2) No one shall be required to perform forced or compulsory labour.

Art. 5. (1) Everyone has the right to liberty and security of person. . . .

Art. 6. (1) In the determination of his civil rights and obligations, or of any criminal charge against him, everyone is entitled to a fair and public hearing within a reasonable time by an independent and impartial tribunal established by law. . . .

Art. 7. (1) No one shall be held guilty of any criminal offence on account of any act or omission which did not constitute a criminal offence under national or international law at the time when it was committed. Nor shall a heavier penalty be imposed than the one that was applicable at the time the criminal offence was committed. . . .

Art. 8. (1) Everyone has the right to respect for his private and family life, his home and his correspondence. . . .

Art. 9. (1) Everyone has the right to freedom of thought, conscience and religion. . . .

Art. 10. (1) Everyone has the right to freedom of expression.

Art. 11. (1) Everyone has the right to freedom of peaceful assembly and to freedom of association with others. . . .

Art. 12. Men and women of marriageable age have the right to marry and to found a family. . . .

Art. 14. The enjoyment of the rights and freedoms set forth in this convention shall be secured without discrimination on any ground such as sex, race, colour, language, religion, political or other opinion, national or social origin, association with a national minority, property, birth or other status. . . .

The *Fourth Protocol* to the convention, which came into force on May 2, 1968, provides for freedom from imprisonment for inability to fulfil a contractual obligation; freedom of movement and residence; freedom from exile; and a guarantee against the collective expulsion of exiles.

The **European Commission of Human Rights** is composed of a number of representatives equal to that of the High Contracting Parties to the convention. It is competent to receive petitions from governments or individuals claiming violation of the provisions of the convention. Before the Commission could begin to exercise its powers, which it did on July 5, 1955, its competence to receive individual petitions had to be recognized by a minimum of six signatory countries.

After it has examined a petition and tried to bring about a settlement, the commission submits a report to the Committee of Ministers of the Council of Europe, which then decides, by a majority of two-thirds of its members, whether there has been a violation of the convention. In some cases, however, the matter is referred to the Court of Human Rights.

The **European Court of Human Rights** consists of a number of judges equal to that of the members of the Council of Europe. Under Article 56 of the convention, the Court of Human Rights could come into being only when eight of the High Contracting Parties had declared acceptance of the Court's compulsory jurisdiction. The Icelandic and Austrian declarations of acceptance

on Sept. 3, 1958, brought the total of acceptances up to the required number.

The Court functions through a chamber composed of seven judges. Only the Commission of Human Rights and the governments of the High Contracting Parties to the convention may bring a case before the Court, and then only after the Commission has acknowledged the failure of efforts to reach a friendly settlement. The judgment of the Court is final.

The original provisions of the convention dealing with the Commission and Court of Human Rights have been amended by the *Second* and *Third Protocols*, which came into force on Nov. 21, 1970. The *Second Protocol* gives the Court of Human Rights advisory powers in legal matters concerning the convention, while the *Third Protocol* amends the original convention to accelerate and simplify procedure before the Commission of Human Rights.

The Court's decisions are accepted as final by all member countries except Malta and Turkey.

A *European Agreement relating to Persons participating in Proceedings of the European Commission and Court of Human Rights*, concluded on May 6, 1969, and in force since April 17, 1971, provides for freedom of movement and of correspondence for such persons and confers immunity with respect to statements or documents submitted to those institutions.

The Sixth Protocol to the convention, signed on April 18, 1983, by 12 of the 21 member countries of the Council of Europe, enshrined the principle of the abolition of the death penalty, although not in respect of acts committed in times of war or of imminent threat of war, when it should be applied only in the instances laid down in the relevant national law and strictly in accordance with its provisions. The death penalty was then retained in law for certain non-military crimes in only six Council member countries—Belgium, Cyprus, Greece, Ireland, Liechtenstein and Turkey; in the last-named country executions of convicted terrorists had been resumed in 1980. The protocol came into force on Feb. 21, 1985 after ratification by Austria, Denmark, Spain, Sweden and Luxembourg.

The Seventh Protocol to the convention, opened for signature on Nov. 22, 1984, protected and guaranteed (i) the rights of aliens to procedural guarantees in the event of expulsion from the territory of a state; (ii) the right of a convicted person to have his sentence reviewed by a higher tribunal; (iii) the right to compensation in the event of a miscarriage of justice; (iv) the right of any person not to be tried or punished in criminal proceedings for an offence of which he had already been acquitted or convicted; and (v) equality of rights and responsibilities of spouses.

Peaceful Settlement of Disputes

The *European Convention for the Peaceful Settlement of Disputes* was signed in Strasbourg on April 29, 1957, and came into force on April 30, 1958, for those countries which had ratified it.

Under this convention the signatories agreed to submit to the International Court of Justice all international legal disputes which might arise between them. For other disputes the convention provided for the establishment of a five-member Conciliation Commission whenever requested by a party to a dispute, and also for an Arbitral Tribunal for such disputes as remained unresolved within one month after the end of the conciliation procedure.

(In an agreement concluded between Austria and Italy on July 17, 1971, the provisions of the convention were made retroactive to before the date of its entry into force for these two countries.)

The European Social Charter

In order to provide protection for social rights, as the Convention for Human Rights protects civil and political rights, the *European Social Charter* was drawn up by a Social Committee of experts in collaboration with the International Labour Office, the Parliamentary Assembly of the Council of Europe, and employers and trade union organizations. After approval by the Committee of Ministers, the charter was signed on Oct. 18, 1961, and came into effect on Feb. 26, 1965.

In Part I of the charter, the signatory governments "accept as the aim of their policy, to be pursued by all appropriate means, both national and international in character, the attainment of conditions in which the following rights and principles may be effectively realized:

"(1) Everyone shall have the opportunity to earn his living in an occupation freely entered upon.

"(2) All workers have the right to just conditions of work.

"(3) All workers have the right to safe and healthy working conditions.

"(4) All workers have the right to a fair remuneration sufficient for a decent standard of living for themselves and their families.

"(5) All workers and employers have the right to freedom of association in national or international organizations for the protection of their economic and social interests.

"(6) All workers and employers have the right to bargain collectively.

"(7) Children and young persons have the right to a special protection against the physical and moral hazards to which they are exposed.

"(8) Employed women, in case of maternity, and other employed women as appropriate, have the right to a special protection in their work.

"(9) Everyone has the right to appropriate facilities for vocational guidance with a view to helping him choose an occupation suited to his personal aptitude and interests.

"(10) Everyone has the right to appropriate facilities for vocational training.

"(11) Everyone has the right to benefit from any measures enabling him to enjoy the highest possible standard of health attainable.

"(12) All workers and their dependants have the right to social security.

"(13) Anyone without adequate resources has the right to social and medical assistance.

"(14) Everyone has the right to benefit from social and welfare services.

"(15) Disabled persons have the right to vocational training, rehabilitation and resettlement, whatever the origin and nature of their disability.

"(16) The family as a fundamental unit of society has the right to appropriate social, legal and economic protection to ensure its full development.

"(17) Mothers and children, irrespective of marital status and family relations, have the right to appropriate social and economic protection.

"(18) The nationals of any one of the Contracting Parties have the right to engage in any gainful occupation in the territory of any one of the others on a footing of equality with the nationals of the latter, subject to restrictions based on cogent economic or social reasons.

"(19) Migrant workers who are nationals of a Contracting Party and their families have the right to protection and assistance in the territory of any other Contracting Party."

Parts II and III of the charter, comprising 38 articles, lay down procedures for the application of the above principles, and include provisions for (i) derogations in time of war or emergency; (ii) the partial or complete application of the charter by a signatory government to non-metropolitan territories for whose international relations it is responsible; and (iii) the granting to refugees of "treatment as favourable as possible". Acceptance of Part I of the charter (the statement of aims) and of a specified minimum of individual articles was laid down as a requirement for ratification by a signatory government.

Suppression of Terrorism

A *European Convention on the Suppression of Terrorism* was adopted by the Council's Committee of Ministers at deputy level on Nov. 10, 1976 (with Ireland abstaining from voting on it). It was formally concluded on Jan. 27, 1977, and came into force on Aug. 4, 1978 [see below].

The aim of the convention was to facilitate the extradition and prosecution of perpetrators of terrorist acts even though such acts might be politically motivated and therefore be excluded from extradition arrangements.

The provisions of the convention are as follows:

Art. 1 stated: "For the purposes of extradition between contracting states none of the following offences shall be regarded as a political offence or as an offence connected with a political offence or as an offence inspired by political motives.

"(*a*) An offence within the scope of the Convention for the Suppression of Unlawful Seizure of Aircraft, signed at The Hague on Dec. 16, 1970 [see page 38];

"(*b*) an offence within the scope of the Convention for the Suppression of Unlawful Acts against the Safety of Civil Aviation, signed at Montreal on Sept. 23, 1971 [ibid.];

"(*c*) a serious offence involving an attack against the life, physical integrity or liberty of internationally protected persons, including diplomatic agents;

"(*d*) an offence involving kidnapping, the taking of a hostage or serious unlawful detention;

"(*e*) an offence involving the use of a bomb, grenade, rocket, automatic firearm or letter or petrol bomb if this use endangers persons;

"(*f*) an attempt to commit any of the foregoing offences or participation as an accomplice of a person who commits or attempts to commit such an offence."

Art. 2 specified that in addition to the offences listed in Article 1, contracting states might also "decide not to regard as a political offence . . . a serious offence involving an act of violence . . . against life, physical integrity or liberty of a person" or one which "created a collective danger for persons". The same option would apply also to "an attempt to commit any of the foregoing offences or participation as an accomplice of a person who commits or attempts to commit such an offence".

Art. 3 stated: "The provisions of all extradition treaties and arrangements applicable between contracting states . . . are modified . . . to the extent that they are incompatible with this convention."

Art. 4 provided that any of the offences mentioned in Articles 1 and 2 which were not listed as extraditable offences in existing extradition arrangements between contracting states "shall be deemed to be included as such therein".

Art. 5 stated: "Nothing in this convention shall be interpreted as imposing an obligation to extradite if the requested state has substantial grounds for believing that the request for extradition for an offence mentioned in Article 1 or 2 has been made for the purpose of prosecuting or punishing a person on account of his race, religion, nationality or political opinion, or that the person's position may be prejudiced for any of these reasons."

Art. 6 committed a contracting state to taking "such measures as may be necessary to establish its jurisdiction over an offence mentioned in Article 1 in the case where the suspected offender is present in its territory and it does not extradite him after receiving a request for extradition from a contracting state whose jurisdiction is based on a rule of jurisdiction existing equally in the law of the requested state".

The article also specified that the convention "does not exclude any criminal jurisdiction exercised in accordance with national law".

Art. 7 stated: "A contracting state in whose territory a person suspected to have committed an offence mentioned in Article 1 is found and which has received a request for extradition under the conditions mentioned in Article 6 . . . shall, if it does not extradite that person, submit the case, without exception whatsoever and without undue delay, to its competent authorities for the purpose of prosecution. Those authorities shall take their decision in the same manner as in the case of any offence of a serious nature under the law of that state."

Art. 8 provided: "(1) Contracting states shall afford one another the widest measure of mutual assistance in criminal matters in connexion with proceedings brought in respect of the offences mentioned in Article 1 or 2. The law of the requested state concerning the mutual assistance in criminal matters shall apply in all cases. Nevertheless this assistance may not be refused on the sole ground that it concerns a political offence or an offence connected with a political offence or an offence inspired by political motives."

Similarly to Article 5, the article also specified that a requested state would be under no obligation to provide such mutual assistance if it had grounds for believing that it might lead to prosecution or punishment on account of a person's race, religion, nationality or political opinion, or that the person's position might be prejudiced for any of these reasons.

Article 8 also stated that all existing mutual assistance treaties and arrangements between contracting states "are modified . . . to the extent that they are incompatible with this convention".

Art. 9 specified that the Council of Europe's European Committee on Crime Problems "shall be kept informed regarding the application of this convention" and "shall do whatever is needful to facilitate a friendly settlement of any difficulty which may arise out of its execution".

Art. 10 stipulated: "(1) Any dispute between contracting states concerning the interpretation or application of this convention which has not been settled in the framework of Article 9 . . . shall, at the request of any party to the dispute, be referred to arbitration. Each party shall nominate an arbitrator and the two arbitrators shall nominate a referee. If any party has not nominated its arbitrator within the three months following the request for arbitration, he shall be nominated at the request of the other party by the President of the European Court of Human Rights. If the latter should be a national of one of the parties to the dispute, this duty shall be carried out by the Vice-President of the court or, if the Vice-President is a national of one of the parties to the dispute, by the most senior judge of the court not being a national of one of the parties to the dispute. The same procedure shall be observed if the arbitrators cannot agree on the choice of referee.

"(2) The arbitration tribunal shall lay down its own procedure. Its decision shall be taken by majority vote. Its award shall be final."

Art. 11 stated (i) that the convention was open to signature by the member states of the Council of Europe and subject to

ratification, acceptance or approval—instruments in respect of the latter procedure to be deposited with the Secretary-General of the Council of Europe; (ii) that it would enter into force three months after the date of the deposit of the third instrument of ratification, acceptance or approval; and (iii) that in respect of a signatory state ratifying, accepting or approving subsequently, the convention would come into force three months after the deposit of appropriate instruments.

Art. 12 stipulated (i) that at ratification contracting states could "specify the territory or territories to which this convention shall apply"; and (ii) that either at ratification or at any later date a contracting state could by means of a declaration "extend this convention to any other territory or territories specified in the declaration and for whose international relations it is responsible or on whose behalf it is authorized to give undertakings".

Art. 13 stated: "(1) Any state may at the time of signature or when depositing its instrument of ratification, acceptance or approval, declare that it reserves the right to refuse extradition in respect of any offence mentioned in Article 1 which it considers to be a political offence, an offence connected with a political offence or an offence inspired by political motives, provided that it undertakes to take into due consideration, when evaluating the character of the offence, any particularly serious aspects of the offence, including:

"(a) That it created a collective danger to the life, physical integrity or liberty of persons; or

"(b) that it affected persons foreign to the motives behind it; or

"(c) that cruel or vicious means have been used in the commission of the offence.

"(2) Any state which has made a reservation in accordance with the foregoing paragraph may wholly or partly withdraw it. Such withdrawal shall be effected by means of a declaration, addressed to the Secretary-General of the Council of Europe, which shall become effective as from the date of its receipt.

"(3) A state which has made a reservation in accordance with paragraph 1 of this article may not claim the application of Article 1 by any other state; it may, however, if its reservation is partial or conditional, claim the application of that article in so far as it has itself accepted it."

Art. 14 provided that any contracting state could denounce the convention by means of a written notification addressed to the Secretary-General of the Council of Europe and that any such denunciation would take effect immediately or at such later date as might be specified in the notice.

Art. 15 stated that the convention "ceases to have effect in respect of any contracting state which withdraws from or ceases to be a member of the Council of Europe".

Art. 16 laid down that the Secretary-General of the Council of Europe should notify member states of all signatures, ratifications, entries into force, declarations, etc., as provided for under the terms of the convention.

Following ratification by Austria (in August 1977), Sweden (in September 1977) and the Federal Republic of Germany (in January 1978), the convention came into force on Aug. 4, 1978. It was later also ratified by Denmark (on Sept. 28, 1978), the United Kingdom (on Oct. 25, 1978), Cyprus (on May 27, 1979), Liechtenstein (on Sept. 14, 1979), Norway (on April 14, 1980), Spain (on Aug. 21, 1980), Iceland (on Oct. 12, 1980), Turkey (on Aug. 20, 1981), Luxembourg (on Dec. 12, 1981), Portugal (on March 15, 1982), Switzerland (on Aug. 20, 1983) and the Netherlands (on July 19, 1985), coming into force for these countries on the dates shown.

Other Conventions and Agreements in Force

	Date of Entry into Force
Social Matters	
Interim Agreements on Social Security	July 1, 1954
Convention and Protocol on Social and Medical Assistance	July 1, 1954
European Code of Social Security and Protocol thereto	March 17, 1968
Convention on the Adoption of Children	April 26, 1968
Agreement on "au pair" Placement	May 30, 1971
Convention on Social Security and Supplementary Agreement for the Application of the European Convention on Social Security	March 1, 1972
Convention on the Social Protection of Farmers	June 17, 1977
Convention on the Legal Status of Children born out of Wedlock	Aug. 11, 1978
Public Health	
Agreement on Exchange of War Cripples for Medical Treatment	Jan. 1, 1956
Agreement on Exchange of Therapeutic Substances of Human Origin (Creation of European "Blood Bank")	Jan. 1, 1959
Agreement on Duty-free Importation of Medical, Surgical and Laboratory Equipment	July 29, 1960
Agreement for Mutual Assistance in Special Medical Treatment and Climatic Facilities	June 15, 1962
Agreement for Exchange of Blood Grouping Reagents	Oct. 14, 1962
Agreement on the Issue to Civil and Military War Disabled of International Vouchers for the Repair of Prosthetic and Orthopaedic Appliances	Dec. 27, 1963
Agreement on the Instruction and Education of Nurses	Aug. 7, 1969
Agreement on the Restriction of the Use of Certain Detergents in Washing and Cleaning Products	Feb. 16, 1971
Convention on the Elaboration of a European Pharmacopoeia	May 5, 1974
Agreement on the Transfer of Corpses	Nov. 11, 1975
Agreement on the Exchange of Tissue-Typing Reagents	April 23, 1977
Cultural Matters	
Convention on Equivalence of Diplomas for Admission to Universities	April 20, 1954
European Cultural Convention (designed "to foster among the nationals of all members . . . the study of the languages, history and civilization of the others and of the civilization which is common to them all")	May 5, 1955
Convention on Equivalence of Periods of University Studies	Sept. 18, 1957
Convention on Academic Recognition of University Qualifications	Nov. 27, 1961
Convention on the Protection of the Archaeological Heritage	Nov. 20, 1970
Agreement on continued Payment of Scholarships to Students studying abroad	Oct. 2, 1971
Patents	
Convention relating to Formalities required for Patent Applications	June 1, 1955
Convention on International Classification of Patents	Aug. 1, 1955
Television and Broadcasting	
Agreement on Programme Exchanges by Means of Television Films	July 1, 1961
Agreements for Protection of Television Broadcasts	July 1, 1961
Agreement for the Prevention of Broadcasts transmitted from Stations outside National Territories	Oct. 19, 1967
International Law	
Convention on Information on Foreign Law	Dec. 17, 1969
Convention on State Immunity	June 11, 1976

[cont. on next page]

Penal Law

Convention on Extradition[1]	April 18, 1960
Convention on Mutual Assistance in Criminal Matters	June 12, 1962
Convention on the Punishment of Road Traffic Offences	Aug. 18, 1972
Convention on the International Validity of Criminal Judgments	July 26, 1974
Convention on the Supervision of conditionally sentenced or conditionally released Offenders	Aug. 22, 1975
Convention on the Transfer of Proceedings in Criminal Matters	March 30, 1978
Convention allowing Prisoners Abroad to serve their Sentences in their Home Country	Aug. 1, 1985

Other Legal Matters

Agreement relating to Application of the European Convention on International Commercial Arbitration	Jan. 25, 1965
Convention on Establishment (laying down common rules for the treatment of nationals of member states on an equal footing when residing in each other's countries)	Feb. 23, 1965
Convention on Liability of Hotel-keepers for Property of their Guests	Feb. 15, 1967
Convention on the Reduction of Cases of Multiple Nationality and on Military Obligations in Cases of Multiple Nationality	March 28, 1968
Convention on Compulsory Insurance against Civil Liability in respect of Motor Vehicles	Sept. 22, 1969
Convention for the Protection of Animals during International Transport	Feb. 20, 1971
Convention on the Establishment of a Scheme of Registration of Wills	March 20, 1976
Agreement on the Transmission of Applications for Legal Aid	Feb. 28, 1977
Convention for the Protection of Animals kept for Farming Purposes	Sept. 10, 1978
Convention relating to Stops on Bearer Securities in International Circulation	Feb. 11, 1979

Movement of Persons

Agreement on Regulations governing Movement of Persons between States	Jan. 1, 1958
Agreement on Abolition of Visas for Refugees	Sept. 3, 1960
Agreement on Travel by Young Persons on Collective Passports	Jan. 1, 1962

[1] This convention, signed on Dec. 13, 1957, was by Dec. 31, 1975, in force for Austria,* Cyprus, Denmark,* Finland, the Federal Republic of Germany, Greece, Iceland, Ireland, Israel, Italy,* Liechtenstein, Luxembourg, the Netherlands,* Norway,* Spain, Sweden,* Switzerland* and Turkey (* with additional agreements).

The European Convention on Extradition provided for the extradition (by the parties to the convention) of persons sought by the requesting state for prosecution, sentence or detention (for offences other than political ones). Under a first additional protocol of Oct. 15, 1979, and in force from Aug. 20, 1979, war crimes and crimes against humanity were excluded from the category of political offences to which extradition did not apply. A second additional protocol, signed on March 17, 1978, and in force from June 5, 1983, inter alia contained new provisions concerning fiscal offences, judgments in absentia and amnesty.

A *Convention on the Elimination of Spectator Violence at Sporting Events with Particular Reference to Football Matches* was opened for signature on Aug. 19, 1985.

The conventions and agreements reflect a general European consensus and may be signed and applied by governments in their territories. It is rare for a convention to be ratified by all the Council's member states, but almost all of them are open to non-member states and thus allow for international co-operation beyond Europe (e.g. under the Convention on the Suppression of Terrorism).

The Nordic Council

Address. Box 19506, 10432 Stockholm 19, Sweden.

Officer. Ilkka-Christian Björklund (sec.).

Founded. Feb. 13, 1953.

Membership. Denmark, Finland (since Oct. 28, 1955), Iceland, Norway and Sweden.

History. The establishment of such a Council had first been advocated by a Danish Foreign Minister in 1939 and had been recommended by the Nordic Interparliamentary Union in 1951. This recommendation was approved by the Foreign Ministers of Denmark, Norway and Sweden and the Icelandic Minister in Copenhagen on March 16, 1952.

Objects. In its relations with the Parliaments of the participating countries, the functions of the Nordic Council are purely advisory and aimed at "stimulating initiative and shaping opinion", though its decisions have no binding character. It was, however, to develop the existing co-operation between the Scandinavian countries; aim at co-ordinating their legislation wherever desirable; as far as possible, try to bring about uniformity in administrative practice as far as the status of their citizens is concerned; deal with all such questions where there is a possibility of co-ordinated action; submit suitable proposals to the governments concerned; and stimulate joint initiative. The sovereignty of the participating countries is not affected.

Structure. The Council meets annually and is composed of 18 members from each of the Parliaments of Denmark, Finland, Norway and Sweden and six from the Icelandic *Althing,* as well as some 40 non-voting government representatives. It has seven standing committees (on economic, on cultural, on legal and on social and environmental affairs, and on communications, on the budget and on information). It has a five-member Presidium in charge of work between Council sessions and with its own secretariat. There are separate secretariats in each member country.

The Nordic Council of Ministers

Address. St. Olavs gate 29, Postboks 6753, Oslo 1 Norway; Snaregade 10, 1205 Copenhagen, Denmark.

Founded. July 1, 1971.

Membership. Denmark, Finland, Iceland, Norway and Sweden.

Objects. This Council implements the co-operation between the five Nordic countries as regulated by the revised *Treaty of Nordic Co-operation* (the *Helsinki Convention*) (see below).

Structure. The Council's meetings are attended by member countries' ministers with responsibility for the subject under discussion. Unanimous decisions taken by the Council are binding on the member countries unless they are subject to parliamentary approval in each member country (which has in its cabinet a Minister for Nordic Co-operation). There are a secretariat with three divisions; a Secretariat for Nordic Cultural Co-operation; and two committees (of ministerial deputies and of senior civil servants).

INSTITUTIONS

The numerous institutions set up under Nordic Council auspices include the following:

The **Nordic Institute for Theoretical Atomic Physics** (NORDITA), established in Copenhagen as a result of a Nordic Council decision taken in February 1957 to promote scientific research, co-operation in theoretical atomic physics and advanced training for physicists from the Council's five member states.

The **Nordic Investment Bank**, set up under an agreement signed by the Council of Ministers on Dec. 4, 1975, with an initial capital equivalent to SDRs 400,000,000 (with Sweden contributing 45 per cent, Denmark 22 per cent, Finland and Norway 16 per cent each and Iceland 1 per cent), and with headquarters in Helsinki, where the bank was inaugurated on June 9, 1976.

NORDIC CO-OPERATION AGREEMENTS AND CONVENTIONS

At its first meeting on Feb. 20–21, 1953, the Council set up committees to deal with economic, cultural, social and legal matters, and a further one to deal with questions of communications. Recommendations of the committees adopted by the Council included the relaxation and eventual abolition of all passport and currency controls for inter-Scandinavian travel by nationals of the Council's member countries, and increased economic, social, cultural and postal co-operation.

On May 22, 1954, representatives of the Council's four member countries signed an agreement creating a single labour market, to come into force on July 1, 1954. They also concluded an agreement exempting Danish, Finnish, Norwegian and Swedish nationals from the need to carry a passport when entering any of the four countries or to obtain residential permits for stays longer than three months (as required hitherto).

A *Convention on Social Security,* adopted in 1955, provided for co-operation in social and health policy, the text being amended in 1975 so as to establish new rights concerning sickness, pregnancy and birth.

Under a convention concluded on July 12, 1957, all identity controls at frontiers between member states were lifted, including that over foreigners who had entered one member country and wished to proceed to another. The provisions concerning foreigners were, however, modified as from Aug. 26, 1979, under an agreement enabling each member country to reserve the right to restore regular and permanent control of foreigners' movements (as had been desired by Sweden in order to stem clandestine immigration via Denmark).

At a meeting held in Helsinki on March 23, 1962, the Council's five member nations initialled a *Treaty of Nordic Co-operation,* also known as the *Helsinki Convention,* covering the principal subjects of Nordic co-operation since 1953. The main provisions of the treaty (which was amended on Feb. 13, 1971, and on March 11, 1974) were as follows:

Cultural Co-operation. Uniformity of vocational training, mutual recognition of the validity of academic degrees and other examinations throughout the area, and joint planning of educational and research centres.

Juridical Co-operation. Mutual law enforcement, making judgments given by courts in one country enforceable also in the others, and co-operation in jurisprudence.

Social Co-operation. Co-operation of labour exchanges throughout the area; unification of vocational guidance; co-ordination of measures to protect workers; and social benefits and welfare measures in each member country to be the same for citizens of the other countries as for its own citizens—the aim of all these measures being the continuation of the existing single labour market.

Economic Co-operation. Mutual consultation on economic policy, with emphasis on the possibility of parallel measures; co-ordination of production and investment, and promotion of direct arrangements between private enterprises in two or more of the Nordic countries; maximum possible freedom of capital investment in the Nordic area; mutual consultation on questions of international trade policy; joint development measures for regions belonging to two or more member countries, if economically desirable; co-operation in trying to find joint solutions on payments and foreign exchange questions; co-ordination of customs legislation; simplification of customs rules to facilitate mutual commercial exchanges; maximum facilities for border traffic; collaboration in projects to assist under-developed countries; and co-ordination of statistics.

Communications. Co-operation in the construction of communications, and joint measures relating to safety of road traffic.

A Nordic agreement relating to the administration of joint assistance projects in developing countries was signed on July 18, 1968, with a supplementary protocol being signed on Dec. 3, 1971, and a protocol on the accession of Iceland on May 25, 1973.

Other Nordic agreements include one on co-operation, concluded on March 23, 1962 (repeatedly amended, most recently on June 15, 1983), and another on cultural co-operation, signed on March 15, 1971 (amended on June 13, 1983).

Harmonization of Nordic Law. The Nordic Council has achieved almost perfect harmonization in certain areas of the law (especially in civil and family law, in mercantile law and in copyright, patents, trade marks and industrial designs) and in the common principles of basic legal rules.

A Nordic Transport Agreement of 1974 provided for both collaboration and division of labour with the object of achieving increased efficiency in transport and communications.

In October 1975 agreement was reached on voting rights, and in 1976 all Nordic citizens who had been resident in Finland and Sweden for the preceding three years obtained the right to vote in local elections.

An environmental protection agreement was concluded between Denmark, Finland, Norway and Sweden on Feb. 19, 1974.

BILATERAL AGREEMENTS BETWEEN NORDIC COUNTRIES

Denmark and Iceland. Agreement on peaceful settlement of Disputes of June 27, 1930.

Trade agreement of June 4, 1948.

Denmark and Sweden. Commerce and navigation treaty of Nov. 2, 1826.

Agreement on peaceful settlement of disputes of Jan. 14, 1926.

Agreement on co-operation in the field of natural gas of Feb. 29, 1980.

Agreement on trade between Sweden and Greenland of Dec. 4, 1984.

Finland and Iceland. Treaty of commerce and navigation of Dec. 12, 1923.

Agreement on peaceful settlement of disputes of June 27, 1930.

Finland and Sweden. Navigation agreement of May 29, 1963.

Convention on peaceful settlement of disputes of Jan. 29, 1926; amended on April 9, 1953.

Trade agreement of Dec. 14, 1927.

Iceland and Norway. Treaty of commerce and navigation of Nov. 2, 1826.

Agreement on peaceful settlement of disputes of June 27, 1930.

Agreement on the continental shelf in the area between Iceland and Jan Mayen of Oct. 22, 1981.

Iceland and Sweden. Treaty of commerce and navigation of Nov. 2, 1826.

Agreement on peaceful settlement of disputes of June 27, 1983.

Norway and Sweden. Convention on peaceful settlement of disputes of Nov. 25, 1925.

Declaration on Sweden's and Norway's maritime territory in the north-eastern Skagerrak of April 5, 1967.

Agreement on economic co-operation (in industry, energy and the supply of electricity by Sweden to Norway in return for Norwegian petroleum products) of March 25, 1981.

Agreement on co-operation in the operation of communication satellites of April 12, 1983.

Belgium-Luxembourg Economic Union (BLEU)

Address. rue de la Loi 81 A, B-1040 Brussels, Belgium.

Founded. May 1922.

History. The BLEU, a monetary and customs union between the two countries, was established under a Brussels Treaty signed on July 25, 1921, and ratified by Belgium on March 5, 1922. After the German occupation of 1940–44 the BLEU was restored on May 1, 1945. It was extended for 10 years in 1977 and for another 10 years on March 9, 1981, when it was decided to set up a Luxembourg Monetary Institute in order to give Luxembourg greater economic autonomy. The Brussels Treaty was not formally ratified by Luxembourg's Parliament until March 9, 1983. After the creation of the Luxembourg Monetary Institute later that year, the proportion of Belgium's fiduciary money actually issued by Luxembourg was increased from 5 per cent to 20 per cent. All decisions on interest rates and foreign exchange rates, however, continued to be made by the Belgian National Bank in Brussels.

Benelux Economic Union

Address. 39 rue de la Régence, 1000 Brussels, Belgium.

Officer. Drs E. D. J. Kruijtbosch (sec. gen.).

Founded. Nov. 1, 1960.

Membership. Belgium, Luxembourg and the Netherlands.

Objects. The free mutual movement of persons, goods, services and capital; the co-ordination of national economic policies; and the pursuance of a common trade policy towards other countries.

History. On Sept. 5, 1944, the Governments of Belgium, Luxembourg and the Netherlands—then in exile in London—signed a treaty establishing Benelux. It was not until Jan. 1, 1948, however, that the London agreement, involving measures to introduce a common customs tariff *vis-à-vis* third countries and to abolish import duties in mutual trade relations, could come into force. The organs provided for in the London agreement—a Customs Regulation Council, a Trade Treaties Council and an Economic Union Council—were set up at the same time.

At a ministerial conference in Luxembourg in October 1949 the three countries concluded the so-called Pre-Union Treaty, as an introductory stage to a fully-fledged economic union. Under this treaty, the exchange of goods between the three countries was made progressively free from quantitative restrictions, except for a special arrangement for agricultural products, and the three countries undertook not to change this liberalization of their mutual trade except by common agreement.

A period of instability for Benelux in the early 1950s was followed on July 24, 1953, by a protocol which laid down that the member countries would in future co-ordinate their economic and social policies. A further protocol was signed on Dec. 9, 1953, under which the three countries started concluding joint trade agreements with third countries.

Further steps in the extension of economic co-operation between the Benelux countries included (a) the treaty of July 8, 1954, which largely liberalized the mutual exchange of capital; (b) a protocol signed on May 3, 1955, on the progressive harmonization of their agricultural policies within a seven-year period; and (c) the setting-up of a common labour market under interim regulations in April 1957, as a transitional stage in the implementation of a Labour Treaty which had been signed on June 7, 1955.

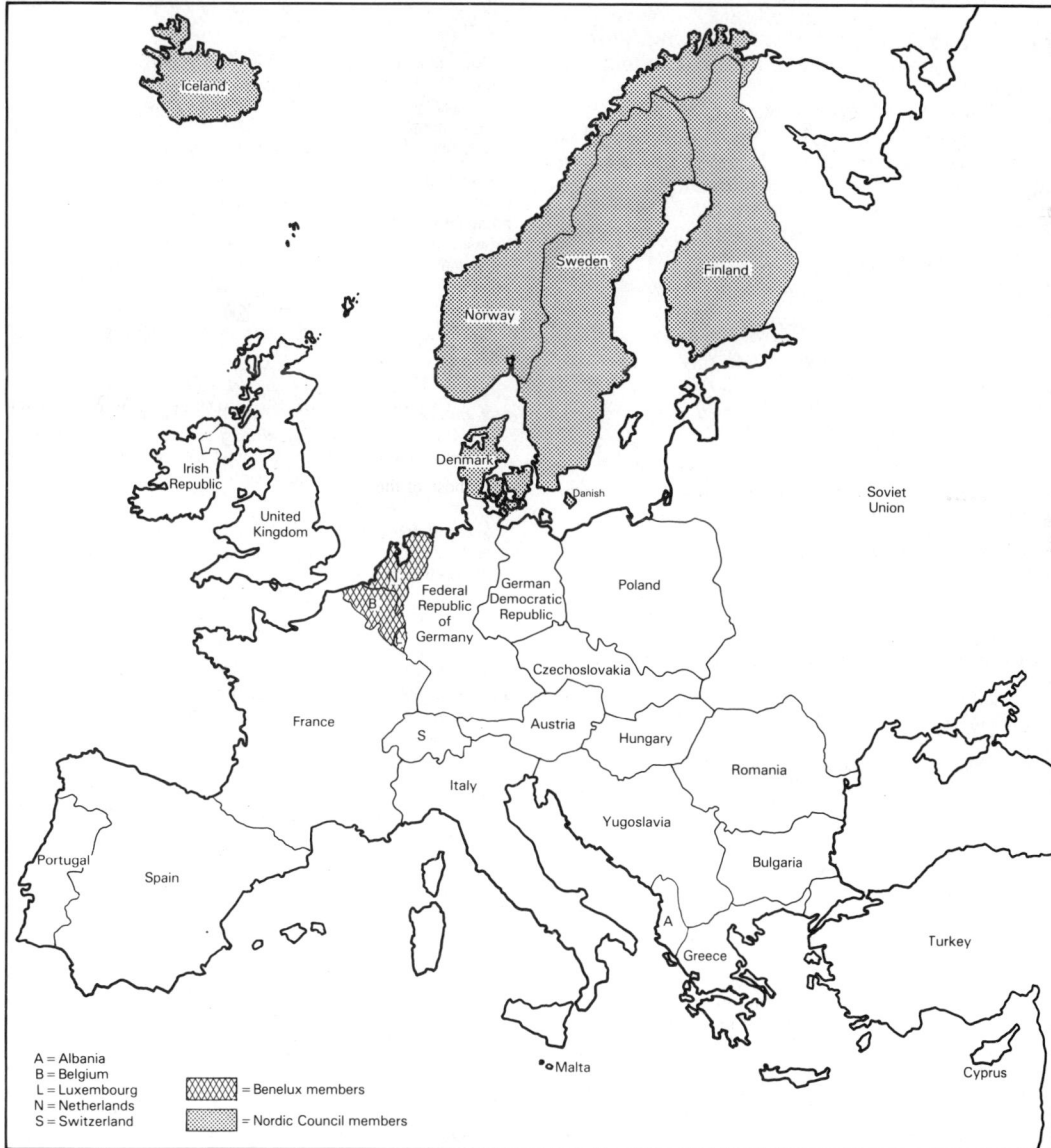

Map 3   Benelux Economic Union and Nordic Council

155

An agreement of Nov. 5, 1955, provided for the establishment of an Interparliamentary Benelux Advisory Council [see below]. The Economic Union Treaty was signed in The Hague on Feb. 3, 1958, and came into force on Nov. 1, 1960. On July 1, 1960, shortly before the treaty came into force, passport controls were abolished for nationals of the Benelux countries travelling between those countries. Foreigners travelling across the inner frontiers of the three countries could also, from that date, obtain a Benelux visa.

From Nov. 1, 1960, all remaining customs duties within the Benelux frontiers were abolished, and from Jan. 1, 1961, all trade agreements with third countries were to be concluded by Benelux as an entity. It was established that, by November 1965, all remaining obstacles to the free flow of goods among the three countries should be eliminated.

Following the "floating" of most of the world's major currencies in 1971, the three Benelux members decided on Aug. 21, 1971, to form a single monetary block whose currency exchange rates would not diverge by more than $1\frac{1}{2}$ per cent in either direction. This arrangement, however, was terminated on March 15, 1976.

BENELUX TREATY

The principal provisions of the treaty are summarized below:

Free Movement of Persons. The nationals of the three member countries will be free to move within the whole territory of the Economic Union, and the nationals of each member country will enjoy in the other two countries the same treatment as is accorded to the nationals of those countries.

Free Exchange of Goods, Capital and Services. Trade between the three countries will be free from all import duties, taxes or levies, as well as from any import or export restrictions of a quantitative, qualitative or currency nature; capital movements from one country to the other will also be free; the exchange of services will be subject to the same principles as merchandise trade.

Co-ordination of Economic, Financial and Social Policies. The three governments will jointly consult on their national economic policies with a view to creating the necessary conditions for the economic integration of their countries.

Co-ordinated and Joint Action towards Third Countries. In addition to co-ordinating their internal economic policies, member countries will also consult each other to determine the Union's attitude at meetings of international bodies and in matters relating to regional economic integration, or in relation to matters with third countries, insofar as these matters affect the aims of the Union. There will also be common policy to cover trade and payments with third countries.

The two principal provisions of Part IV laid down (1) that the scope of the treaty would be limited to the territories of the member countries in Europe, although the interests of Belgian and Dutch overseas territories could be safeguarded in trade agreements concluded with third countries; (2) that the treaty would be concluded for a period of 50 years, but could be tacitly extended by further 10-year terms unless any of the parties wished to terminate it by giving advance notice of one year.

INSTITUTIONS

The institutions of the Benelux Economic Union are as follows:

The Committee of Ministers. This committee, consisting of nine members (three from each member country), is the directing body of the Union, being charged with the implementation of the treaty and the taking of the necessary measures to that end. Decisions must be taken by unanimous vote and be binding on the three governments. The committee also gives directives to the bodies operating under it, and maintains contact with the Consultative Interparliamentary Council.

Interparliamentary Council. Consisting of 21 members each from Belgium and the Netherlands and seven from Luxembourg, the Consultative Interparliamentary Council (first established on Nov. 5, 1955) advises on questions of closer economic, political, cultural and legal co-operation between the three countries.

Council of the Economic Union. This body, which functions under the Committee of Ministers as a co-ordinator of the other institutions, consists of three chairmen appointed by each of the member governments, and of representatives of the committees similarly designated by member governments.

Committees and Special Committees. There are eight committees: on foreign economic relations; on monetary and financial questions; on industry and commerce; on agriculture, foods and fisheries; on customs duties and taxes; on transport; on social questions; and on the movement and establishment of persons.

There are also special committees for co-ordination statistics; comparing the budgets of public and semi-public institutions; public tenders; public health; the "trading middle class" (i.e. small and medium businesses); movement of persons (control at external frontiers); territorial planning; tourism; administrative and judicial co-operation; and the environment.

All these committees are empowered to make proposals to the directing organs of the Union; they also possess executive and supervisory powers regarding the administration of decrees by the member governments.

Secretariat-General. Established at Brussels, it is directed by a Netherlander, its organization and powers agreeing broadly with those of the Secretariat-General already existing under the Customs Agreement of 1944. To the budget of the Secretariat-General, Belgium and the Netherlands each contribute 48.5 per cent and Luxembourg 3 per cent.

Joint Services. The Committee of Ministers is empowered to institute joint services if a need for these should arise. Those set up by 1978 were (i) a Benelux Office for trade marks and brands and (ii) a Joint Service for the registration of medicaments.

Court of Arbitration. The original Board of Arbitrators set up to discuss disputes over the application of the treaty has been superseded by a Court of Arbitration. A convention concerning the establishment of such a court was adopted during a meeting of the Interparliamentary Council at The Hague on Feb. 22, 1964. Composed of three judges from each of the Benelux countries, the court supervises the execution of the Benelux Agreements.

Court of Justice. A Benelux Court of Justice, founded in 1974, consists of senior judges of the three member countries and has power to make binding decisions on the interpretation of common legal rules when requested by a national court, and serves in a consultative capacity when requested by a member government.

Economic and Social Consultative Council. This body (whose members are appointed by the three governments) gives advice—at the request of the Committee of Ministers or on its own initiative—on matters directly related to the operation of the Union. It has 27 members and 27 deputy members from economic and social organizations, with each of the three member countries supplying one-third of these members.

EARLIER TRADE AGREEMENTS

Trade agreements concluded before the estab-

lishment of the Benelux Economic Union by this Union's member countries were signed as follows:

Between the Belgium-Luxembourg Economic Union (BLEU) and Switzerland on Aug. 26, 1929.

Between the BLEU and the Netherlands on the one hand and Switzerland on the other on June 21, 1957 (amended on May 5, 1961).

Between the Benelux countries and Sweden on April 27, 1957.

The European Communities

Address of Commission. 200 rue de la Loi, 1049 Brussels, Belgium.

Officer. Jacques Delors (pres. of Commission).

Founded. July 1, 1967.

Membership. Belgium, Denmark*, France, Federal Republic of Germany, Greece†, Italy, Ireland*, Luxembourg, the Netherlands, Portugal§, Spain§, and the United Kingdom* (* with effect from Jan. 1, 1973; † with effect from Jan. 1, 1981; § with effect from Jan. 1, 1986).

Greenland, which had entered the Communities when it was still under full Danish rule, left the Communities with effect from Feb. 1, 1985, following a referendum held on Feb. 23, 1982, when 12,615 votes were cast for Greenland's withdrawal and 11,180 votes against (there being a 52 per cent majority in favour of withdrawal in a 75 per cent turnout).

With the accession of Portugal and Spain in 1986 the Communities' population was increased to over 320,000,000 and its surface area to 2,255,000 sq. km.

History. The three European Communities— European Coal and Steel Community (ECSC), European Economic Community (EEC), and European Atomic Energy Community (Euratom)—were formed under separate treaties and, until July 1967, were directed by separate organs, while sharing a common European Parliament and Court of Justice. A treaty providing for the merger of the High Authority of the ECSC, the Commission of the EEC, and the Commission of Euratom, and the merger of the Councils of Ministers of all three, was signed on April 8, 1965, the mergers coming into effect on July 1, 1967.

European Coal and Steel Community (ECSC)

The European Coal and Steel Community was set up under a 50-year treaty, providing for the institution of a common market by the abolition of import and export duties, subsidies and other restrictive practices on the movement of coal and steel between the participating countries. The Community is financed by a levy of 0.25 per cent on the value of production.

Creation of the ECSC. On May 9, 1950, the French Foreign Minister, Robert Schuman, issued a declaration approved by the French Cabinet,

proposing the creation of a single authority to control the production of coal and steel in France and the Federal Republic of Germany. The organization would be open for membership to other European countries and would be associated with the United Nations. This plan, known as the "Schuman Plan", represented the first step towards a federation of Europe, since it proposed that individual nations should entrust part of their sovereignty to a supra-national authority. It was felt that economic co-operation in Europe, particularly between France and Germany, which had long been traditional enemies, would form a firm basis for later political federation.

A six-nation conference for the pooling of the coal and steel resources of Western Europe under a supra-national authority, as put forward in the Schuman Plan, was held in Paris on June 20–27, 1950, and attended by delegations from France, the Federal Republic of Germany, Italy, Belgium, Luxembourg, and the Netherlands (the "Six"). Negotiations on the drafting of a treaty for the proposed Community continued throughout the following nine months, culminating in the signing in Paris, on April 18, 1951, of a Joint Declaration formally setting up the European Coal and Steel Community. The treaty entered into force on July 25, 1952, and the High Authority (created as the principal organ of the Community) began operations on Aug. 10, 1952.

Britain was an associate member of the ECSC until Dec. 31, 1972, whereupon it became a full member on its accession to the Communities on Jan. 1, 1973.

ECSC TREATY

The character, aims and functions of the ECSC are contained in Articles 1–6 of the treaty.

Art. 1. By the present treaty the High Contracting Parties institute among themselves a European Coal and Steel Community, based on a common market, common objectives and common institutions.

Art. 2. The mission of the European Coal and Steel Community is to contribute to economic expansion, the development of employment, and the improvement of the standard of living in the participating countries through the institution, in harmony with the general economy of the member states, of a common market as defined in Art. 4.

The Community must progressively establish conditions which will in themselves assure the most rational distribution of production at the highest possible level of productivity, while safeguarding the continuity of employment and avoiding the creation of fundamental and persistent disturbances in the economies of the member states.

Art. 3. Within the framework of their respective powers and responsibilities, the institutions of the Community should: (*a*) See that the common market is regularly supplied, taking account of the needs of third countries; (*b*) assure to all consumers in comparable positions within the common market equal access to the sources of production; (*c*) seek the establishment of the lowest prices which are possible without requiring any corresponding rise either in the prices charged by the same enterprises in other transactions or in the price-level as a whole in another period, while at the same time permitting necessary amortization and providing normal possibilities of remuneration for capital invested; (*d*) see that conditions are maintained which will encourage enterprises to expand and improve their ability to produce and to promote a policy of rational development of natural resources, avoiding inconsiderate exhaustion of such resources; (*e*) promote the improvement of the living and working conditions of the labour force in each of the industries under its jurisdiction so as to make possible the equalization of such conditions in an upward direction; (*f*) further the development of international trade and see that equitable limits are observed in prices charged on external markets; (*g*) promote the regular expansion and the modernization of production, as well as the improvement of its quality, under conditions which preclude any protection against competing industries, except where justified by illegitimate action on the part of such industries or in their favour.

Art. 4. The following were recognized to be incompatible with the common market for coal and steel, and were therefore "abolished and prohibited" within the Community: (*a*) Import and export duties, or charges with an equivalent effect, and quantitative restrictions on the movement of coal and steel; (*b*) measures or practices discriminating among producers, buyers or consumers, specifically as concerned prices, delivery terms and transportation rates, as well as measures or practices which hampered the buyer in the free choice of his supplier; (*c*) subsidies or state assistance, or special charges imposed by the state, in any form whatsoever; (*d*) restrictive practices tending towards the division of markets or the exploitation of the consumer.

Art. 5. The Community would accomplish its mission with "limited direct intervention", and to this end it would: "Enlighten and facilitate the action of the interested parties" by collecting information, organizing consultations and defining general objectives; place financial means at the disposal of enterprises for their investments and participate in the expenses of readaptation; assure the establishment, maintenance and observance of normal conditions of competition, and take direct action with respect to production and the operation of the market only when circumstances made it absolutely necessary; publish the justifications for its action and take the necessary measures to ensure observance of the rules set forth in the treaty. The institutions of the Community should carry out these activities with "as little administrative machinery as possible" and in close co-operation with the interested parties.

Art. 6 provided that the Community should have "juridical personality" and that it should enjoy, in its international relations, "the juridical capacity necessary to the exercise of its functions and the attainment of its ends".

Arts. 7–45 are concerned with the institutions of the Community—the High Authority, the Assembly, the Council and the Court—the functions of which have since been taken over by the European Commission, the European Parliament, the joint Council of Ministers, and the European Court of Justice respectively.

Arts. 46–75 contain the technical details for the realization of the objectives of the treaty. The remaining provisions are concerned, inter alia, with such general matters as the privileges and immunity of the Community in the territory of member states, settlements of disputes and relations with other international organizations.

Among the documents accompanying the treaty was a *Convention on Transitional Provisions*, setting forth the measures necessary for the creation of the common market. These covered a five-year period from the creation of the common market for coal.

DEVELOPMENTS

ECSC Common Market. The common market between the six original member countries of the ECSC was opened for coal, iron ore and scrap on Feb. 10, 1953; for steel on May 1, 1953; and for special steels on Aug. 1, 1954. The market came into full operation on Feb. 10, 1958, when the five-year transitional period of its formation came to an end. By this time all barriers to trade in coal and steel—such as customs duties, currency restrictions and quantitative restrictions—had been abolished, all subsidies had been eliminated and discriminatory practices abolished, and a harmonized external tariff for the whole Community had been introduced.

Trade and Production. In the initial period after the formation of the ECSC the production of all commodities covered by the ECSC treaty (coal, coke, iron ore, pig iron, crude steel and finished rolled products) rose considerably, as also did the volume of trade among Community countries and between Community countries and other countries. Since 1957, however, the coal industry has declined, although steel production continued to rise until 1974.

In view of the ensuing recession in steel production, measures were taken from December 1976 onwards, under a common steel policy drawn up in that year by Henri Simonet (then Belgian Foreign Minister and member of the European Commission with responsibility for the steel industry) to control prices and set limits on the production of steel, and in May 1977 compulsory licensing was introduced for steel imports from third countries. Efforts were also made to rationalize the steel industry.

Labour Aid. The Community plays an active part in overcoming the social problems within its sphere of activity. It has evolved adaptation schemes to protect workers against the risk of unemployment, these being particularly applicable to workers in the coal industry; has carried out programmes of house-building to accommodate workers; has developed vocational training and research in industrial health and medicine; and has made loans for industrial development in certain areas.

European Economic Community (EEC)

The Foreign Ministers of the six ECSC nations met at Messina (Italy) on June 2–4, 1955, to discuss certain proposals for further European economic integration which had been put forward by the three Benelux countries on May 20, 1955.

The Benelux proposals called for (a) the establishment of a "common organization" to study development plans for a European network of roads, canals and railways, and for the co-ordination of civil aviation policies; (b) the study of methods of co-ordinating power policy in Europe; (c) the creation of a "common authority" for the development of atomic energy for peaceful purposes, with the pooling of investment funds, technical knowledge and research facilities; and (d) the progressive integration of the national economies of the six member countries and the harmonization of economic, financial and social policies. To implement this programme the Benelux governments proposed that a conference should be called to work out (a) a treaty on the pooling of transport, power and atomic energy; (b) a treaty on general economic integration;

and (c) a treaty defining the European institutions necessary to carry out the programme.

At the end of their meeting the Foreign Ministers adopted the "Messina Resolution", which included a plan for the creation of "a common European market free from all customs barriers and quantitative restrictions", to be realized by stages. The six ministers also envisaged the creation of a joint organization having "the responsibility and the facilities" for ensuring the development of atomic energy for peaceful purposes. An Intergovernmental Committee was set up to study the problems raised and to prepare draft treaties.

A = Albania
B = Belgium
L = Luxembourg
N = Netherlands
S = Switzerland

= European Community members
= EFTA members

Map 4   European Communities and European Free Trade Association (EFTA)

The final drafts of the treaties establishing the EEC and Euratom were completed by the Intergovernmental Committee on March 9, 1957, and were signed in Rome by Belgium, France, the Federal Republic of Germany, Italy, Luxembourg and the Netherlands on March 25, 1957. Both came into force on Jan. 1, 1958.

EEC TREATY

The main provisions of the original treaty setting up the European Economic Community (the Treaty of Rome) are summarized below (for amendments under the 1986 "Single European Act", see pages 175–76).

Aims

In the preamble to the treaty, the six signatory countries declared their intention of establishing "the foundations of an enduring and closer union between European peoples" by gradually removing the economic effects of their political frontiers. A common market and a common external tariff (customs union) would be established for all goods; common policies would be devised for agriculture, transport, labour mobility and important sectors of the economy; common institutions would be set up for economic development; and the overseas territories and possessions of member states would be associated with the new Community for an experimental five-year period. All these measures would have one "essential aim"—the steady improvement in the conditions of life and work of the peoples of the member countries.

The tasks of the Community were defined in Article 1 of the treaty as the achievement of a harmonious development of the economy within the whole Community, a continuous and balanced economic expansion, increased economic stability, a more rapid improvement in living-standards, and closer relations between the member countries.

Progressive Implementations of Common Market—Procedure during Transitional Period

One of the principal characteristics of the process of creating a common market would be its irrevocable character—i.e. once the process had been set in motion, the ultimate aim would have to be achieved. This constituted an important safeguard for the member countries inasmuch as their sacrifices in adjusting themselves to the new conditions would not be in vain, and would not involve a risk of a complete standstill and a subsequent return to the previous status after a number of years. The change from one stage to the next would thus in principle take place automatically.

The common market would be progressively established in three stages within a transitional period of 12 years, which might be extended to 15 years. Within the basic 12-year period there would be three stages, each lasting in principle four years. However, if at the end of the first four years the Council of Ministers and the Commission were not unanimously agreed that the objectives of that stage had been essentially accomplished, the stage would automatically be extended for one year. At the end of the fifth year there would be another one-year extension on the same condition, whilst at the end of the sixth year (when the decision of the Council of Ministers would no longer require unanimity but would be taken by a weighted majority) a further extension could be granted only if a request by a member state for such an extension was recognized as justified by an ad hoc arbitration tribunal of three members appointed by the Council of Ministers.

The second and third stages could either be prolonged or shortened by unanimous decision of the Council of Ministers, subject to the maximum limit of 15 years for the whole transitional period.

Removal of Tariffs and Quantitative Restrictions—Development of Agriculture

The European Economic Community would be based on a customs union covering the whole trade of member countries and entailing (a) a prohibition on imposing import or export duties or similar levies between member countries; (b) the introduction of a common tariff on imports from non-Community countries; (c) the abolition of all quantitative import and export restrictions and other similar measures between member countries. The free exchange of goods within the Community would apply not only to goods produced in the member countries but also to those which had been imported by a member country from outside the Community, and on which customs duties had been paid on entry. The only exception from the application of the common customs tariff vis-à-vis non-Community countries would be in the case of goods landed in a free trade zone where each member country could apply its own customs tariff.

Internal Tariffs. Tariff restrictions on trade between member countries would have to be abolished entirely by the end of the transitional period at the latest.

All export duties and similar levies on goods destined for other Community countries would be abolished not later than the end of the first stage.

External Tariffs. A common tariff on imports from non-Community countries would be established in full not later than the end of the transitional period.

Quantitative Restrictions. All quantitative restrictions on trade within the Community would be progressively eliminated by a series of quota increases. Thus, one year after the coming into force of the treaty, the member states would convert all their existing bilateral import quotas into global quotas in favour of all other member countries, without any discrimination between them. All these global import quotas would then be increased annually by at least 20 per cent as regards their overall value, and by at least 10 per cent as regards each individual product; bigger increases would be made in the case of quotas amounting initially to less than 3 per cent of the domestic output of a given product.

Agriculture. Agricultural products would be included in the common market, although a special regime would apply in view of the different social structure of agriculture in the various member countries, which made it impossible to introduce a completely liberalized market.

A common agricultural policy would be implemented in the course of the transitional period, aiming at increased agricultural productivity, safeguarding an adequate standard of living for the agricultural population, stabilization of agricultural markets, an assurance of adequate supplies and fair prices for consumers.

A joint organization of agricultural markets would be created, but, because of the diversity of market conditions for individual products, this development would not take place under prearranged rules but through decisions of the organs of the Community, varying from case to case.

Freedom of Movement for Labour, Services and Capital—Joint Transport Policy

Labour, Settlement, Services and Capital. The free circulation of labour, services and capital, as well as the right to settle, work and trade anywhere in the Community, would be fully established by the end of the transitional period.

All restrictions on the right to settle freely in any member country, or the right of nationals of any member country to set up agencies, branches or subsidiary companies in the territory of another, would be gradually removed during the transitional period.

All restrictions on the offering of services by insurance companies, banks, finance houses, the wholesale and retail trade, and by members of the professions would be gradually removed within the Community during the transitional period.

Existing restrictions on the movement of capital between Community countries would be progressively removed. As far as was necessary for the proper working of the common market, restrictions on current payments relating to the movement of capital (e.g. interest, dividends, rents, premiums) would be completely abolished not later than the end of the first stage of the transitional period.

Transport. The Council of Ministers would establish a joint transport policy and common rules for international transport within or through the Community, covering rail, road and inland water transport.

Common Policies

To ensure free and equal competition within the Community, common rules and policies would be introduced in the member countries as summarized below.

Common Rules. Any agreement or association preventing, restraining or distorting competition within the Community would be forbidden—e.g. agreements or associations directly or indirectly fixing prices; regulating or controlling production, investment or technical development; sharing markets; requiring the acceptance of additional goods besides those needed by the customer; or providing for discriminatory conditions of supply.

Dumping practices by any member country within the common market would be prohibited.

Unless otherwise provided by the treaty, state subsidies (of whatever kind) which distorted or threatened to distort competition would be prohibited.

Economic Policy. Member countries would harmonize their general economic, foreign exchange and foreign trade policies.

The general economic policies of member countries would be regarded as a matter of joint interest, and the countries concerned would consult each other as well as the Commission on the measures which should be taken to meet changing circumstances.

A common external trade policy would be established by the end of the transitional period.

The common external trade policy after the end of the transitional period would cover the application of a common customs tariff; the joint conclusion of trade and customs agreements; the unification of trade liberalization measures; the working-out of common export policies; and the joint application of protective measures, e.g. against dumping or subsidies by non-Community countries.

Social Policy. The EEC Commission would promote the co-ordination of the social policies of member countries, with particular reference to employment, labour legislation, conditions of work, vocational training, social security, prevention of industrial accidents and occupational diseases, health protection, trade union rights, and collective bargaining between employers and employed.

Provisions for Association and Future Membership

The overseas territories of Belgium, France, Italy and the Netherlands would be associated with the Community. A special convention annexed to the treaty laid down the details of this association for the initial five-year period.

Any other European country could apply for membership in the Community; the terms of its admission, and any consequential amendments of the treaty which might become necessary, would be agreed between the original member countries and the applicant country.

Agreements might also be concluded with another country or group of countries for their association with the Community, based on certain mutual rights and obligations, joint action and special procedures. Similar agreements of association might be entered into with international organizations.

The treaty was concluded for an unlimited period.

European Atomic Energy Community (EAEC or Euratom)

As described in the section above on the European Economic Community, the European Atomic Energy Community came into being under a separate treaty which, with the March

1957 Rome Treaty, entered into force on Jan. 1, 1958.

EURATOM TREATY

The aims of the Community were defined in the preamble as the raising of living standards in the member countries and the promotion of trade with non-Community countries. The tasks of Euratom were defined in Article 1 of the treaty as the creation, within a short period, of the technical and industrial conditions necessary to utilize nuclear discoveries, and especially to produce nuclear energy on a large scale. This result would be achieved by joint measures of the member countries and through the activities of the institutions of the Community.

The main functions of Euratom, as laid down in the treaty, can be summarized as follows:

(1) The promotion, facilitation, and co-ordination of research in member countries, and the execution of a research programme of its own; (2) the dissemination of information on atomic energy, and the acquisition of information on all patents, patent applications and working models of inventions which would be useful to the Community; (3) the establishment of a code of basic standards governing personal safety against dangers resulting from ionizing radiation; (4) the promotion of a planned development of investments by public and private undertakings in the nuclear energy fields; and (5) the formation of Community undertakings for the development of nuclear industry within Euratom.

Other significant provisions of the treaty are as follows:

Supplies. A joint policy would be pursued with regard to the supply of ores, raw materials and special fissile matter on the basis of the principle of equal access to resources. For this purpose the Commission would set up a Commercial Agency which would be a corporate body, vested with financial independence and able to conduct its affairs according to business rules, but controlled by the Commission. The Agency (the majority of whose capital would have to be owned by the Community and the member countries) would possess (i) an option to purchase any of the materials in question produced in member states; and (ii) the exclusive right to conclude contracts for the purchase or sale of such materials outside the Community.

The Commission would be entitled to make recommendations regarding prospecting and the exploitation of mines, and might participate financially in such activities. Member states would be required to send the Commission annual reports on prospecting, reserves and mining investments.

Security. The Commission would be required to ensure (i) that ores, raw materials and special fissile matter were not diverted from their intended use as declared by their consumers; and (ii) that arrangements for their supply, and any special control measures accepted by the Community in an agreement with a non-Community state or international organization were observed.

To this end, the Commission would:

(*a*) Request declarations from all the undertakings concerned describing the basic technical characteristics of their equipment:

(*b*) request statements of all transactions in order to facilitate accounting of ores, raw materials and special fissile matter;

(*c*) insist, if necessary, on all surplus special fissile matter temporarily not in use being placed in deposit;

(*d*) arrange for its inspectors to carry out checks and, where necessary, impose sanctions ranging from a warning to the complete withdrawal of raw materials or special fissile matter.

Ownership of Special Fissile Matter. All special fissile matter would be the property of the Community. Member states, undertakings or individuals, however, would be entitled to the widest possible utilization and consumption of the special fissile matter which had legitimately come into their possession.

Common Market in Nuclear Materials. A common market in nuclear materials would be set up, involving the following obligations on member countries:

(*a*) To introduce, one year after the coming into force of the treaty, a common customs tariff for nuclear minerals, materials and products imported from non-Community countries:

(*b*) to repeal between each other, after the same one-year period, all import and export duties and taxes on such minerals, materials and products (the non-European territories of member states being entitled, however, to continue to levy duties and taxes of a purely fiscal character);

(*c*) to apply the procedure laid down in the Common Market Treaty for the gradual abolition of internal tariffs and quantitative import restrictions between member countries, and for the introduction of a uniform customs tariff, to all other products which might be used in the nuclear industry;

(*d*) to admit nationals of the other member countries, without discrimination, to all posts and occupations requiring qualifications in the nuclear sphere, as well as to participation in the construction of nuclear undertakings;

(*e*) to set up an insurance scheme covering risks arising from the use of atomic energy;

(*f*) to facilitate the transfer between member countries of capital needed for nuclear projects, and to permit the transfer to other member countries of payments in connexion with nuclear transactions and employment in nuclear industries or research.

Nuclear Research. A Joint Research Centre, set up under the Euratom Treaty, includes four important establishments for nuclear research. These are:

(1) The Nuclear Research Centre at Ispra (Italy), transferred by Italy to Euratom under an agreement signed on July 22, 1959;

(2) the Central Nuclear Measurements Bureau at Geel (Belgium);

(3) the Transuranium Elements Institute at Karlsruhe (Federal Republic of Germany); and

(4) the General Purpose Centre at Petten (Netherlands).

Euratom has signed several hundred research contracts with public and private undertakings in the member countries of the Community. Under these contracts the Community contributes both finance and personnel. One of the most important such agreements is with the Belgian Nuclear Study Centre at Mol, whose high-neutron-flux reactor (BR-2) for the testing of materials is jointly operated by the Centre and by Euratom, the latter bearing two-thirds of the running costs. Other fields of research covered by such agreements include fast-breeder and high temperature gas reactors, nuclear ship propulsion and the uses of nuclear energy in agriculture and medicine.

Part of Euratom's research programme is carried out in conjunction with that of the broader Nuclear Energy Agency of the OECD [see pages 115–16]. The Community also co-operates with the International Atomic Energy Agency of the United Nations.

Information on the various research projects with which Euratom is concerned is disseminated through an atomic information and documentation centre.

Following the completion of a second five-year research programme in December 1967, the member states failed to agree on a further multi-annual programme, and research continued at a reduced level by means of a series of five interim annual programmes until the end of 1972. During this period the emphasis in Euratom research shifted from participation in the development of future generations of nuclear power reactors to more basic studies in the nuclear field and also to work in other scientific sectors.

Promotion of the Atomic Energy Industry. Euratom has adopted a number of measures by which it promotes the development of the peaceful uses of atomic energy in Europe. These include:

(1) The creation of the common market for nuclear materials and equipment (in operation since Jan. 1, 1959);

(2) the introduction of the freedom of movement within the Community for technical workers in the atomic energy industry;

(3) the preparation of an insurance convention under which the Community as a whole will have third-party coverage for damages arising out of the atomic energy industry;

(4) financial assistance for power reactor projects in return for access to all planning, constructional and operational information; and

(5) the creation of special bureau (Eurisotop) to provide information on the use of radio isotopes in industry.

Under a **Joint European Torus** (JET), a thermonuclear fusion programme designed to lead to the provision of virtually unlimited supplies of cheap and "clean" energy by the end of the 20th century, a first prototype reactor was to be built at Culham (near Oxford, England), as decided by the Council of Ministers on Oct. 25, 1977. The decision was formally approved on May 30, 1978, when the project was set up as a joint undertaking comprising Euratom and the then nine member states of the European Community as well as Sweden and Switzerland (under agreements signed on May 10, 1976, and Sept. 14, 1978, respectively). Under another agreement, signed in Madrid on July 14, 1980, Spain was also linked with the JET programme.

Supplies, Health and Security. A Supply Agency, as provided for in the treaty, came into operation on June 1, 1960. This agency, which is a commercially-operating independent department attached to the Commission, has an option to purchase any ores, raw materials and special fissile matter produced in the member countries, and has the exclusive right to conclude contracts for the purchase or sale of such materials outside the Community.

To protect workers in the atomic energy industry, and also the rest of the population, Euratom has drawn up a code of basic health standards (February 1959). The code, which has been made binding on the governments concerned, has been incorporated in the national legislation of each of the member countries of the Community. The regulations, whose coverage includes X-ray installations and the use of radioactive materials in the manufacture of household goods and cosmetics, represented the first attempt anywhere to set up a comprehensive legal system to cover radiation health risks.

A security control system to supervise the proper use of ores, raw materials and special fissile materials, as provided for in the treaty, has been set up by the Commission. The control system is binding on the member governments. (*Note:* Euratom has no control over nuclear materials or installations intended for military purposes.)

In 1985 the Euratom Safeguards Directorate conducted physical and accounting checks on average stocks of some 90 tonnes of plutonium, 13 tonnes of high-enriched uranium, 18,000 tonnes of low-enriched uranium and 111,000 tonnes of natural uranium, depleted uranium, thorium and heavy water. These stocks were held in more than 560 nuclear installations in the Community and gave rise to over 350,000 entry lines, including some 330,000 lines transmitted under the agreement with the International Atomic Energy Agency (IAEA). These lines were fed into the Directorate's computer and processed to ensure confidentiality. The checks also covered equipment subject to external commitments under co-operation agreements with non-member countries.

AGREEMENTS INVOLVING EURATOM MEMBERS

On April 5, 1973, Belgium, the Federal Republic of Germany, Italy, Luxembourg and the Netherlands signed an agreement in Brussels enabling the International Atomic Energy Agency (IAEA) to verify the safeguard system of Euratom as a precondition of their signing the Nuclear Non-Proliferation Treaty.

An agreement signed in Vienna on Sept. 6, 1976, by Euratom, the IAEA and the United Kingdom provided for the submission of UK non-military nuclear installations to international safeguards under IAEA supervision; the agreement entered into force on Aug. 14, 1978.

An agreement which was concluded by Euratom, the IAEA and seven member countries of the European Communities—Belgium, Denmark, the Federal Republic of Germany, Italy, Luxembourg and the Netherlands—and came into force in February 1977 provided for the application of IAEA and Euratom safeguards to the nuclear installations of these countries "with a view to preventing diversion of nuclear energy from peaceful uses to nuclear weapons or other explosive devices".

Under an agreement signed in Vienna on July 27, 1978, between Euratom, the IAEA and France (which is not a signatory of the Nuclear Non-Proliferation Treaty), certain French non-military nuclear installations were to be submitted to international safeguards under IAEA supervision (although France retained the effective right to decide which installations would be open to such inspection).

AGREEMENTS WITH NON-MEMBERS

Agreements made by Euratom with non-member countries concerning the peaceful uses of atomic energy are as follows:

Euratom—USA. The United States has concluded agreements with Euratom as follows:

Agreement relating to co-operation for peaceful applications of atomic energy; May 29 and June 19, 1958; entry into force Aug. 27, 1958.

Agreement for co-operation concerning peaceful uses of atomic energy: Nov. 8, 1958; entry into force Feb. 18, 1959; extended and amended May 21–22, 1962. (Under this agreement the USA promised technical and financial help in the construction and running of from six to eight power-producing reactors with a total capacity of 1,000,000 kilowatts, and provision was made for collaboration of the USA and Euratom in a 10-year nuclear research and development programme.)

Additional agreement for co-operation concerning peaceful uses of atomic energy: June 11, 1960; entry into force July 25, 1960; extended and amended May 21–22, 1962; Aug. 22 and 27, 1963; and Sept. 20, 1972.

Agreement in the field of nuclear material safeguards research and development, Jan. 28, 1982.

Agreement for exchange of information concerning a co-operative programme in the field of management of radioactive wastes, Oct. 6, 1982.

Arrangement in the field of nuclear safety research, Sept. 20, 1984.

Euratom—Britain. An agreement on collaboration in developing nuclear energy for peaceful purposes was signed by Euratom and Britain in February 1959. Under it a standing committee for co-operation was set up. Aspects of nuclear research in which the two parties have co-operated include (i) the study of controlled thermonuclear reactions for peaceful purposes; (ii) fast-breeder reactor techniques; and (iii) advanced gas-cooler reactor systems.

The original 10-year agreement was extended for another two years on Feb. 4, 1969.

Euratom—Canada. Two agreements with Canada were signed on Oct. 5, 1959. An outline agreement concluded with the Canadian Government laid down the conditions under which Canada and Euratom would exchange nuclear data, materials, and equipment between individuals and corporations. The second agreement, a technical agreement between Euratom and Atomic Energy of Canada Ltd., provided for a joint research and development programme in the use of reactors powered by uranium fuel moderated by heavy water.

Under an agreement of Jan. 16, 1978, new safeguards arrangements were established for the supply of nuclear material and equipment by Canada to the member states of the European Communities (which had been suspended by Canada since Jan. 1, 1977).

The agreement was amended by a long-term agreement signed on Dec. 18, 1981, setting out agreed conditions for the transfer, enrichment, processing and storage within the European Community of uranium and plutonium from Canada.

Joint research and environmental assessment of the handling of radioactive waste was provided for under an agreement signed on Nov. 3, 1980, by Euratom and Atomic Energy of Canada Ltd.

Euratom—Australia. A 30-year safeguards agreement signed on Sept. 21, 1981, set out agreed conditions for the transfer of nuclear material from Australia to the European Community and also for any subsequent retransfer of such material (thus clearing the way for the export of Australian uranium to the Community member states).

Euratom—Brazil. A 20-year agreement for co-operation between Euratom and Brazil in the peaceful uses of atomic energy was signed on June 9, 1961. The agreement covered exchange of information on research and development; means of health protection; installations and equipment; utilization of minerals, raw materials, special fissile matter, and nuclear fuels and radio-isotopes; exchange of personnel; and the granting of patent licences.

Euratom—Argentina. A similar agreement to that between Euratom and Brazil was concluded between Euratom and Argentina on Sept. 4, 1962.

Euratom—CMEA. An agreement approved by the International Atomic Energy Agency (IAEA) at its 19th annual conference in Vienna on Sept. 22–26, 1975, provided for co-operation between Euratom and the Council for Mutual Economic Assistance (CMEA) in the peaceful use of nuclear energy, consultation on matters of mutual interest, joint participation in meetings, exchange of information and permanent contact between the two organizations' secretaries.

Euratom—Spain. An agreement relating to nuclear fusion, signed on July 14, 1980, was on Sept. 1, 1983, extended until Dec. 31, 1986.

MULTILATERAL RESEARCH AGREEMENT

On April 10, 1985, the European Commission approved the signing of an agreement covering co-operation on research in the field of nuclear safety between Euratom and nine bodies in six Community countries (Belgium, France, the Federal Republic of Germany, Italy, the Netherlands and the United Kingdom) and in Finland, Sweden and the United States.

Common Organs of the European Communities

European Council. The European Council consists of the heads of government of the member states who, accompanied by their Foreign Ministers, generally meet three times a year in order "gradually to adopt common positions and co-ordinate their diplomatic action in all areas of international affairs which affect the interests of the European Community"—as decided at a conference held in Paris on Dec. 9–10, 1974, by the heads of government of the then nine member states.

At this conference it was also decided to set up an administrative secretariat of the Council, and it was stated that the heads of government considered it "necessary to renounce the practice which consists of making agreement on all questions conditional on the unanimous consent of the member states". Although the European Council possesses no legal standing under the Community treaties, it has nevertheless become the forum where the major strategic decisions affecting the development of the Community are taken.

Conferences of the heads of state or government of the member countries, first of the European Economic Community (EEC) and later of the European Communities, had earlier been held on various occasions to discuss not only future Community policies but also the international economic situation. Such conferences were held:

(1) In Paris on Feb. 10–11, 1961, when the participants expressed their wish to seek agreements aimed at maintaining and developing exchanges with other countries, "in particular with Great Britain".

(2) In Bonn on July 18, 1961, when the leader of the six EEC member states decided to hold regular meetings, inter alia, in order to "further the political unification of Europe and thus to strengthen the Atlantic Alliance".

(3) In Rome on May 29–30, 1967, when it was decided to merge the executives of the EEC, the European Coal and Steel Community (ECSC) and the European Atomic Energy Community (Euratom) in one Commission on July 1, 1967.

(4) In The Hague on Dec. 1–2, 1969, when it was stated in a communiqué that the entry of other countries of Europe into the Communities "would undoubtedly help the Communities to grow to dimensions more in conformity with the present state of world economy and technology"; it was also agreed that "a plan in stages should be worked out . . . with a view to the creation of an economic and monetary union".

(5) In Paris on Oct. 19–20, 1972, attended by the French President and heads of government of eight other countries—including also three "applicant" countries—Denmark, Ireland and the United Kingdom—as well as a delegation of the European Communities, and issuing a lengthy communiqué reaffirming the Communities' objectives and stating in particular (i) that the leaders would establish the Community's position in world affairs as "a distinct entity determined to promote a better international equilibrium"; (ii) that as "the driving force of the European construction" the member states affirmed "their intention to transform before the end of the present decade the whole complex of their relations into a European union"; (iii) that they reaffirmed "the determination of the member states of the enlarged European Communities irreversibly to achieve the economic and monetary union" previously agreed upon in March 1971 and March 1972, for which they laid down a timetable and decided on the use of a European monetary unit of account and on "fixed but adjustable parity" and the general convertibility of member countries' currencies [see page 181].

(6) In Copenhagen on Dec. 14–15, 1973, after which the participants issued a general communiqué, a statement on the energy crisis and a declaration on European identity.

In the communiqué they stated inter alia that they had decided to meet more frequently, that "the growing unity of the Nine" [member countries] would "strengthen the West as a whole and . . . be beneficial for the relationship between Europe and the United States"; and that they had agreed on the establishment of a regional development fund on Jan. 1, 1974.

The statement on the energy crisis envisaged inter alia a comprehensive Community programme on alternative sources of energy (including "a European capacity for enrichment of uranium"), and it "confirmed the importance of entering into negotiations with oil-producing countries on comprehensive arrangements comprising co-operation on a wide scale for the economic and industrial development of these countries, industrial investment, and stable energy supplies to the member countries at reasonable prices".

In the declaration on European identity the heads of state or government described as "fundamental elements of the European identity" "the principles of representative democracy, of the rule of law, of social justice—the ultimate goal of economic progress—and of respect for human rights".

Following a 1974 conference in Paris, the European Council held further conferences as follows:

(1) In Dublin on March 10–11, 1975, when decisions taken included approval of a budgetary correction mechanism to be applied when a member country was "a disproportionate contributor" to the Communities' budget and also in economic difficulties.

(2) In Brussels on July 16–17, 1975, when it was stated that the Community was "prepared to initiate discussions on closer economic and financial co-operation with Portugal" (which was, in October 1975, granted emergency aid by the Communities of up to 150,000,000 units of account).

(3) In Rome on Dec. 1–2, 1975, when it was, inter alia, decided that direct elections to the European Parliament would take place in May or June 1978.

(4) In Luxembourg on April 1–2, 1976.

(5) In Brussels on July 12–13, when the number and distribution of seats in the European Parliament were agreed upon.

(6) In The Hague on Nov. 29–30, 1976.

(7) In Rome on March 25–26, 1977.

(8) In London on June 29–30, 1977. While the London conference and its two predecessors dealt mainly with economic problems, the Council reiterated, at the London conference, its principles for the achievement of a lasting settlement of the Arab-Israeli conflict based on "the inadmissibility of the acquisition of territory by force, the need for Israel to end the territorial occupation which it has maintained since the conflict of 1967, respect for the sovereignty, territorial integrity and independence of every state in the area and their legal right to live in peace within secure and recognized boundaries, and recognition that in the establishment of a lasting peace account must be taken of the legitimate rights of the Palestinians".

(9) In Brussels on Dec. 5–6, 1977, when the Council approved in principle (i) the creation of a new Community facility of 1,000 million European units of account (EUA), to be managed by the European Investment Bank, and (ii) the establishment of a European Foundation to promote understanding and human contacts among the peoples of the Community (as proposed in a report on the overall concept of European union prepared by Léo Tindemans, then Belgian Prime Minister, and published in January 1976).

(10) In Copenhagen on April 7–8, 1978, when it was agreed that the elections to the European Parliament should take place on June 7–10, 1979 (and not in May or June 1978, as previously intended).

(11) In Bremen (Federal Republic of Germany) on July 6–7, 1978, when it was agreed in principle to create a system of closer monetary co-operation leading to a "zone of monetary stability in Europe" and the introduction of the European currency unit (ECU) as the Community's monetary unit within a European monetary system (EMS) [see also page 181].

(12) In Brussels on Dec. 4–5, 1978, when it was resolved to set up the EMS as from Jan. 1, 1979 (with Belgium, Denmark, France, the Federal Republic of Germany, Luxembourg and the Netherlands committing themselves to full participation from the outset and Ireland and Italy deciding in December 1978 to join the EMS but the United Kingdom remaining outside). The implementation of the EMS was, however, deferred after France had decided in December 1978 to block it pending the resolution of a dispute over common agricultural policy prices.

(13) In Paris on March 12–13, 1979, when, after the dispute with France had been resolved, it was decided to implement the EMS from March 13, 1979 (without UK participation), and also to reduce the Community's oil consumption in 1979 to about 500,000,000 tonnes (or about 25,000,000 tonnes less than originally estimated).

(14) In Strasbourg on June 21–22, 1979, when the Council considered a British request to bring about a reduction in the net UK contribution to the Communities' budget.

(15) In Dublin on Nov. 29–30, 1979, when no agreement was reached on the question of the UK contribution to the Communities' budget, mainly because the proposals made contained no guarantees beyond 1980.

(16) In Luxembourg on April 27–28, 1980, when the heads of government (i) stated in a declaration on the international situation that in view of recent events (in Afghanistan, Iran and the Middle East) unity among the Communities' member states was needed more than ever; (ii) reiterated that the problem of Afghanistan should be solved by that country's return to the position of a neutral and non-aligned state; (iii) expressed satisfaction at the stability of the European Monetary System (EMS) during its first year of operation, but (iv) reached no agreement on various items, including fisheries, agriculture and the UK budget contribution.

(17) In Venice on June 12–13, 1980, when agreement was reached on the UK contribution question on the basis of a formula agreed upon by the Communities' Council of (Foreign) Ministers in Brussels on May 29–30, 1980, whereby the UK contribution for 1980–81 was reduced by a total of 2,585 million European units of account (EUA) or then about £1,577 million, while measures were proposed to prevent "the recurrence of unacceptable situations" for member states in later years.

(18) In Luxembourg on Dec. 1–2, 1980, when the heads of government came to the conclusion that the prospects for the European economy had "never required more vigilant attention", especially to the problems of unemployment and of continued payment imbalances.

(19) In Maastricht (Netherlands) on March 23–24, 1981, when unanimous agreement was reached that "in the present difficult economic conditions" the Community remained "an essential achievement and an indispensable instrument for limiting the effects of the recession and bringing about the return . . . of sustained economic growth and satisfactory levels of employment", for the achievement of which, and for the reduction of inflation, "the continuation of prudent monetary policies, a healthy budgetary management, and the reorientation of public and private expenditure in the direction of productive investment" were "major elements".

(20) In Luxembourg on June 29–30, 1981, when it was noted that there were "the first cautious signs of limited improvement in the business cycle" but that "the ravages of inflation and unemployment" had "by no means been brought under control" and called for "co-ordinated action", including "efforts at structural adjustment" by national governments.

(21) In London on Nov. 26–27, 1981, when no specific progress was made on the major issues over which there was disagreement (the milk problem, agricultural expenditure, Mediterranean agriculture and the budget).

(22) In Brussels on March 29–30, 1982, when the Council inter alia emphasized the need to co-ordinate policy to promote investment and to combat unemployment, and a wide range of international problems were discussed.

(23) In Brussels on June 28–29, 1982, when the Council discussed the invasion of Lebanon by Israel earlier that month, as well as relations between the European Community and the United States, in particular in monetary policy, trade relations and the implications of US sanctions against the Soviet Union in connexion with the Polish crisis.

(24) In Copenhagen on Dec. 3–4, 1982, when a lengthy statement was issued, listing "priority goals" in order to restore economic stability and inter alia to strengthen the EMS and international co-operation in all areas, and to pursue a constructive dialogue with the United States.

(25) In Brussels on March 21–23, 1983, when no agreement was reached on a series of operational decisions and the fundamental question of the convergence of economic policies in the Community.

(26) In Stuttgart (Germany) on June 17–19, 1983, when agreement was reached on a comprehensive working programme of negotiations on the future of the Community, centring on the question of financial resources and including the possible restructuring of policies, especially the Common Agricultural Policy; it was also agreed to include 750,000,000 ECUs in the 1984 draft budget for a 1983 rebate to Britain; a "solemn declaration on European union" was signed, providing inter alia for "intensified consultations in the area of foreign policy, including the co-ordination of the positions of member states on the political and economic aspects of security". The Council also issued a lengthy declaration setting out the salient points of a "relaunch" of the Communities on the basis of "more integration".

(27) In Athens on Dec. 4–6, 1983, when no agreement was reached on agriculture, finance or other policy issues; nor was any communiqué issued.

(28) In Brussels on March 19–20, 1984, when agreement was reached on tighter controls on Community spending, based on a revised budgetary procedure, and on keeping the growth in expenditure on the Common Agricultural Policy below the annual rise in the budget income (then around 6 per cent); however, these and other agreements did not come into effect because of continued disagreements on other questions, especially on contributions to the Community budget.

(29) In Fontainebleau (France) on June 25–26, 1984, when agreement in principle was reached on a 1984 rebate for the United Kingdom (as a result of which the agreements reached in Brussels in March could be implemented); the participants also agreed on new guidelines for European co-operation, including approval of the principle of a European passport (to be available to member states' nationals by Jan. 1, 1985, at the latest).

(30) In Dublin on Dec. 3–4, 1984, when agreement was reached on curbing wine production and on common positions in the enlarged Community on fish, fruit and vegetables.

(31) In Brussels on March 29–30, 1985, when "Integrated Mediterranean Programmes" were approved (after acceptance by Greece), and agreement was announced on all issues concerning the accession of Portugal and Spain to the Community.

(32) In Milan on June 28–29, 1985, when discussions were started on a comprehensive constitutional reform of the Communities, while unanimous agreement was reached on the establishment of a unified internal market, co-operation in research and technology, and the creation of a 500,000-tonne cereal store to help combat famine in Africa.

(33) In Luxembourg on Dec. 2–3, 1985, when the areas in which it was intended to initiate changes to the Treaty of Rome were outlined.

(34) In The Hague on June 26–27, 1986, when the leaders of the 12 EC countries (i) called on South Africa to free Nelson Mandela and other political prisoners and to lift the ban on the African National Congress and other political parties; (ii) decided to consult with the other industrialized countries over the next three months on further measures to bring pressure to bear on South Africa (e.g. a ban on new investment and on the import of coal, iron, steel and gold coins from South Africa);

but (iii) agreed meanwhile that Sir Geoffrey Howe (UK Foreign Secretary and incoming President of the EC Council of Foreign Ministers) should visit southern Africa in a further effort to establish conditions in which the necessary national dialogue on South Africa's future could commence.

The Council of Ministers. The common Council of Ministers, with headquarters in Brussels, fulfils the same functions as did the separate organs of the three Communities, and exercises its rights and obligations under the same conditions as provided for in the treaties for each Community.

Each member state is represented by a member of its government, usually the Minister of Foreign Affairs, Finance, Agriculture or Economics, according to the subject to be discussed, and more than one minister from a member state may attend.

The basic function of the Council of Ministers is to co-ordinate the economic policies of the member countries within the framework of the three treaties for the Communities, and to make decisions for the implementation of the treaties.

Most decisions of the Council are taken by a simple majority vote, but in certain cases the treaties require a unanimous vote or a qualified majority. For a qualified majority the votes are as follows: France, Italy, the Federal Republic of Germany and the United Kingdom have 10 votes each; Spain has eight; Belgium, Greece, the Netherlands and Portugal have five votes each; Denmark and Ireland three each; and Luxembourg two.

Where the treaties require a previous proposal of the Commission [see below], at least 54 out of 76 votes are needed to carry a decision, but in all other cases the votes must include a favourable vote by at least six of the member countries. On Jan. 29, 1966, the Council resolved that, in deciding on issues "very important to one or more member countries", the members of the Council would "try within a reasonable time to reach solutions which can be adopted by all members of the Council while respecting their mutual interests and those of the Community"— so that in effect the Council has generally taken decisions by unanimity and not by a majority vote.

The Council is authorized to request the Commission to examine proposals which may be submitted to it, and to make studies towards the achievement of the common objectives.

The European Commission. The European Commission, based in Brussels, exercises its rights and obligations under the same conditions as provided for in the treaties of the Communities for their individual organs.

It has 17 members—two each from France, the Federal Republic of Germany, Italy, Spain and the United Kingdom, and one each from the remaining member countries. The members are appointed for a renewable four-year term by the governments of the member states, but they are independent and neither solicit nor accept instructions from their governments. Each member is responsible for a particular sphere of economic activity.

The President and the five Vice-Presidents of the Commission are appointed for renewable two-year terms of office.

Decisions of the Commission are taken by simple majority vote. The work of the Communities is directed by the Commission through four variously binding types of decision: (*a*) Regulations, which are compulsory and directly applicable in any member state; (*b*) directives, under which member states are obliged to achieve a particular result but are free to choose their own ways and means; (*c*) decisions, which are obligatory on the parties concerned; and (*d*) recommendations and opinions, which have no binding force.

The functions of the Commission are to supervise the application of the treaties and of measures adopted within their framework; to make proposals to the Council which the latter cannot amend except by unanimous vote; to formulate opinions and recommendations on matters within the scope of the treaties; to take decisions for which it has authority; and to publish an annual general report.

The Commission's administration comprises a secretariat, a legal service, a statistical office, an administration of the customs union, an environment and consumer protection service and 19 specialized directorates.

The European Parliament. The European Parliamentary Assembly, usually known as the European Parliament, has, following the accession of Portugal and Spain, a total of 518 members— 81 each from France, the Federal Republic of Germany, Italy and the United Kingdom; 60 from Spain; 25 from the Netherlands; 24 each from Belgium, Greece and Portugal; 16 from Denmark; 15 from Ireland; and six from Luxembourg.

All members of the European Parliament are normally chosen by direct elections in the various member states, with each country making its own decisions on constituencies, voting and the qualifications of election candidates—in particular whether they had to be, or might or might not be, members of national legislatures.

In all member countries except the United Kingdom elections are conducted on a form of proportional representation.

Following the results of elections held on June 14–17, 1984 (according to official sources), subsequent changes and the taking of their seats by Portuguese and Spanish delegates from the respective national parliaments (pending direct elections) on Jan. 13, 1986, the strength of the various political groupings in the European Parliament was as follows: Socialist Group 172, European People's Party (EPP—Christian Democrats) 118, European Democratic Group (Conservatives) 63, Communists and Allies Group 36, Liberal and Democratic Group 42, European Democratic Alliance 34, Rainbow Group 20,

Group of the European Right 16, Non-attached 7.

The Parliament, which has its seat in Luxembourg but also holds sessions in Strasbourg, has 16 committees and five sub-committees, which sometimes meet in Brussels as well as in Strasbourg and Luxembourg.

The European Parliament has no executive powers. Its function is to supervise the work of the executive organs of the three Communities and to guide it by means of resolutions and expressions of opinion. Its members are entitled to request information on all aspects of the Communities' work from the Commission and the Council of Ministers. The latter decided in October 1973 that relations between itself and Parliament should be improved, in particular by granting Parliament the right to debate Community trade agreements with third countries after their signature but before ratification.

As from the end of 1974 the powers of Parliament in respect of the budget were expanded, and Parliament was given the right to reject a draft budget in its entirety, while a conciliation committee (as a joint Parliament-Council of Ministers consultative body) was created in February 1975. The Parliament also has powers to enforce, by a two-thirds majority, the resignation of the Commission.

The Court of Justice. The task of the Court of Justice, based in Luxembourg, is to safeguard the law in the interpretation and application of the treaties under which the Communities have been set up.

The Court is composed of 13 judges (with at least one from each member state), one of whom is President of the Court. There are four chambers, each comprising a president and two judges. There are also a First Advocate-General and four other advocates-general, as well as a registrar. The members of the Court are appointed by the Communities' member governments for renewable six-year terms, and the President of the Court is appointed for a renewable three-year term by the judges from among themselves. A partial renewal of the Court takes place every three years.

The jurisdiction of the Court covers the settlement of all disputes within the Communities. The Court is the final arbiter on the legality of decisions—other than recommendations or opinions—of the executive. It hears appeals on the part of the executive or of a member state on grounds of incompetence, violation of essential rules of procedure, infringement of the treaties or of any rule implementing them, or an abuse of power. Any person or legal entity may, under the same terms, appeal against a decision which affects him.

Other matters which come under the jurisdiction of the Court include compensation for damage, and disputes between the Communities and their employees.

The Court of Auditors. The Court of Auditors, consisting of one member from each of the member countries appointed for six years by the Council of Ministers, was set up under the second Budget Treaty which came into force on June 1, 1977. It replaced an Audit Board established in 1974, as decided at the December 1973 summit conference in Copenhagen, and the auditor of the ECSC. Its functions are to examine not only the revenue and expenditure of the Community and of any body created by it but also those of the European Development Fund. It has to co-operate with national audit bodies which supervise the national authorities responsible for enforcing Community law.

The Economic and Social Committee. This committee assists the Council of Ministers and the Commission in an advisory capacity. It is composed of 189 members (24 each from France, the Federal Republic of Germany, Italy and the United Kingdom, 21 from Spain, 12 each from Belgium, Greece, the Netherlands and Portugal, nine each from Denmark and Ireland and six from Luxembourg) appointed for four-year renewable terms by the Council of Ministers. One-third of its members represent employers, one-third employees and one-third the general economic interest.

Consultative Committee of the ECSC. The European Coal and Steel Community's Consultative Committee has a minimum membership of 60 and a maximum membership of 81. Its members, who are oppointed by the Council of Ministers for a two-year term, include producers, workers, dealers and consumers.

Under the terms of the ECSC treaty the advice of the Consultative Committee must be sought by the Commission in certain cases before a decision can be reached. It may also be consulted on any other relevant matter.

Institutions of the European Communities

European Investment Bank. The European Investment Bank (EIB) was set up under the Treaty of Rome as an independent legal unity. Its members are the governments of the 12 member countries of the European Communities and its headquarters are in Luxembourg.

The functions of the bank are to promote a common investment policy within the Communities and thus to contribute to the smooth functioning of the common market. The EIB grants, on a non-profit basis, loans or guarantees for (i) projects in underdeveloped regions; (ii) the modernization, reorganization or extension of already established enterprises; and (iii) new enterprises of joint interest to several member countries because the size or special character of these enterprises makes it difficult for a single member country to finance them. The EIB is also authorized to grant loans to non-member countries in Europe and to countries and territories with association or co-operation agreements with the European Communities.

The powers of the EIB are vested in a Board of Governors, usually consisting of the Finance Ministers of the member countries. Its executive organ is a Board of Directors comprising 19 members and 11 alternate members, with France, Germany, Italy and the United Kingdom each nominating three members and two alternate members, the three Benelux countries each one member and jointly one alternate member, Denmark, Greece and Ireland each one member and jointly one alternate member, and the European Commission one of each. There is also a Management Committee consisting of a President and four Vice-Presidents.

Following the accession of Greece as from Jan. 1, 1981, the subscribed capital of the EIB totalled 7,200 million EUA.

With effect from Jan. 1, 1982, the EIB's subscribed capital was doubled to 14,400 million European currency units (ECU) (of the European Monetary System, EMS, established in March 1979). This meant an increase from 18,000 million to 36,000 million ECU in the permitted ceiling for outstanding EIB loans and guarantees (i.e. 250 per cent of the subscribed capital). By the end of 1981 these loans and guarantees had reached a total of 16,900 million ECU. To finance its lending in 1981 the EIB had raised the equivalent of 2,309,700,000 ECU in the international capital markets.

On June 11, 1985, the EIB Board of Governors decided once more to double the EIB's subscribed capital from 14,400 million to 28,800 million ECU) with effect from Jan. 1, 1986 (with Portugal and Spain contributing 2,300 million ECU).

Between 1981 and 1985 the EIB made loans totalling 550,000,000 ECU available to Portugal and Spain in order to facilitate their transition to membership of the European Communities. This financing was directed mainly towards small and medium-sized industries, energy supplies, transport links, forestry and tourism.

European Social Fund. The European Social Fund was created under the Treaty of Rome to facilitate employment and the mobility of labour within the Community. By improving opportunities of employment the Social Fund helps to raise the standard of living in the common market countries.

At the request of a member state the Fund pays 50 per cent of the cost incurred by that country or any of its public bodies in (i) retraining or granting resettlement allowances to workers who have become unemployed as a result of common market activities, and (ii) granting aid to workers temporarily forced to work for a short time or suspended as a result of changes in production in the undertaking employing them, so that these workers may maintain their standard of living pending the restoration of their full employment.

The Fund is administered by the Commission assisted by a committee consisting of representatives of member governments, trade unions and employers' associations.

The Council of Ministers on Nov. 26, 1970, approved proposals for changing the Social Fund into a "dynamic instrument" of a common employment policy. The major change under the new reforms was to enable an increasing proportion of the Fund's budget to help workers directly affected, or likely to be affected, by the execution of Community policies.

The Council decided on the same date to establish a Standing Committee on Employment to provide a forum for co-operation between the Council, the Commission, employers and unions. The Committee held its first meeting in Brussels on March 18, 1971.

On Dec. 20, 1977, the Council of (Foreign) Ministers adopted regulations revising the rules of the European Social Fund with effect from Jan. 1, 1978, "to make utilization of the fund's resources more effective and better co-ordinated with the Community's other structure-oriented financial instruments, to increase the rate of the fund's intervention to help projects in backward or declining regions, to increase aid for the vocational training of women and to widen the fund's field of activity".

New rules, adopted by the Council of (Foreign) Ministers on Oct. 17, 1983, and applied from Jan. 1, 1984, provided for new arrangements to promote youth employment and for grants to be made to certain categories of workers, including the unemployed, workers threatened with unemployment or part-time employment, women wishing to resume a career, the handicapped, and migrant workers. Moreover, 40 per cent of the Fund's resources were to be used for schemes to help the less favoured regions—Greece, the French overseas departments, Ireland, the Italian Mezzogiorno, and Northern Ireland.

University Institute. A post-graduate European University Institute was established on April 19, 1972, at the Villa Tolomei, Florence, Italy.

European Regional Development Fund. The ERDF, as endorsed by the heads of state or government of the nine member states in December 1974, was inaugurated as from Jan. 1, 1975, with the aim of providing funds for the development of less-favoured regions within the Community.

The ERDF budget increased from 300,000,000 units of account in 1975 to 2,140 million ECU in 1984. With effect from Jan. 1, 1985, a larger share of the disbursements was to be allocated to specific Community regional development programmes and geared towards mobilizing local resources to promote the indigenous potential of regions, rather than attracting investments from wealthier regions.

With effect from Jan. 1, 1986, the percentage ranges of ERDF disbursement to member states were established as follows: Italy 21.62–28.79 per cent, Spain 17.97–23.93 per cent, United Kingdom 14.50–19.31 per cent, Portugal 10.66–14.20 per cent, Greece 8.36–10.64 per cent, France 7.48–9.96 per cent, Ireland 3.82–4.61 per cent, Federal Republic of Germany 2.55–3.40 per cent, Netherlands 0.68–0.91 per cent, Belgium 0.61–0.82 per cent, Denmark 0.34–0.46 per cent, Luxembourg 0.04–0.06 per cent.

Other Funds. The *European Agricultural Guidance and Guarantee Fund* (EAGGF, or FEOGA) was set up in 1962 to finance the Community's common agricultural policy [see also pages 173–74]. By means of variable import levies it keeps the prices of imports at a threshold level, while the prices of domestic products are supported by the authorities committed to buy at an official intervention price; the Fund also makes grants towards the structural reform of agriculture.

For the year 1985 the appropriation available to the EAGGF was 19,883,100,000 ECU (an increase of 8.2 per cent over 1984).

The *European Monetary Co-operation Fund* (FECOM) was set up in 1973 in the context of moves towards monetary union, its task including the management of the "snake" (i.e. the joint float within permitted fluctuation margins of member countries' currencies) and also of the settlement of debts and credits among member countries and of short-term credits granted by central banks to a member state in temporary balance of payments difficulties. Under the new European Monetary System introduced in 1979 it was envisaged that FECOM would eventually be replaced by a fully-fledged European Monetary Fund [see pages 180–81].

The *European Development Fund* (EDF) is designed mainly to increase production and modernize infrastructures and services in the developing countries by means of the disbursement of aid for specific projects. Such aid is granted mainly to those developing countries associated with the Community under the Lomé Convention [see pages 182–84], but increasing amounts are also allocated to non-associated developing countries, notably those of the Indian sub-continent.

European Foundation. This foundation was set up on March 29, 1982 (upon the 25th anniversary of the signing of the Treaty of Rome establishing the EEC). It was to be based in Paris and to promote understanding of Europe's cultural heritage, foster a deeper perception of European integration and encourage contacts among the peoples of the Community. It was to be financed by a contribution of 4,000,000 ECU from the Community in the first three years, and also by voluntary contributions.

Enlargement of the Community

At the end of protracted negotiations on the enlargement of the European Community—which in the case of Britain had been conducted over a period of more than 10 years—a *Treaty of Accession to the European Communities* (the *Treaty of Brussels*) was signed in Brussels on Jan. 22, 1972, by the Prime Ministers of Britain, Denmark, the Republic of Ireland and Norway. As described below, Norway subsequently decided against accession.

The three principal documents making up the treaty were:

(*a*) The "Treaty concerning the accession of the Kingdom of Denmark, Ireland, the Kingdom of Norway and the United

Kingdom of Great Britain and Northern Ireland to the European Economic Community and the European Atomic Energy Community".

(b) The "Decision of the Council of the European Communities of Jan. 22, 1972, concerning the accession of the Kingdom of Denmark, Ireland, the Kingdom of Norway and the United Kingdom of Great Britain and Northern Ireland to the European Coal and Steel Community".

(c) The "Act concerning the conditions of accession and the adjustments to the treaties", covering under a number of heads the negotiations between Britain, Ireland, Denmark and Norway with the Six over the previous 18 months. Unlike (a) and (b), which were relatively short documents, (c) was an Act of great complexity and detail, embodying 161 articles and with numerous annexes.

As regards (a) and (b), a separate procedure was required for accession to the European Economic Community and Euratom on the one hand, and to the European Coal and Steel Community on the other, because of legal differences between the original treaties—the Treaties of Rome and the Treaty of Paris respectively.

The treaty on accession contained the following provisions:

Art. 1. (1) The Kingdom of Denmark, Ireland, the Kingdom of Norway and the United Kingdom of Great Britain and Northern Ireland hereby become members of the European Economic Community and of the European Atomic Energy Community and parties to the treaties establishing these Communities as amended or supplemented.

(2) The conditions of admission and the adjustments to the treaties establishing the European Economic Community and the European Atomic Energy Community necessitated thereby are set out in the Act annexed to this treaty. The provisions of that Act concerning the European Economic Community and the European Atomic Energy Community shall form an integral part of this treaty.

(3) The provisions concerning the rights and obligations of the member states and the powers and jurisdiction of the institutions of the Communities as set out in the treaties referred to in Paragraph 1 shall apply in respect of this treaty.

Art. 2. This treaty will be ratified by the high contracting parties in accordance with their respective constitutional requirements. The instruments of ratification will be deposited with the Government of the Italian Republic by Dec. 31, 1972, at the latest.

This treaty will enter into force on Jan. 1, 1973, provided that all the instruments of ratification have been deposited before that date and that all the instruments of accession to the European Coal and Steel Community are deposited on that date.

If, however, the states referred to in Article 1(1) have not all deposited their instruments of ratification and accession in due time, the treaty shall enter into force for those states which have deposited their instruments. . . .

The Decision of the Council contained provisions as follows:

Art. 1. (1) The Kingdom of Denmark, Ireland, the Kingdom of Norway and the United Kingdom of Great Britain and Northern Ireland may become members of the European Coal and Steel Community by acceding, under the conditions laid down in this Decision, to the treaty establishing that Community, as amended or supplemented.

(2) The conditions of accession and the adjustments to the treaty establishing the European Coal and Steel Community necessitated thereby are set out in the Act annexed to this Decision. The provisions of that Act concerning the European Coal and Steel Community shall form an integral part of this Decision.

(3) The provisions concerning the rights and obligations of the member states and the powers and jurisdiction of the institutions of the Community as set out in the treaty referred to in Paragraph 1 shall apply in respect of this Decision.

Art. 2. The instruments of accession of the Kingdom of Denmark, Ireland, the Kingdom of Norway and the United Kingdom of Great Britain and Northern Ireland to the European Coal and Steel Community will be deposited with the Government of the French Republic on Jan. 1, 1973.

Accession will take effect on Jan. 1, 1973, provided that all the instruments of accession have been deposited on that date and that all the instruments of ratification of the treaty concerning Accession to the European Economic Community and the European Atomic Energy Community have been deposited before that date.

If, however, the states referred to in the first paragraph of this article have not all deposited their instruments of accession and ratification in due time, accession shall take effect for the other acceding states. . . .

The 161 articles of the Act specified the transitional arrangements agreed upon in the negotiations leading to the conclusion of the treaty. During a transitional period of five years the new member countries undertook:

(a) To reduce customs barriers and non-tariff obstacles for industrial products between them and the old members of the Community in five phases at 20 per cent per annum;

(b) to adopt the Community's common external tariff at the end of the five-year period by adjustment in four phases of 40 per cent on Jan. 1, 1974, and 20 per cent on Jan. 1 of the three succeeding years.

In regard to agriculture the new member countries adopted the Community system of support under the common agricultural policy, with adjustments to full Community price levels in six steps over the five-year transitional period.

Approval of Enlargement in Britain, Denmark and Ireland. In *Britain*, the European Communities Bill, providing for the United Kingdom's entry into the European Economic Community, was given a second reading in the House of Commons on Feb. 17, 1972, by 309 votes (304 Conservatives and five Liberals) to 301 (279 Labour members, 15 Conservatives, six independents, and one Liberal), with eight abstentions and three members absent. The Bill passed its third reading in the House of Commons on July 13, 1972 by 301 votes (296 Conservatives and five Liberals) to 284 (264 Labour members, 16 Conservatives and four independents), with four Conservatives and 13 Labour members abstaining. In the House of Lords the Bill was approved by far larger majorities—189 votes to 19 at its second reading on July 26, and 161 votes to 21 at its third reading on Sept. 20. The Bill became law on Oct. 17, 1972.

In *Denmark*, ratification of the Treaty of Accession was approved by Parliament on Sept. 8, 1972, by 272 votes to 95, with one blank vote. Denmark's entry into the Community was also approved in a referendum on Oct. 3 by 1,958,115 votes (63.3 per cent of the votes cast) to 1,135,691 (36.7 per cent), with 11,907 blank and 7,409 other invalid papers, in a 90.1 per cent poll. Royal Assent was given to the ratification on Oct. 11, 1972.

In the *Republic of Ireland*, the necessary amendment to the Constitution, enabling the

Republic to become a member of the European Communities, was approved by the *Dail* (Lower House of Parliament) on Jan. 26, and by the Senate on March 8, 1972. As required by the Constitution, the proposal to amend it was submitted to a popular referendum on May 10, 1972, with the result that 1,041,880 voters (83 per cent of those voting) voted for the amendment, and 211,888 (17 per cent) against it, in a 71 per cent poll—so that those in favour constituted over 58 per cent of the electorate, and those against about 12 per cent. The Bill was signed by President de Valera on June 8, 1972.

Rejection in Norway. In Norway the decision to join the European Communities was, under the Norwegian Constitution, subject to a three-quarters' majority in the *Storting* (Parliament) being in favour; the Government, which did not command a parliamentary majority, did not expect to gain the required support in Parliament and decided to seek the people's approval of entry in a referendum (which is not provided for in the Norwegian Constitution), in the expectation that a popular majority in favour of entry would enable it subsequently to obtain the necessary parliamentary majority. In the event, the referendum held on Sept. 24–25, 1972, resulted in 1,099,389 votes (53.5 per cent of the poll) being cast against entry and 956,043 (or 46.5 per cent) in favour, in a 77.6 per cent poll.

The Norwegian Government consequently informed the representatives of the European Communities' member countries in Brussels on Sept. 26 that Norway was withdrawing its participation in the consultative negotiating committees, and it was officially announced on the same day that the Government had decided not to submit a proposal for membership of the European Communities to the *Storting*.

Norway's failure to ratify the Treaty of Accession necessitated a number of amendments to the treaty and its attendant documents, and these amendments were subsequently made, including the deletion of special protocols previously agreed upon with the Norwegian Government, and the reduction in the number of judges at the Court of Justice to nine (instead of the 11 previously envisaged).

Approval of Ratification by the Six. In France, ratification of the Treaty of Accession by the French President was approved in a referendum held throughout metropolitan France and the French overseas departments and territories on April 23, 1972, the official result being as follows:

	Actual figure	Percentage of electorate	Percentage of valid votes
"Yes" votes	10,847,554	36.37	68.31
"No" votes	5,030,934	16.87	31.68
Blank or spoilt papers	2,086,119	6.99	—
Abstentions	11,855,857	39.75	—

Ratification of the treaty was approved in Belgium by the Senate on June 30, 1972, and by the Chamber of Deputies on Dec. 8; in Western Germany by the *Bundestag* on June 21 and by the *Bundesrat* on July 7; in Italy by the Chamber of Deputies on Dec. 5 and by the Senate on Dec. 19; in Luxembourg by the Parliament on Dec. 20; and in the Netherlands by the Second Chamber of the States-General on Sept. 14 and by the First Chamber on Nov. 14.

Accession of Britain, Denmark and Ireland. Britain, Denmark and the Republic of Ireland became members of the European Communities on Jan. 1, 1973, in accordance with the provisions of the Treaty of Accession. The transitional period for the three acceding members ended on June 30, 1977.

The Danish Treaty of Accession to the European Communities extended also to Greenland but not to the Faroe Islands for which a special status was provided, with the effect that the Faroes participated in the Communities' free trade arrangements only with a status similar to that of the EFTA member countries, and they were therefore not bound by any other common policy arrangements, including those on fisheries.

UK Renegotiation and Referendum. The British (Labour) Government officially demanded, on April 1, 1974, a renegotiation of the terms of UK membership of the Communities on a number of grounds, including the proposed economic and monetary union to be achieved by 1980 (which the British Government described as "over-ambitious"); the European Union into which the relations of member states were to be transformed by 1980 (which was said to be "not desired . . . by the British people"); the common agricultural policy (which was said "not to take sufficient account of the differing interests and circumstances of member countries" and to confer "privileges on some and unfair burdens on others"); trade with Commonwealth and developing countries, the conditions of which should be improved; and the Communities' budget, to which Britain was making an excessive contribution.

However, on March 18, 1975, the British Government announced that it had decided to recommend to the British people to vote for continued UK membership of the European Communities in a referendum fixed for June 5, 1975, on the grounds that the UK Government had secured a satisfactory result in the response to its renegotiation demands.

These results included revisions in the common agricultural policy; the introduction of a corrective mechanism to deal with unfair contributions to the Communities' budget; the tacit abandonment of achieving economic and monetary union (EMU) by 1980; changes in regional, industrial and fiscal policies; agreements on Commonwealth sugar and New Zealand dairy products; the benefits accruing to developing countries under the Lomé Convention and avoidance of uniformity in the application of value-added tax.

The referendum of June 5, 1975, resulted in 17,378,581 votes (or 67.2 per cent of the total votes cast) in favour of Britain's continued membership of the European Communities, and 8,470,073 votes (32.8 per cent) against it in a poll of about 64 per cent.

Accession of Greece. Under a treaty of accession signed in Athens on May 28, 1979, Greece—which had formally applied for Community membership on June 12, 1975—became the 10th member of the European Communities on Jan. 1, 1981, following ratification of the treaty by all 10 countries concerned.

The treaty provided for a five-year transitional period for Greek adaptation to Community membership, with a seven-year period for the abolition of tariffs in a small number of agricultural products (in particular tomatoes and peaches) and for free movement of labour (although preference would be given, during the transitional period, to Greek workers where it was found necessary to recruit workers from outside the Communities, and Greek workers already legally employed in Community member states would be able progressively to bring in their families).

Greece would appoint a member to the Communities' Council of Ministers and another to the European Commission; it would have 24 seats in the European Parliament; there would be 12 Greek members in the Communities' Economic and Social Committee; and Greece would appoint a representative to the Board of Governors of the European Investment Bank.

A 1962 agreement providing for Greece's associate membership of the EEC had been virtually suspended in 1967 (following the military coup in April of that year) but had been reactivated in December 1974 after the new Greek Government had stated that it wished to transform its existing association into full membership in the very near future. Under a protocol to the association agreement, Greece had on Feb. 27, 1977, been granted loans and aid of 280,000,000 EUA up to Oct. 31, 1981.

Accession of Spain and Portugal. Spain and Portugal acceded to the Communities on Jan. 1, 1986, as provided for under a treaty of accession signed in Brussels on June 12, 1985, and subsequently ratified by all 10 existing member states. The two countries had originally applied for full membership in 1977 and negotiations had commenced with Portugal in October 1978 and with Spain in February 1979.

In general a seven-year transitional period was laid down for the establishment of a common market in industrial and agricultural goods between the two acceding countries and the 10, although provision was made for longer periods in certain sectors, principally in the agricultural and fisheries fields.

Progress of the EEC

Progressive Implementation of the Common Market. The progressive implementation of the common market in three four-year stages, as envisaged in the Treaty of Rome, proceeded

without prolonging any of the stages as provided for in the treaty. The most critical changeover was that from the first to the second stage which took place on Jan. 14, 1962. On this date, after a series of 45 meetings, the Council of Ministers finally reached unanimous agreement on a common policy for agriculture, without which the French Government had refused to agree to the move into the second stage of the common market's transitional period.

During the first stage of the treaty a unanimous decision of the Council of Ministers was required for the settlement of most issues, only a limited number of questions being decided by a qualified majority vote. The application of a qualified majority vote was extended in the second stage, when the unanimous vote was retained only on important questions of economic union and common policies.

The third stage of implementation of the treaty, which began on Jan. 1, 1966, saw yet a further extension of the application of the qualified majority vote, the unanimous vote being retained only for a relatively small number of important decisions. It continued to be true, however, that in practice no major issues were decided without the unanimous agreement of member states.

Acceleration of Economic Integration. From the middle of 1959 economic and political conditions within the Community improved to such an extent that adherence to the programme of economic integration laid down in the Treaty of Rome was no longer necessary. On May 12, 1960, the Council of Ministers therefore agreed on a plan to speed up implementation of the treaty from Jan. 1, 1961.

In connexion with its decision of May 12, 1960, to accelerate the reduction of customs duties between member countries and the adjustment of their duty rates to a common external tariff [see above], the Council of Ministers issued on the same date a "declaration of intention" to carry out such an acceleration also in all other spheres of economic integration, especially in the implementation of social measures, notably vocational training of employees, their freedom to accept employment anywhere, the application of social security schemes, and equal pay for men and women.

Customs duties within the European Economic Community were reduced on Jan. 1, 1962, by a further 10 per cent, making a total of 40 per cent for industrial products, 35 per cent for non-liberalized agricultural products, and 30 per cent for agricultural products liberalized since the formation of the Community. The 40 per cent reduction had been made in four stages of 10 per cent each on Jan. 1, 1959; July 1, 1960; Jan. 1, 1961; and Jan. 1, 1962. The reduction of duty for each industrial product by a minimum of 25 per cent, which was the target under the Treaty of Rome in the first stage of the transitional period up to Jan. 1, 1962, had therefore been substantially exceeded.

The European Economic Community took its first step towards a common external tariff policy on Dec. 31, 1960, i.e. the alignment of individual national tariffs with the proposed common tariff.

The Treaty of Rome originally set the date for this at Dec. 31, 1961 (the end of the first transitional period), but the Council of Ministers decided on May 12, 1960, to bring it forward by one year, i.e. to Dec. 31, 1960. The treaty specified that where individual duties were higher or lower than the common tariff rate by not more than 15 per cent, the common tariff rate was to be introduced at the first stage of alignment; in other cases the individual rates were to be increased or decreased towards the level of the common tariff by 30 per cent of the difference between the common tariff rate and the individual national rate. For the first move on Dec. 31, 1960, which applied only to industrial products while agricultural commodities were expressly excluded, the Community modified the basis of calculation by requiring the alignment to be carried out towards the rates shown in the common tariff nationally reduced by 20 per cent. The downward alignment of national rates on the common tariff, as calculated on this basis, was subject to the proviso that the resultant rate must not be less than that shown in the common tariff before the national 20 per cent reduction.

At its meeting of May 15, 1962, the Council of Ministers decided also to bring forward the second stage of adjustment between national tariffs and the common external tariff, this time by 18 months, i.e. from Dec. 31, 1965 (the end of the second stage), to July 1, 1963. From the latter date, therefore, a second 30 per cent alignment would come into force, reducing the difference between national tariffs and the common external tariff by 60 per cent.

Further Tariff Reductions. Customs duties on industrial and agricultural goods were reduced by 10 per cent on July 1, 1963, Jan. 1, 1965, and Jan. 1, 1966. By the last-named date there had been a total reduction of 80 per cent on industrial goods, 65 per cent on non-liberalized agricultural goods, and 60 per cent on agricultural goods liberalized since the establishment of the Community. A further lowering of customs duties in the industrial sector took place on July 1, 1967, when duties were reduced by another 5 per cent, bringing the total reduction up to 85 per cent. The final abolition of these duties came into force on July 1, 1968, thereby completing the customs union in the industrial sector.

Establishment of Common Agricultural Policy (CAP). The principal cause of disagreement within the EEC has been agricultural policy.

In 1960 the EEC Commission proposed the formation of a common agricultural policy based on common prices, a single fund for price supports, and joint import levies. It was not until Jan. 14, 1962, however, that an agreement for the first stage of a common agricultural policy for the EEC was adopted by the Council of Ministers.

Policy Objectives. The main objectives of the common policy for agriculture were outlined as follows:

(a) To balance supply and demand within the Community and externally by influencing supply by such measures as more regional specialization, stockpiling and structural reforms, and increasing demand by improving the quality of products.

(b) To provide farmers with a fair income by structural and regional improvements, the consolidation of holdings, electricity supplies, better transport and farming methods, information services and education.

(c) To stabilize the market by protecting farmers from speculative price fluctuations while not insulating them from the influence of long-term movements in world markets.

(d) To ensure equitable supplies to consumers by enabling the processing industries to find external outlets at reasonable or competitive prices, and by preventing prices from being fixed on the basis of marginal production costs.

Products. The regulations adopted by the Ministers applied to grain, pigmeat, eggs, poultry, fruit and vegetables, and wine. Fundamental decisions were also taken on the remaining major farm products (rice, beef and veal, dairy produce and sugar) and a time-table was set for the publication of the full regulations on all these items in 1962. The products covered constituted over 46 per cent of the total inter-Community trade in farm produce.

Transition Period. A seven-year transition period pending the full implementation of the common policy was fixed from July 1, 1962, to Dec. 31, 1969, but a decision to shorten this period to six years could be taken in the third year.

Other clauses of the agreement provided for common quality standards, harmonization of prices and a system of levies. The agreement also provided for the setting up of five management committees for grain, pigmeat, eggs and poultry, fruit and vegetables, and wine respectively.

The common agricultural policy would be financed by a European Agricultural Guidance and Guarantee Fund (EAGGF or FEOGA) consisting, for the first three years, of financial contributions by the member states. As soon as a common market system for agricultural products came into force the Community expenditure would be directly financed by receipts from levies on imports from non-member countries.

The common marketing organizations for grain, pigmeat, eggs and poultry, fruit and vegetables, and wine came into operation on July 30, 1962. Agreement on other agricultural marketing organizations was reached on Dec. 23, 1963.

An important agreement on cereal prices was reached by the Council of Ministers on Dec. 15, 1964. The ministers agreed on the settling of common prices for cereals, to be effective from July 1, 1967, and they also agreed to establish a common fund to help in harmonizing agriculture throughout the Community. The agreement was based on a set of proposals presented by the Commission to the Council of Ministers in November 1963. This plan set target prices for the whole Community for all cereals, and provided for compensation from the EEC budget for farmers who would thereby suffer loss of income.

The 1964–66 CAP Crisis. On Dec. 15, 1964, the Council of Ministers asked the EEC Commission for proposals, to be presented before April 1, 1965, on how the common agricultural policy should be financed for the period 1965–70.

The Commission accordingly submitted its proposals to the Council on April 1, 1965. These covered not only the renewal of levies on agricultural goods but also proposed that both these levies and industrial import duties should be paid into the EEC fund. As these receipts represented enormous amounts and constituted the EEC's financial resources, the Commission proposed that the European Parliament should be strengthened by being given powers to determine the Community's revenue, and that it should also receive wider powers over the Community's budget.

The Commission's scheme was considered by the Council of Ministers at a meeting in Brussels which opened on June 28, 1965, under the chairmanship of M. Couve de Murville, the French Foreign Minister, who immediately rejected the Commission's proposals, maintaining that political conditions had been imposed by the Commission which were totally unacceptable to France, and that the sole question to be settled was the renewal of levies after the expiration of the existing agricultural finance regulations on June 30, 1965.

Following the breakdown on July 2, 1965, of talks between the Foreign Ministers of the Six, the French Government announced on July 5, that it was withdrawing its representatives from a number of the Commission's working committees. France also boycotted the next meeting of the Council of Ministers on July 26–27, 1965, and did not in fact meet again with the other five EEC member states until January 1966. The main issues on which France felt unable to co-operate with her fellow-members of the EEC were (i) the granting to the Commission of significant supra-national authority, in particular of a budget of its own, financed from agricultural levies and customs duties, and (ii) the application of majority decisions, to which France could not agree on matters of importance.

These questions were discussed at the two Council meetings held in Luxembourg on Jan. 17–18 and Jan. 28–29, 1966. On the question of the powers of the Commission, the Council adopted a number of points for improving its relations with the Commission. These included the following:

(1) The Commission should consult the member governments at the appropriate level before submitting proposals for Community action of particular importance to the Council.

(2) Commission proposals should not be made known to the European Parliament or the public before their submission to the Council.

(3) The executive powers granted to the Commission in any policy field should be precisely formulated, leaving no room for its discretion.

(4) The Council should exercise a closer control over the Commission's budget.

The question of majority decisions was solved as follows:

(1) When issues very important to one or more member countries were at stake, the members of the Council would try, within a reasonable time, to reach solutions which could be adopted by all members of the Council, while respecting their mutual interests, and those of the Community, in accordance with Article 2 of the Treaty. (This article aimed at approximating the economic policies of EEC members to create a common market.)

(2) The French delegation considered that, when very important issues were at stake, discussion must be continued until unanimous agreement was reached.

(3) The six delegations noted that there was a divergence of views on what should be done in the event of a failure to reach complete agreement.

(4) They considered that this divergence did not prevent the Community's work being resumed in accordance with normal procedure.

On Feb. 2, 1966, the Commission issued a communiqué stating that the Community would resume its normal activities.

1966 Agreement on Agricultural Policy. Following the French delegation's return to the conference table, the Foreign Ministers decided in Luxembourg on Jan. 31, 1966, to proceed with all speed in an effort to reach agreement on the common agricultural policy and the industrial customs union, including the completion of a common external tariff. Accordingly, at their meeting on May 11 the ministers agreed on details of the Farm Fund and set July 1, 1968, as the target date for the coming into force of complete common markets for both industrial and agricultural goods. Finally, following a further series of meetings which opened on July 21 and lasted four days and two nights, full agreement was reached on the outstanding agricultural questions and also on the common external tariff for industrial goods.

Between 1966 and 1970 agreement was reached on common organization of markets in most agricultural sectors and also with respect to fisheries.

Financing of Agricultural Fund. After lengthy discussions, agreement was reached on financing the EAGGF. For the two years 1965–66 and 1966–67 the cost of the common agricultural policy would be met entirely by percentage contributions from the member countries to the Fund. From July 1, 1967 onwards, 90 per cent of the levies on imports of foodstuffs would be handed over by the member governments to the European Fund. This would, in fact, cover some 45 per cent of the Fund's expenditure, and the remainder of the cost would be paid from the national exchequers of the member countries in agreed proportions.

Agreement was also reached by the Council of Ministers on Feb. 5–7, 1970, on a regulation for financing the common agricultural policy as from Jan. 1, 1971, provided the preconditions for the coming into force of the arrangements replacing the contributions by member countries to the Community by the Community's own revenues had been met by that date. When the regulations became effective, the Guarantee Section of the Agricultural Fund took over complete financing responsibility from the national governments.

Adoption of CAP by Acceding Members. The common agricultural policy was officially adopted by Britain, Ireland and Denmark on Feb. 1, 1973. The adoption followed a compromise agreement reached a few days earlier on prices for cereals, pigmeat, poultry and eggs, and sugar. In this context Britain agreed, in view of the de facto devaluation of sterling against the

Community's unit of account, to a new (reduced) reference rate for the purposes of the agricultural policy (involving a devaluation of sterling by 9.2 per cent since June 1972, when sterling had been allowed to float).

Rules for the regulation of the Community's fruit, vegetable and olive oil markets were approved by the Council of (Agriculture) Ministers in Luxembourg on Oct. 17–18, 1983. For Greece (which acceded to the Community in 1981) the CAP was gradually applied over a five-year transitional period, except that a seven-year period was to apply to tomatoes and peaches. The transitional measures covered the progressive elimination of residual customs duties and the alignment of Greek prices to those of the Community. The differences between Greek and Community prices were compensated for during the transitional period by "accession compensatory amounts", but a special mechanism was agreed for certain fresh fruit and vegetables.

The integration of farmers in Portugal and Spain (members from Jan. 1, 1986) in the CAP is being spread over seven to more than 10 years, with customs duties to be abolished in stages while price and subsidy levels gradually rise to those in the rest of the Community, and price gaps during the transitional period are offset by "accession compensatory amounts" to adjust the price of goods crossing the frontier in either direction between the new and the old member countries.

For Spain special transitional measures have been agreed for up to 10 years for wine, olive oil and other fats, fruit and vegetables, and certain northern products (milk and dairy produce, beef and soft wheat). For Portugal the normal transitional rules apply only to 15 per cent of Portuguese production, and transition will be spread over up to 10 years for the biggest sectors (cereals, dairy produce, meat, fresh fruit and vegetables, and wine). In addition to other special measures the Community has undertaken to finance a development programme to assist Portugal's agriculture to cope with the required changes (at a cost of 700,000,000 ECU over 10 years).

CAP Surplus Stocks. The availability of guaranteed prices under the CAP led to the accumulation of vast surplus stocks of certain agricultural products (notably butter, milk powder, grain, beef and wine), as Community farmers were able to maximize production without reference to market requirements. On March 31, 1984, the Council of (Agriculture) Ministers agreed (for the first time) to a limitation on production of milk by introducing a quota system at a total of 98,363,000 tonnes per annum for five years (except for 1984–85, when it was set at 99,235,000 tonnes). Other measures intended to reduce surpluses were subsequently introduced, although all have had only limited effect.

One controversial consequence of the "food mountain" phenomenon has been the regular sale of surplus stocks to non-Community countries (notably to the Soviet Union) at prices well below those applicable in the Community and thus effectively subsidized by Community taxpayers.

Common Fisheries Policy (CFP). A common fisheries policy for the EC was eventually agreed on Jan. 25, 1983, after many years of negotiations. Its four constituent parts are (i) an EC system for the conservation of resources, including a listing of total allowable catches (TACs) each year, the allocation of quotes to individual states, and agreement on exclusive access zones; (ii) structural measures designed to adjust capacity in the fishing industry and to improve productivity; (iii) a common organization of the market; and (iv) fisheries agreements with non-member countries, together with formal consultations between members with a view to concerted action in the context of international agreements.

The accession of Spain (with a fishing fleet larger than that of the 10 existing members combined) and Portugal to the EC as from Jan. 1, 1986, meant that the Community's 200-mile exclusive economic zone was more than doubled (in particular by the inclusion of Atlantic island groups), although the continental shelf area of fishing grounds and commercial stocks was increased only marginally. Under the accession arrangements the CFP was to be applied for Spain and Portugal over a seven-to-10-year transitional period, during which licensing arrangements were to apply to Spanish fishing in Community waters beyond a 12-mile coastal economic zone.

As from Jan. 1, 1985, Greenland (having ceased to be a member of the Community) obtained overseas countries and territories (OCT) status with the Community, which gave Greenland fishery products duty-free access to Community markets, while a 10-year fisheries agreement (setting annual quotas) was automatically renewable for six-year periods.

1986 "Single European Act". After several months of discussion on proposals for reform of Community arrangements, agreement was reached by the Council of Ministers on Dec. 16–17, 1985, on a number of amendments to the Treaty of Rome. These were enshrined in a "Single European Act" which was, on Feb. 17, 1986, signed by nine of the 12 member states, with Denmark, Greece and Italy following suit on Feb. 28. The Act required ratification by the 12 national parliaments before it could enter into force (the first such ratifications coming from Denmark on June 13, 1986, and Belgium on Aug. 25, 1986).

The Danish government had failed to obtain parliamentary support for approval of the Act, but in a referendum held in Denmark on Feb. 27, 1986, 56.2 per cent of the votes cast were in favour of, and 43.8 per cent against, the Community reforms. Greece had initially entered a symbolic protest against the isolation of Denmark, while Italy had been concerned to register its view that the measures were inadequate.

The "Single European Act" contained the following principal amendments to the 1957 Treaty of Rome:

A deadline of Dec. 31, 1992, was set for the establishment of the internal market as "an area without frontiers in which the free movement of goods, persons, services and capital is ensured in accordance with the provisions of the Treaty".

On the Community monetary capacity a new article was added, stating that "member states . . . shall take account of the experience acquired in co-operation in the framework of the EMS and in developing the ECU, and shall respect existing powers in this field".

The Community was to aim at reducing the "disparities between the various regions and the backwardness of the least-favoured regions" (including "declining industrial regions"). The Council was required to act unanimously on the proposals made within one year, with subsequent decisions being taken by a qualified majority.

Proposals were agreed for the "institution of a procedure for co-operation with the European Parliament" by the Council and the Commission.

The aim of the Communities was redefined, so as to include efforts "to strengthen the scientific and technological basis of European industry and to encourage it to become more competitive at international level".

Objectives of action relating to the environment were "to preserve, protect and improve the quality of the environment, to contribute towards protecting human health, and to ensure the prudent and rational use of natural resources"; measures adopted were not to prevent each member state from "maintaining and introducing more stringent protective measures compatible with the Treaty, and with the operation of the internal market in particular".

Member states were also to "pay particular attention to encouraging improvements, especially in the working environment, as regards the health and safety of workers", with the object of "the harmonization of conditions in this area" (but again without preventing member states from "introducing more stringent measures").

Developments in Other Fields

LABOUR QUESTIONS

On July 20, 1960, the EEC Commission sent a formal recommendation to member states on the fulfilment of the principle of equal pay for men and women in return for equal work. The Council approved the reduction of the maximum differences to 15 per cent by June 30, 1962, and to 10 per cent by June 30, 1963, with their complete elimination by Dec. 31, 1964.

The first regulations on the free movement of workers within the Community came into force on Sept. 1, 1961. These were superseded by new regulations effective from May 4, 1964. The principal changes were as follows:

Abandonment of Priority for Home Labour Market. The new regulations provided, in principle, for equal rights of access to employment throughout the Community territory for all wage-earners, and particularly seasonal and frontier workers, who had previously not been covered by any regulation regarding free movement.

To prevent the balance of the labour market from being upset in certain regions, or the aggravation of crises in certain occupations, a member state, if it should consider such action necessary, might provisionally maintain or reinstate priority for the home labour market with specific limits (i.e. lay down that any available vacancies on the national labour market should be filled within three weeks by the domestic administration from its own nationals, but that after this period offers of employment should be transmitted to the other Community countries). A member state must inform the Commission of its decision, giving its reasons for taking such action.

Prolongation of Employment Rights. The period of "assimilation" of foreign workers in the country of employment (making them eligible for any employment within the Community) was reduced from four to two years. A foreign worker who had been in regular employment for two years and who subsequently returned to his country of origin would retain for two years afterwards the rights acquired under the provision for prolongation of employment.

Eligibility of Workers for Election in Representative Bodies in Places of Employment. Hitherto, foreign workers had enjoyed the right to vote for but not the right to election to representative bodies in the firm in which they were working. Under the new regulations foreign workers could be elected to these bodies provided they satisfied the same conditions as national workers and had worked for the firm for three years.

Admission of Foreign Workers' Families. The earlier regulations allowed the worker the right to be accompanied or joined by his wife and children under the age of 21. Under the new regulations this right was extended to all dependent relatives and any other relative living in the worker's home. Admission of a worker's family would continue to depend on whether he could house them in a manner regarded as normal for local workers in the area where he was employed.

FREEDOM OF ESTABLISHMENT AND FREEDOM TO SUPPLY SERVICES

A programme of gradually abolishing restrictions on setting up business and supplying services was adopted by the Council of Ministers on Oct. 25, 1961.

The programme envisaged the abolition of discriminations based on nationality, hitherto restricting access to numerous activities as follows:

(1) By Dec. 31, 1963, for the textile, footwear, paper, basic chemicals and metalworking industries, and for the wholesale trade, banking and dealings in property;

(2) by Dec. 31, 1965, for retail distribution, department stores and the food industry;

(3) by Dec. 31, 1967, for pharmacies (chemists), veterinary surgeons, insurance agents and transport;

(4) by Dec. 31, 1969, for education, film production and publicity material.

Certain general principles on freedom of establishment and freedom to supply services were approved by the Council of Ministers at its meeting in November 1963. They included the following:

(1) Self-employed people who wished to establish themselves or supply services in another member country had the right to membership in Chambers of Commerce and professional associations in that country, and would be eligible to hold office in these organizations provided that such officers would not exercise public authority.

(2) Where specific qualifications were required for certain occupations, the host country would only be able to require that the applicant had passed a supplementary examination if the practice of a profession was subject to special conditions.

(3) Persons who supplied services would have the right to be accompanied by members of their staff in the country in which the service was performed.

FREEDOM OF MOVEMENT FOR CAPITAL

On May 12, 1960, the Council of Ministers approved a directive on freedom of movement for capital, which entered into force on June 27, 1960.

It established:

(1) Unconditional freedom of capital movements connected with the freeing of trade in goods, of services, and of the movement of persons, and also with the free exercise of the right to establishment;

(2) unconditional and irreversible freedom for sale and purchase of stocks and shares quoted in the Community stock markets;

(3) conditional freedom with regard to the issuing and placing of stocks and shares on capital markets, and for the purchase of unquoted stocks and shares. Any Community country might, however, maintain or reimpose existing restrictions if their abolition was likely to hinder the achievement of its economic policy objectives.

The Federal Republic of Germany, Belgium and Luxembourg were not required to take any further liberalization measures in this respect since their foreign currency legislation already went beyond the obligations imposed by the Community directive.

COMMON TRANSPORT POLICY

On Feb. 27, 1962, the Council of Ministers asked the Commission to present detailed proposals for a common transport policy for roads, railway and inland waterways. The programme, which was submitted on June 1, 1962, was based on the principles of equality of treatment; financial independence; freedom of action for transport enterprises; free choice by the user of the means of transport; and co-ordination of investment.

An actual common transport policy was not agreed upon by the Council of Ministers until June 22, 1965. The Community transport system was intended to regulate competition in all sectors by the progressive introduction of fixed-rate limits in two separate stages.

During the first stage—1966 to 1969—only commercial transport between member countries would be subject to EEC regulations. Upper and lower tariff limits would be published for certain classes of road and rail traffic, though contracts could be made outside these rates under certain circumstances provided the details were published. Non-binding reference limits would be fixed for water transport, but contracts made outside these limits would also be published.

In the second stage—1969 to 1972—the reference limit system would be extended to certain categories of national and international traffic of heavy goods (the Council had still to decide on a definition) and also on other forms of national transport. By 1970, therefore, almost all road transportation and a significant part of rail goods traffic in the common market would be covered by a strict system of rate control, while a more flexible system would apply to all waterborne traffic and the remaining section of railway traffic,

though probably to only a small part of road haulage.

The Ministers also agreed that during the two stages of the programme the harmonization of national regulations affecting their transport sectors should be achieved and an attempt made to reach a common position on competition questions, including subsidies for national railways.

On Feb. 1, 1984, the then 10 Community member countries, as well as Hungary and Switzerland, signed an international convention on the harmonization of frontier control of goods (worked out under the auspices of the UN Economic Commission for Europe-ECE).

On the Franco-German border customs formalities were abolished for French and West German citizens from July 16, 1984, and for other Community citizens from Aug. 1, 1984.

On Dec. 18, 1984, the Council of (Internal and Consumer Protection) Ministers reached agreement on a single administrative document for trade in goods within the Community as from Jan. 1, 1988.

On Dec. 19, 1984, the Council of (Transport) Ministers definitively adopted a series of liberalization and harmonization measures which included, as from July 1, 1986, the raising of the maximum weight of lorries generally to 40 tonnes (with Ireland and the United Kingdom being able to maintain their 38-tonne limit until a review in 1987), the doubling of Community road haulage licences by 1989, and the allocation of 950,000,000 ECU from the 1983–84 budgets for road and rail infrastructure projects.

Border controls on road and rail freight between the Federal Republic of Germany and the Benelux countries were lifted from Jan. 1, 1985.

As from June 15, 1985, the Benelux countries, France and the Federal Republic of Germany agreed to abolish customs formalities for Community citizens travelling between the five countries (and to replace them by spot checks only).

Notwithstanding these measures the European Court of Justice found on May 22, 1985, that the Communities Council of Ministers had failed to ensure the freedoms to provide transport services and to carry out transport operations as required by the 1957 Treaty of Rome setting up the EEC.

COMPETITION POLICY

Following a decision of the Council of Ministers on Dec. 19, 1961, to adopt a common anti-trust policy, detailed regulations on monopolistic practices were approved by the Council on Feb. 6, 1962.

The regulations (1) reaffirmed Articles 85–86 of the Treaty of Rome, which places a general ban on agreements, decisions, and concerted practices of an anti-competitive character; (2) required all such agreements, decisions, and practices already in force to be registered with the Commission by Nov. 1, 1962, if they had been made or agreed between more than two participants, and by Feb. 1, 1963, if between two participants; (3) laid down that all agreements etc. entered into after the coming into force of the regulations must be notified to the Commission; (4) exempted, however, from the stipulations under (2) and (3) certain types of agreements, decisions and concerted practices; (5) gave the Commission power with regard to provision of information, control, and, in the cases where the rules were not observed, the imposition of penalties and fines.

It was stated that the rules would apply in principle also to transport, though they might be modified by the common transport policy; that they would apply to agriculture only in so far as they did not affect the aims of the common agricultural policy; and that they applied to oil but not to coal, for which the European Coal and Steel Community was responsible.

On March 14, 1967, the EEC Commission adopted a regulation on block exemption for some 30,000 exclusive dealing agreements between manufacturers and distributors, which had been notified to the Commission in accordance with the regulations of Feb. 6, 1962. Under each of these agreements, which was between a manufacturer and a dealer, the dealer could acquire a sole right of re-sale of products in a specific area of the Community. The new regulation came into force on May 1, 1967.

The achievement of the customs union in July 1968 was followed by rapid development of competition policy with the aim of maintaining the free trade facilitated by the removal of tariff barriers. The application of the relevant articles of the Treaty of Rome and of the 1962 regulations was carried out by means of further block exemptions for certain business agreements and also by means of a series of test cases, designed to identify restrictive business practices which the Commission judged to be in contravention of the Community rules.

On July 29, 1968, the Commission published a list of forms of co-operation between small and medium-sized companies which it actively encouraged, and illustrated its intentions by a number of individual decisions with respect to certain forms of agreement. In parallel with this action the Commission also took a number of decisions forbidding various forms of cartels and in July 1969 for the first time imposed fines against members of two cartels.

The decisions to impose fines and, in one of the two cases, to act against companies based outside the Community, were upheld by the Court of Justice in July 1970 and in July 1972. On Dec. 16, 1972, the Commission announced that it had imposed fines totalling 9,000,000 units of account on members of a sugar cartel, the heaviest penalty thus far inflicted to enforce competition policy.

The first interpretation of Community competition policy with regard to Article 86 (dealing with abuse of a dominant position) was made with a decision against the West German performing rights society on June 2, 1971, and was followed by a further decision against an American metal container company on Dec. 13, 1971. The latter decision was the first in which the Commission had attempted to define Article 86 of the Rome Treaty as an instrument for controlling economic concentrations.

COMMON TURNOVER TAX SYSTEM

On Feb. 9, 1967, the Council of Ministers adopted two directives on the harmonization of the turnover tax system in member countries, to be completed by Jan. 1, 1970. The system adopted by the Six was the "value-added" system (VAT), by which only the value added to a product at different stages of production is liable to taxation, as opposed to the "cascade" system, by which the whole value of the product at different stages of production is taxed.

The system was adopted by three member countries—France, West Germany and the Netherlands—before the deadline; by Luxembourg on Jan. 1, 1970; by Belgium on Jan. 1, 1971; and by Italy on Jan. 1, 1973. VAT had already been in force in Denmark since 1967; was introduced in Ireland on Nov. 1, 1972; and came into force in Britain on April 1, 1973.

COMMON COMMERCIAL POLICY

The European Communities' common commercial policy came into force on Jan. 1, 1970, i.e. at the end of the 15-year transitional period as laid down in the Treaty of Rome.

However, the Council of Ministers decided on Oct. 17, 1969, that member countries would be allowed to conclude bilateral trade agreements with other countries for a three-year period from Jan. 1, 1970, provided such agreements had received prior authorization from the Council, which would have to approve the agreement before signature. [This ruling enabled EEC member states to conclude individual agreements with member states of the Council for Mutual Economic Assistance (CMEA or Comecon), which had declined to negotiate with the EEC as one unit.] After Jan. 1, 1973, all trade negotiations with non-EEC countries had to be conducted by the Commission of the EEC as a whole.

GENERALIZED SYSTEM OF PREFERENCES

The Council of Ministers decided on March 30, 1971, to introduce as from July 1, 1971, a generalized system of preferences (GSP) in favour of manufactured and semi-manufactured goods exported to the EEC by developing countries, involving the abolition of duties on such exports as well as on certain processed agricultural products—within certain limits.

These limits included the imposition of "ceilings" on imports of manufactures from developing countries and the limitation of preferences for the most competitive of the developing countries so as to reserve a substantial quota for the less developed ones.

On Dec. 16, 1980, the Council of Ministers adopted an outline GSP scheme for the five-year period 1981–85 within the context of a commitment to apply such arrangements at least until 1990.

As from the beginning of 1982 a total of 125 countries benefited from GSP concessions.

MONETARY AGREEMENTS

The European Commission on Feb. 12, 1969, sent to EEC member governments a proposal—the so-called "Barre plan" (named after the Commission's Vice-President, M. Raymond Barre)—for co-ordination of economic policies and monetary co-operation.

Under this plan, each member country undertook to place part of its reserves at the disposal of the others, and in the event of difficulties any member might call on its partners for assistance within a ceiling to be fixed subsequently. Joint consultations would then be held with a view to re-establishing equilibrium. If no agreement could be reached, the receiving country's indebtedness should not exceed three months, but if agreement was reached the credits might be renewed or converted into medium-term assistance, all such arrangements having to be accompanied by increased co-ordination of economic policies.

The Council of Ministers approved the plan on March 4, 1969, with the proviso that the arrangements should be between the various central banks rather than between the governments.

COMMUNITY BUDGET

Following a conference of the member countries' heads of state or government at The Hague on Dec. 1–5, 1969, the Council of Ministers reached agreement on Dec. 22, 1969, on the Communities' budget as follows:

From Jan. 1, 1971, all receipts from levies would be allocated to the Communities, and there would be a similar gradual allocation of the receipts from customs duties from the same date. Any deficit during an interim period would be covered by national contributions according to an agreed scale, and after the interim period these contributions would be replaced by receipts corresponding to a uniform rate of the harmonized value-added tax (VAT).

As from the adoption of the 1975 budget the European Parliament would have powers to amend, by a majority vote of its members, any draft budget submitted by the Council of Ministers, although any amendment of the VAT rate would have to remain within the limit set by the Council's decree introducing this tax. Any amendments made by the European Parliament might be altered by the Council by a qualified majority vote; any such alterations by the Council could be changed by the European Parliament by a decision of a majority of its membership and subject to three-fifths of the votes cast being in favour; the Parliament would thus adopt the budget in its final form, but if Parliament failed to reach a decision within a fixed period, the budget would stand as drawn up by the Council.

Procedures for the European Parliament's control of the budget were approved by the Council on April 22, 1970.

The 1979 budget of the Communities was the first to be financed by "own resources" accruing from the Community system of VAT, applied from Jan. 1, 1979, by six of the member states (Belgium, Denmark, France, Italy, the Netherlands and the United Kingdom), while the three other member states (the Federal Republic of Germany, Ireland and Luxembourg) paid financial contributions based on their gross national product. However, these three subsequently also applied the VAT-based system, the Federal Republic of Germany from Jan. 1, 1980.

After a protracted dispute in 1979 and early 1980 over the UK Government's demand for a reduction in its net contribution to the Community budget, the Council of Ministers on May 29–30, 1980, reached agreement on a formula under which:

(i) The United Kingdom would obtain a rebate of about two-thirds of the Commission's estimate of its net contribution of some £2,380 million overall for the two years 1980 and 1981, (ii) the United Kingdom would bear only a portion of any net UK contribution in excess of the Commission's estimates for 1980 and 1981, and (iii) similar arrangements would apply in 1982 if no restructuring of the Community budget had been agreed in the intervening period, the Commission being instructed to put forward detailed proposals in the latter respect.

Under this agreement, the United Kingdom would receive substantial rebates of original payments on the basis of (i) a revision of the budgetary correcting mechanism set up in 1976 in an earlier attempt to solve Britain's difficulties and (ii) special supplementary measures under which Community funds would be available to support certain categories of UK public expenditure programmes.

Annual Community budgets finally approved since 1978 have been as follows:

Year	Date adopted	Appropriation for payment	Appropriation for commitments
		EUA	EUA
1978	Dec. 21, 1977	12,362,004,592	12,702,284,084
1979	Dec. 15, 1978	13,494,353,875	14,576,673,920
1980	July 9, 1980	15,683,097,261	17,318,895,261
		ECU	ECU
1981	Dec. 23, 1980	19,327,630,620	21,122,798,325
1982	Dec. 21, 1981	21,984,441,540	23,260,133,140
1983	Dec. 21, 1982	21,558,923,924	22,988,604,924
1984	Dec. 20, 1983	25,361,000,000	25,404,000,000
1985	June 13, 1985	28,433,190,000	30,616,020,000
1986	July 10, 1986	35,174,000,000	36,052,000,000

Moves towards European Union

Political Union. After the Hague conference of EEC heads of state and government of December 1969 [see page 164] had agreed to an examination of "the best way of achieving progress in the matter of political unification", a group of Foreign Ministry officials under the chairmanship of Vicomte Etienne Davignon (Belgium) subsequently prepared two reports, the final version of the second report being adopted by the EEC Foreign Ministers on Oct. 27, 1970.

Listing the objects of a united Europe, the Davignon Report stated that it should be "based on a common heritage of respect for the liberty and rights of man and bring together democratic states with freely elected parliaments".

Proposals made in the report were inter alia that Foreign Ministers should meet at least once every six months; conferences of heads of state or government should be held when deemed desirable; and "in the event of a serious crisis or special urgency" there should be extraordinary consultation between the member states' governments. The ministerial meetings should be prepared by a Political Committee, and the Council's President-in-office should, once a year, provide the European Parliament with a progress report on the work done in this field.

At the summit conference of heads of government or of state of the Nine held in Paris in October 1972, a communiqué was issued setting out the future policies of the enlarged Community. Member countries agreed as follows:

(i) To create before Dec. 31, 1973, a Regional Development Fund;

(2) to draw up by Jan. 1, 1974, action programmes in the fields of social policy, industrial, scientific and technological policy and environmental policy;

(3) to define guidelines for external relations with developing countries and with Eastern Europe. In this field the Community also attached major importance to the multilateral negotiations in the context of GATT in which it would participate.

(4) With regard to foreign policy, Foreign Ministers would in future meet four times a year instead of twice as hitherto, and would prepare a second stage report on political integration by June 30, 1973.

(5) Support would be given to measures aimed at clarifying relationships between Community institutions and member states, and practical steps towards this end would be taken before June 30, 1973.

The meeting requested the institutions of the Community to draw up a report by the end of 1975 on the incorporation before the end of the decade of "the whole complex of the relations of member states into a European union". However, although by the end of 1980 member states had made some progress towards co-ordinating their foreign policies and also towards greater economic and monetary union [see below], the original aim of a full-scale European union had by the mid-1970s ceased to be regarded as a realistic goal for the foreseeable future. In a further report on European union published in January 1976, the then Belgian Prime Minister, M. Léo Tindemans, "deliberately refused" to draw up a draft constitution for a future union since it was "difficult to lay down at this stage the date of completion of the European union". Instead, the report set out "the objective and methods whereby Europe can be invested with a new vitality and current obstacles can be overcome", stressing in particular the role of a directly-elected European Parliament.

Economic and Monetary Union. With a view to achieving complete economic and monetary union of the EEC member countries by December 1980, the Council endorsed in February 1971

plans for the first of three stages for this scheme. The details were contained in the so-called Werner Report, drawn up by a working party under the chairmanship of M. Pierre Werner, the Luxembourg Prime Minister and Minister of Finance.

The final part of this report, completed on Oct. 8, 1970, restated the objectives of economic and monetary union as affirmed by The Hague conference of EEC heads of state and government in December 1969 [see page 164].

The report made it clear that the proposed union would mean that the principal decisions of economic policy would be taken at Community level, and that the necessary powers would therefore be transferred from the national plane to the Community plane, which would entail the progressive development of political co-operation. In the long run, the report said, this development was bound to lead to political union.

The proposed monetary union would imply, the report continued, "the total and irreversible convertibility of currencies, the elimination of margins of fluctuation in rates of exchange, the irrevocable fixing of parity ratios and the total liberation of movements of capital".

The Community's centre of decision would be politically responsible to a European Parliament.

The report also laid down procedures for the first stage of this programme, covering three years as from Jan. 1, 1971.

After adopting the above plan on Feb. 9, 1971, the Council defined its objectives in a resolution, approved on March 22, 1971, and including the following details:

At the end of the three-stage, 10-year plan, the Community would be:

(1) "An area within which persons, goods, services and capital can circulate freely . . . without leading to structural and regional disequilibrium . . .";

(2) "an individual monetary unit within the international system, . . . comprising a Community organization of the central banks"; and

(3) in possession of institutions empowered to ensure the management of economic and monetary union "subject to the deliberations and control" of the European Parliament.

The resolution also laid down what measures would have to be taken within the first three-year stage. These included the establishment of Community rules determining the uniform assessment of the value-added tax; harmonization in the application, assessment and collection of excise duties; and harmonization of other taxes. It was also stressed that "the Community must progressively adopt common positions in monetary relations with third countries and international organizations".

Another decision by the Council involved approval for a four-year scheme (later renewable every five years) for providing medium-term financial aid for member countries which might be in, or threatened by, balance-of-payments difficulties—this decision being an implementation of the "Barre plan" of 1969 [see above].

At their meeting on Feb. 8–9, 1971, the EEC Ministers of Foreign Affairs and Finance agreed, at a request by the Federal Republic of Germany, to an "escape clause", under which, if progress in the harmonization of the economic policies of the member countries was in the view of one or more members insufficient and further negotiations to reach an agreed solution of the outstanding problems remained unsuccessful, it would become possible for dissatisfied members to demand, by Dec. 31, 1975, the termination of the various measures of monetary co-operation although it was agreed, on French insistence, that the decision not to widen the fluctuation margins between Community currencies could not be revoked.

Joint Currency Float. The Council of Ministers on March 21, 1972, formally approved an agreement in principle on the implementation of the 1971 resolution on economic and monetary union [see above]. The main element of the agreement was that by July 1, 1972, at the latest, the maximum margin of fluctuation between the currencies of any two member states would be fixed at 2.25 per cent, while the longer-term aim was the complete elimination of any fluctuation margin.

This joint currency float—also known as "the snake in the tunnel" or the "snake"—was implemented by the then six member countries of the European Communities as from April 24, 1972, by Denmark and Ireland from May 1, 1972, and by Norway from May 23, 1972.

The "snake", however, did not operate without disturbances. The United Kingdom and Ireland devalued their currencies in the second half of June 1972, when the Danish currency was allowed to float within margins of 4.5 per cent; Denmark, however, rejoined the "snake" on Oct. 10 of that year. France temporarily withdrew from the "snake" from Jan. 19, 1974, until July 10, 1975, and it again withdrew on March 15, 1976. Italy effectively left the "snake" on Jan. 22, 1973, by introducing a two-tier exchange rate. Norway finally left the "snake" on Dec. 12, 1978 (leaving only the three Benelux countries, Denmark and the Federal Republic of Germany within the "snake").

The Swiss National Bank was from December 1975 included in the consultation mechanism linking the central banks of the "snake" countries.

European Monetary System. With effect from March 13, 1979, a European Monetary System (EMS) entered into operation on the basis of new central rates fixed on the previous day for each of the then nine member countries' currencies against the European currency unit (ECU), with fluctuation limits of plus or minus 2.25 per cent (6 per cent for the Italian lira). The United Kingdom decided not to participate in the exchange-rate mechanism, although it became associated with other aspects of the EMS.

The new exchange rates remained in force until Sept. 24, 1979, when the West German mark was revalued by 5 per cent against the Danish currency and by 2 per cent against the currencies of the other EMS participants. The ECU was from the outset of the EMS defined as identical with the European unit of account (EUA).

On March 22, 1981, the Italian lira was devalued by 6 per cent within the EMS.

On April 6, 1986, the European currencies were realigned, with five of them being changed as follows: the Deutsche Mark plus 3 per cent, the Netherlands guilder plus three per cent, the Belgian and Luxembourg francs by plus 1 per cent, the Danish krone by plus 1 per cent and the French franc by minus 3 per cent. The Italian lira and the Irish punt remained unchanged.

Industrial Action Programme. On Dec. 17, 1973, the Council of Ministers adopted proposals relating to an "initial action programme" on industrial policy with a view to initiating a uniform industrial base in the EEC's member countries, with the abolition of technical, fiscal and legal barriers between undertakings in the various member states.

Scientific and Technological Programme. On Jan. 16, 1974, the Council of Ministers adopted proposals for an action programme on scientific and technological policy involving (i) the creation of a Committee for Scientific and Technical Research (CREST) for co-ordinating national policies not subject to military or industrial secrecy; (ii) the promotion of basic research through participation in a proposed European Science Foundation; and (iii) research projects in various fields, including the development of the European Communities over the next 30 years (a "Europe plus 30" project). (CREST held its first meeting in Brussels on Feb. 18–19, 1974.)

On Dec. 10, 1985, agreements on the promotion of high-technology research in super-dense metals were signed in Brussels by France, the Federal Republic of Germany, Italy and the United Kingdom.

Further Activities, 1973–85

Environmental Action Programme. A two-year programme of environmental action, adopted by the Council of Ministers on July 20, 1973, was aimed at the harmonization of national programmes on the basis of a common long-term plan. The programme laid down certain principles, among them that "the cost of preventing and abolishing nuisances (caused by pollution) must be borne by the polluter" and that the interests of the developing countries must be taken into account, with any adverse consequences of measures taken on their economic development being reduced as far as possible.

Social Action Programme. A three-year social action programme, approved by the Council of Ministers on Dec. 11, 1973, and coming into force on Jan. 1, 1964, was aimed inter alia at "appropriate consultation between member states on their employment policies" and "better co-operation by national employment services"; an "action programme for migrant workers"; a "common vocational training policy"; "equality between men and women" in employment, vocational training and advancement, working conditions and pay; consultation on social protection policies; an initial action programme on health and safety at work and the health of workers; and also "specific measures to combat poverty". Also within the context of this programme, a series of directives were adopted in the late 1970s providing for freedom of movement and practice throughout the Community of certain professions, including doctors (June 1975), lawyers (March 1977), dentists (June 1978) and veterinary surgeons (December 1978), and for the mutual recognition of their diplomas in the Community.

Action Committee for Europe. An inaugural session of this Committee was held in Bonn on June 7, 1985, and attended by leading politicians, trade union officials and industrialists. It called for (i) the creation of a true unified European market, (ii) the concentration and rationalization of the development of a technological Europe, and (iii) the adoption of measures to reinforce the European Monetary System (EMS). The Committee based itself on the original Action Committee for the United States of Europe which had been founded by Jean Monnet in 1955, had led to the founding of the European Economic Community and had for 20 years remained a focus for those supporting supranational Community goals.

Harmonization of Age of Majority. On Oct. 21, 1985, the European Parliament adopted a resolution on the harmonization of the age of majority under civil law and the legal capacity of young people in the Community.

THE LOMÉ CONVENTIONS

First Convention. A five-year convention establishing an overall trading and economic co-operation relationship between the EEC and 46 developing African, Caribbean and Pacific (ACP) countries was signed in Lomé (Togo) on Feb. 28, 1975, and came into full force on April 1, 1976, following ratification by all signatory states.

The original ACP countries were (i) 19 mainly French-speaking African states (Benin, Burundi, Cameroon, the Central African Republic, Chad, the Congo, Côte d'Ivoire, Gabon, Madagascar, Mali, Mauritania, Mauritius, Niger, Rwanda, Senegal, Somalia, Togo, Upper Volta and Zaïre), which had earlier been associated with the EEC—all except Mauritius under a First Yaoundé Convention of July 20, 1963, and all 19 under a second Yaoundé Convention of July 29, 1969, which expired on Jan. 31, 1975, but was extended to July 31, 1975; (ii) the then members of the East African Community (Kenya, Tanzania and Uganda), which had been associated with the EEC under an Arusha agreement of July 26, 1968, and later under the Arusha Convention running parallel with the second Yaoundé Convention; (iii) other Commonwealth states in Africa (Botswana, The Gambia, Ghana, Lesotho, Malawi, Nigeria, Sierra Leone, Swaziland and Zambia), in the Caribbean (the Bahamas, Barbados, Grenada, Guyana, Jamaica and Trinidad and Tobago) and in the Pacific (Fiji, Tonga and

Western Samoa); and (iv) other African states (Equatorial Guinea, Ethiopia, Guinea, Guinea-Bissau, Liberia and the Sudan).

As described below, over the next decade a further 20 developing countries acceded to the Community's ACP arrangements, namely (i) Angola, Cape Verde, Comoros, Djibouti, Mozambique, São Tomé and Príncipe, Seychelles and Zimbabwe (in Africa); (ii) Antigua and Barbuda, Belize, Dominica, St Kitts and Nevis, St Lucia, St Vincent and the Grenadines, and Suriname (in the Caribbean); and (iii) Kiribati, Papua New Guinea, Solomon Islands, Tuvalu and Vanuatu (in the Pacific).

The Lomé Convention's main provisions covered:

(i) The granting by the Community of duty-free access on a non-reciprocal basis to all industrial and to 96 per cent of agricultural imports from ACP countries; (ii) the creation of an export stabilization scheme ("Stabex") guaranteeing the ACP countries a certain level of income on exports of their primary products; (iii) increased development aid for the ACP countries from Community sources; (iv) increased industrial co-operation between the Community's member states and the ACP countries; and (v) the creation of three new bodies to provide the institutional framework for the operation of the agreement— a Council of Ministers (comprising members of the Community's Council of Ministers, of the European Commission and of each of the ACP states' governments), a committee of ambassadors and a Consultative Assembly comprising members of the European Parliament and representatives designated by the ACP states, to meet once a year, inter alia to discuss a report by the Council of Ministers.

The convention also contained special arrangements, among them one for continued imports into the Community of up to 1,400,000 tonnes of cane sugar annually from ACP countries, mainly from Commonwealth producers for the UK market.

In addition the convention provided for the accession of any other state of comparable economic structure and production, subject to agreement by the Community's nine member states and the ACP countries themselves.

Total Community aid for the ACP countries during the five-year period was to amount to 3,390 million u.a. (then about $4,270 million, compared with about $918,000,000 under the second Yaoundé Convention), of which 3,000 million u.a. was to be made available through a new European Development Fund (2,100 million of it in grants) and the remainder through the European Investment Bank in the form of ordinary loans. The resources of the European Development Fund were to be financed, at 3,150 million u.a., outside the normal Community budget by contributions from member states in fixed proportions.

The constituent session of the Consultative Assembly, comprising 184 members (two from each of the ACP states and an equal number of members of the European Parliament) was held in Luxembourg on June 1–3, 1976, and the inaugural meeting of the ACP-EEC Council of Ministers in Brussels on July 14–15 of that year, when approval was given to the accession to the Convention of six newly-independent countries (the Cape Verde Islands, the Comoro Islands, Papua New Guinea, São Tomé and Príncipe, Seychelles and Suriname).

The Communities' Council of Ministers had earlier, on June 29, 1976, decided that the Lomé Convention would also apply to the overseas territories still dependent on EEC member states and had allocated a further 160,000,000 u.a. for financial and technical assistance for these dependencies.

These territories comprised (i) Netherlands and French dependencies already associated with the European Communities under the Treaty of Rome and (ii) certain other territories whose eventual association with the Communities was provided for by the UK Treaty of Accession. Of these territories, Djibouti, the Solomon Islands, Tuvalu, Dominica, St Lucia, Kiribati (the Gilbert Islands) and St Vincent and the Grenadines subsequently became independent states, and as such full partners in the EEC-ACP association agreement in 1978–80, as did Zimbabwe on Nov. 4, 1980.

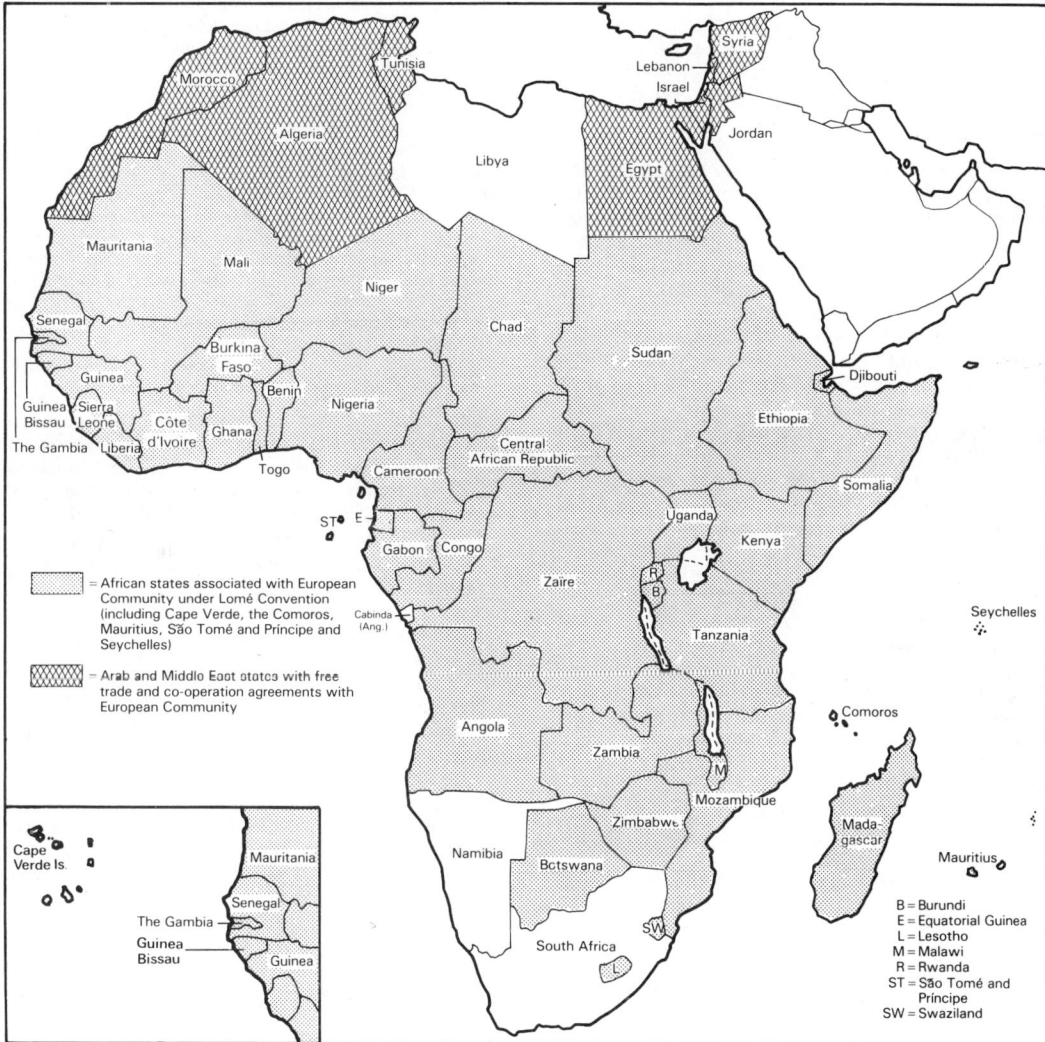

Map 5   African and Middle East states linked with European Community

Second Convention. The 1975 convention, which expired on March 1, 1980, was renewed under a second Lomé Convention, which was signed on Oct. 31, 1979, and entered fully into force on Jan. 1, 1981.

Under this second convention the duty-free arrangements for the bulk of ACP agricultural exports into the European Community were retained, while these concessions were extended to a number of products, mainly coming under the Community's common agricultural policy; existing preferential arrangements for beef and veal were extended; the "Stabex" scheme was expanded to cover a total of 44 products or by-products in order to afford more balanced protection for different countries' exports; and a special fund of 280,000,000 EUA (£174,000,000) was to protect the producers of minerals (copper and cobalt, phosphates, bauxite and aluminium, manganese, tin, iron ore and iron pyrites) against falls in export earnings or other untoward events.

The principal objects of the second convention were to improve and increase industrial development in the ACP countries, in particular in the production of manufactured goods, with technical and financial assistance being given to small and medium enterprises, and to develop new sources of energy, with investment through the European Investment Bank or by private capital. For agriculture, for which 40 per cent of the European Development fund had been allocated under the first Lomé Convention, a new Technical Centre for Agricultural and Rural Co-operation was to be established.

The funds available under the second convention were to be raised to a grand total of 5,607 million EUA (excluding food aid and joint financing given to ACP countries outside the convention).

This convention expired on Feb. 28, 1985.

Third Convention. The third convention, signed in Lomé on Dec. 8, 1984, attempted to provide for more co-ordinated development policies aimed at increasing the self-reliance of the ACP states, and for co-operation in such areas as cultural and social affairs, drought and desertification control, private investment, and services.

Improvements in trade co-operation involved a precise time limit for Community consideration of ACP applications requesting preferential access to Community markets for ACP countries' agricultural products. The rules of origin system for ACP products were considerably simplified and a general tolerance rule of 5 per cent of non-originating components was introduced. The total allocation for the "Stabex" scheme was increased for the five-year duration of the third Lomé Convention to 925,000,000 ECU (the ECU having replaced the EUA from January 1981).

A "Sysmin" special financing facility (first introduced under the second Lomé Convention) was to help re-establish the viability of the mining sector in ACP countries dependent on mining of iron ore, copper and cobalt, phosphates, manganese, tin, bauxite and alumina, for which 415,000,000 ECU were made available. Community aid allocated to EEC-ACP co-operation for the five years was 8,500 million ECU (nearly 60 per cent more than under the second Lomé Convention).

A major institutional change was the amalgamation of the existing consultative assembly with the joint committee, to form a joint assembly which was to meet twice a year.

In a joint declaration of principles, annexed to the convention, reference was made, for the first time, to the question of human rights.

The total number of ACP countries had by April 1985 reached 66 (including all black African states south of the Sahara), following the accession of Vanuatu (March 18, 1981); Belize (March 5, 1982); Antigua and Barbuda (July 30, 1982); St Kitts and Nevis (March 4, 1984); Mozambique (Dec. 8, 1984) and Angola (April 30, 1985).

Other Association Agreements

Turkey. An agreement on Turkey's associate membership in the EEC was signed in Ankara on Sept. 12, 1963, and entered into force on Dec. 1, 1964.

This agreement provided for Turkey's becoming a full member of the EEC when her economic progress should permit this.

The objective of the agreement—the continuous strengthening of the economic and commercial relations between Turkey and the EEC—would be attained by stages.

(1) During a five-year preparatory stage Turkey, with the assistance of the EEC, would continue her efforts to strengthen her economic and commercial position. The assistance would take the form of (i) tariff quotas, to be gradually increased, allowing Turkey to sell specified amounts of tobacco, raisins, dried figs and hazelnuts in the common market; and (ii) loans for economic development granted through the European Investment Bank.

(2) The second or transitional stage, lasting a maximum of 12 years, would see the gradual establishment of a customs union between Turkey and the EEC. Although the details would depend on the situation at the end of the initial phase of the agreement, a framework for the trade and economic arrangements in the second stage was laid down. Under the arrangements, which would cover all trade, Turkey would be expected to adopt the common customs tariff, and to bring her economic policy with regard to free movement of persons, transport policy and rules of competition into line with that of the EEC.

(3) The third or definitive stage would be based on a full customs union, including a common external tariff.

The application of the agreement is supervised by a Council of the Association, the members of which are drawn from the Council of Ministers, the Commission, the governments of the EEC member states and the Turkish Government.

The main developments under the Agreement of Association between the EEC and Turkey took the form of quota increases for Turkish tobacco, raisins, dried figs and hazelnuts as provided for in the initial stage of the agreement. The largest such increases were agreed upon by the Council of the Association on Nov. 23, 1966.

By Dec. 31, 1965, Turkey had received loans amounting to more than $50,000,000 from the European Investment Bank, the money being devoted mainly to infrastructure projects.

A supplementary protocol agreed on July 22, 1970, and signed on Nov. 23, 1971, regulated the transition from the preparatory to the second (transitional) stage. Under an interim agreement, pending ratification of the above protocol, but in any case valid only until Sept. 30, 1972, Turkish industrial goods (except petroleum products and certain textile goods) were able to enter EEC countries without tariff or quantitative restrictions from Sept. 1, 1971, and about 90 per cent of Turkey's agricultural exports were granted preferential treatment. In return Turkey would start to apply tariff reductions for industrial goods from the EEC.

An annex to the protocol provided for loans of $220,000,000 over five years and a 10-year schedule as from 1976 for the free movement and social rights of Turkish workers employed in the EEC. The provisions concerning free movement of labour were not, however, implemented by the Community side.

Under a new agreement signed on July 1, 1980, Turkey's associate membership of the EEC was renewed, with EEC tariffs on Turkish agricultural exports being gradually lowered from 1981 onwards and to be eliminated by 1987, while Turkish workers legally employed in EEC member countries gained full social security benefits. EEC aid to Turkey amounted to $840,000,000—including $455,000,000 in 40-year loans at 1 per cent interest; $70,000,000 in direct loans; and $315,000,000 in loans by the European Investment Bank at market rates of interest.

However, the implementation of further financial protocols was held up in view of Community concern over the political situation in Turkey.

Malta. An association agreement between Malta and the EEC was approved by the EEC Council of Ministers on Nov. 26, 1970, and signed on Dec. 5. It came into force on April 1, 1971, and was aimed at the completion of a customs union by 1981 in two five-year stages.

During the first stage the EEC would grant Malta a 70 per cent reduction in customs duties on industrial products, except petroleum and some textiles which would remain subject to quotas. Malta would reduce its import duties on EEC products by 15 per cent on April 1, 1971; 10 per cent at the start of the third year of the agreement; and another 10 per cent at the start of the fifth year. In the second stage Malta would reduce these duties by at least a further 35 per cent.

On March 4, 1976, this agreement was extended until June 30, 1977; it was adapted to UK, Danish and Irish membership of the European Communities; and provision was made for Community financial aid to Malta of 26,000,000 EUA over a five-year period. On June 29, 1977, agreement was reached on extending the existing association provisions until Dec. 1, 1980, and it was again extended, first for one year and then to June 30, 1982. A bilateral textile agreement was concluded on July 8, 1982.

A new financial protocol, signed on Dec. 4, 1985, provided for aid to Malta of 29,500,000 ECU up to Oct. 31, 1988 (10,500,000 ECU of this being in grants).

Cyprus. An association agreement between Cyprus and the European Economic Community was signed on Dec. 19, 1972, providing for reciprocal tariff reductions on industrial and agricultural products during the course of a first stage ending on June 30, 1977.

For industrial products the EEC agreed to make an immediate 70 per cent reduction in tariffs, while Cyprus undertook to reduce its tariffs by 32 per cent in three steps over a four-year period. In the agricultural sector EEC tariffs would be cut by 40 per cent with regard to citrus fruits, while carobs would enter the EEC duty-free. In addition, special arrangements were made for continuing Cypriot exports of sherry to the United Kingdom and Ireland for a two-year period and within quota limitations.

On June 22, 1977, the existing association arrangements with Cyprus were extended until

Dec. 31, 1979, and provision was made for Community financial aid to Cyprus of 30,000,000 EUA over a five-year period. The arrangements were further extended on an annual basis pending agreement on the content of and transition to the second stage of association, i.e. to June 30, 1982.

An agreement signed in December 1983 provided, for a period of five years from Jan. 1, 1984, for amounts of 44,000,000 ECU in aid, 20,000,000 ECU in grants and 6,000,000 ECU in special loans—designed to benefit "the entire population" of the island.

Trade and Co-operation Agreements

Various agreements have been signed between the EEC and countries outside the Community, as follows:

Iran. A three-year agreement between the EEC and Iran, signed on Oct. 14, 1963, and in force since Dec. 1, 1963, provided inter alia for temporary reductions in the EEC's common external tariff for products of special importance to Iran's economy (such as carpets, dried grapes and apricots) and fixed a tariff quota for raisins imported by the EEC from Iran (at 15 per cent of such imports from non-member and non-associated countries). The agreement was amended in 1967 and extended for a further three years from Dec. 1, 1970, but it was allowed to expire on Nov. 30, 1973, because of the changed economic situation of Iran.

Iceland. A trade agreement between the EEC and Iceland was signed on July 22, 1972, and a supplementary protocol on May 29, 1975.

Israel. A trade agreement between the EEC and Israel, signed on June 4, 1964, was in force from July 1, 1964, for a three-year period with a possible extension. No formal extension was approved, although certain special trade arrangements between Israel and the EEC were continued.

A new trade agreement, for five years, signed on June 29, 1970, provided for mutual tariff reductions as from Oct. 1, 1970.

These agreements included provisions for a 40 per cent reduction in the EEC tariff for citrus and other fruit from Israel, and an immediate 30 per cent reduction on a wide range of industrial products, with further 5 per cent annual reductions so as to reach a total of 50 per cent by Jan. 1, 1974. These measures were expected to benefit about 55 per cent of Israel's industrial exports to the EEC, and about 80 per cent of her agricultural exports. Israel granted tariff preferences ranging from 5 to 30 per cent by 1974 for about half of her industrial and agricultural imports from the EEC subject to duties.

A new agreement was concluded on Jan. 23, 1975, and came into force on July 1, 1975, for the progressive dismantling of all tariff and quota barriers on industrial goods for all Community imports from Israel by July 1, 1977; for 60 per cent of Israeli imports from the Community by

Jan. 1, 1980; and for the remaining 40 per cent by Jan. 1, 1985; the Community would make substantial tariff cuts on about 85 per cent of Israel's agricultural exports; and Israeli tariffs on industrial goods from the Community would be abolished not later than Jan. 1, 1989. This agreement was effectively converted into a full-scale economic co-operation agreement on Feb. 8, 1977, with Israel to receive Community loans and grants of 30,000,000 u.a. up to Oct. 31, 1981.

A five-year financial protocol, agreed on Oct. 16, 1981, to take effect from Nov. 1, 1981, provided for EIB loans totalling 40,000,000 ECU, but was not finally signed by the due date of June 14, 1982 (after the Israeli invasion of Lebanon).

A new agreement signed on June 24, 1983, came into force on Jan. 1, 1984; it provided for loans on market terms of up to 40,000,000 ECU from the EIB to Israel for the period up to Oct. 31, 1986.

Arab Countries. An agreement on trade and technical co-operation between the Community and its member countries on the one hand and Lebanon on the other was signed on May 21, 1965. The agreement was valid for a period of three years and was renewed several times, pending the conclusion of a more comprehensive preferential trade agreement.

Following a financial protocol signed in June 1982, Community aid to Lebanon included some 22,000,000 ECU in 1982 and over 5,000,000 ECU in 1983 (in food and emergency aid); an exceptional EIB loan of up to 50,000,000 ECU in November 1982; and 20,000,000 ECU in 1983 (as a grant towards drinking water supplies to Beirut).

Between the EEC and the ECSC on the one hand and seven Arab countries on the other, free trade and co-operation agreements were signed as follows: (i) with Tunisia on April 25, 1976; (ii) with Algeria on April 26, 1976; (iii) with Morocco on April 27, 1976; (iv) with Egypt, Jordan and Syria on Jan. 18, 1977; and (v) with Lebanon on May 3, 1977.

All these agreements were of indefinite duration except for their financial co-operation provisions which were to extend to Oct. 31, 1981, and which involved loans and grants channelled through the European Investment Bank of 95,000,000 units of account (u.a.) for Tunisia, 114,000,000 u.a. for Algeria, 130,000,000 u.a. for Morocco, 170,000,000 u.a. for Egypt, 40,000,000 u.a. for Jordan, 60,000,000 u.a. for Syria and 30,000,000 u.a. for Lebanon. (The agreements with Tunisia and Morocco replaced earlier association agreements which had been in force since Sept. 1, 1969, and extended pending completion of the new agreements.)

All seven agreements came into full force on Nov. 1, 1978. Financial protocols within the framework of these agreements covered the period up to Oct. 31, 1981. A series of second financial protocols signed in June 1982 covered the period up to Oct. 31, 1986.

Yugoslavia. A trade agreement with Yugoslavia, signed on March 19, 1970, and in force from May 1, 1970, provided for most favoured-nation treatment between the two sides; an acceleration of the import duty concessions proposed under the Kennedy Round; concessions for Yugoslav beef exports; and the establishment of a mixed commission to carry out the agreement. It was replaced by a new agreement for five years, signed in Brussels on June 26, to come into effect on Sept. 1, 1973.

A new preferential trade and co-operation agreement between the EEC and Yugoslavia, signed on April 2, 1980, provided, in the industrial sector, for unrestricted duty-free access to the European Community for five years for the majority of Yugoslav products except for (i) 29 industrial products on which duty would be payable when agreed import quotas had been reached; (ii) certain non-ferrous alloys and metals of which agreed import quotas would be subject to a progressive reduction of Community duties of 40 per cent from July 1, 1980, to 100 per cent on Jan. 1, 1984; and (iii) textile products on which quotas had been agreed under the international Multifibre Arrangement. In the agricultural sector Yugoslavia was granted tariff concessions on a range of special products.

Under this agreement Yugoslavia would continue to benefit from the Community's generalized system of preferences for developing countries and would in turn accord the Community most-favoured-nation status (subject to any measures deemed necessary for Yugoslavia's industrial and economic development). Among the provisions for co-operation was one designed to enable Yugoslav workers in the Community to enjoy the same conditions of work and social security benefits as Community countries' nationals. A joint co-operation council was to be established, and over a five-year period loans totalling 200,000,000 EUA would be available to Yugoslavia from the EIB.

The agreement came into force on April 1, 1983, after its trade and financial provisions had been applied under an interim agreement since July 1, 1980.

Argentina. The first trade agreement of the EEC with a Latin American country was that with Argentina, signed in Brussels on Nov. 8, 1971, for a three-year period from Jan. 1, 1972.

This non-preferential agreement, providing for mutual most-favoured-nation treatment, afforded Argentina tariff advantages for frozen beef exports to the EEC; it also provided for duty-free imports of Argentine industrial and processed farm goods within the EEC's "generalized preferences" scheme for developing nations, which came into effect from July 1, 1971 [see above]. The agreement was implemented by a joint commission set up between Argentina and the EEC and charged with examining possible further tariff concessions.

This agreement was repeatedly renewed, most recently with effect from Dec. 31, 1978, but was allowed to lapse by the Argentinian Government at the end of 1980.

Uruguay. A three-year non-preferential trade agreement with Uruguay was signed in Luxembourg on April 25, 1973. It provided for an effective increase of Uruguayan beef and veal imports by up to 30 per cent and a suspension, as far as possible, of import levies in Uruguayan refrigerated beef products. This agreement, in force since Aug. 1, 1974, is automatically extended from year to year unless denounced by either party three months before the expiry date.

Brazil. A trade agreement with Brazil, signed on Dec. 19, 1973, and in force from Aug. 1, 1974, provided for (i) increased EEC imports of Brazilian beef and veal; (ii) facilitation of Brazilian exports to the EEC of cocoa butter and soluble coffee; (iii) agricultural and commercial co-operation; (iv) the easing of shipment conditions for EEC exports to Brazil; and (v) the creation of a joint committee for the development of economic co-operation.

This agreement was replaced by a five-year non-preferential trade and economic co-operation agreement between the EEC and Brazil, signed on Sept. 18, 1980, and providing for the development and diversification of exchanges between the two sides, the intensification of industrial relations between them and an increase in EEC investment in Brazil.

Mexico. A five-year non-preferential commercial co-operation agreement between the EEC and Mexico, renewable by tacit approval, was signed in Brussels on July 15, 1975. It provided inter alia for the mutual granting of most-favoured-nation status and for the establishment of a joint committee to supervise the functioning of the agreement and to improve it.

India. A trade agreement with India (the first between the EEC and a Commonwealth member state and an Asian developing country), signed in Brussels on Dec. 17, 1973, covering a five-year period from April 1, 1974 and renewable by tacit consent, provided for (i) the mutual granting of most-favoured-nation status; (ii) consolidation of certain tariff suspensions operated by the EEC on Indian goods; (iii) possible amendments to the system of generalized preferences as it affected India; and (iv) the creation of a joint commission for economic and commercial co-operation. Commodity agreements in operation are one for handicraft products (from Jan. 1, 1973), and one for cane sugar (for five years from July 18, 1975).

A new five-year non-preferential commercial and economic co-operation agreement was signed on June 23, 1981, and came into effect on Dec. 31, 1981. It covered industrial, technological and scientific co-operation and the promotion of mutually beneficial investment, as well as trade relations, and contained a protocol extending co-operation to the coal and steel sectors. A joint commission for trade promotion and sectoral agreements first met on Jan. 22–23, 1982, to discuss inter alia ways of reducing India's growing trade deficit with the Community.

Sri Lanka, Pakistan and Bangladesh. Comprehensive five-year commercial co-operation agreements were signed between the EEC and (i) Sri Lanka on July 22, 1975, effective Dec. 1, 1975; (ii) Pakistan on June 1, 1976, effective July 1, 1976; and (iii) Bangladesh on Oct. 19, 1976, effective Dec. 1, 1976.

These agreements were closely modelled on that between the EEC and India. In a Declaration of Intent annexed to the British Treaty of Accession to the European Communities it had been stated that a solution would be sought to the problems arising for Asian Commonwealth countries from Britain's entry into the EEC, and limited commodity agreements had been operated by the EEC with the above three countries since 1973–74, especially for textiles and jute.

The 1976 agreement with Pakistan was amplified by a new five-year agreement for commercial, economic and development co-operation signed on July 23, 1985, designed in particular to increase the effectiveness of Community aid to Pakistan and to be administered by a joint commission.

Canada. A framework agreement for non-preferential commercial and economic co-operation between the European Communities and Canada was signed in Ottawa on July 6, 1976, and it came into force on Oct. 1 of that year for an indefinite period (although either side was empowered to terminate it after five years, subject to one year's notice). In this agreement the two sides confirmed their wish to accord each other most-favoured-nation treatment on an equal and reciprocal basis, and they agreed that economic co-operation should be promoted inter alia by joint ventures and increased two-way investment; that there should be joint co-operation by the private sectors in third countries; and that a joint co-operation committee should be set up and meet at least once a year.

China. A five-year preferential trade agreement, which was signed on April 3, 1978, and came into force on June 1 of that year, provided for most-favoured-nation treatment between China and the EEC, for trading at "market-related prices" and for the establishment of a joint committee to ensure the satisfactory working of the agreement. A reduction of EEC tariffs on 20 items was approved by the Council of Ministers on Sept. 19, 1978. A preliminary agreement of July 17, 1979, effectively allowed China to double its textile exports to the EEC from 21,000 to 41,000 tonnes a year. The 1978 agreement was renewable by tacit agreement.

A new textile agreement, to replace one which had expired at the end of 1983, was initialled on March 29, 1984, and laid down import quotas for Chinese textiles for 1984.

A trade and economic co-operation agreement signed on May 21, 1985, largely reinforced the 1978 agreement, under which most-favoured-nation status between the parties had been established, but it also provided for increased exchanges of economic information, transfers of technology and joint ventures. It came into force on Oct. 1, 1985.

Association of South East Asian Nations (ASEAN). A framework non-preferential five-year agreement on co-operation between the EEC and the five member states of the ASEAN (Indonesia, Malaysia, the Philippines, Singapore and Thailand), signed in Kuala Lumpur on March 7, 1980, provided for (i) the mutual granting of most-favoured-nation status; (ii) commercial co-operation involving the removal of trade barriers, improved access to each other's markets and promotion and consultation in trade matters; (iii) economic co-operation in all fields deemed suitable by the two parties in order to create closer industrial and technological links between private enterprises; (iv) development co-operation; and (v) the establishment of a joint co-operation committee. The agreement was ratified by both sides on Sept. 25, 1980, and came into force on Oct. 1, 1980.

Thailand. In September 1982 a co-operation agreement was signed on the production, marketing and trading of manioc (cassava).

Andean Pact. A non-preferential co-operation agreement was signed with the Andean Pact on Dec. 17, 1983, with a protocol relating to the European Coal and Steel Community. The five-year agreement was automatically renewable for two-year periods. The two sides also granted each other most-favoured-nation treatment under the GATT.

New Zealand. A three-year agreement reached on June 19, 1984, provided for import quotas for New Zealand butter at 83,000 tonnes, falling by 2,000 tonnes each year in 1985 and 1986.

Zimbabwe. An agreement concluded under the third Lomé Convention and signed on Oct. 31, 1985, provided that Zimbabwe should receive aid totalling 73,000,000 ECU over five years (over half of this being in grants and the rest in special loans).

Central America. A five-year multilateral co-operation agreement concluded on Nov. 12, 1985, by the Community member countries, Portugal and Spain on the one hand and the six Central American countries (including Panama) covered trade and economic development co-operation but did not go beyond according most-favoured-nation treatment to those countries (and did not provide preferential treatment as afforded to the APC countries).

Romania. Between the EEC and Romania a five-year non-preferential trade agreement and an agreement of unlimited duration for the establishment of a joint committee were signed on July 28, 1980, and entered into force on Jan. 1, 1981. The industrial trade agreement—the first to be concluded between the EEC and a full member of the CMEA—covered about two-thirds of current exchanges between the two sides.

EFTA Member Countries. A special relations agreement signed on May 14, 1973, provided for both the EEC and Norway to establish all tariffs on industrial goods in five successive reductions of 20 per cent each between July 1, 1973, and July 1, 1977, and for concessions to Norway in respect of fish, a number of sensitive products and semi-manufactured agricultural products. A separate agreement signed at the same time provided for free trade for ECSC products by July 1, 1977.

A special relations agreement between Finland (an associate member of EFTA) on the one hand and the EEC and the ECSC on the other, signed on Oct. 5, 1973, was ratified by the Finnish Diet on Nov. 16, 1973, and entered into force on Jan. 1, 1974. It provided for free trade in industrial goods within four years, with a longer transition period for certain sensitive products.

Under trade agreements concluded by the EEC with Austria, Iceland, Portugal, Sweden and Switzerland duty-free trade in most industrial goods was also reached by July 1, 1977.

On Jan. 1, 1984, free trade in industrial goods (with few minor exceptions) was established between the EFTA member countries and the then 10 member countries of the European Communities, thus creating the largest free trade area in industrial goods in the world (with 312,000,000 consumers). Minor exceptions to the final tariff abolition on Jan. 1, 1984, concerned Finland, where the final abolition was to take place on Jan. 1, 1985, and Iceland, where certain customs duties were allowed to be maintained temporarily.

A first ministerial-level meeting between the Communities and EFTA, held in Luxembourg on April 9, 1984, with Liechtenstein being included in the Swiss delegation, agreed on the need for co-operation in other areas, especially in the reduction of non-tariff barriers to trade. (EFTA subsequently established a committee on technical barriers to trade to follow up the Luxembourg decision.)

During 1985 agreements on general co-operation in research and development were concluded between the EEC on the one hand and Sweden and Switzerland on the other.

RELATIONS WITH THE CMEA

Until 1972 the Soviet Union, as the principal partner in the Council for Mutual Economic Assistance (CMEA, or Comecon) evinced hostility to the European Communities, but on March 20 of that year Leonid Brezhnev (the General Secretary of the Communist Party of the Soviet Union) recognized the Communities' existence and stated that Soviet relations with their member states would depend on the extent to which they recognized "the realities obtaining in the socialist part of Europe" and particularly the interests of the member countries of the CMEA.

Several CMEA member countries had earlier concluded limited technical agreements with the Communities, mainly concerning their agricultural exports (thus Poland in 1965 and Bulgaria, Hungary and Romania in 1969). In 1973 EEC member countries accounted for 25 per cent of the CMEA's external trade (although the Communities' trade with the CMEA countries was only 4 per cent of its total).

Protracted negotiations begun in February 1975 on the drafting of a framework agreement on co-operation between the EEC and the CMEA were broken off by the EEC at the end of March 1980 because no agreement was in sight on certain points considered fundamental by the EEC.

Whereas the CMEA desired a global agreement to cover the economic and trade co-operation, the EEC insisted that it should be free to negotiate trade agreements with individual CMEA member countries because, in the opinion of the EEC, the CMEA had no organizational powers comparable to those held by the EEC over its members. The EEC had accepted (in November 1979) that such individual agreements should include most-favoured-nation treatment. The CMEA, however, had

asked for the collective application of this treatment to the CMEA as a whole and had proposed the creation of a joint commission which would supervise economic and trade relations between the two sides and their members—but this proposal was not accepted by the EEC.

However, on June 8, 1985, the Foreign Ministers of the Communities' member states agreed to open an informal dialogue with the CMEA, and in September 1985 V. Sychev (the CMEA executive secretary) proposed a joint declaration which would establish official relations with the Communities "within their respective fields of competence". On Jan. 31, 1986, the European Commission responded by specifying its readiness to open negotiations. The Commission was also reported to have proposed "a normalization of relations" with the seven individual CMEA member states.

European Free Trade Association (EFTA)

Address. 9–11 rue de Varembé, 1211 Geneva 20, Switzerland.

Officer. Per Kleppe (sec. gen.).

Founded. May 3, 1960.

Membership. Austria, Finland, Iceland, Norway, Sweden and Switzerland.

History. The first definite moves toward the creation of a European free trade area, comprising the then six EEC member countries and the 11 other members of the OEEC (Organization for European Economic Co-operation, see page 111), were made at ministerial meetings of the OEEC on Feb. 13, March 8, and Oct. 17, 1957.

At the last-mentioned meeting a resolution was unanimously passed expressing the Council's "determination to secure the establishment of a European free trade area which would comprise all member countries of the Organization (i.e. the OEEC); which would associate, on a multilateral basis, the European Economic Community with the other member countries; and which, taking fully into consideration the objectives of the Euorpean Economic Community, would in practice take effect parallel with the Treaty of Rome."

Discussions were continued throughout the next year, but little progress was made because of the French Government's opposition to some aspects of the free trade area as proposed in a working paper then being considered. A complete breakdown in negotiations finally took place at a session of the Inter-Governmental Committee of the OEEC on Nov. 13–14, 1958, when the French Minister of Information stated that the French Cabinet saw no possibility of establishing a free trade area on the lines proposed, since there were no provisions for a common external tariff nor for harmonization of social and economic systems.

With the imminent threat of an economic rift between the EEC members of the OEEC and the 11 other member countries, a conference of senior trade officials of the so-called "Outer Seven" countries (Austria, Britain, Denmark,

Norway, Portugal, Sweden and Switzerland) was held on Dec. 1–2, 1958, at Geneva.

A statement was issued after the meeting by the chairman of the conference, Dr. Schaffner (of the Swiss Ministry of Economics), which (i) expressed the identity of views of the Governments represented on both the short-term and long-term objectives of the free trade area negotiations with the six EEC countries; and (ii) reaffirmed their intention to pursue their efforts to find a satisfactory formula of multilateral association between the Six and the other members of the OEEC.

A further meeting of experts of the "Outer Seven" countries was held on March 17–18, 1959, at Saltsjøbaden, Sweden. The delegates decided that the Hallstein Report—a memorandum of the EEC Commission on possible measures to overcome the crisis between the two economic groups in Europe—did not constitute a satisfactory basis for negotiations with the European Community countries. It was decided that investigations into the possibilities of stimulating trade between the "Outer Seven" countries, by the gradual removal of tariffs and quantitative import restrictions, should be opened.

These investigations led to a meeting of experts of the "Outer Seven" countries to draw up a plan for a "trading association". The draft plan was examined by ministers at a meeting in Stockholm on July 20–21, 1959, and it was finally announced that the ministers would recommend to their governments "that a European Free Trade Association among the seven countries should be established".

The ensuing Treaty of Stockholm was signed between Dec. 29, 1959, and Jan. 4, 1960. It established the association of the "Outer Seven" with effect from May 3, 1960.

Iceland joined EFTA on March 1, 1970, whereas Britain and Denmark left it on Dec. 31, 1972, and Portugal on Dec. 31, 1985 (these three countries joining the European Communities).

Finland, having been an associate member of the EFTA, became a full member on Jan. 1, 1986.

THE EFTA CONVENTION

The *Convention of the European Free Trade Association* was drafted between Oct. 8 and Nov. 5, 1959, and initialled at a ministerial meeting in Stockholm on Nov. 20, 1959. On Dec. 12, 1959, the seven EFTA states decided on the establishment of a permanent Secretariat which, it was subsequently announced, would have its headquarters in Geneva.

Art. 2 of the Convention of the European Free Trade Association described the Association's objectives as (*a*) "to promote within the area of the association and within each member state a sustained expansion of economic activity, full employment, increased productivity and the rational use of resources, financial stability, and a continuous improvement in living standards"; (*b*) to secure that trade between member states took place in conditions of fair competition; (*c*) to avoid significant disparity in the supply of raw materials; and (*d*) to contribute to the harmonious development and expansion of world trade.

Art. 3 laid down that as from the dates shown below no member state might apply an import duty on any product at a level exceeding the percentage of the basic duty as applied by that country on Jan. 1, 1961—or March 1, 1960, in the case of Denmark—as follows:

	Percentage of basic duty
July 1, 1960	80 per cent
Jan. 1, 1962	70 per cent
July 1, 1963	60 per cent
Jan. 1, 1965	50 per cent
Jan. 1, 1966	40 per cent
Jan. 1, 1967	30 per cent
Jan. 1, 1968	20 per cent
Jan. 1, 1969	10 per cent

All import duties were to be eliminated by Jan. 1, 1970.

Each member state declared its willingness to apply import duties at lower levels if it considered that its economic and financial position and the position of the sector concerned so permitted.

The actual rate of tariff reduction is shown in the following table:

	Percentage of basic duty
Jan. 1, 1960	80 per cent
Jan. 1, 1961	70 per cent
March 1–Sept. 1, 1962	60 per cent
Oct. 31-Dec. 31, 1962	50 per cent
Dec. 31, 1963	40 per cent
Jan. 1, 1965	30 per cent
Dec. 31, 1965	20 per cent
Jan. 1, 1967	0 per cent

The first decision to accelerate tariff reductions was made at a meeting of the Ministerial Council in Geneva on Feb. 14–16, 1961. At the Council's meeting in Lisbon on May 9–11, 1963, it was decided that the tariff reduction should be complete by Dec. 31, 1966. Almost all remaining tariffs and quotas on trade in industrial goods between the seven EFTA countries were in fact abolished with effect from Dec. 31, 1966, with only a few exceptions under special arrangements.

Art. 4. Goods would qualify for area tariff treatment if (*a*) they had been wholly produced within the area of the association, or (*b*) they had been produced by certain processes within the area of the association (the "process rule"), or (*c*) not more than 50 per cent of their value consisted of non-area materials (the "percentage rule"). Provision was made for certain materials of which there were large imports from outside the area (i.e. basic materials) to be treated as if they had originated from within the area.

The main provisions of the remainder of the convention are summarized below:

Safeguards. Member countries will be free to take action which they consider necessary for the protection of their essential security interests and, consistently with their other international obligations, their balance of payments. In certain circumstances a member state may also take special safeguarding action where the application of the convention leads to serious difficulties in a particular sector of industry.

Competition. The convention contains provisions to ensure that the benefits which are expected from the removal of tariffs and quotas are not nullified through the use of other measures by governments, public undertakings or private industries. These include provisions about subsidies, restrictive business practices and discriminatory restrictions against nationals of member states wishing to establish businesses anywhere in the area.

Agriculture and Fish. Special arrangements have been made for agricultural goods and fish and other marine products. The objective is to facilitate reasonable reciprocity to those member states whose economies depend to a great extent on agricultural or fish exports. Arrangements have also been concluded between several member countries in respect of trade in agricultural goods.

The Council. The convention establishes a Council charged with the general oversight of the application of the convention and with the task of considering what further action should be taken to promote the objectives of the Association and to facilitate close association with other countries or groups of countries. The Council is empowered to establish relationships with other international organizations. Each member state has one vote on the Council. Decisions and recommendations are to be made by unanimous vote where new obligations are involved. On a wide range of issues, and particularly in dealing with any complaints which may be made by member states, decisions will be by majority vote.

Consultation and Complaints. The procedure for consultation and complaints is an important part of the convention, and a member country may refer to the Council any case in which it considers that a benefit conferred upon it by the convention or an objective of the Association is being or may be frustrated. Member states intend to pursue economic and financial policies in a manner which will promote the objectives of the Association, and to exchange views about them from time to time.

Extension. The Council is empowered to make arrangements for the accession of other countries, and member states may propose the extension of the convention to cover non-European territories for which they are responsible.

After the Danish Government had proposed, in December 1967, that the convention should be made applicable to the Faroe Islands, this territory was included in the EFTA area as from Jan. 1, 1968.

Annex on Portugal. Special arrangements concerning Portugal were contained in Annex G of the Convention. By these arrangements Portugal was permitted to apply a slower rate of import duty reduction than other EFTA members. The planned reduction of the percentage of the basic duty was to 50 per cent by 1970. An accelerated rate of duty reduction was provided for in the case of exporting industries.

ORGANS OF EFTA

In addition to the Council, which consists of delegations led by ministers and which normally meets twice a year, there are standing committees for customs, trade, the budget, economic development and economic problems. There are also (i) a consultative committee consisting of employers' representatives, trade union leaders and other individuals and (ii) a committee of members of parliament of the EFTA member countries. EFTA's secretariat is headed by a Secretary-General assisted by a Deputy Secretary-General.

BUDGET CONTRIBUTIONS

For 1985–86 the national contributions to EFTA's budget were as follows (in percentages): Switzerland 26.61; Sweden 24.92; Austria 15.85; Norway 13.54; Finland 12.31; Portugal 5.23; Iceland 1.54.

AGREEMENTS AND ACTIVITIES

Industrial Development Fund. The Council of EFTA approved, on April 7, 1976, the statutes of a $100,000,000 Industrial Development Fund (based in Geneva) to help develop Portuguese industry over a five-year period (with Sweden and Switzerland contributing 30 and 25 per cent respectively).

Yugoslav Observers. It was announced on Dec. 11, 1967, that it had been agreed that Yugoslavia could send observers to EFTA technical meetings, including those on double taxation, patents, and probably customs.

On June 20, 1978, it was decided to replace an existing working group established between EFTA and Yugoslavia by a full joint committee to promote intensified economic co-operation between the two sides. The committee held its first meeting at ministerial level on June 6, 1983.

Iceland's Accession. Iceland became a full member of EFTA, and also a party to the Finland-EFTA agreement, on March 1, 1970.

Iceland's protective import duties on EFTA industrial products were reduced immediately by 30 per cent, with seven further annual reductions by 10 per cent to follow from Jan. 1, 1974, so that all such tariffs would be abolished by Jan. 1, 1980.

Special Relations Agreements. Following the withdrawal of Britain and Denmark from EFTA on Jan. 31, 1972, Special Relations Agreements entered into force between four of the seven remaining members or associates of EFTA—Austria, Portugal, Sweden and Switzerland—on the one hand and the EEC on the other, thus inaugurating a programme of tariff reductions

and other measures which would lead to a free trade area embracing the 13 countries involved.

The agreements, concluded in Brussels on July 22, 1972, provided for the gradual achievement of free trade in industrial goods between the six original members of the EEC and Ireland on the one hand and each of the six EFTA countries which had not applied for full EEC membership on the other, while at the same time preserving the existing free trade among all countries which were members of EFTA at the time of signature of the agreements, including Britain, Norway and Denmark. The agreements differed fundamentally from the terms reached for full membership with the other three EFTA countries and Ireland in that the six countries would have no power of decision in Community affairs, and they would not take part in any institutions except in a joint executive committee which would meet twice a year to manage the free trade arrangements.

The free trade area was further extended when (i) the Finnish Government had signed the terms of a Special Relations Agreement initialled in July 1972 but not formally signed by the end of that year; (ii) a similar agreement had been negotiated by Norway with the Communities, following the Norwegian decision not to become a full member [see page 171]; and (iii) the Icelandic Parliament had approved the agreement signed in July 1972 with the Communities.

Vienna Declaration. At a meeting held in Vienna on May 13, 1977, the Council adopted a declaration in which it was stated *inter alia*: "The EFTA governments recognize that their economies react with particular sensitivity to problems in the world economy. The share of external trade in their economies is considerable; while representing only 1 per cent of world population the EFTA countries together account for 7 per cent of total world trade." The declaration welcomed the achievement, on July 1, 1977, of a free trade system for industrial products between the 16 countries of EFTA and the European Communities, constituting a market of 300,000,000 people; it stressed, however, that it was "important to ensure that the advantages deriving from free trade are not jeopardized as a result of diverging economic developments and policies" and that it was desirable to "develop the existing co-operation within EFTA and . . . between EFTA countries and the European Communities". [See also page 188.]

EFTA and Spain. A multilateral free trade agreement between Spain and the seven EFTA member states (including Finland, then an associated member) was initialled in Geneva on Dec. 7, 1978, and signed on June 26, 1979. It provided mainly for the application of the same rules for industrial trade as existed between Spain and the European Communities, and also for any future concessions on industrial products made by Spain to the European Communities to apply similarly to EFTA member countries.

Bilateral agreements with Spain were reached at the same time by Austria, Finland, Norway, Sweden and Switzerland to facilitate trade in agricultural products.

All these agreements came into force on May 1, 1980.

The multilateral free trade agreement between Spain and EFTA expired on Dec. 31, 1985 (with Spain entering the European Community on Jan. 1, 1986). Bilateral trade agreements between Spain and individual EFTA member countries were to be phased out during a seven-year transitional period.

Ending of Portuguese Membership. Portugal ceased to be an EFTA member on Dec. 31, 1985, after which date trade relations with individual EFTA member countries were to be replaced by the special relations agreements between these countries and the European Community.

Finland's Full Accession. Finland became a full member of EFTA on Jan. 1, 1986, having been an associated member since June 26, 1961, under an agreement (signed in Helsinki on March 27, 1961) which had contained special provisions in respect of Finland's trade relations with the Soviet Union.

EFTA SHARE OF WORLD TRADE

EFTA's share in world exports was 5.6 per cent in 1984 and 5.7 per cent in 1985. Its share in world imports was 5.9 per cent in 1983 and 5.5 per cent in 1984. (The population of EFTA member countries is only 0.9 per cent of the world's population.)

Imports of the European Communities and EFTA together accounted for 35.1 per cent of world imports in 1984, and their joint exports in that year represented 35.2 per cent of the world total.

European Co-operation in Other Spheres

Bank for International Settlements (BIS)

Address. Centralbahnplatz 2, 4002 Basel, Switzerland.

Officers. Jean Godeaux (ch. of board of directors); Prof. Alexandre Lamfalussy (gen. man.).

Founded. 1930.

Objects. To promote co-operation among European central banks, to provide additional facilities for international financial operations, and to act as trustees or agents in connection with international financial settlements entrusted to it.

Structure. The BIS has a Board of Directors composed of the governors or presidents of the central banks of Belgium, France, the Federal Republic of Germany, Italy, the Netherlands, Sweden, Switzerland and the United Kingdom and five other members nominated by some of these governors.

Central Commission for the Navigation of the Rhine

Address. Palais du Rhin, Strasbourg, France.

Officers. M. Riphagen (pres.); R. Doerflinger (sec. gen.).

Founded. 1815.

Object. To ensure free movement of traffic and standard river facilities for ships of all nations.

Structure. The commission has an administrative centre for social security for boatmen and a tripartite commission for labour conditions.

Membership. Belgium, France, the Federal Republic of Germany, the Netherlands, Switzerland and the United Kingdom.

Eureka Programme

A meeting of representatives of the then 10 member states of the European Communities as well as of Austria, Norway, Portugal, Spain, Sweden and Switzerland, and also of the European Commission, held in Paris on July 17, 1985, endorsed a Eureka programme involving research in technologies similar to those of the US strategic defence initiative (SDI or "Star Wars") but directed towards non-military use. The meeting expressed its firm support for the programme, which it declared to have been created on that date (July 17, 1985).

European Centre for Medium-Range Weather Forecasts (ECMWF)

Address. Fitzwilliam House, Skimped Hill, Bracknell, Berks, UK.

Founded. Oct. 11, 1973.

Membership. Austria, Belgium, Denmark, Finland, France, the Federal Republic of Germany, Greece, Ireland, Italy, the Netherlands, Portugal, Spain, Sweden, Switzerland, Turkey, the United Kingdom and Yugoslavia.

European Company for the Financing of Railway Equipment (EUROFINA)

Address. Rittergasse 20, 4001 Basel, Switzerland.

Officer. Dr W. Vaerst (pres.).

Founded. Oct. 20, 1955.

History. The company was established by the European Conference of Ministers of Transport (ECMT) with the participation of the railway administrations of Austria, Belgium, Denmark, France, the Federal Republic of Germany,

Greece, Italy, Luxembourg, the Netherlands, Norway, Portugal, Spain, Sweden, Switzerland, Turkey and Yugoslavia.

European Conference of Ministers of Transport (ECMT)

Address. 19 rue Franqueville, 75775 Paris Cédex 16, France.

Officer. B. Billet (sec. gen.).

Founded. Oct. 17, 1953.

Membership. Austria, Belgium, Denmark, Finland, France, the Federal Republic of Germany, Greece, Ireland, Italy, Luxembourg, the Netherlands, Norway, Portugal, Spain, Sweden, Switzerland, Turkey, the United Kingdom and Yugoslavia.

Associate Members. Australia, Canada, Japan and the USA.

History. The ECMT was set up at a conference of Transport Ministers from a number of European countries, held in Brussels between Oct. 12 and 17, 1953. The aim of the organization is to achieve the best use and most economical development of the means of transport for inter-European communications. It has adopted a general transport policy, based on common principles, in the fields of railways, roads, inland waterways, forecasting of transport demand, co-operation between surface and air transport, and research in transport economics.

Structure. The organs of the ECMT are:

(1) A Council of Ministers, composed of the Ministers of Transport of the member countries, meeting twice a year.

(2) A Committee of Deputies, composed of officials of the member countries acting as the ministers' deputies. The committee, which meets six times a year, prepares—with the assistance of a number of specialized subsidiary bodies—the material to be discussed at meetings of the Council of Ministers.

(3) A Secretariat, which is responsible for the everyday administration of the Conference.

Although it is an autonomous institution, the ECMT works in close co-operation with other international organizations, in particular with the OECD, the Council of Europe and the United Nations Economic Commission for Europe (ECE).

European Conference of Postal and Telecommunications Administrations
Conférence européenne des administrations des postes et des télécommunications (CEPT)

Address. c/o PTT, 52 rue du Louvre, 75001 Paris, France.

Founded. 1959.

Membership. 26 countries.

Objects. To foster relations between member administrations and to harmonize and improve their technical services.

Activities. In 1963 member governments of the CEPT set up a European Conference on Satellite Communication (CETS) as a medium of consultation on global telecommunications. The main objectives of the CETS were achieved by the conclusion of two agreements on the establishment of an international communications satellite system, signed in Washington on Aug. 20, 1964, by the United States, Britain and nine other countries. The first, an intergovernmental agreement, outlined the general organizational principles of the system, while the second agreement, concluded between the "designated communications entities of each country" (e.g. the US Communications Satellite Corporation) dealt with the commercial, financial and technical operations, and provided for the setting up of a management committee.

The provisions of the intergovernmental treaty included the following:

(1) The design, development, construction and establishment of satellites, and the ground installations for their control, would be a co-operative international enterprise. The telecommunications ground stations would be owned by the countries or groups of countries in which they were located.

(2) The US Communications Satellite Corporation (COMSAT) would be responsible for the management of the satellite system, and would bear the greatest part of the cost.

(3) Part ownership of the system would be open to any member of the International Telecommunication Union [see page 39].

A supplementary agreement on arbitration was concluded in Washington on June 4, 1965.

The CEPT has also set up a Eurodata Foundation (for research and publishing).

European Fighter Aircraft Agreement

A meeting of arms procurement directors held in Turin (Italy) on Aug. 1–2, 1985, resulted in an agreement between the Federal Republic of Germany, Italy and the United Kingdom on the development of a European fighter aircraft (to replace such aircraft which would become obsolete by the mid-1990s). Spain decided on Sept. 3, 1985, to take part in the project.

European Organization for Astronomical Research in the Southern Hemisphere, also known as
European Southern Observatory (ESO)

Address. Karl-Schwarzschild-Str. 2, D-8046 Garching b. München, Fed. Rep. of Germany.

Officer. Prof. L. Woltjer (dir.).

Founded. Oct. 5, 1962.

Membership. Belgium, Denmark, France, the Federal Republic of Germany, Italy, the Netherlands, Sweden and Switzerland.

History. Until 1981 the ESO was based at the CERN (Geneva). Its first telescope was opened at La Silla (Chile) in 1977. by 1985 it had 13 telescopes in the southern hemisphere.

European Organization for Nuclear Research
(CERN)

Address. 1211 Geneva 23, Switzerland.
Officer. Prof. H. Schopper (dir.-gen.).
Founded. Sept. 29, 1954.
Membership. Austria, Belgium, Denmark, France, the Federal Republic of Germany, Greece, Italy, the Netherlands, Norway, Spain, Sweden, Switzerland and the United Kingdom.
Observers. Poland, Turkey and Yugoslavia.
History. On May 8, 1952, a European Council for Nuclear Research was set up under the auspices of UNESCO, as a result of an agreement signed by Denmark, France, West Germany, Greece, Italy, the Netherlands, Sweden, Switzerland and Yugoslavia on Feb. 15, 1952. Norway and Belgium later adhered to the agreement.

At a meeting on June 21, 1952, the Council decided to build a nuclear research institute which would house two of the world's largest particle accelerators—a proton-cyclotron and a synchro-cyclotron. The project would be a co-operative venture. On Oct. 6, 1962, the Council decided that the European Nuclear Research Laboratory should be sited at Geneva.

The preparation of a convention transforming the European Council for Nuclear Research into a full international organization took place at meetings of the Council in January, March and June 1953. The Convention of the European Organization for Nuclear Research (Conseil Européen pour la Recherche Nucléaire, or CERN) was signed in Paris on July 1, 1953, by representatives of Belgium, Britain, Denmark, France, the Federal Republic of Germany, Greece, Italy, the Netherlands, Norway, Sweden, Switzerland and Yugoslavia. It entered into force on Sept. 29, 1954.

Spain was a party to the convention from June 6, 1962, to Dec. 31, 1968, and did not rejoin CERN until June 24, 1982. In 1963 Yugoslavia withdrew from membership of CERN, but remained associated with the organization as an observer. Poland and Turkey also became observers in 1963.

The Convention. The functions of the organization are defined in the basic programme outlined in the convention.

These are "the construction and operation of an international laboratory for research on high energy particles, including work in the field of cosmic rays" and "organizing and sponsoring international co-operation in nuclear research, including co-operation outside the laboratory". Specifically, mention is made of co-operative work in nuclear physics and cosmic rays, the promotion of contacts between and interchange of scientists, the dissemination of information, the provision of advanced training for research workers, and collaboration with national research institutes. The work is carried out on a purely theoretical basis and solely for non-military purposes, and its results are published for general distribution.

Provision is made for the entry into the organization of other states by the unanimous vote of the existing member states.

The funds to finance the organization are provided by the member states on a relative scale based on their average net national incomes.

The Organs. The governing body of CERN is the Council, on which each member state is represented by two delegates. The Council meets at least once a year to determine policy, approve plans and adopt the budget. The Council is assisted by a Scientific Policy Committee, a Finance Committee and a European Committee for Future Accelerators.

Developments. The construction programme undertaken by CERN was completed in 1961, the foundation-stone for the laboratory at Meyrin near Geneva having been laid on June 10, 1955. The installations include a 600 million electron volt synchro-cyclotron, which entered into operation on Aug. 17, 1957, and a 30,000 million electron volt proton-synchrotron, brought into operation in November 1959. These two machines form the basis of CERN's experimental research programme, which is primarily concerned with high-energy particles. The experiments are conducted by mixed teams of scientists from the member countries of the organization.

The organization's Council decided on Feb. 19, 1971, that a 300,000 million electron volt particle accelerator (proton-synchrotron) for high-energy nuclear physics should be built on a site adjacent to CERN's existing installations at Meyrin.

Under an agreement of October 1965 the area of the CERN laboratory was extended across the Swiss border into France.

On June 16, 1960, it was announced that an agreement had been made with the USSR for the exchange of scientists from CERN with scientists from the Nuclear Research Centre at Dubna near Moscow.

By 1979 the major experimental facilities of CERN were a synchro-cyclotron (of 600 MeV), a proton-synchrotron (of 25-28 GeV), intersecting storage rings (ISR) and a super proton-synchrotron (of 400 GeV).

At an extraordinary session held on Oct. 31, 1981, the then 12 member states of CERN unanimously approved a plan to build, during the next five to eight years, a 30-kilometre-long circular tunnel for a new particle accelerator (electron-positron ring, LEP) in the Gex area (on the Franco-Swiss border) which would eventually replace earlier accelerators.

CERN has a special arrangement for collaboration with the USSR State committee for the Utilization of Atomic Energy at Serpukhov (south of Moscow).

European Organization for the Safety of Air Navigation (EUROCONTROL)

Address. 72 rue de la Loi, 1040 Brussels, Belgium.
Officer. Jean Lévèque (dir.-gen.).
Founded. 1963.

Membership. Belgium, France, the Federal Republic of Germany, Ireland, Luxembourg, the Netherlands and the United Kingdom.

History. The Aviation Ministers of the then six member countries of the European Economic Community approved, at a meeting in Rome on June 9–10, 1960, a draft convention and protocol for a unified air traffic control system for Western Europe. The convention was signed in Brussels on Dec. 13, 1960, by the above six countries and the United Kingdom.

Activities. EUROCONTROL is headed by a permanent commission consisting of the ministers responsible for civil and military aviation in each of the member states, and its budget makes provision, inter alia, for the joint financing of the operating costs of traffic control services for the upper airspace of the Benelux countries and the Federal Republic of Germany.

Co-operation agreements were signed in 1964 by Denmark, Norway, Sweden and the US Federal Aviation Administration; in 1965 by Switzerland; in 1966 by Italy; in 1967 by Austria; in 1971 by Spain; and in 1976 by Portugal.

European Patent Office (EPO)

Address. 8000 Munich 2, Erhardstr. 27, Federal Republic of Germany.

Officers. J. B. van Benthem (pres.); I. G. J. Davis (ch. of admin. board).

Founded. Oct. 19, 1977.

Membership. Austria, Belgium, France, the Federal Republic of Germany, Italy, Liechtenstein, Luxembourg, the Netherlands, Sweden, Switzerland and the United Kingdom.

History. The office was established under the 1973 Convention on the Grant of European Patents [see page 4].

European Science Foundation (ESF)

Address. 1 quai Lezay-Marnésia, Strasbourg, France.

Officers. Prof. Eugen Seibold (pres.); J. Goormaghtigh (sec. gen.).

Founded. 1973.

Membership. Austria, Belgium, Denmark, France, the Federal Republic of Germany, Greece, Ireland, Italy, the Netherlands, Norway, Portugal, Spain, Sweden, Switzerland, the United Kingdom and Yugoslavia.

Object. Co-operation among national research programmes.

Structure. The ESF has an executive council and, as its main decision-making body, an assembly of representatives of 48 national organizations meeting once a year in Strasbourg. It also has standing committees for medical sciences, natural sciences, space sciences, humanities and social sciences and an astronomy committee. It has set up a European Training Programme for Brain and Behaviour Research (ETP).

European Space Operations Centre (ESOC)

Address. Robert-Bosch-Str. 5, D-6100 Darmstadt, Federal Republic of Germany.

Membership. Belgium, Denmark, France, the Federal Republic of Germany, Ireland, Italy, the Netherlands, Spain, Sweden, Switzerland and the United Kingdom; *associate members*: Austria and Norway; *observer*: Canada.

European Telecommunications Satellite Organization (EUTELSAT)

Founded. Sept. 1, 1985.

Membership. Austria, Belgium, Cyprus, Denmark, Finland, France, the Federal Republic of Germany, Greece, the Holy See, Iceland, Ireland, Italy, Liechtenstein, Luxembourg, Malta, Monaco, the Netherlands, Norway, Portugal, San Marino, Spain, Sweden, Switzerland, Turkey, the United Kingdom and Yugoslavia.

Object. To provide a regional satellite system for telecommunications and television transmissions in Western Europe, i.e. in the member countries of the European Conference of Postal and Telecommunications Administrations (CEPT).

History. EUTELSAT was given a definitive statute under a convention of July 7, 1982 (which came into force on Sept. 1, 1985). Its first satellite, *ECS-1*, was launched by *Ariane L06* on June 16, 1983.

Group for Co-operation in Scientific and Technical Research

A Group for European Co-operation in the Field of Scientific and Technical Research (COST Group) formed by 19 European countries held a conference in Brussels on Nov. 22–23, 1971, when co-operation agreements were concluded between various groups of countries.

These agreements covered

(i) The creation of a European data processing network; (ii) a research programme on telecommunications aerials; (iii) joint action on material for gas turbines and sea-water desalination plants with respect to metallurgical research; (iv) three programmes on technical aspects of air, water and waste pollution; and (v) agreement in principle on a European computer programme information centre and on a European centre for medium-term weather forecasting.

The last-named centre was established under a convention signed on Oct. 23, 1973, by its members—Austria, Belgium, Denmark, Finland, France, the Federal Republic of Germany, Greece, Italy, the Netherlands, Portugal, Spain, Sweden, Switzerland and Yugoslavia.

Institut Max von Laue—Paul Langevin (ILL)

Address. 38042 Grenoble Cédex, France.

Directors. Prof. R. Haensel, Prof. J. Enderby, Dr A. Michaudon.

Founded. 1967.

Membership. France, the Federal Republic of Germany and the United Kingdom (since 1973).

Activities. There is an ILL laboratory with a nuclear reactor (in Grenoble) the cost of which is shared by the three member countries.

Intergovernmental Committee for European Migration (ICEM)

Address. 16 ave. Jean Tremblay, 1211 Geneva 19, Switzerland.

Officer. James L. Carlin (dir.).

Founded. Oct. 2, 1951.

Membership. Argentina, Austria, Belgium, Bolivia, Brazil, Chile, Colombia, Costa Rica, Cyprus, Denmark, the Dominican Republic, Ecuador, El Salvador, the Federal Republic of Germany, Greece, Honduras, Israel, Italy, Luxembourg, Malta, the Netherlands, Nicaragua, Norway, Panama, Paraguay, Peru, Portugal, South Africa, Spain, Switzerland, the United States, Uruguay and Venezuela.

Activities. The ICEM was established as a Provisional Intergovernmental Committee for the Movement of Migrants from Europe by representatives of 16 governments attending an international migration conference in Brussels in 1951. The ICEM adopted its present name on Nov. 15, 1952. Its objects have been to effect the movement of refugees to countries offering final settlement and also to promote social and economic advancement of Latin American countries through selective migration. Between 1952 and 1978 it moved over 2,000,000 migrants overseas.

Structure. The ICEM has a Council, which determines policy, and an Executive Committee assisted by sub-committees on the budget and finance and on co-ordination of transport.

Nations without a State

At a first conference of representatives of 16 of Western Europe's small nations, held in Barcelona at the end of 1985, the European Community was accused of "endangering the survival of the small nations" by failing to take into account their economic and cultural interests, which were deemed to be already menaced by the Community's member states denying them the right of self-determination.

Those who attended the conference included representatives of organizations in Alsace, the Basque country (*Herri Batasuna* or United People), Brittany, Catalonia, Corsica, Flanders, the Friesian Islands, Friuli, Ireland (*Sinn Féin*), Sardinia, the Val d'Aosta and Wales (*Plaid Cymru*). (The Scottish National Party, though invited, did not attend.)

The conference demanded inter alia that the small nations' languages should gradually, over a 30-year period, officially and socially be taken over in their respective geographical areas.

The conference established a permanent secretariat in Barcelona. It avoided to pronounce itself on the legitimacy of small nations resorting to violence in pursuit of self-determination.

Bilateral Treaties and Agreements between Countries in Northern, Southern and Western Europe

The date of entry into force is shown in parentheses where it differs from the date of signature.

Andorra and Spain. Cultural convention, July 8, 1981.

Austria and the Federal Republic of Germany. A treaty supplementing the European extradition convention of Dec. 13, 1957, and facilitating its application, Jan. 31, 1972 (Feb. 1, 1977).

Austria and Iceland. Treaty of commerce and navigation, April 6, 1938.

Austria and Spain. Extradition treaty, Feb. 1, 1978. Convention on scientific co-operation, March 22, 1983.

Austria and Sweden. Agreement on commerce and navigation, Jan. 26, 1934.
Notes on co-operation in peaceful uses of nuclear energy, Aug. 21 and 25, 1970.

Austria and Switzerland. Exchange of notes concerned with extradition, March 6, 1926.
Extradition agreement, June 13, 1972.
Agreement on trade exchanges and payments service, Sept. 15, 1954.

Belgium and the Federal Republic of Germany. A treaty dealing with the ratification of the two countries' common border and other questions concerning mutual relations, Sept. 24, 1956 (Aug. 28, 1958), with the border being demarcated under a protocol of Dec. 6, 1960; amended, March 29 and June 22, 1984.
A treaty providing for extradition and legal assistance in criminal cases, Jan. 17, 1958 (May 30, 1959); partly superseded by the European extradition convention in force from Jan. 1, 1977.
A cultural agreement, Sept. 9, 1956 (March 22, 1957).
An agreement for compensation for Belgian nationals persecuted by the Nazi regime, Sept. 28, 1960 (Aug. 25, 1961).
An agreement on mutual secrecy in regard to defence-related inventions and technical knowledge, Feb. 1, 1963 (March 1, 1963).

Belgium and Iceland. Extradition treaty, March 25, 1876.

Treaty of commerce and navigation, June 18, 1895.

Belgium and the Netherlands. A treaty on the formation of a Netherlands language union was signed in Brussels on Sept. 9, 1980, by the Governments of Belgium and of the Netherlands.

The union was to achieve integration between the Netherlands and the Netherlands-speaking community in Belgium in the field of the Netherlands language (in Belgium also referred to as Flemish) and literature and to provide a legal framework for establishing uniformity in the use of the language. The union's policy was to be formulated and implemented by a ministerial committee consisting of at least two Belgian and two Netherlands ministers with responsibility for education and culture. This committee would seek the advice of a Council of the Netherlands Language and Literature composed of 45 experts from the Netherlands and the Netherlands-speaking community in Belgium. The treaty also provided for the establishment of an interparliamentary commission which would deliberate on all matters concerning the union and would advise the ministerial committee. The preparation and implementation of the union's policy would be carried out by a general secretariat.

The treaty was subject to ratification by the Netherlands Parliament and the Netherlands-language Cultural Council in Belgium.

A further treaty, signed on Jan. 27, 1982, called for the "integration of the Netherlands and the Flemish-speaking community in Belgium in matters of Dutch language and letters in the broadest sense".

Belgium and Spain. Cultural agreement, Oct. 11, 1980.

Belgium and Sweden. Extradition agreement, Feb. 25, 1976; amended Nov. 18 and 25, 1980.

Agreement on the use of nuclear material, equipment, installations and information, Sept. 27, 1977; amended Dec. 18, 1981.

Belgium and Switzerland. Extradition convention, May 13, 1874; amended 1977; Sept. 6, 1983; Aug. 14, 1984.

Denmark and the Federal Republic of Germany. A treaty on the delimitation of the North Sea continental shelf near the coast, June 9, 1965 (May 27, 1966). A further treaty on the delimitation of the continental shelf below the North Sea, Jan. 28, 1971 (Dec. 7, 1972).

Agreements on the two countries' borderline in Flensburg, Oct. 26 and 28, 1970; supplementary protocols, Aug. 25 and Sept. 14, 1971.

A cultural co-operation agreement, June 18, 1974 (Dec. 2, 1975).

A treaty on compensation for Danish nationals persecuted under the Nazi regime, Aug. 29, 1979 (June 3, 1980).

Denmark and Spain. Convention on cultural co-operation, Aug. 18, 1978.

Denmark and Switzerland. Treaty of friendship, establishment and commerce, Feb. 10, 1875.

Agreement on regulation of trade exchanges, Sept. 15, 1951.

Finland and the Federal Republic of Germany. A joint declaration on the normalization of relations between the two countries, signed in Bonn on Sept. 19, 1974, covered the mutual renunciation of the use of force and a West German agreement to respect Finland's policy of neutrality, and it also settled part of financial and legal questions outstanding since the end of World War II (Finland having requested compensation for damage caused by German troops in 1944–45).

Agreement on cultural co-operation, Sept. 27, 1978 (April 25, 1979).

Finland and Spain. Cultural convention, Dec. 10, 1979.

Finland and Switzerland. Trade agreement, June 24, 1927.

France and the Federal Republic of Germany. Extradition treaty, Nov. 29, 1951 (Oct. 22, 1959).

Cultural agreement, Oct. 23, 1954 (July 28, 1959); additional protocol, Feb. 2, 1973 (Jan. 6, 1976).

Treaty on compensation for French nationals persecuted under the Nazi regime, July 15, 1960 (Aug. 4, 1961).

Agreement on mutual secrecy in the treatment of defence-related inventions and technical knowledge, Sept. 28, 1961.

Treaty of co-operation, providing for the co-ordination of the two countries' policies in foreign affairs, defence, information and cultural affairs, Jan. 22, 1963 (July 2, 1963).

The principal provisions are summarized below.

There would be regular meetings of the heads of state, Foreign and Defence Ministers, and Chiefs of Staff of the two countries. An inter-ministerial commission would be set up in each country to supervise questions of co-operation. Under the programme of co-operation set forth in the treaty, the two governments undertook to "consult each other before taking any decision on all major questions of foreign policy".

In the sphere of defence the treaty provided for the setting up of Franco-German operational research institutes, for the exchange of personnel between the two armed forces, and for the organization of joint activities in the field of armaments.

The cultural programme outlined in the treaty included: The extension of reciprocal language-teaching; the adoption of arrangements for equivalent values of periods of education, examinations, degrees and diplomas; and an increase in co-operation in scientific research.

Except for the clauses concerning defence, the treaty also applies to West Berlin.

As part of the process of reactivating the security clauses of the treaty, agreement was reached on Feb. 28, 1986, on consultations over the use of French tactical nuclear weapons against targets in the Federal Republic of Germany in the event of East-West conflict (France thus emphasizing its commitment to defence of West German territory as essential to its own security). There were then some 17,000 French troops stationed in the FRG.

Agreement on the construction and operation of a fast-breeder nuclear reactor, Jan. 19, 1967 (May 26, 1967); amended July 6, 1971; on July 19, 1974, it was joined, as agreed, by the United Kingdom with effect from Jan. 7, 1976;

supplementary agreements were concluded on July 7, 1976, and Dec. 9, 1982.

An agreement signed on Feb. 2, 1971, empowered West German legal authorities to bring to trial alleged Nazi war criminals already convicted in absentia by French courts, this agreement being finally ratified by the German Federal Parliament on Feb. 21, 1975.

Agreement on research and development in prospecting for, and exploitation and processing of, manganese nodules, April 26, 1974.

An agreement signed in Bonn on May 18, 1976, by the French Atomic Energy Commission and two West German companies provided for co-operation in the development, production and sale of fast-breeder nuclear reactors.

Agreement on exchange and co-operation in safety research on light-water reactors, Sept. 28, 1978; supplementary agreement, Sept. 29, 1983.

Under an agreement signed on March 31, 1981, the Federal Republic undertook to pay DM250,000,000 (about £53,000,000) in indemnity to French citizens forcibly recruited into the German Army during World War II.

On May 29, 1984, a series of bilateral co-operation measures were agreed, including the development of a military observation satellite and the joint development of an anti-tank helicopter.

An agreement signed on July 13, 1984, provided for the abolition of customs formalities for European Community citizens at the Franco-German border.

On Feb. 5, 1985, the two governments announced the establishment of a "joint operational group" of police experts and a telex "hot line" between the Paris and Bonn Interior Ministries to combat terrorism.

Joint Franco-German manoeuvres were held on June 18–20, 1985, at Münsingen near Stuttgart.

France and Iceland. Treaty of commerce, navigation and establishment, Aug. 23, 1742.

Extradition treaty, March 28, 1877.

Treaty of commerce and payments, Dec. 6, 1951; supplementary agreement, May 24, 1966.

France and Italy. On June 14, 1985, it was agreed to set up a joint commission to deal with differences over the wine trade, and to co-operate in technology, defence and cultural projects.

France and Spain. A five-year military co-operation agreement was signed in Madrid on June 22, 1970, and was automatically renewable for two years unless six months' notice was given by either side. It provided for close co-operation in defence and armaments, involving joint defence exercises, exchanges of personnel and units, and collaboration in respect of equipment, "including missiles, munitions and spare parts".

Two agreements on the delimitation of the continental shelf and territorial waters in the Bay of Biscay, signed on Jan. 29, 1974, provided inter alia for the designation of a special zone, about 50 kilometres square (some 200 kilometres off the north coast of Spain), where the two countries would co-operate in the exploitation of hydrocarbon reserves.

Agreement on oceanographic co-operation, Dec. 11, 1975.

Agreement on co-operation in radio-astronomy, June 1, 1980.

Agreement on co-operation in defence, Oct. 7, 1983.

Friendship and co-operation agreement, providing for the holding of annual summit meetings, July 9, 1985.

France and Sweden. Trade agreement, March 3, 1949.

France and Switzerland. Extradition treaty, July 9, 1869; amended April 20, 1959.

Convention on the protection against pollution of the waters of the Lake of Geneva (Lac Léman), Nov. 16, 1962; expanded May 5, 1977.

Trade convention, March 31, 1967.

Agreement on co-operation in the use of nuclear energy for peaceful purposes, May 14, 1970.

The Federal Republic of Germany and Greece. Agreements on economic co-operation, Nov. 11, 1953, and Nov. 27, 1958.

Cultural agreement, May 17, 1956 (June 16, 1957).

Agreement on scientific and technical co-operation, Nov. 30, 1958.

Agreement on compensation for Greek nationals persecuted by the Nazi regime, March 18, 1960 (Oct. 21, 1961).

Agreement on mutual secrecy on defence-related inventions and technical knowledge, Oct. 5 and Dec. 15, 1971 (Jan. 1, 1974).

Agreement on scientific and technical co-operation, Nov. 30, 1978.

The Federal Republic of Germany and Iceland. Treaty on extradition of merchant seamen deserters, June 14, 1881.

Provisional commerce and navigation agreement, Dec. 19, 1950; extended (until Dec. 31, 1986), Dec. 10, 1984.

Commercial treaty, May 20, 1954; supplementary agreement, July 4 and Sept. 26, 1966.

Agreement on the formation of a governmental committee on economic affairs, Nov. 27, 1984.

The Federal Republic of Germany and Ireland. Treaty of commerce and navigation, May 12, 1930 (Dec. 12, 1931).

Agreement on cultural co-operation, Feb. 10, 1983 (Feb. 17, 1984).

The Federal Republic of Germany and Italy. Treaty of friendship, commerce and navigation, Nov. 21, 1957 (Nov. 19, 1961).

Agreement on mutual secrecy in the treatment of defence-related inventions and technical knowledge, Jan. 27, 1960 (March 28, 1972).

Treaty on compensation for Italian nationals persecuted under the Nazi regime, June 2, 1961 (July 31, 1963).

The Federal Republic of Germany and Luxembourg. Extradition treaty, March 9, 1876 (Nov.

11, 1876); expanded by a supplementary treaty, May 6, 1912 (Sept. 2, 1912); except for its Art. 13, paragraph 1, first sentence, it was superseded by the European extradition convention.

Treaty on cultural co-operation, Oct. 28, 1980 (March 1, 1982).

The Federal Republic of Germany and Monaco. Extradition treaty May 21, 1962 (March 14, 1965); correction of Art. 21, Oct. 12 and 16, 1965.

The Federal Republic of Germany and the Netherlands. Treaty on the lateral delimitation of the continental shelf near the coast, Dec. 1, 1964 (Aug. 27, 1965), and a treaty on the delimitation of the continental shelf below the North Sea, Jan. 28, 1971 (Dec. 7, 1972).

Treaty supplementing the European extradition convention of Dec. 13, 1979, and facilitating its application, Aug. 30, 1979 (Jan. 30, 1983).

Treaty on cross-border co-operation in the utilization of the estuary of the River Ems, Sept. 10, 1984.

The Federal Republic of Germany and Norway. Agreement on the deportation of persons, March 18, 1955.

Cultural agreement, May 29, 1956 (March 9, 1957).

Treaty on compensation for Norwegian nationals persecuted under the Nazi regime, Aug. 7, 1959 (April 23, 1960).

Protocol on increased co-operation in industry and energy, Aug. 19, 1976; followed by a further protocol of June 6, 1977.

Agreement on the formation of a new government committee for economic affairs, Aug. 24, 1977.

The Federal Republic of Germany and Portugal. Trade agreement, March 20, 1926 (April 1, 1926); extended (until Dec. 31, 1986) on Dec. 10, 1984.

Agreement on commerce and navigation, on Aug. 24, 1950; amended June 29, 1953, and extended on Dec. 10, 1984, until Dec. 31, 1986.

A protocol of May 13, 1961, provided for increased economic co-operation.

Treaty on extradition and legal assistance in criminal cases, June 15, 1964, came into force on March 29, 1968.

Cultural agreement, Oct. 22, 1965 (Dec. 29, 1966).

Agreement on co-operation in research and technological development, June 15, 1981 (Sept. 21, 1981).

The Federal Republic of Germany and Spain. Extradition treaty, May 2, 1978 (Aug. 1, 1978).

A cultural agreement signed on Dec. 10, 1954 (March 14, 1956).

A trade agreement signed on June 6, 1960, and in force since May 1, 1961, was repeatedly amended, most recently on Oct. 9, 1964, and was extended on Nov. 22, 1984, until April 30, 1986.

An agreement on economic co-operation was signed and came into force on May 9, 1961.

A framework agreement on co-operation in scientific research and technological development, April 23, 1970 (March 10, 1971).

An agreement on co-operation in the field of solar energy and an agreement on co-operation in the peaceful use of nuclear energy, Dec. 3, 1978 (Dec. 13, 1978).

Agreement on scientific and technical co-operation in agricultural research, Oct. 22, 1979.

Agreement on co-operation in radio-astronomy, May 16, 1980 (Aug. 3, 1981).

Agreement on scientific and technical co-operation, Dec. 6, 1983.

The Federal Republic of Germany and Sweden. Agreement on the deportation of persons, May 31, 1954 (June 1, 1954).

Treaty on compensation for Swedish nationals persecuted by the Nazi regime, Aug. 3, 1964.

Agreement on the formation of a new governmental committee for economic affairs, Jan. 1, 1977.

Agreement (relating to Art. 5 of the European extradition convention of Dec. 13, 1957) on extradition in cases of fiscal offences, Feb. 7 and March 16, 1978.

The Federal Republic of Germany and Switzerland. Trade agreement, Dec. 2, 1954; repeatedly amended, most recently by a protocol of Sept. 13, 1977; on Sept. 18, 1985, it was extended to Dec. 31, 1986.

Treaty amplifying the European extradition convention of Dec. 13, 1957, and facilitating its application, Nov. 13, 1969 (Jan. 1, 1977).

Agreement on the formation of a new governmental committee on economic affairs, Dec. 15, 1977.

Agreement providing for the two countries' foreign ministers to hold annual consultations with each other, October 1979.

Agreement on mutual notification of the construction and operation of nuclear installations near the two countries' common border, Aug. 10, 1982 (Sept. 9, 1983).

The Federal Republic of Germany and Turkey. Trade treaty, July 26, 1930 (Sept. 25, 1930); amended May 19, 1936; partly reapplied May 29, 1952, and extended, on Dec. 10, 1984, until Dec. 31, 1986.

Extradition treaty, Sept. 3, 1930 (June 19, 1932); reapplied May 29, 1952, but terminated (except for its Art. 23) upon the entry into force of the European extradition convention on Jan 1, 1977.

Cultural agreement, May 8, 1957 (June 9, 1958).

Agreement on co-operation in tourism, March 3, 1980 (July 30, 1980).

Greece and Iceland. Treaty of commerce and navigation, Jan. 28, 1930.

Greece and Italy. Agreement on the delimitation of the two countries' common border on the continental shelf, May 24, 1977.

This agreement laid down that the border was to be based on a median line between the two countries' coasts, with the proviso that in the area of the Ionian Islands equidistance was to be measured from the western end of the shelf of these islands. (Italy had not signed the 1958 Convention on the Continental Shelf—see page 55.)

Greece and Sweden. Trade agreements, Sept. 10, 1926, and June 25, 1948.

Iceland and Ireland. Trade agreement, Dec. 2, 1954.

Iceland and Italy. Treaty of commerce and navigation, May 1, 1864; additional article, Sept. 17, 1902.
Extradition treaty, July 19, 1873.

Iceland and Luxembourg. Extradition treaty, April 8, 1879.

Iceland and the Netherlands. Treaty of friendship, mutual understanding and commerce, June 15, 1701; supplementary declaration, July 10, 1817.
Extradition treaty, January 1895.

Iceland and Portugal. Declaration on commerce and navigation, March 14, 1896.

Iceland and Spain. Extradition treaty, Oct. 12, 1889.
Treaty of commerce and navigation, Aug. 26, 1929.
Commercial treaty, June 29 and July 16, 1934.
Trade agreement, Nov. 29, 1960.
Cultural agreement, July 27, 1980.

Iceland and Switzerland. Treaty of friendship, commerce and establishment, Feb. 2, 1875; additional article, May 2, 1875.
Exchange of letters on the conclusion of a trade agreement, Dec. 26, 1951.

Italy and Spain. Agreement on defence matters, July 16, 1980.
Agreement on mutual co-operation in the protection of classified material, Dec. 2, 1983.

Italy and Sweden. Commerce and navigation agreement, June 14, 1862; amended Dec. 15, 1967.
Trade agreement, Dec. 18, 1961.

Italy and Switzerland. Trade treaty, Jan. 27, 1923; additional protocol, Dec. 30, 1933.
Trade agreement, Oct. 21, 1950; exchange of letters, July 18, 1969.
Convention on the protection of Italo-Swiss waters against pollution, April 20, 1972.
(On Jan. 7–18, 1985, the Swiss Air Force conducted exercises at Decomonnu, Sicily, a base previously used for NATO exercises.)

Liechtenstein and Switzerland. Under an agreement on the movement of Swiss citizens in Liechtenstein, signed in November 1981, Swiss citizens had no automatic right to settle in Liechtenstein.

Luxembourg and Spain. Agreement on cultural exchanges, March 18, 1982.

Monaco and Switzerland. Extradition convention, Dec. 10, 1885.

The Netherlands and Spain. Trade agreement, Nov. 29, 1976.
Convention on cultural and scientific co-operation, Feb. 27, 1978.

The Netherlands and Sweden. Treaty of commerce and navigation, Sept. 25, 1847; amplified, Dec. 15, 1908.

The Netherlands and Switzerland. Treaty of friendship, establishment and commerce, Aug. 19, 1975.

Portugal and Spain. Conventions on the delimitation of (i) the territorial sea and the contiguous zone and (ii) the continental shelf, Feb. 12, 1976.
A 10-year treaty of friendship and co-operation (superseding an Iberian Pact signed on March 17, 1939, by Portugal and Spain and due to expire in 1980) was signed in Madrid on Nov. 22, 1977. It was approved by the Spanish *Cortes* (Parliament) on March 9 and by the Portuguese Legislative Assembly on April 18, 1978, and was ratified on May 5, 1978 (during a visit to Portugal by the King of Spain).

The treaty provided for the establishment of a Hispano-Portuguese council under the chairmanship of the two countries' Foreign Ministers; mutual preferential trade arrangements; co-ordination of economic policies; and the development of border areas. Both countries undertook not to interfere in each other's internal affairs and to extend to each other military and economic co-operation (with the resumption of joint military exercises, which had been suspended since 1974).

Agreement on co-operation in safety of nuclear installations near the two countries' common border, and protocol, March 31, 1980.
Agreement on the relations between the two countries during the 10-year period after their accession to the European Communities, April 30, 1985.

The agreement covered fisheries as well as bilateral trade, in which (inter alia) Spanish import duties and restrictions were to be abolished from Jan. 1, 1986, except for textiles, cork and some petrochemicals for which quotas were to be kept for four or five years.

Portugal and Sweden. Declaration on trade and navigation, Oct. 19, 1935.
Protocol on expanded co-operation, Dec. 8, 1978.

Portugal and Switzerland. Extradition convention, Oct. 30, 1873.
Trade agreement, Dec. 20, 1905.

Spain and Sweden. Treaty of navigation, March 15, 1883; extended, June 23, 1887; amended, July 13, 1900.
Trade agreement, May 4, 1925; expanded, May 28, 1928.
Trade agreement, April 6, 1960.
Military co-operation agreement, July 1985.

Spain and Switzerland. Trade agreement, April 2, 1960.

Sweden and Switzerland. Provisional convention on trade relations, March 20, 1924.

Agreement on regulation of trade exchanges, June 20, 1951.

Ministerial note on co-operation in defence technology, Aug. 4, 1966.

Agreement on co-operation in peaceful uses of nuclear energy, Feb. 14, 1968.

Sweden and Turkey. Friendship treaty, May 31, 1924.

Treaty of commerce and navigation, Sept. 29, 1929; additional agreement, March 24, 1939; amended, Dec. 28, 1960, Jan. 27 and Feb. 19, 1962.

Treaty on extradition and legal assistance, Feb. 13, 1932.

Trade agreement, June 7, 1948; extended, June 30, 1953.

Switzerland and Turkey. Treaty of friendship, Sept. 19, 1925.

Trade agreement, March 17, 1948.

9. North Atlantic Treaty Organization (NATO)

This section covers the origins, formation, aims and structure of NATO. It also traces the development and activities of the organization since 1949 and surveys the principal multilateral and bilateral agreements concluded by member states within the NATO framework.

North Atlantic Treaty Organization (NATO)

Address. 1110 Brussels, Belgium.
Officer. Lord Carrington (sec. gen.).
Founded. April 4, 1949.
Membership. Belgium, Canada, Denmark, France, the Federal Republic of Germany, Greece, Iceland, Italy, Luxembourg, the Netherlands, Norway, Portugal, Spain,* Turkey, the United Kingdom and the United States (* since May 30, 1982).

Origins

The necessity for the creation of a defence alliance of Western powers was acknowledged by the governments concerned soon after the end of World War II. The tension which had arisen between the Allied nations of Western Europe and the Soviet bloc came to a head in 1948 with the Communist coup d'état in Czechoslovakia and the Soviet blockade of Berlin.

In addition, the authority of the United Nations, as guardian of world peace and security, had shown itself to be severely restricted by the use of the veto in the Security Council, which precluded the settlement of many important questions.

In the years immediately following the war the Soviet Union formed a close network of military alliances in Eastern Europe. In answer to this Belgium, Britain, France, Luxembourg and the Netherlands created their own defence system in the Western Union, based on the Brussels Treaty of March 17, 1948 [see page 143]. It was, however, apparent that, without the participation of the United States, such an alliance would in no way counterbalance the defence system of Eastern Europe.

The Vandenberg Resolution. The principles upon which the USA would be willing to join a defensive alliance of Western nations were set out in a resolution introduced in the US Senate Foreign Relations Committee by Senator Vandenberg, the Republican Party's foreign affairs specialist, and approved on May 19, 1948. The resolution committed the United States, in principle, to military assistance to regional alliances and other collective arrangements entered into within the framework of the United Nations. It was stressed, however, that the USA would not enter into any "automatic commitments"; that any action associating the USA with defence pacts such as the Western Union would require congressional approval; and that any regional defence arrangements must provide for the "continuous and effective self-help" of the countries concerned before the question of US participation could be considered.

A report commending the policy outlined in the Vandenberg Resolution was formally adopted by the Senate Foreign Relations Committee on May 27, 1948, and approved by the full Senate on June 11.

The report declared that "certainty in advance concerning the intentions of the USA should constitute a vital factor in deterring aggression", and stressed that regional alliances or other "collective arrangements" should be promised the "association and help" of the USA, subject to final approval by Congress, if they guaranteed among themselves "continuous and effective self-help and mutual aid". Senator Vandenberg, speaking on the necessity for a plain declaration by the USA that aggression would mean war, declared: "The experience of World War I and World War II suggests that the best deterrent to aggression is the certainty that immediate and effective counter-measures will be taken against those who violate the peace. The principle of individual and collective self-defence is fundamental to the independence and integrity of the members of the United Nations. This is recognized in Art. 51 [of the UN Charter]. By reaffirming now its allegiance to this principle, the USA would take an important step in the direction of removing any dangerous uncertainties that might mislead potential aggressors. Such a reaffirmation is directed against no one and threatens no one. It is directed solely against aggression."

The report pointed out that peace-loving people everywhere were "concerned over the present inability of the United Nations to assure international peace" and were troubled by the excessive use of the veto and the failure of arms control, and went on: "The present sense of insecurity in many parts of the world retards and hampers the efforts which the USA is making to promote international economic recovery. It is clear that the security aspects of world economic recovery cannot be ignored. The people of the world look to the USA, as the strongest free nation, for leadership in making the United Nations an effective instrument for peace and security."

The North Atlantic Treaty

On the basis of the Vandenberg Resolution negotiations were opened in July 1948 between the members of the Western Union on the one hand and the USA and Canada on the other. Further exploratory talks on the proposed North Atlantic Alliance were held in December 1948 and January 1949, but it was only after several weeks of discussions that, in March 1949, the final draft treaty was agreed upon by the USA, Canada, Belgium, Britain, France, Luxembourg, the Netherlands and Norway (which had taken part in the later stages of the negotiations). The treaty was signed on April 4, 1949, by the eight nations listed above and by Denmark, Iceland, Italy and Portugal, which had received invitations to join the pact. After ratification by all parliaments concerned, it came into force on Aug. 24, 1949.

Later adherents to the North Atlantic Treaty were Greece and Turkey (Feb. 18, 1952), the Federal Republic of Germany (May 6, 1955) and Spain (May 30, 1982).

The text of the treaty, which entered into force on Aug. 24, 1949, is given below:

"**Preamble.** The parties to this treaty reaffirm their faith in the purposes and principles of the UN Charter and their desire to live in peace with all peoples and all governments.

"They are determined to safeguard the freedom, common heritage and civilization of their peoples, founded on the principles of democracy, individual liberty and the rule of law.

A = Albania
B = Belgium
L = Luxembourg
N = Netherlands
S = Switzerland

▨ = European members of NATO (which also includes Canada and the United States)

▨ = Members of Warsaw Treaty Organization

Map 6   North Atlantic Treaty Organization (NATO) and the Warsaw Treaty Organization

"They seek to promote stability and well-being in the North Atlantic area.

"They are resolved to unite their efforts for collective defence for the preservation of peace and security.

"They therefore agree to this North Atlantic treaty.

"**Art. 1.** The parties undertake, as set forth in the UN Charter, to settle any international dispute in which they may be involved by peaceful means in such a manner that international peace and security and justice are not endangered, and to refrain in their international relations from the threat or use of force in any manner inconsistent with the purposes of the United Nations.

"**Art. 2.** The parties will contribute towards the further development of peaceful and friendly international relations by strengthening their free institutions, by bringing about a better understanding of the principles upon which these institutions are founded, and by promoting conditions of stability and well-being. They will seek to eliminate conflict in their international economic policies and will encourage economic collaboration between any or all of them.

"**Art. 3.** In order more effectively to achieve the objectives of this treaty, the parties, separately and jointly, by means of continuous and effective self-help and mutual aid, will maintain and develop their individual and collective capacity to resist armed attack.

"**Art. 4.** The parties will consult together whenever, in the opinion of any of them, the territorial integrity, political independence or security of any of the parties is threatened.

"**Art. 5.** The parties agree that an armed attack against one or more of them in Europe or North America shall be considered an attack against them all, and consequently agree that, if such an armed attack occurs, each of them, in exercise of the right of individual or collective self-defence recognized by Art. 51 of the UN Charter, will assist the party or parties so attacked by taking forthwith, individually and in concert with the other parties, such action as it deems necessary, including the use of armed force, to restore and maintain the security of the North Atlantic area. Any such armed attack, and all measures taken as a result thereof, shall immediately be reported to the Security Council. Such measures shall be terminated when the Security Council has taken the measures necessary to restore and maintain international peace and security.

"**Art. 6.** For the purpose of Art. 5 an armed attack on one or more of the parties is deemed to include an armed attack on the territory of any of the parties in Europe or North America, on the Algerian Departments of France, on the occupation forces of any party in Europe, on the islands under the jurisdiction of any party in the North Atlantic area north of the Tropic of Cancer, or on the vessels or aircraft in this area of any of the parties."

[To provide for the accession to NATO of Greece and Turkey, Article 6 was reworded in a protocol to the treaty (signed on Oct. 22, 1951) as follows:

"For the purpose of Art. 5 an armed attack on one or more of the parties is deemed to include an armed attack—(i) on the territory of any of the parties in Europe or North America, on the Algerian Departments of France, on the territory of Turkey, or on the islands under the jurisdiction of any of the parties in the North Atlantic area north of the Tropic of Cancer; (ii) on the forces, vessels, or aircraft of any of the parties, when in or over these territories or any other area in Europe in which occupation forces of any of the parties were stationed on the date when the treaty entered into force, or the Mediterranean Sea, or the North Atlantic area north of the Tropic of Cancer."

In January 1963 the clauses of this article referring to the Algerian Departments of France were recognized by the North Atlantic Council as having become inapplicable since July 3, 1962 (the date of Algerian independence).]

"**Art. 7.** This treaty does not affect, and shall not be interpreted as affecting, in any way the rights and obligations under the Charter of the parties which are members of the United Nations, or the primary responsibility of the Security Council for the maintenance of international peace and security.

"**Art. 8.** Each party declares that none of the international engagements now in force between it and any other of the parties or any third state is in conflict with the provisions of this treaty, and undertakes not to enter into any international engagement in conflict with this treaty.

"**Art. 9.** The parties hereby establish a Council, on which each of them shall be represented, to consider matters concerning the implementation of this treaty. The Council shall be so organized so as to be able to meet promptly at any time. It shall set up such subsidiary bodies as may be necessary; in particular, it shall establish immediately a Defence Committee, which shall recommend measures for the implementation of Arts. 3 and 5.

"**Art. 10.** The parties may, by unanimous agreement, invite any other European state in a position to further the principles of the treaty, and to contribute to the security of the North Atlantic area, to accede to this treaty. Any state so invited may become a party to the treaty by depositing its instrument of accession with the US Government.

"**Art. 11.** This treaty shall be ratified and its provisions carried out by the parties in accordance with their respective constitutional processes. The instruments of ratification shall be deposited as soon as possible with the US Government, which will notify all the other signatories of each deposit. The treaty shall enter into force between the states which have ratified it as soon as the ratifications of the majority of the signatories, including those of Belgium, Canada, France, Luxembourg, the Netherlands, the United Kingdom and the United States, have been deposited, and shall come into effect with respect to other states on the date of deposit of their ratifications.

"**Art. 12.** After the treaty has been in force for 10 years, or at any time thereafter, the parties shall, if any of them so requests, consult together for the purposes of reviewing the treaty, having regard for the factors then affecting peace and security in the North Atlantic area, including the development of universal as well as regional arrangements under the UN Charter for the maintenance of international peace and security.

"**Art. 13.** After the treaty has been in force for 20 years, any party may cease to be a party one year after notice of denunciation has been given to the US Government, which will inform the governments of the other parties of the deposit of each notice of denunciation.

"**Art. 14.** This treaty, of which the English and French texts are equally authentic, shall be deposited in the archives of the US Government. Duly certified copies will be transmitted by that government to the governments of the other signatories."

In an official NATO analysis of the treaty it is pointed out that the treaty is of unlimited duration, and in connection with Art. 6 (as amended) it is stated: "The definition of the military area in which the treaty is applicable in no way implies that political events occurring outside it cannot be the subject of consultations within the Council, for it is the overall international situation which is liable to affect the preservation of peace and security in the area in question, and it is to consideration of this situation that the Council must, and indeed does, devote its attention as a matter of course."

Accession of West Germany. A Protocol to the North Atlantic Treaty on the Accession of the

Federal Republic of Germany formed one of the Paris Agreements of Oct. 23, 1954. The document was signed by the 14 North Atlantic Treaty countries. A Resolution of Association, welcoming and recapitulating a Declaration made by the Federal Republic of Germany and a Joint Declaration issued by the United States, British and French Governments at the London Nine-Power Conference of Sept. 28–Oct. 3, 1954, was signed at the same time [see also Western European Union, pages 143–44]. The German declaration ran as follows:

"The Federal Republic of Germany has agreed to conduct its policy in accordance with the principles of the United Nations Charter.

"Upon her accession to the North Atlantic Treaty and the Brussels Treaty, the Federal Republic of Germany declares that she will refrain from any action inconsistent with the strictly defensive character of the two treaties. In particular, the Federal Republic of Germany undertakes never to have recourse to force to achieve the reunification of Germany or the modification of the present boundaries of the Federal Republic of Germany, and to resolve by peaceful means any disputes which may arise between the Federal Republic and other states."

In the tripartite Joint Declaration the three governments, after stating their resolution to devote their efforts to the strengthening of peace in accordance with the UN Charter, declare that:

(1) They consider the Government of the Federal Republic as the only German Government freely and legitimately constituted, and therefore entitled to speak for Germany as the representative of the German people in international affairs.

(2) In their relations with the Federal Republic they will follow the principles set out in Article 2 of the UN Charter.

(3) A peace settlement for the whole of Germany, freely negotiated between Germany and her former enemies, which should lay the foundation of a lasting peace, remains an essential aim of their policy. The final determination of the boundaries of Germany must await such a settlement.

(4) The achievement through peaceful means of a fully free and unified Germany remains a fundamental goal of their policy.

(5) The security and welfare of Berlin and the maintenance of the position of the three powers there are regarded by the three powers as essential elements of the peace of the free world in the present international situation. Accordingly they will maintain armed forces within the territory of Berlin as long as their responsibilities require it. They therefore reaffirm that they will treat any attack against Berlin from any quarter as an attack upon their forces and themselves.

(6) They will regard as a threat to their own peace and safety any recourse to force which, in violation of the principles of the UN Charter, threatens the integrity and unity of the Atlantic Alliance or its defensive purposes. In the event of any such action the three governments will consider the offending government as having forfeited its rights to any guarantee and any military assistance provided for in the North Atlantic Treaty and its protocols. They will act in accordance with Article 4 of the North Atlantic Treaty with a view to taking other measures which may be appropriate.

The provision in Paragraph (1) above must be considered as superseded by the 1972 Basic Treaty between the Federal Republic of Germany and the German Democratic Republic (see Section 11 on East-West Treaties).

North Atlantic Council

The supreme authority of the Atlantic Alliance is the North Atlantic Council, a political assembly composed of representatives of the governments of the 15 member countries. The Council meets at the level of ministers or of permanent representatives.

Ministerial meetings, which are generally held twice a year, are attended by Ministers for Foreign Affairs, Defence or Economic Affairs from each of the member countries. The agenda of each meeting determines which ministers should attend. Member countries are occasionally represented by their heads of state.

The Council functions continuously at the level of permanent representatives who are of ambassadorial rank and who lead national delegations accredited to NATO. The permanent representatives meet at least once a week.

The Chairman of the Council, at both ministerial and permanent representatives' level, is the Secretary General of NATO. The presidency, held by the Foreign Minister of each member country in turn, rotates annually.

Council Committees. Much of the work of the North Atlantic Council is carried out through permanent and temporary committees, which give advice and make recommendations on technical matters.

The committees are those for:
Political Affairs
Science
Defence Review
Armaments
Nuclear Planning
Civil Emergency Planning
Air Defence
Economics
Budget
Infrastructure
Logistics
Communications
Challenges of Modern Society
Crisis Management

The Council has a number of civilian agencies under its authority, as follows:

(1) **Central Europe Operating Agency** (CEOA), established in 1957 to act as the central co-ordinating and controlling body for the Central European Pipelines System, with the participation of eight nations and located at Versailles (France).

(2) **NATO Maintenance and Supply Organization** (NAMSO), established in 1958 for the supply of spare parts and logistic support for a number of jointly-used weapon systems or equipment, especially missiles and electronic systems, with the participation of all member nations except Iceland, and located in Luxembourg.

(3) **NATO Hawk Production and Logistics Organization** (NHPLO), established in 1959 to supervise the multinational production of the Hawk surface-to-air missile system in Europe and subsequently to supervise the Hawk European Limited Improvement Programme, with the participation of seven nations, and located at Rueil-Malmaison (France).

(4) **NATO Multi-Role Combat Aircraft Development and Production Management Organization** (NAMMO), established in 1969 as an intergovernmental body supported by the Federal

Republic of Germany, Italy and the United Kingdom, and located in Munich (Germany).

(5) **NATO Integrated Communications System Organization** (NICSO), established in 1971 to supervise the planning and management of NATO's Integrated Communications System (NICS), a voice, telegraph and data communications network designed to improve the Alliance capability for crisis management and for the command and control of NATO forces, comprising the NATO Joint Communications-Electronics Committee (NJCEC)—also acting as the NICS Policy Committee—and the NICS Management Agency (NICSMA), and located in Brussels.

(6) **NATO Airborne Early Warning and Control Programme Management Organization** (NAPMO), established in 1978 to manage the procurement aspects of the NATO Airborne Warning and Control System, located at Brunssum (Netherlands).

International Staff

NATO's International Staff consists of the Office of the Secretary General, which includes the Office of the Executive Secretary, the Office of Security and the Press Service. It comprises five divisions as follows:

(1) The Division of Political Affairs (whose Assistant Secretary General is chairman of the Political Affairs Committee) with three separate directorates—the Political Directorate, the Economics Directorate and the Information Directorate.

(2) The Division of Defence Planning and Policy with three directorates—the Directorate of Force Planning and Policy, the Directorate of Nuclear Planning and the Directorate of Civil Emergency Planning. (The Assistant Secretary General for Defence Planning and Policy is chairman of the Defence Review Committee, composed of all member countries participating in NATO's integrated military structure, and vice-chairman of the Executive Working Group of the Defence Planning Group Staff Group and of the Civil Emergency Planning Committee.)

(3) The Division of Defence Support with four directorates—the Directorate of Armaments and Defence Research, the Directorate of Command, Control and Communications (responsible for the establishment of the NATO Integrated Communications System and to the NATO Joint Communications-Electronics Committee), the Directorate of Air Defence (providing inter alia support for the NATO Air Defence Committee), and the Directorate of Planning and Support (with the Assistant Secretary General for Defence Support serving as permanent chairman of the Conference of National Armaments Directors).

(4) The Division of Infrastructure, Logistics and Council Operations, with three directorates—the Infrastructure Directorate, the Logistics Directorate and the Council Operations Directorate.

(5) The Scientific Affairs Division (with the Assistant Secretary General for Scientific and Environmental Affairs serving inter alia as acting chairman of the Committee on the Challenges of Modern Society).

There are also an Office of Management, an Office of the Financial Controller and a Board of Auditors.

Military Committee

NATO's highest military authority is its Military Committee composed of the Chiefs of Staff of all member countries except France and Iceland. France is represented by the Chief of the French Military Mission to the Military Committee.

Iceland has no military forces but can be represented by a civilian. The Chiefs of Staff meet at least twice a year or whenever deemed necessary. To enable the Military Committee to function on a continuous basis with effective powers of decision, each Chief of Staff appoints a Permanent Military Representative. The chairman of the Military Committee is elected by the Chiefs of Staff normally for a period of three years, and he represents the Military Committee at meetings of the North Atlantic Council.

The Military Committee is assisted by an Integrated International Military Staff headed by a director selected from one of the member nations. It is the executive agency of the Military Committee and has divisions for Intelligence; Plans and Policy; Operations; Logistics and Resources; Command, Control and Communications Systems; and Armaments, Standardization and Interoperability.

The Military Committee has a number of military agencies under its authority, as follows:

(1) **Allied Communications Security Agency** (ACSA), created in 1953 to advise on all matters relating to communications security, and located in Brussels.

(2) **Allied Long Lines Agency** (ALLA), created in 1951 to formulate policies and plans for NATO's long lines requirements, and located in Brussels.

(3) **Allied Naval Communications Agency** (ANCA), established in 1951 and located in London.

(4) **Allied Radio Frequency Agency** (ARFA), formed in 1951, providing inter alia engineering assistance to all nations and NATO commands in the selection of suitable radio frequencies, and located in Brussels.

(5) **Allied Tactical Communications Agency** (ATCA), established in 1972, inter alia effecting liaison with ANCA for joint operations involving naval forces, and located in Brussels.

(6) **Allied Data Systems Interoperability Agency** (ADSIA), inaugurated in 1979 to plan, develop and maintain common data systems interoperability standards in order to improve interoperability within the NATO Command, Control and Information Systems (NCCIS) and to provide advice and assistance to the main groups of the Conference of National Armaments Directors (CNAD) and the Military Committee and its agencies, and located in Brussels.

(7) **Advisory Group for Aerospace Research and Development** (AGARD), created in 1952 and located in Neuilly-sur-Seine (France).

(8) **Military Agency for Standardization** (MAS), set up in 1951 to enable NATO forces to operate together in the most effective manner, and located in Brussels.

(9) **NATO Defence College** (NADEFCOL), founded in 1951 for the training of civilian and military officials for key posts in NATO or in national ministries and located in Rome.

(10) **SACLANT Anti-Submarine Warfare Research Centre** (SACLANTCEN), created in 1962 for research in submarine detection and oceanographic problems, and located at La Spezia (Italy).

(11) **SHAPE Technical Centre** (STC), created in 1960 to provide scientific and technical advice to the Supreme Allied Commander Europe (to whom it is responsible) and located in The Hague.

The following agencies are also under the control of the Military Committee:

The Military Command, Control and Information Systems Working Group (MCCISWG).

The Military Committee Meteorological Group (MCMG).

The NATO Command, Control and Information Systems and Automatic Data Processing Committee (NCCDPC).

The NATO Communications-Electronics Board (NCEB).
The NATO Electronic Warfare Advisory Committee (NEWAC).
The NATO Training Group.

Defence Planning Committee (DPC)

NATO's military policy is discussed in its Defence Planning Committee (DPC) composed of representatives of the member countries taking part in NATO's integrated defence system. Whether at ministerial or at permanent representative level, the DPC meets (like the Council) under the chairmanship of the Secretary General.

The DPC works with the Council's committees and also other committees. An Executive Working Group (EWG) is responsible to the DPC for the principal aspects of defence and the overall conduct of the long-term defence programme.

Nuclear Planning Group

The Nuclear Planning Group, set up in 1966 to discuss nuclear matters, consists of representatives of 14 countries and meets, under the chairmanship of the Secretary General, as required at the level of Permanent Representatives and twice a year at the level of Ministers of Defence.

Eurogroup

The Eurogroup, formed in 1968, is an informal group of Defence Ministers open to all European NATO member countries and currently consisting of the Defence Ministers of Belgium, Denmark, the Federal Republic of Germany, Greece, Italy, Luxembourg, the Netherlands, Norway, Portugal, Spain, Turkey and the United Kingdom.

Its object is to make the European contribution to the common defence strong and cohesive and also to encourage and support the continuing (and vital) presence in Europe of Canadian and US forces. In 1970 it launched a **European Defence Improvement Programme** (EDIP) extending over five years and involving a cost exceeding $1,000 million, this being supplementary to existing national plans; the programme was designed to procure extra aircraft (both combat and transport) and additional funds for the NATO integrated communications system and the building of some 1,600 hardened aircraft shelters.

At a meeting held on May 21, 1985, the group pointed out that the European allies provided 90 per cent of the ground forces, 80 per cent of the air forces and 70 per cent of the warships of NATO's standing forces in Western Europe.

North Atlantic Assembly

A North Atlantic Assembly (created in 1955 as the NATO Parliamentarians' Conference, which assumed its present name in 1966) is an informal assembly of 184 members delegated by the NATO member countries' parliaments (with each country's representation being weighted according to its population and thus ranging from 36 from the United States to three each from Iceland and Luxembourg). The purpose of the Assembly is to promote the aims of the North Atlantic Treaty and to encourage solidarity and co-operation in national parliaments. It meets once a year; it has five committees and an International Secretariat; and it is based in Brussels.

Independent European Programme Group (IEPG)

Founded. December 1975.
Membership. Defence Ministers of Belgium, Denmark, France, the Federal Republic of Germany, Greece, Italy, Luxembourg, the Netherlands, Norway, Portugal, Spain, Turkey and the United Kingdom.
Object. To secure collaboration in the development and production of arms.
Structure. The group has an advisory Committee of National Armaments Directors (CNAD).
Activities. The group held its first meeting in February 1976 but was virtually moribund until it held further meetings on Nov. 22–23, 1984, and on June 17–18, 1985, when the Defence Ministers made progress in collaborating on projects for transport aircraft, a medium-range surface-to-air missile and a main battle tank.

On the development of a European fighter aircraft (EFA), see page 193.

NATO's Military Forces

The military forces of NATO consist of three interlocking elements (known as the NATO Triad) as follows:

(1) Conventional forces strong enough to resist and repel a conventional attack on a limited scale and to sustain a conventional defence in the forward areas against large-scale conventional aggression.

(2) Intermediate- and short-range nuclear forces to enhance the deterrent and, if necessary, the defensive effort of NATO's conventional forces against a conventional attack; to deter and defend against an attack with nuclear forces of the same kind; and to provide a linkage to the strategic nuclear forces of the Alliance with the aim of convincing an aggressor that any form of attack against NATO could result in very serious damage to his interests, and of emphasizing the dangers implicit in continuing a conflict.

(3) United States and United Kingdom strategic nuclear forces which provide the ultimate deterrent. The strategic nuclear forces comprise three elements—intercontinental ballistic missiles (ICBMs), submarine-launched ballistic missiles (SLBMs) and heavy bombers.

The reported strength of the NATO member countries' armed forces (excluding para-military units) in mid-1985 was as follows:

NATO's Military Structure

Military Committee
(*Chairman:* NATO Secretary General)

International Military Staff

Major Commands

Canada-US Regional Planning Group

Allied Command Atlantic (ACLANT) Norfolk, Virginia (USA) *Commander:* Supreme Allied Commander Atlantic (SACLANT)

Allied Command Europe (ACE) Supreme Headquarters Allied Powers Europe, (SHAPE) Mons (Belgium) *Commander:* Supreme Allied Commander Europe (SACEUR)

Allied Command Channel (ACCHAN) Northwood (UK) *Commander:* Supreme Allied Commander-in-Chief, Channel Command (CINCHAN)

Western Atlantic, Norfolk (USA)
Submarine Force Western Atlantic Area Command
Ocean Sub-Area Command
Canadian Atlantic Sub-Area Command
Bermuda Command
Azores Command
Greenland Island Command

Eastern Atlantic, Northwood (UK)
Commander Maritime Air Eastern Atlantic Area
Commander Northern Sub-Area
Commander Maritime Air Northern Sub-Area
Commander Central Sub-Area
Commander Maritime Air Central Sub-Area
Commander Submarine Force Eastern Atlantic Area
Island Commanders of Iceland and the Faroes

Striking Fleet, Afloat
Commander Carrier Striking Force
Commanders Carrier Striking Groups I and II

Submarines, Norfolk (USA)

Iberian Atlantic (IBERLANT), Lisbon (Portugal)
Island Command of Madeira

Standing Naval Force Atlantic (STANAVFORLANT), Afloat

Northern Europe, Kolsaas (Norway)
Allied Forces North Norway
Allied Forces South Norway
Allied Forces Baltic Approaches

Central Europe, Brunssum (Netherlands)
Northern Army Group
Central Army Group
Allied Air Forces Central Europe
2nd Allied Tactical Air Force
4th Allied Tactical Air Force

Southern Europe, Naples (Italy)
Allied Land Forces Southern Europe
Allied Land Forces South-Eastern Europe
Allied Air Forces Southern Europe
Allied Naval Forces Southern Europe
Naval Striking and Support Forces Southern Europe

UK Air Forces, High Wycombe (UK)

Allied Command Europe Mobile Force, Heidelberg (Germany)

Early Warning and Control Force, Geilenkirchen, (Germany)

Nore Channel, Rosyth (UK)

Plymouth Channel, Plymouth (UK)

Benelux Channel, Walcheren (Netherlands)

Allied Maritime Air Force Channel Command (COMMAIRCHAN), Northwood (UK)

Standing Naval Force Channel (Mine Counter Measures) (STANAVFORCHAN), Afloat

208

Country	Numbers
Belgium	92,000
Denmark	27,000
*France	477,000
Federal Rep. of Germany	478,000
*Greece	201,000
Italy	385,000
Luxembourg	750
Netherlands	106,000
Norway	37,000
Portugal	73,000
*Spain	320,000
Turkey	630,000
United Kingdom	327,000
NATO in Europe	3,144,750
Canada	83,000†
United States	2,150,000‡
Total NATO	5,377,750

* France, Greece and Spain do not participate in NATO's integrated military structure.
† Including 5,000 stationed in Western Europe.
‡ Including 350,000 stationed in Western Europe.

According to a statement by President Reagan of the United States, published on Feb. 24, 1986, there were considerable imbalances in both nuclear and conventional weapons between Warsaw Pact and NATO forces, in particular in central Europe where the Warsaw Pact nations were said to have 200,000 more troops than NATO and to enjoy a superiority of 2.1 to 1 in tanks, 1.3 to 1 in anti-tank guided weapons, 2.7 to 1 in artillery and 2 to 1 in fixed-wing tactical aircraft.

Development and Activities of NATO

1949–1955

The first phase of NATO's existence, roughly covering the period from its inception to the mid-1950s, saw the evolution of the organization's complex military and civilian structure.

The first meeting of the NATO Council, set up under Article 9 of the North Atlantic Treaty, was held on Sept. 17, 1949. The Council, which consisted of the Foreign Ministers of the member countries, decided to set up a Defence Committee. This Committee, to be composed of the Ministers of Defence of the NATO countries, was to have the initial function of drawing up unified defence plans for the North Atlantic area. Other bodies formed at this meeting were the Military Committee, composed of high military representatives of each member country, to advise on military matters; a Standing Group, comprising one representative each of Britain, France and the USA, to provide military information and guidance; and five Regional Planning Groups to prepare plans for the defence of each region (Northern Europe, Western Europe, Southern Europe, the Western Hemisphere and the North Atlantic).

At its second session, held on Nov. 18, 1949, the Council created a Defence Financial and Economic Committee and a Defence Production Board. The function of the latter was to promote the co-ordinated production, standardization and further technical development of armaments.

Two important organizational decisions were made at the fourth session of the Council (the second at ministerial level), held on May 15–18, 1950. It was decided to form a Permanent Council of Deputies to the Foreign Ministers and to create a North Atlantic Planning Board for Ocean Shipping.

In December 1950, after a meeting of the Foreign and Defence Ministers of the 12 NATO countries, it was announced that arrangements had been completed for an integrated defence force under centralized control and command, to which all the participating governments would contribute contingents. The Supreme Headquarters Allied Powers in Europe (SHAPE) was set up in Paris in 1951.

In May 1951 a reorganization of the North Atlantic Council was announced. The Defence Committee and the Defence Financial and Economic Committee [see above] ceased to exist as separate organs, but were incorporated in the North Atlantic Council, which thus became the sole ministerial body of NATO. Henceforth the Ministerial Council might be formed by Foreign, Defence or Finance Ministers according to the agenda of the meeting. The functions of the Council of Deputies were defined as being to co-ordinate and guide all other permanent organs of NATO and to exchange views on political matters within the scope of the treaty. A new body set up at this time was the Financial and Economic Board to make recommendations on financial and economic matters.

At a meeting of the North Atlantic Council in September 1951 it was agreed, inter alia, to support the entry into NATO of Greece and Turkey. A Temporary Committee of the Council (TCC) was set up to study the problems of reconciling the requirements for the fulfilment of a militarily acceptable defence plan with the realistic politico-economic capabilities of the member countries. The final report of the TCC was adopted by the Council at its session in February 1952, after which the Committee was wound up. On the basis of the report the Council agreed on a "definite programme of measures to increase defensive strength in following years". Organizational changes agreed upon were the creation of the post of Secretary General to head a unified international Secretariat, and the formation of a North Atlantic Council in permanent session through the appointment of permanent representatives. The Council would assume the functions hitherto performed by the Council of Deputies, the Defence Production Board and the Financial and Economic Board.

Early 1952 also saw the formation of the other two main NATO military commands: the Atlantic Ocean Command, headed by the Supreme Allied Commander Atlantic (SACLANT), and the Channel Command, headed by the Allied Commander-in-Chief Channel (CINCHAN).

In the same year the North Atlantic Council agreed upon close association with the proposed European Defence Community (EDC) of Belgium, France, the Federal Republic of Germany, Italy, Luxembourg and the Netherlands. After the French rejection of the EDC treaty in August 1954, however, the integration of the Federal Republic of Germany into a defence system of the West had to be reconsidered. The results of these considerations, carried out at the nine-power London conference of September 1954, were embodied in the Paris Agreements which included the protocol on the entry of Western Germany into NATO [see page 143].

1956–1965

In the decade from 1955 to 1965 the actual structure of NATO underwent relatively little alteration, the main developments within the organization being an increase in its political role, and the improvement and adaptation of its defensive system.

Political Development. At a North Atlantic Council meeting in May 1956 it was decided, inter alia, to set up a committee of three ministers (known as the "three wise men") to examine "ways and means to improve and extend NATO co-operation in non-military fields and develop greater unity within the Atlantic community". The report of this committee, which was adopted by the Council on Dec. 13, 1956, recommended full and timely consultation between NATO member governments on issues of common concern. The following points were given as a guideline to such consultation:

(1) Members should inform the Council of any development which significantly affected the Alliance. They should do this not merely as a formality but as a preliminary to effective political consultation.

(2) Both individual member governments and the Secretary General should have the right to raise for discussion in the Council any subject which was of common NATO interest, and not of a purely domestic character.

(3) A member government should not, without adequate advance consultation, adopt firm policies or make major political announcements on matters which significantly affected the alliance or any of its members, unless circumstances made such prior consultation obviously and demonstrably impossible.

(4) In developing their national policies, members should take into consideration the interests and views of other governments—particularly those most directly concerned—as expressed in NATO consultation, even where no community of view or consensus of opinion had been reached in the Council.

(5) Where consensus had been reached, it should be reflected in the formation of national policies. When for national reasons the consensus was not followed, the government concerned should offer an explanation to the Council. It was even more important that, where an agreed and formal recommendation had emerged from the Council's discussions, governments should give it full weight in any national actions or policies related to the subject of that recommendation.

(6) To strengthen the process of consultation it was recommended that at each spring meeting the Foreign Ministers should make an appraisal of the political progress of the Alliance and consider the lines along which it should advance.

(7) To prepare for this discussion, the Secretary General should submit an annual report analysing the major political problems of the Alliance; reviewing the extent to which member governments had consulted and co-operated in such problems; and indicating the problems and the possible developments which might require consultation, so that difficulties might be resolved and positive and constructive initiatives taken.

(8) To assist the permanent representatives (of member countries) and the Secretary General in discharging their responsibilities for political consultation, a committee of political advisers from each delegation should be constituted under the Council, aided when necessary by specialists.

Settlement of Members' Disputes. It was further recommended that NATO members should submit any dispute between them which had not proved capable of direct settlement to "good offices" procedures under NATO before resorting to any other international agency. Exceptions to this procedure would be legal questions which could be dealt with more appropriately by a judicial tribunal, or economic questions which could more appropriately be dealt with in the specialized economic organizations.

All member countries, as well as the Secretary General, had the right and the duty to bring to the Council's attention matters which in their opinion might threaten the solidarity or effectiveness of the Alliance. The Secretary General should be empowered to offer his good offices informally to the parties to a dispute and, with their consent, "to initiate or facilitate procedures of inquiry, mediation, conciliation or arbitration". For this purpose, he should be able to use the assistance of not more than three permanent representatives chosen by him in each instance.

While approving the report, the United States informed the North Atlantic Council that it could not subject its policies or actions throughout the world to prior consultation within NATO.

The NATO Political Committee was formed in January 1957, meeting once a week to discuss questions of political interest to the members of the Atlantic Alliance.

At the ministerial meeting of the North Atlantic Council held in December 1959 in Paris, proposals were adopted for long-term planning, to cover the following ten years, on the objectives of the Alliance in the political, military, scientific and economic fields and in regard to arms control.

An "Atlantic Convention", attended by 98 delegates (private citizens appointed by their governments) of all NATO member countries, was held in Paris between Jan. 8 and Jan. 20, 1962, to make recommendations for the further political development of the Atlantic Community. The convention finally adopted the *Declaration of Paris*, calling for "the creation of a true

Atlantic Community within the next decade". The declaration included recommendations for the creation of new political, judicial and cultural organs; for the harmonization of political, military and economic policy on matters affecting the Atlantic Community as a whole; and for closer economic co-operation with developing countries. The declaration was endorsed by the Parliamentarians' Conference in November 1962, but its proposals have not been adopted by the North Atlantic Council.

Military and Defence Developments. From Dec. 16 to 19, 1957, the heads of government of the NATO countries met in conference in Paris. Their most important decision was to establish stocks of nuclear warheads in the treaty area, and to place intermediate-range ballistic missiles (IRBMs) at the disposal of the Supreme Allied Commander Europe (SACEUR). They also decided to set up the Science Committee composed of qualified representatives of each NATO country, and to appoint a scientist of outstanding qualifications as science adviser to the Secretary General of NATO.

In December 1957 the United States stated its willingness to participate in a NATO atomic stockpile, and also to make available to other NATO members intermediate-range ballistic missiles for deployment according to the plans of SACEUR. Each country concerned would have to make a separate agreement with the United States with respect to material, training of personnel and other necessary arrangements. Agreements on co-operation in the field of atomic weapons were signed by the USA with Canada, France, the Federal Republic of Germany, Greece, the Netherlands, Turkey and the United Kingdom in May 1959. A similar agreement was signed with Italy in December 1960.

On March 2, 1960, it was announced by SACEUR that a multi-national Allied task force, to be equipped with both conventional and atomic weapons, would be established. The constituent units would be brought together occasionally for joint training, but would generally remain with their national formations. The multi-national task force came officially into existence in July 1961, when it comprised five reinforced infantry battalions.

Meanwhile, the new Anti-Submarine Warfare Research Centre at La Spezia, Italy, had been formally inaugurated in May 1959. This was completely reorganized to receive full NATO support as an international military organization in January 1963.

Nuclear Force for NATO. At a Ministerial Council meeting held in Athens in May 1962, the United States made two important announcements on defence matters: (i) That it would not remove or diminish its nuclear stockpiles in Europe without prior consultation; and (ii) that five Polaris submarines would be immediately committed to NATO (these had already been promised in December 1960). At this meeting the Council

decided to set up a special committee of all member countries "to receive and exchange information about NATO's nuclear defences".

In December 1962 President Kennedy of the United States and the British Prime Minister, Harold Macmillan, met at Nassau (Bahamas), where they signed an agreement on US provision of Polaris missiles to Britain. In a joint statement issued at the time the two leaders put forward a suggestion for a NATO multilateral nuclear force, which would initially consist of some part of the force already in existence. "This would include allocations from US strategic forces, from UK Bomber Command and from tactical nuclear forces now held in Europe. Such forces would be assigned as part of a NATO nuclear force and targeted in accordance with NATO plans.

At the Ministerial Council meeting in Ottawa in May 1963 it was decided to set up such a multinational nuclear force by reorganizing the nuclear forces already assigned to SACEUR. The principal steps approved by the Council were: (1) The assignment of the British V-bomber force and three US Polaris submarines to SACEUR; (2) the appointment by SACEUR of a Deputy responsible to him for nuclear affairs; (3) arrangements for broader participation by NATO officers in nuclear activities in Allied Command, Europe, and in co-ordination of operational planning; and (4) fuller information to national authorities. The Ministerial Council also directed the Council in Permanent Session to undertake studies towards a satisfactory balance between nuclear and conventional forces.

At the Kennedy-Macmillan meeting at Nassau in December 1962 [cf. above] the US President put forward a plan for the formation of a mixed-manned seaborne nuclear force to be assigned to NATO and to which non-nuclear powers could contribute. Discussions on the technical details of such a force were opened in October 1963 and continued throughout 1964. In addition, the United States made available a destroyer for an experiment in mixed manning which began in May 1964. No agreement on the mixed-manned nuclear force (MNF) has, however, been concluded, as the new British Labour Government opposed the idea of a mixed-manned nuclear surface fleet. Britain proposed, as an alternative, an Atlantic Nuclear Force (ANF) comprising the British V-bomber force; a British fleet of Polaris submarines; at least an equal number of US Polaris submarines; and some kind of mixed-manned or jointly-owned element in which the non-nuclear powers could participate.

An agreement concluded between all 15 NATO member states on co-operation in the field of nuclear information was signed on June 18, 1964, and came into force on March 12, 1965.

New Committees. It was announced on Aug. 25, 1964, that a NATO Defence Research Directors' Committee had been set up with the aim of attempting to "establish a more direct relevance between science and the military needs" of the organization. It would supplement the work of the NATO Science Committee (established in 1957, see above), which devoted most of its activities to civilian science.

At a NATO Defence Ministers' meeting in Paris on May 31–June 1, 1965, the US Defence Secretary Robert McNamara proposed the creation of a "select committee" of a few member countries to study ways of extending nuclear planning and consultation within the alliance. This proposal led, in November 1965, to the creation of a ten-member "special committee" of Defence Ministers, i.e. the Defence Ministers of all NATO countries except France, Luxembourg, Norway, Portugal and Iceland (which has none). The committee set up three working groups to deal with Communications, Data Exchange, and Nuclear Planning.

1966–1967

The years 1966–67 saw the withdrawal of France from the military side of NATO, and the subsequent removal of all NATO installations from French soil.

French Withdrawal from NATO. French opposition to the integrated military organization was already of several years' standing, the French President, General de Gaulle, having repeatedly affirmed since 1959 that, although she was in favour of the Atlantic Alliance, France could no longer support an integrated defence system which deprived her of sovereignty over her own military forces.

In March 1959 the French Mediterranean Fleet was withdrawn from the integrated command, and French naval units were withdrawn from the Atlantic and Channel Commands from Jan. 1, 1964. In April 1964 the French Government gave formal notification of the withdrawal of all French naval officers serving in NATO naval command posts or on NATO naval staffs.

In February and March 1966 the French Government made it clear that France intended to withdraw completely from the integrated organization, while remaining a member of the Atlantic Alliance. She was, however, ready to conclude arrangements for liaison between French and NATO forces, and also to retain French forces in the Federal Republic of Germany under new terms.

On March 29, 1966, the French Government, in an aide-mémoire to the other NATO members, set a timetable for France's withdrawal. The withdrawal of French forces in West Germany from NATO command, and of French personnel from Allied commands and staffs, was timed for July 1, 1966; the removal of SHAPE, the Allied Forces Central Europe (AFCENT) command and the NATO Defence College from French territory was to be carried out by April 1, 1967; and the withdrawal of most US and Canadian military installations was also to completed by April 1, 1967. This timetable was, in fact, adhered to.

On Sept. 7, 1966, France stated her intention of stopping her financial contributions to the military budget from Jan. 1, 1967, but expressed a wish to continue participation in the NATO Air Defence Ground Environment System, or NADGE, an automatic air defence system due for completion in 1971; in SHAPE's technical research centre at The Hague; in the anti-submarine warfare centre at La Spezia; and in the management organization of the Hawk missile (produced by a consortium of five European NATO countries). At the end of September France withdrew from the NATO Military Committee.

Removal of NATO Institutions from French Territory. (1) The new headquarters of SHAPE, near Mons in southern Belgium, were officially opened by the Supreme Allied Commander Europe on March 31, 1967.

(2) The headquarters of Allied Forces Central Europe (AFCENT) were removed from Fontainebleau to Brunssum, a site in the Netherlands province of Limburg, at the beginning of April 1967.

(3) Formerly located at the Ecole Militaire in Paris, the NATO Defence College opened its first session in the Palazzo Fondiaria, on the outskirts of Rome, on Jan. 18, 1967.

(4) In October 1966 it was decided to move the headquarters of the NATO Council from Paris to Brussels.

Reorganization of Military Structure. The Standing Group, which was formed in 1949, was abolished on July 1, 1966, as a result of France's withdrawal from NATO's military organization [see above]. It was replaced by a temporary international staff.

The removal of the Military Committee from Washington to Brussels was authorized in November 1966.

The Allied Land Forces Central Europe (LANDCENT) and Allied Air Forces Central Europe (AIRCENT) lost their individual identity to be merged with AFCENT from Nov. 15, 1966.

Changes in the naval organization which were made in 1966–67 were as follows:

(1) In January 1966 the Commander-in-Chief Eastern Atlantic assumed the additional NATO post of Commander-in-Chief Channel.

(2) On Feb. 22, 1967, a new Command, the Iberian Command Atlantic (IBERLANT), was inaugurated. IBERLANT, based in Lisbon, is attached to Allied Command Atlantic.

(3) Another new Command, Naval Command South (NAVSOUTH), was inaugurated on June 5, 1967. This Command, responsible to the Commander-in-Chief Allied Forces Southern Europe, replaced the Commander-in-Chief Allied Forces Mediterranean.

The 1967 Harmel Report. In a Report on the Future Tasks of the Alliance, prepared on an initiative by the Belgian Minister of Defence (then Pierre Harmel), and approved by the Council's ministerial meeting in Brussels on Dec. 12–13, 1967, NATO's future tasks were defined as being directed towards guaranteeing military security while at the same time pursuing a policy of détente. The meeting adopted these two tasks as being "not contradictory but complementary".

1968–1971

In 1968–71 the NATO Council's decisions were designed to counteract growing Soviet power both on the continent of Europe and in the Mediterranean, and any proposals for a reduction of armed forces were treated with reserve.

The NATO Nuclear Planning Group declared on April 19, 1968, that the deployment of an anti-ballistic missile system in Europe was not justified at that time, although developments in that field should be kept under constant review.

On June 25, 1968, the Council issued a *Declaration on Mutual and Balanced Force Reductions* (MBFR), in which its Ministers affirmed that "the overall military capability of NATO should not be reduced except as part of a pattern of mutual force reductions balanced in scope and timing". At the same time they agreed that "it was desirable that a process leading to mutual force reductions should be initiated". (For MBFR talks, see page 221 below.)

The Ministers also decided that, in view of the recent expansion of Soviet activity in the Mediterranean, measures should be taken to enhance the effectiveness and co-ordination of allied surveillance in that area.

The Brussels Council meeting of Nov. 15–16, 1968, was strongly influenced by the Soviet invasion of Czechoslovakia on Aug. 20–21, 1968.

The Ministers' communiqué stated inter alia: "World opinion has been profoundly shocked by this armed intervention carried out against the wishes of the Government and people of Czechoslovakia. . . . The contention of the Soviet leadership that there exists a right of intervention in the affairs of other states deemed to be within a so-called 'Socialist Commonwealth' runs counter to the basic principles of the UN Charter [and] is dangerous to European security. . . . Applied to Germany [these] policies . . . would be contrary to the four-power agreements relating to Germany as a whole." In this context the Ministers reaffirmed "the determination of the Alliance to persevere in its efforts to contribute to a peaceful solution of the German question based on the free decision of the German people and on the interests of European security", and they reiterated their governments' non-recognition of the German Democratic Republic.

In response to the Soviet action, the Ministers declared:

"The quality, effectiveness and deployment of NATO's forces will be improved in terms of both manpower and equipment in order to provide a better capability for defence as far forward as possible. The quality of reserve forces will also be improved and their ability to mobilize rapidly will be increased.

"Renewed attention will be directed to the provision of reinforcements for the flanks and the strengthening of local forces there.

"The conventional capability of NATO's tactical air forces will be increased. Certain additional national units will be committed to the major NATO Commanders. Specific measures have been approved within these categories of action for improving the conventional capability of NATO's forces."

They added: "Prospects for mutual balanced force reductions have suffered a severe setback."

At a meeting of the Defence Planning Committee on Nov. 14, 1968, increased military contribu-

tions by member governments were announced by Defence Ministers of most member countries.

The Canadian Government, on the other hand, decided in April 1969 to reduce the size of Canadian forces in Europe.

The Defence Planning Committee approved on Dec. 3, 1969, provisional political guidelines for the initial defensive use of tactical nuclear weapons, as drawn up by the Nuclear Planning Group in November. The group had also completed a review of procedures for consultation on the possible use of nuclear weapons in defence of NATO.

On May 27, 1970, the Council issued a further *Declaration on Mutual and Balanced Force Reductions*, calling for exploratory talks by interested states and stating inter alia that any reduction agreed upon should include "stationed and indigenous forces and their weapons systems in the area concerned", with "adequate verification and controls".

A European Defence Improvement Programme was announced in Brussels on Dec. 1, 1970, after a meeting of Defence Ministers of the European NATO member countries except France, Iceland and Portugal. Based on the assumption that US forces in Europe would be maintained "at substantially current levels", the programme comprised a "special European scheme" involving a contribution of about $420,000,000 towards the acceleration and extension of (i) the NATO Integrated Communications System (NICS) and (ii) aircraft survival measures to improve the ability of NATO Air Forces to survive enemy strikes on their bases.

At its meeting on Dec. 3–4, 1970, the Council discussed in detail a comprehensive study *AD-70* setting out the problems for allied defence in the 1970s, with NATO's approach to security continuing to be "based on the twin concepts of defence and détente", and with the "special military and political role of US forces in Europe as an irreplaceable contribution to the common defence".

The Defence Planning Committee, in a communiqué issued on May 28, 1971, stated inter alia that, in view of "the continuing increase in real terms in the allocation of resources to military and military-related programmes by the Soviet Union and other Warsaw Pact countries", and "in order to continue providing modern and sufficient nuclear and conventional forces and to improve the situation in the important areas highlighted in the *AD-70* Study, some overall increase in defence outlay was needed". The Committee had therefore given the NATO Military Authorities the necessary guidance for the planning period 1973–78.

Command Changes. A Standing naval Force Atlantic (STANAVFORLANT), consisting of destroyers and frigates, under the overall command of SACLANT and responsible, when in European waters, to CINCHAN and C.-in-C. Eastern Atlantic, was established at Portland (UK) on Jan. 13, 1968.

A new command called Maritime Air Forces Mediterranean (MARAIRMED), subordinated to Allied Naval Forces Southern Europe (NAVSOUTH), was inaugurated in Naples on Nov. 21, 1968.

The Council's Defence Planning Committee decided on May 28, 1969, that NATO's Military Authorities should establish a naval on-call force for the Mediterranean, the concept of which had been approved by the Council on Jan. 16, 1969.

It was announced at NATO headquarters in Brussels on Aug. 20, 1971, that in accordance with the wishes of the government of Malta and also with long-term planning aims agreed upon in 1965, the headquarters of Allied Naval Forces, Southern Europe, should be moved from Malta to Naples.

NATO Air Defence System. A programming and training centre forming part of a computerized underground control point for NATO's air defence system, was opened at Glons (Belgium) on April 9, 1968, for eventual incorporation in NADGE.

NATO Communications Satellite. The first NATO communications satellite, *NATO-1*, was launched from Cape Kennedy (USA) on March 20, 1970; it was to link NATO headquarters in Brussels, national capitals, and NATO land and sea commands.

Committee on Challenges of Modern Society. The Council decided on Nov. 6, 1969, upon a proposal made by President Nixon on April 10, to establish a Committee on the Challenges of Modern Society (CCMS) to consider problems of the human environment, and at its first meeting on Dec. 8–10, 1969, the new committee recommended pilot studies to be carried out on road safety, disaster relief, air and water pollution, and problems of individual and group motivations in a modern industrial society, as well as of the transmission of scientific knowledge to the decision-making sectors of government.

Exchange of Defence Information. An agreement on exchange of defence information between NATO member countries and for compensation of owners of such information who suffer damages through unauthorized further disclosure, concluded on Oct. 19, 1970, came into force on Feb. 7, 1971.

1972–1978

At a meeting of the North Atlantic Council on Dec. 7–8, 1972, the Defence Planning Committee noted with concern the growing military capability of the Soviet Union and her allies, which it described as "greatly in excess of that required for purely defensive purposes", and endorsed the principle that "the overall military capability of NATO should not be reduced except as part of a pattern of mutual force reductions, balanced in scope and timing". The committee adopted a five-year NATO Force Plan for 1973–77 in the light of each nation's force commitment for 1973.

The Eurogroup Ministers met on Dec. 5, 1972. They reviewed the European Defence Improvement Programme [see page 207] and noted with satisfaction that its implementation was well under way.

The Committee on the Challenges of Modern Society met on Nov. 14–15, 1972. It endorsed a new project on urban transportation and sponsored the signing of a memorandum on the development of "clean" automobile engines by France, the Federal Republic of Germany, Italy, the United Kingdom and the USA.

A Standing Naval Force Channel (STANAVFORCHAN) was commissioned on May 11, 1973, to be under the operational command of the Commander-in-Chief, Channel Command.

A ministerial meeting of the Defence Planning Committee was held in Brussels on June 7, 1973, during which the committee reviewed the capabilities of NATO in the light of a further report on the Allied Defence Problems in the 1970s (*AD-70*). The report summarized progress in the preceding two years in improving NATO's effectiveness in each region, and also identified areas requiring further improvement. The committee undertook to concentrate on these areas and to allocate more resources for the modernization and re-equipment of NATO forces. An increased need was recognized to improve co-operation in logistics and in the research, development and production of armaments.

Following a meeting of the Nuclear Planning Group in The Hague on Nov. 6–7, 1973, the ministers stated in a communiqué inter alia: "Ministers emphasized the important bearing which the strength and readiness of NATO's conventional forces, particularly those located in Europe, have upon NATO's overall deterrent posture. The Ministers also discussed a report by the NATO military authorities describing the operational concepts and doctrine that currently govern their military planning, and which reflect the NATO strategy of flexibility in response."

At a Ministerial Council meeting in Brussels on Dec. 10–11, 1973, ministers noted progress by the CCMS, in particular in the fields of the development of supplemental energy resources through the use of solar and geothermal energy and of the disposal of hazardous wastes and toxic industrial effluents.

Ottawa Declaration. At the Council's ministerial meeting in Ottawa on June 18–19, 1974, ministers adopted, on the occasion of the 25th anniversary of the establishment of the Alliance, an "Ottawa Declaration" reaffirming the aims and ideals of the North Atlantic Treaty.

In the declaration it was noted in particular: "The members of the Alliance . . . realize that the circumstances affecting their common defence have profoundly changed in the last 10 years. The strategic relationship between the United States and the Soviet Union has reached a point of near equilibrium. Consequently, although all the countries of the Alliance remain vulnerable to attack, the nature of the danger to which they are exposed has changed. . . . The European members, who provide three-quarters of the conventional strength of the

Alliance in Europe, and two of whom possess nuclear forces capable of playing a deterrent role of their own contributing to the overall strengthening of the deterrence of the Alliance, undertake to make the necessary contribution to maintain the common defence at a level capable of deterring and if necessary repelling all actions directed against the independence and territorial integrity of the members of the Alliance.

"The United States, for its part, reaffirms its determination not to accept any situation which would expose the Allies to external political or military pressure likely to deprive them of their freedom and states its resolve, together with its allies, to maintain forces in Europe at the level required to sustain the credibility of the strategy of deterrence and to maintain the capacity to defend the North Atlantic area should deterrence fail. . . .

"All members of the Alliance agree that the continued presence of Canadian and substantial US forces in Europe plays an irreplaceable role in the defence of North America as well as of Europe. Similarly, the substantial forces of the European allies serve to defend Europe and North America as well. It is also recognized that the further progress towards unity, which the member states of the European Community are determined to make, should in due course have a beneficial effect on the contribution to the common defence of the Alliance of those of them who belong to it. . . ."

Withdrawal of Greek Forces. As a result of the occupation of about one-third of the territory of Cyprus by Turkish troops on Aug. 14, 1974, the Government of Greece decided to withdraw its armed forces from NATO and to remain a member of NATO "only in connexion with its political aspects" on the ground of NATO's "inability to prevent Turkey from creating a state of conflict between two allies".

The US Congress, on Dec. 10, 1974, passed legislation which in effect suspended US military aid to Turkey pending "substantial progress" towards a negotiated settlement of the Cyprus problem, and on Dec. 30 of that year the US President signed foreign aid legislation further suspending US military assistance as well as arms deliveries to Turkey with effect from Feb. 5, 1975. (See also US-Turkish bilateral agreements, page 224.)

(Greece rejoined NATO's military activities in October 1980, but a year later again suspended its participation—see page 218.)

Strengthening of NATO Forces. At a meeting of NATO's Nuclear Planning Group in London on Nov. 17–18, 1976, ministers inter alia discussed "the need to maintain an adequate defence and deterrent capability in the light of recent developments and deployments over the full spectrum of Soviet forces"; drew attention to "interdependencies between developments in the threat, new weapons technologies and arms control measures"; "stressed the importance of maintaining the essential linkage between the three elements of the NATO triad—strategic nuclear, theatre nuclear and conventional forces— and especially the importance of strong conventional forces"; and discussed "improvements in the effectiveness of NATO's theatre nuclear force posture considered necessary to support the Alliance's strategy of flexibility in response".

At a meeting of the Defence Planning Committee on Dec. 7–8, 1976, ministers approved a NATO force plan for the period 1977–81 involving

in particular the procurement or development of additional modern aircraft by Canada, the United Kingdom and the United States and the restructuring of US and German forces.

Arrangements for the purchase of new aircraft by four other NATO member countries had in April–June 1976 resulted in firm orders for a total of 306 US F-16 fighter aircraft (72 for Norway, 84 for the Netherlands, 48 for Denmark and 102 for Belgium) to replace the ageing US F-104G Starfighter aircraft in use since the early 1960s.

Under a memorandum of understanding signed on July 29, 1976, by the Governments of the Federal Republic of Germany, Italy and the United Kingdom, a full production programme was launched for 809 multirole combat aircraft (MRCA) known as the Tornado (385 for the UK Royal Air Force, 324 for the West German Air Force and Navy and 100 for the Italian Air Force), production contracts being signed on behalf of the three Governments by NATO's MRCA Development and Production Management Organization (NAMMO).

At a Ministerial Council meeting held in London on May 10–11, 1977, and attended by the Presidents of the United States and of Portugal and the heads of government of 11 other member governments (with France and Iceland being represented by their respective Foreign Ministers), the "essential purpose" of NATO was strongly reaffirmed as follows:

"The essential purpose of the Alliance is to safeguard the independence and security of its members, enabling them to promote the values of democracy and respect for human rights, individual freedom, justice and social progress, and to make possible the creation of a lasting structure of peace. The Allies are firmly resolved to maintain and enhance the effectiveness of the Alliance and the ties which unite them."

The leaders also reaffirmed "their support for an equitable world system in which all countries, developing as well as developed, will see their best interests served and which can sustain the economic progress of all". They expressed their intention of mobilizing their efforts towards the attainment of that objective in the appropriate form, and they invited the Warsaw Pact countries to do the same.

At a Defence Planning Committee meeting in Brussels on May 17–18, 1977, approval was given to ministerial guidance on the development of force proposals for 1979–84 "designed to correct current deficiencies" in NATO defence.

This guidance was summarized as follows:

"**NATO Objectives.** The overall strategic concept of NATO is to preserve peace and to provide for the security of the North Atlantic Treaty area primarily by a credible deterrence effected by confronting any possible threatened or actual aggression with adequate NATO forces, within the concept of forward defence and flexibility in response.

"**Recent Developments in the Threat.** The Warsaw Pact forces are increasingly offensive in posture and capable of projecting Soviet power on a global scale. Soviet nuclear forces continue to improve with the appearance of new nuclear missile systems equipped with multiple warheads, including the expected deployment of the SS-20 mobile intermediate range system capable of striking targets in the whole of Europe and beyond. It is in the conventional field, however, where the growth of the Warsaw Pact capability has been most pronounced. In particular, the Warsaw Pact ground forces have the capability to stage a major offensive in Europe without reinforcement. The improved offensive and deep penetration capabilities of the Warsaw Pact tactical air forces now permit the Warsaw Pact to conduct the initial stages of an air attack to a greater extent than hitherto with in-place forces. The capabilities of the Soviet Union to exercise sea power all around the world have been enhanced by the introduction of new and improved ships, submarines and aircraft.

"The steady growth in military power is backed in the Soviet Union by an allocation of resources for defence estimated at between 11 per cent and 13 per cent of gross national product (nearly three times the NATO average) and by an annual increase in real terms in defence expenditure of about 5 per cent. The heavy investment by the Soviet Union in military research and development has begun to erode the qualitative advantage in military equipment long enjoyed by NATO.

"**Implications for NATO.** The Allies are undertaking significant equipment replacement and modernization programmes. However, many deficiencies remain in NATO forces, and the disparity in conventional military capabilities between NATO and the Warsaw Pact continues to widen. This adverse trend points to certain areas of critical importance that should be taken into account in both national and NATO planning.

"**NATO Strategy and Crisis Management.** NATO's strategic concept for deterrence and forward defence remains valid. However, if NATO is to retain the ability to carry out this strategy and to avoid the need to use nuclear weapons at an early stage of a conflict, a balanced force improvement programme should be carried out with emphasis placed on conventional force improvements. While NATO should be capable of dealing with the entire spectrum of possible Warsaw Pact aggressions, particular attention should be paid to NATO's ability to respond to an attack by ready forces after very little warning. For deterrence as well as defence, NATO governments need to be able to take prompt political decisions in times of tension, so that NATO can deploy its forces in a timely and orderly fashion.

"**NATO Forces.** The enhanced ability of the Warsaw Pact to launch an attack at short notice places additional emphasis on NATO's need for adequate, fully trained and exercised in-place forces. Reserve forces should be capable of being deployed rapidly as organized, equipped and sufficiently trained units. Systems for rapid call-up should be maintained and exercised. Reinforcement and augmentation forces should reach an area of potential conflict before an aggression takes place or, if warning time is very short, early enough to affect the initial course of hostilities. Special emphasis should be placed on prestocking, on the timely provision of sea and airlift capabilities and on adequate reception facilities. All the forces committed to NATO should be brought up to standards established by the major NATO commanders as soon as possible.

"**Defence against Armour.** Although the Alliance has improved its anti-armour capabilities, a gap persists between these capabilities and the threat posed by the Warsaw Pact's armoured forces, and more anti-armour weapons should be acquired.

"**Maritime.** If the Alliance is to maintain the ability to cope with the emerging threat at sea, and to protect the sea lanes for the timely reinforcement and resupply of Europe, it is imperative that the rate of improvement of NATO's maritime forces be increased.

"**Air Defence.** The increasing offensive capability of Warsaw Pact air forces emphasizes the need to improve NATO's air defences over land and at sea. To enhance the survivability of NATO forces, the Alliance's integrated air defence system needs to be expanded and modernized.

"**Regional Aspects.** The defence of the North Atlantic area is indivisible. On the flanks an adequate allocation of forces and a balanced military effort must be assured; continued efforts must be made to strengthen local mobilization capabilities, advance the arrival times of external reinforcements and improve reception and other logistic arrangements. For some countries assistance from external sources is required as well as the need for improved reinforcement capabilities.

"**New Technology.** Efficient application of modern technology, while not offering any inexpensive solutions, can provide opportunities, if applied through co-operative and timely efforts, for substantial improvement to the deterrent and defence capabilities of the Alliance.

"**Alliance Co-operation.** NATO resources can be employed to best effect if, in the development of national plans and programmes, greater account is taken of the collective needs of the Alliance, recognizing that the prerogatives of sovereign governments and national systems of finance are bound to place limits on the pace and degree to which integration can be achieved. Some progress has been made but there is still much room for a better allocation of defence resources, especially through greater Alliance co-operation. This process would be greatly facilitated by the establishment of a more comprehensive framework for defence planning incorporating a longer-term approach. Only thus would it be possible to establish in a timely and orderly way the necessary requirements, set the priorities, reconcile demands on resources for co-operative efforts with those required for national efforts, and identify areas for co-operation.

"**Armaments Planning.** The trend for the cost of equipment to increase disproportionately in relation to most other defence costs has continued. In many cases the cost of major defence projects is beyond the capability of most member nations to finance alone. The cost of equipment is also of major importance for potential buyers among Allies because of the budgetary impact on their defence planning. Interested countries should therefore be involved in relevant projects as early as possible. Separate research, development and production of different weapon systems for similar roles has led to problems of non-standardization and the lack of interoperability between forces and equipment of member nations.

"On-going studies should therefore be pursued with a view to harmonizing national defence equipment planning procedures and developing NATO long-term armaments planning. The aim of these efforts should be standardization and, where this is not possible, full interoperability. In pursuing these objectives a better balance in the traffic in the 'two-way street' between Europe and North America in weapons and equipment procurement will be necessary.

"**Impact on NATO Planning.** In developing more rational procedures for NATO's long-term planning for defence, the Alliance must seek to harmonize planning mechanisms for the various co-operative and supporting programmes, and to dovetail the results of this effort with the present NATO force planning procedures into a comprehensive approach for Alliance defence planning. The need for early identification of the resource implications for major co-operative projects will be of special importance. The activities of regional groups, such as the Eurogroup, will have an important contribution to make in this context.

"**Resources for Defence.** Against the background of adverse trends in the NATO-Warsaw Pact military balance and in order to avoid a continued deterioration in the relative force capabilities, an annual increase in real terms in defence budgets should be aimed at by all member countries. This annual increase should be in the region of 3 per cent, recognizing that for some individual countries economic circumstances will affect what can be achieved; present force contributions may justify a higher level of increase. Specific target figures for each country will need to be determined in the normal course of the defence planning review. Nations should provide full compensation for the inflationary impact of rising pay and price levels to ensure that planned real increases are achieved. It is, moreover, imperative that nations increase the cost effectiveness of their defence expenditures, in particular the percentage of such expenditure devoted to major equipment, but without detriment to combat readiness. The effective use of resources will depend to a large extent on progress in Alliance co-operation.

"**Priorities.** Priority should be given to those capabilities which contribute directly to deterrence and to NATO's ability to withstand the initial phases of attack and, in particular, to measures which will enhance readiness and reinforcement capabilities and promote a collective approach to equipping, supporting and training Alliance forces."

At a meeting in Brussels on Dec. 8–9, 1977, the Ministerial Council approved a NATO force plan for the period up to 1982.

The Defence Planning Committee, at a meeting in Brussels on May 18–19, 1978, adopted a long-term defence programme and endorsed new force goals for 1979–84 to cover the whole spectrum of NATO's forces. The main elements of the long-term defence programme were summarized under the headings of readiness, reinforcement, reserve mobilization, maritime posture, air defence, communication, command and control, electronic warfare, consumer logistics, rationalization and theatre nuclear modernization.

1977–78 US Decisions on Nuclear Weapons. In July 1977 President Carter announced the following modifications in the context of the US defence programme: (i) The cancellation of plans for a strategic B-1 intercontinental bomber (to replace the B-52 in use since the mid-1950s) with a top speed of 1,350 miles per hour (Mach 2.1) and capable of flying at the speed of sound at very low altitudes (and thus difficult to detect by radar); (ii) the continued development of the advanced cruise missile, a small jet-propelled missile with a "terrain contour matching" (Tercon) guidance system enabling it to fly at very low altitudes at subsonic speeds and with projected ranges of some 300 miles in the tactical (conventional) role and 2,000 miles in the strategic (nuclear) role (different versions being either sea-launched or air-launched); and (iii) the allocation of funds for the development of "neutron" warheads, an "enhanced radiation" weapon or thermonuclear fusion device with a nuclear fission detonator (in effect a small hydrogen bomb triggered by a smaller atomic bomb) which, because of its "limited collateral damage", would be especially effective against tanks and armoured personnel carriers in areas where other nuclear explosives would cause much damage to "friendly" forces, civilians and buildings.

On April 7, 1978, however, President Carter announced that he had decided to defer the production of the enhanced radiation weapon (i.e. the neutron bomb); that the ultimate decision on the "incorporation of enhanced radiation features into our modernized battlefield" would be made later; and that it would be "influenced by the degree to which the Soviet Union shows restraint in its conventional and nuclear arms programmes and force deployments affecting the security of the United States and Western Europe". (The Supreme Commander of NATO forces in Europe had, however, said on March 21, 1978, that "from the purely military point of view" the neutron bomb was "a most desirable

modernization step to be undertaken by the Alliance".)

In April 1978 President Carter was reported to have suggested, during a visit to Warsaw on Dec. 30, 1977, that the United States might be prepared to enter into an agreement with the Soviet Union which would prevent the European NATO member countries from obtaining the cruise missile.

However, on Oct. 18, 1978, the US Government announced that the President had endorsed the production of tactical nuclear warheads for the Lance missile and an eight-inch artillery weapons system adaptable for use as enhanced radiation weapons (neutron bombs).

1978–1980

At a meeting in Washington on May 30–31, 1978, the NATO Ministerial Council inter alia welcomed a US intention to pre-position heavy equipment for three additional US divisions in the central region of Allied Command Europe by 1982.

At a Defence Planning Committee meeting in Brussels on Dec. 5–6, 1978, ministers again expressed their concern at the military strength of the Warsaw Pact countries and in particular the introduction of the SS-20 mobile intermediate-range ballistic missile with multiple warheads and the Backfire (Tupolev V-G) bomber systems capable of striking targets in the whole of Europe and beyond, also from locations far in the interior of the Soviet Union. The ministers inter alia approved the programme for a NATO airborne early warning and control system (AWACS) and the NATO force plan for 1979–83. (The AWACS was to consist of 16 to 18 modified Boeing 707 aircraft, renamed E3A, equipped with radar and computers capable of monitoring military activities up to 300 or 400 miles inside Eastern Europe, and stationed in West Germany from early in 1982.)

At a further Defence Planning Committee meeting in Brussels on May 15–16, 1979, ministers again expressed concern at recent developments in the Warsaw Pact countries' military capabilities, stating: "Specifically, the SS-20 missile introduces a new dimension of threat in the theatre nuclear field. For the first time a weapon on the continental scale can reach all the territories of Western Europe with multiple warheads from mobile launchers based in the Soviet Union. . . . Ministers also noted improvements in new Soviet intercontinental and submarine-launched ballistic missiles, all with multiple independently targetable, re-entry vehicles (MIRVs), which have enhanced substantially the Soviet strategic capability."

A White Paper on national security issued by the Ministry of Defence of the Federal Republic of Germany on Sept. 4, 1979, recorded that West Germany currently maintained 495,000 servicemen and contributed half of the total NATO land forces manpower in central Europe, half of its ground-based air defence resources, 30 per cent of its combat aircraft [see also below] and 70 per cent of its naval resources in the Baltic region. In the 10 years since 1969, it said, over 27,000 million Deutschemarks (DM)—about $15,700 million at end-1979 exchange rate—had been spent on new equipment for the Army, DM 17,000 million for the Air Force and DM 10,000 million for the Navy, while further investment of DM 15,000 million was planned for the Army in the period up to the mid-1980s. It was subsequently announced in late September 1979 that the Army was to be equipped with 1,800 (West German) *Leopard 2* tanks by 1986, raising its total tank force to about 5,000 (the first *Leopard 2* tanks coming into service in October 1979).

December 1979 "Twin-track" Decision. In December 1979 NATO Foreign and Defence Ministers (i) decided to install new long-range theatre nuclear weapons (Pershing II launchers and ground-launched cruise missiles) in Western Europe; (ii) called for negotiations between the United States and the Soviet Union on reducing the numbers of such weapons on both sides; and (iii) made new proposals on mutually and balanced force reductions (MBFR) in Central Europe.

In particular the ministers decided on Dec. 12 to deploy in Europe 108 Pershing II launchers (replacing existing Pershing I-A launchers) and 464 ground-launched cruise missiles (GLCM), all with single warheads. At the same time 1,000 US warheads were to be withdrawn from Europe as soon as possible and the above 572 long-range theatre nuclear force (LRTNF) warheads would be accommodated within the reduced level. (All 108 Pershing II launchers were to be deployed in the Federal Republic of Germany, and of the cruise missiles 160 were to be placed in the United Kingdom, 112 in Italy, 96 in Germany and 48 each in Belgium and the Netherlands.)

A special consultative group on arms control, the establishment of which had been announced at the same meeting, stated after its first session on Jan. 25, 1980, that NATO was still firmly committed to the parallel approach of modernizing its LRTNF in Europe while seeking agreement with the Soviet Union on limiting the number of such weapons on either side.

The Defence Planning Committee, meeting on Dec. 11–12, 1979, adopted a NATO force plan for 1980–84, and at a meeting in Brussels on May 13–14, 1980, it endorsed NATO force goals for the 1981–86 period.

At a meeting of the (Foreign Ministers') Council in Ankara on June 25–26, 1980, the ministers condemned as "unacceptable" the Soviet armed intervention in Afghanistan ("a traditionally neutral and non-aligned country of the Third World") and reaffirmed a UN General Assembly resolution calling for the "immediate, unconditional and total withdrawal of foreign troops from Afghanistan". They declared inter alia: "It is vital that the Soviet Union should be left in no doubt as to the extremely grave view which the

Allies take of this situation which jeopardizes world peace." Of the Soviet activities in the field of LRTNF systems the ministers noted that, in addition to the existing force of 450 SS-4 and SS-5 medium and intermediate-range ballistic missiles, the Soviet Union had "deployed approximately 450 warheads on 150 SS-20 launchers" (i.e. new intermediate or limited range missiles), and that the USSR was in the process of deploying for its SS-20 force alone more warheads than were planned for the entire modernization programme agreed to in December 1979 (whereas deployments in Allied countries would not begin until late in 1983).

A meeting of the Nuclear Planning Group held on Nov. 13–14, 1980, discussed inter alia a new US "countervailing strategy" which had been set out in a Presidential Directive (which became known in August 1980) requiring US nuclear forces to be able to undertake precise, limited nuclear strikes against military facilities in the Soviet Union rather than concentrating their efforts on destroying Soviet cities as in the past.

A meeting of the Defence Planning Committee on Dec. 9–10, 1980, adopted the NATO force plan for 1981–85.

In the communiqué issued at the end of the North Atlantic Council's meeting on Dec. 11–12, 1980, it was stated inter alia that the Soviet Union's bases for mobile intermediate-range ballistic missiles (SS-20) already identified would alone support more warheads than were planned under NATO's entire modernization programme, and that the withdrawal of 1,000 nuclear warheads as an integral part of this modernization had been completed.

Position of Greece. The Government of Greece announced on Oct. 20, 1980, that it had decided to rejoin the military organization of NATO (which it had left in 1974—see above), and this decision was approved by the Greek Parliament on Oct. 24 by 182 votes to 20, with the opposition Pan-Hellenic Socialist Movement—PASOK) having left the Chamber before the vote.

In October 1981 PASOK came to power on a platform of renegotiating Greece's military participation in NATO, removing US bases from Greece and seeking in the longer term the dissolution of both NATO and the Warsaw Pact. Although in September 1983 the PASOK government signed a new five-year defence and economic co-operation agreement with the United States [see page 370], Greece maintained its boycott of NATO military exercises in the eastern Mediterranean, principally because of its unresolved dispute with Turkey over Cyprus and the Aegean Sea continental shelf.

1981–1986

In a report to the Central Committee of the Communist Party of the Soviet Union (CPSU) on Feb. 23, 1981, President Brezhnev (General Secretary of the CPSU) claimed inter alia that there was "military and strategic equilibrium" between the Soviet Union and the United States and between the Warsaw Treaty Organization and NATO, which he saw as "objectively a safeguard of world peace". He rejected Western suggestions of a Soviet military advantage and alleged (i) that, although the Soviet Union had more tanks than the NATO member countries, the latter had more anti-tank weapons, (ii) that the overall NATO troop strength exceeded that of the Soviet Union, and (iii) that "whether we take strategic nuclear arms or medium-range nuclear weapons in Europe, in both cases there is approximate parity between the sides" (this assertion being sharply disputed in the West).

The NATO Nuclear Planning Group, meeting in Bonn on April 7–8, 1981, expressed concern at the "continued growth in Soviet forces, and in particular their preponderance of theatre nuclear forces". It claimed that the Soviet Union had maintained some 380 SS-4 and SS-5 medium-range and intermediate-range missiles and deployed about 220 launchers for SS-20 MIRVed missiles (i.e. equipped with multiple independently targeted re-entry vehicles) and that, with SS-20 missiles alone, the Soviets had deployed some 660 warheads (i.e. more than planned for NATO's long-range nuclear force modernization programme).

In a British Defence White Paper (Cmnd. 8212) published on April 15, 1981, NATO's conventional forces deployment was described as follows:

"In the Federal Republic of Germany the UK provides some 55,000 men in four armoured divisions and one artillery division as part of the central region forces, which also include some 155,000 regulars and 180,000 conscripts from the Federal German Army, about 200,000 US Army personnel and about 80,000 from the armies of Belgium, Canada and the Netherlands. As part of NATO's Second Allied Tactical Air Force the Royal Air Force has 11 fast-jet squadrons based in Germany; the Federal German Air Force contributes 23 combat squadrons to the Second and the Fourth Allied Tactical Air Force, as well as four squadrons in the Baltic Approaches; and the US 17th Air Force is divided between Germany and the Netherlands. Belgium, Canada and the Netherlands also provide air force contributions. In the EASTLANT (Eastern Atlantic) area of naval operations the UK provides some 70 per cent of the ready forces and operates alongside forces from Denmark, the Netherlands, Norway and Portugal. The UK, Belgium and the Netherlands also assign ships to the Allied C.-in-C. Channel (CINCHAN) and the UK and the Netherlands assign Marine units to the UK/Netherlands Amphibious Force under the Supreme Allied Commander Atlantic (SACLANT). Certain of these forces are under NATO command all the time, notably air defence fighter aircraft, missiles and radars, and the Standing Naval Force Atlantic (STANAVFORLANT), to which nine countries contribute ships. In peacetime most NATO forces remain under national command, only in times of tension or war coming under the direct command of a major NATO commander—Supreme Allied Commander Europe (SACEUR), SACLANT or CINCHAN."

In the central region of Europe the immediate threat to NATO's forces was posed by the Warsaw Pact forces in Czechoslovakia, East Germany and Poland; these comprised 26 Soviet and 31 other Warsaw Pact divisions, which in a period of tension could be reinforced from the 30 further divisions in the Soviet western military districts; all the Soviet divisions stationed in other Warsaw Pact countries, and certain other Warsaw Pact divisions, were almost fully manned in peacetime,

but most of those in the western military districts would need the addition of reservists to make them combat-ready.

A meeting of the North Atlantic Council held in Rome on May 4–5, 1981, in its final communiqué (i) reaffirmed that Soviet forces must be withdrawn from Afghanistan and "a political settlement must be found enabling the Afghan people to exercise fully their rights of independence and self-determination and permitting the 2,000,000 refugees to return to their homes" and (ii) declared that "Poland must be left free to resolve its own problems".

The NATO Defence Planning Committee, meeting in Brussels on May 12–13, 1981, emphasized in its communiqué that measures taken outside the NATO area by NATO member states (e.g. by the newly established US rapid deployment force) had implications for allied capabilities to deter aggression and to defend Europe.

The Italian government decided on Aug. 7, 1981, that the Italian site for cruise missiles was to be at Magliocco military airport near Comiso (Sicily), but that installation would not commence before 1984.

A NATO Foreign Ministers' session held on Jan. 11, 1982, issued a Declaration on Events in Poland, condemning the imposition of martial law in that country and "the massive violation of human rights and the suppression of fundamental civil liberties"; calling on the Soviet Union to respect Poland's fundamental right to solve its own problems free from foreign interference; stating that the Soviet Union would "bear full responsibility if its actions with regard to Poland and its failure to live up to existing international obligations damage the arms control process"; suggesting appropriate national action by each ally, covering further restrictions on the movements of Soviet and Polish diplomats and reduction of scientific and technical activities or non-renewal of exchange agreements; and recognizing the importance of economic measures, including the placing in abeyance of future commercial credits to Poland (other than for food) and of negotiations on Poland's official debts.

A meeting of the Nuclear Planning Group held in Colorado Springs (USA) on March 23–24, 1982, effectively rejected a Soviet offer (made on March 15) of a Soviet freeze on the deployment of SS-20 missiles in the European region as it would perpetuate the Soviet monopoly in such weapons. The meeting supported the US position—to cancel the proposed deployment of Pershing II and cruise missiles if the Soviet Union eliminated its SS-20, SS-4 and SS-5 missiles worldwide.

Following the accession of Spain as the organization's 16th member on May 30, 1982, the Spanish Foreign Minister emphasized on the following day that, while Spain was allied to Britain in the context of defending democracy, it was "absolutely not allied to Britain in the Malvinas" (i.e. the Falkland Islands).

The first summit meeting of NATO member countries' heads of state or government since 1978, held in Bonn on June 10, 1982, reaffirmed NATO's "twin-track" decision of December 1979, viz. (i) the deployment of Pershing II and cruise missiles in Western Europe and (ii) the continuation of arms control negotiations to achieve a more stable overall balance and lower levels of nuclear weapons on both sides, in particular through Strategic Arms Reduction Talks (START) as proposed by the United States. The meeting issued a communiqué which contained a "programme for peace in freedom" listing its aims inter alia as to prevent war while safeguarding democracy, to preserve the security of the North Atlantic area, to have a stable balance of forces at the lowest possible level, to develop substantial and balanced East-West relations aimed at genuine détente, to contribute to peaceful progress worldwide, and to "ensure economic and social stability for our countries".

The "twin-track" decision of December 1979 received continued support at NATO meetings late in 1982 (of the Nuclear Planning Group on Nov. 30, the Defence Planning Committee on Dec. 1–2, and the NATO Foreign Ministers on Dec. 9–10).

Gen. Bernard Rogers, then Supreme Allied Commander Europe, stated inter alia on Dec. 15, 1982, that there was a widening gap between the force capabilities of NATO and those of the Warsaw Pact Organization which, he said, must be closed by enhancing NATO's conventional forces; that a reduction of US troop strength in Europe would be "disastrous" and against the "vital interests of the United States . . . inextricably linked with Western Europe"; and that such a step would "unravel" the Atlantic Alliance.

On Dec. 5, 1984, the NATO Defence Planning Committee adopted a six-year $7,850 million programme for improving NATO's structural facilities and increasing its war stocks.

A commissioned assessment of the threats to Western security over the next 20 years, and measures needed to counter them, was submitted to NATO defence ministers on May 22, 1985. This report, known as Conceptual Military Framework (CMF), was said to show that the Soviet Union had initiated measures which could, and probably would, lead within 15 years to the capability required to challenge the conventional military strength of NATO without necessarily taking the risk of escalation.

A US-Netherlands treaty on the stationing of 48 cruise missiles in the Netherlands was approved for ratification by the lower house of the Dutch Parliament on Feb. 27, 1986 (by 79 votes to 69).

The continued NATO membership of Spain—although without participation in the organization's military structure, with the maintenance of a ban on the installation, storage or introduction of nuclear weapons, and with a progressive reduction of the US military presence in Spain—was supported in a referendum held on March 12, 1986, when 9,054,509 votes were cast in favour of continued membership, and 6,872,421 votes against, with 1,127,673 blank papers and 191,855 spoilt papers, in a 59.4 per cent poll. (For 1982 US-Spain friendship, defence and co-operation agreement, see page 373.)

The NATO Defence Planning Committee decided, on May 22, 1986, to endorse plans for the eventual resumption of US production of chemical weapons.

Co-ordinating Committee for Multilateral Export Controls (COCOM)

Membership. All NATO member countries except Iceland, and also Japan.

An embargo on the shipment to areas under communist control of "arms, ammunition and implements of war, atomic energy materials, petroleum and items useful in the production of implements of war" was first recommended by the UN General Assembly on May 18, 1951.

An embargo of this type was subsequently agreed upon by the COCOM member states, but with effect from Aug. 15, 1958, this was reduced to a prohibition of shipments of "strictly strategic goods". Since then COCOM has held regular meetings to discuss restrictions on East-West trade in technology deemed useful to the Warsaw Pact military forces. It has laid down three international lists of commodities which would be subject to control—(i) a strict embargo list, (ii) a qualitative control list and (iii) a surveillance list, and it has also introduced a control system of granting permits for imports.

A COCOM meeting held on Oct. 4–5, 1982, agreed to update the list of items the export of which to the Eastern bloc was prohibited, but at a meeting held on April 28, 1983, it was agreed only "that the joint system of checking sensitive technology exports should be as effective as possible and continually adapted to developments in technology and equipment"; it did not approve a US proposal for the establishment of a military subcommittee to oversee dual-purpose exports (i.e. of items of both civil and military use).

In December 1983 COCOM members agreed to an embargo on the sale of silicon and silicon-making equipment to the Soviet bloc (this embargo being expected to retard the Soviet Union's military modernization plans). (The United States imposed controls on sensitive exports far in excess of those approved by COCOM.)

On July 12, 1984, COCOM decided to revise, for the first time since the 1970s, COCOM computer export controls, but most Western COCOM members subsequently refused to observe the newly imposed restrictions.

A COCOM meeting held on Feb. 6–7, 1985, decided to update about one-third of the embargo lists each year (instead of every three years as until then).

On Sept. 18, 1985, the Spanish Council of Ministers approved Spain's incorporation into

COCOM (Spain having become a member of NATO in May 1982).

Vienna Talks on Mutual and Balanced Force Reductions in Central Europe

Talks between representatives of NATO and Warsaw Pact countries with troops in Central Europe on mutual and balanced force reductions (MBFR) in that area—which had first been suggested in the North Atlantic Council's MBFR Declaration of June 25, 1968 [see page 213]—were conducted in Vienna from 1973 onwards.

At the first such talks, held on Oct. 30–31, 1973, policy statements made by the two sides revealed, according to a NATO spokesman, the following divergencies: (1) Whereas NATO wanted to start with US and Soviet force reductions, the Warsaw Pact powers were pressing for cuts affecting both national and other troops; (2) NATO wished to limit reductions to ground forces, while the Warsaw Pact powers aimed to reduce both ground and air forces; (3) while the Warsaw Pact powers wanted to reduce nuclear arms, NATO preferred to concentrate on conventional armaments; and (4) NATO insisted that the Warsaw Pact powers should make the biggest cuts because of their superiority in manpower and armaments, while these powers challenged this concept.

During the following years the talks continued without leading to agreement.

On July 17, 1975, a NATO spokesman defined the object of the talks as "the achievement of approximate parity between the two sides in ground forces in Central Europe in the form of a common ceiling on ground force manpower plus reductions of Soviet tanks", whereas the Warsaw Pact side wanted force reductions to apply also to air forces and nuclear-equipped units.

On Dec. 16, 1975, the US representative submitted a proposal for the withdrawal of 1,000 tactical nuclear warheads (out of NATO's total of 7,000) and of 29,000 US troops, against a reduction of Soviet troops by 68,000 men and 1,700 tanks (out of 15,000), to achieve a "common ceiling" of about 700,000 men on either side. The Warsaw Pact side, however, continued to insist on "an equal percentage reduction of ground and air forces"—a proposal which had been criticized by NATO because it failed to state any figures on which these percentages should be calculated.

At the ministerial meeting of the North Atlantic Council held on Dec. 13–14, 1979, new proposals were made, envisaging a two-phase reduction in NATO and Warsaw Pact forces levels, under which about 13,000 US and 30,000 Soviet troops were to be withdrawn from Central Europe, with the aim of achieving "a common collective ceiling in ground force manpower for each side at approximately 900,000". Although these proposals were subsequently discussed in Vienna, the North Atlantic Council's ministerial meeting held in Brussels on December 11–12, 1980, found that the Eastern countries had "regrettably still not provided the information necessary to reach agreement on the size of the forces of the Soviet Union in Central Europe which is an essential prerequisite to a Phase 1 agreement", and that they had not responded adequately to Western proposals concerning associated measures designed to ensure verification of force reductions and limitation and to enhance stability.

Survey of Agreements Basic to the NATO Structure

NORTH ATLANTIC TREATY AND SUBSEQUENT ACCESSIONS

(1) North Atlantic Treaty between Belgium, Canada, Denmark, France, Iceland, Italy, Luxembourg, the Netherlands, Norway, Portugal, the United Kingdom and the USA, signed on April 4, 1949 (in force from Aug. 24, 1949) (for text see pages 203–04).

(2) Protocol to the North Atlantic Treaty on the accession of Greece and Turkey, signed on Oct. 22, 1951 (in force from Feb. 15, 1952).

(3) Protocol to the North Atlantic Treaty on the accession of the Federal Republic of Germany, signed on Oct. 23, 1954 (in force from May 5, 1955).

(4) Resolution of the North Atlantic Council on Implementation of Section IV of the Final Act of the London Conference, signed on Oct. 23, 1954. This document, one of the Paris Agreements, provided for the placing of the armed forces of the NATO countries stationed on the continent of Europe under the authority of the Supreme Allied Commander Europe (SACEUR); the location and integration of the forces; closer co-ordination of logistics; the right of inspection of forces in Europe by SACEUR; and the indefinite duration of the North Atlantic Treaty.

(5) Resolution of Association with the Tripartite Declaration of Oct. 3, 1954, signed on Oct. 23, 1954 [see page 205].

(6) Protocol to the North Atlantic Treaty on the accession of Spain, signed on Dec. 10, 1981.

AGREEMENT ON THE STATUS OF NATO

Agreement on the Status of the North Atlantic Treaty Organization, National Representatives, and the International Staff, signed on Sept. 20, 1951 (in force from May 18, 1954).

AGREEMENTS ON THE STATUS OF FORCES

(1) Agreement between member states of the North Atlantic Treaty on the Status of their Forces, signed on June 19, 1951 (in force from Aug. 23, 1953).

(2) Agreement between the USA and Canada relating to the application of the NATO Status of Forces Agreement to the US forces in Canada, signed on April 28 and 30, 1952, in effect since Sept. 27, 1953.

(3) Agreement on the status of NATO forces stationed in Germany, signed on Aug. 3, 1959 (in effect for Germany since July 1, 1963).

AGREEMENTS ON THE STATUS OF INTERNATIONAL MILITARY HEADQUARTERS

(1) Agreement concerning the employment by the International Military Headquarters of US nationals, signed on Feb. 25, 1953.

(2) Agreement concluded by the United States regarding the headquarters of the Supreme Allied Commander Atlantic, signed on Oct. 22, 1954 (operative since April 10, 1954).

(3) Agreement between the Government of the Turkish Republic and the Supreme Allied Commander Europe, signed on Feb. 22, 1956.

(4) Agreement between the Government of the Italian Republic and SACEUR regarding special conditions of establishment and operation on Italian territory of International Military Headquarters which are or might be located there, signed on July 26, 1961.

(5) Agreement between the Government of the Kingdom of the Netherlands and SACEUR regarding special conditions of establishment and operation on Dutch territory of International Military Headquarters, signed on May 25, 1964.

AGREEMENTS SIGNED IN THE FRAMEWORK OF NATO

(1) Agreement between the 15 member countries for co-operation regarding atomic information, signed on June 18, 1964 (approved by the North Atlantic Council on April 13, 1955, and in force from March 12, 1965).

(2) Agreement concluded by the 15 member countries for the mutual safeguarding of secrecy of inventions relating to defence, for which applications for patents have been made, signed on Sept. 21, 1960 (in force from Jan. 12, 1961).

COMMUNICATIONS AGREEMENTS

(1) Agreement concerning the NATO satellite communications earth terminal in the United States, signed on July 10 and Aug. 20, 1970.

(2) Memorandum of understanding concerning interconnection of NICS TARE network and US AUTODIN, signed on Sept. 14 and 28, 1984.

Military Assistance Agreements concluded by the USA with NATO Partners

On Oct. 6, 1949, the US President signed the Mutual Defence Assistance Act of 1949 providing for military aid from the USA to the signatory governments of the North Atlantic Treaty. An amended form of this Act, known as the Mutual Security Act, was passed in 1951.

Bilateral agreements between the USA and NATO member countries, within the framework of the Mutual Security Act of 1951, can be broadly classified into the following categories: Mutual defence agreements including military aid; agreements relating to the assurances required

under the Mutual Security Act; facilities assistance agreements; offshore procurements agreements; agreements for the return of military equipment; agreements allowing members of the Land, Naval and Air Force Missions to act as a military Advisory Group, and agreements relating to military missions; mutual security military sales agreements; and weapons production agreements.

Agreements Relating to Defence concluded between NATO Countries

The NATO defence system has been strengthened by the many agreements concluded between the various NATO countries. US defence agreements with NATO countries may be found in the chapter "Defence Treaties of the USA", pages 367ff.

Agreements among the other NATO countries are given below.

AGREEMENTS CONCLUDED BY BRITAIN

The United Kingdom has concluded agreements within the NATO framework with:

(1) *Belgium and Canada:* on transit and stationing in Belgium of Canadian forces, signed on March 30, 1953; in force from July 29, 1953.

(2) *Belgium:* on the establishment of a military base at Campine, Nov. 12, 1952.

(3) *Denmark:* relating to the Agreement on the Status of Forces of June 19, 1951 [see page 221], Oct. 8, 1956.

(4) *France:* (i) a military air transit agreement governing flights by military aircraft over both countries and their servicing at British and French airfields, signed on April 19, 1948; (ii) an agreement in principle, concluded in Paris on Oct. 6, 1976, on the exchange of information on the world naval situation, including the size and movements of third-country navies.

(5) *The Federal Republic of Germany:* (i) on British bases in the German Federal Republic, Sept. 9, 1952; Oct. 15 and 18, 1954; May 22 and 31, 1957; (ii) relating to the Convention on Foreign Forces stationed in Germany [see below], April 11, 1957; and (iii) on the maintenance cost of British forces stationed in Germany, June 7, 1957; Oct. 3, 1958; April 28, 1967. Under an agreement signed on Oct. 18, 1977, the Federal Republic was to pay no further support costs for British troops in Germany after 1980.

(6) *The Netherlands:* relating to the Convention on Foreign Forces stationed in Germany [see below], June 11 and 13, 1956. Extension signed on June 7, 1957.

(7) *Turkey:* on the sale of destroyers to Turkey, Aug. 16, 1957. Amended on Jan. 12, 1959.

AGREEMENTS CONCLUDED BY CANADA

Canada has concluded agreements within the NATO framework with:

(1) *Belgium and Britain* (see above under "Agreements concluded by Britain").

(2) *Denmark:* on aircrew training for NATO, April 17, 1957. Renewed on March 25, 1960; extended on June 30, 1964.

(3) *France:* (i) pursuant to the Convention on Foreign Forces stationed in Germany: April 19, 1955; Jan. 26, 1956; and (ii) on the exchange of defence-science information, May 25, 1962.

(4) *The Federal Republic of Germany:* (i) on the training of German aircrews in Canada, Sept. 17 and Dec. 10, 1956; (ii) on the use of the Churchill Research Range, July 8, 1969, amended and extended on April 28, 1972, and June 7–29, 1973.

(5) *Greece:* on the exchange of defence-science information, July 17 and 18, 1962.

(6) *The Netherlands:* on the extension of the NATO aircrew training programme, April 12 and 13, 1957.

(7) *Norway:* (i) on the transfer of three *Prestonian* class frigates to Norway, July 1, 1958; (ii) on the continuation of Canada's NATO air training programme, June 30, 1964; and (iii) on the exchange of information on defence, May 24, 1960.

AGREEMENTS CONCLUDED BY FRANCE

France has concluded agreements within the NATO framework with:

(1) *Belgium and Luxembourg:* on co-operation between the three countries for internal defence, July 25, 1959.

(2) *Canada* [see above].

(3) *Federal Republic of Germany:* (i) on logistics and training of German forces, Oct. 25, 1960; and (ii) on co-operation in the field of political, defence, information, cultural and scientific matters, Jan. 22, 1963 [see page 197].

(4) *Portugal:* on the setting up, by France, of a tracking station for ballistic missiles in the Azores, April 9, 1964. On April 5, 1985, it was reported that the agreement had been extended for a further 12 years, during which France would provide 300,000,000 escudos per annum for development projects and 200,000,000 escudos for purchases of French military equipment.

(5) *The Netherlands:* on close co-operation in the production, purchase and maintenance of armaments, June 5, 1984 (the Netherlands having similar agreements with Denmark, Greece, the Federal Republic of Germany, Italy, Spain and the United Kingdom).

AGREEMENTS CONCLUDED BY THE FEDERAL REPUBLIC OF GERMANY

The Federal Republic of Germany has concluded agreements within the NATO framework as follows:

(i) *Convention on Relations between the Three Powers* (the USA, Britain and France) and the Federal Republic of Germany and related conventions, signed on May 26, 1952. Amended by the Paris Agreements of Oct. 23, 1954.

[For bilateral agreements pursuant to these conventions see above under "Agreements concluded by Britain" and "Agreements concluded by Canada".]

(2) *Agreements with the Netherlands* on (i) mutual defence assistance, Jan. 27, 1950; (ii) supplementing the NATO agreement of Sept. 21, 1960, on mutual secrecy of defence-related inventions on which patents have been applied for, May 16, 1961, in force from Oct. 8, 1971; (iii) stationing of West German military units in the Netherlands, Jan. 17, 1963, in force from May 17, 1963.

(3) *Agreement with Norway* on the delivery of armaments spare parts, Oct. 30, 1957.

(4) *Agreement with Britain* on the development and production of a howitzer, Aug. 9, 1968.

(5) *Agreement with Portugal* on West German use of Beja air base, announced on Dec. 27, 1968. An earlier agreement on training and storage facilities for West German forces in Portugal had been concluded on June 12, 1964.

(6) A *wartime host nations support agreement* signed on April 15, 1982, committed the Federal Republic of Germany to providing increased military and civilian support for six extra US divisions to be sent to Germany in the event of a military emergency (at an estimated cost of $570,000,000 to be shared equally between the two governments).

AGREEMENTS CONCLUDED BY BELGIUM

Belgium has concluded agreements within the NATO framework with:

(1) *Luxembourg and France* (see above under "Agreements concluded by France").

(2) *Luxembourg:* on an alarm network, Feb. 19 and 21, 1955.

Important Agreements related to Military Bases and Nuclear Weapons

The more significant defence agreements between NATO partners are described below.

USA-Britain [see also page 374]. During 1948 the USA and Britain concluded an agreement on the use of air bases in Eastern England by the US Strategic Air Command. Details of this agreement were, however, not made public. In 1952, after a meeting in Washington between President Truman and the British Prime Minister, Winston Churchill, it was stated that "the use of these bases in an emergency would be a matter for joint decision by HM Government and the US Government in the light of the circumstances prevailing at the time".

An unpublished agreement of October 1951 regulated the use of US bases in Britain.

In 1960 the USA and Britain concluded an informal agreement under which the British Government agreed to provide facilities for US Polaris nuclear submarines at a floating-base in Holy Loch on the Clyde (Scotland).

On Dec. 21, 1962, a joint communiqué was issued by President Kennedy and the British Prime Minister, Harold Macmillan, after their meeting at Nassau where, inter alia, the question of nuclear missiles was discussed. The communiqué announced that the US Government would make available to Britain, "on a continuing basis", Polaris missiles without warheads; that Britain would provide the necessary submarines;

and that these forces, together with at least equal US forces, would be made available for inclusion in a NATO multilateral nuclear force. An agreement on the terms of sale by the United States of up to 100 Polaris missiles in Britain was signed on April 6, 1963. The Polaris agreement superseded an earlier agreement, concluded during 1960, for the development of the Skybolt missile by the US Government for the joint use of the US and British air forces.

USA-Canada. On Aug. 16, 1963, it was announced that Canada and the United States had reached agreement on "the conditions under which nuclear warheads will be made available for Canadian forces engaged in North American defence and assigned to NATO". The terms of the agreement were not made public, but it was stated that stockpiles of nuclear warheads would be stored at Canadian bases under Canadian command and control, but would remain under US custody. The warheads could only be used operationally with the joint authorization of the US and Canadian Governments.

However, the Canadian Government later withdrew its consent to the storage of nuclear weapons in Canada, and by July 1984 all such weapons were removed from Canadian territory.

USA-Italy. On March 30, 1959, it was announced that an agreement between the USA and Italy had been signed in Rome under which the Italian armed forces would be equipped with American intermediate-range ballistic missiles (IRBMs). Italian personnel would receive training in the use of the missiles, but the nuclear warheads would remain under US control. It was stressed that any decision to use the missiles and warheads would need the approval of both the Italian Government and SHAPE.

USA-Turkey. A similar agreement on the supply of IRBMs to Turkey came into force on Oct. 29, 1959.

Under an agreement between the United States and Turkey, signed in Ankara on July 3, 1969, and replacing over 50 earlier agreements concluded since 1959, Turkey's absolute sovereignty over all military installations in Turkey was emphasized; the agreement also laid down that Turkey would not lease or rent territory to the USA, that Turkish personnel would not be excluded from the bases, and that Turkey would, within the general framework of NATO defence policies, have co-determination with the USA on the number of US troops and their weapons and equipment to be stationed in Turkey.

In 1974, however, the US Government suspended military aid to Turkey and imposed an arms embargo against that country [see page 215]. After an attempt to reverse this decision had failed in the US House of Representatives on July 24, 1975, the Turkish Government declared on the following day that the 1960 joint US-Turkish defence co-operation agreement and other agreements connected with it had lost their validity, and that the activities of all joint US-Turkish defence installations in Turkey would be suspended and the installations placed under full Turkish control. (This did not apply to the Incirlik joint defence installation, which would be reserved for its NATO task alone.)

The US arms embargo was, however, lifted under legislation signed by President Carter on Sept. 26, 1978, but this legislation did not authorize the resumption of military aid to Turkey. On Oct. 9, 1978, the Turkish Government reopened four of the 26 US military bases closed down in July 1975, these four being three intelligence gathering stations and a navigational base.

During the 1979 US-Soviet negotiations on a second strategic arms limitation treaty (SALT II—see pages 291–96) the Turkish Government took the view that this was a bilateral agreement which did not directly involve NATO and in which Turkey wished to remain neutral.

A US House of Representatives-Senate conference committee agreed on Sept. 26, 1979, to include in the 1980 US foreign aid authorization bill a total of $450,000,000 of economic and military aid for Turkey, of which $252,000,000 would constitute military aid—(i) a long-term low-interest loan of $50,000,000 to Turkey for the purchase of US military equipment; (ii)

$200,000,000 in other military loans; and (iii) $2,000,000 for the training in Turkey and in the United States of Turkish military officers. (At the same time a long-term low-interest loan of $42,000,000 was to be made available to Greece for military expenditure.)

A new five-year defence and economic co-operation agreement, renewable annually, was concluded in Ankara on March 29, 1980.

The agreement laid down that defence co-operation between the two countries would be limited to the obligations arising from the North Atlantic Treaty, and that a total of 12 military bases in Turkey, incuding the four reopened by Turkey on Oct. 9, 1978 [see above], were to be used again by the United States (although only within the framework of NATO and each being under the command of a Turkish officer).

Three supplementary agreements were concluded at the same time for (i) mutually agreed US financial and technical assistance to Turkey; (ii) enhanced co-operation in the production of defence material and a listing of Turkish projects under consideration; and (iii) US participation in joint defence measures in specified Turkish armed forces installations (with 13 implementing agreements concerning the technical arrangements in each installation). [See also page 374.]

The military element of US aid to Turkey for the 1984 fiscal year was put at $755,000,000, and this was to be increased to $934,000,000 for 1985. On June 7, 1983, it was disclosed that Turkey was to buy 600 kits with which to upgrade its obsolete M-48 tanks, with larger guns and new engines. Arrangements finalized in December 1983 were for a deal worth $4,200 million under which Turkey would buy 40 F-16 C/D fighter bombers and build another 160 such aircraft under licence in 1985–87. The US air bases in Turkey have been modernized since 1982.

USA-Portugal. An agreement between the USA and Portugal was signed on Sept. 6, 1951, defining the facilities in the Azores granted by Portugal to the USA for the purposes of the common defence. Under the agreement these facilities were integrated into the NATO framework. The agreement has been extended on various occasions, most recently on Dec. 13, 1983 [see below].

The lease of a US air base in the Azores under the US-Portuguese agreement of Jan. 5, 1951, was on Nov. 15, 1957, extended to Dec. 31, 1962, and on Jan. 4, 1963, until a new lease was agreed. A new agreement was subsequently signed in Brussels on Dec. 9, 1971, granting the USA the continued use until Feb. 4, 1974, of air and naval bases on the island of Terceira, in the Azores, in return for economic assistance to Portugal by the USA.

Under a further agreement signed on June 18, 1979, the USA was allowed continued use of the strategic Lajes base on Terceira until February 1983 in return for US economic and military aid to Portugal. This agreement was extended for one year from February 1983 pending renegotiation of terms, which was finally accomplished with the signature on Dec. 13, 1983, of an agreement under which the United States was to have continued use of the Lajes base for a seven-year period to February 1991 in return for US economic and military aid to Portugal, set at $40,000,000 and $90,000,000 respectively for the 1984–85 fiscal year, and with military aid of $105,000,000 also being agreed for the 1985–86 fiscal year. The new agreement stressed that no nuclear weapons were to be installed on Portuguese territory. The US side noted the importance of Lajes for refuelling aircraft and for monitoring Soviet submarine movements and also confirmed that it wished to negotiate for the use of bases on the Portuguese mainland.

USA-Greece. An agreement giving American forces the use of air and naval bases in Greece, and authorizing the USA to develop Greek roads and railways for military purposes under the NATO defence pact, was signed on Oct. 12, 1953. This agreement was partially abrogated by the agreement on the status of US forces in Greece of Sept. 7, 1956.

Under a new defence co-operation agreement between the USA and Greece, initialled on July 28, 1977, the operation of

US military bases in Greece was to be limited to those which (in the Greek Prime Minister's words) "served Greek national defence needs", i.e. a naval-air base (in Crete), monitoring and communications bases (also in Crete and near Athens) and an air base at Athens, with these four bases being Greek installations under Greek command and with up to 50 per cent Greek personnel; the USA would not be permitted to store nuclear weapons at these bases or use them for war purposes without the express consent of the Greek Government. The agreement, however, remained unsigned owing to Greek objections to massive US aid granted to Turkey which the Greek Government regarded, by 1980, as upsetting the Greek-Turkish military balance.

A defence and economic co-operation agreement signed on Sept. 9, 1982, and to come into force on Dec. 31, 1983, provided for continued US military presence until the end of 1988 at four bases (in Athens and Crete) and 20 auxiliary installations, but with clauses permitting Greece to suspend US operations at the bases "to safeguard its vital national security interests in an emergency". The agreement would be extended after December 1988 unless written notice of termination was given five months beforehand by either party. At the same time the United States undertook to maintain the balance of power in the region (between Greece and Turkey), and for 1983 a sum of $500,000,000 was allocated to Greece in aid.

10. The Communist World

Aspects of international co-operation involving the states of the Communist world dealt with in this section include (i) the early international organizations of Communist parties, the more recent international conferences of such parties and the development of serious divisions within the world Communist movement, (ii) the Warsaw Treaty Organization, (iii) the Council for Mutual Economic Assistance, (iv) the major bilateral treaties between Communist states and (v) certain bilateral treaties concluded by the Soviet Union, China, and other Communist states.

International Communist Organizations and Contacts

The Comintern (1919–1943)

The Comintern, the Third (Communist) International, was founded in 1919 by Lenin in Moscow. The First International had been founded in 1864 by Karl Marx and Friedrich Engels, but broke up in 1874 on account of internal dissensions. The Second International was formed in 1889, but collapsed on the outbreak of war in 1914. The Comintern served as a roof organization of the Communist parties of the world, the individual national Communist parties being in effect sections of the world revolutionary Communist party.

On June 8, 1943, the Presidium of the Executive Committee of the Communist International met to dissolve the Comintern formally with the approval of the majority of world Communist parties and without any of the existing sections of the Communist International having raised any objections to the dissolution.

The proposal for the dissolution of the Comintern, as put before the Executive Committee at a meeting on May 15, 1943, was worded as follows:

"(1) The Communist International, as the directing centre of the international working-class movement, is to be dissolved.

"(2) The sections of the Communist International are to be freed from the obligations of their rules and regulations and from the decisions of the congress of the Communist International.

"(3) The Presidium calls on all supporters of the Communist International to concentrate their energies on whole-hearted support for and active participation in the war of liberation waged by the peoples and states of the anti-Hitlerite coalition for the speediest defeat of the deadly enemy of the working-class—German fascism and its associates and vassals."

The Cominform (1947–1956)

On Oct. 5, 1947, it was announced that the Communist parties of Bulgaria, Czechoslovakia, France, Hungary, Italy, Poland, Romania, the Soviet Union and Yugoslavia had decided to set up a Communist Information Bureau (the Cominform), with its headquarters in Belgrade. Its purpose was stated to be to "organize the exchange of experience" and "where necessary to co-ordinate the activities of the Communist parties on the basis of mutual agreement".

On June 28, 1948, it was disclosed that Yugoslavia had been expelled from the Cominform on grounds, inter alia, of deviation from Marxism-Leninism, of nationalism and of hostility towards the Soviet Union.

The official announcement of the dissolution of the Cominform appeared on April 18, 1956, signed by the eight national Communist parties which then formed the membership of the organization. It was stated that the eight had unanimously agreed that the Cominform had "exhausted its function".

International Communist Conferences of 1957 and 1960

Since the dissolution of the Cominform in 1956 there has been no co-ordinating body for the Communist parties in various countries. Conferences held in 1957 and 1960 failed to preserve the unity of the communist movement.

THE 1957 CONFERENCE

This conference, which was held in Moscow on Nov. 14–16, 1957, issued the *Moscow Declaration* approved by 12 parties:—The Communist parties of the USSR, China, Bulgaria and Czechoslovakia, the Polish United Workers' Party, the Hungarian Socialist Workers' Party, the Romanian Workers' Party, the Socialist Unity Party in East Germany, the Albanian Party of Labour, the (North) Korean Party of Labour, the Working People's Party of (North) Vietnam and the Mongolian People's Revolutionary Party.

This declaration, drawn up without the participation of the League of Communists of Yugoslavia, was expressly rejected by the latter on Dec. 7, 1957.

The declaration consisted of four sections:

(1) **Denunciation of "Imperialism".** This section described the USA as "the centre of world reaction"; accused "American, British, French and other imperialists and their stooges" of waging wars in various parts of the world; blamed the "aggressive imperialist forces" for their "flat refusal" to reduce armaments or prohibit nuclear weapons; attacked NATO, SEATO and "West German militarism and revanchism"; and asserted that "the cause of peace is upheld by . . . the invincible camp of socialist countries headed by the Soviet Union". It added that other "powerful peace forces" were "the peace-loving countries of Asia and Africa taking an anti-imperialist stand"; the "international working class and above all its vanguard, the Communist Party"; the "liberation movement of the peoples of colonies and semi-colonies"; the "peoples of the European countries which have proclaimed neutrality"; and "the peoples of Latin America". This section also affirmed that the 12 Communist parties signing the declaration adhered to the "Leninist principles of peaceful coexistence . . . which . . . coincide with the Five Principles put forward jointly by China and India and with the programme adopted at the Bandung conference of Afro-Asian countries" [see pages 461–62].

(2) **Co-operation between Communist Countries.** The declaration described the principles, upon which collaboration among the Communist states should be constructed, in these terms:

"The socialist countries base their relations on principles of complete equality, respect for territorial integrity, state independence and sovereignty, and non-interference in one another's affairs. These are vital principles. However, they do not exhaust the essence of the relations among them. Fraternal mutual aid is part and parcel of these relations. . . . The socialist countries also advocate all-round expansion of economic and cultural relations with all other countries, provided they desire it, on a basis of equality, mutual benefit and non-interference in internal affairs. . . ."

(3) **"Revisionism" and "Sectarianism".** In this section the "international phenomena" of "revisionism", "sectarianism" and "dogmatism" were attacked, and it was claimed that Marxism-Leninism, "deriving from historical materialism", was a "world outlook reflecting the universal law of development of nature, society and human thinking" and was "valid for the past, present and future".

The declaration continued: "In condemning dogmatism, the Communist parties believe that the main danger at present is revisionism—in other words, right-wing opportunism as a manifestation of bourgeois ideology paralysing the revolutionary energy of the working-class and demanding the preservation or restoration of capitalism. However, dogmatism and sectarianism can also be the main danger at different phases of development in one party or another. It is for each Communist party to decide what danger threatens it more at a given time. . . . Modern revisionism seeks to smear the teaching of Marxism-Leninism, declares that it is 'out-moded', and alleges that it has lost its significance for social progress. . . . The revisionists deny the historical necessity for a proletarian revolution and the dictatorship of the proletariat during the period of transition from capitalism to socialism; reject the principles of proletarianism; and call for the rejection of Leninist principles of party organization and democratic centralism. Above all, they call for the transformation of the Communist party from a militant revolutionary party into some kind of debating society. . . ."

(4) **Relations with Non-Communist Parties.** A section on this theme was worded as follows:

". . . The working class and its vanguard—the Marxist-Leninist party—seek to achieve the socialist revolution by peaceful means. . . . In a number of capitalist countries the working-class today has the opportunity—given a united working-class and people's front, or other workable forms of political co-operation between the different parties and organizations—to unite a majority of the people, win power without civil war, and ensure the transfer of the basic means of production to the hands of the people . . . [The] . . . working-class . . . can secure a firm majority in parliament, transform parliament from an instrument serving the class interests of the bourgeoisie into an instrument serving the working people, launch a non-parliamentary mass struggle, smash the resistance of the reactionary forces, and create the necessary conditions for the peaceful realization of the socialist revolution. . . .

"In the event of the ruling classes resorting to violence against the people, the possibility of non-peaceful transition to socialism should be borne in mind. Leninism teaches, and experience confirms, that the ruling classes never relinquish power voluntarily. In this case the degree of bitterness and the forms of the class struggle will depend not so much on the proletariat as on the resistance put up by the reactionary circles. . . . The possibility of one or another way to socialism depends on the concrete conditions in each country. . . .

"In the struggle for winning power and building socialism, the Communist parties seek co-operation with the socialist parties. Although right-wing socialist party leaders are doing their best to hamper this co-operation, there are increasing opportunities for co-operation between communists and socialists on many issues. The ideological differences between the Communist and socialist parties should not keep them from establishing unity of action on the many pressing issues that confront the working-class movement. . . ."

THE 1960 CONFERENCE

This, the largest conference since the seventh world congress of the Communist International held in 1935, took place in Moscow in November 1960, and was attended by delegations of 81 countries, excluding Yugoslavia, whose League of Communists had not been invited. The conference was not attended by Chairman Mao Tse-tung (Mao Zedong) of the Chinese Communist Party, nor by Palmiro Togliatti, then general secretary of the Italian Communist Party—although both these parties were represented by delegations.

The 1960 conference was faced with the possibility of a split in the international communist movement as a result of the controversy between the Soviet and Chinese parties on questions of theory and policy. The main issues of this controversy may be summarized as follows:

(1) The Soviet party upheld the view, put forward by Nikita Khrushchev (then First Secretary of the party's Central Committee) at its 20th congress in 1956, that Lenin's theory of the inevitability of war under capitalism was no longer valid because of the growing strength of the socialist bloc, the neutral policy pursued by many former colonial countries, and the strength of "anti-war" movements in capitalist countries. Chinese spokesmen, on the other hand, maintained that it was a "naive illusion" to think that war could be avoided before capitalism had been abolished.

(2) The Soviet party emphasized that nuclear war would prove equally disastrous to all concerned, and used this argument in favour of peaceful coexistence between countries with different social systems. The Chinese Communists, however, maintained that China could survive a nuclear war and that a third world war would result in further victories for communism.

(3) The Chinese Communists rejected the policy of peaceful coexistence as involving a rejection of the class struggle and an attitude of "peace at any price".

(4) The Chinese Communists also rejected as "very wrong" the view that nationalist movements in colonial and underdeveloped countries might possibly endanger world peace and should therefore not necessarily be supported by the Soviet Union and international communism.

(5) Soviet theoreticians contended that in underdeveloped countries communists should ally themselves with the "bourgeoisie" in the struggle for national independence, which would prepare the way for the transition to socialism. The Chinese Communists, however, declared in August 1960: "If we view the movement led by the bourgeoisie in colonial countries as the mainstream of the national liberation movement and give full support to it, while ignoring, or expressing contempt for, the anti-imperialist struggle waged by the revolutionary masses, it will in fact mean the adoption of bourgeois viewpoints."

(6) The Chinese Communists did not accept the Soviet view, then expressed by N. Khrushchev, that in certain countries it was possible for Communist parties to attain power by parliamentary means without violent revolution.

(7) Against the accepted Marxist theory that intensive industrialization was an essential prerequisite for the transition from socialism to full communism, the Chinese Communists contended that agricultural expansion was "the one essential base".

(8) The Chinese party continued to uphold the assertion of the 1957 Moscow declaration [see above] that "revisionism" was "the main danger" to the international communist movement and rejected the Soviet party's relaxation (since 1959) of its campaign against the "revisionism" of the Yugoslav Communists.

The declaration of the Moscow conference published on Dec. 5, 1960, reflected the Soviet view, although with some concessions made in its wording to the Chinese position. It contained the following significant passages:

War and Peace. "The aggressive nature of imperialism has not changed, but real forces have appeared that are capable of foiling its plans of aggression. War is not fatally inevitable. . . . World war can be prevented by the joint efforts of the world socialist camp, the international working class, the national liberation movement, all the countries opposing war, and all peace-loving forces. . . . The policy of peaceful coexistence is also favoured by a definite section of the bourgeoisie of the developed capitalist countries, which takes a sober view of the relationship of forces and of the dire consequences of a modern war. . . . But should the imperialist maniacs start war, the peoples will sweep capitalism out of existence and bury it. . . .

"The near future will bring the forces of peace and socialism new successes. The USSR will become the leading industrial power of the world. China will become a mighty industrial state. The socialist system will be turning out more than half the world's industrial product. The peace zone will expand. . . . In these conditions a real possibility will have arisen of excluding world war from the life of society even before socialism achieves complete victory on earth, with capitalism still existing in a part of the world. . . .

"Peaceful coexistence of countries with different social systems does not mean conciliation of the socialist and bourgeois ideologies. On the contrary, it implies intensification of the struggle of the working class, of all the Communist parties, for the triumph of socialist ideas. But ideological and political disputes between states must not be settled through war. . . ."

Colonial and Under-developed Countries. "Communists have always recognized the progressive, revolutionary significance of national liberation wars. . . . The peoples of the colonial countries win their independence both through armed struggle and by non-military methods, depending on the specific conditions in the country concerned. . . .

"The urgent tasks of national rebirth facing the countries that have shaken off the colonial yoke cannot be effectively accomplished unless a determined struggle is waged against imperialism and the remnants of feudalism by all the patriotic forces of the nation, united in a single national democratic front. . . . The alliance of the working class and the peasantry is the most important force in winning and defending national independence, accomplishing far-reaching democratic transformations, and ensuring social progress. . . . The extent to which the national bourgeoisie participates in the liberation struggle depends to no small degree upon its strength and stability. . . . In present conditions the national bourgeoisie of the colonial and dependent countries unconnected with imperialist circles is objectively interested in the accomplishment of the principal tasks of the anti-imperialist, anti-feudal revolution, and therefore retains the capacity of participating in the revolutionary struggle against imperialism and feudalism. In that sense it is progressive. But it is unstable, and is inclined to compromise with imperialism and feudalism. . . .

"The socialist countries are true and sincere friends of the peoples fighting for liberation and of those who have thrown off the imperialist yoke. While rejecting on principle any interference in the internal affairs of young national states, they consider it their internationalist duty to help the peoples in strengthening their independence. . . ."

Moving on to another major area of international communist policy, the declaration also called for joint action on a national and international scale between Communist and social democratic parties in support of complete disarmament under international control, the abolition of military bases on foreign soil, assistance to the nationalist movements in colonial and dependent countries, and the improvement of living standards.

Forms of Transition to Socialism. "The imperialist reactionaries", the declaration continued, "intimidate the masses by alleging that the communists need wars between states to overthrow the capitalist system and establish a socialist system. The Communist parties emphatically reject this slander. The fact that both World Wars, which were started by the imperialists, ended in socialist revolutions by no means implies that the way to social revolution is necessarily through world war. . . . The choice of its social system is the inalienable right of the people of each country. Socialist revolution is not an item of export, and cannot be imposed from without. . . .

"Today in a number of capitalist countries the working class, headed by its vanguard, has the opportunity . . . to unite a majority of the people, win state power without civil war, and ensure the transfer of the basic means of production to the hands of the people. . . . The working class can defeat the reactionary anti-popular forces, secure a firm majority in parliament . . . and create the necessary conditions for peaceful realization of the socialist revolution. . . . In the event of the exploiting classes resorting to violence against the people, the possibility of non-peaceful transition to socialism should be borne in mind. . . . The actual possibility of the one or the other way of transition to socialism in each individual country depends on the concrete historical conditions."

Revisionism and Dogmatism. After condemning "the personality cult, which shackles creative thought and initiative", the declaration denounced "the Yugoslav variety of international opportunism" and asserted that "further exposure of the leaders of the Yugoslav revisionists, and active struggle to safeguard the communist and working-class movement from the anti-Leninist ideas of the Yugoslav revisionists, remains an essential task of the Marxist-Leninist parties". It repeated the formula of the 1957 declaration that "revisionism . . . remains the main danger" but that "dogmatism and sectarianism in theory and practice can also become the main danger at some stage of development of individual parties", and called for "a determined struggle" against both. In conclusion, the declaration referred to the Soviet party as "the universally recognized vanguard of the world communist movement", and described the decisions of its 20th congress as initiating "a new stage in the world communist movement".

Intensification of the Sino-Soviet Dispute

During 1961 China concluded agreements with Albania providing for increased trade between the two countries and including a declaration on the two Governments' "complete agreement on ideological questions". During the same year Albania's relations with the Soviet Union began to deteriorate, and at the 22nd congress of the Soviet Communist Party on Oct. 17–31, 1961, Khrushchev openly broke with Albania, alleging that its leaders had "begun to depart from the common agreed line of the communist movement of the whole world on major issues" and were "using the same methods as were current in our country at the time of the personality cult" (i.e. under Stalin).

The break between the USSR and China was widened at this congress, with Chou En-lai (Zhou Enlai, the Chinese Foreign Minister) leaving Moscow before the end of the conference after blaming the Soviet party for "laying bare a dispute between fraternal parties or fraternal countries, openly in the face of the enemy"— which, he said, was "not a serious Marxist-Leninist attitude".

The congress was followed by the breaking-off of diplomatic relations between the USSR and Albania and open expression of support for Albania by the Chinese Communist Party in December 1961.

During the years 1962–64 the Sino-Soviet conflict intensified. The Chinese Government disapproved of N. Khrushchev's approaches to Yugoslavia in May 1962; of his compromise with the USA over the Cuban issue in October 1962; and of Soviet military aid given to India in the Sino-Indian War of October-November 1962.

On June 14, 1963, the Chinese party approved a letter to the Soviet party, in which it put forward "25 points" for discussion at talks to be held in Moscow. These points included:

(3) "If the general line of the international communist movement is one-sidedly reduced to 'peaceful coexistence', 'peaceful competition' and 'peaceful transition', this is to violate the revolutionary principles of the 1957 declaration and the 1960 statement. . . .

(4) "The fundamental contradictions in the contemporary world . . . are: The contradiction between the socialist camp and the imperialist camp; the contradiction between the proletariat and the bourgeoisie in the capitalist countries; the contradiction between the oppressed nations and imperialism; and the contradictions among imperialist countries and among monopoly capitalist groups. . . .

(5) "The following erroneous views should be repudiated . . .: (a) The view which blots out the class content of the contradiction between the socialist and imperialist camps . . .; (b) the view which recognizes only the contradiction between the socialist and imperialist camps . . .; (c) the view which maintains . . . that the contradiction between the proletariat and the bourgeoisie can be resolved without a proletarian revolution in each country and that the contradiction between the oppressed nations and imperialism can be resolved without revolution . . .; (d) the view which denies that the development of the inherent contradictions in the contemporary capitalist world inevitably leads to a new situation in which the imperialist countries are locked in an intense struggle, and asserts that the contradictions among the imperialist countries can be reconciled

or even eliminated by 'international agreements among the big monopolies'; and (e) the view which maintains that the contradiction between the two world systems of socialism and capitalism will automatically disappear in the course of 'economic competition', . . . and that a 'world without wars', a new world of 'all-round co-operation', will appear. . . .

(9) "The oppressed nations and peoples of Asia, Africa and Latin America are faced with the urgent task of fighting imperialism and its lackeys. . . . In these areas extremely broad sections of the population refuse to be slaves of imperialism. They include not only the workers, peasants, intellectuals and petty bourgeoisie, but also the patriotic national bourgeoisie and even certain kings, princes and aristocrats. . . . The proletariat and its party must . . . organize a broad united front against imperialism. . . . The proletarian party should maintain its ideological, political and organizational independence and insist on the leadership of the revolution. The proletarian party and the revolutionary people must learn to master all forms of struggle, including armed struggle. . . . The policy of the proletarian party should be . . . to unite with the bourgeoisie, in so far as they tend to be progressive, anti-imperialist and anti-feudal, but to struggle against their reactionary tendencies to compromise and collaborate with imperialism and the forces of feudalism. . . .

(10) "In the imperialist and capitalist countries the proletarian revolution and the dictatorship of the proletariat are essential. . . . It is wrong to refuse to use parliamentary and other legal forms of struggle when they can and should be used. However, if a Marxist-Leninist party falls into legalism or parliamentary cretinism, confining the struggle within the limits permitted by the bourgeoisie, this will inevitably lead to renouncing the proletarian revolution and the dictatorship of the proletariat.

(11) "Marx and Lenin did raise the possibility that revolutions may develop peacefully. But, as Lenin pointed out, the peaceful development of revolution is an opportunity 'very seldom to be met with in the history of revolution'. As a matter of fact, there is no historical precedent for peaceful transition from capitalism to socialism. . . . The proletarian party must never base its thinking, its policies for revolution and its entire work on the assumption that the imperialists and reactionaries will accept peaceful transformation. . . .

(14) ". . . Certain persons now actually hold that it is possible to bring about 'a world without weapons, without armed forces, and without wars' through 'general and complete disarmament' while the system of imperialism and of the exploitation of man by man still exists. This is sheer illusion. . . .

(15) "The emergence of nuclear weapons does not and cannot resolve the fundamental contradictions in the contemporary world, does not and cannot alter the law of class struggle, and does not and cannot change the nature of imperialism and reaction. It cannot, therefore, be said that with the emergence of nuclear weapons the possibility and the necessity of social and national revolutions have disappeared, or that the basic principles of Marxism-Leninism, and especially the theories of proletarian revolution and the dictatorship of the proletariat . . . have become out-moded. . . .

(21) "Relations between socialist countries, whether large or small, and whether more developed or less developed economically, must be based on the principles of complete equality. . . .

(22) "If the principle of independence and equality is accepted in relations among fraternal parties, then it is impermissible for any party to place itself above others, to interfere in their internal affairs and to adopt patriarchal ways in relations with them. . . ."

The central committee of the Soviet party answered the above "25 points" on July 14, 1963.

In their reply the Soviet party blamed the Chinese for having themselves caused the deterioration in relations and described their views as "erroneous". In particular, the Soviet party claimed that the Chinese "obviously underestimated the whole danger of nuclear war", and also the importance of "the struggle for disarmament". The Soviet party emphasized that "the nuclear bomb does not distinguish between the imperialists and working people" and that it would not be possible, as suggested by Mao Tse-tung, "to build a bright future on the ruins of a destroyed imperialism".

The Soviet party also accused the Chinese leaders of "organizing and supporting various anti-party groups of renegades", including dissident communist groups in various countries, and of having "pushed the Albanian leaders on to the road of open struggle against the Soviet Union".

Following bitter polemics in the press of the two countries, the Chinese party rejected on May 7, 1964, a Soviet proposal for a world conference to be held in the autumn of 1964 to end the dispute.

After N. Khrushchev's removal from office on Oct. 14, 1964, the dispute was aggravated by disagreements on communist policy on Vietnam during 1965. The Chinese party refused to attend a meeting of Communist parties in Moscow in March 1965 and also to send a delegation to the 23rd Soviet party congress in March–April 1966.

During the period of the "Great Proletarian Cultural Revolution" in China the conflict was further intensified, and on Dec. 13, 1966, the Soviet party for the first time condemned the policy of "Mao Tse-tung and his group", whose actions, it said, had "nothing in common with Marxism-Leninism" and "objectively" assisted imperialism. Further fierce criticism of Mao Tse-tung and his policies followed in the Soviet press from February 1967 onwards.

The Soviet invasion of Czechoslovakia on Aug. 20–21, 1968, was condemned by Chou En-lai on Aug. 23 as "the most barefaced and typical specimen of fascist power politics played by the Soviet revisionist clique against its so-called allies"—a clique which had, he claimed, "degenerated into a gang of social-imperialists and social-fascists". At the same time Chinese statements strongly denounced the Dubcek regime in Czechoslovakia for its "revisionism" and its failure to organize armed resistance to the invasion.

The Sino-Soviet dispute was further aggravated by Chinese claims on Soviet territory, arising out of the fact that large areas formerly under Chinese suzerainty had been annexed by Tsarist Russia between 1858 and 1881.

These areas included over 75,000 square miles north and west of Lake Balkhash, ceded to Russia in 1864 and 1881; 230,000 square miles of territory north of the river Amur, acquired by Russia under the Treaty of Aigun (1858); and 150,000 square miles east of the Ussuri river, incorporated into the Russian Empire under the Treaty of Peking (1860).

China regarded these treaties as being two of nine "unequal treaties" which were forced upon the Chinese Empire between 1842 and 1901. These also included the 1881 Treaty of St. Petersburg confirming Russia's annexations of 1864; the 1895 Treaty of Shimonoseki, under which Japan obtained control of Taiwan (Formosa) and the Pescadores; and an 1898 Convention on the expansion of the territory of Hong Kong.

In addition, the Soviet Union and China disagreed on the exact demarcation of their common frontier, and boundary negotiations were intermittently conducted by the two Governments from 1964 onwards without reaching final conclusions.

Meanwhile armed clashes had taken place along the border between March and August 1969, and the press and radio on both sides continued their polemics from time to time.

Despite their dispute, negotiations between the two Governments led to (a) an agreement concluded on Aug. 8, 1969, on navigation on the Amur and Ussuri rivers, and (b) a trade and payments agreement concluded on Nov. 22, 1970.

The Chinese Government announced on April 3, 1979, that it would not extend its 1950 treaty of friendship, alliance and mutual assistance with the Soviet Union, due to expire in April 1980.

Since then the Sino-Soviet border dispute has remained basically unresolved, although the two sides have recently improved their bilateral relations.

In a speech made in Tashkent on March 24, 1982, L. Brezhnev (then President of the Presidium of the Supreme Soviet) said inter alia that the Soviet Union had no territorial claims against China and was ready to continue talks on "existing border questions" and "possible measures to strengthen mutual trust in the border area", but he also said that many aspects of the policy of the Chinese leaders (and especially their foreign policy) were "at variance with socialist principles and standards". He added: "We have not denied, and do not deny now, the existence of a socialist system in China."

During 1982 the Chinese side repeatedly listed three "major obstacles" to improved relations with the Soviet Union—the deployment of large numbers of Soviet troops on the Chinese border and in Mongolia, the Soviet intervention in Afghanistan, and Soviet support for the Vietnamese occupation of Kampuchea.

President Brezhnev, on the other hand, said in Baku on Sept. 26, 1982: "We would deem it very important to achieve a normalization and gradual improvement of relations between the USSR and the People's Republic of China on a basis which I would describe as common sense, mutual respect and mutual advantage."

Yury Andropov, L. Brezhnev's successor, said on Nov. 22, 1982, that the USSR wished to "improve relations with all socialist states, including our great neighbour, the People's Republic of China".

In response to Soviet allegations (made on Jan. 14, 1983) that China claimed 1,500,000 square kilometres of Soviet territory (said to have been annexed by the Russian Tsars under "unequal treaties"), it was officially stated in China on Jan. 23: "China has no territorial claims whatsoever on the Soviet Union, nor does it demand the return of territories ceded to Tsarist Russia under a series of unequal treaties, but stands for an overall solution to the border issue through peaceful negotiations by taking into consideration the actual conditions, and on the basis of the above-mentioned treaties. . . ."

However, on Dec. 7, 1983, the Chinese Foreign Minister (Wu Xueqian) said that talks held on normalizing relations with the USSR had made no headway because the Soviets refused to discuss the "three obstacles".

The "Brezhnev Doctrine"

Leonid Brezhnev, then General Secretary of the Soviet Communist Party, in an address to a Polish United Workers' Party congress in Warsaw on Nov. 12, 1968, put forward the doctrine of "limited sovereignty" in an attempt to justify the Soviet intervention in Czechoslovakia earlier in that year.

L. Brezhnev declared inter alia:

"When internal and external forces that are hostile to socialism try to turn the development of some socialist country towards the restoration of a capitalist regime, when socialism in that country and the socialist community as a whole are threatened, it becomes not only a problem of the country concerned, but a common problem and concern of all socialist countries. Naturally, an action such as military assistance to a fraternal country designed to avert the threat to the social system is an extraordinary step, dictated by necessity." Such a step, he added, "may be taken only in case of direct actions of the enemies of socialism within a country and outside it, actions threatening the common interests of the socialist camp".

In China, Marshal Lin Piao (Lin Biao, then party vice-chairman) commented on the theory on April 1, 1969, in his report to the ninth congress of the Chinese Communist Party, and prophesied that the Soviet Government would be overthrown by its own people.

"Since Brezhnev came to power," he said, ". . . the Soviet revisionist renegade clique has been practising social-imperialism and social-fascism more frantically than ever. Internally, it has intensified its suppression of the Soviet people and speeded up the all-round restoration of capitalism. Externally, it has stepped up its collusion with US imperialism and its suppression of the revolutionary struggles of the people of various countries, intensified its control over and its exploitation of various East European countries and the People's Republic of Mongolia, and intensified its threat of aggression against China. . . .

"In order to justify its aggression and plunder, the Soviet revisionist renegade clique trumpets the so-called theory of 'limited sovereignty', the theory of 'international dictatorship' and the theory of 'socialist community'. What does all this stuff mean? It means that your sovereignty is 'limited', while his is unlimited. . . . We firmly believe that the proletariat and the broad masses of the people in the Soviet Union, with their glorious revolutionary tradition, will surely rise and overthrow this clique consisting of a handful of renegades."

In another passage of his report, in which he reaffirmed the party's views on the inevitability of war, Marshal Lin Piao opposed the "social-imperialist" countries (i.e. the USSR) to the socialist countries (i.e. China and Albania), and suggested that a conflict existed in the former between the proletariat and the "bourgeoisie", implying that the USSR had ceased to be a socialist country.

L. Brezhnev, however, denied during a visit to Yugoslavia on Sept. 22, 1971, that the so-called "doctrine of limited sovereignty" existed. The story of this "doctrine", he said, had been circulated by forces intent upon "driving a wedge between Yugoslavia and the USSR", and it was not worth wasting time on denying "the slanderous inventions".

The 1969 Conference

A further conference of Communist parties in Moscow on June 5–17, 1969, with 66 of the 75 parties taking part, approved a document entitled "Tasks at the present stage of the struggle against imperialism and united action of the Communist and Workers' parties and all anti-imperialist forces".

Parties not taking part in this conference included those of Albania, Iceland, the Netherlands and Yugoslavia.

L. Brezhnev declared on June 7: "We cannot afford to ignore the divergencies existing in the communist movement today". In particular, he attacked the Chinese Communist Party for classifying as "revisionists" the "overwhelming majority of the socialist countries and Communist parties" and for organizing "subversive splinter groups" against these parties. He also accused Maoism of calling for war, instead of for a struggle against war, and of directing its spearhead of foreign policy chiefly "against the Soviet Union and the other socialist countries".

During the conference the Soviet intervention in Czechoslovakia in August 1968 was criticized by representatives of the British, Italian, Spanish and Swedish Communist parties.

The document finally approved by the conference (a) reaffirmed the communist movement's support for the policy of peaceful coexistence of states with different social systems, which did "not contradict the right of any oppressed people to fight for its liberation" (in which context the document called for "all-round support for the heroic Vietnamese people . . . in order to compel US imperialism to withdraw its interventionist troops from Vietnam"); (b) expressed the view that the Communist countries made their "primary contribution to the struggle against capitalism" by their economic development, though it emphasized that this did not mean abandonment of support for revolutionary movements; (c) accepted the possibility of a peaceful transition to socialism in certain countries, while accepting the use of force as inevitable in others; and (d) asserted that there was "no leading centre of the international communist movement" (thus in effect repudiating the 1960 Moscow conference statement that the Soviet party was "the universally recognized vanguard of the world communist movement").

Soviet-Yugoslav Reconciliation

A normalization of relations between the Soviet Union and Yugoslavia—which had been expelled from the Cominform in 1948 [see above]—was effected by a visit to Yugoslavia in May 1955 by a delegation led by Nikita Khrushchev. In a joint Belgrade declaration signed on June 2, 1955, the two sides expressed "their determination to develop their future relations in the spirit of friendly co-operation". This reconciliation was further strengthened by a visit to Moscow by President Tito in June 1956, after N. Khrushchev had included a friendly reference to the Yugoslav leader in his denunciation of the Stalin regime at the 20th congress of the Communist Party of the Soviet Union (CPSU) in February 1956.

An agreement on increased co-operation between the Soviet Union and Yugoslavia in the use of atomic energy for peaceful purposes was signed in Belgrade on Jan. 10, 1963, and trade and co-operation agreements were signed in 1964 and 1965.

However, the 1968 Soviet action in Czechoslovakia was strongly condemned by President Tito, his Government and the League of Communists of Yugoslavia as constituting a violation of the sovereignty of an independent socialist state, and in October 1968 President Tito repudiated L. Brezhnev's "limited sovereignty" doctrine.

Three years later, after an "unofficial friendly visit" to Yugoslavia by L. Brezhnev on Sept. 22–25, 1971, Soviet-Yugoslav relations were again placed on a basis of "equality and mutual respect" as well as "non-interference in internal affairs", as expressed in the Belgrade declaration of 1955 and also a declaration signed in Moscow by the two sides in June 1956. This reconciliation was confirmed during a visit to Moscow by President Tito on July 5–10, 1972.

Conferences of European Communist Parties, 1974–80

The 1974 Conference. A conference of 20 West European Communist parties, held in Brussels on Jan. 26–28, 1974, adopted a political declaration on future policy strategy, in particular with reference to the European Community.

Parties represented at the conference were those of Austria, Belgium, Denmark, Finland, France, the Federal Republic of Germany, Greece, Ireland, Italy, Luxembourg, Portugal, San Marino, Spain, Turkey and the United Kingdom, as well as the Socialist Unity Party of West Berlin, the Cyprus Progressive Party of Working People, the Communist Left Party of Sweden and the Swiss Party of Labour (while the Netherlands Communist Party was represented as an observer and the Norwegian Communist Party did not send a delegate).

In the declaration the parties noted that the Communist parties of the six original member states of the European Communities were "fighting against its monopolistic orientation and also for its democratization", whereas the parties of the three new member countries of the Communities (Denmark, Ireland and the United Kingdom) were "campaigning for complete withdrawal" and those of non-member or associated states "against attempts to include their countries in the sphere of influence of the monopolies which dominate the Communities". Nevertheless the parties reaffirmed that "a joint response to the policy of monopolistic economic integration" was "possible and necessary", and that they intended "to campaign together to secure acceptance, in the light of the problems which confront the peoples of Western Europe as a whole, of solutions which correspond to the interests of all these peoples, as well as for European co-operation which is genuinely democratic, responding to the interests of each of their countries and of all". All participating parties expressed their total opposition to European Communities membership or association for the "fascist regimes" of Europe and condemned any attempt to establish a European Defence Community. The declaration also called for a "broad alliance of all workers' and democratic forces" and for efforts by the parties to seek "convergencies and joint actions and initiatives" with socialist, social-democratic and Christian democratic forces.

Among differences of view which became apparent at the conference was that between the French party, which expressed serious reservations about working within the existing framework of the European Communities, and the Italian party, which stressed the possibility of using the Communities' institutions to further working-class interests.

The 1976 Conference. A conference of European Communist parties held in East Berlin on June 29–30, 1976, was attended by 29 party delegations.

These represented (i) the parties of the Soviet bloc (the CPSU, the Communist parties of Bulgaria, Czechoslovakia and Romania, the Socialist Unity Party of the German Democratic Republic, the Hungarian Socialist Workers' Party and the Polish United Workers' Party), (ii) the League of Communists of Yugoslavia; and (iii) West European Communist parties (of Austria, Belgium, Denmark, Finland, France, the Federal Republic of Germany, Greece—the "exterior" party, Ireland, Italy, Luxembourg, the Netherlands, Norway, Portugal, San Marino, Spain, Turkey and the United Kingdom) as well as the Socialist Unity Party of West Berlin, the Cyprus Progressive Party of the Working People, the Swedish Left Communist Party and the Swiss Party of Labour.

The conference adopted a declaration entitled *For Peace, Security, Co-operation and Social Progress in Europe*, which was a compromise involving acceptance of the principles that the declaration must be approved by all participants; must recognize the complete independence of all Communist parties and their right to decide their own policies; and must not criticize or condemn the policies of the Chinese or any other Communist party. These principles also covered the use of the phrase "international co-operation" in the place of "proletarian internationalism" which was objected to—by a group of parties led by those of France, Italy, Romania, Spain and Yugoslavia—as being associated with the acceptance of Soviet leadership.

During the debate the concept of "proletarian internationalism" and the condemnation of any criticism of the Soviet Union were supported by the Austrian, West German, Greek, Luxembourg, Norwegian, Portuguese and Turkish representatives.

The declaration adopted by the conference stated in its preamble inter alia:

"The participants in the conference emphasize that their parties, on the basis of a political line worked out and adopted by every party in complete independence in accordance with the socio-economic and political conditions and the specific national features prevailing in the country concerned, are firmly resolved to continue waging a consistent struggle in order to achieve the objectives of peace, democracy and social progress. . . . They state with all clarity that the policy of peaceful coexistence, active co-operation between states irrespective of their social systems, and international détente correspond both to the interests of each people as well as to the cause of progress for the whole of mankind, and in no way mean the maintenance of the political and social status quo in the various countries, but on the contrary create optimum conditions for the development of the struggle of the working class. . . .

"The parties participating in the conference . . . will develop their internationalist, comradely and voluntary co-operation and solidarity on the basis of the great ideas of Marx, Engels and Lenin, strictly adhering to the principles of equality and sovereign independence of each party, non-interference in internal affairs, and respect for their free choice of different roads in the struggle for social change of a progressive nature and for socialism. The struggle of each party for socialism in its own country and its responsibility towards the working class and the people of that country are bound up with mutual solidarity among working people of all countries and all progressive moments and peoples. . . ."

Among its concrete proposals the declaration listed (i) measures to be taken to achieve disarmament and security in Europe; (ii) the removal of impediments to full civil and democratic rights (e.g. in Northern Ireland) and the achievement of independence and territorial integrity for Cyprus; and (iii) settlements leading to peace and security in the Middle East, Indo-China, Latin America and southern Africa.

On the other hand adherence to the concepts of "proletarian internationalism", the "dictatorship of the proletariat" and the leadership of the CPSU was expressed by speakers at a conference of Soviet bloc countries held in Sofia (Bulgaria) on Dec. 15–17, 1976, and attended by party officials from the USSR as well as Bulgaria, Cuba, Czechoslovakia, the German Democratic Republic, Hungary, Mongolia, Poland and Romania. (The concept of the "dictatorship of the proletariat" had been abandoned by the French Communist Party in February 1976 and by the Japan Communist Party in July of that year.)

The 1980 Conference. Convened on the initiative of the French Communist Party and the Polish United Workers' Party, a further conference of European Communist parties was held in Paris on April 28–29, 1980, and devoted to the theme of peace and disarmament. It was attended by delegations of six Soviet-bloc parties (those of Bulgaria, Czechoslovakia, the German Democratic Republic, Hungary, Poland and the Soviet Union) and of 14 West European parties (of Austria, Cyprus, Denmark, Finland, France, the Federal Republic of Germany, Greece, Ireland, Luxembourg, Malta, Norway, Portugal, Turkey and West Berlin), while the Belgian Communist Party and the Swiss Party of Labour sent observers. Among those parties not represented were the Romanian Communist Party, the League of Communists of Yugoslavia and the Italian and Spanish Communist parties.

The principal outcome of the conference was the issuing of an appeal for co-operation between "Communists, Socialists, Social Democrats, Christians and believers of other faiths" to promote peace and disarmament, to which end it was stated that Communists were "ready for any dialogue, for any talks and for any joint action".

The specific aims of such co-operation, said the appeal, would be to prevent the deployment of new US nuclear missiles in Europe as decided by NATO; to work for the earliest possible ratification of the SALT II treaty between the Soviet Union and the United States and the continuation of negotiations on a further reduction of strategic armaments; to seek "decisive progress" at the Vienna talks on mutual and balanced force reductions in Europe (MBFR) and the "establishment of nuclear-free zones in our continent"; to ensure "further progress in the implementation by all states of all the provisions of the Helsinki Final Act [i.e. of the 1975 Conference on Security and Co-operation in Europe], especially through complementing political détente with military détente" to work for "the convocation in Warsaw of a European conference on military détente and disarmament"; to "demand the practical implementation of the decisions of the [1978] UN special disarmament session"; and to ensure that the funds thereby released would be used for development purposes.

The Concept of "Eurocommunism"

At the 1976 Sofia conference Bulgarian representatives in particular attacked as "incorrect" the policies of certain West European Communist parties (notably those of France, Italy and Spain), which had become known as "Eurocommunism".

These parties had in recent years openly stated that they favoured a non-violent road to socialism through co-operation with other parties and the achievement of a parliamentary majority by democratic means and even with the retention of a multi-party system.

In 1972 the French Communist Party entered into an electoral agreement with the Socialist and Left Radical parties (but by October 1978 this agreement had effectively lapsed). In November 1975 the party opted for respecting the people's verdict in all circumstances and for ruling out "categorically all recourse to oppression, totalitarianism and personal rule".

For the Italian Communist Party (PCI) its then secretary, Palmiro Togliatti, had stated in June 1956 that the Soviet model could not and should no longer be obligatory for other Communist parties, and of the communist movement he had said: "The whole system is becoming polycentric . . .; we cannot speak of a single guide but rather of progress which is achieved by following paths which are often different." In February 1976 Enrico Berlinguer, the PCI's secretary, declared: "The accession of the working classes to political power can and must be achieved in Italy in a manner fully consistent with democratic institutions, the principles of freedom and the procedures for change embodied in our Constitution." He repeatedly called for the formation of a broadly-based government of "democratic unity" with PCI participation, and the party has sought to come to an understanding with the ruling Christian Democratic Party on a long-term strategy of co-operation. In August 1978 Berlinguer emphasized that Lenin had not excluded "the possibility of a peaceful development of the socialist revolution and of a continuation of a plurality of parties".

For the Spanish party underground leaders called, on Jan. 28, 1976, for a "Spanish road to socialism characterized by democracy and a multi-party system".

In a Madrid Declaration, signed on March 3, 1977, Berlinguer, Georges Marchais (secretary-general of the French Communist Party) and

Santiago Carrillo (then secretary-general of the Communist Party of Spain, PCE) stated that their three parties intended

"To work on behalf of creating a new society on the principle of pluralism of social and political forces, respecting, guaranteeing and developing all collective and individual freedoms; freedom of thought and of the press, association and assembly, demonstration, unrestrained movement of persons in their own country and abroad, the right to unionize, the independence of union organizations and the right to strike, the inviolability of private life, observance of general elections and the possibility of making changes by the majority carried out in a democratic manner, freedom of religion, freedom of culture, freedom to profess various philosophical, cultural and artistic views and trends. . . ."

The declaration continued:

"In the future the three parties also intend to develop international solidarity and friendship on the basis of the independence of each party, equal rights, non-interference, respect for the free choice of their own party and solutions in forming socialist societies suitable to the conditions of each country. This meeting in Madrid is also an opportunity for French, Italian and Spanish Communists to affirm the great significance which they attach to new steps forward on the road to détente and peaceful co-existence, to real progress in the reduction of armaments, to a full realization by all countries of all of the resolutions of the Helsinki Final Act and to a positive outcome of the meeting in Belgrade, to action in support of liquidating the division of Europe into opposing military blocs, to the establishment of new relations between the developed and developing countries, and to a new international economic order.

"In this way the three parties see the prospect for a democratic and independent Europe without military bases and an armaments race and the prospect for a Mediterranean Sea of peace and co-operation between the countries of this region."

The Soviet intervention in Afghanistan in December 1979 was opposed by the Communist parties of Italy, Spain and the United Kingdom, but not by those of France and Portugal. It was also opposed by the parties of Romania and Yugoslavia. The declaration of martial law in Poland on Dec. 13, 1981, was condemned by the Communist parties of Belgium, Greece (i.e. the KKK interior), Italy, the Netherlands, Spain, Sweden and the United Kingdom.

The most outspoken protagonists of Eurocommunism were the Communist parties of Italy (the CPI) and of Spain (the PCE).

From March 1978 to January 1979 the PCI was, under a "historic compromise", part of the official parliamentary majority supporting the Christian Democratic government, but it did not enter this government. Thereafter the PCI sought an accommodation with other left-wing parties (the "third way" or "democratic alternative") but this did not come about.

Relations between the CPI and the Communist Party of China (CPC) had been suspended in 1966, and in 1979 the CPI condemned the Chinese invasion of Vietnam. However, on a visit to China by Enrico Berlinguer (then general secretary of the PCI) it was agreed to resume relations between the two parties "on the basis of complete equality, independence and mutual respect". At the same time E. Berlinguer confirmed that the PCI continued to reject the CPC's thesis of the inevitability of war and the idea of an international united front of China, Japan, Western Europe and the United States against the Soviet Union, and to disapprove of China's offensive against Vietnam.

On Dec. 21, 1981, E. Berlinguer was reported to have said that the Soviet October (1917) revolution had proved itself to be a spent force because it had failed to promote renewal in Poland.

In a 17-page resolution adopted by the PCI central committee on Dec. 29, 1981, it was stressed inter alia that trade unions must be independent, even in a socialist society; democracy and socialism were inextricably linked; the Polish crisis was due to the hierarchical rigidity and dogmatism of the Polish United Workers' (i.e. Communist) Party, the sluggishness, insecurity and wavering of its leadership and the conduct of the other Warsaw Treaty states; the Soviet model of socialism had proved inapplicable to Eastern Europe; the existence of military power blocs should not be used as a pretext for the suppression of demands for freedom; the striving for socialism was a historical necessity and the current crisis called more than ever for the search for new ways to attain socialism; and the PCI maintained normal relations with all communist parties and with socialist, revolutionary and progressive forces without preference for any one partner, on the basis of absolute autonomy regarding ideology or political action.

This resolution was bitterly condemned by the French Communist Party and by the organs of the parties of the Warsaw Treaty states.

Relations between the (Spanish) PCE, and the Communist Party of China, also suspended since 1966, were likewise resumed in 1980. During a visit to China on Nov. 11–25, 1980, Santiago Carrillo (then secretary-general of the PCE) stated inter alia that Spain should not join any military bloc, but Deng Xiao Ping (the Chinese party's chief theoretician and policy-maker) said on Nov. 24 that China had no objection to Spain becoming a member of NATO. (Like the CPI, the PCE had condemned the Chinese invasion of Vietnam.)

By 1981 the PCE was divided into four factions—the Eurocommunists led by S. Carrillo, the "renovators" standing for more forthright endorsement of Eurocommunism, and "Afghans" (a pro-Soviet section) and "Leninists" supporting the theory of the dictatorship of the proletariat. The pro-Soviet group broke away and founded, on Jan. 15, 1984, a new Communist Party, which opposed Spain's entry into the European Community and into NATO.

After the PCE had, with its allied Catalan party, been reduced from 23 to four seats in the Congress of Deputies in the 1982 general elections, S. Carrillo resigned as PCE secretary-general and was on Nov. 7, 1982, succeeded by Gerardo Iglesias, who reaffirmed the party's commitment to Eurocommunism. S. Carrillo, however, continued to be active in the party. Although he advocated independence of Spain from both power blocs he said (on Dec. 15, 1983) that the United States was "the greatest enemy of peace today". By January 1984 his opposition to the policies of G. Iglesias (who intended to form a new broad left-wing front) had led to an open split in the PCE, with supporters of Carrillo forming a separate party in 1985.

In all officially Eurocommunist parties there have been dissident pro-Soviet minorities. The French Communist Party, which had Eurocommunist tendencies between 1966 and 1980, has since reverted to its former pro-Soviet attitude in international affairs.

1980 East Berlin Conference

An "international scientific conference" of representatives of 116 Communist parties, revolutionary organizations and national liberation movements, organized by the Socialist Unity Party (SED) of the German Democratic Republic and the Prague review *Problems of Peace and Socialism*, was held in East Berlin on Oct. 20–24, 1980, on the subject of "the common struggle of the workers' movement and the national liberation movements against imperialism and for social co-operation".

According to Erich Honecker, the General Secretary of the SED, the "three principal revolutionary currents of our time" were "the world socialist system, the workers' movements in capitalist countries and the national liberation movements".

A report by the principal working group of the conference stressed the need "to pursue the struggle against the policy of confrontation followed by imperialism" and to fight for "arms limitation and disarmament", and it denounced in particular "the expansionist and neo-colonialist tendencies of West German imperialism" which was leading the Federal Republic of Germany to support for the nuclear arms race and to the adoption of "a revanchist posture towards the German Democratic Republic and other socialist countries".

At the end of the conference it was admitted (inter alios by Hermann Axen, a member of the Politburo of the SED, and Maxime Granetz, secretary of the central committee of the French Communist Party) that the conference had shown up "differences of conception and of fighting conditions" and also on the role of China.

The Warsaw Treaty Organization

Headquarters of Joint Command: Moscow.

Members. Bulgaria, Czechoslovakia, the German Democratic Republic, Hungary, Poland, Romania and the Soviet Union.

History. The East European Mutual Assistance Treaty, or Warsaw Pact as it is generally known, is the counterpart, in Communist Eastern Europe, of the North Atlantic Treaty in the West. The 20-year *Treaty of Friendship, Co-operation and Mutual Assistance* was signed in Warsaw on May 14, 1955, by Albania, Bulgaria, Czechoslovakia, the German Democratic Republic, Hungary, Poland, Romania and the Soviet Union. It came into force in the following month.

The first move towards a military alliance of the Communist bloc countries in Europe was made at a conference held in Moscow from Nov. 29 to Dec. 2, 1954, and attended by the eight countries listed above. At this conference on "the safeguarding of peace and collective security in Europe", the London and Paris Agreements establishing the Western European Union and providing for West Germany's entry into NATO [see page 143], were condemned as encouraging a revival of German militarism. A declaration published at the end of the conference stated that, if the Paris Agreements were ratified, the countries represented at the Moscow conference would again meet "to adopt measures for safeguarding their security".

On March 21, 1955, agreement was announced between the eight nations on the principles of a mutual defence treaty and the organization of a unified command.

Six days after the Paris Agreements came into force, representatives of the eight nations met again in Warsaw, where they signed a treaty of mutual assistance and decided on the creation of a unified military command for their armed forces with the exception of those of the German Democratic Republic.

The Warsaw Treaty

The preamble to the treaty reiterates the criticism of the Paris Agreements as creating a danger of renewed war through the re-militarization of West Germany.

The principal provisions of the treaty are:

"**Art. 1.** The contracting parties undertake, in accordance with the UN Charter, to refrain in their international relations from the threat or use of force, and to settle their international disputes by peaceful means so as not to endanger international peace and security.

"**Art. 2.** The contracting parties declare their readiness to take part, in a spirit of sincere co-operation, in all international undertakings designed to safeguard international peace and security, and to use all their energies for the realization of these aims. Moreover, they shall work for the adoption, in agreement with other states desiring to co-operate in this matter, of effective measures towards a general reduction of armaments and the prohibition of atomic, hydrogen and other weapons of mass destruction.

"**Art. 3.** The contracting parties shall consult among themselves on all important international questions relating to their common interests. In the interests of organizing their joint defence, and of upholding peace and security, the contracting parties shall immediately consult together whenever, in the opinion of any of them, there has arisen the threat of an armed attack on one or several states that are signatories of the treaty.

"**Art. 4.** In the event of an armed attack in Europe on one or several states that are signatories of the treaty by any state or group of states, each party to this treaty shall, in the exercise of the right to individual or collective self-defence in accordance with Article 51 of the UN Charter, render the state or states so attacked immediate assistance, individually and in agreement with other states parties to this treaty, by all the means it may consider necessary, including the use of armed force. The parties to this treaty shall immediately consult among themselves on the necessary joint measures to be adopted for the purpose of restoring and upholding international peace and security.

In accordance with the UN Charter, the Security Council shall be advised of the measures taken on the basis of this article. These measures shall be discontinued as soon as the Security Council has taken the necessary steps to restore and uphold international peace and security.

"**Art. 5.** The contracting parties have agreed to set up a unified command to which certain elements of their armed forces shall be allocated by agreement among the parties, and which shall function on the basis of jointly defined principles. They shall also take other agreed measures to strengthen their defensive capacity, in order to safeguard the peaceful labour of their peoples, to guarantee the inviolability of their frontiers and territories, and to provide safeguards against possible aggression.

"**Art. 6.** For the purpose of holding the consultations provided for in the present treaty between the states parties thereto, and for considering problems arising out of the implementation of this treaty, a Political Consultative Committee shall be formed in which each state party to this treaty shall be represented by a member of the government, or any other specially appointed representative. This committee may set up any auxiliary organs which may be necessary.

"**Art. 7.** The contracting parties undertake not to participate in any coalitions and alliances, and not to conclude any agreements, the purposes of which would be at variance with those of the present treaty. They declare that their obligations under existing international treaties are not at variance with the provisions of the present treaty.

"**Art. 8.** The contracting parties declare that they will act in a spirit of friendship and co-operation with the object of furthering and strengthening the economic and cultural ties between them, adhering to the principles of mutual respect for their independence and sovereignty, and of non-interference in their internal affairs.

"**Art. 9.** This treaty may be open for accession by other states—irrespective of their social and state systems—who declare their readiness to assist the efforts of the peace-loving states for the purpose of safeguarding the peace and security of nations. . . .

"**Art. 11.** The present treaty shall remain in force for 20 years. For contracting parties which do not, one year before the expiration of that term, give notice of termination of the treaty to the Government of the Polish People's Republic, the treaty shall remain in force for a further 10 years. In the event of the establishment of a system of collective security in Europe and the conclusion for that purpose of a general European treaty concerning collective security, a goal which the contracting parties shall steadfastly strive to achieve, the present treaty shall cease to have effect as from the date on which the general European treaty comes into force."

Formation of Unified Military Command

The decisions of the eight nations relating to the creation of a unified military command were contained in a separate statement declaring inter alia that:

(1) Questions relating to the joint force would be considered by the Political Consultative Committee set up by the Warsaw Treaty.
(2) Ministers of Defence and military leaders would have command of the armed forces of each state allotted to the joint armed forces, and would act as deputies of the Commander-in-Chief.
(3) A General Staff, with its headquarters in Moscow, would include representatives of the general staffs of all the participating countries.
(4) Deployment of the joint armed forces in the territories of member states would be carried out "in accordance with the requirements of mutual defence and by agreement between these states".
(5) The participation of the German Democratic Republic would be examined later.

At the first meeting of the Political Consultative Committee on Jan. 27–28, 1956, it was decided to incorporate contingents of a new East German Army in the joint command of the Warsaw Treaty powers.

Political Consultative Committee

Other important decisions taken at the first meeting of the Political Consultative Committee related to the organization of the committee itself. It was decided that (i) the committee would meet as often as necessary, but at least twice a year (meetings have, in fact, been less

frequent); and (ii) two subsidiary bodies—a Permanent Commission to make recommendations on foreign policy, and a Secretariat—should be set up.

Delegations sent by member countries to the Political Consultative Committee generally include the First Secretary of the Party, the Chairman of the Council of Ministers, the Minister of Defence and the Foreign Minister of each country.

The Political Consultative Committee decided in Budapest on March 17, 1969, to endorse new statutes on:

(1) The permanent committee of member-countries' Defence Ministers;
(2) the joint supreme command;
(3) the appointment of deputy supreme commanders from the national general staffs to the joint supreme command;
(4) participation of generals and other officers from member countries in the various commands of the armed forces in proportion to the member countries' share in the combined forces; and
(5) the establishment of a co-ordinating authority for warfare and types of armament.

Early Developments

Membership. Although the membership of the Warsaw Treaty Organization has not formally changed since the treaty's inception in 1955, one member, Albania, did not participate in the activities of the organization after the severance of relations with the Soviet Union in 1961, and announced its withdrawal from the Warsaw Pact on Sept. 12, 1968, on the ground that by the Soviet invasion of Czechoslovakia on Aug. 20–21, 1968, the Pact had been turned "from a treaty of defence against imperialist aggression into an aggressive treaty against the socialist countries themselves".

Hungary briefly withdrew from the Warsaw Pact on Oct. 31, 1956, at the time of the popular uprising in Hungary, but returned to the organization under the Soviet-oriented regime which replaced the revolutionary government after the insurrection had been put down.

Declarations and Communiqués. A considerable number of declarations and communiqués have been issued by the Political Consultative Committee, embodying the views of the Warsaw Pact organization. The most significant of these are listed below:

January 1956. A joint declaration, issued after the meeting held on Jan. 27–28, contained the recommendations that neither East nor West Germany should possess atomic weapons, and that NATO and the Warsaw Treaty Powers should sign a collective security treaty.
May 1958. Documents published after the meeting on May 24 included the draft of a proposed non-aggression pact between the Warsaw Treaty Organization and NATO.
August 1961. On Aug. 13 the text of a communiqué was issued in which the member countries of the Warsaw Pact "addressed to the . . . Government of the German Democratic

Republic a proposal to establish such control on the borders of West Berlin as would securely block the way for subversive activities against the socialist countries", thus advocating the building of the wall between East and West Berlin.

July 1966. Two important declarations were issued after the meeting of July 4–6:

(1) *Declaration on Strengthening Peace and Security in Europe.* This included proposals for the recognition of peaceful coexistence; for the relaxation of military tension in Europe, towards which all military alliances should be simultaneously dissolved; for the setting-up of nuclear-free zones; for a German peace settlement; and for a general European conference on European co-operation and security.

(2) *Declaration on the Aggression of the USA in Vietnam.*

Developments, 1969–1986

1969 Budapest Meeting. At a meeting held in Budapest on March 17, 1969, the Political Consultative Committee approved a reorganization of the Warsaw Treaty Organization and its military structure, involving the establishment of several new bodies.

(1) A **Committee of Defence Ministers** was to act as a permanent organ and to meet annually, with each member country providing the chairman and the venue in turn, and with the task of considering a report by the Commander-in-Chief of the Joint Armed Forces.

(2) A **Military Council** would function as a consultative committee and be composed of national chiefs of staff or Deputy Defence Ministers with the status of Deputy Commanders-in-Chief of the Joint Armed Forces. This Council was to meet generally twice a year in each member country in turn and with the Commander-in-Chief of the Joint Armed Forces in the chair.

(3) A **Technical Committee of the Joint Armed Forces** was set up at the same time.

As a result of these changes the Joint Command of the Armed Forces (set up in 1955 under the general supervision of the Political Consultative Council) consisted of the Commander-in-Chief, a Chief of Staff and First Deputy Commander-in-Chief, and all the members of the Military Council as Deputy Commanders-in-Chief.

1974 Warsaw Meeting. At a meeting of the Political Consultative Committee in Warsaw on April 17–18, 1974, the participants stated that they were "ready to disband the Warsaw Treaty Organization simultaneously with the disbanding of the North Atlantic Treaty Organization (NATO) or, as an initial step, the liquidation of their military organization". However, they also declared that "as long as the NATO bloc exists and effective disarmament measures have not been implemented, the Warsaw Treaty countries will consider it necessary to strengthen their defences and to develop close co-operation among themselves in the sphere".

1976 Bucharest Meeting. At a further meeting, held in Bucharest on Nov. 25–26, 1976, the Political Consultative Committee set up a Committee of Foreign Ministers as a permanent organ, in parallel with the Committee of Defence Ministers, with consultative functions, its decisions having to be reached by consensus and to be approved by the legislatures of each member state.

A Combined General Staff, set up in 1955 with headquarters in Moscow, and composed of representatives of the organization's seven member states, was given the functions of serving the meetings of both the Military Council and of the Committee of Foreign Ministers, and of planning and evaluating manoeuvres and exercises of the Joint Armed Forces.

At the same time the organization's Joint Secretariat (set up in Moscow in January 1956) was given a higher status by being charged with servicing the Committee of Foreign Ministers and placed under a Soviet director-general.

At the 1976 Bucharest meeting the Political Consultative Committee also adopted a lengthy declaration "for fresh advances in international relaxation, the strengthening of security and the development of co-operation in Europe" as well as a draft treaty designed to promote disarmament and to be submitted to the participants in the 1975 (Helsinki) Conference on Security and Co-operation in Europe [see pages 268–79].

In the declaration it was stated that, following the East Berlin conference of European Communist and Workers' parties in June 1976 [see above], the political atmosphere in Europe was "increasingly being freed of the remnants and vestiges of the cold war". The declaration continued, however: "The cause of strengthening peace in Europe, like universal peace and the process of détente, also encounters big difficulties. There are still forces of reaction, militarism and revanchism which seek to create situations of conflict, spur on the arms race, seek to call in question the sovereignty of states and the inviolability of existing frontiers. ... These forces provoke intervention in the domestic affairs of states and they would like to dictate to the peoples which internal system must exist in this or that country and which parties can or cannot take part in governmental activities. ..."

The declaration went on: "In our time peace and security in Europe are indivisible, they cannot be a question of choice. There is no sane alternative to the policy of détente; it is needed equally by all states, irrespective of their social system. This is the firm and immutable point of departure of the Warsaw Treaty member countries in all their foreign policy actions."

In connexion with disarmament, the responsibility for the continuing arms race was laid on "the most aggressive imperialist circles and world reaction", and it was asserted: "If our countries have to take steps to strengthen their armed forces ... this is done exclusively in the interest of the reliable defence of the peaceful labour of our peoples and to deter the forces of militarism and war."

After reiterating previously-made proposals for general disarmament, including a call for a special session of the UN General Assembly on disarmament, the declaration went on: "The conclusion of a world treaty on the renunciation of force in international relationships could be a major step forward in strengthening the relaxation of world tensions and world peace." Such a treaty, it was stated, had been submitted for discussion by the United Nations, and the Warsaw Treaty member countries were ready to discuss and to sign it.

Moreover, the participants in the meeting again expressed their readiness to "disband the Warsaw Treaty Organization simultaneously with the disbandment of the North Atlantic Treaty Organization and to abolish their military organizations as the first step". The declaration continued: "They urge all states not to undertake any action that could lead to the expansion of existing closed groupings and military political alliances, or to the establishment of new ones. The simultaneous suspension of Article 9 in the Warsaw Treaty and Article 10 in the North Atlantic Treaty [see page 204], which allow the expansion of the number of participants by the acceptance of new states, could be a practical move in this direction."

The declaration also called for the removal of all remaining "artificial barriers" to the development of mutually profitable economic co-operation between states on the European continent, in particular in the fields mentioned in the Final Act of the Helsinki conference. The participants in the meeting further urged "the restructuring of international economic relationships on a just democratic foundation and on the basis of equality for all states, big and small, socialist and capitalist, industrialized and developing". However, the declaration added: "It has been discovered that certain forces wish to use the development of . . . contacts [between East and West] for purposes that are hostile to understanding and friendship between peoples, and to interfere in the domestic affairs of states. The states participating in the Warsaw Treaty Organization find it necessary to reaffirm that this is a road without a future and that they reject it."

Of co-operation among the socialist states the declaration stated that the Warsaw Treaty member countries reaffirmed "their resolve constantly to strengthen mutual co-operation on the basis of Marxism-Leninism and international solidarity, respect for equality and sovereignty of each state, non-intervention in internal affairs and comradely mutual understanding".

The *draft treaty* contained the following provisions:

Art. 1. All participants of the Helsinki conference would pledge themselves "not to be the first to use nuclear weapons, one against the other, either on land, on the sea, in the air or in outer space".

Art. 2. This commitment would apply "not only to the territory of the states but also to their armed forces in whatever area of the world they may be".

Art. 3. The treaty would be for an unlimited period.

Art. 4. The treaty would be open for signature by any state which signed the Final Act of the Helsinki conference.

Art. 5. The treaty would "enter into force for each of the contracting parties from the time of deposition of its instruments of ratification".

(The NATO Foreign Ministers, however, rejected on Dec. 10, 1976, both the above draft treaty and the proposal for "freezing" the membership of the two military alliances on the ground that they were "a diversionary tactic designed to divert attention from the Soviet Union's poor record in implementing the agreements of the Helsinki conference—notably the provisions for free movement and creating confidence".)

1978 Moscow Meeting. A meeting of the Political Consultative Committee held in Moscow on Nov. 22-23, 1978, unanimously adopted a *Moscow Declaration* on the international situation, which was to be circulated within the United Nations and to be brought to the notice of the participants in the 1975 Helsinki conference (CSCE). The main points of this declaration were as follows:

The declaration stated that discussions at the meeting had centred on "further steps in the struggle to develop the process of détente and disarmament". Significant changes for the better had taken place on the continent of Europe with regard to strengthening security and developing co-operation, and this had been facilitated by the development of relations between the states of the continent in the spirit of the principles contained in the CSCE Final Act and by the general recognition of the existing frontiers between the European states and their inviolability. The trend towards the relaxation of international tension had emerged and had begun to have an impact on the general development of world affairs.

After stating that "the Warsaw Treaty countries attach great importance to attainment of USSR-USA accords on strategic arms limitation" and stressing the "tremendous importance" of the early conclusion of Soviet-US talks on the second agreement on the limitation of strategic offensive arms (SALT II) and the subsequent conclusion of new agreements on a reduction of these arms with the participation of other nuclear powers, the declaration called for the implementation of the following measures: (i) The conclusion of a world treaty on the non-use of force in international relations which would commit all states to renouncing the threat or use of force and would include a ban on the use of nuclear weapons; (ii) the strict observance by all CSCE states of a commitment not to use or threaten force in their relations with one another; (iii) the implementation of a proposal that the CSCE states would commit themselves not to be the first to use nuclear weapons against each other, that the NATO and Warsaw Treaty states should not increase the number of participants in their alliances, that the scale of military exercises by the respective sides in Europe should be limited to the level of 50,000-60,000 men, and that the measures of trust on which agreement was reached at the Helsinki conference should also be applied to the area of the Mediterranean; and (iv) the reinforcement of security guarantees for non-nuclear states, including the renunciation of the use of nuclear weapons against states which did not possess them and did not have them on their own territory, and the renunciation of the deployment of nuclear weapons on the territories of states where there were none at present.

Further, the declaration called on all the states and peoples of the world (i) "to press for holding early negotiations between the five nuclear powers—the USSR, the USA, Britain, France and China—in order to remove nuclear weapons of all types from the arsenals of states and turn nuclear energy to peaceful uses only"; (ii) "to insist firmly that the countries possessing the most considerable military and economic potential, primarily the five powers which are permanent members of the UN Security Council [i.e. the five nuclear powers] . . . , should reach agreement without delay on a reduction of their military budgets by a certain percentage or by magnitudes of the same order, as a first step, for the next three years"; (iii) "to step up the efforts of states and governments with a view to the earliest conclusion of the current talks on the limitation and cessation of the arms race along its main lines, and to pool efforts by all states in the drafting and implementation of disarmament measures"; and (iv) "undeviatingly to pursue the policy of peaceful coexistence".

The declaration also called for an end to the "last vestiges of colonialism" and to national and racial oppression, a restructuring of international economic relations on a just and democratic basis, and the establishment of a "new international economic order".

With regard to human rights, the declaration said that "dangerous trends . . . are engendered by the policy of imperialist circles . . . to try to use the problem of human rights for interference in the internal affairs of socialist and other states and for attacks on the socialist social system"; the socialist countries "reject the slander heaped on them by the ruling classes of states whose peoples have to endure all the hardships of mass unemployment, national and social inequality, racial discrimination, organized crime and moral degradation", and they "do not and will not allow any interference in their internal affairs". The participant countries "stress that they are guided in this respect by concern for the further positive development of international relations and for the removal of the obstacles artificially complicating them".

President Ceausescu of Romania revealed after the meeting that he had refused to agree to Soviet proposals for an increase in defence spending by the individual member countries of the organization and for the integration of each country's national armed forces under a unified command. He later reaffirmed his government's policy of defending the right of each nation "to decide its own destiny without interference from outside". Since the early 1960s Romania had not allowed Warsaw Pact forces to conduct exercises in Romanian territory; it was the only Warsaw Treaty country in which no Soviet troops or advisers were stationed; and since 1969 it had not taken part in Warsaw Pact forces' manoeuvres (except at the level of staff officers).

1979 Budapest Meeting. At a meeting of the Committee of Foreign Ministers in Budapest on May 14–15, 1979, an appeal was launched to all European countries as well as the United States and Canada to convene a general conference with the aim of taking practical measures in order to reduce military forces in Europe. In this context the ministers quoted a paragraph from a "programme for further co-operation between the Soviet Union and France" signed on April 28, 1979, during a visit to Moscow by the French President.

The Ministers also made five specific proposals for (i) the conclusion and implementation of the SALT II agreement and transition to the next stage (SALT III); (ii) the fixing of dates and modalities for talks on ceasing the manufacture of all types of nuclear weapons and for the progressive reduction of stocks of such weapons until their complete elimination; (iii) the definitive prohibition of the use of nuclear weapons; (iv) the conclusion of an agreement on a total and general ban on nuclear weapon tests; and (v) the adoption of measures to strengthen guarantees for the security of non-nuclear countries.

1979 East Berlin Meeting. Meeting in East Berlin on Dec. 5–6, 1979, the Foreign Ministers of the Warsaw Pact countries appealed to NATO not to proceed with the proposed modernization of its long-range theatre nuclear forces (LRTNF)—involving the deployment in Europe of Pershing II launchers and cruise missiles [see page 218]—as the implementation of this proposal would "destroy the basis for negotiations" and would "signify an attempt by NATO to engage in negotiations from positions of strength which is, as a matter of principle, unacceptable to the Warsaw Treaty states" and "the governments of the NATO countries cannot be unaware of this".

1980 Warsaw Meeting. A meeting of the Political Consultative Committee, held in Warsaw on May 14–15, 1980 (to celebrate the 25th anniversary of the founding of the Warsaw Treaty Organization), and also attended by President Brezhnev of the USSR, issued a statement calling for a world conference on international problems and a lengthy declaration proposing a European conference on disarmament and détente.

The statement proposed the convening in the immediate future of "a top-level meeting of the leaders of states of all the regions of the world" who would focus their attention on "the task of removing the hotbeds of international tension and preventing war"; particular attention should be paid to "the issues of European security and the preservation of peace on the European continent". The statement concluded that such a meeting could be arranged by means of consultations between states, and that "the present situation and the peril it evokes . . . suggest that it is precisely such a top-level meeting which would provide the safest road to mutual understanding and lasting peace".

The declaration proposed: (i) That as from an agreed date no state or grouping of states in Europe should increase the size of its armed forces in the area defined by the Final Act of the CSCE; (ii) that all the provisions of the Final Act should be strictly observed; (iii) that exchanges of views should be "intensified and deepened" in preparation for the 1980 Madrid follow-up CSCE conference; (iv) that the preparation of a conference on military détente and disarmament in Europe should be accelerated; (v) that efforts should be made to bring about the ratification of the SALT II treaty and to reach swift agreements on the complete prohibition of nuclear weapon tests, radiological weapons and chemical weapons (and on the destruction of stockpiles of the latter), and on the renunciation of the use of nuclear weapons in the territories of non-nuclear states which did not have such weapons on their territory; (vi) that talks should immediately begin on concluding a world treaty on the renunciation of force, on ending the production of nuclear weapons and gradually reducing their stocks until their complete liquidation, on banning the development of new types and systems of weapons of mass destruction, and on the reduction of military budgets, particularly of the major powers; and (vii) that an examination should begin, possibly within a UN framework, of the question of limiting and reducing the level of military presence and activity in the Atlantic, the Indian and Pacific oceans, the Mediterranean and the Persian Gulf.

The participants in the meeting also "stressed the need for a political settlement" of the Afghanistan situation with reliable guarantees for the termination of external interference against that country so that the Soviet Union could commence withdrawing its troops (which had entered that country in December 1979).

1983 Prague Meeting. A meeting of the Prime Ministers, Foreign and Defence Ministers and communist party leaders of the Warsaw Treaty Organization's member states, which took place in Prague on Jan. 4–5, 1983, issued a joint declaration calling inter alia for (i) the drafting of a non-aggression treaty between the member countries of the Warsaw Pact and of NATO; (ii) a commitment by both sides to renounce the first use of nuclear weapons; (iii) the maintenance and further development of talks between member states of the two organizations on arms reduction; and (iv) the strengthening of the role of the United Nations in the maintenance of global security.

In the declaration it was stated that it was "nonsensical" to believe (as allegedly was the case in the United States) that it would be possible to win a war through the first use of nuclear weapons, and that strategies (said to be central to US defence policy) based on a "first disarming strike", a "limited nuclear war" or a "protracted nuclear conflict" all ignored the real likelihood that a nuclear war would lead to complete catastrophe. The declaration also contained an attack on the NATO decision of December 1979 to deploy a new range of US medium-range nuclear missiles in Europe from the end of 1983 unless US-Soviet arms reduction talks in Geneva had by then produced agreement. The position of the Warsaw Pact member states was that the best solution would be to rid Europe completely of nuclear weapons, both medium-range and tactical, and that, if this "truly zero" decision could not be reached at the moment, it was "feasible to proceed to the radical reduction of medium-range missiles in Europe on the basis of the principle of equality and equal security". In the declaration it was reiterated that the Warsaw Pact member states did not seek "military superiority over the NATO member states" and did not have "any intention to attack them or any other country in Europe or elsewhere".

1985 Extension of Warsaw Pact. In a protocol signed by communist party leaders of the seven member countries on April 26, 1985, the Warsaw Pact was extended for a further 20 years. The protocol came into effect on May 30, 1985.

1985–86 Arms Control Proposals. A meeting of the Political Consultative Committee, held in Sofia on Oct. 22–23, 1985, proposed a freeze, as from Jan. 1, 1986, of both US and Soviet conventional armed forces, including those stationed outside their national territories. The final communiqué of the meeting also restated Soviet negotiating positions, notably an end to the testing, production and stationing of "offensive" space weapons; a moratorium on nuclear weapon testing; a ban on the development of new intermediate-range nuclear missiles; a ban on chemical weapons; the creation of nuclear-weapon-free zones in north and central Europe as well as the Balkans; and a non-aggression

agreement between the nations of the Warsaw Pact and of NATO.

A meeting of Warsaw Pact foreign ministers, held in Warsaw on March 19–20, 1986, issued a communiqué calling for the phased elimination of nuclear and chemical weapons until the year 2000 and the renunciation of space armaments, and it appealed to the NATO states, in particular the United States, the United Kingdom and France, to declare their readiness to conclude agreements on a radical reduction of nuclear weapons, a first step towards which would be a reduction of medium-size missiles in Europe. The minimum result of a new US-Soviet summit meeting, the communiqué stated, should be agreements on the renunciation of nuclear weapons tests and the removal of US and Soviet medium-range missiles from Europe. In return for such a removal by the USA the Soviet side would withdraw its short-range missiles from the German Democratic Republic and Czechoslovakia.

Military Strength of Warsaw Pact

According to the Institute of Strategic Studies (in London), the mid-1985 strengths of the combined armed forces of the Warsaw Pact states (excluding para-military units) were as follows:

Country	Number
Bulgaria	148,500
Czechoslovakia	203,300
German Democratic Republic	174,000
Hungary	106,000
Poland	319,000
Romania	189,500
Soviet Union	5,300,000
Total	6,440,300

Council for Mutual Economic Assistance (CMEA or Comecon)

Address. Prospekt Kalinina 54, 121206 Moscow, USSR.

Officer. Vyacheslav Sychev (exec. sec.).

Founded. Jan. 25, 1949.

Membership. Bulgaria, Cuba, Czechoslovakia, the German Democratic Republic, Hungary, Mongolia, Poland, Romania, the Soviet Union and Vietnam.

Associate member. Yugoslavia.

Observers. Afghanistan, Angola, Ethiopia, The People's Democratic Republic of Korea, Laos, Mozambique, Nicaragua and the People's Democratic Republic of Yemen.

History

The decision to establish a Council for Mutual Economic Assistance was made at an economic conference held in Moscow in January 1949 and attended by representatives of Bulgaria, Czechoslovakia, Hungary, Poland, Romania and the Soviet Union. These countries were the founder-members of the CMEA. The purpose of

the CMEA would be "the exchange of experience in the economic field, and mutual assistance in regard to raw materials, foodstuffs, machinery, equipment, etc." Each of the participating countries would be equally represented on the Council.

It was further stated that the Council would be open for membership to "other countries in Europe which share its principles and desire broad economic co-operation with the countries already represented in it".

Albania was admitted to membership in February 1949, but left the Council in 1961 as a result of ideological differences. The German Democratic Republic entered in October 1950, and the Mongolian People's Republic in June 1962; Mongolia entered the CMEA under an amendment to the Charter [see below] permitting the admission of non-European countries to membership. Cuba became a full member on July 12, 1972, and Vietnam on June 29, 1978.

Yugoslavia was admitted to associate membership under an agreement concluded on Sept. 17,

1964. By the terms of this agreement, Yugoslavia would be able to share in the work of the CMEA, on a basis of equality and mutual benefit, in the fields of foreign trade, currency and financial relations, ferrous and non-ferrous metallurgy, engineering, the chemical industry, and co-ordination of scientific and technical research. Yugoslavia's participation became effective on April 24, 1965. By 1982 Yugoslavia had signed some 120 agreements within this framework.

The CMEA Charter

At its 12th session in December 1959, the Council drafted a *Charter*, which was signed on Dec. 14, 1959, and came into force on April 13, 1960. A summary of the document is given below:

In the preamble the signatories state their determination "to continue developing all-round economic co-operation on the basis of the consistent implementation of the international socialist division of labour in the interests of building socialism and communism in their countries and ensuring a lasting peace throughout the world". They also state their "readiness to develop economic relations with all countries, irrespective of their social and state systems".

Art. 1. The purpose of the CMEA is to facilitate, by uniting and co-ordinating the efforts of the Council's member countries, the planned development of the national economy, acceleration of economic and technical progress in these countries, a rise in the level of industrialization in countries with less developed industries, uninterrupted growth of labour productivity, and a steady advance of the welfare of the peoples in the Council's member countries.

Art. 2 deals with membership of the CMEA. Membership is open to any European country sharing the Council's aims and principles. Any member country may leave the Council with six months' notice. This article was amended at the 16th session of the Council, when admission to membership was extended to non-European countries.

Art. 3 states the functions of the CMEA to be to:
(1) "Organize all-round economic, scientific and technical co-operation of all the Council's member countries in the most rational use of their natural resources and acceleration of the development of their productive forces"; and
(2) "assist the Council's member countries in elaborating and carrying out joint measures for (i) the development of the industry and agriculture of the Council's member countries; (ii) the development of transport . . . ; (iii) the most efficient use of principal capital investments allocated by the Council's member countries for the development of the mining and manufacturing industries and for the construction of major projects which are of interest to two countries or more; (iv) the development of trade and exchange of services between the Council's member countries and between them and other countries; (v) the exchange of scientific and technical achievements and advanced production experience".

Art. 4 states that "recommendations shall be made on questions of economic, scientific and technical co-operation" and on "decisions on organizational and procedural matters". Recommendations and decisions apply only to those members who have declared an interest in the question from which they arise.

Art. 5 names the constituent organs of the Council as the Session of the Council; the Conference of Members' Representatives (since replaced by the Executive Committee); the standing Commissions; and the Secretariat.

Arts. 6, 7, 8 and 9 give details of the composition and functions of the organs of the Council.

The remaining articles deal with the Council's international relations and financial arrangements, and with such matters as the ratification and amending of the Charter.

Organization of the Council

Summit Conferences. Since June 1962 the First or General Secretaries of the Central Committees of the Communist and Workers' Parties and the heads of government of the member countries of the CMEA have met in conference from time to time to discuss the expansion and consolidation of economic co-operation among CMEA countries. At these summit conferences the general lines of the CMEA's work are laid down.

Session of the Council. The supreme permanent organ of the CMEA is the Session of the Council, which meets at least once a year in the capital of each member country in turn, the host-country providing the chairman for each session. The programme of work discussed at the summit conferences is here determined in greater detail. Recommendations, which must be passed unanimously, are put into effect by intergovernmental agreements.

Executive Committee. The Executive Committee was set up at the 16th Session of the Council on June 7, 1962. It consists of Deputy Prime Ministers of the CMEA member countries, their deputies and advisers. Meetings are held at least every three months, the function of the Committee being to co-ordinate national economic development plans and to supervise collaboration in scientific and technical research. A branch of the Executive Committee is the Bureau for Common Questions of Economic Planning, in which each CMEA country is represented by the Deputy Chairman of its State Planning Organization.

Secretariat. The Secretariat consists of the Secretary of the Council and five Deputy Secretaries. It is responsible for preparation of material for the Council, the Committee and the Permanent Commissions, and for the drafting of reports and the compiling of statistics.

Permanent Commissions. Twenty-three Permanent Commissions were set up at various times between 1956 and 1963 to study different aspects of the CMEA's work. All the CMEA member countries are represented on each of the committees and sub-committees of the Permanent Commissions.

The commissions are listed below, together with their date of foundation and present headquarters.

Agriculture	(May 1956; Sofia)
Forestry	(May 1956; Bucharest)
Power	(May 1956; Moscow)
Coal Industry	(May 1956; Warsaw)
Machine Building	(May 1956; Prague)
Oil and Gas	(May 1956; Bucharest)
Ferrous Metals	(May 1956; Moscow)
Non-Ferrous Metals	(May 1956; Budapest)
Chemical Industry	(May 1956; Berlin)
Wood, Cellulose, Paper	(May 1956; Budapest)
Transport	(June 1958; Warsaw)
Construction	(June 1958; Berlin)

Light Industry	(July 1963; Prague)	Created as a single commission in December 1958
Food Industry	(July 1963; Sofia)	

Economic Questions	(1958; Moscow)
Foreign Trade	(May 1959; Moscow)
Peaceful Uses of Atomic Energy	(Sept. 1960; Moscow)
Standardization	(June 1962; Berlin)
Co-ordination of Scientific and Technical Research	(June 1962; Moscow)
Statistics	(June 1962; Moscow)
Finance and Currency	(Dec. 1962; Moscow)
Radio and Electronics Industries	(July 1963; Budapest)
Geology	(July 1963; Ulan-Bator)

The creation of a Permanent Commission for Posts and Telecommunications was decided upon by the Council at its 25th session held in Bucharest on July 27–29, 1971, The Permanent Commission for the Co-ordination of Scientific and Technical Research was at the same time replaced by a Committee for Scientific and Technical Co-operation, and a Committee for Co-operation in the Sphere of Planning was also set up. Permanent commissions have also been set up for health and for civil aviation.

Other permanent bodies created by the Council are a working party for the co-ordination and delivery of finished articles (founded in 1959) and a central dispatcher administration (founded in 1962).

A Standardization Institute was established in 1964, its function being the creation of a progressive standardization of industrial products among the CMEA member countries.

The creation of an International Institute of Economic Problems of the World Socialist System was approved by the CMEA's Executive Committee on July 24, 1970.

CMEA Industrial Organizations

Industrial organizations designed to promote specialization and co-operation in production were set up by CMEA member countries as follows:

(1) Central Control Administration of the United Power Grids of European CMEA Member Countries (CCA), set up in Prague in 1962.

(2) Intermetall, set up in Budapest in 1964 for ferrous metallurgy.

(3) Intershipnik (Bearings), established in Warsaw in 1964 for the anti-friction bearings industry.

(4) Computers, formed in Moscow in 1969 for computer engineering, a standardized computer technology and the joint planning of an international industrial complex.

(5) Interchim, founded in Halle (German Democratic Republic) in 1970 for branches of the chemical industry.

(6) Interatominstrument, set up in Warsaw in 1972 for nuclear-technical apparatus construction.

(7) Interatomenergo, established in Moscow in 1973 for nuclear power plant production.

(8) Intertextilmasch, founded in Moscow in 1973 for branches of textile machinery construction.

(9) Interelektro, also founded in Moscow in 1973, for branches of electro-technology.

(10) Assofoto, established in Moscow in 1973 for the photochemical industry.

(11) Interchimvolokno, established in Bucharest in 1973 for the chemical fibres industry.

CMEA Transport Organizations

The following organizations have been set up for transport on land and at sea:

(1) OPW for railway freight transport, set up in Prague in 1963.

(2) Conference of Chartering and Ship-owning Organizations (CCSO) of the CMEA member countries, established in Moscow in 1963.

(3) "Interlighter" International Shipping Company, set up in Budapest in 1978 by Bulgaria, Czechoslovakia, Hungary and the Soviet Union.

(4) International Organization for Seaports (INTERPORT), established in Szczecin (Poland) in 1973 by the German Democratic Republic and Poland.

(5) International Shipowners' Association (INSA), established in Gdynia (Poland) in 1970 as the CMEA joint maritime traffic organization.

CMEA Transport Agreements

Transport agreements have been concluded on the dates shown under the following headings:

International Direct Mixed Rail-Water Freight Transport, Dec. 14, 1959.

Joint Planning of the Material Technical Base of the Container Transport System and Co-operation in the Creation of Future Development, Dec. 14, 1959.

Questions of Co-operation in the Operational Commercial and Financial Activity between Air Transport Enterprises, Dec. 14, 1959.

Introducing a Uniform Container Transport System, Dec. 3, 1971.

Joint Use of Containers in International Transport, June 24, 1974.

Other Joint CMEA Bodies

The following joint research institutes and associations have been set up within the framework of the CMEA.

(1) International Centre for Scientific and Technological Information, set up in Moscow in 1969.

(2) Interkosmos, founded in Moscow in 1970 for space research. (A programme for international exploration of space was first established by Warsaw Pact member states in 1963. Artificial satellites for scientific exploration were first launched as follows: Interkosmos I on Oct. 14, 1969; Interkosmos II on Dec. 25, 1969; Interkosmos III on Dec. 7, 1970; and Interkosmos Copernicus 500 on April 19, 1973.)

(3) Intersputnik—International System and Organization for Space Communications, founded in Moscow on Nov. 15, 1971. This system includes a space complex of communications satellites (*Molniya*), ground steering elements and earth stations for contact through satellites.

(4) Intertalonpribor, formed in Moscow in 1972 for measurement technology.

(5) International Organization for Marine Geology (INTERMORGEO), set up in Riga in 1973.

(6) Intervodochistka, founded in Sofia on Feb. 8, 1978, for co-operation in rational water utilization and protection of water resources.

A *Convention on the Transfer and Use of Data of the Remote Sensing of the Earth from Outer Space*, signed in Moscow on May 19, 1978, by Bulgaria, Cuba, Czechoslovakia, the German Democratic Republic, Hungary, Mongolia, Poland, Romania and the Soviet Union laid down procedures for co-operation among the signatories. It was to be in force for five years and automatically renewable for further five-year periods.

Scientific Co-operation

Joint Institute for Nuclear Research. A preliminary agreement on the establishment of a Joint Institute for Nuclear Research, made on March 26, 1956, was implemented on July 12, 1956, the institute being established at Dubna in the Soviet Union. The members of the institute are Bulgaria, Cuba, Czechoslovakia, the German Democratic Republic, Hungary, the Democratic People's Republic of Korea, the Mongolian People's Republic, Poland, Romania, the Soviet Union and Vietnam. The People's Republic of China, formerly a member, withdrew its scientists in July 1966.

On its inception the institute comprised the former Institute of Nuclear Problems and Electrophysical Laboratory of the Soviet Academy of Sciences. Other sections of the institute, which have come into operation since its establishment, are the laboratory of high energies, which began operating in 1957; the laboratory of neutron physics, equipped with an experimental fast neutron pulse reactor (in operation since 1960); a laboratory of nuclear reactions equipped with a cyclotron for accelerating multicharged ions (also coming into operation in 1960); and laboratories for nuclear problems, theoretical physics and computing and automation. The joint institute also has a computing centre and a radiochemical laboratory.

The supreme authority of the joint institute is the Committee of Government Plenipotentiaries, the members of which are the heads of the atomic energy authorities of the member countries. The committee is responsible for policy and finance. The programme of work is the responsibility of a Scientific Council, while the practical administration is carried out by a management consisting of a director, two vice-directors and an administrative manager.

Other Scientific Centres. Agreements signed in Moscow on April 28, 1971, provided for the establishment of seven new scientific centres to study such matters as new chemical compounds, prevention of pollution, control of weeds and agricultural pests, automated systems for medical institutions, anti-corrosion measures, research in biological physics, and uses of timber.

CMEA Financial Institutions

International Bank for Economic Co-operation.

An International Bank for Economic Co-operation, formed by the CMEA's eight member countries with an initial capital of 60,000,000 roubles (to be increased to 300,000,000 roubles within five years) came into being on Jan. 1, 1964.

The bank has a Council consisting of representatives of all its member countries (which are the same as those of the International Investment Bank) and a similarly composed Board.

Its functions are mainly to undertake multilateral settlements on transferable roubles and to grant credits for the financing of foreign trade and other operations of its members, which now include Cuba and Vietnam.

International Investment Bank. An International Investment Bank, with its seat in Moscow, was set up on July 10, 1970, by seven countries as founder-members (Bulgaria, Czechoslovakia, the German Democratic Republic, Hungary, Mongolia, Poland and the Soviet Union). Romania became a member of the bank on Jan. 12, 1971, Cuba on Jan. 22, 1974, and Vietnam in May 1977.

The bank's highest authority is its Council which meets at least twice a year, on which each member has one vote, and which has to take decisions by unanimous vote. The bank's executive body is its Board, consisting of a chairman and three deputies appointed by the Council.

Starting operations on Jan. 1, 1971, with initial capital subscriptions totalling 175,000,000 roubles (increased by another 175,000,000 roubles in 1972 and rising to a total of 1,071,300,000 transferable roubles of authorized capital by Jan. 1, 1979), the bank was to concentrate resources for capital construction and for co-ordinated expenditure through the granting of long- and medium-term credits. Membership subscriptions were based on the volume of members' exports in mutual trade turnover, with the Soviet Union providing nearly 40 per cent and the German Democratic Republic about 17.6 per cent of the capital. The bank was also authorized to use loans and investments from third countries.

In 1974 a special fund was set up by the bank for the financing of economic and technical assistance programmes for developing countries.

The bank repeatedly took up credits from Western banks, including a loan, early in 1976, of $600,000,000 from the Dresdner Bank (of the Federal Republic of Germany) for the financing of capital projects; a loan of $500,000,000 granted on June 15, 1977, largely to finance the construction of the natural gas pipeline from Orenburg (Urals) to the Czechoslovak border; and another loan of $500,000,000 granted in September 1978 by a consortium headed by the Dresdner Bank, mainly towards financing the above pipeline.

Co-operation Agreements with Non-Member Countries

Finland. An agreement between the CMEA and Finland—the first with a non-socialist country—was signed on May 16, 1973. It provided for the establishment of a joint commission, with representatives from all the CMEA members and from Finland, to study the possibilities for the development of economic, scientific and technological co-operation.

Iraq. An agreement with Iraq on multilateral economic, scientific and technical co-operation, signed on July 4, 1975, was the first of its kind to be concluded by the CMEA and a developing country (although Iraq had, since 1973, signed various co-operation agreements with individual CMEA member countries). The agreement was approved at the 30th session of the CMEA in East Berlin on July 7–9, 1976, and ratified on July 23, 1976.

Mexico. A similar agreement was signed with Mexico on Aug. 13, 1975, and likewise approved on July 7–9, 1976, and ratified on July 23, 1976.

Mozambique. A co-operation agreement with Mozambique was ratified on June 27, 1985.

Nicaragua. Several co-operation agreements concluded in October 1985 covered inter alia Soviet aid towards an irrigation project on Nicaragua's Pacific coast and a Soviet loan (equivalent to about £300,000,000) to be used for purchases of Soviet oil and agricultural equipment (in equal parts).

CMEA Decisions and Operations

Division of Labour. The work of the CMEA is largely based on the principle of the division of labour. In sessions of the Council from 1956 to 1961 a number of plans were approved for specialization, in various industries, among the CMEA countries. At the session of the Council from Dec. 12–15, 1961, the draft of the "Fundamental Principles of International Socialist Division of Labour" was adopted. The details of the document were published on June 17, 1962. Described as "a planned and consciously moulded process, which takes into consideration the objectively operating economic laws of socialism", the Principles are contrasted with the competitive system of capitalist international division. All later resolutions of the CMEA in the field of the division of labour are based on this document.

"Complex Programme". The Council published on Aug. 7, 1971, a *Complex Programme for the Further Deepening and Improvement of Co-operation and Development of the Socialist Economic Integration of the CMEA Member Countries.*

The purpose of the programme was stated to be "the promotion of the growth of the economic power of the socialist world system and the strengthening of the economic system of each country". Socialist economic integration, however, was to take place on the basis of "complete voluntariness" and would not be linked with the creation of supranational organs. There would be intensified co-operation in planning, with joint forecasts for energy, petrochemicals and automotive systems in the period 1971–75, and also in joint research projects in science and technology.

The programme further provided for a new form of trading, i.e. trade in non-quota goods which would not need to be balanced bilaterally but would, for clearing purposes, be counted in the total trade of the respective countries.

The "transferable rouble" (the collective currency used for accounting in the internal CMEA clearing accounts but not transferable otherwise) was to be strengthened so as to attain "real transferability" and be used in clearings with non-CMEA countries, and new parities would be established between the currencies of the member states and in relation to the "transferable rouble".

The proposed increased co-operation was to include the creation of a network of express trains and of long-distance roads, joint shipping enterprises, and the introduction of standardized container transport systems.

The negotiations on the programme during the Council's 25th session in Bucharest, July 27–29, 1971, revealed "serious controversy on questions of integration", and, in particular, strong reservations on any surrender of a country's sovereignty to the CMEA were expressed by Romania.

Further Activities, 1975–80

Oil Prices. It was disclosed in Budapest on March 18, 1975, that the CMEA had agreed that in coming years oil prices would no longer be "determined five years in advance but annually on the basis of five-year average prices in the world markets". This meant that by 1978 prices of Soviet oil would approximate those obtaining in the Western world.

29th CMEA Session. At the 29th session of the CMEA held in Budapest on June 24–26, 1975, a co-ordinated plan for multinational integration was approved with a view to implementing the "complex programme" [see above].

The plan provided mainly for joint investments in developing Soviet raw material resources during 1976–80 at a cost of 9,000 million transferable roubles (then about £6,000 million). The projects included the construction of the natural gas pipeline from the Orenburg fields (in the Urals) to the Czechoslovak border and a power transmission line from the Ukraine to Hungary.

The session also decided to draw up a joint long-term co-operation programme for 1976–90 for the raw material, fuel, energy, engineering, farming and food industries.

The Romanian Prime Minister expressed opposition to plans for supranational integration, including the creation of a uniform electrical power system, and he emphasized that his country wanted co-operation based on the co-ordination of national plans rather than a joint plan for integration. The national identity of each economy, he said, should be preserved while co-operation should be improved "in the industrially less developed countries" such as Romania.

Outer Space Agreement. On July 14, 1976, the CMEA member countries signed an agreement on co-operation in exploration and the use of outer space for peaceful purposes.

31st CMEA Session. At the end of the CMEA's 31st session in Warsaw on June 21–23, 1977, it was stated that the socialist countries had become "the world's most dynamic economic force" and that in 1976 the national income of the CMEA member countries had reached nine and a half times the 1948 level (whereas in the industrialized capitalist countries the increase was said to be about three and one-third times).

32nd CMEA Session. The 32nd session, held in Bucharest on June 27–29, 1978, approved long-term target programmes for (i) energy, fuel and raw materials, (ii) machine-building and (iii) agriculture and the food industry for 1981–90. Ten joint projects to be completed under the co-ordinated five-year plan for 1976–80 included the natural gas complex at Orenburg (Urals) and the Soyuz gas pipeline to the Czechoslovak border, which was to reach a maximum capacity of 28,000 million cubic metres in 1980, of which 15,500 million cubic metres would be supplied to the other East European members of the CMEA annually.

Assistance to Developing Countries. In a survey of its activities in 1977, circulated by the CMEA at the 33rd regular session of the UN General Assembly in 1978, the CMEA member countries were stated to have rendered, and to be continuing to render, economic and technical assistance to 78 developing countries in Asia, Africa and Latin America in the construction of a total of 3,560 industrial enterprises and other projects in various fields of these countries' national economies, including 2,685 which had been completed and had gone into service.

Trade and Output Statistics. In connexion with a session of the CMEA's Executive Committee in Moscow on March 30, 1979, it was claimed that trade between CMEA member countries had, in 1978, reached 103,000 million roubles and their foreign trade nearly 174,000 million roubles, and that industrial output in CMEA member countries was twice that of the countries of the European Economic Community.

33rd CMEA Session. The 33rd session of the CMEA held in Moscow on June 26–28, 1979, approved "long-term specific programmes" for satisfying the national requirements of CMEA member countries in manufacturing consumer goods and for developing transport communications. A total of 14 agreements were signed on the implementation of specific programmes. The final communiqué stated that since the 32nd session the CMEA member countries had concluded 22 agreements on the implementation of "five long-term specific programmes of co-operation and co-ordination of the national economic development plans for 1981–85".

The session also unanimously approved amendments to the CMEA Charter, with the effect that it was no longer necessary for important decisions to obtain the approval of all members; that the statutes provided for mutual consultation on the main aspects of the economic policy of member countries and on the elaboration of long-term co-operation programmes; and that multilateral and bilateral co-operation among individual CMEA member countries would be bound up with the overall long-term programmes.

The session further decided to apply to Vietnam special measures, as previously applied to Cuba and Mongolia, to accelerate that country's economic development.

1980 Prague Summit. A session of the CMEA held at the level of heads of government in Prague on June 17–19, 1980, approved further extensive programmes.

In a communiqué issued at the end of the session it was emphasized that it was "the invariable striving of CMEA member countries to develop co-operation with other states in the interests of deepening the international division of labour on a just, equitable and mutually beneficial basis" and also that the CMEA was ready "to expand relations of co-operation with countries which are not members of the CMEA and with international economic organizations for the good of peace and progress".

The communiqué also noted that during 1979 there had been a further deepening and improvement of co-operation between the CMEA and Yugoslavia, which was taking part in the work of CMEA bodies in 22 fields of co-operation and was a party to 22 multinational agreements.

The session noted that national income in CMEA countries in 1979 had been 19 per cent higher than in 1975, and industrial output 23 per cent higher; that the average agricultural output in 1976–79 had been 9 per cent higher than in 1971–75; and that the foreign trade turnover of the CMEA countries had increased in 1979 by almost 13 per cent as against 1978 and had reached 196,000 million roubles, of which mutual trade turnover among CMEA members had accounted for 110,000 million roubles and had met the bulk of import needs in respect of key fuels, raw materials, machinery and equipment.

Agreements signed by the participants of the session included one on specialization and co-ordination in the manufacture of computers and another on co-operation in improving oil refining. It was reported that the Soviet Union had undertaken to provide 400,000,000 tons of oil over the next five years. It was also agreed to promote further development of nuclear energy while making a concerted effort to economize on energy and raw material consumption.

The Soviet Government stated, with reference to a US embargo imposed on trade with the Soviet Union following the latter's intervention in Afghanistan in December 1979: "Such measures may cause some temporary difficulties in the construction of individual projects, but no one has succeeded, and no one will succeed, in preventing us from going forward and implementing the plans which we have drafted, even if the US Administration includes all American products in its lists of banned goods."

35th CMEA Session. The 35th CMEA session, held in Sofia on July 2–4, 1981, agreed on a co-ordinated economic plan for multilateral economic integration in 1981–85 (i.e. a third five-year plan) and also on further assistance to be offered to the economies of Cuba, Mongolia and Vietnam.

The Chairman of the USSR Council of Ministers said on July 2 that the overall national income of the CMEA member countries had risen during the 1970s by 66 per cent and their industrial output by 84 per cent. Mutual trade between the member countries had, he said, in 1980 covered 69 per cent of their machinery, oil and iron ore import requirements, 94 per cent of coal and timber imports, and 60 per cent of imports of consumer goods. During 1981–85, he stated, the Soviet Union's trade with the other CMEA countries would increase by 40 per cent over the 1976–80 level, Soviet exports of electric power, fuel and raw materials to the CMEA countries by more than one-third, exports of Soviet machinery and equipment by 25 per cent, and Soviet imports of engineering products from those countries by over 50 per cent.

36th CMEA Session. The 36th session of the CMEA was held in Budapest on June 8–10, 1982, when it was stated that the CMEA countries had increased their economic co-operation in 1981 despite sanctions imposed by the United States and other countries against Poland and the Soviet Union and an "illegal blockade" imposed by Western countries against "fraternal Cuba"; that the co-ordination of economic plans for 1986–90 had been reviewed and approved; that it had been agreed to develop further the plans for scientific, technical and economic policies; and that it had been agreed to expedite the development of the economies of Vietnam, Cuba and Mongolia and to increase the level of these countries' involvement in the CMEA's division of labour.

37th and 38th CMEA Sessions. The 37th session of the CMEA, held in East Berlin on Oct. 18–20, 1983, stated in its communiqué that the member states had "carried out intensive work for the fulfilment of the tasks of the current five-year plan" (for 1981–85); that national incomes had increased despite "worsened external conditions and the rise in the cost of raw materials and power"; and that the member countries' mutual trade had grown more rapidly than their overall exports.

Unofficial reports on the session referred to differences over the price and quantity of crude oil deliveries from the USSR and over the price of foodstuffs (with Romania calling for a review of the export price system to enable it to import more foodstuffs at subsidized prices, whereas net food exporters, such as Bulgaria and Hungary, protested that food prices, frozen for some 10 years, should in fact increase).

The 38th (special) session, held in Moscow on June 12–14, 1984, issued a declaration "on the main directions of further developing the economic, scientific and technological co-operation of the CMEA member states". The proposals listed were (inter alia) to allow individual enterprises in different countries to deal with each other directly; to draft a comprehensive programme of scientific and technical progress for a period of 15 to 20 years; to take measures to conserve energy and raw materials by using "progressive technical processes . . . and equipment"; for member states, in return for assurances of continued deliveries of raw materials and fuel from the Soviet Union, to develop their production of exports "with the aim of supplying the Soviet Union with the products it needs, in particular foodstuffs and manufactured consumer goods, construction materials, machines and equipment".

In a survey published in March 1985 the (UN) Economic Commission for Europe (ECE) noted that despite the CMEA's call for increased economic integration there was "no evidence of a turning away by the CMEA from the markets of the rest of the world" and that in fact its external economic policy continued to be dominated by the need to maximize exports to, and to maintain a low level of imports from, Western countries in order to reduce further the CMEA countries' foreign debt. (According to the Vienna Institute for International Economic Studies, the net hard-currency debt of the Eastern bloc had fallen from US$64,800 million at the end of 1983 to $54,900 million at the end of 1984).

41st CMEA Session. The 41st (special) CMEA session, held in Moscow on Dec. 17–18, 1985, unanimously approved a Comprehensive Programme for the Scientific and Technological Progress of the CMEA member countries up to the year 2000.

The programme detailed five priority areas of co-operation "for the creation and utilization of fundamentally new types of machinery": (i) the use of electronics in the national economy; (ii) comprehensive automation; (iii) nuclear power; (iv) raw materials and technologies for their production and processing; and (v) bio-engineering. There was to be "at least a two-fold increase in the productivity of social labour in the CMEA countries in general by the year 2000 and a sharp decrease in the proportional expenditure of energy and raw materials per unit of national income". The programme was to benefit the three less developed CMEA members (Cuba, Mongolia and Vietnam) by promoting the "acceleration of the process of gradual evening-out of levels of development" within the CMEA and improving the effectiveness of assistance from European member states.

The programme also contained a commitment to developing co-operation with other socialist countries and to giving scientific and technical assistance to the developing world.

The implementation of the programme was to be promoted by (i) a general agreement on multilateral co-operation in the design and introduction of automatic design systems; (ii) a general agreement on multilateral co-operation in the design, manufacture and exploitation of a single system of light-conductor facilities for transmitting information; and (iii) an agreement on instituting an international scientific and production organization, "Interrobot", to develop robotics facilities.

Distribution of CMEA Member Countries' Trade

In 1983 the trade turnover of the European CMEA member countries was distributed over four groups of countries as follows (in approximate percentages of national trade):

	CMEA member countries	Other socialist countries	Non-socialist countries developing	developed
Bulgaria	77.4	1.3	9.3	12.0
Czechoslovakia	72.0	4.6	7.3	16.1
German Democratic Republic	62.2	2.3	6.9	28.6
Hungary	51.3	2.8	14.0	31.9
Poland	69.5	2.8	6.7	21.0
Romania	47.1	6.5	20.4	26.0
Soviet Union	51.7	4.0	13.6	30.7

Danube Commission

Address. Benczúr utca 25, 1068 Budapest, Hungary.

Officers. V. N. Bazovsky (pres.); O. Durej (sec.).

Founded. May 11, 1949.

Membership. Bulgaria, Czechoslovakia, Hungary, Romania, the Soviet Union, the Ukraine and Yugoslavia.

History. The commission was set up under a convention signed on Aug. 18, 1848, to ensure that "navigation on the Danube will be free and open for citizens, vessels and the goods of all states on the principle of equality".

Other Treaties and Agreements of Communist States

East European Agreements

Prior to the conclusion of the Warsaw Pact the Soviet Union had concluded bilateral agreements with Czechoslovakia, Yugoslavia and Poland, and after 1947 the USSR made similar bilateral agreements with Romania, Hungary and Bulgaria.

Later, the Warsaw Pact was supplemented by treaties on the stationing of Soviet troops in East European countries and by bilateral treaties of friendship and mutual assistance concluded among members of the Warsaw Treaty Organization.

Under the Warsaw Treaty the air defences of the Soviet Union are extended to other East European countries, whose forces are provided with advanced air defence radar systems, surface-to-air missiles and fighter interceptors. Nuclear warheads and weapons, however, are kept in Soviet hands.

BILATERAL AGREEMENTS OF THE USSR CONCLUDED BEFORE 1950

Earlier bilateral treaties between the USSR and East European countries, although not formally abrogated, have been superseded by the Warsaw Pact and new bilateral agreements of 1966.

These were the "treaties of friendship, co-operation and mutual assistance" between the USSR and:

Czechoslovakia .... Dec. 12, 1943
Yugoslavia .... April 11, 1945, abrogated by the USSR on Sept. 28, 1949
Poland.................. April 21, 1945
Romania................ Feb. 4, 1948
Hungary .... Feb. 18, 1948
Bulgaria................ March 18, 1948

An agreement on political co-operation and economic aid concluded with Albania on April 17, 1957 (of unlimited duration) has been inoperative since 1961.

Under a treaty signed by the USSR and Czechoslovakia on June 29, 1945, and in force from Jan. 30, 1946, Czechoslovakia renounced its claim to Transcarpathia, which became part of the Ukrainian Soviet Socialist Republic.

TREATIES ON STATIONING OF SOVIET TROOPS IN EAST EUROPEAN COUNTRIES

Treaties on the stationing of Soviet troops, in amplification of the Warsaw Pact, were concluded by the USSR in 1956–57 with:

(1) **Poland** on Dec. 17, 1956;

(2) the **German Democratic Republic** on March 12, 1957;

(3) **Romania** on April 15, 1957 (but, as decided by the Political Consultative Committee of the Warsaw Pact in Moscow on April 24, 1958, all Soviet troops were withdrawn from Romania in that year); and

(4) **Hungary** on May 27, 1957.

While the treaty with Hungary was of unlimited duration, the three others were limited to the period during which Soviet troops would be stationed in the country concerned, or until the conclusion of a new agreement by the contracting partners.

The treaties were similar in content, that with Poland specifying inter alia that: (i) The numbers and locations of Soviet troops in Poland would be defined by special agreements between the two countries; (ii) no troop movements outside these locations would be permitted without Polish authorization; (iii) Soviet troops in Poland, and their families, would have to respect Polish law and would be subject to the Polish courts; (iv) persons committing crimes against Soviet military personnel would bear the same responsibility as for crimes committed against the Polish forces; (v) the Soviet Government would pay for any material damage which might be caused by the actions or negligence of Soviet military personnel in Poland; (vi) the Polish Government, in return, could compensate the USSR for damage to Soviet property caused by Polish nationals; (vii) any disputes would be examined by a mixed commission; (viii) the two Governments would appoint representatives to deal with any current problems arising out of the presence of Soviet troops in Poland.

The agreement stressed that "the temporary stay of Soviet troops in Poland can in no way affect the sovereignty of the Polish state and cannot lead to any interference in the domestic affairs of Poland".

Between **Czechoslovakia** and **Poland** an agreement on the final demarcation of the frontier between the two countries and a treaty on legal relations at the frontier and co-operation and mutual assistance in frontier matters were signed on June 13, 1958.

1968 Soviet-Czechoslovak Treaty. Following the invasion of Czechoslovakia on Aug. 20, 1968, by troops of the Soviet Union and three other Warsaw Pact member states, a treaty on the "temporary stationing" of Soviet troops in Czechoslovakia was signed in Prague on Oct. 16, 1968, and came into effect on Oct. 18 after ratification by the two countries.

Article 1 of the treaty stated that the Soviet troops would "remain temporarily on the territory of Czechoslovakia in order to ensure the security of the countries of the socialist community against the increasing revanchist strivings of the West German militarist forces".

Bilateral Treaties of Friendship and Mutual Assistance between the USSR and East European States and among the Latter, concluded in 1964–1972

Partners	Date of Signature	Duration (years)	Automatic Extension
USSR and German Democratic Republic	June 12, 1964	20	once for 10 years
USSR and Poland	April 8, 1965	20	every 5 years
Poland and Czechoslovakia	March 1, 1967	20	once for 5 years
Poland and German Democratic Republic	March 15, 1967	20	once for 10 years
Czechoslovakia and German Democratic Republic	March 17, 1967	20	once for 10 years
Poland and Bulgaria	April 6, 1967	20	every 5 years
USSR and Bulgaria	May 12, 1967	20	every 5 years
Hungary and German Democratic Republic	May 18, 1967	20	once for 10 years
Bulgaria and German Democratic Republic	Sept. 7, 1967	20	once for 10 years
USSR and Hungary	Sept. 7, 1967	20	every 5 years
Bulgaria and Czechoslovakia	April 26, 1968	20	every 5 years
Poland and Hungary	May 16, 1968	20	every 5 years
Hungary and Czechoslovakia	June 14, 1968	20	every 5 years
Romania and Czechoslovakia	Aug. 16, 1968	20	every 5 years
Hungary and Bulgaria	July 10, 1969	20	every 5 years
USSR and Czechoslovakia	May 6, 1970	20	every 5 years
USSR and Romania	July 7, 1970	20	every 5 years
Poland and Romania	Nov. 12, 1970	20	every 5 years
Bulgaria and Romania	Nov. 19, 1970	20	every 5 years
Hungary and Romania	Feb. 24, 1972	20	every 5 years
Romania and German Democratic Republic	May 12, 1972	20	once for 5 years

The treaties concluded by the German Democratic Republic contain references to (i) rejection of the Federal Republic of Germany's claim to represent the whole of Germany, and (ii) recognition of West Berlin as "an independent political unit" (i.e. not part of the Federal Republic of Germany). Other provisions contained in the various bilateral treaties are: A reference to the principles of peaceful coexistence and those of the UN Charter; guarantees of the postwar frontiers in Europe (including the Oder-Neisse frontier between Germany and Poland and the frontier between East and West Germany); rejection of the 1938 Munich Agreement on Czechoslovakia as "invalid ab initio"; a refusal to permit access to nuclear weapons by the Federal Republic of Germany; in the event of an armed attack on either of the contracting parties, immediate assistance, including military aid; and an undertaking to "communicate and consult with one another on all important international problems which concern them".

With reference to the 1970 treaty between the USSR and Romania the two countries' leaders signed, on Nov. 24, 1976, a "statement on the further development of co-operation and fraternal friendship" between the two countries and their Communist parties in "comradely co-operation on the basis of the principles of Marxism-Leninism and proletarian internationalism and equality and in the spirit of mutual trust and respect".

The bilateral treaties concluded by the Soviet Union since 1967, contrary to Article 4 of the Warsaw Treaty, do not limit the obligation of mutual assistance to an attack in Europe but call for all-round military assistance against aggression by "any state or combination of states".

IMPORTANT TREATIES CONCLUDED BY GERMAN DEMOCRATIC REPUBLIC

Agreement on the Oder-Neisse Frontier. On June 7, 1950, it was announced that agreement had been reached between the Polish and East German Governments on the recognition of the Oder-Neisse line as the permanent frontier between the German Democratic Republic and Poland. This agreement was implemented on July 6, 1950, when a frontier demarcation agreement was signed at the town of Zgorzelec (Görlitz) on the River Neisse.

Soviet-East German Treaty of 1955. By this treaty, which was signed on Sept. 20, 1955, and came into force on Oct. 6, 1955, the USSR recognized the German Democratic Republic as a sovereign state. The main provisions are given below:

Art. 1. Both governments "solemnly confirmed" that their relations were based "on complete equality of rights, mutual respect of sovereignty and non-interference in domestic affairs". In accordance with this principle, the German Democratic Republic was henceforth "free to decide questions concerning its internal and foreign policy, including its relations with the Federal Republic of Germany as well as its relations with other states".

Art. 4. (1) The Soviet forces at present stationed in East Germany under international (i.e. four-power) agreements would continue to be stationed there temporarily with the approval of the Government of the German Democratic Republic, and on conditions to be settled by an additional agreement between the two governments.

(2) Soviet forces stationed in East Germany would not interfere in the internal affairs of the German Democratic Republic or in the social and political life of the country.

Art. 5. Both governments were agreed that it was "their main aim to bring about a peaceful settlement for the whole of Germany by means of appropriate negotiations". To this end they would "make the necessary efforts towards a settlement by a peace treaty and towards the restoration of the unity of Germany on a peaceful and democratic basis".

At the same time it was agreed that the German Democratic Republic would take over responsibility for the control of its frontiers and of lines of communications between the Federal

Republic of Germany and West Berlin crossing East German territory.

Soviet-East German Treaty of 1975. The Soviet Union and the German Democratic Republic concluded, on Oct. 7, 1975, a new Treaty of Friendship, Co-operation and Mutual Assistance, which was to be in force for 25 years and would be automatically extended for 10-year periods unless one of the parties expressed, 12 months before the expiry of the current term, its wish to terminate the treaty.

The principal articles of the treaty read as follows:

"**Art. 1.** The high contracting parties will, in accordance with the principles of socialist internationalism, continue to strengthen the relations of eternal and inviolable friendship and fraternal mutual assistance in all spheres. They will systematically and unswervingly develop and deepen all-round co-operation and render each other every assistance and support on the basis of mutual respect of national sovereignty and independence, equality and non-interference in internal affairs.

"**Art. 2.** The high contracting parties will unite their efforts for the effective use of the material and spiritual potential of their peoples and states for the establishment of socialist and communist society and the consolidation of the socialist community. In accord with the principles and aims of socialist economic integration and in order better to meet the material and cultural needs of their peoples, they will strengthen and broaden mutually beneficial bilateral and multilateral economic and scientific-technical co-operation, including co-operation within the framework of the Council for Mutual Economic Assistance. Both sides will continue the long-term co-ordination and harmonization of economic plans, extend specialization and co-operation in production and research, harmonize long-term measures for the development of the most important branches of economy, science and technology, exchange knowledge and experience accumulated in the establishment of socialism and communism, and in the interests of raising the efficiency of social production secure an ever closer co-operation of the national economies of both states.

"**Art. 3.** The high contracting parties will advance co-operation between the organs of state power and the social organizations, develop extensive contacts in the fields of science and culture, education, literature and art, the press, radio, film and television, public health, environmental protection, tourism, physical culture and sports as well as in other fields. They will also develop contact between workers of both countries.

"**Art. 4.** The high contracting parties will advance the further development of fraternal relations between all states of the socialist community to the maximum and always act in the spirit of the strengthening of their unity and cohesion. They declare their willingness to take the necessary measures to protect and defend the historical achievements of socialism and the security and independence of both countries.

"**Art. 5.** The high contracting parties will continue to take all measures incumbent upon them towards the consistent implementation of the principles of peaceful coexistence between states of differing social systems and towards the expansion and deepening of the process of détente in international relations, and will strive to banish war finally from the life of all nations. They will do their utmost to protect international peace and the security of nations against the encroachments of the aggressive forces of imperialism and reaction, to end the arms race, to contribute to general and complete disarmament, finally to abolish colonialism in all forms and manifestations and to support states freed from colonial oppression in the strengthening of their national independence and sovereignty.

"**Art. 6.** The high contracting parties regard the inviolability of state frontiers in Europe as the most important prerequisite for the guarantee of European security and express their firm determination jointly and in alliance with the other participant states of the Warsaw Treaty of Friendship, Co-operation and Mutual Assistance of May 14, 1955, to ensure, in accordance with it, the inviolability of the frontiers of the participant states of this treaty, as they emerged as a result of the 1939–45 war and post-war developments, including the borders between the German Democratic Republic and the Federal Republic of Germany. Both sides will undertake joint efforts to counteract any manifestations of revanchism and militarism, and aspire to the strict observance of treaties concluded with the aim of strengthening European security.

"**Art. 7.** In accordance with the Four-Power Agreement of Sept. 3, 1971 [see page 281], the high contracting parties will maintain and develop their ties with West Berlin on the basis that it is not a constituent part of the Federal Republic and will not be governed by it in the future.

"**Art. 8.** In the event of an armed attack by any state or any group of states on one of the high contracting parties, the other high contracting party will regard this as an attack on itself and will immediately lend it every assistance and support it with all the means at its disposal in the exercise of its right to individual and collective self-defence in accordance with Article 51 of the United Nations Charter. The high contracting parties will immediately inform the UN Security Council of the measures taken on the basis of this article and act in accordance with the provisions of the UN Charter.

"**Art. 9.** The high contracting parties will in all important international questions inform each other, consult each other and act on the basis of their joint position, agreed upon in accordance with the interests of both states.

"**Art. 10.** This treaty does not affect the rights and duties of the high contracting parties under valid bilateral and multilateral agreements. . . ."

The new treaty contained no indication of any termination of either the 1955 treaty on relations between the German Democratic Republic and the Soviet Union or the 1964 Treaty of Friendship, Mutual Assistance and Co-operation concluded for 20 years [see above]. Like other treaties concluded by the Soviet Union with other Communist countries since 1967, the new treaty did not limit the obligation to render military assistance in case of attack to any such attack in Europe. Contrary to the 1955 treaty, the new treaty contained no reference to the reunification of Germany.

Other East German Treaties with Communist States. Treaties with the same provisos as to duration and termination were subsequently concluded by the German Democratic Republic as follows:

(1) With **Hungary** on March 24, 1977;
(2) with **Poland** on May 28, 1977;
(3) with **Bulgaria** on Sept. 14, 1977;
(4) with **Czechoslovakia** on Oct. 3, 1977.

In the treaty with Hungary both sides undertook inter alia to continue their long-term co-ordination and harmonization of economic plans; to act always in the spirit of strengthening unity and cohesion of all states of the socialist community; to expand and deepen the process of détente in international relations and "to contribute to general and complete disarmament"; to guarantee, together with other partners of the Warsaw Treaty Organization, the inviolability of the frontiers between member states, including those between the Federal

Republic of Germany and the German Democratic Republic; and to afford each other instant mutual aid, including military assistance, in the event of an armed attack on either side by any country or group of countries.

The treaty with Poland contained, in its preamble, a special reference to the fulfilment by the German Democratic Republic of the provisions of the 1945 Potsdam Agreement [see page 9] and to the Zgorzelec (Görlitz) treaty of 1950 [see page 248] on the demarcation of the frontier between the two countries.

The treaty with Czechoslovakia was followed, on Dec. 3, 1980, by a joint border treaty providing for easier access across the two countries' common border and for increased economic co-operation in view of a shortfall of imports from Poland.

(For later treaties and agreements of the German Democratic Republic with other communist states see below.)

Later Soviet-East German Treaties

On Oct. 5, 1979, a trade agreement was signed on the sale of Soviet oil, natural gas, and nuclear energy equipment to the German Democratic Republic until 1990 in exchange for ships, machine tools and chemical plant.

An agreement signed on Jan. 28, 1980, provided for an annual supply of 19,000,000 tonnes of Soviet oil in 1980–84.

A further five-year agreement of early February 1980 dealt with the co-ordination of the Soviet and East German national economic plans and envisaged a total trade turnover worth 48,000 million roubles.

A five-year trade agreement signed on March 19, 1981, provided for exchanges of goods worth 58,000 million roubles during 1981–85, with the Soviet Union to supply 95,000,000 tonnes of oil and 37,500 million cubic metres of natural gas during that period, in return for East German machinery and other technological products.

In mid-June 1982 a series of economic co-operation agreements were signed on the supply of advanced East German technology to the Soviet Union. Further industrial co-operation agreements were signed in June and December 1983. Under agreements for oil supplies during 1984 and 1985 such supplies, reduced by 10 per cent in 1982, were to be maintained at the 1983 level.

An agreement signed on Oct. 6, 1984, provided for co-operation in science, technology and production until the year 2000 (with emphasis on microelectronics and data-processing industries). There followed the signing of 14 co-operation agreements on Dec. 17, 1984.

A 1985 trade protocol, signed on Dec. 8, 1984, provided for a turnover of goods worth 15,000 million roubles.

On Dec. 27, 1985, a new long-term trade agreement was concluded, providing for bilateral trade in 1986–90 worth more than the equivalent of £97,000 million.

(The German Democratic Republic has consistently conducted about 40 per cent of its foreign trade with the Soviet Union and has been the latter's main trading partner with a 10 per cent share in Soviet foreign trade.)

Soviet Agreements with Other Communist States in Europe

With **Bulgaria**. An agreement on economic, scientific and technical co-operation until the year 2000, June 7, 1985.

With **Czechoslovakia**. An agreement on co-operation in science, technology and production until the year 2000, May 31, 1985.

An agreement on Czechoslovak participation in the construction of a pipeline from the Yamburg gas field in Western Siberia to Eastern Europe, January 1986.

With **Hungary**. Co-operation agreement, April 1, 1985.

With **Poland**. A major trade and payments protocol, reported on Jan. 6, 1982, guaranteed Poland Soviet supplies during 1982 worth the equivalent of about $6,000 million. (The Soviet Union was subsequently reported to have granted Poland large-scale long-term credits at low interest rates.)

A trade agreement for 1983, reported on Dec. 26, 1982, was designed to increase the volume of trade by 8 to 9 per cent over its 1982 level.

A 15-year economic, scientific and technological co-operation agreement, May 5, 1984.

A long-term programme of scientific and technical co-operation for 1986–90, Sept. 19, 1985.

A protocol signed on Oct. 7, 1985, provided that Poland's debt to the Soviet Union of about 5,000 million roubles (£4,500 million) was to be rescheduled until after 1990, while the economic plans of the two countries for 1986–90 envisaged a 31 per cent increase in trade turnover and a further "reorientation" of the Polish economy towards closer co-operation with the Soviet Union.

Agreements between the Soviet Union and Cuba

A number of agreements for economic co-operation between the Soviet Union and Cuba were signed on Dec. 23, 1972. "Extraordinary assistance" provided by the Soviet Union for Cuba under these agreements included a deferment of payment of Cuba's accumulated debt; new credits for the years 1973–75; payment of special concessionary prices for Cuban sugar, nickel and cobalt; and for capital development.

Under a five-year trade agreement signed for 1976–80 by the Soviet Union and Cuba on Feb. 6, 1976, the volume of trade foreseen in a previous agreement of September 1975 was to be doubled.

A five-year economic and technical co-operation agreement, signed by the two countries on April 14, 1976, included provision for the construction of a Soviet-built nuclear power station in Cuba.

According to US sources quoted in August 1979, Soviet military co-operation with Cuba had included the supply of the following equipment: (i) Up to 20 MiG fighter-bombers received by Cuba between July and November 1978; (ii) a first Soviet submarine and two high-speed torpedo boats delivered to Cuba in February 1979, while submarine facilities were being built at Cienfuegos (on Cuba's south coast); and (iii) 20 An-26 transport aircraft delivered by July 1979 under a 1977 agreement. A Soviet brigade stationed in Cuba in 1979 was described by the US Government as a combat unit and by President Castro of Cuba as a training centre which had been in Cuba since October 1962. (In September 1979 the Soviet Government stated that this training centre would not be enlarged or given additional capabilities; that Soviet personnel in Cuba would not be a threat to the USA or any other nation; and that the Soviet Union would abide by the understanding reached with the USA in 1962 and by its mutually agreed confirmation in 1970, under which the Soviet Union had undertaken, in 1962, not to place any offensive missiles in Cuba and, in 1970, not to establish a military naval base on the island.)

An economic co-operation agreement, signed in Moscow on Oct. 31, 1980, for 1981–85 provided for bilateral trade to be increased by about 50 per cent as against the 1976–80 period, for the extension of economic co-operation beyond 1985, and for the joint preparation of plans for the general development of the Cuban economy until 1990 and for other fields until the year 2000.

A further co-operation agreement was signed on Oct. 31, 1984.

A trade agreement worth about 8,200 million roubles (almost $10,000 million) was signed on June 22, 1985.

Bilateral Treaties Between the USSR and Asian Communist or "Friendly" Countries

Since before World War II the Soviet Union has concluded a number of treaties and agreements with Asian Communist countries.

Early Treaties with the People's Republic of Mongolia. (i) 10-year treaty of mutual assistance, signed on March 28, 1936; (ii) 20-year treaty of friendship and mutual assistance, signed on Feb. 27, 1946; and (iii) 20-year treaty of friendship, co-operation and mutual assistance, signed on Jan. 15, 1966.

1961 Treaty with the Democratic People's Republic of Korea. A treaty of friendship, co-operation and mutual assistance was signed on July 6, 1961, for the duration of ten years.

Common Provisions of Above Treaties. These Soviet treaties of friendship and mutual assistance, although they each contain clauses relating to the particular country forming the second party, have certain provisions in common. These are:

(1) Automatic mutual assistance in the event of one of the parties being an object of armed attack.
(2) An agreement not to conclude any alliance directed against the other party.
(3) An agreement on mutual consultation on all important international problems affecting the common interests of both.
(4) The development and consolidation of economic and cultural ties between the two countries.

Treaties and Agreements with Afghanistan. A 20-year treaty of friendship, good-neighbourliness and co-operation between the USSR and Afghanistan was signed in Moscow on Dec. 5, 1978,

following the establishment of the Democratic Republic of Afghanistan through the assumption of power by the (communist) People's Democratic Party of Afghanistan in April 1978.

The principal provisions of the 15-article treaty were as follows:

After reaffirming their commitment to the aims and principles of Soviet-Afghan treaties of 1921 and 1931, the two countries agreed to develop and strengthen bilateral co-operation in a wide range of matters on the basis of "equality, national sovereignty, territorial integrity and non-interference in each other's internal affairs" and to aid one another in the "training of national personnel and in planning the development of the national economy".

They pledged that they would respect each other's foreign policies (including "the policy of non-alignment which is pursued by ... Afghanistan"), would not engage in any military aggression against each other and would consult one another about all issues which might affect the security, independence and territorial integrity of either country; furthermore, in accordance with Article 4, they agreed that "in the interests of strengthening their defence capacity" they would continue to develop military co-operation "on the basis of appropriate agreements concluded between them".

Both sides declared that they would continue their efforts to promote peace and co-operation in all parts of the world and would "actively contribute towards general and complete disarmament, including nuclear disarmament, under effective international control". With regard to Asia, they stated in Article 8 that they would "facilitate the development of co-operation among Asian states and the establishment of relations of peace, good-neighbourliness and mutual confidence among them" and the establishment in the area of an "effective security system . . . on the basis of joint efforts by all countries of the continent".

An agreement on the establishment of a permanent Soviet-Afghan intergovernmental commission of economic co-operation, signed at the same time, had been preceded by the conclusion of numerous trade and co-operation agreements by the two sides since April 1978 and also by a 12-year agreement on economic co-operation, signed in April 1977.

The Soviet-Afghan treaties of 1921 and 1931, referred to above, had been treaties of neutrality and mutual non-aggression, and that of 1931 had been three times extended for a further 10 years (on Dec. 18, 1955; on Aug. 6, 1965; and on Dec. 10, 1975).

A mutual trade programme for 1981–85, agreed in April 1981, was to treble the trade volume of 1976–80, with Afghanistan supplying raw materials, natural gas and food products in return for industrial equipment and machinery.

A border treaty of June 16, 1981, confirmed the two countries' existing frontier north of the Wakhan salient (where an area was in dispute between China and the Soviet Union).

The agreement on the development of mutual trade, covering the above programme and signed on Feb. 1, 1982, also provided for direct Soviet assistance to Afghanistan worth about $10,000,000.

The conclusion of an agreement on the construction of a railway line from the Amu Darya (Oxus) River to a supply depot on the road to Kabul was reported on March 21, 1983.

Agreements with China. With China agreements have been concluded since 1977 as detailed below (although the 30-year Sino-Soviet treaty of friendship, alliance and mutual assistance signed on Feb. 14, 1950, was allowed to lapse by both sides on the expiry of its term).

A limited agreement on navigation on the Amur and Ussuri rivers was reached between July and October 1977, and a joint commission for navigation has held annual meetings since 1979.

Annual trade and payments agreements between the two countries have covered a fluctuating volume of trade, falling from $516,000,000 in 1978 to $200,000,000 in 1981, but under an agreement signed on April 20, 1982, the value of bilateral trade (involving decreasing Chinese purchases of Soviet capital goods and rising imports of raw materials by China) was set at $302,000,000.

Under an agreement signed on Feb. 6, 1982, Chinese exports to Europe and Iran were allowed to cross Soviet territory by rail.

A trade and payments agreement for 1983, signed on March 10, 1983, was to increase the value of trade from $300,000,000 to $800,000,000.

Two agreements were signed in Khabarovsk (in the Soviet Far East) on April 10, 1983, on local cross-border trade (suspended since 1969).

A trade and payments agreement for 1984, signed on Feb. 10, 1984, was expected to raise two-way trade to $1,200 million.

Three agreements signed on Dec. 28, 1984, provided for (i) increased economic and technical co-operation, (ii) an expansion of scientific and technological exchanges, and (iii) the establishment of a Sino-Soviet joint committee to promote and supervise economic, trade, scientific and technical co-operation. It was also formally agreed to increase trade exchanges to about $1,750 million in 1985.

A five-year trade agreement and a further economic co-operation agreement were signed on July 10, 1985.

A protocol on economic relations was signed on Oct. 29, 1985.

Agreements with Kampuchea. Agreements on non-reimbursable Soviet aid to Kampuchea, commercial co-operation and the establishment of and air service between Moscow and Phnom-Penh were signed in Moscow on July 24, 1979.

Agreements on Soviet aid, cultural and scientific co-operation and economic and technical co-operation were signed during an official visit to Moscow by the President of the People's Republic of Kampuchea on Feb. 3–11, 1980.

1984 Agreement with the Democratic People's Republic of Korea. An agreement of May 25, 1984, was designed to strengthen defences in East Asia and the Pacific region against the "intensified militarist policies" of the United States and Japan. (On Nov. 12, 1984, a previously unreported border dispute between the two countries was reported to have been settled.)

Agreements with Laos. Four agreements signed by the USSR with Laos on April 22, 1976, included a trade treaty and a cultural and scientific co-operation agreement. An agreement on economic and technical co-operation between the two countries in 1979–80 was signed in Vientiane on Feb. 10, 1979.

Soviet aid to Laos in 1981–82 included assistance in the construction of an oil pipeline between the Vietnamese port of Vinh and Vientiane (the capital of Laos), expansion of hydroelectric capacity, and delivery of construction material and an Intersputnik satellite liaison station.

Later Agreements with Mongolia. A trade protocol for 1984 was signed in December 1983.

An agreement on economic, scientific and technical co-operation until the year 2000 was concluded on Aug. 29, 1985.

Treaty and Agreements with Vietnam. A treaty of friendship and co-operation between Vietnam and the Soviet Union was signed in Moscow on Nov. 3, 1978, together with six economic agreements.

The treaty provided inter alia that the parties would consult each other on all important international issues affecting their interests, and that in the event of either becoming the object of attack or of threats of attack they would "immediately begin mutual consultations for the purpose of removing that threat and taking appropriate effective measures to ensure the peace and security of their countries"; that they would strengthen their economic, scientific and technical co-operation and co-ordinate their national economic plans; that they would "wage all-out and consistent struggle for the further strengthening of fraternal relations and of unity and solidarity among socialist countries on the basis of Marxism-Leninism and socialist internationalism"; and that they would promote the development of relations between countries with different social systems on the basis of the principles of peaceful coexistence and the process of détente in international relations. The treaty was to remain in force for 25 years and to be automatically extended for another 10 years unless either party wished to end it. Instruments of ratification of the treaty were exchanged in Hanoi on Dec. 13, 1978.

In May 1979 Soviet warships began to use (the former US base of) Cam Ranh Bay, a Soviet Deputy Foreign Minister stating on May 14 that the Soviet fleet was using Vietnamese harbours "to carry out its obligations under the Soviet-Vietnamese treaty of friendship and alliance".

An agreement on Soviet co-operation in exploration for and exploitation of oil and natural gas on the Vietnamese continental shelf was signed in Moscow on July 3, 1980.

Agreements signed in 1981–82 were a protocol on the co-ordination of economic plans for 1981–85 (June 1981); an agreement on insurance in connexion with oil and gas exploration in Vietnamese waters (reported on May 7, 1982); and an agreement on scientific and technical co-operation in the peaceful uses of atomic energy (announced on June 14, 1982, with Vietnam having decided to adhere to the 1968 Nuclear Non-Proliferation Treaty).

A new accord on labour co-operation was signed on Dec. 26, 1983.

Treaty and Agreements with the People's Democratic Republic of Yemen. A 20-year treaty of friendship and co-operation between the Soviet Union and the People's Democratic Republic of Yemen was signed in Moscow on Oct. 25, 1979, and ratified by the Soviet Union on Dec. 26, 1979. It stated in regard to military co-operation that the two countries would "act on the basis of the relevant agreements concluded between them for the purpose of strengthening their defence capability"; that each country would fully respect the territorial integrity and independence of the other and would neither "enter into military or other alliances" nor "take part in any grouping of states and undertakings" directed against the other party; and that in the case of situations arising which would "threaten peace or violate international peace" the two countries would contact each other "for the purpose of removing a threat to peace or restoring peace".

At the same time the two sides signed (i) a "plan of contacts" between the two countries' political parties for 1980–83 and (ii) a protocol on economic and technical co-operation.

On May 28, 1980, agreements were signed on the formation of a standing committee for technical and economic co-operation and on co-operation in the construction of a thermal power station, and also a protocol agreement on the further expansion of economic and technical co-operation.

An economic and technical co-operation agreement signed on Jan. 5, 1985, provided for Soviet project aid in the agricultural, transport, geological and power-generation fields.

Bilateral Treaties and Agreements between the USSR and African Countries

The Soviet Union has signed 20-year treaties of friendship and co-operation with the following African countries:

(1) **Angola** on Oct. 8, 1976, when the two sides undertook inter alia to develop co-operation in the military sphere "in the interests of strengthening their defence capacity"—while a co-operation agreement was also signed between the Popular Movement for the Liberation of Angola (MPLA) and the Communist Party of the Soviet Union (CPSU).

(2) **Mozambique** on March 31, 1977, this treaty providing in Art. 4 that "in the interests of reinforcing the defence potential" of the two countries they would "continue to develop co-operation in the military sphere on the basis of the relevant military agreements" and in Art. 9 that "in the event of situations arising that threaten peace or lead to an outbreak of war" the two contries would "immediately get in touch with each other in order to co-ordinate their positions in the interests of eliminating the threat that has arisen or of restoring peace" (this treaty being ratified by the Supreme Soviet of the USSR on June 15, 1977).

(3) **Ethiopia** on Nov. 20, 1978, when the two sides stated that they would (i) "develop and deepen the relations of unbreakable friendship and co-operation" in the political, economic, trade, scientific, technical and cultural spheres "on the basis of equality, non-interference in each other's internal affairs, respect for sovereignty, territorial integrity and the inviolability of borders" and also respecting each other's foreign policies; (ii) consult each other on "important international questions directly involving the interests of the two countries" and in situations which "constitute a threat to or a breach of international peace"; (iii) work "actively" for the complete elimination of colonialism, neocolonialism and racism; (iv) continue to work towards safeguarding and securing international détente and settling "international controversial issues by peaceful means without prejudice to the legitimate rights of states to defend themselves, individually or collectively, in accordance with the UN Charter"; and (v) "continue to co-operate in the military field in the interests of ensuring the defence capacity" of the two countries. Following ratification by both sides, this treaty entered into force in April 1979.

Earlier, an agreement had been concluded in March 1977 for the supply to Ethiopia of Soviet weapons, including MiG fighters, missiles and tanks. A Soviet-Ethiopian trade agreement was signed on July 22, 1977, and on Sept. 3 of that year it was reported that an agreement concluded in July 1977 provided for the supply of Soviet aircraft, tanks and equipment and of 3,000 Soviet and Cuban experts. (The participation of Cuban forces in Ethiopia's armed conflict with Somalia was officially admitted in Cuba on March 14, 1978, as "following an urgent call by the Ethiopian Government to the Cuban Communist Party".)

(4) **The Congo** on May 13, 1981. Unlike the three treaties listed above, this treaty contained no commitment to bilateral military co-operation but provided instead that "in the event of situations emerging which create a threat to peace or a violation of peace the USSR and the People's Republic of the Congo will enter into contact with each other without delay in order to co-ordinate their position with a view to eliminating a threat or restoring peace". (The USSR was said to have the use of a military base at Pointe Noire.)

ABROGATION OF SOVIET TREATIES WITH EGYPT AND SOMALIA

Two important treaties of friendship and co-operation concluded by the Soviet Union were abrogated in 1976 and 1977 respectively.

Egypt. Such a treaty, concluded with Egypt for 15 years on May 27, 1971, was abrogated by Egypt on March 15, 1976, on the grounds that (as stated by the Egyptian President) the USSR had refused to supply Egypt with arms and to grant a moratorium for Egypt's debts.

Somalia. A similar treaty, which the USSR had signed with Somalia on July 11, 1974, and under which the USSR had not only supplied that country with defence equipment but had also established a naval base in Somalia, was abrogated by the latter on Nov. 13, 1977, after the Somali President had, on Oct. 21 of that year, condemned the Soviet Union for its "all-out armed support of the Ethiopian regime" with which Somalia was then at war.

OTHER SOVIET-AFRICAN AGREEMENTS

Other Soviet agreements with countries in Africa have been concluded as follows.

Angola. On Jan. 24, 1981, an agreement on a programme of economic and technical co-operation was reported to have been signed, providing inter alia for the building of several dams and a second oil refinery in Luanda. (On Nov. 27, 1981, it was reported that the Soviet Union was setting up a new fleet to be based on Luanda.)

The Congo. Co-operation agreements relating to the economy, technology, agriculture and culture were signed in March 1975.

Egypt. A trade protocol for 1984, signed on Dec. 1, 1983, provided for an increase in the volume of trade by 25 per cent.
A further agreement to increase the volume of trade was signed in June 1985.

Ethiopia. A co-operation agreement concluded on Aug. 11, 1981, was designed to speed up the implementation of economic, technical, trade and scientific co-operation agreements signed in 1978 and 1979.
A long-term economic co-operation agreement signed on Sept. 8, 1984, covered Soviet participation in Ethiopia's 10-year plan as well as Soviet assistance in oil and gold exploration, irrigation and power projects, and training. The conclusion of a further co-operation agreement was reported on Dec. 18, 1984.

Ghana. An economic co-operation agreement signed in early 1982 was renewed in August 1984.
The signing of a cultural and scientific co-operation agreement was announced on April 14, 1984.

Guinea. Bilateral agreements were signed on Sept. 11, 1984, on the financing of projects in agriculture and mining and were followed by two Soviet loans respectively equivalent to $102,000,000 and $130,000,000.

Guinea-Bissau. Agreements on economic, technical, cultural and scientific co-operation and on trade and air services were signed in February 1975.

Libya. An agreement signed in May 1975 provided for co-operation in the use of nuclear energy for peaceful purposes. At the same time it was disclosed that the Soviet Union had agreed to supply Libya with military equipment worth $800,000,000.

Mauritius. Agreement on cultural and scientific co-operation, Sept. 16, 1969.
Trade agreement, July 25, 1979.

Mozambique. Agreements were signed on Nov. 22, 1980, on the promotion of trade in the areas of agriculture, fishing and mining.
Under an economic agreement of Jan. 20, 1983, the value of bilateral trade was to be doubled by 1985.

Nigeria. The signing of a two-year cultural agreement was announced on Aug. 13, 1983.

Tanzania. Agreements signed on March 25, 1977, provided for trade and for cultural, scientific and technical co-operation.

Tunisia. An agreement on cultural and scientific co-operation was concluded in 1971.
A five-year trade agreement was signed on Sept. 18, 1985.

Uganda. An agreement on the supply of Soviet military equipment, including long-range aircraft, was said to have been signed on Sept. 28, 1976.

An agreement on co-operation in trade and technology was signed on Jan. 25, 1978.
On May 11, 1978, further co-operation agreements were reported to have been signed.

Zambia. Agreement on purchases of arms (including MiG fighter bombers, personnel carriers, artillery and armoured cars) was reported to have been reached in February 1980 as part of a package worth about £39,000,000.

Zimbabwe. The first bilateral trade agreement between the two countries was signed on Jan. 18, 1984.
A wide-ranging economic and technical co-operation agreement was signed on Dec. 4, 1985 (when military aid was also discussed, with specific agreements to follow).

Treaties and Agreements concluded by Communist States in Europe (other than the Soviet Union) with Other Communist or "Friendly" States

ALBANIA

Albania has concluded agreements with other communist countries as follows:

China. Trade protocol, March 9, 1985.
Trade agreement for 1986–90, Dec. 3, 1985.

German Democratic Republic. Trade protocol, Oct. 1, 1984.

Hungary. Trade protocol, Oct. 3, 1984.

Democratic People's Republic of Korea. A 1986–90 agreement on mutual commodity delivery and payments, Nov. 23, 1985.

Vietnam. Trade protocol, Feb. 5, 1985.

Yugoslavia. Five-year trade agreement, July 14, 1980 (superseding a trade protocol of Nov. 2, 1978).
Agreement on the construction of a railway link between Shkoder (northern Albania) and Titograd, reported on April 7, 1982. (This link, the first rail connexion between Albania and the rest of Europe, was opened on Aug. 6, 1986.)
Agreement on exemption from visa requirements for Albanian and Yugoslav personnel working on common engineering projects in the border areas, Oct. 2, 1984.
Trade agreement on exchange of goods (worth $121,000,000) in 1985, Oct. 5, 1984.
Protocol on transport of goods by road in 1985, Feb. 7, 1984.

BULGARIA

Bulgaria has concluded treaties and agreements with other communist or "friendly" countries as follows:

Angola. Treaty of friendship and co-operation, Oct. 22, 1978.

China. Protocol on scientific and technical co-operation, Aug. 30, 1985.
Trade agreement for 1986–90 and barter and payments agreement for 1986, Dec. 21, 1985.

Czechoslovakia. A 25-year treaty of friendship and co-operation.

Democratic People's Republic of Korea. Treaty of friendship and co-operation, June 1984.

Laos. A 25-year treaty of friendship and co-operation, providing for economic, scientific and technical co-operation, and for co-operation in culture, education, sport and tourism, Oct. 4, 1979.

Mongolia. Treaty of friendship and co-operation, July 23, 1967, and May 5, 1977.

Vietnam. Treaty of friendship and co-operation, Oct. 1, 1979.

People's Democratic Republic of Yemen. Protocol agreements (i) for co-operation in defence, April 2, 1980; (ii) for the expansion of economic co-operation, the development of trade in 1981–83 and co-operation in foreign affairs, Dec. 2, 1980.

A 20-year treaty of friendship and co-operation, automatically renewable for five-year periods and providing for economic and technical-scientific co-operation and the expansion of trade and shipping, including most-favoured-nation treatment, Nov. 11, 1981.

Yugoslavia. A 1984 programme for bilateral trade exchanges worth $312,000,000.

CZECHOSLOVAKIA

Czechoslovakia has concluded treaties and agreements with other communist or "friendly" countries as follows:

China. A five-year agreement on trade exchanges worth the equipment of £1,700 million, December 1985.

German Democratic Republic. Trade agreement for 1986–90, Oct. 25, 1985.

Ethiopia. A 20-year treaty of friendship and co-operation and an aide-mémoire ratifying the establishment of a joint commission for economic, scientific and technical co-operation, Sept. 13, 1981.

Laos. A 25-year treaty of friendship and co-operation, Feb. 17, 1980.

Mozambique. Friendship agreement for closer economic and political co-operation, Oct. 21, 1981.

People's Democratic Republic of Yemen. A 20-year treaty of friendship and co-operation in commerce, science, culture, education, health and the media, providing also for agreement to "continue their active fight against the aggressive policy of world imperialism and hegemonism and for the elimination of colonialism, Zionism and racism", signed in September 1981, together with an agreement for co-operation in trade in 1982–83.

GERMAN DEMOCRATIC REPUBLIC

The German Democratic Republic has concluded treaties and agreements with other communist and with "friendly" states as follows:

Afghanistan. Treaty of friendship and co-operation (for 20 years), May 23, 1982.

Agreement on the construction of a railway line from the river Amu Darya (Oxus) to a supply depot on the route to Kabul, reported on March 21, 1983.

Angola. Treaty of friendship and co-operation (for 20 years), Feb. 19, 1979.

Undertaking to increase military co-operation, Nov. 9, 1982 (when there were an estimated 2,500 military and security advisers from the German Democratic Republic in Angola).

China. Trade agreement for 1979, January 1979.

Economic co-operation agreement, September 1984.

Five-year trade agreement (to increase bilateral trade to 2½ times that of 1981–85), July 15, 1985.

A working plan for cultural and scientific co-operation, June 1986.

Cuba. Treaty of friendship and co-operation (for 25 years, without provision for military co-operation), June 1, 1980.

Ethiopia. Treaty of friendship and co-operation (for 20 years), Nov. 15, 1979 (ratified on Aug. 14, 1980), and a military co-operation protocol, May 31, 1979.

Hungary. Treaty of friendship, co-operation and mutual assistance (for 25 years), March 24, 1977 [see page 249].

A long-term programme for the development of economic, scientific and technological co-operation up to the year 2000, Oct. 29, 1985.

Democratic People's Republic of Korea. Treaty of friendship and co-operation, May 1984.

Laos. A 25-year treaty of friendship and co-operation (together with a communiqué on increased aid for the mechanization of agriculture in Laos), Sept. 22, 1982.

Mongolia. A 25-year treaty of friendship and co-operation (without provision for mutual assistance in the event of armed attack, and replacing earlier treaties of Aug. 22, 1957, and Sept. 12, 1968), May 6, 1977.

Mozambique. A 20-year treaty of friendship and co-operation, with military co-operation protocol, May 26, 1979.

Poland. Agreement on plan co-ordination and trade for 1986–90, 1985.

Romania. Treaty of friendship and mutual assistance (for 20 years, renewable once for five years), May 12, 1972.

Agreement on plan co-ordination and trade for 1986–90, 1985.

Long-term programme of economic, scientific and technical co-operation up to the year 2000, May 30, 1985.

People's Democratic Republic of Yemen. Treaty of friendship and co-operation (for 20 years), with a military co-operation protocol, Nov. 17, 1979; instruments of ratification exchanged on Nov. 24, 1980.

Economic and technical co-operation protocol and agreement on facilitating travel between the two countries, Nov. 8, 1981.

Yugoslavia. Agreement on co-operation in scientific, educational, cultural and technical matters, Oct. 3, 1985.

HUNGARY

Hungary has concluded such agreements as follows:

Angola. A general agreement in the military field, Oct. 25, 1982.

An agreement on cultural, educational and scientific co-operation for 1986–88, Sept. 30, 1985.

China. Trade protocol for 1986, Dec. 16, 1985.

Mongolia. Agreement on the development of cultural and scientific co-operation in 1981–85, Oct. 29, 1981.

Romania. A long-term trade agreement for 1986–90, Oct. 22, 1985.

People's Democratic Republic of Yemen. A treaty of friendship and collaboration, Oct. 29, 1983.

POLAND

Poland concluded a treaty of friendship and co-operation with **Ethiopia** on Dec. 12, 1979.

ROMANIA

Romania has concluded treaties of friendship and co-operation with other communist states or with "friendly" countries as follows:

Angola, for a 20-year period, April 14, 1979.

China, agreements on the establishment of an intergovernmental committee for economic and technical co-operation, on regular shipping services and on trade, Aug. 21, 1979.

Kampuchea (i.e. the Pol Pot regime), May 28, 1978.

Mongolia, June 17, 1983.

Mozambique, for 20 years, together with a programme for economic co-operation until 1990, April 20, 1979.

Vietnam, a declaration of permanent consolidation of friendship, solidarity and the development of co-operation, May 25, 1978.

Treaties and Agreements of Asian Communist Countries with Other Communist or "Friendly" Countries

Afghanistan and Czechoslovakia. A 25-year treaty of friendship and co-operation signed in Prague on June 25, 1981, provided for "all-round co-operation, mutual assistance and support" and the expansion of "mutually advantageous economic, scientific and technical co-operation" (this being the first such treaty between Afghanistan and an East European country).

Kampuchea and Vietnam. A treaty of peace, friendship and co-operation signed in Phnom-Penh on Feb. 18, 1979, by Vietnam with the Government set up in Cambodia by the "People's Revolutionary Council" (established with Vietnamese support as the provisional Government of the People's Republic of Kampuchea on Jan. 8, 1979) contained the following provisions:

The two sides would develop their traditional solidarity, friendship and co-operation and would assist each other in all fields on the basis of respect for independence, non-interference in internal affairs and equality; assist each other to strengthen their capacity to defend their independence against "all schemes and acts of sabotage by the imperialist and reactionary forces"; would resolve all differences which might arise between them by peaceful negotiations and would negotiate a treaty delineating the frontier between them on the basis of the present border line; and would pursue a foreign policy of independence, peace, friendship, co-operation and non-alignment, and of friendship and good-neighbourliness with Thailand and the other South-East Asian countries. The treaty was not aimed at opposing any third country, and it would be valid for 25 years and automatically renewed every 10 years, unless either party gave a year's notice of its intention to cancel it.

An agreement signed on July 7, 1982, defined the two countries' territorial waters and stated that negotiations would be held to delimit their maritime frontier.

A border treaty signed in Phnom Penh on July 20, 1983, defined the two countries' common border as shown on a 1:100,000 scale map in use before 1954.

Democratic People's Republic of Korea and Angola. Treaty of friendship and co-operation, Oct. 19, 1981.

Democratic People's Republic of Korea and Mozambique. A commitment to increased political, military and economic support for Mozambique, announced on Feb. 17, 1983.

Democratic People's Republic of Korea and People's Democratic Republic of Yemen. A treaty of friendship and co-operation providing for a wide range of co-operation in economic, political and cultural matters, Oct. 11, 1984.

Laos and Mongolia. A 25-year treaty of friendship and co-operation, Dec. 8, 1979.

Laos and Vietnam. A treaty of friendship and co-operation signed in Vientiane on July 18, 1977, between Vietnam and the Lao People's Democratic Republic provided inter alia that both sides would "protect and develop the special Vietnam-Laos relationship"; would "co-operate closely in increasing their capability of defending and protecting their independence, sovereignty and territorial integrity"; would "strive to strengthen the militant solidarity and co-operative relations with other fraternal socialist countries"; and would "positively contribute together with the other socialist countries and the international communist movement to intensifying their solidarity and mutual support and assistance"; "strengthen the militant solidarity, lasting co-operation with and mutual assistance to fraternal Cambodia"; and "establish and develop relations of friendship and co-operation with the countries in this area". The treaty would be valid for 20 years and automatically renewed for further 10-year periods unless one of the signatories gave a year's written notice of intention to cancel it.

(In a joint statement issued at the same time the two sides undertook to "do everything in their power to strengthen their militant solidarity and relations of co-operation with the USSR, China and the other fraternal socialist countries" and "strengthen solidarity and mutual support and assistance on the basis of Marxism-Leninism and proletarian internationalism".)

A co-operation agreement for 1981–85 was signed in March 1982 (when it was also agreed to conclude a treaty delimiting the Lao-Vietnamese border).

Mongolia and Vietnam. A treaty of friendship and co-operation, concluded for 25 years and automatically renewable every 10 years, was signed in Hanoi on Dec. 3, 1979, between the Socialist Republic of Vietnam and the Mongolian People's Republic. In this treaty it was stated inter alia that the two sides supported "the South-East Asian peoples' aspiration to turn the region into one of peace, independence, freedom, neutrality, stability and prosperity".

Soviet Agreements with Non-Communist Countries in Europe, Asia and the Pacific

Australia. An agreement on the development of trade and economic relations was concluded on May 16, 1973.

Agreements on cultural and on scientific and technical co-operation between the Soviet Union and Australia were signed on Jan. 15, 1975.

Austria. A trade and payments agreement of Aug. 5, 1970, replacing a twice-renewed 1955 agreement, was itself renewed to the end of 1985 at the end of May 1975.

A 1973 agreement on the development of economic, scientific, technical and industrial co-operation was on Jan. 19, 1981, replaced by a 10-year agreement giving detailed lists of joint products and of mutual trading interests.

Under a 20-year agreement signed in September 1982, the Soviet and Austrian power grids were to be linked from 1985 (this being the first such Soviet agreement with a Western country).

Following agreements of 1968, 1974 and 1975 on Austrian imports of Soviet gas, an agreement was signed on March 30, 1984, providing for such imports to be increased from 2,400 million to 3,800 million cubic metres per year.

Bangladesh. A one-year barter trade agreement was signed on April 28, 1985.

Finland. A Treaty of Friendship, Co-operation and Mutual Assistance between the Soviet Union and Finland was signed on April 6, 1948, and was concluded for 10 years. A protocol extending the treaty for a further 20 years was signed on Sept. 19, 1955, and it is automatically renewable for five-year periods after 1975, unless abrogated by one party one year before the date of expiration.

The treaty differs from other treaties of mutual assistance made by the Soviet Union in that the obligation to intervene with military assistance in the event of aggression by a third party is restricted to the USSR. Finland is obliged only to fight any aggression on her own territory.

The main provisions of the treaty are given below:

Art. 1. In the event of Finland or the Soviet Union, across the territory of Finland, becoming the object of military aggression on the part of Germany or any state allied to the latter, Finland, loyal to her duty as an independent state, will fight to repulse the aggression. In doing so, she will direct all the forces at her disposal to the defence of the inviolability of her territory on land, on sea and in the air, acting within her boundaries in accordance with her obligations under the present treaty with the assistance, in case of need, of the Soviet Union or jointly with the latter.

In the cases indirected above, the Soviet Union will render Finland the necessary assistance, in regard to the granting of which the parties will agree between themselves.

Art. 6. The parties undertake to observe the principles of mutual respect for their state sovereignty and independence, as well as of non-interference in the domestic affairs of the other state.

On July 20, 1970, the treaty was extended for another 20 years (i.e. until 1990), and on April 20, 1971, a further treaty was signed in Moscow on economic, technical and industrial co-operation between the two countries.

The treaty was again renewed for 20 years on June 6, 1983 (i.e. before its scheduled expiry in 1990). At the same time a protocol was signed on agricultural co-operation, as were several engineering contracts. The renewed treaty was ratified by the two countries' respective legislatures on Oct. 29 and Nov. 11, 1983. A Permanent Intergovernmental Committee for Economic Co-operation was also established.

A new five-year trade agreement for 1986–90, signed on Sept. 29, 1984, provided for a trade turnover worth the equivalent of $31,500 million. (The balance of trade has remained firmly in Finland's favour.)

France. Under an agreement signed on Jan. 23, 1982, the Soviet Union was to supply France for 25 years as from 1984–85 with an annual volume of 8,000 million cubic metres of natural gas.

A five-year economic co-operation agreement signed on Feb. 3, 1984, provided inter alia for the Soviet purchase of 10,000 million French francs worth of French capital goods and F 40,000 million worth French steel products.

Greece. On Jan. 18, 1982, the Greek government confirmed the renewal of a 1979 agreement on the repair and maintenance of Soviet commercial and naval supply ships on the island of Syros in the Aegean Sea.

An agreement on the purchase of 2,000,000 tonnes of Soviet oil in 1982 in exchange for agricultural products was concluded early in February 1982; a general 10-year accord on economic co-operation on Feb. 22, 1983; and a further economic agreement on the construction of an aluminium plant in Greece and other co-operation in early October 1983. For the aluminium plant agreement was reached in March 1984 on its joint financing and on its processing an annual 1,500,000 tonnes of bauxite.

Iceland. An agreement on commerce and navigation was signed on May 25, 1927.

An agreement on trade and payments of Aug. 1, 1953, was followed by a protocol of Oct. 31, 1975, and a protocol on exchange of goods of Sept. 11, 1980.

An agreement on co-operation in culture, science and technology was signed on April 25, 1961.

An agreement on economic co-operation was concluded on July 2, 1982.

India. A 20-year treaty of peace, friendship and co-operation between the Soviet Union and India, automatically renewable for five-year periods unless either party gave prior notice of termination, was signed in New Delhi on Aug. 9, 1971.

The treaty included the following articles:

"**Art. 2.** Guided by the desire to contribute in every possible way towards ensuring the lasting peace and security of their peoples, the high contracting parties declare their determination to continue efforts to preserve and strengthen peace in Asia and throughout the world, end the arms race, and achieve general and complete disarmament, covering both nuclear and conventional weapons, under effective international control.

"**Art. 3.** Guided by their devotion to the noble ideal of equality of all peoples and states, irrespective of race or creed, the high contracting parties condemn colonialism and racialism in all their forms and manifestations and reaffirm their determination to strive for their final and complete elimination.

"The high contracting parties will co-operate with other states in achieving these aims and support the just aspirations of the peoples in their struggle against colonialism and racial domination.

"**Art. 4.** The Union of Soviet Socialist Republics respects India's policy of non-alignment and reaffirms that this policy is an important factor for maintaining world peace and international security and for lessening tensions in the world.

"The Republic of India respects the peaceful policy of the USSR aimed at strengthening friendship and co-operation with all peoples.

"**Art. 8.** In accordance with the traditional friendship established between the two countries, each of the high contracting parties solemnly declares that it will not enter into or participate in any military alliances directed against the other party.

"Each high contracting party undertakes to refrain from any aggression against the other party and not to allow the use of its territory for the commission of any act that might inflict military damage on the other high contracting party.

"**Art. 9.** Each high contracting party undertakes to abstain from giving any assistance to any third party that engages in an armed conflict with the other party. In the event of either party being subjected to attack or threat thereof, the high contracting parties shall immediately enter into mutual consultations with a view to eliminating this threat and taking appropriate effective measures to ensure the peace and security of their countries.

"**Art. 10.** Each high contracting party solemnly declares that it will not enter into any commitment, secret or public, with one or more states which is incompatible with the present treaty. Each high contracting party further declares that no commitment exists, nor shall any be entered into between itself or any other state or states, that might cause military damage to the other party."

In a communiqué issued at the time when the treaty was signed the Indian Minister of External Affairs referred to "a heavy burden . . . placed on India by the influx of more than seven million refugees" from East Pakistan (now Bangladesh), and India's "gratitude for the Soviet Union's understanding of the problem", as shown by an appeal by President Podgorny to the President of Pakistan in April 1971.

The treaty was ratified in New Delhi on Aug. 9 and in Moscow on Aug. 13, 1971.

In a joint communiqué issued in New Delhi at the end of a meeting between the Soviet Foreign Minister and India's Minister of External Affairs on April 27, 1977, it was stated: "The two sides expressed their satisfaction with the development of the time-tested relations of traditional friendship and co-operation, of mutual respect and confidence, that have been established between the Soviet Union and India. The determination of both sides was stressed to continue to follow the course towards the further strengthening of equal and mutually beneficial co-operation in the spirit of the Soviet-Indian treaty of peace, friendship and co-operation of August 1971. . . . The two sides noted with satisfaction that the positions of the Soviet Union and India on many important questions are identical or close." The communiqué also said that the two sides were ready to participate with all the states concerned in "efforts leading to the early establishment of the Indian Ocean as a zone of peace" and called for "the elimination of all existing foreign military bases from the Indian Ocean and the prohibition of new ones".

A 15-year economic and trade agreement, providing for far-reaching economic, technical and scientific co-operation between the Soviet Union and India, was signed on Nov. 29, 1973.

Agreements were signed on Dec. 8–11, 1980, (i) on Soviet aid to India worth £337,000,000 and (ii) on trade in 1981–86, involving inter alia increased Indian imports of crude oil and refined petroleum products.

An agreement signed in May 1981 provided for the supply of Soviet military equipment worth $1,600 million payable over 17 years.

An agreement on co-operation in research and development was signed on June 13, 1982.

An agreement signed on May 12, 1983, provided for Soviet credit for the second stage of a steel plant in Andhra Pradesh.

An agreement announced on July 23, 1983, covered the licensed production of the (Soviet) MiG-27 aircraft (and on Aug. 6, 1984, it was disclosed that India had agreed to buy the MiG fighter-bomber).

Two economic agreements were signed on May 22, 1985, involving (i) a credit of 1,000 million roubles for specific Indian projects and (ii) long-term co-operation in economic affairs, trade, science and technology.

On Nov. 22, 1985, the 1973 trade agreement was extended until 1990.

Indonesia. A protocol on economic relations was signed on Oct. 29, 1985.

Iran. A 15-year treaty on the development of economic and technical co-operation between the Soviet Union and Iran was signed in Moscow on Oct. 12, 1972. A further economic co-operation agreement, signed on Feb. 25, 1975, covered projects with an estimated value of $3,000 million. (For earlier Soviet-Iranian treaties, see page 6.)

In February 1982 an economic agreement was officially stated to have been signed on the construction of two gas-powered electricity plants in Iran. (Trade between the two countries was said to have reached a record level of $1,000 million in 1981.)

Iraq. A 15-year treaty of friendship and co-operation between the Soviet Union and Iraq, automatically renewable for periods of five years, was signed in Baghdad on April 9, 1972.

Art. 1 of the treaty provided for all-round co-operation in the political, economic, trade, scientific, technical and other fields "on the basis of respect for state sovereignty, territorial integrity, and non-interference in one another's internal affairs".

In Art. 4 both countries condemned "imperialism and colonialism in all their forms and manifestations" and undertook to "continue to wage an undeviating struggle against imperialism and Zionism . . .".

Art. 8 laid down that "in the event of situations which threaten the peace of either of the sides or create a threat to peace or the danger of a violation of peace" both countries would "immediately contact each other with the aim of co-ordinating their positions . . .".

In Art. 9 the two sides undertook to "continue to develop co-operation in the strengthening of their defence capabilities".

In Art. 10 each of the two sides declared that it would "not enter into alliances or take part in any groupings of states or actions or undertakings" directed against the other side, and would "not permit the use of its territory for any act capable of doing military harm to the other side".

The treaty came into force after the exchange of ratification documents in Moscow on July 20, 1972.

In December 1978 agreement was reached on the supply to Iraq of Soviet arms "to reinforce the defence capacity of Iraq".

At talks held in Moscow in December 1982 an understanding was said to have been reached on the resumption of deliveries of sophisticated Soviet weapons to Iraq.

Japan. A number of agreements signed between June 1974 and July 1975 provided for the joint development of natural resources in Siberia and the Soviet Far East, involving inter alia large-scale supplies to Japan of Soviet coal, oil, gas and timber in return for credits to be granted by Japan to the Soviet Union.

On May 30, 1977, an earlier trade and payments agreement was extended to cover the 1976–80 period. (Later exchanges were, however, affected by sanctions applied by Japan in connection with its condemnation of the Soviet involvement in Afghanistan, but these sanctions were relaxed in June 1981.)

An agreement on co-operation between Japan and the Soviet Union in the peaceful uses of atomic energy, signed in November 1977, provided for exchanges of visits by experts and also for regular exchanges of scientific information.

A financial agreement for 1986–90 was concluded on Jan. 18, 1986.

Jordan. In November 1981 King Hussein of Jordan confirmed that his government had reached agreement with the Soviet Union on arms purchases worth $200,000,000, including SAM-6 surface-to-air missiles (later reported to include 320 SAM missiles at a total cost of $360,000,000).

The conclusion of an agreement on the purchase by Jordan of a Soviet air defence system was announced on Jan. 5, 1985.

Kuwait. An arms sales agreement worth $327,000,000 and concluded in July 1984 was reported to involve the purchase by Kuwait of air defences, surface-to-surface missiles and tanks. (10 Soviet military officers later arrived in Kuwait to assist in training activities.)

Malta. Under an agreement signed on Jan. 26, 1981, the Soviet Union was to have oil storage and refuelling facilities in Malta (while Soviet warships would continue to have no access to Maltese ports).

Agreements signed on March 2, 1984, related to an expansion of economic and technical co-operation, including a three-year counter trade agreement worth $265,000,000 and the construction by Malta of eight cargo ships for the Soviet Union.

Nepal. Under an agreement on economic and technical co-operation signed on Nov. 19, 1976, the Soviet Union undertook to supply Nepal with machines and other equipment as well as with specialists for the building of factories.

The Philippines. An agreement on the expansion of scientific and cultural exchanges between the two countries was signed early in January 1975. A trade agreement was signed on June 2, 1976.

Another agreement on scientific and technical co-operation was signed on July 8, 1982.

An agreement signed on Oct. 15, 1982, provided for continuing co-operation in trade and in cultural and technological matters.

Spain. Agreements signed on Jan. 19, 1979, provided for (i) cultural co-operation and (ii) scientific and technical co-operation, with a protocol on the latter being signed on Oct. 27, 1982.

New agreements signed on March 1, 1985, included one on cultural and scientific co-operation.

Sweden. A trade agreement was concluded on March 15, 1924.

An agreement on co-operation in the use of nuclear energy for peaceful purposes was signed on Jan. 12, 1970, together with an agreement on economic, technical and scientific co-operation.

A navigation agreement was signed on April 5, 1973.

A long-term trade agreement was concluded on April 7, 1976.

A treaty on border trade and a protocol on credits were signed on Feb. 13, 1985.

Switzerland. An extradition convention signed with Russia on Nov. 17, 1873, is still in force.

An agreement on exchange of goods was concluded on March 17, 1948.

An agreement on the development of economic, industrial, scientific and technical co-operation was signed on Jan. 12, 1978, and followed by a long-term programme signed on July 9, 1979.

Syria. In a joint communiqué issued at the end of a meeting between the Soviet and Syrian Presidents in Moscow on Oct. 6, 1978, it was recorded that "relevant decisions" had been taken with a view to strengthening Syria's defence capacity, and on Oct. 17, 1979, an agreement was concluded providing for "substantial military aid" to Syria by the USSR, with details still to be worked out.

A protocol on economic, scientific and technical co-operation between the Soviet Union and Syria was signed on May 15, 1980.

A treaty of friendship and co-operation in various fields, including military affairs, was signed in Moscow on Oct. 8, 1980, during a visit by the Syrian President, and the treaty was approved by the Syrian Government on Oct. 13, 1980. Instruments of ratification were signed on Dec. 2, 1980.

Five-year agreements on trade and economic co-operation were signed in April–May 1985.

Turkey. An economic and technical co-operation agreement signed on July 9, 1975, provided inter alia for a Soviet credit of $700,000,000 mainly to finance Soviet-built projects and to be repaid with Turkish exports.

Agreement was reached in June 1984 on the construction of a new natural gas pipeline from Bulgaria, to be ready by the end of 1986.

An agreement concluded on Dec. 27, 1984, provided for trade exchanges worth the equivalent of $6,000 million during 1986–90.

The **Yemen Arab Republic.** A treaty of friendship was concluded on March 21, 1964.

A plan for cultural and scientific co-operation between the two countries was signed on Oct. 27, 1981, and in a joint communiqué issued on Oct. 28 the 1964 treaty was expressly recalled and the desire was expressed to continue, expand and improve mutual beneficial co-operation in the economic, military, scientific-technical, trade and cultural spheres and in those of health care, education and the training of national cadres in the Yemen Arab Republic.

A 20-year treaty of friendship and co-operation was signed on April 9, 1984, as a successor to treaties signed in 1927, 1955 and 1964. The treaty also provided for increased trade and economic co-operation within the framework of a joint economic commission, as well as for consultation on important issues of foreign policy.

Treaties and Agreements concluded by Communist States in Europe (other than the Soviet Union) with Non-Communist Countries

ALBANIA

Albania has concluded agreements with non-communist countries as follows:

Finland. A five-year trade agreement, May 1986.

France. Trade exchange agreement, March 11, 1983.
Greece. Agreements on road transport, postal services, telecommunications, and educational and scientific exchanges, Dec. 3–6, 1984.
Economic co-operation agreement for 1985, Jan. 25, 1985.
Cultural exchange programme, agreed on March 8, 1985.

Italy. Trade agreement, March 17, 1984.

Morocco. Trade protocol, Oct. 30, 1984.

Sweden. Trade agreement, Dec. 6, 1984.

Switzerland. Trade agreement, Oct. 28, 1974.

Turkey. Agreements on air links and trade, Feb. 13 and 22, 1984.
Trade protocol, Feb. 5, 1985.

BULGARIA

Bulgaria has concluded agreements with non-communist countries as follows:

Algeria. Economic, technical and scientific protocol, Jan. 9, 1985.

Australia. Trade agreements, June 22, 1966, and Dec. 5, 1974.

Egypt. Agreement on cultural and scientific co-operation, January 1982.
Cultural co-operation agreement, May 13, 1984.

France. A five-year economic co-operation agreement, March 19, 1976.

Federal Republic of Germany. A 10-year agreement on the development of economic, industrial and technological co-operation, May 14, 1975; extended to May 14, 1995, on March 8, 1985.
Cultural co-operation agreement, Nov. 25, 1975 (in force from Nov. 12, 1976).

Iceland. Commercial agreement, Oct. 29, 1963.

Italy. Long-term agreement on the development of economic, industrial, scientific and technical co-operation, May 27, 1974.
Agreement on economic co-operation in 1975–79, June 23, 1975.
A 10-year economic co-operation agreement, Jan. 22, 1981.

Libya. Friendship and co-operation treaty, January 1983.

Malaysia. Technical and economic co-operation agreement, June 14, 1971.

Spain. Conventions on cultural, educational and scientific co-operation and on scientific and technical co-operation, March 7, 1980.

Switzerland. Agreement on economic exchanges, Nov. 23, 1972.

Syria. A 20-year treaty of friendship and co-operation (to be extended automatically for a further five years unless countermanded by either party), and agreements on improving economic co-operation, April 30, 1985.

United Kingdom. Agreements on the development of economic, industrial, scientific and technological co-operation, May 14, 1974.
Agreement on a programme for the development of co-operation, 1975.
(For agreements between Bulgaria and the United States see page 298.)

Yemeni Republic (now the Yemen Arab Republic). Treaty of friendship and co-operation, April 4, 1964.

CZECHOSLOVAKIA

Czechoslovakia has concluded agreements with non-communist countries as follows:

Australia. Treaty of commerce, Aug. 3 and 19, 1936 (in force from Jan. 1, 1937); amended Oct. 30, 1947, and April 7, 1948.
Agreement on trade relations, May 16, 1972 (in force from Dec. 19, 1972).
(For extradition treaty see page 322.)

France. A 10-year trade and technological co-operation agreement, covering in particular co-operation in the motor industry, chemical engineering, machine tools, electronic and energy industries, as well as farming and food-processing machinery, Nov. 14, 1975.

Federal Republic of Germany. Agreement on the further development of economic, industrial and technical co-operation, Jan. 22, 1975.
Cultural co-operation agreement, April 11, 1978.
(For 1973 treaty see page 286.)

Iceland. Exchange of notes on commerce and navigation, May 8, 1924.
Long-term trade and payments agreement, Sept. 1, 1977.
Exchange of notes on cultural and scientific co-operation, Sept. 19, 1979.

Libya. Treaty of friendship and co-operation, Sept. 9, 1982.

Pakistan. Cultural agreement, Jan. 29, 1976.
Barter agreement, July 12, 1979.

South Africa. Preliminary commercial agreement, Jan. 27, 1937.

Spain. Long-term agreement on trade exchanges and development of economic and industrial co-operation, Dec. 12, 1977; protocols, May 26, 1978, and May 24, 1979.
Cultural co-operation treaty, March 7, 1979.
Basic agreement on scientific and technical co-operation, Jan. 16, 1980.

Sweden. Agreement on trade and navigation, April 18, 1925.
Agreement on scientific and technical co-operation, Oct. 13, 1971.
Long-term trade agreement, March 30, 1973.

Switzerland. Trade agreement, Nov. 24, 1953.
Agreement on economic exchanges, May 7, 1971.

Syria. Treaty of friendship and co-operation, October 1985.

United Kingdom. An agreement on the restitution to Czechoslovakia of some 10 tonnes of gold held by the Bank of England since World War II, in return for payment of compensation (about $45,000,000 or £24,000,000) in respect of British claims arising mainly from post-war property expropriation in Czechoslovakia, initialled on Dec. 16, 1981.

United States. A similar agreement on the restitution to Czechoslovakia of some 8.4 tonnes of gold held in New York since World War II, in return for payment of compensation (at about $6,500,000) by Czechoslovakia in respect of US claims arising mainly from post-war property expropriation in Czechoslovakia, initialled on Nov. 6, 1981, and approved by the US Congress on Dec. 16, 1981.

Yemeni Republic (now the Yemen Arab Republic). Treaty of friendship and co-operation, May 20, 1964.

Zaïre. Agreement on mutual exchange of goods and on industrial, scientific and technical co-operation, Oct. 31, 1985.

Zambia. Co-operation agreement, May 17, 1982.

GERMAN DEMOCRATIC REPUBLIC

The German Democratic Republic has concluded treaties and agreements with non-communist countries as follows:

Australia. Trade agreement, Feb. 28, 1974; additional protocol, Feb. 22, 1977.

Austria. A 10-year trade and payments agreement (replacing an earlier five-year agreement and providing for payments to be made in Austrian or other convertible currency), Nov. 13, 1980.
An agreement on environmental co-operation (providing also for increased exchanges of information on nuclear installations), October 1985.

Finland. Trade agreement, October 1984.

France. A five-year trade agreement, Feb. 1, 1980.
A 10-year economic co-operation agreement, April 24, 1980.
Agreement on the opening of cultural centres, June 16, 1980.
Agreement on increasing bilateral trade (from French frs. 4,000 million in 1984 to at least frs. 15,000 million in 1988 and frs. 20,000 million by 1990), June 1984.

Federal Republic of Germany. Treaty on questions of traffic, May 12, 1972, and Basic Treaty, Dec. 21, 1972—see pages 282–84.

Greece. A long-term economic co-operation agreement, Oct. 10, 1985.

Iceland. Trade agreement, Feb. 6, 1973. Exchange of notes on cultural and scientific co-operation, May 17, 1979.

India. A six-year economic co-operation agreement (providing for an increase in bilateral trade from about $125,000,000 to at least $250,000,000 per annum), Jan. 9, 1979.
Trade agreement (providing for a 10 per cent increase in 1984), reported on Nov. 6, 1983.

Iran. Economic and trade agreement, April 23, 1980.
Protocol on economic co-operation, May 22, 1985.

Iraq. Agreement on economic, scientific and technical co-operation, 1985.

Italy. Treaty on legal assistance and agreements on cultural and economic co-operation, July 10, 1984.
A 10-year agreement on economic, industrial and technical co-operation, April 24, 1985.

Japan. Several economic co-operation agreements, May 28, 1981.

Mexico. Agreements on economic, scientific and technical co-operation, Sept. 11, 1981.

Nigeria. Long-term trade agreement based on most-favoured-nation treatment, initialled on Nov. 29, 1980.

Pakistan. Agreement on cultural, educational and scientific co-operation, April 3, 1975.

Spain. Agreement on cultural and scientific co-operation, Oct. 3, 1978.
Trade agreement, Dec. 17, 1979.
Joint communiqué on economic and industrial co-operation, Jan. 20, 1982.
Agreement on economic and industrial co-operation, Oct. 20, 1983.

Sweden. Long-term trade agreement, July 26, 1973; annual protocol for 1985, Nov. 29, 1984.
Agreement on economic, industrial and technical co-operation, Jan. 15, 1976.
Agreement on environmental co-operation, May 27, 1976.
Agreement on the delimitation of the continental shelf, June 22, 1978.

Switzerland. Trade and economic agreement, June 27, 1975.

Tanzania. Treaty of friendship and co-operation, May 17, 1964.

United Kingdom. Agreement on the development of economic, industrial, scientific and technological co-operation, Dec. 19, 1973.
A three-year cultural, educational and scientific co-operation agreement, Dec. 10, 1981; renewed Oct. 12, 1984.

HUNGARY

Hungary has concluded treaties and agreements with non-communist countries as follows:

Australia. Treaty of commerce and navigation, July 23, 1926; revised, Feb. 10, 1947, with effect from July 10, 1948.
Trade agreement, Sept. 30, 1974.
(For extradition treaty see page 322.)

Austria. An agreement enabling citizens of either country convicted in the other country of a crime (other than political) to serve their prison sentences in their native country, July 1985.
An agreement on environmental co-operation (providing also for increased exchanges of information on nuclear installations), Sept. 10, 1985.

Federal Republic of Germany. Agreement on economic, industrial and technical co-operation, Nov. 11, 1974; extended until Nov. 10, 1994, Aug. 13, 1984.

Agreement on cultural co-operation, July 6, 1977 (in force from April 19, 1978).

Iceland. Treaty of commerce and navigation, March 14, 1887.

Trade and payments agreement, May 19, 1970.

Italy. Agreement on the development of economic, industrial and technical co-operation, May 25, 1974.

Joint declaration on development and deepening of co-operation in the political, economic, scientific, technical and cultural fields, Nov. 12, 1975.

Pakistan. Cultural and scientific co-operation agreement, Nov. 12, 1974.

Spain. Long-term agreement on trade exchanges, navigation, transport and development of economic, industrial and technical co-operation, April 8, 1976; additional protocols, April 14, 1978, and June 21, 1979.

Convention on cultural and scientific co-operation, and basic convention on scientific and technical co-operation, Nov. 27, 1979.

Agreement on scientific co-operation and promotion of commerce, science and technology, July 15, 1981.

Extradition treaty, May 11, 1985 (the first to be concluded by Spain with an Eastern bloc country).

Sweden. Agreement on commerce and navigation, Nov. 8, 1928.

Agreement on economic, industrial and technical co-operation, May 12, 1969.

Long-term trade agreement, Feb. 23, 1982.

Switzerland. Extradition treaty, March 10, 1896 (originally for Austria-Hungary, but abrogated for Austria in 1970).

Trade treaty (with Austria-Hungary), March 9, 1900.

Agreement on economic exchanges, Oct. 30, 1973.

United Kingdom. Agreement on economic, industrial and technological co-operation, 1972.

Agreement on co-operation in medicine and public health, Nov. 1, 1978.

Memorandum of understanding on co-operation in the production of coal, oil and gas, in power generation and increased energy efficiency, Oct. 5, 1985.

United States. Agreement on co-operation in culture, education, science and technology, April 6, 1977; in force from May 21, 1977.

Agreement on trade relations (granting Hungary most-favoured-nation status), March 17, 1978; in force from July 7, 1978.

Agreement on scientific and technological co-operation, July 7, 1982 (with Annex III entering into force on Nov. 1, 1982).

Yemeni Republic (now the Yemen Arab Republic). Treaty of friendship and co-operation, May 20, 1964.

POLAND

Poland has concluded treaties and agreements with non-communist countries as follows:

Australia. Trade agreement, June 20, 1966.

Agreement on trade and technical co-operation, Aug. 16, 1978.

(For extradition treaty see page 323.)

France. Three agreements—(i) a declaration on the principles of friendly co-operation, providing inter alia for annual political consultation at the level of ministers or their representatives and reserving a "special place" for cultural

co-operation; (ii) a declaration on the principles and means of cultural and scientific co-operation, information and human relations between the two countries; and (iii) a five-year economic co-operation agreement; June 20, 1975.

Additional co-operation agreements, Sept. 14, 1977.

Agreement on French credit (worth $800,000,000), March 31, 1981.

French food aid and credit arrangement, Aug. 5, 1981.

Federal Republic of Germany. Agreement on economic, industrial and technical co-operation, Nov. 1, 1974 (in force from Jan. 15, 1975).

Long-term programme of co-operation, Oct. 9, 1975.

Agreements and a protocol on (i) a reciprocal pensions arrangement; (ii) a long-term West German credit to Poland of DM1,000 million payable in three annual instalments in 1975, 1976 and 1977; and (iii) the resettlement in the Federal Republic of between 120,000 and 125,000 ethnic Germans from Poland; signed on Oct. 9, 1976; approved by the Federal German Parliament on March 12, 1976, after Poland had agreed that further emigration of ethnic Germans beyond the above figures would eventually be permitted; approved by the Polish Council of State March 15, 1976; and instruments of ratification exchanged on March 24.

Agreement on the further development of economic co-operation, June 11, 1976.

(For 1970 treaty on mutual relations see pages 280–81.)

Greece. Agreements on long-term economic, scientific and technological co-operation, trade exchanges (worth $40,000,000) and shipbuilding (worth $100,000,000), Oct. 22–24, 1984.

Iceland. Treaty of commerce and navigation, March 22, 1924.

Exchange of notes on the development of cultural, scientific and technical contacts, May 23, 1970.

Long-term trade and payments agreement, April 30, 1975.

Italy. Agreement on economic co-operation in 1975–79, Oct. 28, 1975.

A joint political statement in which the two sides inter alia confirmed that "respect for human rights and fundamental freedoms" was "one of the important foundations for good inter-state relations", and four economic co-operation agreements, Nov. 28, 1977.

Pakistan. Agreements on commodity exchanges, Feb. 8 , 1977, and April 12, 1979.

Spain. Convention on cultural and scientific co-operation, May 27, 1977.

Basic convention on scientific and technical co-operation, Nov. 15, 1979.

Sweden. Treaty of commerce and navigation, Dec. 2, 1924.

Long-term agreement on development of economic, industrial, technical and scientific co-operation, June 5, 1975.

Long-term trade agreement, April 13, 1978.

Switzerland. Agreement on extradition and legal assistance in penal matters, Nov. 19, 1937.

Agreement on economic exchanges, June 25, 1973.

United Kingdom. Long-term agreement on the development of economic, industrial, scientific and technical co-operation, to remain in force until Dec. 21, 1982, and to continue thereafter subject to six months' notice by either side, March 20, 1973. (This agreement extended the functions of a joint commission set up under an agreement on April 21, 1971, and to remain in force until Dec. 31, 1975, subject to mutual agreement on its further extension.)

A 10-year programme under the 1973 agreement, Sept. 9, 1975.

Declaration on the development of friendly relations between the two countries, laying down the principles of their bilateral relations in conformity with the UN Charter and of their international activities in working for détente and disarmament, with the provision that their Foreign Ministers or their representatives should meet at least once a year, July 15, 1975.

A five-year agreement on economic co-operation, Dec. 16, 1976.

Convention on co-operation in education, science and culture, Nov. 7, 1978.

United States. Memorandum of understanding on scientific and technological co-operation, Dec. 11, 1981.

(For extradition treaty see page 387.)

ROMANIA

Romania has concluded agreements with non-communist countries as follows:

Australia. Trade agreement, May 18, 1967.

Agreement on trade and industrial and technical co-operation, May 29, 1975 (in force from June 26, 1975).

Cultural agreement, Nov. 17, 1977 (in force from Sept. 7, 1978).

(For extradition treaty see page 323.)

Botswana. Programme of long-term economic and technical co-operation, September 1984.

Burundi. Treaty of friendship and co-operation for an indefinite period, together with several co-operation agreements, including one on development of mineral resources, April 23, 1979.

Egypt. Agreement on joint production of Romanian tanks for the Egyptian Army, reported on Aug. 11, 1983.

France. Agreements on joint production of 50 Alouette helicopters (1970) and on purchase from France of 100 Puma helicopters (1974).

Long-term agreement on economic, industrial and technical co-operation, July 28, 1975; new such agreements, July 24–28, 1978.

Four economic co-operation agreements, covering Romania's adoption of the French SECAM colour television system, a contract for 40 Alouette-III helicopters, the building of motor vehicles and co-operation in electronics and computer technology, March 10, 1979.

Joint declaration on trade exchanges to be doubled by 1985, July 25, 1980.

Gabon. Treaty of friendship and co-operation for an indefinite period, with several co-operation agreements, April 11, 1979,

Federal Republic of Germany. Four agreements on (i) economic, industrial and technical co-operation, (ii) co-operation in scientific research and technological development, (iii) co-operation in the peaceful use of nuclear energy, and (iv) cultural and scientific co-operation, June 29, 1973 (in force from March 4, 1974); agreement (i) extended, on Aug. 3, 1983, until June 29, 1993.

Iceland. Treaty of commerce and navigation, May 8, 1931. Long-term trade agreement, June 16, 1972.

Iran. Protocol on the sale of Iranian oil in exchange for Romanian foodstuffs (worth over $1,000 million), October 1981.

Libya. Long-term commercial agreement, April 9, 1979. Treaty of friendship and co-operation, Jan. 24, 1983.

Malaysia. Agreement on cultural and scientific co-operation, Oct. 10, 1975.

Pakistan. Agreement on co-operation in science and technology, Oct. 24, 1971.

Somalia. Economic co-operation agreement, July 24, 1983.

Spain. Long-term treaty on trade and economic, industrial and technological co-operation, Jan. 19, 1977 (in force from April 28, 1977).

Conventions on scientific co-operation and on cultural and scientific co-operation, May 24, 1979.

Agreement on scientific and technical co-operation, March 4, 1980.

Sudan. Treaty of friendship and co-operation for an indefinite period, April 25, 1979.

Sweden. Agreement on settlement, trade and navigation, Oct. 7, 1931.

Agreement on economic, industrial and technical co-operation, April 9, 1968.

Long-term trade agreement, Nov. 8, 1980.

Switzerland. Economic agreement, Dec. 13, 1972.

Turkey. Agreement on Romanian assistance for major Turkish projects (mainly in the energy and heavy engineering sector), mid-1984.

United Kingdom. A 10-year agreement on economic, industrial and technical co-operation, Sept. 18, 1975.

Long-term programme for further development of co-operation, 1977.

Zaïre. Treaty of friendship and co-operation, March 19, 1980.

Zambia. Treaty of friendship and co-operation for an unlimited period, April 17, 1979.

YUGOSLAVIA

Yugoslavia has concluded treaties and agreements with non-communist countries as follows (with dates of entry into force shown in parentheses where it differs from the date of signature):

Austria. Extradition treaty, Dec. 6, 1900. Trade Agreement, July 21, 1970 (May 10, 1971).

Agreement on cultural co-operation, Sept. 14, 1976 (March 31, 1977).

Treaty providing for bilateral legal assistance in criminal cases and permitting nationals of either country to be repatriated to serve prison sentences, in force from Jan. 1, 1984 (after exchange of ratification documents on Oct. 21, 1983).

Federal Republic of Germany. Economic co-operation agreement, March 10, 1956 (Jan. 22, 1957).

Exchange of letters on technical and economic co-operation, July 16, 1965.

Agreement on economic, industrial and technical co-operation, Feb. 10, 1969 (June 19, 1969).

Agreement on cultural and scientific co-operation, July 28, 1969 (Jan. 26, 1970).

Extradition treaty, Nov. 26, 1970.

Agreement on co-operation in scientific research and technological development, May 23, 1975.

Iceland. Trade agreement, June 9, 1965.

Pakistan. Protocol on the establishment of a joint commission for economic, scientific, technical, cultural and educational co-operation, May 30, 1977.

Spain. Trade agreement, July 30, 1976.

Sweden. Trade and navigation agreement signed on May 14, 1937.

Trade agreement signed on April 12, 1947.

Agreement on economic, industrial and technical co-operation, signed on June 9, 1970.

Switzerland. Extradition agreement, Nov. 28, 1887 (between Switzerland and Serbia).

Technical co-operation agreement, Dec. 1, 1966.

Protocol on the formation of a mixed commission for economic, commercial, industrial and scientific-technical co-operation, April 5, 1977.

Soviet Agreements with Countries in Latin America and the Caribbean

Argentina. A 10-year agreement which was initialled in 1974 and came into force on Aug. 11, 1977, provided for increased trade and technical and scientific co-operation between the two countries, with the Soviet Union supplying mainly machinery in exchange for Argentinian meat, wool, grain, citrus fruit, leather, shoes, chemicals and machinery.

Agreements were signed (i) on July 1, 1980, for the sale of 22,500,000 tonnes of Argentine grain and oilseeds to the Soviet Union in 1981–85 and (ii) on April 22, 1981, for the annual sale of 60,000 to 100,000 tonnes of Argentine beef to the Soviet Union in 1981–85. (In January 1980 it had been agreed that Argentina would supply up to 5,000,000 tonnes of grain to the Soviet Union in 1980, compared with 2,200,000 tonnes in 1979.)

Jamaica. The first economic and technical co-operation agreement between the two countries was signed on Dec. 7, 1977 (with the Soviet Union assisting in the construction of a cement plant and carrying out prospecting for nickel, copper and other minerals in Jamaica).

A number of further economic agreements were signed during the Jamaican Prime Minister's first visit to Moscow on April 9–13, 1979, providing inter alia for alumina exports from Jamaica to the Soviet Union, the establishment of a joint fisheries company and a long-term Soviet loan to finance Jamaican imports from the Soviet Union.

Nicaragua. In May 1985 the Nicaraguan President announced that the Soviet Union had agreed to guarantee up to 90 per cent of Nicaragua's oil needs, for the rest of 1985.

Peru. Under an agreement reached in mid-1976 Peru purchased 36 Soviet Su-22 (Su-20) fighter-bombers to be paid for at $250,000,000 over 10 years. (It was, however, officially denied in Peru on Jan. 7, 1977, that the two sides had signed a military treaty.)

Venezuela. Economic co-operation agreements between the two countries were signed in Moscow in November 1976, among them one on oil sales (signed on Nov. 26) to Venezuela's neighbours (including Cuba) against Soviet supplies to Venezuela's more distant customers (e.g. Spain).

Treaties and Agreements between Communist Countries in Asia and Non-Communist Countries

NORTH KOREA

The Democratic People's Republic of Korea has concluded treaties or agreements as follows:

Guinea. A 20-year treaty of friendship and co-operation, Oct. 11, 1980.

Guinea-Bissau. Treaty of friendship and co-operation, Nov. 9, 1979.

Malaysia. A trade agreement, June 9, 1979.

Nigeria. Agreement on a programme of joint defence, reported on Oct. 24, 1984.

Pakistan. A protocol on economic and technical co-operation signed in May 1976, and a trade and payments agreement on Sept. 10, 1979.

Sweden. A trade agreement on Nov. 20, 1973.

Zimbabwe. A 10-year treaty of friendship and co-operation on Oct. 12, 1980.

LAOS

Laos has concluded agreements as follows:

Sweden. An agreement on Swedish aid for forestry, industry, communications and transport, signed in Vientiane in December 1981.

An agreement on development co-operation from July 1, 1984, to June 30, 1986, signed on May 26, 1984.

VIETNAM

Vietnam has concluded agreements with non-communist countries as follows:

Australia. A trade agreement on Nov. 26, 1974.

France. An agreement on commercial credits worth $40,000,000 on Dec. 23, 1981.

India. Agreements to provide Indian aid, including a loan and provision of training for technical and scientific personnel in Vietnam, in February 1982.

Malaysia. Agreement on trade and economic and technical co-operation, 1980.

Sweden. A trade agreement on Dec. 1, 1976. An agreement on development co-operation from July 1, 1983, to June 30, 1985, signed on May 26, 1983.

Cuban Agreements with African Countries

Angola. In addition to the military support given to Ethiopia [see page 353], Cuba also sent military forces to Angola in November 1975 (upon a unilateral decision by the Cuban Communist Party). During a visit to Angola Dr Castro, the Cuban leader, stated on March 28, 1977, that Cuba would place no limits on its "international duty" to collaborate with Angola and that Cuba's military presence in Angola would be maintained until the Angolan armed forces were organized, trained and equipped. In May 1977 he said that the Cuban presence was "in accordance with a strict international principle and in full agreement with the Luanda Government". Within the framework of an Angolan-Cuban mixed commission bilateral agreements were signed early in November 1977 on a "supplementary contingent" of Cuban civilians to be sent to Angola. By May 1978 the total of Cuban military personnel in Angola was estimated at 21,000.

On Nov. 30, 1978, a total of 35 agreements on co-operation between Cuba and Angola in economic affairs, defence and political assistance were signed in Havana.

An agreement on economic, scientific and technical co-operation was signed on Sept. 27, 1982.

The Congo. With the Congo, Cuba signed four co-operation agreements, including one relating to foreign affairs, in May 1978.

Ghana. Four co-operation agreements were concluded in 1982.

An agreement signed in March 1984 provided for an exchange of diplomatic and foreign intelligence.

Mozambique. With Mozambique, Cuba signed, on June 4, 1977, agreements on co-operation in the fields of health, public works, transport, agriculture and fisheries, and on Oct. 21, 1978, an agreement on economic and scientific co-operation.

Other Cuban Agreements

Cuba has concluded agreements with other countries as follows:

Iceland. Trade agreement, Nov. 24, 1975.

Mexico. An energy co-operation agreement, signed on Jan. 21, 1981, to provide for Mexican assistance to Cuba in offshore oil and gas prospecting, increasing liquefied gas production and the acquisition of equipment in third countries.

Nigeria. The conclusion of an agreement to strengthen cultural, economic and scientific ties between the two countries was reported on March 30, 1981.

Saharan Arab Democratic Republic (Western Sahara). An economic co-operation agreement and a trade protocol were signed on March 6, 1984.

Spain. Basic convention on scientific and technical co-operation, Sept. 10, 1978.

Trade agreement, with four protocols, Jan. 23, 1979.

Cultural and educational agreement, Jan. 28 and March 17, 1982.

Agreement on scientific and technical co-operation, April 1983.

A five-year economic and scientific co-operation agreement and a one-year financial aid agreement, Oct. 3, 1985.

Sweden. Trade agreement, Sept. 12, 1957; extended Dec. 12 and 28, 1978, and Jan. 19 and Feb. 25, 1982.

Switzerland. Trade agreement, March 30, 1954.

Tanzania. A co-operation agreement of March 1980 provided inter alia for Cuban doctors and advisers on agriculture and fisheries to work in Tanzania.

Uganda. A technical co-operation agreement was concluded on Oct. 1, 1980.

United States. Agreement on normalization of migration procedures, Dec. 14, 1984 (but abrogated by Cuba the following year).

Chinese Agreements with Other Communist States

With other communist states in China has concluded agreements as follows:

Democratic People's Republic of Korea. Treaty of friendship, co-operation and mutual assistance, July 11, 1961.

This treaty is similarly worded to the treaties of mutual assistance made by the USSR with Mongolia, the People's Republic of China and North Korea [see above].

Laos. With Laos an economic and technical co-operation agreement was signed by China on Oct. 3, 1977, involving Chinese aid of about £25,000,000.

Mongolia. A protocol signed in Beijing on July 14, 1984, marked the completion of the first joint survey of the Sino-Mongolian border.

A frontier trade agreement signed by the People's Republic of Mongolia and the Chinese region of Inner Mongolia early in November 1985 covered Chinese exports of light industrial products and imports of paper and shoes, as well as exchanges of rice and flour.

Yugoslavia. A trade agreement was signed by China on March 17, 1983, providing for a 24-fold increase in mutual barter exchanges (from $50,000,000 in 1982 to $1,200 million in 1984). On May 10, 1983, China granted Yugoslavia a loan of $120,000,000.

Chinese Agreements with Developed Countries

Chinese agreements with developed countries are listed below.

(For agreements with NATO member countries see pages 301ff.)

Australia. Trade agreements, April 22, 1968, and July 24, 1973.

Agreement on co-operation in science and technology, May 6, 1980.

Agreement on cultural co-operation, April 29, 1981.

Agreement on a programme for technical co-operation for development, Oct. 2, 1981.

Agreement on agricultural co-operation, May 17, 1984.

Agreement on economic and technical co-operation in the iron and steel industry, Aug. 7, 1984.

Protocol on a programme of co-operation in agricultural research for development, Sept. 14, 1984.

Finland. A scientific, technical, industrial and economic co-operation agreement, May 29, 1979.

Japan. Prior to the entry into force of the Sino-Japanese treaty of peace and friendship of 1978 [see page 12], an eight-year mutual trade agreement had been signed by the two countries in February 1978, and there followed a succession of detailed agreements within the framework of the agreement. An extension until 1990 of the trade agreement was agreed in principle in September 1978 and finalized on March 29, 1979.

An agreement on scientific and technical co-operation signed on May 28, 1980, involved the setting-up of a joint committee. However, China subsequently cancelled a substantial number of joint projects.

In March 1984 agreement was reached on the purchase by China of a pressure vessel for a 300 MW nuclear power plant near Shanghai, and on May 22, 1984, an accord was signed on prospecting for uranium in Yunnan province.

An atomic power co-operation agreement signed on July 31, 1985, did not include nuclear reprocessing technology and stipulated that activities would be limited to peaceful uses and that China's nuclear facilities would be regularly inspected by the International Atomic Energy Agency.

Sweden. Treaty of peace, friendship and commerce, March 20, 1847.

Treaty of friendship, commerce and navigation, July 2, 1908.

Agreement on industrial, scientific and technical co-operation, Dec. 5, 1978.

Trade agreement, May 15, 1979; amended Oct. 14, 1984.

Switzerland. Trade agreement, Dec. 20, 1974.

Turkey. Agreement to set up a joint economic commission and business council, April 1986.

Chinese Agreements with Non-Communist Developing Countries

China has concluded agreements with third-world (non-communist) countries as follows:

Bangladesh. An economic and technical agreement and a trade and payments agreement, Jan. 4, 1977.

A long-term trade agreement providing for exchanges worth from £200,000,000 to £250,000,000 in 1985–89, Dec. 21, 1984.

An agreement on economic and technical co-operation, July 6, 1985.

Brazil. A five-year trade agreement on exchange of Brazilian iron ore against Chinese oil, Nov. 9, 1978.

An agreement on joint uranium prospecting and the construction of power stations, May 1984.

A barter agreement on the exchange of Brazilian goods against 59,000 barrels per day of Chinese oil, while Brazilian iron ore exports to China would be increased over the next six years in exchange for Brazilian imports of oil and coal from China, September 1985.

A trade agreement to grant China a licence to manufacture military aircraft and vehicles in exchange for Chinese electronic components and guidance systems, reported on Nov. 3, 1985.

Burma. Treaty of friendship and non-aggression and agreement on the settlement of border problems, Jan. 28, 1960.

Chad. An agreement on economic and technical co-operation, Sept. 23, 1978.

The **Congo.** Treaty of friendship, Oct. 2, 1964. Military aid agreements have been signed since 1970.

Egypt. Following the abrogation of the Soviet-Egyptian treaty of friendship and co-operation in March 1976 by Egypt [see above], the latter requested China to supply Egypt with military equipment. Under a protocol signed on April 21, 1976, China agreed to supply such equipment and also to erect a munitions factory in Egypt and possibly to send Chinese technicians for the maintenance of Egypt's Soviet-built MiG fighter aircraft. In the same year China was said to have delivered to Egypt, free of charge, 30 MiG engines and other spare parts. In the first half of 1979 Egypt received 40 Shenyang F-6 jet aircraft (the Chinese version of the Soviet MiG 19), while another 40 or 50 were still to be supplied.

In October 1982 agreement was reached on the supply to Egypt of two Soviet-designed *Romeo*-class diesel-electric submarines and the provision of Chinese technicians to assist in the refitting of similar submarines already in the Egyptian Navy.

On Dec. 21, 1982, it was announced that China would supply Egypt with from 60 to 80 F-7 fighters.

Agreements on agricultural, trade, scientific and technical co-operation were signed on April 3, 1983, and a trade agreement for 1984 on Dec. 24, 1983.

Fiji. In April 1985 Fiji was promised Chinese aid equivalent to $800,000 and increased Chinese purchases of Fijian sugar (later stated to be for at least 40,000 tonnes a year). In May 1985 the aid offer was increased to include a further grant of $1,000,000 or an interest-free loan of about $5,000,000.

Gabon. A technical and economic co-operation agreement, Oct. 7, 1974.

Ghana. Treaty of friendship, Aug. 18, 1961.

Guinea. Treaty of friendship, Sept. 13, 1960.

India. Treaty on trade and border affairs, June 28, 1954.

Trade agreement providing for mutual most-favoured-nation treatment, Aug. 15, 1984.

Indonesia. Treaty of friendship, April 1, 1961. (There have, however, been no diplomatic relations between the two countries since October 1967.)

Jamaica. An outline co-operation agreement, mid-1983.

Kenya. Loan agreement, September 1980.

Libya. Agreement to expand economic ties, Nov. 6, 1985.

Madagascar. Two agreements on trade and economic and technical co-operation, Jan. 19, 1974.

Mali. Treaty of friendship, Nov. 3, 1964.

Malta. In 1972 China granted Malta a loan equivalent to almost £17,000,000 over six years, whereafter a number of Chinese-backed development projects were initiated in Malta, including the construction of a new graving dock capable of accommodating 300,000-ton tankers. An economic and technical aid agreement was signed in Peking on Nov. 6, 1977.

Mauritius. Technical co-operation agreement, July 25, 1969.

Agreement on economic and technical co-operation, Aug. 9, 1970.

Cultural agreement, Sept. 4, 1980.

Mexico. Agreements on tourism and cultural relations between the two countries, Oct. 24–30, 1978.

Mozambique. Arrangements for a Chinese soft loan of $13,000,000 repayable over 10 years, and for a gift of consumer goods worth $2,000,000, July 1984.

Nepal. (i) Agreement on settlement of border problems (March 21, 1960); (ii) treaty of peace and friendship (April 28, 1960); and (iii) boundary treaty (Oct. 5, 1961).

A protocol providing for Chinese aid towards road construction in Nepal was signed by a joint economic and trade committee at its first meeting on Dec. 24, 1984.

Nigeria. A five-year economic and technical co-operation agreement and a trade agreement, late in 1972.

The signing of a two-year cultural agreement was announced on Aug. 13, 1983.

Pakistan. Treaty on the delimitation of the frontier between Kashmir and Sinkiang, May 3, 1962.

Treaty of friendship and co-operation, providing inter alia for the possibility that, on the settlement of the Kashmir dispute between India and Pakistan, a border area might come under other than Pakistani rule, March 2, 1963.

Protocol on the final demarcation of the frontier, March 26, 1965.

Trade protocol, July 27, 1974.

Agreements on scientific and technical co-operation, May 30, 1976; June 10, 1978; June 14, 1979.

Border trade agreement, June 9, 1976.

Trade protocols, Dec. 28, 1977; April 21, 1979.

Agreement on the delivery of fighter bombers and ground-to-air missiles by China, reported in June 1981.

The Philippines. A five-year trade agreement signed in July 1978 provided for Philippine imports of 1,200,000 tonnes of crude oil per annum from China as from January 1979 (making the Philippines the second largest importer of Chinese oil after Japan). Among further agreements concluded in July 1979 was an eight-year trade agreement providing for two-way trade between the two countries amounting to $2,000 million.

Rwanda. Economic and technical co-operation agreement, June 10, 1978.

São Tomé and Príncipe. Agreements on trade and economic and technical co-operation, Dec. 24, 1975.

Senegal. By 1984 Senegal was receiving Chinese aid worth $60,000,000 per annum (mainly for the development of water resources).

Seychelles. Agreement on economic and technical co-operation, May 2, 1978.

Sierra Leone. Economic and technical co-operation agreement, March 28, 1985.

Singapore. Trade agreement, December 1979.

Somalia. A technical aid agreement was signed on Oct. 23, 1966, and under an agreement of May 1972 China was to finance and build a 600-mile road between Mogadishu and Hargeisa (in northern Somalia).

The Sudan. Agreement on technical and economic co-operation, June 9, 1977.

Tanzania. Treaty of friendship, Feb. 20, 1965.

Under subsequent Sino-Tanzanian agreements, China sent to Tanzania (i) some 13,000 technicians to work on the construction of a railway line from Tanzania to the copperbelt in Zambia, as agreed in July 1970, and (ii) military equipment, including tanks and aircraft. China also undertook to build in Tanzania a naval base, for which the foundation stone was laid in May 1971.

The railway line was completed in July 1976, having been financed by an interest-free Chinese loan equivalent to $415,000,000 repayable over a 30-year period from 1983. A technical co-operation agreement signed in July 1976 provided inter alia for some 1,000 Chinese technicians to continue to train indigenous railway staff over a two-year period.

On Aug. 19, 1983, the Chinese government agreed to the postponement for 10 years of the repayment of then almost $500,000,000 lent to Tanzania and Zambia for the building of the railway line.

Thailand. Agreements signed on March 12, 1985, were (i) on the promotion and protection of investments and (ii) on the establishment of a ministerial-level joint committee for economic co-operation, trade and investment.

United Arab Emirates. An economic, trade and technical co-operation agreement, Nov. 14, 1985.

Vanuatu. In 1984 China agreed to finance the construction of Vanuatu's Parliament House, and a team of Chinese agricultural experts arrived subsequently for a two-year technical assistance project.

Yemeni Republic (Yemen Arab Republic). Treaty of friendship, June 9, 1964.

Zaïre. The President of Zaïre stated in March 1980 that, under the terms of an existing agreement on military co-operation, China would train 3,000 Zaïrean commandos.

A military sales credit agreement for about $3,500,000 was concluded on June 2, 1982.

11. East-West Treaties of 1970-86

This section covers the major East-West treaties and agreements entered into over the past two decades, including (i) the Final Act of the 1975 Conference on Security and Co-operation in Europe, (ii) agreements concluded in the first phase of East-West détente in 1970-73, (iii) further US-Soviet agreements of 1974-79, including those relating to strategic arms limitation and limitation of nuclear tests, (iv) other recent Soviet agreements with Western states and (v) major agreements entered into with Western states by the People's Republic of China.

Conference on Security and Co-operation in Europe (CSCE)

1975 Helsinki Conference

The Conference on Security and Co-operation in Europe (CSCE) was held in three stages—respectively (i) in Helsinki on July 3–7, 1973, (ii) in Geneva from Sept. 19, 1973 to July 21, 1975, and (iii) again in Helsinki from July 30 to Aug. 1, 1975. It was attended by representatives of Canada, the United States and 32 countries of Europe—i.e. all except Albania and Andorra (the latter's foreign affairs being handled by France).

A *Final Act* drawn up by officials of the 35 countries (Austria, Belgium, Bulgaria, Canada, Cyprus, Czechoslovakia, Denmark, Finland, France, the German Democratic Republic, the Federal Republic of Germany, Greece, the Holy See, Hungary, Iceland, Ireland, Italy, Liechtenstein, Luxembourg, Malta, Monaco, the Netherlands, Norway, Poland, Portugal, Romania, San Marino, the Soviet Union, Spain, Sweden, Switzerland, Turkey, the United Kingdom, the United States and Yugoslavia) was signed at the third session of the CSCE in Helsinki on Aug. 1, 1975, by representatives of the above 35 participating countries, the majority of the signatories being heads of state or of government.

The *Final Act* comprised four main sections, described as "baskets", on subjects agreed to at the first stage of the CSCE—on questions relating to security in Europe; co-operation in the fields of economics, science, technology and environment; co-operation in humanitarian and other fields; and a follow-up to the conference. In addition the *Final Act* contained a section on questions relating to security and co-operation in the Mediterranean.

The material passages of the *Final Act* were worded as follows:

"BASKET ONE"
Questions Relating to Security in Europe

"The states participating in the Conference on Security and Co-operation in Europe,

"*Reaffirming* their objective of promoting better relations among themselves and ensuring conditions in which their people can live in true and lasting peace free from any threat to or attempt against their security;

"*Convinced* of the need to exert efforts to make détente both a continuing and an increasingly viable and comprehensive process, universal in scope, and that the implementation of the results of CSCE will be a major contribution to this process;

"*Considering* that solidarity among peoples, as well as the common purpose of the participating states in achieving the aims as set forth by the CSCE, should lead to the development of better and closer relations among them in all fields and thus to overcoming the confrontation stemming from the character of their past relations, and to better mutual understanding;

"*Mindful* of their common history and recognizing that the existence of elements common to their traditions and values can assist them in developing their relations, and desiring to search, fully taking into account the individuality and diversity of their positions and views, for possibilities of joining their efforts with a view to overcoming distrust and increasing confidence, solving the problems that separate them and co-operating in the interest of mankind;

"*Recognizing* the indivisibility of security in Europe as well as their common interest in the development of co-operation throughout Europe and among themselves and expressing their intention to pursue efforts accordingly;

"*Recognizing* the close link between peace and security in Europe and in the world as a whole and conscious of the need for each of them to make its contribution to the strengthening of world peace and security and to the promotion of fundamental rights, economic and social progress and well-being for all peoples;

"*Have adopted the following:*

(A) Declaration on Principles Guiding Relations between Participating States

"The participating states,

"*Reaffirming* their commitment to peace, security and justice and the continuing development of friendly relations and co-operation;

"*Recognizing* that this commitment, which reflects the interest and aspirations of peoples, constitutes for each participating state a present and future responsibility, heightened by experience of the past;

"*Reaffirming*, in conformity with their membership in the United Nations and in accordance with the purposes and principles of the United Nations, their full and active support for the United Nations and for the enhancement of its role and effectiveness in strengthening international peace, security and justice, and in promoting the solution of international problems, as well as the development of friendly relations and co-operation among states;

"*Expressing* their common adherence to the principles which are set forth below and are in conformity with the Charter of the United Nations as well as their common will to act, in the application of these principles, in conformity with the purposes and principles of the Charter of the United Nations;

"*Declare* their determination to respect and put into practice, each of them in its relations with all other participating states, irrespective of their political, economic or social systems as well as of their size, geographical location or level of economic development, the following principles, which are all of primary significance, guiding their mutual relations:

"I. Sovereign Equality, Respect for the Rights Inherent in Sovereignty. The participating states will respect each other's sovereign equality and individuality as well as all the rights inherent in and encompassed by its sovereignty, including in particular the right of every state to juridical equality, to territorial integrity and to freedom and political independence. They will also respect each other's right freely to choose and develop its political, social, economic and cultural systems as well as its right to determine its laws and regulations.

"Within the framework of international law, all the participating states have equal rights and duties. They will respect each other's right to define and conduct as it wishes its relations with other states in accordance with international law and in the spirit of the present Declaration. They consider that their frontiers can be changed, in accordance with international law, by peaceful means and by agreement. They also have the right to belong or not to belong to international organizations, to be or not to be a party to bilateral or multilateral treaties including the right to be or not to be a party to treaties of alliance; they also have the right to neutrality.

"II. Refraining from the Threat or Use of Force. The participating states will refrain in their mutual relations, as well as in their international relations in general, from the threat or use of force against the territorial integrity or political independence of any state, or in any other manner inconsistent with the purposes of the United Nations and with the present Declaration. No consideration may be invoked to serve to warrant resort to the threat or use of force in contravention of this principle.

"Accordingly, the participating states will refrain from any acts constituting a threat of force or direct or indirect use of force against another participating state. Likewise they will refrain from any manifestation of force for the purpose of inducing another participating state to renounce the full exercise of its sovereign rights. Likewise they will also refrain in their mutual relations from any act of reprisal by force.

"No such threat or use of force will be employed as a means of settling disputes, or questions likely to give rise to disputes, between them.

"III. Inviolability of Frontiers. The participating states regard as inviolable all one another's frontiers as well as the frontiers of all states in Europe and therefore they will refrain now and in the future from assaulting these frontiers.

"Accordingly, they will also refrain from any demand for, or act of, seizure and usurpation of part or all of the territory of any participating state.

"IV. Territorial Integrity of States. The participating states will respect the territorial integrity of each of the participating states.

"Accordingly, they will refrain from any action inconsistent with the purposes and principles of the Charter of the United Nations against the territorial integrity, political independence or the unity of any participating state, and in particular from any such action constituting a threat or use of force.

"The participating states will likewise refrain from making each other's territory the object of military occupation or other direct or indirect measures of force in contravention of international law, or the object of acquisition by means of such measures or the threat of them. No such occupation or acquisition will be recognized as legal.

"V. Peaceful Settlement of Disputes. The participating states will settle disputes among them by peaceful means in such a manner as not to endanger international peace and security, and justice.

"They will endeavour in good faith and a spirit of co-operation to reach a rapid and equitable solution on the basis of international law.

"For this purpose they will use such means as negotiation, enquiry, mediation, conciliation, arbitration, judicial settlement or other peaceful means of their own choice including any settlement procedure agreed to in advance of disputes to which they are parties.

"In the event of failure to reach a solution by any of the above peaceful means, the parties to a dispute will continue to seek a mutually agreed way to settle the dispute peacefully.

"Participating states, parties to a dispute among them, as well as other participating states, will refrain from any action which might aggravate the situation to such a degree as to endanger the maintenance of international peace and security and thereby make a peaceful settlement of the dispute more difficult.

"VI. Non-Intervention in Internal Affairs. The participating states will refrain from any intervention, direct or indirect, individual or collective, in the internal or external affairs falling within the domestic jurisdiction of another participating state, regardless of their mutual relations.

"They will accordingly refrain from any form of armed intervention or threat of such intervention against another participating state.

"They will likewise in all circumstances refrain from any other act of military, or of political, economic or other coercion designed to subordinate to their own interest the exercise by another participating state of the right inherent in its sovereignty and thus to secure advantages of any kind.

"Accordingly, they will, inter alia, refrain from direct or indirect assistance to terrorist activities, or to subversive or other activities directed towards the violent overthrow of the regime of another participating state.

"VII. Respect for Human Rights and Fundamental Freedoms, including the Freedom of Thought, Conscience, Religion or Belief. The participating states will respect human rights and fundamental freedoms, including the freedom of thought, conscience, religion or belief, for all without distinction as to race, sex, language or religion.

"They will promote and encourage the effective exercise of civil, political, economic, social, cultural and other rights and freedoms all of which derive from the inherent dignity of the human person and are essential for his free and full development.

"Within this framework the participating states will recognize and respect the freedom of the individual to profess and practise, alone or in community with others, religion or belief acting in accordance with the dictates of his own conscience.

"The participating states on whose territory national minorities exist will respect the right of persons belonging to such minorities to equality before the law, will afford them the full opportunity for the actual enjoyment of human rights and fundamental freedoms and will, in this manner, protect their legitimate interests in this sphere.

"The participating states recognize the universal significance of human rights and fundamental freedoms, respect for which is an essential factor for the peace, justice and well-being necessary to ensure the development of friendly relations and co-operation among themselves as among all states.

"They will constantly respect these rights and freedoms in their mutual relations and will endeavour jointly and separately, including in co-operation with the United Nations, to promote universal and effective respect for them.

"They confirm the right of the individual to know and act upon his rights and duties in this field.

"In the field of human rights and fundamental freedoms, the participating states will act in conformity with the purposes and principles of the Charter of the United Nations and with the Universal Declaration of Human Rights. They will also fulfil their obligations as set forth in the international declarations and agreements in this field, including, inter alia, the International Covenants on Human Rights, by which they may be bound.

"**VIII. Equal Rights and Self-Determination of Peoples.** The participating states will respect the equal rights of peoples and their right to self-determination, acting at all times in conformity with the purposes and principles of the Charter of the United Nations and with the relevant norms of international law, including those relating to territorial integrity of states.

"By virtue of the principle of equal rights and self-determination of peoples, all peoples always have the right, in full freedom, to determine, when and as they wish, their internal and external political status, without external interference, and to pursue as they wish their political, economic, social and cultural development.

"The participating states reaffirm the universal significance of respect for and effective exercise of equal rights and self-determination of peoples for the development of friendly relations among themselves as among all states; they also recall the importance of the elimination of any form of violation of this principle.

"**IX. Co-operation among States.** The participating states will develop their co-operation with one another and with all states in all fields in accordance with the purposes and principles of the Charter of the United Nations. In developing their co-operation the participating states will place special emphasis on the fields as set forth within the framework of the CSCE, with each of them making its contribution in conditions of full equality.

"They will endeavour, in developing their co-operation as equals, to promote mutual understanding and confidence, friendly and good-neighbourly relations among themselves, international peace, security and justice. They will equally endeavour, in developing their co-operation, to improve the well-being of peoples and contribute to the fulfilment of their aspirations through, inter alia, the benefits resulting from increased mutual knowledge and from progress and achievement in the economic, scientific, technological, social, cultural and humanitarian fields. They will take steps to promote conditions favourable to making these benefits available to all; they will take into account the interest of all in the narrowing of differences in the levels of economic development, and in particular the interest of developing countries throughout the world.

"They confirm that governments, institutions, organizations and persons have a relevant and positive role to play in contributing towards the achievement of these aims of their co-operation.

"They will strive, in increasing this co-operation as set forth above, to develop closer relations among themselves on an improved and more enduring basis for the benefit of peoples.

"**X. Fulfilment in Good Faith of Obligations under International Law.** The participating states will fulfil in good faith their obligations under international law, both those obligations arising from the generally recognized principles and rules of international law and those obligations arising from treaties or other agreements, in conformity with international law, to which they are parties.

"In exercising their sovereign rights, including the right to determine their laws and regulations, they will conform with their legal obligations under international law; they will furthermore pay due regard to and implement the provisions in the Final Act of the CSCE.

"The participating states confirm that, in the event of a conflict between the obligations of the members of the United Nations under the Charter of the United Nations and their obligations under any treaty or other international agreement, their obligations under the Charter will prevail, in accordance with Article 103 of the Charter of the United Nations.

"All the principles set forth above are of primary significance and, accordingly, they will be equally and unreservedly applied, each of them being interpreted taking into account the others.

"The participating states express their determination fully to respect and apply these principles, as set forth in the present Declaration, in all aspects, to their mutual relations and co-operation in order to ensure to each participating state the benefits resulting from the respect and application of these principles by all.

"The participating states, paying due regard to the principles above and, in particular, to the first sentence of the tenth principle, 'Fulfilment in good faith of obligations under international law', note that the present Declaration does not affect their rights and obligations, nor the corresponding treaties and other agreements and arrangements.

"The participating states express the conviction that respect for these principles will encourage the development of normal and friendly relations and the progress of co-operation among them in all fields. They also express the conviction that respect for these principles will encourage the development of political contact among them which in turn would contribute to better mutual understanding of their positions and views.

"The participating states declare their intention to conduct their relations with all other states in the spirit of the principles contained in the present Declaration.

(B) Matters Related to giving Effect to Certain of the Above Principles

"(i) The participating states,

"*Reaffirming* that they will respect and give effect to refraining from the threat or use of force and convinced of the necessity to make it an effective norm of international life,

"*Declare* that they are resolved to respect and carry out, in their relations with one another, inter alia, the following provisions which are in conformity with the Declaration on Principles Guiding Relations between Participating States [see above]:

"To give effect and expression, by all the ways and forms which they consider appropriate, to the duty to refrain from the threat or use of force in their relations with one another.

"To refrain from any use of armed forces inconsistent with the purposes and principles of the Charter of the United Nations and the provisions of the Declaration on Principles Guiding Relations between Participating States, against another participating state, in particular from invasion of or attack on its territory.

"To refrain from any manifestation of force for the purpose of inducing another participating state to renounce the full exercise of its sovereign rights.

"To refrain from any act of economic coercion designed to subordinate to their own interest the exercise by another participating state of the rights inherent in its sovereignty and thus to secure advantages of any kind.

"To take effective measures which by their scope and by their nature constitute steps towards the ultimate achievement of general and complete disarmament under strict and effective international control.

"To promote, by all means which each of them considers appropriate, a climate of confidence and respect among peoples consonant with their duty to refrain from propaganda for wars of aggression or for any threat or use of force inconsistent with the purposes of the United Nations and with the Declaration on Principles Guiding Relations between Participating States, against another participating state.

"To make every effort to settle exclusively by peaceful means any dispute between them, the continuance of which is likely to endanger the maintenance of international peace and security in Europe, and to seek, first of all, a solution through the peaceful means set forth in Article 33 of the United Nations Charter.

"To refrain from any action which could hinder the peaceful settlement of disputes between the participating states.

"(ii) The participating states,

"*Reaffirming* their determination to settle their disputes as set forth in the Principle of Peaceful Settlement of Disputes [see above];

"*Convinced* that the peaceful settlement of disputes is a complement to refraining from the threat or use of force, both being essential though not exclusive factors for the maintenance and consolidation of peace and security;

"*Desiring* to reinforce and to improve the methods at their disposal for the peaceful settlement of disputes;

"(1) Are resolved to pursue the examination and elaboration of a generally acceptable method for the peaceful settlement of disputes aimed at complementing existing methods, and to continue to this end to work upon the 'Draft Convention on a European System for the Peaceful Settlement of Disputes' submitted by Switzerland during the second stage of the CSCE, as well as other proposals relating to it and directed towards the elaboration of such a method.

"(2) Decide that, on the invitation of Switzerland, a meeting of experts of all the participating states will be convoked in order to fulfil the mandate described in paragraph 1 above within the framework and under the procedures of the follow-up to the conference laid down in the chapter 'Follow-up to the Conference' [see below].

"(3) This meeting of experts will take place after the meeting of the representatives appointed by the Ministers of Foreign Affairs of the participating states, scheduled according to the chapter 'Follow-up to the Conference' for 1977; the results of the work of this meeting of experts will be submitted to governments.

Document on Confidence-building Measures and Certain Aspects of Security and Disarmament

"The participating states,

"*Desirous* of eliminating the causes of tension that may exist among them and thus of contributing to the strengthening of peace and security in the world;

"*Determined* to strengthen confidence among them and thus to contribute to increasing stability and security in Europe.

"*Determined* further to refrain in their mutual relations, as well as in their international relations in general, from the threat or use of force against the territorial integrity or political independence of any state, or in any other manner inconsistent with the purposes of the United Nations and with the Declaration on Principles Guiding Relations between Participating States as adopted in this Final Act [see above];

"*Recognizing* the need to contribute to reducing the dangers of armed conflict and of misunderstanding or miscalculation of military activities which could give rise to apprehension, particularly in a situation where the participating states lack clear and timely information about the nature of such activities;

"*Taking into account* considerations relevant to efforts aimed at lessening tension and promoting disarmament;

"*Recognizing* that the exchange of observers by invitation at military manoeuvres will help to promote contacts and mutual understanding;

"*Having studied* the question of prior notification of major military movements in the context of confidence-building;

"*Recognizing* that there are other ways in which individual states can contribute further to their common objectives;

"*Convinced* of the political importance of prior notification of major military manoeuvres for the promotion of mutual understanding and the strengthening of confidence, stability and security;

"*Accepting* the responsibility of each of them to promote these objectives and to implement this measure, in accordance with the accepted criteria and modalities, as essentials for the realization of these objectives;

"*Recognizing* that this measure deriving from political decision rests upon a voluntary basis;

"*Have adopted the following:*

I

"**Prior Notification of Major Military Manoeuvres.** They will notify their major military manoeuvres to all other participating states through usual diplomatic channels in accordance with the following provisions:

"Notification will be given of major military manoeuvres exceeding a total of 25,000 troops, independently or combined with any possible air or naval components (in this context the word 'troops' includes amphibious and air-borne troops). In the case of independent manoeuvres involving them, these troops will be included in this total. Furthermore, in the case of combined manoeuvres which do not reach the above total but which involve land forces together with significant numbers of either amphibious or air-borne troops, or both, notification can also be given.

"Notification will be given of major military manoeuvres which take place on the territory, in Europe, of any participating state as well as, if applicable, in the adjoining sea area and air space.

"In the case of a participating state whose territory extends beyond Europe, prior notification need be given only of manoeuvres which take place in an area within 250 kilometres from its frontier facing or shared with any other European participating state. The participating state need not, however, give notification in cases in which that area is also contiguous to the participating state's frontier facing or shared with a non-European non-participating state.

"Notification will be given 21 days or more in advance of the start of the manoeuvre or in the case of a manoeuvre arranged at shorter notice at the earliest possible opportunity prior to its starting date.

"Notification will contain information of the designation, if any, the general purpose of and the states involved in the manoeuvre, the type or types and numerical strength of the forces engaged, the area and estimated time-frame of its conduct. The participating states will also, if possible, provide additional relevant information, particularly that related to the components of the forces engaged and the period of involvement of these forces.

"**Prior Notification of Other Military Manoeuvres.** The participating states recognize that they can contribute further to strengthening confidence and increasing security and stability, and to this end may also notify smaller-scale military manoeuvres to other participating states, with special regard for those near the area of such manoeuvres.

"To the same end, the participating states also recognize that they may notify other military manoeuvres conducted by them.

"**Exchange of Observers.** The participating states will invite other participating states, voluntarily and on a bilateral basis, in a spirit of reciprocity and goodwill towards all participating states, to send observers to attend military manoeuvres.

"The inviting state will determine in each case the number of observers, the procedures and conditions of their participation, and give other information which it may consider useful. It will provide appropriate facilities and hospitality.

"The invitation will be given as far ahead as is conveniently possible through usual diplomatic channels.

"**Prior Notification of Major Military Movements.** In accordance with the final recommendations of the Helsinki consultations [the preparatory talks for the CSCE], the participating states studied the question of prior notification of major military movements as a measure to strengthen confidence.

"Accordingly, the participating states recognize that they may, at their own discretion and with a view to contributing to confidence building, notify their major military movements.

"In the same spirit, further consideration will be given by the states participating in the CSCE to the question of prior notification of major military movements, bearing in mind, in particular, the experience gained by the implementation of the measures which are set forth in this document.

"Other Confidence-building Measures. The participating states recognize that there are other means by which their common objectives can be promoted.

"In particular, they will, with due regard to reciprocity and with a view to better mutual understanding, promote exchanges by invitation among their military personnel, including visits by military delegations.

"In order to make a fuller contribution to their common objective of confidence-building the participating states, when conducting their military activities in the area covered by the provisions for the prior notification of major military manoeuvres, will duly take into account and respect this objective.

"They also recognize that the experience gained by the implementation of the provisions set forth above, together with further efforts, could lead to developing and enlarging measures aimed at strengthening confidence.

II

"Questions relating to Disarmament. The participating states recognize the interest of all of them in efforts aimed at lessening military confrontation and promoting disarmament which are designed to complement political détente in Europe and to strengthen their security. They are convinced of the necessity to take effective measures in these fields which, by their scope and by their nature, constitute steps towards the ultimate achievement of general and complete disarmament under strict and effective international control, and which should result in strengthening peace and security throughout the world.

III

"General Considerations. Having considered the views expressed on various subjects related to the strengthening of security in Europe through joint efforts aimed at promoting détente and disarmament, the participating states, when engaged in such efforts, will, in this context, proceed, in particular, from the following essential considerations:

"The complementary nature of the political and military aspects of security; the inter-relation between the security of each participating state and security in Europe as a whole and the relationship which exists, in the broader context of world security, between security in Europe and security in the Mediterranean area; respect for the security interests of all states participating in the CSCE inherent in their sovereign equality; the importance that participants in negotiating fora see to it that information about relevant developments, progress and results is provided on an appropriate basis to other states participating in the CSCE and, in return, the justified interest of any of those states in having their views considered.

"BASKET TWO"

Co-operation in the Field of Economics, of Science and Technology and of the Environment

"The participating states . . . have adopted the following:

1. Commercial Exchanges

"General Provisions. The participating states . . . are resolved to promote, on the basis of the modalities of their economic co-operation, the expansion of their mutual trade in goods and services, and to ensure conditions favourable to such development; recognize the beneficial effects which can result for the development of trade from the application of most-favoured-nation treatment; will encourage the expansion of trade on as broad a multilateral basis as possible, thereby endeavouring to utilize the various economic and commercial possibilities; recognize the importance of bilateral and multilateral intergovernmental and other agreements for the long-term development of trade; note the importance of monetary and financial questions for the development of international trade, and will endeavour to deal with them with a view to contributing to the continuous expansion of trade; will endeavour to reduce

or progressively eliminate all kinds of obstacles to the development of trade; will foster a steady growth of trade while avoiding as far as possible abrupt fluctuations in their trade;

"Consider that their trade in various products should be conducted in such a way as not to cause or threaten to cause serious injury—and, should the situation arise, market disruption—in domestic markets for these products and in particular to the detriment of domestic producers of like or directly competitive products; as regards the concept of market disruption, it is understood that it should not be invoked in a way inconsistent with the relevant provisions of their international agreements; if they resort to safeguard measures, they will do so in conformity with their commitments in this field arising from international agreements to which they are parties and will take account of the interests of the parties directly concerned; will give due attention to measures for the promotion of trade and the diversification of its structure; note that the growth and diversification of trade would contribute to widening the possibilities of choice of products; consider it appropriate to create favourable conditions for the participation of firms, organizations and enterprises in the development of trade.

"Business Contacts and Facilities. The participating states . . . will take measures further to improve conditions for the expansion of contacts between representatives of official bodies, of the different organizations, enterprises, firms and banks concerned with foreign trade, in particular, where useful, between sellers and users of products and services, for the purpose of studying commercial possibilities, concluding contracts, ensuring their implementation and providing after-sales service; will encourage organizations, enterprises and firms concerned with foreign trade to take measures to accelerate the conduct of business negotiations; will further take measures aimed at improving working conditions of representatives of foreign organizations, enterprises, firms and banks concerned with external trade, particularly as follows:

"By providing the necessary information, including information on legislation and procedures relating to the establishment and operation of permanent representation by the above-mentioned bodies; by examining as favourably as possible requests for the establishment of permanent representation and of offices for this purpose, including, where appropriate, the opening of joint offices by two or more firms; by encouraging the provision, on conditions as favourable as possible and equal for all representatives of the above-mentioned bodies, of hotel accommodation, means of communication, and of other facilities normally required by them, as well as of suitable business and residential premises for purposes of permanent representation;

"Recognize the importance of such measures to encourage greater participation by small and medium-sized firms in trade between participating states.

"Economic and Commercial Information. The participating states . . . will promote the publication and dissemination of economic and commercial information at regular intervals and as possible, in particular: Statistics concerning production, national income, budget, consumption and productivity; foreign trade statistics drawn up on the basis of comparable classification, including breakdown by product with indication of volume and value, as well as country of origin or destination; laws and regulations concerning foreign trade; information allowing forecasts of development of the economy to assist in trade promotion, for example, information on the general orientation of national economic plans and programmes; other information to help businessmen in commercial contacts, for example, periodic directories, lists, and where possible, organizational charts of firms and organizations concerned with foreign trade;

"Will in addition to the above encourage the development of the exchange of economic and commercial information through, where appropriate, joint commissions for economic, scientific and technical co-operation, national and joint chambers of commerce, and other suitable bodies; will support a study, in the framework of the UN Economic Commission for Europe

[ECE], of the possibilities of creating a multilateral system of notification of laws and regulations concerning foreign trade and changes therein; will encourage international work on the harmonization of statistical nomenclatures, notably in the ECE.

"**Marketing.** The participating states . . . will encourage organizations, enterprises and firms concerned with foreign trade to develop further the knowledge and techniques required for effective marketing; will encourage the improvement of conditions for the implementation of measures to promote trade and to satisfy the needs of users in respect of imported products, in particular through market research and advertising measures as well as, where useful, the establishment of supply facilities, the furnishing of spare parts, the functioning of after-sales services, and the training of the necessary local technical personnel; will encourage international co-operation in the field of trade promotion, including marketing, and the work undertaken on these subjects within the international bodies, in particular the ECE.

2. Industrial Co-operation and Projects of Common Interest

"**Industrial Co-operation.** The participating states . . . propose to encourage the development of industrial co-operation between the competent organizations, enterprises and firms of their countries; consider that industrial co-operation may be facilitated by means of intergovernmental and other bilateral and multilateral agreements between the interested parties; note that in promoting industrial co-operation they should bear in mind the economic structures and the development levels of their countries; note that industrial co-operation is implemented by means of contracts concluded between competent organiz-ations, enterprises and firms on the basis of economic considerations; express their willingness to promote measures designed to create favourable conditions for industrial co-operation; recognise that industrial co-operation covers a number of forms of economic relations going beyond the framework of conventional trade, and that in concluding contracts on industrial co-operation the partners will determine jointly the appropriate forms and conditions of co-operation, taking into account their mutual interests and capabilities;

"Recognize further that, if it is in their mutual interest, concrete forms such as the following may be useful for the development of industrial co-operation: joint production and sale, specialization in production and sale, construction, adaptation and modernization of industrial plants, co-operation for the setting up of complete industrial installations with a view to thus obtaining part of the resultant products, mixed companies, exchanges of 'know how', of technical information, of patents and of licences, and joint industrial research within the framework of specific co-operation projects;

"Recognize that new forms of industrial co-operation can be applied with a view to meeting specific needs; consider it desirable to improve the quality and the quantity of information relevant to industrial co-operation, in particular the laws and regulations, including those relating to foreign exchange, general orientation of national economic plans and programmes as well as programme priorities and economic conditions of the market; and to disseminate as quickly as possible published documentation thereon;

"Will encourage all forms of exchange of information and communication of experience relevant to industrial co-operation, including through contacts between potential partners and, where appropriate, through joint commissions for economic, industrial, scientific and technical co-operation, national and joint chambers of commerce, and other suitable bodies; consider it desirable, with a view to expanding industrial co-operation, to encourage the exploration of co-operation possibilities and the implementation of co-operation projects and will take measures to this end, inter alia, by facilitating and increasing all forms of business contacts between competent organizations, enterprises and firms and between their respective qualified personnel; note that the provisions adopted by the conference relating to business contacts in the economic and commercial fields also apply to foreign organizations, enterprises and firms

engaged in industrial co-operation, taking into account specific conditions of this co-operation, and will endeavour to ensure, in particular, the existence of appropriate working conditions for personnel engaged in the implementation of co-operation projects;

"Consider it desirable that proposals for industrial co-operation projects should be sufficiently specific and should contain the necessary economic and technical data, in particular preliminary estimates of the cost of the project, information on the form of co-operation envisaged, and market possibilities, to enable potential partners to proceed with the initial studies and to arrive at decisions in the shortest possible time; will encourage the parties concerned with industrial co-operation to take measures to accelerate the conduct of negotiations for the conclusion of co-operation contracts;

"Recommend further the continued examination—for example within the framework of the ECE—of means of improving the provision of information to those concerned on general conditions of industrial co-operation and guidance on the preparation of contracts in this field; consider it desirable to further improve conditions for the implementation of industrial co-operation projects, in particular with respect to: the protection of the interests of the partners in industrial co-operation projects, including the legal protection of the various kinds of property involved; the consideration, in ways that are compatible with their economic systems, of the needs and possibilities of industrial co-operation within the framework of economic policy and particularly in national economic plans and programmes;

"Consider it desirable that the partners, when concluding industrial co-operation contracts, should devote due attention to provisions concerning the extension of the necessary mutual assistance and the provision of the necessary information during the implementation of these contracts, in particular with a view to attaining the required technical level and quality of the products resulting from such co-operation; recognize the usefulness of an increased participation of small and medium-sized firms in industrial co-operation projects.

"**Projects of Common Interest.** The participating states . . . regard it as necessary to encourage, where appropriate, the investigation by competent and interested organizations, enterprises and firms of the possibilities for the carrying out of projects of common interest in the fields of energy resources and of the exploitation of raw materials, as well as of transport and communications; regard it as desirable that organizations, enterprises and firms exploring the possibilities of taking part in projects of common interest exchange with their potential partners, through the appropriate channels, the requisite economic, financial and technical information pertaining to these projects;

"Consider that the fields of energy resources, in particular, petroleum, natural gas and coal, and the extraction and processing of mineral raw materials, in particular, iron ore and bauxite, are suitable ones for strengthening long-term economic co-operation and for the development of trade which could result; consider that possibilities for projects of common interest with a view to long-term economic co-operation also exist in the following fields: Exchanges of electrical energy within Europe with a view to utilizing the capacity of the electrical power stations as rationally as possible; co-operation in research for new sources of energy and, in particular, in the field of nuclear energy; development of road networks and co-operation aimed at establishing a coherent navigable network in Europe; co-operation in research and the perfecting of equipment for multimodal transport operations and for the handling of containers;

"Recommend that the states interested in projects of common interest should consider under what conditions it would be possible to establish them, and if they so desire, create the necessary conditions for their actual implementation.

3. Provisions concerning Trade and Industrial Co-operation

"Harmonization of Standards. The participating states . . . reaffirm their interest to achieve the widest possible international harmonization of standards and technical regulations; express their readiness to promote internatiomal agreements and other appropriate arrangements on acceptance of certificates of conformity with international co-operation on standardization, in particular by supporting the activities of intergovernmental and other appropriate organizations in this field.

"Arbitration. The participating states . . . recommend, where appropriate, to organizations, enterprises and firms in their countries to include arbitration clauses in commercial contracts and industrial co-operation contracts, or in special agreements; recommend that the provisions on arbitration should provide for arbitration under a mutually acceptable set of arbitration rules, and permit arbitration in a third country, taking into account existing intergovernmental and other agreements in this field.

"Specific Bilateral Arrangements. The participating states . . . will consider favourably the conclusion, in appropriate cases, of specific bilateral agreements concerning various problems of mutual interest in the fields of commercial exchanges and industrial co-operation, in particular with a view to avoiding double taxation and to facilitating the transfer of profits and the return of the value of the assets invested.

4. Science and Technology

"Possibilities for improving Co-operation. [The participating states] recognize that possibilities exist for further improving scientific and technological co-operation and, to this end, express their intention to remove obstacles to such co-operation, in particular through: the improvement of opportunities for the exchange and dissemination of scientific and technological information among the parties interested in scientific and technological research and co-operation, including information related to the organization and implementation of such co-operation; the expeditious implementation and improvement in organization, including programmes, of international visits of scientists and specialists in connexion with exchanges, conferences and co-operation; the wider use of commercial channels and activities for applied scientific and technological research and for the transfer of achievements obtained in this field while providing information on and protection of intellectual and industrial property rights.

"Fields of Co-operation. [The participating states] consider that possibilities to expand co-operation exist within the areas given below as examples, noting that it is for potential partners in the participating countries to identify and develop projects and arrangements of mutual interest and benefit:

"Agriculture. Research into new methods and technologies for increasing the productivity of crop cultivation and animal husbandry; the application of chemistry to agriculture; the design, construction and utilization of agricultural machinery; technologies of irrigation and other agricultural land improvement works;

"Energy. New technologies of production, transport and distribution of energy aimed at improving the use of existing fuels and sources of hydro-energy, as well as research in the field of new energy sources, including nuclear, solar and geothermal energy;

"New Technologies, Rational Use of Resources. Research on new technologies and equipment designed in particular to reduce energy consumption and to minimize or eliminate waste;

"Transport Technology. Research on the means of transport and the technology applied to the development and operation of international, national and urban transport networks including container transport as well as transport safety;

"Physics. Study of problems in high energy physics and plasma physics; research in the field of theoretical and experimental nuclear physics;

"Chemistry. Research on problems in electro-chemistry and the chemistry of polymers, of natural products, and of metals

and alloys, as well as the development of improved chemical technology, especially materials processing; practical application of the latest achievements of chemistry to industry, construction and other sectors of the economy;

"Meteorology and Hydrology. Meteorological and hydrological research, including methods of collection, evaluation and transmission of data and their utilization for weather forecasting and hydrology forecasting;

"Oceanography. Oceanographic research, including the study of air/sea interactions;

"Seismological Research. Study and forecasting of earthquakes and associated geological changes; development and research of technology of seism-resisting constructions;

"Research on Glaciology, Permafrost and Problems of Life under Conditions of Cold. Research on glaciology and permafrost; transportation and construction technologies; human adaptation to climatic extremes and changes in the living conditions of indigenous populations;

"Computer, Communications and Information Technologies. Development of computers as well as of telecommunications and information systems; technology associated with computers and telecommunications, including their use for management systems, for production processes, for automation, for the study of economic problems, in scientific research and for the collection, processing and dissemination of information;

"Space Research. Space exploration and the study of the earth's natural resources and the natural environment by remote sensing, in particular with the assistance of satellites and rocket probes;

"Medicine and Public Health. Research on cardiovascular, tumour and virus diseases, molecular biology, neurophysiology; development and testing of new drugs; study of contemporary problems of paediatrics, gerontology and the organization and techniques of medical services;

"Environmental Research. Research on specific scientific and technological problems related to human environment."

Forms and Methods of Co-operation. The document enumerated a wide range of forms and methods by which scientific and technological co-operation should be promoted, including the exchange of publications, exchange of visits, international conferences and seminars, joint programmes, use of commercial channels and more effective use of existing international organizations.

5. Environment

"Aims of Co-operation. [The participating states] agree to the following aims of co-operation, in particular:

"To study, with a view to their solution, those environmental problems which, by their nature, are of a multilateral, bilateral, regional or sub-regional dimension; as well as to encourage the development of an interdisciplinary approach to environmental problems; to increase the effectiveness of national and international measures for the protection of the environment by the comparison and, if appropriate, the harmonization of methods of gathering and analysing facts, by improving the knowledge of pollution phenomena and rational utilization of natural resources, by the exchange of information, by the harmonization of definitions and the adoption, as far as possible, of a common terminology in the field of the environment; to take the necessary measures to bring environmental policies closer together and, where appropriate and possible, to harmonize them; to encourage, where possible and appropriate, national and international efforts by their interested organizations, enterprises and forms in the development, production and improvement of equipment designed for monitoring, protecting and enhancing the environment.

"Fields of Co-operation. To attain these aims, the participating states will make use of every suitable opportunity to co-operate in the field of environment and, in particular, within the areas described below as examples."

These areas included control of air pollution; water pollution control and fresh water utilization; protection of the marine environment; land utilization and soils; nature conservation and nature reserves; improvement of environmental conditions in areas of human settlement; fundamental research, monitoring, forecasting and assessment of environmental changes; legal and administrative measures.

"Forms and Methods of Co-operation. The participating states . . . agree on the following recommendations on specific measures:

"To develop through international co-operation an extensive programme for the monitoring and evaluation of the long-range transport of air pollutants, starting with sulphur dioxide and with possible extension to other pollutants, and to this end to take into account basic elements of a co-operation programme which were identified by the experts who met in Oslo in December 1974 at the invitation of the Norwegian Institute of Air Research;

"To advocate that within the framework of the ECE a study be carried out of procedures and relevant experience relating to the activities of Governments in developing the capabilities of their countries to predict adequately environmental consequences of economic activities and technological development."

6. Co-operation in Other Areas

Development of Transport. The document outlined various ways in which the participating states would seek to develop co-operation in the field of transport, including the simplification of frontier formalities, the harmonization of safety provisions, the elimination of disparities arising from the legal provisions applied to traffic on inland waterways subject to international conventions and the improvement of international rail transport.

Promotion of Tourism. The participating states expressed their intention "to encourage increased tourism on both an individual and group basis", the document specifying a number of ways to achieve this end.

"Economic and Social Aspects of Migrant Labour. The participating states . . . are of the opinion that the problems arising bilaterally from the migration of workers in Europe as well as between the participating states should be dealt with by the parties directly concerned in order to resolve these problems in their mutual interest, in the light of the concern of each state involved to take due account of the requirements resulting from its socio-economic situation, having regard to the obligation of each state to comply with the bilateral and multilateral agreements to which it is party, and with the following aims in view:

"To encourage the efforts of the countries of origin directed towards increasing the possibilities of employment for the nationals in their own territories, in particular by developing economic co-operation appropriate for this purpose and suitable for the host countries and the countries of origin concerned; to ensure through collaboration between the host country and the country of origin the conditions under which the orderly movement of workers might take place, while at the same time protecting their personal and social welfare and, if appropriate, to organize the recruitment of migrant workers and the provision of elementary language and vocational training; to ensure equality of rights between migrant workers and nationals of the host countries with regard to conditions of employment and work and to social security, and to endeavour to ensure that migrant workers may enjoy satisfactory living conditions, especially housing conditions;

"To endeavour to ensure, as far as possible, that migrant workers may enjoy the same opportunities as nationals of the host countries of finding other suitable employment in the event of unemployment; to regard with favour the provision of vocational training to migrant workers and, as far as possible, free instruction in the language of the host country, in the framework of their employment; to confirm the right of migrant workers to receive, as far as possible, regular information in their own language, covering both their country of origin and the host country; to ensure that the children of migrant workers established in the host country have access to the education

usually given there, under the same conditions as the children of that country and, furthermore, to permit them to receive supplementary education in their own language, national culture, history and geography; to bear in mind that migrant workers, particularly those who have acquired qualifications, can by returning to their countries after a certain period of time help to remedy any deficiency of skilled labour in their country of origin; to facilitate, as far as possible, the reuniting of migrant workers with their families; to regard with favour the efforts of the countries of origin to attract the savings of migrant workers with a view to increasing, within the framework of their economic development, appropriate opportunities for employment, thereby facilitating the reintegration of these workers on their return home."

Training of Personnel. The document stressed "the importance of the training and advanced training of professional staff and technicians for the economic development of every country" and outlined ways of promoting co-operation in this field.

"BASKET THREE"
Co-operation in Humanitarian and Other Fields
1. Human Contacts

"The participating states . . . express their intention now to proceed to the implementation of the following:

"(a) Contacts and Regular Meetings on the Basis of Family Ties. In order to promote further development of contacts on the basis of family ties the participating states will favourably consider applications for travel with the purpose of allowing persons to enter or leave their territory temporarily, and on a regular basis if desired, in order to visit members of their families. Applications for temporary visits to meet members of their families will be dealt with without distinction as to the country of origin or destination; existing requirements for travel documents and visas will be applied in this spirit. The preparation and issue of such documents and visas will be effected within reasonable time limits; cases of urgent necessity—such as serious illness or death—will be given priority treatment. They will take such steps as may be necessary to ensure that the fees for official travel documents and visas are acceptable. They confirm that the presentation of an application concerning contacts on the basis of family ties will not modify the rights and obligations of the applicant or of members of his family.

"(b) Reunification of Families. The participating states will deal in a positive and humanitarian spirit with the applications of persons who wish to be reunited with members of their family, with special attention being given to requests of an urgent character—such as requests submitted by persons who are ill or old. They will deal with applications in this field as expeditiously as possible. They will lower where necessary the fees charged in connexion with these applications to ensure that they are at a moderate level. Applications for the purpose of family reunification which are not granted may be renewed at the appropriate level and will be reconsidered at reasonably short intervals by the authorities of the country of residence or destination, whichever is concerned; under such circumstances fees will be charged only when applications are granted.

"Persons whose applications for family reunification are granted may bring with them or ship their household and personal effects; to this end the participating states will use all possibilities provided by existing regulations. Until members of the same family are reunited meetings and contacts between them may take place in accordance with the modalities for contacts on the basis of family ties. The participating states will support the efforts of Red Cross and Red Crescent societies concerned with the problems of family reunification. They confirm that the presentation of an application concerning family reunification will not modify the rights and obligations of the applicant or of members of his family. The receiving participating state will take appropriate care with regard to employment for persons from other participating states who take up permanent residence in that state in connexion with family reunification with its citizens and see that they are afforded opportunities equal to those enjoyed by its own citizens for education, medical assistance and social security.

"(c) Marriage between Citizens of Different States. The participating states will examine favourably and on the basis of humanitarian considerations requests for exit or entry permits from persons who have decided to marry a citizen from another participating state. The processing and issuing of the documents required for the above purposes and for the marriage will be in accordance with the provisions accepted for family reunification. In dealing with requests from couples from different participating states, once married, to enable them and the minor children of their marriage to transfer their permanent residence to a state in which either one is normally a resident, the participating states will also apply the provisions accepted for family reunification.

"(d) Travel for Personal or Professional Reasons. The participating states intend to facilitate wider travel by their citizens for personal or professional reasons, and to this end they intend in particular: Gradually to simplify and to administer flexibly the procedures for exit and entry; to ease regulations concerning movement of citizens from the other participating states in their territory, with due regard to security requirements. They will endeavour gradually to lower, where necessary, the fees for visas and official travel documents. They intend to consider, as necessary, means—including, in so far as appropriate, the conclusion of multilateral or bilateral consular conventions or other relevant agreements or understandings—for the improvement of arrangements to provide consular services, including legal and consular assistance.

"They confirm that religious faiths, institutions and organizations, practising within the constitutional framework of the participating states, and their representatives can, in the field of their activities, have contacts and meetings among themselves and exchange information.

"(e) Improvement of Conditions for Tourism on an Individual or Collective Basis. The participating states consider that tourism contributes to a fuller knowledge of the life, culture and history of other countries, to the growth of understanding among peoples, to the improvement of contacts and to the broader use of leisure. They intend to promote the development of tourism on an individual or collective basis and, in particular, they intend: To promote visits to their respective countries by encouraging the provision of appropriate facilities and the simplification and expediting of necessary formalities relating to such visits; to increase on the basis of appropriate agreements or arrangements where necessary co-operation in the development of tourism, in particular by considering bilaterally possible ways to increase information relating to travel to other countries and to the reception and service of tourists, and other related questions of mutual interest.

"(f) Meetings among Young People. The participating states intend to further the development of contacts and exchanges among young people by encouraging: increased exchanges and contacts on a short- or long-term basis among young people, training or undergoing education through bilateral or multilateral agreements or regular programmes in all cases where it is possible; study by their youth organizations of the question of possible agreements relating to frameworks of multilateral youth co-operation; agreements or regular programmes relating to the organization of exchanges of students, of international youth seminars, of courses of professional training and foreign language study; the further development of youth tourism and the provision to this end of appropriate facilities; the development, where possible, of exchanges, contacts and co-operation on a bilateral or multilateral basis between their organizations which represent wide circles of young people working, training or undergoing education; awareness among youth of the importance of developing mutual understanding and of strengthening friendly relations and confidence among peoples.

"(g) Sport. In order to expand existing links and co-operation in the field of sport the participating states will encourage contacts and exchanges of this kind, including sports meetings and competitions of all sorts, on the basis of the established international rules, regulations and practice.

"(h) Expansion of Contacts. By way of further developing contacts among governmental institutions and non-governmental organizations and associations, including women's organizations, the participating states will facilitate the convening of meetings as well as travel by delegations, groups and individuals.

2. Information

"The participating states . . . express their intention in particular:

"(a) Improvement of the Circulation of, Access to, and Exchange of Information. (i) *Oral Information*. To facilitate the dissemination of oral information through the encouragement of lectures and lecture tours by personalities and specialists from the other participating states, as well as exchanges of opinions at round-table meetings, seminars, symposia, summer schools, congresses and other bilateral and multilateral meetings.

"(ii) *Printed Information*. To facilitate the improvement of the dissemination on their territory of newspapers and printed publications, periodical and non-periodical, from the other participating states. For this purpose: They will encourage their competent firms and organizations to conclude agreements and contracts designed gradually to increase the quantities and the number of titles of newspapers and publications imported from the other participating states; these agreements and contracts should in particular mention the speediest conditions of delivery and the use of the normal channels existing in each country for the distribution of its own publications and newspapers, as well as forms and means of payment agreed between the parties making it possible to achieve the objectives aimed at by these agreements and contracts; where necessary, they will take appropriate measures to achieve the above objectives and to implement the provisions contained in the agreements and contracts.

"To contribute to the improvement of access by the public to periodical and non-periodical printed publications imported on the bases indicated above. In particular: They will encourage an increase in the number of places where these publications are on sale; they will facilitate the availability of these periodical publications during congresses, conferences, official visits and other international events and to tourists during the season; they will develop the possibilities for taking out subscriptions according to the modalities particular to each country; they will improve the opportunities for reading and borrowing these publications in large public libraries and their reading rooms as well as in university libraries.

"They intend to improve the possibilities for acquaintance with bulletins of official information issued by diplomatic missions and distributed by those missions on the basis of arrangements acceptable to the interested parties.

"(iii) *Filmed and Broadcast Information*. To promote the improvement of the dissemination of filmed and broadcast information. To this end: They will encourage the wider showing and broadcasting of a greater variety of recorded and filmed information from the other participating states, illustrating the various aspects of life in their countries and received on the basis of such agreements or arrangements as may be necessary between the organizations and firms directly concerned; they will facilitate the import by competent organizations and firms of recorded audio-visual material from the other participating states.

"The participating states note the expansion in the dissemination of information broadcast by radio, and express the hope for the continuation of this process, so as to meet the interest of mutual understanding among peoples and the aims set forth by this conference.

"(b) Co-operation in the Field of Information. To encourage co-operation in the field of information on the basis of short-

or long-term agreements or arrangements. In particular: They will favour increased co-operation among mass media organizations, including press agencies, as well as among publishing houses and organizations; they will favour co-operation among public or private, national or international radio and television organizations, in particular through the exchange of both live and recorded radio and television programmes, and through the joint production and the broadcasting and distribution of such programmes; they will encourage meetings and contacts both between journalists' organizations and between journalists from the participating states; they will view favourably the possibilities of arrangements between periodical publications as well as between newspapers from the participating states for the purposes of exchanging and publishing articles; they will encourage the exchange of technical information as well as the organization of joint research and meetings devoted to the exchange of experience and views between experts in the field of the press, radio and television.

"(c) Improvement of Working Conditions for Journalists. The participating states, desiring to improve the conditions under which journalists from one participating state exercise their profession in another participating state, intend in particular to:

"Examine in a favourable spirit and within a suitable and reasonable time-scale requests from journalists for visas; grant to permanently accredited journalists of the participating states, on the basis of arrangements, multiple entry and exit visas for specified periods; facilitate the issue to accredited journalists of the participating states of permits for stay in their country of temporary residence and, if and when these are necessary, of other official papers which it is appropriate for them to have; ease on a basis of reciprocity procedures for arranging travel by journalists of the participating states in the country where they are exercising their profession, and to provide progressively greater opportunities for such travel, subject to the observance of regulations relating to the existence of areas closed for security reasons; ensure that requests by such journalists for such travel receive, in so far as possible, an expeditious response, taking into account the time-scale of the request;

"Increase the opportunities for journalists of the participating states to communicate personally with their sources, including organizations and official institutions; grant to journalists of the participating states the right to import, subject only to its being taken out again, the technical equipment (photographic, cinematographic, tape recorder, radio and television) necessary for the exercise of their profession; enable journalists of the other participating states, whether permanently or temporarily accredited, to transmit completely, normally and rapidly by means recognized by the participating states to the information organs which they represent the results of their professional activity, including tape recordings and undeveloped film, for the purpose of publication or of broadcasting on the radio or television. The participating states reaffirm that the legitimate pursuit of their professional activity will neither render journalists liable to expulsion nor otherwise penalize them. If an accredited journalist is expelled, he will be informed of the reasons for this act and may submit an application for re-examination of his case."

3. Co-operation and Exchanges in the Field of Culture

This section of the document covered the extension of relations between participating states in the field of culture, the promotion of mutual knowledge, exchanges and dissemination in the field of culture, fuller access to the culture of other participating states, the development of contacts and co-operation and the identification of fields and forms of co-operation. It also stated that the participating states recognized and intended to facilitate the "contribution that national minorities or regional cultures can make to co-operation among them in various fields of culture".

4. Co-operation and Exchanges in the Field of Education

The participating states expressed their intention "to expand and improve . . . co-operation and links in the fields of education and science", in particular by extending relations, promoting access and exchanges, promoting co-operation in the field of science, encouraging the study of foreign languages and promoting the exchange of information of teaching methods.

"BASKET FOUR"

Follow-Up to the Conference

"The participating states . . .

"1. *Declare their resolve*, in the period following the conference, to pay due regard to and implement the provisions of the Final Act of the conference: (*a*) unilaterally, in all cases which lend themselves to such action; (*b*) bilaterally, by negotiations with other participating states; (*c*) multilaterally, by meetings of experts of the participating states, and also within the framework of existing international organizations, such as the ECE and UNESCO, with regard to educational, scientific and cultural co-operation.

"2. *Declare furthermore their resolve* to continue the multilateral process initiated by the conference: (*a*) By proceeding to a thorough exchange of views both on the implementation of the provisions of the Final Act and of the tasks defined by the conference, as well as, in the context of the questions dealt with by the latter, on the deepening of their mutual relations, the improvement of security and the development of co-operation in Europe, and the development of the process of détente in the future; (*b*) by organizing to these ends meetings among their representatives, beginning with a meeting at the level of representatives appointed by the Ministers of Foreign Affairs. This meeting will define the appropriate modalities for the holding of other meetings which could include further similar meetings and the possibility of a new conference.

"3. The first of the meetings indicated above will be held at Belgrade in 1977. A preparatory meeting to organize this meeting will be held at Belgrade on June 15, 1977. The preparatory meeting will decide on the date, duration, agenda and other modalities of the meeting of representatives appointed by the Ministers of Foreign Affairs. . . ."

SECTION ON MEDITERRANEAN

Questions Relating to Security and Co-operation in the Mediterranean

"The participating states,

"*Conscious* of the geographical, historical, cultural, economic and political aspects of their relationship with the non-participating Mediterranean states,

"*Convinced* that security in Europe is to be considered in the broader context of world security and is closely linked with security in the Mediterranean area as a whole, and that accordingly the process of improving security should not be confined to Europe but should extend to other parts of the world, and in particular to the Mediterranean area,

"*Believing* that the strengthening of security and the intensification of co-operation in Europe would stimulate positive processes in the Mediterranean region, and expressing their intention to contribute towards peace, security and justice in the region, in which ends the participating states and the non-participating Mediterranean states have a common interest;

"*Recognizing* the importance of their mutual economic relations with the non-participating Mediterranean states, and conscious of their common interest in the further development of co-operation,

"*Noting* with appreciation the interest expressed by the non-participating Mediterranean states in the conference since its inception, and having duly taken their contributions into account,

"*Declare their intention*: to promote the development of good-neighbourly relations with the non-participating Mediterranean states in conformity with the purposes and principles of the Charter of the United Nations, on which their relations are based, and with the UN Declaration on Principles of International Law concerning Friendly Relations and Co-operation among States [see page 48] and accordingly, in this context, to conduct their relations with the non-participating Mediterranean states in the spirit of the principles set forth in the Declaration of Principles Guiding Relations between Participating States [see above];

"To seek by further improving their relations with the non-participating Mediterranean states to increase mutual confidence, so as to promote security and stability in the Mediterranean area as a whole; to encourage with the non-participating Mediterranean states the development of mutually beneficial co-operation in the various fields of economic activity, especially by expanding commercial exchanges, on the basis of a common awareness of the necessity for stability and progress in trade relations, of their mutual economic interests, and of differences in the levels of economic development, thereby promoting their economic advancement and well-being;

"To contribute to a diversified development of the economies of the non-participating Mediterranean states, whilst taking due account of their national development objectives, and to co-operate with them, especially in the sectors of industry, science and technology, in their efforts to achieve a better utilization of their resources, thus promoting a more harmonious development of economic relations; to intensify their efforts and their co-operation on a bilateral and multilateral basis with the non-participating Mediterranean states directed towards the improvement of the environment of the Mediterranean, especially the safeguarding of the biological resources and ecological balance of the sea by appropriate measures, including the prevention and control of pollution; to this end, and in view of the present situation, to co-operate through competent international organizations and in particular within the UN Environment Programme (UNEP); to promote further contacts and co-operation with the non-participating Mediterranean states in other relevant fields.

"In order to advance the objectives set forth above the participating states also declare their intention of maintaining and amplifying the contacts and dialogue as initiated by the CSCE with the non-participating Mediterranean states to include all the states of the Mediterranean with the purpose of contributing to peace, reducing armed forces in the region, strengthening security, lessening tensions in the region, and widening the scope of co-operation, ends in which all share a common interest, as well as with the purpose of defining further common objectives. The participating states would seek in the framework of their multilateral efforts to encourage progress and appropriate initiatives and to proceed to an exchange of views on the attainment of the above purposes."

Follow-Up Meetings

At the first follow-up meeting of representatives of the CSCE Final Act signatories held in Belgrade from Oct. 4, 1977, until March 9, 1978, over 80 proposals were submitted for improving the implementation of the Helsinki Final Act. However, no consensus was reached on any of the substantive proposals, and this was reflected in the agreed concluding document.

It was nevertheless stated in the document that the representatives had "stressed the political importance of the CSCE and reaffirmed the resolve of their governments to implement fully, unilaterally, bilaterally and multilaterally all the provisions of the Final Act"; that the second follow-up meeting of the CSCE would commence in Madrid on Nov. 11, 1980; and that it was agreed to hold meetings of experts (i) in Montreux

(Switzerland) from Oct. 31, 1978, to examine and elaborate a generally acceptable method of peaceful settlement of disputes (as proposed by Switzerland); (ii) in Bonn from June 20, 1978, to prepare a "Scientific Forum"; and (iii) in Valletta (Malta) from Feb. 13, 1979, on co-operation in the Mediterranean region.

The Montreux conference ended on Dec. 11, 1978, without reaching agreement on three different concepts of settlement procedures (presented respectively by the neutral and non-aligned, the East European and the Western countries) but it agreed on an eight-point basis for the future elaboration of a method of settling international disputes and it recommended that the Madrid follow-up meeting of the CSCE should consider the holding of a further conference of experts on the subject.

The Bonn conference decided to hold a Scientific Forum in Hamburg from Feb. 18, 1980. At this conference a number of Western scientists strongly defended civil liberties and criticized the Soviet Union for violating provisions of the Helsinki Final Act. The conference, attended by some 400 scientists, nevertheless fulfilled its purpose of exchanging scientific knowledge and thus extending scientific co-operation, notably in medicine and the protection of the environment. It agreed on a final document (issued on March 3, 1980), that "respect for human rights and fundamental freedoms by all states" was "one of the bases for a significant improvement in mutual relations and international scientific co-operation".

The Valletta conference, to which Mediterranean countries outside Europe were also invited (of which, however, only Egypt, Israel and Syria attended the conference), was confined to discussing questions of economic, scientific and cultural co-operation, and it ended on March 28, 1979, with the adoption of 23 recommendations on increased co-operation in the region.

The second follow-up meeting of representatives of the CSCE Final Act signatories was held in Madrid, where negotiations were protracted over eight separate sessions (Nov. 11 to Dec. 19, 1980; Jan. 27 to April 10, 1981; May 5 to July 28, 1981; Oct. 27 to Dec. 18, 1981; Feb. 9 to March 12, 1982; Nov. 9 to Dec. 17, 1982; Feb. 8 to March 25, 1983; and April 19 to Sept. 9, 1983).

In an agreed concluding document the participants reaffirmed their commitment to the CSCE process, emphasized the importance of the implementation of all the provisions of the 1975 Final Act and stressed the importance which they attached to security and genuine détente "while deploring the deterioration of the international situation since the Belgrade meeting of 1977". They noted "certain progress" since 1975 but expressed concern at the serious deficiencies in the implementation of the Final Act, deplored serious violations of a number of its principles and "considered it necessary to state that strict application of and respect for these principles

. . . are essential for the improvement of mutual relations between the participating states".

The participants decided that a third follow-up meeting would be held in Vienna from Nov. 4, 1986.

The participants also decided that a conference on confidence- and security-building measures should be convened in Stockholm on Jan. 17, 1984, with its first stage being devoted to the negotiation and adoption of a set of mutually complementary measures designed to reduce the risk of military confrontation in Europe, covering the whole of Europe as well as the adjoining sea (and ocean) area and air space, with these measures being of military significance and politically binding, with adequate forms of verification corresponding to their content.

1986 Stockholm Agreement

The Stockholm conference was held in phases from January 1984 to September 1986, during which a total of 12 sessions were held, some of them in other capitals. At the conclusion of the 12th session (Aug. 19 to Sept. 22, 1986) agreement was reached on a set of confidence- and security-building measures including the following:

Notification. Countries agreed to give 42 days' advance warning, with detailed information on all military ground-based exercises involving more than 13,000 troops or 300 tanks.

Observation. Countries would invite observers from other nations to observe the manoeuvres of their ground forces involving more than 17,000 troops.

Verification and Inspection. Any nation doubting another's adherence to the Stockholm agreement was given the right to make a ground and aerial inspection of the military exercises in question. No state was required to allow more than three inspections a year. Members of military alliances could not inspect each other. An inspection must take place within 36 hours of a request.

Calendars. Each state would, by Nov. 15 each year, exchange a calendar of military exercises being carried out in Europe within the following calendar year.

Constraints. Countries should, by Nov. 15 each year, give two years' warning of exercises using more than 75,000 troops and one year's warning of manoeuvres with more than 40,000.

Non-Use of Force. The participating states reaffirmed their commitment to refrain from the threat or use of force against the territory or political independence of any state, in accordance with the 1975 Final Act and the UN Charter. The right of self-defence was noted.

Further paragraphs reaffirmed the significance of human rights and the necessity to take action against terrorism, "including terrorism in international relations".

Other Conferences

A conference on cultural issues held by representatives of the CSCE parties in Budapest and concluded on Nov. 25, 1985, ended without reaching agreement on the nature of the arts (with the Soviet side emphasizing the role of the state in making culture serve peace and security,

whereas the West insisted on individual freedom in the arts).

A conference of experts on human contacts was held in Berne (Switzerland) from April 15 to May 26, 1986, to discuss the issues of the reunion of families, marriages between citizens of different states and the crossing of borders for personal or professional reasons. It ended with a call for simplified regulations for travel for family reasons, including family reunions, an end to interference in mail and telephone calls, and speedy travel formalities in cases of serious illness or death.

US-Soviet Summit Meeting, November 1985

A summit meeting held in Geneva on Nov. 19–21, 1985, by President Reagan of the United States and Mikhail Gorbachov, General Secretary of the Communist Party of the Soviet Union, ended with the issuing of a joint statement in which the two leaders, while acknowledging the differences in their systems and approaches to international issues, agreed on the need to improve US-Soviet relations and the international situation as a whole.

Conscious of their responsibility for maintaining peace they agreed that a nuclear war could not be won and must not be fought. Recognizing that any conflict between their two countries would have catastrophic consequences, they emphasized the importance of preventing any war between them, whether nuclear or conventional, and stated that they would not seek to achieve nuclear superiority.

They also stated that their governments would accelerate the pace of negotiations on both nuclear arms and space weapons "to prevent arms race in space and to terminate it on earth, to limit and reduce nuclear arms and enhance strategic stability". In this context they called for early progress in areas where there was common ground, such as the principle of 50 per cent reductions in their nuclear arms appropriately applied and the idea of an interim agreement on intermediate-range nuclear weapons. They added that in these negotiations effective verification measures would be agreed upon.

Both leaders reaffirmed their desire for the general and complete prohibition of chemical weapons and the destruction of existing stockpiles and agreed to accelerate efforts to conclude an effective and verifiable international convention. They also agreed on the need to intensify the dialogue between the two countries through regular meetings at summit and ministerial level, to continue regular exchanges on regional issues and to expand bilateral cultural, educational and scientific-technical exchanges and the development of trade and economic ties.

The US President was also reported to have promised the Soviet Union that, if US research (on the US Strategic Defence Initiative, SDI) showed that a defence against ballistic missiles was possible, the United States would discuss with the Soviet Union how they would replace all strategic ballistic missiles with such a defensive system in space.

(According to a paper released by the British Ministry of Defence on Nov. 26, 1985, the Soviet Union had research programmes underway on such defence, including research on high-energy lasers, particle-beam weapons, surveillance and target detection, and pointing and tracking, and the Soviet Union also had the world's only deployed anti-satellite system—a space-based orbital interceptor, though of limited capability.)

East-West Treaties and Agreements, 1970-73

In the pursuit of a policy of negotiation rather than confrontation between Western Governments and those of communist countries, a number of treaties and agreements designed to increase détente and to normalize relations were concluded in 1970-73.

The Federal Republic of Germany and the Soviet Union

A treaty on the renunciation of the use of force in relations between the West German and Soviet Governments was signed in Moscow on Aug. 12, 1970. The operative articles of the treaty were as follows:

Art. 1. The Union of Soviet Socialist Republics and the Federal Republic of Germany regard the maintenance of international peace and the achievement of the relaxation of tension as a major objective of their policies.

They affirm their desire to promote the normalization of the situation in Europe and the development of peaceful relations between all European states, and in so doing proceed from the actual situation existing in this region.

Art. 2. The Federal Republic of Germany and the USSR shall be guided in their mutual relations, as well as in matters concerning the safeguarding of European and international security, by the aims and principles set out in the Charter of the United Nations. Accordingly, they will settle their disputes exclusively by peaceful means and undertake, in accord with Article 2 of the UN Charter, to refrain from the threat of force or the use of force in any matters affecting security in Europe and international security, as well as in their mutual relations.

Art. 3. In conformity with the foregoing aims and principles set out above, the USSR and the Federal Republic of Germany share the realization that peace in Europe can only be maintained if no one disturbs the present frontiers.

They undertake to respect the territorial integrity of all states in Europe within their existing frontiers.

They declare that they have no territorial claims whatsoever against anybody, and will not assert such claims in the future.

They regard as inviolable now and in the future the frontiers of all states in Europe as they are on the date of the signing of this treaty, including the Oder-Neisse line, which forms the western frontier of the People's Republic of Poland, and the frontier between the Federal Republic of Germany and the German Democratic Republic.

Art. 4. The present treaty between the USSR and the Federal Republic of Germany does not affect any bilateral or multilateral treaties and agreements previously concluded by them.

Art. 5. The present treaty is subject to ratification and shall come into force on the date of exchange of the instruments of ratification, which will take place in Bonn.

The West German government, also on Aug. 12, 1970, published the following letter sent by the West German Foreign Minister to his Soviet counterpart:

"In connection with today's signature of the treaty between the Federal Republic of Germany and the Union of Soviet Socialist Republics, the Government of the Federal Republic of Germany has the honour to state that this treaty does not conflict with the political objective of the Federal Republic of Germany to work for a state of peace in Europe in which the German nation will recover its unity in free self-determination."

The West German government simultaneously advised the governments of Britain, France and the USA that it had been made clear in the negotiations that the treaty did not affect the rights of the four powers "reflected in the known treaties and agreements" (i.e. the Potsdam Agreements).

The West German government also advised the governments of France, the United Kingdom and the USA that its Foreign Minister had declared:

"The question of the rights of the four powers is in no way connected with the treaty which the Federal Republic of Germany and the Union of Soviet Socialist Republics intend to conclude, and is not affected by it."

It added that the Soviet Foreign Minister had declared:

"The question of the rights of the four powers will also not be affected by the treaty which the Union of Soviet Socialist Republics and the Federal Republic of Germany intend to conclude. This is the attitude of the Soviet Government in this matter."

The treaty was ratified in the Federal Republic of Germany on May 23, 1972, and by the Presidium of the Supreme Soviet on May 31, and it entered into force on June 3, 1972.

An agreement on the development of economic, industrial and technical co-operation between the two countries came into force on May 19, 1973, and long-term perspectives of the above co-operation were agreed on Jan. 18, 1974.

An agreement on cultural co-operation was signed on May 19, 1973, and came into force on Nov. 2 of that year.

The Federal Republic of Germany and Poland

A treaty normalizing relations between the Federal Republic of Germany and Poland was published on Nov. 20, 1970, the two governments having agreed as follows:

Art. 1. (1) The Federal Republic of Germany and the People's Republic of Poland state in mutual agreement that the existing boundary line, the course of which is laid down in Chapter IX of the decisions of the Potsdam conference of Aug. 2, 1945, as running from the Baltic Sea immediately west of Swinemünde, and thence along the Oder river to the confluence of the western Neisse river and along the western Neisse to the Czechoslovak frontier, shall constitute the western state frontier of the People's Republic of Poland.

[The Polish text defined Poland's western frontier as "running from the Baltic Sea immediately west of Swinoujscie and thence along the Odra river to the confluence of the Lusatian Nysa river and along the Lusatian Nysa to the Czechoslovak frontier."]

(2) They reaffirm the inviolability of their existing frontiers now and in the future and undertake to respect each other's territorial integrity without restriction.

(3) They declare that they have no territorial claims whatsoever against each other and that they will not assert such claims in the future.

Art. 2. (1) The Federal Republic of Germany and the People's Republic of Poland shall in their mutual relations, as well as in matters of ensuring European and international security, be guided by the purposes and principles embodied in the Charter of the United Nations.

(2) Accordingly they shall, pursuant to Articles 1 and 2 of the UN Charter, settle all their disputes exclusively by peaceful means and refrain from any threat or use of force in matters affecting European and international security and in their mutual relations.

Art. 3. (1) The Federal Republic of Germany and the People's Republic of Poland shall take further steps towards full normalization and a comprehensive development of their mutual relations, of which the present treaty shall form the solid foundation.

(2) They agree that a broadening of their co-operation in the sphere of economic, scientific, technological, cultural and other relations is in their mutual interest.

Art. 4. The present treaty shall not affect any bilateral or multilateral international arrangements previously concluded by either contracting party or concerning them.

Art. 5. The present treaty is subject to ratification and shall enter into force on the date of exchange of the instruments of ratification, which shall take place in Bonn.

The treaty was signed in Warsaw on Dec. 7, 1970, by Willy Brandt, the German Federal Chancellor, and Jozef Cyrankiewicz, the President of Poland. It was ratified by the Federal Republic of Germany on May 23, 1972, and by the Polish Council of State on May 26, 1972, and entered into force on June 3, 1972.

Simultaneously with the approval, on May 17, 1972, of this treaty and of that concluded between the German Federal Government and the Soviet Union of Aug. 12, 1970, the parties represented in the *Bundestag* (the West German Lower House of Parliament) adopted, with only five abstentions, a resolution specifying that the treaties did not affect "the [German people's] inalienable right to self-determination" and declaring: "The policy of the Federal Republic of Germany, which aims at a peaceful restoration of national unity within the European framework, is not inconsistent with the treaties." The resolution also reiterated the *Bundestag*'s view that "the final settlement of the German question as a whole" was "still outstanding", but emphasized that the Federal Republic advocated the normalization of relations with the German Democratic Republic.

It was only after agreement on the above resolution that the Opposition (of the Christian Democratic and Christian Social Unions) decided to abstain from voting on the treaties rather than against their approval.

Canada and the Soviet Union

A *Protocol on Consultations* signed in Moscow on May 19, 1971, provided for regular consultation between the two countries on "important international problems of mutual interest . . . with the aim of facilitating a relaxation of tension, the development of co-operation, and the strengthening of security", and for such consultation to be held "without delay" in "the event of a situation which, in the opinion of the two Governments, endangers the maintenance of peace or involves a breach of the peace".

Four-Power Agreement on Status of Berlin

Talks between the ambassadors of Britain, France and the United States to the Federal Republic of Germany and the Soviet ambassador to the German Democratic Republic led to the conclusion of an agreement on Berlin, the first part of which was signed on Sept. 3, 1971.

The four powers agreed "to promote the elimination of tension" in the area, to settle disputes solely by peaceful means, and to "respect their individual and joint rights and responsibilities". They declared that transit traffic between West Berlin and the Federal Republic would be "unimpeded", be facilitated so as to take place in "the most simple and expeditious manner" and "receive preferential treatment".

The agreement reiterated that the Western Sectors of Berlin continued "not to be a constituent part of the Federal Republic of Germany and not to be governed by it".

The Government of the USSR declared: "Communications between the Western sectors of Berlin and areas bordering on these sectors and those areas of the German Democratic Republic which do not border on these sectors will be improved. Permanent residents of the Western sectors will be able to travel to and visit such areas for compassionate, family, religious, cultural or commercial reasons, or as tourists, under conditions comparable to those applying to other persons entering these areas. . . ."

On the status of West Berlin the three Western powers agreed as follows:

"(1) The ties between the Western sectors of Berlin and the Federal Republic of Germany will be maintained and developed, taking into account that these sectors continue not to be a constituent part of the Federal Republic of Germany and not to be governed by it. The provisions of the Basic Law of the Federal Republic of Germany and of the Constitution operative in the Western sectors of Berlin which contradict the above have been suspended and continue not to be in effect.

"(2) The Federal President, the Federal Government, the *Bundesversammlung* (joint session of Parliament), the *Bundesrat* (Upper House), and the *Bundestag* (Lower House), including their committees and *Fraktionen* (parliamentary party groups), as well as other state bodies of the Federal Republic of Germany, will not perform in the Western sectors of Berlin constitutional or official acts which contradict the provisions of Paragraph (1).

"(3) The Government of the Federal Republic of Germany will be represented in the Western Sectors of Berlin to the authorities of the three governments and to the Senate by a permanent liaison agency."

On the question of diplomatic representation the three Western powers declared:

"The Governments of the French Republic, the United Kingdom and the United States of America maintain their rights and responsibilities relating to the representation abroad of the interests of the Western sectors of Berlin and their permanent residents, including those rights and responsibilities concerning matters of security and status both in international organizations and in relations with other countries.

"The three governments will authorize the establishment of a Soviet consulate-general in the Western sectors of Berlin accredited to the appropriate authorities of the three governments."

In a final *Quadripartite Protocol* the four governments agreed that they would proceed on the basis that the agreement and arrangements concluded between the competent German authorities would enter into force simultaneously with the quadripartite agreement. The protocol was finally signed in West Berlin on June 3, 1972, on which date it entered into force. (For treaty between Federal Republic of Germany and German Democratic Republic signed a week earlier, see below.)

Other Berlin Agreements

Further agreements on Berlin were signed in 1971 as follows:

(1) An agreement on transit traffic between the Federal Republic of Germany and West Berlin, concluded by the West and East German governments and signed in Bonn on Dec. 17, 1971;

(2) an agreement between the Senate of West Berlin and the German Democratic Republic on "facilitation and improvement of travelling and visiting", signed in East Berlin on Dec. 19, 1971;

(3) an agreement between the Senate of West Berlin and the German Democratic Republic on the "settlement of the question of enclaves by exchange of territories", also signed in East Berlin on Dec. 19, 1971.

Under an agreement of Dec. 30, 1983, the operation of the loss-making sector of the Berlin S-Bahn (city railway) was transferred from the East German Reichsbahn to West Berlin, which would pay an annual rent to the Reichsbahn.

France and the Soviet Union

In a document laying down *The Principles of Co-operation between the USSR and France*, signed in Paris on Oct. 29, 1971, the two governments declared that their co-operation was based on reciprocity of advantages, was not directed against the interests of any people, and did not affect commitments of either country in respect of third states. In the event of situations creating a threat to peace, both governments would "immediately contact each other with the object of concerting their positions on all aspects of those situations" and on steps which would make it possible to cope with them (as agreed in a protocol signed in Paris on Oct. 13, 1970). Both sides would co-operate closely in Europe, together with other states concerned, "in the maintenance of peace and the pursuit of détente, and in the strengthening of security, peaceful relations and co-operation of all European states, on the basis of unswerving respect for the following principles: Inviolability of the present frontiers, non-interference in internal affairs, equality, independence and renunciation of the use or threat of force". Both parties would also work for "general and complete disarmament, and first of all nuclear disarmament", and "the overcoming of the division of the world into military-political groupings".

The United States and the Soviet Union

Two agreements signed in Washington on Sept. 30, 1971, were:

(1) An agreement designed to reduce the risk of outbreak of nuclear war, in which both parties undertook to notify each other immediately in the event of an "accidental, unauthorized, or any other unexplained incident involving a possible detonation of a nuclear weapon which would create a risk of outbreak of nuclear war"; "to take necessary measures to render harmless or destroy any such weapon"; and to notify the other "in advance of any planned missile launches" extending "beyond its national territory in the direction of the other party".

(2) An agreement amending an earlier agreement signed in Geneva on June 20, 1963, by the heads of the US and Soviet delegations at the Geneva disarmament conference, known as the "Hot Line" agreement and providing for the establishment of "a direct communications link between the two governments" for use in an emergency, e.g. an abrupt shift in the East-West military balance. Under the 1971 agreement the communications link was improved by the proposed replacement of cable and teleprinter links by a satellite communication system comprising two circuits and a number of ground stations.

In a note formally initialled by both sides on July 17, 1984, a facsimile capability was added to the direct communications link.

On July 5, 1985, it was announced that an agreement had been signed on consultation by way of the "Hot Line" in the event of a nuclear explosion or threat by a third party.

The Federal Republic of Germany and the German Democratic Republic

(1) A *Treaty between the Federal Republic of Germany and the German Democratic Republic on Questions of Traffic* was initialled in Bonn on May 12, 1972, and signed on May 26, 1972.

The contracting states undertook "to the greatest possible extent to allow, to facilitate and to organize as expeditiously as possible the traffic in and through their sovereign territories, corresponding to normal international practice on the basis of reciprocity and non-discrimination". Traffic would be subject to the law of the state in which it occurred, as far as the treaty did not provide otherwise.

The treaty included provisions for road and rail traffic and inland navigation. The text was supplemented by protocol notes, which stated that "at the proper time" further discussions on passenger and goods traffic would take place, as well as negotiations on an air traffic agreement. A "Notification of the GDR on Travel Facilitations" stated that at the invitation of the GDR citizens of the Federal Republic would be permitted to visit the GDR.

The treaty was approved by the West German *Bundestag* (Lower House) on Sept. 22, with no opposing votes and with nine abstentions; unanimous approval was given by the *Bundesrat* (Upper House) on Oct. 6. The East German *Volkskammer* approved the treaty on Oct. 16, and the treaty came into force on the following day.

Simultaneously with the traffic treaty a number of new East German travel regulations came into force, setting out conditions under which citizens of the two German states might be permitted to visit the other.

(2) After the signing of the above traffic treaty, the State Secretaries of the Federal Republic of Germany (FRG) and the German Democratic Republic (GDR) succeeded in negotiating the terms of a *Basic Treaty* establishing the basis of relations between the two German states, which was initialled on Nov. 8, 1972, and signed on Dec. 21. The two governments agreed as follows:

Art. 1. The FRG and the GDR will develop normal good-neighbourly relations with each other on the basis of equality of rights.

Art. 2. The FRG and the GDR will let themselves be guided by the aims and principles which are laid down in the Charter of the United Nations, in particular those of the sovereign equality of all states, respect for independence, sovereignty and territorial integrity, the right of self-determination, the protection of human rights, and non-discrimination.

Art. 3. In accordance with the Charter of the United Nations, the FRG and the GDR will solve their differences solely by peaceful means and refrain from the threat of force or the use of force. They affirm the inviolability, now and in the future, of the border existing between them, and pledge themselves to unrestricted respect for each other's territorial integrity.

Art. 4. The FRG and the GDR proceed on the assumption that neither of the two states can represent the other internationally or act in its name.

Art. 5. The FRG and the GDR will promote peaceful relations among the European states and contribute to security and co-operation in Europe. They support the efforts towards a reduction of armed forces and armaments in Europe provided this does not adversely affect the security of the parties concerned. With a view to achieving general and complete disarmament under effective international control, the FRG and the GDR will support efforts serving international security and designed to bring about arms limitation and disarmament, in particular in the field of nuclear arms and other weapons of mass destruction.

Art. 6. The FRG and the GDR proceed from the principle that the sovereign power of each of the two states is confined to its [own] state territory. They respect the independence and sovereignty of each of the two states in its internal and external affairs.

Art. 7. The FRG and the GDR declare their readiness, in the course of the normalization of their relations, to settle practical and humanitarian questions. They will conclude agreements in order—on the basis of this treaty and for their mutual advantage—to develop and promote co-operation in the economic field, science and technology, transport, juridical relations, posts and telecommunications, public health, culture, sport, the protection of the environment and in other spheres.
. . .

Art. 8. The FRG and the GDR will exchange permanent representative missions. They will be established at the seat of the respective governments. Practical questions connected with the establishment of the missions will be settled separately.

Art. 9. The FRG and the GDR are agreed that bilateral and multilateral international treaties and agreements previously concluded by or concerning them are not affected by this treaty.

In a *Supplementary Protocol* it was proposed to set up a commission of representatives of the two governments to "examine and, so far as is necessary, renew or supplement the demarcation of the border existing between the two states" and to "compile the necessary documentation on the line of the border".

In separate declarations on the protocol the Federal Republic stated that questions of nationality had not been settled by the treaty, and the German Democratic Republic stated that it proceeded on the assumption that the treaty would facilitate a settlement of these matters.

The documents were accompanied by a series of exchanges of letters and declarations:

(1) In the course of the normalization of relations after the entry into force of the treaty, the Government of the GDR would take steps for the settlement of questions related to (*a*) problems arising out of the separation of families; (*b*) the improvement of border and tourist passenger traffic; and (*c*) the improvement of non-commercial merchandise traffic.

(2) With the entry into force of the treaty the following improved arrangements would take effect:
Reunion of Families. Married couples would be reunited and parents who were in need of the care of their children could rejoin them, the same applying in the case of grandparents and grandchildren. In special cases the contraction of marriages would be permitted.
Travel Arrangements. These comprised (*a*) an extension of the list of urgent family matters, in the case of which East German citizens might be permitted to pay visits to the Federal Republic of Germany; (*b*) the inclusion of half-brothers and half-sisters having the same mother among those East German citizens entitled to apply for permission to pay visits to the FRG in cases of urgent family matters; (*c*) the extension of the procedure for the issuing of visas in transit traffic between the FRG and West Berlin to other transit traffic by rail and inland navigation; and (*d*) the possibility of breaks in transit journeys (with the exception of Berlin traffic).

(3) At the time of the entry into force of the treaty, four additional border crossing-points on the frontier between the GDR and the FRG would be opened for passenger traffic.

(4) Each side took note that the other would initiate the necessary measures to seek membership of the United Nations; both governments would inform each other of the date of their application.

(5) The Federal Government stated in a declaration that after the reassembly of the *Bundestag* [after the forthcoming general election] it would take steps for the creation of the necessary internal preconditions for application for FRG membership of the United Nations. The leaders of both delegations declared that the above-mentioned reciprocal notification had as its objective that both applications should take place at approximately the same time.

(6) A "declaration on signing" stated that both governments had agreed that in the course of the normalization of relations between the two states they would consult each other on questions of mutual interest, in particular on those which were of importance for the safeguarding of peace in Europe.

The Basic Treaty between the FRG and the GDR was ratified by the German Federal Parliament on May 25 and by the East German *Volkskammer* on June 13, and came into force at midnight on June 20, 1973.

Talks between the British, French and US ambassadors in the FRG and the Soviet ambassador to the GDR on the maintenance of the rights and responsibilities of the four powers in Germany after the conclusion of the Basic Treaty and the entry of the two German states into the United Nations opened in West Berlin on Oct. 23, 1972.

The text of the joint declaration agreed upon by them and published on Nov. 9, 1972, was worded as follows:

"The Governments of the United Kingdom of Great Britain and Northern Ireland, the French Republic, the Union of

Soviet Socialist Republics and the United States of America, having been represented by their ambassadors who held a series of meetings in the building formerly occupied by the Allied Control Council, are in agreement that they will support the applications for membership in the United Nations, when submitted, by the Federal Republic of Germany and the German Democratic Republic, and affirm in this connection that this membership shall in no way affect the rights and responsibilities of the four powers and the corresponding related quadripartite agreements, decisions and practices."

Article 8 of the Basic Treaty was implemented on March 14, 1974, when documents were signed on the establishment of "permanent representative missions" by the two states in East Berlin and Bonn respectively, with the FRG mission in East Berlin representing also the interests of West Berlin (this being the first occasion on which such a provision was included in any agreement by the FRG with a Warsaw Treaty Organization member state).

The United States and the Soviet Union

During a visit to Moscow by President Nixon on May 22–29, 1972, a treaty on the limitation of anti-ballistic missile systems, an interim agreement of certain measures with respect to the limitation of strategic offensive arms and six different co-operation agreements were signed by the two sides.

TREATY ON THE LIMITATION OF ANTI-BALLISTIC MISSILE SYSTEMS

The *Treaty on the Limitation of Anti-Ballistic Missile Systems*, signed on May 26, 1972, was the culmination of over two years of talks on strategic arms limitation (SALT) held between the two Governments. The treaty, also known as SALT I, and concluded for an unlimited duration, consisted of 16 articles, including the following:

Art. 1. (1) Each party undertakes to limit anti-ballistic missile (ABM) systems and to adopt other measures in accordance with the provisions of this treaty.

(2) Each party undertakes not to deploy ABM systems for a defence of the territory of its country and not to provide a base for such a defence, and not to deploy ABM systems for defence of an individual region except as provided for in Article 3 of this treaty.

Art. 2. (1) For the purpose of this treaty an ABM system is a system to counter strategic ballistic missiles or their elements in flight trajectory currently consisting of:

(*a*) ABM interceptor missiles, which are interceptor missiles constructed and deployed for an ABM role, or of a type tested in an ABM mode;

(*b*) ABM launchers, which are launchers constructed and deployed for launching ABM interceptor missiles; and

(*c*) ABM radars, which are radars constructed and deployed for an ABM role, or of a type tested in an ABM mode.

(2) The ABM system components listed in paragraph 1 of this article include those which are: (*a*) operational; (*b*) under construction; (*c*) undergoing testing; (*d*) undergoing overhaul, repair or conversion; or (*e*) mothballed.

Art. 3. Each party undertakes not to deploy ABM systems or their components except that:

(*a*) Within one ABM system deployment area having a radius of 150 kilometres and centred on the party's national capital, a party may deploy: (1) No more than 100 ABM

launchers and no more than 100 ABM interceptor missiles at launch sites; and (2) ABM radars within no more than six ABM radar complexes, the area of each complex being circular and having a diameter of no more than three kilometres; and

(*b*) within one ABM system deployment area having a radius of 150 kilometres and containing ICBM silo launchers, a party may deploy: (1) No more than 100 ABM interceptor missiles at launch sites; (2) two large phased-array ABM radars comparable in potential to corresponding ABM radars operational or under construction on the date of signature of the treaty in an ABM system deployment area containing ICBM silo launchers; and (3) no more than 18 ABM radars each having a potential less than the potential of the smaller of the above-mentioned two large phased-array ABM radars.

Art. 4. The limitations provided for in Article 3 shall not apply to ABM systems or their components for development or testing, and located within current or additionally agreed test ranges. Each party may have no more than a total of 15 ABM launchers at test ranges.

Art. 5. (1) Each party undertakes not to develop, test, or deploy ABM systems or components which are sea-based, space-based or mobile land-based.

(2) Each party undertakes not to develop, test or deploy ABM launchers for launching more than one ABM interceptor missile at a time from each launcher, nor to modify deployed launchers to provide them with such a capability, nor to develop, test, or deploy automatic or semi-automatic or other similar systems for rapid reload of ABM launchers.

Art. 6. To enhance assurance of the effectiveness of the limitations on ABM systems and their components provided by this treaty, each party undertakes:

(*a*) Not to give missiles, launchers, or radars, other than ABM interceptor missiles, ABM launchers, or ABM radars, capabilities to counter strategic ballistic missiles or their elements in flight trajectory, and not to test them in an ABM mode; and

(*b*) not to deploy in the future radars for early warning of strategic ballistic missile attack except at locations along the periphery of its national territory and oriented outwards.

Art. 8. ABM systems or their components in excess of the numbers or outside the areas specified in this treaty, as well as ABM systems or their components prohibited by this treaty, shall be destroyed or dismantled under agreed procedures within the shortest possible agreed period of time.

Art. 9. To assure the viability and effectiveness of this treaty, each party undertakes not to transfer to other states, and not to deploy outside its national territory, ABM systems or their components limited by this treaty.

Art. 12. (1) For the purpose of providing assurance of compliance with the provisions of this treaty, each party shall use national technical means of verification at its disposal in a manner consistent with generally recognized principles of international law.

(2) Each party undertakes not to interfere with the national technical means of verification of the other party operating in accordance with Paragraph (1) of this article.

(3) Each party undertakes not to use deliberate concealment measures which impede verification by national technical means of compliance with the provisions of this treaty. This obligation shall not require changes in current construction, assembly, conversion or overhaul practices.

After approval by the US Senate, President Nixon ratified the treaty on Sept. 29–30, 1972; the Supreme Soviet of the USSR approved it and President Podgorny ratified in on Sept. 29; and instruments of ratification were exchanged in Washington on Oct. 3, 1972.

At a review of the treaty by the US-Soviet Standing Consultative Commission in November

1977 the two sides agreed that the treaty was operating effectively, had decreased the risk of outbreak of war, facilitated progress in the further limitation and reduction of strategic offensive arms and required "no amendment at this time".

INTERIM AGREEMENT ON CERTAIN MEASURES WITH RESPECT TO THE LIMITATION OF STRATEGIC OFFENSIVE ARMS

Under the *Interim Agreement*, to be valid for five years, and also signed on May 26, 1972, both parties undertook:

In Article 1, "not to start construction of additional fixed land-based intercontinental ballistic missile (ICBM) launchers after July 1, 1972";

in Article 2, "not to convert land-based launchers for light ICBMs, or for ICBMs of older types deployed prior to 1964, into land-based launchers for heavy ICBMs of types deployed after that time"; and

in Article 3, "to limit submarine-launched ballistic missile (SLBM) launchers and modern ballistic missile submarines to the numbers operational and under construction on the date of signature of this Interim Agreement, and in addition launchers and submarines constructed under procedures established by the parties as replacements for an equal number of ICBM launchers of older types deployed prior to 1964 or for launchers on older submarines".

A protocol to the Interim Agreement contained the following provisions:

The United States may have no more than 710 ballistic missile launchers on submarines (SLBMs) and no more than 44 modern ballistic missile submarines. The Soviet Union may have no more than 950 ballistic missile launchers on submarines and no more than 62 modern ballistic missile submarines.

Additional ballistic missile launchers on submarines up to the above-mentioned levels—in the United States over 656 ballistic missile launchers on nuclear-powered submarines, and in the USSR over 740 ballistic missile launchers on nuclear-powered submarines, operational and under construction—may become operational as replacements for equal numbers of ballistic missile launchers of older type deployed prior to 1964 or of ballistic missile launchers on older submarines.

The deployment of modern SLBMs on any submarine, regardless of type, will be counted against the total level of SLBMs permitted for the USA and the USSR.

The Interim Agreement also came into force on Oct. 3, 1972.

SOVIET-US CO-OPERATION AGREEMENTS

The Soviet-US co-operation agreements signed at the same time were:

(1) An *Environmental Protection Agreement* on measures to prevent pollution and to protect environmental quality;

(2) a *Medicine and Public Health Agreement*;

(3) a *Space Co-operation Agreement* providing notably for the first joint space-flight by astronauts of the two countries in 1975 [see page 92];

(4) a *Scientific and Technological Co-operation Agreement*;

(5) an *Agreement on Prevention of Incidents at Sea*, aimed at ensuring safety of navigation by warships and aircraft of the two countries; and

(6) a communiqué announcing the two parties' intention to establish a joint Commercial Commission.

In addition, the two parties issued on May 29, 1972, a statement on the *Basic Principles of Relations between the United States of America and the Union of Soviet Socialist Republics*, in which they expressed their agreement as follows:

(1) They [the USA and the USSR] will proceed from the common determination that in the nuclear age there is no alternative to conducting their mutual relations on the basis of peaceful coexistence. Differences in ideology and in the social systems of the USA and the USSR are not obstacles to the bilateral development of normal relations based on the principles of sovereignty, equality, non-interference in internal affairs and mutual advantage.

(2) The USA and the USSR attach major importance to preventing the development of situations capable of causing a dangerous exacerbation of their relations. Therefore, they will do their utmost to avoid military confrontations and to prevent the outbreak of nuclear war. They will always exercise restraint in their mutual relations, and will be prepared to negotiate and settle differences by peaceful means. Discussions and negotiations on outstanding issues will be conducted in a spirit of reciprocity, mutual accommodation and mutual benefit.

Both sides recognize that efforts to obtain unilateral advantage at the expense of the other, directly or indirectly, are inconsistent with these objectives. The prerequisites for maintaining and strengthening peaceful relations between the USA and the USSR are the recognition of the security interests of the parties based on the principle of equality and the renunciation of the use or threat of force.

In May 1984 it was agreed to extend the Agreement on Prevention of Incidents at Sea—see under (5) above—for a further three years.

SETTLEMENT OF LEND-LEASE DEBT

Under an agreement concluded on Oct. 18, 1972, the Soviet Union undertook to pay the United States the balance of $722,000,000 which it owed for civil supplies under the (US) Lend-Lease Act of 1941 (payment to be made in annual instalments of $24,000,000 from 1972 to 2001).

INEFFECTUAL US-SOVIET TRADE AGREEMENTS OF 1972

At a session of the US-Soviet Joint Commercial Commission (established under the Soviet-American co-operation agreements of May 1972—see above) held from Oct. 12–16, 1972, a series of agreements was reached covering trade and lend-lease obligations. The trade agreement provided inter alia for most-favoured-nation treatment between the two countries—this, however, being subject to congressional approval, without which the agreement would not enter into force. Under a congressional move known as the Jackson Amendment, led by Senator Henry Jackson, the granting of most-favoured-nation status to the Soviet Union would be made conditional on the removal of restrictions on Jewish emigration from the Soviet Union. The US Ways and Means Committee on Sept. 27, 1973, also voted to deny most-favoured-nation status until this condition was fulfilled.

(A "Jackson Amendment" was also adopted in regard to the ABM treaty [see page 284], in this case President Nixon being urged to seek a future treaty on the limitation of offensive nuclear weapons "which would not limit the United States to levels of intercontinental strategic forces inferior to the limits provided for the Soviet Union".)

Following the passing of a Trade Reform Bill by the US Congress on Dec. 20, 1974, and its enactment on Jan. 3, 1975, the Soviet Government informed the US government on Jan. 10 of that year that it would not put the 1972 bilateral trade agreement into effect because it considered the US legislation as contravening the agreement and as representing interference in the Soviet Union's domestic affairs (the bill having been amended so as to prevent the US President from granting most-favoured-nation status to any communist country unless he certified that that country did not restrict emigration).

The Federal Republic of Germany and Czechoslovakia

A treaty normalizing relations between the Federal Republic of Germany and Czechoslovakia and declaring the Munich Agreement of 1938 to be null and void was initialled on June 20, 1973, by the Foreign Ministers of the two states. The text of the treaty is given below.

"The Federal Republic of Germany and the Czechoslovak Socialist Republic;

"In the historic recognition that the harmonious coexistence of the peoples of Europe constitutes a prerequisite for peace;

"In the firm determination once and for all to put an end to the disastrous past in their relations, above all in connexion with the Second World War, which has inflicted immeasurable sufferings on the European peoples;

"Recognizing that the Munich Agreement of Sept. 29, 1938, was imposed on the Czechoslovak Republic by the National Socialist regime under the threat of force;

"In view of the fact that in both countries a new generation has grown up, which has a right to a secure [and] peaceful future;

"With the intention of creating lasting foundations for the development of good-neighbourly relations;

"Endeavouring to strengthen peace and security in Europe;

"Convinced that peaceful co-operation on the basis of the aims and principles of the Charter of the United Nations is in accordance with the wishes of the peoples as well as the interest of peace in the world;

"Have agreed as follows:

"**Art. 1.** The Federal Republic of Germany and the Czechoslovak Socialist Republic consider the Munich Agreement of Sept. 29, 1938, as null and void under the terms of this treaty in regard to their mutual relations.

"**Art. 2.** (1) This treaty does not affect the legal consequences arising with regard to private persons and legal entities from the laws applied in the period Sept. 30, 1938, to May 9, 1945. Excepted from this are the consequences of measures which both contracting parties consider as null and void by reason of their irreconcilability with the fundamental principles of justice.

"(2) This treaty leaves unaffected the citizenship of persons alive and dead resulting from the legal system of each of the two contracting parties.

"(3) This treaty with its declarations on the Munich Agreement does not constitute a legal basis for material claims on the part of the Czechoslovak Socialist Republic and its natural and juristic persons.

"**Art. 3.** (1) The Federal Republic of Germany and the Czechoslovak Socialist Republic are guided in their mutual relations, as well as in questions of guaranteeing security in

Europe and in the world, by the aims and principles which are laid down in the Charter of the United Nations.

"(2) Accordingly, in conformity with Articles 1 and 2 of the Charter of the United Nations, they will resolve all their differences by exclusively peaceful means, and in questions which concern European and international security, as well as in their mutual relations, will abstain from the threat of force or the use of force.

"**Art. 4.** (1) In conformity with the foregoing aims and principles the Federal Republic of Germany and the Czechoslovak Socialist Republic reaffirm the inviolability of their common frontier at present and in the future, and reciprocally commit themselves to the unrestricted respect of their territorial integrity.

"(2) They declare that they have no territorial claims of any kind against each other and likewise in the future will not raise any such claims.

"**Art. 5.** (1) The Federal Republic of Germany and the Czechoslovak Socialist Republic will take further steps for the comprehensive development of their mutual relations.

"(2) They are in agreement that an expansion of neighbourly co-operation in the fields of the economy, science, scientific and technological relations, culture, the protection of the environment, sport, traffic and their other relations is in their mutual interest.

"**Art. 6.** This treaty requires ratification and enters into force on the day of the exchange of the ratification documents, which is to take place in Bonn. . . ."

In an exchange of letters the two ministers stated that Article 2 would be extended to cover West Berlin. However, owing to disagreement over the West German claim to represent West Berlin, the signature of the treaty was delayed, but it was eventually signed on Dec. 11, 1973. Despite objections by the *Bundesrat* (Upper House of the West German Parliament) the treaty was finally ratified by the Federal Republic of Germany on June 30, 1974, when the *Bundestag* (Lower House) passed a bill to that effect, and instruments of ratification were exchanged on July 14, 1974.

The United States and the Soviet Union

During a visit to the USA on June 17–25, 1973, by Leonid Brezhnev, General Secretary of the Communist Party of the Soviet Union (CPSU), a series of agreements between the USA and the Soviet Union was signed, the most important being an agreement on the basic principles of negotiation on the further limitation of strategic offensive arms, and an agreement on the prevention of nuclear war.

(1) The *Agreement on the Basic Principles of Negotiation on the Further Limitation of Strategic Offensive Arms*, signed on June 21, 1973, was worded as follows:

"The President of the United States of America, Richard Nixon, and the General Secretary of the Central Committee of the CPSU, L. I. Brezhnev;

"Having thoroughly considered the question of the further limitation of strategic arms, and the progress already achieved in the current negotiations;

"Reaffirming their conviction that the earliest adoption of further limitation of strategic arms would be a major contribution in reducing the danger of an outbreak of nuclear war and in strengthening international peace and security;

"Have agreed as follows:

"(1) The two sides will continue active negotiations in order to work out a permanent agreement on more complete measures on the limitation of strategic offensive arms, as well as their subsequent reduction, proceeding from the Basic Principles of Relations between the USA and the USSR signed in Moscow on May 29, 1972 [see page 285], and from the Interim Agreement between the USA and the USSR of May 26, 1972, on Certain Measures with Respect to the Limitation of Strategic Offensive Arms [ibid.].

"Over the course of the next year the two sides will make serious efforts to work out the provisions of the permanent agreement on more complete measures on the limitation of strategic offensive arms with the objective of signing it in 1974.

"(2) New agreements on the limitation of strategic offensive armaments will be based on the principles of the American-Soviet documents adopted in Moscow in May 1972 and the agreements reached in Washington in June 1973; and in particular, both sides will be guided by the recognition of each other's equal security interests and by the recognition that efforts to obtain unilateral advantage, directly or indirectly, would be inconsistent with the strengthening of peaceful relations between the USA and the USSR.

"(3) The limitations placed on strategic offensive weapons can apply both to their quantitative aspects as well as to their qualitative improvement.

"(4) Limitations on strategic offensive arms must be subject to adequate verification by national technical means.

"(5) The modernization and replacement of strategic offensive arms would be permitted under conditions which will be formulated in the agreements to be concluded.

"(6) Pending the completion of a permanent agreement on more complete measures of strategic offensive arms limitation, both sides are prepared to reach agreements on separate measures to supplement the existing interim agreement of May 26, 1972.

"(7) Each side will continue to take necessary organizational and technical measures for preventing the accidental or unauthorized use of nuclear weapons under its control in accordance with the agreement of Sept. 30, 1971, between the USA and the USSR.

(2) The text of the *Agreement on the Prevention of Nuclear War*, signed on June 22, 1973, was as follows:

"The United States of America and the Union of Soviet Socialist Republics, hereinafter referred to as the parties;

"Guided by the objectives of strengthening world peace and international security;

"Conscious that nuclear war would have devastating consequences for mankind;

"Proceeding from the desire to bring about conditions in which the danger of an outbreak of nuclear war anywhere in the world would be reduced and ultimately eliminated;

"Proceeding from their obligations under the Charter of the United Nations regarding the maintenance of peace, refraining from the threat or use of force, and the avoidance of war, and in conformity with the agreements to which either party has subscribed;

"Proceeding from the Basic Principles of Relations between the United States and the USSR signed in Moscow on May 29, 1972;

"Reaffirming that the development of relations between the USA and the USSR is not directed against other countries and their interests;

"Have agreed as follows:

"**Art. 1.** The United States and the Soviet Union agree that an objective of their policies is to remove the danger of nuclear war and of the use of nuclear weapons.

"Accordingly, the parties agree that they will act in such a manner as to prevent the development of situations capable of causing a dangerous exacerbation of their relations, as to avoid military confrontations, and as to exclude the outbreak of nuclear war between them and between either of the parties and other countries.

"**Art. 2.** The parties agree, in accordance with Article 1 and to realize the objective stated in that article, to proceed from the premise that each party will refrain from the threat or use of force against other countries, in circumstances which may endanger international peace and security. The parties agree that they will be guided by these considerations in the formulation of their foreign policies and in their actions in the field of international relations.

"**Art. 3.** The parties undertake to develop their relations with each other and with other countries in a way consistent with the purposes of this agreement.

"**Art. 4.** If at any time relations between the parties or between either party and other countries appear to involve the risk of a nuclear conflict, or if relations between countries not parties to this agreement appear to involve the risk of nuclear war between the USA and the USSR or between either party and other countries, the United States and the Soviet Union, acting in accordance with the provisions of this agreement, shall immediately enter into urgent consultations with each other and make every effort to avert this risk.

"**Art. 5.** Each party shall be free to inform the UN Security Council, the Secretary-General of the United Nations, and the Governments of allied or other countries of the progress and outcome of consultations initiated in accordance with Article 4 of this agreement.

"**Art. 6.** Nothing in this agreement shall affect or impair:

"(*a*) The inherent right of individual or collective self-defence as envisaged by Article 51 of the Charter of the United Nations;

"(*b*) the provisions of the Charter of the United Nations, including those relating to the maintenance or restoration of international peace and security; and

"(*c*) the obligations undertaken by either party towards its allies or other countries in treaties, agreements and other appropriate documents.

"**Art. 7.** This agreement shall be of unlimited duration.

"**Art. 8.** This agreement shall enter into force upon signature."

(3) A 10-year agreement on scientific and technical co-operation in the peaceful uses of atomic energy was signed on June 21, 1973.

This provided for co-operation to be concentrated in the spheres of controlled thermonuclear fission, fast-breeder reactors, and research on the fundamental properties of matter. Under the terms of the agreement a US-Soviet Joint Committee on Co-operation in the Peaceful Uses of Atomic Energy would be established.

(4) Other agreements signed were:

(i) *On June 19*—an agreement on agricultural co-operation; an agreement on transportation; an agreement on studies of the world ocean; a six-year agreement on cultural and scientific exchanges;

(ii) *on June 20*—a convention on taxation (enabling nationals of either country to avoid paying double taxation in the other);

(iii) *on June 22*—a protocol on the establishment of a Soviet trade mission in Washington and a US commercial bureau in Moscow; a protocol on the establishment of a US-Soviet chamber of commerce; and

(iv) *on June 23*—a protocol on co-operation in air traffic.

The agreements on agricultural co-operation, transportation and studies of the world ocean, all for five years, stated that co-operation would be "on the basis of mutual benefit, equality and reciprocity". Each provided for the setting up of a US-Soviet joint committee for its implementation.

Further US-Soviet Agreements, 1974-85

During a further visit to the Soviet Union by President Nixon from June 27 to July 3, 1974, the US President and L. I. Brezhnev signed (i) a US-Soviet treaty on the limitation of underground nuclear weapon tests and (ii) a protocol to the Treaty on the Limitation of Anti-Ballistic Missile Systems of May 1972 [see page 284].

Treaty on Limitation of Underground Nuclear Weapon Tests

The full text of this treaty was as follows:

"**Art. I.** (1) Each party undertakes to prohibit, to prevent, and not to carry out any underground nuclear weapon test having a yield exceeding 150 kilotons at any place under its jurisdiction or control, beginning March 31, 1976.

"(2) Each party shall limit the number of its underground nuclear weapon tests to a minimum.

"(3) The parties shall continue their negotiations with a view towards achieving a solution to the problem of the cessation of all underground nuclear weapon tests.

"**Art. II.** (1) For the purpose of providing assurance of compliance with the provisions of this treaty, each party shall use national technical means of verification at its disposal in a manner consistent with the generally recognized principles of international law.

"(2) Each party undertakes not to interfere with the national technical means of verification of the other party operating in accordance with Paragraph 1 of this article.

"(3) To promote the objectives and implementation of the provisions of this treaty the parties shall, as necessary, consult with each other, make inquiries and furnish information in response to such inquiries.

"**Art. III.** The provisions of this treaty do not extend to underground nuclear explosions carried out by the parties for peaceful purposes. Underground nuclear explosions for peaceful purposes shall be governed by an agreement which is to be negotiated and concluded by the parties at the earliest possible time.

"**Art. IV.** This treaty shall be subject to ratification in accordance with the constitutional procedures of each party. This treaty shall enter into force on the day of the exchange of instruments of ratification.

"**Art. V.** (1) This treaty shall remain in force for a period of five years. Unless replaced earlier by an agreement in implementation of the objectives specified in Paragraph 3 of Article 1 of this treaty, it shall be extended for successive five-year periods unless either party notifies the other of its termination no later than six months prior to the expiration of the treaty. Before the expiration of this period the parties may, as necessary, hold consultations to consider the situation relevant to the substance of this treaty and to introduce possible amendments to the text of the treaty.

"(2) Each party shall, in exercising its national sovereignty, have the right to withdraw from this treaty if it decides that extraordinary events related to the subject-matter of this treaty have jeopardized its supreme interests.

"It shall give notice of its decision to the other party six months prior to withdrawal from this treaty. Such notice shall include a statement of the extraordinary events the notifying party regards as having jeopardized its supreme interests.

"(3) This treaty shall be registered pursuant to Article 102 of the Charter of the United Nations."

A protocol to the treaty said that the two countries had agreed as follows:

"(1) For the purpose of ensuring verification of compliance with the obligations of the parties under the treaty by national technical means, the parties shall, on the basis of reciprocity, exchange the following data:

"(*a*) The geographic co-ordinates of the boundaries of each test site and of the boundaries of the geophysically distinct testing areas therein.

"(*b*) Information on the geology of the testing areas of the sites (the rock characteristics of geological formations and the basic physical properties of the rock—i.e., density, seismic velocity, water saturation, porosity and depth of water table).

"(*c*) The geographic co-ordinates of underground nuclear weapon tests, after they have been conducted.

"(*d*) Yield, date, time, depth and co-ordinates for two nuclear weapons tests for calibration purposes from each geophysically distinct testing area where underground nuclear weapon tests have been and are to be conducted.

"In this connexion the yield of such explosions for calibration purposes should be as near as possible to the limit defined in Article I of the treaty, and not less than one-tenth of that limit.

"In the case of testing areas where data are not available on two tests for calibration purposes, the data pertaining to one such test shall be exchanged, if available, and the data pertaining to the second test shall be exchanged as soon as possible after a second test having a yield in the above-mentioned range. The provisions of this protocol shall not require the parties to conduct tests solely for calibration purposes.

"(2) The parties agree that the exchange of data pursuant to Sub-paragraphs *a*, *b* and *d* of Paragraph 1 shall be carried out simultaneously with the exchange of instruments of ratification of the treaty, as provided in Article IV of the treaty, having in mind that the parties shall, on the basis of reciprocity, afford each other the opportunity to familiarize themselves with these data before the exchange of instruments of ratification.

"(3) Should a party specify a new test site or testing area after the entry into force of the treaty, the data called for by Sub-paragraphs *a* and *b* of Paragraph 1 shall be transmitted to the other party in advance of use of that site or area. The data called for by Sub-paragraph *d* of Paragraph 1 shall also be transmitted in advance of use of that site or area if they are available; if they are not available, they shall be transmitted as soon as possible after they have been obtained by the transmitting party.

"(4) The parties agree that the test sites of each party shall be located at places under its jurisdiction or control and that all nuclear weapon tests shall be conducted solely within the testing areas specified in accordance with Paragraph 1.

"(5) For the purposes of the treaty, all underground nuclear explosions at the specified test sites shall be considered nuclear weapon tests and shall be subject to all the provisions of the treaty relating to nuclear weapon tests. The provisions of Article III of the treaty apply to all underground nuclear explosions conducted outside of the specified test sites, and only to such explosions."

PROTOCOL TO TREATY ON LIMITATION OF ABM SYSTEMS

A final paragraph of the above treaty stated that the following protocol "shall be considered an integral part of the treaty".

"**Art. I.** (1) Each party shall be limited at any one time to a single area out of the two provided in Article III of the Treaty for Deployment of Anti-Ballistic Missile (ABM) Systems or their Components, and accordingly shall not exercise its right to deploy an ABM system or its components in the second of the two ABM system deployment areas permitted by Article III of the treaty, except as an exchange of one permitted area for the other in accordance with Article II of this Protocol.

"(2) Accordingly, except as permitted by Article II of this Protocol: The United States of America shall not deploy an ABM system or its components in the area centred on its capital, as permitted by Article III(*a*) of the treaty, and the Soviet Union shall not deploy an ABM system or its components in the deployment area of intercontinental ballistic missile (ICBM) silo launchers permitted by Article III(*b*) of the treaty.

"Art. II. (1) Each party shall have the right to dismantle or destroy its ABM system and the components thereof in the area where they are presently deployed and to deploy an ABM system or its components in the alternative area permitted by Article III of the treaty, provided that, prior to initiation of construction, notification is given in accord with the procedure agreed to by the Standing Consultative Commission during the year beginning Oct. 3, 1977, and ending Oct. 2, 1978, or during any year which commences at five-year intervals thereafter, those being the years for periodic review of the treaty, as provided in Article XIV of the treaty. This right may be exercised only once.

"(2) Accordingly, in the event of such notice, the United States would have the right to dismantle or destroy the ABM system and its components in the deployment area of ICBM silo launchers and to deploy an ABM system or its components in an area centred on its capital, as permitted by Article III(*a*) of the treaty, and the Soviet Union would have the right to dismantle or destroy the ABM system and its components in the area centred on its capital and to deploy an ABM system or its components in an area containing ICBM silo launchers, as permitted by Article III(*b*) of the treaty.

"(3) Dismantling or destruction and deployment of ABM systems or their components and the notification thereof shall be carried out in accordance with Article VIII of the ABM treaty and procedures agreed to in the Standing Consultative Commission.

"Art. III. The rights and obligations established by the treaty remain in force and shall be complied with by the parties except to the extent modified by this Protocol. In particular, the deployment of an ABM system or its components within the area selected shall remain limited by the levels and other requirements established by the treaty.

"Art. IV. This Protocol shall be subject to ratification in accordance with the constitutional procedures of each party. It shall enter into force on the day of the exchange of instruments of ratification and shall thereafter be considered an integral part of the treaty."

The above Protocol to the Treaty on the Limitation of ABM Systems was ratified by the US Senate on Nov. 11, 1975, and the relevant instruments of ratification were exchanged in Washington on May 24, 1976.

EXPLANATORY "FACT SHEET"

A "fact sheet" on the ABM Treaty Protocol was released in Moscow on July 3 by the White House Press Secretary, briefly explaining the provisions of the protocol in non-technical language.

"In 1972," the fact sheet recalled, "The United States and the Soviet Union signed an ABM Treaty limiting each side to one ABM site for defence of their national capital and one site for the defence of an ICBM [inter-continental ballistic missile] field. Each side was permitted 100 ABM interceptors at each site. The US has deployed 100 interceptors around a *Minuteman* site at Grand Forks, North Dakota. The Soviets have deployed their ABMs around Moscow. Neither side has initiated construction of the second site permitted under the 1972 ABM Treaty."

It was explained that the Protocol to the ABM Treaty had the following effect:

(1) Each side would be limited to one ABM site for the defence of their national capital (Moscow and Washington) or for the defence of an ICBM field.

(2) Each party would have the right to dismantle its ABM system and components in the area where they were presently deployed, and to deploy an ABM system and its components in the alternative area during the year beginning Oct. 3, 1977, and ending Oct. 2, 1978, and during any year which commenced at five-year intervals thereafter.

(3) The Soviet Union would have the right to dismantle its ABM system centred in its capital and deploy an ABM system in an area containing ICBM silo launchers, at least 1,300 kilometres from Moscow.

(4) The United States would have the right to dismantle the ABM system in the deployment area of ICBM silo launchers and to deploy an ABM system in an area centred on the capital.

(5) Prior notification must be given of the desire to switch ABM defences in accord with procedures agreed to by the SALT Standing Consultative Commission.

OTHER 1974 US-SOVIET AGREEMENTS

Also during President Nixon's visit to the Soviet Union, three US-Soviet agreements were signed on June 28, 1974, relating to co-operation in (i) housing and construction, (ii) energy research and (iii) the development of an artificial heart.

A long-term agreement to facilitate economic, industrial and technical co-operation was signed in Moscow on June 29, 1974, and entered into force on the same day. On June 27, 1984, it was agreed to extend this agreement for a further 10 years.

1974 Agreement to proceed to SALT II

At the end of a meeting in Vladivostok on Nov. 23–24, 1974, President Ford and L. I. Brezhnev agreed that a new agreement should be concluded between the USA and the Soviet Union on the limitation of strategic offensive arms to last until Dec. 31, 1985. The two leaders agreed on the provisions on which further negotiations should be based, in particular that the new agreement should "include the following limitations: (*a*) Both sides will be entitled to have a certain agreed aggregate number of strategic delivery vehicles; (*b*) both sides will be entitled to have a certain agreed aggregate number of ICBMs [inter-continental ballistic missiles] and SLBMs [submarine-launched ballistic missiles] equipped with multiple independently targeted warheads [MIRVs]". President Ford gave the numbers agreed under (*a*) as up to 2,400 and under (*b*) as up to 1,320 missiles on either side.

1975 US-Soviet Trade and Shipping Agreements

President Ford of the United States announced on Oct. 20, 1975, that two parallel agreements had been concluded on the supply of US grain to the Soviet Union and of Soviet oil to the USA, providing for Soviet purchases, between Oct, 1,

1975, and Sept. 30, 1981, of an annual 6,000,000 tonnes of grain (which might be increased by up to 2,000,000 tonnes per annum unless US grain supplies were not expected to reach 225,000,000 tonnes in the year concerned), and for US purchases of up to 10,000,000 tonnes of crude oil and petroleum products per annum over a period of five years.

A new six-year shipping agreement, effective from Jan. 1, 1976, was signed on Dec. 29, 1975, covering inter alia the fixing of freight charges and the mutual opening of ports to vessels of either country.

The supply of grain under the above agreement was embargoed by the United States between Jan. 4, 1980, and April 24, 1981, but on Aug. 25, 1983, it was renewed by a new five-year agreement providing for a minimum of 9,000,000 tonnes of grain to be supplied to the Soviet Union every year, with an optional additional 3,000,000 tonnes to be purchased by the Soviet Union without prior consultation.

1976 US-Soviet Treaty on Limitation of Underground Nuclear Explosions for Peaceful Purposes

A new treaty, signed on May 28, 1976, by President Ford for the United States and L. I. Brezhnev for the Soviet Union, completed and complemented the 1974 treaty on the limitation of underground nuclear weapon tests [see above] which had remained unratified—in which connection Article IX of the new treaty laid down that both treaties should be ratified simultaneously.

The nine operative articles of the treaty were as follows:

"Art. I. (1) The parties enter into this treaty to satisfy the obligations in Article III of the Treaty on the Limitation of Underground Nuclear Weapon Tests and assume additional obligations in accordance with the provisions of this treaty.

"(2) This treaty shall govern all underground nuclear explosions for peaceful purposes conducted by the parties after March 31, 1976.

"Art. II. For the purposes of this treaty:

"(a) 'Explosion' means any individual or group underground nuclear explosion for peaceful purposes;

"(b) 'explosive' means any device, mechanism or system for producing an individual explosion;

"(c) 'group explosion' means two or more individual explosions for which the time interval between successive individual explosions does not exceed five seconds and for which the emplacement points of all explosives can be interconnected by straight line segments, each of which joins two emplacement points and each of which does not exceed 40 kilometres.

"Art. III. (1) Each party, subject to the obligations assumed under this treaty and other international agreements, reserves the right to:

"(a) Carry out explosions at any place under its jurisdiction or control outside the geographical boundaries of test sites specified under the provisions of the Treaty on the Limitation of Underground Nuclear Weapon Tests; and

"(b) carry out, participate or assist in carrying out explosions in the territory of another state at the request of such other state.

"(2) Each party undertakes to prohibit, to prevent and not to carry out at any place under its jurisdiction or control, and further undertakes not to carry out, participate or assist in carrying out anywhere:

"(a) Any individual explosion having a yield exceeding 150 kilotons;

"(b) any group explosion:

"(i) having an aggregate yield exceeding 150 kilotons except in ways that will permit identification of each individual explosion and determination of the yield of each individual explosion in the group in accordance with the provisions of Article IV and the Protocol to this treaty;

"(ii) having an aggregate yield exceeding one and one-half megatons;

"(c) any explosion which does not carry out a peaceful application;

"(d) any explosion except in compliance with the provisions of the Treaty banning Nuclear Weapon Tests in the Atmosphere, in Outer Space and Under Water, the Treaty on the Non-Proliferation of Nuclear Weapons, and other international agreements entered into by that party.

"(3) The question of carrying out any individual explosion having a yield specified in Paragraph (2)(a) of this article will be considered by the parties at an appropriate time to be agreed.

"Art. IV. (1) For the purpose of providing assurance of compliance with the provisions of this treaty, each party shall:

"(a) Use national technical means of verification at its disposal in a manner consistent with generally recognized principles of international law; and

"(b) provide to the other party information and access to sites of explosions and furnish assistance in accordance with the provisions set forth in the Protocol to this treaty.

"(2) Each party undertakes not to interfere with the national technical means of verification of the other party operating in accordance with Paragraph (1)(a) of this article, or with the implementation of the provisions of Paragraph (1)(b) of this article.

"Art. V. (1) To promote the objectives and implementation of the provisions of this treaty, the parties shall establish promptly a Joint Consultative Commission within the framework of which they will:

"(a) Consult with each other, make enquiries and furnish information in response to such enquiries, to assure confidence in compliance with the obligations assumed;

"(b) consider questions concerning compliance with the obligations assumed and related situations which may be considered ambiguous;

"(c) consider questions involving unintended interference with the means for assuring compliance with the provisions of this treaty;

"(d) consider changes in technology or other new circumstances which have a bearing on the provisions of this treaty; and

"(e) consider possible amendments to provisions governing underground nuclear explosions for peaceful purposes;

"(2) The parties through consultation shall establish, and may amend as appropriate, regulations for the Joint Consultative Commission governing procedures, composition and other relevant matters.

"Art. VI. (1) The parties will develop co-operation on the basis of mutual benefit, equality and reciprocity in various areas related to carrying out underground nuclear explosions for peaceful purposes.

"(2) The Joint Consultative Commission will facilitate this co-operation by considering specific areas and forms of co-operation which shall be determined by agreement between the parties in accordance with their constitutional procedures.

"(3) The parties will appropriately inform the International Atomic Energy Agency of results of their co-operation in the field of underground nuclear explosions for peaceful purposes.

"Art. VII. (1) Each party shall continue to promote the development of the international agreement or agreements and procedures provided for in Article V of the Treaty on the Non-Proliferation of Nuclear Weapons, and shall provide appropriate assistance to the International Atomic Energy Agency in this regard.

"(2) Each party undertakes not to carry out, participate or assist in the carrying out of any explosion in the territory of another state unless that state agrees to the implementation in its territory of the international observation and procedures contemplated by Article V of the Treaty on the Non-Proliferation of Nuclear Weapons and the provisions of Article IV and the Protocol to this treaty, including the provision by that state of the assistance necessary for such implementation and of the privileges and immunities specified in the Protocol.

"**Art. VIII.** (1) This treaty shall remain in force for a period of five years, and it shall be extended for successive five-year periods unless either party notifies the other of its termination no later than six months prior to its expiration. Before the expiration of this period the parties may, as necessary, hold consultations to consider the situation relevant to the substance of this treaty. However, under no circumstances shall either party be entitled to terminate this treaty while the Treaty on the Limitation of Underground Nuclear Weapon Tests remains in force.

"(3) Termination of the treaty on the Limitation of Underground Nuclear Weapon Tests shall entitle either party to withdraw from this treaty at any time.

"(3) Each party may propose amendments to this treaty. Amendments shall enter into force on the day of the exchange of instruments of ratification of such amendments.

"**Art. IX.** (1) This treaty, including the Protocol which forms an integral part hereof, shall be subject to ratification in accordance with the constitutional procedures of each party. This treaty shall enter into force on the day of the exchange of instruments of ratification, which exchange shall take place simultaneously with the exchange of instruments of ratification of the Treaty on the Limitation of Underground Nuclear Weapon Tests.

"(2) This treaty shall be registered pursuant to Article 102 of the Charter of the United Nations."

The Protocol to the treaty contained details of procedures for on-site inspection.

In a statement signed on May 13 the two parties to the treaty agreed, with reference to Sub-paragraph 2(*c*) of Article III of the treaty, as follows:

"(*a*) Development testing of nuclear explosives does not constitute a 'peaceful application' and any such development tests shall be carried out only within the boundaries of nuclear weapon test sites specified in accordance with the treaty between the USA and the USSR on the Limitation of Underground Nuclear Weapon Tests;

"(*b*) Associating test facilities, instrumentation or procedures related only to testing of nuclear weapons or their effects with any explosion carried out in accordance with the treaty does not constitute a 'peaceful application'."

However, like the treaty of 1974 on the limitation of underground nuclear weapons tests, this treaty also has remained unratified.

1977 Scientific Co-operation Agreement

An agreement on co-operation in the fields of science and technology between the United States and the Soviet Union was signed in Washington on July 8, 1977, and entered into force on the same day.

Second Strategic Arms Limitation Treaty (SALT II)

The 1972 Interim Agreement between the USA and the Soviet Union, concluded in connexion with the SALT I treaty [see pages 284ff.], formally lapsed on Oct. 3, 1977, but both sides undertook to continue to observe its main provisions pending the conclusion of a further strategic arms limitation (SALT II) treaty.

After several years of negotiations such a treaty was eventually signed in Vienna on June 18, 1979, by President Carter for the USA and President Brezhnev for the Soviet Union. The principal provisions of the main SALT II treaty were as follows:

(1) Upon entry into force of the treaty, each side would limit to 2,400 the number of intercontinental ballistic missile (ICBM) launchers, submarine-launched ballistic missile (SLBM) launchers, heavy bombers and air-to-surface ballistic missiles (ASBMs)—i.e. the level agreed by President Ford and L. I. Brezhnev in Vladivostok in November 1974 [see page 289]—and would dismantle or destroy any excess within a period of three to six months; these aggregate numbers would be further reduced to 2,250 for each side in the course of 1981.

(2) Within these aggregates, each side would limit to 1,320 the number of launchers of ICBMs and SLBMs equipped with multiple independently targetable re-entry vehicles (MIRVs), of MIRVed ASBMs and of heavy bombers equipped for cruise missiles capable of a range of over 600 kilometres (about 373 miles); not more than 1,200 might be launchers of MIRVed ICBMs and SLBMs or ASBMs equipped with MIRVs, while within this total the number of launchers of MIRVed ICBMs might not exceed 820.

(3) No more than 10 re-entry vehicles might be placed on any one ICBM or ASBM, nor more than 14 on any one SLBM. Bombers equipped for cruise missiles with a range of over 600 kilometres might not carry more than an average of 28 such missiles.

(4) Neither side might start the construction of additional fixed ICBM launchers, relocate fixed ICBM launchers or convert launchers of light or older types of ICBMs into launchers of heavy or later ICBMs.

(5) Neither side might flight-test or deploy new types of ICBMs, except one new type of light ICBM each, nor might they increase the number of re-entry vehicles on any type of ICBM.

(6) Neither side might develop, test or deploy (i) ICBMs heavier than those currently deployed by either party, (ii) mobile launchers of heavy ICBMs or (iii) fractional orbital missiles; nor might they flight-test or deploy on aircraft MIRVed cruise missiles with a range in excess of 600 kilometres.

(7) The Soviet Union would not produce, test or deploy RS-14 (SS-16) light ICBMs.

(8) The USA and the Soviet Union would seek to conclude a further SALT agreement well in advance of 1985 (the date of expiry of the SALT II treaty).

Under a protocol, which would expire on Dec. 31, 1981, the two sides undertook (i) not to deploy mobile ICBM launchers or to flight-test ICBMs from such launchers; (ii) not to deploy cruise missiles capable of a range in excess of 600 kilometres on sea-based or land-based launchers, nor to flight-test MIRVed cruise missiles capable of such a range from such launchers; and (iii) not to flight-test or deploy ASBMs.

The articles of the treaty were worded as follows:

"**Art. 1.** Each party undertakes, in accordance with the provisions of this treaty, to limit strategic offensive arms quantitatively and qualitatively, to exercise restraint in the development of new types of strategic offensive arms, and to adopt other measures provided for in this treaty.

"**Art. 2.** For the purposes of this treaty:

"(1) Intercontinental ballistic missile (ICBM) launchers are land-based launchers of ballistic missiles capable of a range in excess of the shortest distance between the north-eastern border of the continental part of the territory of the USA and the north-western border of the continental part of the territory of the USSR, that is, a range in excess of 5,500 kilometres [i.e. about 3,418 miles].

"(2) Submarine-launched ballistic missile (SLBM) launchers are launchers of ballistic missiles installed on any nuclear-powered submarine or launchers of modern ballistic missiles installed on any submarine, regardless of its type.

"(3) Heavy bombers are considered to be:

"(a) Currently, for the USA, bombers of the B-52 and B-1 types and, for the USSR, Tupolev-95 and Myasishchev types;

"(b) in the future, types of bombers which can carry out the mission of a heavy bomber in a manner similar or superior to that of bombers listed in Sub-paragraph (a) above;

"(c) types of bombers equipped for cruise missiles capable of a range in excess of 600 kilometres; and

"(d) types of bombers equipped for ASBMs.

"(4) Air-to-surface ballistic missiles (ASBMs) are any such missiles capable of a range in excess of 600 kilometres and installed in an aircraft or on its external mountings.

"(5) Launchers of ICBMs and SLBMs equipped with multiple independently targetable re-entry vehicles (MIRVs) are launchers of the types developed and tested for launching ICBMs or SLBMs equipped with MIRVs.

"(6) ASBMs equipped with MIRVs are ASBMs of the types which have been flight-tested with MIRVs.

"(7) Heavy ICBMs are ICBMs which have a launch-weight greater or a throw-weight greater than that of the heaviest—in terms of either launch-weight or throw-weight respectively—of the light ICBMs deployed by either party as of the date of signature of this treaty.

"(8) Cruise missiles are unmanned, self-propelled, guided weapon-delivery vehicles which sustain flight through the use of aerodynamic lift over most of their flight path and which are flight-tested from or deployed on aircraft, that is, air-launched cruise missiles, or such vehicles which are referred to as cruise missiles in Sub-paragraph 1(b) of Article 9.

"**Art. 3.** (1) Upon entry into force of this treaty, each party undertakes to limit ICBM launchers, SLBM launchers, heavy bombers and ASBMs to an aggregate number not to exceed 2,400.

"(2) Each party undertakes to limit, from Jan. 1, 1981, strategic offensive arms referred to in Paragraph 1 of this article to an aggregate number not to exceed 2,250, and to initiate reductions of those arms which as of that date would be in excess of this aggregate number.

"(3) Within the aggregate numbers provided for in Paragraphs 1 and 2 of this article and subject to the provisions of this treaty, each party has the right to determine the composition of these aggregates.

"(4) For each bomber of a type equipped for ASBMs, the aggregate numbers provided for in Paragraphs 1 and 2 of this article shall include the maximum number of such missiles for which a bomber of that type is equipped for one operational mission.

"(5) A heavy bomber equipped only for ASBMs shall not itself be included in the aggregate numbers provided for in Paragraphs 1 and 2 of this article.

"(6) Reductions of the numbers of strategic offensive arms required to comply with the provisions of Paragraphs 1 and 2 of this article shall be carried out as provided for in Article 11.

"**Art. 4.** (1) Each party undertakes not to start construction of additional fixed ICBM launchers.

"(2) Each party undertakes not to relocate fixed ICBM launchers.

"(3) Each party underakes not to convert launchers of light ICBMs, or of ICBMs of older types deployed prior to 1964, into launchers of heavy ICBMs of types deployed after that time.

"(4) Each party undertakes in the process of modernization and replacement of ICBM silo launchers not to increase the original internal volume of an ICBM silo launcher by more than 32 per cent. Within this limit each party has the right to determine whether such an increase will be made through an increase in the original diameter or in the original depth of an ICBM silo launcher, or in both of these dimensions.

"(5) Each party undertakes:

"(a) Not to supply ICBM launcher deployment areas with ICBMs in excess of a number consistent with normal deployment, maintenance, training and replacement requirements;

"(b) not to provide storage facilities for or to store ICBMs in excess of normal deployment requirements at launch sites of ICBM launchers;

"(c) not to develop, test or deploy systems for rapid reload of ICBM launchers.

"(6) Subject to the provisions of this treaty, each party undertakes not to have under construction at any time strategic offensive arms referred to in Paragraph I of Article 3 in excess of numbers consistent with a normal construction schedule.

"(7) Each party undertakes not to develop, test or deploy ICBMs which have a launch-weight greater or a throw-weight greater than that of the heaviest—in terms of either launch-weight or throw-weight respectively—of the heavy ICBMs deployed by either party as of the date of signature of this treaty.

"(8) Each party undertakes not to convert land-based launchers of ballistic missiles which are not ICBMs into launchers for launching ICBMs, and not to test them for this purpose.

"(9) Each party undertakes not to flight-test or deploy new types of ICBMs—that is, types of ICBMs not flight-tested as of May 1, 1979—except that each party may flight-test and deploy one new type of light ICBM.

"(10) Each party undertakes not to flight-test or deploy ICBMs of a type flight-tested as of May 1, 1979, with a number of re-entry vehicles greater than the maximum number of re-entry vehicles with which an ICBM of that type has been flight-tested as of that date.

"(11) Each party undertakes not to flight-test or deploy ICBMs of the new type permitted pursuant to Paragraph 9 of this article with a number of re-entry vehicles greater than the maximum number of re-entry vehicles with which an ICBM of either party has been flight-tested as of May 1, 1979—that is, 10.

"(12) Each party undertakes not to flight-test or deploy SLBMs with a number of re-entry vehicles greater than the maximum number of re-entry vehicles with which an SLBM of either party has been flight-tested as of May 1, 1979—that is, 14.

"(13) Each party undertakes not to flight-test or deploy ASBMs with a number of re-entry vehicles greater than the maximum number of re-entry vehicles with which an ICBM of either party has been flight-tested as of May 1, 1979—that is, 10.

"(14) Each party undertakes not to deploy at any one time on heavy bombers equipped for cruise missiles capable of a range in excess of 600 kilometres a number of such cruise missiles which exceeds the product of 28 and the number of such heavy bombers.

Art. 5. (1) Within the aggregate number provided for in Paragraphs 1 and 2 of Article 3, each party undertakes to limit launchers of ICBMs and SLBMs equipped with MIRVs, ASBMs equipped with MIRVs, and heavy bombers equipped for cruise missiles capable of a range in excess of 600 kilometres to an aggregate number not to exceed 1,320.

"(2) Within the aggregate number provided for in Paragraph 1 of this article, each party undertakes to limit launchers of ICBMs and SLBMs equipped with MIRVs, and ASBMs equipped with MIRVs, to an aggregate number not to exceed 1,200.

"(3) Within the aggregate number provided for in Paragraph 2 of this article, each party undertakes to limit launchers of ICBMs equipped with MIRVs to an aggregate number not to exceed 820.

"(4) For each bomber of a type equipped for ASBMs equipped with MIRVs, the aggregate numbers provided for in Paragraphs 1 and 2 of this article shall include the maximum number of ASBMs for which a bomber of that type is equipped for one operational mission.

"(5) Within the aggregate number provided for in Paragraphs 1, 2 and 3 of this article and subject to the provisions of this treaty, each party has the right to determine the composition of these aggregates.

"**Art. 6.** (1) The limitation provided for in this treaty shall apply to those arms which are:

"(a) Operational;

"(b) in the final stage of construction;

"(c) in reserve, in storage or mothballed;

"(d) undergoing overhaul, repair, modernization or conversion.

"(2) Those arms in the final stage of construction are:

"(a) SLBM launchers on submarines which have begun sea trials;

"(b) ASBMs after a bomber of a type equipped for such missiles has been brought out of the shop, plant or other facility where its final assembly or conversion for the purpose of equipping it for such missiles has been performed;

"(c) other strategic offensive arms which are finally assembled in a shop, plant or other facility after they have been brought out of the shop, plant or other facility where their final assembly has been performed.

"(3) ICBM and SLBM launchers of a type not subject to the limitation provided for in Article 5, which undergo conversion into launchers of a type subject to that limitation, shall become subject to that limitation as follows:

"(a) Fixed ICBM launchers when work on their conversion reaches the stage which first definitely indicates that they are being so converted;

"(b) SLBM launchers on a submarine when that submarine first goes to sea after their conversion has been performed.

"(4) ASBMs on a bomber which undergoes conversion from a bomber of a type equipped for ASBMs which are not subject to the limitation provided for in Article 5 into a bomber of a type equipped for ASBMs which are subject to that limitation shall become subject to that limitation when the bomber is brought out of the shop, plant or other facility where such conversion has been performed.

"(5) A heavy bomber of a type not subject to the limitation provided for in Paragraph 1 of Article 5 shall become subject to that limitation when it is brought out of the shop, plant or other facility where it has been converted into a heavy bomber of a type equipped for cruise missiles capable of a range in excess of 600 kilometres. A bomber of a type not subject to the limitation provided for in Paragraph 1 or 2 of Article 3 shall become subject to that limitation and to the limitation provided for in Paragraph 1 of Article 5 when it is brought out of the shop, plant or other facility where it has been converted into a bomber of a type equipped for cruise missiles capable of a range in excess of 600 kilometres.

"(6) The arms subject to the limitations provided for in this treaty shall continue to be subject to these limitations until they are dismantled, are destroyed, or otherwise cease to be subject to these limitations under procedures to be agreed upon.

"(7) In accordance with the provisions of Article 17, the parties will agree in the Standing Consultative Commission upon procedures to implement the provisions of this Article.

"**Art. 7.** (1) The limitations provided for in Article 3 shall not apply to ICBM and SLBM test and training launchers or to space vehicle launchers for exploration and use of outer space, ICBM and SLBM test and training launchers are ICBM and SLBM launchers used only for testing or training.

"(2) The parties agree that:

"(a) There shall be no significant increase in the number of ICBM or SLBM test and training launchers or in the number of such launchers of heavy ICBMs;

"(b) construction or conversion of ICBM launchers at test ranges shall be undertaken only for purposes of testing and training;

"(c) there shall be no conversion of ICBM test and training launchers or of space vehicle launchers into ICBM launchers subject to the limitations provided for in Article 3.

"**Art. 8.** (1) Each party undertakes not to flight-test cruise missiles capable of a range in excess of 600 kilometres or ASBMs from aircraft other than bombers or to convert such aircraft into aircraft equipped for such missiles.

"(2) Each party undertakes not to convert aircraft other than bombers into aircraft which can carry out the mission of a heavy bomber as referred to in Sub-paragraph 3(b) of Article 2.

"**Art. 9.** (1) Each party undertakes not to develop, test or deploy:

"(a) Ballistic missiles capable of a range in excess of 600 kilometres for installation on waterborne vehicles other than submarines, or launchers of such missiles;

"(b) fixed ballistic or cruise missile launchers for emplacement on the ocean floor, on the seabed, or on the beds of internal waters and inland waters, or in the subsoil thereof, or mobile launchers of such missiles which move only in contact with the ocean floor, the seabed, or the beds of internal waters and inland waters, or missiles for such launchers;

"(c) systems for placing into earth orbit nuclear weapons or any other kind of weapons of mass destruction [already banned under the 1966 Outer Space Treaty, whose signatories included the United States and the Soviet Union and which had entered into force on Oct. 10, 1967—see pages 87–89], including fractional orbital missiles;

"(d) mobile launchers of heavy ICBMs;

"(e) SLBMs which have a launch-weight greater or a throw-weight greater than that of the heaviest—in terms of either launch-weight or throw-weight, respectively—of the light ICBMs deployed by either party as of the date of signature of this treaty, or launchers of such SLBMs; or

"(f) ASBMs which have a launch-weight greater or a throw-weight greater than that of the heaviest—in terms of either launch-weight or throw-weight respectively—of the light ICBMs deployed by either party as of the date of signature of this treaty.

"(2) Each party undertakes not to flight-test from aircraft cruise missiles capable of a range in excess of 600 kilometres which are equipped with multiple independently targetable warheads and not to deploy such cruise missiles on aircraft.

"**Art. 10.** Subject to the provisions of this treaty, modernization and replacement of strategic offensive arms may be carried out.

"**Art. 11.** (1) Strategic offensive arms which would be in excess of the aggregate numbers provided for in this treaty as well as strategic offensive arms prohibited by this treaty shall be dismantled or destroyed under procedures to be agreed upon in the Standing Consultative Commission.

"(2) Dismantling or destruction of strategic offensive arms which would be in excess of the aggregate number provided for in Paragraph 1 of Article 3 shall begin on the date of the entry into force of this treaty and shall be completed within the following periods from that date: four months for ICBM launchers; six months for SLBM launchers; and three months for heavy bombers.

"(3) Dismantling or destruction of strategic offensive arms which would be in excess of the aggregate number provided for in Paragraph 2 of Article 3 shall be initiated no later than Jan. 1, 1981, shall be carried out throughout the ensuing 12-month period, and shall be completed no later than Dec. 31, 1981.

"(4) Dismantling or destruction of strategic offensive arms prohibited by this treaty shall be completed within the shortest possible agreed period of time, but not later than six months after the entry into force of this treaty.

"**Art. 12.** In order to ensure the viability and effectiveness of this treaty, each party undertakes not to circumvent the provisions of this treaty, through any other state or states or in any other manner.

"**Art. 13.** Each party undertakes not to assume any international obligations which would conflict with this treaty.

"**Art. 14.** The parties undertake to begin, promptly after the entry into force of this treaty, active negotiations with the objective of achieving, as soon as possible, agreement on further measures for the limitation and reduction of strategic arms. It is also the objective of the parties to conclude well in advance of 1985 an agreement limiting strategic offensive arms to replace this treaty upon its expiration.

"**Art. 15.** (1) For the purpose of providing assurance of compliance with the provisions of this treaty, each party shall use national technical means of verification at its disposal in a manner consistent with generally recognized principles of international law.

"(2) Each party undertakes not to interfere with the national technical means of verification of the other party operating in accordance with Paragraph 1 of this article.

"(3) Each party undertakes not to use deliberate concealment measures which impede verification by national technical means of compliance with the provisions of this treaty. This obligation shall not require changes in current construction, assembly, conversion or overhaul practices.

"**Art. 16.** (1) Each party undertakes, before conducting each planned ICBM launch, to notify the other party well in advance on a case-by-case basis that such a launch will occur, except for single ICBM launches from test ranges or from ICBM launcher deployment areas which are not planned to extend beyond its national territory.

"(2) The parties shall agree in the Standing Consultative Commission upon procedures to implement the provisions of this article.

"**Art. 17.** (1) To promote the objectives and implementation of the provisions of this treaty, the parties shall use the Standing Consultative Commission established by the Memorandum of Understanding between the Government of the USA and the Government of the USSR regarding the Establishment of a Standing Consultative Commission of Dec. 21, 1972.

"(2) Within the framework of the Standing Consultative Commission, with respect to this treaty, the parties will:

"(a) Consider questions concerning compliance with the obligations assumed and related situations which may be considered ambiguous;

"(b) provide on a voluntary basis such information as either party considers necessary to assure confidence in compliance with the obligations assumed;

"(c) consider questions involving unintended interference with national technical means of verification, and questions involving unintended impeding of verification by national technical means of compliance with the provisions of this treaty;

"(d) consider possible changes in the strategic situation which have a bearing on the provisions of this treaty;

"(e) agree upon procedures for replacement, conversion and dismantling or destruction of strategic offensive arms in cases provided for in the provisions of this treaty and upon procedures for removal of such arms from the aggregate numbers when they otherwise cease to be subject to the limitations provided for in this treaty, and, at regular sessions of the Standing

Consultative Commission, notify each other in accordance with the aforementioned procedures, at least twice annually, of actions completed and those in process;

"(f) consider, as appropriate, possible proposals for further increasing the viability of this treaty, including proposals for amendments in accordance with the provisions of this treaty;

"(g) consider, as appropriate, proposals for further measures limiting strategic offensive arms.

"(3) In the Standing Consultative Commission the parties shall maintain by category the agreed data base on the numbers of strategic offensive arms established by the Memorandum of Understanding between the USA and the USSR regarding the Establishment of a Data Base on the Numbers of Strategic Offensive Arms of June 19, 1979 [see below].

"**Art. 18.** Each party may propose amendments to this treaty. Agreed amendments shall enter into force in accordance with the procedures governing the entry into force of this treaty.

"**Art. 19.** (1) This treaty shall be subject to ratification in accordance with the constitutional procedures of each party. This treaty shall enter into force on the day of the exchange of instruments of ratification and shall remain in force through Dec. 31, 1985, unless replaced earlier by an agreement further limiting strategic offensive arms.

"(2) This treaty shall be registered pursuant to Article 102 of the Charter of the United Nations.

"(3) Each party shall, in exercising its national sovereignty, have the right to withdraw from this treaty if it decides that extraordinary events related to the subject matter of this treaty have jeopardized its supreme interests. It shall give notice of its decision to the other party six months prior to withdrawal from the treaty. Such notice shall include a statement of the extraordinary events the notifying party regards as having jeopardized its supreme interests.

"Done at Vienna on June 18, 1979, in two copies, each in the English and Russian languages, both texts being equally authentic."

PROTOCOL TO SALT II TREATY

The protocol to the SALT II treaty, valid to Dec. 31, 1981, was worded as follows:

"The USA and USSR, hereinafter referred to as the parties,

"Having agreed on limitations on strategic offensive arms in the treaty,

"Have agreed on additional limitations for the period during which this protocol remains in force, as follows:

"**Art. 1.** Each party undertakes not to deploy mobile ICBM launchers or to flight-test ICBM's from such launchers.

"**Art. 2.** (1) Each party undertakes not to deploy cruise missiles capable of a range in excess of 600 kilometres on sea-based launchers or on land-based launchers.

"(2) Each party undertakes not to flight-test cruise missiles capable of a range in excess of 600 kilometres which are equipped with multiple independently targetable warheads from sea-based launchers or from land-based launchers.

"(3) For the purposes of this protocol, cruise missiles are unmanned, self-propelled, guided weapon-delivery vehicles which sustain flight through the use of aerodynamic lift over most of their flight and which are flight-tested from or deployed on sea-based or land-based launchers—that is, sea-launched cruise missiles and ground-launched cruise missiles respectively.

"**Art. 3.** Each party undertakes not to flight-test or deploy ASBMs.

"**Art. 4.** This protocol shall be considered an integral part of the treaty. It shall enter into force on the day of the entry into force of the treaty and shall remain in force through Dec. 31, 1981, unless replaced earlier by an agreement on further measures limiting strategic offensive arms.

"Done at Vienna on June 18, 1979, in two copies, each in the English and Russian languages, both texts being equally authentic."

AGREED STATEMENTS AND COMMON UNDERSTANDINGS REGARDING SALT II TREATY

Agreed statements and common understandings signed by President Carter and L. I. Brezhnev comprised principally definitions of terms used in the treaty and protocol and further details and elaborations of the provisions of the treaty and protocol. The length of these agreed statements and common understandings was approximately twice that of the treaty and protocol themselves, details of the most important being given below.

Art. 2. *Para. 1.* The 177 former US Atlas and Titan 1 ICBM launchers, which were no longer operational and were partially dismantled, should not be considered as subject to the limitations provided for in the treaty.

After the date on which the protocol ceased to be in force, mobile ICBM launchers should be subject to the relevant limitations in the treaty which were applicable to ICBM launchers, unless the parties agreed that mobile ICBM launchers should not be deployed after that date.

Para. 3. Soviet Tupolev-142 aircraft in their current configuration—i.e. for anti-submarine warfare—were considered to be aeroplanes of a type different from types of heavy bombers referred to in Sub-paragraph 3(a) of Article 2.

Not later than six months after entry into force of the treaty, the Soviet Union would give its 31 Myasishchev aeroplanes used as tankers in existence as of the date of the signature of the treaty functionally related observable differences which indicated that they could not perform the mission of a heavy bomber.

The Soviet Tupolev-95 heavy bombers were known in the United States as Bears and the Myasishchev heavy bombers as Bisons.

Para. 5. MIRVed ICBMs and SLBMs as of the date of signature of the treaty were: For the United States Minuteman III light ICBMs, Poseidon C-3 SLBMs and Trident C-4 SLBMs; for the Soviet Union RS-16, RS-18 and RS-20 ICBMs and RSM-50 SLBMs (these Soviet missiles being known in the United States as, respectively, the SS-17 light ICBM, the SS-19 light ICBM, the SS-18 heavy ICBM and the SS-N-18 SLBM).

All ICBM launchers in the Derazhnya and Pervomaysk areas of the Soviet Union were included in the aggregate numbers provided for in Article 5 of the treaty.

Art. 4. *Para. 8.* During the term of the treaty, the Soviet Union would not produce, test or deploy ICBMs of the type designated by the Soviet Union as RS-14 (known to the USA as SS-16)—a light ICBM first flight-tested after 1970 and flight-tested only with a single re-entry vehicle; the Soviet Union would not produce the third stage of that missile, the re-entry vehicle of that missile or the appropriate device for targeting the re-entry vehicle of that missile.

Para. 9. Every ICBM of the one new type of light ICBM permitted to each party under this paragraph should have the same number of stages and the same type of propellant (i.e. liquid or solid) of each stage as the first ICBM of the one new type of light ICBM launched by that party. In addition, after the 25th launch of an ICBM of that type, or after the last launch before deployment began of ICBMs of that type, whichever occurred earlier, ICBMs of the one new type of light ICBM permitted to that party should not be different in any one or more of the following respects: Length, largest diameter, launch-weight or throw-weight of the missile. A party which launched ICBMs of the one new type of light ICBM permitted under this paragraph should promptly notify the other party of the date of the first launch and of the date of either the 25th or the last launch before deployment began of ICBMs of that type, whichever occurred earlier.

Para. 10. Types of ICBMs and SLBMs equipped with MIRVs had been flight-tested with the maximum number of re-entry vehicles as follows. United States: Minuteman III ICBMs—seven re-entry vehicles; Poseidon C-3 SLBMs—14 re-entry vehicles; Trident C-4 SLBMs—seven re-entry vehicles. Soviet Union: RS-16 ICBMs—four re-entry vehicles; RS-18—six re-entry vehicles; RS-20 ICBMs—10 re-entry vehicles; RSM-50 SLBMs—seven re-entry vehicles. Minuteman III ICBMs had been deployed with not more than three re-entry vehicles; during the term of the treaty the USA had no plans to and would not flight-test or deploy missiles of this type with more than three re-entry vehicles.

Para. 11. Each party undertook not to flight-test or deploy the one new type of light ICBM permitted to each party under Paragraph 9 of Article 4 with a number of re-entry vehicles greater than the maximum number of re-entry vehicles with which an ICBM of that type had been flight-tested as of the 25th launch before deployment began of ICBMs of that type, whichever occurred earlier.

Para. 14. During the term of the treaty no bomber of the B-52 or B-1 types of the USA or of the Tupolev-95 or Myasishchev types of the Soviet Union would be equipped for more than 20 cruise missiles capable of a range in excess of 600 kilometres.

Art. 6. *Para. 6.* The procedures for removal of strategic offensive arms from the aggregate numbers provided for in the treaty which were referred to in this paragraph and were to be agreed upon in the Standing Consultative Committee should include (i) procedures for removal from the aggregate numbers, provided for in Article 5, of ICBM and SLBM launchers which were being converted from launchers of a type subject to the limitation provided for in Article 5 into launchers of a type not subject to that limitation and (ii) procedures for removal from the aggregate numbers provided for in Articles 3 and 5 of bombers which were being converted from bombers of a type subject to the limitations provided for in Article 3 or in Articles 3 and 5 into aeroplanes or bombers of a type not so subject.

Art. 7. *Para. 2.* Current test ranges where ICBMs were tested were located in the United States near Santa Maria (California) and at Cape Canaveral (Florida), and in the Soviet Union in the areas of Tyura-Tam and Plesetskaya. In the future, each party should provide notification in the Standing Consultative Commission of the location of any other test range used by that party to test ICBMs.

Of the 18 launchers of fractional orbital missiles at the test range where ICBMs were tested in the area of Tyura-Tam, 12 launchers should be dismantled or destroyed within eight months of the treaty entering into force and should not be replaced; the other six might be converted after entry into force of the treaty to launchers for testing missiles undergoing modernization; after entry into force of the treaty fractional orbital missiles should be removed and should be destroyed, pursuant to the provisions of Sub-paragraph 1(c) of Article 9, and should not be replaced by other missiles, except in the case of conversion of these six launchers for testing missiles undergoing modernization.

Art. 8. *Para. 1.* For the purposes of testing only, each party had the right, through initial construction or (as an exception to this paragraph) by conversion, to equip for cruise missiles capable of a range in excess of 600 kilometres or for ASBMs no more than 16 aeroplanes, including aeroplanes which were prototypes of bombers equipped for such missiles. None of these 16 aeroplanes might be replaced, except in the event of the involuntary destruction of any such aeroplane or in the case of the dismantling or destruction of any such aeroplane.

Art. 15. *Para. 3.* Each party was free to use various methods of transmitting telemetric information during testing, including encryption, except that, in accordance with the provisions of this paragraph, neither party should engage in deliberate denial of telemetric information, such as through the use of telemetry encryption, whenever such denial impeded verification of compliance with the provisions of the treaty.

RELATED UNDERSTANDINGS AND STATEMENTS

(1) The following Memorandum of Understanding between the USA and the Soviet Union regarding the Establishment of a Data Base on the Numbers of Strategic Offensive Arms was signed by President Carter and L. I. Brezhnev.

"For the purposes of the Treaty between the USA and the USSR on the Limitation of Strategic Offensive Arms, the parties have considered data on numbers of strategic offensive arms and agree that as of Nov. 1, 1978, there existed the following numbers of strategic offensive arms subject to limitations provided for in the treaty which is being signed today:

	USA	USSR
Launchers of ICBMs	1,054	1,398
Fixed launchers of ICBMs	1,054	1,398
Launchers of ICBMs equipped with MIRVs	550	576
Launchers of SLBMs	656	950
Launchers of SLBMs equipped with MIRVs	496	128
Heavy bombers	574	156
Heavy bombers equipped for cruise missiles capable of a range in excess of 600 kilometres	0	0
Heavy bombers equipped only for ASBMs	0	0
ASBMs	0	0
ASBMs equipped with MIRVs	0	0

"At the time of entry into force of the treaty the parties will up-date the above agreed data in the categories listed in this memorandum.

"Done at Vienna on June 18, 1979, in two copies, each in the English and Russian languages, both texts being equally authentic."

(2) Statements of data on the number of strategic offensive arms as of the date of signature of the treaty were made by both the United States and the Soviet Union, declaring the numbers of arms possessed at June 18, 1979. These showed arms equal to the numbers as of Nov. 1, 1978, except that (i) the USA had only 573 heavy bombers but three heavy bombers equipped for cruise missiles capable of a range in excess of 600 kilometres; and (ii) the Soviet Union had 608 launchers of MIRVed ICBMs and 144 launchers of MIRVed SLBMs.

(3) In a Joint Statement on Principles and Basic Guidelines the two sides agreed to continue negotiations on the further limitation and reduction of strategic arms and to "strengthen verification and to perfect the operation of the Standing Consultative Commission", and they laid down their precise objectives to be pursued in such negotiations.

(4) A written Soviet statement on the TU-22M (Backfire) aircraft, handed to President Carter on June 16, 1979, read as follows:

"The Soviet side informs the US side that the Soviet TU-22M aeroplane, called Backfire in the USA, is a medium-range bomber, and that it does not intend to give this aeroplane the capability of operating at intercontinental distances. In this connexion, the Soviet side states that it will not increase the radius of action of this aeroplane in such a way as to enable it to strike targets on the territory of the USA. Nor does it intend to give it such a capability in any other manner, including by in-flight refuelling. At the same time, the Soviet side states that it will not increase the production rate of this aeroplane as compared to the present rate."

L. I. Brezhnev confirmed that the Soviet Backfire production rate would not exceed 30 per year.

US DEFERMENT OF SALT II RATIFICATION

As a result of Soviet intervention in Afghanistan in December 1979, President Carter on Jan. 3, 1980, formally requested the US Senate to delay its consideration of the ratification of the SALT II treaty.

On the following day the US President also announced a number of measures to be taken by the USA against the Soviet Union, including the curtailment of grain sales by 17,000,000 tonnes and the suspension of sales of high technology equipment to the USSR; however, it was officially stated in Washington on April 30, 1980, that the United States would honour the existing five-year US-Soviet grain agreement [see page 290] until its expiry on Sept. 30, 1981.

RESUMPTION OF ACTIVITIES OF JOINT COMMISSION

In March 1985 it was agreed to resume sessions of the joint US-Soviet commission, which had met seven times between 1972 and 1979, but which had been suspended in 1980.

TRIPARTITE AIR TRAFFIC AGREEMENT

An agreement was signed by Japan, the United States and the Soviet Union in Tokyo on Oct. 8, 1985, on "co-operative measures" to increase the safety of air traffic over the north-west Pacific (on which preliminary agreement had been reached on July 29). It provided for a new communications network between air traffic control centres in Toyko, Anchorage (Alaska) and Khabarovsk (USSR).

Further East-West Agreements, 1974–86

Soviet Agreements

Belgium. On June 25, 1975, agreements between the two countries were signed in Moscow on environmental protection and co-operation in tourism, while in a joint declaration the two sides expressed their determination "to contribute to the process of international relaxation of tension" and to seek to make this process "irreversible".

Canada. A 10-year agreement to facilitate economic, industrial, scientific and technical co-operation between the two countries was signed in Ottawa on July 14, 1976, and an existing trade agreement was extended for a further five years.

Denmark. A 10-year Soviet-Danish agreement on economic, industrial and technical co-operation was signed in Moscow on Aug. 28, 1975.

France. During a first visit to the Soviet Union by President Giscard d'Estaing of France a joint declaration was signed on Oct. 17, 1975, both sides stating in particular that they were "convinced of the need to prevent the proliferation of nuclear arms . . . and determined to assume the responsibilities incumbent upon them in this respect as nuclear powers" and that they would "display concern to ensure that their supplies of fissile material or equipment to non-nuclear states are used exclusive for the peaceful purposes". [France was not a signatory to the 1968 Nuclear Non-Proliferation Treaty—see page 71.] Co-operation agreements were signed at the same time, covering the fields of energy, civil aviation, the aircraft industry and tourism.

In an exchange of letters dated July 16, 1976, France and the Soviet Union agreed that they would carry out and if possible improve measures to prevent accidental or unauthorized use of nuclear weapons; to notify each other immediately about any incident which might lead to the explosion of combat nuclear devices; and, in the event of an unexplained nuclear incident, to act in such a way as to avoid, as far as possible, its actions being misinterpreted by the other side. [For similar Soviet agreements (i) with the United States in 1971 see page 282; and (ii) with the United Kingdom in 1977 see page 298.]

During a visit to France by President Brezhnev, six documents were signed on June 22, 1977, including three joint statements emphasizing that bilateral talks had taken place "in an atmosphere of great cordiality which accords with the friendly relations and historic ties which exist between the two countries"; stating inter alia that all states should promote détente, which should "not be hampered by considerations of bloc policy"; reaffirming that "respect for human rights and basic freedoms by all states represents one of the fundamental principles for a radical improvement of their relations"; and also reaffirming their determination to prevent the proliferation of nuclear weapons and their "readiness to contribute to improvement of control by the International Atomic Energy Agency".

Three other documents signed at the same time were agreements on co-operation in the economic field, in transportation and in chemistry.

An agreement on relations between the French and Soviet armed forces during the 1977–78 period had been signed earlier by the chiefs of staff of the two countries' armed forces.

During a further visit to Moscow by the French President, seven documents were signed on April 28, 1979—(i) a programme for further co-operation in promoting peace and détente; (ii) a long-term development programme for economic, industrial and technical co-operation for the 1980–90 period; (iii) an economic co-operation agreement for the 1980–85 period; (iv) an agreement on scientific, technical and industrial co-operation in the fields of computer technology and electronics; (v) an agreement on oceanic research; (vi) an agreement on the study of the French and Russian languages in the two countries; and (vii) an exchange of letters extending until December 1990 the agreement on the development of economic, technical and industrial co-operation concluded in 1971 [see page 282].

An agreement concluded by France with the Soviet Gas Export company on Jan. 23, 1982, provided for the supply from 1984–85, for a period of 25 years, of an annual volume of 8,000 million cubic metres of natural gas to France.

A five-year economic and industrial co-operation agreement was signed at the end of January 1984.

Germany. An agreement concluded on, and in force from, Oct. 30, 1974, provided for the further development of mutual economic co-operation with the Federal Republic.

During a visit to the Federal Republic of Germany by President Brezhnev of the Soviet Union a long-term economic co-operation agreement was signed on May 6, 1978.

This agreement provided for the further development of co-operation between the Federal Republic and the Soviet Union, in particular in "the creation, expansion and modernization of industrial complexes and enterprises, the joint development of certain types of equipment and other products; the extraction and processing of certain types of raw materials, including the development of minerals on the seabed; co-operation in the field of energy, . . . in banking and insurance, transport and other services", and also in engineering, the chemical industry, electronics and the consumer goods industry. The two sides further agreed to grant medium-term and long-term credits on as favourable terms as possible.

The agreement was concluded for 25 years, with an initial term of 10 years, to "be extended by agreement between the contracting parties for a five-year period each time".

On the basis of the above agreement a "long-term programme of main lines of co-operation" was signed in Moscow on July 1, 1980.

Under an agreement signed on Nov. 20, 1981, the Soviet Union was to supply the Federal Republic, from 1984–85, for a period of 25 years, with an annual volume of 10,500 million cubic metres of natural gas, and West Berlin with an annual volume of 700,000,000 cubic metres (equivalent to the city's current requirements), also for 25 years.

An agreement on general questions of trade and navigation concluded on April 25, 1958, in force from April 4, 1959, and extended on Dec. 31, 1960, with effect from July 26, 1962, was on Dec. 10, 1984, extended until Dec. 31, 1986.

After a meeting of the Soviet-West German joint economic commission on Jan. 21–22, 1985, it was stated that the Federal Republic could compete for contracts worth DM20,000 million within the framework of the 1986–90 Soviet five-year plan. (By 1984 the increase of West German imports of Soviet oil and gas had turned the Federal Republic's surplus in trade with the Soviet Union into a deficit of DM3,600 million.)

Italy. An agreement on scientific and technological co-operation was signed on Feb. 19, 1974, and a long-term agreement on the development and deepening of co-operation in the political, scientific, technical and cultural fields on May 27, 1974.

A joint declaration signed in Moscow on Nov. 20, 1975, provided for the development and deepening of co-operation in the political, economic, scientific, technical and cultural fields, while an economic co-operation agreement for 1975–79 was signed at the same time and notes were exchanged on the application of general principles laid down in a treaty on commerce and maritime navigation signed on Dec. 11, 1948.

Luxembourg. Among agreements signed in Moscow on June 5, 1975, was one on scientific, technical and cultural co-operation between the two countries.

Turkey. With Turkey the Soviet Union signed a number of agreements on June 25, 1978—(i) a "political document on the principles of good-neighbourly and friendly co-operation"; (ii) an agreement on the delimitation of the Black Sea continental shelf; and (iii) a two-year programme of cultural and scientific exchange. Under further agreements concluded at the same time the Soviet Union was to supply Turkey with 3,000,000 tonnes of oil a year from 1979 in exchange for Turkish wheat.

Agreement was reached in June 1984 on the construction of a new gas pipeline running from Bulgaria and expected to be completed by the end of 1986.

The United Kingdom. A 10-year economic, scientific, technical and industrial co-operation agreement between the Soviet Union and the United Kingdom was signed in London on May 6, 1974. In implementation of this agreement a long-term programme for the development of economic and industrial co-operation was agreed upon during a visit to Moscow by a delegation led by Harold Wilson, the UK Prime Minister, on Feb. 13–17, 1975. At the same time a 10-year programme for scientific and technological co-operation was also approved. These programmes were to involve British credit arrangements for the USSR for £950,000,000.

An agreement on co-operation in the field of environmental protection was signed in London on May 21, 1974.

An agreement on Anglo-Soviet co-operation in the scientific, educational and cultural fields was signed in Moscow on Feb. 25, 1977.

On the prevention of any accidental outbreak of nuclear war, similar to those concluded by the Soviet Union with France in July 1976 [see page 297] and with the United States in September 1971 [see page 282] was signed in Moscow on Oct. 10, 1977.

(An agreement on the establishment of a direct British-Soviet communications line had been signed on Aug. 25, 1967, and had come into force on Oct. 27, 1967.)

An agreement on relations in the scientific, educational and cultural fields for 1979–91 was signed in London on March 1, 1979.

On Feb. 6, 1986, the 1975 10-year programme was replaced by a five-year economic and industrial co-operation programme.

Agreements concluded by Other East European Countries

East European states concluded co-operation agreements with Western countries as follows:

Bulgaria and France. A five-year economic co-operation agreement was signed in Paris on March 19, 1976.

Bulgaria and the Federal Republic of Germany. A 10-year agreement on economic, industrial and technological co-operation was signed on May 14, 1975.

Bulgaria and Italy. A long-term agreement on the development of economic, industrial, scientific and technical co-operation was concluded on May 27, 1974, and an agreement on economic co-operation in 1975–79 was signed on June 23, 1975. (An earlier scientific and technical co-operation agreement had been signed on May 30, 1963.)

Bulgaria and the United Kingdom. Agreements on the development of economic, industrial, scientific and technological co-operation were signed on May 14, 1974, and an agreement on a programme for the development of this co-operation in 1975.

Bulgaria and the United States. An agreement on exchanges and co-operation in cultural, scientific, educational, technological and other fields was signed on June 13, 1977, and came into force on March 23, 1978.

A programme of cultural, educational, scientific and technological exchanges for 1985 and 1986 was signed on Dec. 14, 1984.

Czechoslovakia and France. At the conclusion of a visit to France by the Czechoslovak Prime Minister on Nov. 14, 1975, a 10-year trade and technological co-operation agreement was signed, covering in particular co-operation in the motor industry, chemical engineering, machine tools, electronic and energy industries and in farming and food-processing machinery.

Czechoslovakia and the Federal Republic of Germany. An agreement on the further development of economic, industrial and technical co-operation was signed and came into force on Jan. 22, 1975.

An agreement on cultural co-operation was signed on April 11, 1978, and came into force on March 16, 1979.

Czechoslovakia and the United Kingdom. A co-operation agreement was signed in 1972.

The German Democratic Republic and the Federal Republic of Germany. A cultural agreement was concluded on May 6, 1986.

The German Democratic Republic and the United Kingdom. An agreement on the development of economic, industrial, scientific and technological co-operation was signed on Dec. 18, 1973.

A three-year cultural and scientific co-operation agreement was signed on Dec. 10, 1981, and was renewed on Oct. 12, 1984.

The German Democratic Republic and the United States. A consular convention, signed on Sept. 4, 1979, allowed US officials automatic access to US citizens arrested in the GDR; it came into force on Feb. 19, 1981.

Hungary and the Federal Republic of Germany. An agreement on economic, industrial and technical co-operation was signed in Budapest and came into force on Nov. 11, 1974.

Hungary and Italy. An agreement on the development of economic, industrial and technical co-operation was signed on May 25, 1974, and a joint declaration signed in Rome on Nov. 12, 1975, provided for the development and deepening of co-operation in the political, economic, scientific, technical and cultural fields.

Hungary and the United Kingdom. An economic, industrial and technological co-operation agreement was concluded in 1972, and an agreement on co-operation in medicine and public health was signed in Budapest on Nov. 1, 1978.

Hungary and the United States. An agreement providing for consultations should exports of cotton, wool and man-made fibre textiles and apparel products from Hungary cause market disruption in the United States was signed on Feb. 12 and 18, 1976, and came into force on the latter date.

An agreement on co-operation in culture, education, science and technology, signed on April 6, 1977, entered into force on May 21, 1979.

A trade agreement providing for most-favoured-nation treatment for Hungary was signed on March 17, 1978, and came into force on July 7, 1978.

An agreement within the context of multilateral trade negotiations on non-tariff matters, concluded on May 30, 1980, was effective from Jan. 1, 1980. A similar agreement relating to tariff matters, concluded on Nov. 18, 1978, came into force on Jan. 1, 1980; it was amended on June 13, 1979, May 30, 1980, and Sept. 4 and 18, 1980.

A joint statement on the development of agricultural trade and co-operation was signed and came into force on May 13, 1981.

An agreement relating to trade in wool textile products was concluded and came into force on Feb. 3, 1983. It was effective from Oct. 1, 1982, and was amended on Feb. 13 and 24, 1984.

A programme of co-operation and exchanges in culture, education, science and technology for 1984 and 1985 was signed on Dec. 12, 1983.

A memorandum of understanding for scientific and technical co-operation in earth sciences was signed on Jan. 6 and 20, 1984, and came into force on the latter date.

Poland and France. Agreement was expressed in three documents signed in Warsaw on June 20, 1975, during a visit to Poland by the French President—(i) a declaration on the principles of friendly co-operation between the two countries, providing inter alia for annual political consultation at the level of ministers or their representatives and reserving "a special place" for cultural co-operation; (ii) a declaration on the principles and means of cultural and scientific co-operation, information and human relations between the two countries; and (iii) a five-year economic co-operation agreement. At the same time provision was made for the opening of a French credit line of F7,000 million (then about £800,000) to Poland for the next three years.

Additional co-operation agreements with France were signed on Sept. 14, 1977, during a visit to France by Edward Gierek, then First Secretary of the Polish United Workers' Party.

Poland and the Federal Republic of Germany. An agreement on economic, industrial and technical co-operation was signed on Nov. 1, 1974; it came into force on Jan. 15, 1975, and was followed by a long-term programme of such co-operation, which was agreed and came into force on Oct. 9, 1975.

Two agreements and a protocol, initialled in Bonn on Aug. 7, 1975, related to (i) a reciprocal pensions arrangement, under which the FRG would pay Poland, for pension insurance claims arising from World War II, a lump sum of DM1,300 million in three annual instalments; (ii) a long-term credit by the FRG to Poland of DM1,000 million to be paid in three annual instalments in 1975, 1976 and 1977; and (iii) the resettlement in the FRG of between 120,000 and 125,000 ethnic Germans who would be allowed to leave Poland. The agreements were signed in Warsaw on Oct. 9, 1975; effectively ratified by the West German Parliament by March 12, 1976, after the Polish Government had agreed that further emigration of ethnic Germans from Poland beyond the 120,000 to 125,000 would eventually be permitted; and approved by the Polish Council of State on March 15, 1976, whereafter instruments of ratification were exchanged on March 24.

Agreements of June 11, 1976, provided for the further development of co-operation between the two countries in the economic field and for cultural co-operation.

Poland and Italy. An agreement on economic co-operation in 1975–79 was signed in Rome on Oct. 28, 1975.

A visit to Rome by E. Gierek on Nov. 28, 1977, resulted in the signing of (i) a joint political statement in which the two sides inter alia confirmed that "respect for human rights and basic freedoms" was "one of the important foundations for good inter-state relations" and (ii) four economic co-operation agreements.

Poland and the United Kingdom. A long-term agreement on the development of economic, industrial, scientific and technical co-operation was signed in London on March 20, 1973, to remain in force until Dec. 31, 1982, and to continue thereafter subject to six months' notice by either side. This agreement extended the tasks of a UK-Polish joint commission established under an economic and trade agreement signed in London on April 21, 1971, and to remain in force until Dec. 31, 1974, subject to mutual agreement on its further extension. A 10-year programme of co-operation under the 1973 agreement was signed in London on Sept. 9, 1975.

During a visit to Poland by the UK Foreign and Commonwealth Secretary on July 13–15, 1975, a declaration on the development of friendly relations between the two countries was signed, laying down the principles of their bilateral relations in conformity with the UN Charter and of their international activities in working for détente and disarmament, with the provision that their Ministers of Foreign Affairs or their representatives should meet at least once a year.

A five-year agreement on economic co-operation was concluded on Dec. 16, 1976.

A convention on co-operation in education, science and culture was signed in London on Nov. 7, 1978.

Poland and the United States. An agreement relating to co-operation in the field of health and a joint statement on the development of agricultural trade were signed and came into force on Oct. 8, 1974.

An agreement relating to tariff and non-tariff matters within the framework of multilateral trade negotiations, with effect from Jan. 1, 1980, was concluded on June 27 and Oct. 20, 1980.

A memorandum of understanding on scientific and technological co-operation was signed and entered into force on Dec. 11, 1981.

An agreement relating to limitation of imports of specialty steel from Poland was signed and entered into force on Oct. 18, 1983.

An agreement relating to trade in cotton, wool, and man-made fibre textiles and textile products was signed on Dec. 5 and 31, 1984, and became effective on Jan. 1, 1985.

Romania and France. After the President of Romania (which had had close relations with France since 1964) had first visited France in June 1970, Franco-Romanian agreements were concluded (i) in 1970 (with the state-owned Société nationale industrielle aérospatiale—SNIAS) on the joint production of 50 Alouette helicopters and (ii) in 1974 on the purchase from France of 100 Puma helicopters, part of them to be assembled in Romania under licence from SNIAS.

A long-term agreement on economic, industrial and technical co-operation between France and Romania was signed in Bucharest on July 28, 1975, and new such agreements were concluded on July 24–28, 1978.

At the end of a visit to Romania by the French President, four economic agreements were signed on March 10, 1979, (i) on the adoption by Romania of the French SECAM colour television system; (ii) on the early signing of a contract for 40 Alouette-III helicopters to be supplied to Romania; (iii) on the building of motor vehicles; and (iv) on co-operation in electronics and computer technology.

During a further visit to Paris by President Ceausescu of Romania a nine-page joint declaration was published on July 25, 1980, reaffirming an earlier similar declaration of 1979, noting that trade exchanges between the two countries had been doubled between 1975 and 1979 and stating that a further doubling by 1985 constituted "a realistic target".

Romania and the Federal Republic of Germany. A "joint solemn declaration" and eight co-operation agreements were signed on June 29, 1973, during a visit to the Federal Republic by President Ceausescu. In the joint declaration the two sides undertook to intensify their relations of friendship and co-operation in the fields of politics, the economy, industry, science, technology, culture, education and the media and tourism.

During a visit to Romania by the German Federal Chancellor on Jan. 6–7, 1978, agreement was reached (i) on the continued emigration of ethnic Germans from Romania (at the rate of about 11,000 persons a year over the next five years) and (ii) additional credit guarantees to Romania by the Federal Republic.

Romania and the United Kingdom. A 10-year agreement on economic, industrial and technical co-operation was signed during a visit to Bucharest by Harold Wilson, the UK Prime Minister, on Sept. 16–18, 1975. A long-term programme for the further development of this co-operation was agreed upon in 1977.

An agreement on co-operation in education, science and culture was signed in London on June 15, 1978.

Romania and the United States. President Ceausescu of Romania signed on Dec. 5, 1973, during a visit to the USA, (i) a joint statement laying down principles for their bilateral relations to be based on the provisions of the UN Charter and expressing their determination "to encourage the expansion of trade as well as industrial, scientific and technical co-operation" and "to develop friendly relations between the two peoples", and (ii) a joint declaration on economic, industrial and technical co-operation, to include most-favoured-nation treatment of Romania by the United States.

An agreement on co-operation and exchanges in the cultural, educational, scientific and technological fields, signed on Dec. 13, 1974, came into force on Jan. 1, 1975. A trade agreement, signed on April 2, 1975, incorporated the granting of most-favoured-nation treatment, which was approved by the US Congress on July 25–28 of that year (subject to the proviso that during the first 18 months the agreement would be under scrutiny in regard to Romania's policy on emigration, as laid down in the 1975 US Trade Reform Act—see page 286). This agreement came into force on Aug. 3, 1975.

Protocols on co-operation in agriculture and on development of agricultural trade were signed and came into force on Sept. 11, 1975.

A long-term agreement on economic, industrial and technological co-operation of Nov. 21, 1976, came into force on May 5, 1977.

An agreement clarifying certain understandings relating to the supply of enriched uranium to Romania was signed and came into force on Feb. 13, 1978.

A memorandum of understanding on scientific and technical co-operation was signed and came into force on Feb. 27, 1979; it was extended on Jan. 14 and Feb. 26, 1982.

An agreement relating to tariff and non-tariff matters within the framework of multilateral trade negotiations was concluded on March 2 and Nov. 8, 1979, and came into force on Jan. 1, 1980.

An agreement relating to trade in cotton textiles, with effect from Jan. 1, 1983, was concluded on Jan. 28 and March 31, 1983, and came into force on the latter date.

A programme of co-operation and exchanges in educational, cultural, scientific, technological and other fields for the years 1984 and 1985 was signed and came into force on Dec. 23, 1983.

An agreement relating to trade in wool and man-made fibre textiles and textile products, effective Jan. 1, 1985, was signed on March 8 and 16, 1984, when it entered into force.

Agreements between China and Western States

Belgium. Investment accord guaranteeing legal protection for Belgian investments in China, repatriation of profits and compensation for possible nationalization, June 2, 1984.

Agreements on (i) nuclear energy co-operation, (ii) taxation and (iii) government loans, April 18, 1985.

Canada. Several agreements, covering inter alia trade and co-operation in science and technology, Oct. 10–17, 1973. A protocol on economic co-operation between the two countries, Oct. 19, 1979.

France. A long-term agreement on the development of economic relations and co-operation (during the seven-year period from 1979 to 1985), signed in Peking on Dec. 4, 1978, by China and France, envisaged trade worth F60,000 million ($13,600 million). Within the framework of the agreement China placed orders for the construction of two 900-MW nuclear reactors by

a French subsidiary of a US firm at a cost of F10,000 million. It was officially confirmed in Paris on Oct. 20, 1978, that negotiations had been completed for the sale to China of substantial quantities of French arms, including anti-tank missiles and Crotalle anti-aircraft missiles (worth at least $350,000,000), subject to approval by the Inter-Allied Co-ordinating Committee for East-West Trade (COCOM, see page 220).

A seven-year agreement on the development of economic relations and co-operation was signed on Dec. 4, 1978.

In an agreement on economic relations between the two countries, signed in Paris on Oct. 17, 1979, it was stated that all useful measures would be taken to develop bilateral economic and commercial relations.

Further agreements were concluded as follows:

Agreement in principle on the sale to China of four French nuclear reactors, May 5, 1983.

A memorandum on nuclear co-operation, signed on May 5, 1984, providing for the supply of equipment and technology by France for nuclear power stations planned in China, a protocol on radio and television co-operation being also signed.

Agreement signed by a French company on the preliminary development of the first oil field in the South China Sea, May 26, 1984.

Three accords on economic, scientific and technical co-operation in the agricultural and food sectors, July 13, 1984.

Further agreement in principle on French supplies for and supervision of the construction of China's first nuclear reactor, Dec. 13, 1985.

The Federal Republic of Germany. Agreement on the formation of a mixed commission for promoting mutual economic relations, Oct. 31, 1975.

Agreement on scientific and technological co-operation, Oct. 9, 1978 (in force from Nov. 10, 1978).

Agreement on co-operation in research on raw and other materials, Nov. 20, 1978.

Cultural co-operation agreement, Oct. 24, 1979 (in force from Aug. 29, 1980).

Agreement on scientific and technical co-operation in geodesy, Sept. 24, 1980.

Agreement on co-operation in geological sciences and technology, June 19, 1979 (supplemented on April 15, 1980).

Agreement on co-operation in scientific and technical research in agriculture, Nov. 23, 1981.

Agreement on co-operation in civil space sciences and technology, March 7, 1984.

Agreement on co-operation in peaceful uses of nuclear energy, May 9, 1984.

Three economic co-operation agreements and a long-term nuclear energy co-operation agreement, June 10, 1985.

Italy. Economic co-operation agreement, April 23, 1979.

Declarations of intent on expansion of co-operation in the economy, trade, industry and technology as well as on co-operation in the cultural and scientific-technological fields, Nov. 6, 1979.

Civil space research and technology co-operation agreement, March 1984.

A military agreement under which Italy undertook to supply China with a range of weapons and with training in the use of advanced weapons systems, April 6, 1985.

The United Kingdom. An agreement and a protocol on scientific and technological co-operation were signed in London on Nov. 15, 1978.

Two agreements signed on June 3, 1985, were (i) an economic co-operation agreement, replacing one of March 4, 1979, and to run to at least 1990, and (ii) an agreement on peaceful uses of nuclear energy.

The United States. New principles of the relations between the United States and China were agreed upon during a visit to China by President Nixon and laid down in a joint communiqué issued in Shanghai on Feb. 27, 1972. These principles included in particular the provisions that "neither side should seek hegemony in the Asia-Pacific region and each is opposed to efforts by any other country or group of countries to establish such hegemony", and that "neither is prepared to negotiate on behalf of any third party or to enter into agreements or understandings with the other directed at other states".

These principles were reaffirmed in a joint communiqué issued on Dec. 15–16, 1978, to announce the establishment of diplomatic relations between the two countries with effect from Jan. 1, 1979.

Agreements signed on Jan. 31, 1979, were (i) an agreement on the establishment of consular relations; (ii) a cultural agreement; and (iii) an agreement on co-operation in science and technology (which was extended on Jan. 12, 1984).

Under an agreement which was signed in Peking on March 2, 1979, and entered into force on May 11 of that year, China was to pay the US Treasury $80,500,000 in settlement of some 400

US claims totalling $196,800,000 while the United States would release $80,500,000 of Chinese assets frozen in the USA during the Korean war in 1950.

An agreement on trade relations, signed on July 7, 1979, came into force on Feb. 1, 1980.

Under a US-Chinese trade agreement of Jan. 24, 1980, China was granted most-favoured-nation status (as provided for in an agreement initialled in China on May 14, 1979, signed in Peking on July 7, 1979, and approved by the US Congress on Oct. 23, 1979). The trade agreement came into force on Feb. 1, 1980.

Also on Jan. 24, 1980, the US Defence Department announced that it was prepared to sell military equipment (though excluding offensive weapons) to China—this being a reversal of US policy under the rules of the Inter-Allied Co-ordinating Committee for East-West Trade (COCOM, see page 220).

Furthermore it was agreed on the same day (Jan. 24, 1980) in a memorandum of understanding that a ground receiving station would be built in China for data transmitted by the US Landsat-D satellite system (which had possible military applications).

In March 1980 an agreement was signed opening the way for large-scale US assistance in the development of China's hydroelectric industry.

A four-year agreement on US grain supplies to China of 6,000,000 tons per annum was concluded on Oct. 22, 1980.

A protocol on co-operation in nuclear safety matters was signed and came into force on Oct. 17, 1981.

An agreement relating to trade in cotton, wool and man-made fibre textiles and textile products, effective Jan. 1, 1983, was signed and came into force on Aug. 19, 1983.

An accord on industrial and technological co-operation was signed and came into force on Jan. 12, 1984.

A nuclear co-operation agreement initialled in April 1984 was finally concluded on July 22, 1985.

Under an agreement announced on April 8, 1986, China was to purchase military equipment worth about $550,000,000, including avionics sets for 55 F8 fighter aircraft.

12. The Commonwealth

This section covers (i) the membership, structure and historical development of the Commonwealth, (ii) the various regional groupings and organizations which have been created within the Commonwealth framework, (iii) various treaties and agreements concluded by the United Kingdom and (iv) treaties and agreements concluded by other Commonwealth member countries.

Structure and Development of the Commonwealth

The Commonwealth is an association of independent sovereign states all of which have been, at some time, British territories. It is neither a formal alliance nor a federation of states since there exists no written Commonwealth constitution and no central political authority. Any former British territory, on attaining independence, may seek membership of the Commonwealth; this is granted only by the unanimous consent of the members.

The head of the Commonwealth is the British monarch, who is recognized, even by those member countries which have their own heads of state, as the symbol of the free association of member nations of the Commonwealth. In those countries which owe allegiance to her as their head of state, the Queen is represented by a Governor-General whom she appoints on the recommendation of the country in question.

One of the principal factors binding together the member nations of the Commonwealth is the use of English Common Law as a basis for most judicial systems. Exceptions are the Canadian province of Quebec, where the judicial system is based on French law; Sri Lanka, where Roman Dutch law is applied (this is also the case in Zimbabwe); and the Moslem countries of Africa and Asia, where Moslem civil law is applied.

Commonwealth Members

The members of the Commonwealth are the United Kingdom, together with its dependent territories, protectorates and protected states, and 48 other independent states. The membership is given in the table below.

Since the merging of the Colonial Office and the Commonwealth Relations Office in August 1966, to form the Commonwealth Office, and its subsequent merger with the Foreign Office to form the Foreign and Commonwealth Office on Oct. 17, 1968, the dependent territories of Britain (listed below) have become the responsibility of this office.

BRITISH DEPENDENT TERRITORIES

Colonies with Internal Self-Government. Belize; Bermuda; British Virgin Islands; Cayman Islands; Gibraltar; Montserrat; St Helena and Dependencies; Turks and Caicos Islands.

Other Colonies. Anguilla (formerly part of the Associated State of St Kitts-Nevis-Anguilla); British Antarctic Territory; British Indian Ocean Territory; Falkland Islands and their dependencies; Hong Kong (Colony and Leased Territories); Pitcairn Islands Group.

OTHER DEPENDENCIES

Other dependencies which are members of the Commonwealth are (i) *of Britain*—the Channel Islands and the Isle of Man; (ii) *of Australia*—the Australian Antarctic Territory, Christmas Island, the Cocos (Keeling) Islands, the Coral Sea Islands Territory, the Heard and McDonald Islands and Norfolk Island; and (iii) *of New Zealand*—the Cook Islands, Niue, the Ross Dependency and Tokelau.

Commonwealth Organs

Summit Meetings. Meetings of the heads of government of Commonwealth member countries are held every two years at different capitals in the Commonwealth. These meetings are private and informal, and decisions are taken by consensus (and not by voting). Matters discussed include the international political situation, regional problems (in particular the developments in southern Africa), conflicts affecting Commonwealth members (e.g. Cyprus), economic affairs (with particular reference to assistance for developing Commonwealth countries) and special Commonwealth programmes. A detailed communiqué is issued at the end of each meeting.

Finance Ministers' Meetings. Meetings of Commonwealth Ministers of Finance take place once a year to discuss the world economic situation

Countries within the Commonwealth

Country	Date of Independence	Political Status
United Kingdom	—	Monarchy
Canada	July 1, 1867	Monarchy
Australia	Jan. 1, 1901	Monarchy
New Zealand	Sept. 26, 1907	Monarchy
India	Aug. 15, 1947	Republic since Jan. 26, 1950
Sri Lanka	Feb. 4, 1948	Republic since May 22, 1972
Ghana	March 6, 1957	Republic since July 1, 1960
Cyprus	Aug. 16, 1960	Republic since Aug. 16, 1960
Nigeria	Oct. 1, 1960	Republic since Oct. 1, 1963
Sierra Leone	April 27, 1961	Republic since April 19, 1971
Tanzania	Dec. 9, 1961	Republic since Dec. 9, 1962 (in union with Zanzibar since April 27, 1964)
Western Samoa	Jan. 1, 1962	Independent state under two chiefs
Jamaica	Aug. 6, 1962	Monarchy
Trinidad and Tobago	Aug. 31, 1962	Republic since Aug. 1, 1976
Uganda	Oct. 9, 1962	Independent sovereign state on Oct. 9, 1963. Republic (officially) since Sept. 8, 1967
Malaysia	Sept. 16, 1963	Monarchy*
Kenya	Dec. 12, 1963	Republic since Dec. 12, 1964
Malawi	July 6, 1964	Republic since July 6, 1966
Malta	Sept. 21, 1964	Republic since Dec. 13, 1974
Zambia	Oct. 24, 1964	Republic since Oct. 24, 1964
The Gambia	Feb. 18, 1965	Republic since April 24, 1970
Maldives	July 26, 1965	Republic since January 1968
Singapore	Oct. 16, 1965	Republic since Dec. 22, 1965
Guyana	May 26, 1966	Republic since Feb. 23, 1970
Botswana	Sept. 30, 1966	Republic since Sept. 30, 1966
Lesotho	Oct. 4, 1966	Monarchy*
Barbados	Nov. 30, 1966	Monarchy
Nauru†	Jan. 31, 1968	Republic
Mauritius	March 12, 1968	Monarchy
Swaziland	Sept. 6, 1968	Monarchy*
Tonga	June 4, 1970	Monarchy*
Fiji	Oct. 10, 1970	Monarchy
Bangladesh	Dec. 16, 1971	Republic
Commonwealth of the Bahamas	July 10, 1973	Monarchy
Grenada	Feb. 7, 1974	Monarchy
Papua New Guinea	Sept. 16, 1975	Monarchy
Seychelles	June 29, 1976	Republic
Solomon Islands	July 7, 1978	Monarchy
Tuvalu†	Oct. 1, 1978	Monarchy
Commonwealth of Dominica	Nov. 3, 1978	Republic
St Lucia	Feb. 22, 1979	Monarchy
Kiribati	July 12, 1979	Republic
St Vincent and the Grenadines	Oct. 27, 1979	Monarchy
Zimbabwe	April 18, 1980	Republic
Vanuatu	July 31, 1980	Republic
Belize	Sept. 21, 1981	Monarchy
Antigua and Barbuda	Nov. 1, 1981	Monarchy
St Christopher and Nevis	Sept. 19, 1983	Monarchy
Brunei	Jan. 1, 1984	Monarchy*

* These monarchies are headed by their own monarchs. All other Commonwealth countries described as monarchies owe allegiance to the British Queen.

† Special member without representation at Commonwealth heads of government conferences.

Maldives became a full member of the Commonwealth on June 20, 1985, having been a special member since July 1982.

St Vincent and the Grenadines became a full member on June 20, 1985, having been a special member since its attainment of independence.

Antigua and Barbuda as well as St Christopher and Nevis, and also Brunei, had previously participated in Commonwealth meetings concerned with matters over which they had jurisdiction. (Such participation is still exercised by the New Zealand associated states of the Cook Islands and Niue.)

Pakistan—a Commonwealth member since Aug. 15, 1947, and a Republic since March 23, 1956—withdrew from the Commonwealth on Jan. 30, 1972, in protest against recognition of the independence of Bangladesh (formerly East Pakistan) by Britain, Australia and New Zealand.

and to agree on Commonwealth proposals to be made in international economic and financial fora.

Secretariat. The Commonwealth Secretariat was set up in London in July 1965 in pursuance of a recommendation made by the heads of government meeting of July 1964. The Secretariat was to be "a visible symbol of the spirit of co-operation which animates the Commonwealth". Divided into departments dealing with administration, applied studies in government, economic affairs, education, export market development, food production and rural development, information, international affairs, legal matters, medical affairs, youth, and finance and personnel services, the Secretariat is responsible for disseminating information on questions of common interest; for aiding the various Commonwealth agencies, both official and unofficial, in the promotion of Commonwealth links in all fields; and for preparing and servicing the heads of government and other ministerial meetings.

The Secretariat is headed by a Secretary-General (elected by the heads of government for a five-year term and re-eligible), two Deputy Secretaries-General and two Assistant Secretaries-General.

Conferences of Heads of Government of Asian and Pacific Commonwealth Member States

A first regional conference of heads of government of Asian and Pacific Commonwealth member countries was held in Sydney (Australia) on Feb. 13–16, 1978, with the principal object of

Map 7   African members of Commonwealth

encouraging co-operation for regional development. The participants in the conference acknowledged their collective responsibility for rendering special assistance to the small Commonwealth member states in the region.

A second such conference, held in New Delhi on Sept. 4–8, 1980, expressed its "full support for the independence, sovereignty, territorial integrity and non-aligned status of Afghanistan and other countries of the region". It also called for an opportunity to be afforded to all peoples of the South Pacific "to exercise their right to self-determination" and "commended the desire of Pacific island countries for greater self-reliance through increased mutual co-operation among themselves".

The third conference, held in Suva (Fiji) on Oct. 14–18, 1982, issued a lengthy communiqué in which the participants inter alia "reaffirmed their commitment to the goal of establishing a zone of peace in the Indian Ocean and noted with alarm the increasing build-up of the great power military presence in the arca . . . against the wishes of the littoral and hinterland states". They also noted with approval "efforts to establish a zone of peace, freedom and neutrality in South-East Asia".

The fourth conference, held in Port Moresby (Papua New Guinea) on Aug. 8, 1984, issued only a brief communiqué in which the participants "condemned French nuclear testing in the Pacific and expressed their united opposition to any proposal to dump nuclear waste in the Pacific" without commenting on other aspects of proposals to declare the Pacific a nuclear-free zone. The conference also decided to hold future meetings only as the occasion warranted, and no longer every two years.

Commonwealth Organizations

The main Commonwealth organizations active in various fields are listed below.

Commonwealth Fund for Technical Co-operation (CFTC). The CFTC was established in April 1971 to provide technical assistance for economic and social development in Commonwealth developing countries. It is financed by contributions from all member states, and its controlling board comprises one representative from each participating government. Its expenditure has grown from £400,000 in 1971 to some £23,000,000 in 1985–86, the major contributors being Canada, the United Kingdom, Australia, India, New Zealand and Nigeria.

Its programmes include one for fellowship and training, an industrial development unit and an export market development division.

Under the CFTC a programme for technical assistance to the Government of Mozambique was set up in April 1976 with an initial target of £1,000,000 (as a sequel to a recommendation by a Commonwealth Sanctions Committee to compensate Mozambique for losses incurred through its participation in sanctions against the then White minority regime in Rhodesia). By November 1977 the Commonwealth Fund for Mozambique had initiated technical assistance and training projects costing £300,000.

Agriculture and Forestry. The Commonwealth Agricultural Bureaux—four institutes and 10 bureaux, each concerned with a particular aspect of agricultural science—collect and supply specialized information on agricultural science for research workers. The structure was founded in 1929.

The bodies concerned with co-operation in the field of forestry are: (i) The Commonwealth Forestry Association, founded in 1921; and (ii) the Standing Committee on Commonwealth Forestry, founded in 1923.

Commonwealth Studies. (i) The Institute of Commonwealth Studies, formed in London in 1949 to promote advanced study of the Commonwealth; and (ii) the Institute of Commonwealth Studies at the University of Oxford.

Communications. (i) The Commonwealth Air Transport Council, formed in London in 1945; (ii) the Commonwealth Telecommunications Organization, with a secretariat known as the Commonwealth Telecommunications Bureau, established in London in 1968; and (iii) Conferences of Commonwealth Postal Administrations, held at various times since 1971.

Education. (i) The Association of Commonwealth Universities, founded in London in 1913 as the Universities Bureau of the British Empire; (ii) the Commonwealth Association of Science, Technology and Mathematics Educators (CASME), established in London in 1974; (iii) the Commonwealth Education Liaison Committee (CELC), founded in 1959; and (iv) the League for the Exchange of Commonwealth Teachers, formed in London in 1901.

Health. (i) The Commonwealth Medical Association, formed in London in 1962; (ii) the Commonwealth Regional Health Secretariat for East, Central and Southern Africa, founded in Arusha (Tanzania) in 1974; (iii) the Commonwealth Society for the Deaf, London; (iv) the Royal Commonwealth Society for the Blind (at Haywards Heath, Sussex), formed in 1950; and (v) the West African Health Secretariat (Yaba, Nigeria), founded in 1972 as the Commonwealth West African Health Secretariat, which was joined by Liberia in 1974, when it assumed its present name.

Information and the Media. (i) The Commonwealth Broadcasting Association, formed in London in 1945; (ii) Commonwealth Institute, London, established in 1887 as the Imperial Institute; (iii) the Commonwealth Institute, Scotland (Edinburgh); and (iv) the Commonwealth Press Union, formed in London in 1909.

Law. (i) The Commonwealth Legal Advisory Service (c/o British Institute of International and

Comparative Law, London); (ii) the Commonwealth Legal Bureau, Auckland (New Zealand); (iii) the Commonwealth Legal Education Association, formed in London in 1971; and (iv) the Commonwealth Magistrates' Association, London.

Parliamentary Affairs. (i) The Commonwealth Parliamentary Association, formed in London in 1911; and (ii) the Conference of Speakers and Presiding Officers of Commonwealth Parliaments, Ottawa (Canada), held every two years.

Professions. (i) The Commonwealth Association of Architects, formed in London in 1964; and (ii) the Commonwealth Foundation, established in London in 1965 to administer a fund for promoting interchanges between Commonwealth professional organizations. In February 1983 the foundation was reconstituted as an international organization of the Commonwealth.

Science and Technology. (i) The Commonwealth Advisory Aeronautical Research Council (Teddington, Middlesex), formed in 1946; (ii) the Commonwealth Committee on Mineral Resources and Geology, formed in London in 1948; (iii) the Commonwealth Consultative Space Research Committee, formed in London in 1960; (iv) the Commonwealth Engineers' Council, formed in London in 1946; and (v) the Commonwealth Science Council, formed in London in 1946 for collaboration between Commonwealth government civil science organizations in joint projects.

Sport. The Commonwealth Games Federation (London), which holds games every four years (the first having been held in 1930).

Youth. (i) The Commonwealth Expedition (COMEX), London, for organizing international expeditions; (ii) the Commonwealth Youth Exchange Council, formed in London in 1970; and (iii) the Duke of Edinburgh's Award Scheme (London), enabling young people to gain awards for a programme of activities.

Other Organizations. (i) The British Commonwealth Ex-Services League, London; (ii) the Commonwealth Countries League, formed in London in 1925 to work for equality of status and opportunities between women and men and for mutual understanding throughout the Commonwealth; (iii) the Commonwealth War Graves Commission (Maidenhead, Berks), formed in 1917 as the Imperial War Graves Commission; (iv) the Joint Commonwealth Societies Council, London; (v) the Royal Commonwealth Society, established in London to promote knowledge and understanding among the peoples of the Commonwealth; (vi) the Royal Over-Seas League, formed in London in 1910 with similar objects; and (vii) the Victoria League for Commonwealth Friendship, formed in London in 1901 to further personal friendship between Commonwealth peoples.

Development of the Commonwealth

The Commonwealth began to evolve with the formation of self-governing dominions. The first of these was the Dominion of Canada, created, under the British North America Act of 1867, out of the provinces of Ontario, Quebec, Nova Scotia and New Brunswick. Additional provinces acceded to the Dominion, in accordance with the provisions of the Act, as follows: Manitoba (1869), British Columbia (1871), Prince Edward Island (1873), Alberta (1905), Saskatchewan (1905) and Newfoundland (1949).

The six self-governing provinces of Australia formed a dominion in 1900 known as the Commonwealth of Australia. New Zealand, which had obtained a unitary form of government in 1876, was designated a dominion in 1907, but did not adopt the principal sections of the Statute of Westminster [see below] until 1947. The Union of South Africa was formed from four self-governing colonies in 1910. Southern Ireland became in effect a self-governing dominion when the Irish Free State was established in 1921.

An *Imperial Conference of 1926*, adopting a report by an Inter-Imperial Relations Committee, defined the Dominions and Great Britain as "autonomous communities within the Empire, equal in status, in no way subordinate to one another in any aspect of their domestic or external affairs, though united by a common allegiance to the Crown, and freely associated as members of the British Commonwealth of Nations . . . Every self-governing member of the Empire is now the master of its destiny. In fact, if not always in form, it is subject to no compulsion whatever. . . . The British Empire is not founded upon negations. It depends essentially, if not formally, on positive ideals. Free institutions are its lifeblood. Free co-operation is its instrument."

The *Statute of Westminster of 1931* gave effect to the above definition and offered all former colonies the undisputed right to secede from the Commonwealth. Other provisions of the statute are:

(1) The Parliament of Westminster ceases to have the right of revision with regard to the legislation of the Parliaments of the Dominions.
(2) A Dominion possesses full authority to make laws possessing extra-territorial validity.
(3) When there are discrepancies between a Dominion law and an existing law of the United Kingdom, this fact shall not render the Dominion law invalid.

Steps in the gradual decentralization of powers within the Commonwealth were:

(1) The granting of complete independence in 1947 to Burma, Ceylon (later Sri Lanka), India and Pakistan—with Burma seceding from the Commonwealth and the other three states becoming independent members of it.
(2) British recognition of the secession of the Irish Republic in 1949—although citizens of the Republic continued to enjoy in Britain substantially all rights and privileges of British subjects.
(3) The acceptance of India as a Republic in 1949, with the British sovereign being acknowledged as head of the Commonwealth. (The monarchy remained merely a unifying symbol for the Commonwealth, but no longer had valid

constitutional significance. Relations among Commonwealth members are no longer based on constitutional law, but on international law—i.e. multilateral treaties which also embrace non-Commonwealth states.)

(4) The Canadian Citizenship Act of 1946 by which Canadians became Canadian citizens first, and British subjects only by consequence. This act forced the other independent members of the Commonwealth to follow suit by establishing their own citizenships.

South Africa left the Commonwealth in 1961, not because it had become a Republic the previous year, but because its racial policies were at variance with the principles of all other Commonwealth members.

1971 Singapore Declaration. At the Commonwealth conference held in January 1971 in Singapore, a *Declaration of Commonwealth Principles* was unanimously agreed on by the 31 delegations on Jan. 22. The declaration stated inter alia:

"... We believe in the liberty of the individual, in equal rights for all citizens regardless of race, colour, creed or political belief, and in their inalienable right to participate by means of free and democratic political processes in framing the society in which they live. We therefore strive to promote in each of our countries those representative institutions and guarantees for personal freedom under the law that are our common heritage.

"We recognize racial prejudice as a dangerous sickness threatening the healthy development of the human race and racial discrimination as an unmitigated evil of society. Each of us will vigorously combat this evil within our own nation.

"No country will afford to regimes which practise racial discrimination assistance which in its own judgment directly contributes to the pursuit or consolidation of this evil policy. We oppose all forms of colonial domination and racial oppression and are committed to the principles of human dignity and equality.

"We will therefore use all our efforts to foster human equality and dignity everywhere, and to further the principles of self-determination and non-racialism. . . ."

1973 Ottawa Conference. At the Ottawa conference of Commonwealth heads of government, held from Aug. 2 to 10, 1973, the Prime Minister of Canada, Pierre Trudeau, opened with the following speech on the nature of the Commonwealth:

"Within the Commonwealth we have the opportunity and the means for both communication and understanding. In this forum of discussion each Commonwealth member is equal. None is senior; none is superior. None is distinguished by economic self-sufficiency; none is possessed of all political virtue. In our discussions during the next few days, I have no doubt that we will be able to demonstrate to one another and to the world the advantages of our dissimilarity, the richness of our diversity, the excitement of our variety. We will be able to do so because we are members of an association, not an institution. In this Commonwealth there is no structure to contain us, there are no fetters to chafe us. The Commonwealth is a reflection of its [then] 32 members and of their desire to consult and co-operate with one another. There is no artificial adhesive. Nor is there any voting, any constitution, any flag, any headquarters. This association is neither regional in nature, nor specialized in its interests. The Commonwealth is an organism and this fact guarantees both its vitality and its flexibility. . . .

"None of us in the Commonwealth is so powerful or so self-sufficient that he is able to act independently of the opinion or the assistance of others. None of us disregards the value of

consultation and co-operation. We are able in these gatherings of heads of government, and by extension, in those other groupings to which we belong, to ensure that we understand one another's problems and one another's aspirations. That, to me, is the significance of our association. I am not, at this meeting, in search of a new role for the Commonwealth, or indeed any role. The Commonwealth is for many of us our window on the world. Over the years its importance will deepen largely because it has no specific role, but emphasizes instead the value of the human relations. . . ."

1977 Gleneagles Agreement on Apartheid in Sport. At the end of the 21st meeting of the heads of government of Commonwealth countries, held in London on June 8–15, 1977, the participants issued, separately from a final communiqué, a statement on apartheid in sport agreed upon at informal discussions at Gleneagles (Scotland) on June 11–12 and reading as follows:

"The member countries of the Commonwealth, embracing peoples of diverse races, colours, languages and faiths, have long recognized racial prejudice and discrimination as a dangerous sickness and an unmitigated evil and are pledged to use all their efforts to foster human dignity everywhere. At their London meeting, heads of government reaffirmed that apartheid in sport, as in other fields, is an abomination and runs directly counter to the Declaration of Commonwealth Principles which they made at Singapore on Jan. 22, 1971 [see above].

"They were conscious that sport is an important means of developing and fostering understanding between the people, and especially between the young people, of all countries. But they were also aware that, quite apart from other factors, sporting contacts between their nationals and the nationals of countries practising apartheid in sport tend to encourage the belief (however unwarranted) that they are prepared to condone this abhorrent policy or are less than totally committed to the principles embodied in their Singapore Declaration. Regretting past misunderstandings and difficulties and recognizing that these were partly the result of inadequate intergovernmental consultations, they agreed that they would seek to remedy this situation in the context of the increased level of understanding now achieved.

"They reaffirmed their full support for the international campaign against apartheid and welcomed the efforts of the United Nations to reach universally accepted approaches to the question of sporting contacts within the framework of that campaign.

"Mindful of these and other considerations, they accepted it as the urgent duty of each of their governments vigorously to combat the evil of apartheid by withholding any form of support for, and by taking every practical step to discourage, contact or competition by their nationals with sporting organizations, teams or sportsmen from South Africa or from any other country where sports are organized on the basis of race, colour or ethnic origin.

"They fully acknowledged that it was for each government to determine in accordance with its laws the methods by which it might best discharge these commitments. But they recognized that the effective fulfilment of their commitments was essential to the harmonious development of Commonwealth sport hereafter.

"They acknowledged also that the full realization of their objectives involved the understanding, support and active participation of the nationals of their countries and of their national sporting organizations and authorities. As they drew a curtain across the past they issued a collective call for that understanding, support and participation with a view to ensuring that in this matter the peoples and governments of the Commonwealth might help to give a lead to the world.

"Heads of government specifically welcomed the belief, unanimously expressed at their meeting, that in the light of their consultations and accord there were unlikely to be future sporting contacts of any significance between Commonwealth countries or their nationals and South Africa while that country continues to pursue the detestable policy of apartheid. On that basis, and having regard to their commitments, they looked forward with satisfaction to the holding of the [1978] Commonwealth Games in Edmonton [Canada] and to the continued strengthening of Commonwealth sport generally."

1979 Lusaka Conference. At the 22nd meeting of the heads of government of Commonwealth countries, held in Lusaka (Zambia) on Aug. 1–7, 1979, a framework agreement was unanimously approved for a peaceful settlement of Rhodesia's transition to an independent Zimbabwe under Black majority rule, while a strong Commonwealth declaration on racism was also approved.

On the Rhodesian issue the participants of the meeting agreed inter alia that (i) it was "the constitutional responsibility of the British Government to grant legal independence to Zimbabwe on the basis of majority rule"; (ii) "the search for a lasting settlement must involve all the parties to the conflict"; and (iii) "independence on the basis of majority rule requires the adoption of a democratic constitution including appropriate safeguards for minorities", with the government being "chosen through free and fair elections properly supervised under British Government authority and with Commonwealth observers".

Stating that the Commonwealth was "an institution devoted to the promotion of international understanding and world peace, and to the achievement of equal rights for all citizens regardless of race, colour, sex, creed or political belief, and . . . committed to the eradication of the dangerous evils of racism and racial prejudice", the participants of the meeting proclaimed the following *Lusaka Declaration of the Commonwealth on Racism and Racial Prejudice:*

"United in our desire to rid the world of the evils of racism and racial prejudice, we proclaim our faith in the inherent dignity and worth of the human person and declare that:

"(1) The peoples of the Commonwealth have the right to live freely in dignity and equality, without any distinction or exclusion based on race, colour, sex, descent or national or ethnic origin;

"(2) while everyone is free to retain diversity in his or her culture and lifestyle, this diversity does not justify the perpetuation of racial prejudice or racially discriminatory practices;

"(3) everyone has the right to equality before the law and equal justice under the law;

"(4) everyone has the right to effective remedies and protection against any form of discrimination based on the grounds of race, colour, sex, descent, or national or ethnic origin.

"We reject as inhuman and intolerable all policies designed to perpetuate apartheid, racial segregation or other policies based on theories that racial groups are or may be inherently superior or inferior.

"We reaffirm that it is the duty of all the peoples of the Commonwealth to work together for the total eradication of the infamous policy of apartheid which is internationally recognized as a crime against the conscience and dignity of mankind and the very existence of which is an affront to humanity.

"We agree that everyone has the right to protection against acts of incitement to racial hatred and discrimination, whether committed by individuals, groups or other organizations.

"We affirm that there should be no discrimination based on race, colour, sex, descent or national or ethnic origin in the acquisition or exercise of the right to vote; in the field of civil rights or access to citizenship; or in the economic, social or cultural fields, particularly education, health, employment, occupation, housing, social security and cultural life.

"We attach particular importance to ensuring that children shall be protected from practices which may foster racism or racial prejudice. Children have the right to be brought up and educated in a spirit of tolerance and understanding so as to be able to contribute fully to the building of future societies based on justice and friendship.

"We believe that those groups in societies who may be especially disadvantaged because of residual racist attitudes are entitled to the fullest protection of the law. We recognize that the history of the Commonwealth and its diversity require that special attention should be paid to the problems of indigenous minorities. We recognize that the same special attention should be paid to the problems of immigrants, immigrant workers and refugees.

"We agree that special measures may in particular circumstances be required to advance the development of disadvantaged groups in society. We recognize that the effects of colonialism or racism in the past may make desirable special provisions for the social and economic enhancement of indigenous populations.

"Inspired by the principles of freedom and equality which characterize our association, we accept the solemn duty of working together to eliminate racism and racial prejudice. This duty involves the acceptance of the principle that positive measures may be required to advance the elimination of racism, including assistance to those struggling to rid themselves and their environment of the practice.

"Being aware that legislation alone cannot eliminate racism and racial prejudice, we endorse the need to initiate public information and education policies designed to promote understanding, tolerance, respect and friendship among peoples and racial groups.

"We are particularly conscious of the importance of the contribution the media can make to human rights and the eradication of racism and racial prejudice by helping to eliminate ignorance and misunderstanding between people and by drawing attention to the evils which afflict humanity. We affirm the importance of truthful presentation of facts in order to ensure that the public are fully informed of the dangers presented by racism and racial prejudice.

"In accordance with established principles of international law and, in particular, the provisions of the International Convention on the Elimination of All Forms of Racial Discrimination [of 1965—see page 48], we affirm that everyone is, at all times and in all places, entitled to be protected in the enjoyment of the right to be free of racism and racial prejudice.

"We believe that the existence in the world of apartheid and racial discrimination is a matter of concern to all human beings. We recognize that we share an international responsibility to work together for the total eradication of apartheid and racial discrimination.

"We note that racism and racial prejudice, wherever they occur, are significant factors contributing to tension between nations and thus inhibit peaceful progress and development. We believe that the goal of the eradication of racism stands as a critical priority for governments of the Commonwealth, committed as they are to the promotion of the ideals of peaceful and happy lives for their people.

"We intend that the Commonwealth, as an international organization with a fundamental and deep-rooted attachment to principles of freedom and equality, should co-operate with other organizations in the fulfilment of these principles. In particular the Commonwealth should seek to enhance the co-ordination of its activities with those of other organizations similarly committed to the promotion and protection of human rights and fundamental freedoms."

1981 Melbourne Conference. A meeting of the heads of government of the Commonwealth member states held in Melbourne (Australia) from Sept. 30 to Oct. 7, 1981, adopted a 16-point *Melbourne Declaration* (published on Oct. 4).

It reaffirmed Commonwealth policies and stated in particular: "The gross inequality of wealth and opportunity currently existing in the world, and the unbroken circle of poverty in which the lives of millions in developing countries are confined, are fundamental sources of tension and instability in the world. . . . There must be determined and dedicated action at national and international level to reduce that inequality and to reduce that circle. . . . The choice is not between change and no change but between timely, adequate, managed change and disruptive, involuntary change imposed by breakdown and conflict; . . . in the process of negotiations nations must cast aside inhibitions and habits which have thwarted progress in the past and find new ways of talking constructively to one another as to reach the larger moral, political and strategic discussion of what is at stake; . . . the issues are so important that they require the personal commitment and involvement of political leaders who, representing the will of their people, have the greatest power to advance the common cause of mankind."

The declaration was appended to the final communiqué of the meeting, which noted with deep concern the deterioration of the situation in southern Africa, where the apartheid system of South Africa "gravely endangered international peace and security" and where no progress had been made towards independence for Namibia.

The communiqué also called for greater assistance to the Southern African Development Co-ordination Conference (SADCC—see page 433). The leaders further agreed that the level of activities carried out by the Commonwealth Fund for Technical Co-operation (CFTC) should by 1983–84 be restored to that attained in 1978–79 as a basis for future agreements.

1983 New Delhi and Goa Conference. A meeting of Commonwealth heads of government held in New Delhi and Goa on Nov. 23–29, 1983, issued a *Goa Declaration on International Security* and a *New Delhi Statement on Economic Action.*

In the Goa Declaration the heads of government expressed concern that "relationships between the world's major military alliances" were "becoming more confrontational" and their belief that it was "imperative that the Soviet Union and the United States should summon up the political vision of a world in which their nations can live in peace". They emphasized the supreme importance of political will, in particular to stop the nuclear arms race. They deplored "the diminishing capacity of international institutions to play an effective role in world affairs" and "the vulnerability of small states to external attack and interference in their affairs". They stressed their "belief that an ethic of non-violence must be at the heart of all efforts to ensure peace and harmony in the world", an ethic which required "close adherence to the principle of peaceful settlement".

The Statement on Economic Action contained a decision to establish a Commonwealth consultative group for the purpose of promoting a consensus on the issues of a reform of the Bretton Woods institutions [see page 36], on a comprehensive review of the international monetary, financial and relevant trade problems, and on the threat of the rising level of protectionism.

The final communiqué of the meeting contained a survey by regions of international problems and inter alia condemned the creation of a separatist Turkish state in northern Cyprus. On

southern Africa it was stated in the communiqué: "The overwhelming majority of heads of government rejected the proposals of the South African government for 'constitutional' change, since the African majority was wholly excluded from their scope and the proposals were designed not to eradicate but to entrench and strengthen apartheid."

1985 Nassau Conference. A further meeting of Commonwealth heads of government, held in Nassau (Bahamas) on Oct. 16–22, 1985, issued a *Nassau Declaration on World Order* and an *Accord on Southern Africa.*

In the declaration the leaders of the Commonwealth, "comprising 1,000 million people and one-third of the world's nations", proclaimed:

"We commit ourselves and our nations to work tirelessly in the pursuit of a world marked not by disorder and the use of competitive power but one governed by the principles of collective international co-operation and respect for the rights of all nations and peoples as the necessary foundation for lasting peace and assured economic and social development.

"We reaffirm our commitment to the principles and precepts of the Charter of the United Nations and to the goal of strengthening the United Nations system as the central instrument of peace, security and co-operation among nations. As we ourselves categorically reject the use or threat of force as a means of settling disputes, we appeal to all governments to work to strengthen the institutions which contribute to orderly resolution of differences between nations and which sustain peace.

"We rededicate ourselves to the principles of self-determination, non-racialism, human freedom and equality, and co-operation between nations in the service of international understanding, development and world peace, which have guided the Commonwealth throughout its evolution.

"We pledge ourselves to play a full part in revitalizing international co-operation for development and concerted action to confront the crucial issues of international economic inequality.

"We call upon the world community to construct a framework of collective security based on mutual trust and shared interest. All nations have a stake in disarmament. We therefore look for urgent agreement in reversing the arms race and on significant reductions, and eventual elimination, of nuclear and other weapons of mass destruction.

"We invite all peoples and nations to join in a universal effort to fulfil these objectives."

In conclusion the leaders stated: "We place the Commonwealth's proven qualities of understanding and bridge-building across the divides of race, religion and economic and political systems at the service of the United Nations and of all efforts to make it more effective."

In their *Accord on Southern Africa* the Commonwealth leaders called on the South African Government to take five specific steps, including the opening of a dialogue with a view to establishing a representative, non-racial government; decided to set up a group of eminent Commonwealth persons to facilitate such a dialogue; agreed on a series of economic measures to signal their opposition to apartheid, and, decided to review the position in six months and, in the absence of sufficient progress, to consider further measures of economic pressure.

As announced on Nov. 25, 1985, the Group of Eminent Persons (EPG) consisted of the following members: Malcolm Fraser (Australia), Gen. Olusegun Obasanjo (Nigeria) (both co-chairmen of the group), Lord Barber of Wentbridge (United Kingdom), Dame Nita Barrow (Barbados), John

Malecela (Tanzania), Sardar Swaran Singh (India) and Archbishop Edward W. Scott (Canada).

After visiting South Africa the EPG produced a unanimous report which inter alia concluded that at present there was "no genuine intention on the part of the South African government to dismantle apartheid and no present prospect of a process of dialogue leading to the establishment of a non-racial and representative government".

The report was the central document considered at a meeting of leaders of seven Commonwealth member states (Australia, the Bahamas, Canada, India, the United Kingdom, Zambia and Zimbabwe) in London on Aug. 3–5, 1986, which resulted in a final communiqué setting out the decision of six of the participants and also the "different view" of the British government.

In the communiqué it was stated: "We continue to believe with the EPG that the cycle of violence in South Africa must end. It is clearly established that the situation in South Africa constitutes a serious threat to regional peace and security. It is thus clear to us that since our meeting in Nassau there has not been the adequate concrete progress that we looked for there. Indeed, the situation has deteriorated." The six leaders therefore decided to call for the urgent adoption and implementation of all the measures listed in the Nassau Accord and, in addition, of new measures, including a ban on all new bank loans to South Africa and a ban on the import of uranium, coal, iron and steel from South Africa. The British government, on the other hand, declared that it would "(i) put a voluntary ban on new investment in South Africa; (ii) put a voluntary ban on the promotion of tourism to South Africa; and (iii) accept and implement any EEC decisions to ban the import of coal, iron and steel and of gold coins from South Africa".

Commonwealth Regional Groupings

Colombo Plan

(The Colombo Plan for Co-operative, Economic and Social Development in Asia and the Pacific)

Address. 12 Melbourne Ave., P.O.B. 596, Colombo 4, Sri Lanka.

Officer. Donald R. Toussaint (dir. of Colombo Plan Bureau).

Founded. July 1, 1951.

Membership within the Area. Afghanistan, Bangladesh, Bhutan, Burma, Fiji, India, Indonesia, Iran, Kampuchea, Korea, Laos, Malaysia, Maldives, Nepal, Pakistan, Papua New Guinea, Philippines, Singapore, Sri Lanka, Thailand.

Membership outside the Area. Australia, Canada, Japan, New Zealand, United Kingdom, United States.

History. The Colombo Plan for Co-operative Economic and Social Development in Asia and the Pacific was drawn up by a Commonwealth Consultative Committee on South and South-East Asia, and published on Nov. 28, 1950. This plan, originally adopted for a six-year period, was based on detailed development programmes for India, Pakistan, Ceylon, Malaya, Singapore, North Borneo (Sabah), and Sarawak, and formally came into operation on July 1, 1951. Already by February 1951 the scope of the scheme had been widened to include non-Commonwealth countries, and the USA had agreed to join Australia, Canada, New Zealand and the United Kingdom in making available aid within the framework of the Colombo Plan.

Originally known as the Colombo Plan for Co-operative Economic Development in South and South-East Asia, the Plan adopted its present name after the accession of Papua New Guinea in 1976.

Organization. The principal organ of the Colombo Plan is the Consultative Committee, which directs the working of the plan. The committee, consisting of ministers of the member countries, meets annually to discuss the annual reports of the individual members, and to co-ordinate the schemes for aid. The meetings of the committee are also attended by representatives of the Asian Development Bank, the World Bank (IBRD), the International Labour Organization, the UN Economic and Social Commission for Asia and the Pacific, the UN Development Programme, the Asian Productivity Organization, the Commonwealth Secretariat and the Colombo Plan Bureau.

The *Council for Technical Co-operation in Asia and the Pacific* is a consultative organ concerned specifically with the problems of technical co-operation. It is also responsible for the dissemination of information on the Colombo Plan as a whole. The council, which meets in Colombo several times a year, is composed of representatives of the member countries' governments.

The decisions of the Council for Technical Co-operation are executed by the *Colombo Plan Bureau.* The work of the bureau includes the keeping of records of all technical assistance given and received and of capital aid projects; the provision of information to member governments, in particular on the training facilities, experts and equipment available; and the issuing of progress reports and statistics.

A *Staff College for Technical Education* was established in Singapore in 1974.

The technical co-operation plan activities during 1983 included the training of 17,490 students and trainees, and disbursements in that year totalled over $598,000,000. Over three-fifths of the experts were financed by Japan and the remainder by Australia, the United States, the United Kingdom, New Zealand and Canada. The total value of co-operation during the period from 1950 to December 1983 was $5,310 million.

Forms of Aid. Although the bulk of aid within the framework of the Colombo Plan is provided by Australia, Britain, Canada, Japan and the United States, economic co-operation among the other members of the plan is encouraged.

Economic assistance is provided through capital aid in the form of grants and loans for national projects, and through technical aid in the form of experts, facilities for technical training and the supply of special equipment.

Assistance from major donors between 1950 and 1984 totalled US$75,668,200,000.

In 1973 the Colombo Plan launched a Drug Advisory Programme (financed by the United States) with the object of eliminating the causes of drug abuse and remedying its effects in member states.

Caribbean Community (CARICOM)

Address. P.O.B. 10827, Georgetown, Guyana.
Officer. Roderick Rainford (sec. gen.).
Founded. Aug. 1, 1973.
Membership. Antigua and Barbuda, the Bahamas, Barbados, Belize, Dominica, Grenada, Guyana, Jamaica, Montserrat, St Christopher and Nevis, St Lucia, St Vincent and the Grenadines, and Trinidad and Tobago. *Observers* (in "non-sensitive" ministerial committees): Dominican Republic, Haiti and Suriname.

History. CARICOM was formed under the Treaty of Chaguaramas (Trinidad) signed on July 4, 1973, with the object of achieving economic integration in a Caribbean Common Market; the latter replaced an earlier Caribbean Free Trade Association (CARIFTA) set up in 1968 by Antigua, Barbados, Dominica, Grenada, Guyana, Jamaica, Montserrat, St Christopher-Nevis-Anguilla, St Lucia, St Vincent and Trinidad and Tobago, and joined by Belize (then British Honduras) in 1971 and by the Bahamas in 1973.

The organs of CARICOM are (i) a heads of government conference, which is the organization's final authority and determines its policies; (ii) a Common Market Council consisting of one minister from each member state and responsible for the development and management of the Common Market and for the settlement of any disputes; and (iii) a secretariat with five divisions (for trade, economics and statistics; sectoral policy and planning, functional co-operation; legal affairs; and general services and administration). There are also a conference of ministers responsible for health, and standing committees of other ministers (responsible for education, labour, foreign affairs, finance, agriculture, mines, industry and transport).

The decision to establish the CARICOM had been reached at a conference of the heads of government of Commonwealth Caribbean countries in Georgetown (Guyana) on April 9–12, 1973, when a Georgetown Accord was signed on the deepening of the integration process within CARIFTA with a view to enabling all member states to share equitably in the benefits of integration. (The CARIFTA members had been grouped as "more developed countries"—MDCs, i.e. Barbados, Guyana, Jamaica, and Trinidad and Tobago—and "less developed countries"—

LDCs, i.e. the other CARIFTA member countries.)

At a meeting of the Prime Ministers of Barbados, Guyana, Jamaica and Trinidad and Tobago in Port of Spain (Trinidad) on June 9, 1976, it was agreed inter alia to grant Jamaica short- and long-term loans and credits to alleviate economic difficulties which had arisen in that country, to introduce a common protective policy including quantitative restrictions on imports from outside the region, to encourage further joint industrial projects, and to set up a **Caribbean Food Corporation** in September 1976.

Trinidad and Tobago, economically the strongest member of CARICOM, had during 1978–79 favoured the conclusion of bilaterally agreed arrangements involving financial and economic aid and had not supported economic arrangements between CARICOM member states and third countries nor helped to establish or develop institutions or enterprises in competition with Trinidad and Tobago interests. A more balanced picture of CARICOM's internal relations emerged by June 1979, when Guyana announced that its imports from other member states had in 1978 returned to the level of 1976 and Jamaica removed all quota restrictions on intra regional trade which it had previously imposed. However, no new policy decisions were taken as the heads of government conference was not convened, having held its last meeting in 1976.

A third meeting of the CARICOM heads of government conference (the first since a special meeting held in March 1976) was held in Ocho Rios (Jamaica) on Nov. 16–18, 1982. It agreed on an *Ocho Rios Declaration* which contained a general commitment to "political, civil, economic, social and cultural rights" while recognizing "the emergence of ideological pluralism" within CARICOM.

In the declaration the heads of government inter alia reaffirmed that the CARICOM member states would "aim at the fullest possible co-ordination of their foreign policies and should seek to adopt as far as possible common positions on major international issues". They also asserted their "commitment to the maintenance of absolute respect for defined borders, and demarcated and traditional lines of jurisdiction of states of the region". With regard to economic assistance the declaration stated: "The principle of international social justice requires that such assistance be given in consultation with, and with the fullest respect for, the sovereign wishes of the recipient countries."

The declaration was attached to the final communiqué of the meeting, in which the participants deplored "the sharp deterioration in international relations", the failure to reach any significant disarmament agreement, and "the eruption of regional conflicts in a number of areas". With regard to Caribbean affairs the participants welcomed a Caribbean Basin Initiative proposed by President Reagan of the United States on Feb. 24, 1982, and, inter alia, stressed the need to expand intra-regional trade as a means of stimulating economic growth.

The fourth meeting of the heads of government conference was held in Port of Spain (Trinidad) on July 4–8, 1983, when the Bahamas became the 13th member of CARICOM. The meeting decided inter alia to revive a Caribbean Multilateral Clearing Facility (CMCF) which had been established in 1976, had had a credit limit of US$100,000,000 and had been suspended in April 1983 after Guyana had accumulated a debt to other CARICOM member states of $98,000,000 (of which $65,000,000 were owed to Barbados).

The fifth meeting, held in Nassau (Bahamas) on July 4–7, 1984, agreed on a package of economic measures set out in a "Nassau understanding" and to be implemented by Jan. 1, 1985. These measures provided for (i) the raising of common external tariffs for a range of "sensitive" products, (ii) the dismantling of intra-regional trade barriers, and (iii) the attraction of funds to the CMCF. Although the deadline for implementing the understanding was subsequently postponed (first to June 1, 1985, and later to Aug. 31, 1985), the understanding was not implemented, largely because of protectionist measures taken by individual member states, in particular Trinidad and Tobago.

The sixth meeting of heads of government, held in Barbados on July 1–4, 1985, failed to find solutions to these problems. However, at the seventh meeting held in Georgetown (Guyana) on July 1–4, 1986, agreement was reached on the creation of a new CARICOM trade credit facility of $75,000,000 ($15,000,000 in equity and $60,000,000 in loans) to replace the CMCF with effect from Jan. 1, 1987.

Co-operation with Mexico and Canada. A Mexico-CARICOM Joint Commission, established in July 1974, held its first meeting in Barbados on Oct. 20–22, 1980.

A Canada-CARICOM Joint Trade and Economic Committee, established under an agreement signed in April 1979, held meetings in Canada on Nov. 21–22, 1979, and in Jamaica on Jan. 15–17, 1981, when the Prime Minister of Jamaica explained details of a "Marshall Plan" for the Caribbean region. In response the Canadian Secretary of State for External Affairs announced that his government had "approved an action plan for a regional policy approach which directed that the Commonwealth Caribbean should be accorded priority in the overall external policy of Canada", with an increase of Canadian aid to at least $55,200,000 by the mid-1980s.

In July 1986 a new "Caribcan" trade preference scheme came into effect, allowing CARICOM members and other English-speaking Caribbean states duty-free access to the Canadian market for 98 per cent of their exports (by category).

Associate institutions. Such institutions operating under the Treaty of Chaguaramas are: The Caribbean Development Bank [see below], the Caribbean Examinations Council; the Caribbean Investment Corporation; the Caribbean Meteorological Council [see below]; the Council of Legal Education; the West Indies Shipping Corporation; and the Universities of Guyana and of the West Indies.

Caribbean Development Bank

Address. P.O.B. 408, Wildey, St Michael, Barbados.
Officer. William Demas (pres.).
Founded. 1969.
Membership. The CARICOM member states and also Canada, Colombia, Mexico, Venezuela, the United Kingdom as well as Anguilla, the British Virgin Islands, the Cayman Islands and the Turks and Caicos Islands.
Object. To promote regional economic growth by supporting agriculture, industry, transport, tourism and education.
Finance. Paid-up capital £57,200,000 (November 1983).

Caribbean Meteorological Council

Address. c/o Caribbean Community Secretariat, P.O. Box 10827, Bank of Guyana Building, Georgetown, Guyana.
Activities. This council has as its training and research arm a Caribbean Meteorological Institute which has been engaged in various projects involving inter alia (i) a Caribbean Operational Hydrology Institute (COHI), funded mainly by the UN Development Programme, for the training of personnel for hydrological units to carry out data collection and analysis, (ii) a wind assessment project and (iii) hurricane detection systems. There are meteorological stations in Antigua, Barbados, Belize, Guyana, Jamaica, St Lucia and Trinidad and Tobago.

Organization of Eastern Caribbean States (OECS)

Address. Bridge St., Castries, St Lucia.
Officer. Dr Vaughan Lewis (dir.-gen.).
Founded. July 2, 1981.
Membership. Antigua and Barbuda, Dominica, Grenada, Montserrat, St Christopher and Nevis, St Lucia, and St Vincent and the Grenadines.
Associate membership. The British Virgin Islands.
History. The OECS was established under a treaty concluded on June 18, 1981.
Objects. To promote unity and solidarity among its members, the defence of their sovereignty, the harmonization of their foreign policy, and their economic integration.
Structure. The supreme organ of the OECS is its Authority of Heads of Government. An **Eastern Caribbean Central Bank** was set up, with effect from Oct. 1, 1983, in Basseterre (St Christopher) under an agreement signed by OECS member states in July; it superseded an earlier Eastern Caribbean Currency Authority. (The Eastern Caribbean dollar was linked to the US dollar at the rate of US$1.00 = EC$2.70.)
Defence developments. In October 1982 a regional defence agreement was concluded by Antigua and Barbuda, Barbados, Dominica, St Lucia and St Vincent and the Grenadines, and this agreement was adhered to by St Christopher

and Nevis on Feb. 8, 1984. Following an appeal for help made on Oct. 21, 1983, by the Governor-General of Grenada, the Prime Minister of which had been killed in a coup, contingents from Antigua and Barbuda, Dominica, St Lucia and St Vincent and the Grenadines took part in the military intervention by US and Caribbean combat forces which began on Oct. 25 and eventually resulted in the installation of a new government in Grenada. (The last US and Caribbean forces were withdrawn from Grenada by September 1985.)

Progress towards an Eastern Caribbean regional defence system (with the participation of Barbados) was tested in a joint US-Caribbean military exercise held on St Lucia on Sept. 11–15, 1985.

British Treaties and Agreements with Commonwealth and Other Countries

ANZUK Agreements

In succession to an Anglo-Malaysian Defence Treaty (of Oct. 12, 1957), which was terminated on Oct. 31, 1971, agreements were signed between Australia, Britain and New Zealand to implement as from Nov. 1, 1971, a decision made on April 16, 1971, to set up a joint ANZUK force for the defence of Malaysia and Singapore.

Under these agreements the five Governments decided to establish (1) an Integrated Air Defence System for Malaysia and Singapore under the responsibility of a joint Air Defence Council; (2) a Joint Consultative Council; and (3) continued stationing of Australian, New Zealand and United Kingdom armed forces in Malaysia and Singapore.

However, the United Kingdom withdrew its ANZUK forces in 1975–76, the last of them leaving Singapore on March 31, 1976.

Other UK Agreements with Commonwealth States

The United Kingdom and Australia. An agreement on the construction of a rocket-testing range in central Australia (the Woomera range) was announced on May 13, 1947. The cost of maintaining the range, used in a joint British-Australian scheme for the development of guided weapons, is shared by the two governments under an agreement of Sept. 13, 1953.

On April 4, 1955, it was announced that the Australian and British Governments had agreed on the establishment of a new atomic testing ground, to be known as Maralinga, in the South Australian desert.

A trade agreement signed on Feb. 26, 1957, was effective from Nov. 9, 1956.

An agreement concerning nuclear transfers between the two countries, signed on July 24, 1979, entered into force on the same day.

In a British-Australian treaty of 1956 (officially filed closed until 1999, but disclosed in *The Observer* of London on Aug. 12, 1984), the British government undertook to take "all practical measures . . . to ensure that any tests carried out there do not cause injury or damage . . . and to indemnify the Australian government of all valid claims arising out of death or injury due to tests carried out at the site" (with Australian soldiers and government employees being, however, excluded from this clause).

The United Kingdom and Belize. It was agreed in 1981 that British troops would remain in Belize for an appropriate time after the country's independence and would provide military training.

A British independence aid package of £12,000,000 (half in grants and half in interest-free loans) was announced on Sept. 9, 1981 (while an existing technical co-operation programme costing about £600,000 per annum would continue to operate). (On Sept. 21, 1981, the United Kingdom and six other Commonwealth member states—the Bahamas, Barbados, Canada, Guyana, Jamaica and Trinidad and Tobago—pledged to consult together in the event of an armed attack against Belize.)

The United Kingdom and Brunei. A treaty of friendship and co-operation, superseding an agreement concluded in 1959 (when Brunei's first written Constitution was promulgated) and amended in 1971 (when Brunei was given full internal self-government, with responsibility for public order) was initialled in London on Sept. 28, 1978, and signed in Brunei on Jan. 7, 1979.

The treaty laid down that by the end of 1983 the Sultanate of Brunei would "assume its full international responsibilities as a sovereign and independent state" and Britain's remaining responsibility for Brunei's defence and external affairs would be terminated. Until that time, however, Britain would keep in Brunei a Gurkha battalion, the costs of which had been met by the Brunei Government since 1968.

On Sept. 22, 1983 (i.e. shortly before Brunei attained full independence on Jan. 1, 1984) it was agreed that the garrison in Brunei of one battalion of regular British Army Gurkhas would be maintained, with this decision to be reviewed after five years if desired by either party.

The United Kingdom and India. Five agreements signed on Jan. 4, 1978, provided for British aid to India worth £164,000,000 for the 1977–78 financial year.

Under an agreement signed on Nov. 23, 1979, India purchased eight Sea Harrier jump jets for the Indian Navy, and on July 19, 1983, contracts were exchanged for India's purchase of 12 Sea King helicopters equipped with anti-ship missiles.

The United Kingdom, Kenya and Uganda. After British troops had helped to put down mutinies in the Uganda and Kenya Armies in January 1964, two new defence agreements were concluded by the British Government on March 3 and March 6, 1964, with the Governments of Uganda and Kenya respectively. The agreements provided for the continuation of British assistance in the command and training of the Uganda and Kenya Armies. Under the agreement with Kenya, Britain was granted training facilities for the Army, overflying and staging rights for the RAF, and port maintenance facilities at Mombasa for the Royal Navy.

The agreements between Britain and Uganda became inoperative by 1975, when Uganda was receiving considerable supplies of Soviet weapons.

The United Kingdom and Malawi. On Oct. 30, 1980, the (British) Overseas Development Administration agreed to provide £55,500,000 in development aid to Malawi over four years.

The United Kingdom and Mauritius. A six-year defence agreement signed on March 12, 1968 (when Mauritius attained its independence) provided for joint consultations on any request for assistance by the Government of Mauritius in the event of a threat to the island's internal security and also, inter alia, for the continuation of British facilities on the island.

An agreement signed on July 7, 1982, provided for a British payment of £4,000,000 in resettlement assistance for families moved in 1965–73 from the Chagos Archipelago (the British Indian Ocean Territory, BIOT). (The Mauritian government, however, reserved its position on the Diego Garcia atoll, claiming that it had been wrongfully detached from the BIOT in 1965.)

The United Kingdom and Singapore. An agreement regarding UK assistance for the armed forces of Singapore and the arrangement for a UK force in Singapore, signed on Dec. 1, 1971, was amended on July 26, 1978. (see also ANZUK Agreements above.)

The United Kingdom and Tonga. A treaty of friendship between Britain and Tonga was signed on Aug. 25, 1958, to replace the treaty of 1900 by which Tonga became a British-protected state while remaining self-governing. The treaty provided for greater autonomy for Tonga, which became a sovereign and independent member of the Commonwealth on June 4, 1970.

The United Kingdom and Tuvalu. At a 1978 constitutional conference it was agreed that Britain's aid to Tuvalu after the latter's achievement of independence would include capital grants for development projects (£2,620,000 for 1978–80), budgetary support (about £875,000 in 1979) and a special development fund (£2,500,000).

In July 1980 the British government agreed to extend the £2,620,000 grant beyond Dec. 31, 1980, and also to provide aid not exceeding 810,000 Australian dollars in 1981 and $A900,000 in 1982.

The United Kingdom and Uganda. An agreement signed on Aug. 17, 1984, formalized a British military training operation which had functioned since March 19, 1984, and in April 1985 this was extended to June 1986.

British Treaties with Countries outside the Commonwealth

Treaties concluded by the United Kingdom within the NATO framework may be found in the section on the North Atlantic Treaty Organization [pages 202–25] except for those with the USA, which are included in the section on US Defence Treaties [pages 374–75]. A number of other treaties involving Britain, not mentioned elsewhere in this book, are given below.

Anglo-Portuguese Alliance. A treaty of alliance concluded between King Edward III of England and King Ferdinand and Queen Eleanor of Portugal in 1373 provided for "perpetual friendship" between the two countries and mutual assistance "by sea and by land against all men".

This treaty, variously reinforced between 1386 and 1815, was reaffirmed by the Portuguese Government early in World War II and was invoked by the British Government in connexion with a temporary agreement, announced on Oct. 12, 1943, on the use by Britain of facilities in the Azores.

Treaty of Utrecht. Under the Treaty of Utrecht of 1713, which ended the War of the Spanish Succession and by which Spain's power in Europe was greatly reduced, Britain obtained the "full and intire propriety of the Town and Castle of Gibraltar, together with the port fortifications and forts thereunto belonging". However, if Britain should wish to "grant, sell or by any means alienate" ownership of Gibraltar, the treaty stated that Spain should be given first preference to it.

While the provisions of the treaty have not been challenged by Spain, there have been repeated disputes between Britain and Spain, e.g. in 1854 and 1908, when Spain alleged that Britain had moved Gibraltar's frontier farther north, and since 1950 when Britain first granted increased rights of internal government to the people of Gibraltar—the Spanish Government considering the new political institutions in Gibraltar to be incompatible with the Treaty of Utrecht.

The Cyprus Agreements. Agreement on the future of Cyprus was reached in London on Feb. 19, 1959, between the British, Greek and Turkish Governments and representatives of the Greek and Turkish communities in Cyprus. This agreement followed a previous agreement reached in Zürich on Feb. 11, 1959, between the Governments of Greece and Turkey.

The documents embodying these agreements, published on Feb. 23, 1959, included:

(1) A Greco-Turkish declaration on the "Basic Structure of the Republic of Cyprus";

(2) a Treaty of Guarantee between Cyprus on the one hand, and Britain, Greece and Turkey on the other, whereby Britain,

Greece and Turkey undertook to recognize and maintain "the independence, territorial integrity and security" of the Republic of Cyprus;

(3) a Treaty of Alliance between Greece, Turkey and Cyprus, whereby the three countries undertook to "co-operate for their common defence" and to "resist any attack or aggression, direct or indirect, against the independence and territorial integrity of the Republic of Cyprus";

(4) a Declaration by the British Government in which it relinquished sovereignty over the island to the Republic of Cyprus, except for two areas [see below].

It was not until July 1960 that the British and Cypriot Governments reached final agreement on the areas of the bases remaining under British sovereignty, the agreement being embodied in the Treaty of Establishment, published on July 7, 1960. This treaty defined the areas of the two bases, Akrotiri and Dhekelia, and gave Britain the right to use 31 defence sites and installations, and 10 training areas and ranges in other parts of the island.

On April 14, 1964, Cyprus unilaterally abrogated the Treaty of Alliance with Turkey.

Following the invasion of Cyprus by Turkish forces on July 20, 1974, new agreements were reached by the Foreign Ministers of Greece, Turkey and the United Kingdom in Geneva on July 30, 1974, on (i) a ceasefire, (ii) the establishment of a security zone with UN participation, (iii) the evacuation and protection by the UN Peacekeeping Force (UNFICYP—see page 22) of Turkish Cypriot enclaves occupied by Greek or Greek Cypriot forces, (iv) an exchange of prisoners of war and (v) implementation "in the shortest possible time" of a UN Security Council resolution of June 20, 1974, calling inter alia for the withdrawal from Cyprus of foreign forces other than those present under international agreements. The three powers, however, reached no agreement on the constitutional future of Cyprus, nor did the new Geneva agreements lead to the withdrawal of Turkish forces from the island.

The United Kingdom and Argentina. A treaty of amity, commerce and navigation came into force on May 12, 1825.

The United Kingdom and Bahrain. A treaty of friendship, signed on Aug. 15, 1971, replaced earlier treaties of 1882 and 1892.

The United Kingdom and Brazil. (1) Economic co-operation agreements signed on May 6, 1976, covered the supply and financing of about £300,000,000 worth of British capital goods to Brazil.

(2) A trade agreement was signed in October 1981.

The United Kingdom and Chile. Under an agreement concluded in 1984 the use of a British base on Adelaide Island (Antarctica) was transferred to Chile (although without prejudice to the two parties' positions on sovereignty in Antarctica).

The United Kingdom and China. A Joint Declaration on the ending of British sovereignty over Hong Kong was signed in Beijing on Dec. 19, 1984.

In this declaration the British government agreed to restore Hong Kong to the People's Republic of China with effect from July 1, 1997, whereupon China would establish a Hong Kong Special Administrative Region directly under the authority of China's central people's government and with "a high degree of autonomy, except in foreign and defence affairs" which were the responsibility of the central people's government. The laws currently in force in Hong Kong would remain basically unchanged. The government of the Hong Kong region would be composed of local inhabitants but have a chief executive appointed by the people's central government on the basis of the results of local elections or consultations. British and other foreign nationals might be employed as advisers or in certain public posts. The current social and economic system and the lifestyle of Hong Kong would remain unchanged. British property, ownership of enterprises, legitimate rights of inheritance and foreign investment would be protected by law. The region would retain the status of a free port and a separate customs territory, and that of an international financial centre, with a free flow of capital and the Hong Kong dollar continuing to circulate and remain freely convertible. The declaration also contained provisions for co-operation between the two sides during a transitional period until June 30, 1997.

In Annex I to the declaration it was specified that "the socialist system and socialist policies shall not be practised and Hong Kong's previous capitalist system and lifestyle shall remain unchanged for 50 years" after July 1, 1997, and that Chinese military forces in Hong Kong would be paid for by the central government and would not interfere in the internal affairs of the region.

In Annex II it was laid down that Britain and China would co-operate until the year 2000 in a Joint Liaison Group (a forum for discussion of matters arising from the transition to Chinese rule).

Annex III covered Chinese acceptance of the validity of agreements on the sale of land leases as practised in Hong Kong.

An exchange of memoranda dealt with the question of nationality. The British memorandum stated that after July 1, 1997, the estimated 2,500,000 British dependent territory citizens of the United Kingdom would continue to be entitled to travel abroad under a special new British passport (which would not entail the right to abode in Britain). The Chinese memorandum stated that they would be regarded as Chinese citizens from 1997 even if they used British travel documents.

The United Kingdom and Colombia. A treaty of friendship, commerce and navigation, signed on Feb. 16, 1866, came into force on Oct. 17, 1866, and was prolonged on Dec. 30, 1938.

The United Kingdom and Costa Rica. A treaty of friendship, commerce and navigation was signed on Nov. 27, 1849, and came into force on Feb. 20, 1850.

The United Kingdom and Denmark (then including Iceland). A treaty of peace and commerce was concluded on Feb. 13, 1666, and July 11, 1670, and was revised on Jan. 14, 1814.

The United Kingdom and France. A provisional treaty covering safety, environmental and legal aspects of a proposed cross-Channel link was signed on Feb. 12, 1986.

The United Kingdom and the Federal Republic of Germany. A cultural agreement, signed on April 18, 1958, came into force on April 17, 1959.

An agreement on compensation for British citizens persecuted by the Nazi regime was signed and came into force on June 9, 1964.

A treaty on the delimitation of the continental shelf below the North Sea between the two countries was signed on Nov. 25, 1971, and came into force on Dec. 7, 1972.

The United Kingdom, the Federal Republic of Germany and the Netherlands. Atomic energy co-operation agreements between the three countries were concluded on Nov. 24, 1968, and Dec. 19, 1969.

The United Kingdom and Guatemala. A treaty laying down the frontier between Guatemala and the then British Honduras (now Belize) was signed on April 30, 1859.

The United Kingdom and Iceland. An agreement on trade and commerce was signed on May 19, 1933.

The United Kingdom and the Republic of Ireland. The British-Irish peace treaty signed on Dec. 6, 1921, and ratified by the Irish and British parliaments on Dec. 6, 1922, recognized the independence of the Irish Free State and granted it dominion status within the British Commonwealth. The treaty laid down that Northern Ireland would not be subject to the rule of the parliament and government of the Irish Free State. (The latter became the Republic of Ireland under a new constitution on Dec. 21, 1949, and left the Commonwealth.)

An Anglo-Irish free trade agreement of 1965 came into force on July 1, 1966.

On Nov. 6, 1981, it was agreed by the British and Irish governments to set up an Anglo-Irish Inter-Governmental Council which would meet regularly at ministerial and official level to discuss matters of common concern.

On Nov. 15, 1985, the Council signed, at Hillsborough (Northern Ireland), an agreement designed to "promote peace and stability in Northern Ireland". The agreement, the terms of which had been agreed by the two governments on the previous day, principally (i) affirmed that any change in the status of Northern Ireland would only come about with the consent of the majority of the people of Northern Ireland, while recognizing that the present wish of a majority there was for no change in that status, and (ii) established, within the framework of the Anglo-Irish Inter-Governmental Council, an Intergovernmental Conference concerned with Northern Ireland and with relations between the two parts of the island of Ireland, which would deal on a regular basis with political matters, with security and related matters, with legal matters (including the administration of justice) and with the promotion of cross-border co-operation. The Hillsborough Agreement was approved by the Irish and British parliaments on Nov. 21 and 27, 1985, respectively.

The United Kingdom and Japan. An atomic energy co-operation agreement was signed on March 6, 1968.

The United Kingdom and Liberia. A treaty of friendship and commerce was signed on July 23, 1908.

The United Kingdom and Mexico. A treaty laying down the frontier between Mexico and Belize was signed on July 8, 1983.

The United Kingdom and Mozambique. Under a £500,000 military aid programme announced on July 2, 1985, Britain was to provide military training for Mozambican forces (to take place in Zimbabwe).

The United Kingdom and Nepal. (1) An agreement on the employment of Gurkha troops in the British Army was signed on Nov. 9, 1947.

(2) A treaty of peace and friendship was signed on Oct. 30, 1950. The treaty, which laid down that each country would acknowledge and respect the independence of the other, replaced an earlier treaty of 1923, which had been made partially invalid through the independence of India and Pakistan.

The United Kingdom and Norway. An atomic energy co-operation agreement was signed in March 1968.

The United Kingdom and Oman. A treaty of friendship, commerce and navigation, signed on Dec. 20, 1951, came fully into force on May 19, 1952.

The United Kingdom and Pakistan. An atomic energy co-operation agreement was signed on July 26, 1970.

The United Kingdom and Qatar. A treaty of friendship came into force on Sept. 1, 1971, replacing a treaty of 1916 under which Britain had been responsible for Qatar's defence and foreign relations.

The United Kingdom and Saudi Arabia. An agreement signed on Sept. 26, 1985, on the sale of 132 British-made military aircraft was said to be worth US$5,640 million. The British government was also reported to have promised to participate in a number of industrial and technical projects in Saudi Arabia.

The United Kingdom and South Africa. A commercial agreement was signed on Aug. 31, 1935.

The United Kingdom and Spain. Under an agreement signed on Nov. 27, 1984, the frontier between Gibraltar and Spain, closed to all traffic since June 1969, was re-opened on Feb. 4–5, 1985. In a note to the agreement the Spanish government claimed that Britain had inter alia agreed to discuss "both the theme of sovereignty of the territory referred to in the Treaty of Utrecht [see page 315] as well as the sovereignty of the isthmus, which was never ceded to Britain".

An agreement on economic and cultural co-operation was signed on Feb. 5, 1985.

The United Kingdom and Sweden. Early treaties were signed as follows: A treaty of peace and commerce on April 11, 1654; a trade treaty on July 17, 1656; another treaty of peace and commerce on Oct. 16, 1661; a treaty of alliance on Feb. 5, 1766; a treaty of peace, union and friendship at Örebro on July 18, 1812; and a treaty on commerce and navigation on March 18, 1826.

An agreement on co-operation in the use of nuclear energy for peaceful purposes, signed on Sept. 20, 1957, was amended on Feb. 14, 1964, extended on Sept. 19, 1967, and again amended on April 25, 1975.

The United Kingdom and Switzerland. A treaty of friendship, commerce and reciprocal establishment was signed on Sept. 6, 1855, in force from March 6, 1856, and applied to Liechtenstein on April 26, 1924, and July 14, 1947.

A co-operation agreement on the use of atomic energy for peaceful purposes was signed on Aug. 11, 1964.

The United Kingdom and Thailand. A treaty of commerce and navigation signed in Bangkok on Nov. 23, 1937, was temporarily prolonged by an exchange of notes on Sept. 24–Nov. 15, 1973.

The United Kingdom and the United Arab Emirates. A treaty of friendship, concluded on Dec. 2, 1971, replaced earlier 150-year-old treaties with the Trucial Coast sheikhdoms.

The United Kingdom and Venezuela. (1) A treaty of friendship, commerce and navigation, originally signed on April 18, 1825, with Colombia (of which Venezuela was then an integral part), was applied to Venezuela under a convention of Oct. 29, 1934.

(2) An agreement on procedure for the settlement of a territorial dispute between Britain and Venezuela, relating to some 60,000 square miles of territory in British Guiana (now Guyana), was signed on Feb. 17, 1966.

The agreement was supplemented by a Protocol of Port of Spain (Trinidad) signed on June 18, 1970, by the United Kingdom, Guyana and Venezuela, which placed a 12-year moratorium on the territorial dispute, to be renewable for successive 12-year periods. (On Dec. 11, 1981,

Venezuela notified the United Kingdom that it would not renew the moratorium, which was due to expire in June 1982.)

(3) An agreement on economic and industrial co-operation was initialled in London on Nov. 23, 1976, and signed in Caracas on Aug. 12, 1977.

The United Kingdom and Zaïre. A general agreement on co-operation in development matters was signed on Oct. 11, 1976.

The British Government disclosed on Nov. 2, 1978, that it had agreed to supply Zaïre with military equipment (at a cost of about £10,000,000) for defence purposes only.

British Extradition Treaties

The United Kingdom has concluded extradition treaties or agreements on the dates shown with the following countries:

Austria, Dec. 3, 1873.

Belgium, Oct. 29, 1901; supplemented March 5, 1907.

Brazil, Nov. 11, 1872.

Denmark, March 31, 1873.

France, Aug. 14, 1876.

Germany (now the Federal Republic of Germany), May 14, 1872; in force from July 18, 1872; partly reapplied and amended, Feb. 23, 1960, with effect from Sept. 1, 1960; continued by a new agreement signed on Dec. 5, 1983, and Jan. 1, 1985, and in force from Jan. 25, 1985. (It also applied to former British dependencies, now independent countries—Dominica, Fiji, Grenada, Jamaica, Kenya, Lesotho, Malawi, Malta, Mauritius, St Lucia, St Vincent and the Grenadines, Swaziland, Tonga and Uganda.)

Greece, Sept. 24, 1910.

Hungary, Dec. 3, 1873.

Iceland, March 31, 1873; extended, Nov. 25, 1937; supplemented, Oct. 25, 1938.

Italy, Feb. 5, 1873.

The Netherlands, Sept. 26, 1898.

Norway, June 26, 1873.

Paraguay, Sept. 12, 1908, supplemented Sept. 13/30, 1933; Oct. 2, 1940; Oct. 2, 1944.

Portugal, Oct. 17, 1892; supplemented Jan. 20, 1932; extended July 16/Aug. 14, 1934.

Spain, July 22, 1985.

Sweden, April 26, 1963; amended Dec. 6, 1965; June 6, 1966; April 19, 1979; and Feb. 19, 1980.

Switzerland, Nov. 26, 1880 (terminated for Ireland on Dec. 19, 1934).

The United States, see under US extradition treaties, page 388.

Treaties and Agreements among Commonwealth Countries other than the United Kingdom

Australia and Canada. Agreements on the peaceful uses of nuclear energy were signed on Aug. 4, 1959, and on March 9, 1981.

Trade agreements were signed on Feb. 12, 1960, and Oct. 24–25, 1973.

An agreement on the launching of a Canadian scientific rocket from Woomera was signed on Aug. 26–27, 1981.

Australia and Cyprus. A trade agreement was signed and came into force on Dec. 9, 1983.

Australia and India. An agreement on Australian aid in the defence of India with effect from Dec. 1, 1962, was signed in New Delhi on Dec. 3, 1963. It related to the Sino-Indian border conflict at the time.

A cultural agreement was signed and came into force on Oct. 21, 1971.

An agreement on co-operation in science and technology was signed and came into force on Feb. 26, 1975.

A trade agreement was signed and came into force on Aug. 2, 1975.

Australia and Malaysia. A trade agreement was signed and came into force on Aug. 26, 1958, and was amended on July 25, 1968, and on Feb. 21, 1975.

A cultural agreement was signed on Oct. 16, 1975.

Australia and New Zealand. A trade agreement of Sept. 5, 1933, was amended on April 27, 1970.

A free trade agreement, signed on Aug. 31, 1965, in force from Jan. 1, 1966, was extended on June 30, 1977.

A closer economic relations and trade agreement, concluded on March 28, 1983, with effect from Jan. 1, 1983, provided for a bilateral free-trade area with the immediate removal of tariffs of less than 5 per cent, the gradual removal of other tariffs and export incentives, and the removal of import licensing by 1995.

Australia and Papua New Guinea. An agreement on trade and commercial relations, signed on Nov. 6, 1976, came into force on Feb. 1, 1977, and was continued on March 7, 1983.

An agreement regarding the status of forces in each state in the territory of the other state, signed on Jan. 26, 1977, came into force on Sept. 14, 1978.

A treaty on the demarcation of the Torres Strait border between Australia and Papua New Guinea was signed in Sydney (New South Wales) on Dec. 18, 1978. The treaty involved agreement on a seabed resources delimitation line between the two countries to the north of several islands under Australian sovereignty and the recognition of a "protected zone" which included islands on both sides of the above delimitation line and in which the inhabitants would enjoy freedom of movement in pursuit of their traditional way of life, mining and oil drilling would be prohibited for 10 years, and there would be an "equitable division" of fishing rights. The treaty came into force on Feb. 15, 1985.

Australia and Singapore. A cultural agreement was signed on Sept. 26, 1975.

From 1982 onwards it was agreed that Singapore's armed forces would exercise extensively in Australia (with a Singapore military attaché or adviser to be appointed to Australia).

Australia and Sri Lanka. A trade agreement was signed on Aug. 20, 1932.

Bangladesh and Canada. A general agreement concerning development co-operation was signed on Dec. 14, 1979.

Bangladesh and India. (1) A 25-year treaty of friendship and co-operation, signed in Dhaka on May 19, 1972, provided inter alia that neither country would participate in any military alliance directed agianst the other; both would refrain from aggression against each other; neither would give any assistance to a third party involved in an armed conflict against the other; and, in the event of an attack or threat of attack against either, both parties would immediately enter into consultations in order to take measures to eliminate the threat.

(2) Among other agreements concluded between Bangladesh and India was one (of April 9, 1972) providing for the establishment of a permanent Joint River Commission to formulate plans for flood control, irrigation projects and the linking of power grids, and on April 29, 1972, it was officially announced that complete agreement on these and other matters had been reached.

(3) A border demarcation agreement signed in May 1974, provided for the exchange of 125 Indian enclaves in Bangladesh for 75 Bangladesh enclaves in India without payment of compensation for the additional areas going to Bangladesh. In a joint declaration issued on the same day agreement was announced on economic co-operation between the two countries, with India granting credits for various projects in Bangladesh and also for Indian imports from that country.

(4) An agreement on the division of the Ganges waters at the Farakka barrage (on the Indian side of the two countries' border), which had come into operation on April 21, 1975, was signed on Nov. 5, 1977. The agreement, due to expire on Nov. 4, 1982, was on Oct. 7, 1982, extended for 18 months.

(5) A protocol signed on Aug. 1, 1982, covered water transit and fixed India's contributions for maintaining waterways and installing navigation aids for Indian vessels in transit to and from Assam through Bangladesh.

(6) Agreements signed on Oct. 7, 1982, covered the creation of a joint economic commission at ministerial level; the leasing by India of the Tin Bigha corridor to Bangladesh in perpetuity (to connect Bangladesh with four enclaves in the Indian state of West Bengal).

(7) An understanding on the sharing of river waters was reached on Oct. 17, 1985, and included a long-term scheme for augmenting the flow of water at the Farakka barrage (see (4) above).

Bangladesh and Malaysia. A trade agreement was signed on Dec. 1, 1977, and an economic and technical agreement on April 11, 1979.

Bangladesh and Zambia. An agreement on cultural, economic and technical co-operation was signed on Nov. 19, 1983.

Canada and Ghana. A technical assistance agreement on military training was signed on Feb. 14, 1978.

Canada and India. (1) An exchange of notes implementing a statement of principles for co-operative economic development of India took place on Sept. 10, 1951.

(2) A nuclear reactor agreement was concluded on April 28, 1956.

(3) An agreement on the construction of the Kundah hydroelectric projects (under the Colombo Plan—see page 311) was signed on Dec. 29, 1956.

(4) An atomic energy co-operation agreement was signed on Nov. 15, 1963.

Canada and Sri Lanka. An exchange of notes implementing a statement of principles for co-operative development of Ceylon (now Sri Lanka) took place on July 11, 1952.

Canada and Tanzania. An agreement concerning the provision of military training and advisory assistance was signed on Nov. 4, 1965.

India and Malaysia. An agreement on economic and technical co-operation was signed on Jan. 24, 1979, and a cultural agreement in 1980.

India and Mauritius. Cultural agreements were signed on Feb. 6, 1973, and on Feb. 18, 1984.

India and Sri Lanka. (1) An agreement on the demarcation of the boundary between India and Sri Lanka in the waters of the Palk Strait (between the two countries) was signed on June 28, 1974. Under this agreement India recognized Sri Lanka's claim to the (uninhabited) island of Kachchativu (which had been in dispute since 1910).

(2) An agreement on the maritime boundary between the Gulf of Mannar (west of Sri Lanka) and the Bay of Bengal was signed on March 23, 1976, and came into force on May 10 of that year. It supplemented the above agreement on the Palk Strait and recognized each country's economic zone extending to 200 miles from the coastline, or to the median line where these zones overlapped.

Kenya and Tanzania and **Kenya and Uganda** concluded economic co-operation agreements with each other in 1983.

Kenya and Zambia. An agreement concluded on Sept. 8, 1982, provided for the formation of a permanent commission responsible for the planning and implementation of a bilateral programme of co-operation.

Malaysia and New Zealand. A trade agreement of 1961 was amended on Jan. 14, 1975.

Malaysia and Singapore. To strengthen bilateral relations a joint intergovernmental committee, directly responsible to the Prime Ministers of the two countries, was established in December 1980.

Agreement was reached in December 1981 on a fixed boundary line in the Strait of Johore and on the use of more land for the Royal Malaysian Navy's Woodlands base.

On Aug. 23, 1982, it was agreed that Malaysia would supply liquefied natural gas to cover between 30 and 50 per cent of Singapore's energy needs and that there would be a joint air shuttle service as well as greater economic co-operation and investment.

Malaysia and Sri Lanka. A cultural agreement was signed on April 21, 1983.

Mauritius and Seychelles. An agreement on economic, commercial, technical and cultural co-operation was concluded on July 18, 1982.

New Zealand and Western Samoa. A treaty of friendship between the two countries, signed on Aug. 1, 1962, provided for New Zealand to represent Western Samoa in foreign and diplomatic relations except at the United Nations. The treaty was expanded by a protocol (drawn up as a result of an agreement of Aug. 21, 1982) providing inter alia for the relinquishment of Western Samoans' right to New Zealand citizenship but also for the granting of the right to acquire New Zealand citizenship to all Western Samoans currently living in New Zealand.

Tanzania and Uganda. An agreement providing for military co-operation was on Aug. 23, 1981, reported to have been signed but was later said to have been confined to the training of Ugandan troops by Tanzanians (who were not to be involved in security operations).

Tanzania and Zambia. Under an agreement signed on March 14, 1982, a joint commission on co-operation was established. It was also agreed to take measures to improve operations on the Tazara railway (completed in 1975 with Chinese aid and linking the port of Dar es Salaam with Zambia).

Tanzania and Zimbabwe. Among several agreements signed on Dec. 5, 1980, were a friendship and co-operation agreement and an agreement on economic, technical and scientific co-operation.

Zambia and Zimbabwe. On June 27, 1980, it was agreed in principle to establish a joint co-operation commission.

Treaties and Agreements of Commonwealth Member States (other than the United Kingdom) with Countries outside the Commonwealth

Australian Treaties and Agreements

Australia has concluded treaties or agreements with the following countries outside the Commonwealth on the dates stated:

Argentina. Treaty of amity, commerce and navigation: Feb. 2, 1825.

Belgium. Provisional commercial agreement, Oct. 3, 1936; in force from Jan. 1, 1937; amended Feb. 16–March 26, 1954.

Brazil. Trade agreement, Feb. 23, 1978; in force from Aug. 25, 1978.

Ecuador. Treaty of amity, commerce and navigation: April 18, 1825.

Ethiopia. Treaty of friendship: May 14, 1897.

Finland. Agreement on the transfer of nuclear material between Australia and Finland: July 20, 1978; entry into force on Feb. 9, 1980.

France. Commercial agreement, Nov. 27, 1936; in force from Jan. 1, 1937; applied Sept. 21, 1949.
Cultural agreement, June 20, 1977; in force from April 27, 1978.
Transitional agreement on conversion and/or enrichment in France of Australian-origin nuclear material supplied to Japan, Oct. 30, 1980.
Agreement on nuclear transfers between Australia and France (in respect of the latter's Pacific territories), Jan. 7, 1981; in force from Sept. 12, 1981.
Agreement on maritime delimitation between Australia and France, Jan. 4, 1982; in force from Jan. 10, 1983.

The Federal Republic of Germany. Trade agreement, Oct. 14, 1959; in force from July 1, 1960; with protocols of Feb. 18, 1961, Aug. 11, 1961, and Dec. 22, 1961.
Agreement on launching of a Skylark vehicle and payload at Woomera for scientific purposes, Dec. 19, 1974, and Feb. 11, 1975.
Agreement on scientific and technical co-operation, Aug. 24, 1976; in force from Oct. 25, 1976.
Agreement on launching of two scientific payloads from Woomera for scientific purposes, Feb. 16, 1979.
Agreement on reciprocal safeguarding of classified material, Nov. 27, 1979.

Greece. Agreement on cultural co-operation, Nov. 20, 1979; in force from April 29, 1981.

Iceland. Exchange of notes on most-favoured-nation tariff treatment, Nov. 13, 1952; in force from Nov. 17, 1952.

Indonesia. Cultural agreement, June 14, 1968. An agreement on the establishment of seabed boundaries between the two countries, May 18, 1971; supplemented by a further agreement of Oct. 9, 1972, on such boundaries in the area of the Timor and Arafura Seas. Both agreements came into force on Nov. 8, 1973.
Agreement for the extension of a trade agreement of Dec. 17, 1959, Jan. 28, 1972 (with effect from July 1, 1970).
Agreement on certain boundaries between Indonesia and Papua New Guinea, Feb. 12, 1973; in force from Nov. 26, 1974. (See also page 329.)

Iran. Cultural agreement, Sept. 25, 1974; in force from June 2, 1975.
Trade agreement, Sept. 25, 1974; in force from Nov. 11, 1974.

Iraq. Agreement on trade and economic and technical co-operation, March 11, 1980; in force from April 29, 1980.

Israel. Agreement on most-favoured-nation treatment, Sept. 6, 1951; in force from Sept. 17, 1951.

Italy. Cultural co-operation agreement, Jan. 8, 1975; in force from May 28, 1975.
Economic and commercial co-operation agreement, Sept. 26, 1984.

Japan. Agreement on commerce, July 6, 1957.
Agreement on co-operation in civil uses of atomic energy, Aug. 7, 1962.
Agreement for co-operation in peaceful uses of atomic energy, Feb. 21, 1972; in force from July 28, 1972.
Cultural agreement, Nov. 1, 1974; in force from Feb. 9, 1976.
Basic treaty of friendship and co-operation, June 16, 1976; in force from Aug. 21, 1977. Under this treaty the two sides agreed (i) to "endeavour to facilitate, strengthen and diversify mutual understanding and co-operation in . . . the political, economic, labour relations, human rights, legal, scientific, technological, social, cultural, professional, sporting and environmental fields"; (ii) to promote the further strengthening and development of trade on a fair and stable basis, recognizing each other as a "stable and reliable" supplier and market; (iii) to accord to each other's nationals "fair and equitable treatment" with respect to their entry, stay, departure and business and professional activities; and (iv) to review periodically the general operation of the treaty at ministerial level.
Agreement on co-operation in research and development in science and technology, Nov. 27, 1980.
Agreement for co-operation in peaceful uses of nuclear energy, March 5, 1982; in force from Aug. 17, 1982.

Jordan. Agreement on co-operation: Oct. 21, 1977; entry into force on Sept. 5, 1978.

The Republic of Korea. Trade agreement, Sept. 21, 1965.

Cultural agreement, May 11, 1971; in force from July 9, 1972.

Agreement on the development of trade and economic relations, June 17, 1975.

Agreement on co-operation in peaceful uses of nuclear energy and the transfer of nuclear material, May 2, 1979.

Kuwait. Agreement on economic and technical co-operation, April 22, 1982; in force from Nov. 8, 1982.

Liberia. Agreement providing for the maintenance of mutual most-favoured-nation treatment, July 23, 1908.

Luxembourg. Commercial agreement, Oct. 8, 1936; in force from Jan. 1, 1937.

Mexico. Basic agreement on scientific and technical co-operation, June 24, 1981; in force from March 4, 1982.

Monaco. Commercial agreement, Nov. 27, 1936; in force from Jan. 1, 1937.

Morocco. Convention of commerce and navigation, Dec. 9, 1856.

Oman. Agreement on trade and economic and technical co-operation, Oct. 20, 1981; in force from Feb. 13, 1982.

Peru. Treaty of friendship, commerce and navigation, April 10, 1850.

The Philippines. Trade agreements, June 16, 1965, and June 25, 1975; the latter in force from May 11, 1979.

Cultural agreement, April 15, 1977; in force from Feb. 20, 1980.

Agreement on co-operation in peaceful uses of nuclear energy and the transfer of nuclear material, Aug. 8, 1978; in force from May 11, 1982.

Saudi Arabia. Agreement on economic and technical co-operation, March 23, 1980; in force from May 18, 1981.

South Africa. Trade agreement, Aug. 31–Sept. 3, 1935; in force from July 1, 1935.

Sweden. Agreement on conditions and controls for nuclear transfers for peaceful purposes between Australia and Sweden, March 1, 1981; in force from May 22, 1981; amended July 12, 1982.

Switzerland. Treaty of friendship, commerce and reciprocal establishment; Sept. 26, 1855, with additional convention signed on March 30, 1914. (On Jan. 9, 1920, Australia withdrew from Articles 9 and 10 of the treaty.)

Thailand. Cultural agreement, Dec. 16, 1974. Trade agreement, Oct. 5, 1979.

The United Arab Emirates. Agreement on trade and economic relations, March 6, 1985.

The United States. Agreement relating to scientific and technical co-operation, Oct. 16, 1968; extended Oct. 8 and Dec. 11, 1984.

Venezuela. Treaty of amity, commerce and navigation (concluded with Colombia), April 18, 1825; a convention of Oct. 29, 1834, applied it to Venezuela.

Nuclear safeguards agreements were signed by Australia with Finland (in July 1978), France (on Jan. 7, 1981), the Republic of Korea (on May 2, 1979), the Philippines (on Aug. 8, 1978) and Sweden (in mid-March 1981). (For agreement with the United States see page 384.)

EXTRADITION TREATIES

Australia has concluded extradition treaties with the following countries on the dates shown. The date of entry into force is shown in parenthesis where it differs from the date of signature.

Albania, July 22, 1926; exchange of notes, Dec. 11, 1955, and May 16, 1936.

Argentina, May 22, 1889.

Austria, March 29, 1973 (Feb. 5, 1975).

Belgium, Oct. 29, 1901; repeatedly expanded, most recently on July 2, 1928.

Bolivia, Feb. 22, 1892.

Chile, Jan. 26, 1897 (Jan. 13, 1928).

Colombia, Oct. 27, 1888; supplementary convention, Dec. 2, 1929.

Cuba, Oct. 3, 1904; extended April 17, 1930.

Czechoslovakia, Nov. 11, 1924 (July 12, 1927).

Ecuador, Sept. 20, 1880 (Jan. 19, 1928); supplementary convention, June 4, 1934 (Nov. 8, 1937).

El Salvador, June 23, 1881.

Finland, June 7, 1984 (June 23, 1985).

France, Aug. 14, 1876; amending conventions, Feb. 13, 1896; Oct. 17, 1908.

The Federal Republic of Germany, May 14, 1872 (Aug. 17, 1930); new treaty, May 8, 1984.

Greece, Sept. 24, 1910 (April 19, 1928).

Guatemala, July 4, 1885; amended May 30, 1914.

Haiti, Dec. 7, 1874.

Hungary, Dec. 3, 1873; supplementary treaty, Sept. 18, 1936; treaty revived, Feb. 10, 1947 (July 10, 1948).

Iceland, March 31, 1873; amended Oct. 25, 1938 (Dec. 31, 1939).

Iraq, May 2, 1932 (Aug. 31, 1934).

Israel, Dec. 4, 1975 (Jan. 3, 1976).

Italy, Nov. 28, 1973 (May 10, 1976).

Liberia, Dec. 16, 1892.

Luxembourg, Nov. 24, 1880; supplementary convention, Jan. 23, 1937 (Aug. 1, 1938); amended May 29, 1939.

Mexico, Sept. 7, 1886.

Monaco, Dec. 17, 1891.

The Netherlands, Sept. 26, 1898.

Nicaragua, April 19, 1905.

Norway, June 26, 1873; supplementary agreement, Feb. 18, 1907.

Panama, Aug. 25, 1906.

Paraguay, Sept. 12, 1908; supplementary convention, Sept. 30, 1933 (Nov. 22, 1942).

Peru, Jan. 26, 1905.

Poland, Jan. 11, 1932.

Portugal, Oct. 17, 1892; supplementary convention, Jan. 20, 1932.

Romania, March 21, 1893; explanatory protocol, March 13, 1894.

San Marino, Oct. 16, 1899.

Spain, June 4, 1878; amended Feb. 19, 1889.

Sweden, March 20, 1973 (March 10, 1974).

Switzerland, Nov. 26, 1880; supplement, June 29, 1904; supplementary treaty, Dec. 19, 1974.

Thailand, March 4, 1911.

The United States, Dec. 22, 1931.

Uruguay, March 26, 1884; amended March 20, 1891.

Yugoslavia. Dec. 6, 1900.

Other Commonwealth Countries' Agreements

The Bahamas and Haiti. An immigration treaty signed on Sept. 2, 1985, provided inter alia that illegal Haitian immigrants in the Bahamas were required to register with the Bahamas authorities by Nov. 27, 1985, and that only those who had arrived before Dec. 31, 1980, or were married to a Bahamian or owned real estate would be permitted to remain in the Bahamas (where up to 40,000 Haitians were thought to be liable to expulsion).

The Bahamas and Iceland. Agreement on the validity of an extradition treaty, March 3, 1978; in force from July 22, 1980.

Bangladesh and Bhutan. Trade agreement and economic and technical co-operation agreement, Feb. 5, 1984.

Bangladesh and Burma. The common border of the two countries was formally agreed on Aug. 12, 1985, on the basis of a map prepared by a joint survey department under a 1979 agreement.

Bangladesh and Japan. On June 20, 1985, Japan agreed to lend Bangladesh about $100,000,000 for commodity purchases, a telecommunications project and a steel mill project.

Bangladesh and Pakistan. A first trade agreement, providing for most-favoured-nation treatment in trade between the two countries, April 30, 1976.
Cultural agreement, Oct. 10, 1979.

Bangladesh and Sweden. An agreement on development co-operation from July 1, 1983, to June 30, 1985, June 10, 1983.

Bangladesh and Switzerland. A technical co-operation agreement, April 7, 1976.

Bangladesh and the United Arab Emirates. Agreement on cultural co-operation, March 1978.

Botswana and France. An agreement on cultural, scientific and technical co-operation was signed on Nov. 17, 1982.

Botswana and the Federal Republic of Germany. Technical co-operation agreement, Oct. 3, 1974.

Botswana and South Africa. Boundary agreement, March 8–9, 1973.

Botswana, Lesotho and Swaziland with South Africa. Customs union agreement, Dec. 11, 1967; amended Oct. 27, Nov. 10 and 27, and Dec. 18, 1975.
Monetary agreement, Dec. 5, 1974.

Canada and France. (1) Exchange of notes on exchange of defence science information (May 25, 1962).
(2) Agreement on a wide-ranging programme of industrial and technological co-operation (Oct. 22, 1974).
(Agreements on co-operation between France and the Province of Quebec were signed on Dec. 5, 1974.)

Canada and the Federal Republic of Germany. Agreement on co-operation in peaceful uses of nuclear energy, Dec. 11, 1957; in force from Dec. 18, 1957.
Agreement on defence scientific information, Aug. 21–28, 1964; in force from Sept. 28, 1964.
Agreement on scientific and technological co-operation, April 16, 1971; in force from June 30, 1971.
Agreement on cultural co-operation, March 3, 1975; in force from Nov. 6, 1975.
Extradition treaty, July 11, 1977; in force from Sept. 30, 1979.

Canada and Iceland. Treaties of peace and commerce, Feb. 13, 1660–61, and July 11, 1670.
Extradition convention, March 3, 1873.
Extradition agreement on merchant seamen deserters, June 21, 1881.

Canada and Japan. An agreement for co-operation in the peaceful uses of atomic energy, signed on July 2, 1979, provided inter alia for Canadian supplies of uranium to Japan; amended on Aug. 22, 1980.
An interim agreement initialled in Tokyo on Jan. 26, 1978, had provided for the resumption of Canadian uranium supplies to Japan, which had been suspended by Canada since Jan. 1, 1977.

Agreement on limitation of Japanese car exports to Canada, May 29, 1981.

Canada and the Republic of Korea. An agreement for the purchase of a heavy-water nuclear reactor from Canada, Jan. 26, 1976.

Canada and Norway. Exchange of notes concerning the organization of a "Canada-Norway defence science information exchange project" (May 24, 1960).

Canada and Pakistan. (1) An agreement on the peaceful uses of atomic energy, May 14, 1959.
(2) An exchange of notes implementing a statement of principles for co-operative economic development of Pakistan, Sept. 10, 1951.

Canada and Sweden. Agreement concerning defence research, development and production (Feb. 3, 1975).

Canada and Switzerland. Agreement on co-operation in the peaceful uses of nuclear energy, March 6, 1958; renewed, Dec. 1, 1971.

Canada and Turkey. A 15-year nuclear energy co-operation agreement, June 18, 1985.

Canada and the United States. The Webster-Ashburton Treaty to settle and define the boundaries between the United States and British possessions in North America, Aug. 9, 1842; in force from Oct. 13, 1842.
The Oregon Treaty establishing the boundary on the north-west coast westwards of the Rocky Mountains, June 15, 1846; in force from July 17, 1846.
Treaties concerning the boundary between the two countries, April 11, 1908, in force from June 4, 1908, and Feb. 4, 1925, in force from July 17, 1925.
Agreement relating to the Upper Columbia River Basin, Feb. 25, and March 3, 1944; in force from latter date.
Agreements relating to the St Lawrence seaway project, June 30, 1952; Nov. 12, 1953; and Aug. 17, 1954 (followed by numerous related agreements and amendments).
Treaty relating to co-operative development of the water resources of the Columbia River Basin, Jan. 17, 1961; in force form Sept. 16, 1964; with related agreements of Jan. 22 and Sept. 16, 1964, and Oct. 4, 1965.
Extradition treaty, Dec. 3, 1971; amended June 28 and July 9, 1974; in force from March 22, 1976.
(For US-Canadian agreements on defence and co-operation, see pages 367–68 and 377 respectively.)

Canada and Zaïre. A general agreement for development co-operation was signed on Nov. 11, 1977.

The Cook Islands and the United States. In a treaty signed in June 1980 the United States formally relinquished claims to four northern islands in the Cook Islands group (dating back to 1856), while provisions were also agreed on the overlap area of the respective offshore economic zones of American Samoa and the Cook Islands. The treaty was ratified by the US Senate on June 21, 1983.

Cyprus and the Federal Republic of Germany. Trade agreement, agreement on economic co-operation and agreement on technical assistance, Oct. 30, 1961.
Cultural agreement, Feb. 4, 1971; in force from Feb. 5, 1971.

Cyprus and Greece. From 1982 onwards Greece gave Cyprus annual aid equivalent to £834,500,000.

Cyprus and Spain. Cultural, scientific and educational agreement, July 16, 1980.

Dominica and Venezuela. An economic co-operation agreement was signed late in January 1979.

Fiji and Iceland. Extradition treaty on merchant seamen deserters, June 21, 1881.

Fiji and Switzerland. Exchange of letters concerning the application of the Anglo-Swiss extradition treaty of Nov. 26, 1880, July 14, 1972, and Jan. 31, 1974.

The Gambia and the Federal Republic of Germany. Agreement on economic and technical co-operation, March 5, 1976.

The Gambia and Liberia. A 1974 treaty of friendship and co-operation in the political, economic and cultural fields was renewed on May 27, 1984, when it was decided to establish a joint committee to meet annually at foreign ministerial level.

The Gambia and Senegal. Agreements concluded upon The Gambia's achievement of independence on Feb. 17, 1965, provided for co-operation between the two countries in foreign affairs, defence and economic matters, and under a treaty of association signed during a visit to The Gambia by the President of Senegal on April 17–20, 1967, a permanent ministerial inter-state committee with an executive secretariat was created.
(For formation of Senegambia see Section 16.)

The Gambia and the United States. Extradition treaty between the United States and the United Kingdom, July 6, 1948; applicable to The Gambia from that date.

Ghana and the Federal Republic of Germany. An agreement on economic and technical co-operation was signed on July 3, 1975.

Guyana and Venezuela. Agreement was reached on Feb. 9, 1985, on Venezuelan purchases of bauxite from Guyana in 1985 and an exchange of information and assistance within a wide range of economic and other activities.

India and Afghanistan. A treaty of peace and friendship, providing for closer commercial, cultural, industrial and agricultural relations between the two countries, was signed on Jan. 4, 1950. Valid in the first instance for five years, the treaty can be terminated by either party at six months' notice.

India and Algeria. An agreement on Indian oil purchases from Algeria was concluded on June 11, 1985.

India and Bhutan. A treaty of "perpetual peace and friendship" was signed on Aug. 8, 1949. It provided, inter alia, that India would not interfere in the internal administration of Bhutan; the Government of Bhutan would be guided by the advice of the Indian Government in its external relations; India would return to Bhutan an area of 32 square miles in the Dewangiri district; and there would be freedom of trade and commerce between the two countries.

A bilateral agreement on trade and commerce, Dec. 27, 1983.

India and Burma. An agreement providing for the demarcation of the frontier between India and Burma, March 19, 1967.

India and Egypt. An atomic energy co-operation agreement, September 1962.

India and France. An agreement on the Indian purchase of French Mirage-2000 aircraft, April 1982.

Agreement on Indian purchase of French long-range air-to-air Magic-2 seeker missiles for the Mirage-2000 fighter jets.

Agreement on cleaning up the Ganges River, announced on June 6, 1985.

India and the Federal Republic of Germany. Trade agreements (i) of March 19, 1952, in force from Nov. 1, 1952, extended on Dec. 10, 1984, until Dec. 31, 1986; (ii) of March 31, 1955, with later exchange of letters and protocol, also extended on Dec. 10, 1984, until Dec. 31, 1986.

Cultural agreement, March 20, 1969; in force from Sept. 11, 1969.

Technical co-operation agreement, Dec. 31, 1971; amended Feb. 8–March 7, 1979.

Agreement on Indian purchase of two sub-marines from the Federal Republic, with further submarines to be assembled in India, December 1981.

India and Iceland. Treaty of peace and commerce, Feb. 13, 1660–61.

Extradition convention, March 31, 1873; supplementary convention, Oct. 25, 1938.

Treaty on extradition of merchant seamen deserters, June 21, 1881.

India and Indonesia. An agreement delimiting the continental shelf boundary between India and Indonesia was signed on Aug. 8, 1974, and came into force on Dec. 17 of that year.

Under an agreement signed in New Delhi on Jan. 14, 1977, the two countries redefined their respective sea boundaries, extending the existing median line 48 nautical miles off the coasts of both the (Indian) Nicobar Islands and Sumatra

(established under the 1974 agreement) north-eastwards into the Andaman Sea (towards the Isthmus of Kra) to a possible trijunction point between the waters of India, Indonesia and Thailand, and south-westwards into the Indian Ocean up to a distance of 200 miles from the two countries' respective coasts—with each country exercising sovereignty and exclusive jurisdiction over the continental shelf and the seabed resources within the newly agreed boundaries. Instruments of ratification of this agreement were exchanged on Aug. 15, 1977.

India, Indonesia and Thailand. A trilateral agreement, determining the trijunction point of the seabed boundaries of the three countries in the Andaman Sea (roughly 100 nautical miles from the nearest point of their respective coastlines), was signed in New Delhi on June 22, 1978 (thus complementing the bilateral agreements concluded between the three countries on their common seabed boundaries in the Andaman Sea).

India and Iran. An agreement to increase Iranian exports to India in 1984–85 to US$225,000,000, May 1984.

India and Italy. An exchange of notes on economic co-operation took place in New Delhi on Oct. 30, 1975.

India and Maldives. An agreement signed on Dec. 28, 1976, defined the maritime boundary between the two countries as running mainly along the median line between the west coast of India and Maldives and embracing an area extending westwards into the Arabian Sea up to 200 nautical miles from the western atoll of Maldives. It also provided for exclusive jurisdiction over the continental shelf and the exclusive economic zone and their resources for each state on its own side of the boundary.

India and Nepal. A treaty providing for "everlasting peace and friendship" between the Governments of India and Nepal was signed on July 31, 1950. The treaty states, inter alia, that the two countries recognize the "complete sovereignty, territorial integrity and independence" of each other; that Nepal should be free to import from and through Indian territory the arms, ammunition, material and equipment necessary for her security; and that each government would "give, to nationals of the other in its territory, national treatment with regard to participation in the industrial and economic development of such territory . . .".

Cancellation of the arms agreement by Nepal was announced on June 24, 1969.

Two treaties which were signed on March 17, 1978, and came into force on March 25 of that year were (i) a seven-year treaty on transit, providing Nepal and Bangladesh with free access across Indian territory to each other's markets and (ii) a five-year trade treaty (including preferences for a wider range of Nepalese-manufactured goods in Indian markets). At the same time agreement was reached on the control of unauthorized trade between the two countries.

Further co-operation agreements were signed in April and September 1978, involving the promotion of Nepal's industrialization and the construction of a hydroelectric project.

An Indian-Nepalese intergovernmental committee decided on March 21, 1983, to extend the trade treaty for another five years and to maintain co-operation in controlling unauthorized trade.

India and Pakistan. (1) *Settlement of Border Disputes.* Agreements were concluded between the Governments of India and Pakistan in September 1958 and October 1959 in regard to a number of border disputes. The latter agreement also laid down "ground rules" governing the conduct of army and police forces on both sides, and principles for provisional demarcation.

(2) *The Indus Waters Treaty.* A treaty settling the long-standing dispute between India and Pakistan regarding the allocation of the waters of the Indus river system was signed on Sept. 19, 1960. Under the treaty, the waters of the three eastern Rivers (Ravi, Beas and Sutlej) are in general allocated to India, those of the three western Rivers (Indus, Jhelum and Chenab) to Pakistan. The treaty states that "both countries recognize their common interest in the optimum development of the rivers, and declare their intention to co-operate by mutual agreement to the fullest possible extent". Provision was made for the setting up of a Permanent Indus Commission, composed of one member appointed by each government and with responsibility for implementing the provisions of the treaty.

(3) *The Tashkent Declaration* was signed at the end of a meeting between Prime Minister Shastri of India and President Ayub Khan of Pakistan, held at Tashkent in Uzbekistan (USSR) on Jan. 4–10, 1966, in an attempt to solve the Indo-Pakistan dispute which had reached a crisis with the outbreak of hostilities over Kashmir in August 1965. Under the declaration India and Pakistan pledged themselves, inter alia, to restore "normal and peaceful relations" between the two countries; to withdraw their armed forces, not later than Feb. 25, 1966, to the positions they held before the outbreak of hostilities; to repatriate captured prisoners of war; to restore diplomatic and economic relations between the two countries; to end hostile propaganda; and to deal with the question of refugees and illegal immigrants.

(4) *The Simla Agreement*, signed on July 3, 1972, and ratified by Pakistan on July 15 and by India on Aug. 1–3, came into effect on Aug. 4, 1972. It was designated to end conflict and confrontation between the two countries after the war which had led to the secession of Bangladesh from Pakistan. The agreement provided in particular for the withdrawal of armed forces to their side of the international border between the two countries, while in Jammu and Kashmir both sides would respect the line of control which had resulted from a ceasefire on Dec. 17, 1971—"without prejudice to the recognized position of either side" on the status of Jammu and Kashmir.

(5) *The 1973 Repatriation Agreement.* An agreement was signed by India and Pakistan on Aug. 28, 1973, in New Delhi on the repatriation of Pakistani prisoners of war and civilian internees held since the 1971 conflict, as well as nationals of Bangladesh in Pakistan and Pakistanis in Bangladesh, with the exception of 195 prisoners of war. It was agreed that no trials of these 195 should take place during the repatriation period, but that on completion of repatriation Bangladesh, India and Pakistan would discuss and settle their fate.

(6) *Agreements on Normalization of Relations.* Agreements on the resumption of trade links between the two countries (which had been severed since the 1965 war) were (i) a protocol on the resumption of shipping services signed on Jan. 15, 1975, and (ii) a trade agreement of Jan. 23, 1975. Agreement on the restoration of air links, rail traffic and diplomatic relations was reached in Islamabad on May 14, 1976.

(7) An agreement on economic, scientific and technical co-operation was signed on March 10, 1983.

(8) An agreement not to attack each other's nuclear facilities was announced on Dec. 17, 1985.

(9) An agreement on bilateral economic co-operation, allowing Pakistan's private sector to trade in 42 items until then restricted to the state trading corporation, was reached on Jan. 10, 1986, when it was also agreed to set up a joint committee to consider possible joint ventures in each other's country.

India and the Philippines. A treaty affirming that there should be "perpetual peace and everlasting amity" between the two countries was signed on July 11, 1952. It is to remain in force unless terminated by either side at one year's notice.

India and Portugal. Under an agreement signed in New York on Sept. 24, 1974, Portugal expressed its readiness to relinquish all claims to Portugal's former Indian territories (Goa, Daman, Diu, Dadra and Nagar Haveli), over which India would have full sovereignty while co-operating with Portugal to preserve the Portuguese culture, language and religious monuments in these areas.

India and Spain. Agreement on cultural co-operation, Sept. 16, 1982, and a cultural agreement, April 11, 1983.

India and Sweden. Agreement on development co-operation from Oct. 1, 1983, to June 30, 1985, Sept. 15, 1983.

India and Switzerland. A technical and scientific co-operation agreement, Sept. 26, 1966.

India and Thailand. An agreement defining the seabed boundary between the two countries in the Andaman Sea, generally on the principle of the median line, June 22, 1978.

India and Turkey. An agreement on economic and technical co-operation between the two countries, July 13, 1978.

India and the United Arab Emirates. Agreement on cultural co-operation, July 1976.

India and the People's Democratic Republic of Yemen. Agreement on a number of joint ventures and other measures to improve economic co-operation, Oct. 28, 1984.

Jamaica and the Dominican Republic. Agreements on co-operation in trade, tourism, and energy, signed in the latter half of 1983.

Jamaica and the Federal Republic of Germany. Bilateral co-operation agreement, 1982 (West German aid having risen to the equivalent of US$49,055,000 in 1981).

Jamaica and Japan. Various co-operation agreements, 1981.

Jamaica and the Republic of Korea. Co-operation agreements, 1981.

Jamaica and Mexico. Outline co-operation agreement, mid-1983.

Jamaica and Mozambique. It was agreed on Oct. 11, 1977, that the two countries would strengthen their bilateral relations through trade, economic and cultural co-operation.

Jamaica and the United States. Various aid and co-operation agreements signed with Puerto Rico, 1982–83.

Jamaica and Venezuela. A trade agreement concluded in April 1975 included a bilateral arrangement on Jamaican bauxite and alumina to be supplied to Venezuela in return for fertilizer supplies by Venezuela to Jamaica. Early in 1977 a new agreement was signed on intensifying co-operation between the two countries.

Kenya and Denmark, Finland, Iceland, Norway and Sweden. Agreement on development co-operation in the co-operative sector, May 29, 1981; extended July 24/Aug. 1, 1984.

Kenya and Ethiopia. A defence agreement, providing for mutual aid in the case of attack by a third party, was concluded between Ethiopia and Kenya in November 1963 and ratified by both countries on Dec. 27, 1963.

A treaty delimitating the entire frontier between both countries was signed on June 9, 1970.

A treaty of friendship and co-operation was signed on Jan. 31, 1979, for a period of 10 years and for a further five years thereafter unless one year's notice was given by either party. The treaty contained a reference to the parties' "unwavering opposition to any country or countries which pursue an expansionist policy" (Art. 5) and also stated that they would "continue their co-operation in the political, diplomatic and military fields" and "meet for consultation from time to time" (Art. 6). The treaty also dealt with co-operation in various other fields and envisaged

the conclusion of additional agreements on matters of common interest.

Kenya and the Federal Republic of Germany. A trade and economic agreement and an agreement on technical co-operation, Dec. 4, 1964; the former agreement extended Sept. 16, 1985, until Dec. 31, 1986.

Kenya and Italy. Agreement on technical and scientific co-operation, July 8, 1981.

Kenya and Somalia. Under a memorandum of agreement signed at Arusha (Tanzania) on Oct. 28, 1967, Kenya and Somalia agreed to end border fighting (which had been in progress for many months), to restore normal relations, gradually to suspend emergency regulations in force on both sides, and to cease hostile propaganda. A co-operation agreement signed in June 1981 put an end to several years of hostility between the two states.

A border security agreement signed on Dec. 2, 1984, was to facilitate the free movement of people across the two countries' common border. It was also agreed to increase bilateral trade and to seek international aid for joint projects.

Kenya and the Sudan. A border security agreement recommending that local tribesmen on both sides of the border should be disarmed to prevent cattle rustling and to increase the security of travellers, August 1981.

Kenya and Switzerland. Technical and scientific co-operation agreement, May 5, 1970.

Kiribati and United States. Under a treaty of friendship signed by the Republic of Kiribati and the United States in September 1979, the USA formally relinquished its claim to the eight Phoenix Islands, the five Southern Line Islands and Kiritimati (Christmas) Island in the Northern Line Islands, with the treaty also providing for consultation on any military use of these 14 islands by third parties, and for the use by third parties for military purposes of the facilities constructed by the United States on three of these islands (Enderbury, Kanton and Orona) to be subject to US agreement. The treaty was ratified by the US Senate on June 21, 1983.

Lesotho and the Federal Republic of Germany. Agreement on technical co-operation, March 3, 1975.

Lesotho and South Africa. A non-aggression and mutual security agreement was signed on Jan. 25, 1986.

Lesotho and Sweden. Agreement on development co-operation from July 1, 1983, until June 30, 1985; April 14, 1983.

Malawi and South Africa. Trade agreement, Feb. 2, 1967; amended Feb. 1, 1971, and Dec. 13 and 18, 1974.

Extradition treaty, Feb. 25, 1972.

Malaysia and Bahrain. Cultural and scientific co-operation agreement, Jan. 26, 1975.

Malaysia and Egypt. Trade agreement, cultural and scientific co-operation agreement, and economic and technical co-operation agreement, Jan. 8, 1977.

Malaysia and Indonesia. Peace treaty concluding hostilities between 1964 and 1966, signed on June 1, 1966.

A treaty of friendship between Indonesia and Malaysia and another treaty establishing a boundary through the Straits of Malacca (between Sumatra and the Malay Peninsula) were signed in Kuala Lumpur on March 17, 1970. The treaty of friendship replaced an earlier treaty of April 17, 1959, and formally ended a period of "confrontation" between the two countries.

On Nov. 16, 1971, both governments issued a declaration claiming sovereignty of the Straits, which they no longer considered to be an international waterway.

(While Malaysia had extended its territorial waters limit to 12 nautical miles in August 1969, Indonesia had, in a proclamation issued on Dec. 14, 1957, claimed that all waters "around, between and connecting the islands or part of the islands of the Indonesian archipelago" were "an integral part of the inland waters subject to the absolute sovereignty of Indonesia" and had at the same time fixed the limit of Indonesia's territorial waters at 12 nautical miles "measured from straight base lines connecting the outermost points of the Republic of Indonesia", thus adding about 660,000 nautical square miles to the country's territory and thereby doubling it. This proclamation had, however, been rejected by the principal sea-faring nations of the world.)

An extradition treaty was signed on June 7, 1974.

Under a maritime treaty, signed on Feb. 25, 1982, Malaysia became the first country formally to recognize Indonesia's "archipelagic principle" whereby the latter country's 13,000 scattered islands were enclosed within territorial seas delineated by straight base lines drawn from the outermost points of the outer islands. Under the treaty, relating to parts of the South China Sea separating Peninsular Malaysia from Sabah and Sarawak, Malaysia recognized Indonesia's sovereignty and exclusive economic rights, while Indonesia undertook to respect Malaysia's traditional fishing rights, rights of free sea and air passage between Peninsular Malaysia and the Borneo states and rights to lay submarine cables and pipelines.

A revised security agreement signed on Dec. 3, 1984, contained new provisions concerning the two countries' navies, air forces and ground forces.

Malaysia, Indonesia and Thailand. Tripartite agreement on boundaries of continental shelves in the northern part of the Malacca Straits, Dec. 21, 1971.

Malaysia and Iraq. Trade, economic and technical co-operation agreement, and cultural and scientific co-operation agreement, Feb. 17, 1977.

Cultural agreement, Aug. 29, 1981.

Malaysia and Italy. Agreement on economic and technical co-operation, July 27, 1983.

Malaysia and Japan. During a visit to Malaysia by the Prime Minister of Japan it was agreed on Aug. 10, 1977, to promote co-operative relations between the two countries in the political, economic and cultural fields, with Japan granting loans to assist Malaysia's economic development plan for 1976–80 (this assistance including a credit equivalent to $80,000,000 for 1977).

Malaysia and Kuwait. Economic and technical co-operation agreement, and cultural and scientific co-operation agreement, Jan. 21, 1975.

Malaysia and Libya. Economic, scientific and technical co-operation agreement and trade agreement, Jan. 18, 1977.

Malaysia and the Netherlands. Economic co-operation treaty, June 15, 1971.

Malaysia and Norway. Agreement on economic and technical co-operation, March 1, 1982.

Malaysia and Oman. Cultural and scientific co-operation agreement, Jan. 22, 1975.

Malaysia and Pakistan. Cultural agreement, Jan. 26, 1979.

Agreement on economic and cultural co-operation, Nov. 9, 1982.

Malaysia and Qatar. Agreement on economic, technical, cultural and information co-operation, Jan. 25, 1975.

Malaysia and Saudi Arabia. Agreement on economic and technical co-operation, Jan. 29, 1975.

Malaysia and Sweden. Agreement on co-operation in family planning, July 3, 1968.

Malaysia and Thailand. Agreement on border co-operation, providing for combined operations by both countries' security forces against communist guerrillas, March 4, 1977.

Memorandum of understanding on the establishment of a joint authority for the exploitation of the resources of the seabed on the continental shelf in the Gulf of Thailand, Feb. 21, 1979.

Treaty on the delimitation of the territorial seas (with memorandum of understanding on the continental shelf boundary), Oct. 24, 1979.

Agreement on setting up a regional border commission and conducting joint counter-insurgency operations along the border against communist guerrillas, June 1983.

Malaysia and Turkey. Trade agreement, economic and technical co-operation agreement and cultural agreement, Feb. 13, 1977.

Cultural agreements, May 13, 1983, and Sept. 8, 1983.

Malaysia and the United Arab Emirates. Cultural and scientific co-operation agreement and economic and technical co-operation agreement, Jan. 25, 1975.

Malta and the Federal Republic of Germany. Agreement on cultural co-operation, Feb. 27, 1974.

Malta and Italy. In an agreement formalized on Sept. 15, 1980, (i) the government of Malta declared its neutrality and undertook not to allow foreign forces or military bases on its territory and to make its shipbuilding yards available neither to the US Navy nor to the Soviet Navy; (ii) Italy called on all countries to respect Malta's neutrality and undertook to enter into immediate consultations in the event of this neutrality being threatened or violated, and to afford Malta military assistance if deemed necessary "by the Italian side also"; and (iii) Italy promised to provide Malta, during the first few years of its neutrality, with credit facilities and technical co-operation. All clauses of the agreement except those relating to the Italian guarantees of Malta's neutrality were due for renewal in 1984, but the Maltese government announced on Dec. 4, 1984, that the agreement had not been renewed. (Malta's neutrality was recognized by the Soviet Union on Oct. 9, 1981, and by Algeria and France on Dec. 1, 1981.)

Malta and Libya. A five-year treaty of economic and security co-operation, with Malta undertaking not to permit any foreign military bases on its soil and Libya to assist in the training of Maltese forces and to provide military aid if Malta were attacked, was signed on Nov. 19, 1984.

Malta and Spain. Cultural convention, June 11, 1976.

Malta and Switzerland. Agreement on trade, protection of investments and technical co-operation, Jan. 20, 1965.

Mauritius and Egypt. Agreement on cultural, technical and scientific co-operation, March 9, 1972.
General agreement on economic, scientific and technical co-operation, Dec. 12, 1980.

Mauritius and France. Agreement on cultural and technical co-operation, June 20, 1970.
Convention on the delimitation of the Mauritian and French economic zones between the islands of Mauritius and Réunion, April 2, 1980.

Mauritius and Gabon. Trade agreement, June 22, 1984.

Mauritius and the Federal Republic of Germany. Agreement on technical co-operation, Oct. 31, 1980; in force from July 10, 1981.

Mauritius and Libya. Cultural agreement, Feb. 22, 1979.
Agreement on bilateral co-operation, Feb. 20, 1983.

Mauritius and Madagascar. Trade agreement, Dec. 14, 1984.

Mauritius and Pakistan. Cultural agreement, May 13, 1975.
Trade agreement, Dec. 2, 1984.

New Zealand and the Federal Republic of Germany. Trade agreement, April 20, 1959; in force from April 1, 1959 (list of commodities partly superseded by EEC regulations); extended Sept. 16, 1985, until Dec. 31, 1986.
Agreement on scientific and technical co-operation, Feb. 12, 1977; in force from Aug. 23, 1978.
Agreement on scientific co-operation in Antarctica, June 26, 1981.

New Zealand and Iceland. Extradition convention, March 31, 1873; supplementary convention, Oct. 25, 1938.
Treaty on extradition of merchant seamen deserters, June 21, 1881.

New Zealand and Switzerland. Trade agreement, May 5, 1938; exchange of letters, March 6, 1957.

New Zealand and the United States. Under a treaty signed in 1980 New Zealand relinquished, on behalf of its dependent territory of Tokelau, a claim to Swain's Island (administered by the United States as part of American Samoa), while the United States formally relinquished its claim to three islands which were part of Tokelau. The treaty was ratified by the US Senate on June 21, 1983.

Nigeria and Cameroon. An agreement on scientific and technical co-operation, providing for the creation of a new joint commission, April 21, 1983.

Nigeria and Chad. A treaty of friendship, co-operation and mutual assistance, together with an extradition treaty and an agreement on cultural relations, was initialled on Dec. 11, 1972. On May 15, 1984, the two sides agreed to set up a joint economic commission.

Nigeria and the Federal Republic of Germany. Trade agreement, March 25, 1963; in force from Nov. 1, 1963; extended Sept. 16, 1985, until Dec. 31, 1986.

Nigeria and Guinea. (1) An agreement on economic, scientific and technical co-operation, Feb. 14, 1973.
(2) An agreement on commercial, agricultural and industrial co-operation, April 1978.

Nigeria and Mali. A treaty of friendship, co-operation and mutual assistance was signed on March 3, 1973. It was agreed that a joint commission should be set up to plan for increased co-operation between the two countries. Agreement was also reached on cultural co-operation, a convention on the free movement of persons and goods and the expansion of an existing trade agreement.

Nigeria and Sweden. Agreement on economic, industrial, technical and scientific co-operation, Jan. 7, 1980.

Papua New Guinea and Indonesia. A border agreement designed to end the frontier problem between Inidonesia on the one hand and Australia and Papua New Guinea on the other was signed on Feb. 13, 1974. A further agreement, dealing with the administration of the border between Papua New Guinea and West Irian (Indonesia), was signed on Nov. 13, 1973, and came into force on May 26, 1974. These agreements were replaced by a new one signed on Dec. 17, 1979.

A three-year technical co-operation agreement between Papua New Guinea and Indonesia was signed on June 5, 1979.

A new border agreement, providing that Indonesia would not take reprisals against returning refugees, was signed on Oct. 29, 1984.

Papua New Guinea and Japan. Under an agreement reached on Dec. 8, 1977, Japan undertook to extend loans equivalent to US$15,000,000 for various development projects in Papua New Guinea, with Japan regarding this agreement as marking "the establishment of a new development co-operation relationship between the two countries".

Papua New Guinea and Switzerland. Exchange of letters concerning the application of the Anglo-Swiss extradition treaty of Nov. 26, 1880, Sept. 22, 1976, and Feb. 25, 1977.

St Lucia and Venezuela. (1) A treaty of friendship and co-operation was signed in February 1980, when it was announced that Venezuela would provide St Lucia with technical assistance in agriculture, education, sports, transport, tourism and energy.
(2) In September 1981 Venezuela granted St Lucia aid worth US$1,500,000 for development projects and the establishment of a joint commission to promote bilateral private-sector co-operation.

Seychelles and the Federal Republic of Germany. Agreement on technical co-operation, Nov. 24, 1978; in force from July 31, 1979.

Sierra Leone and the Federal Republic of Germany. Economic agreement, Sept. 13, 1963; extended Sept. 16, 1985, until Dec. 31, 1986.
Agreement on technical co-operation, Sept. 13, 1963; amended and extended, July 3, 1970.

Sierra Leone and Guinea. Under a defence agreement signed on March 26, 1971, Guinean troops were temporarily sent to Sierra Leone to prevent the latter country's government from being overthrown.

Singapore and France. Agreement on economic and industrial co-operation, May 26, 1982 (with a joint committee holding its first meeting in October 1982).

Singapore and Indonesia. A five-year economic co-operation agreement (tacitly renewable for further five-year periods) was signed on Oct. 31, 1980, with Singapore to contribute to the industrial development of the Indonesian island of Batam (20 km south of Singapore).

Singapore and the Republic of Korea. Agreement on setting up a South Korean military attaché's post in Singapore, on mutual exchanges of senior military personnel, on co-operation in technology and military education, and on the expansion of trade and economic co-operation, July 2, 1981.

Singapore and Thailand. Agreement to further intensify co-operation in trade and in defence industry, with Singapore supplying Thailand with petroleum products at open-market prices, April 20, 1980.

Sri Lanka and the Federal Republic of Germany. Protocol on trade (general questions) and supplementary protocol, Nov. 22, 1952, and Jan. 1, 1954; in force from Aug. 8, 1955.
Trade agreement, April 1, 1955; amended April 1, 1959; extended Sept. 16, 1985, until Dec. 12, 1986.
Agreements on technical co-operation, Oct. 18, 1973, in force from Sept. 28, 1974, and June 6, 1983.

Sri Lanka and Iceland. Treaties of peace and commerce, Feb. 13, 1660–61, and July 11, 1670.
Extradition convention, March 13, 1873; supplementary convention, Oct. 25, 1939.
Treaty on extradition of merchant seamen deserters, June 21, 1981.

Sri Lanka and Sweden. Agreement on development co-operation from July 1, 1984, to June 30, 1986; June 15, 1984.

Swaziland and the Federal Republic of Germany. Agreement on technical co-operation, Sept. 7, 1973.

Swaziland and South Africa. Extradition treaty, Sept. 4–5, 1968.

Tanzania and Denmark, Finland, Norway and Sweden. Agreement on co-operation on co-operatives, Dec. 13, 1971; joined by Iceland on Feb. 26–27, 1974; new agreement, April 25, 1984.
Agreement on development co-operation from July 1, 1983, to June 30, 1985; May 19, 1983.

Tanzania and the Federal Republic of Germany. Trade and economic agreement, Sept. 6, 1962; extended, Sept. 16, 1985, until Dec. 31, 1986.
Agreement on technical co-operation, May 29, 1975.

Tanzania and Madagascar. Bilateral agreements signed on June 22, 1973, provided for commercial and cultural links between the two countries.

Tanzania and Mozambique. In an agreement signed on Sept. 7, 1975, the heads of state of the two countries agreed on a broad basis of co-operation both ideologically and in the economic fields, with the economies of the two countries to be made complementary while accelerating their development.
New political, military and economic agreements between the two countries were signed in December 1976.
An agreement on the strengthening of military and economic co-operation was reported on Feb. 15, 1982. (Under this agreement a detachment of

200 Tanzanian troops was to be sent to Mozambique to replace Soviet instructors to the Mozambican Army.)

Tanzania and Sweden. An agreement on development co-operation between July 1, 1983, and June 30, 1985, was signed on May 19, 1983.

Tanzania and Switzerland. Technical and scientific co-operation agreement, Oct. 21, 1966.

Tonga and the Federal Republic of Germany. A treaty of friendly relations and co-operation was signed on June 1, 1977, and came into force on Jan. 2, 1978. An agreement on technical co-operation, signed also on June 1, 1977, came into force on Jan. 31, 1978.

Trinidad and Tobago and Haiti. A trade agreement signed by the two countries in 1974 was the first of its kind to be concluded between a Commonwealth Caribbean state and Haiti.

Tuvalu and the United States. A treaty of friendship was signed in April 1979, including a renunciation by the United States of any claim (dating back to 1856) to the four southernmost of Tuvalu's nine islands and providing for consultation on security and marine resources.

Uganda and the Federal Republic of Germany. Agreement on technical co-operation, March 3, 1964, in force from Nov 24, 1964; extended on Nov. 20, 1969.
Trade agreement March 17, 1964: in force from Jan. 28, 1967; extended, Sept. 16, 1985, until Dec. 31, 1986.

Uganda and Rwanda. A treaty on the joint management of the navigable part of the Kagera River was signed in April 1971.
Under an agreement reported on March 9, 1983, Rwanda agreed to settle more than 30,000 refugees from Uganda who had entered Rwanda in October 1982, while Uganda agreed to take back any refugees who could prove that they were Ugandan citizens.

Uganda and the Sudan. A mutual defence agreement between the Sudan and Uganda, providing for military aid against aggression by any external enemies, was signed in Khartoum on June 28, 1972.

Uganda, the Sudan and Zaïre. An agreement was concluded on June 8, 1981, on co-operation

in countering any activities directed against any one of the three countries and on forming a security committee at ministerial level to deal with the problems of refugees, illicit trade and poaching.

Uganda and Sweden. Agreement on technical co-operation, Sept. 30, 1970.

Western Samoa and American Samoa. A committee to discuss communications, trade, economic co-operation, migration and other issues was set up in mid-1985.

Western Samoa and the Federal Republic of Germany. An agreement on technical co-operation, signed on Dec. 8, 1978, came into force on June 7, 1979.

Zambia and Egypt. Agreement to set up a joint co-operation committee, Feb. 12, 1985.

Zambia and the Federal Republic of Germany. Economic agreement, Dec. 10, 1966; extended Sept. 16, 1985, until Dec. 31, 1986.
Agreement on technical co-operation, June 11, 1981; in force from April 4, 1982.

Zambia and Sweden. Agreement on development co-operation from Jan. 1, 1984, to Dec. 31, 1985; Sept. 30, 1983.

Zimbabwe and the Federal Republic of Germany. Agreement on technical co-operation, March 26, 1981; in force from March 15, 1984.

Zimbabwe and Mozambique. (1) An agreement was reached on May 23, 1980, on joint military action against armed rebels opposed to the Government of Mozambique.
(2) During a visit to Zimbabwe by the President of Mozambique on Aug. 4–9, 1980, a total of eight agreements were signed on co-operation in the fields of information, tourism, telecommunications, aviation, land transport, energy, trade and banking.
(3) On Oct. 20, 1980, it was agreed to conclude a security pact designed to prevent possible guerrilla activities in both countries.

Zimbabwe and South Africa. Trade agreement, Nov. 30, 1964; amended Dec. 4, 1965; revised, July 31, 1986.

Zimbabwe and Sweden. Agreement on development co-operation from July 1, 1983, to June 30, 1985; June 17, 1983.

13. The French Community ("*Communauté*") and Other Francophone Co-operation

Covered in this section are the French Community, its constitution, membership, historical development and related organizations, together with other major multilateral and bilateral co-operation agreements between France and francophone countries.

The French Community ("*Communauté*")

Membership: The French Republic (including Overseas Departments and Overseas Territories), the Central African Republic, Chad, Gabon, Senegal.

Constitution and Membership

The French Union, as defined under the 1946 Constitution of the Fourth Republic of France, was reconstituted as the French Community ("*Communauté*") under the new Constitution of the Fifth Republic, published on Sept. 4, 1958.

Section XII of the Constitution deals with the Community. Its most important provisions are the following:

Art. 77. In the Community established by the present Constitution, the member states enjoy autonomy; they administer themselves and manage their own affairs democratically and freely. There is only one citizenship in the Community. All citizens are equal before the law, whatever their origin, their race or religion. They have the same duties.

Art. 78. The competence of the Community comprises foreign policy, defence, currency, and common economic and financial policy, as well as policy concerning strategic raw materials.

In addition, it comprises (unless excluded by special agreement) control of justice, higher education, the general organization of external and common transport, and telecommunications.

Special agreements may establish other common spheres of competence or regulate the transfer of competences from the Community to one of its members.

Art. 80. The President of the Republic presides over and represents the Community. The organs of the Community are an Executive Council, a Senate, and a Court of Arbitration.

Art. 86. A change in the status of a member state may be requested either by the Republic or by a resolution of the Legislative Assembly of the state concerned which has been confirmed in a local referendum, the organization and supervision of which is carried out by the organs of the Community. The terms of such a change in status are regulated by an agreement approved by the Parliament of the Republic and the Legislative Assembly concerned.

Under the same conditions a member state of the Community may become independent. It then ceases to belong to the Community.

Each overseas territory of France was given the choice of: (i) Becoming a *département* of the French Republic; or (ii) retaining the territorial status it then enjoyed; or (iii) entering the French Community as an autonomous unit.

The Central African Republic, Chad, the Congo, Côte d'Ivoire, Dahomey (now Benin), Gabon, Madagascar, Mauritania, Niger, Senegal, French Sudan (now Mali) and Upper Volta (now Burkina Faso) chose to join the Community.

Guinea, until then a member of the French Union, voted, in a referendum held on Sept. 28, 1958, against joining the French Community and opted for complete independence which was granted on Oct. 2, 1958. (A treaty of co-operation with France was nevertheless signed on March 22, 1963.)

Early in 1960 the Mali Federation (comprising the Republics of Senegal and the Sudan) and Madagascar decided to ask for full independence while retaining membership in the Community. An amendment to the Constitution, enabling member states to remain in the Community after attaining full independence, was approved by the French National Assembly on May 11, 1960.

Altogether six members of the Community in Africa gained their independence in June and August of 1960. The five remaining members of the old Community—Côte d'Ivoire, Dahomey, Mauritania, Niger and Upper Volta—chose to leave the Community on attaining independence and the Congo and Madagascar withdrew from the Community in 1973. [For dates of independence see table on page 334.] [See also *Conseil de l'entente*, page 429.]

Development of the Community

The character of the French Community was radically altered by the new, independent status of all its members. This was recognized by the French Government which, on May 18, 1961, agreed upon the creation of new governmental machinery for dealing with the relations of France with French-speaking Africa and Madagascar. The new posts of Minister of Co-operation (to deal with technical assistance), Secretary of State for Political Affairs and Secretary-General for Community, African and Malagasy Affairs were created. The function of the latter was to co-ordinate the activities of the President relating to the countries in question. A Council for African and Malagasy Affairs was also created. The powers exercised by the Community, as laid down in Article 78 of the French Constitution [see above], were transferred to each member country on its attaining independence.

In January 1974 many of the responsibilities of the Secretary-General for Community, African and Malagasy Affairs were transferred to the French Foreign Ministry, and on May 31, 1974, his remaining functions were entrusted to the Minister of Co-operation.

The practical functions of the Community have thus been greatly reduced, its varous organs [see above] have fallen into abeyance, and the bond between France and other Community members is now mainly restricted to a co-ordination of foreign policy in certain matters, and to co-operation in the fields of economy and education.

Mutual Defence Agreements

Agreements for co-operation between France and the newly-independent states were signed immediately after the various proclamations of independence. These agreements contained important provisions for mutual military aid. The mutual defence agreement between France and the Mali Federation, which may be taken as typical, stated that France and Mali would assist each other in defence matters; Mali would share with France in the defence of the Community and possibly of other African states; a Franco-Malian defence committee would be set up; Mali would obtain military equipment exclusively from France; and Malian nationals would be free to enlist in the French armed forces.

The defence agreements with the Central African Republic, Chad, the Congo and Gabon were supplemented in 1961, when these four states joined to form, with French co-operation, a "Defence Council of Equatorial Africa".

France also had defence agreements with African countries outside the Community, namely Cameroon, Côte d'Ivoire, Dahomey (now Benin), Mauritania, Niger and Togo.

The French military presence in Africa was drastically reduced in the year 1964–65. It was announced on Sept. 29, 1964, that by July 1965 it was intended to reduce the total of French forces in African states and Madagascar to about 6,000 officers and men, from an official total of 27,800 on Oct. 1, 1964. The remaining troops would be regrouped, and there would be four "support points", these being Dakar (Senegal), Abidjan (Côte d'Ivoire), Fort-Lamy (now N'Djaména, Chad) and Diégo-Suarez, Ivato and Antsirabé in Madagascar.

The independence agreements signed by these states included no agreements on their continued membership in the Community.

[For further defence and military co-operation agreements, see pages 338–40.]

By 1985 contingents of French troops remained stationed in the following African countries: Cameroon, the Central African Republic, Côte d'Ivoire, Djibouti, Gabon and Senegal.

Evian Agreements between France and Algeria

After being a member of the French Community—divided into five autonomous territories comprising a total of 13 *départements* (as well as two *départements* of the Saharan territory under the control of the French Minister for the Sahara)—Algeria achieved its independence in 1962 after many years of warfare between French forces and the Algerian National Liberation Front.

On March 18, 1962, after several months of negotiations, a ceasefire agreement between France and the "Provisional Government of the Algerian Republic" was signed at Evian in France, together with a general declaration summarizing the agreements reached on the future of Algeria. The latter agreements included provision for a referendum on self-determination for the people of Algeria (held on July 1, 1962), and outlined the terms of Algerian independence.

Under the provisions concerning Franco-Algerian co-operation, Algeria guaranteed the interests of France and the rights acquired by individuals and organizations, while France, in exchange, undertook to provide technical, cultural and financial assistance to Algeria. Preferential treatment would be applied in certain spheres of trade, and Algeria would be part of the Franc Zone. In the *départements* of the Oases and Sahara the development of subsoil wealth would be carried on under Franco-Algerian co-operation, to be ensured by a technical body for co-operation which would include an equal number of French and Algerian representatives.

The military arrangements laid down in the agreements included the withdrawal of French troops from Algeria, and the leasing to France by Algeria of the naval base of Mers-el-Kébir and the air base of Bou-Sfer for a 15-year period. France was also granted the use of a number of other military areas required by her (including rocket and nuclear-testing installations in the Sahara).

The French Government, however, evacuated the Mers-el-Kébir base on Jan. 31, 1968, and the air base at Bou-Sfer on Dec. 29, 1970.

A convention signed in December 1967 provided for continued Franco-Algerian co-operation.

Bilateral Agreements with France, 1960–64

The table below shows the independence and other bilateral agreements which France concluded with its former African dependencies in the period 1960–64.

	Independence Agreement signed on	Proclamation of Independence	Co-operation and Mutual Defence Agreements signed on
Community Members			
Mali Federation*	April 4, 1960	June 20, 1960	June 22, 1960
Chad	July 12, 1960	Aug. 10, 1960	Aug. 11, 1960 May 1, 1964
Central African Republic	July 12, 1960	Aug. 12, 1960	Aug. 13, 1960
Gabon	July 15, 1960	Aug. 16, 1960	Aug. 17, 1960
Former Members			
Madagascar	April 2, 1960	June 26, 1960	June 27, 1960
Dahomey (Benin)	July 11, 1960	Aug. 1, 1960	
Niger	July 11, 1960	Aug. 2, 1960	
Upper Volta (Burkina Faso)	July 11, 1960	Aug. 5, 1960	
Ivory Coast (Côte d'Ivoire)	July 11, 1960	Aug. 6, 1960	
Congo	July 12, 1960	Aug. 14, 1960	Aug. 15, 1960
Mauritania	Oct. 19, 1960	Nov. 27, 1960	

* After the secession of Senegal from the Federation of Mali (Aug. 20, 1960) and the subsequent French recognition of Senegal on Sept. 11, 1960, the Republic of Mali declared itself free from all links with France, claiming that the Franco-Malian agreements had been broken by France's recognition of Senegal. Senegal remained within the Community.

The Franc Zone

Address. Secrétariat du Comité de la Zone Franc, Banque de France, 39 rue Croix-des-Petits-Champs, Paris 1er, France.

Membership. Benin, Burkina Faso, Cameroon, the Central African Republic, Chad, the Comoros, the Congo, Côte d'Ivoire, Equatorial Guinea, the French Republic (Metropolitan France, Mayotte and the Overseas Departments and Territories), Gabon, Mali, Niger, Senegal and Togo.

History. Mauritania withdrew from the Franc Zone on Feb. 15, 1973, following the Mauritanian Government's decision, first announced on Nov. 28, 1972, to create a national currency. The Malagasy Republic announced its withdrawal from the Franc Zone on May 22, 1973.

The Mali franc became fully convertible on March 29, 1968, following the ratification of Franco-Malian agreements signed in Paris on Dec. 19, 1967, under which France had undertaken to guarantee the Malian franc after a transitional period during which Mali would carry out a monetary and economic reorganization with intensive French technical, economic and financial aid. During a visit to Mali by the French President on Feb. 13–15, 1977, it was agreed that the 1967 monetary agreement would be renewed and that France would give aid to Mali towards railways and road programmes and would take part in mineral exploration.

Object. To provide for the free movement of currency among its members and a guaranteed franc exchange rate.

Other Co-operation between France and Francophone Countries

Central African Countries' Monetary Co-operation

A convention of monetary co-operation was signed with France in 1972 by Cameroon, the Central African Republic, Chad, the Congo and Gabon. The central issuing bank for these countries is the Banque des états de l'Afrique centrale at Yaoundé (Cameroon) [see page 427.]

West African Monetary Union
Union monétaire ouest-africaine (UMOA)

Founded. 1962

Membership. Benin, Burkina Faso, Côte d'Ivoire, Mali, Niger, Senegal and Togo.

History. The UMOA was set up under an agreement initialled on May 12, 1962, by France as well as Côte d'Ivoire, Dahomey (now Benin), Mali, Mauritania, Niger, Senegal and the Voltaic Republic (now Burkina Faso). It was reorganized

under a treaty which was concluded with France in November 1973 and came into force in 1974.

Mali, which had been a member of the UMOA until 1962, applied for readmission to the union in 1981, but owing to opposition by Burkina Faso (then involved in a border dispute with Mali) Mali's readmission was delayed until it had, on Feb. 17, 1984, signed a treaty of readmission which became effective on June 1, 1984 (with a conversion rate of 2 Mali francs to 1 CFA franc).

Activities. The central issuing bank of the UMOA is the Banque centrale des états de l'Afrique de l'ouest in Dakar (Senegal), founded in 1955 as the Institut d'émission de l'Afrique de l'ouest française et du Togo. Its currency is the CFA (=Communauté Financière Africaine) franc tied to the French franc at the rate of 50 CFA francs to one French franc.

In 1973 the heads of state of the union set up a **West African Development Bank** (Banque ouest-africaine de développement, BOAD) in Lomé

(Togo) to promote balanced economic development and integration in West Africa.

Franco-African Conferences

Conferences of the head of state of France and representatives of African states were held from 1973 onwards, and annually from 1975.

First Conference. The first of these conferences, called on the initiative of the President of Niger, took place in Paris on Nov. 13, 1973, under the chairmanship of the French President and was attended by the Presidents of the Central African Republic, Côte d'Ivoire, Gabon, Niger, Senegal and Upper Volta (now Burkina Faso), the Foreign Ministers of Dahomey (later Benin) and Mali. It was decided inter alia to hold regular consultations in the future.

Second Conference. The second such conference, held in Bangui (Central African Republic) on March 7–8, 1975, had new participants in the Presidents of Burundi and Rwanda, the Prime Minister of Mauritius and a state commissioner from Zaïre, while the Chief Minister of Seychelles attended as an observer and another observer represented Somalia. The object of the conference was defined by the French President as being the creation of "a new, more equitable economic order" which would require industrialized countries to allocate a fixed percentage of their gross national product to the Third World, which should be added to (and not replaced by) aid from the petroleum-producing countries.

In a final communiqué the participants in the conference expressed their agreement on the need for a thorough reform of the international monetary system and on their wish to follow new guidelines on co-operation, with special account to be taken of the problems of land-locked countries in Africa and of those affected by drought. The participants were also determined to present a united front at a proposed international energy conference, and they stressed that their countries constituted one cultural area and monetary zone, and that they would try to channel Arab oil revenues to the under-developed countries of Africa (through a French fund).

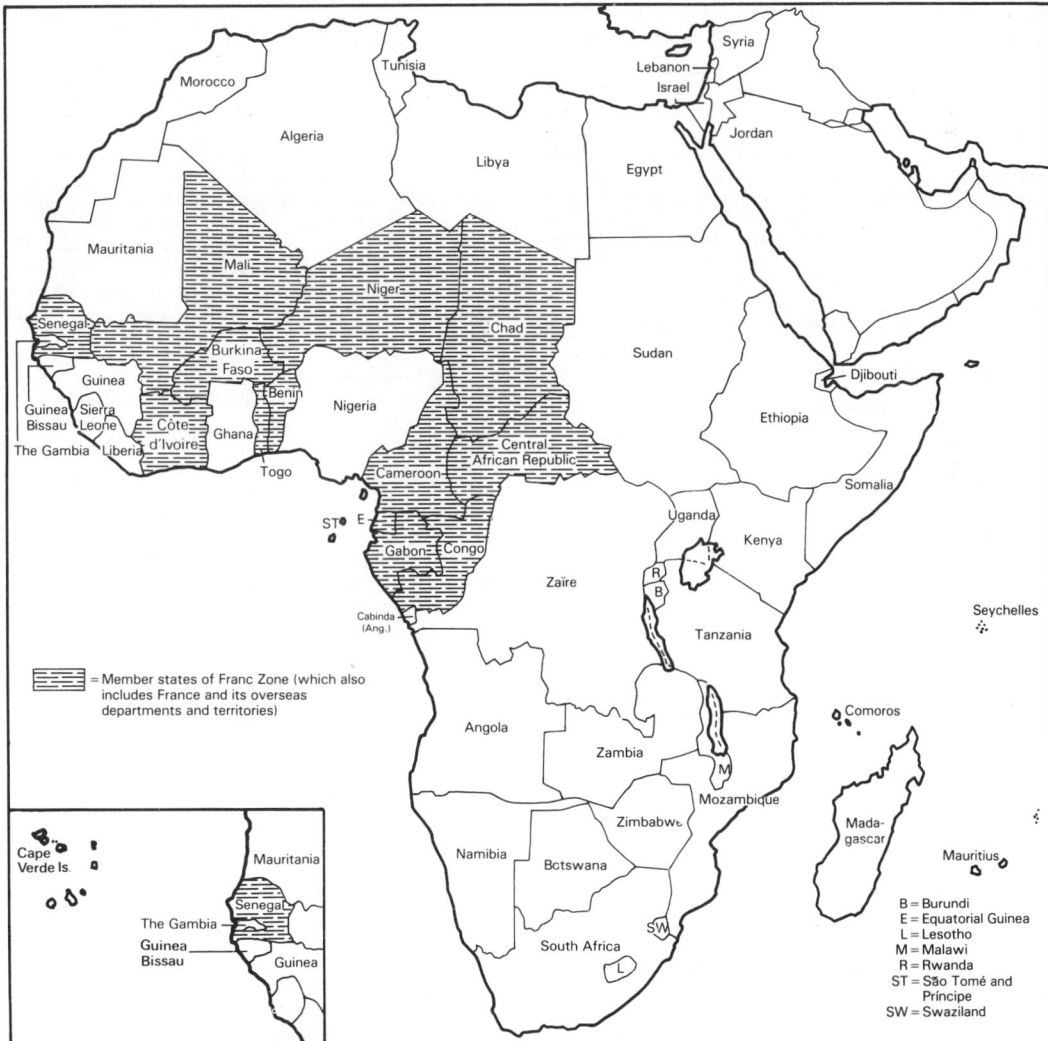

Map 8   African members of Franc Zone

Third Conference. The third conference, held in Paris and Versailles on May 10–11, 1976, had among its participants also ministers from the Cape Verde Islands, Chad, the Comoros, Guinea-Bissau and São Tomé and Principe. It was principally concerned with economic problems and decided that an African Solidarity Fund should be set up. In a final communiqué it was stated that "a convergence of views" had been established "on world inflation, the international monetary system, the problem of raw materials, the north-south dialogue and development aid".

The proposed African Solidarity Fund was established under an agreement reached on Dec. 21, 1976, signed by representatives of France, Benin, Burundi, the then Central African Empire, Chad, Côte d'Ivoire, Gabon, Mali, Mauritania, Niger, Rwanda, Senegal, Togo, Upper Volta and Zaïre, and providing for a fund totalling the equivalent of 100,000,000 French francs (or $20,000,000), of which it was reported that France would contribute one-half.

Fourth Conference. The fourth conference was held in Dakar on April 20–21, 1977, after Guinea-Bissau, the Cape Verde Islands and Seychelles had acceded to the African Solidarity Fund. (Proposals made earlier by the President of Senegal for the conclusion of defence agreements between certain West African states were, however, not discussed at the conference.)

Fifth Conference. The fifth conference took place in Paris on May 22–23, 1978 (the participants including, inter alia, the Presidents of Djibouti and of Zaïre and a representative of the Congo). At this conference the French President clarified his country's policy in regard to military assistance to African states, saying that France had been asked more and more frequently "for military support to poorly-armed countries which are victims of external aggression"; that in each case France's intervention had amounted to "limited technical assistance"; but that the main responsibility for their security rested with the states directly concerned, that "we must not allow the politics of power blocs to play havoc with Africa" and that "in the political domain Africa must remain for the Africans".

After the conference the French President urged the expansion of the West African Economic Community (CEAO—see page 432) to central African countries in the field of defence, with defence and non-aggression agreements to be signed first with Burundi, Rwanda, Gabon and Zaïre, and later with other countries.

Sixth Conference. The sixth conference was held at Kigali (Rwanda) on May 21–22, 1979. Among the observers present at this conference was the Foreign Minister of Liberia. During the session it was announced that France had decided to increase by $50,000,000 its contribution to the African Development Bank [see page 424] and to 12 per cent its share in the African Development Fund.

The African participants in this conference asked France to be their spokesman at the European Communities and other industrialized countries, and they endorsed a French call for greater solidarity between European, African and Arab states (the French President having on Feb. 15, 1979, proposed a meeting of leaders of the European Communities, the Organization of African Unity and the Arab League).

Seventh Conference. The seventh conference was held in Nice (France) on May 9–10, 1980, and was attended by representatives of France and 25 African countries (comprising the Presidents of France, Burundi, the Central African Republic, the Comoros, Djibouti, Gabon, Equatorial Guinea, Mali, Niger, Rwanda, Senegal, Sierra Leone, Somalia, Togo and Zaïre; the Prime Minister of Mauritius; ministers from Benin, the Cape Verde Islands, Chad, the Congo, Guinea-Bissau and Morocco; and the Mauritanian ambassador to France).

At the conference the French President again defined his policy as one of "non-interference and solidarity" and of responding to requests for aid.

At the end of the conference the President of Senegal announced that agreement had been reached on the establishment of an "organic community" (comparable to the Commonwealth) with a permanent secretariat to be based in Paris.

Eighth Conference. The eighth conference, held in Paris on Nov. 3–4, 1981, was attended by representatives of France and 19 African countries as full participants (Benin, Burundi, Cape Verde, the Central African Republic, Chad, the Comoros, the Congo, Côte d'Ivoire, Djibouti, Gabon, Mali, Mauritania, Mauritius, Niger, Rwanda, Senegal, Togo, Upper Volta—later Burkina Faso, and Zaïre); by six observers (from Equatorial Guinea, Guinea-Bissau, Morocco, São Tomé and Príncipe, Sierra Leone and Somalia); and by delegates of seven invited countries (Angola, Egypt, Kenya, the Sudan, Tanzania, Tunisia and Zimbabwe). During the conference Col. Moamer al Gadaffi, the Libyan leader, announced that he had ordered the withdrawal of Libyan troops from Chad (which they had entered in 1980).

The conference issued an appeal for improved international economic relations, in particular for the full implementation and extension of the commodity price arrangements agreed within the framework of UNCTAD and for adjustments to the provisions of the second Lomé Convention (see page 183).

Ninth Conference. The ninth conference was held in Kinshasa (Zaïre) on Oct. 8–9, 1982, when the countries represented were those which had taken part in the eighth conference, and also The Gambia, Mozambique, Nigeria, Seychelles and Zambia. At the conference the French President reiterated some of the principal aims of French policy towards the Third World—the achievement of self-sufficiency in food, independence in the field of energy, suitably adapted industrialization and interdependence between North and South—and he promised that the proportion of France's gross national product devoted to aid to the Third World would be increased by one-fifth between 1982 and 1983.

Tenth Conference. The tenth conference was held in Vittel (France) on Oct. 3–4, 1983, with the participation of 19 heads of state (of Benin, Burkina Faso, Burundi, Chad, the Comoros, the Congo, Côte d'Ivoire, Djibouti, France, Gabon, Guinea, Mali, Mauritania, Niger, Rwanda, Senegal, Seychelles, Togo and Zaïre) and of representatives of two others (the Central African Republic and Mauritius). Observers attended from 18 other nations (Angola, Botswana, Cape Verde, Egypt, Equatorial Guinea, the Gambia, Guinea-Bissau, Kenya, Liberia, Morocco, São Tomé and Príncipe, Sierra Leone, Somalia, the Sudan, Tanzania, Tunisia, Zambia and Zimbabwe). The conference failed, however, to find a solution to the civil war in Chad.

11th Conference. The 11th conference took place in Bujumbura (Burundi) on Dec. 11–12, 1984, and was attended by leaders from 20 states (not including Burkina Faso) and by observers from 17 others. The French President announced on this occasion that France was ready to contribute 500,000,000 French francs (about £50,000,000) to a Special Assistance Facility for Sub-Saharan Africa proposed by the World Bank.

12th Conference. The 12th conference, held in Paris on Dec. 11–13, 1985, was attended by representatives of altogether 35 African states (but again not including Burkina Faso). As at previous meetings, regional conflicts (in particular in Chad) dominated the debates, with the French President stating that France would not act as the "gendarme of Africa". It was agreed to hold a conference on the debt repayment problems facing African countries. No concrete decisions were made on the situation in South Africa, despite the presence of six southern African "front-line states".

Agency for Cultural and Technical Co-operation
Agence de coopération culturelle et technique (ACCT)

Address. 13, quai André Citroën, 75015 Paris, France.

Officer. Paul Okumba d'Okouatségué (sec. gen.).

Founded. 1970.

Membership. 39 governments (of Belgium, Benin, Burkina Faso, Burundi, Cameroon, Canada, the Central African Republic, Chad, the Comoros, the Congo, Côte d'Ivoire, Djibouti, Dominica, Egypt, France, Gabon, Guinea, Guinea-Bissau, Haiti, Laos, Lebanon, Luxembourg, Mali, Mauritania, Mauritius, Monaco, Morocco, Niger, Rwanda, St Lucia, Senegal, Seychelles, Togo, Tunisia, Vanuatu, Vietnam and Zaïre, as well as of the Canadian provinces of New Brunswick and Quebec).

Observers. Equatorial Guinea and Madagascar

History. The decision to form the agency was taken at a conference held in Niamey (Niger) on Feb. 17–20, 1969, and attended by representatives of some 30 countries where French was either the official language or widely spoken. The agency has since been involved in projects in Benin, Chad, Laos and Vietnam. At a general conference held in Dakar on Dec. 16–18, 1985, it elected a new secretary-general, but it was not directly involved in preparations for the holding of the Conference of Francophone Countries scheduled for February 1986 [see below].

High Council of Francophony
Haut Conseil de la francophonie

Address. 72, rue de la Varenne, 75700 Paris, France.

Officers. President F. Mitterrand (pres.); Stélio Farandjis (sec. gen.).

Founded. March 1984.

Membership. 28 representatives of various French-language regions (including Black Africa, Québec, the Maghreb and the Near East).

History. The creation of the council was first proposed by the French Prime Minister on Aug. 24, 1983, as one of three organs for the propagation of the use of the French language. It held its first meeting in Paris on March 6, 1985, and its second meeting, also in Paris, on Dec. 9–10, 1985, when it discussed the teaching of the French language as well as teaching in French. At its third meeting, held on May 28–30, 1986, the council called for the establishment of a "special status for French-speaking people", involving freedom to enter or leave countries for students and businessmen as well as for manual workers (modelled to some extent on Commonwealth practices).

Associated organs. The other two organs for promoting the use of the French language are as follows:

The General Commissariat of the French Language (*Commissariat général de la langue française*), which has inter alia issued a list of anglicisms which it wishes to see suppressed and which created, in September 1985, a *groupement intérêt public* (GIP) *de la terminologie et de la traduction.*

The Consultative Committee of the French Language (*Comité consultatif de la langue française*), comprising 28 members and headed by a secretary of state at the Prime Minister's office appointed on May 6, 1986, with the task of promoting the development, use and enrichment of the French language.

Conference of Francophone Countries

A conference of leaders of francophone countries and regions was held in Versailles on Feb. 17–19, 1986.

Of the 42 delegations taking part, 16 were led by heads of state (Burundi, the Central African Republic, the Comoros, Côte d'Ivoire, Djibouti, France, Gabon, Guinea-Bissau, Lebanon, Madagascar, Mali, Mauritania, Rwanda, Senegal, Togo and Zaïre). Those represented by their Prime Ministers were Belgium, Canada, Luxembourg, Monaco, Niger, St Lucia, Tunisia and Vanuatu. Delegations from other countries or regions were those of Benin, Burkina Faso, Chad, the Congo, Dominica, Egypt, Guinea, Haiti, Morocco, Mauritius, New Brunswick, Québec, Seychelles and Wallonia (Belgium). Delegations attending as observers were those of Laos, Louisiana (USA), Switzerland and Vietnam.

Countries or regions considered partially francophone but not represented at the conference were Algeria, Cambodia, Cameroon, Pondicherry, Syria and the Val d'Aosta (Italy).

President Mitterrand said in his opening speech that the identity of the 120,000,000 members of the French-speaking community in the world was threatened and that vis-à-vis other world language communities it was seeing itself "too often condemned to the role of subcontractor, translator or interpreter". He called for "ambition and imagination" so that francophone countries could become "the creators of a new era". At the same time he stressed the need for "active solidarity" between industrialized and developing countries, saying: "How to bridge the gap between North and South is our number one problem."

The conference approved a total of 28 concrete measures, inter alia to set up an international francophone television agency which would distribute 20 minutes of news a day in French, to which France would contribute 5,000,000 French francs (£416,000) of the F16,000,000 needed to finance it over three years; to make available one of the four channels of the French TDF-1 satellite for francophone programmes and to spend F29,000,000 on extending the French programmes put out in Europe through the TV-5 cable network; to launch a project to catalogue data banks in French (with Canada taking a leading part); to hold an international French book fair; to set up a French-language energy institute; to establish an international French baccalauréat (secondary school-leaving certificate) examination; and to implement programmes for training technicians in the developing countries, in particular in agriculture.

The conference also set up a follow-up committee (of 11 members: Burundi, Canada, the Comoros, France, Lebanon, Mali, Morocco, Québec, Senegal, Wallonia and Zaïre). It was to meet every month and held its first meeting in Paris on April 24, 1986.

Other Agreements between France and Francophone Countries

Algeria. An agreement signed on Sept. 18, 1980, was designed to encourage Algerian immigrant workers in France to return home. In this context agreement was reached on Dec. 1, 1981, on co-operation between the Algerian and French police forces.

Two protocols were signed on Jan. 19, 1982, on co-operation in certain economic projects in Algeria.

A contract providing for the supply of Algerian liquefied gas to France was signed on Feb. 3, 1982, with agreement being reached on the price to be paid by France.

Benin. An agreement on co-operation in various fields, including military technology, was signed on Feb. 23, 1975, between France and Dahomey (which changed its name to Benin in December 1975).

Cameroon. A set of co-operation agreements between France and Cameroon, signed on Feb. 21, 1974, covered inter alia technical, cultural, economic, financial and military co-operation.

The Central African Republic. In September 1979 French parachute troops, at the request of opponents of the then Emperor Bokassa, took part in an operation leading to the overthrow of the Emperor and the restoration of the Central African Republic; of the three companies involved, one was withdrawn on Dec. 16, 1979.

A joint plan for the recovery of the Central African Republic's economy was approved by the Governments of France and the Central African Republic in February 1980, and the latter's President asked the French Government on May 16, 1980, to maintain in his country a French army detachment in order to train the forces of the Central African Republic.

Two agreements signed at the end of September 1981 provided for French aid for transport and for the printing of maps for the planning of economic development.

Two financial agreements were signed on March 13, 1982, covering the allocation of the equivalent of about $50,000,000 for rural sector development and public works.

Chad. After the Government of Chad had, on Sept. 28, 1975, accused France of interfering in the country's internal affairs and had demanded the withdrawal of French troops stationed there under the 1964 agreement, the evacuation of all French military bases in Chad was completed by Oct. 27, 1975.

New civil and military agreements signed between France and Chad on March 6, 1976, provided inter alia for co-operation in various fields, including military technology, but they comprised no automatic clause for the defence of Chad in the event of an attack, and it was officially stated at the same time that French military personnel would "not intervene directly" against the rebellion (then in progress in northern Chad). Following these agreements the French military personnel in Chad was said to number only about 300 men. However, in March 1978 more French forces were sent to Chad "to ensure the safety of French nationals" (during the civil war in Chad) and also "to block" any advance by Libyan-backed rebels. During 1979 the number of these French forces was reduced from 2,500 to about 1,100, and at the request of the President of Chad all of them were withdrawn between April 28 and May 16, 1980, after most Europeans had been evacuated from the country.

A co-operation agreement signed on Aug. 2, 1982, provided for France to finance the construction of a dam on the Chari River and to assist with the provision of health services and the re-establishment of the country's administrative infrastructure.

A protocol agreement on co-operation worth the equivalent of $2,750,000 was signed on Nov. 2, 1982.

Under the 1976 military agreement, France again supplied, in 1983–84, military aid to Chad, i.e. to the Habré regime, for defence against Libyan and Libyan-backed rebel forces. This was ended under a Franco-Libyan agreement announced on Sept. 17, 1984, providing for the withdrawal from Chad of both Libyan and French forces; all French troops were withdrawn from Chad by Nov. 10, 1984 (largely to the Central African Republic where there were some 1,100 French troops in 1985). France undertook, however, to continue its co-operation with Chad and in particular to supply arms to Chad's armed forces.

The Comoros. Five agreements signed on Nov. 10, 1978, by France and the Comoros included a treaty of friendship and co-operation, an economic, monetary and financial agreement, a cultural agreement and a military agreement, under which France would supply the Comoros with aid in the event of external aggression and provide technical assistance in the training of the Comoro Army.

An agreement was signed in December 1983 on a French subsidy equivalent to $1,000,000 to balance the Comoros' current budget. It was also announced that the French government had doubled its aid to the Comoros and would assume full responsibility for the defence of the islands.

The Congo. New co-operation agreements between France and the Congo were signed in Brazzaville on Jan. 1, 1974, including one on French technical assistance to the Congo's armed forces.

Djibouti. Seven bilateral agreements—including a treaty of friendship and co-operation, an agreement on economic and financial co-operation and a provisional military protocol—were signed between France and the Republic of Djibouti on June 27, 1977 (when Djibouti achieved independence). (France maintained some 5,000 troops in Djibouti and assisted in the formation of a Djibouti national Army, but it would not intervene militarily unless requested by Djibouti in the event of aggression against it.)

Gabon. A new co-operation agreement between France and Gabon, signed on Feb. 12, 1974, and renewing that of 1960, provided for the partial maintenance of the 1960 defence arrangements and the continued presence in Gabon of a small French force.

Two agreements signed in October 1980 covered, inter alia, reciprocal social security measures.

Agreements on economic aid signed on April 1–2, 1984, included provisions for the supply by France of a nuclear power station, assistance for the Air Gabon airline, the renovation of Libreville airport and an increase in French imports of minerals from Gabon.

Guinea. (1) Following the normalization (on July 14, 1975) of relations between France and Guinea (which had been severed in 1958 when Guinea had opted for complete independence outside the French Community), an agreement was concluded in Paris on Jan. 27, 1977, on the final settlement of financial relations between the two countries, entailing the promotion of economic co-operation between them.

(2) In September 1984 it was announced that France would double its aid to Guinea to the equivalent of $4,300,000. A permanent French aid mission was established in October 1984.

Madagascar. Eight new co-operation agreements between France and the Malagasy Republic were signed on June 4, 1973, replacing those in force since June 27, 1960. An agreement on military co-operation provided for the withdrawal of French ground forces based at Ivato by Sept. 1, 1973; the training of Malagasy units to run the naval installations at Diégo-Suarez; and unlimited French landing and harbouring rights for refuelling and repairs, renewable every year. The withdrawal of all French forces from Madagascar was completed by June 3, 1975.

Three further co-operation agreements were signed in Antananarivo on July 4, 1975.

Mauritania. Three new agreements, covering cultural, technical and economic co-operation between France and Mauritania, were signed on Feb. 15, 1973. Mauritania regarded its 1960 defence agreement with France as void.

Later, however, France gave assurances of support for the territorial integrity of Mauritania, and under a new military co-operation convention there were, by early 1985, at least 70 French military instructors in Mauritania.

Morocco. On March 11, 1982, it was announced that the sale of certain military arms to Morocco had been temporarily suspended as Morocco owed France about 2,000 million francs (or about US$310,000,000) for military supplies, but new arrangements for payment of this debt were agreed on April 9, 1982. At the same time French aid to Morocco amounted to 1,300 million francs, and in addition France supported Morocco's phosphate development programme (at an estimated 6,000 million francs).

An agreement reached in May 1985 related to the sale of 250,000 tonnes of French wheat on credit terms to Morocco.

Niger. Agreement was reached on July 18, 1982, on a loan of 5,000 million CFA francs (about $10,000,000) from the French Caisse centrale de coöpération économique for improving budgetary and supervisory procedures and the reorganization of the finances of enterprises in Niger.

Rwanda. Under an agreement concluded in February 1982 France decided to increase its aid to Rwanda by 30 per cent.

Senegal. Four separate documents signed on March 29, 1974, comprised a general treaty of friendship and co-operation; an agreement on economic and financial co-operation; a cultural convention; and a military agreement providing for the transfer to Senegal of the French base in Dakar, with France retaining certain facilities, and for the phased reduction of French forces in Senegal from 2,250 to 1,300 men by April 1975.

New co-operation agreements were signed in March and October 1979, and joint military manoeuvres were held in November of that year.

Co-operation agreements signed on April 26, 1982, involved French aid commitments (of the equivalent of about £9,000,000 from the Fonds d'aide et de coopération and of about £45,000,000 from the Caisse centrale de coopération économique).

In February 1984 it was announced that French aid to Senegal in 1984–85 would amount to 68,000,000 French francs (about £7,000,000), plus an additional grant of 280,000,000 French francs towards Senegal's budget deficit and 10,000 tonnes of wheat in food aid. In November 1984 six French military aircraft and a large amount of military equipment were delivered to Senegal.

Togo. New co-operation agreements, to replace earlier ones concluded in 1963, were signed between France and Togo in Lomé on March 23, 1976, covering mainly co-operation in economic, technical and cultural affairs, scientific research and military technology. In September 1975 it had been agreed that France would supply Togo with five training aircraft and two coastal patrol boats and would provide training for Togolese pilots and technicians.

Tunisia. In January–February 1980 France responded to an appeal by Tunisia for help against rebels, and provided transport and military advisers.

On July 6, 1981, France undertook to expand and intensify its co-operation with Tunisia on the basis of a "true policy of association", eventually to reach the stage of "integration and complementarity" and also to secure "military security in regions which included Tunisia". France also contributed to the capital of a newly-established investment bank.

Two agreements signed on March 19, 1982, related to judicial matters and military service.

An agreement concluded on Dec. 29, 1982, was to facilitate free passage and movement of people and goods.

Zaïre. In early May 1984 it was announced that France had agreed to make available to Zaïre 100,000,000 French francs (about $12,000,000) in credits for economic development, and also to provide continued military assistance.

14. The Americas

This section deals with treaties, alliances and other agreements concluded by the states of the American continents, covering in particular (i) early manifestations of pan-Americanism and the first regional security arrangements, (ii) the development of the Organization of American States, (iii) other inter-American co-operation agencies and agreements, (iv) the major treaties and agreements concluded by the United States in the fields of defence, economic co-operation and peaceful use of nuclear energy, and (v) other important agreements involving American states.

Pan-Americanism and the First Regional Security Arrangements

The Monroe Doctrine

The idea of the unity of interests of the countries of the American continents, or of Pan-Americanism, received its first impetus from the so-called Monroe Doctrine which rejected all interference in American affairs by outside powers.

The doctrine was proclaimed by President James Monroe in a Message to Congress delivered on Dec. 2, 1823, stating inter alia:

"The American continents, by the free and independent condition which they have assumed and maintain, are henceforth not to be considered as subject for future colonization by any European power. . . . We would not view any interposition for the purpose of oppressing" the former colonies in the Americas or "controlling in any other manner their destiny by any European power in any other light than as the manifestation of an unfriendly disposition toward the United States".

The doctrine was restated by President James K. Polk on Dec. 2, 1845, and by other US Presidents later in the 19th century. It was formally recognized by Great Britain after President Theodore Roosevelt had pronounced the following corollary to the doctrine in May 1904: "In the Western Hemisphere the adherence of the United States to the Monroe doctrine may force the United States, however reluctantly, in flagrant cases of such wrongdoing or interference, to the exercise of an international police power."

Earliest Pan-American Organizations

The first manifestation of Pan-Americanism was the **First Congress of American States** convened in Panama City by Simón Bolívar in 1826 which led to the signing of a *Treaty of Permanent Union, League and Confederation* of Colombia, Central America, Mexico and Peru.

An **International Union of American Republics** was set up at a First International Conference of American States in Washington in 1889–90. The fourth conference of this organization decided in Washington in 1910 to change its name to **Union of American Republics**, and at the fifth conference in Santiago de Chile in 1923 it was decided to adopt the name of **Union of the Republics of the American Continents** and to establish the **Pan-American Union** as its permanent organ. This conference also formulated the *Gondra Treaty* providing for procedures for the peaceful prevention of conflicts.

At the 7th conference of the Union of the Republics of the American Continents in Montevideo in 1933 the United States joined the other member states in signing a convention on the *Rights and Duties of States* declaring explicitly: "No state has the right to intervene in the internal or external affairs of another."

A *Convention on Extradition*, signed on Dec. 26, 1933, came into force on Jan. 25, 1935. The parties to it are Argentina, Chile, Colombia, the Dominican Republic, Ecuador, El Salvador, Guatemala, Honduras, Mexico, Nicaragua, Panama and the United States. (An Inter-American Convention on Extradition signed on Feb. 28, 1981, has not yet entered into force.)

A Conference of American States held in Buenos Aires in December 1936 adopted:

(1) A *Pan American Peace Pact*, providing for consultation in the event of the peace of the American Republics being threatened or in case of war between American nations;

(2) a *Pact for Co-ordination of Treaties*, endorsing and amplifying existing treaties between American states; and

(3) a non-intervention convention named the *"Declaration of Inter-American Solidarity and Co-operation"*.

A further conference held in Lima in December 1938 issued the *Declaration of Lima* on inter-American solidarity, under which regular meetings of American Foreign Ministers were agreed upon. A first such meeting, held in Panama on Sept. 23–Oct. 3, 1939, adopted an *Act of Panama* as a multilateral declaration of neutrality (following the outbreak of World War II).

The act contained decisions (i) to establish a committee of experts for the duration of the war to study and make recommendations on problems of neutrality; (ii) to proclaim a neutral zone on the high seas up to 300 miles from the coasts of American Republics; and (iii) to call, in the event of any territory in the Americas belonging to a European state changing sovereignty and thereby endangering American security, for an urgent consultative meeting. (The decision on the 300-mile neutral zone was later invalidated by the doctrine of the freedom of the seas, as embodied in the UN Convention of the High Seas of 1958—see page 55.)

At a further meeting held in Havana on July 21–30, 1940, the Foreign Ministers of the American Republics adopted a *Convention on the Provisional Administration of European Colonies and Possessions in the Americas.*

In this convention it was laid down that, if a non-American state attempted, directly or indirectly, to replace another non-American state in the sovereignty or control over any territory in the Americas, thus threatening the peace of the continent, such territory would automatically be submitted to a provisional administrative regime to be exercised by one or more American states, until such time as the territory would be able to govern itself or be restored to its former status, whenever the latter was compatible with the security of the American Republics.

However, no unanimity on the question of neutrality was maintained among American Republics in subsequent years. When a third meeting of the Republics' Foreign Ministers was held in Rio de Janeiro on Jan. 15–28, 1941, nine Central American and Caribbean states had declared war on the Axis powers, and it was only near the end of the war in 1945 that all American Republics had declared war on Germany and Japan.

Act of Chapultepec

The basis of later alliances between American states is the so-called *Act of Chapultepec* of 1945. This declaration on "reciprocal assistance and American solidarity" was issued on March 3, 1945, during an Inter-American Conference on the Problems of War and Peace, convened by the Pan-American Union in Mexico City.

The declaration of the Act of Chapultepec contained the following provisions:

(1) All sovereign states are juridically equal amongst themselves.

(2) Every state has the right to the respect of its individuality and independence on the part of the other members of the international community.

(3) Every attack against the integrity, territorial inviolability, sovereignty or political independence of an American state shall be considered as an act of aggression against the other states which sign this declaration. Invasion by armed forces of one state into the territory of another, trespassing boundaries established by treaty and marked in accordance therewith, shall constitute an act of aggression.

(4) In the case that acts of aggression occur or that there may be reasons to believe that an aggression is being prepared by any other state against an American state, the states signatory to this declaration will consult amongst themselves in order to agree upon measures they think it may be advisable to take.

(5) This laid down that during the war against the Axis the American nations would, in the event of interference with the war effort of the United Nations, take any or all of the following actions: Recall of diplomatic missions, breaking of diplomatic relations, interruption of economic, financial and commercial relations, breaking off of postal, telegraphic, radiotelephonic, etc., communications, and the use of armed force to prevent or repel aggression.

The signatories were Bolivia, Brazil, Chile, Colombia, Costa Rica, Cuba, the Dominican Republic, Ecuador, Guatemala, Haiti, Honduras, Mexico, Nicaragua, Panama, Paraguay, Peru, the USA, Uruguay and Venezuela. Argentina signed the Act on April 4, 1945.

Treaty of Rio

A mutual defence treaty in pursuance of the Act of Chapultepec was adopted on Aug. 30, 1947, at an inter-American defence conference held at Petropolis near Rio de Janeiro. The treaty—known as the *Treaty of Rio*, or *Inter-American Treaty of Reciprocal Assistance*—was signed on Sept. 2, 1947, by 19 of the 21 American Republics, only Ecuador and Nicaragua—both of which had suffered recent coups d'état—withholding their signatures; both acceded to the treaty later (on Nov. 7, 1950, and Nov. 12, 1948, respectively). The treaty was also adhered to by Trinidad and Tobago (on June 12, 1967) and the Bahamas (on Nov. 24, 1982). Cuba withdrew from the treaty on March 29, 1960.

The treaty came into force on Dec. 3, 1948. Its principal terms are summarized below:

Art. 1. The signatories "formally condemn war and undertake in their international relations not to resort to the threat or use of force in any manner inconsistent with the UN Charter or of this treaty".

Art. 2. Consequently, they "undertake to submit every controversy which may arise between them to methods of peaceful settlement and endeavour to settle such controversies among themselves by means of procedures in force in the inter-American system before referring them to the UN General Assembly or the Security Council".

Art. 3. (1) The signatories "agree that an armed attack by any states against an American state shall be considered as an attack against all the American states", and consequently each of the signatories "undertake to assist in meeting the attack in exercise of the inherent right of individual or collective self-defence recognized by Art. 51 of the UN Charter".

(2) "On the request of the state or states directly attacked and until the decision of the organ of consultation of the inter-American system", each of the signatories "may determine immediate measures which it may individually adopt in fulfilment of the obligation contained in the preceding paragraph and in accordance with the principle of continental solidarity. The organ of consultation shall meet without delay for the purpose of examining these measures and agreeing upon measures of a collective character that should be adopted".

(3) These provisions shall apply "in case of any armed attack which takes place within the region described in Art. 4 or within the territory of an American state. When an attack takes place outside this area the provisions of Art. 6 shall be applied".

(4) The above measures of self-defence "may be taken until the UN Security Council has taken measures necessary to maintain international peace and security".

Art. 4. This article defines the region to which the treaty refers, which extends from the North Pole to the South Pole, and includes Canada, Alaska, the Aleutians, Greenland, the Falklands, the South Orkneys and Antarctica.

Art. 6. "If the inviolability or the integrity of the territory or sovereignty or political independence of any American state should be affected by an aggression which is not an armed attack or by an intra-continental or extra-continental conflict, or by any other fact or situation that might endanger the peace of America, the organ of consultation shall meet immediately in order to agree on the measures which must be taken in case of aggression to assist the victim of the aggression or, in any case, the measures which should be taken for the common defence and for the maintenance of the peace and security of the continent."

Art. 7. "In the case of a conflict between two or more American states, without prejudice to the right of self-defence in conformity with Art. 51 of the UN Charter", the signatories, "meeting in consultation, shall call upon the contending states to suspend hostilities and restore matters to the *status quo ante bellum*, and shall take in addition all other necessary measures to re-establish or maintain inter-American peace and security and for the solution of the conflict by peaceful means. The rejection of the pacifying action will be considered in the determination of the aggressor and in the application of the measures which the consultative meeting may agree upon."

Art. 8. "The measures on which the organ of consultation may agree will comprise one or more of the following: Recall of chiefs of diplomatic missions, breaking of diplomatic relations, breaking of consular relations, complete or partial interruption of economic relations or of rail, sea, air, postal, telegraphic, telephonic, radio-telephonic or radio-telegraphic communications, and the use of armed force."
(The taking of such sanctions required a two-thirds majority in the organ of consultation.)

Art. 11. "The organ of consultation referred to in this treaty shall be, until a different decision is taken, the meeting of the Ministers of Foreign Affairs of the signatory states."

Art. 20. "Decisions which require the application of the measures specified in Art. 8 shall be binding upon all the signatory states . . . except that no state shall be required to use armed force without its consent."

The Treaty of Rio formed the basis of a series of bilateral treaties of assistance concluded by the USA with Brazil, Chile, Colombia, Cuba, Peru and Uruguay after 1951 (see below under "Defence Treaties of the USA").

It also provided that sanctions taken under Art. 8 of the Treaty could be rescinded by a simple majority of votes in the organ of consultation, whereas the imposition of such sanctions required, under Art. 17 of the Treaty, a two-thirds majority. Moreover, under the protocol contracting states were not (as in 1947) obliged to come to the assistance of a state which

was not a party to the Treaty. However, if any of these states were victims of aggression or of a conflict which might endanger the peace of the hemisphere, the organ of consultation was to meet immediately to agree on measures for the common defence of the hemisphere.

There have been differences of interpretation of the Treaty of Rio.

A US State Department statement of Aug. 18, 1967, contained the claim that "in keeping with [the Treaty's] provisions each of the parties renders assistance in face of attack". An official Mexican statement of Aug. 21, 1967, read inter alia: "Consistently with the explicit text of the Treaty of Rio no state may claim the right to defence by forces of another American state, unless it was called for." The Government of Ecuador, on Aug. 22, 1967, called the US interpretation "extremely dangerous" because "no state of the Western hemisphere has been assailed from outside the continent; however, many of them have been victims of armed interventions made by the USA".

APPLICATIONS OF THE TREATY OF RIO

The Treaty of Rio has been applied in the following disputes and civil conflicts in Latin America:

1948. Dispute between Costa Rica and Nicaragua.
1950. Dispute between the Dominican Republic and Cuba and Guatemala.
Dispute between Haiti and the Dominican Republic.
1954. Civil war in Guatemala.
1955. Dispute between Costa Rica and Nicaragua.
1957. Border dispute between Honduras and Nicaragua.
1959. Attempted invasion of Panama.
Attempted coup d'état in Nicaragua.
1960. Dispute between Venezuela and the Dominican Republic.
1962. Events in Cuba caused the treaty to be invoked twice in this year.
1963. Dispute between Haiti and the Dominican Republic.
Dispute between Venezuela and Cuba.
1964. Dispute between Panama and the USA.
Venezuelan accusation of aggression by Cuba.
1965. Civil war in the Dominican Republic.

The treaty was amended by the *Protocol of San José*, unanimously approved on July 25, 1975, by the 21 signatories of the treaty. The amendment inter alia expanded the treaty's provisions for dealing with aggression against an OAS member country and defined aggression as "the use of armed force by a state against the sovereignty, territorial integrity or political independence of another state, or in any form incompatible with the UN Charter or the OAS Charter or the present treaty".

The OAS and its Related Structures

Organization of American States (OAS)

Address. 17th Street and Constitution Avenue, N.W. Washington, D.C. 20006, USA.

Officer. João Clemente Baena Soares (sec. gen.).

Founded. 1948.

Membership. Antigua and Barbuda, Argentina, the Bahamas, Barbados, Bolivia, Brazil, Chile, Colombia, Costa Rica, Dominica, the Dominican Republic, Ecuador, El Salvador, Grenada, Guatemala, Haiti, Honduras, Jamaica, Mexico, Nicaragua, Panama, Paraguay, Perú, St Christopher and Nevis, St Lucia, St Vincent and the Grenadines, Suriname, Trinidad and Tobago, the United States, Uruguay and Venezuela.

Permanent observers. Austria, Belgium, Canada, Egypt, France, the Federal Republic of Germany, Greece, Guyana, Israel, Italy, Japan, the Republic of Korea, the Netherlands, Portugal, Saudi Arabia, Spain, Switzerland and the Vatican (Holy See). (British applications for permanent observer status were rejected in 1973 and 1979.)

History. The Organization of American States was formed in 1948 as a regional alliance, under the United Nations, to foster mutual understanding and co-operation among the nations of the Western Hemisphere. The Charter of the OAS was drawn up in treaty form at the ninth Inter-American Conference, held in Bogotá in April 1948, and was signed by 21 American Republics, including Cuba, which was later excluded from the organization [see below]. The Charter gave permanent legal form to the hitherto loosely and indefinitely organized pan-American system.

The organization was joined by Trinidad and Tobago in February 1967, Barbados in October 1967, Jamaica in June 1969, Grenada in May 1974, Suriname in February 1977, and Dominica and St Lucia in May 1979, Antigua and Barbuda, as well as St Vincent and the Grenadines, in December 1981, the Bahamas in March 1982 and St Christopher and Nevis in March 1984.

The Charter of the OAS, drafted in Bogotá in 1948, was amended by a supplementary protocol signed in Buenos Aires on March 27, 1967. The amended Charter contained the following provisions:

"Part One. Chapter I. Nature and Purposes

"Art. 1. The American States establish by this Charter the international organization that they have developed to achieve an order of peace and justice, to promote their solidarity, to strengthen their collaboration, and to defend their sovereignty, their territorial integrity, and their independence. Within the United Nations, the Organization of American States is a regional agency.

"Art. 2. The Organization of American States, in order to put into practice the principles on which it is founded and to fulfil its regional obligations under the Charter of the United Nations, proclaims the following essential purposes:

(a) To strengthen the peace and security of the continent;

(b) To prevent possible causes of difficulties and to ensure the pacific settlement of disputes that may arise among the Member States;

(c) To provide for common action on the part of those States in the event of aggression;

(d) To seek the solution of political, juridical, and economic problems that may arise among them; and

(e) To promote, by co-operative action, their economic, social and cultural development.

"Chapter II. Principles

"Art. 3. The American States reaffirm the following principles:

(a) International law is the standard of conduct of States in their reciprocal relations;

(b) International order consists essentially of respect for the personality, sovereignty, and independence of States, and the faithful fulfilment of obligations derived from treaties and other sources of international law;

(c) Good faith shall govern the relations between States;

(d) The solidarity of the American States and the high aims which are sought through it require the political organization of those States on the basis of the effective exercise of representative democracy;

(e) The American States condemn wars of aggression: victory does not give rights;

(f) An act of aggression against one American State is an act of aggression against all the other American States;

(g) Controversies of an international character arising between two or more American States shall be settled by peaceful procedures;

(h) Social justice and social security are bases of lasting peace;

(i) Economic co-operation is essential to the common welfare and prosperity of the peoples of the continent;

(j) The American States proclaim the fundamental rights of the individual without distinction as to race, nationality, creed, or sex;

(k) The spiritual unity of the continent is based on respect for the cultural values of the American countries and requires their close co-operation for the high purposes of civilization;

(l) The education of peoples should be directed toward justice, freedom, and peace.

"Chapter III. Members

"Art. 4. All American States that ratify the present Charter are Members of the Organization."

Articles 5–8 laid down procedures for admission to OAS membership and stated in particular (in Art. 7) that admission should be subject to approval by two-thirds of the member states and (in Art. 8) that no recommendation or decision should be made "with respect to a request for admission on the part of a political entity whose territory became subject, in whole or in part, prior to Dec. 18, 1964, the date set by the First Special Inter-American Conference, to litigation or claim between an extracontinental country and one or more Member States of the Organization, until the dispute has been ended by some peaceful procedure."

"Chapter IV. Fundamental Rights and Duties of States

"Art. 9. States are juridically equal, enjoy equal rights and equal capacity to exercise these rights, and have equal duties. The rights of each State depend not upon its power to ensure the exercise thereof, but upon the mere fact of its existence as a person under international law.

"Art. 10. Every American State has the duty to respect the rights enjoyed by every other State in accordance with international law.

"Art. 11. The fundamental rights of States may not be impaired in any manner whatsoever.

"Art. 12. The political existence of the State is independent of recognition by other States. Even before being recognized, the State has the right to defend its integrity and independence, to provide for its preservation and prosperity, and consequently to organize itself as it sees fit, to legislate concerning its interests, to administer its services, and to determine the jurisdiction and competence of its courts. The exercise of these rights is limited only by the exercise of the rights of other States in accordance with international law.

"Art. 13. Recognition implies that the State granting it accepts the personality of the new State, with all the rights and duties that international law prescribes for the two States.

"Art. 14. The right of each State to protect itself and to live its own life does not authorize it to commit unjust acts against another State.

"Art. 15. The jurisdiction of States within the limits of their national territory is exercised equally over all the inhabitants, whether nationals or aliens.

"Art. 16. Each State has the right to develop its cultural, political, and economic life freely and naturally. In this free development, the State shall respect the rights of the individual and the principles of universal morality.

"Art. 17. Respect for and the faithful observance of treaties constitute standards for the development of peaceful relations among States. International treaties and agreements should be public.

"Art. 18. No State or group of States has the right to intervene, directly or indirectly, for any reason whatever, in the internal or external affairs of any other State. The foregoing principle prohibits not only armed force but also any other form of interference or attempted threat against the personality of the State or against its political, economic, and cultural elements.

"Art. 19. No State may use or encourage the use of coercive measures of an economic or political character in order to force the sovereign will of another State and obtain from it advantages of any kind.

"Art. 20. The territory of a State is inviolable; it may not be the object, even temporarily, of military occupation or of other measures of force taken by another State, directly or indirectly, on any grounds whatever. No territorial acquisitions or special advantages obtained either by force or by other means of coercion shall be recognized.

"Art. 21. The American States bind themselves in their international relations not to have recourse to the use of force, except in the case of self-defense in accordance with existing treaties or in fulfilment thereof.

"Art. 22. Measures adopted for the maintenance of peace and security in accordance with existing treaties do not constitute a violation of the principles set forth in Articles 18 and 20.

"Chapter V. Pacific Settlement of Disputes

"Art. 23. All international disputes that may arise between American States shall be submitted to the peaceful procedures set forth in this Charter, before being referred to the Security Council of the United Nations."

Articles 24–26 laid down procedures for the peaceful settlement of disputes and provided for the drafting of a special treaty to establish "adequate procedures" for such settlement.

"Chapter VI. Collective Security

"Art. 27. Every act of aggression by a State against the territorial integrity or the inviolability of the territory or against the sovereignty or political independence of an American State shall be considered an act of aggression against the other American States.

"Art. 28. If the inviolability or the integrity of the territory or the sovereignty or political independence of any American State should be affected by an armed attack or by an act of aggression that is not an armed attack, or by an extra-continental conflict, or by a conflict between two or more American States, or by any other fact or situation that might endanger the peace of America, the American States, in furtherance of the principles of continental solidarity or collective self-defense, shall apply the measures and procedures established in the special treaties on the subject.

"Chapter VII. Economic Standards

"Art. 29. The Member States, inspired by the principles of inter-American solidarity and co-operation, pledge themselves to a united effort to ensure social justice in the Hemisphere and dynamic and balanced economic development for their peoples, as conditions essential to peace and security.

"Art. 30. The Member States pledge themselves to mobilize their own national human and material resources through suitable programs, and recognize the importance of operating within an efficient domestic structure, as fundamental conditions for their economic and social progress and for assuring effective inter-American co-operation.

"Art. 31. To accelerate their economic and social development, in accordance with their own methods and procedures and within the framework of the democratic principles and the institutions of the inter-American system, the Member States agree to dedicate every effort to achieve the following basic goals:

(a) Substantial and self-sustained increase in the per capita national product;

(b) Equitable distribution of national income;

(c) Adequate and equitable systems of taxation;

(d) Modernization of rural life and reforms leading to equitable and efficient land-tenure systems, increased agricultural productivity, expanded use of underdeveloped land, diversification of production; and improved processing and marketing systems for agricultural products; and the strengthening and expansion of facilities to attain these ends;

(e) Accelerated and diversified industrialization, especially of capital and intermediate goods;

(f) Stability in the domestic price levels, compatible with sustained economic development and the attainment of social justice;

(g) Fair wages, employment opportunities, and acceptable working conditions for all;

(h) Rapid eradication of illiteracy and expansion of educational opportunities for all;

(i) Protection of man's potential through the extension and application of modern medical science;

(j) Proper nutrition, especially through the acceleration of national efforts to increase the production and availability of food;

(k) Adequate housing for all sectors of the population;

(l) Urban conditions that offer the opportunity for a healthful, productive, and full life;

(m) Promotion of private initiative and investment in harmony with action in the public sector; and

(n) Expansion and diversification of exports.

"Art. 32. In order to attain the objectives set forth in this Chapter, the Member States agree to co-operate with one another, in the broadest spirit of inter-American solidarity, as far as their resources may permit and their laws may provide."

Articles 33–42 listed details of methods suitable for achieving the objectives set out in previous articles, including the eventual establishment of a Latin American common market (Art. 40).

Chapter VIII. Social Standards

In this chapter Articles 43 and 44 laid down principles of labour relations, including the harmonization of social legislation of the developing countries.

Chapter IX. Educational, Scientific and Cultural Standards

Articles 45–50 provided for co-operation in these fields, with special attention to be given to the elimination of illiteracy (Art. 48).

Part Two. Chapters X–XXII

In this part Articles 51–136 listed the organs of the OAS and defined their functions and procedures. These organs were:

1. The General Assembly (which meets annually and is the supreme organ of the OAS).

2. The Meetings of Consultation of the Ministers of Foreign Affairs (which take place as necessary, or when requested).

3. The Permanent Council (which comprises one representative of each member state and which is assisted by an Inter-American Committee on Peaceful Settlement).

4. The Inter-American Economic and Social Council (with a Permanent Executive Committee).

5. The Inter-American Council for Education, Science and Culture (also with a Permanent Executive Committee).

6. The Inter-American Juridical Committee (consisting of 11 jurists elected for four years and with its seat in Rio de Janeiro).

7. The Inter-American Commission on Human Rights.

8. The General Secretariat (with a Secretary-General and an Assistant Secretary-General).

9. The Specialized Inter-American Conferences.

10. The Specialized Organizations.

Chapter XXII

Art. 137. In this article it was laid down that "none of the provisions of this Charter shall be construed as impairing the rights and obligations of the Member States under the Charter of the United Nations".

Chapters XXIII to XXV

Articles 138–150. These chapters contained miscellaneous and transitional provisions.

The 1967 Protocol of Amendment of the Charter was signed with reservations by Argentina, Ecuador and Panama. It came into force on Feb. 27, 1970.

The protocol was the result of deliberations during 1965–66 on a reform of the 1948 version of the OAS Charter. Suggestions for reforms were contained in an *Act of Rio de Janeiro* signed by all delegates of the then 19 OAS member states except Venezuela at a special Inter-American Conference held on Nov. 17–30, 1965.

A *Declaration of Bogotá*, signed on Aug. 16, 1966, was the result of further deliberations on such reforms to the Charter. This declaration inter alia reasserted the principle of non-intervention in the internal affairs of American states; called on the rich nations of the world to assist in Latin American development; demanded "greater respect by the United States for the rules of international trade"; and advocated economic integration in the Americas, particularly in the form of closer relations between the Latin American Free Trade Association (LAFTA) and the Central American Common Market [see below].

1985 AMENDMENTS TO THE CHARTER

Under a Protocol of Cartagena, adopted on Dec. 5, 1985, Article 8 of the Charter was to expire in 1990 and be replaced by new rules under which eligibility for OAS membership was extended to all independent American states which were members of the United Nations as at Dec. 10, 1985, and to certain specified currently non-autonomous territories, including Martinique, Guadeloupe, French Guiana, Montserrat and Bermuda (but not the Falkland/Malvinas Islands) in the event of their attaining independence.

The protocol also extended the powers of the OAS Secretary-General who was enabled to bring to the attention of the OAS Assembly or Permanent Council any matter which "could affect the peace and security of the continent and the development of its member countries". The Permanent Council was, in addition, allowed to provide peacekeeping services to assist in dealing with crises in the region.

1948 BOGOTÁ DECLARATIONS

Declaration on European Colonies. A declaration condemning the existence of European colonies in the Western Hemisphere and establishing an inter-American body to study the problem and seek peaceful means of solving it was adopted at the Bogotá conference; the declaration was approved by 17 of the 21 countries represented, those abstaining being the USA, Brazil, Chile and the Dominican Republic.

The declaration considered "that the historical process of emancipation of America will not be completed so long as there remain on the continent peoples and regions subjected to colonial regimes or territories occupied by non-American countries", and described as a "just aspiration" that an end be put to colonialism and to occupation of American territories by extracontinental countries. There would be created, the declaration continued, an "American Commission of Dependent Territories" to centralize the study of the colonial problem, composed of one representative from each member state, and it would be considered to be installed when two-thirds of those representatives had been named. Its site would be Havana and its functions would include study of the "colonial situation" and the seeking of peaceful means for "the abolition of colonialism as well as the occupation of American territories by extra-continental countries". It would submit a report on each territory to the Council, which would inform the member states, the reports being subsequently considered at the first meeting of the Foreign Ministers. "The creation of this Commission," the declaration concluded, "and the exercise of its functions, shall not exclude or limit the rights and actions of interested states in seeking directly and by peaceful means the solution of problems affecting them."

Declaration on Democracy and Communism. Another declaration reaffirming the faith of the American states in democracy and condemning communism was also adopted.

This declaration said inter alia that "the present international situation demands urgent measures to safeguard peace and defend mutual respect among states, proscribing tactics of totalitarian hegemony irreconcilable with the tradition of the American countries and preventing agents at the service of international communism or any totalitarianism from seeking to distort the free world of the peoples of this hemisphere." It reiterated "the faith that the peoples of the New World have placed in the ideal and reality of democracy"; condemned the "interference of any foreign power, or any political organization serving the interests of a foreign power, in the public life of the nations of the American continent"; and promised that the American states would adopt within their respective territories the necessary measures to prevent and uproot activities directed or instigated by foreign governments which tended to subvert their institutions through violence or to promote disorder in their internal political life.

Pact of Bogotá. In fulfilment of Article 23 of the OAS Charter, the Bogotá conference also adopted an *American Treaty on Pacific Settlement* (known as the *Pact of Bogotá*) on procedures for settling disputes (on which reservations were, however, expressed by the United States and also by Argentina, Bolivia, Ecuador, Nicaragua, Paraguay and Peru).

The first special Inter-American Conference—this conference then being the supreme authority of the organization—was held in Washington on Dec. 16–18, 1964, and was limited to establishing, in an *Act of Washington*, procedures for the admission of new members to the organization.

Under the terms of this Act any country against which a member state of the OAS had a territorial claim was excluded from OAS membership, and this was applied to Belize because of Guatemala's claim against it, and to Guyana because of a longstanding claim by Venezuela.

Special Organizations, Agencies and Commissions

The OAS also embraces the following specialized organizations:

(1) **Inter-American Institute of Agricultural Sciences (IAIAS)**, founded in 1942 and based in San José (Costa Rica); its members include Canada.

(2) **Pan-American Health Organization (PAHO)**, founded in 1902 and based in Washington; it acts as a regional organization of the World Health Organization (WHO); and its members include Canada and also France, the Netherlands and the United Kingdom (for their departments and territories in America).

(3) **Inter-American Commission of Women (IACW)**, founded in 1928 and based also in Washington, with the object of extending civil, political, economic, social and cultural rights of women in the Americas.

(4) **Inter-American Children's Institute (IACI)**, based in Montevideo and founded in 1927 to improve the health and living conditions of mothers and children.

(5) **Pan-American Institute of Geography and History (PAIGH)**, based in Mexico, with Canada being one of its members, and with its objects including the opening-up of natural resources available in individual countries of the Americas.

(6) **Inter-American Indian Institute (IAII)**, based in Mexico and founded in 1940; its members are the following OAS member states: Argentina, Bolivia, Brazil, Chile, Colombia, Costa Rica, Ecuador, El Salvador, Guatemala, Honduras, Mexico, Nicaragua, Panama, Paraguay, Peru, the United States and Venezuela.

In addition there are the following special agencies and commissions, all based in Washington:

(1) **Inter-American Defence Board (IADB)**, founded in 1942; it has as one of its institutions an Inter-American Defence College, established in 1962 to provide special education for high-ranking officers of the Latin American armed forces.

(2) **Inter-American Statistical Institute (IASI)**, founded in 1940; Canada is one of its members.

(3) **Inter-American Nuclear Energy Commission (IANEC)**, established in 1959 to assist in the development and coordination of research in the peaceful uses of atomic energy.

(4) **Administrative Tribunal**.

(5) **Inter-American Emergency Aid Fund (FONDEM)**.

(6) **Pan-American Highway Congresses**, established in 1925 to promote highway development and progress; they also serve as an advisory body on highways in the American hemisphere.

The Inter-American Economic and Social Council (IA-ECOSOC) established a **Special Development Assistance Fund** in 1965 and an **Inter-American Export Promotion Centre** in 1969.

Protection of American States against Communism

In pursuance of the policies expressed in the Declaration on Communism of 1948 adopted at the Bogotá Conference [see above], further declarations were approved by OAS members as follows:

(1) The *Declaration of Solidarity for Preservation of the Political Integrity of the American States against International Communist Intervention*, presented by John Foster Dulles (then US Secretary of State) and adopted by 17 votes to one (Guatemala), with Argentina and Mexico abstaining, at the 10th conference of the OAS held in Caracas, March 1–28, 1954.

In its final form the declaration specified that:

(1) The conference condemned the activities of international communism as constituting intervention in American affairs; expressed the determination of the American states "to take the necessary measures to protect their political independence against the intervention of international communism"; reiterated "the faith of the peoples of America in the effective exercise of representative democracy as the best means to promote their social and political progress"; and declared that "the domination or control of the political institutions of any American state by the international communist movement, extending to this hemisphere the political system of an extra-continental power, would constitute a threat to the sovereignty and political independence of the American states . . . and would call for consultation and appropriate action in accordance with existing treaties".

(2) The governments agreed to take the following steps "for the purpose of counteracting the subversive activities of the international communist movement within their respective jurisdictions": (i) To require "the disclosure of the identity, activities and source of funds of those who are spreading propaganda of the international communist movement, or who travel in the interests of that movement, or who act as its agents or on its behalf"; (ii) to exchange information with a view to implementing the resolutions adopted on this subject at inter-American conferences.

(3) "This declaration of foreign policy made by the American Republics in relation to dangers originating outside this hemisphere is designed to protect, and not to impair, the inalienable right of each American state freely to choose its own form of government and economic system, and to live its own social and cultural life."

(2) The *Declaration of Santiago de Chile*, adopted at a meeting of OAS Foreign Ministers at Santiago de Chile on Aug. 14–20, 1959, and laying down the following principles:

"(1) The principle of the rule of law should be assured by the separation of powers and by the control of the legality of governmental acts by competent organs of the state;

"(2) the Governments of the American Republics should be derived from free elections;

"(3) perpetuation in power, or the exercise of power without fixed term and with the manifest intent of perpetuation, is incompatible with the effective exercise of democracy;

"(4) the Governments of the American states should ensure . . . freedom for the individual and social justice based on respect for fundamental human rights;

"(5) the human rights incorporated in the legislation of the various American states should be protected by effective judicial procedures;

"(6) the systematic use of political proscription is contrary to American democratic order;

"(7) freedom of the press, of radio and television, and, in general, of information and expression, are essential conditions for the existence of a democratic regime;

"(8) the American states . . . should co-operate . . . to strengthen and develop their economic structure and achieve just and humane living conditions for their peoples."

(3) The *Declaration of San José*, adopted unanimously (after the withdrawal of the Cuban delegation from the conference) at the meeting

of OAS Foreign Ministers in San José (Costa Rica) on Aug. 16–28, 1960.

The declaration contained the following points:

(1) An "emphatic condemnation" of "intervention or the threat of intervention . . . from an extra-continental power in the affairs of the American Republics", coupled with a declaration that "the acceptance of a threat of extra-continental intervention by any American state jeopardizes American solidarity and security".

(2) Rejection of "the attempt of the Sino-Soviet powers to make use of the political, economic or social situation of any American state, inasmuch as any such attempt is capable of destroying hemispheric unity and jeopardizing the peace and security of the hemisphere".

(3) Reaffirmation of "the principle of non-intervention by any American state in the internal or external affairs of other American states", and of the right of each state "to develop its cultural, political and economic life freely and naturally, respecting the rights of the individual and the principles of universal morality. As a consequence, no American state may intervene for the purpose of imposing upon another American state its ideology or political, economic or social principles".

(4) "The inter-American system is incompatible with any form of totalitarianism and . . . democracy will achieve the full scope of its objectives in the hemisphere only when all the American Republics conduct themselves in accordance with the principles stated in the Declaration of Santiago de Chile [see above]".

(5) A declaration that "all member states (of the OAS) are under obligation to submit to the discipline of the inter-American system, voluntarily and freely agreed upon . . .".

(6) A declaration that "all controversies between member states should be resolved by the measures of peaceful solution contemplated in the inter-American system".

(7) Reaffirmation of "faith in the regional system" and of "confidence in the Organization of American States, created to achieve an order of peace and justice that excludes any possible aggression, to promote solidarity among its members, to strengthen their collaboration, and to defend their sovereignty, territorial integrity and political independence . . .".

(4) A resolution dealing with *The Offensive of Communist Governments* in America, approved unanimously, in the absence of the Cuban delegation, at the conference of OAS Foreign Ministers in Punta del Este (Uruguay) held on Jan. 22–31, 1962.

The resolution stated inter alia:

"The Ministers of Foreign Affairs of the American Republics . . . declare that the continual unity and the democratic institutions of the hemisphere are now in danger.

"The ministers have been able to verify that the subversive offensive of Communist governments, their agents and the organizations which they control has increased in intensity. The purpose of this offensive is the destruction of democratic institutions and the establishment of totalitarian dictatorships at the service of extra-continental powers. The outstanding facts in this intensified offensive are the declarations, set forth in official documents of the directing bodies of the international communist movement, that one of its principal objectives is the establishment of Communist regimes in the underdeveloped countries and in Latin America; and the existence of a Marxist-Leninist government in Cuba which is publicly aligned with the doctrine and foreign policy of the Communist powers.

"In order to achieve their subversive purposes and hide their true intentions, the Communist governments and their agents exploit the legitimate needs of the less-favoured sectors of the population and the just national aspirations of the various peoples. With the pretext of defending popular interests, freedom is suppressed, democratic institutions are destroyed, human rights are violated, and the individual is subjected to materialistic ways of life imposed by the dictatorship of a single

party. Under the slogan of "anti-imperialism", they try to establish an oppressive, aggressive imperialism, which subordinates the subjugated nations to the militaristic and aggressive interests of the extra-continental powers. By maliciously utilizing the principles of the inter-American system, they attempt to undermine democratic institutions and to strengthen and protect political penetration and aggression. The subversive methods of Communist governments and their agents constitute one of the most subtle and dangerous forms of intervention in the internal affairs of other countries.

"The ministers . . . alert the peoples of the hemisphere to the intensification of the subversive offensive of Communist governments, their agents and the organizations that they control and to the tactics and methods they employ, and also warn them of the dangers this situation represents to representative democracy, to respect for human rights, and to the self-determination of peoples.

"The principles of communism are incompatible with the principles of the inter-American system.

"Convinced that the integrity of the democratic revolution of the American states can and must be preserved in the face of the subversive offensive of communism, the ministers . . . proclaim the following basic political principles:

"(a) The faith of the American peoples in human rights, liberty and national independence as a fundamental reason for their existence, as conceived by the founding fathers who destroyed colonialism and brought the American republics into being.

"(b) The principle of non-intervention and the right of peoples to organize their way of life freely in the political, economic and cultural spheres, expressing their will through free elections, without foreign interference. The fallacies of communist propaganda cannot and should not obscure or hide the difference in philosophy which these principles represent when they are expressed by a democratic American country, and when Communist governments and their agents attempt to utilize them for their own benefit.

"(c) The repudiation of repressive measures which, under the pretext of isolating or combating communism, may facilitate the appearance or strengthening of reactionary doctrines and methods which attempt to repress ideas of social progress and to confuse truly progressive and democratic labour organizations and cultural and political movements with communist subversion.

"(d) The affirmation that communism is not the way to achieve economic development and the elimination of social injustice in America. On the contrary, a democratic regime can encompass all the efforts for economic advancement and all measures for improvement and social progress without sacrificing the fundamental values of the human being. The mission of the peoples and governments of the hemisphere during the present generation is to achieve an accelerated development of their economies and to put an end to poverty, injustice, illness and ignorance as was agreed in the Charter of Punta del Este [see below].

"(e) The most essential contribution of each American state in the collective effort to protect the inter-American system against communism is a steadily greater respect for human rights, improvement in democratic institutions and practices, and the adoption of measures that truly express the impulse for a revolutionary change in the economic and social structures of the American Republics."

The conference decided on Jan. 31, 1962, by 14 votes to one (Cuba), with Argentina, Bolivia, Brazil, Chile, Ecuador and Mexico abstaining— i.e. with the bare two-thirds majority required by the OAS Charter—to exclude Cuba from the Inter-American system, and this resolution was ratified by the Council of the OAS of Feb. 14 by 17 votes (including Argentina, Bolivia, and Ecuador) to three (Brazil, Chile and Mexico). Cuba was also excluded "immediately" from the Inter-American Defence Board.

(5) A resolution approved by the OAS Council in Washington on Oct. 23, 1962, by 19 votes to none (with Uruguay abstaining for lack of government instructions).

This resolution, inter alia, (i) called for "the immediate dismantling and withdrawal from Cuba of all missiles and other weapons with offensive capability"; and (ii) recommended that the OAS member states, in accordance with Articles 6 and 8 of the Inter-American Treaty of Reciprocal Assistance, should "take all measures, individually and collectively, including the use of armed force, which they may deem necessary to ensure that Cuba cannot continue to receive from the Sino-Soviet powers military material and related supplies which may threaten the peace and security of the continent, and to prevent the missiles in Cuba with offensive capability from ever becoming an active threat to the peace and security of the continent".

(6) A report by the OAS Council, issued on Feb. 24, 1964, indicting the Government of Cuba for "a series of actions . . . openly intended to subvert Venezuelan institutions and to overthrow the democratic Government of Venezuela through terrorism, sabotage, assault and guerrilla warfare".

(7) A resolution adopted by the ninth consultative meeting of American Foreign Ministers in Washington on July 26, 1964, by 15 votes to four (Bolivia, Chile, Mexico and Uruguay) with Venezuela, having brought a charge of aggression against Cuba, taking no part in the vote.

This resolution, based on a report by an investigating committee appointed by the OAS Council in December 1963, inter alia,
(1) declared "that the acts verified by the investigating committee constitute an aggression and an intervention on the part of the Government of Cuba in the internal affairs of Venezuela, which affects all of the member states";
(2) condemned "energetically the present Government of Cuba for its act of aggression and intervention against the territorial inviolability, sovereignty and political independence of Venezuela";
(3) requested member-countries, "in accordance with the provisions of Articles 6 and 8 of the Inter-American Treaty of Reciprocal Assistance, . . . (i) not [to] maintain diplomatic or consular relations with the Government of Cuba", (ii) to "suspend all trade, whether direct or indirect, with Cuba, except in foodstuffs, medicines and medical equipment that may be sent to Cuba for humanitarian reasons", and (iii) to "suspend all sea transportation between their countries and Cuba" except for transportation "necessary for reasons of a humanitarian nature".

Promotion of Economic and Social Co-operation among American States

An inter-American economic conference held under the auspices of the OAS in Buenos Aires from Aug. 15 to Sept. 4, 1957, approved the *Economic Declaration of Buenos Aires*, which expressed the intention of the participating states to increase the volume of mutual trade, to reduce trade barriers, to endeavour jointly to solve the problems of producers of basic raw materials subject to excessive price fluctuations, to take measures to attract foreign capital and stimulate private investment, to establish sound financial and monetary systems in Latin America, and to increase technical co-operation through the OAS.

On Aug. 16, 1958, the Brazilian Government proposed to all Latin American countries a plan known as *Operation Pan-America* for increased economic co-operation with a view to establishing, inter alia, an Inter-American Development Bank and eventually a Latin American Common Market. A conference of Foreign Ministers of the OAS decided in Washington on Sept. 24, 1958, to recommend the establishment of a **Special Commission for Economic Co-operation,** and such a commission was constituted in Buenos Aires from April 28 to May 9, 1959.

1960 ACT OF BOGOTÁ

At a meeting in Bogotá Sept. 5–12, 1960, the commission approved the *Act of Bogotá*, signed on Sept. 13, 1960, by all American Republics except Cuba and the Dominican Republic which, however, signed it later. Considering it opportune to give further practical expression to the spirit of Operation Pan-America, the act contained the following recommendations:

Measures for Social Development. (1) Modernization and improvement of the legal and institutional systems of land tenure, agricultural credit and taxation; acceleration of projects for land reclamation and improvement, land settlement, and the construction of farm-to-market and access roads; and governmental programmes particularly designed to help small farmers.
(2) Expansion and improvement of schemes of housing and community services; strengthening of the existing facilities for mobilizing financial resources for housing, or, if necessary, the creation of new institutions for this purpose; expansion of those industries engaged in house-building; encouragement of pilot projects of "self-help" housing; and the purchase of land for low-cost and industrial housing projects.
(3) Development of all aspects of the educational system, particularly mass education aimed at eradicating illiteracy; instruction in agricultural, technical and scientific subjects; and the training of professional personnel "of key importance to economic development".
(4) Improvement of health services, including the provision of medical services in remote areas, development of health insurance schemes, campaigns for the control or elimination of communicable diseases, especially malaria, and the provision of adequate water-supply facilities.
(5) More equitable and effective measures to achieve maximum domestic savings; improvement of fiscal and financial practices; and the allocation of tax revenues to an extent adequate for the above-mentioned measures of social development.

Creation of Special Social Development Fund. The Latin American countries welcomed the decision of the US Government to establish a special inter-American fund for social development, with the Inter-American Development Bank as the primary mechanism for administering the fund.

Measures for Economic Development. (1) Provision of additional domestic and external resources for financing plans and projects of basic economic and industrial development, with special attention to loans on flexible terms and conditions, including repayment in local currency whenever advisable because of balance-of-payments conditions, and the strengthening of credit facilities for small and medium private business, agriculture and industry.
(2) Special attention to the expansion of long-term lending.

(3) Examination of methods to deal with the problem of the instability of exchange earnings in countries relying heavily on exports of primary products.

ALLIANCE FOR PROGRESS
ALIANZA PARA EL PROGRESO (CIAP)

In a message to Congress on March 14, 1961, President John F. Kennedy declared that the Act of Bogotá marked "an historic turning point in the evolution of the Western Hemisphere", and he requested massive aid to Latin America. The previous day, March 13, he had outlined a broad development plan for Latin America, which he called the *Alliance for Progress.*

This plan contained proposals for a "vast new 10-year plan for the Americas". It was to be administered by the (OAS) Inter-American Economic and Social Council (IA-ECOSOC) through a permanent executive, the Inter-American Committee on the Alliance for Progress (Comisión Interamericana de la Alianza para el Progreso).

A **First Punta del Este Conference** of the IA-ECOSOC held on Aug. 5–17, 1961, issued two documents—(a) a *Declaration to the Peoples of America* and (b) a *Charter of Punta del Este* setting out the aims, methods and execution of the Alliance for Progress.

The declaration established the goals of the plan as being to apply the principle of self-determination by the people; to produce "a substantial and steady increase in the average income as quickly as possible"; to carry out housing programmes; to encourage programmes of integral agrarian reform; to "wipe out illiteracy"; to improve health and sanitation; "to assure workers fair wages and satisfactory working conditions"; to reform tax laws; to "protect the purchasing power of the many"; to stimulate private enterprise; to find "a rapid and lasting solution to the grave problem created by excessive price fluctuations in the basic exports of Latin American countries"; and to accelerate the integration of Latin America, already begun through the General Treaty of Economic Integration of Central America [see page 364] and the Latin American Free Trade Association.

Developments in 1963–64. During the following two years, however, the Alliance for Progress failed to achieve many of its objectives. Experts and leaders from the Latin American states criticized the United States for not having lived up to its promises, while US spokesmen placed the blame on the Latin American countries themselves.

The annual report of the Alliance for Progress published on Nov. 11, 1963, showed that the actual growth rate of per capita income in Latin America in 1962 had been between 0.6 and 1 per cent—as against 2.5 per cent aimed at by the Alliance for Progress; this development had been due to a decline in Argentina's gross national product and a fall in Brazil's growth rate.

Second Inter-American Conference at Rio (1965). At a second special Inter-American Conference in Rio de Janeiro the US Secretary of State on Nov. 22, 1965, read a message from President Johnson pledging US support for the Alliance for Progress—which had until then totalled $4,000 million—beyond 1971, the terminal

date agreed at Punta del Este in 1961. In return, the Latin American nations agreed to do more to promote their own economic development.

The conference also adopted the *Economic and Social Act of Rio de Janeiro*, reaffirming the principles and objectives of the Declaration to the Peoples of America and the Charter of Punta del Este [see above].

However, a report issued by the Inter-American Committee on the Alliance for Progress in Washington on March 31, 1967, stated that during 1966 the per capita growth in goods and services in Latin America had been little more than 1 per cent on average, and that economic growth had barely kept ahead of Latin America's increasing population, which was expected to reach 250,000,000 by the end of 1967.

President Johnson asked the US Congress on March 13, 1967, to increase aid to the Alliance for Progress by $1,500 million over the next five years, in addition to the $1,000 million already provided by the USA annually since 1961.

Second Punta del Este Conference (1967). The Punta del Este conference of American Presidents on April 14, 1967, adopted a *Declaration of the American Presidents* embodying an *Action Plan for Latin American Economic Integration and Industrial Development.*

The aims of this plan were defined as follows:

"(A) Beginning in 1970, to establish progressively the Latin American Common Market, which should be substantially in operation within a period of no more than 15 years.

"(B) The Latin American Common Market will be based on the improvement of the two existing integration systems: the Latin American Free Trade Association (LAFTA) and the Central American Common Market (CACM). The two systems will initiate simultaneously a process of convergence by stages of co-operation, by closer ties and integration, taking into account the interests of Latin American countries not yet associated with these systems, in order to provide their access to one of them."

The plan envisaged a system of programmed elimination of duties and other restrictions from 1970 to not later than 1985 within the Latin American Free Trade Area, and of working towards integration in the Central American Common Market countries.

The declaration also pointed out that the economic development of Latin America was seriously affected by the adverse conditions of international trade, which prejudiced exports and other income from outside Latin America, impeded its growth and retarded the integration process, and that there was a "serious and growing imbalance between the standard of living in Latin American countries and that of the industrialized nations".

It outlined a programme for overcoming these difficulties, inter alia by "the greatest reduction or the elimination of tariffs and other restrictions" without the more highly developed countries expecting reciprocity.

The plan also listed proposals for the modernization of agricultural activities and for the adjustment of education to the demands of economic, social and cultural development.

1980 Ending of Programme. Having fallen far short of achieving its targets the Alliance of Progress was formally ended in 1980.

OAS Conventions

Major conventions adopted by the OAS are described below.

Convention on Territorial Asylum. This convention, which inter alia defined the rights and duties of political refugees, was signed on March 22, 1954, and came into force on Dec. 29, 1954, after being ratified by Brazil, Colombia, Costa Rica, Ecuador, El Salvador, Haiti, Panama, Paraguay, Uruguay and Venezuela.

Latin American Convention on Human Rights. This convention, drawn up in 1969, forbade torture and maltreatment of prisoners, guaranteed freedom of expression and of religion, and provided for the creation of an **Inter-American Court of Human Rights.** It entered into force on July 18, 1978, upon ratification by Grenada (as the eleventh country, the other 10 being Colombia, Costa Rica, the Dominican Republic, Ecuador, El Salvador, Guatemala, Haiti, Honduras, Panama and Venezuela—with Nicaragua ratifying it in September 1979).

The Inter-American Court of Human Rights was accordingly established formally in San José (Costa Rica) on Sept. 3, 1979, with a membership of seven judges. Its mandate was to deal with violations of civil and political rights, but its decisions would not be legally binding and states which had not ratified the 1969 convention would be able to ask the court for an advisory opinion but not to have cases tried by it.

Convention on Kidnapping of Diplomats. A draft convention outlawing the kidnapping of foreign diplomats was approved by the Foreign Ministers of the OAS member states on Feb. 2, 1971, by 13 votes to one (Chile), with Bolivia and Peru abstaining and Barbados absent.

The convention defined criminal acts against persons with diplomatic status as common crimes and not political acts; their perpetrators would therefore not be entitled to political asylum in any country whose government had ratified the convention but would be liable to extradition or trial.

A Convention on the Protection of the Archaeological, Historic and Artistic Heritage of the American Nations was signed in San Salvador on June 16, 1976, and came into force on Sept. 27, 1978. By Dec. 31, 1985, only Costa Rica, Ecuador, El Salvador, Guatemala, Haiti, Honduras, Nicaragua, Panama and Peru were parties to the convention.

Decisions by OAS General Assembly and Ministerial Meetings

Inaugural Assembly Session. The OAS General Assembly, which normally meets annually to decide on general action and policy, held its first regular session in San José (Costa Rica) in April 1971, when a Canadian initiative for closer co-operation in social and economic development between Canada and the Latin American countries was considered. (Canada was on Feb. 2, 1972, admitted to the OAS as an observer.)

April 1972 Assembly Session. At the second regular session of the General Assembly, which took place in Washington in April 1972, ministers adopted two resolutions (i) condemning all forms of interference in the internal affairs of the 23 OAS member states, in particular "political and economic coercion" and "imported subversion and terrorism" and (ii) undertaking to limit military expenditure by Latin American countries in order that a maximum of financial resources should be devoted to social and economic development. The Assembly endorsed the principle of "ideological pluralism" as advocated by the Foreign Minister of Venezuela, according to which "each nation may realize its own destiny within the framework created by its people's will, their tradition, their temperament and their specific interests", but it did not favour the readmission of Cuba to OAS activities (from which Cuba had been excluded in 1962—see above).

The Assembly also adopted (with the USA abstaining) two resolutions (i) calling on the US Government to prevent large corporations from intervening in the internal affairs of Latin American countries and (ii) urging the US Government to take all possible measures to prevent a fall in prices of vital exports (from Latin American countries).

1974 Declaration of Tlatelolco. In subsequent years the OAS continued to be beset by marked divergencies in the economic interests and policies of the USA and the other OAS member states. At a conference of 24 Foreign Ministers of Latin American and English-speaking Caribbean countries held in Tlatelolco (Mexico) on Feb. 21–23, 1974, with the object of conferring with the US Secretary of State, a *Declaration of Tlatelolco* was agreed to, stating inter alia that "inter-American relations must be sustained on the basis of effective equality between the states" and must be based on "non-intervention, the reduction of the use of force and coercive measures, and on respect for the right of those countries to choose their own political, economic and social systems".

In the declaration the ministers emphasized the need to intensify work on the restructuring of the inter-American system and in particular "to speed up the development of the countries on the Latin American continent and to promote the well-being of all its peoples", while the United States accepted a special responsibility and the most developed nations of the region recognized that special attention would have to be paid to the needs of the less developed. The USA offered to seek congressional approval for legislation relating to generalized tariff preferences for Latin America and the avoidance of new restrictions on market access to the United States for Latin American products. The USA also undertook to maintain present levels of aid "despite rising prices" and to facilitate the flow of new resources to the countries most affected by the rising cost of energy.

Opposition to US Trade Act. A special session of the Permanent Council of the OAS, held on Jan. 20, 1975, expressed overwhelming opposition to the 1975 US Trade Reform Act because of its provisions enabling the US President to exclude from proposed special measures relating to developing countries those states which belonged to producers' cartels—i.e. not only the Organization of Petroleum Exporting Countries (OPEC) but also producer organizations covering coffee, bauxite, copper and bananas. On Jan. 23, 1975, the OAS condemned the US Act as discriminatory and coercive and also as being in conflict with the UN Charter of the Economic Rights and Duties of States [see pages 49ff.].

Relations with Cuba. At a special consultative meeting of OAS ministers held in San José (Costa Rica) on July 29, 1975, a resolution was adopted by 16 votes to three (with two abstentions and with the USA voting in favour) stating that the 21 signatories of the Inter-American Treaty of Reciprocal Assistance would henceforth be free to normalize, or conduct in accordance with national policy and interests, relations with the Republic of Cuba at the level and in the form each state deemed advisable.

Human Rights Issue. At a session of the OAS General Assembly, held in Grenada on June 14–23, 1977, the US Secretary of State declared that US economic aid to and trade with Latin American countries would continue to be linked to observance of human rights by those countries.

On the grounds of documented human rights violations, the USA had in 1976 limited its military aid to Chile and cancelled that to Uruguay; in February 1977 the US President had decided to reduce US economic aid to Argentina and Uruguay, and this had led to the rejection of various forms of US aid by Argentina, Uruguay, Brazil, El Salvador, Guatemala and Chile. As a result the OAS member states were divided, on this issue, into two major blocs—those opposing the US attitude as constituting interference in their internal affairs (including Argentina, Chile, Brazil, Uruguay, Bolivia, Nicaragua and Paraguay) and those which supported it (notably Venezuela, Costa Rica, Mexico, Colombia and the English-speaking Caribbean countries).

A resolution introduced by the USA, Venezuela, Costa Rica and the Dominican Republic, calling for a strengthening of the resources and the competence of the OAS Human Rights Commission, was approved, on June 18, by 14 states (with eight abstentions and three members being absent from the vote).

The 10th General Assembly of the OAS, held in Washington on Nov. 19–27, 1980, was preoccupied with the question of human rights in Latin America, in particular with a report presented by the Inter-American Human Rights Commission (IAHRC) which noted "grave violations of fundamental human rights" in Argentina, and also criticized the governments of Chile, El Salvador, Paraguay and Uruguay for failing

adequately to guarantee political and judicial rights (while special IAHRC reports dealt with alleged rights violations in Cuba and Haiti). As a number of states objected to the condemnation of individual countries, the Assembly adopted, by consensus, a compromise resolution undertaking to consider responses from the governments accused in the IAHRC reports and referring to the need to "put an immediate end, in the countries where it may occur, to any practice that leads to the disappearance of persons".

Transnational Corporations. At a session of the OAS General Assembly held in Washington from June 21 to July 1, 1978, a *Code of Conduct for Transnational Corporations* was approved by 20 votes to four, with the United States abstaining from voting.

The code, said to be based on the 19th-century Calvo doctrine, laid down that foreign companies (i) must be subject to the exclusive jurisdiction of the host country, (ii) must not serve as instruments of the foreign policy of another state, (iii) must accept the sovereignty of the host country over natural resources and economic activities, and (iv) must not interfere in the host country's internal affairs or its relations with other countries. The code also stipulated that transnational corporations should operate in a manner such as to produce financial resources for the host country, should supply the host country with the information necessary to ensure that their activities were in accordance with national policies and development programmes, and must refrain from restrictive trade practices and contribute to the scientific and technological capacity of the host country. (In an accompanying document the USA inter alia contested the exclusive jurisdiction of the host country over a foreign company.)

1979 Declaration of La Paz. A session of the General Assembly, held in La Paz (Bolivia) on Oct. 22–31, 1979, unanimously adopted, on Oct. 30, a *Declaration of La Paz*, calling for democracy, respect for human rights, ideological pluralism and disarmament in the region; condemning the use of torture; urging military governments to introduce democratic systems; expressing "deep concern at the heightening of tensions as the result of recent increases in military activity in the Caribbean" (this being a reference to US manoeuvres at the US Guantánamo naval base in Cuba in mid-October); and repudiating "the concept of the region as a sphere of influence of any power" (this concept having earlier been rejected by the Governments of Jamaica, Guyana, Grenada and St Lucia). In connexion with a report to the Assembly by the IA-ECOSOC accusing the USA of having restricted the growth of some developing countries of the region by applying protectionist measures, the declaration urged all OAS member states to refrain from adopting such measures.

11th General Assembly Session. At the 11th General Assembly session, held in St Lucia on Dec. 2–11, 1981, the US Secretary of State attempted to convince the OAS member states of the need to take action against the growing influence of Cuba and Nicaragua as "sources of subversion" in the Central American region. He also presented the outline of a Caribbean Basin

Initiative whereby the United States was planning to join Canada, Mexico and Venezuela in giving large-scale assistance to the region by means of investments, trade arrangements and financial measures (as explained later by President Reagan on Feb. 24, 1982).

The Assembly unanimously approved a Mexican-sponsored resolution allowing the OAS Secretary-General to seek an extended loan to help finance the OAS. (Brazil, Mexico and the United States—the three wealthiest member states—had failed to pay their contributions in time, and the US government had indicated that it wanted to reduce its contribution by two-thirds.)

OAS Resolution on the Falklands/Malvinas Issue. Upon an initiative by Argentina a special meeting of the OAS Council of Foreign Ministers, held on April 26–28, 1982, adopted by 17 votes to none (with four abstentions – Chile, Colombia, Trinidad and Tobago and the United States) a

Map 9   Organization of American States (OAS) and Organization of Central American
States (OCAS)

resolution recognizing Argentinian sovereignty over the Falkland/Malvinas Islands and calling on Britain to cease hostilities in the South Atlantic. The resolution made no mention of invoking the 1947 Inter-American Treaty of Reciprocal Assistance (the Treaty of Rio), which would have required the votes of two-thirds of the 21 signatories of the treaty. (The eight OAS members which were not signatories of the Treaty of Rio did not participate in the vote.)

Other Inter-American, Latin and Central American Co-operation

Inter-American Development Bank (IDB)

Address. 808 17th Street, N.W., Washington, D.C. 20577, USA.

Officer. Antonio Ortiz Mena (pres.).

Founded. April 1959.

Membership. All members of the Organization of American States and also Guyana and Canada, as well as (from outside the region) Austria, Belgium, Denmark, Finland, France, the Federal Republic of Germany, Israel, Italy, Japan, the Netherlands, Norway, Portugal, Spain, Sweden, Switzerland, the United Kingdom and Yugoslavia.

History. The Inter-American Development Bank and a Fund for Special Operations were set up in April 1959. They represented the culmination of prolonged efforts by the Latin American countries for the creation of a development bank backed by the USA, ever since the Marshall Plan was initiated in 1948 for the recovery of Western Europe. Until August 1958, however, the US Government had always opposed such a scheme on the ground that private banks, the World Bank and the US Export-Import Bank were able to provide sufficient credit for sound development projects. The change in US policy was the direct result of a meeting of the Foreign Ministers of the American Republics (then numbering 21) in September 1958.

Activities. The Inter-American Development Bank, founded to finance economic and social development projects and to provide technical assistance in member countries, opened with an authorized capital stock of US$850,000,000, of which US$400,000,000 was to be paid in, the remaining US$450,000,000 to be payable on call. The United States provided 37.5 per cent of the payable capital, and 44.5 per cent of that payable on call. By 1979 the paid-in capital amounted to US$1,484 million and another US$10,538 million was callable.

The IDB also administers funds set up by several donor countries, the largest of these funds being the Social Progress Trust Fund of US$525,000,000 established in June 1961 by the United States under the Alliance for Progress programme.

Loans from the capital resources are made for particular economic projects, and are repayable in the currencies lent.

The powers of the IDB are vested in a Board of Governors, on which each member country is represented by one Governor and one alternate. Executive powers are delegated to an Executive Board of 12 Directors, eight of whom are elected by Latin American countries, two by member countries not in the region, one by Canada and one by the USA.

At the bank's 11th anniversary meeting at Punta del Este (Uruguay) on April 22, 1970, its achievements were criticized by the Peruvian Minister of Economic Affairs and Finance as "disheartening and incommensurate with what Latin America expected of economic and social progress", as the disparities in production, income and living standards were "even more marked than at the beginning of the decade".

The Fund for Special Operations opened with a capital of US$150,000,000, of which the United States contributed US$100,000,000. The fund makes loans on economically and socially useful projects which would not normally be acceptable to a bank. Repayments may be made in local currency.

Between 1961 and 1984 the IDB granted loans totalling US$27,772 million, of which US$3,566,600,000 were granted in the year 1984.

The total of outstanding borrowings was, at the end of 1984, US$6,131,700,000 (composed of US$2,496,500,000 in ordinary capital and US$3,635,200,000 in inter-regional capital).

At the annual conference of the IDB held on March 26–28, 1984, differences emerged on the role of the IDB in the context of foreign debts. A bloc of regional members, led by the three largest debtors (Argentina, Brazil and Mexico) called for the IDB to increase its capital resources and provide "flexible" lending programmes in cases of need. In contrast the United States (the largest shareholder in the IDB) and the West European countries supported the retention of the role of the bank as a regional development agency and argued that it should not become "a balance-of-payments financing organization". The IDB's annual report, issued on March 25, 1984, estimated that the total of outstanding debts at the end of 1983 was equivalent to 56 per cent of Latin America's gross domestic product and 325 per cent of its exports. The report also stated that in 1983 living standards in some Latin American countries had dropped to the level of the 1960s and that average gross domestic product had fallen by more than 3 per cent, so that per capita for the region as a whole it was now below the level of 1977.

An **Institute for Latin American Integration** was established in Buenos Aires in 1963 as a permanent department of the IDB with the object of conducting research into problems of the regional integration process, organizing training courses on its various aspects and providing advisory services.

Other Organizations for Inter-American Co-operation

International Regional Organization of Plant Protection and Animal Health
Organismo Internacional Regional de Sanidad Agropecuaria (OIRSA)
Address. Edificio Carbonell 2, Carretera a Sta Tecla, San Salvador, El Salvador
Officer. Dr Carlos Meyer Arevalo (exec. dir.)
Founded. 1953
Membership. Costa Rica, El Salvador, Guatemala, Honduras, Mexico, Nicaragua and Panama

Latin American Institute of Educational Communication
Address. Apdo. Postal 94-328, Mexico 10, D.F., Mexico.
Officer. Dr José Manual Alvarez (dir.-gen.).
Founded. 1956.
Membership. Governments of Latin American and Caribbean states.
Objects. Founded by UNESCO and the Mexican government, the institute was to produce audiovisual aids, in particular film strips, and to train Latin American teachers in the production of film strips with scholarships granted by UNESCO, the OAS and Latin American governments.

Latin American Confederation of Tourist Organizations
Address. Viamonte 640, 8° piso, 1053 Buenos Aires, Argentina.
Officer. Mario W. Amestoy (sec. gen.).
Founded. 1957.
Membership. 19 countries and affiliate members in 70 countries.

Caribbean Group for Co-operation in Economic Development (CGCED)

Founded. June 1978.
History. The CGCED was set up at a conference on economic development in the Caribbean in Washington in December 1977. At the CGCED's inaugural meeting held in June 1978 and attended by representatives of some 31 governments and 16 international and regional agencies, it was decided to establish, under World Bank auspices, a Caribbean Development Facility, the initial size of which was fixed at US$125,000,000 on the basis of pledges made by Canada, Colombia, France, the Netherlands, Norway, the United Kingdom, the United States and Venezuela, as well as the World Bank and the OPEC Special Fund; the largest beneficiaries of this facility were Jamaica and Guyana. Additional aid pledges totalling US$183,000,000 were made in June 1979 for the year commencing July 1 of that year. For the year commencing July 1, 1981, pledges totalled US$700,000,000,

the main donors being Mexico and Venezuela and the main recipients Jamaica and Guyana.

Conference of American Armies

This conference was held in camera on Nov. 3–5, 1981, at Fort McNair (near Washington, USA) and was attended by military commanders from the United States and Latin American and Caribbean countries including Chile, El Salvador, Haiti, Honduras and Paraguay. It was addressed by the US Defence Secretary and by the Defence Minister of El Salvador, and it was officially stated to have been concerned with "countering terrorism, subversion and armed insurgency" in the region.

Latin American Parliament
Parlamento Latinoamericano

Address. Carrera 7a, No. 12–25, P.&. Bogotá, Colombia.
Officer. Andres Townsend Ezcurra (sec. gen.).
Founded. 1965.
Membership. Delegations of members of the parliaments of Argentina, Bolivia, Brazil, Chile, Colombia, Costa Rica, Cuba, Ecuador, El Salvador, Guatemala, Honduras, Mexico, Nicaragua, Panama, Paraguay, Peru, Uruguay and Venezuela.
History. The decision to set up this parliament was taken at a meeting of representatives of Latin American countries and institutions held in Lima (Peru) on Dec. 6–11, 1964, and the first session of this parliament was held on July 17–18, 1965. At its 17th meeting held on June 19, 1985, it decided inter alia to admit a delegation from Cuba (by 145 votes to 25) and to readmit Nicaragua (which had been suspended in 1979) against some opposition from Costa Rica and Paraguay.
Objects. To promote contacts between national legislative bodies, to further Latin American integration in all fields, to oppose any form of colonialism and to defend the peace.
Structure. Under its statutes approved at its first session the Latin American Parliament is a permanent unicameral body which meets in ordinary session once a year and in extraordinary session at the request of a majority of its members.
Activities. Among declarations issued by the Latin American Parliament was one (approved in Caracas on April 18, 1984) criticizing the International Monetary Fund (IMF) for imposing conditions which had "profoundly negative effects on the countries which accept them"; calling on the IMF "to accept innovative and creative formulas to solve the foreign debt problem"; and giving a warning that the alternative was a "serious threat to peace, democracy and stability in the continent".

At a special session which opened on April 3, 1986, the parliament agreed, with the exception of El Salvador and Honduras, on a motion condemning US policy towards Nicaragua.

Andean Group (or Pact)
Grupo Andino

Address. Av. Paseo de la República 3895, Casilla Postal 3237, Lima, Peru.

Founded. 1969.

Membership. Bolivia, Colombia, Ecuador, Peru and Venezuela.

Associate Member. Panama.

Observers. Costa Rica, the Dominican Republic, Panama and Spain.

History. Under the *Cartagena Agreement* signed in Bogotá (Colombia) on May 26, 1969, the governments of Bolivia, Chile, Colombia, Ecuador and Peru set up an Andean Common Market, in which all internal customs tariffs between the five member countries were to be abolished by 1980. This agreement came into force on Nov. 24, 1969.

Structure. The supreme authority of the organization is the Andean Group Commission consisting of one representative from each member country. The Commission's policies are formulated, and their implementation supervised, by a three-member Junta.

The institutional structure of the organization also comprises (i) a Consultative Committee responsible for liaison between the Junta and the member countries, (ii) an Economic and Social Committee, (iii) the Andean Development Corporation, (iv) the Andean Reserve Fund, (v) a Court of Justice, (vi) the Andean Parliament and (vii) the Andean Council of Foreign Ministers (the last three bodies having been set up in 1979—see also below).

Activities. Under Decision 24 taken by the group's Commission in December 1970, foreign investments in the group's five founder member countries were subject to the following conditions: As from July 1971, wholly foreign-owned companies wishing to qualify for preferential treatment in the Andean group market would, within three years, have to sign an agreement to transfer 51 per cent of their shares to local investors over a period of 15 years in Chile, Colombia and Peru, and of 20 years in Bolivia and Ecuador, and such companies would be allowed to repatriate not more than 14 per cent of the invested capital (unless specially exempted from this condition).

In May 1971 the member states agreed on the pooling of their merchant fleets, and in October of the same year agreement was reached on the gradual removal of customs duties as envisaged in the Cartagena Agreement.

In October 1972 Mexico became a working partner in the group, co-operating with it in joint financial and industrial development.

An application by Venezuela for full membership of the group was agreed to on Feb. 13, 1973, and became effective on Jan. 1, 1974. Venezuelan legislation applying the provisions of Decision 24 was published on April 29 of that year, although under special concessions made to Venezuela 450 products were exempted from having to be free of duty by 1985.

Chile formally withdrew from the group on Oct. 30, 1976. Chilean legislation of July 1974 had failed to comply with major conditions laid down in Decision 24. In April 1976 a ministerial conference had ratified a protocol (known as Decision 100) amending the Cartagena Agreement by extending by two years the group's original industrial tariff deadlines and common external tariff programme, but Chile refused to sign this protocol. It subsequently persisted in this refusal even though the group had in August 1976 made special concessions to Chile in an attempt to prevent its defection from the group.

Also on Oct. 30, 1976, Decision 100 was amended by a protocol extending the deadlines by a further year, and at the same time changes in the foreign investment regulations were confirmed, as had been contained in a *Declaration of Sochagota* of Aug. 15, 1976. In particular, the 14 per cent limit on repatriation of profits by foreign companies was raised to 20 per cent; capital from individual member countries was to be treated as national investment within the region as a whole; investments by official international finance organizations were to be treated as "neutral capital" with no restrictive legislation; and foreign companies were to be allowed to increase from 5 to 7 per cent their annual reinvestment in countries in which they operated.

Under the *Arequipa Protocol* signed on April 21, 1978, further amendments were made to the Cartagena Agreement, including the following: (i) In Colombia, Peru and Venezuela the full adoption of the common external tariff would be completed by Dec. 31, 1983 (instead of 1982), and in Bolivia and Ecuador by Dec. 31, 1989 (instead of 1987); and (ii) internal tariffs between Bolivia and Ecuador would be eliminated in 1989 instead of 1988 (although the deadline for the removal of internal tariffs on goods traded between Colombia, Venezuela and Peru remained at 1983).

At a meeting of the heads of state of Bolivia, Colombia, Ecuador, Venezuela and also Panama (not then a member of the group) and the Prime Minister of Peru in Bogotá on Aug. 8, 1978, a *Declaration of Bogotá* was signed in which, inter alia, (i) it was decided to update development programmes in the metal-working and petrochemical industries; (ii) concern was expressed over the situation in less developed Andean nations, notably Bolivia; (iii) greater attention was called to the Andean Development Corporation [see below]; and (iv) it was pointed out that action was needed in facilitating international road transport and implementing joint schemes for border integration.

At a meeting of the Presidents of the group's five member countries in Cartagena on May 26–28, 1978, a *Mandate of Cartagena* was signed, calling for (i) the fostering of greater economic and political co-operation in the 1980s and the encouragement of more subregional development programmes, especially industrial ones; (ii) the promotion of the goals of the Latin American Economic System (SELA, see page 358); (iii) the creation of an Andean judicial tribunal which would seek to resolve problems arising over the interpretation of and compliance with Andean Group decisions; and (iv) the holding of regular summit meetings. It was also agreed to give the private sector of the economy a greater role in planning.

A memorandum of understanding with the United States concerning trade, financing, science and technology, development of industry, agriculture and infrastructure was signed in Washington and entered into force on Nov. 21, 1979.

A consultative Council of Ministers, established under an agreement signed by all Andean Group member states except Bolivia on Nov. 13, 1979, to formulate and co-ordinate the external policy of the region, held its first meeting in Santa Cruz (Bolivia) on Jan. 14–15, 1980, when it declared its support for Bolivia's quest for access to the sea.

A memorandum of understanding on the promotion of mutual relations and the stimulation of Latin American co-operation was signed by the Andean Group and Brazil on Jan. 17, 1980.

In February 1980 it was announced that the target for a common Andean Group customs tariff had been set at about 28 per cent, to be effected by Jan. 1, 1981, with phased approach to this target to be completed by 1983 in Colombia, Peru and Venezuela, and later in Bolivia and Ecuador.

An emergency plan for the future operation of the *Cartagena Agreement* was drafted in May 1983 and proposed inter alia the encouragement of trade negotiations, the promotion of regional trade by the identification of goods manufactured within the Pact region but which members continued to purchase from outside exporters, the establishment of a "food security system" to provide details of current surpluses and shortages within the region, the holding of meetings between the central banks of the member countries to reduce delays in payments, and the implementation of a plan which would "harmonize" the currencies by fixing a maximum and a minimum rate for fluctuation of any Andean currency against another.

On July 20, 1983, the five member states agreed to establish an Andean Court of Justice in Quito (Ecuador) to deal with disputes arising out of failure of the signatories of the Cartagena Agreement to comply with its stipulations.

On Dec. 18, 1984, the Andean Pact countries launched a new currency, the Andean peso, to be used in commercial and financial transactions between member countries. It was not brought out as a note and was initially fixed at par with the US dollar. To support the new currency Colombia, Peru and Venezuela each contributed US$20,000,000 and Bolivia and Ecuador each US$10,000,000.

At the same time Colombia and Ecuador began to seek modification of Andean Pact rules. The President of Colombia, speaking at a session of the Andean Parliament on Dec. 17, 1984, called for a fundamental reform of foreign investment rules. The Ecuadorean Minister of Industry, Trade and Integration declared that his country would leave the Andean Pact if there were no reforms, and on March 16, 1985, the President of Ecuador called for the repeal of Decision 24. In direct contravention of this decision he issued, on May 14, 1985, a decree considerably liberalizing the rules governing foreign investment in Ecuador. These developments led to a meeting of the Foreign and Trade Ministers of the Andean Pact countries in Cartagena on Sept. 14–15, 1985, when they were reported to have reached agreement on an "emergency adjustment plan".

ANDEAN DEVELOPMENT CORPORATION AND ANDEAN RESERVE FUND

The **Andean Development Corporation (Corporación Andina de Fomento)**, with headquarters in Caracas, was formed in 1968 to act as the development-financing arm of the Andean Group, mainly for industrial development and for the creation of basic services. Its authorized capital was (in 1976) US$400,000,000.

The **Andean Reserve Fund**, with headquarters in Bogotá, was established in 1977 and began its operations in July 1978. Its organs are an Assembly consisting of the Ministers of Economy or Finance of the Andean Group's member countries; a Board of Directors comprising the Governors of the member countries' central banks; and an Executive President. Its initial capital was US$240,000,000 subscribed by the five member countries, and it was authorized inter alia to invest in the Andean Development Corporation.

Latin American Energy Organization
Organización Latinoamericana de Energía
(OLADE)

Address. Av. 10 de Agosto 5133 y Naciones Unidas, P.O.B. 6413 C.C.I., Quito, Ecuador.

Officer. Ulises Ramírez Olmos (exec. sec.).

Founded. Nov. 19, 1974.

Membership. Argentina, Barbados, Bolivia, Brazil, Chile, Colombia, Costa Rica, Cuba, the Dominican Republic, Ecuador, El Salvador, Grenada, Guatemala, Guyana, Haiti, Honduras, Jamaica, Mexico, Nicaragua, Panama, Paraguay, Peru, Suriname, Trinidad and Tobago, Uruguay and Venezuela.

History. The OLADE was formed under a treaty signed by 22 Latin American and Caribbean countries on Nov. 2, 1973, with the object of providing a co-operative (but not a supranational) organization constituting a framework for the integration, conservation, sale, defence and development of oil and other energy resources in the region.

At a ministerial meeting held in Mexico City on Sept. 8–12, 1975, a work programme was approved for the organization's permanent secretariat to (i) establish the basis for a regional inventory of energy resources; (ii) define general outlines of national energy programmes and a regional energy plan; (iii) draw up national legislation on the transfer of technology; and (iv) study the creation of a financial institution for the OLADE. It was also agreed that the oil-exporting member countries (among which Ecuador and Venezuela were members of the Organization of Petroleum Exporting Countries—OPEC, while other significant oil producers included Argentina, Brazil, Colombia, Mexico, and Trinidad and Tobago) would establish a $6,000 million loan fund to assist those countries of the region which were experiencing balance-of-payments difficulties.

At another ministerial meeting held in Mexico City on Sept. 5–8, 1978, it was decided to create, as from January 1980, a financing system enabling those Latin American countries which were poor in energy resources to finance their energy research programmes. (This decision was endorsed by Bolivia, Chile, Costa Rica, Cuba, the Dominican Republic, Ecuador, Haiti, Honduras, Jamaica, Panama and Peru but opposed by Brazil, while Venezuela abstained from voting.)

Latin American Economic System
Sistema Económico Latinoamericano (SELA)

Address. Apdo. 17035, El Conde, Caracas 1010, Venezuela.

Officer. Sebastián Alegrett (exec. sec.).

Founded. Oct. 18, 1975.

Membership. Argentina, Barbados, Bolivia, Brazil, Chile, Colombia, Costa Rica, Cuba, the Dominican Republic, Ecuador, El Salvador, Grenada, Guatemala, Guyana, Haiti, Honduras, Jamaica, Mexico, Nicaragua, Panama, Paraguay, Peru, Spain, Suriname, Trinidad and Tobago, Uruguay and Venezuela.

Objects. To formulate common economic strategies among member states, to encourage the formation of Latin American multinational companies and to develop a code of conduct for transnational companies operating in the region.

Structure. SELA's supreme body is the Latin American Council, which consists of one member from each member country and holds ordinary sessions once a year. It elects the organization's permanent secretary, but it has no powers to make decisions affecting the national policies of member states. SELA has action committees on fertilizer manufacturing (in Mexico City), marine and freshwater products (in Lima, Peru), handicrafts (in Panama City), housing and public works (in Quito, Ecuador), tourism (at San José, Costa Rica), Nicaragua's reconstruction programme (in Managua), technological information (in Rio de Janeiro) and the sale and distribution of highly nutritional food supplements.

Activities. At a meeting of the Latin American Council held at Carabellada (Venezuela) on April 3–5, 1978, ministers condemned "restrictions applied by the capitalist countries on raw materials produced by underdeveloped countries" and called for an end to "discriminatory measures by the US foreign trade law".

Spain became a member of SELA under an agreement concluded on Sept. 21, 1979.

At a meeting of the Latin American Council in Lima on April 10–11, 1980, it was decided to create a new financing organization which would make Latin America independent of the International Monetary Fund which (according to the Finance Minister of Peru) was applying credit policies which did not always take due account of the circumstances of the recipient countries.

SELA was granted observer status at the United Nations General Assembly on Oct. 13, 1980.

The first consultative meeting of SELA was held in Panama on Nov. 30–Dec. 2, 1981, and discussed a new collective strategy for Latin America's economic relations with the United States. It adopted a *Declaration of Panama* calling for "significant changes" in US-Latin American relations.

The declaration stated that "the acceleration of the process of development and the strengthening of the Latin American external sectors are urgent priorities and must not be subordinated to the prior execution of US internal policies", and that private foreign investment must not be "considered as aid or calculated as part of financial co-operation for development". It urged the United States to eliminate "the causes which generate high interest rates" and claimed the right of SELA member states to defend the prices of the region's basic products and access for these products to US markets. The member states agreed not to use exports of food or any other products as a political weapon and opposed "any attempt to bring pressure to bear on international financial institutions to bring about discrimination on political grounds against any member country". The declaration claimed "the right of each Latin American nation to go its own way in the economic and social field in peace and liberty, free from external threats and pressures".

On Jan. 22, 1982, it was reported that SELA and the Economic Community of West African States (ECOWAS) had signed a joint communiqué in Caracas on promoting trade between member countries of the two organizations.

In May 1983 SELA and the (UN) Economic Commission for Latin America (ECLA) jointly issued a survey entitled *Bases for a Latin American Response to the International Economic Crisis*, which concluded that "Latin America must organize itself economically as a unit, [since] in the face of the crisis and of concerted action by the industrialised countries, Latin American dispersion is ineffective for defending our interests".

At its annual meeting held on March 22, 1984, SELA confirmed its support for the *Declaration of Quito* (q.v.), and its executive secretary proposed that not more than 20 per cent of export revenue should be devoted to debt payments and that periods of repayment should be no less than 15 years with a seven-year grace period.

Trinidad
and Tobago

Venezuela

Guyana

Colombia

Suriname

Fr.
Guiana

Ecuador

Peru

Brazil

Bolivia

Paraguay

Uruguay

Chile

Argentina

= Member states of ALADI (also Mexico)

= Member states of ALADI and of Andean Group

Map 10   Latin American Integration Association (ALADI) and Andean Group

Latin American Integration Association
Asociación Latinoamericana de Integración
(ALADI)

Address. Cebolati 1461, Casilla de Correo 577, Montevideo, Uruguay.

Officer. Julio César Schupp (sec. gen.).

Founded. Jan. 1, 1981.

Membership. Argentina, Bolivia, Brazil, Chile, Colombia, Ecuador, Mexico, Paraguay, Peru, Uruguay and Venezuela.

History. The ALADI was established under an agreement signed in Montevideo on Aug. 12, 1980, by the above 11 states. The decision to create the ALADI in the place of the Latin American Free Trade Association (LAFTA) had been taken at a meeting of LAFTA's Council of Ministers in Acapulco (Mexico) on June 16–27, 1980. LAFTA had been set up under a Treaty of Montevideo of Feb. 18, 1960, by Argentina, Brazil, Chile, Mexico, Paraguay, Peru and Uruguay and had later been joined by Bolivia, Colombia, Ecuador and Venezuela. It had come into force on Jan. 2, 1962, but its timetable for the gradual reduction of tariff barriers between member countries (to be completed by 1972) fell into arrears; under a Caracas protocol of 1969 the deadline for completion was extended to 1980, but no substantial progress was made towards this goal, largely owing to the disparate level of development among member countries, problems of communications and transport, protectionism, conflicting economic systems and political and economic changes (notably in Brazil and Argentina), and also to the creation of the Andean group as a subregional grouping within LAFTA [see page 356].

In the new association preferential treatment was to be given by the richer countries to the poorer, and to this end member countries were classified in three groups according to their level of development—(i) less developed (Bolivia, Ecuador, Paraguay); (ii) medium developed (Chile, Colombia, Peru, Uruguay, Venezuela) and (iii) more developed (Argentina, Brazil, Mexico).

The 1980 Montevideo agreement came into force on March 18, 1981, having been ratified by Argentina, Mexico, Paraguay and Uruguay. It was subsequently ratified by the seven other ALADI members.

The transition from the LAFTA to the ALADI was completed in August 1983 with a renegotiation of tariff reductions agreed in 1962-80 and the retention of certain LAFTA arrangements, notably an accord on reciprocal payments and credits and a multilateral accord for the attenuation of transitory deficiencies in liquidity (which had been expanded in 1981).

In April 1984 the ALADI approved in principle a series of proposals designed to increase interregional trade—the implementation of a system of preferential tariffs, a programme for the reduction of all non-tariff barriers within the region, the revival of a 1969 accord for co-operation between central banks on the settlement of trade payments, and the promotion of bilateral reciprocal trade agreements as a means of saving foreign exchange at times of balance-of-payments difficulties.

Tripartite Commission for Economic Co-operation, Trade and Integration (Urupabol)

Founded. May 29, 1981.

Membership. Bolivia, Paraguay and Uruguay.

History. This commission had existed informally since 1963, when the three countries had agreed to rotate a seat on the Inter-American Development Bank among themselves.

Forum for Peace and Democracy

Founded. Oct. 4, 1982.

Membership. Belize, Colombia, Costa Rica, the Dominican Republic, El Salvador, Honduras, Jamaica and Panama.

History. The Forum was established at a meeting of the Foreign Ministers of the above countries in San José (Costa Rica), with the US Assistant Secretary of State for Inter-American Affairs being present as an observer and Nicaragua being excluded. In a Declaration of San José the ministers criticized "the disastrous near-sightedness of totalitarian forces of all trends, especially the Marxist-Leninist trend", and advocated a "verifiable and reciprocal" regional accord banning arms trafficking, subversion and the presence of foreign military advisers. In April 1983, however, the President of Costa Rica stated that the Forum had failed because of the exclusion of Nicaragua and that consequently "we have to find other formulas which are more viable in the current circumstances".

The Contadora Group

Address. c/o Secretaría de Asuntos Exteriores, Mexico, D.F., Mexico.

Founded. January 1983.

Membership. Colombia, Mexico, Panama and Venezuela.

Object. To find a political solution to the Central American conflict, in particular along the Nicaraguan border and in El Salvador.

History. The Foreign Ministers of the four above-mentioned countries, meeting on the island of Contadora (in the Gulf of Panama), issued, on Jan. 8, 1983, a statement calling on the Central American states involved in conflict to institute multilateral negotiations, on neighbouring countries to help them by means of economic initiatives, and on all foreign powers to withdraw their advisers from the region.

At a second meeting, held in Panama on April 11, 1983, the four ministers made more detailed proposals, involving also the cessation of arms sales to places suffering from armed conflict;

the implementation of a plan for economic reactivation; the resolution of internal conflicts by democratic means with the inclusion of all political parties in each country; and representation at peace talks for the region of all ethnic minorities.

At a meeting held in Panama City on April 20–21, 1983, with the participation of representatives from Costa Rica, the Dominican Republic, El Salvador, Guatemala, Honduras and Nicaragua, an agenda for negotiations was agreed. At a further meeting on May 11–15 it was agreed that 11 civilian observers should be sent to Costa Rica to inspect the border with Nicaragua.

A summit meeting of the Presidents of the four Contadora Group member countries held in Panama City on July 14–17, 1983, issued a statement containing a programme suggesting that commitments should be made by the parties involved, inter alia on a "freeze on existing offensive weapons"; to start talks on agreements on arms control; "to prohibit the existence of foreign military installations in their territories"; "to give previous notice of troop movements near the border" if the contingents were in excess of the number stated in the agreement; to co-operate in various joint measures, involving international supervision of borders, "in order to prevent armed conflict and to generate an atmosphere of reciprocal trust".

By this time Cuba had begun to give public support to the Contadora Group's programme.

At another meeting, held in Panama City on Sept. 7, 1983, and attended also by the Foreign Ministers of the five Central American states, the Group drafted a 21-point programme, which was approved by the heads of state of Costa Rica, El Salvador, Guatemala, Honduras and Nicaragua during the first week of October 1983.

This programme contained additional proposals on (i) the banning of the installation of foreign military bases and of any form of military interference; (ii) a commitment to refrain from fostering or supporting acts of terrorism, subversion or sabotage in the region and from supporting anyone trying to overthrow a government in the region; (iii) the establishment of direct means of communications between the two sides; and (iv) the continuation of humanitarian aid to refugees (of whom there were, according to the UN High Commissioner for Refugees, some 328,000 in Central America).

This programme was supported also by the US administration, and on Nov. 16 the OAS offered the "firmest support" for the Contadora Group's initiative. However, on Oct. 20, 1983, Nicaragua had submitted to the United States its own proposals (involving four draft treaties), which were formally rejected by the United States on the following day.

As confrontation between Nicaragua and the United States intensified, the Contadora Group, at a further meeting held on Jan. 7–8, 1984, and attended also by the Foreign Ministers of the five Central American states, produced a compromise draft treaty which did not include the clause providing for the withdrawal of all foreign troops and military advisers, would not be binding on the countries involved, provided no framework for ensuring compliance with its provisions, and took no account of a Nicaraguan suggestion of mutual non-aggression pacts.

Meeting again in Panama City on April 9, 1984, the Contadora Group Foreign Ministers noted "the actions of irregular forces, supported and supplied by communications centres located in neighbouring countries, which were seeking to destabilize the region", operations which were carried out, "such as the mining of ports, which impaired the economy, disrupted trade and hindered freedom of navigation", and the "increasingly open presence of foreign troops and advisers" and the "proliferation of weapons and military actions and exercises". (The Ministers also announced the establishment of an Action Committee for the Social and Economic Development of Central America.)

On June 10, 1984, the Contadora Group issued a 15-point Act for Peace and Co-operation in Central America which was based on the draft treaty of January 1984.

This Act bound the signatories (i) not to allow their own territory to be used by foreign irregular forces, (ii) to stop terrorist activities or destabilization attempts, (iii) to expel all foreign military advisers, (iv) to limit their acquisition of defence material, (v) to allow for the verification and control of their arsenals, (vi) to ban the installation of foreign military bases, (vii) to establish and improve institutions of representative and pluralist democracy, (viii) to guarantee full respect for human rights to make national reconciliation possible. (ix) to provide guarantees for those taking up amnesty offers; (x) to open the election process to all citizens and establish the autonomy of the judicial system, (xi) to collaborate on the regional refugee problem, (xii) to negotiate a regional stance on foreign finance, (xiii) to promote trade, (xiv) to undertake joint investment projects, and (xv) to establish more equitable regional economic structures.

Although by the third week of August 1984, all five Central American republics had accepted the Act "in principle", there followed further open disagreements. After a Honduran call for changes in the Act, Costa Rica and El Salvador withdrew their acceptance of the Act early in October 1984. The Contadora Group therefore decided on Jan. 8–9, 1985, to prepare a revised treaty.

Following a number of meetings held by the Group between April and September 1985, a new draft treaty was presented to the Central American Foreign Ministers by the Group on Sept. 12–13, 1985, but no agreement on its acceptance was reached during the following two months. Nicaragua announced on Nov. 17, 1985, that it would not sign the draft treaty and proposed "a new protocol directed solely at the US government" and requiring it to "cease its aggression in all forms against Nicaragua".

Within the framework of another Contadora Group meeting Costa Rica and Nicaragua signed, on March 12, 1986, an agreement to establish an international border commission which would limit the activities in Nicaragua of anti-Sandinista "contra" forces operating from Costa Rican territory.

At a meeting held in Esquipulas (Guatemala) on May 24–26, 1986, the Presidents of the five Central American states failed to reach any agreement on a peace treaty for the region but decided to establish a Central American parliament.

The Lima Group

Founded. July 28, 1985.

Membership. Argentina, Brazil, Peru and Uruguay.

History. This group was established on the occasion of the signing of the *Declaration of Lima* (q.v.) with the object of helping to find "Latin American solutions to Latin American problems". The group took part in a meeting held by the Contadora Group (q.v.) in Cartagena (Colombia) on Aug. 24–26, 1985.

River Plate Basin Development

A treaty for the economic integration and joint development of the Rio de la Plata region was signed in Brasilia on April 23, 1969, by the Foreign Ministers of Argentina, Bolivia, Brazil, Paraguay and Uruguay. The treaty provided for the establishment of an Inter-governmental Co-ordinating Committee as the permanent body responsible for promoting and co-ordinating assistance from international institutions and for implementing decisions made by the Foreign Ministers of the five countries.

However, no full agreement was reached in later years on the exploitation of waters, in particular by means of hydroelectric works, in the region as each of the participating states insisted on retaining its sovereignty over its natural resources and the right to dispose freely of them. (Early in 1977 Argentina revoked an 1857 bilateral treaty with Brazil on river transport in the River Plate basin.)

Amazon Co-operation Treaty

A treaty on economic co-operation in the Amazon basin area was signed in Brasília on July 3, 1978, by the Foreign Ministers of Bolivia, Brazil, Colombia, Ecuador, Guyana, Peru, Suriname and Venezuela.

The object of this Amazon Pact was to promote the harmonious development of the Amazon territories of the eight signatory states by joint efforts to their common benefit; to protect the environment; to preserve and make rational use of natural resources; and to maintain full freedom of commercial navigation on the Amazon and other international rivers of the region as guaranteed by each signatory. In particular the treaty provided for the preservation of species of flora and fauna and the maintenance of the ecological balance; co-ordination of health services to fight endemic diseases; increased scientific and technical co-operation; and the establishment of adequate transport and communications facilities. National sovereignty was safeguarded by a number of clauses in the treaty, reserving

for each signatory the sovereign right of exploitation and use of its own natural resources with no restrictions other than those established by international law, and stating that "nothing in the treaty can be regarded as having any bearing upon a border dispute or controversy". According to the President of Brazil, the pact's principal aim was to emphasize that the development and preservation of the region was the exclusive responsibility of the Amazon basin countries and to protect the area from "foreign interference".

On Oct. 24, 1980, the parties to the treaty signed a 17-point *Declaration of Belém*, in which it was emphasized that the development of the Amazon region and the conservation of its environment were inseparably linked to each other; that these objectives were the sole responsibility of the Amazon states; and that a programme would be worked out for scientific and technical co-operation in the development and exploration of the region.

A newly established **Amazon Co-operation Council** has been holding annual meetings since July 1, 1981, its major task being to seek improvements in communications in the region by studying ways of linking rivers in the Amazon basin, the construction of ports and the adjustment of river courses.

Organization of Central American States (OCAS)
Organización de los Estados Centroamericanos (ODECA)

Address. Oficina Centroamericana, Pino Alto, Paseo Escalón, San Salvador, El Salvador

Officer. Ricardo Suárez Márquez (gen. sec.)

Founded. Oct. 14, 1951

Membership. Costa Rica, El Salvador, Guatemala, Honduras and Nicaragua

History. The organization was set up at the end of a conference held in San Salvador on Oct. 10-14, 1951, to discuss measures for common action by the five Central American republics in regard to problems of mutual interest. It came into being with the signing, by the five republics (listed above), of the *Charter of San Salvador.*

It was officially stated that the object of the organization would be "to promote by group action the strengthening of the bonds of fraternity among the Central American states, and to serve as an instrument for the study and solution of their common problems"; that periodic meetings of Foreign Ministers would be held; that special committees, with representatives from each country, would be set up to study and report on matters of mutual interest; that these bodies would include a committee on economic relations (comprising the Finance Ministers of the five countries), which would report on the possibility of a Central American customs union, and a committee on educational and cultural matters (consisting of the Ministers of Education), which would consider the eventual standardization of educational courses and methods, together with the possibility of establishing a Central American university; and that the organization would have a permanent secretariat with its headquarters in San Salvador.

On Nov. 30, 1961, at a conference of the Foreign Ministers of the organization's member countries, it was decided to prepare for the creation of a common supreme command with an integrated Latin American army; integrated organs for security; a common defence council; and common organs to deal with economic and social matters.

At a meeting of Foreign Ministers of the five member countries held on Nov. 15–17, 1962, and attended also by an observer from Panama, it was provisionally agreed to set up a new Organization of Central American States superseding the organization of the same name which had been set up in October 1951. The Charter of the new organization, known as the *San Salvador Charter* (the same name as the Charter of the previous organization), was formally signed at a further meeting of Foreign Ministers held in Panama City on Dec. 12–14, 1962.

The new San Salvador Charter provided for the setting up of: (i) A Supreme Council of heads of member states; (ii) a Council of Foreign Ministers; (iii) an Executive Council with permanent headquarters in San Salvador; (iv) a Legislative Council comprising three legislators from each member country, to standardize legislation; (v) an Economic Council to pursue actively the aim of a common market similar to the European Economic Community; (vi) a Cultural and Educational Council; (vii) a Council of Defence Ministers to maintain collective security; and (viii) a Central American Court of Justice.

The new Charter, which came into force in 1965, was not signed by Panama, because of "international commitments and economic problems". [See also USA-Panama relations, page 375.] In addition to the organs mentioned above, there is a General Secretariat (the Central American Bureau), which serves to co-ordinate the work of the various organs and to prepare information.

On March 18–19, 1963, a meeting between the Presidents of the member countries of OCAS and the Presidents of the USA and Panama took place in San José (Costa Rica). At the end of the meeting a *Declaration of Central America* was issued, in which it was stated:

"The Presidents of the Republics of Central America and Panama are determined to improve the well-being of their peoples, and are aware that such a task demands a dynamic economic and social development programme based on the carefully planned use of human, natural and financial resources. It also depends on important changes of the economic, social and administrative structure, within the framework of the principles that govern our democratic institutions."

The Presidents continued by pledging:

"To accelerate establishment of a customs union to perfect the functioning of the Central American Common Market; to formulate and implement national economic and social development plans, co-ordinating them at the Central American level, and progressively to carry out regional planning for the various sectors of the economy; to establish monetary union and common fiscal, monetary and social policies within the programme of economic integration; to cooperate in programmes to improve the prices of primary export commodities; to complete as soon as possible the reforms needed to achieve the objectives set forth in the Act of Bogotá and the Charter of Punta del Este, especially in the fields of agriculture, taxation, education, public administration and social welfare; to take the above measures with a view to achieving the creation of a Central American economic community which will establish relationships with other nations or regional groups having similar objectives."

In 1969–80 OCAS was preoccupied with two problems—(i) the conflict between El Salvador and Honduras, which had led to the severance of their diplomatic relations following the "football" war between them in 1969, and (ii) Guatemala's claim to sovereignty over Belize (the former British Honduras, currently still a British dependency).

In the conflict between El Salvador and Honduras, these two states agreed at a meeting held in San José on June 4, 1970, to the creation of a demilitarized zone along their common frontier, while the three other OCAS member states undertook to police such a zone. However, this agreement was not implemented until after the two Presidents (of El Salvador and Honduras) had on June 14, 1976, agreed on this zone as proposed and a definitive ceasefire agreement, guaranteed by Costa Rica, Guatemala and Nicaragua, had been signed on July 30, 1976. The conflict was, however, settled by a peace treaty signed on Oct. 30, 1980 [see page 390].

The Guatemalan claim to Belize was supported as "legitimate" by the heads of state of Costa Rica, El Salvador, Honduras, Nicaragua and Panama, meeting in Guatemala City on Nov. 3, 1975, and on Aug. 25, 1977, the Foreign Ministers of Costa Rica, El Salvador, Honduras and Nicaragua again expressed their support for Guatemala's Belize policy. These four countries were the only UN member states to vote against a UN General Assembly resolution of Nov. 28, 1977, calling for early independence for Belize. On the other hand the President of Costa Rica agreed, at a meeting held in Bogotá (Colombia) on Aug. 5-6, 1977, with the heads of state of Colombia, Jamaica, Mexico, Panama and Venezuela that "the conflict should be settled by the peaceful means prescribed in the OAS and UN Charters with respect for [Belize's] territorial integrity and the principle of self-determination".

Central American Common Market (CACM)

Mercado Común Centroamericano

Address. 4a Avenida 10–25, Apdo. Postal 1237, Guatemala City, Guatemala

Officer. Raúl Sierra Franco (sec. gen.)

Founded. June 1961

Membership. Costa Rica, El Salvador, Guatemala, Honduras and Nicaragua.

History. The Ministers of Economy of Costa Rica, Guatemala, Honduras, Nicaragua and El Salvador, meeting in Guatemala City on Feb. 24, 1957, approved in principle two treaties designed to create a free trade area in Central America and a system of regional industries.

A 10-year multilateral trade treaty was designed to eliminate import and export duties on certain products embracing about 49 per cent of intra-Central American trade on the basis of 1955 figures. In its original form the treaty laid down two lists of member countries' products: (i) Those which would have unhindered circulation within the projected free trade zone, and (ii) those that might be subjected to quantitative export and import controls by member countries. To this, the Ministers of Economy added a third classification—viz., products whose tariffs might be lowered gradually over several years to lessen the economic impact of the change. The treaty stated that the five countries would form a customs union after the creation of a free trade zone, "as soon as conditions are propitious".

The second treaty provided for the establishment of regional industries in areas where the most efficient use could be made of local resources and transport, and in such a manner as not to duplicate existing industries. It laid down, inter alia, that the industries concerned would have access to the free trade zone; that conflicting national interests would be resolved by a separate five-nation pact to be signed for every regional industry established; and that such pacts would include the specific amounts of tariff reductions, tax-exemptions, fiscal benefits and subsidies.

A common market for Central America first came into effect on Jan. 8, 1959, when three out of the five countries which had signed the five-nation treaty on the establishment of a free trade area had ratified it. It was brought within the framework of the Organization of Central American States in 1960.

On Dec. 13, 1960, representatives of the governments of El Salvador, Guatemala, Honduras and Nicaragua signed, in Managua, the *General Treaty of Central American Economic Integration*. The 20-year treaty, which came into force between June 4, 1961, and Nov. 16, 1962, established the Central American Common Market, and took precedence over all earlier free trade agreements between the contracting parties. The treaty provided for the immediate removal of internal duties on 95 per cent of product classifications, and for the abolition of all tariff restrictions by June 1966. Provision was also made for the free movement of labour and capital throughout the treaty area.

Costa Rica entered the common market in 1962, while Honduras withdrew from active participation in December 1970, although it continued to regard itself as a de jure member.

On May 16, 1976, the text of a draft treaty was published in Nicaragua providing for the eventual establishment of a Central American Economic and Social Community (*Comunidad Económica y Social de Centroamérica*) to replace the CACM. According to the draft treaty, all products of the Central American region would circulate duty-free among the member countries and their sale would be liable to restrictions only for health or internal security reasons. It was envisaged that the new community would initially comprise the five CACM member countries and that Panama would have the opportunity of joining at a later date.

CACM TREATIES

The treaties on which the Central American Common Market system of equalization of duties and reduction of tariffs is based are the following:

(1) *Tratado Multilateral de Libre Comercio e Integración Económica Centroamericana*. This was signed on June 10, 1958, by El Salvador, Guatemala, Honduras and Nicaragua, and in 1962 by Costa Rica. It came into force on June 2, 1959, and provided for the equalization of customs duties between the signatory countries, and for the removal of duties from regionally-produced goods, the latter to be completed by 1972.

(2) *Tratado de Integración Económica Centroamericana*. This was signed on Feb. 6, 1960, by El Salvador, Guatemala and Honduras; Nicaragua signed in December 1960, and Costa Rica in July 1962. When Costa Rica had added her signature in 1962, all five partners signed supplementary agreements establishing uniform duties for some 95 per cent of all goods imported into their countries.

(3) *Tratado de Asociación Económica*. This treaty, between El Salvador, Guatemala and Honduras, was signed in February 1960 and came into force in April 1960. It removed tariffs on groups of commodities in the trade between the three states, to the value of 50 per cent of the total trade. The treaty was valid for 20 years with unlimited extension. A Development and Welfare Fund, with a capital of $5,500,000, was set up under its terms.

(4) *Tratado de Intercambio Preferencial y de Libre Comercio*. This treaty, signed by Costa Rica, Nicaragua and Panama in 1961 and ratified in 1962, was simed at speeding up economic integration through tariff reductions between the members.

By 1967 internal tariff dismantlement had been applied to 95 per cent of all items of trade. The rates of a common external tariff had by then entered into force for more than 90 per cent of items of trade.

ORGANIZATION

The principal organ of the CACM is the Central American Economic Council, consisting of the Ministers of Economy of the member countries, which meets every three months. Its other organs are the Executive Council, composed of two government delegates from each of the member countries, and the Permanent Secretariat in Guatemala City.

INSTITUTIONS

There are a considerable number of institutions which now function within the framework of the CACM. The most important of these is the *Banco Centroamericano de Integración Económica* (BCIE). Founded in 1960, the Central American Integration Bank came into operation on Sept. 2, 1961, with a capital of $40,000,000, which by 1972 was raised to $200,000,000. On July 29, 1965, a Central American Integration Fund, to finance regional infrastructure projects, was established when the USA placed a loan of $35,000,000 at the disposal of the members of the bank. Each CACM member also contributed $1,400,000 to the fund. In 1966 Mexico made a loan to the bank of $5,000,000.

A *Cámara Centroamericana de Compensación de Monedas* (Central American Clearing House) was set up within the framework of the BCIE to encourage the use of Central American currencies within the area. The clearing house began operations on Oct. 1, 1961.

The *Unión Monetaria Centroamericana*, a union of the central banks of the five Central American Republics, has been effective as a formal union since 1964. Its main organ is the *Consejo Monetario Centroamericano*.

Other institutions are listed below with their dates of foundation:

(1) *Federación de Cámaras de Comercio del Istmo Centroamericano*, founded 1961.

(2) *Federación de Cámaras y Asociaciones Industriales de Centroamérica*, founded 1960.

(3) *Federación de Asociaciones de Banqueros de Centroamérica y Panama*, founded 1965.

(4) *Instituto Centroamericano de Investigación y Tecnologia Industrial*, founded 1955.

(5) *Instituto Centroamericano de Administración de Empresas*, founded 1964.

(6) *Instituto Centroamericano de Administración Publica*, founded 1954 (Panama being a member).

(7) *Confederación Universitaria Centroamericana*, founded 1948.

(8) *Instituto de Nutrición de Centroamérica y Panama*, founded 1949.

(9) *Corporación Centroamericana de Servicios de Navegación Aérea*, founded 1960.

(10) *Secretaria de Integración Turistica Centroamericana*.

(11) *Comisión Técnica de las Telecomunicaciones de Centroamérica*.

Declaration of Guayana on Venezuelan Aid

Under a Declaration of Guayana, signed in Puerto Ordaz (Venezuela) on Dec. 14, 1974, by the Presidents of Costa Rica, El Salvador, Guatemala, Honduras, Nicaragua and Venezuela and the "supreme leader" of Panama, Venezuela undertook to supply financial aid and investments to the six other countries in order to compensate them for their heavy oil import bills.

Under this agreement the Central American states would purchase Venezuelan oil, paying approximately half the current price to Venezuela and depositing the difference in their central banks in their own currencies; the resulting funds were to be held in interest-bearing accounts at Venezuela's disposal in each country. Venezuela would also contribute between $60,000,000 and $80,000,000 over two years to finance a coffee-stockpiling scheme in Central America, with a multinational coffee organization being created [see page 132], and Venezuela would make a further $60,000,000 available to the Central American Bank for Economic Integration.

Central American Defence Council
Consejo de Defensa Centroamericana
(CONDECA)

Founded. Dec. 14, 1963

Membership. El Salvador, Guatemala and Honduras

History. The council was first established by the governments of El Salvador, Guatemala, Honduras and Nicaragua. These four governments decided on July 2, 1965, to create a military bloc for the co-ordination of all defence measures against possible communist aggression. CONDECA, which co-operated closely with the US

Southern Command, was subsequently joined by Panama, which, however, withdrew from the organization after the assumption of power by Lt. Col. Omar Torrijos Herrera in 1968. Honduras left CONDECA in 1973, and after the overthrow of the Somoza regime in Nicaragua in 1979, only El Salvador and Guatemala were left as CONDECA members. (El Salvador, however, had rejected US military aid in March 1977.)

The council was revived on Oct. 2, 1983, by El Salvador, Guatemala and Honduras in order to achieve a joint approach to any "extra-continental aggression of a Marxist-Leninist character".

At a meeting held in Tegucigalpa (Honduras) on Oct. 22–23, 1983, the three partners discussed inter alia substantial US military aid in the form of advice, training, communications, intelligence-sharing and logistic support and "in case of extreme crisis" direct participation by the United States, with all its resources, in "the pacification of Nicaragua".

Central American Democratic Community (CDC)
Comunidad Democrática Centroamericana

Founded. Jan. 19, 1982

Membership. Costa Rica, El Salvador and Honduras

Objects. The stated aims of the CDC are to promote security and democracy in the region, to provide mutual solidarity in the case of external aggression against a member country, and to further economic development, notably in the private sector. The CDC's declared political objectives were "to state that free elections are the highest expression of the people's will and participation"; to condemn all foreign intervention; to defend human rights as the cornerstone of the policy of the CDC member countries; to conform to the principles and norms of the Inter-American system; and to reiterate their individual right to resort to collective security measures within the framework of existing treaties. Its economic objectives were inter alia "to create an economic community in Central America based on the overall and balanced development of its members, for which they agree to strive to obtain more favourable access to the markets of countries with greater resources and to request the political support of such countries".

History. The formation of the CDC was endorsed by the Presidents of Colombia and Venezuela and by the US Assistant Secretary of State for Latin American Affairs on Jan. 27, 1982. It was opposed by Guatemala, Nicaragua and Panama, which had not been invited to participate. In Nicaragua the CDC was (on Feb. 15, 1982) denounced as being "anti-democratic" and a further manoeuvre by the United States for "greater aggression against Nicaragua and for the invocation of the 1947 Treaty of Rio".

Other Latin American Declarations

The 1974 Declaration of Ayacucho. At a meeting of representatives of eight Latin American countries—Argentina, Bolivia, Colombia, Cuba, Ecuador, Panama, Peru and Venezuela—held in Lima on Dec. 7–9, 1974, to mark the 150th anniversary of the battle of Ayacucho (in which the last of the Spanish royal armies was defeated by South American troops in 1824), the participants signed a *Declaration of Ayacucho* in which they expressed their commitment to the establishment of a permanent state of internal peace and co-operation, to the eventual effective attainment of effective arms limitation and to the dedication of all possible resources to the economic and social development of each country. They condemned the use of nuclear power for other than peaceful purposes and they deplored the "economic dependence" imposed on their continent.

The declaration dealt in particular with the following items:

Latin American Nationalism. The declaration described Latin American nationalism as the awareness of the peoples of their true personality, which was the result of cross-breeding, the fusion of cultures, and common historical, social and economic backgrounds. To strengthen their unity it was necessary, in the present international situation, to solve regional problems without external interference, to act jointly to promote the interests of the nations, and to prevent the prospering in Latin America of policies which might impair the personality of the peoples and the sovereignty of the states.

Inter-State Relations. The signatories reiterated their adherence to the principles of, inter alia: the juridical equality of states; their territorial integrity and right of self-determination; ideological pluralism; respect for human rights; and the renunciation of the threat or use of force or of armed, economic or financial aggression in relations between states.

Economic Questions. The signatories also stated that the concerted efforts of all the nations of Latin America were essential to promote the formation and strengthening of associations between the producer and exporter countries; to obtain the best terms of access for Latin American products to international markets; to obtain the best conditions for the transfer and interchange of technology for their particular needs; to ensure adequate supplies of essential commodities, particularly food; to establish multinational Latin American concerns; and to co-operate in monetary matters, transport and communications.

Other Contents. The declaration also included a pledge to give the fullest understanding to the land-locked position of Bolivia, and condemned the colonial enclaves still existing in Latin America, which were said to constitute a potential threat to peace.

The 1980 Declaration of Santa Marta. This declaration signed on Dec. 18, 1980, by the Presidents of Colombia, Costa Rica, the Dominican Republic, Ecuador, El Salvador, Honduras, Panama, Peru and Venezuela and by the Prime Minister of Spain, called for Latin American democracy to be upheld and reaffirmed that "the sovereign will of the people, freely expressed by a vote, is the only legitimate source of authority", and it noted that the unity of Latin American nations was "a firm requirement not only for their progress and development but also for the maintenance of their historical identity and common destiny". In particular the declaration urged Bolivia, then under a military regime, to "return to the path of democratic institutionality" and not to leave the Andean Group (which it had threatened to do).

The 1984 Declaration of Quito. This declaration, issued by an economic conference of Latin American and Caribbean countries held in Quito (Ecuador) on Jan. 9–14, 1984, contained proposals to alleviate the foreign debt problem which affected the 26 participating countries.

Under these proposals debt negotiations were to take into account the social and development aims of each country; debtors and creditors were to share responsibility for the debt burden; the debt-servicing payments should not exceed a "reasonable percentage" of the inflow of foreign assets on the grounds that economic development was crucial to the long-term settlement of the debt; payments were to "reconcile the demands of the servicing of the debt with the development aims of each country by reducing as much as possible the social costs of the adjustment process"; short-term debts might be converted into long-term debts, with extended grace periods, reduced renegotiation fees and lower interest rates; and creditor countries were to reduce protectionist barriers obstructing exports from Latin American and Caribbean states.

The points of the declaration were ratified by a conference held in Cartagena on June 21–22, 1984, by the Foreign and Finance Ministers of Argentina, Bolivia, Brazil, Chile, Colombia, the Dominican Republic, Ecuador, Mexico, Peru and Venezuela, which suggested concrete proposals to ease the payment of debt and reached a "Consensus of Cartagena" on the origins, impact and management of the debt crisis. The deliberations were continued at a further conference held in Mar del Plata (Argentina) on Sept. 13–14, 1984.

The 1985 Declaration of Lima. A declaration signed in Lima (Peru) by representatives of 20 Latin American countries on July 28, 1985, in favour of continental integration expressed support for the actions of the Contadora Group in its search for a political solution to Central American conflicts, called for a reduction in arms spending in the region, and supported Argentina in its dispute with the United Kingdom over the Falkland (Malvinas) Islands.

Treaties and Agreements of the United States

Defence Treaties of the USA

Many bilateral and multilateral agreements relating to defence have been concluded by the United States with partners throughout the world. Of these a number are direct defence treaties, while others are merely agreements on defence assistance.

BILATERAL TREATIES

The bilateral agreements are listed below in alphabetical order of countries. Where only one date is given, the agreement entered into force immediately after signature, otherwise dates of entry into force are shown in parentheses.

Antigua and Barbuda. Agreement on US defence areas and facilities in Antigua, Dec. 14, 1977 (Jan. 1, 1978). (Late in 1978 it was reported that the United States intended gradually to phase out the use of one of the two bases in Antigua and to reduce its payments to Antigua accordingly from 1982 onwards.)

Argentina. (1) Agreement relating to a military assistance programme, May 10, 1964.
(2) Armed forces co-operative projects agreement, May 5, 1970.

Australia. (1) Mutual defence assistance agreement, Feb. 1 and Feb. 20, 1951 (Feb. 20, 1951).
(2) Agreement on co-operation regarding atomic information for mutual defence purposes, July 12, 1957, (Aug. 14, 1957).
(3) Agreement to facilitate the interchange of patent rights and techical information for defence purposes, Jan. 24, 1958.
(4) Agreement on a mutual weapons development programme, Aug. 23, 1960.
(5) Agreement relating to the establishment of a United States naval communication station in Australia, May 9, 1963 (June 28, 1963); amended on July 12, 1968, with effect from July 1, 1968, on March 21, 1974, and on Nov. 24, 1982.
(6) Agreement relating to the establishment of a joint defence space research facility, Dec. 9, 1966, extended on Oct. 19, 1977.
(7) Agreement relating to the establishment of a joint defence space communications station in Australia, Nov. 10, 1969.

Austria. (1) Exchange of notes on mutual security agreement (Dec. 14, 1951, and Jan. 5, 1952; entry into force on latter date).
(2) Exchange of notes relating to the purchase by Austria of certain military equipment, materials and services, Aug. 9, 1957.

The Bahamas. Agreements between the United States and the United Kingdom (i) on naval and airbases, Sept. 2, 1940; (ii) on leased naval and air bases, March 27, 1941; amended July 19 and Aug. 1, 1950; (iii) on the Bahamas long-range proving ground for guided missiles, July 21, 1950; (iv) on the establishment by the United States of a high-altitude interceptor range in connexion with (iii) above, Feb. 24 and March 2, 1953; (v) on other related matters, as well as on the establishment of an Atlantic underwater test and evaluation centre, Oct. 11, 1967; on the transfer of part of Eleuthera Island to the US Navy, Aug. 9, 1971, and Feb. 17, 1972; and on the use of land at the US Navy base in Georgetown, Great Exuma Island, June 19, Sept. 12 and Nov. 2, 1972; (vi) on US defence facilities in the Bahamas, April 5, 1984 (effective Jan. 26, 1985). The agreements listed under (i) to (v) above continue to apply under an exchange of notes of July 10 and 20, 1973.

Bahrain. During 1984 Bahrain received US assistance in the construction of a new military airport, and it was reported to have ordered advanced fighter aircraft from the United States.

Belgium. (1) Mutual defence agreement under the North Atlantic Treaty, Jan. 27, 1950 (March 30, 1950); amended June 19 and 29, 1976. (See also agreements with Denmark, France, Italy, Luxembourg, the Netherlands, Norway and the United Kingdom.)
(2) Exchange of notes relating to the assurances required under the (US) Mutual Security Act of 1951, Jan. 7, 1952.
(3) Exchange of notes relating to a weapons production programme April 6 and 22, 1960.
(4) Agreement for co-operation in the use of atomic energy for mutual defence purposes, May 17, 1962 (Sept. 5, 1962).
(5) Memorandum of understanding concerning the principles governing mutual co-operation in the research, development, production, procurement and logistic support of defence equipment, Dec. 12, 1979.
(6) Agreement on the status of a US ground launched cruise missile (GLCM) unit to be located in Belgium, Feb. 13, 1984.

Benin. Agreement on the furnishing of military equipment, materials and services to Dahomey (now Benin) to help assure its security and independence, June 5 and 13, 1962 (June 13, 1962).

Bolivia. (1) Military assistance agreement, March 21 and April 22, 1958 (April 22, 1958).
(2) Agreement on the furnishing of defence articles and services to Bolivia, April 26, 1962.

Brazil. (1) Agreement for the establishment of a joint group on emergency supply problems, July 24, 1951.
(2) Military assistance agreement, March 15, 1952 (May 19, 1953); terminated March 11, 1977, except for safeguard clauses.
(3) Exchange of notes on understanding relating to military assistance, Jan. 30, 1964.
(4) Agreement of Dec. 1, 1982, relating to a US loan of US$1,230 million to Brazil and to nuclear and military co-operation, with Brazilian military equipment to be supplied to the United States and certain members of the Brazilian armed forces to be offered training in the United States.
(5) Under two economic protocols signed on Feb. 6, 1984, Brazil was to receive US military equipment (including 10 destroyers and 60 helicopters), the Brazilian Navy would carry out "certain duties in the South Atlantic", and the United States would be allowed to monitor the sale by Brazil of arms containing US technology.
(6) Master data exchange arrangement for the mutual development of military equipment, Nov. 14, 1984.

Canada. (1) The Ogdensburg declaration regarding the establishment of a permanent joint board on defence, Aug. 18, 1940.
(2) Arrangement relating to naval and air bases, Sept. 2, 1940.
(3) Agreement regarding leased naval and air bases, March 27, 1941; modified, Feb. 13 and March 19, 1952.
(4) Protocol concerning the defence of Newfoundland, March 27, 1941.
(5) Joint statement concerning defence co-operation providing for the permanent joint board on defence to continue collaboration for security purposes, Feb. 12, 1947.
(6) Agreement relating to the leased naval base at Argentia, Newfoundland, Aug. 13 and Oct. 22, 1947.
(7) Exchange of notes on the establishment of a joint industrial mobilization committee, April 12, 1949.
(8) Exchange of notes relating to economic co-operation for defence, Oct. 26, 1950.
(9) Exchange of notes regarding the extension and co-ordination of the continental radar defence system (Pine Tree), Aug. 1, 1951, partly superseded by agreement of Aug. 16, 1971; related agreements, May 25, 1964; Sept. 30, 1966; June 30, 1971; and March 22, 1974. (See also agreements of June 13, 1955; June 15, 1955; and Sept. 27, 1961.)

(10) Agreement relating to the application of the NATO status of forces agreement to US forces in Canada, including those at the leased bases in Newfoundland and Goose Bay, Labrador (except for certain arrangements under the leased bases agreement), April 28 and 30, 1952, (Sept. 27, 1953).

(11) Exchange of notes governing the establishment of a distant early warning system in Canadian territory (DEW Line) May, 5, 1955. (See also agreements of April 13, 1959, and July 13, 1959, below.)

(12) Agreement relating to the establishment and operation of certain radar stations in the Newfoundland-Labrador area, June 13, 1955.

(13) Agreement relating to the construction and operation of certain radar stations in British Columbia, Ontario and Nova Scotia, June 15, 1955 (provided the provisions are not inconsistent with financial arrangements of Aug. 16, 1971).

(14) Agreement for co-operation regarding atomic information for mutual defence purposes, June 15, 1955 (July 22, 1955); amended May 22, 1959.

(15) Agreement on the organization and operations of the North American Air Defence Command (NORAD), May 12, 1958; extended March 30, 1968, May 12, 1973, for two years; May 8, 1975, for five years until May 1980; May 12, 1980, for one year; March 11, 1981, for five years, with the deletion of a clause forbidding any steps which violated the 1972 US–Soviet Anti-Ballistic Missile (ABM) Treaty; and March 19, 1986, for a further five years from May 1986: see also (31) below.

In 1975 it was decided to extend NORAD by the establishment, in addition to the existing control centre at North Bay (Ontario), of another control centre at Edmonton (Alberta), with the result that all Canadian air space would be controlled from centres located in Canada and manned by Canadian personnel.

(16) Agreement providing for the establishment of a Canada–United States committee on joint defence, Aug. 29 and Sept. 2, 1958.

(17) Agreement relating to communications facilities at Cape Dyer, Baffin Island, to support the Greenland extension of the distant early warning system, April 13, 1959 (operative Jan. 15, 1959).

(18) Agreement relating to the establishment, maintenance and operation of short range tactical air navigation (TACAN) facilities in Canada, May 1, 1959; amended Sept. 19 and 23, 1961.

(19) Exchange of notes concerning the establishment of an integrated communications system to support the ballistic missiles early warning system, July 13, 1959.

(20) Exchange of notes concerning the cost-sharing and related arrangements with respect to planned improvements in the continental air defence system (CADIN), Sept. 27, 1961; amended May 6, 1964; Nov. 24, 1965.

(21) Exchange of notes concerning the establishment, operation and maintenance of improved ground-to-air military communications facilities in northern Canada, Dec. 1, 1965.

(22) Agreement relating to the use of certain facilities at the US Air Force Pine Tree radar site at Hopedale, Labrador, June 11, Sept. 19, 1969, and Feb. 24, 1970.

(23) Lease of three radar sets to Canada, with general provisions, Nov. 18, 1975.

(24) Agreement relating to the installation, operation and maintenance of a circuit for narrative record traffic between the defence agencies, Jan. 7 and 19, 1976; entry into force on latter date.

(25) Agreement relating to the continued operation and maintenance of the torpedo test range in the strait of Georgia and the installation and utilization of an advanced underwater acoustic measurement system at Jervis Inlet, Jan. 13 and April 14, 1976.

(26) Agreement relating to the continued use of facilities at Goose Bay airport by the United States, Nov. 10 and 24, 1976.

(27) Memorandum of understanding concerning region operations control centre, March 5 and April 11, 1977.

(28) Agreement relating to performance evaluation of a variable depth sonar system in conjunction with a high speed surface vessel (Project Hytow), Sept. 12 and Oct. 12, 1977.

(29) Memorandum of understanding concerning NAVSTAR global positioning system, Aug. 7 and Oct. 5, 1978.

(30) Memorandum of understanding pertaining to co-ordination of co-operative research and development, Feb. 1, 1979.

(31) Agreement regarding continued co-operation in the North American Aerospace Defence Command (previously known as the North American Air Defence command, NORAD), March 11, 1981 (effective May 12, 1981).

(32) Letter of agreement concerning narrative record telecommunication interface arrangements, Sept. 15 and Oct. 22, 1981.

(33) Agreement concerning the test and evaluation of US defence weapons systems in Canada, Feb. 10, 1983.

(34) Mutual logistical support agreement, Feb. 11, 1983.

(35) Agreement regarding the establishment of a new chain of 52 ground radar stations across the Canadian Arctic and northern Alaska (to replace the obsolescent DEW line established in 1955), March 18, 1985.

Chile. Military assistance agreement, April 9, 1952 (July 11, 1952).

China. On Jan. 12, 1985, it was announced in Washington that preliminary agreement had been reached to supply China with US military equipment (defensive in nature), including anti-submarine weapons, torpedoes and ship-defence systems.

Colombia. (1) Agreement relating to the procurement of strategic materials, March 21, 1943.

(2) Military assistance agreement, April 17, 1952.

(3) Agreement on Army, Navy and Air Force advisers, July 13 and Sept. 16, 1955 (Sept. 20, 1955).

(4) Agreement relating to the furnishing of military equipment, materials and services to Colombia, (April 3, 1961).

(5) Agreement concerning general security of military information, Dec. 26, 1981.

Costa Rica. (1) Agreement on the furnishing of defence articles and services to Costa Rica for the purpose of contributing to its internal security, May 21 and June 18, 1962 (June 18, 1962).

(2) On May 6, 1985, it was announced that on a Costa Rican request 24 US Special Forces advisers were being sent to Costa Rica to train civil guard officers "to counter Nicaraguan subversive activities".

Cuba. (1) Agreement for the lease to the USA of lands in Cuba for coaling and naval stations, Feb. 16 and Feb. 23, 1903 (Feb. 23, 1903).

Under this agreement, confirmed by a treaty of 1934, the United States was granted complete jurisdiction and control over a military base on Guantánamo Bay at the southern tip of Cuba, in return for which the United States would recognize Cuban sovereignty over the area. After the deterioration in US–Cuban relations in 1960, President Eisenhower issued a statement in November of that year, saying that the agreement on the Guantánamo Bay military base could be modified or abrogated only by agreement between the two parties, and that the US Government had no intention of agreeing to modification or abrogation.

(2) Military assistance agreement, March 7, 1952.

Cyprus. Exchange of notes between the United States and the United Kingdom relating to the assurances required under the (US) Mutual Security Act of 1951, made applicable to Cyprus, Jan. 8, 1952.

Denmark. (1) Mutual defence assistance agreement under the North Atlantic Treaty, Jan. 27, 1950. (See also agreements with Belgium, France, Italy, Luxembourg, the Netherlands, Norway and the United Kingdom.)

(2) Exchange of notes relating to the assurances required by the (US) Mutual Security Act of 1951, Jan. 8, 1952.

(3) Exchange of notes relating to a weapons production programme, April 12, 1960.

(4) Two agreements concerning the defence of Greenland (the first signed April 27, 1951 and in force June 8, 1951; the second signed and in force Dec. 2, 1960).

(5) Agreement on general security of military information, Jan. 23 and Feb. 27, 1981.

(6) Mutual logistic support agreement, June 1 and 4, 1982.

The Dominican Republic. Military assistance agreement, March 8, 1962 (June 10, 1964); terminated June 20, 1966, except for paragraphs 2–6 of article 1.

Ecuador. Exchange of notes relating to eligibility for US military assistance and training pursuant to the (US) International Security and Arms Export Control Act of 1976, Aug. 17 and Sept. 3, 1976.

Egypt. (1) Exchange of notes relating to mutual defence assistance, April 29, 1952; amended Dec. 9–10, 1952.

(2) Memorandum of understanding on the production in Egypt of US-designed defence equipment, Oct. 21, 1979.

(3) General security of military information agreement, Feb. 10, 1982.

The conclusion of the Egyptian–Israeli peace treaty [see page 415] was followed by comprehensive US arms supplies to Egypt and by related decisions, as detailed below.

(i) In 1979 the US Government proposed to supply $1,500 million in military aid to Egypt over three years. (ii) An agreement in co-operation in the production and assembly of electronic equipment and armoured vehicles was concluded on Oct. 21, 1979. (iii) The US State Department announced on Feb. 25, 1980, that the United States would sell to Egypt 244 M-60 tanks and 40 advanced F-16 fighters, and had agreed in principle to sell F-15 fighters to Egypt later, and by April 1980 this sale was approved by the US Congress. On July 25, 1980, the US Defence Department announced that a further 67 M-60 tanks would be sold to Egypt. (iv) It was announced in Washington on Aug. 26, 1980, that an airfield at Ras Banas (on the Red Sea) would be expanded so as to serve as a launching pad for a US rapid-deployment force (for the Middle East region).

Joint naval exercises were held in November 1984 and August 1985. US aid to Egypt in 1985 totalled US$2,200 million, of which US$1,200 million were for military purposes. At the end of 1984 Egypt's current debt to the US lenders was estimated at about US$8,000 million.

El Salvador. Agreement on the furnishing of defence articles and services to El Salvador to contribute to its internal security, April 10 and 13, 1962 (April 13, 1962).

US military aid to El Salvador has included the following amounts per fiscal year since 1981: US$5,000,000 and US$5,400,000 for 1981; US$26,000,000 and US$17,000,000 for 1982; US$64,800,000 for 1983; US$70,000,000 and (in emergency aid) US$35,000,000 in 1984; US$128,000,000 for 1985; and US$113,000,000 for 1986. Some 1,000 Salvadorean troops have been trained at Fort Bragg, North Carolina. By February 1984 there were 97 US military advisers in El Salvador. By March 1985 the Salvadorean Air Force had received from the United States at least two C-74 gunships, 39 Huey UH-1H helicopters, nine A-37 Dragonfly ground assault fighters and four Hughes 500 helicopter gunships.

Ethiopia. (1) Exchange of notes relating to mutual defence assistance, June 12-13, 1952.

(2) Exchange of notes relating to a special programme of facilities assistance, Dec. 26, 1957.

France. (1) Mutual defence assistance agreement under the North Atlantic Treaty, Jan. 27, 1950. (See also agreements with Belgium, Denmark, Italy, Luxembourg, the Netherlands, Norway and the United Kingdom.)

(2) Mutual security agreement, Jan. 5, 1952.

(3) Agreement for co-operation on uses of atomic energy for mutual defence purposes, May 7, 1959 (July 20, 1959).

(4) Exchange of notes relating to a weapons production programme, Sept. 19, 1960.

(5) Agreement for co-operation in the operation of atomic weapons systems for mutual defence purposes, July 27, 1961 (Oct. 9, 1961); renewed in a revised version, Aug. 1, 1985.

(6) Memorandum of understanding relating to military procurement, Dec. 20, 1961.

(7) General security of information agreement, Sept. 7, 1977.

The Gambia. Exchange of notes between the United States and the United Kingdom relating to the assurances required under the (US) Mutual Security Act of 1951, Jan. 8, 1952.

The Federal Republic of Germany. (1) Exchange of letters relating to the assurances required under the (US) Mutual Security Act of 1951, Dec. 19 and 28, 1951.

(2) Mutual defence assistance agreement, June 30, 1955 (Dec. 27, 1955).

(3) Agreements on the training of German army and navy personnel, Dec. 12, 1956.

(4) Agreement relating to a weapons production programme, May 27, 1960.

(5) Agreement for co-operation in uses of atomic energy for mutual defence purposes, May 5, 1959 (July 27, 1959).

(6) Agreement relating to the AIM-9L Sidewinder air-to-air missile, Feb. 14, 1974.

(7) Memorandum of understanding relating to co-operative tests for the ROLAND 2 all-weather short-range air defence system, Feb. 18 and 28, 1975.

(8) Memorandum of understanding concerning co-operative development of an advanced surface-to-air missile system, July 16 and 22, 1976.

(9) Agreement on the release and testing of strebo submunitions and on the exchange of information, Aug. 4 and Nov. 4, 1976.

(10) Agreement relating to the security of information on the JT-10D aircraft engine, Feb. 24 and March 18, 1977.

(11) Memorandum of understanding for co-production and sale of the Sidewinder AIM-9L missile system, Oct. 7, 1977.

(12) Memorandum of understanding for co-production and sale of modular thermal imaging systems (MOD FLIR) and their components, Feb. 27 and March 3, 1978 (April 20, 1978); supplement signed March 26, 1979.

(13) Memorandum of understanding concerning the principles governing mutual co-operation in the research and development, procurement and logistic support of defence equipment, Oct. 17, 1978.

(14) Memorandum of understanding for co-operation in arms tactical data systems for the purpose of standardization and interoperability, Jan. 6 and April 14, 1980.

(15) Agreement concerning the support of USAFE A-10 aircraft at forward operations locations (FOLS) in the Federal Republic of Germany, Nov. 5 and 9, 1981; effective Oct. 1, 1979.

(16) Agreement concerning host nation support during crisis or war, April 15, 1982 [see page 223].

(17) Two agreements on the participation of West German industry in the US Strategic Defence Initiative (SDI or "Star Wars") research programme and on technology transfers, March 27, 1986. (The agreements were not to be published. The West German Economic Minister stated afterwards that he had made it clear to the US side that the Federal Republic would not take part in the SDI programme.)

Ghana. Mutual defence assistance agreement between the United States and the United Kingdom, Jan. 27, 1950 (made applicable to the Gold Coast—now Ghana—on July 19, 1952).

Greece*. (1) Agreement on the use of certain Greek islands for training exercises by the US fleet in the Mediterranean, Feb. 11 and Feb. 21, 1949.

(2) Exchange of notes relating to the assurances required under the (US) Mutual Security Act of 1951, Dec. 21, 1951 and Jan. 7, 1952.

---

* See also pages 224–25.

(3) Agreement concerning military facilities, Oct. 12, 1953; Art. III, Para. 1 partly abrogated Sept. 7, 1956.

(4) Agreement concerning the status of US forces in Greece, Sept. 7, 1956.

(5) Exchange of notes on co-operation in the uses of atomic energy for mutual defence purposes, May 6, 1959 (Aug. 11, 1959).

(6) Exchange of notes on a weapons production programme, Feb. 15, 1960.

(7) Agreement relating to the status of US Navy personnel and the establishment of a joint standing committee, Sept. 1, 13 and 29, 1972.

(8) Exchange of notes concerning the grant of defence articles and services under the military assistance programme, Aug. 30, 1979.

(9) Agreement on defence and economic co-operation, Sept. 8, 1983 (Dec. 20, 1983).

Grenada. Agreement concerning the status of US forces in Grenada, March 12-13, 1984.

Guatemala. (1) Exchange of notes providing for the transfer of equipment and material to the Government of Guatemala, July 27 and 30, 1954.

(2) Military assistance agreement, June 18, 1955.

(3) Exchange of notes relating to the furnishing of defence articles and services for the purpose of contributing to its internal security, May 25 and Aug. 2, 1962.

(4) Announcement by the US State Department that arms sales to Guatemala, suspended in 1977, would be resumed, Jan. 7, 1983. (They were said to be worth US$3,600,000, chiefly for spare parts for US-made UH-IH helicopters. On Jan. 27, 1984, it was announced that Guatemala would be allowed to buy helicopter spare parts worth US$2,000,000.)

Guinea. Exchange of notes relating to military assistance, June 29, 1965.

Haiti. (1) Military assistance agreement, Jan. 28, 1955 (Sept. 12, 1955).

(2) Exchange of notes relating to the transfer of military equipment, materials and services to Haiti, Sept. 1, 1960.

(In 1981 the United States acquired the use of a military base at Mole St Nicolas (Haiti's nearest point to Cuba) against the reported payment of US$600,000,000. (US aid to Haiti was US$43,500,000 for the 1983 fiscal year, US$44,600,000 for 1984 and US$54,050,000 for 1985.)

Honduras. (1) Military assistance agreement, May 20, 1954.

(2) Exchange of notes for performance by members of army and air force missions of duties of military advisory group specified in the above agreement, April 17 and 25, 1956 (April 26, 1956).

(3) Exchange of notes relating to military assistance (Oct. 24, 1962).

(4) Agreement relating to the military assistance agreement of May 20, 1954, concerning the use of certain facilities in Honduras by the United States, May 6–7, 1982.

(By March 19, 1982, there were nearly 100 US military advisers in Honduras, as stated by the US State Department, which gave US "security aid" to Honduras at $8,900,000 in 1981 and US$68,100,000 in 1982, with US$40,300,000 being requested for 1983 and a separate grant of US$21,000,000 for the improvement and extension of three airports to accommodate US transport aircraft and jet fighters. Joint manoeuvres were held in July 1982 and February 1983. In May 1983 it was announced that a US training base for Salvadorean soldiers would be established in Honduras at Puerto Castilla (with a budget of US$7,000,000).

On March 11, 1983, the US Defence Department announced that Honduras would be provided with radar stations to track small aircraft suspected of carrying arms for Nicaragua, and a month later it was stated that the United States would provide Honduras with airborne warning and control systems (AWACS) aircraft for similar purposes. For exercises involving US and Honduran troops an advance team of US forces arrived in

Honduras on Oct. 3, 1983. Further joint military exercises took place in 1984 and 1985 and were to be continued until 1988.)

Iceland. (1) Defence agreement pursuant to North Atlantic Treaty, May 5, 1951.

(2) Exchange of notes relating to the assurances required under the (US) Mutual Security Act of 1951, Jan. 7 and 8, 1952.

(3) Exchange of notes concerning the sale to Iceland of certain military equipment, materials and services, Oct. 4 and Dec. 10, 1954.

(4) Exchange of notes relating to the presence of defence forces in Iceland and setting up an Iceland defence standing group, Dec. 6, 1956.

(5) Exchange of notes relating to the continuation of the defence agreement of May 5, 1951, Oct. 22, 1974.

(6) Arrangement for Icelandic operation of Loran-C monitor facility at US Naval Station at Keflavik, Iceland, Sept. 9, 1975 (effective July 1, 1976).

India. (1) Exchange of notes relating to a military sales agreement, March 7 and 16, 1951.

(2) Exchange of notes concerning an understanding that the assurances contained in the above military sales agreement are applicable to equipment, materials, information and services furnished under the (US) Mutual Security Act of 1951 as amended and such other applicable US laws as might come into effect, April 16 and Dec. 17, 1958.

(3) Exchange of notes supplementing the 1951 military sales agreement, Nov. 14, 1962.

(4) Exchange of notes relating to military assistance, Jan. 13, 1965.

Indonesia. (1) Exchange of notes relating to the sale to Indonesia of military equipment, materials and services, Aug. 13, 1958.

(2) Exchange of notes relating to the furnishing of military equipment, materials and services for a programme of civic action, April 14, 1967.

(3) Exchange of notes relating to the provision by the United States of basic pilot training aircraft, April 9 and 17, 1969.

(4) Exchange of notes relating to the furnishing of combat equipment to Indonesia as additional military assistance, Aug. 18–19, 1970.

(5) Exchange of notes relating to eligibility for US military assistance and training pursuant to the International Assistance and Arms Export Act of 1976, Aug. 3 and 24, 1976.

Iran. (1) Exchange of notes concerning a mutual defence assistance agreement, May 23, 1950.

(2) Exchange of notes relating to agreement on the continuation of military assistance to Iran, April 24, 1952.

(4) Exchange of notes relating to the safeguarding of classified information, May 28 and June 6, 1974.

(5) Memorandum of understanding concerning revisions of foreign military sales letters of offer and acceptance between the United States and Iran, Feb. 3, 1979.

Iraq. Agreement on the sale to Iraq of six Lockheed L-130 civilian transport aircraft (convertible into Hercules C-130 military transport aircraft), May 1982.

Israel. (1) Exchange of notes relating to assurance and economic assistance as authorized in the US Mutual Security Act of 1951, Dec. 7, 1951.

(2) Exchange of notes relating to mutual defence assistance, July 1 and 23, 1952.

(3) Exchange of notes relating to general procurement arrangements for goods and services, July 15 and 20, 1965.

(4) Agreement regarding payment for tooling costs of accelerated production of M-60 A1 tanks, Aug. 22 and Oct. 23, 1975.

(5) Memorandum of agreement concerning the principles governing mutual co-operation in research and development,

scientist and engineer exchange, and procurement and logistic support of selected defence equipment, March 19, 1979.

(6) Agreement concerning construction of airbase facilities and agreement on funding of this construction, April 6, 1979.

(7) General security of information agreement, July 30 and Dec. 10, 1982.

(8) A strategic co-operation agreement concluded on Nov. 28–29, 1983, provided for the creation of a joint military-political group "to establish ways to enhance US–Israeli co-operation". The United States also undertook to resume the supply of cluster bombs to Israel (suspended in 1982). US aid to Israel for the 1984 fiscal year was approved at US$2,610 million—including economic grants at US$910,000,000, with the remainder being military credits, half as grants and half repayable with interest. Under the above agreement joint US–Israeli naval exercises were held on June 20, 1984.

(9) Agreement on Israeli participation in the US Strategic Defence Initiative (SDI or "Star Wars") research programme, May 6, 1986.

Italy*. (1) Exchange of notes on mutual defence assistance agreement, Jan. 27, 1950. (See also agreements with Belgium, Denmark, France, Luxembourg, the Netherlands, Norway and the United Kingdom.)

(2) Exchange of notes relating to the assurances required by the (US) Mutual Security Act of 1951, Jan. 7, 1952.

(3) Exchange of notes relating to a weapons production programme, July 7, 1960.

(4) Agreement for co-operation on uses of atomic energy for mutual defence purposes, Dec. 3, 1960 (May 24, 1961).

(5) Exchange of notes relating to the safeguarding of classified information, Aug. 4, 1964.

(6) Memorandum of understanding concerning the principles governing mutual co-operation in the research, development, production and procurement of defence equipment, Sept. 11, 1978.

(7) Mutual logistics support agreement, Feb. 23, 1983.

Jamaica. (1) Exchange of notes between the United States and the United Kingdom relating to the assurances required under the (US) Mutual Security Act of 1951, Jan. 8, 1952.

(2) Exchange of notes relating to the furnishing of defence articles and services to Jamaica, June 6, 1963.

Japan. (1) Mutual defence assistance agreement, March 8, 1954, (May 1, 1954); exchange of notes, Jan. 19, 1960.

(2) Exchange of notes relating to the transfer of military equipment and supplies to Japan, Nov. 19, 1954.

(3) Exchange of notes relating to a programme of aircraft assembly or manufacture in Japan, June 3, 1955; exchange of notes, April 13, 1956.

(4) Exchange of notes relating to a cost-sharing programme for the production and development in Japan of P2V anti-submarine and sea patrol aircraft, Jan. 25, 1958.

(5) Treaty of mutual co-operation and security, Jan. 19, 1960 (June 23, 1960—see page 448).

(6) Various agreements for the production and acquisition of defence equipment, including aircraft as well as Hawk, Nike and Sparrow missiles, concluded since 1960.

(7) Agreement for the transfer of defence-related technologies, No. 8, 1983.

(8) Agreement concerning Japan's financial contribution for US administrative and related expenses for the Japanese fiscal year 1984 (pursuant to the mutual defence agreement of March 8, 1954), July 20, 1984.

Jordan. (1) Exchanges of notes relating to the furnishing of defence articles and services to Jordan, Oct. 20, 1976, and Feb. 23, 1977, and also Aug. 14 and 30, 1980 (effective Aug. 28, 1980).

(2) Exchange of notes concerning the grant of defence articles and services under the military assistance programme, Aug. 27, 1979 (entry into force on the following day).

Kenya. Exchange of notes relating to eligibility for US military assistance and training pursuant to the International Security Assistance and Arms Export Control Act of 1976, Aug. 10 and 24, 1976.

Republic of Korea. (1) Mutual defence assistance agreement, Jan. 26, 1950.

(2) Exchange of notes relating to the assurances required under the (US) Mutual Security Act of 1951, Jan. 4 and 7, 1952.

(3) Agreement for the establishment of minimum facilities for an arsenal and the reworking of ammunition, May 29, 1955.

(4) Mutual defence treaty, Oct. 1, 1953 (Nov. 17, 1954) [see page 447].

(5) Memorandum of understanding relating to the establishment of an M-16 rifle production programme in Korea, March 31 and April 2, 1971; amended July 30, 1976; Oct. 14, 1977.

(6) Memorandum of agreement concerning conventional ammunition logistics, Nov. 25, 1974.

(7) Memorandum of understanding concerning constructing, equipping and operating a combined hardened tactical air control centre facility at Osan Air Base, June 19 and July 20, 1981.

(8) Memorandum of understanding concerning establishing a permanent Taegu operation location, Dec. 31, 1981, and Jan. 20, 1982.

(9) Memorandum of understanding regarding the construction of facilities at 2nd ID USA to improve combined defence capabilities, Feb. 2, 1982.

Kuwait. (1) Exchange of notes concerning the procurement of defence articles and services by Kuwait and the establishment of a US liaison office in Kuwait, Feb. 24 and April 15, 1975.

(2) Technical security arrangement, Jan. 18, 1976; amended June 26, 1977.

Lebanon. Exchange of notes relating to reimbursable military aid, March 6 and 23, 1953.

(2) Exchange of notes on military assistance agreement, June 3 and 6, 1957; amended June 9 and 12, 1958.

(3) Agreement on the supply to Lebanon arms worth US$50,000,000, including 36 M-68 tanks, 12 155 mm field guns and 24 armoured personnel carriers, announced on Dec. 2, 1982.

Liberia. (1) Exchange of notes relating to mutual defence assistance, Nov. 16 and 19, 1951.

(2) Exchange of notes on an understanding that the assurances contained in the above agreement are applicable to equipment, materials, information and services furnished under the (US) Mutual Security Act of 1951 as amended and such other applicable US laws as may come into effect, April 10 and July 19, 1958.

(3) Agreement of co-operation, July 8, 1959.

(4) Exchange of notes concerning the furnishing of military equipment and materials to Liberia, May 23 and June 17, 1961; amended Jan. 18 and 23, 1962.

(5) Agreement on construction of additional facilities at Roberts International Airport, Feb. 3, 1983; amended March 25 and April 4, 1983.

Luxembourg. (1) Mutual defence assistance agreement, Jan. 27, 1950 (March 28, 1950); amended Jan. 19 and 31, 1977. (See also agreements with Belgium, Denmark, France, Italy, the Netherlands, Norway and the United Kingdom.)

(2) Exchange of notes relating to the assurances required under the (US) Mutual Security Act of 1951, Jan. 8, 1952.

(3) Agreement concerning general security of military information, Sept. 17, 1981.

(4) Mutual logistics support agreement, Dec. 15, 1983.

Malaysia. (1) Exchange of notes relating to the purchase by Malaya of military equipment, materials and services from the United States, June 30 and July 9, 1958.

(2) Exchange of notes relating to eligibility for US military assistance and training pursuant to the International Security

---

* See also page 224.

and Arms Export Control Act of 1976, Feb. 11 and March 14, 1977.

Mali. Exchange of notes on military assistance agreement, May 20, 1961.

Morocco. Agreement concerning the use of certain facilities in Morocco by the United States, May 27, 1982. (Joint naval exercises were carried out in January 1985.)

The Netherlands. (1) Mutual defence assistance agreement, Jan. 27, 1950. (See also agreements with Belgium, Denmark, France, Italy, Luxembourg, Norway and the United Kingdom.)

(2) Agreement relating to the assurances required by the (US) Mutual Security Act of 1951, Jan. 8, 1952.

(3) Exchange of notes on the stationing of US armed forces in the Netherlands, Aug. 13, 1954 (Nov. 16, 1954).

(4) Exchange of notes on establishing an air defence technical centre, with cost reimbursement contract attached, Dec. 14, 1954.

(5) Agreement for co-operation on uses of atomic energy for mutual defence purposes, May 6, 1959 (July 27, 1959).

(6) Exchange of notes relating to a weapons production programme, March 24, 1960 (definitive entry into force Jan. 2, 1962).

(7) Memorandum of understanding concerning principles governing mutual co-operation in research and development, production and procurement of conventional defence equipment, July 25 and Aug. 24, 1978.

(8) Agreement relating to storage of pre-positioned war readiness materials by US forces, Jan. 15, 1981 (Aug. 20, 1981).

(9) Agreement establishing a television transmitter at Soesterberg Airfield, Dec. 7, 1981, and March 4, 1982 (July 19, 1983).

(10) Mutual logistics support agreement, Feb. 22, 1983.

New Zealand. (1) Exchange of notes relating to mutual defence assistance (June 19, 1952).

(2) Exchange of notes on an understanding that the assurances contained in the above agreement are applicable to equipment, materials, information and services furnished under the (US) Mutual Security Act of 1951 as amended and such other applicable US laws as may come into effect (March 25, 1960).

(3) Memorandum of understanding on logistic support, May 13 and June 21, 1982.

Niger. Exchange of notes relating to the furnishing of military equipment, materials and services to Niger to help assure its security and independence, May 22 and June 14, 1962.

Norway. (1) Mutual defence assistance agreement, Jan. 27, 1950 (Feb. 24, 1950). (See also agreements with Belgium, Denmark, France, Italy, Luxembourg, the Netherlands and the United Kingdom.)

(2) Agreement relating to the assurances required under the (US) Mutual Security Act of 1951, Jan. 8, 1952.

(3) Exchange of notes relating to a weapons production programme, Feb. 13, 1960; amended April 26 and Sept. 16, 1960.

(4) Exchanges of notes relating to a shipbuilding programme for the Norwegian Navy, July 6, 1960, and Nov. 29, 1960 (entry into force of the latter Jan. 31, 1961).

(5) Exchange of notes relating to the safeguarding of classified information, Feb. 26, 1970.

(6) Memorandum of understanding concerning the principles governing mutual co-operation in the research and development, production and procurement of defence equipment, May 19, 1978.

(7) Agreement on stockpiling of heavy equipment for a 10,000-strong US Marines brigade to be sent to Norway in the event of a Soviet attack, Jan. 16, 1981.

(8) Mutual logistic support agreement, Jan. 29 and Aug. 20, 1982.

Oman. An exchange of diplomatic notes on June 4, 1986, provided for co-operation between the two countries in economic development, trade and security "designed to enhance the ability of Oman to develop its economy and to safeguard its territorial integrity and to foster peace and security in the region". (The US State Department explained that under the agreement the USA would obtain land and naval facilities "similar to those enjoyed by other friendly countries", but that the USA would not "seek permission to station any military units in Oman", although it would provide Oman with certain items "appropriate to its defence".)

Pakistan. (1) Exchange of notes relating to transfer of military supplies and equipment to Pakistan, Nov. 29 and Dec. 15, 1950.

(2) Mutual defence assistance agreement, May 19, 1954.

(3) Defence support assistance agreement, Jan. 11, 1955; amended March 11, 1961.

(4) Agreement of co-operation, March 5, 1959.

(5) Agreement on Pakistan's purchase of 40 US-made F-16 aircraft, Dec. 4, 1981. (This agreement was part of a package of US economic and military assistance said to be worth $3,200 million over a six-year period from Oct. 1, 1981, accepted by Pakistan in September 1981, though with Pakistan reaffirming its Islamic foreign policy principles and its commitment to non-alignment.)

(6) Agreement concerning general security of military information, April 6, June 21 and 24, 1982.

Panama. (1) Exchange of notes relating to the sale of military equipment, materials and services to Panama, May 20, 1959; operative from April 27, 1959.

(2) Exchange of notes relating to the furnishing of defence articles and services to Panama for the purpose of contributing to its internal security, March 26 and May 23, 1962.

(3) Exchange of notes relating to economic and military co-operation, Sept. 7, 1978.

(4) Agreement concerning general security of military information, Aug. 17, 1984.

Paraguay. (1) Exchange of notes concerning the furnishing of assistance to Paraguay for the purpose of increasing the air transport capability of the Paraguayan Air Force, Aug. 25, 1962.

(2) Exchange of notes providing for assistance to increase the road construction and maintenance capability of the Paraguayan Army, Feb. 10, 1964.

(3) Exchange of notes relating to the furnishing of additional military assistance to Paraguay, April 11, 1966.

Peru. (1) Military assistance agreement, Feb. 22, 1952 (April 26, 1952).

(2) Exchange of notes relating to the furnishing of defence articles and services to Peru, Dec. 17 and 20, 1962.

The Philippines. (1) Agreement on military bases, March 14, 1947 (March 26, 1947); amended on numerous occasions between 1947 and 1983; and followed by related agreements between 1957 and 1974 (see also pages 447–48).

(2) Mutual defence treaty, Aug. 30, 1951 (Aug. 27, 1952).

(3) Agreement relating to the assurances under the (US) Mutual Security Act of 1951, Jan. 4 and 7, 1952.

(4) Exchange of notes relating to military assistance, June 26, 1953 (July 5, 1953).

(5) Exchange of notes relating to military assistance, April 27, 1955; amended April 20, 1956; June 14, 1957; and April 14, 1958.

(6) Exchange of notes for the establishment of a mutual defence board and the assignment of Philippine liaison officers to US military bases in the Philippines, May 15, 1958.

(7) Agreement relating to the establishment of a US communications facility at Mt. Cabuyao, March 16, 1965.

(8) Agreements concerning the grant of defence articles and services under the military assistance programme (i) Aug. 23 and 30, 1979, (ii) Aug. 12 and 22, 1980, and (iii) Aug. 19 and 30, 1981—all three amended Aug. 16 and Sept. 30, 1982.

Portugal. (1) Mutual defence assistance agreement, Jan. 5, 1951.

(2) Exchange of notes relating to the assurances required by the (US) Mutual Security Act of 1951, Jan. 8, 1952.

(3) Exchange of notes relating to a weapons production programme, Sept. 26, 1960.

(4) Memorandum of understanding concerning the principles governing mutual co-operation in the research, development, production, procurement and logistic support of defence equipment, Dec. 18, 1978, and March 28, 1979.

(5) Agreements concerning the grant of defence articles and services under the military assistance programme, (i) Aug. 14 and 27, 1979, (ii) Aug. 12 and 28, 1980, and (iii) Aug. 24 and 28, 1981—all three amended Aug. 16 and Sept. 29, 1982.

(6) Agreement concerning general security of military information, Sept. 10, 1982.

(7) Agreement relating to economic and military assistance, Dec. 13, 1983 [see page 224].

(8) Agreement concerning the installation in Portugal of a ground-based electro-optical deep space surveillance (GEODSS) station, March 27, 1984.

São Tomé and Príncipe. The signing of a military training agreement was reported in April 1985.

Saudi Arabia. (1) Exchange of notes relating to the extending of procurement assistance to Saudi Arabia for the transfer of military supplies and equipment, June 18, 1951.

(2) Agreement relating to the transfer of F-86 aircraft to Saudi Arabia, May 16 and Nov. 11, 1960.

(3) Exchange of notes relating to the construction of certain military facilities in Saudi Arabia, May 24 and June 5, 1965; operative May 24, 1965; extended Nov. 25, 1981, and May 10, 1982.

(4) Agreement on co-operation in the fields of economics, technology, industry and defence, June 8, 1974.

(5) Exchange of notes relating to a US military training mission in Saudi Arabia Feb. 8 and 27, 1977.

(6) Agreement on the supply to Saudi Arabia of four E3-A AWACS (Airborne Warning and Control System) aircraft (in addition to two AWACS aircraft sent in 1979), announced on Sept. 30, 1980 (to enable Saudi Arabia to observe the border conflict between the two Yemens and to obtain advance warning of any Iranian attack).

Senegal. Exchange of notes relating to the furnishing of military equipment, materials and services to Senegal for the purpose of assuring its security and supporting its development, July 20, 1962.

Seychelles. Exchange of notes between the United States and the United Kingdom relating to the assurances required under the (US) Mutual Security Act of 1951, Jan. 8, 1952; applicable to Seychelles on that date.

Singapore. (1) Agreement relating to the purchase by Malaya of military equipment, materials and services from the United States, June 30 and July 9, 1958.

(2) Agreement relating to the establishment of a US Air Force assistance team in Singapore, Feb. 23–24, 1977.

(3) Agreement concerning general security of military information, June 25, 1982, and March 9, 1983.

Solomon Islands. Exchange of notes between the United States and the United Kingdom relating to the assurance required under the (US) Mutual Security Act of 1951, Jan. 8, 1952; applicable to Solomon Islands on that date.

Somalia. Exchange of notes concerning the furnishing of defence articles and services to Somalia, March 22–23 and April 19 and 29, 1978 (April 29, 1978).

(On June 24, 1982, it was officially confirmed in Washington that the United States was giving Somalia emergency military aid, consisting of rifles, ammunition and communications equipment for use against Ethiopia, and that the supply of previously ordered anti-aircraft guns and radar had been accelerated. In 1982–83 US servicemen took part in joint military exercises with Somali forces. In June 1983 it was officially announced that the United States was funding and

managing a project to improve facilities at the Red Sea port of Berbera.)

South Africa. Exchange of notes relating to mutual defence assistance, Nov. 9, 1951.

Spain. (1) Mutual defence assistance agreement, Sept. 26, 1953.

(2) Exchange of notes confirming the bilateral arrangements for a facilities assistance programme pursuant to the above mutual defence assistance agreement, April 9 and May 11 and 19, 1954 (May 19 1954); supplementary agreements: May 25, 1955; Sept. 17, 1956.

(3) Agreements concerning the grant of defence articles and services under the military assistance programme, (i) Aug. 30, 1979, and (ii) Aug. 28–29, 1981.

(4) Master data exchange agreement for the mutual development of weapons systems, June 19, 1980.

(5) Cover agreement on the territorial command net, July 24, 1980.

(6) Agreement on friendship, defence and co-operation, July 2, 1982 (May 14, 1983). (During the five-year term of this agreement, the United States was entitled to continued use of three air bases in Spain, the naval base at Rota and a military firing range, while established bans on the stationing of US nuclear submarines at Rota, and on the storage of nuclear devices on Spanish soil, were maintained.)

(7) Memorandum of understanding pertaining to installation of satellite ground terminal at Rota (Spain), Nov. 3, 1982.

(8) General security of military information agreement, with protocol on security procedures for industrial operations, March 12, 1984.

(9) Memorandum of understanding concerning mutual logistic support between the US European Command and the Spanish armed forces, Nov. 5, 1984.

Sri Lanka. Exchange of notes relating to the purchase by Ceylon (now Sri Lanka) of certain military equipment, materials and services, Oct. 25 and Nov. 2, 1956.

The Sudan. (1) Mutual defence assistance agreement, April 8 and 22, 1981.

(2) Agreement concerning the grant of defence articles and services under the military assistance programme, Aug. 24 and 30, 1981; amended Aug. 30 and Sept. 25, 1982.

Suriname. Exchange of notes between the United States and the Netherlands relating to the assurances required by the (US) Mutual Security Act of 1951, Jan. 8, 1952.

Sweden. (1) Exchange of notes relating to the procurement of reimbursable military equipment, materials or services, June 30 and July 1, 1952.

(2) Agreement concerning general security of military information, Dec. 4 and 23, 1981.

Switzerland. Memorandum of understanding offsetting the amount to be paid by Switzerland for the aircraft and supporting equipment under an F-5 aircraft programme, July 2 and 9, 1975.

Thailand. (1) Agreement respecting military assistance, Oct. 17, 1950.

(2) Exchange of notes relating to the assurances required by the (US) Mutual Security Act of 1951, Dec. 27 and 29, 1951.

(3) Memorandum of agreement on an integrated communications system, Jan. 10, 1977.

(4) Memorandum of agreement on storage of ammunition in Thailand, March 22, 1977.

[As demanded by Thailand, all US forces (which had in 1969 numbered about 48,000 men) were withdrawn from Thailand by July 20, 1976, except for a 263-strong Military Advisory Group stationed in Thailand under the 1950 defence assistance agreement.]

[However, US military aid to Thailand was worth $80,000,000 in 1983, $91,000,000 in 1984 and $110,000,000 in 1985, and included supplies of medium tanks and F-16 fighter bombers.

Joint exercises were held regularly, e.g. in the Gulf of Siam in 1985, involving 7,400 US marines, 3,000 Thai troops, 20 US and 17 Thai warships and more than 100 aircraft.]

(5) General security of military information agreement, March 30 and April 5, 1983.

Trinidad and Tobago. Agreement between the United States and the United Kingdom relating to the assurances required under the (US) Mutual Security Act of 1951, Jan. 8, 1952.

Tunisia. Exchange of notes relating to a programme of grants of military equipment and material to Tunisia, Oct. 25, 1974; effective July 1, 1974.

Turkey*. (1) Exchange of notes relating to the assurances required by the (US) Mutual Security Act of 1951, Jan. 7, 1952.

(2) Agreement relating to implementation of the agreement between the parties to the North Atlantic Treaty regarding the status of their forces of June 19, 1951, signed on June 23, 1954; amended April 22 and July 21, 1955.

(3) Agreement of co-operation, March 5, 1959.

(4) Exchange of notes for co-operation in uses of atomic energy for mutual defence purposes, May 5, 1959 (July 27, 1959).

(5) Agreement relating to the introduction of modern weapons into NATO defence forces in Turkey, Sept. 18 and Oct. 28, 1959.

(6) Agreement for the establishment of a facility for repairing and rebuilding M-12 range finders in Turkey, Nov. 30, 1959.

(7) Agreement on a weapons production programme, March 2, 1960.

(8) Exchange of notes concerning the grant of defence articles and services under the military assistance programme, Aug. 15 and 31, 1979; amended Aug. 13 and Sept. 24, 1982.

(9) Agreement for co-operation on defence and economy; supplementary agreements (i) on defence support, (ii) on defence industrial co-operation, and (iii) on installations, with implementing agreements, March 29, 1980 (Dec. 18, 1980).

This agreement, concluded for five years and renewable annually, laid down that defence co-operation would be limited to the obligations arising from the North Atlantic Treaty, and that 12 military bases in Turkey (including three intelligence gathering stations and a navigational base) would be used by the United States only within the framework of NATO and each being under the command of a Turkish officer. The supplementary agreements provided (i) for mutually agreed financial and technical assistance to Turkey, (ii) for enhanced co-operation in the production of defence material and a listing of Turkish projects under consideration: and (iii) for US participation in joint defence measures in specified Turkish armed forces installations.

On Oct. 5, 1984, the US Congress was reported to have agreed to a military allocation of US$700,000,000 for Turkey (and to additional economic assistance worth US$175,000,000).

The United Arab Emirates. Agreement relating to the sale of defence articles and services to the United Arab Emirates, June 15 and 21, 1975.

The United Kingdom [see also pages 223–24]. (1) Exchange of notes on an arrangement relating to naval and air bases, Sept. 2, 1940.

(2) Agreement regarding leased naval and air bases, March 27, 1941; and amended July 19 and Aug. 1, 1950, with effect from Aug. 1, 1950; and amended with regard to land and facilities on Bermuda on Dec. 5-6, 1978.

(3) Protocol on the defence of Newfoundland (March 27, 1941).

(4) Mutual defence assistance agreement, of which Art. IV is applicable to the Falkland Islands, Gibraltar, Hong Kong, the Leeward Islands, St Helena and Western Pacific dependencies, Jan. 27, 1950. (See also agreements with Belgium, Denmark, France, Italy, Luxembourg, the Netherlands and Norway.)

(5) Agreement relating to the assurances required under the (US) Mutual Security Act of 1951, Jan. 8, 1952.

(6) Exchange of notes relating to the supply by the United States to the United Kingdom of intermediate-range ballistic missiles, Feb. 22, 1958.

The arrangements under this agreement were made "in consonance with the North Atlantic Treaty and in pursuance of the mutual defence assistance agreement of Jan. 27, 1950", and it was laid down that, although ownership of the missiles would eventually pass to the United Kingdom, all nuclear warheads would "remain in full US ownership and control", and that the decision to launch the missiles would be a matter for joint decision of the two governments.

(7) Agreement for co-operation in the uses of atomic energy for mutual defence purposes, July 3, 1958 (entry into force Aug. 4, 1958); amended May 7, 1959; Sept. 27, 1968; Oct. 16, 1969; July 22, 1974; Dec. 5, 1979; and June 5, 1984.

(8) Exchange of notes relating to the establishment and operation of a ballistic missile early warning station at Fylingdales Moor Feb. 15, 1960.

(9) Exchange of notes on the setting-up of a missile defence alarm system station in the United Kingdom, July 18, 1961.

(10) Exchange of notes relating to a weapons production programme, June 29, 1962.

(11) Polaris sales agreement, April 6, 1963.

(12) Memorandum of arrangement between the United States, Australia and the United Kingdom to cover re-entry experiments in Australia (Project SPARTA), March 30 1966.

(13) Memorandum of understanding relating to the principles governing co-operation in research and development, production and procurement of defence equipment, Sept. 24, 1975.

(14) Letter of agreement concerning narrative record telecommunication interface arrangements, Sept. 2 and 21, 1977.

(15) Memorandum of understanding regarding support to the Royal Air Force detachment at Hickam Air Force Base, April 21, 1981.

(16) Memorandum of understanding on the shared use of communications facilities in the northern Federal Republic of Germany, May 11 and June 2, 1981.

(17) Agreement extending the Polaris sales agreement to cover the sale of Trident II weapon system, Oct. 19, 1982.

(18) Memorandum of understanding concerning the provision of mutual logistic support, supplies and services, Oct. 5 and 11, 1984.

(19) Agreement concerning certain communications facilities in the Turks and Caicos Islands, Dec. 18, 1984.

(20) Confidential memorandum of understanding regarding British participation in the US Strategic Defence Initiative (SDI or "Star Wars") research programme designed to eliminate the threat posed by nuclear-armed ballistic missiles by intercepting and destroying them in flight, Dec. 6, 1985.

United Kingdom Dependencies. (1) Agreement concerning the extension of the Bahamas long range proving ground by the establishment of additional sites in Ascension Island, June 25, 1956, and Aug. 24–25, 1959.

(2) Exchange of notes relating to the use of the airfield at Widewake on Ascension Island by the Royal Air Force, Aug. 29, 1962.

(3) Exchange of notes concerning the availability of certain Indian Ocean islands for the defence purposes of both Governments, Dec. 30, 1966; amended June 22 and 25, 1976, to allow for the expansion of the US facility on Diego Garcia, one of the islands in the territory.

(4) Agreement for the construction by Bermuda of the proposed road through the US Naval Air Station, Bermuda, Jan. 28, 1971.

(5) Exchange of notes relating to the lease of certain land to the US Navy on the island of Anegada in the British Virgin Islands for use as a drone-launching facility, Feb. 1, 1973.

(6) Exchange of notes relating to the expanded use of Ascension Island, March 30, 1973.

---

* See also page 224.

(7) Exchange of notes concerning a US naval support facility on Diego Garcia, British Indian Ocean Territory, Feb. 25, 1976.

(8) Agreement concerning US defence areas in the Turks and Caicos Islands, Dec. 12, 1979; effective Jan. 1, 1979.

(8) Agreement concerning the turnover of the airfield at Grand Turk Auxiliary Air Base to the Government of the Turks and Caicos Islands and its use by the US Government, Dec. 12, 1979.

Uruguay. Military assistance agreement, June 30, 1952 (entry into force June 11, 1953).

Venezuela. (1) Exchange of notes relating to eligibility for US military assistance and training pursuant to the International Security Assistance and Arms Export Control Act of 1976, June 16 and 30, 1977.

(2) General security of military information agreement, July 15, 1983.

Yugoslavia. Exchange of notes relating to the purchase by Yugoslavia of military equipment, materials and services, Aug. 25, 1959.

The US Defence Department announced in September 1978 that it had agreed to expand bilateral military co-operation with Yugoslavia in the next few years. (Yugoslavia was reported to have received, since 1948, more than US$1,700 million worth of US military aid, but in 1961 President Tito of Yugoslavia had refused to renew an earlier US-Yugoslavia military agreement, and thereafter US military aid had been confined mainly to spare parts.)

Zambia. Exchange of notes relating to the assurances required under the (US) Mutual Security Act of 1951, Jan. 8, 1952.

Panama Canal Treaties

After 13 years of negotiations between the Governments of the United States and Panama, agreement was reached in principle on Aug. 10, 1977, on the conclusion of (i) a basic treaty between the two countries on the gradual transfer to Panama, to be completed by the year 2000, of the Panama Canal and the Panama Canal Zone (which the USA had leased in perpetuity from the Republic of Panama since 1903) and (ii) a treaty guaranteeing the canal's permanent neutrality.

Basic Treaty. This treaty laid down that upon its entry into force all previous treaties and agreements relating to the canal would be terminated and superseded, among them an Isthmian Canal Convention of Nov. 18, 1903, and a Treaty of Friendship and Co-operation signed on March 2, 1936, as well as a Treaty of Mutual Understanding and Co-operation and related memorandum of Jan. 25, 1955. Under the treaty Panama granted to the USA, "for the duration of this treaty [i.e. until Dec. 31, 1999], the rights necessary to regulate the transit of ships through the Panama Canal, and to manage, operate, maintain, improve, protect and defend the canal", while Panama guaranteed "to the USA the peaceful use of the land and water areas which it has been granted to use for such purposes pursuant to this treaty and related agreements", with Panama participating increasingly in the management, protection and defence of the canal.

The treaty also contained details of the operations, Panama's sovereignty rights (under which Panama would, upon the treaty's entry into force, assume general territorial jurisdiction over the Canal Zone), and the joint defence of the canal. It also provided that Panama would receive exclusively from canal revenues an annual average of US$80,000,000 for 23 years, and in addition the USA undertook to make the best possible efforts to arrange, outside the treaty, loan guarantees and credits to Panama totalling US$345,000,000, as well as military sales credits of up to US$50,000,000 over a 10-year period to improve Panama's ability to assist in the canal's defence.

It was also agreed that during the duration of the treaty no new interoceanic canal would be constructed in the territory of Panama except in accordance with the provisions of the treaty or as otherwise agreed, and that the USA was granted the right to add a third lane of locks to the existing canal.

Neutrality Treaty. The *Treaty on the Permanent Neutrality and Operation of the Canal* contained the following material provisions:

"**Art. 1.** The Republic of Panama declares that the canal, as an international transit waterway, shall be permanently neutral in accordance with the regime established in this treaty. The same regime of neutrality shall apply to any other international waterway that may be built either partially or wholly in the territory of the Republic of Panama.

"**Art. 2.** The Republic of Panama declares the neutrality of the canal in order that both in time of peace and in time of war it shall remain secure and open to peaceful transit by the vessels of all nations on terms of entire equality, so that there will be no discrimination against any nation or its citizens or subjects, concerning the conditions or charges of transit or for any other reason, and so that the canal, and therefore the isthmus of Panama, shall not be the target of reprisals in any armed conflict between other nations of the world. . . .

"**Art. 3.** For purposes of the security, efficiency and proper maintenance of the canal the following rules shall apply:

"(*a*) The canal shall be operated efficiently in accordance with conditions of transit through the canal and rules and regulations that shall be just, equitable and reasonable and limited to those necessary for safe navigation and efficient, sanitary operation of the canal;

(*b*) ancillary services necessary for transit through the canal shall be provided;

(*c*) tolls and other charges for transit and ancillary services shall be just, reasonable and equitable, consistent with the principles of international law; . . .

(*e*) vessels of war and auxiliary vessels of all nations shall at all times be entitled to transit the canal, irrespective of their internal operation, means of propulsion, origin, destination or armament, without being subjected, as a condition of transit, to inspection, search or surveillance. . . .

"**Art. 4.** The United States of America and the Republic of Panama agree to maintain the regime of neutrality established in this treaty, which shall be maintained in order that the canal shall remain permanently neutral, notwithstanding the termination of any other treaties entered into by the two contracting parties.

"**Art. 5.** After the termination of the Panama Canal treaty, only the Republic of Panama shall operate the canal and maintain military forces, defence sites and military installations within its national territory.

"**Art. 6.** (*a*) In recognition of the important contributions of the United States of America and of the Republic of Panama to the construction, operation, maintenance and protection and defence of the canal, vessels of war and auxiliary vessels of those nations shall, notwithstanding any other provisions of this treaty, be entitled to transit the canal irrespective of their internal operation, means of propulsion, origin, destination, armament or cargo carried. Such vessels of war and auxiliary vessels will be entitled to transit the canal expeditiously.

(*b*) The United States of America, so long as it has responsibility for the operation of the canal, may continue to provide the Republic of Colombia toll-free transit through the canal for its troops, vessels and materials of war. Thereafter, the Republic of Panama may provide the Republic of Colombia and the Republic of Costa Rica with the right of toll-free transit. . . ."

Under a protocol to the treaty, which was open to signature by all states of the world and would enter into force at the time of deposit of the relevant instrument of accession with the Secretary-General of the Organization of American States, its signatories were able to acknowledge the regime of permanent neutrality of the canal and to agree to observe its rules.

Signature, Ratification and Entry into Force. The two treaties were signed by the US President and the "supreme leader" of Panama on Sept. 7, 1977. They were approved in a referendum held in Panama on Oct. 23, 1977, with about 66 per cent of the valid votes cast being in favour. They were approved by the US Senate (with the required two-thirds majority) on March 16 and April 18, 1978, respectively. The US Senate, however, also approved a number of amendments and reservations to the neutrality treaty, introduced by opponents to the treaty.

One of these reservations (approved on March 16), inserted at the end of the Senate's resolution of ratification, stated that, notwithstanding the provisions of Article 5 of the treaty [see above], "if the canal is closed or its operations are interfered with, the USA and the Republic of Panama shall each independently have the right to take such steps as it deems necessary . . . , including the use of military force in Panama to reopen the canal or restore the operations of the canal. . . ."

Another reservation (approved on March 15) stated that nothing in the treaty was to preclude Panama and the USA from making any agreement or arrangement between them "to facilitate performance at any time after Dec. 31, 1999, of their responsibilities to maintain the regime of neutrality established in the treaty, including agreements or arrangements for the stationing of any US forces or maintenance of defence sites after that date in the Republic or Panama that Panama and the USA may deem necessary or appropriate".

The US bill implementing the ratification of the treaties was not finally passed by the US Senate until Sept. 25, 1979, and by the House of Representatives until the following day, whereupon the bill was signed by the President on Sept. 27, 1979.

The treaties came into force on Oct. 1, 1979, when the Panama Canal Zone formally ceased to exist as Panama assumed general territorial jurisdiction over it and 11 out of the 14 US military bases in the zone reverted to Panama (although about 40 per cent of the former Canal Zone would remain under effective US control until Dec. 31, 1999).

In December 1984 the United States, Japan and Panama agreed on a four-year programme (to start in 1985) to consider proposals to improve the Panama Canal or to build a new canal to handle ships of up to 300,000 tonnes.

US Bilateral Co-operation Agreements

Bilateral treaties and agreements on co-operation in various fields have been concluded by the United States with other countries as follows:

Algeria. An agricultural co-operation agreement was signed on Feb. 2, 1984.

During talks on economic co-operation held in April 1985 it was agreed to establish a joint committee (to meet every two years).

Antigua and Barbuda. General agreement for economic, technical and related assistance, June 17, 1983.

Argentina. (1) Treaty of friendship, commerce and navigation (July 27, 1853; entry into force Dec. 20, 1854).

(2) Trade agreement, Oct. 14, 1941; in force from Jan. 8, 1943; supplementary agreement, July 24, 1963; amended, Dec. 18 and 27, 1967; further supplementary agreement, Aug. 3 and 8, 1966; amended, Dec. 18 and 27, 1967.

(3) General agreement for a programme of technical co-operation, June 3, 1957.

(4) Exchange of notes relating to a co-operation programme for the optical satellite tracking station at Villa Dolores, Argentina, March 16, 1962.

(5) Agreement for scientific and technical co-operation, April 7, 1972; entry into force Aug. 11, 1972.

(6) Agreement on limitation of imports of specialty steel from Argentina, Nov. 8, 1983.

Austria. (1) Treaty of friendship, commerce and consular rights, June 19, 1928; in force from May 27, 1931.

(2) Economic co-operation agreement, July 2, 1948; amended Oct. 21 and Nov. 30, 1949; Feb. 20, 1950; Jan. 16 and March 7, 1951; May 11 and 15, 1951; and Oct. 15 and Dec. 6, 1952.

(3) Memorandum of understanding on scientific and technological co-operation, Feb. 24, 1984.

Bangladesh. (1) Economic, technical and related assistance agreement, May 21, 1974.

(2) Numerous (US) Agency for International Development agreements between 1972 and 1981.

Barbados. General agreement for economic, technical and related assistance, Sept. 14, 1983.

Belgium. (1) Economic co-operation agreements, July 2, 1948; entry into force July 29, 1948; amended Nov. 22 and 29, 1948; June 29, 1950; Sept. 10, 1951; Dec. 11, 1952; and March 5, 1953.

(2) Treaty of friendship, establishment and navigation, Feb. 21, 1961; entry into force Oct. 3, 1963.

(3) Memorandum of understanding for the development of a co-operative programme in the sciences, June 2, 1980.

Belize. Agreement relating to economic and technical co-operation, March 3, 1983.

Benin. Agreement relating to economic, technical and related assistance, May 27, 1961.

Bolivia. (1) Treaty of peace, friendship, commerce and navigation, May 13, 1958; in force from Nov. 9, 1962 (Art. 34 terminated July 1, 1976).

(2) General agreement for technical co-operation, March 14, 1951; amended Dec. 14, 1951; Jan. 2, 7 and 8, 1952; Aug. 27, 1953; and Jan. 15, 1954.

(3) Agreement providing economic assistance to Bolivia, Nov. 6, 1953; amended Aug. 24 and Nov. 11, 1959.

(4) Numerous agreements by the (US) Agency for International Development between December 1975 and January 1978.

Botswana. (1) Agreement by (US) Agency for International Development, Sept. 19, 1975.

(2) Agreement on the establishment of a space vehicle communications facility in connection with the space shuttle, Dec. 4, 1980.

Brazil. (1) Treaty of peace, friendship, commerce and navigation, Dec. 12, 1828; entry into force March 18, 1829; operative Dec. 12, 1928, but all articles were terminated on Dec. 12, 1841, except those relating to peace and friendship.

(2) Agreement relating to the mobilization of productive resources in Brazil, March 3, 1942.

(3) Agreement relating to technical co-operation, Dec. 19, 1950; amended Jan. 8, 1952.

(4) Special services programme agreement, May 30, 1953; extended Dec. 27 and 30, 1963.

(5) Agreement relating to a programme of joint participation in international testing in connexion with experimental communications satellites, Oct. 27, 1961.

(6) Agreement on co-operation for the promotion of economic and social development in the Brazilian North-East, April 13, 1963.

(7) Agreement relating to trade in cotton and man-made fibre textiles and textile products, March 31, 1982; amended, Aug. 3 and 9, 1984; Aug. 20 and Sept. 10, 1984; Oct. 19 and 24, 1984.

(8) Co-operative project agreement concerning the conduct of a joint geophysical and oceanographic investigation in the South Atlantic, June 10 and 14, 1982.

(9) Agreement for the use of the geostationary operational environmental satellite in the Brazilian national plan for data collection platforms, June 14, 1982.

(10) Memorandum of understanding concerning co-operation in aerospace experiments employing sounding rockets, Jan. 31, 1983.

(11) Memorandum of understanding for scientific and technical co-operation in geological sciences and earth resources, April 12, 1983.

(12) Five technical and scientific agreements, covering inter alia Brazil's purchase of nuclear fuel and a US undertaking to put a Brazilian astronaut into space by 1989, and an economic protocol committing Brazil to buy US equipment worth $500,000,000 over five years for a hydroelectric project, Feb. 6, 1984.

(13) Memorandum of understanding concerning the Landsat system of remote sensing, May 8, 1984.

Brunei. Treaty of peace, friendship, commerce and navigation, June 23, 1850; entry into force July 11, 1853.

Burkina Faso. (1) Agreement providing for the furnishing of economic, technical and related assistance, June 1, 1961.

(2) Economic and technical co-operation agreements by (US) Agency for International Development, June 30 and July 1, 1977; Sept. 9, 1977; and June 8, 1978.

Burma. Economic co-operation agreement, March 21, 1957; entry into force Oct. 9, 1957; amended Sept. 12, 1959, and June 29, 1960.

Burundi. General agreement for special development assistance, Feb. 13 and 18, 1970; entry into force on latter date.

Cameroon. (1) Agreement providing for the furnishing of economic, technical and related assistance, May 26, 1961; amended Dec. 8, 1961.

(2) (US) Agency for International Development agreements, May 18 and Aug. 30, 1978.

Canada. (1) Exchange of notes on co-operation in intercontinental testing in connexion with experimental communication satellites, Aug. 1 and 23, 1963; entry into force on latter date.

(2) Agreement relating to co-operation in civil emergency planning, Aug. 8, 1967.

(3) Exchange of notes regarding an experimental communications technology satellite project, April 21 and 27, 1971; entry into force on latter date.

(4) Agreement concerning liability for loss or damage resulting from certain rocket launches in Canada (Operation Tordo), Dec. 31, 1974.

(5) Exchange of notes relating to a co-operative programme concerning the development and procurement of a space shuttle attached remote manipulator system, June 23, 1976.

(6) Agreement on Great Lakes water quality, Nov. 22, 1978.

(7) Agreement concerning support of US activities at the Canadian National Research Council, March 19 and Sept. 20, 1979; entry into force on latter date.

(8) Memorandum of understanding on co-operation in geological sciences, April 2, 1981.

(9) Memorandum of understanding on co-operation in remote sensing, April 2, 1981.

(10) Agreement relating to limitation of imports of specialty steel from Canada, Oct. 19, 1983.

Cape Verde. Economic and technical co-operation agreements by the (US) Agency for International Development between June 1975 and May 1978.

The Central African Republic. Agreement relating to economic, technical and related assistance, Feb. 10, 1963.

Chad. Economic and technical co-operation agreements by the (US) Agency for International Development between August 1976 and August 1978.

Chile. (1) Treaty of peace, amity, commerce and navigation, May 16, 1932; entry into force April 29, 1934; articles relating to commerce and navigation were terminated on Jan. 20, 1950.

(2) Basic agreement for technical co-operation, Jan. 16, 1951; entry into force July 27, 1951; amended Jan. 8 and Oct. 17, 1952.

(3) (US) Agency for International Development co-operation agreements, Oct. 23, 1975; Jan. 26, 1976; and July 26, 1976.

(4) Exchange of notes concerning a co-operative programme for tracking and receiving radio signals from earth satellites and space vehicles, Feb. 16 and 19, 1959; operative from Dec. 31, 1958.

(5) Memorandum of understanding for scientific co-operation in the earth sciences, Aug. 2 and 26, 1982; in force from latter date.

(6) Agreement on the use of Easter Island as an emergency landing facility for space shuttle for eight years, automatically to be extended for four-year periods, promulgated Nov. 6, 1985.

Colombia. (1) Treaty of peace, amity, navigation and commerce, Dec. 12, 1846; in force from June 10, 1948 (Art. 33 terminated July 1, 1916).

(2) General agreement for economic, technical and related assistance, July 23, 1962.

(3) Treaty concerning the status of Quitasueño, Roncador and Serrana (recognizing Colombia's sovereignty over these islands), Sept. 8, 1972; in force from Sept. 17, 1972; ratified by the US Senate on July 31, 1981; instruments of ratification exchanged Sept. 17, 1981.

(4) (US) Agency for International Development agreements concluded between Dec. 24, 1975, and Nov. 29, 1976.

(5) Memorandum of understanding for scientific and technical co-operation in the earth sciences, Dec. 12, 1978, and Jan. 30, 1979; entry into force on latter date.

Costa Rica. (1) Treaty of friendship, commerce and navigation, July 10, 1851; in force from May 26, 1852.

(2) General agreement for economic, technical and related assistance, Dec. 22, 1961; entry into force Sept. 7, 1962.

(3) (US) Agency for International Development agreements, April 26, 1976; Aug. 30, 1978.

Côte d'Ivoire. Agreement providing for economic, technical and related assistance, May 17, 1961.

Cyprus. (1) Economic co-operation agreement between the United States and the United Kingdom of July 6, 1948, made applicable to Cyprus, July 6, 1948; amended Jan. 3, 1950; May 25, 1951; and Feb. 25, 1953.

(2) General agreement for technical co-operation, June 29, 1961.

Denmark. (1) Economic co-operation agreement, June 29, 1948; entry into force July 2, 1948, applicable to Greenland; amended Nov. 4 and 18, 1948; Feb. 7, 1950; Feb. 2 and 9, 1951; and Nov. 24, 1952.

(2) Treaty of friendship, commerce and navigation, Oct. 1, 1951; in force from July 30, 1961 (not applicable to Greenland).

Djibouti. Economic and technical co-operation agreement by (US) Agency for International Development, Jan. 9, 1978.

Dominica. General agreement for economic, technical and related assistance, Sept. 16, 1983.

The Dominican Republic. (1) General agreement for economic, technical and related assistance, Jan. 11, 1962.

(2) Economic and technical co-operation agreements by (US) Agency for International Development, between Oct. 16, 1974, and April 7, 1977.

(3) Agreement relating to trade in cotton, wool and man-made fibre textiles and textile products, Dec. 30, 1983; effective June 1, 1983.

(4) Memorandum of understanding concerning co-operation in geological sciences, Jan. 23, 1984.

Ecuador. (1) Treaty of peace, friendship, navigation and commerce (June 13, 1839; entry into force April 9, 1842; articles relating to commerce and navigation terminated on Aug. 25, 1892).

(2) General agreement for economic, technical and related assistance (April 17, 1962).

(3) Co-operative scientific and technical project for joint oceanographic research, March 17, 1983.

Egypt. (1) Arrangements and agreements relating to assistance in the clearance of the Suez Canal and coastal waters areas, April 13 and 25, 1974—entry into force on latter date; June 11, 1974; June 16 and 29, 1975—entry into force on latter date; and subsequent amendments effective Aug. 21, 1975, and Dec. 17, 1977.

(2) Agreement concerning principles of relations and co-operation, June 14, 1974.

(3) Economic and technical co-operation agreements by the (US) Agency for International Development between Feb. 13, 1975, and Sept. 26, 1984.

(4) Agreement relating to trade in textiles and textile products, Dec. 7 and 28, 1977; effective Jan. 1, 1978.

(5) Economic, technical and related assistance agreement, Aug. 16, 1978; entry into force Oct. 15, 1978.

(6) Agreement relating to co-operation in science and technology, Jan. 11, 1981.

(7) Statement relating to greater support to economic progress in Egypt, Feb. 4, 1981.

El Salvador. (1) General agreement for economic, technical and related assistance, Dec. 19, 1961; entry into force Jan. 16, 1962.

(2) Economic and technical co-operation agreements by the (US) Agency for International Development, May 3 and Aug. 30, 1978.

(3) Memorandum of understanding covering co-operative investigations in earthquake research, April 16 and 24, 1984; in force from latter date.

Ethiopia. (1) General agreement for technical co-operation, June 16, 1951; extended and amended Dec. 17 and 27, 1951; Jan. 8 and Dec. 24, 1952; March 30, 1953; May 18 and June 12, 1954; April 4 and June 12, 1956.

(2) Treaty of amity and economic relations, and related notes, Sept. 7, 1951; in force from Oct. 8, 1953; amended, Sept. 12, 1965, and Oct. 20, 1972; amendments in force from May 3, 1973.

(3) Exchanges of notes providing for economic assistance to Ethiopia (April 25, 1957).

(4) Economic and technical co-operation agreements by the (US) Agency for International Development between Feb. 20, 1975, and Sept. 22, 1978.

Finland. (1) Treaty of friendship, commerce and consular rights, Feb. 13, 1934; in force from Aug. 10, 1934; amended, Dec. 4, 1952; amendment in force from Sept. 24, 1953.

(2) Memorandum of understanding for the development of a co-operative programme in the sciences, Aug. 27, 1980.

(3) Memorandum of understanding for co-operation in cold regions engineering and scientific and technological research, Dec. 12, 1983.

France. (1) Convention of navigation and commerce, June 24, 1822; in force from Feb. 2, 1823; operative Oct. 1, 1822; amended July 17, 1919; amendment in force from Jan. 10, 1921.

(2) Economic co-operation agreements, also applicable to French overseas departments and territories, June 28, 1948; entry into force July 10, 1948; amended Sept. 21 and Oct. 8, 1948; Nov. 17 and 20, 1948; Jan. 9, 1950; May 22, 1951; Sept. 25 and 27, 1951; and Sept. 11, 1953.

(3) Exchange of notes on co-operation in intercontinental testing in connexion with experimental communications satellites, March 31, 1961.

(4) Exchange of notes concerning development of satellites and balloon techniques and instrumentation for the study of meteorological phenomena (Project EOLE), June 16–17, 1966.

(5) Memorandum of understanding concerning a co-operative programme in science and technology, May 30, 1978.

(6) Memorandum of understanding covering co-operation in the field of geological sciences, July 8 and 23, 1982; in force from latter date.

(7) Memorandum of understanding on environmental co-operation, June 21, 1984.

(8) Agreement concerning emergency use of the Combined Forces Base at Hao, French Polynesia, by the US space shuttle, Sept. 6, 1984.

Gabon. (1) Economic and technical co-operation agreement by (US) Agency for International Development, Feb. 21, 1976.

(2) Memorandum of understanding for a joint programme of demonstration of solar photovoltaic power in Gabon, Feb. 4, 1982.

The Gambia. (1) Economic co-operation agreement between the United States and the United Kingdom, July 6, 1948; amended Jan. 3, 1950; May 25, 1951; Feb. 25, 1953; June 26 and Aug. 20, 1959.

(2) Economic and technical co-operation agreements by (US) Agency for International Development (Oct. 26 and 28, 1977; Jan. 12 and Feb. 20, 1978).

The Federal Republic of Germany. (1) Economic co-operation agreement, Dec. 15, 1949; definitive entry into force Feb. 6, 1950; amended, Feb. 27 and March 28, 1951, and Nov. 14 and Dec. 30, 1952.

(2) Treaty of amity, commerce and navigation, Oct. 29, 1954; entry into force July 14, 1956; extended Dec. 10, 1984, until Dec. 31, 1986.

(3) Exchange of notes on co-operation in intercontinental testing in connexion with experimental communications satellites, Sept. 5 and 29, 1961; entry into force on latter date.

(4) Agreement on co-operation in environmental affairs, May 9, 1974; in force from March 26, 1975; continued March 22, 1985.

(5) Agreement on co-operation in the field of coal hydrogenation technology, Oct. 7, 1977.

(7) Memorandum of understanding on the project of active magnetospheric particle tracer explorers, Oct. 15, 1981.

(8) Memorandum of understanding on the Roentgensatellit programme, Aug. 8, 1982.

Ghana. (1) Economic co-operation agreement between the United States and the United Kingdom of July 6, 1948, made applicable to the Gold Coast (now Ghana), July 6, 1948, amended Jan. 3, 1950; May 25, 1951; and Feb. 25, 1953.

(2) General agreement for technical co-operation, June 3, 1957.

(3) Economic and technical co-operation agreements by (US) Agency for International Development, Sept. 29, 1976; May 24, 1977; and March 31, 1978.

Greece. (1) Agreement regarding commercial relations, Jan. 2 and 11, 1946; in force from latter date.

(2) Agreement on aid to Greece, June 20, 1947.

(3) Economic co-operation agreement, July 2, 1948; entry into force July 3, 1948; amended Dec. 15 and 24, 1949; March 6 and 30, 1951; Oct. 14, 1952; Dec. 2, 1953; April 19, 1963.

(4) Treaty of friendship, commerce and navigation, Aug. 3, 1951; in force from Oct. 13, 1954.

(5) Memorandum of understanding for scientific and technological co-operation, Sept. 16, 1978.

(6) A five-year framework agreement on economic, scientific and technological, education and cultural co-operation, April 22, 1980.

Grenada. General agreement for economic, technical and related assistance, May 7, 1984.

Guatemala. (1) Treaty of peace, amity, commerce and navigation, March 3, 1849; entry into force May 13, 1852; articles relating to commerce and navigation terminated Nov. 4, 1874.

(2) General agreement for technical co-operation, Sept. 1, 1954.

(3) Development assistance agreement, Dec. 13, 1954.

(4) Economic and technical co-operation agreements by (US) Agency for International Development, Nov. 3, 1975; April 8, 1976; Sept. 20, 1976; Sept. 14, 1977; May 18, 1978.

Guinea. (1) Cultural relations agreement, Oct. 28, 1959.

(2) Exchange of notes providing for the furnishing of economic, technical and related assistance, Sept. 30, 1960.

(3) Economic and technical co-operation agreements by (US) Agency for International Development, Sept. 27, 1977; March 31, 1978; April 14 and June 5, 1978.

Guinea-Bissau. Economic and technical co-operation agreements by (US) Agency for International Development, Nov. 10, 1977; Jan. 8, 1978.

Guyana. (1) (US) Agency for International Development (AID) co-operation agreements between Nov. 9, 1971, and July 13, 1977. (Following Guyana's default on repayments since March 1982 the termination of all AID assistance was announced on June 17, 1985.)

(2) General ageeement for economic, technical and related assistance, Nov. 8, 1979.

Haiti. (1) Exchange of notes on general agreement for technical co-operation, May 2, 1951; amended Dec. 15, 1951 and Jan. 8, 1952.

(2) Economic and technical co-operation agreements by (US) Agency for International Development, June 29, Sept. 28 and 30, 1976; April 27 and Aug. 30, 1977.

Honduras. (1) Treaty of friendship, commerce and consular rights, Dec. 7, 1927; in force from July 19, 1928.

(2) General agreement for economic and technical co-operation, April 12, 1961; entry into force May 27, 1961.

(3) Economic and technical co-operation agreements by (US) Agency for International Development, Feb. 19, 1975; Nov. 28, 1977; and Sept. 24, 1982.

(4) Treaty on the cession to Honduras of the Swan Islands, three small islands in the Caribbean which had been under US sovereignty since 1856, Nov. 22, 1971; entry into force Sept. 1, 1972.

Iceland. (1) Economic co-operation agreement, July 3, 1948; amended: Feb. 7, 1950; Feb. 23, 1951; Oct. 9, 1952; and Oct. 1, 1953.

(2) Exchange of notes concerning special economic assistance to Iceland on a loan basis, June 23, 1959.

(3) Exchange of notes providing for an assistance grant in support of Iceland's economic stabilization programme, Dec. 30, 1960.

(4) Memorandum of understanding for scientific and technical co-operation in earth sciences, Jan. 28 and April 9, 1982; in force from latter date.

India. (1) General agreement for technical co-operation, Dec. 28, 1950.

(2) Agreement relating to the technical co-operation programme, Jan. 5, 1952; extended June 29, 1957.

(3) Agreement to establish a joint commission on economic, commercial, scientific, technological, educational and cultural co-operation, Oct. 28, 1974.

(4) Economic and technical co-operation agreements by (US) Agency for International Development between Aug. 26, 1978, and Sept. 29, 1984.

(5) Exchange of notes concerning the furnishing of launching and associated services for Indian national satellite system-I spacecraft, July 18, 1978.

(6) Agreement relating to trade in cotton, wool and man-made fibre textiles and textile products, Dec. 21, 1982; effective Jan. 1, 1983.

Indonesia. (1) Economic co-operation agreement, Oct. 16, 1950.

(2) Exchange of notes relating to continuation of the above agreement, Jan. 5 and 12, 1953; entry into force on latter date.

(3) Agreement relating to the assumption by Indonesia of all responsibilities of the Netherlands incurred under economic and loan agreements of 1948–49, Feb. 11, 1952.

(4) Economic and technical co-operation agreements by (US) Agency for International Development between June 30, 1975, and Aug. 31, 1978.

(5) Exchange of notes concerning the furnishing of launching and associated services by the (US) National Aeronautics and Space Administration for Indonesian satellites, March 26, 1975.

(6) Exchange of notes concerning the furnishing of launching and associated services for Palapa-B spacecraft, April 11, 1979.

(7) Agreement for co-operation in scientific research and technological development, Dec. 11, 1978; in force from Oct. 5, 1979.

(8) Agreement relating to trade in cotton, wool and man-made fibre textiles and textile products, Oct. 13 and Nov. 9, 1982; in force from latter date.

Iran. (1) Treaty of amity, economic relations and consular rights, Aug. 15, 1955; in force from June 16, 1957.

(2) General agreement for economic co-operation, Dec. 21, 1961.

Iraq. (1) Treaty of commerce and navigation, Dec. 3, 1938; in force from June 19, 1940.

(2) General agreement for technical co-operation, April 10, 1951; entry into force June 2, 1951; amended Dec. 18, 1951, and Feb. 21, 1952.

(3) Cultural agreement, Jan. 23, 1961; in force from Aug. 13, 1963.

Israel. (1) General agreement for technical co-operation, Feb. 26, 1951; amended June 21, 1954.

(2) Treaty of friendship, commerce and navigation, Aug. 23, 1951; in force from April 3, 1954.

(3) Agreement relating to emergency economic assistance, May 1, 1952.

(4) Agreement relating to economic assistance, May 9, 1952.

(5) Exchange of notes relating to special economic assistance, Nov. 25, 1953; amended Jan. 31, 1955.

(6) Agreement on the US-Israel binational science foundation, Sept. 27, 1972.

(7) Agreement establishing the Israel-US Binational Industrial Research and Development Foundation, March 3, 1976; entry into force May 18, 1977.

(8) Economic and technical co-operation agreements by the (US) Agency for International Development between June 27, 1975, and Oct. 31, 1984.

(9) A free trade agreement signed on April 23, 1985, providing for the removal of all tariffs between the two countries within 10 years.

Italy. (1) Treaty of friendship, commerce and navigation, Feb. 2, 1948; in force from July 26, 1949; supplementary agreement, Sept. 26, 1951; in force from March 2, 1961.

(2) Economic co-operation agreement, June 28, 1948; amended Sept. 28 and Oct. 2, 1948; Feb. 7, 1950; May 21, 1951; and Jan. 13, 1953.

(3) Exchange of notes providing for a programme of joint participation in the testing of experimental communications satellites, Nov. 14, 1962.

(4) Exchange of notes concerning co-operation in a scientific experiment for the purpose of launching a scientific satellite into an equatorial orbit, Sept. 5, 1962.

(5) Exchange of notes confirming a memorandum of understanding regarding the launching of NASA satellites from the San Marco range, April 30 and June 12, 1969; entry into force on latter date.

(6) Exchange of notes confirming a memorandum of understanding concerning the furnishing of certain services by NASA for Italian satellites, June 15 and 20, 1970; entry into force on latter date.

(7) Agreement for scientific and technological co-operation, July 22, 1981.

(8) Memorandum of understanding concerning furnishing of satellite-launching and associated services for the IRIS payload, July 23 and 29, 1981; in force from Sept. 21, 1981.

(9) Memorandum of understanding concerning furnishing of launch and associated services for ITALSAT programme, Sept. 29 and Oct. 10, 1983; in force from March 5, 1984.

(10) Memorandum of understanding on co-operation in earth sciences, Nov. 7 and Dec. 1, 1983; in force from latter date.

(11) Memorandum of understanding for a co-operative programme in regional digital seismic studies, June 7, 1984.

Jamaica. (1) General agreement for economic, technical and related assistance, Oct. 24, 1963.

(2) Economic and technical co-operation agreements by (US) Agency for International Development between Nov. 13, 1974, and Dec. 17, 1982.

Japan. (1) Treaty of friendship, commerce and navigation, April 2, 1953; in force from Oct. 30, 1953.

(2) Productivity agreement, April 7, 1955.

(3) Exchange of notes providing for a programme of co-operation in the testing of experimental communications satellites, Nov. 6, 1962.

(4) Exchange of notes relating to the establishment by Japan of a satellite tracking station in Okinawa, Sept. 2, 1968; amended Sept. 25, 1969.

(5) Exchange of notes concerning co-operation in space activities for peaceful purposes, July 31, 1969.

(6) Convention for the protection of migratory birds and birds in danger of extinction, March 4, 1972; in force from Sept. 19, 1974.

(7) Exchange of notes concerning the furnishing of launching and associated services by NASA for Japanese satellites, May 23, 1975.

(8) Agreement for co-operation in the field of environmental protection, Aug. 5, 1975; extended and amended, Aug. 5, 1980.

(9) Agreement on co-operation in research and development in energy and related fields, May 2, 1979; related agreements, May 7, 1982; Jan. 24, 1983.

(10) Arrangement concerning trade in cotton, wool and man-made fibre textiles, Aug. 17, 1979; effective Jan. 1, 1979.

(11) Agreement on co-operation in research and development in science and technology, May 1, 1980.

(12) Memorandum of understanding relating to the operation of the Landsat system, July 5 and Aug. 11, 1983; in force from the latter date.

Jordan. (1) Exchange of notes relating to economic assistance, June 29, 1957.

(2) General agreement providing for economic, technical and related assistance to Jordan, June 25 and 27, 1957; entry into force: July 1, 1957.

(3) Economic and technical co-operation agreements by (US) Agency for International Development between June 28, 1975, and Jan. 25, 1979.

Kenya. (1) Economic co-operation agreement between the United States and the United Kingdom of July 6, 1948, made applicable to Kenya, July 6, 1948; amended Jan. 3, 1950; May 25, 1951; and Feb. 25, 1953.

(2) Agreement between the United States and the United Kingdom for technical co-operation in respect of the territories for the international relations of which the United Kingdom was responsible, July 13, 1951, applicable to Kenya on July 14, 1961.

(3) Economic and technical co-operation agreements by (US) Agency for International Development, Sept. 11, 1974; Nov. 10, 1975; June 30, 1976; July 1 and 20 and Sept. 30, 1977; and Aug. 29, 1978.

Republic of Korea. (1) Treaty of friendship, commerce and navigation, Nov. 28, 1956; in force from Nov. 7, 1957.

(2) Exchange of notes providing for economic, technical and related assistance, Feb. 8, 1961; entry into force Feb. 28, 1961.

(3) Agreement concerning supplemental economic assistance, Oct. 16, 1971.

(4) Economic and technical co-operation agreements by (US) Agency for International Development between Sept. 11, 1974, and Jan. 19, 1977.

(5) Agreement relating to scientific and technical co-operation, Nov. 22, 1976.

(6) Agreement relating to trade in cotton, wool and man-made fibre textiles and textile products, Dec. 1, 1982; effective Jan. 1, 1982; amended Oct. 21 and Nov. 4, 1983; July 26–27, 1984; and Oct. 23 and Nov. 28, 1984.

Kuwait. Memorandum of understanding for scientific and technical co-operation, Jan. 26 and April 29, 1983; in force from latter date.

Laos. (1) Economic co-operation agreement, Sept. 9, 1951.

(2) Exchange of notes providing for additional direct economic assistance, July 6 and 8, 1955, operative from Jan. 1, 1955.

Lebanon. (1) General agreement for technical co-operation, May 29, 1951; entry into force Dec. 13, 1951.

(2) Technical co-operation programme agreement, June 26, 1952; amended April 14, 1953; April 30, 1954.

(3) Exchange of notes relating to special economic assistance, June 11 and 18, 1954; entry into force on latter date.

(4) Exchange of notes granting special assistance to Lebanon for budgetary support, Sept. 2 and 3, 1958; entry into force on latter date.

(5) Economic and technical co-operation agreements by (US) Agency for International Development, March 21 and June 22, 1978.

Lesotho. (1) Economic and technical co-operation agreement by (US) Agency for International Development, Aug. 31, 1978.

(2) Agreement for economic, technical and related assistance, Oct. 17, 1984.

Liberia. (1) Treaty of friendship, commerce and navigation, Aug. 8, 1938; in force from Nov. 21, 1939.

(2) Memorandum of understanding on the joint Liberian-US commission for economic development, Oct. 6, 1955; operative Feb. 3, 1956.

(3) General agreement for technical assistance and co-operation, Oct. 6, 1955; entry into force Feb. 3, 1956.

(4) Economic and technical co-operation agreements by (US) Agency for International Development, Aug. 12, 1977.

Luxembourg. (1) Economic co-operation agreement, July 3, 1948; amended, Nov. 17 and Dec. 22, 1948; Jan. 17 and 19, 1950; Aug. 30 and Oct. 17, 1951; Dec. 31, 1952; and Feb. 26, 1953.

(2) Treaty of friendship, establishment and navigation, Feb. 23, 1962; in force from March 28, 1963.

Madagascar. (1) Exchange of notes providing for the furnishing of economic, technical and related assistance, June 22, 1961.

(2) Economic and technical co-operation agreement by (US) Agency for International Development, July 25, 1973.

Malawi. Economic and technical co-operation agreement by (US) Agency for International Development, April 29, 1976.

Malaysia. (1) Economic co-operation agreement between the United States and the United Kingdom, July 6, 1948; made applicable to the then Federation of Malaya on July 20, 1948; amended Jan. 3, 1950; May 25, 1951; and Feb. 25, 1953.

(2) Agreement relating to trade in cotton, wool and man-made fibre textiles and textile products, Dec. 5, 1980, and Feb. 27, 1981; effective Jan. 1, 1981.

Mali. (1) Exchange of notes providing for the furnishing of economic, technical and related assistance, Jan. 4, 1961.

(2) (US) Agency for International Development co-operation agreements between Jan. 28, 1974, and Aug. 26, 1978.

Malta. (1) Economic co-operation agreement between the United States and the United Kingdom, July 6, 1948, applicable to Malta on the same date; amended Jan. 3, 1950; May 25, 1951; and Feb. 25, 1953.

(2) Economic and technical co-operation agreement by (US) Agency for International Development, June 15, 1973.

Mauritania. (1) General agreement for special development assistance, March 23, 1971.

(2) Economic and technical co-operation agreements by (US) Agency for International Development, Feb. 26, 1974; May 28, 1976; and April 18, 1978.

Mauritius. (1) Economic co-operation agreement between the United States and the United Kingdom, July 1948; amended Jan. 3, 1950; May 25, 1951; and Feb. 25, 1953.

(2) Agreement concerning trade in cotton, wool and man-made fibres, Oct. 2 and 5, 1981; in force from latter date.

Mexico. (1) Treaty relating to the boundary line, transit of persons, etc., across the Isthmus of Tehuantepec (Gadsden Treaty), Dec. 30, 1853; in force from June 30, 1854.

(2) Convention providing for the equitable distribution of the waters of the Rio Grande for irrigation purposes, May 21, 1906; in force from Jan. 16, 1907.

(3) Convention for the protection of migratory birds and game mammals, Feb. 7, 1936; in force from March 15, 1937; supplementary agreement, March 10, 1972.

(4) Treaty relating to the utilization of waters of the Colorado and Tijuana Rivers and of the Rio Grande, Feb. 3 and Nov. 14, 1944; in force from Nov. 8, 1945.

(5) Agreement establishing a US-Mexican Commission on Cultural Co-operation, Dec. 28, 1948, and Aug. 30, 1949; in force from latter date; amended, June 15, 1972; Oct. 30, 1978; and Jan. 23, 1979.

(6) Exchange of notes on general agreement for technical co-operation, June 27, 1951; amended Jan. 21–22, 1952; and April 13, 1954.

(7) Exchange of notes relating to a programme of industrial productivity in Mexico, Feb. 21 and Nov. 15, 1961; entry into force on latter date.

(8) Agreement for participation by Mexican scientists in certain programmes of space research by the (US) National Aeronautics and Space Administration, Feb. 27, 1965.

(9) Treaty of co-operation providing for the recovery and return of stolen archaeological, historical and cultural properties, July 17, 1970; in force from March 24, 1971.

(10) Treaty to resolve pending boundary differences and maintain the Rio Grande and Colorado Rivers as the international boundary between the United States and Mexico, Nov. 23, 1970; in force from April 18, 1972.

(11) Agreement for scientific and technical co-operation, June 15, 1972.

(12) Joint statement relating to the problem of illegal entry into the United States by Mexican migratory workers, July 18, 1973.

(13) Agreement relating to trade in cotton, wool and man-made fibre textiles and textile products, Feb. 26, 1979; effective May 1, 1979.

(14) Agreement on natural gas, Sept. 21, 1979.

(15) Agreement on co-operation in cases of natural disasters, Jan. 15, 1980; entered into force provisionally Jan. 15, 1980, definitively March 18, 1981.

(16) Agreement of co-operation regarding pollution of the marine environment by discharges of hydrocarbons and other hazardous substances, July 24, 1980; definitively in force from March 30, 1981.

(17) Memorandum of understanding covering scientific co-operation in earth resources, Jan. 19, 1981.

(18) Memorandum of understanding concerning the furnishing of launch and associated services for the MEXSAT project, Nov. 18, 1982; in force from March 18, 1983.

(19) Agreement for co-operation on environmental programmes and transboundary problems, Aug. 14, 1983; in force from Feb. 16, 1984.

Morocco. (1) Exchange of notes providing for economic, technical and related assistance, April 1, 1957; entry into force on the following day; amended May 19, 1958.

(2) Economic and technical co-operation agreements by (US) Agency for International Development, Nov. 7, 1975; June 14, 1976; and Aug. 14 and 31, 1978.

(3) Memorandum of understanding for technical co-operation in the earth sciences, June 7 and July 16, 1984; in force from latter date.

Mozambique. Economic and technical co-operation agreements by (US) Agency for International Development, Sept. 14, 1976; and Dec. 2, 1977.

Nepal. (1) General agreement for technical co-operation, Jan. 23, 1951; amended Jan. 2 and 8, 1952.

(2) Economic and technical co-operation agreements by (US) Agency for International Development between June 5, 1975, and Aug. 31, 1980.

(3) Five agreements providing for grant assistance to Nepal worth US$23,569,000, Dec. 23, 1984.

The Netherlands. (1) Economic co-operation agreement applicable to Curaçao, July 2, 1948; amended Jan. 16 and Feb. 2, 1950; March 7 and April 3, 1951; and Nov. 28, 1952.

(2) General agreement for technical co-operation for Suriname and Netherlands Antilles, Jan. 22, 1954; entry into force April 21, 1954.

(3) Treaty of friendship, commerce and navigation, March 27, 1956; in force from Dec. 5, 1957.

New Zealand. (1) Exchange of notes relating to co-operation in scientific and logistical operations in Antarctica, Dec. 24, 1958.

(2) Exchange of notes concerning a programme of research on aerospace disturbance, May 15, 1963.

(3) Agreement for a space vehicle tracking programme, July 9, 1968.

(4) Agreement for scientific and technological co-operation, Feb. 27, 1974.

Nicaragua. (1) Exchange of notes on general agreement for economic, technical and related assistance, March 30, 1962; entry into force May 14, 1962.

(2) Economic and technical co-operation agreement by (US) Agency for International Development, Aug. 30, 1978; and Oct. 17, 1980.

Niger. (1) Exchange of notes providing for the furnishing of economic, technical and related assistance, May 26, 1961.

(2) Economic and technical co-operation agreements by (US) Agency for International Development between Sept. 17, 1975, and June 1, 1978.

(3) On Dec. 10–12, 1984, it was agreed that Niger would receive $25,000,000 in US development aid in 1985 (i.e. US$4,000,000 more than in 1983 and 1984).

Nigeria. (1) Economic co-operation agreement between the United States and the United Kingdom, July 6, 1948; made applicable to Nigeria on the same day; amended Jan. 3, 1950; May 25, 1951; and Feb. 25, 1953.

(2) Agreement providing for the establishment and operation of a space vehicle tracking and communications station within the Federation of Nigeria, Oct. 19, 1960; extended and amended April 28 and May 21, 1964.

(3) Agreement for scientific and technological co-operation, Sept. 22, 1980.

(4) Memorandum of understanding on environmental protection, Sept. 22, 1980.

Norway. (1) Treaty of friendship, commerce and consular rights, June 5, 1928; additional article, Feb. 25, 1929; in force from Sept. 13, 1932.

(2) Economic co-operation agreement, July 3, 1948; amended Jan. 17, 1950; July 5, 1951; and Jan. 8, 1953.

(3) Exchange of notes relating to the installation, operation and management of a seismic array facility in Norway, June 15, 1968.

Oman. (1) Treaty of amity, economic relations and consular rights, Dec. 20, 1958; in force from June 11, 1960.

(2) Agreement to establish a joint commission on economic and technical co-operation, Aug. 19, 1980.

(3) Economic and technical co-operation agreement, Sept. 4, 1980.

Pakistan. (1) Agreement for technical co-operation, Feb. 9, 1951; amended Jan. 8, 1952.

(2) Supplementary agreement for technical co-operation, Feb. 2, 1952; amended March 27 and Dec. 28, 1953; June 24, 1954; and Jan. 18, 1955.

(3) Treaty of friendship and commerce, Nov. 12, 1959; in force from Feb. 12, 1961.

(4) Economic and technical co-operation agreements by (US) Agency for International Development between Oct. 10, 1975, and Dec. 19, 1983.

Panama. (1) General agreement for technical and economic co-operation, Dec. 11, 1961; entry into force March 5, 1962.

(2) Economic and technical co-operation agreements by (US) Agency for International Development between May 6, 1969, and Aug. 23, 1978.

Paraguay. (1) Treaty of friendship, commerce and navigation, Feb. 4, 1859; in force from March 7, 1860.

(2) General agreement for economic, technical and related assistance, Sept. 26, 1961.

(3) Economic and technical co-operation agreements by (US) Agency for International Development, June 30, 1975; Dec. 7, 1976, and Aug. 15, 1977.

Peru. (1) General agreement for technical co-operation, Jan. 25, 1951; entry into force Jan. 15, 1953; amended Jan. 7, 1952; Feb. 21 and 28, 1952; and Jan. 15, 1953.

(2) Economic and technical co-operation agreements by (US) Agency for International Development between Sept. 29, 1976, and May 11, 1984.

The Philippines. (1) Economic and technical co-operation agreement, April 27, 1951; entry into force May 21, 1951.

(2) Economic and technical co-operation agreements by (US) Agency for International Development between Dec. 23, 1975, and Aug. 18, 1978.

(3) Agreement relating to trade in cotton, wool and man-made fibre textiles and textile products, Nov. 24, 1982; in force from Jan. 1, 1983.

Poland. (1) Agreement relating to economic and financial co-operation, April 24, 1946.

(2) Memorandum of understanding on scientific and technological co-operation, Dec. 11, 1981.

(3) Agreement relating to imports of specialty steel from Poland, Oct. 18, 1983.

(4) Agreement relating to trade in cotton, wool and man-made fibre textiles and textile products, Dec. 5 and 31, 1984; effective Jan. 1, 1985.

Portugal. (1) Economic co-operation agreement, Sept. 28, 1948, amended Feb. 14, 1950; May 17, 1951; and March 9 and 18, 1953.

(2) Exchange of letters relating to provision of economic assistance to Portugal, Dec. 9, 1971.

(3) Economic and technical co-operation agreements by (US) Agency for International Development between Feb. 28, 1975, and March 1, 1978.

Romania. * (1) Agreement on co-operation and exchanges in the cultural, educational, scientific and technological fields, Dec. 13, 1974, entry into force Jan. 1, 1975.

(2) Long-term agreement on economic, industrial and technical co-operation, Nov. 21, 1976; entry into force May 5, 1977.

(3) Programme of co-operation and exchanges in educational, cultural, scientific, technological and other fields for the years 1979 and 1980, Dec. 7, 1978; effective Jan. 1, 1979.

(4) Memorandum of understanding on scientific and technical co-operation, Feb. 27, 1979.

(5) Agreement relating to trade in cotton textiles, Jan. 28 and March 31, 1983; effective Jan. 1, 1983.

(6) Agreement relating to trade in wool and man-made fibre textiles and textile products, Nov. 7 and 16, 1984; effective Jan. 1, 1985.

Rwanda. Economic and technical co-operation agreements by (US) Agency for International Development, April 26 and 29, 1977.

St Lucia. General agreement for economic, technical and related assistance, Oct. 20, 1983.

St Vincent and the Grenadines. General agreement for economic, technical and related assistance, Sept. 30, 1983.

Saudi Arabia. (1) Agreement on co-operation in the fields of economics, technology, industry and defence, June 8, 1974.

(2) Technical co-operation agreement, Feb. 13, 1975; in force from May 12, 1975; extended, Sept. 25, 1984.

(3) Numerous project agreements concluded between 1975 and 1979.

(4) Agreement for technical co-operation in desalination, May 3, 1977; entry into force Aug. 30, 1977.

Senegal. (1) Agreement providing for economic, financial, technical and related assistance, May 13, 1961.

(2) Economic and technical co-operation agreements by (US) Agency for International Development between March 23, 1974, and March 29, 1978.

(3) Agreement for scientific and technical co-operation, Sept. 30, 1980; in force from Aug. 17, 1982.

(4) Agreement regarding the establishment and operation of a space vehicle tracking and communication facility in connection with the space shuttle, Jan. 30 and Feb. 5, 1981; in force from latter date.

(5) Agreement providing for an emergency landing site in Senegal for the space shuttle, Dec. 15, 1982, and Jan. 31, 1983; in force from latter date.

Seychelles. (1) Economic co-operation agreement between the United Kingdom and the United States, applicable to Seychelles, July 6, 1948; amended, Jan. 3, 1950; May 25, 1951; and Feb. 25, 1953.

(2) Agreement relating to the establishment, operation and maintenance of a tracking and telemetry facility on the island of Mahé, June 29, 1976; amended March 16 and June 19, 1981.

---

* See also page 300–01

Sierra Leone. General agreement for a programme of economic, technical and related assistance (May 5, 1961).

Singapore. (1) Economic co-operation agreement between the United States and the United Kingdom, July 6, 1948; amended Jan. 3, 1950; May 25, 1951; and Feb. 25, 1953.

(2) Agreement relating to cotton, wool and man-made fibre textiles and textile products, Aug. 21, 1981; effective Jan. 1, 1982.

The Solomon Islands. Economic co-operation agreement between the United Kingdom and the United States, applicable to the Solomon Islands, July 6, 1948; amended, Jan. 3, 1950; May 25, 1951; and Feb. 25, 1953.

Somalia. (1) Economic and technical co-operation agreements by (US) Agency for International Development, June 7, 1976, and Dec. 18, 1977.

(2) Agreement on economic and technical co-operation, June 14 and Oct. 12–13, 1981; in force from last-named date.

South Africa. Memorandum of understanding relating to the operation of the Landsat system for remote sensing, Sept. 19 and Oct. 19, 1983; in force from latter date.

Spain. (1) Treaty of friendship and general relations, July 3, 1902; entry into force April 14, 1903; amended as from July 1, 1916, by abrogation of Arts. XXIII and XXIV.

(2) Economic aid agreement, Sept. 26, 1953.

(3) Exchange of notes providing for the establishment and operation of a tracking and data acquisition station, Jan. 29, 1964; extended and amended Oct. 11, 1965, and Feb. 1 and May 2, 1983.

(4) Exchange of notes providing for a project in Spain to measure winds and temperatures at high altitudes and for continuing other co-operative space research projects, April 14, 1966.

(5) Exchange of notes establishing a joint Spanish-US economic committee to consult with regard to financial and other economic matters of mutual interest, July 15, 1968.

(6) Complementary agreement to agreement on friendship, defence and co-operation of July 2, 1982 (see page 373), concerning scientific, technological, cultural, educational and economic co-operation, July 2, 1982; in force from May 14, 1983.

(7) Agreement relating to limitation of imports of specialty steel from Spain, Oct. 18, 1983.

(8) Agreement on space co-operation, Aug. 31 and Sept. 4, 1984; in force from latter date.

Sri Lanka. (1) General agreement for technical co-operation, Nov. 7, 1950.

(2) Exchange of notes relating to development assistance programme to Ceylon, now Sri Lanka, April 28, 1956.

(3) Agreements for economic and technical co-operation of (US) Agency for International Development concluded between Nov. 9, 1977, and Aug. 31, 1978.

(4) Agreement relating to trade in cotton, wool and man-made fibre textiles and textile products, May 10, 1983; effective May 1, 1983.

(5) Agreement on co-operation in science and technology, June 18, 1984.

Sudan. (1) Exchange of notes providing for economic, technical and related assistance to the Sudan, March 31, 1958.

(2) Economic and technical co-operation agreements by (US) Agency for International Development, May 12, 1977; Aug. 30, 1978; and Dec. 31, 1979.

Suriname. (1) Economic co-operation agreement between the United States and the Netherlands, July 2, 1948; amended Jan. 16, and Feb. 2, 1950; March 7 and April 3, 1951; and Nov. 28, 1952.

(2) General agreement between the United States and the Netherlands for technical co-operation for Suriname and the Netherlands Antilles, Jan. 22, 1954; entry into force April 21, 1954.

(3) Treaty of friendship, commerce and navigation between the United States and the Netherlands, March 27, 1956; applicable to Suriname Feb. 10, 1963.

Swaziland. (1) General agreement on special development assistance, June 3, 1970.

(2) Economic and technical co-operation agreement by (US) Agency for International Development, Aug. 31, 1978.

Sweden. Economic co-operation agreement, July 3, 1948; entry into force July 21, 1948; amended Jan. 5 and 17, 1950; Feb. 8 and 23, 1951.

Syria. (1) Exchange of notes with the United Arab Republic (UAR) extending to the Syrian region of the UAR application of the general agreement for technical co-operation with Egypt of May 5, 1951, and the economic development programme of Nov. 6, 1954 (April 2, 1960).

(2) Economic and technical co-operation agreements by (US) Agency for International Development between Feb. 27, 1975, and Sept. 12, 1979.

(3) Cultural agreement, May 12, 1977.

Tanzania. (1) Exchange of notes providing for the furnishing of economic, technical and related assistance, Feb. 8, 1968.

(2) Economic and technical co-operation agreements by (US) Agency for International Development, Aug. 12–13, 1975; April 13, 1976; Aug. 15, 1977; Dec. 28–29, 1977; and July 6, 1978.

Thailand. (1) Economic and technical co-operation agreements, June 2, 1977.

(2) Economic and technical co-operation agreements by (US) Agency for International Development, Dec. 11, 1975; March 31 and Sept. 8, 1976; May 31 and Aug. 24 and 29, 1977; and May 4, 1978.

(3) Agreement relating to trade in cotton, wool and man-made fibre textiles and textile products, July 7 and Aug. 8, 1983; effective Jan. 1, 1983.

(4) Agreement on co-operation in science and technology April 13, 1984.

Togo. (1) Exchange of notes providing for economic, technical and related assistance, Dec. 22, 1960.

(2) Treaty of amity and economic relations, Feb. 8, 1966; in force from Feb. 5, 1967.

(3) Economic and technical co-operation agreement by (US) Agency for International Development, Oct. 12, 1977.

Trinidad and Tobago. (1) Economic co-operation agreement between the United States and the United Kingdom, July 6, 1948, applicable to Trinidad and Tobago on March 17, 1949; amended Jan. 3, 1950; May 25, 1951; Feb. 23, 1953; and June 26 and Aug. 20, 1959.

(2) Agreement between the United States and the United Kingdom for technical co-operation in respect of the territories for the international relations of which the United Kingdom was responsible, July 13, 1951, applicable to Trinidad and Tobago on Aug. 14, 1954.

Tunisia. (1) Exchange of notes providing for economic, technical and related assistance, March 26, 1957.

(2) Exchange of notes supplementing the above agreement, Oct. 8, 1958.

(3) Economic and technical co-operation agreements by (US) Agency for International Development, Dec. 29, 1977; Jan. 12, March 24 and Aug. 31, 1978.

(4) Agreement concerning cultural co-operation, Sept. 28, 1979.

Turkey. (1) Agreement for the regularization of relations between the United States and Turkey, Feb. 17, 1927.

(2) Treaty of commerce and navigation, Oct. 1, 1929; in force from April 22, 1930.

(3) Agreement on aid to Turkey, July 12, 1947.

(4) Economic co-operation agreement, July 4, 1948; amended Jan. 31, 1950; Aug. 16, 1951; and Dec. 30, 1952.

(5) Economic and technical co-operation agreements by (US) Agency for International Development between Dec. 5, 1978, and Dec. 24, 1984.

(6) Agreement regarding scientific and technical co-operation, Feb. 21, 1983; in force from Oct. 11, 1983.

(7) Memorandum of understanding for a co-operative programme in strong-motion data acquisition and analysis, March 8 and April 16, 1983; in force from latter date.

Uganda. Exchange of notes relating to economic, technical and related assistance, Dec. 3 and 11, 1971; entry into force on latter date.

The United Kingdom. (1) Treaty of amity, commerce and navigation, of which only three articles are still in force, Nov. 19, 1794; entry into force Oct. 28, 1795.

(2) Economic co-operation agreement applicable to Channel Islands, Falkland Islands, Western Pacific High Commission territories, Gibraltar, British Virgin Islands, Hong Kong, Isle of Man and St Helena and Dependencies, and also, except for Art. IV, to Turks and Caicos Islands, Cayman Islands, Montserrat and Anguilla, July 6, 1948; amended Jan. 3, 1950; May 25, 1951; Feb. 21, 1953; and June 26 and Aug. 20, 1959.

(3) Agreement for technical co-operation in respect of the territories for the international relations of which the United Kingdom was responsible, applicable to British Virgin Islands, Montserrat, Anguilla, Turks and Caicos Islands and Cayman Islands, July 13, 1951.

(4) Exchange of notes providing for the establishment and operation of a space vehicle tracking and communication station in Bermuda, March 15, 1961; extended and amended Sept. 23, 1963; Jan. 17, 1968.

(5) Exchange of notes on co-operation in intercontinental testing in connexion with experimental communications satellites, March 29, 1961.

(6) Agreement relating to the establishment of a joint programme of space research, Sept. 8, 1961.

(7) Exchange of notes providing for the establishment of a lunar and planetary spacecraft tracking facility on Ascension Island, July 7, 1965.

(8) Exchange of notes providing for the establishment and operation of space vehicle tracking and communications stations in the United Kingdom, Dec. 8, 1966, and Jan. 1, 1967; entry into force on latter date.

(9) Exchange of notes concerning the establishment and operation of a space vehicle tracking and communications station on Antigua, Jan. 17 and 23, 1967; entry into force on latter date.

(10) Exchange of notes confirming a memorandum of understanding concerning the furnishing of launching and associated services by the (US) National Aeronautics and Space Administration for UK satellites, Jan. 17, 1973.

(11) Memorandum of understanding on co-operation in earth sciences and environmental studies, Sept. 21 and 26, 1979; entry into force on latter date.

(12) Memorandum of understanding relating to a satellite-aided maritime distress alert system, July 23, 1981.

(13) Memorandum of understanding on the participation of the United Kingdom in the ocean drilling programme, Aug. 30, 1983.

Uruguay. (1) General agreement for a programme of technical co-operation, March 23, 1956; entry into force March 22, 1960.

(2) Economic and technical co-operation agreements by (US) Agency for International Development (Sept. 3, 1975).

Venezuela. (1) Treaty of peace, friendship, navigation and commerce, Jan. 20, 1836; entry into force May 31, 1836; articles on commerce and navigation terminated Jan. 3, 1851.

(2) Exchange of notes on general agreement on technical co-operation, Sept. 29, 1952.

(3) Agreement for scientific and technical co-operation, Jan. 11, 1980; in force from July 22, 1983.

(4) Memorandum of understanding on co-operation in earth resources and geological phenomena, Feb. 5 and 7, 1980; in force from July 22, 1983.

(5) Agreement in the field of energy research and development, March 6, 1980.

Yemen Arab Republic. (1) Agreement relating to friendship and commerce, May 4, 1946.

(2) Economic, technical and related assistance agreement, April 20, 1974.

Yugoslavia. (1) Economic co-operation agreement, Jan. 8, 1952; amended, Feb. 25 and March 10, 1953.

(2) Agreement on scientific and technical co-operation, April 2, 1980; in force from June 24, 1980.

Zaïre. Economic and technical co-operation agreements by (US) Agency for International Development, June 29 and Sept. 30, 1976; Jan. 27, 1977; and July 10 and Aug. 9, 1978.

Zambia. (1) Economic co-operation agreement between the United States and the United Kingdom of July 6, 1948, made applicable to Northern Rhodesia, now Zambia, July 20, 1948; amended Jan. 3, 1950; May 25, 1951; and Feb. 25, 1953.

(2) Agreement for technical co-operation in respect of the territories for the international relations of which the United Kingdom was responsible of July 13, 1951; made applicable to the Federation of Rhodesia and Nyasaland, April 8, 1960.

(3) Economic and technical co-operation agreements by (US) Agency for International Development, Dec. 3, 1976, and March 30, 1978.

Zimbabwe. (1) Agreement for scientific and technical co-operation, Sept. 25, 1980.

(2) General agreement for economic, technical and related assistance, Feb. 10 and March 22, 1982; in force from latter date.

Bilateral US Agreements on the Peaceful Use of Nuclear Energy

Agreements on co-operation in the peaceful uses of atomic (or nuclear) energy have been concluded by the United States with the following countries. The dates given are those of the signature and, unless otherwise stated, of entry into force of the agreements. Where no further particulars are given, the agreements refer only to "co-operation in the civil uses of atomic energy".

Argentina. (1) Exchange of notes providing for a grant to assist in the acquisition of certain nuclear resources and training equipment and materials, Sept. 9, 1959, and May 23, 1960; entry into force on latter date.

(2) Exchange of notes providing for equipment to be used in nuclear research and training programme at La Plata University, Argentina, Nov. 8, 1962, and Nov. 30, 1963; entry into force on latter date.

(3) Agreement, June 25, 1969; entry into force July 25, 1969.

Australia. Agreement, July 5, 1979; in force from Jan. 16, 1981.

Austria. Agreement, July 11, 1969; in force from Jan. 24, 1970; extended and amended, June 14, 1974.

Belgium. (1) Agreement in the field of radioactive waste management, Jan. 7 and 19, 1981; in force from latter date.

(2) Agreement relating to severe nuclear accident research, March 29 and April 18, 1983; in force from April 18, 1983; effective Feb. 10, 1983.

Brazil. (1) Exchanges of notes providing for grants to assist in the acquisition of nuclear research and training equipment and materials (a) Oct. 20, 1959 and Feb. 27, 1960; entry into force on latter date; (b) Oct. 10, 1960, and March 17, 1962; entry into force on latter date; and (c) Oct. 10, 1962, and March 29, 1963; entry into force on latter date.

(2) Agreement, July 17, 1972; entry into force Sept. 20, 1972.

(3) Arrangement for the exchange of technical information and co-operation in safety research, Jan. 14, 1982.

Canada. (1) Agreement, June 15, 1955; entry into force July 21, 1955; extended and amended June 26, 1956; May 22, 1959; June 11, 1960; May 22, 1959; and April 23, 1980.

(2) Agreement respecting co-operation in radioactive waste management, Aug. 25, 1982.

(3) Agreement for co-operation in severe (nuclear) accident research, March 2 and 16, 1984; in force from latter date; effective Feb. 10, 1984.

Chile. Exchange of notes providing for a grant for the acquisition of certain nuclear research and training equipment and materials, July 23, 1959, and Feb. 19, 1960; entry into force on latter date.

Colombia. (1) Exchange of notes providing for a grant for the acquisition of nuclear training and research equipment and materials, July 31, 1959 and Jan. 11, 1960; entry into force on latter date.

(2) Agreement, Jan. 8, 1981; in force from Sept. 7, 1983.

Denmark. Arrangement for exchange of technical information and co-operation in nuclear safety matters, Sept. 29, 1980.

Egypt. (1) Arrangement for the exchange of technical information and co-operation in nuclear safety matters, April 27 and June 8, 1981; in force from latter date.

(2) Agreement, June 29, 1981; in force from Dec. 29, 1981.

Finland. (1) Agreement, April 8, 1970; entry into force July 7, 1970.

(2) Arrangement for the exchange of technical information and co-operation in nuclear safety matters, Sept. 26, 1980.

France. (1) Technical exchange arrangement in the field of research on light water reactor safety, Sept. 12, 1980.

(2) Agreement concerning the retransfer of nuclear power light water reactor technology, Jan. 22, 1981; in force from March 13, 1981.

(3) Agreement regarding the nuclear qualification of polymer base materials, April 23 and May 14, 1982; in force from latter date.

(4) Agreement regarding participation in the USNRC steam generator safety research project, March 18 and June 8, 1982; in force from latter date; amended Oct. 8 and 22, 1982.

(5) Technical exchange and co-operation arrangement in the field of fast-breeder reactor safety research, June 7 and 21, 1983; in force from latter date.

(6) Agreement for co-operation in the field of radioactive waste management, July 26, 1983.

(7) Technical exchange and co-operation arrangement in the field of safety of radioactive waste management, Jan. 3 and 10, 1984; in force from latter date.

(8) Arrangement for the exchange of technical information and co-operation in the regulation of nuclear safety, Sept. 17, 1984.

The Federal Republic of Germany. (1) Technical exchange and co-operative arrangement in the field of management of radioactive wastes, Dec. 20, 1974; extended and amended, March 19, 1980.

(2) Agreement for research and development in the field of liquid metal-cooled fast-breeder reactors, applicable also to West Berlin, June 8, 1976.

(3) Agreement in the field of gas-cooled reactor concepts and technology, Feb. 11, 1977.

(4) Technical exchange and co-operative arrangement in the field of reactor safety research and development, April 30, 1981.

(5) Agreement concerning the listing of reactors supplied from the Federal Republic of Germany to the Taiwan Power Company on the inventory of the IAEA safeguards agreement of Dec. 6, 1971, Nov. 5, 1981.

(6) Agreement relating to severe nuclear accident research programmes, March 29 and April 15, 1983, in force from latter date.

Greece. Arrangement for the exchange of technical information and co-operation in nuclear safety matters, Oct. 17 and Dec. 16, 1983, and Feb. 24, 1984; in force from last-named date; effective Oct. 17, 1983.

Guatemala. Exchange of notes providing for a grant to assist in the acquisition of certain nuclear research and training equipment and materials, April 7 and 23, 1960; entry into force on latter date.

India. (1) Exchange of notes providing for a grant of nuclear research equipment in the field of agriculture, April 22 and June 13, 1960; entry into force on latter date.

(2) Exchange of notes providing for a grant for assistance in obtaining materials and equipment for establishing a radiation medicine centre at a Bombay hospital, Jan. 4 and Feb. 1, 1963; entry into force on latter date.

(3) Agreement, Aug. 8, 1963; entry into force Oct. 25, 1963; amended Nov. 30, 1982.

Indonesia. Agreement, June 30, 1980.

Ireland. Exchange of notes providing for a grant to assist in the acquisition of certain nuclear research and training equipment and materials, March 24, 1960; entry into force April 7, 1960.

Israel. (1) Exchange of notes providing for a grant to Israel to assist in the acquisition of certain nuclear research and training equipment and materials, Oct. 19 and Dec. 19, 1960; entry into force on latter date.

(2) Exchange of notes continuing in effect safeguards and guarantee provisions of an agreement of July 12, 1955, as amended, for co-operation concerning civil uses of atomic energy, April 7–8, 1977; entry into force on latter date.

(3) Arrangement for the exchange of technical information and co-operation in nuclear safety matters, April 11, 1983.

Italy. (1) Arrangement for the exchange of technical information and co-operation in nuclear safety matters, April 1, 1981.

(2) Agreement relating to participation in the programme of severe nuclear accident research, Dec. 23, 1982, and Feb. 25, 1983; in force from latter date; effective Dec. 23, 1982.

Japan. (1) Agreement, Feb. 26, 1968; entry into force July 10, 1968; amended Feb. 24, 1972, and March 28, 1973.

(2) Agreement in the field of liquid metal-cooled fast-breeder reactors, Jan. 31, 1979.

(3) Technical exchange arrangement in the field of regulatory matters, Sept. 12 and 29, 1980; in force from latter date.

(4) Joint determination for reprocessing of special nuclear material of US origin, Oct. 30, 1981; extended, Oct. 30, 1984; additional joint determination, July 23, 1982.

(5) Agreement on co-operation in fast-reactor safety research, Sept. 20, 1983.

(6) Agreement concerning severe nuclear accident research, Sept. 27 and Oct. 1, 1984; in force from latter date.

The Republic of Korea. (1) Agreement providing for a grant to the Government of Korea to assist in the acquisition of certain nuclear research and training equipment and materials, Oct. 14 and Nov. 18, 1960; entry into force on latter date.

(2) Agreement, Nov. 24, 1972; in force from March 19, 1973; extended and amended, May 15, 1974.

(3) Arrangement for exchange of technical information and co-operation in regulatory and safety research matters, Nov. 10, 1981.

(4) Agreement relating to participation in the programme of severe (nuclear) accident research, Aug. 23, 1984.

Lebanon. Exchange of notes providing for a grant to the Government of Lebanon to assist in the acquisition of nuclear research and training equipment and supplies, Sept. 16, 1959.

Mexico. Arrangement for the exchange of technical information and co-operation in nuclear safety matters, April 8, 1981.

The Netherlands. (1) Arrangement for the exchange of information and co-operation in regulatory and safety research matters, Sept. 15, 1982.

(2) Agreement relating to severe nuclear accident research programmes, March 29 and April 1, 1983; in force from latter date; effective Feb. 15, 1983.

New Zealand. Exchange of notes providing for a grant to assist in the acquisition of nuclear research and training equipment and materials, March 23, 1960.

Norway. Revised agreement, Jan. 12, 1984; in force from July 2, 1984.

Peru. (1) Agreement providing for a grant to the Government of Peru to assist in the acquisition of nuclear research and training equipment and materials, July 12 and Aug. 22, 1959; entry into force on latter date.

(2) Agreement, June 26, 1980; in force from April 15, 1982.

The Philippines. (1) Agreement, June 13, 1968; in force from July 19, 1968.

(2) Arrangement for the exchange of technical information and co-operation in nuclear safety matters, March 28 and April 28, 1980; in force from latter date.

Portugal. Agreement, May 16, 1974; entry into force June 26, 1974.

Romania. Agreement clarifying certain understandings relating to the supply of enriched uranium to Romania for the TRIGA reactor, Feb. 13, 1978.

South Africa. Agreement, July 8, 1957; entry into force Aug. 22, 1957; extended and amended June 12, 1962; July 17, 1967; and May 22, 1974.

Soviet Union. Agreement, June 21, 1973; extended and amended. July 5 and Aug. 1, 1983.

Spain. (1) Agreement, March 20, 1974; entry into force June 28, 1974.

(2) Arrangement for the exchange of technical information and co-operation in nuclear safety matters, Sept. 28, 1984.

Sweden. (1) Arrangement for the exchange of technical information and co-operation in nuclear safety matters, Oct. 30, 1979.

(2) Technical exchange and co-operative arrangement in the field of nuclear safety research and development, Jan. 27 and Feb. 23, 1981; in force from latter date.

(3) Agreement, Dec. 19, 1983; in force from April 11, 1984.

Switzerland. (1) Agreement, Dec. 30, 1965; entry into force Aug. 8, 1966; amended Nov. 2, 1973.

(2) Agreement on research participation and technical exchange in the US loss of fluid test programme and the Swiss emergency core cooling systems-reflood programme, June 15 and July 9, 1979; entry into force on latter date; extended and amended, March 27 and May 2, 1984.

(3) Agreement on research participation and technical exchange in the US heavy section steel technology programme and the Swiss research programme in fracture mechanics, June 15 and July 9, 1979; entry into force on latter date; extended and amended, May 7 and 14, 1984.

(4) Arrangement for the exchange of technical information and co-operation in nuclear safety matters, July 20 and Aug. 10, 1982; in force from latter date.

(5) Agreement in the area of carbide fuel development, Nov. 15, 1982.

Taiwan. Agreement, April 4, 1972; in force from June 22, 1972; extended and amended, March 15, 1974.

Thailand. Agreement, May 14, 1974; in force from June 27, 1974.

Turkey. Agreement continuing in effect safeguards and guarantee provisions of an agreement of June 10, 1955, as amended, April 15 and June 9, 1981; in force from latter date.

United Kingdom. (1) Articles of agreement governing collaboration between the authorities of the United States and the United Kingdom in the matter of tube alloys, Aug. 19, 1943.

(2) Agreement in the field of liquid metal-cooled fast-breeder reactors, Sept. 20, 1976; amended and extended, Aug. 14 and 18, 1978, and April 30 and Aug. 12, 1981.

(3) Arrangement in the field of nuclear safety research and development, July 20 and Aug. 3, 1977; entry into force on latter date; extended, Feb. 18 and June 11, 1982.

(4) Arrangement for the exchange of technical information and co-operation in nuclear safety matters, May 15, 1981.

Venezuela. Agreement continuing in effect safeguard and guarantee provisions of an agreement of Oct. 8, 1958, as amended, Feb. 18, 1981.

Yugoslavia. Exchange of notes providing for a grant to assist in the acquisition of certain nuclear research and training equipment and materials, April 19, 1961.

US Extradition Treaties

The United States has extradition treaties with the following states, concluded on the dates given (with the dates of their entry into force shown in parentheses):

Albania, March 1, 1933 (Nov. 14, 1935).

Antigua, June 8, 1972 (with the United Kingdom) (Jan. 21, 1977).

Argentina, Jan. 21, 1972 (Sept. 15, 1972).

Australia, May 14, 1974 (May 8, 1976).

Austria, Jan. 31, 1930 (Sept. 11, 1930); supplementary convention, May 19, 1934 (Sept. 5, 1934).

The Bahamas and **Barbados,** UK-US treaty of Dec. 22, 1931; continued as agreed on March 7, June 19 and Aug. 17, 1978 (June 24, 1983).

Belgium, Oct. 24, 1901 (July 14, 1902).

Belize, UK-US treaty of June 8, 1972 (Jan. 21, 1977).

Bolivia, April 21, 1900 (Jan, 22, 1902).

Brazil, Jan. 13, 1961 (Dec. 17, 1964).

Bulgaria, March 19, 1924 (June 24, 1924); supplementary treaty, June 8, 1934 (Aug. 15, 1935).

Burma, UK-US treaty of Dec. 22, 1931; applicable to Burma, Nov. 1, 1941.

Canada, Dec. 3, 1971; amended, June 28 and July 9, 1974 (March 22, 1976).

Chile, April 17, 1900 (June 26, 1902).

Colombia, Sept. 14, 1979 (March 4, 1982).

The Congo, US-French treaty of Jan. 6, 1909 (July 7, 1911); supplementary conventions, Jan. 15, 1929 (May 19, 1929); April 23, 1936 (Sept. 24, 1936).

Costa Rica, Nov. 10, 1922 (April 27, 1923).

Cuba, April 6, 1904 (March 2, 1905); additional treaty, Jan. 14, 1926 (June 18, 1926).

Cyprus, UK-US treaty of Dec. 22, 1931; applicable to Cyprus, June 24, 1935.

Czechoslovakia, July 2, 1925 (March 29, 1926); supplementary treaty, April 29, 1935 (Aug. 28, 1935).

Denmark, June 22, 1972 (July 31, 1974).

Dominica, UK-US treaty of June 8, 1972 (Jan. 21, 1977).

The Dominican Republic, June 19, 1909 (Aug. 2, 1910).

Ecuador, June 28, 1872 (Nov. 12, 1873); supplementary treaty, Sept. 22, 1939 (May 29, 1941).

Egypt, US-Ottoman Empire treaty, Aug. 11, 1874 (April 22, 1875).

El Salvador, April 18, 1911 (July 10, 1911).

Fiji, UK-US treaty of Dec. 22, 1931 (June 24, 1935).

Finland, June 11, 1976 (May 11, 1980).

France, Jan. 6, 1909 (July 27, 1911); supplementary convention, Feb. 12, 1970 (April 3, 1971).

The Gambia, UK-US treaty of Dec. 22, 1931 (June 24, 1935).

The Federal Republic of Germany, June 20, 1978 (Aug. 29, 1980).

Ghana, UK-US treaty of Dec. 22, 1931; applicable to the Gold Coast, June 24, 1935.

Greece, May 6, 1931 (Nov. 1, 1932); protocol, Sept. 2, 1937.

Grenada, UK-US treaty of Dec. 22, 1931 (June 24, 1935).

Guatemala, Feb. 27, 1903 (Aug. 14, 1903).

Guyana, UK-US treaty of Dec. 22, 1931 (June 24, 1935).

Haiti, Aug. 9, 1904 (June 28, 1905).

Honduras, Jan. 15, 1909 (July 10, 1912); supplementary convention, Feb. 21, 1927 (June 5, 1928).

Hungary, July 3, 1856 (Dec. 13, 1856).

Iceland, US-Danish treaty of Jan. 6, 1902; supplementary treaty, Nov. 6, 1905 (Feb. 19, 1906).

India, UK-US treaty of Dec. 22, 1931; applicable to India, March 9, 1942.

Iraq, June 7, 1934 (April 23, 1936).

Ireland, July 13, 1983 (Dec. 15, 1984).

Israel, Dec. 10, 1962 (Dec. 5, 1963); exchange of notes, April 4 and 11, 1967.

Italy, Oct. 13, 1983 (Sept. 24, 1984).

Jamaica, UK-US treaty of Dec. 31, 1931; applicable to Jamaica, June 24, 1935.

Japan, March 3, 1978 (March 26, 1980).

Kenya, UK-US treaty of Dec. 22, 1931; applicable to Kenya, June 24, 1935; continued, May 14 and Aug. 19, 1965.

Kiribati, June 8, 1972 (Jan. 21, 1977).

Lesotho, UK-US treaty of Dec. 22, 1931 (June 24, 1935).

Liberia, Nov. 1, 1937 (Nov. 21, 1939).

Liechtenstein, May 20, 1936 (June 28, 1937).

Luxembourg, Oct. 29, 1883 (Aug. 13, 1884).

Malawi, UK-US treaty of Dec. 22, 1931; applicable to Nyasaland, June 24, 1935; continued, Dec. 17, 1966; Jan. 6 and April 4, 1967.

Malaysia, UK-US treaty of Dec. 22, 1931; applicable to Federated and Unfederated Malay states, Aug. 10, 1939.

Malta, UK-US treaty of Dec. 22, 1931; applicable to Malta, June 24, 1935.

Mauritius, UK-US treaty of Dec. 22, 1931 (June 24, 1935).

Mexico, May 4, 1978 (Jan. 25, 1980).

Monaco, Feb. 15, 1939 (March 28, 1940).

Nauru, UK-US treaty of Dec. 22, 1931; applicable inter alia to Nauru, Aug. 30, 1935.

The Netherlands, June 24, 1980 (Sept. 15, 1983); also for the Netherlands Antilles.

New Zealand, Jan. 12, 1970 (Dec. 8, 1970).

Nicaragua, March 1, 1905 (July 14, 1907).

Nigeria, UK-US treaty of Dec. 22, 1931; applicable to Nigeria, June 24, 1935.

Norway, June 9, 1977 (March 7, 1980).

Pakistan, UK-US treaty of Dec. 22, 1931; applicable to India, March 9, 1942.

Panama, May 25, 1904 (May 8, 1905).

Papua New Guinea—as for Nauru.

Paraguay, May 24, 1973 (May 7, 1974).

Peru, Nov. 28, 1899 (Feb. 22, 1901).

Poland, Nov. 22, 1927 (July 6, 1929).

Portugal, May 7, 1908 (Nov. 14, 1908).

Romania, July 23, 1924 (April 7, 1925); supplementary treaty, Nov. 10, 1936 (July 27, 1937).

St Christopher and Nevis, UK-US treaty of June 8, 1972 (Jan. 21, 1977).

St Lucia—as for St Christopher and Nevis.

St Vincent and the Grenadines—do.

San Marino, Jan. 10, 1906 (July 8, 1908).

Seychelles, UK-US treaty of Dec. 22, 1931 (June 24, 1935).

Sierra Leone—as for Seychelles.

Singapore, UK-US treaty of Dec. 22, 1931 (June 24, 1935); confirmed in force between USA and Singapore, April 23 and June 10, 1969.

The Solomon Islands, US-UK treaty of June 8, 1972 (Jan. 21, 1977).

South Africa, Dec. 18, 1947 (April 30, 1951).

Spain, May 29, 1970 (June 16, 1971); supplementary treaty, Jan. 25, 1975 (June 2, 1978).

Sri Lanka, UK-US treaty of Dec. 22, 1931 (June 24, 1935).

Suriname, US-Netherlands treaty of June 2, 1887 (July 11, 1889); extended to Netherlands possessions, Jan. 18, 1904 (Aug. 28, 1904).

Swaziland, UK-US treaty of Dec. 22, 1931 (June 24, 1935); continued, May 13 and July 28, 1970.

Sweden, Oct. 24, 1961 (Dec. 3, 1963).

Switzerland, May 14, 1900 (March 28, 1901); supplementary treaties, (i) Jan. 10, 1935 (May 16, 1935); (ii) Jan. 31, 1940 (April 8, 1941).

Tanzania, UK-US treaty of Dec. 22, 1931 (June 24, 1935); continued, Nov. 30 and Dec. 6, 1965.

Thailand, Dec. 30, 1922 (March 24, 1924).

Tonga, UK-US treaty of Dec. 22, 1931 (June 24, 1935), applicable to Tonga, Aug. 1, 1966; continued, March 14 and April 13, 1977.

Trinidad and Tobago, UK-US treaty of Dec. 22, 1931; applicable to Trinidad and Tobago, June 24, 1935.

Turkey, June 7, 1979 (Jan. 1, 1981).

Tuvalu, UK-US treaty of June 8, 1972 (Jan. 21, 1977).

United Kingdom, June 8, 1972 (Jan. 21, 1977); supplementary treaty, June 25, 1985, which as subsequently revised and ratified by the US Senate on July 17, 1986, specified that those accused or convicted of certain violent crimes (but not conspiracy or possession of firearms) could not avoid extradition solely on the grounds that their offences were of a political nature.

Uruguay, April 6, 1973 (April 11, 1984).

Venezuela, Jan. 19 and 21, 1922 (April 14, 1923).

Yugoslavia, Oct. 25, 1901 (June 12, 1902).

Zambia, UK-US treaty of Dec. 22, 1931 (June 24, 1935).

Other Agreements involving American States

Agreements between States in Latin America and the Caribbean

Argentina and Bolivia. Agreements signed in November 1976 provided for the supply to Argentina of 1,400,000 cubic feet of Bolivian gas per day from 1979 onwards.

Argentina and Brazil. (1) Agreements were signed on May 26, 1981, between the Argentine National Atomic Energy Commission and the Brazilian state nuclear concern Nuclébras on closer co-operation in nuclear technology and Argentine deliveries of uranium to Brazil.

(2) A bilateral trade agreement was signed in August 1985.

(3) A general agreement on integration and development, signed, with 11 protocols, on July 29, 1986, and to come into effect on Jan. 1, 1987, provided inter alia for expanding and balancing trade, in particular in capital goods and primary products; increased Brazilian grain purchases from Argentina; the establishment of a mechanism for creating stocks of foodstuffs in order to help control supply and pricing; the establishment of co-operation in biotechnology; the study of policies for import duties for third countries; the setting-up of a commission to study the exchange of technology, increasing trade and other areas of co-operation; and the setting-up of means for immediate communication and assistance in the event of a nuclear accident.

Argentina, Brazil and Paraguay. A treaty on the sharing of the waters of the Paraná River was signed on Oct. 19, 1979.

Argentina and Chile. (1) An arbitration agreement signed in Buenos Aires on April 5, 1972, between Argentina and Chile provided for reference to the International Court of Justice of any bilateral dispute not resolved by direct negotiation. The agreement superseded a 1902 treaty which had provided for arbitration by the British Crown in territorial disputes between the two countries. Being due to expire, the treaty was extended on Sept. 15, 1982.

(2) A number of co-operation agreements were signed during a visit of the Argentine President to Chile on Nov. 11–13, 1976, covering land transport links, the annual supply by Argentina to Chile of 500,000 tons of wheat during 1977–79 and increased sales of Chilean natural gas to Argentina.

(3) Under an *Act of Puerto Montt* signed by the two countries' Presidents on Feb. 20, 1978, it was agreed to seek to create a "harmonious atmosphere" which might lead to a peaceful solution of the controversies existing between the two sides and subsequently to determining the two nations' respective rights under the legal system.

(4) A treaty of peace and friendship signed on Jan. 23, 1984, contained a commitment by both parties to abide by a final settlement of their dispute over the Beagle Channel [see below].

(5) A 19-article treaty of peace and friendship, signed on Nov. 29, 1984, had been ratified by the Chilean military junta and approved in a referendum held in Argentina on Nov. 25, when 77 per cent of the votes were cast in favour of the treaty (in a 73 per cent turnout).

The treaty ended a long-standing dispute over three islands (Picton, Lennox and Nueva) off Tierra del Fuego and over territorial waters in the area. The treaty gave Chile sovereignty over the three islands and over territorial waters around these islands, but it preserved the "bi-oceanic principle" under which a line drawn south from Cape Horn would be the boundary between the Argentine and Chilean claims to 200-mile territorial waters; this principle also entailed Chile's giving-up of any claim to waters east of the Magellan Straits; and it was also stated that the treaty's stipulations in no way affected the Antarctic continent, where Argentina and Chile had overlapping claims. The two sides also agreed to create a permanent binational commission which would inter alia promote the establishment of duty-free ports and zones. A first annex to the treaty provided for conciliation and arbitration procedures for the solution of any controversy. A second annex laid down rules for navigation, Argentina having expressed concern over access to the port of Ushuaia (the main port in the Argentine part of Tierra del Fuego).

On May 2, 1985, the instruments of ratification of the treaty were formally exchanged at the Vatican, which had been instrumental in achieving the final conclusion of the treaty.

Argentina and El Salvador. Under an agreement signed on June 5, 1981, Argentina granted El Salvador a loan of US$15,000,000 in economic aid and technical assistance and for the purchase of locally manufactured goods.

Argentina and Paraguay. A treaty on the construction of a hydroelectric project on the Paraná River (constituting part of the border between the two countries) at the Yaciretá-Agipé falls was signed on Dec. 3, 1973. An agreement on the final specifications of this scheme was, however, not signed until Aug. 30, 1979, when it was agreed that Argentina would pay Paraguay up to $50,000,000 a year in compensation for the flooding of an area in Paraguay by the scheme.

A permanent office for co-operation in investment and industry had been officially opened in Asunción (Paraguay) on June 15, 1974.

Argentina and Peru. At the end of a visit to Peru by Argentina's President on March 3–5, 1977, it was announced that Argentinian technology and equipment would be used to build Peru's first nuclear reactor.

Argentina and Uruguay. (1) A treaty on equal rights in navigation on the River Plate (Rio de la Plata) was signed in Montevideo on Nov. 19, 1973. It provided for freedom of navigation in perpetuity for the vessels of both Argentina and Uruguay on the river; for mutual guarantees for the maintenance of access to the ports of Buenos Aires and Montevideo; and for the use of all shipping lanes by the two countries under conditions of equality. (Under the *Ramírez-Saenz Pena Protocol* of 1910, the frontier between the two countries had been defined as the line of the river's greatest depth—and not the median line as demanded by Uruguay.)

(2) A commercial treaty abolishing most customs duties in bilateral trade was signed on June 19, 1985.

Belize and Costa Rica. A bilateral friendship agreement was concluded in November 1981.

Bolivia and Brazil. An agreement on friendship and co-operation between the two countries, signed by their Presidents during a visit to Brazil by Bolivia's President on Aug. 13–17, 1977, provided inter alia for delivery to Brazil of 240,000,000 cubic feet of natural gas daily for 20 years and of 410,000 tonnes of rolled steel and 100,000 tonnes of urea per annum, in return for which Brazil would invest an estimated $1,000 million for industrial development in Bolivia and for a pipeline to transport the gas.

Bolivia and Paraguay. A treaty of peace, friendship and borders (ending the Chaco War) was signed on July 21, 1938, and was followed by a protocol of Oct. 10, 1938.

Brazil and Guyana. Under a military agreement signed on Oct. 1, 1982, Guyana was granted a US$50,000,000 credit to enable it to buy from Brazil two reconnaissance aircraft, six armoured vehicles as well as arms and ammunition and to obtain military training for some Guyanese troops in Brazil.

Brazil and Paraguay. The Itaipú Treaty, signed on April 26, 1973, provided for the construction, within eight to 10 years, of a dam on the Paraná River. It was amended by a series of agreements signed on Jan. 29, 1986, providing inter alia for currency adjustments.

Brazil and Peru. Agreements were concluded between the two countries on Nov. 5, 1976, on trade, navigation and communications, while a period of "greater rapprochement" was envisaged with "more effective guidelines" to be laid down "for mutual understanding and economic co-operation" between the two sides.

Brazil and Suriname. Under an agreement signed on June 1, 1983, Brazil was to supply some US$25,000,000 worth of arms to Suriname,

and a similar amount was to be spent on training Surinamese soldiers with the Brazilian armed forces, while mutual trade was to be substantially expanded. (This agreement was said to result from Brazilian efforts to limit Cuban influence in Suriname.)

Brazil and Uruguay. Six agreements covering inter alia co-operation in science, technology and agriculture were signed on Aug. 14, 1986.

Chile and Peru. Under a 1929 Treaty of Ancón it was agreed that no Chilean territory which had earlier been part of Peru could be surrendered to a third party without Peru's consent. (This related to territory annexed by Chile as a result of the 1879-93 War of the Pacific, through which Bolivia, which had been joined by Peru in fighting against Chile, lost its access to the sea.)

Chile and Uruguay. An agreement on co-operation in the peaceful uses of nuclear energy, including the training of Uruguayan scientists, was signed by the two countries in July 1979.

Colombia and Ecuador. A treaty on the integration of borderland, known as the Rumichaca Act, was signed on March 12, 1966.

Colombia and Nicaragua. A Barcenas-Meneses-Esguerra treaty of 1930 provided inter alia for the cession, by Nicaragua to Colombia, of five islands in the Caribbean Sea—Providencia, Quitasueño, Roncador, San Andrés and Serrana. The treaty was unilaterally abrogated by Nicaragua on Feb. 5, 1980, but Colombia rejected the abrogation and maintained its sovereignty over the islands (which were believed to contain oil reserves).

Colombia and Panama. An agreement was signed on Nov. 20, 1976, on the delimitation of the two countries' marine and submarine territories.

Colombia and Peru. A treaty on the two countries' common boundary was concluded in 1922.

Colombia and Suriname. A commercial and financial co-operation agreement signed on Feb. 22, 1985, involved a US$15,000,000 credit line to finance imports from Colombia and Suriname.

Costa Rica and Venezuela. A co-operation and mutual aid agreement was signed on Sept. 15, 1978.

The Dominican Republic and Haiti. Under an agreement said to have been concluded in January 1980 Dominican Republic forces were to intervene in Haiti if serious guerrilla warfare erupted there.

The Dominican Republic and Venezuela. An economic agreement signed in December 1976 involved the purchase of sugar from the Dominican Republic by Venezuela and a Venezuelan loan of $60,000,000 for oil purchases by the Dominican Republic.

Ecuador and Venezuela. On March 17, 1975, the Presidents of Ecuador and Venezuela signed a 22-point declaration on intensive co-operation between their countries, with Venezuela (i) placing the equivalent of US$23,000,000 in Ecuadorean national bonds on the Venezuelan financial market and (ii) providing capital and technology to finance industrial projects in Ecuador.

El Salvador, Guatemala and Honduras. A meeting held in Tegucigalpa (Honduras) by the Presidents of the three countries on Aug. 12–13, 1981, led to the establishment of a Honduran naval base on Amapala, an island in the Gulf of Fonseca (between El Salvador, Honduras and Nicaragua).

El Salvador and Honduras. El Salvador and Honduras agreed to the establishment of a demilitarized zone along their common frontier at a meeting of the Foreign Ministers of five Central American States under OAS auspices at San José (Costa Rica) on June 4, 1970. The OAS had previously mediated in hostilities between the two countries in July 1969 [see also page 363].

A peace treaty between the two countries, signed in Lima (Peru) on Oct. 30, 1980, ended the effective state of war which had existed between them since 1969. It reopened their common border, provided for the resumption of diplomatic relations, committed both parties to the reactivation of the Central American Common Market [see pages 363ff.] and demarcated two-thirds of the common frontier, with an undertaking to settle within five years the question of disputed border areas, which formed part of the demilitarized zone. The treaty was ratified by the Constituent Assembly of Honduras at the end of November 1980 and instruments of ratification were exchanged on Dec. 10, 1980. The treaty also provided for a bilateral trade treaty which was signed on Oct. 30, 1981.

Mexico and El Salvador. An economic and technical co-operation agreement between the two countries was signed in January 1979.

Mexico and Venezuela. (1) A total of 15 agreements covering co-operation between state enterprises in the two countries were signed during a visit of the President of Venezuela to Mexico on March 17–22, 1975.

(2) In an agreement signed in San José (Costa Rica) on Aug. 3, 1980, the two governments agreed to supply oil at concessionary prices to nine countries—Barbados, Costa Rica, the Dominican Republic, El Salvador, Guatemala, Honduras, Jamaica, Nicaragua and Panama—for their total requirements of about 8,000,000 tonnes a year. These countries would pay the current market price less 30 per cent returned to them in the form of a five-year loan at 4 per cent interest; if these loans were used for primary development, particularly in the energy field, they would be extended over 20 years at 2 per cent interest. In April 1981 the agreement was extended to cover also Belize and Haiti. On Aug. 5, 1984, it was agreed to extend the agreement for another five

years in modified form and with the addition of a clause stating that concessionary supplies of oil would be suspended in respect of any country initiating military action or intervention against any other regional state.

Late in 1983 Venezuela suspended its side of the agreement with Nicaragua because of Nicaragua's outstanding debt of $30,000,000, and Mexico followed suit in February 1985 when Nicaragua owed it $500,000,000. However, a new oil agreement between Mexico and Nicaragua reached on May 29, 1985, provided for shipment of 320,000 barrels of oil to Nicaragua in July-September of that year on preferential terms, and for a further 410,000 barrels in October-December on terms still to be negotiated.

Panama and Peru. On June 13, 1984, a naval co-operation agreement was signed for the training of the Panamanian Navy by Peru.

Major Agreements between Latin American and Caribbean Countries and Countries outside Latin America

Argentina and France. An agreement to strengthen economic, industrial and financial co-operation was signed on Sept. 2, 1985.

Argentina and the Federal Republic of Germany. (1) A treaty of friendship, commerce and navigation signed on Sept. 18, 1857, and in force from June 3, 1859, was, on Dec. 10, 1984, extended until Dec. 31, 1986.

(2) A trade and payments agreement signed on Nov. 25, 1950, and in force from Oct. 27, 1951, and another such agreement signed on Nov. 25, 1957, and in force from Dec. 2, 1957, were both, on Sept. 16, 1985, extended until Dec. 31, 1986.

(3) A framework agreement on co-operation in scientific research and technological development was signed on March 31, 1969, and came into force on Oct. 22, 1969.

(4) A treaty on entry into Argentine waters of reactor ships and their sojourn in Argentine ports was signed on May 21, 1971, and came into force on Nov. 3, 1977.

(5) An agreement on cultural co-operation was signed on June 29, 1973, and came into force on Aug. 24, 1978.

(6) An agreement on exchange of technical information and co-operation in safety of nuclear installations was signed and came into force on Oct. 8, 1981.

Argentina and Spain. (1) A protocol on commercial and financial co-operation was signed on Dec. 3, 1976.

(2) A protocol on economic, commercial, industrial and technological co-operation was signed on Nov. 30, 1978.

(3) A special agreement on co-operation in the development and application of peaceful uses of nuclear energy was signed on Nov. 30, 1978.

(4) A protocol on economic and financial co-operation was signed on June 22, 1981.

Argentina and Sweden. A treaty of amity, commerce and navigation was signed on July 17, 1885.

Argentina and Switzerland. (1) An extradition agreement was signed on Nov. 21, 1906.
(2) A trade and payments agreement was signed on Nov. 25, 1957.

Bolivia and the Federal Republic of Germany. A cultural agreement was signed on Aug. 4, 1966, and came into force on Sept. 21, 1970.

Bolivia and Iceland. A treaty of commerce was signed on Nov. 9, 1931.

Bolivia and Spain. (1) A convention on co-operation in Bolivia's rural development was signed on March 23, 1982.
(2) A cultural agreement was signed on Jan. 15, 1983.

Bolivia and Switzerland. A technical and scientific co-operation agreement was signed on Nov. 30, 1973.

Brazil and France. Protocols signed on Feb. 1, 1981, provided for French loans and financing to Brazil worth US$1,000 million.

Brazil and the Federal Republic of Germany. (1) An agreement on extradition and other legal assistance in criminal cases was signed on April 8 and June 16, 1926, and was confirmed on April 22, 1953.
(2) A framework agreement on technical co-operation concluded on Feb. 4, 1964, came into force on May 25, 1965. Another framework agreement on co-operation in scientific research and technological development of June 9, 1969, came into force on Aug. 12, 1969.
(3) A cultural agreement was signed on June 9, 1969, and came into force on Dec. 17, 1970.
(4) An agreement on entry of reactor ships into Brazilian waters and their sojourn in Brazilian ports was signed on June 7, 1972, and came into force on Sept. 4, 1974.
(5) A framework agreement on co-operation in agriculture was signed and came into force on Jan. 21, 1975.
(6) An agreement approved by the German Federal Cabinet on April 30, 1975, and signed in Bonn on June 27, 1975, provided for the supply to Brazil, over a 15-year period, of eight West German nuclear reactors and for the erection in Brazil of a plant for the retreatment of irradiated fuels and a uranium enrichment plant at a total cost said to be equivalent to about $5,000 million. The agreement came into force on Nov. 18, 1975.

According to US officials quoted on June 3 of that year, the US Government had persuaded the two sides to sign a special-safeguards treaty with the International Atomic Energy Agency (IAEA), while the Brazilian Foreign Minister pointed out on June 27 that his country had not signed the Treaty of Tlatelolco (on a nuclear-weapon-free zone in Latin America—see page 71) but also explained that Brazil refused to sign the Nuclear Non-Proliferation Treaty because this treaty legalized the possession of atomic weapons by specified countries.

Under an agreement signed by Brazil with the IAEA on Jan. 16, 1976 (to take effect from March 2 of that year), Brazil accepted international inspection and supervision of the reactors and all other installations in the same way as signatories of the NPT were bound to accept.

Notwithstanding attempts by the US Government to force the German Federal Government to abrogate or alter its nuclear agreement with Brazil, the German Federal Chancellor stated on Jan. 25, 1977, that his Government intended to fulfil all its existing treaty obligations, including those with Brazil.

(7) On March 8, 1978, Brazil and the Federal Republic of Germany signed new agreements on co-operation in nuclear research, covering safety precautions for nuclear reactors, protection against radiation, disposal of nuclear waste, research on the vaporization of coal, and studies in metallurgy and welding technology. In a joint declaration signed by the President of Brazil and the German Federal Chancellor on March 10, 1978, the two sides affirmed that they were pursuing "exclusively peaceful" ends in implementing their nuclear agreement, which was based on a policy of "non-proliferation of nuclear weapons", and they agreed to intensify their contacts at all levels, to work towards a just and balanced world economic system, and to expand mutual exchanges in the fields of the economy and industry, science and technology.

(8) On the supply to Brazil of enriched uranium (under a system of strict safeguards) an agreement was formalized by an exchange of notes in Brasília on Sept. 1, 1978, by Brazil, the Federal Republic of Germany, the Netherlands and the United Kingdom (the three latter states being involved as a result of the enriched uranium being supplied by Urenco, a consortium of Dutch, West German and UK interests).

(9) An agreement on exchange of technical information and co-operation in safety of nuclear installations, signed on and in force from March 10, 1978, was extended on May 30 and July 27, 1983.

Brazil and Iceland. (1) A treaty of commerce and navigation was signed on July 30, 1936.
(2) A commercial agreement was signed on May 10, 1956.

Brazil and Iran. A barter agreement signed in September 1982 provided for the supply of Brazilian goods and services in return for Iranian oil.

Brazil and Iraq. Under an agreement signed in January 1980 Brazil undertook to supply Iraq with raw and slightly enriched uranium and also with equipment and construction services for building nuclear reactors (while purchasing about 40 per cent of its oil imports from Iraq). In 1981 Brazil also supplied Iraq with armaments in return for Iraqi oil.

Brazil and Portugal. (1) In a joint communiqué issued at the end of a visit to Brazil by the Portuguese Prime Minister on Dec. 15–18, 1977, the two sides undertook to reactivate trade between them (with the help of a Brazilian credit equivalent to $50,000,000 to finance Portuguese purchases in Brazil), to establish co-operation and friendship with the new Portuguese-speaking states in Africa, and to form joint commissions on economic, scientific and technical co-operation.

(2) Agreements signed on Feb. 4, 1981, provided for financial and commercial co-operation worth US$280,000,000 covering inter alia Portuguese imports of Brazilian raw materials and technology and also the purchase by Brazil of two oil tankers from Portugal.

Brazil and Spain. (1) An agreement on technical co-operation and assistance was signed on April 23, 1981.

(2) A convention on technical co-operation was signed on Aug. 26, 1982.

(3) An agreement on nuclear co-operation was signed on May 12, 1983.

Brazil and Switzerland. (1) An extradition treaty was signed on July 23, 1932.

(2) A provisional trade agreement was signed on July 24, 1936.

(3) An agreement on co-operation in the use of nuclear energy for peaceful purposes was signed on May 26, 1965.

(4) A technical and scientific co-operation agreement was signed on April 26, 1968.

Chile and the Federal Republic of Germany. (1) A trade agreement signed on Feb. 2, 1951, and in force from April 1, 1953, was, on Dec. 10, 1984, extended until Dec. 31, 1986.

(2) An agreement on exchange of goods and payments signed on Nov. 2, 1956, and in force from Oct. 1, 1956, was, on Sept. 9, 1985, extended until Dec. 31, 1986.

(3) A cultural agreement signed on Nov. 20, 1956, and in force from May 24, 1959, was supplemented on April 4, 1959.

(4) A framework agreement on economic and technical co-operation was signed on Oct. 18, 1968, and came into force on Oct. 3, 1969.

(5) An agreement on co-operation in scientific research and technological development was signed on Aug. 28, 1970, and came into force on Oct. 23, 1970.

Chile and Iceland. A treaty of commerce and navigation was signed on Feb. 2, 1899, and additional articles were signed on Nov. 30, 1905.

Chile and Spain. (1) An agreement on trade and economic co-operation was signed on March 9, 1977.

(2) An agreement on technical co-operation was signed on May 27, 1982.

(3) A basic agreement on technological assistance was signed on Dec. 27, 1982.

Chile and Sweden. A trade and navigation agreement was signed on Oct. 30, 1936.

Chile and Switzerland. (1) A trade agreement was signed on Oct. 31, 1897, and a supplementary agreement on June 17, 1955.

(2) A framework agreement on scientific and technical co-operation was signed on Dec. 5, 1968.

Colombia and the Federal Republic of Germany. (1) A treaty of amity, commerce and navigation, signed with the German Reich on July 23, 1892, and in force from July 12, 1894, was on Dec. 18, 1978, extended until Dec. 31, 1980.

(2) A trade agreement signed on Nov. 9, 1957 and in force from Nov. 11, 1957, was amended on Aug. 11 and Nov. 20, 1969, and extended, on April 30, 1985, until Nov. 10, 1986.

(3) A cultural agreement was signed on Nov. 11, 1960, and came into force on Nov. 18, 1965.

(4) An agreement on technical co-operation, signed on March 2, 1965, came into force on April 26, 1965, and was amended with effect from Aug. 10, 1973.

Colombia and Spain. (1) A long-term agreement on economic, industrial and technical co-operation and a long-term trade agreement were signed on Jan. 24, 1979.

(2) A basic agreement on scientific and technical co-operation and a trade agreement were signed on June 27, 1979.

(3) A supplementary agreement on the use of nuclear energy for peaceful purposes was signed on Dec. 20, 1980.

(4) An agreement on scientific and technical co-operation was signed on Dec. 29, 1983.

Colombia and Sweden. An agreement on scientific, industrial and technical co-operation was signed on Feb. 14, 1984.

Colombia and Switzerland. (1) A treaty of friendship, establishment and commerce was signed on March 14, 1908.

(2) A technical and scientific co-operation agreement was signed on Feb. 1, 1967.

Costa Rica and the Federal Republic of Germany. (1) A technical co-operation agreement signed on July 23, 1965, came into force on Jan. 18, 1966.

(2) A cultural co-operation agreement signed on Aug. 29, 1979, came into force on May 21, 1981.

Costa Rica and Israel. In 1983 Israel provided training for security and intelligence units of the Costa Rican civil guard. Further Israeli security assistance for Costa Rica was reported subsequently (which led to the rupture of diplomatic relations with Costa Rica by six Islamic countries in April-May 1984).

Costa Rica and Spain. A technical co-operation agreement was signed on July 22, 1983.

Costa Rica and Switzerland. An agreement on technical and scientific co-operation was signed on Nov. 17, 1971.

The Dominican Republic and the Federal Republic of Germany. A treaty of amity, commerce and navigation was signed on Dec. 23, 1957, and came into force on June 3, 1960; on Dec 10, 1984, it was extended until Dec. 31, 1986.

The Dominican Republic and Spain. (1) A convention on extradition and judicial assistance in personal matters was signed on May 4, 1981.

(2) A convention on technical co-operation was signed on July 2, 1983.

Ecuador and France. Under a contract to purchase 18 French Mirage F-1 aircraft, concluded in November 1977, Ecuador became the first Latin American country to obtain this type of aircraft (although Mirage III or V aircraft were then already in the possession of Peru, Brazil, Argentina, Colombia and Venezuela).

Ecuador and the Federal Public of Germany. (1) A cultural agreement signed on March 13, 1969, came into force on March 22, 1970.

(2) A trade treaty signed on Aug. 1, 1953, and in force from Oct. 15, 1954, was, on Dec. 10, 1984, extended until Dec. 31, 1986.

(3) Another trade treaty signed on Aug. 1, 1953, and in force from Oct. 1, 1953, was, on April 30, 1985, extended until Oct. 15, 1986.

Ecuador and Spain. An agreement on the use of nuclear energy for peaceful purposes was signed on May 10, 1977.

(2) A technical co-operation agreement was signed on April 28, 1981.

Ecuador and Sweden. An agreement on economic, industrial, and technical co-operation was signed on July 2, 1981.

Ecuador and Switzerland. (1) A treaty of friendship, establishment and commerce and a provisional agreement on extradition were signed on June 22, 1888.

(2) A trade agreement was signed on Oct. 8, 1957.

(3) A technical and scientific co-operation agreement was signed on July 4, 1969, and was amended on Nov. 23–25, 1977.

El Salvador and the Federal Republic of Germany. (1) An agreement on most-favoured-nation treatment was signed on Oct. 31, 1952, and came into force on Jan. 3, 1953; it was extended on Dec. 10, 1984, until Dec. 31, 1986.

(2) An agreement on technical co-operation, signed on Sept. 24, 1963, and in force from Sept. 24, 1963, was, on July 8, 1964, extended until July 10, 1984.

(3) A cultural agreement signed on Dec. 2, 1971, came into force on June 30, 1972.

(4) Agreement was reached in July 1984 on West German financial and technical assistance worth $18,000,000.

El Salvador and Switzerland. (1) An extradition convention was signed on Oct. 30, 1883.

(2) A trade agreement was signed on Feb. 11, 1954.

Guatemala and the Federal Republic of Germany. Agreements on technical co-operation were concluded (i) on April 26, 1966, in force from May 24, 1966, and extended on June 24, 1971, (ii) on June 8, 1979, in force from Sept. 26, 1979.

Guatemala and Spain. A basic convention on technical co-operation was signed on Sept. 12, 1977, and ratified on Feb. 8, 1979.

Guatemala and Switzerland. A trade agreement was signed on April 1, 1955.

Haiti and the Federal Republic of Germany. A technical co-operation agreement was signed and came into force on April 25, 1978.

Haiti and Iceland. A treaty of commerce was signed on Oct. 21, 1937.

Haiti and Switzerland. A provisional trade agreement was signed on Dec. 23, 1936.

Honduras and the Federal Republic of Germany. An agreement on technical co-operation was signed on April 18, 1964, and came into force on Nov. 23, 1965.

Honduras and Switzerland. A technical co-operation agreement was signed on Dec. 7, 1978.

Mexico and France. An industrial and technical co-operation agreement signed on Dec. 11, 1978, and ratified early in February 1979, provided for French purchases of 5,000,000 tonnes of Mexican crude oil per annum for 10 years from Jan. 1, 1980. Economic, scientific and cultural co-operation agreements signed at the same time included one on "scientific and industrial development in the utilization of nuclear energy for exclusively peaceful ends". France also agreed to grant Mexico credits amounting to F1,000 million (or US$230,000,000).

Mexico and the Federal Republic of Germany. (1) A framework agreement on scientific and technological co-operation was signed on Feb. 6, 1974, and came into force on Sept. 4, 1975.

(2) An agreement on cultural co-operation was signed on Feb. 1, 1977, and came into force on March 3, 1978.

Mexico and Japan. Agreements concluded on Oct. 30–Nov. 4, 1978, including one of Japanese aid for economic and petroleum projects in Mexico.

Mexico and Spain. (1) An agreement on economic and commercial co-operation, a basic convention on scientific and technical co-operation, and a convention on cultural and educational co-operation were all signed on Oct. 14, 1977, with an additional protocol to the above basic convention being signed on Nov. 18, 1978.

(2) A supplementary agreement on co-operation in peaceful uses of nuclear energy was signed on Nov. 18, 1978.

(3) A treaty on extradition and mutual assistance in penal matters was signed on Nov. 21, 1978, and ratified on March 14, 1980.

(4) An agreement on co-operation in industry, energy and mining was also signed on Nov. 21, 1978.

(5) A cultural convention was signed on Dec. 12, 1980.

(6) An agreement on technical assistance was signed on Feb. 8, 1982.

(7) A further cultural agreement was signed on May 23, 1983.

Mexico and Sweden. (1) A memorandum on co-operation was signed on Jan. 30, 1979.

(2) An agreement on scientific and technical co-operation was signed on May 24, together with a memorandum on industrial and economic co-operation.

Mexico and Switzerland. A trade agreement was signed on Sept. 2, 1950.

Nicaragua and France. An agreement on the sale of French arms worth about $15,000,000 was concluded in January 1982.

Nicaragua and the Federal Republic of Germany. An agreement on technical co-operation signed on April 8, 1965, came into force on June 9, 1965.

Nicaragua and Spain. (1) An agreement on technical co-operation was signed on Dec. 20, 1974, and a supplementary agreement on Nov. 6, 1981.

(2) An agreement reached on July 5, 1983, provided for a Spanish loan worth US$41,300,000 to facilitate Nicaraguan purchases of equipment, fuel and raw materials.

Nicaragua and Sweden. An agreement on development co-operation from July 1, 1984, to June 30, 1986, was signed on May 10, 1984.

Panama and the Federal Republic of Germany. An agreement on technical co-operation was signed and came into force on Sept. 30, 1964.

Panama and Spain. (1) A convention on cultural co-operation was signed on May 2, 1979.

(2) A basic convention on scientific and technical co-operation was signed on June 3, 1983.

Paraguay and the Federal Republic of Germany. (1) An agreement on commercial traffic signed on July 25, 1955, came into force on Oct. 1, 1955; the addition of an EEC clause was agreed on Feb. 10–27, 1970; the agreement was, on Sept. 16, 1985, extended until Dec. 31, 1986.

(2) An agreement on most-favoured-nation treatment and legal protection, signed on July 30, 1957, and in force from March 6, 1959, was, on Dec. 10, 1984, extended until Dec. 31, 1986.

(3) An agreement on technical co-operation, signed on Nov. 21, 1967, and in force from June 11, 1968, was amended on Dec. 10, 1971, with effect from March 2, 1972.

Paraguay and South Africa. Agreements on cultural exchanges, co-operation in science and technology, economic co-operation and investment were signed on April 3, 1974 (with South Africa agreeing to provide technical assistance in oil, gas, bauxite and iron-ore prospecting in Paraguay).

Paraguay and Switzerland. (1) An extradition convention was signed on June 30, 1906.

(2) A trade agreement was signed on April 2, 1969.

(3) A technical and scientific co-operation agreement was signed on May 20, 1971.

Peru and the Federal Republic of Germany. (1) A trade agreement signed on July 7, 1951, and in force from June 14, 1962, was, on Dec. 10, 1984, extended until Dec. 31, 1986.

(2) A cultural agreement was signed on Nov. 20, 1964, and came into force on Jan. 14, 1966.

Peru and Spain. (1) A supplementary agreement on the use of nuclear energy for peaceful purposes was signed and came into force on July 19, 1976; an exchange of notes on Art. IV took place on Feb. 2, 1977.

(2) An agreement on economic co-operation was signed on March 22, 1982.

Peru and Switzerland. (1) A trade agreement was signed on July 20, 1953.

(2) A technical co-operation agreement was signed on Sept. 9, 1964.

Uruguay and the Federal Republic of Germany. (1) A trade agreement on most-favoured-nation treatment, signed on April 18, 1953, and in force from Oct. 10, 1954, was, on Dec. 10, 1984, extended until Dec. 31, 1986.

(2) An agreement on technical co-operation signed on July 22, 1974, came into force on Aug. 15, 1974.

Uruguay and Spain. (1) A supplementary agreement on co-operation in the use of nuclear energy for peaceful purposes was signed on March 30, 1979.

(2) An agreement on scientific and technological co-operation was signed on March 30, 1982.

Uruguay and Sweden. An agreement on commerce and navigation was signed on Aug. 13, 1936.

Uruguay and Switzerland. (1) An extradition treaty was signed on Feb. 27, 1923.

(2) A trade agreement was signed on March 4, 1938.

Venezuela and the Federal Republic of Germany. A framework agreement on scientific and technological co-operation was signed on Oct. 10, 1978, and came into force on Dec. 28, 1978.

Venezuela and Portugal. (1) During a visit to Portugal by the President of Venezuela on Nov. 29–30, 1976, a credit agreement was signed to assist Portuguese payment for shipments of Venezuelan oil, and Venezuela also agreed in principle to receive refugees from Portugal's former territories in Africa.

(2) During a visit to Venezuela by the President of Portugal in May 1978, agreements were signed on emigration and on economic and industrial co-operation between the two countries.

Venezuela and Spain. A supplementary agreement on scientific co-operation was signed on Jan. 21, 1983.

The 35 Independent States in the Americas

Countries	OAS	Commonwealth	ALADI	SELA	OCAS	Central American Common Market	Andean Group	NATO	Defence Treaty or Military Assistance Agreement with USA
Antigua and Barbuda	☆	☆							☆
Argentina	☆		☆	☆					☆
Bahamas	☆	☆							☆
Barbados	☆	☆		☆					
Belize		☆							
Bolivia	☆		☆	☆			☆		☆
Brazil	☆		☆	☆					☆
Canada		☆						☆	☆
Chile	☆		☆	☆					☆
Colombia	☆		☆	☆			☆		☆
Costa Rica	☆			☆	☆	☆			
Cuba				☆					
Dominica	☆	☆							
Dominican Republic	☆			☆					☆
Ecuador	☆		☆	☆			☆		
El Salvador	☆			☆	☆	☆			☆
Grenada	☆			☆					☆
Guatemala	☆			☆	☆	☆			☆
Guyana		☆		☆					
Haiti	☆			☆					☆
Honduras	☆			☆	☆	☆			☆
Jamaica	☆	☆		☆					
Mexico	☆		☆	☆					
Nicaragua	☆			☆	☆	☆			
Panama	☆			☆					☆
Paraguay	☆		☆	☆					☆
Peru	☆		☆	☆			☆		☆
St Christopher and Nevis	☆	☆							
St Lucia	☆	☆							
St Vincent and the Grenadines	☆	☆							
Suriname	☆			☆					
Trinidad and Tobago	☆	☆		☆					
United States	☆							☆	
Uruguay	☆		☆	☆					☆
Venezuela	☆		☆	☆			☆		

Dependent Territories in the Americas

United Kingdom. (1) Colonies with Executive Councils and Legislatures: Bermuda; British Virgin Islands; Cayman Islands; Falkland Islands (Malvinas); Montserrat; Turks and Caicos Islands.*

(2) Colony under direct British rule: Anguilla (since July 28, 1971).

France. French overseas departments and members of French Community: French Guiana; Guadeloupe; Martinique; St Pierre and Miquelon.

---

* The Turks and Caicos Executive Council was dissolved by the British Governor in July 1986 as an interim measure, after a public inquiry had found evidence of serious maladministration.

Denmark. Greenland (with a Legislative Council in West Greenland and two members of the Danish Parliament).

Netherlands. Integral parts of the Kingdom of the Netherlands with internal autonomy: Netherlands Antilles (Bonaire, Curaçao, Saba, St Eustatius, St Maarten); Aruba.

United States. Puerto Rico (an autonomous commonwealth since 1952 and associated with the USA, which has responsibility for defence and external affairs); US Virgin Islands (governed under the Revised Organic Act of the Virgin Islands of July 22, 1954, and having a US-appointed Governor and an elected Legislature).

15. The Middle East and Islamic States

This section covers the main multilateral and bilateral agreements concluded by Middle East and Islamic states and deals in particular with (i) the Arab League and its related organizations, (ii) co-operation between Islamic states and (iii) other treaties and agreements concluded by Middle East states, notably the 1979 Egyptian-Israeli peace treaty. (For environmental protection organizations and agreements relating to this area, see Section 5.)

Organizations of Arab States

The League of Arab States (the Arab League) and its Related Organizations

Address. 37 avenue Khereddine Pacha, Tunis, Tunisia.

Officer. Chedli Klibi (sec. gen.).

Founded. March 1945.

Membership. Algeria, Bahrain, Djibouti, Iraq, Jordan, Kuwait, Lebanon, Libya, Mauritania, Morocco, Oman, the Palestine Liberation Organization, Qatar, Saudi Arabia, Somalia, Sudan, Syria, Tunisia, the United Arab Emirates, the Yemen Arab Republic, and the People's Democratic Republic of Yemen. (The membership of Egypt was suspended in March 1979.)

History. A union of the Arab peoples was envisaged during World War I, when the Arabs rose in revolt against their Turkish rulers. Under the Peace Treaty of 1919, however, the Arab-populated former Turkish territories were split into separate states and, with the exception of the Hedjaz and Yemen, placed under British or French mandate. The Hedjaz was subsequently conquered in 1925 by King Ibn Saud, ruler of Nejd, and his enlarged realm renamed Saudi Arabia in 1932.

Between 1932 and 1946 the British and French mandated territories (Iraq, Lebanon, Syria and Transjordan) succeeded in gaining de facto independence. In 1943 and 1944 a series of bilateral meetings on the formation of an Arab

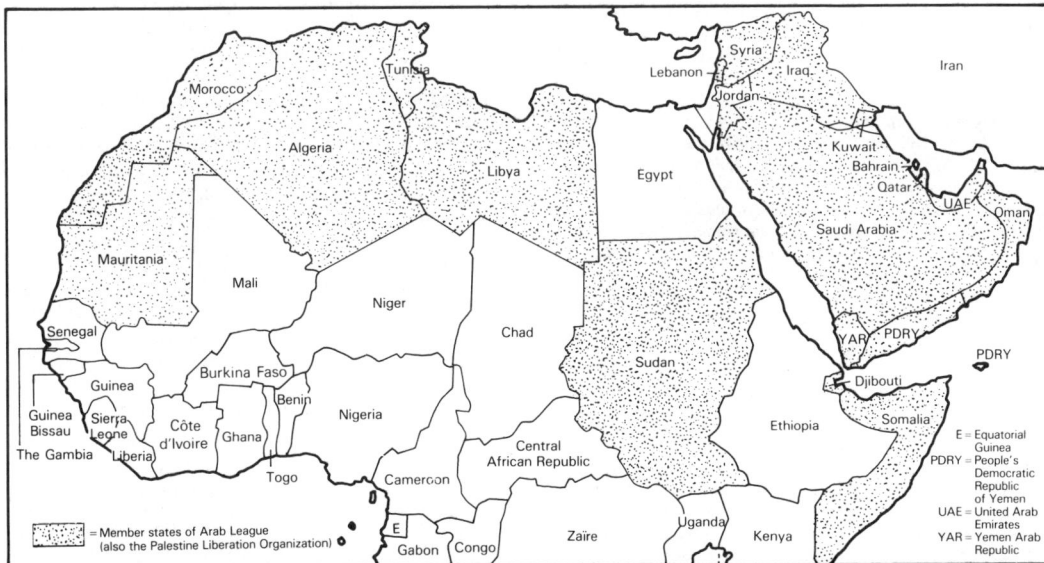

Map 11   Arab League

union took place between the various Arab states. This revival of Pan-Arabism differed in its aims from the movement against the Turks during World War I in that it envisaged the mutual co-operation of individual Arab states rather than the formation of a single Arab realm.

A sufficient measure of agreement was reached in these bilateral talks to make possible the convening of a conference of Arab nations. The conference was held at Alexandria from Sept. 25 to Oct. 7, 1944, and was attended initially by delegates from Egypt, Iraq, Lebanon, Syria and Transjordan, and later also by delegates from Saudi Arabia and Yemen and a representative of the Palestinian Arabs. On Oct. 7, 1944, a protocol providing for the establishment of a League of Arab States was signed by the Egyptian, Iraqi, Lebanese, Syrian and Transjordanian delegates.

A Pan-Arab Union Preparatory Committee, formed at the Alexandria conference and consisting of the Foreign Ministers of Egypt, Iraq, Lebanon, Saudi Arabia, Syria and Transjordan, and a Palestinian representative, met on Feb. 14, 1945, to approve and sign a constitution for the proposed Arab League.

The *Pact of the Union of Arab States* was finally signed on March 22, 1945, by representatives of Egypt, Iraq, Lebanon, Saudi Arabia, Syria, Transjordan and Yemen. It came into force on May 10, 1945. Later adherents to the pact were Libya (March 28, 1953); the Sudan (Jan. 9, 1956); Tunisia and Morocco (Oct. 1, 1958); Kuwait (July 20, 1961); Algeria (Aug. 16, 1962); People's Democratic Republic of Yemen (i.e. South Yemen) (December 1967); Bahrain and Qatar (Sept. 11, 1971); Oman (Sept. 29, 1971); the United Arab Emirates (Dec. 6, 1971); Mauritania (Oct. 13, 1973); Somalia (Feb. 14, 1974); Palestine (represented by the Palestine Liberation Organization, Sept. 9, 1976); and Djibouti (Sept. 3, 1977).

The main provisions of the pact are summarized below:

The League of Arab States. It was laid down that "a League of Arab States will be formed by those independent Arab countries who wish to join it"; that it would possess a Council on which all member states would be on an equal footing; that the Council would organize periodical meetings to improve and strengthen mutual relations, co-ordinate their political programmes with a view to mutual co-operation, and "safeguard by every possible means their independence and sovereign rights against all aggression"; that decisions of the Council would be binding on all member states (disputes between member states being referred to it for arbitration); that resort to force between member states in settling disputes was forbidden; and that no state would be permitted to follow a policy prejudicial to the League of Arab States as a whole.

Co-operation. The Arab states would co-operate closely on questions of economics and finance (commercial exchanges, customs duties, currency, agriculture and industry), communications (by land, sea and air), cultural matters, social and hygiene questions, and matters relating to nationality, passports and visas, extradition of criminals, etc. For these questions, commissions of experts would be formed, with a co-ordinating committee to direct their work.

Lebanon. The Arab states unanimously affirmed their respect for the independence and sovereignty of Lebanon within its existing frontiers.

Palestine. The declaration on Palestine stated: "The Committee considers that Palestine forms an important integral part of the Arab countries and the rights of the Arabs there cannot be infringed without danger to the peace and security of the Arab world. At the same time it considers that the engagements entered into by Great Britain, which include the cessation of Jewish immigration, the safeguarding of land belonging to the Arabs and the guiding of Palestine along the road to independence, constitute a portion of the rights acquired by the Arabs and that their execution will be a step towards the goal to which they aspire, towards the establishment of peace and security. It proclaims its support of the Palestine cause for the realization of legitimate aspirations and the safeguarding of lawful rights. It sympathizes as deeply as anyone with the Jews for the horrors and sufferings they have endured in Europe through the actions of certain dictatorial states. But it is careful not to confuse the case of these Jews with Zionism, for nothing would be more arbitrary or unjust than to wish to resolve the question of the Jews of Europe by another injustice of which the Arabs of Palestine, no matter to what religion or confession they belong, would be the victims."

It was also laid down that the Arab League would study means of collaboration with international organizations; that its permanent headquarters would be in Cairo (though the Council could meet in other cities); that the Council would hold biennial meetings (in March and October); that member states could withdraw from the League on one year's notice, or be expelled by unanimous vote for not fulfilling their obligations; and that the Pact could be modified by a two-thirds majority vote.

Organization. The Council is the supreme organ of the Arab League. It is composed of representatives of all the member states, each of which has one vote, and a representative of the Palestinian Arabs. The Council is responsible for the functioning of the League and the realization of its objectives. It meets twice a year; its unanimous decisions are binding on all member states; but majority decisions are binding only on those member states which have accepted them.

The Council is assisted by 16 committees dealing respectively with political, cultural, economic, social, legal and women's affairs, and with communications, information, health and human rights; grouping Arab oil experts and experts on co-operation; and including also two permanent committees (i) for administrative and financial affairs and (ii) for meteorology, as well as an organization for youth welfare and a conference of liaison officers (to co-ordinate activities among commercial attachés at Arab embassies).

The other organ of the Arab League is the Secretariat, whose main officers are the Secretary-General and five Assistant Secretaries-General. Among the functions of the Secretary-General are the preparation of a draft budget, which he submits to the Council, and the convening of the Council sessions.

Collective Security Pact

On June 17, 1950, a *Collective Security Pact* was signed by Egypt, Syria, Lebanon, Saudi Arabia and Yemen (i.e. the present Yemen Arab Republic). The draft of the pact had been unanimously approved by the Arab League Council on April 13, 1950.

The main provisions of the pact were as follows: (1) An armed attack on one of the signatories would be regarded as aggression against all. In the event of such an aggression, the other signatories would provide, individually or collectively, all military and other aid consistent with existing obligations under the League Charter and Art. 51 of the UN Charter. (2) A permanent Joint Defence Council, consisting of the Foreign Ministers and Defence Ministers of the signatories, would be set up to co-ordinate defensive measures. Its decisions, reached by majority vote, would be binding on all members. (3) A permanent committee composed of the signatories' Chiefs of Staff would draft joint defence plans and give technical advice on measures of collective defence. (4) An economic committee composed of the Ministers of National Economy would carry out economic measures complementary to the military decisions reached. (5) The signatories would give one another priority in the exchange of goods and services, and would co-operate in raising the economic level of the Arab world as a whole, measures envisaged for this purpose including the establishment of an Arab Central Bank and a Bureau of Statistics, the improvement of communications, the joint exploitation of the mineral wealth of the Arab countries, and the modernization of agricultural equipment.

The pact came into force on Aug. 22, 1964. Other Arab states became parties to it as follows: Jordan on March 31, 1952; Iraq on Aug. 7, 1952; Tunisia and the United Arab Emirates on Oct. 11, 1953; Morocco on June 13, 1961; Kuwait on Aug. 12, 1961; Algeria, Libya and Sudan on Sept. 11, 1964; Bahrain and Qatar on Nov. 14, 1971; the People's Democratic Republic of Yemen on Nov. 23, 1971; and Somalia on May 20, 1974. The Palestine Liberation Organization became a party on Nov. 21, 1976.

Arab Summit Conferences

Since 1964 the heads of Arab states have repeatedly met in conference to discuss questions of common political interest.

(1) The first such conference, which took place in Cairo on Jan. 13–16, 1964, styled itself the "Council of the Kings and Heads of State of the Arab League". All 13 Arab League members were represented. A communiqué issued at the end of the conference stated, inter alia, that the meetings had resulted in "unanimous agreement . . . to stop all campaigns by information media, to consolidate relations among the sister Arab states in order to ensure constructive joint co-operation, and to ward off expansionist aggressive ambitions threatening all Arabs alike". It was decided that a meeting of kings and heads of state should be held at least once a year.

(2) At the second Arab summit conference, held at Alexandria on Sept. 5–11, 1964, the organization of the meetings of heads of state was worked out in some detail. It was agreed that a conference of Arab heads of state should be held each year in September. A control commission, meeting monthly, would supervise the implementation of conference decisions. Every third meeting of this commission would be attended by the Prime Ministers of the Arab countries or their representatives.

Other decisions of the Alexandria conference included the setting up of a unified Arab military command, an Arab Court of Justice, and an Arab council for research into the use of atomic energy for peaceful purposes.

(3) In the course of their third conference, held in Casablanca on Sept. 13–17, 1965, the Arab heads of state signed a "solidarity pact" which was intended to put an end to propaganda attacks by one Arab state against another, and to bind the signatories not to support "subversive movements of any kind" against one another.

(4) The fourth summit conference, scheduled to open in Algiers on Sept. 5, 1966, was indefinitely postponed, after it had been announced that the United Arab Republic (i.e. Egypt) would not take part in a conference with "the reactionary Arab forces". However, it was eventually held in Khartoum from Aug. 28 to Sept. 3, 1967 but was boycotted by the Government of Syria. The conference dealt mainly with the aftermath of the Arab-Israeli war of June 1967. It reached agreement inter alia on the consolidation of Arab military strength, the need to eliminate "all foreign military bases from Arab territory" and "the principles of non-recognition and non-negotiation" in relations with Israel.

(5) The fifth summit conference, held in Rabat (Morocco) on Dec. 21–23, 1969, ended without agreement after President Nasser of the United Arab Republic had failed to obtain general Arab support for his proposal of a mobilization of all Arab resources against Israel.

(6) The sixth summit conference, held in Algiers on Nov. 26–28, 1973, without participation by Iraq and Libya, issued several declarations, including a political declaration in which it was stated that peace in the Middle East could be achieved only after fulfilment of two "paramount and unchangeable" conditions—(i) the evacuation by Israel of all occupied Arab territories and (ii) the re-establishment of the full national rights of the Palestinian people.

In a declaration on Africa it was stated that several decisions taken included (i) the severance by all African countries which had not already done so of diplomatic and other relations with South Africa, Portugal and Rhodesia; (ii) a strict embargo on deliveries of Arab oil to these countries; (iii) intensification of relations with "fraternal" African countries and the creation of an Arab fund for economic, social and technical assistance to these countries; and (iv) diplomatic and material support for African national liberation movements.

A resolution on Arab oil policy contained the decision "to continue the use of oil as a weapon . . . until the withdrawal from occupied Arab lands is realized and the rights of the Palestinian people are assured", in particular by maintaining an oil embargo against all states supporting Israel.

(7) At the seventh summit conference, held in Rabat on Oct. 26–29, 1974, it was unanimously decided to support the Palestine Liberation

Organization (PLO) as "the sole legitimate representative of the Palestinian people" in carrying out "its national and international responsibility within the framework of Arab obligations".

(8) The eighth summit conference was held in Cairo on Oct. 25–26, 1976, when all member countries except Iraq and Libya endorsed an agreement reached in Riyadh (Saudi Arabia) on Oct. 18 of that year by the heads of state of Lebanon, Syria, Egypt, Kuwait and Saudi Arabia and the PLO leader on a ceasefire in the civil war in Lebanon. The agreement provided inter alia for the establishment of an Arab security force of 30,000 men to secure observance of the ceasefire.

(9) The ninth summit conference, which took place in Baghdad on Nov. 2–5, 1978, and was attended by all Arab League member states except Egypt, agreed that all Arab countries would give "all forms of support, aid and facilities" to the PLO and that it was "not permitted for any side to act unilaterally in solving the Palestinian question in particular and the Arab-Zionist conflict in general". The conference accordingly rejected the agreements reached between Egypt and Israel at Camp David (USA) and all effects of these agreements [see page 415]. Moreover, it agreed (with only Morocco, Oman and the Sudan dissenting) that, if Egypt proceeded to the signature of a peace treaty with Israel, steps should be taken to remove the headquarters of the Arab League from Cairo and to impose economic sanctions on Egypt. It was also decided to establish a 10-year fund with annual resources of US$3,500 million to finance Jordan and Syria as well as the PLO in opposing the Camp David agreements.

Following the signing of the peace treaty between Egypt and Israel on March 26, 1979 [ibid.], Egypt announced on March 27 the "freezing" of its membership of the Arab League. Mahmoud Riad, the League's (Egyptian) Secretary-General, had already announced his resignation from this post on March 22.

A conference of Foreign and Economy Ministers of all Arab League member states except Egypt, Oman and the Sudan, held in Baghdad on March 27–31, 1979, imposed a wide-ranging political and economic boycott (including an oil embargo) by Arab states on Egypt. The measures agreed to by the conference included the withdrawal of Arab ambassadors from Egypt; the suspension of Egypt from the Arab League and all its specialized bodies as well as from a large number of joint Arab projects and undertakings, with effect from the date of Egypt's signing of the peace treaty; the temporary transfer of the Arab League's headquarters from Cairo to Tunis; and the eventual suspension of Egypt's membership of the non-aligned movement, of the Islamic Conference Organization and of the Organization of African Unity. The economic boycott was, however, not to apply to "those private national Egyptian institutions which are

confirmed as not to be dealing with the Zionist enemy".

Following this conference, diplomatic relations were broken off by Egypt with all other Arab countries with which it still had such relations, except with Somalia. Organizations which suspended Egypt's membership included the Organization of Arab Petroleum Exporting Countries (OAPEC) and its subsidiary organizations, the Arab Monetary Fund and the Islamic Conference Organization. Saudi Arabia announced on May 14, 1979, that the Arab Military Industries Organization (AMIO), which it had set up in May 1975 with Egypt, the United Arab Emirates and Qatar, would cease to exist as from July 1, 1979.

(10) At the tenth summit conference, held in Tunis on Nov. 19–21, 1979, the measures taken against Egypt were confirmed but no agreement was reached on a framework for a peace initiative which would constitute an alternative to the Egyptian-Israeli peace treaty.

(11) The eleventh summit conference, held in Amman on Nov. 25–27, 1980, showed the Arab League to be in disarray, as the conference was boycotted by six of its members (Syria, Algeria, Lebanon, Libya, the PLO and the People's Democratic Republic of Yemen) and no effective decision was taken on the question of Palestine.

The 15 member countries attending the conference agreed unanimously on the establishment of a long-term economic development fund aimed at reducing the unevenness of wealth among the Arab countries by making available $500,000,000 a year over the next decade from Iraq, Kuwait, Saudi Arabia, the United Arab Emirates and Qatar for financing social and economic projects, improving economic relations between Arab states and raising the standard of living of the less developed Arab countries.

In its final communiqué the conference inter alia called for an end to the war which had broken out in September 1980 between Iraq and Iran and also for recognition of Iraq's right to sovereignty over its territories and waters.

(12) The twelfth summit conference held in Fez (Morocco) on Sept. 6–9, 1982, concluded with the unanimous adoption of a peace plan (for the Arab-Israeli conflict) based largely on an earlier Saudi Arabian proposal (the Fahd plan). The Fez plan reaffirmed the League's recognition of the PLO as the "sole legitimate representative of the Palestinian people" and listed among its provisions the withdrawal of Israel from all Arab territories occupied in 1967, including Arab Jerusalem; the placing of the West Bank and the Gaza Strip under United Nations control for a transitional period of a few months; the establishment of an independent Palestinian state with Jerusalem as its capital; and a UN Security Council guarantee of peace among all states of the region.

The Fez conference also expressed support for the Arab side in the two wars in the Middle

East, i.e. for Iraq in the Iran-Iraq war and for Somalia in the Ethiopian-Somali conflict.

(The PLO endorsed the Fez peace plan at a meeting of the Palestinian National Council in Algeria on Feb. 14–23, 1983, as "the minimal programme" to be "complemented by military action".)

(13) A further summit conference held in Casablanca on Aug. 7–9, 1985, welcomed a joint peace initiative agreed in February 1985 between King Hussein of Jordan and Yassir Arafat, chairman of the PLO, and considered it to be compatible with the Fez peace plan of 1982.

Arab League Subsidiary Bodies

In addition to the bodies established under the above Collective Security Pact numerous subsidiary institutions and agencies have been set up by the Arab League, including the following:

(1) The **Council of Arab Economic Unity** (CAEU), with headquarters in Cairo, was set up on June 3, 1957, by a resolution of the Arab Economic Council of the Arab League and became operative on May 30, 1964. Following the suspension of Egypt's membership in 1979 [see page 400], its remaining members were Iraq, Jordan, Kuwait, Libya, Mauritania, the Palestine Liberation Organization, Somalia, the Sudan, Syria, the United Arab Emirates, the Yemen Arab Republic, and the People's Democratic Republic of Yemen. Its headquarters were moved to Amman (Jordan) in 1979.

The council has set up four Arab joint companies (for drug industries and medical appliances, for industrial investment, for livestock development and for mining); 10 specialized Arab federations (for cement and building materials, for chemical fertilizers producers, for engineering industries, for leather industries, for paper industries, for shipping industries, for textile industries, for railways, for seaports and for sugar); as well as three Arab unions (of fish producers, of food industries and of land transport).

(2) Under a resolution adopted by the Council in August 1964, an **Arab Common Market** was to be established in stages between Egypt, Iraq, Jordan and Syria, with customs duties and other taxes on trade between the four countries to be abolished by 1971 and with a full customs union and free movement of capital goods and people to follow later. Libya and the Sudan joined the project in June 1977.

(3) The **Arab League Educational, Cultural and Scientific Organization,** with headquarters in Tunis, was founded in 1964 to promote intellectual unity of the Arab countries through education. Within the organization's framework there are several institutions, among them an Institute for Arab Studies and Research Work, an Arab Literacy and Adult Education Organization, an Institute of Arab Manuscripts and a Permanent Bureau of Arabization (in Rabat, Morocco). In October 1974 it set up a workshop on a

marine science programme for the Red Sea in Bremerhaven (Federal Republic of Germany).

(4) The **Arab Labour Organization,** with headquarters in Baghdad, was established in 1965 to co-ordinate labour conditions throughout the Arab world.

(5) The **Arab Fund for Economic and Social Development,** established in Kuwait in 1968, began its operations in 1972. Its capital is subscribed by the member states of the Arab League, and its object is to participate in the financing of economic and social development projects in the Arab states.

(6) An **Arab Industrial Development Organization,** with headquarters in Baghdad, was originally set up in 1968 as the Industrial Development Centre for Arab States. It has inter alia assisted the development of sugar industries in Somalia and in the Yemen Arab Republic and of leather processing in Djibouti.

(7) The **Arab Bank for Economic Development in Africa (Banque Arabe pour le développement économique en Afrique, BADEA),** with headquarters in Khartoum, has as its subscribing countries the members of the Arab League except Djibouti, Somalia and the two Yemen Republics. It was set up under a decision taken at the sixth summit conference of the Arab League in Algiers in November 1973 [see above] to assist in the financing of development projects in African countries and to supply them with technical aid; it began its operations in 1975. As at Dec. 31, 1984, it had a paid-up capital of US$985,500,000.

(8) Integrated with the bank is the **Special Arab Assistance Fund for Africa** (originally the Arab Loan Fund for Africa), set up under a resolution adopted in January 1974 by a meeting of Arab Oil Ministers and the Oil Committee of the Organization of African Unity. The fund's object is to provide aid to African countries in serious balance-of-payments difficulties (including those caused by natural disasters and by the rise in oil prices since 1973).

(9) The **Arab Monetary Fund,** with headquarters in Abu Dhabi, was set up under an agreement approved by the Arab Economic Unity Council in Rabat in April 1976, and commenced operations on Feb. 2, 1977. Under its Articles of Agreement the fund was to function both as a fund and as a bank, and it was inter alia to correct balance-of-payments disequilibria among member states; to promote stability of exchange rates and also Arab economic integration; to pave the way for the creation of a unified Arab currency; and to co-ordinate the monetary policies of member states. The fund's unit of account is the Arab Accounting Dinar (AAD) equivalent to 3 Special Drawing Rights (SDR) of the International Monetary Fund. The fund grants loans at concessionary and uniform rates of interest. Each loan is normally not to exceed 400 per cent of a member's paid-up contribution. By the end of 1984 the total of approved loans amounted to AAD 248,060,000, with its total paid-up capital being AAD 268,250,000.

In 1981 the fund introduced an Inter-Arab Trade Facility to encourage trade among member countries. It enabled a member to borrow an amount of up to 100 per cent of its subscription paid in convertible currencies, but not more than its trade deficit with other members; such loans were to be repayable within three years.

Egypt's membership of the fund was suspended in April 1978.

(10) Other specialized agencies of the Arab League are an Arab Academy of Maritime Transport (in Sharjah), an Arab Centre for the Study of Dry Regions and Arid Territories (in Damascus), an Arab Civil Aviation Council (in Rabat), an Arab Organization of Administrative Sciences (in Amman), an Arab Organization for Agricultural Development (in Khartoum), an Arab Organization for Standardization and Metrology (in Amman), an Arab Postal Union (in Dubai), an Arab Satellite Communication Organization (in Riyadh), an Arab States Broadcasting Union (in Tunis), an Arab Telecommunications Union (in Baghdad), an Arab Organization for Social Defence against Crime (in Rabat), and an Inter-Arab Investment Guarantee Corporation (in Safat, Kuwait).

Arab Authority for Agricultural Investment and Development (AAAID)

Address. P.O.B. 2102, Khartoum, Sudan.
Founded. 1977.
Objects. To accelerate agricultural development in Arab countries and to ensure food security.
Membership. States providing capital: Algeria, Egypt, Iraq, Kuwait, Mauritania, Morocco, Qatar, Saudi Arabia, Somalia, the Sudan, Syria, and the United Arab Emirates.
Activities. In 1981–82 the AAAID launched companies to deal with dairy produce, poultry, starch and glucose, the processing of oil seeds, production of animal feed, and rehabilitation of an existing state farm.

Co-operation Council of the Arab States of the Gulf (Gulf Co-operation Council, GCC)

Address. P.O.B. 7153, Riyadh, Saudi Arabia.
Officer. Abdullah Yacoub Bishara (sec. gen.).
Founded. May 25, 1981.
History. The formation of the Council had first been suggested at an Islamic summit meeting in Taib (Saudi Arabia) in January 1981 and was agreed on Feb. 4–5, 1981, by Bahrain, Kuwait, Oman, Qatar, Saudi Arabia and the United Arab Emirates (UAE). The heads of state of the six countries held their first summit meeting in Abu Dhabi (UAE) on May 25–26, 1981, and approved the Council's statutes.
Objects. The Council's aims were defined in its statutes as follows:

"(i) To achieve co-ordination, integration and co-operation among the member states in all fields in order to bring about

their unity; (ii) to deepen and strengthen the bonds of co-operation existing among their peoples in all fields; (iii) to draw up similar systems in all fields . . . including economic and financial, trade, customs and transport, educational and cultural, health and social, information and tourism, and judicial and administrative; and (iv) to promote scientific and technical progress in the fields of industry, minerals, agriculture, sea wealth and animal wealth and to establish scientific research centres and collective projects and to encourage the private sector's co-operation for the good of the peoples of the member states."

Structure. The council's highest authority is its Supreme Council consisting of the six heads of state. There is a Ministerial Council composed of the Foreign Ministers of the member states. A secretary-general is appointed by the Supreme Council for three-year renewable terms. There are special committees for (i) economic and social planning; (ii) financial, economic and trade co-operation; (iii) industrial co-operation; (iv) oil; and (v) social and cultural services.

Further developments. In the Iran-Iraq war, which broke out in September 1980, the GCC supported Iraq. This eventually led to open threats against the independence of the GCC member states by the government of Iran.

At its second session held on Nov. 10–11, 1981, the GCC Supreme Council proposed to invite its Defence Ministers to set the priorities required to secure the member states' independence and sovereignty. The ensuing meeting of these ministers, held on Jan. 25–27, 1982, was reported to have agreed (in order to "combat the Iranian threat") to set up a rapid deployment force for the Gulf and to have recommended the establishment of (i) a joint air defence system based on the Saudi Arabian AWACS aircraft and (ii) a Gulf arms industry.

On Feb. 7, 1982, the GCC announced that its members would counter "Iranian sabotage acts aimed at wrecking the stability of the Gulf region" and urged Iran to "respond to international efforts for an equitable settlement of the war".

The GCC Council of (Foreign) Ministers agreed at a meeting held on March 7–9, 1982, that the GCC member states should sign a general security agreement between them.

On May 31, 1982, the GCC Foreign Ministers meeting in Riyadh issued a communiqué stating that "the achievement of a unified Arab position" (i.e. including that of Syria, which supported Iraq) was "the basic factor in ending the bloodshed between two Moslem countries".

A meeting of GCC Defence Ministers held on Oct. 11–12, 1982, was reported to have discussed the formation of a joint air defence system and arms industry (whereas the proposed establishment of a Gulf multinational force was said to have been opposed by Oman and Saudi Arabia). However, no formal agreements on these proposals were reached at the third session of the GCC Supreme Council held on Nov. 9–11, 1982.

This session, on the other hand, approved a number of economic measures discussed at a meeting of GCC Finance Ministers on June 19–20, 1982. These measures included a package constituting the first phase of a "unified economic agreement", providing inter alia for the abolition of customs duties on domestic products, greater freedom of nationals of member states to carry out economic activities in any of the member states, and an easing of travel regulations. The session also endorsed a proposal to set up a Gulf Investment Corporation with a capital of US$1,200 million and the conversion of the Saudi Arabian Foundation for Specifications and Measures into an establishment covering all the GCC states.

A meeting of Oil Ministers held under GCC auspices on Oct. 14, 1982, strongly criticized overproduction and price-cutting by OPEC member states, and destabilizing influences on the oil market resulting from the refusal of African oil producers to lower their price differentials and the undercutting of OPEC prices by Mexico and the North Sea producers.

At a meeting of GCC Communications Ministers held on May 30, 1983, it was decided to establish an integrated telecommunications network between all member states and to form a permanent ministerial communications committee.

At a meeting held on Aug. 22–23, 1983, the GCC Council of (Foreign) Ministers issued a warning that GCC member states would "sever political, economic and other ties" with any state which resumed diplomatic relations with Israel (as some African countries had done or were about to do).

The fourth session of the GCC Supreme Council, held on Nov. 7–9, 1983, approved the expansion of the joint economic agreement to include tourism, maintenance, pharmacy and craft industries (which subsequently came into effect on March 1, 1984) and the unification of utilities charges.

GCC Interior Ministers approved, at a meeting on Nov. 28–29, 1983, the standardization of passports and free movement for GCC citizens between member states.

At a meeting of Oil Ministers held on Nov. 1, 1984, plans were approved for the construction of a pipeline to carry oil from the Northern United Arab Emirates to Fujairah (on the Gulf of Oman) to bypass the Strait of Hormuz.

The fifth session of the GCC Supreme Council, held on Nov. 22–29, 1984, noted with approval a proposal by the six heads of state that priority should be given to the use of products from GCC states when allocating contracts for major projects. Although no mention was made of a joint defence strategy, the session agreed to establish a joint defence force as a temporary expedient to be reviewed periodically. (During 1984 the GCC navies carried out a number of joint exercises.)

The sixth session of the GCC Supreme Council, held on Nov. 3–6, 1985, took decisions on economic, defence and regional issues. It reaffirmed the principle that the security of the GCC countries was "indivisible"; it called on Iran to respect UN Security Council resolutions on freedom of navigation; and it declared the "readiness of GCC states to continue their endeavours with the parties concerned to end this destructive war [between Iran and Iraq] in a manner that safeguards the legitimate rights and interests of the two sides, in order to bring about the establishment of normal relations among the Gulf states".

Gulf Organization for Industrial Consulting

Address. P.O.B. 5114, Doha, Qatar.
Officer. Dr Abdullah al-Moajil (sec. gen.).
Founded. 1976.
Membership. Bahrain, Iraq, Kuwait, Oman, Qatar, Saudi Arabia and the United Arab Emirates.

Maghreb Permanent Consultative Committee

At a conference held in Tangiers on Nov. 26 and 27, 1964, the Economy Ministers of Algeria, Libya, Morocco and Tunisia decided to establish a permanent joint consultative committee to harmonize economic development plans. Libya withdrew from the committee in 1970, and Mauritania joined it in 1975.

The highest authority of the committee (with headquarters in Tunis) is the conference of Ministers of Economy. There is a permanent committee consisting of a President and a delegate from each of the member countries, and there is also a secretariat.

The committee has set up specialized groups located in various cities in the member countries, for industrial studies, administrative studies and research, tourism, co-ordination of posts and telecommunications, transport and communications, co-ordination of national accounts and statistics, employment and labour, normalization, insurance and reinsurance, electric energy, and development of stockbreeding.

Co-operation between Islamic Countries

Organization of the Islamic Conference

Address. P.O.B. 178, Jeddah, Saudi Arabia.
Officer. Habib Chatti (sec. gen.).
Founded. May 1971.
Membership. Algeria, Bahrain, Bangladesh, Brunei, Burkina Faso, Cameroon, Chad, the Comoros, Djibouti, Egypt, Gabon, The Gambia, Guinea, Guinea-Bissau, Indonesia, Iran, Iraq, Jordan, Kuwait, Lebanon, Libya, Malaysia, Maldives, Mali, Mauritania, Morocco, Niger, Oman, Pakistan, the Palestine Liberation Organization, Qatar, Saudi Arabia, Senegal, Sierra Leone, Somalia, the Sudan, Syria, Tunisia, Turkey, Uganda, the United Arab Emirates, the Yemen Arab Republic and the People's Democratic Republic of Yemen.
Observers. The Turkish Republic of Northern Cyprus (known as the Turkish Federated State of Cyprus until Nov. 15, 1983) and Nigeria. (The membership of Egypt was suspended from May 1978 until January 1984, and that of Afghanistan in January 1980.)
Objects. As set out in the organization's charter adopted in 1972, its aims included the promotion of Islamic solidarity among its member states and the consolidation of co-operation among them; the elimination of racial segregation and discrimination and of colonialism in all its forms; and support for the people of Palestine in their struggle to regain their rights and to liberate their land.
History. A non-governmental Afro-Asian Islamic Organization had been established in Jakarta (Indonesia) in 1965, with delegates from the Soviet Union and China participating; the Chinese Moslems, however, had left this organization in 1966. The first congress of the organization was held by delegates from 25 countries meeting in Bandung (Indonesia) on Oct. 6–10, 1970, when it was decided to change the organization's name to International Islamic Organization, as it included Moslems from outside Africa and Asia. Soviet Moslems were not invited to this congress, which adopted resolutions condemning communism in Moslem countries as "unjust and unlawful" and demanding religious freedom for the Moslem minorities in the Soviet Union and China.

An Islamic summit conference held in Rabat on Sept. 22–25, 1969, was attended by representatives of 25 countries out of 36 invited. Those present included Iran and Turkey but not Iraq and Syria; India was, upon a decision by the conference, admitted as a full member but was subsequently asked to withdraw because the President of Pakistan had refused to attend a conference at which India would be represented.

A first conference of Islamic Foreign Ministers was held in Jeddah on March 23–26, 1970, when it was decided to set up, in Jeddah, a permanent secretariat under a Secretary-General of what was to become the Organization of the Islamic Conference.

The second conference of Foreign Ministers, held in Karachi (Pakistan) on Dec. 26–28, 1970, condemned the Israeli occupation of the territory of three Arab countries as a violation of the UN Charter, and denounced Zionism as a "racial, aggressive and expansionist movement . . . constituting a permanent threat to world peace".

The fourth conference of the organization's Foreign Ministers, held in Benghazi (Libya) on March 24–27, 1973, decided inter alia to send a mission to the Philippines and to the Vatican with a view to ending the Philippine Government's alleged persecution of Philippine Moslems; however, this and later efforts made in this respect by the organization failed to end the armed confrontation between the (Moslem) Moro National Liberation Front and the Philippine armed forces.

An Islamic summit meeting, held in Lahore (Pakistan) on Feb. 22–24, 1974, affirmed the solidarity of the Islamic peoples and issued a *Declaration of Lahore* expressing full support for all Arab countries "to recover, by all means available, all their occupied land" and calling for "the complete Israeli withdrawal from occupied Arab territories and the full restitution of the national rights of the Palestinian people". The meeting also called for the extension of support and solidarity by Moslem countries to each other in their national development efforts and appointed a committee to devise ways and means of inter alia ending the exploitation of developing countries by developed ones and achieving mutual economic co-operation.

The sixth conference of Foreign Ministers, held in Jeddah on July 12–16, 1975, unanimously decided to seek Israel's expulsion from the United Nations; called on all Moslem states to break off political, economic and cultural relations with Israel and for the recovery of the Arab sector of Jerusalem from Israel; and decided to form a permanent committee to pursue the question of the future of Jerusalem.

The seventh conference of Foreign Ministers, held in Istanbul on May 12–15, 1976, re-affirmed earlier resolutions on the Middle East and also adopted a resolution on Cyprus, stating that the two communities in that island were "equal partners in an independent and non-aligned Republic of Cyprus" and that the Islamic Turkish community in Cyprus, which would seek a political and peaceful solution on the basis of a federal constitution, had the right to participate in and address every international meeting at which the Cyprus question was discussed.

Resolutions adopted at the eighth conference of Foreign Ministers in Tripoli (Libya) on May 16–21, 1977, included (i) a condemnation of France for holding "sham referendums" in Mayotte (in the Comoros) which had resulted in a majority favouring Mayotte's continued status as part of France (and rejecting its adherence to the—Islamic—Republic of the Comoros); and (ii) a call for the establishment of nuclear-free zones in Africa, the Middle East and South-East Asia, and the Indian Ocean.

At the ninth conference of Foreign Ministers, which ended in Dakar (Senegal) on April 28, 1978, the organization's support for the Palestinian cause was reaffirmed and the United States was condemned for its military and financial aid to Israel and was asked to grant recognition to the Palestine Liberation Organization. The conference also decided to open a permanent bureau of the organization for West Africa in Dakar.

At an extraordinary meeting of Islamic Foreign Ministers, called on a proposal by Saudi Arabia, held in Islamabad (Pakistan) on Jan. 27–29, 1980, and attended by all member states of the organization except Afghanistan, Guinea-Bissau, Syria, the Turkish Federated State of Cyprus, Upper Volta (now Burkina Faso) and the People's Democratic Republic of Yemen, the 36 member states represented unanimously approved a resolution which strongly condemned the Soviet Union's intervention in Afghanistan and suspended the latter's membership of the organization.

The resolution inter alia (i) condemned the "Soviet military aggression against the Afghan people" as a flagrant violation of international laws, "an aggression against human rights and a violation of the freedoms of people which cannot be ignored"; (ii) demanded the immediate and unconditional withdrawal of all Soviet troops from Afghanistan; (iii) urged support for the Afghan people and aid for Afghan refugees; and (iv) declared complete solidarity with the Islamic countries neighbouring Afghanistan against any threat to their security and wellbeing.

The meeting also adopted various other resolutions, in particular:

(i) A resolution condemning "the efforts of certain great powers to exert various forms of pressures on the Islamic states, threatening the use of force against them to interfere in their internal affairs and to establish military bases on their territories to protect the interests of those great powers and their strategic plans in the context of the struggle raging between them"; (ii) a resolution on the "increasing tension" between the United States and Iran, affirming "the vital stake of the Islamic Conference in the sovereignty, territorial integrity and political independence" of Iran, expressing the sincere wish that the outstanding problems between the two countries should be solved by peaceful means, and declaring "solidarity with the Moslem people of Iran in choosing whatever system it prefers on the tenets of Islam as a system of social and political life"; and (iii) a resolution condemning "armed aggression" against Somalia, denouncing the presence of "the military forces of the Soviet Union and some of its allies" in the Horn of Africa, calling for the total and unconditional withdrawal of these foreign troops and for the liquidation of foreign bases in the Horn of Africa and the Red Sea, and urging the material and moral strengthening of the Islamic peoples in the Horn of Africa and provision of assistance to refugees in the area, particularly the Eritrean people.

The 11th conference of Islamic Foreign Ministers, held in Islamabad (Pakistan) on May 17–22, 1980, adopted—with objections lodged by Libya, the Palestine Liberation Organization, Syria and the People's Democratic Republic of Yemen—a resolution reaffirming the resolutions approved at the extraordinary session in January 1980 and reiterating the demand for the immediate, total and unconditional withdrawal of all Soviet forces from Afghanistan. The session also appointed a three-member committee (comprising The Gambia, Pakistan and Saudi Arabia) to administer a fund for assistance to Afghan insurgents and refugees, to which the Saudi Arabian Government had contributed US$25,000,000.

The session also adopted a resolution calling upon all Moslem nations to guard against efforts to establish foreign military bases on their territories and reaffirming their determination to remain outside the influence of (both Eastern and Western) foreign powers. In another resolution the session denounced "the continued presence of Soviet, Cuban and other troops from outside the continent in the Horn of Africa" and undertook to "support and strengthen the Somali Democratic Republic morally, politically and materially to enable it to withstand foreign pressure and aggression" (with reservations being expressed by Algeria, Libya, Mali, the Palestine Liberation Organization and both Yemens).

Following the outbreak of the Iran-Iraq war the organization's Foreign Ministers decided on Dec. 26, 1980, to charge the President of Pakistan with leading a good offices committee to Iran and Iraq. This committee visited both Tehran and Baghdad on Sept. 28–30, 1980, but was unable to achieve any reconciliation between the two sides.

On June 20–21, 1980, the committee met representatives of the (anti-Soviet) Islamic Alliance for the Liberation of Afghanistan who, however, refused to negotiate with the Soviet Union or the Soviet-backed regime in Afghanistan. The two sides therefore reached no agreement, with the committee restating its aim of seeking a political solution to the Afghan conflict on the basis of the immediate and unconditional withdrawal of Soviet troops and the achievement of political independence and non-alignment of Afghanistan.

The third Islamic summit conference, held in Taif (Saudi Arabia) on Jan. 25–29, 1981 (and attended neither by Iran nor by Libya), issued, on Jan. 28, a Mecca declaration which affirmed the organization's determination to find a political solution to the Afghanistan issue and called for co-operation with the UN Secretary-General and his special envoy to find a just solution. On the Iran-Iraq conflict the conference decided to enlarge the good offices committee and to set up an Islamic force to implement a ceasefire if necessary.

The enlarged good offices committee, led by the President of Guinea, visited Baghdad and Tehran in March 1982, but its mediation attempt was also unsuccessful, as were further such visits made in April, June and September 1982.

The fourth summit conference of the organization was held in Casablanca on Jan. 16–19, 1984, again without Iran being represented. The conference decided to invite Egypt to resume its membership of the organization, suspended since May 1979; to express support for the Turkish Republic of Northern Cyprus in its efforts to secure equal status with the Greek Cypriots; and to send a delegation to Tehran to try to persuade the Iranian government to consider a peaceful solution to its conflict with Iraq.

The conference also adopted a Casablanca charter which stressed the need for improved solidarity between Islamic states; provided for the creation of committees for "regional reconciliation and concord" to "settle differences and conflicts" between members of the organization; and reaffirmed the organization's commitment to work for the liberation of Jerusalem and other Arab lands occupied by Israel.

Egypt subsequently rejoined the organization on Jan. 30, 1984, when its President explained that Egypt would respect its commitments (which was interpreted as involving continued adherence to its treaty with Israel—see below).

On the basis of an earlier resolution of the organization instructing all member states to sever all diplomatic, political, economic and cultural ties with any country which had an embassy in Jerusalem or which recognized Israeli sovereignty over the city, the organization's Al-Quds (Jerusalem) Committee recommended on April 20, 1984, that all member states should sever diplomatic relations with Costa Rica and El Salvador, both of which had chosen to locate their embassies in Jerusalem.

The Syrian Foreign Ministry announced on May 21, 1984, that it had suspended its membership of the Jerusalem committee in protest against contacts between the governments of Morocco and Israel.

The good offices committee, pursuing its efforts to move towards an end to the Iran-Iraq war, met on July 18–19, 1984, when it called on both sides to end attacks on shipping in the Gulf and authorized the President of The Gambia (its chairman) to visit Baghdad and Tehran to seek common ground between the two countries. However, this further attempt was also unsuccessful.

Subsidiary bodies. The organization has set up the following bodies:

The **Al-Quds (Jerusalem) Committee,** established in 1975, to publicize the Islamic point of view on the status of Jerusalem.

The **Committee of Islamic Solidarity** with the People of the Sahel, to provide food aid to drought-stricken countries in that region.

The **International Commission for the Islamic Heritage,** founded in 1980.

The **International Islamic Law Commission,** founded in 1982.

The **International Islamic News Agency,** founded in December 1972.

The **Islamic Capitals Organization.**

The **Islamic Centre for Development of Trade,** set up in 1981.

The **Islamic Centre for Statistical, Economic and Social Research,** formed in 1978.

The **Islamic Centre for Technical and Vocational Training and Research,** established in 1979.

The **Islamic Chamber of Commerce, Industry and Commodity Exchange,** founded in 1979.

The **Islamic Civil Aviation Council.**

The **Islamic Commission for Economic, Cultural and Social Affairs,** which meets twice a year.

The **Islamic Commission for the International Crescent.**

The **Islamic Development Bank,** which was set up in Jeddah in 1974 and began operations in 1975. Its capital is contributed by oil-producing member coutries; adhering to Islamic principles, the bank does not grant loans and credits for interest (except at a nominal commission) but takes up equity participation in development projects, while it also finances foreign trade. The bank's unit of account is the Islamic Dinar (ID), equal to 1 Special Drawing Right of the International Monetary Fund. As at June 30, 1984, the bank had subscriptions totalling ID 1,952,020,000.

The **Islamic Foundation for Science, Technology and Development (IFSTAD),** founded in 1981.

The **Islamic Jurisprudence Academy.**

The **Islamic Shipowners' Association.**

The **Islamic Solidarity Fund,** set up in 1977. Contributions to this fund, announced in May 1977, included $15,000,000 from Saudi Arabia, $6,000,000 from Libya and $3,000,000 from the United Arab Emirates.

The **Islamic States Broadcasting Organization,** established in 1975.

The **Research Centre for Islamic History, Art and Culture,** set up in 1982.

The **World Centre for Islamic Education,** founded in 1980.

Regional Economic Co-operation

Address. P.O.B. 3273, Tehran, Iran.
Officer. Behcet Tureman (sec. gen.).
Founded. 1964 (under the name of Regional Co-operation for Development, RCD).
Membership. Iran, Pakistan and Turkey.
Activities. Results of co-operation by the three member countries of the RCD—Iran, Pakistan and Turkey—included a Regional Cultural Institute, a tripartite Shipping Conference and a joint Chamber of Commerce and Industry. A tripartite agreement on tourism and bilateral agreements on the abolition of visas for tourists were concluded at the first meeting of the Ministerial Council held in October 1964.

A joint declaration signed by the Shah of Iran, the Prime Minister of Pakistan and the President of Turkey in Izmir (Turkey) on April 22, 1976, provided for increased economic, trade, industrial and cultural co-operation between the three nations and for the establishment of (i) a free trade area through the gradual reduction of tariffs within 10 years and (ii), under a protocol on trade, an RCD investment bank promoting and financing projects of a regional character with participation by the private sector. A *Treaty of Izmir*, implementing the above declaration, was signed in Tehran on March 12, 1977.

It was, however, not until July 1984, that officials of the three countries met again to discuss plans to revitalize the organization under its new name.

Turkish-Pakistani Agreement on "Friendly Co-operation"

An agreement on "friendly co-operation" between Turkey and Pakistan had been signed in Karachi on April 2, 1954. The agreement, which remains valid for consecutive periods of five years if no notice of denunciation is given one year before the end of a five-year period, is open to other countries. It came into force on June 12, 1954.

The main provisions of the agreement are given below:

Art. 1. The contracting parties undertake to refrain from intervening in any way in the internal affairs of each other, and from participating in any alliance or activities directed against the other.

Art. 2. They will consult on international matters of mutual interest and, taking into account international requirements and conditions, co-operate to the maximum extent.

Art. 4. Consultation and co-operation between the contracting parties in the field of defence shall cover the following points:

(*a*) Exchange of information for the purpose of deriving joint benefit from technical experience and progress.

(*b*) Endeavours to meet, as far as possible, the requirements of the parties in the production of arms and ammunition.

(*c*) Studies and determination of the manner and extent of co-operation which might be effected between them, in accordance with Article 51 of the UN Charter, should an unprovoked attack occur against them from outside.

Art. 5. Each contracting party declares that none of the international engagements in force between it and any third state is in conflict with the provisions of this agreement, and that this agreement shall not affect, and cannot be interpreted as affecting, the aforesaid engagements. They undertake not to enter into any international engagement in conflict with this agreement.

A new economic and technical co-operation agreement between the two countries was signed on Nov. 20, 1975.

Treaties and Agreements concluded by Middle East States

Agreements between Arab Countries

Algeria and Libya. (1) At a meeting between the Algerian and Libyan leaders in Tripoli on Dec. 28–29, 1975, it was agreed that "any attack against either of the two revolutions [of Algeria and Libya] will be considered by the other as an attack against itself" and that efforts should be intensified to establish institutional links between the two countries.

(2) An agreement reached in January 1982 provided for the co-ordination of development, economic and social plans; a programme of action for industrial integration involving new joint industrial projects; development of passenger and goods transport and of communications; increased research in irrigation (with the formation of a joint company for drilling wells); and co-operation in many other areas, including banking, insurance, foreign trade, hydrocarbons, manpower supply, energy, and agriculture in arid areas.

(3) On March 27, 1983, agreement was reached on "co-ordinating efforts to confront the imperialist onslaught against the Arab nations" by means of joint meetings of the Algerian National Assembly and the Libyan General People's Congress as well as the two countries' cabinets and party committees.

Algeria and Mauritania. An agreement on border demarcation (superseding an earlier agreement of December 1983) was signed on April 9, 1983.

Algeria and Morocco. A treaty on the delimitation of the two countries' common frontier was signed on June 25, 1972.

Algeria and Tunisia. (1) A 20-year "treaty of brotherhood, good neighbourliness, and co-operation" between Algeria and Tunisia was signed in Tunis on Jan. 6, 1970. In September 1980 the two Governments agreed on the immediate reactivation of the joint commission established under the 1970 treaty with a view to promoting closer political, economic and cultural relations between the two countries.

(2) A 20-year treaty of friendship and concord, signed on March 20, 1983, was to lay the foundations for co-operation between the two states and to resolve a dispute over the delineation of their common border. In the treaty the parties undertook to abstain from the threat or use of force to settle their differences and not to tolerate the presence on their territory of any group aiming at the overthrow of the other regime. The treaty was to be open to adhesion by other states of the Maghreb (i.e. Morocco). Mauritania acceded to this treaty later in 1983.

Bahrain and Jordan. An economic co-operation agreement was signed in February 1985.

Bahrain and Kuwait. As from March 1, 1979, Bahrain and Kuwait abolished all customs duties on goods produced in the other country, and a permanent joint organization was established for the importation of goods from all Gulf countries.

Bahrain, Oman and the United Arab Emirates. Agreements were reached in December 1978 on the establishment of a unified economic system between the three states.

Bahrain and Saudi Arabia. After Bahrain had foiled an attempted coup (which the Saudi Arabian Foreign Minister described as "engineered by Iran and directed against Saudi Arabia"), a security agreement was concluded by the two countries on Dec. 20, 1981.

Djibouti and Somalia. A co-operation agreement was signed on Jan. 22, 1986.

Egypt and Iraq. In an agreement reached in Paris in early December 1982 it was decided to organize "joint resistance" to Iran.

Egypt and Jordan. (1) A trade agreement was concluded in December 1983.
(2) In October 1984 it was decided to set up a "higher joint committee" under the joint chairmanship of the two countries' Prime Ministers to discuss co-operation in trade, agriculture, labour and transport.
(3) Agreements were concluded on Oct. 23, 1984, on the establishment of a development bank and of a joint shipping enterprise.
(4) A trade protocol signed on Oct. 25, 1984, provided for free trade worth US$150,000,000 between the two countries.
(5) A number of agreements were reached on April 20–22, 1985, on improving co-operation in trade, information, tourism and culture.

Egypt and Saudi Arabia. A mutual defence treaty was signed on Oct. 27, 1955.

Egypt and the Sudan. (1) A 25-year joint defence agreement was signed in Alexandria on July 15, 1976; it provided (i) for the two countries to regard an attack on either of them as aggression against both and (ii) for the setting-up of a common defence council and a joint committee of chiefs of staff. The agreement was activated on Jan. 5, 1977, by a declaration of the two countries' Ministers of War.
(2) At a meeting of the Presidents of Egypt, the Sudan and Syria in Khartoum a joint declaration was signed on Feb. 28, 1977, whereby the Sudan joined an Egyptian-Syrian unified political command agreed upon on Dec. 21, 1976 (but since superseded by Syria's rejection of the 1979 Egyptian-Israeli peace treaty—see page 415).
A first joint congress of the Egyptian and Sudanese People's Assemblies (Parliaments) was held in Cairo on Oct. 24-31, 1977, and agreed on a political action programme and economic integration between the two countries.
(Following the signing of the Egyptian-Israeli peace treaty co-operation between Egypt and the Sudan was temporarily interrupted in 1979–81.)
(3) A charter of integration of the two countries was signed by their Presidents in Khartoum on Oct. 12, 1982, to last for a 10-year trial period

and to provide for political and economic integration and close co-ordination in foreign policy, security and development. Institutions to be established under the charter were (i) a Higher Council for Integration, to deal with economic, political, military, social and cultural policies and to approve projects to be endorsed by (ii) a Nile Valley Parliament of 60 members (20 from each of the two legislatures and 10 appointed by each President), which would meet twice a year from December 1982 alternately in Khartoum and Cairo and which would submit its recommendations to the Higher Council and to the Egyptian and Sudanese People's Assemblies (if legislation were required); and (iii) a Joint Fund with a budget to be approved by the Nile Valley Parliament.
Following the deposition of President Jafaar al Nemery of the Sudan on April 6, 1985, the new Sudanese Prime Minister was on May 22, 1985, reported to have stated that the existing accords with Egypt would be abrogated as they did "not reflect the will of the people". However, on March 30, 1986, the Sudanese government reaffirmed the principle of integration with Egypt but decided at the same time to dissolve the existing integration bodies in the Sudan.

Egypt and the United Arab Emirates. An agreement on co-operation in agricultural sciences and technology was concluded in June 1973.

Iraq and Saudi Arabia. (1) A 10-year treaty of alliance between the two countries was signed in Baghdad on April 3, 1936. (It was open to accession by other independent Arab countries and was in fact joined by Yemen on April 7 of that year—see below.)
(2) An agreement was concluded on July 2, 1975, on the equal division between Iraq and Saudi Arabia of a neutral zone of about 2,500 square miles to the west of the western end of Kuwait's frontier with the two states. (The frontier between Iraq and Saudi Arabia had been defined by the Treaty of Mohammar in May 1922; the neutral zone had been established later, and in May 1938 Iraq and Saudi Arabia had signed an agreement on its administration.) The agreement remained unratified, but it was confirmed in a frontier treaty signed on Dec. 26, 1981.

Iraq and the United Arab Emirates. A cultural agreement was signed in September 1975, and a trade and economic agreement in June 1978.

Jordan and Saudi Arabia. On Aug. 29, 1962, it was announced that King Hussein of Jordan and King Saud of Saudi Arabia had concluded agreements on military, political and economic co-operation. The agreements included the establishment of joint Saudi-Jordanian military command. In a communiqué the two countries pledged themselves to work for the achievement of Arab rights in Palestine.

Kuwait and Saudi Arabia. (1) An agreement signed in 1942 with the United Kingdom, acting on behalf of Kuwait, provided for friendship and neighbourly relations as well as control of the frontier between Saudi Arabia and Kuwait.

(2) The Kuwaiti Foreign Minister acknowledged on June 19, 1984, that the two sides were co-operating fully in air defence matters and that Kuwait was benefiting from information gathered by Saudi Arabia's AWACS aircraft.

Kuwait and the United Arab Emirates. An agreement on cultural and health co-operation was signed in 1972, and an economic co-operation agreement in July 1973.

Lebanon and Saudi Arabia. In September 1984 it was reported that Lebanon had received at least US$450,000,000 in reconstruction aid from Saudi Arabia.

Libya and Morocco. A treaty of federation between Libya and Morocco was signed in Oudja (Morocco) on Aug. 13, 1984.

The treaty provided inter alia that the federation would be known as the Arab-African Federation, would have a presidency jointly held by King Hassan II of Morocco and Col. Gadaffi, the Libyan leader, and would also have a general secretariat, presidential advisory councils on defence, economic, educational and political affairs, a federal assembly, an executive committee comprising the Moroccan cabinet and the Libyan General People's Committee, a federal court to adjudicate on any disputes and administrative and development budgets. It was to have "absolute respect" for the sovereignty of both countries; any aggression against one of the two countries was to be regarded as aggression against the other; and both parties were allowed to sign similar or identical pacts with third parties, "other states of the Arab nation or the African community" being invited to join the federation. The treaty was declared ratified by both parties on Sept. 1, 1984.

The federal assembly, composed of 60 members each from the Moroccan parliament and the Libyan General People's congress, held its inaugural meeting in Rabat (Morocco) on July 6–10, 1985, and elected a 10-member permanent bureau and also committees on political, economic, social and defence affairs respectively.

(On May 9, 1985, Libya had been reported to have made a loan of $100,000,000 to Morocco to facilitate its cereal purchases.)

The 1984 treaty of federation was abrogated by Morocco on Aug. 29, 1986, after Libya and Syria had issued a joint statement condemning as "an act of treason" a proposed meeting between the King of Morocco and the Prime Minister of Israel. On the following day the Libyan People's Bureau for Foreign Liaison (i.e. Foreign Ministry) issued a statement regretting the Moroccan move and describing the abrogation of the treaty as "illegal".

Libya and the Sudan. On July 8, 1985, it was announced that an agreement had been signed providing the Sudan with Libyan military logistical support, training and assistance in air and naval defence. (The agreement was not to constitute a strategic alliance and Libya was not to interfere in the Sudan's internal affairs or foreign policy.)

Libya and Syria. The Governments of Libya and Syria announced on Oct. 10, 1980, that their countries were to merge in a unitary state under a single (as yet undefined) leadership with the object of intensifying Arab military confrontation with Israel. The new state was to have full political, economic and military union, and other Arab states were invited to join it. At the conclusion of talks between the two leaderships in December 1980, however, it was disclosed that the countries had agreed only to form a joint "revolutionary leadership" to supervise unification efforts until "the plans for unity and its institutions" had been elaborated.

Libya and Tunisia. (1) An agreement on a merger between Libya and Tunisia, concluded on Jan. 12, 1974, was not implemented owing to subsequent disagreement by Tunisia. Nevertheless agreement was reached on Oct. 25, 1977, on the co-ordination of industrial development plans and the expansion of transport facilities between the two countries.

(2) A co-operation agreement covering economic, industrial and cultural matters was signed on Feb. 27, 1982.

(3) A mixed committee on political co-operation, the establishment of which had been decided on Jan. 22, 1981, and which was composed of members of the Tunisian Council of Ministers and of the Libyan General People's Congress, held its first meeting in Tripoli on July 19–20, 1983. It decided to set up ministerial and lower-level committees to discuss co-operation in economic and foreign affairs and also a Tunisian-Libyan Bank.

(4) In mid-July 1984 the Tunisian government agreed to participate in a mixed security commission.

Morocco and the United Arab Emirates. An industrial co-operation agreement was concluded in November 1974.

Oman and the People's Democratic Republic of Yemen. An agreement on a "declaration of principles" between the two sides, signed on Oct. 27, 1982, and in force from Nov. 15, 1982 (after ratification by the two countries' legislative bodies), contained commitments "to establish normal relations" and to form a technical committee to discuss border problems, "not to allow any foreign forces to use their territories for aggression or provocation against the other country", to "stop hostile media campaigns" and to exchange diplomatic representatives.

Saudi Arabia and the Sudan. An agreement "in principle" on the exploitation of the resources of the Red Sea was reached between the two countries on Jan. 14, 1975. A joint Red Sea Commission was subsequently set up to explore the possibilities of the exploitation of mineral resources.

Saudi Arabia and the United Arab Emirates. A cultural agreement was signed in September 1976.

Saudi Arabia and the Yemen Arab Republic. The *Treaty of Taif*, concluded in May 1934 for a 20-year period to end an armed conflict between Saudi Arabia and Yemen (later the Yemen Arab

Republic), provided inter alia for a common foreign policy and mutual support in the event of foreign aggression; in March 1953 it was extended for a further 20 (lunar) years. Another agreement signed in November 1937 provided for the final settlement of the dispute and the delimitation of the two states' common border.

A defence treaty was concluded on April 21, 1956.

On April 7, 1936, Yemen joined the treaty of alliance concluded by Saudi Arabia with Iraq on April 3 [see above].

(In May 1982 Saudi Arabian aid to the Yemen Arab Republic was running at £400,000,000 a year and included the supply of ammunition.)

Somalia and the United Arab Emirates. A trade and economic co-operation agreement was signed in November 1974.

The Sudan and the United Arab Emirates. A cultural agreement was concluded in April 1975.

The Sudan and the People's Democratic Republic of Yemen. On March 22, 1977, agreements were signed in Aden on economic and technical co-operation between the two countries and on the establishment of a joint high ministerial council to co-ordinate this co-operation.

Tunisia and the United Arab Emirates. A cultural agreement was signed in June 1974 and an economic and technological co-operation agreement in November 1974.

The Yemen Arab Republic and the People's Democratic Republic of Yemen. Proposals for a merger between the two states were first made in October 1972 and were revived in October 1979. Talks held by the two sides in late 1981 resulted in the compilation of statutes for the executive functioning of a united state and the draft of a constitution. An agreement on further co-operation and co-ordination, signed in Aden on Dec. 2, 1981, provided inter alia for the creation of a Yemen Council comprising the two countries' Presidents, of a joint ministerial committee and of a six-member secretariat. The duties of these bodies were discussed at meetings during 1982.

The Yemen Council held its first meeting in Sana'a (Yemen Arab Republic) on Aug. 15–20, 1983, and set up a Yemen unity special committee, which in turn decided to form a "permanent joint committee" at ministerial level with the task of increasing trade and abolishing customs duties between the two countries. The second meeting of the Yemen Council was held in Aden on Feb. 15–17, 1984, and noted agreement on a number of foreign policy issues, in particular "absolute support for fraternal Syria".

Among further discussions which took place in 1984 was a meeting of a joint economic committee which decided in late November on measures providing for animal and crop exchanges and calling for a feasibility study on a possible link of electricity supplies. In January 1985 the two governments approved the delineation of a zone across their border for joint oil exploration.

Agreements between Arab and non-Arab Countries

Algeria and Argentina. The conclusion of an agreement on the construction in Algeria of a nuclear reactor for research and training purposes was reported in Argentina on May 27, 1985.

Algeria and Canada. A general scientific and technical co-operation agreement was signed on Feb. 13, 1983.

Algeria and Greece. On the basis of an agreement concluded in 1982 it was agreed on Jan. 10, 1985, to expand economic co-operation.

Algeria and Guinea-Bissau. An economic and commercial co-operation agreement was signed in April 1975.

Algeria and Italy. An agreement concluded in early February 1985 provided for co-operation in the economic, scientific, technical and cultural fields and accelerated transfer of technology to Algeria.

Algeria and Mali. An agreement on the demarcation of the 800-mile border between the two countries in the Sahara was concluded on May 8, 1983, and was finally signed on April 26, 1984.

Algeria and Mexico. On May 10, 1985, it was agreed to set up a joint economic co-operation committee.

Algeria and Niger. A treaty defining the 600-mile border between the two countries was signed on Jan. 5, 1983 (this border having previously been an imaginary line across the Sahara).

Algeria and Spain. An agreement on co-operation in professional and technical training was signed on Jan. 21, 1975.

A number of agreements on economic, trade and cultural co-operation were signed in February 1985.

An economic and industrial co-operation agreement signed on July 3, 1985, provided for a significant increase in trade.

Algeria and Sweden. An agreement on economic, industrial, scientific and technical co-operation was signed on Nov. 15, 1974.

Algeria and Yugoslavia. An industrial co-operation protocol was signed on March 27, 1985.

Bahrain and Australia. An agreement on trade and economic relations and technical co-operation was signed on May 15, 1979.

Djibouti and the Federal Republic of Germany. A technical co-operation agreement signed on Feb. 22, 1979, came into force on Dec. 1, 1979.

Djibouti and Pakistan. A protocol on technical and cultural co-operation was signed on Dec. 12, 1979.

Egypt and Chad. A treaty of friendship between Egypt and Chad was signed on Feb. 22, 1973.

Egypt and France. Two framework nuclear co-operation agreements were signed on March 23, 1981.

Under an agreement signed in January 1982 France was to supply Egypt with 20 Mirage 2000 combat aircraft; a joint working group would be set up on defence co-operation; and a number of Egyptian officers, pilots and technicians would be trained in France. (Egypt already had 60 French Mirage 5 aircraft, Gazelle helicopters and Crotale surface-to-air missiles and was assembling 30 French-designed Alpha jet trainers.)

Egypt and the Federal Republic of Germany. An agreement on co-operation in scientific research and technological development was signed on April 11, 1979, and came into force on Feb. 20, 1980.

An agreement on co-operation in the peaceful use of atomic energy was signed on Oct. 26, 1981, and came into force on March 15, 1982.

Egypt and Italy. An agreement signed on March 8, 1984, provided for the supply of Italian equipment to the Egyptian nuclear power industry.

Egypt and Pakistan. A trade agreement was signed on Dec. 13, 1975.

Egypt and Spain. A major agreement providing for the supply to Egypt of Spanish naval vessels, military trucks and armoured personnel carriers (worth the equivalent of £581,000,000) was concluded in July 1982.

A trade agreement was signed on May 19, 1976, and a cultural agreement on Feb. 20, 1981.

Egypt and Sweden. An agreement on economic, industrial and technical co-operation was signed on Feb. 23, 1975.

Egypt and Switzerland. A provisional trade agreement was signed on April 19, 1930.

A treaty of friendship was concluded on June 7, 1934.

A payments agreement of April 6, 1950, was amended on Dec. 26, 1951, and on Aug. 19/Sept. 8, 1954.

Egypt and Turkey. An agreement on a joint programme of arms manufacture in the fields of aircraft, tank and submarine construction was announced in August 1984.

Egypt and Yugoslavia. A military protocol was signed on Feb. 4, 1984.

An agreement to increase technical co-operation was reached on June 9, 1985.

Egypt and Zaïre. A technical military co-operation agreement was on Feb. 7, 1980, reported to have been signed between the two countries.

Egypt and Zambia. An agreement to form a joint co-operation committee was signed on Feb. 12, 1985.

Iraq and Brazil. An agreement providing inter alia for Brazilian exports of raw and slightly enriched uranium to Iraq was signed in January 1980.

Iraq and France. Under a nuclear energy co-operation agreement signed on Nov. 18, 1975, France undertook to supply to Iraq (which had in 1968 built a nuclear research centre with Soviet help) a nuclear research centre containing a 70-megawatt Osirak reactor and an 800-kilowatt Isis reactor, which were to be operational by 1981–82. In Iraq these two reactors, both located in a complex near Baghdad, were known as Tamuz-1 and Tamuz-2. In the agreement Iraq undertook to submit the material, equipment and installations received from France to inspection by the International Atomic Energy Agency (IAEA) in accordance with the provisions of the Nuclear Non-Proliferation Treaty, of which Iraq was a signatory (whereas France was not).

In March 1980 France undertook to supply 72 kilogrammes of 93 per cent enriched nuclear fuel to Iraq.

Under an agreement concluded on Aug. 20, 1981, France agreed in principle to co-operate in the rebuilding of Iraq's Osirak reactor (severely damaged in an air raid in September 1980).

Iraq and the Federal Republic of Germany. A trade agreement signed on Oct. 7, 1951, and in force from Jan. 13, 1954, was, on Sept. 16, 1985, extended until Jan. 31, 1987.

An agreement on economic, scientific and technical co-operation, signed on March 25, 1981, came into force on July 15, 1981.

An agreement on cultural co-operation, signed on May 5, 1982, came into force on Feb. 7, 1983.

Iraq and Italy. On March 4, 1981, Italy was reported to have authorized the export to Iraq of warships worth the equivalent of £829,000,000.

Iraq and the Netherlands. An economic, commercial and technical co-operation agreement, with the provision of the establishment of a joint committee to supervise relations in these fields, was signed on Oct. 31, 1983.

Iraq and the Republic of Korea. An agreement on trade and technical and scientific co-operation was signed on March 7, 1983.

Iraq and Sweden. An agreement on trade and economic and technical co-operation was signed on May 30, 1978.

Iraq and Switzerland. An agreement on trade and economic and technical co-operation was signed on Feb. 11, 1978.

Iraq and Turkey. An agreement signed in October 1984 provided for the pursuit of "subversive groups" (i.e. Kurdish rebels) across the Iraqi-Turkish border.

Jordan and Ethiopia. An agreement to increase bilateral trade and to set up a feasibility study on maritime transport links was concluded in mid-October 1984.

Jordan and France. On Sept. 10, 1984, it was announced that France had supplied Jordan with 33 Mirage fighter aircraft, with a further 13 to be delivered, and the French Defence Minister agreeing to the formation of a joint military committee to study Jordanian requests for French armaments.

A credit agreement announced on March 5, 1985, provided for a French loan to Jordan equivalent to $64,000,000, mainly for the completion of a telephone network begun in 1981 with the aid of a similar loan.

Jordan and the Federal Republic of Germany. A technical co-operation agreement signed on June 14, 1977, came into force on Nov. 2, 1977.

An agreement on cultural co-operation signed on Aug. 29, 1979, came into force on Feb. 2. 1982.

Jordan and Spain. A trade agreement was concluded on Dec. 16, 1980.

Jordan and Switzerland. An Anglo-Swiss extradition treaty of Nov. 26, 1880, was applied to Jordan on Jan. 28/May 9, 1932.

An agreement on trade and economic co-operation was signed on Nov. 11, 1976.

Kuwait and France. It was announced in France on Feb. 23, 1983, that the Kuwaiti Defence Minister had signed a contract for the purchase of 12 Mirage F-1 C aircraft (which would bring Kuwait's total F-1 C Air Force strength to 32).

An agreement announced on July 31, 1983, provided for the supply to Kuwait of six French-made Super-Puma helicopters armed with exocet missiles. (Kuwait already had 10 squadrons of Puma helicopters and three of Gazelle helicopters.) Further purchases of French air defence installations worth US$140,850,000 were agreed in November 1983.

An agreement concluded in early October 1984 provided for the training of Kuwaiti Air Force pilots by French officers.

Kuwait and the Federal Republic of Germany. An agreement on scientific and technological co-operation was signed on Dec. 13, 1979, and came into force on Nov. 4, 1980.

Libya and Afghanistan. On Feb. 7, 1982, it was reported that Libya had agreed to finance a number of (unspecified) Afghan development projects.

Libya, Algeria and Niger. Under an agreement reached in Tripoli on Nov. 20, 1976, by the Presidents of Algeria and Niger and the Libyan leader, a tripartite commission was to be set up to study the possibilities of increased regional co-operation between the three countries, as decided in principle on April 8, 1976.

Libya and Benin. A co-operation agreement was signed on Sept. 28, 1980.

Libya and Burundi. A 10-year treaty of friendship and co-operation, automatically renewable, was signed in Tripoli on Aug. 24, 1973.

Libya and Cameroon. A treaty of friendship and co-operation was signed in Tripoli on Oct. 29, 1975.

Libya and Chad. In a treaty of friendship signed on June 15, 1980, both parties undertook to "mutually defend each other in the event of one of the two parties being threatened by direct or indirect external aggression" and to "exchange information regarding military plans and plans for internal and external security"; Libya would contribute to the reconstruction of Chad in the sphere of its "economic and military plan"; and Chad would not permit the installation of any "foreign base" or "military, colonialist or imperialist troops on its territory". The treaty was ratified by a session of the Libyan General People's Congress on Jan. 3–7, 1981. (However, the conclusion of the treaty was followed by civil war in Chad which by 1982 brought an anti-Libyan government to power.)

Libya, Ethiopia and the People's Democratic Republic of Yemen. At a summit meeting of the leaders of these three countries held in Aden on Aug. 17–19, 1981, a treaty of friendship and co-operation was signed, providing in particular for closer political and economic co-ordination. The treaty stated inter alia that the three parties agreed to co-operate to "guarantee the common struggle of the three revolutionary countries" against the "conspiracies of imperialism, Zionism and reactionary forces"; rejected the 1978 Camp David agreements (which led to the Egyptian-Israeli peace treaty); set up a political committee of Foreign Ministers and a Supreme Council consisting of the three countries' leaders and chairmen of committees (to meet once a year); and provided for mutual assistance "in the case of an aggression against any one" of the three countries. The three leaders also agreed to form a defence committee.

Libya and France. An agreement reached on Sept. 17, 1984, provided for the withdrawal from Chad of French and Libyan troops (supporting opposite sides in the civil war) to commence on Sept. 25 of that year. It was later agreed that the withdrawal was to be monitored by a mixed Franco-Libyan commission. The Chad government approved the proposal on Oct. 10.

Libya and Ghana. Scientific, cultural and educational co-operation agreements were signed on Feb. 24, 1982.

Libya and Greece. An agreement on the establishment of joint investment companies was signed on June 22, 1984.

Under an agreement of Sept. 24, 1984, the Greek government undertook to increase the volume of Greek exports to Libya and to purchase more Libyan oil.

On Jan. 11, 1985, it was announced that agreement had been reached on the purchase by Libya, for defensive purposes only, of Greek military equipment worth US$500,000,000.

Libya and Mozambique. Agreements on friendship and co-operation, on economic and technical co-operation and trade exchanges, and on military co-operation were signed in August 1982.

Libya and Niger. A defence and security treaty was ratified on March 9, 1974, with provisions for mutual defence against "direct or indirect aggression" and against "internal or external danger" and for "complete co-operation and co-ordination" between the two countries' armed and security forces.

Libya and Pakistan. An agreement on technical and scientific co-operation was signed on Jan. 9, 1975.

Libya and Suriname. An agreement on an aid package to Suriname, worth $100,000,000 and covering oil supplies and exploration as well as financial, economic and military aid, was reached early in March 1985.

Libya and Sweden. An agreement and a protocol on the possible expansion of economic and industrial co-operation were signed on March 6, 1976.

Libya and Togo. A treaty of mutual defence and assistance was announced on Jan. 5, 1976. (On Dec. 24, 1973, it had been decided to set up a joint Libyan-Togolese bank with headquarters in Lomé, Togo.)

Mauritania and Pakistan. A trade agreement was signed on March 13, 1975.
A general co-operation agreement and a cultural agreement were signed on Aug. 13, 1975.

Mauritania and Spain. Agreements on economic co-operation were signed on Oct. 26, 1977, and on April 6, 1982.

Mauritania and Switzerland. An agreement on trade, promotion and protection of investments and economic and technical co-operation was signed on Sept. 9, 1976.

Morocco and France. An agreement on the sale by France of 250,000 tonnes of wheat on credit terms was concluded in May 1985.

Morocco and the Federal Republic of Germany. A trade agreement of April 15, 1961, in force from Jan. 1, 1964, and a protocol of Jan. 20, 1964, were both extended, on Sept. 16, 1985, until Dec. 31, 1986.
An agreement on technical and scientific co-operation was signed and came into force on Nov. 24, 1966.

Morocco and Guinea. Several agreements on economic, scientific, cultural and technical co-operation were signed in Rabat in January 1979, when the heads of state of the two countries agreed to work for the elimination of tension and the installation of détente in the region.

Morocco and Spain. A convention on scientific and technical co-operation was signed on Nov. 8, 1979, and a cultural agreement on Oct. 14, 1980.

On Nov. 2, 1984, the two sides agreed to increase defence co-operation.
In mid-January 1985 agreement was reached in principle on the construction of a fixed transport link across the Strait of Gibraltar.

Morocco and Sweden. A trade agreement was signed on Feb. 8, 1960.

Morocco and Switzerland. A protocol on the most-favoured nation clause was signed on Aug. 29, 1957.

Oman and the Federal Republic of Germany. An agreement on the development of economic and industrial co-operation was signed on Nov. 25, 1978, and came into force on Dec. 21, 1978.

Saudi Arabia and Brazil. A five-year military co-operation agreement signed on Oct. 14, 1985 (within the framework of an April 1975 agreement), provided for joint ventures in manufacturing Brazilian military equipment in Saudi Arabia.

Saudi Arabia and France. An agreement concluded on Jan. 15, 1984, provided for the supply to Saudi Arabia over the next three years of an air defence system including electronic surveillance equipment and low-altitude surface-to-air missiles.

Saudi Arabia and the Federal Republic of Germany. A treaty of friendship concluded on April 26, 1929, between Germany and Hedjaz, Nejd and Dependencies (now Saudi Arabia) and effective from Nov. 6, 1930, was renewed by Saudi Arabia and the Federal Republic of Germany on July 7, 1952, and extended on Dec. 10, 1984, until Dec. 31, 1986.
An agreement on co-operation in scientific research and technological development, signed on Jan. 7, 1980, came into force on March 24, 1982.

Somalia and the Federal Republic of Germany. A trade agreement signed on Jan. 19, 1962, came into force on Aug. 23, 1962, and was, on Sept. 16, 1985, extended until Dec. 31, 1986.
An agreement on technical co-operation signed on June 28, 1979, came into force on Oct. 30, 1979.

Somalia and Italy. Under a three-year economic and technical co-operation agreement announced on Aug. 6, 1981, Italy was to provide Somalia with aid worth over US$200,000,000, and an increase in Italian food aid was announced at the same time.

The Sudan and the Central African Republic. An agreement on good-neighbourliness and border security was on Nov. 6, 1984, reported to have been approved by the President of the Sudan.

The Sudan and France. A military co-operation agreement signed on Sept. 17, 1980, provided inter alia for Sudanese arms purchases on credit terms.

The Sudan and the Federal Republic of Germany. A framework agreement on technical co-operation, signed on March 3, 1972, and in force from Aug. 17, 1972, was amended on Jan. 15/Sept. 28, 1976.

The Sudan and Spain. An agreement on economic, cultural and technical co-operation and a trade agreement were signed on Oct. 11, 1978.

The Sudan and Sweden. An agreement on technical, scientific and cultural co-operation was signed on July 3, 1982.

Syria and France. In November 1984 it was reported that France had agreed to replace 15 Syrian anti-tank helicopters destroyed by Israeli forces in 1982.

Syria and the Federal Republic of Germany. A framework agreement on technical co-operation was signed on Jan. 26, 1976, and came into force on Aug. 7, 1976.

Syria and Switzerland. An agreement on trade and technical co-operation was signed on Nov. 29, 1976.

Syria and Turkey. A number of economic co-operation agreements were signed in March 1986.

Tunisia and the Federal Republic of Germany. A trade agreement, signed on and in force from Jan. 29, 1960, was amended on Dec. 20, 1963, and was on Sept. 16, 1985, extended until Dec. 31, 1986.
A cultural agreement was signed on July 19, 1966, and came into force on March 13, 1967.
A treaty on extradition and legal assistance in penal affairs was signed on July 19, 1966, and came into force on March 13, 1970.
An agreement on technical co-operation was signed and came into force on April 23, 1970.

Tunisia and Italy. An agreement on the delimitation of the continental shelf on the basis of the median line (as defined in a protocol of Jan. 23, 1975) between the two countries was concluded on Aug. 20, 1971.

Tunisia and Senegal. Under an agreement reached on May 16, 1984, it was decided to establish a joint trade, development and investment bank in Dakar and a joint company for foreign trade, with a two-year trading programme being drawn up.

Tunisia and Sweden. A general agreement on financial and technical co-operation was signed on May 12, 1973.
A trade agreement was concluded on Sept. 20, 1977.

Tunisia and Switzerland. A technical and scientific co-operation agreement was signed on Oct. 27, 1972, and a trade agreement on Dec. 23, 1976.

The United Arab Emirates and Austria. An agreement on economic and technical co-operation was signed in July 1976.

The United Arab Emirates and Chad. An agreement on cultural and scientific co-operation and a friendship treaty were signed in June 1973.

The United Arab Emirates and France. A cultural and technical co-operation agreement was signed in November 1975.

The United Arab Emirates and Gabon. A co-operation protocol was signed in December 1974.

The United Arab Emirates and the Federal Republic of Germany. A technical co-operation agreement was signed in November 1975.

The United Arab Emirates and Pakistan. A co-operation protocol was signed in January 1974.

The United Arab Emirates and Senegal. An agreement on cultural and economic co-operation was signed in March 1976.

The Yemen Arab Republic and the Federal Republic of Germany. A framework agreement on technical co-operation was signed on July 4, 1978, and came into force on July 6, 1979.

The People's Democratic Republic of Yemen and Ethiopia. A 15-year treaty of friendship and co-operation between the two countries was signed on Dec. 2, 1979, together with a six-year "action programme" which would "further strengthen economic, scientific and technical co-operation".
In the treaty the two sides undertook inter alia to work together to "strengthen the unity of the non-aligned movement" (of which they were both members); to continue their efforts to bring about the establishment of a new international economic order; and not to "enter into military alliances or other alliances . . ., join any blocs of states or engage in any actions or measures directed against the other".
On Jan. 17, 1980, the two countries signed a protocol expressing their intention to "continue their co-operation in the political, economic, military and other fields".
A co-operation agreement between the two countries' political parties was signed on Feb. 27, 1985.

Agreements concluded by Qatar

Qatar has concluded agreements, in force by December 1985, as follows:
(1) On commercial and economic co-operation with Iraq, Jordan, the Republic of Korea, Somalia and Tunisia.
(2) On cultural and educational co-operation with the Yemen Arab Republic.
(3) On cultural and information co-operation with Bahrain.
(4) On cultural and technical co-operation with India, Morocco and Tunisia.
(5) On cultural, technical and scientific co-operation with Chad.
(6) On economic co-operation with Saudi Arabia.

(7) On economic, educational and information co-operation with Kuwait.

(8) On economic and financial co-operation with France.

(9) On economic and technical co-operation with Australia, India, Pakistan and Turkey.

(10) On economic, technical and commercial co-operation with Japan.

(11) On information and cultural co-operation with Jordan, Saudi Arabia, Somalia and the Sudan.

(12) On information, cultural and educational co-operation with Oman, Syria and the United Arab Emirates.

(13) On information, cultural and technical co-operation with France.

(14) On information, cultural and tourism co-operation with Iraq.

Treaties and Agreements concluded by Israel

THE 1979 EGYPTIAN-ISRAELI PEACE TREATY

A peace treaty between Egypt and Israel was signed in Washington on March 26, 1979, by President Sadat of Egypt and Menahim Begin, the Israeli Prime Minister, in the presence of President Carter of the USA.

The signing of the treaty was the outcome of protracted negotiations which had been conducted with US participation and had led to the conclusion at Camp David (near Washington, D.C.) on Sept. 17, 1978, of two framework agreements in which the Egyptian President and the Israeli Prime Minister had agreed on certain principles for negotiations between the two sides which would lead to the conclusion of a peace treaty—with this treaty constituting a basis for the eventual peace between Israel and all its neighbours.

The Camp David agreements had, however, been rejected by almost all other Arab states and had been followed, in particular, (i) by the signing of a charter of joint national action by the Presidents of Iraq and Syria (in Baghdad on Oct. 26, 1978), providing inter alia for the establishment of a full military union between these two countries, and (ii) by the ninth Arab summit conference held in Baghdad on Nov. 2–5, 1978 [see page 400].

The first five operative articles of the peace treaty read as follows:

"**Art. I.** (1) The state of war between the parties will be terminated and peace will be established between them upon the exchange of instruments of ratification of this treaty.

"(2) Israel will withdraw all its armed forces and civilians from the Sinai behind the international boundary between Egypt and mandated Palestine, as provided in the annexed protocol (Annex I), and Egypt will resume the exercise of its full sovereignty over the Sinai.

"(3) Upon completion of the interim withdrawal provided for in Annex I, the parties will establish normal and friendly relations, in accordance with Article III (3).

"**Art. II.** The permanent boundary between Egypt and Israel is the recognized international boundary between Egypt and the former mandated territory of Palestine as shown on the map at Annex II, without prejudice to the issue of the status of the Gaza Strip. The parties recognize this boundary as inviolable. Each will respect the territorial integrity of the other, including their territorial waters and airspace.

"**Art. III.** (1) The parties will apply between them the provisions of the Charter of the United Nations and the principles of international law governing relations among states in times of peace. In particular:

"A. They recognize and will respect each other's sovereignty, territorial integrity and political independence.

"B. They recognize and will respect each other's right to live in peace within their secure and recognized boundaries.

"C. They will refrain from the threat or use of force, directly or indirectly, against each other and will settle all disputes between them by peaceful means.

"(2) Each party undertakes to ensure that acts or threats of belligerency, hostility or violence do not originate from and are not committed from within its territory, or by any forces subject to its control or by any other forces stationed on its territory, against the population, citizens or property of the other party. Each party also undertakes to refrain from organizing, instigating, inciting, assisting or participating in acts or threats of belligerency, hostility, subversion or violence against the other party, anywhere, and undertakes to ensure that perpetrators of such acts are brought to justice.

"(3) The parties agree that the normal relationship established between them will include full recognition, diplomatic, economic and cultural relations, termination of economic boycotts and discriminatory barriers to the free movement of people and goods, and will guarantee the mutual enjoyment by citizens of the due process of law. The process by which they undertake to evolve such a relationship parallel to the implementation of other provisions of this treaty is set out in the annexed protocol (Annex III).

"**Art. IV.** (1) In order to provide maximum security for both parties on the basis of reciprocity, agreed security arrangements will be established including limited-force zones in Egyptian and Israeli territory, and United Nations forces and observers, described in detail as to nature and timing in Annex I, and other security arrangements the parties may agree upon.

"(2) The parties agree to the stationing of United Nations personnel in areas described in Annex I. The parties agree not to request withdrawal of the United Nations personnel and that these personnel will not be removed unless such removal is approved by the Security Council of the United Nations, with the affirmative vote of the five permanent members [i.e. China, France, the Soviet Union, the USA and the United Kingdom], unless the parties otherwise agree.

"(3) A joint commission will be established to facilitate the implementation of the treaty, as provided for in Annex I.

"(4) The security arrangements provided for in Paragraphs 1 and 2 of this article may, at the request of either party, be reviewed and amended by mutual agreement of the parties.

"**Art. V.** (1) Ships of Israel, and cargoes destined for or coming from Israel, shall enjoy the right of free passage through the Suez Canal and its approaches through the Gulf of Suez and the Mediterranean Sea on the basis of the Constantinople Convention of 1888, applying to all nations. Israeli nationals, vessels and cargoes, as well as persons, vessels and cargoes destined for or coming from Israel, shall be accorded non-discriminatory treatment in all matters connected with usage of the canal.

"(2) The parties consider the Strait of Tiran [at the mouth of the Gulf of Aqaba] and the Gulf of Aqaba to be international waterways open to all nations for unimpeded and non-suspendible freedom of navigation and overflight. The parties will respect each other's right to navigation and overflight for access to either country through the Strait of Tiran and the Gulf of Aqaba."

In the protocol to the treaty Israel undertook to complete its withdrawal from the Sinai (in two phases) not later than three years from the date of exchange of instruments of ratification of the treaty. The protocol also laid down the modalities of this withdrawal.

In an accompanying letter addressed to President Carter the Governments of Egypt and Israel agreed to proceed, within a month after the exchange of instruments of ratification of the peace treaty, to negotiate on implementing the provisions of the framework agreements relating to the West Bank and the Gaza Strip with the object of providing "full autonomy to the inhabitants" of these two areas.

In letters addressed to Egypt and Israel the US Government confirmed that in the event of actual or threatened violation of the treaty the USA would, on request of one or both of the parties, consult with them and "take such other action as it may deem appropriate and helpful to achieve compliance with the treaty"; that the USA would "conduct aerial monitoring as requested by the parties"; and that, if the UN Security Council failed to establish and maintain the arrangements called for in the treaty (through the deployment of UN forces), the US President would "be prepared to take those steps necessary to ensure the establishment and maintenance of an acceptable alternative multinational force".

In a memorandum of understanding signed on March 26, 1979, between the United States and Israel, the USA undertook to give strong support to Israel in certain circumstances, stating in particular: "The United States will provide support it deems appropriate for proper actions taken by Israel in response to . . . demonstrated violations of the treaty of peace. In particular, if a violation of the treaty of peace is deemed to threaten the security of Israel, including, inter alia, a blockade of Israel's use of international waterways, a violation of the provisions of the treaty of peace concerning limitation of forces or an armed attack against Israel, the United States will be prepared to consider, on an urgent basis, such measures as the strengthening of the US presence in the area, the providing of emergency supplies to Israel, and the exercise of maritime rights in order to put an end to the violation."

The Egyptian Government stated subsequently that it would not recognize the legality of this memorandum and considered it null and void, and it listed 16 reasons for rejecting it. Among these reasons were the fact that the US rights referred to in the memorandum had never been mentioned or negotiated with Egypt; that the memorandum could "be construed as an eventual alliance between the United States and Israel against Egypt"; and that it gave the United States "the right to impose a military presence in the region for reasons agreed between Israel and the United States".

The US Secretary of State explained on April 11, 1979, that in connexion with the peace treaty the United States would make available to Egypt and Israel additional financial assistance totalling US$4,800 million over three years—approximately US$3,000 million for Israel and $1,500 million for Egypt.

The peace treaty was ratified (i) in Israel by the Cabinet on April 1, 1979 (with one Cabinet member abstaining from voting), and (ii) in Egypt by the People's Assembly on April 10 (by 328 votes to 15, with one abstention and 16 members being absent) and in a national referendum held on April 19 (by 99.5 per cent of the valid votes cast in a poll of about 90 per cent). The instruments of ratification were exchanged on April 25, 1979 (at a US surveillance post in the Sinai).

OTHER ISRAELI AGREEMENTS

Israel and Bophuthatswana. In October 1983 it was reported that Israel was assisting Bophuthatswana in agricultural projects and in the development of a television service.

Israel and Ciskei. In October 1983 it was reported that Ciskei, which had opened a trade mission in Israel in late 1982, was buying a number of new aircraft from Israel.

Israel and El Salvador. In March 1984 it was announced that Israel had promised an unspecified quantity of military aid to El Salvador.

Israel and the Federal Republic of Germany. Agreements on economic aid were signed and came into force respectively (i) on May 12, 1966, and (ii) on July 18, 1968.

An agreement on scientific and technical co-operation in agricultural research was signed and came into force on Jan. 22, 1985.

Israel and Iceland. A treaty of commerce and payments was concluded on Oct. 19, 1960.

An exchange of notes on cultural and scientific co-operation took place on Oct. 10, 1980.

Israel and Liberia. An economic co-operation agreement signed in August 1983 covered Israeli aid to Liberia in economic development, defence, national security, road construction, housing, agriculture, communications, shipping, air transport, marketing, manpower development and banking; Israel was also to send medical, agricultural and technical advisers to Liberia.

Israel and Romania. A cultural and scientific co-operation agreement was signed on Sept. 17, 1979.

A trade protocol worth US$90,000,000 was signed in late February 1984.

Israel and South Africa. An extradition treaty signed on Sept. 18, 1959, was amended on May 2 and 26, 1976.

Israel and Switzerland. A protocol on trade exchanges was signed on Sept. 14, 1956, and was followed by an exchange of letters on March 28, 1957.

Treaties and Agreements concluded by Iran

Iran and the Federal Republic of Germany. A treaty of friendship, concluded on Feb. 17, 1929, came into force on Dec. 11, 1930.

A trade, customs and navigation agreement, also signed on Feb. 17, 1929, came into force on Jan. 11, 1931; it was followed by a protocol of April 11, 1954, and was on Dec. 10, 1984, extended until Dec. 31, 1986.

A treaty on economic and technical co-operation, signed on Nov. 4, 1954, came into force on March 27, 1964.

An agreement on co-operation in scientific research and technological development of June 30, 1975, came into force on Nov. 21, 1977.

An agreement on the peaceful use of nuclear energy of July 4, 1976, came into force on Nov. 11, 1977.

Iran and Iceland. A treaty of friendship was signed on July 15, 1950.

Iran and Libya. A military co-operation agreement providing for the establishment of a joint political and military committee, an "Islamic Revolutionary League" and an "Army of Jerusalem" to liberate Palestine was concluded on June 23, 1985. (On June 15, 1983, it had been decided to set up a framework for industrial and economic co-operation and also an "Islamic Liberation Army".)

Iran and Oman. An agreement on joint control over the Strait of Hormuz concluded in January 1975 empowered Iran to conduct exclusive naval and air force patrols.

An agreement on the delimitation of the continental shelf between the two countries was signed on May 25, 1975.

Iran and Saudi Arabia. An agreement on the demarcation of the continental shelf between Iran and Saudi Arabia was signed in Tehran on Oct. 24, 1968.

Iran and Sweden. A settlement, trade and navigation agreement was signed on May 10, 1929.

A friendship treaty was concluded on May 27, 1929.

A protocol on commercial, industrial and technical co-operation was signed on April 20, 1974.

Iran and Switzerland. A treaty of friendship between the two countries was signed on April 25, 1934. An exchange of letters on economic relations took place on Feb. 1, 1964.

Iran and Syria. A preliminary agreement concluded on March 14, 1982, provided for the sale of Iranian crude oil to Syria's two refineries in exchange for the sale of Syrian phosphates to Iran. In April 1984 it was agreed that Iran would continue to supply Syria with 150,000 barrels per day of light crude oil.

Iran and Turkey. An economic and commercial protocol signed in January 1982 provided for the exchange of Iranian oil for Turkish foodstuffs, wood, textile products and electrical equipment.

An economic, technical and industrial co-operation agreement concluded on March 5, 1982, involved the sale of Iranian oil and gas in return for agricultural and industrial goods; agreement was also reached on the construction of three pipelines (one for oil and two for gas). A further agreement concluded in September 1982 provided for the supply of natural gas for Turkey's needs. Another agreement for the supply of Iranian oil to Turkey was signed in January 1983.

Iran and the United Arab Emirates. A co-operation protocol was signed in March 1977.

Iran and Uruguay. A nine-month trade agreement was concluded in March 1982 on Iranian oil supplies worth $80,000,000 to Uruguay in exchange for meat, grain and rice.

Iran and the People's Democratic Republic of Yemen. A political and economic co-operation agreement was signed on April 12, 1982, and an agreement on the refining of Iranian oil in Aden, as well as on the purchase of Iranian crude oil by South Yemen, was reported on July 21, 1982.

(A "reconciliation" treaty between Iran and Iraq, signed in Baghdad on June 13, 1975, and based on an Algiers agreement of March 6, 1975, on the two countries' common border, was unilaterally abrogated by Iraq on Sept. 17, 1980. This decision was followed by the outbreak of war between Iraq and Iran, with the latter insisting on the reactivation of the treaty.)

16. Africa

This section deals with the main international associations, treaties and other agreements entered into by African states, including (i) the Organization of African Unity; (ii) other continental and regional organizations in Africa; and (iii) treaties and agreements concluded between individual African states or between African states and states outside Africa.

Organization of African Unity (OAU)

Address. P.O.B. 3242, Addis Ababa, Ethiopia.
Officer. Ide Oumarou (sec. gen.).
Founded. May 25, 1963.
Membership. 50 independent states of Africa (all except Morocco and South Africa, as well as Bophuthatswana, Ciskei, Transkei and Venda)— see list on page 442. (Morocco withdrew from the OAU in 1984 after the admission of the Saharan Arab Democratic Republic in 1982.)

The OAU Charter. The African heads of state and government attending a conference in Addis Ababa on May 23–26, 1963 signed a Charter of the OAU, the principal provisions of which are as follows:

Establishment

Art. 1. The high contracting parties do by the present Charter establish an organization to be known as the Organization of African Unity.

The organization shall include the continental African states, Madagascar and all the islands surrounding Africa.

Purposes

Art. 2. (1) The organization shall have the following purposes:

(*a*) To promote the unity and solidarity of the African and Malagasy states;

(*b*) to co-ordinate and intensify their co-operation and efforts to achieve a better life for the peoples of Africa;

(*c*) to defend their sovereignty, their territorial integrity and independence;

(*d*) to eradicate all forms of colonialism from Africa; and

(*e*) to promote international co-operation, having due regard to the UN Charter and the Universal Declaration of Human Rights.

(2) To these ends, the member states shall co-ordinate and harmonize their general policies, especially in the following fields:

(*a*) Political and diplomatic co-operation;

(*b*) economic co-operation, including transport and communications;

(*c*) educational and cultural co-operation;

(*d*) health, sanitation, and nutritional co-operation;

(*e*) scientific and technical co-operation; and

(*f*) co-operation for defence and security.

Principles

Art. 3. The member states, in pursuit of the purposes stated in Article 2, solemnly affirm and declare their adherence to the following principles:

(1) The sovereign equality of all member states;

(2) non-interference in the internal affairs of states;

(3) respect for the sovereignty and territorial integrity of each member state and for its inalienable right to independent existence;

(4) peaceful settlement of disputes by negotiation, mediation, conciliation or arbitration;

(5) unreserved condemnation, in all its forms, of political assassination, as well as of subversive activities on the part of neighbouring states or any other states;

(6) absolute dedication to the total emancipation of the African territories which are still dependent;

(7) affirmation of a policy of non-alignment with regard to all blocs.

Institutions

Art. 7. The organization shall accomplish its purposes through the following principal institutions:

(1) The Assembly of Heads of State and Government;

(2) the Council of Ministers;

(3) the General Secretariat;

(4) the Commission of Mediation, Conciliation and Arbitration.

The Assembly of Heads of State and Government

Art. 8. The Assembly of Heads of State and Government shall be the supreme organ of the organization. It shall, subject to the provisions of this Charter, discuss matters of common concern to Africa with a view to co-ordinating and harmonizing the general policy of the organization. It may in addition review the structure, functions and acts of all the organs and any specialized agencies which may be created in accordance with the Charter.

Art. 9. The Assembly shall be composed of the heads of state or government, or their duly accredited representatives, and shall meet at least once a year. At the request of any member state, and upon approval by the majority of the member states, the Assembly shall meet in extraordinary session.

The Council of Ministers

Art. 12. The Council of Ministers shall consist of Foreign Ministers or such other ministers as are designated by the governments of member states.

The Council of Ministers shall meet at least twice a year. When requested by any member state and approved by two-thirds of all member states, it shall meet in extraordinary session.

Art. 13. The Council of Ministers shall be responsible to the Assembly of Heads of State and Government. It shall be entrusted with the responsibility of preparing conferences of the Assembly.

General Secretariat

Art. 16. There shall be an Administrative Secretary-General of the organization, who shall be appointed by the Assembly of Heads of State and Government on the recommendation of the Council of Ministers. The Administrative Secretary-General shall direct the affairs of the Secretariat.

Commission of Mediation, Conciliation and Arbitration

Art. 19. Member states pledge to settle all disputes among themselves by peaceful means and, to this end, decide to establish a Commission of Mediation, Conciliation and Arbitration, the composition and the condition of service of which shall be defined by a separate protocol to be approved by the Assembly of Heads of State and Government.

Specialized Commissions

Art. 20. The Assembly shall establish such Specialized Commissions as it may deem necessary, including the following: (1) Economic and Social Commission; (2) Educational and Cultural Commission; (3) Health, Sanitation, and Nutrition Commission; (4) Defence Commission; (5) Scientific, Technical, and Research Commission.

OAU Institutions

General Secretariat. The OAU's Secretary-General is assisted by five Assistant Secretaries-General—one each for West, Central, North, East and Southern Africa.

Scientific, Technical and Research Commission. The OAU Scientific, Technical and Research Commission (established in Lagos under Art. 20 of the OAU Charter) on Jan. 1, 1965, absorbed the Commission for Technical Co-operation in Africa (CTCA), which had been established in Paris in January 1950.

The CTCA had reconstituted itself in Abidjan (Côte d'Ivoire) on Feb. 8–16, 1962, so as to comprise all independent African member states, ending the full membership of Britain, France, and Belgium (which had founded the Commission and were to be invited to participate in the Commission's work at technical level), and excluding Portugal and South Africa.

OAU Liberation Committee. A Co-ordinating Committee for Liberation Movements in Africa was established in 1963 with headquarters in Dar es Salaam. Since March 1976 it has consisted of representatives of 21 OAU member states. Its function is to provide financial and military aid to national liberation movements which, on the Liberation Committee's proposal, may be recognized by the OAU as the legitimate representatives of the peoples of territories still to be decolonized.

Specialized agencies of the OAU are: The African Civil Aviation Commission, founded in 1969 and based in Dakar; the Organization of African Trade Union Unity (OATUU), founded in 1973 and based in Accra, Ghana; the Pan-African News Agency, founded in 1979; the Pan-African Postal Union, founded in 1980 and based in Arusha, Tanzania; the Pan-African Communications Union, based in Kinshasa, Zaïre; the Supreme Council for Sports in Africa, based in Yaoundé, Cameroon; and the Union of African Railways, founded in 1972 and based in Kinshasa.

Assemblies of Heads of State and Government

1964. The first Assembly of Heads of State and Government, held in Cairo on July 17–21, 1964, decided inter alia (i) to make Addis Ababa the seat of the Organization's permanent headquarters; (ii) to approve a protocol providing for mediation, conciliation, and finally, arbitration in disputes between member countries, as well as an undertaking by member states to respect their frontiers as existing at the achievement of independence; and (iii) to set up two permanent commissions—one of African jurists and another on communications.

1965. The second Assembly of Heads of State and Government, held in Accra on Oct. 21–26, 1965, issued a *Declaration on Subversive Activities* containing the following main provisions:

(1) The OAU pledged itself to oppose collectively and firmly, by every means at its disposal, every form of subversion conceived, organized or financed by any foreign power against Africa as a whole or against OAU member states.

(2) The declaration emphasized that member states would tolerate neither subversion by one state against another nor the use of their territory for subversive activity directed from outside Africa against another member state.

(3) All differences between two or more member states should be settled by bilateral or multilateral consultations, on the basis of a protocol of mediation, conciliation and arbitration as laid down in the OAU Charter, and there should be no reaction against a member state by means of a radio or press campaign.

(4) Member states should not give cause for dissension among themselves by fomenting or aggravating racial, religious, linguistic, ethnic or other differences, and should combat all forms of activity of this kind.

(5) In regard to political refugees, the declaration enjoined member states to observe strictly the principles of international law towards all nationals of member states; to try to promote through bilateral or multilateral consultations the return of refugees to their home country with the consent both of the refugees themselves and of their country of origin; and to continue to guarantee the safety of political refugees from dependent territories and support them in their struggle for the liberation of their countries.

It also adopted a resolution on political refugees which recalled the member states' pledge to prevent refugees living in their territories from carrying out by any means whatsoever any acts harmful to the interests of member states; requested all member states never to allow the refugee question to become a source of disagreement among them; appreciated the assistance given to the refugee programmes of African governments by the UN High Commissioner for Refugees (UNHCR); requested African members of the UN Economic and Social Council to seek an increase in African representation on the executive committee of the UNHCR programme on refugees; and requested those member states which had not already done so to ratify the UN convention on refugees and to apply meanwhile the provisions of that convention to refugees in Africa.

1966. The third Assembly of Heads of State and Government, held in Addis Ababa on Nov. 5–9, 1966, decided inter alia to replace the

Liberation Committee in Dar es Salaam by a new committee of 10 members, the executive of which would be placed under the direct control of the OAU Secretariat-General and would be excluded from any initiative of a political nature in its activities.

1967. The fourth Assembly of Heads of State and Government was held in Kinshasa on Sept. 11–14, 1967, without Malawi being represented.

1968. The fifth Assembly of Heads of State and Government, attended by representatives of all 40 member states except Malawi, was held in Algiers on Sept. 13–16, 1968.

1969. The sixth Assembly, at which all 41 member states (including Equatorial Guinea, independent since Oct. 12, 1968) were represented, took place in Addis Ababa on Sept. 6–9, 1969.

1970. The seventh Assembly, held in Addis Ababa from Sept. 1 to 3, 1970, was marked by the reconciliation of the Federal Military Government of Nigeria and the Governments of Côte d'Ivoire, Gabon, Tanzania, and Zambia, all of which had in 1967 recognized the secessionist regime in "Biafra", since defeated by the Federal Nigerian forces.

1971. The eighth Assembly, which took place in Addis Ababa from June 21 to 23, 1971, was not attended by the Central African Republic and Uganda, the latter being absent in protest against the transfer of the Assembly's venue from Kampala to Addis Ababa as the result of opposition to President Amin of Uganda by several member states. The Assembly adopted, by 28 votes to six, with five abstentions, a declaration rejecting a "dialogue" with the Government of South Africa as suggested by President Houphouët-Boigny of Côte d'Ivoire.

1972. The ninth Assembly, held in Rabat on June 11–15, 1972, reaffirmed its support for the OAU liberation committee by increasing its budget by 50 per cent and its membership to 15 countries—Algeria, the Congo, Egypt, Ethiopia, Guinea, Libya, Mauritania, Morocco, Nigeria, Senegal, Somalia, Tanzania, Uganda, Zaïre and Zambia. The Assembly also adopted a resolution strongly supporting Egypt's demand for the evacuation by Israel of all Egyptian territory occupied since July 1967.

During the years 1971-72 the OAU was instrumental in achieving reconciliation in a number of disputes between member states, including those between Senegal and Guinea (on Senegal's alleged failure to suppress activities against the Guinean Government), between Guinea and Ghana (over the burial of the late ex-President Kwame Nkrumah), and between rival Angolan liberation movements.

1973. The 10th Assembly was held in Addis Ababa on May 27–29, 1973. In the course of the meeting the disputes between Ethiopia and Somalia and between Uganda and Tanzania were

the subject of OAU mediation. An eight-member "good offices committee" was formed to seek ways of reconciling Ethiopia and Somalia in their territorial dispute. In the case of Uganda and Tanzania, whose conflict dated from the previous September, when armed followers of former President Obote of Uganda had invaded Uganda from Tanzania, an agreement was reached, which was signed by the two Presidents on May 28.

Under the terms of the agreement, the Ugandan Government agreed to pay to Tanzania compensation for the deaths of 24 Tanzanian nationals in Uganda; both parties agreed to adhere strictly to the terms of the Mogadishu peace agreement [see below], and in particular to prevent their territories from being used as bases for subversion against each other; the Tanzanian Government assumed responsibility that ex-President Obote would not interfere in Uganda's affairs; and the Ugandan Government would not demand Dr Obote's expulsion from Tanzania.

[The Mogadishu peace agreement, signed on Oct. 5, 1972, provided for the withdrawal of troops from the Ugandan-Tanzanian border and for a cessation of all military activities by the two sides against each other.]

1974. The 11th Assembly was held in Mogadishu (Somalia) on June 12–16, 1974 (with Malawi being represented for the first time in several years). Among resolutions adopted by the Assembly was one confirming acceptance of a loan of US$200,000,000 from Arab League member states and the decision to place this amount in a special account with the African Development Bank (in Abidjan) for subsequent distribution among non-oil-producing African countries in need. The Assembly, however, made no progress towards a solution of the dispute between Ethiopia and Somalia, notwithstanding a private meeting between the two heads of state on June 13.

1975. The 12th Assembly, held in Kampala (Uganda) on July 28–Aug. 1, 1975, elected President Amin of Uganda as President of the OAU (for the customary one-year term), despite strong opposition to President Amin's policies by the Presidents of Botswana, Mozambique, Tanzania and Zambia.

In connection with the admission of the Comoros to the OAU the Assembly called on France to respect the territorial integrity of the newly-independent state (i.e. with the inclusion of the island of Mayotte which, however, remained under French control).

The Assembly declined to demand the expulsion of Israel from the United Nations (as called for in particular by Libya, whereas in Egypt it was argued that the object should be to pressurize Israel into implementing UN resolutions on the Middle East and not induce it to renounce its commitment to these UN resolutions).

This session of the Assembly was also addressed by Yassir Arafat, the leader of the Palestine Liberation Organization (PLO), who declared inter alia that there could be no peace in the Middle East without a Palestine; that the PLO was confident of ultimate victory; and that Africa should be given increased Arab aid. He did not, however, refer to the PLO's earlier call for the expulsion of Israel from the United Nations.

The Assembly endorsed a Dar es Salaam declaration agreed to at an extraordinary meeting of the OAU Council of Ministers on April 11, 1975, expressing "unqualified support for the freedom fighters" led by the African National Council (ANC) of Rhodesia, and also support for the ANC's efforts to achieve a peaceful change until they were convinced that talks had irretrievably failed. As for South Africa, the declaration stated that the Whites had had "ample time to change their attitude on apartheid" and that armed struggle was the only way left. In two supplementary resolutions to the declaration it was proposed that (i) a special OAU committee, to be appointed from among African members of the UN Council for Namibia, should have special responsibility for facilitating contracts between the South African Government and the South West Africa People's Organization (SWAPO), the national liberation movement recognized by the OAU for Namibia, and (ii) further measures should be taken to isolate the White minority Government in South Africa, including enforcement of sanctions and the denial of port and airport facilities not only to all South African ships and aircraft but also to naval vessels and military aircraft from other countries which used South Africa's facilities.

1976. The 13th regular Assembly was held in Port Louis (Mauritius) on July 2–6, 1976, but was only poorly attended. It approved strong resolutions against the Government of South Africa, including a call for intensified armed struggle (but not mobilization of the armies of Africa's independent countries, as called for by Guinea) and for a possible Arab oil boycott against South Africa. The Assembly also proposed the holding of an OAU emergency summit meeting to discuss the dispute between Algeria and Morocco (supported by Mauritania) over the Western Sahara.

1977. The 14th Assembly, held in Libreville (Gabon) on July 2–5, 1977, was not attended by Benin (formerly Dahomey), whose Government accused that of Gabon of having been involved in an attempted coup by mercenaries who attacked Benin on Jan. 16, 1977.

The Assembly was marked by strong attacks made by several African leaders, notably the President of the Sudan, on Soviet interference in African affairs, and it was overshadowed by numerous disputes among African states during 1976-77 (between Egypt and Libya, Libya and the Sudan, Ethiopia and its neighbours, the member states of the East African Community—which had eventually distintegrated, and Mauritania and Morocco on the one hand and Algeria and the Polisario Front of the Western Sahara on the other, in connection with which the Government of Morocco had on Feb. 25, 1977, decided to suspend its participation in the OAU temporarily).

On the conflict between Ethiopia and Somalia an OAU eight-member mediation committee set up in 1973 reaffirmed on Aug. 9, 1977, the inviolability of frontiers inherited from the colonial era (in accordance with the UN Charter) and the condemnation of all subversive activities on the part of neighbouring states or other states, and it invited President Bongo of Gabon to take

up contact with the two sides with a view to "halting hostilities".

On the question of foreign intervention the Assembly approved a draft resolution submitted by Senegal which (i) appealed to all African states to abstain from having recourse to foreign intervention in internal African problems; (ii) invited OAU member states to prohibit the use of their territory as a base for aggression against another African state; (iii) requested powers outside Africa "to abstain from interfering in the internal affairs of African states" and (iv) recommended member states to reach "a peaceful settlement of their disputes by way of negotiation and mediation". (The resolution referred in particular to Cuban intervention in Angola and to Sudanese support for the insurrection in Eritrea.)

1978. The 15th Assembly took place in Khartoum on July 18–22, 1978, and was attended by representatives of all OAU member states except the Comoros (whose delegation was not admitted on the ground that the existing Comoro Government had been installed with the aid of a White mercenary in May 1978). This session of the Assembly revealed wide differences of opinion on the question of foreign troops and bases in Africa.

At the Council of Ministers' meeting preceding the session, the Foreign Minister of Libya denounced Mauritania, Chad and Zaïre for having invited French troops into their countries, and the Congolese Foreign Minister accused African countries which had made up a pan-African force for intervention in Zaïre (viz. Morocco, Senegal, the Central African Empire, Togo, Côte d'Ivoire, Gabon and Egypt), calling their action a flagrant violation of the OAU Charter.

After the countries thus accused had defended their actions, the Assembly adopted a resolution in which it (i) condemned the conclusion of military pacts and alliances with non-African powers but reaffirmed the right of each country to choose its own ideological system and to call on any country for assistance if its sovereignty or territorial integrity was threatened; (ii) rejected the idea of an African intervention force which was not formed within the context of the objectives and priorities defined by the OAU and called for the reactivation of the OAU defence committee to consider the establishment of a force supervised by the OAU; (iii) reaffirmed its adherence to the principle of respect for territorial integrity and sovereignty of states and its desire to resort to peaceful ways of settling differences between African states in order not to pave the way for foreign intervention; (iv) condemned the policy of force and intervention in Africa regarding of its source, and opposed all plans to recolonize the continent; (v) demanded that differences between African states should be resolved peacefully and within the African framework; (vi) proclaimed that the maintenance of peace in Africa was the responsibility of Africans alone; (vii) repeated its unanimous strong condemnation of some (unspecified) non-African countries which had resorted to the use of mercenaries to jeopardize the security and independence of African countries; and (viii) reaffirmed the desire to eliminate foreign military bases.

With implied reference to Cuban intervention in Africa, the Assembly also called on the African members of the non-aligned movement to abide by the agreed objectives and principles of the movement, condemned strongly any foreign intervention in the affairs of the African continent and called on all member states to settle their differences within the African framework.

1979. The 16th Assembly was held in Monrovia (Liberia) on July 17–21, 1979. It was attended by representatives of all OAU member states except Chad (which had sent two delegations, neither of which was admitted to the session). This session was again marked by disputes among member states. Tanzania's role in the overthrow of the Amin regime in Uganda in April 1978 was strongly criticized, notably by the Sudan and Nigeria; a resolution calling for a ceasefire and a UN-supervised referendum in the Western Sahara caused the Moroccan delegation to leave the session; and during a speech by the Egyptian President in defence of the 1979 Egyptian-Israeli peace treaty several other Arab delegations also walked out.

In his opening speech President Tolbert of Liberia said on July 16 that as a result of "fratricidal conflicts" there were over 4,000,000 refugees in Africa and that the OAU Charter should be revised by making the provisions concerning the protection of fundamental human rights explicit, and by creating a mechanism for setting up a pan-African force to enable the OAU to respond rapidly to problems which threatened the peace, security and stability of Africa.

Resolutions adopted by the Assembly included one involving approval, in principle, of the establishment of a joint African defence force. It was also announced that a Pan-African News Agency would begin work on Oct. 1, 1979, with headquarters in Dakar and with regional news pools to be set up in the Sudan, Libya, Nigeria, Zaïre and Zambia.

1980. A special conference of the heads of state and government held in Lagos on April 28–30, 1980, adopted a *Lagos Plan of Action* for the implementation of a strategy (previously proposed by Nigeria) for the economic development of Africa, setting out guidelines (i) for 1980–90 on strengthening subregional groupings in central, eastern, northern and southern Africa and (ii) for 1990–2000 on closer integration between such groupings. In a protocol the heads of state and government reaffirmed their commitment to establish, by the year 2000, an African Economic Community.

The proposals were aimed at achieving food self-sufficiency for the continent by 1990; improving communications; harmonizing industrial development so as to increase Africa's share of the world's industrial production from the current estimated 0.6 per cent to 1 per cent by 1985 and to 2 per cent by the year 2000; and expanding inter-African trade, with the elimination of all trade barriers in Africa by 1990.

The 17th Assembly of Heads of State and Government, held in Freetown (Sierra Leone) on July 1–4, 1980, referred the question of the Western Sahara to an ad hoc committee (appointed earlier) which was to convene a meeting of all interested parties within three months. It also called on all OAU member states to contribute to a required budget of $60,000,000 to finance an African peace-keeping force to end the civil war in Chad.

The meeting on the Western Sahara, which took place in Freetown on Sept. 9–12, 1980, formulated a six-point plan for a ceasefire under UN supervision and a referendum under OAU auspices. The Moroccan Foreign Minister, however, stated that the plan would have to be approved by a two-thirds majority of the Assembly of Heads of State and Government (due in Nairobi in July 1981).

1981. The 18th Assembly of Heads of State and Government, held in Nairobi on June 24–28, 1981, was divided over the unresolved question of the Western Sahara, for which King Hassan II of Morocco had proposed the holding of a referendum. On the problem of Chad (to which Libya had sent troops under a "treaty of friendship" of June 1980) the Assembly reaffirmed the need for a pan-African peace-keeping force to be sent to that country.

The Assembly also approved a Charter of Human and People's Rights.

In the preamble to this Charter the OAU affirmed its "duty to achieve the total liberation of Africa" and its "undertaking to eliminate colonialism, neocolonialism [and] apartheid"—to which it added "Zionism" (at the request of Algeria and Libya). The Charter itself provided inter alia that every individual had the right to express and disseminate his opinions, but only "within the law" (Art. 9), and that the right of an individual to leave any country could be restricted "by law for the protection of national security, law and order, public health or morality" (Art. 12). It defined the individual's duties towards his family, society and state and required every African to "preserve the harmonious development of the family and . . . respect his parents at all times and maintain them in case of need", "to place his abilities at the service of his national community", and to "preserve and strengthen positive African values" (Art. 29).

The text of the Charter was opposed by a number of "moderate" African governments, including that of Senegal.

1982. On the proposed holding of a referendum in the Western Sahara, however, no agreement was reached during 1982 between Morocco and the Polisario Front which had in 1976 set up the Saharan Arab Democratic Republic (SADR). Having been recognized by 26 of the then 50 OAU member states, the SADR was admitted to a meeting of the OAU Council of Ministers on Feb. 22, 1982. This step led to a severe crisis in the organization.

The 19th Assembly of the Heads of State and Government, scheduled for Aug. 5–8, 1982, could not be held because the required two-thirds quorum could not be achieved as a result of a boycott by Morocco and those states which supported its opposition to the SADR's admission to the OAU. The crisis was aggravated by a dispute over the representation of Chad (where civil war had broken out), from which two rival delegations sought admission to OAU meetings. Adjourned until Nov. 23, 1982, the 19th Assembly again failed to open for lack of a quorum. However, those representatives who had travelled to Tripoli for the occasion issued, on Nov. 25, 1982, a Tripoli declaration which included resolutions on two issues—(1) reaffirming the OAU's total support for the armed struggle of the South West Africa People's Organization (SWAPO) in Namibia and (2) condemning "the continuing co-operation" between the Reagan Administration and South Africa in the economic, military and nuclear fields and also the International Monetary Fund's decision of Nov. 3, 1982, on a standby arrangement for South Africa.

1983. The SADR declared in June 8, 1983, that it had decided "voluntarily and temporarily" not to particiapte in the OAU's 19th Assembly. Opening in Addis Ababa on the same day, the Assembly was again dominated by the Western Sahara question and adopted, by consensus on Nov. 21, a draft resolution calling on Morocco and the Polisario Front to undertake direct negotiations with a view to bringing about a ceasefire and creating the necessary conditions for a fair referendum in the territory in December 1983. However, no agreement was subsequently reached on such negotiations.

1984. The 20th Assembly of Heads of State and Government was held in Addis Ababa on Nov. 12–15, 1984. At this session the SADR was again represented. In protest Morocco withdrew from membership of the OAU.

The session dealt in particular with Africa's "critical economic situation", including the problems of recurring drought and desertification and a total foreign debt of some $150,000 million owed by African countries as at June 1984. In a declaration adopted on Nov. 15 a call was made for the lifting at international level of the "externally induced constraints" on African countries which had prevented them from effectively mobilizing resources to relieve areas in need, and the OAU's commitment to the 1980 Lagos Plan of Action [see above] was reaffirmed.

A resolution was also adopted on the creation of a special fund for Africa under the auspices of the World Bank, to be financed by voluntary contributions, and also a special assistance fund for victims of drought and famine.

1985. The 21st Assembly of Heads of State and Government was held in Addis Ababa on July 18–21, 1985. Prior to this session it was disclosed that only 26 per cent of dues owed by member countries for the current financial year had been paid, and that members owed some $39,000,000 ($21,000,000 of this from previous years). (The budget proposed for 1985—86 was for about $23,250,000.)

The outgoing chairman (President Nyerere of Tanzania) referred, in his speech to the session, to the problem of some 5,000,000 refugees in Africa who, he said, should not be forcibly returned to their countries, and to the related problem of human rights, noting that a majority of OAU member states had not completed the process of ratifying the OAU Charter of Human and People's Rights adopted in 1981 [see above] and urging them to do so.

An Addis Ababa declaration adopted on July 20, 1985, contained a survey of the economic situation and a five-year draft programme of measures to achieve a recovery in the short, medium and long term. It reaffirmed that the development of Africa was the primary responsibility of African governments and peoples. The programme called for accelerated implementation of the Lagos Plan of Action, for the improvement of the food situation and the rehabilitation of agricultural development, measures for alleviating the external debt burden, and measures for action against the effects of the destabilization policy of South Africa on the economies of southern African states. [It was noted that 26 of the 36 UN-designated least developed countries (LDCs) were in Africa, and that the external debt of many of them was beyond their capacity to pay.]

1986. The 22nd Assembly of Heads of State and Government was held in Addis Ababa on July 28–30, 1986. In a series of resolutions adopted on the recommendation of an OAU Council of Ministers' meeting earlier in the month, the Assembly (i) repeated its call for the immediate imposition of mandatory economic sanctions on South Africa and condemned Western nations which maintained economic relations with South Africa; (ii) called for "voluntary sanctions" against the United Kingdom for its opposition to economic sanctions on South Africa; (iii) condemned the United States for its military and financial support for the "UNITA bandits" in Angola and asserted the "sovereign right" of Angola to decide "if and when the Cuban forces in that country could be withdrawn"; and (iv) established a special committee of heads of state to monitor the situation in southern Africa.

In other decisions the Assembly (i) requested the OAU Secretary-General to propose "practical ways and means of ensuring the establishment of an African economic community"; (ii) expressed full support for the convening of an international conference on Africa's external debt; (iii) requested the Secretary-General to prepare the groundwork for a first Afro-Arab ministerial conference so that it could be convened before the end of the year; (iv) established a "council of wise men", to include former heads of state "whose authority is still respected at national and international level", charged with seeking to reconcile disputes between OAU member states; and (v) approved an "OAU anthem" (composed by a Kenyan, with words by an Ethiopian and a Nigerian) subject to a suggestion by Prime Minister Mugabe of Zimbabwe that it should have an additional verse on the African struggle against colonialism and foreign domination.

Other International Groupings of African States

African Development Bank (AfDB)

Address. Ol B.P. 1387, Abidjan Ol, Côte d'Ivoire.

Officer. Willa D. Mung'omba (exec. pres. and ch. of board of directors).

Founded. Aug. 4, 1963.

Membership. All members of the Organization of African Unity and some 30 non-African states.

History. The decision to set up an African Development Bank was reached by representatives of 32 independent African states and Kenya in Khartoum on Aug. 4, 1963, when the Finance Ministers of 31 of these countries signed an agreement which came into force on Sept. 10, 1964. The bank was formally constituted on Sept. 25, 1964, with its capital being subscribed exclusively by African states, and it began operations in 1966. Loans granted to member countries by the bank to Dec. 31, 1981, totalled $3,106,597.

The bank has six associated institutions as follows:

African Development Fund (ADF). This fund was set up in November 1972 on a proposal by the AfDB and under an agreement signed by Belgium, Brazil, Canada, Denmark, Finland, the Federal Republic of Germany, Japan, the Netherlands, Norway, Spain, Switzerland, the United Kingdom and Yugoslavia. The fund began operations on Aug. 1, 1973, with initial resources of about $100,000,000 (its first contributors including Canada, the Federal Republic of Germany and Sweden). The fund was also to administer a Special Swiss Fund for Africa of 12,000,000 Swiss francs (about £2,000,000) set up by the Swiss Government on Sept. 14, 1974. By 1985 there were some 30 non-African states participating in the ADF.

Nigeria Trust Fund (NTF). This fund was set up under an agreement which was signed by the ADF and the Government of Nigeria in February 1976 and came into force in April of that year. The NFT provides loans for projects in co-operation with other lending institutions.

Société internationale financière pour les investissements et le développement en Afrique (SIFIDA). SIFIDA was set up in Geneva in November 1970 with the object of promoting the establishment and growth of productive enterprises in Africa.

Africa Reinsurance Corporation (AFRICARE). Established under an agreement signed in February 1976 and in force from January 1977, AFRICARE was formally constituted in March of that year with headquarters in Lagos and with the object of fostering the development of the insurance and reinsurance industry in Africa.

Shelter Afrique, a housing corporation set up in 1983 and based in Nairobi.

Association of African Development Finance Institutions (AADFI), established in 1975 and based in Abidjan.

African Regional Organization for Standardization

Address. P.O.B. 57363, Nairobi, Kenya.

Officer. Zawdu Felleke (sec. gen.).

Founded. 1977.

Membership. 23 states.

African Training and Research Centre in Administration and Development
Centre africain de formation et de recherches administratives pour le développement (CAFRAD)

Address. B.P. 310, Tangier, Morocco.

Officers. Mohamed Tougani (pres.); Aliou Samba Diallo (dir.-gen.).

Founded. 1964.

Membership. 33 African countries.

Activities. The centre provides a consultative service for governments and organizations and holds frequent seminars.

Association of African Trade Promotion Organizations (AATPO)

Address. B.P. 23, Tangier, Morocco.

Officer. Demeke Zewolde (sec. gen.).

Founded. 1975.

Membership. 26 states.

History. The AATPO was established under the auspices of the Organization of African Unity and the (UN) Economic Commission for Africa.

Industrial Property Organization for English-Speaking Africa (ESARIPO)

Address. P.O.B. 30552, Nairobi, Kenya.

Founded. Dec. 7, 1976.

Membership. Botswana, The Gambia, Ghana, Kenya, Malawi, Sierra Leone, Somalia, the Sudan, Tanzania, Uganda, Zambia and Zimbabwe.

Activities. A protocol on the granting of patents and the registration of industrial designs was adopted on Dec. 10, 1982, and came into force on April 25, 1984.

Co-operation between former Portuguese Colonies

At the end of a meeting in Maputo (Mozambique) on March 30, 1980, of the Presidents of Angola, Cape Verde, Guinea-Bissau, Mozambique and São Tomé and Príncipe (all former

Portuguese territories), a general agreement was signed on co-operation, defining the bases of mutual assistance in the fields of trade, transport, finance, banking and insurance. The five Presidents also decided to meet annually in order to analyse how the agreement was being implemented and to define new guidelines for strengthening the existing relations between the five countries. In the field of foreign policy the five Presidents inter alia expressed their solidarity with "the South African people led by the African National Congress", with the Polisario Front in the Western Sahara, with the Fretilin liberation movement of East Timor (Indonesia) and with the Palestine Liberation Organization.

A first summit conference of the five countries' heads of state had been held in Luanda (Angola) on June 9–10, 1979, when it had been agreed to adopt similar policies for the economic and social development of these countries.

At a third summit conference held in Praia (Cape Verde) on Sept. 21–22, 1982, it was decided to increase the exchange of information on the foreign policy of each of the five countries, to intensify policy harmonization within international organizations, to improve the co-ordination of diplomatic efforts, especially for the denunciation of aggression against Angola and Mozambique, and to take action to have Portuguese recognized as a language of international organizations.

A further meeting of heads of state, held in Bissau on Dec. 18–20, 1983, discussed inter alia a Portuguese proposal to create a special link between Portugal, Brazil and the former Portuguese African colonies.

African-Arab Conferences

A first conference of Foreign Ministers from African and Arab countries was held in Cairo on July 9–10, 1975, and was attended by representatives of 23 countries and of the Palestine Liberation Organization (PLO). The participants expressed their desire "to expand and intensify co-operation in trade, mining, industry, agriculture, energy, water resources, transport and communications", and they agreed on the formation of a permanent joint ministerial committee.

A second such conference, held in Dakar on April 19–22, 1976, was attended by 40 ministers and also by representatives of the African Development Bank, the Arab Development Bank and several liberation movements, including the PLO. The conference prepared a draft charter for submission to an Afro-Arab summit meeting to be held in 1977.

This charter provided inter alia for the establishment of direct trade relations between African and Arab countries, with priority to be given to supplying each other's respective markets and mutual preferential treatment to be accorded in trade.

A first conference of heads of state and government of African and Arab states took place in Cairo on March 7–9, 1977, under the joint auspices of the Arab League and the OAU.

It was attended by a total of 60 delegations (from all OAU member states except Malawi and from the 21 members of the Arab League, including the PLO), among them 36 heads of state. Admitted as observers were six national liberation movements—two from Djibouti, SWAPO of Namibia, the African National Congress and the Pan-Africanist Congress (both from South Africa) and the Patriotic Front of Zimbabwe. The Eritrean Liberation Front was admitted in a semi-official capacity, but the Polisario Front of the Western Sahara was not represented.

During the conference leaders of Arab oil-producing countries announced that they would make grants-in-aid and loans to Black African states. These undertakings included $1,200 million from Saudi Arabia for economic and social development in Africa; $240,000,000 from Kuwait; $76,000,000 from Qatar; and $135,000,000 from the United Arab Emirates.

The conference issued three declarations—including a *Declaration and Action Programme for African-Arab Co-operation* to be known as the *Cairo Declaration*—and a resolution on the organization and methods of future African-Arab co-operation. The contents of these documents are summarized below.

The "Cairo Declaration". In the Declaration and Action Programme the participants in the conference listed the basic principles of their co-operation as being respect for the sovereignty of all their states, equality among them, permanent sovereignty over their natural resources, the rejection of all aggression and the illegality of forcible occupation or annexation of the land of others, non-interference in the domestic affairs of other states, preservation of mutual interests on the basis of reciprocal treatment and equality, the peaceable settlement of differences, and "joint struggle against hegemony, racialism and exploitation in all their forms".

In this declaration the African and Arab states undertook to co-operate in the fields of politics and diplomacy, economy and finance, trade, education, culture, science, technology and information, with a detailed action programme being outlined for all these fields. It was also decided to establish a permanent joint committee at ministerial level to ensure the implementation of the programme. [For this "standing commission" see below under "Future African-Arab Relations".]

Political Declaration. The political document expressed the participants' commitment to the principles of non-alignment and of peaceful coexistence; called for the establishment of "a just international economic order"; and demanded "the intensification, on an international scale, of the political and economic isolation of Israel, South Africa and Rhodesia as long as these countries have not changed their policies". The document emphasized the need for an oil embargo, in particular against South Africa (notwithstanding the fact that several states represented at the conference had continued to supply oil to that country), and it also proclaimed support for "the territorial integrity of the Comoros". [Reservations on this declaration had been expressed by Chad, the Congo, Ethiopia and Kenya because it contained no condemnation of "secessionist and counter-revolutionary movements".]

Economic and Financial Co-operation. The Declaration on Economic and Financial Co-operation retraced the development of African-Arab co-operation, which was stated to have increased sevenfold during the past three years, and provided inter alia for (i) encouragement of technical and financial aid for studying the feasibility of development projects and basic structures in Africa and for the financing of such projects; (ii) an expansion of the resources of the Arab Bank for Economic Development in Africa (ABEDA) to enable it to play a greater role; (iii) a strengthening of trade relations between African and Arab countries by mutual preferential treatment; and (iv) encouragement of Arab investment through the creation of a system of investment guarantees in African states. [The development projects to be studied included four sponsored by the UN Economic Commission for Africa which would require total finance of $1,327 million—(i) a trans-African road system of 30,000 kilometres (about 19,000 miles), comprising roads from Algiers to Gao (eastern Mali), from Mombasa (Kenya) to Lagos (Nigeria), from Dakar (Senegal) to N'Djaména (Chad), along the Atlantic coast from Lagos to Nouakchott (Mauritania), from Cairo (via East Africa) to Gaborone (Botswana), and 82 secondary roads of a total length of 47,000 kilometres (28,000 miles) in 40 African countries; (ii) an assessment of Africa's natural resources, in particular of water basins and hydrocarbons; (iii) a pan-African telecommunications network (PANAFTEL), for which 90 per cent of the $250,000,000 required was said to be already available; and (iv) the creation of a computerized data bank (at a cost of $7,000,000).]

Future African-Arab Relations. The resolution on the modalities of African-Arab relations laid down (i) that the Afro-Arab "summit" conference would be held once every three years, and the ordinary meeting of the Afro-Arab Council of Ministers once every 18 months; (ii) that a standing commission would be formed from ministers of the states which were members of the 12-member committees of the OAU and the Arab League, or their representatives, together with the Secretaries-General of the OAU and the Arab League, under the co-chairmanship of the chairmen of these two 12-member committees; (iii) that this standing commission, which would hold ordinary meetings twice a year, would supervise Afro-Arab co-operation and development and would study and direct co-operation in achieving the political, social, technological and economic aims set out in the Declaration and Action programme; (iv) that working groups and specialized committees would be formed when necessary in a number of fields; (v) that a co-ordinating committee, comprising the chairmen of the two 12-member committees and the two Secretaries-General (of the OAU and the Arab League) and responsible to the standing commission, would co-ordinate the activities of the working groups and supervise the implementation of any decisions taken; (vi) that an ad hoc Afro-Arab court, or arbitration and conciliation commission, would settle any dispute arising; and (vii) that a special fund, financed on a 50-50 basis from the budgets of the OAU and the Arab League, would be established to run the work of the executive organs of Afro-Arab co-operation.

Regional Organizations in Africa

East and Central Africa

Conferences of East and Central African States

Heads of state or government of East and Central African states began in 1966 to hold regular conferences to discuss problems of mutual interest.

The first of these conferences, held in Nairobi from March 31 to April 2, 1966, was attended by heads of state, ministers or other representatives of 11 states—Burundi, Congo-Kinshasa (Zaïre), Ethiopia, Kenya, Malawi, Rwanda, Somalia, Sudan, Tanzania, Uganda and Zambia.

The second conference, held in Kinshasa on Feb. 12–14, 1967, was also attended by representatives of the Central African Republic and the Congo (Brazzaville), whereas Ethiopia, Malawi and Somalia were not represented. It issued a "Declaration of Kinshasa" expressing solidarity on African problems and in particular support for the "liberation movement in Africa" and the use of force against the Smith regime in Rhodesia.

The fifth conference, held in Lusaka on April 14–16, 1969, and attended by representatives of 14 countries—i.e. those present at the first conference and also the Central African Republic, Chad and Congo (Brazzaville), issued the "Lusaka Manifesto", defining the 14 states' attitude to "colonialism and racial discrimination . . . practised in southern Africa".

The document contained inter alia the following passages:

"Our stand towards southern Africa involves . . . a rejection of racialism, not a reversal of existing racial domination. . . .

"If peaceful progress to emancipation were possible, or if changed circumstances were to make it possible in the future, we would urge our brothers in the resistance movements to use peaceful methods of struggle, even at the cost of some compromise on the timing of change. But while peaceful progress is blocked by the actions of those at present in power in the states of southern Africa, we have no choice but to give to the peoples of those territories all the support of which we are capable in their struggle against their oppressors. . . .

"The actions of the South African Government are such that the rest of the world has a responsibility to take some action in defence of humanity.

"South Africa should be excluded from the United Nations' agencies and even from the United Nations itself. It should be ostracized by the world community. It should be isolated from world trade patterns and left to be self-sufficient if it can.

"The South African Government cannot be allowed both to reject the very concept of mankind's unity and to benefit by the strength given through friendly international relations."

The seventh conference, held in Mogadishu on Oct. 18–19, 1971, when all 14 countries were represented, approved the "Mogadishu Declaration" condemning any "dialogue" with the Government of South Africa (as had been advocated by President Houphouët-Boigny of Côte d'Ivoire) and reaffirming support for "armed struggle . . . for the liberation of southern Africa". The conference also adopted a "Declaration on Aggression against Zambia" pledging "all material and other aid" to that country against "aggressive actions on the part of the minority and colonialist regimes in southern Africa".

The eighth conference was held in Dar es Salaam on Sept. 7–10, 1972, with 16 countries being represented (i.e. the 14 participants in the previous conference and also Equatorial Guinea and Gabon). The conference adopted a "pledge of solidarity" whereby all member states would grant liberation movements guaranteed access through their territories provided this did not impair national security, and would come to the

426

military assistance of any member state which might be attacked or be subjected to economic pressure by White minority regimes, with aid to be given in particular to Zambia as "the main support base" for the liberation organizations.

At the ninth conference held in Brazzaville on Aug. 31–Sept. 2, 1974, Cameroon was admitted as the 17th member of the conference.

Conferences of East and Central African Leaders

With the object of intensifying mutual co-operation in all fields the Presidents of Burundi, Kenya, Rwanda, Tanzania and Uganda and the Prime Minister of the Sudan have held a number of meetings, the first of them in Kinshasa (Zaïre) in January 1986, the second in Entebbe (Uganda) in March 1986 and the third in Khartoum (Sudan) on July 14–15, 1986. At the third of these meetings they emphasized the need for maintaining security in the region, describing it as "indivisible". They also called for mandatory sanctions to be imposed against South Africa and warned the West that the peoples of Africa would never forgive those who failed to join in the struggle against the apartheid system "at this decisive moment".

Customs and Economic Union of Central Africa
Union douanière et économique de l'Afrique centrale (UDEAC)

Address. B.P. 969, Bangui, Central African Republic.

Officer. Vincent Efon (sec. gen.).

Founded. Dec. 8, 1964.

Membership. Cameroon, the Central African Republic, Chad, the Congo, Equatorial Guinea, and Gabon. (Chad withdrew from the UDEAC on Dec. 31, 1968, but was readmitted on Dec. 17, 1984; Equatorial Guinea was admitted on Dec. 18, 1983.)

History. The UDEAC was formed under a Brazzaville Convention which came into force on Jan. 1, 1966. Trade between member countries was made duty-free, and freedom of movement of nationals of member states was established in 1972. At a summit meeting held in Brazzaville on Dec. 17–19, 1984, decisions were taken on industrial integration, the training of statisticians, the harmonization of taxation, and investment in joint projects, especially in road transport.

Affiliated organizations. The UDEAC's issuing bank is the Banque des états de l'Afrique centrale in Yaoundé, and its development bank is the Banque de développement des états de l'Afrique centrale in Brazzaville.

Economic Community of Central African States
Communauté économique des états de l'Afrique centrale (CEEAC)

Address. B.P. 969, Bangui, Central African Republic.

Founded. Oct. 18, 1983.

Membership. Burundi, Cameroon, the Central African Republic, Chad, the Congo, Equatorial Guinea, Gabon, Rwanda, São Tomé and Príncipe, and Zaïre.

Objects. The CEEAC was to promote co-operation between its member states by abolishing trade restrictions and establishing a common external customs tariff and a development fund over a 12-year period.

History. A declaration of intent to form the CEEAC was issued by the Customs and Economic Union of Central Africa (UDEAC) in December 1981. The CEEAC was subsequently established by ministers of its member countries, the UDEAC secretary-general and the executive secretary of the Economic Community of the Countries of the Great Lakes [see below] and with the collaboration of the Secretary-General of the Organization of African Unity and the executive secretary of the (UN) Economic Commission for Africa (ECA).

The second ordinary summit meeting was held in Yaoundé (Cameroon) on Jan. 23–24, 1986, when Angola took part as an observer. The meeting passed a 1986 budget of some 1,141 million CFA francs (US$1.00=CFA francs 377.72). Contributions, to be paid in dollars, were to be made in the following proportions: Cameroon, the Congo, Gabon and Zaïre 18 per cent each; the Central African Republic 9 per cent; Burundi, Chad, Equatorial Guinea, Rwanda and São Tomé and Príncipe 3.8 per cent each. A shortfall of about 20 per cent of the 1985 budget contributions was to be covered by special contributions from the richer member countries.

Economic Community of the Great Lakes Countries
Communauté économique des pays des grands lacs (CEPGL)

Address. P.O.B. 58, Gisenyi, Rwanda.

Officers. Antoine Nduwayo (exec. sec.).

Founded. Sept. 26, 1976.

Membership. Burundi, Rwanda and Zaïre.

History. The CEPGL was set up under a convention signed by the Presidents of Burundi, Rwanda and Zaïre who, at the same time, concluded a treaty of friendship and co-operation between their three countries.

On Dec. 24, 1976, the three Presidents appointed a permanent executive secretary of the community; granted full powers to the community's Council of Ministers to approve an annual budget; and decided to set up a US$3,000,000 fund for the community.

On Sept. 8–9, 1977, the three Presidents agreed inter alia on various development programmes designed to lead to regional economic integration.

On June 16–17, 1984, the three Presidents agreed to co-operate in the areas of customs duties and commercial operations, to reduce inter-community trade restrictions, and also to maintain security on their common borders.

The community has set up a Banque de développement des états des grands lacs (BDEGL) at Goma (Zaïre), an energy centre at Bujumbura (Burundi) and an Institute of

Agronomic and Zootechnical Research at Gitega (Burundi).

Indian Ocean Commission (IOC)

This commission was established on July 17, 1982, by the governments of Madagascar, Mauritius and Seychelles with the object of examining all possibilities of their co-operation. At the third session of the IOC, held in Antananarivo (Madagascar) on Jan. 16–17, 1985, it was decided to admit the Comoros as the fourth member of the IOC.

Organization for the Management and Development of the Kagera River Basin

Address. B.P. 297, Kigali, Rwanda.
Officer. Dr David S. O. Wache (exec. sec.).
Founded. August 1977.
Membership. Burundi, Tanzania, Uganda (which joined the organization on May 19, 1981) and Rwanda.
Objects. Established by Burundi, Rwanda and Tanzania, the organization was to continue projects begun in 1971 and to develop irrigation, electric power (to enable Burundi to become independent of outside sources for its electricity), navigation and mining in the basin.

Permanent Inter-Governmental Authority on Drought and Development in East Africa (PIGADD)

Officer. Moumin Bahdoun Farah (co-ordinator).
Founded. Feb. 5–6, 1985.
Membership. Ethiopia, Kenya, Somalia, the Sudan and Uganda.

Eastern and Southern Africa

Eastern and Southern African Preferential Trade Area (PTA)

Address. Lusaka, Zambia.
Officer. Rex Nomvete (acting sec. gen.).
Founded. Dec. 21, 1981.
Membership. Burundi, the Comoros, Djibouti, Ethiopia, Kenya, Lesotho, Malawi, Mauritius, Rwanda, Somalia, Swaziland, Tanzania, Uganda, Zambia and Zimbabwe (observers, with a view to continued negotiations on membership, were: Angola, Botswana, Madagascar, Mozambique and Seychelles).
History. The PTA was established under a preferential trade agreement signed in Lusaka by the Comoros, Djibouti, Ethiopia, Malawi, Mauritius, Somalia, Uganda and Zambia (but not by Angola, Botswana, Lesotho, Swaziland and Tanzania). Zimbabwe signed the agreement on June 19, 1982. It covered a wide range of measures for freer regional trade and for co-operation in industry, transport and communications. In June 1982 the Council of Ministers set up under the agreement adopted a programme of work for the next 18 months. In 1984 it announced tariff reductions for nine categories of goods traded between member countries with payment being made in their own currencies through the Reserve Bank of Zimbabwe. At a summit meeting held in Lusaka on Dec. 18, 1985 (when Tanzania became the 15th member of the PTA), it was found that only Zambia had fulfilled all its obligations under the agreed action plan (for the reduction and standardization of tariffs and customs duties for over 200 items) and that the clearing house facilities at the Reserve Bank of Zimbabwe had been used by only six member states during the first year of operation (involving the equivalent of US$47,000,000, whereas total interregional trade was worth US$1,083 million).

West Africa

Confederation of Senegambia

Officers. Abdou Diouf (pres.); Sir Dawda Jawara (vice-pres.).
Founded. Feb. 1, 1982.
History. The plan to form the Confederation of the two states of Senegal and The Gambia was announced on Aug. 19, 1981, and a pact to institute the new Confederation was signed in Dakar on Dec. 19, 1981, by the Presidents of the two states.
Objects. According to a joint communiqué issued on Nov. 14, 1981, the Confederation was to be based on (i) the integration of the armed forces and the security forces of the two states to defend the sovereignty, territorial integrity and independence of the Confederation; (ii) economic and monetary union; (iii) co-ordination of policy in external relations and in communications and all other fields where the confederate state might agree to exercise its jurisdiction jointly; and (iv) joint instructions.
Structure. The Confederation has as its President the President of Senegal, and as its Vice-President the President of The Gambia. There is a Council of Ministers consisting of the two Presidents as well as five Senegalese and four Gambian ministers. A Confederal Assembly consists of 60 members, of whom one-third are chosen from the Gambian Parliament and two-thirds from the Senegalese Parliament. Each of the two confederal states was to maintain its independence and sovereignty (as explicitly stated in the communiqué of Nov. 14, 1981).

Conferences of Heads of State and Government of Countries bordering the Sahara

A conference of heads of state and government of countries bordering the Sahara was held in Bamako (Mali) on March 8-9, 1980, and was attended by the Presidents of Algeria, Chad, Mali, Mauritania and Niger and a member of the General Secretariat of the General People's Congress of Libya.

With a view to "making the subregion a zone of peace, security, stability and co-operation", the participants in the conference adopted several documents, including (i) a programme of economic, technical, cultural and social co-operation and (ii) a political declaration. They also decided that a Ministerial Council would meet every year, and they set up five special commissions to foster development, independence and social progress.

In their political declaration the participants expressed inter alia "absolute support for the struggle of the peoples of Namibia, South Africa, occupied Palestine and the Western Sahara to recover their national rights and for self-determination"; they condemned the 1978 Camp David agreements as aggravating "the violation of the firm rights of the Palestinian people"; they urged "the non-aligned countries to redouble their efforts to lessen tension in the world and to consolidate world peace and security"; and they stressed their determination to work for solidarity among the member states of the Group of 77 [see page 470] in order to bring about the legitimate aspirations of the developing countries.

Earlier meetings between the heads of state of Algeria, Libya and Niger had taken place at Ouargla (Algeria) on April 8, 1976, and in Tripoli on Nov. 23–24, 1976, and the heads of state of Algeria, Chad, Mali and Niger and the Libyan Prime Minister had held a conference in Niamey (Niger) on March 20–21, 1977. The outcome of the Ouargla and Tripoli meetings was the creation of (i) a tripartite commission to study possibilities of increased regional co-operation between the three states concerned and (ii) a Trans-Saharan Road Committee (of which Nigeria became a member in May 1977).

The sixth summit conference, attended by heads of state or government of Algeria, Chad, Mali and Mauritania and by representatives of Libya and Niger, took place in Nouakchott (Mauritania) on March 28–29, 1982.

In their final communiqué the conference participants stated: "African countries must be careful not to become targets for extra-African interests, which will only endanger their independence, security and development." The Mauritanian head of state (as incoming chairman of the conference organization) stressed the need to improve the lot of the rural population affected by persistent drought and to promote a progressive integration of economies by pooling common resources and implementing economic ventures of common interest, which would lead to the establishment of an "inter-Saharan common market"; he also called for "extinction of all hot-beds of tension, especially in Western Sahara".

(For Libya's defence agreements with Algeria and Niger see pages 407 and 413).

Entente Council
Conseil de l'entente

Address. B.P. 3747, Abidjan Ol, Côte d'Ivoire.
Officer. Paul Kaya (admin. sec.).
Founded. May 29–30, 1959.
Membership. Benin, Burkina Faso, Côte d'Ivoire, Niger and Togo
History. The *Conseil de l'entente* (Entente Council) was established by Côte d'Ivoire, Dahomey (later Benin), Niger and Upper Volta (later Burkina Faso) at Abidjan as the supreme organ of a union which would involve (i) a

customs union; (ii) co-ordination of the four countries' legislation in the spheres of finance, justice, public service, labour, communications and public health; (iii) harmonization of tax legislation; and (iv) the creation of a "Solidarity Fund".

Togo—which had been in a customs union with Dahomey after concluding an agreement on Aug. 20, 1960—became associated with the *Conseil de l'entente* in 1966.

The four members of the council achieved full independence outside the French Community in July 1960 and later signed co-operation agreements with France in economic matters and also in defence in April 1961—except in the case of Upper Volta, which declined to sign a defence agreement.

The council has set up a Mutual Aid and Loan Guarantee Fund through which it promotes economic development in the five member countries. By 1978 it was carrying out a rural development programme covering stock-breeding, food production and water supply, with contributions to its cost being received from France, the Netherlands and the United States. The council also co-operates with the West African Development Bank, the West African Economic Community (CEAO) and the Economic Community of West African States (ECOWAS).

Upon the expulsion of unskilled foreigners from Nigeria, begun in January 1983, the heads of state of the *Conseil de l'entente* declared on Feb. 9 of that year that "the African states affected should have been notified in advance so that they could organize the reception of their nationals beforehand".

A summit meeting held at Yamoussoukrou (Côte d'Ivoire) on Feb. 12–13, 1985 confirmed the council's priorities as being the achievement of self-sufficiency in food and the implementation of a water supply programme.

Economic Community of West African States (ECOWAS)
Communauté économique des états de l'Afrique de l'ouest (CEDEAO)

Address. 6 King George V Road, Lagos, Nigeria.
Officer. Momodu Munu (exec. sec.).
Founded. May 26, 1976.
Membership. Benin, Burkina Faso, Cape Verde, Côte d'Ivoire, The Gambia, Ghana, Guinea, Guinea-Bissau, Liberia, Mali, Mauritania, Niger, Nigeria, Senegal, Sierra Leone and Togo.
History. The community was established under a Treaty of Lagos signed by the heads of state of 15 West African countries (i.e. all current member states except Cape Verde, which did not join ECOWAS until 1977).

The treaty, drawn up as a result of an initiative by Nigeria and Togo, had first been approved in draft form by a meeting of delegates of the 15 countries held in Monrovia (Liberia) in January 1975. By the end of June 1975 it had been ratified by seven states—the minimum required before it could enter into force, but it did not finally become operative until after a further summit meeting held in Lomé (Togo) on Nov. 4–5, 1976, when a number of functional protocols were signed.

The treaty's principal objectives, which were to be achieved in stages, were the ending of customs duties and other restrictions on trade between member states; the establishment of a common external customs tariff and commercial policy; and the "harmonization of the economic and industrial policies of member states and the elimination of the disparities in the level of development of member states". The treaty called for the abolition of obstacles to the free movement of people, services and capital, the harmonization of agricultural policies, and the promotion of joint development projects, particularly in the spheres of agriculture (including "agro-industrial" enterprises), transport, communications and energy. Provision was made for the establishment of a community fund for "co-operation, compensation and development", and attention was drawn to the desirability of the harmonization of member states' monetary policies.

The treaty included a timetable for the abolition of barriers to intra-community trade and for the harmonization of external tariffs—the former objective to be fully achieved within 10 years and the latter within 15 years—and proposed that the first step towards the harmonization of economic policy should take the form of a full exchange of information on planned development projects, leading wherever possible to the joint financing of research and feasibility studies.

The principal institutions of the community would be (i) a Supreme Authority of Heads of State, with a rotating chairmanship, to meet at least once a year; (ii) a Council of Ministers, with two representatives from each member state and also with a rotating chairmanship, to meet at least twice a year; (iii) an Executive Secretariat, headed by an executive secretary appointed for a four-year period; (iv) a minimum of four specialized commissions dealing with different aspects of co-operation; and (v) a Community Tribunal which would ensure "the observance of law and justice", would interpret the provisions of the treaty and would settle disputes referred to it.

The treaty also provided that ECOWAS members could belong to other regional or subregional organizations (such as the *Communauté économique de l'Afrique de l'ouest*—CEAO), where such membership did "not abrogate from the provisions of the treaty".

At the Lomé summit meeting it was decided that the community's Fund for Co-operation, Compensation and Development (FCCD) should be based in Lomé; that the first Executive Secretary of ECOWAS should come from Côte d'Ivoire; and that the first managing director of the FCCD should come from Liberia.

It was also agreed that common tariff treatment should be accorded to goods wholly produced by enterprises with headquarters in the community, being at least 51 per cent locally controlled in terms of equity capital and having at least 50 per cent local representation on their boards of directors.

A Trade, Customs, Immigration, Monetary and Payments Commission of ECOWAS was inaugurated in April 1978.

At the third ECOWAS summit meeting, held in Lagos on April 21–22, 1978, it was agreed that as from May 28, 1979, member states should not increase their customs tariff on goods originating within the community (as a first step towards the elimination of all internal tariff barriers).

The meeting also approved a protocol on non-aggression (which had been discussed by the ECOWAS Council of Ministers in November 1977), under which the heads of state undertook inter alia to refrain from attacking each other and to recognize as definitive the present borders of their territories.

Immediately after the meeting an agreement was signed by Guinea and Nigeria, providing for commercial, agricultural and industrial co-operation between the two countries.

By May 1978 the FCCD had a capital of US$20,000,000, of which US$6,700,000 had been contributed by Nigeria (by far the strongest partner in ECOWAS).

The fourth ECOWAS summit meeting was held in Dakar on May 28–29, 1979, when it was decided inter alia to set up a commission to study problems connected with mutual defence assistance.

At the fifth ECOWAS summit meeting, held in Lomé on May 27–28, 1980, it was decided that a free trade area for the member states' raw materials (i.e. unprocessed goods) should be established from May 28, 1981, while for the reduction of tariffs on industrial products an eight-year plan was adopted.

The meeting also approved a protocol on the free movement of persons, to come into force after ratification by at least seven member states. (By the end of July 1980 it had been ratified by eight—The Gambia, Ghana, Guinea, Liberia, Niger, Nigeria, Senegal and Togo.) The protocol's provisions, to be implemented over a 15-year period, laid down that in the first stage (which took immediate effect) an ECOWAS citizen had the right to visit any member state other than his own for up to 90 days without visa; in the second stage he would obtain the right of residence; and in the third stage he would have the right to establish a business in another member country.

At the sixth summit meeting, held in Freetown (Sierra Leone) on May 27–30, 1981, a defence protocol on mutual assistance was signed by Benin, Côte d'Ivoire, The Gambia, Ghana, Guinea, Liberia, Mauritania, Niger, Nigeria, Senegal, Sierra Leone, Togo and Upper Volta (Burkina Faso), with Cape Verde, Guinea-Bissau and Mali expressing reservations. The protocol provided inter alia for the establishment of (i) a council consisting of the ECOWAS heads of state and (ii) a commission of Defence Ministers and chiefs of staff, and for the appointment of a military officer as a deputy executive secretary in charge of defence matters.

The meeting also decided that within eight years all trade barriers were to be eliminated and a common external tariff was to be agreed. The trade liberalization programme included in particular a progressive increase in indigenous ownership of industries to 51 per cent by May 28, 1989; the elimination of all tariffs by May 28, 1981, by the industrially more advanced states

(Côte d'Ivoire, Ghana, Nigeria and Senegal) for all products manufactured in a member state already accorded preferential treatment in an existing regional organization (e.g. the Mano River Union or the West African Economic Community), and by May 28, 1989, by all states.

The promotion of trade between ECOWAS and the Latin American Economic System (SELA—see page 358) was provided for in a joint communiqué reported on Jan. 22, 1982, to have been signed in Caracas.

The seventh summit meeting (also described as the fifth ordinary session of the ECOWAS heads of state), held in Cotonou (Benin) on May 28–29, 1982, approved the creation of a fund for the development of energy resources and adopted a regional strategy for agricultural development in ECOWAS countries, for which the President of Nigeria had proposed a community target of self-sufficiency in food production within the next five years.

The sixth ordinary session of the ECOWAS heads of state, held in Conakry (Guinea) on May 28–30, 1983, reaffirmed the determination of all member states to work towards a customs union and economic integration of all West African states and decided to create a single monetary zone, and also to further industrial development co-operation by giving priority to industries supporting the development of rural sectors (to achieve self-sufficiency in food production), transport and communications, and the natural resources and energy.

A special summit meeting held in Lomé (Togo) on July 6, 1985, decided inter alia to introduce a travel document which would harmonize and simplify border formalities. However, it was also decided to postpone until June 1986 the implementation of the 1980 agreement giving nationals of all member states residential rights anywhere in the Community (due to come into effect in July 1985).

The seventh (ordinary) session, held in Lomé on Nov. 22–23, 1985, resolved inter alia (i) to adopt a common economic strategy based on co-ordinated planning for better utilization of available resources, and (ii) to create the proposed ECOWAS monetary zone as well as a new regional commercial bank (Ecobank).

Gambia River Basin Development Organization
Organisation de la mise en valeur du fleuve Gambia (OMVG)

Address. B.P. 2353, Dakar, Senegal.

Officers. Samba Yella Diop (pres. of Council of Ministers); Malick John (high commissioner).

Founded. 1978.

Membership. The Gambia, Guinea, Guinea-Bissau and Senegal.

Objects. To improve cross-river communications between northern and southern Senegal and to implement irrigation schemes.

Activities. Plans of the OMVG include one for an anti-saltwater dam in The Gambia and another for a dam for irrigation and hydroelectric power in Senegal.

Lake Chad Basin Commission

Address. B.P. 727, N'Djaména, Chad.

Founded. May 23, 1964.

Membership. Cameroon, Chad, Niger and Nigeria.

History. The commission was set up at a conference held in Chad by the four member states, and at a further conference held in Lagos on Aug. 20–22, 1968, the heads of state of these four countries signed an agreement on the joint development of the Lake Chad basin, and a quadripartite commission was established under an executive secretary with eight commissioners (two from each of the participating countries), to be located in Chad.

In July 1972 it was decided to create a development fund for the Lake Chad basin and two specialized agencies—for livestock and meat and for agricultural products.

The commission's programme for 1982-86 has emphasized studies on the development of water resources and control of rinderpest.

Liptako-Gourma Integrated Development Authority

Address. B.P. 619, N'Gourma, Burkina Faso.

Officer. Bakary Touré (sec. gen.).

Founded. 1972.

Membership. Burkina Faso, Mali and Niger.

Object. To foster co-operation in the development of the Liptako-Gourma region (straddling the border between Burkina Faso and Niger), its main organ being a Ministerial Council.

Mano River Union

Address. Private Post Bag 113, Freetown, Sierra Leone.

Officer. Dr Augustus Caine (sec. gen.).

Founded. Oct. 3, 1973.

Membership. Guinea, Liberia and Sierra Leone.

History. The union was formed under a declaration by the Presidents of Liberia and Sierra Leone on co-operation between their two countries, between which the Mano River forms part of their common boundary. Guinea acceded to the union on Oct. 3, 1980.

Activities. The achievements of the Mano River Union include the completion of a new bridge across the Mano River in February 1976, the complete liberalization of bilateral trade by the end of 1976, and the harmonization of the two countries' external customs tariffs by October 1977. Among further projects were the construction of (i) a new highway between the two countries' capitals and (ii) a hydroelectric power dam as part of a Mano River Basin Development Project intended to promote industrial development on both sides of the border. Free trade between the three countries was officially introduced in May 1981.

On Sept. 11, 1986, the Justice Ministers of the three members states, meeting in Freetown (the capital of Sierra Leone), signed a treaty of non-aggression and security co-operation, which was to be submitted for final approval by the three heads of state. The treaty committed the signatories to peaceful coexistence, respect for the territorial integrity of the other parties and prevention of their respective territories being used for any act of subversion or aggression against the others.

Niger Basin Authority
Autorité du bassin du Niger

Address. B.P. 729, Niamey, Niger.
Officer. J. I. Olunu (acting exec. sec.).
Founded. Nov. 25, 1964.
Membership. Benin, Burkina Faso, Cameroon, Chad, Côte d'Ivoire, Mali, Niger and Nigeria.
History. The authority was established as the Niger River Commission under an agreement which came into force on April 12, 1966. An act of navigation and economic co-operation between the states of the Niger basin had previously been signed in Niamey on Oct. 26, 1963, and came into force on Feb. 1, 1966. The commission assumed its present name in 1980.
A new Niger River Development Agreement was signed on Nov. 22, 1983.

Permanent Inter-State Committee on Drought Control in the Sahel (CILSS)

Address. B.P. 7049, Ouagadougou, Burkina Faso.
Officer. Brah Mahamane (exec. sec.).
Founded. Sept. 12, 1974.
Membership. Burkina Faso, Cape Verde, Chad, The Gambia, Guinea, Guinea-Bissau, Mali, Mauritania, Niger, Nigeria and Senegal.
History. The committee was established under a convention signed on Dec. 23, 1973, and in force from July 1, 1974.
Activities. With the help of a Club of the Friends of the Sahel (formed in 1976) a working group was set up in March of that year, and this group subsequently drew up a *Sahel Development Plan* (1978-2000) designed to "enable the Sahel states to achieve food self-sufficiency whatever the climatic hazard" and to lead to "self-sustaining development" in these countries.
The committee has co-operated with the UN Sudano-Sahelian Office (UNSO), has supported efforts to combat desertification, and has aimed at building up a grain reserve for regional food security.
At a meeting of the CILSS council held in Nouakchott (Mauritania) on Jan. 14-17, 1985, the executive secretary pointed out that the CILSS had not yet achieved its primary aim of food self-sufficiency for the region; that food production as a percentage of actual needs had fallen from 98 per cent in 1960 to 60 per cent in 1984; that in 1984 the region had received 1,200,000 tonnes of food aid; and that for 1985 an estimated 1,750,000 tonnes would be needed.
The Club of the Friends of the Sahel, at a meeting held in Milan on Dec. 11-12, 1985, brought together representatives of the CILSS member states and of 11 donor countries, and it called for a 40 per cent increase in aid to the Sahel region over the next 10 years—the population of 35,000,000 being expected to double over the next 25 years and 128,000 square kilometres of land becoming arid each year through the advancement of the Sahara desert.

Organization for the Development of the Senegal River
Organisation pour la mise en valeur du fleuve Sénégal (OMVS)

Address. B.P. 3152, Dakar, Senegal.
Officer. Ely Ould Allaf (sec.).
Founded. March 12, 1972.
Object. The joint economic development of the Senegal River and its tributaries by Mali, Mauritania and Senegal.
History. The OMVS superseded an earlier Organization of Riparian States of the River Senegal of which Guinea had also been a member, in addition to the above three countries, and which had been disbanded on Nov. 30, 1971.
At a conference held in Nouakchott in May 1974, a 40-year development plan was adopted with a proposed investment equivalent to about £1,400 million and involving inter alia the construction of two hydroelectric dams within the first seven years, agricultural development to achieve self-sufficiency in food and the elimination of the risk of drought, the building of 232 factories for the processing of agricultural produce, and the exploitation and processing of iron ore and bauxite in Mali and of iron ore in Senegal.
By May 1982 the dams were constructed (i) at Diama (at the mouth of the Senegal River) and (ii) at Manatali (in Mali, on the Bafing tributary of the Senegal River).

West African Economic Community
Communauté économique de l'Afrique de l'ouest (CEAO)

Address. B.P. 643, Ouagadougou, Burkina Faso.
Officer. Drissa Keita (sec. gen.).
Founded. April 1973.
Membership. Benin, Burkina Faso, Côte d'Ivoire, Mali, Mauritania, Niger and Senegal.
History. The CEAO came into effect in January 1974, superseding an earlier West African Customs Union (UDEAO) established on June 3, 1966, by Côte d'Ivoire, Dahomey (Benin), Mali, Mauritania, Niger, Senegal and Upper Volta (now Burkina Faso) and in force since Dec. 15, 1966. An agreement to form the CEAO had been signed in Bamako (Mali) on June 3, 1972.
Structure. The supreme organ of the CEAO is its Conference of Heads of State, which meets

once a year. The CEAO Council of Ministers meets at least twice a year, and there is also a General Secretariat (with several directorates).

The CEAO is a "zone of organized exchanges" with two unique institutions—(i) a regional co-operation tax designed to encourage exchanges within the community and (ii) a community development fund to finance development projects and to compensate for certain types of trade loss.

Activities. At the first summit conference of the CEAO held in Niamey (Niger) on April 7–8, 1975, the member states' leaders solemnly proclaimed their willingness to co-operate with all heads of state of the region to form a larger West African community.

At the end of the second summit conference, held in Dakar on April 8–9, 1976, it was stated that the regional system of customs co-operation had been applied effectively and that this had strengthened preferential development in trade within the CEAO, and that other proposed developments would include the financing of joint exploitation of mineral resources through the CEAO's development fund (which for 1976 had a budget equivalent to about £5,000,000).

At the third summit conference, held in Abidjan on June 8–9, 1977, the heads of state of the six CEAO member countries and of Togo signed an agreement on non-aggression and mutual assistance among their countries, with a permanent secretariat to be set up in Abidjan for supervising the agreement, which was to be open to accession by other countries in the region. It was also decided to establish a $20,000,000 Solidarity and Intervention Fund to guarantee loans for development projects, in particular in the land-locked member states (Mali, Niger and Upper Volta), with Côte d'Ivoire contributing $10,000,000, Senegal $6,000,000 and each of the four other member states $1,000,000.

In January 1978 an agreement was signed on co-operation with the *Conseil de l'entente* [see page 429].

At the fourth summit conference, held in Bamako on Oct. 27, 1978, an agreement was signed on the free movement of persons and their right to establish residence within the community.

The fifth summit meeting, held in Nouakchott (Mauritania) on Oct. 19–20, 1979, was mainly concerned with a reorganization of the organization's General Secretariat and the adoption of a *Charter of Regional Co-operation*, but it was also pointed out at the conference that the establishment of CEAO organizations and institutions should be in harmony with those of the Economic Community of West African States (ECOWAS) [pages 429ff.].

On July 26, 1980, a co-operation agreement was signed in Ouagadougou between the CEAO and the Mano River Union [page 431].

At the sixth summit meeting, held in Niamey (Niger) on Oct. 27, 1980, with the participation of Togo, it was decided inter alia to extend the freedom of movement of member countries'

nationals; to improve the economic development, and in particular the water supply, of villages; and to convene a committee on the implementation of the non-aggression and mutual assistance agreement with Togo [see above].

At a conference held in Dakar on Dec. 14, 1981, the signatories of the agreement adopted three protocols providing for its implementation and the functions of its secretary-general.

The ninth summit meeting held in Niamey (Niger) on Oct. 29, 1983, voted the equivalent of US$2,012,000 for states affected by drought, fixed the annual endowment of its Solidarity and Intervention Fund (Fosidec, created in December 1977) at the equivalent of about $2,515,000 for 1984, and reaffirmed the full membership of the CEAO within the ECOWAS.

The 10th summit meeting, held in Bamako (Mali) on Oct. 27–29, when Benin (until then an observer) was admitted to full CEAO membership, adopted a "second generation programme" of development projects, primarily in rural water supply, livestock breeding, a common agricultural policy and regional transport schemes.

Southern Africa

Southern African Development Co-ordination Conference (SADCC)

Address. Gaborone, Botswana
Officer. F. A. Blumeris (sec. gen.)
Founded. July 1979
Membership. Angola, Botswana, Lesotho, Malawi, Mozambique, Swaziland, Tanzania, Zambia and Zimbabwe
History. A first Southern African Development Co-ordination Conference was held in Arusha (Tanzania) on July 3–4, 1979, and attended by ministers from Angola, Botswana, Mozambique, Tanzania and Zambia as well as by representatives of nine Western potential donor countries (Belgium, Canada, Denmark, the Federal Republic of Germany, the Netherlands, Norway, Sweden, the United Kingdom and the United States) and six international organizations. This conference prepared a draft declaration on "Southern Africa—towards Economic Liberation".

At a meeting of heads of state and government held in Lusaka (Zambia) on April 1–2, 1980, and attended by leaders from Angola, Botswana, Lesotho, Malawi, Mozambique, Swaziland, Tanzania, Zambia and Zimbabwe, the participants adopted a Lusaka declaration on economic liberation and a programme of action designed to achieve the liberation.

The declaration defined a strategy for closer integration of the nine countries' economies in order to accelerate their development and to reduce their economic dependence on the Republic of South Africa.

The programme of action included proposals for the creation of a southern African transport and communications commission based in Maputo; measures to control foot-and-mouth disease in cattle throughout the region (for which Botswana would be responsible); the preparation of a food security plan for the region (by Zimbabwe); the establishment of a regional agricultural research centre specializing in drought-prone areas; plans for the harmonzation of industrialization (to be prepared by Tanzania) and of energy policies (for which Angola would be responsible); sharing of national training facilities within the region (with Swaziland making recommendations in this respect); and studies leading to proposals for the establishment of a southern African development fund (to be undertaken by Zambia).

The second Southern African Development Co-ordination Conference was held by the nine states in Maputo (Mozambique) on Nov. 27–28, 1980, to discuss development projects with representatives of potential donor countries and of 17 international organizations.

The conference considered a list of 97 projects estimated to cost a total of $2,000 million, mainly for the improvement of railways, roads, ports and telecommunications, with over 40 per cent of the total to be devoted to railway improvements and port developments in Mozambique. Aid pledged by donors amounted to US$650,000,000 over five years, including US$380,000,000 from the African Development Bank, US$100,000,000 from the European Communities and US$50,000,000 from Italy. (It was pointed out by the European Commissioner responsible for development co-operation policy that Community funds provided within the context of the Lomé Convention could not be spent in Angola or Mozambique as they were not signatories of the convention.)

A further summit meeting was held in Salisbury (later Harare), Zimbabwe, on July 20, 1981, when the nine countries' leaders signed a memorandum of understanding codifying decisions on institutional arrangements (but rejected a request for membership by Zaïre).

The second annual meeting of the SADCC Council of Ministers, held in Blantyre (Malawi) on Nov. 19–20, 1981, was preceded by the publication of a joint statement condemning South Africa's alleged "economic destabilization" of southern Africa in general and its 1981 "invasion" of Angola in particular. The meeting was also attended by representatives of 12 international agencies and of a number of aid-giving countries (including Australia, Belgium, Denmark, Finland, the Federal Republic of Germany, Italy and the Netherlands), several of which promised further aid. The council agreed to establish a permanent secretariat in Botswana.

The third annual meeting of the SADCC, held in Maseru (Lesotho) on Jan. 27–28, 1983, strongly condemned "deliberate interference by South Africa in the region", in particular a South African commando raid on Maseru on Dec. 9,

1981, the destruction of fuel storage facilities in Beira (Mozambique) on Dec. 8–9, 1982, and the sabotage of Angola's biggest dam in Benguela Province on Jan. 17, 1983. It was reported that 29 governments and 23 aid organizations and development agencies had promised to make a further US$206,000,000 available for development schemes in the region over the next four years.

A meeting of the SADCC Council of Ministers held in Lusaka on Feb. 2–3, 1984, registered agricultural and drought relief commitments amounting to US$72,000,000 from Ireland, Canada, France, Norway, Switzerland, the United States and the International Fund for Agricultural Development (IFAD), and an EEC spokesman said that US$175,000,000 had been allocated to the SADCC for regional rural development.

The fifth annual summit meeting held in Gaborone (Botswana) in July 1984 considered a report for the period from July 1983 to June 1984 stating that agriculture remained the priority of most member states while in the context of regional co-operation priority had been given to the development of transport and communications.

By August 1985 some US$2,300 million (out of a total of US$4,000 million required) had been obtained or was under negotiation. South Africa's "destabilization policy" was said to have cost the SADCC region some US$10,000 million over the past five years.

The "Front-Line States"

The governments of six African states (Angola, Botswana, Mozambique, Tanzania, Zambia and Zimbabwe), regarding their countries as standing in the front-line against South African hegemony in southern Africa, have held regular consultations in order to co-ordinate their policies. In particular they have supported the armed struggle of the South West African People's Organization (SWAPO) against South Africa's presence in Namibia and (ii) the policies of the African National Congress (ANC) of South Africa. They have strongly condemned South African attacks on targets in five of the above states and what they regard as South African attempts to destabilize the region and to threaten the independence of its northern neighbours.

Co-operation involving African Countries

Treaties and Agreements between African States*

Angola and Cape Verde. A co-operation agreement between the two countries was signed in Luanda (Angola) on Dec. 15, 1976.

* For agreements of francophone countries in Africa, see pages 338–40; for agreements of Arab countries in Africa, see pages 407–16; for agreements between African and Communist states, see pages 253–56 and 260–66.

Angola, Mozambique, Tanzania and Zambia. An agreement announced on Nov. 20, 1976 provided for a joint defence strategy against an external attack on any one or several of these four states.

Angola and South Africa. Under a Lusaka Accord concluded on Feb. 6, 1984, it was agreed to formalize a ceasefire unilaterally declared by South Africa with effect from Feb. 1, 1984, in its operations against SWAPO guerrillas in Angola and to extend it beyond the original 30 days should all parties so wish. However, the implementation of the accord (involving the progressive withdrawal of South African forces from Angola) by a joint monitoring commission was delayed, and after the South African government had registered 60 alleged violations of the accord the South African withdrawal was halted at Ngiva (southern Angola) by mid-October 1984.

Angola and Zaïre. On Feb. 9, 1985, agreements were signed on defence and security, the movement of people and goods, border trade and customs co-operation, the conservation of common natural resources, health and medical co-operation and an education programme (as part of an existing cultural and scientific agreement). A joint commission was to be set up to monitor the security of the two countries' common border (with neither country allowing its territory to be used for attacks against the other).

Angola, Zaïre and Zambia. A trilateral non-aggression pact was signed at Ndola (Zambia) on Oct. 12, 1979, by the Presidents of Angola, Zaïre and Zambia. Under this agreement the three Presidents undertook to end any support which they had given to one another's political opponents, and they also declared their readiness

Map 12   Economic Community of West African States (ECOWAS), West African Economic Community (CEAO) and Economic Community of Central African States (CEEAC)

to co-operate with each other, especially in the field of transport.

Angola and Zambia. (1) Framework agreements on co-operation between the two countries were signed by their Presidents on Oct. 17, 1978, when relations between them were normalized and they undertook to respect the UN and OAU Charters and the principles of non-aggression, non-interference and respect for each other's territorial integrity.

(2) On May 10, 1979, the Presidents of the two countries agreed at a meeting in Ndola (Zambia) to regard an attack on one of them as an attack on both and to set up a joint security force to repel incursions (from Rhodesia or South Africa).

Benin, Ghana, Nigeria and Togo. An extradition treaty, an agreement on police co-operation and an agreement on customs, trade and immigration co-operation were signed by the heads of state of the four countries on Dec. 10, 1984.

Bophuthatswana and South Africa. On the achievement of Bophuthatswana's (internationally unrecognized) independence on Nov. 15, 1977, a total of 71 agreements were signed, to be followed by a further 28 agreements concluded between Nov. 23, 1979, and Nov. 25, 1983.

Burkina Faso and Ghana. Under a military agreement joint manoeuvres were held in the border area on Nov. 4, 1982.

Burkina Faso and Mali. Under an agreement concluded on June 18, 1975, a border dispute between the two countries was settled, and on July 11, 1975, the two countries' Presidents signed a further agreement in which they undertook "definitely to renounce the use of force" in any dispute between them.

Burkina Faso and Togo. In April 1984 it was agreed to establish joint border patrols and to take over measures to eliminate any attempt to "destabilize the revolution in either country".

Burundi, Rwanda and Zaïre. A mutual security pact between the three countries was signed in Kinshasa on Aug. 30, 1966, and this agreement was reaffirmed on June 12, 1974, when additional provisions were agreed—inter alia on identical treatment of persons declared undesirable in any one of the three countries and on the settlement of refugees (at least 150 kilometres from the border of their country of origin). (For formation of Economic Community of the Great Lakes' Countries, see above.)

Burundi and Zambia. On April 8, 1982, agreements were reported to have been signed on trade, air services and cultural co-operation, with a bilateral co-operation commission to be established.

Cameroon and Côte d'Ivoire. A treaty of friendship and co-operation for development of mutual relations was signed on Feb. 24–March 4, 1978.

Cape Verde and Gabon. A treaty of friendship and co-operation signed on Feb. 23, 1985, provided for the creation of a joint commission for economic co-operation.

Cape Verde and Togo. A co-operation agreement was signed on March 7, 1985.

The Central African Republic and Chad. Agreement by the two countries to pursue close co-operation in defence, security and economic affairs was reached on May 30, 1984. (In April 1985 the two countries' armies co-operated in a counter-insurgency operation along their common border.)

The Central African Republic and Equatorial Guinea. A 10-year treaty of friendship and co-operation was signed on Jan. 24, 1975.

The Central African Republic and Senegal. A 10-year treaty of friendship and co-operation was signed on March 24, 1975.

The Central African Republic and Zaïre. A military co-operation agreement was signed on July 9, 1985 (Zaïrean forces having entered Chad at the request of the Habré government of Chad in mid-1983).

Ciskei and South Africa. In connection with the achievement of Ciskei's (internationally unrecognized) independence on Dec. 3, 1981, a total of 82 agreements were signed between Nov. 20, 1981, and June 26, 1985.

Côte d'Ivoire and Ghana. A treaty of co-operation was concluded in 1971.

Côte d'Ivoire and Senegal. A treaty of friendship and co-operation was signed on Dec. 15, 1971, together with an agreement on the establishment of a joint co-operation commission.

Djibouti and Ethiopia. A treaty of friendship and co-operation, as well as agreements on economic, technical and scientific co-operation and a general agreement on transport (including arrangements relating to the Djibouti-Addis Ababa railways), were signed on March 21, 1981.

An agreement concluded in February 1983 provided for the voluntary repatriation of Ethiopian refugees (estimated at 30,000, most of whom had fled from Ethiopia in 1971-78).

The two countries' heads of state agreed on March 26, 1984, to co-ordinate activities against any destabilizing elements and to establish a joint ministerial council and administrative commission on the border regions.

Ethiopia, Kenya and the Sudan. A joint ministerial consultative committee established in 1973 agreed on April 30, 1981, to strengthen and expand co-operation in all fields.

Ethiopia and the Sudan. A trade protocol for 1981 was signed in November 1980.

An agreement signed on May 30, 1982, provided for the removal of "all obstructions to good relations between the two countries" by stopping "all facilities used by secessionists or elements which work for destabilization" and by expelling "groups of individuals working to inflict damage on the neighbouring state". (The Sudanese President, however, still insisted that the Sudan supported "the Eritreans in resolving the Eritrean question".)

In June 1985 both sides agreed to abide by a policy of non-interference in each other's affairs.

Guinea and Côte d'Ivoire. A treaty of friendship and co-operation was signed on April 14, 1978.

Guinea and Guinea-Bissau. A treaty of co-operation and friendship was signed on Aug. 6, 1974.

An agreement reported on March 7, 1985, provided for joint offshore oil prospecting in the border area.

Guinea and Liberia. A non-aggression and mutual defence treaty was concluded in Monrovia on Jan. 23, 1979.

Guinea and Senegal. A treaty of friendship and co-operation was signed on April 14, 1978.

Ten co-operation agreements were concluded in October 1979.

Guinea-Bissau and Mali. A treaty of friendship and co-operation was signed on Nov. 3, 1983, when it was agreed to set up a joint commission.

Guinea-Bissau and Senegal. A treaty of friendship and co-operation signed in Dakar was ratified by the National Assembly of Senegal on July 4, 1974. A series of 11 co-operation agreements was signed in Bissau on Jan. 8, 1975.

Mozambique and São Tomé and Príncipe. A protocol on future military co-operation was signed on Dec. 17, 1984.

Mozambique and South Africa. A railway co-operation agreement was signed on Feb. 26, 1979 (superseding an earlier agreement between Portugal and South Africa), providing for mutual assistance in operating the railway line to and from the ports of Maputo and Matola in Mozambique.

A treaty of non-aggression, good neighbourliness (the Nkomati Accord) was signed on March 16, 1984, when both sides agreed "not to allow their respective territory, territorial waters or air space to be used as a base by another state's government, foreign military forces, organizations or individuals which plan to prepare to commit acts of violence, terrorism or aggression" against the other country. The pact also included commitments (i) to forbid and prevent the organization of armed bands, including mercenaries, (ii) to eliminate all bases used by each other's enemies: and (iii) to prohibit recruitment, abduction or acts of propaganda inciting a war of aggression or acts of terrorism. The treaty was to be monitored by a joint security commission.

Mozambique, South Africa and Swaziland. Under an agreement reported on Feb. 18, 1983, a permanent technical committee was to be established to ensure the most beneficial utilization of the three countries' common rivers.

Senegal and Zaïre. The proposed creation of a joint co-operation commission and of a "friendship group" to promote consultation between the two countries' parliaments was announced on June 13, 1984.

South Africa and Transkei. A total of 59 agreements covering the transition to Transkei's independence (not internationally recognized) and co-operation were signed between Sept. 17, 1976, and Dec. 11, 1980.

Venda and South Africa. In connection with Venda's achievement of independence (not internationally recognized) a total of 80 agreements were signed between Aug. 13, 1979, and Dec. 10, 1985.

Treaties and Agreements of African States with Non-African Countries*

Treaties and agreements concluded by African states with states outside the continent included the following:

Angola and Portugal. A three-year agreement on friendship and co-operation was signed in Guinea-Bissau on June 26, 1978; it provided inter alia for technical, economic, financial, educational and cultural exchanges. In a joint communiqué issued at the same time the two heads of state undertook to promote the mutual rapprochement between their countries and to prevent acts of hostility against each other. A trade agreement was signed in Luanda on Jan. 22, 1979.

Angola and Spain. An agreement on economic and commercial co-operation was signed on March 18, 1983.

An agreement on scientific and technical co-operation was signed on June 14, 1983.

Angola and Sweden. An agreement on development co-operation for the period from Jan. 1, 1983, to Dec. 31, 1984, was signed on Jan. 29, 1983.

Benin and the Federal Republic of Germany. An economic co-operation agreement signed on June 19, 1961, and in force from July 1, 1961, was extended in August 1963 and again on Sept. 16, 1985 (until Dec. 31, 1986).

An agreement on technical co-operation was signed and came into force on June 29, 1978.

Benin and Switzerland. An agreement on trade, protection of investments and technical co-operation was signed on April 20, 1966, and a technical co-operation agreement on Jan. 23, 1981.

Burkina Faso and the Federal Republic of Germany. An economic co-operation agreement signed on June 8, 1961 and in force from July 1, 1961 was extended on Oct. 23/Nov. 13, 1963.

* For agreements of francophone countries in Africa, see pages 338–40; for agreements of Arab countries in Africa see pages 407–16; for agreements between African and Communist states, see pages 253–55 and 260–67.

437

An agreement on economic and technical co-operation signed on Aug. 8, 1973, came into force on April 30, 1974.

Burkina Faso and Switzerland. An agreement on trade, protection of investments and technical co-operation was signed on May 6, 1969.

A technical co-operation agreement was concluded on June 20/Sept. 22, 1978.

Burundi and the Federal Republic of Germany. A technical co-operation agreement signed on July 16, 1984, came into force on Nov. 12, 1984.

Burundi and Switzerland. An agreement on technical and scientific co-operation was signed on Nov. 19, 1969.

Cameroon and the Federal Republic of Germany. A trade agreement was signed and came into force on March 8, 1962.

Cameroon and Switzerland. An agreement on trade, protection of investments and technical co-operation was signed on Jan. 28, 1963, and applied on Jan. 26, 1967.

Cape Verde and the Federal Republic of Germany. An agreement on technical co-operation signed on Oct. 31, 1977, came into force on May 11, 1979.

Cape Verde and Portugal. A friendship and co-operation agreement was signed on July 5, 1975.

An agreement to increase co-operation in the military and technical spheres was announced in late May 1984.

Cape Verde and Sweden. Agreements on development co-operation were signed (i) on Dec. 18, 1982 (for the period from Jan. 1, 1983, to Dec. 31, 1984) and (ii) on Dec. 8, 1984 (for the period from Jan. 1, 1985, to Dec. 8, 1986).

The Central African Republic and Switzerland. An agreement on trade promotion and protection of investments was signed on Feb. 28, 1973.

Chad and the Federal Republic of Germany. An economic agreement of May 31, 1963, was extended on Sept. 16, 1985 (until Dec. 31, 1986).

An agreement on technical co-operation signed on and in force from Feb. 26, 1970, was amended on July 17, 1978.

Chad and Switzerland. An agreement on trade, protection of investments and technical co-operation was signed on Feb. 21, 1967, and a protocol on its application on July 25, 1977.

The Comoros and the Federal Republic of Germany. An agreement on financial co-operation was signed and came into force on Dec. 10, 1983.

The Congo and the Federal Republic of Germany. An economic agreement signed on Oct. 30, 1962, and in force from Nov. 30, 1962, was, on Sept. 16, 1985, extended until Dec. 31, 1986.

An agreement on technical co-operation signed on Oct. 22, 1981, came into force on June 15, 1982.

The Congo and Switzerland. An agreement on trade, protection of investments and technical co-operation was signed on Oct. 18, 1962.

Côte d'Ivoire and the Federal Republic of Germany. An economic co-operation agreement was signed and came into force on Dec. 18, 1961; on Sept. 9, 1985, it was extended until Dec. 31, 1986.

An agreement on technical co-operation was signed on Aug. 21, 1975.

Côte d'Ivoire and Sweden. A trade agreement was signed on Aug. 27, 1965.

Côte d'Ivoire and Switzerland. An agreement on trade, protection of investments and technical co-operation was signed on June 26, 1962.

Equatorial Guinea and the Federal Republic of Germany. An agreement on technical co-operation signed on Jan. 1, 1981, came into force on Dec. 7, 1982.

Equatorial Guinea and Spain. A protocol on technical assistance in defence and security was signed on Oct. 17, 1980, and a treaty of friendship and co-operation on Oct. 23, 1980.

A military assistance agreement was signed in September 1981, and a package of economic co-operation agreements was signed on Nov. 19, 1981.

Ethiopia and the Federal Republic of Germany. An agreement on economic relations was signed on April 21, 1964, and came into force on Dec. 31, 1964; on Sept. 16, 1985, it was extended until Dec. 31, 1986.

Ethiopia and Italy. An agreement signed in April 1981 provided for increased Italian aid to Ethiopia and a trade credit worth £8,600,000.

Ethiopia and Sweden. An agreement on development co-operation for the period from July 1, 1984, until June 30, 1986, was signed on June 15, 1984.

Ethiopia and Switzerland. A treaty of friendship and commerce was signed on May 24, 1933.

Gabon and the Federal Republic of Germany. An economic co-operation agreement, signed on, and in force from, July 11, 1962, was on Sept. 16, 1985, extended until Dec. 31, 1986.

An agreement on financial co-operation was signed and came into force on March 28, 1978.

Gabon and Spain. An agreement on economic and commercial co-operation was signed on Feb. 6, 1976, and a cultural agreement on Nov. 9, 1977.

Gabon and Switzerland. An agreement on trade, protection of investments and scientific and technical co-operation was signed on Jan. 8, 1972.

Guinea and the Federal Republic of Germany. An agreement on economic and technical co-operation was signed and came into force on March 18, 1959, and an economic co-operation agreement of April 19, 1962, in force since Jan. 1, 1962, was on Sept. 1979, extended until Dec. 31, 1980.

Guinea and Switzerland. An agreement on trade, protection of investments and technical co-operation was signed on April 26, 1962, and a protocol on technical co-operation on Oct. 31, 1964.

Guinea-Bissau and the Federal Republic of Germany. An agreement on technical co-operation was signed on Sept. 29, 1982, and came into force on March 14, 1983.

Guinea-Bissau and France. A co-operation agreement was signed in April 1976.

Guinea-Bissau and Portugal. Trade, military assistance and technical co-operation agreements were signed, together with a treaty granting Portugal preferential fishing rights in the coastal waters of Guinea-Bissau, in January 1978.

A financial protocol, reported on June 8, 1984, provided for a range of Portuguese loans and export credits and a restructuring of existing debt. Agreement was also reported to have been reached on the return of former Portuguese property nationalized in Guinea-Bissau since its attainment of independence.

Guinea-Bissau and Sweden. An agreement on development co-operation between Jan. 1, 1984, and Dec. 31, 1985, was signed on Dec. 9, 1983.

Liberia and France. Two economic and technical co-operation agreements were signed on March 23, 1979.

Liberia and the Federal Republic of Germany. An agreement on economic and technical co-operation was signed and came into force on Sept. 27, 1974.

Liberia and Iceland. A treaty of amity, commerce and navigation was signed on May 21, 1860.

Liberia and Sweden. A treaty of amity, commerce and navigation was signed on Sept. 1, 1863, and an agreement on technical co-operation on May 15, 1971.

Liberia and Switzerland. A treaty of friendship and commerce was signed on July 23, 1963.

Madagascar and the Federal Republic of Germany. An economic agreement signed on, and in force from June 6, 1962, was on Sept. 16, 1985, extended until Dec. 31, 1986.

An agreement on economic and technical co-operation, signed also on June 6, 1962, was amended on Jan. 5, 1977.

Madagascar and Sweden. A trade agreement was signed on April 2, 1966.

Madagascar and Switzerland. An agreement on trade, protection of investments and technical co-operation was signed on March 17, 1964, and a protocol on its application on Dec. 11, 1968.

Mali and the Federal Republic of Germany. An agreement on economic and technical co-operation was signed on Oct. 11, 1977.

Mali and Switzerland. A technical co-operation agreement was signed on Oct. 6, 1977, and an agreement on trade and economic co-operation on March 8, 1978.

Mozambique and Denmark, Finland, Iceland, Norway and Sweden. An agreement on co-operative development co-operation was signed on Nov. 7, 1977.

A three-year economic co-operation agreement signed on Nov. 28, 1980, involved Nordic aid of $66,000,000.

Mozambique and the Federal Republic of Germany. An economic aid agreement was signed at the end of July 1982.

Mozambique and India. Agreements on technical co-operation were signed on Aug. 25–27, 1982.

Mozambique and Portugal. A treaty on general co-operation, inter alia in the economic, scientific and technological fields, was concluded in October 1975.

A protocol signed on April 27, 1982, covered technical and military co-operation, including training of Mozambican military personnel in Portugal and possibly the working of Portuguese military instructors in Mozambique.

Several co-operation agreements were signed on June 27–30, 1982.

Mozambique and Spain. An agreement on scientific and technical co-operation was signed on Dec. 12, 1980.

Mozambique and Sweden. A trade agreement and a two-year economic co-operation agreement were signed on Aug. 19, 1981.

An agreement on development co-operation between July 1, 1983, and June 30, 1985, was signed on May 21, 1983.

Mozambique and Switzerland. An agreement on trade and economic co-operation was signed on Oct. 22, 1979.

Niger and the Federal Republic of Germany. An economic agreement signed on June 14, 1961, and in force from July 1, 1961, was extended on Sept. 12, 1963, March 26, 1964, and Sept. 16, 1985 (until Dec. 31, 1986).

An agreement on technical co-operation was signed and came into force on June 18, 1977.

Niger and Switzerland. An agreement on trade, investments and technical co-operation was signed on March 28, 1962.

Rwanda and the Federal Republic of Germany. An agreement on technical co-operation signed on Nov. 22, 1979, came into force on April 1, 1980.

Rwanda and Switzerland. A Belgian-Swiss extradition convention of May 13, 1874, was applied to Rwanda from June 30, 1971.

A technical and scientific co-operation agreement of Oct. 22, 1963, was amended on March 3/7, 1967.

São Tomé and Príncipe and Portugal. Four co-operation agreements (on trade, shipping, emigration and culture) were signed in São Tomé in July 1978. On April 20, 1979, instruments of ratification were exchanged in Lisbon in respect of an agreement on friendship and co-operation and other agreements on scientific, technical and judicial matters, while both countries granted each other most-favoured-nation treatment in trade.

Senegal and the Federal Republic of Germany. An agreement on economic and technical co-operation was signed and came into force on June 27, 1961.

A cultural agreement signed on Sept. 23, 1968, came into force on July 1, 1969.

Senegal and Japan. An aid agreement was signed in April 1979.

Senegal and Spain. A trade agreement was signed on Nov. 15, 1978.

Senegal and Sweden. A trade agreement was signed on Feb. 24, 1967.

Senegal and Switzerland. An agreement on trade, protection of investments and technical co-operation was signed on Aug. 16, 1962.

South Africa and Belgium-Luxembourg. A trade agreement signed on Nov. 2/Dec. 10, 1935, was on July 13, 1937, extended until Dec. 31, 1982.

South Africa and France. An agreement on co-operation in the construction of the Koeberg nuclear power plant was signed on Oct. 15, 1976.

South Africa and the Federal Republic of Germany. A treaty of commerce and navigation signed on Sept. 1, 1928, was amended on Oct. 13, 1932.

A general economic agreement signed on Aug. 28, 1951, was followed by an exchange of notes on April 30, 1962.

A cultural agreement signed on June 11, 1962, came into force on Dec. 25, 1963.

South Africa and Ireland. A trade agreement was concluded on Aug. 20, 1932.

South Africa and Italy. A commercial agreement was signed on May 21, 1935, and supplementary notes were signed on Jan. 21, 1936.

South Africa and the Netherlands. A treaty of commerce and navigation signed on Feb. 20, 1935, was extended until Dec. 31, 1982.

South Africa and Portugal. An agreement on the settlement of the boundary between South Africa and Mozambique was reached on Feb. 18, 1926.

A Mozambique Convention on the introduction of native labour into the Transvaal, railway matters and commercial intercourse was signed on Sept. 11, 1928; it was followed by a working agreement of Nov. 10, 1928, and it was repeatedly amended between Nov. 17, 1934, and Aug. 3–5, 1970.

South Africa and Taiwan. A trade agreement was signed on Feb. 26, 1975.

An agreement on scientific and technological co-operation was signed on March 11, 1980.

An exchange of notes on agreement for co-operation in agricultural science and technology took place on Feb. 5, 1982.

An agreement on co-operation in mineral and energy affairs was signed on April 4, 1985.

An agreement on economic co-operation, covering banking, health, fishing, forestry, shipping, energy, biotechnology and solar energy was signed on Sept. 4, 1986.

Togo and the Federal Republic of Germany. An agreement on technical co-operation was signed and came into force on Feb. 17, 1977.

Togo and Switzerland. An agreement on trade, protection of investments and technical co-operation was signed on Jan. 17, 1964.

Zaïre and Belgium. A general co-operation agreement was signed between the two countries in Kinshasa on March 28, 1976, together with protocols on economic, technical, scientific and industrial co-operation. At Zaïre's request Belgium later supplied that country with military aid, notably in March 1977 and in May 1978. The President of Zaïre stated in March 1979 that under existing agreements Belgium would train 3,000 Zaïrean infantrymen.

On March 19, 1983, the Belgian government agreed to grant Zaïre an interest-free loan equivalent to about $10,000,000 (repayable over 20 years after a 10-year grace period) for the purchase of Belgian equipment. In July 1983 it was announced that Belgian aid to Zaïre would run to the equivalent of about US$612,000,000 in 1983 and a similar amount in 1984.

Zaïre and France. A military co-operation agreement signed in May 1974 was not given final approval by the French National Assembly until Nov. 22, 1978. France subsequently rendered military assistance to Zaïre, in particular by providing transport for Moroccan troops in April 1977 and by sending troops and assisting in the dispatch to Zaïre of an African peace-keeping force in May-June 1978. In 1979 France was to train 3,000 Zaïrean paratroopers.

Zaïre and the Federal Republic of Germany. An agreement on technical co-operation and training, concluded on March 18, 1969, and provisionally implemented from that date, entered into force on Aug. 4, 1975.

Zaïre and Israel. Agreements concluded on Nov. 21–Dec. 1, 1982, were inter alia for (i) an arms sale to Zaïre worth about US$8,000,000; (ii) co-operation in Zaïre's agriculture, development of water and fishing resources and improvement of health services; (iii) the provision of scholarships in Israel; and (iv) the renewal of commercial and cultural exchange agreements abrogated in 1973.

Zaïre and Spain. Agreements on economic and industrial co-operation were signed on Nov. 21, 1983.

Zaïre and Switzerland. A trade agreement was concluded on March 10, 1972.

Zaïre and the United States. At the request of the Government of Zaïre the USA supplied, in March 1977, limited military assistance to that Government (threatened by an invasion of opponents from Angola) and again in May 1979. US military aid to Zaïre was worth $30,200,000 in 1976–77 and $32,500,000 in 1977–78 (in addition to economic and food aid).

Groupings in Africa

INDEPENDENT COUNTRIES

The independent countries of Africa and their major international links are shown in the table on the following page.

Four additional countries whose independence is not internationally recognized except by the Republic of South Africa and mutually among themselves are Bophuthatswana, Ciskei, Transkei and Venda, all former Black "homelands" within South Africa.

Among 66 treaties concluded by South Africa with Bophuthat-swana, signed on Nov. 15, 1977, and in force since Dec. 6, 1977, is a non-aggression pact between the two countries.

An earlier non-aggression pact between South Africa and Transkei, which had come into force on the latter's achievement of "independence" on Oct. 26, 1976, was abrogated by Transkei on May 10, 1978.

DEPENDENT TERRITORIES

France

French overseas department: Réunion.

Territory with special status as a *"collectivité territoriale"*: Mayotte.

South Africa

(1) Namibia (South West Africa), administered by the Government of South Africa as an integral part of the Republic of South Africa under a mandate granted by the League of Nations in 1919. The UN General Assembly decided on Oct. 27, 1966, to terminate South Africa's mandate and to take steps to establish an interim administration to prepare the territory for complete independence.

(2) The following territories (Black "home-lands") have, in varying degrees, been granted internal self-government by South Africa: Gazan-kulu, KaNgwane, KwaZulu, Lebowa, Ndebele and Qwaqwa.

Spain

The towns of Ceuta and Melilla on the North African coast are integral parts of Spain.

United Kingdom

Colonies: British Indian Ocean Territories; St Helena and dependencies (Ascension Island and Tristan da Cunha).

The Independent Countries of Africa

	OAU*	Commonwealth	Conseil de l'Entente	Defence Pact with France	West African Monetary Union	UDEAC	CEEAC	West African Economic Community	ECOWAS	Associate of EEC	Arab League
Algeria	X									X	X
Angola	X									X	
Benin	X		X		X			X	X	X	
Botswana	X	X								X	
Burkina Faso	X		X		X			X	X	X	
Burundi	X						X			X	
Cameroon	X			X		X	X			X	
Cape Verde	X								X	X	
Central African Republic	X			X		X	X			X	
Chad	X			X		X	X			X	
Comoros	X									X	
Congo	X			X		X	X			X	
Côte d'Ivoire	X		X	X	X			X	X	X	
Djibouti	X			X						X	X
Egypt	X										S
Equatorial Guinea	X					X	X			X	
Ethiopia	X									X	
Gabon	X			X		X	X			X	
The Gambia	X	X							X	X	
Ghana	X	X							X	X	
Guinea	X								X	X	
Guinea-Bissau	X								X	X	
Kenya	X	X								X	
Lesotho	X	X								X	
Liberia	X								X	X	
Libya	X										X
Madagascar	X									X	
Malawi	X	X								X	
Mali	X							X	X	X	
Mauritania	X							X	X	X	X
Mauritius	X	X								X	
Morocco										X	X
Mozambique	X									X	
Niger	X		X	X	X			X	X	X	
Nigeria	X	X							X	X	
Rwanda	X						X			X	
São Tomé and Príncipe	X						X			X	
Senegal	X			X	X			X	X	X	
Seychelles	X	X								X	
Sierra Leone	X	X							X	X	
Somalia	X									X	X
South Africa											
Sudan	X									X	X
Swaziland	X	X								X	
Tanzania	X	X								X	
Togo	X		X	X	X				X	X	
Tunisia	X									X	X
Uganda	X	X								X	
Zaïre	X						X			X	
Zambia	X	X								X	
Zimbabwe	X	X								X	

S=Suspended

*The Saharan Arab Democratic Republic (SADR), not generally regarded as an independent country, is also a member of the OAU.

17. South and East Asia and the Pacific Area

This section deals with (i) defence and security agreements of the South and East Asia and Pacific area; (ii) bilateral mutual defence treaties and other agreements concluded by the United States; (iii) intergovernmental organizations and institutions of the region; and (iv) other major agreements concluded by states of the region.

Regional Defence and Security Agreements

Australian-New Zealand Agreement (ANZAC)

After a conference held in January 1944 in Canberra between Australia and New Zealand to discuss their common interests, and in particular joint policy regarding the South-West Pacific region, a joint declaration, the Australian-New Zealand Agreement, 1944 (ANZAC), was signed on Jan. 21.

The two governments agreed that a "regional zone of defence comprising the South-West and South Pacific areas shall be established and that this zone should be based on Australia and New Zealand, stretching through the arch of islands north and north-east of Australia to Western Samoa and the Cook Islands".

In regard to dependent territories, the two governments declared that "the interim administration and ultimate disposal of enemy territories in the Pacific is of vital importance to Australia and New Zealand and that any such disposal should be effected only with their agreement and as part of a general Pacific agreement", and that "no change in the sovereignty . . . of any of the islands of the Pacific should be effected except as the result of an agreement to which they are parties".

In implementation of a further decision of the ANZAC Agreement, a South Pacific Commission was set up on Feb. 6, 1947 [see below].

ANZUS Pact

A tripartite security treaty between Australia, New Zealand and the United States was signed on Sept. 1, 1951, in San Francisco, and came into force on April 29, 1952. The treaty is known as the Pacific Security Treaty or, more usually, the ANZUS Pact. The latter name derives from the initials of the three signatory countries.

The possibility of a pact between Australia, New Zealand and the United States had been discussed in February 1951, when the US President's adviser on foreign affairs, John Foster Dulles, visited the Australian and New Zealand capitals. On April 18, 1951, President Truman announced from Washington that the Australian and New Zealand Governments, in view of the

impending re-establishment of peace with Japan (the Japanese peace treaty was signed on Sept. 8, 1951), had suggested to the United States an arrangement between the three countries which would "make it clear that no one of the three would be indifferent to an armed attack upon the others in the Pacific", and which would "establish consultation to strengthen security on the basis of continuous and effective self-help and mutual aid".

THE TREATY

The text of the Pacific Security Treaty was released on July 12, 1951. The preamble runs as follows:

"The parties to this treaty:
"reaffirming their faith in the purposes and principles of the UN Charter and their desire to live in peace with all peoples and governments, and desiring to strengthen the fabric of peace in the Pacific area;
"noting that the United States has already arrangements pursuant to which its armed forces are stationed in the Philippines, and has armed forces and administrative responsibilities in the Ryukyus, and, upon the coming into force of the Japanese peace treaty, may also station armed forces in and about Japan to assist in the preservation of peace and security in the Japan area;
"recognizing that Australia and New Zealand, as members of the British Commonwealth of Nations, have military obligations outside as well as within the Pacific area;
"desiring to declare publicly and formally their sense of unity, so that no potential aggressor could be under the illusion that any of them stand alone in the Pacific area; and
"desiring further to co-ordinate their efforts for collective defence for the preservation of peace and security pending the development of a more comprehensive system of regional security in the Pacific area;
"declare and agree as follows . . .".

The terms of the treaty are contained in 11 articles summarized below:

Art. 1. The parties undertook, in conformity with the UN Charter, to settle by peaceful means any international disputes in which they might be involved, and to refrain in their international relations from the use of force in any manner inconsistent with the purposes of the United Nations.

Art. 2. In order more effectively to achieve the objectives of the treaty, the parties would maintain and develop their individual and collective capacity to resist armed attack "by means of continuous self-help and mutual aid".

Art. 3. The parties would consult together, when, in the opinion of any one of them, the territorial integrity, political independence or security of any of them was threatened in the Pacific.

Art. 4. "Each party recognizes that an armed attack in the Pacific area on any of the other parties would be dangerous to its own peace and safety, and declares that it would act to meet the common danger in accordance with its constitutional processes." Any such attack, and all measures taken as a result of such attack, would be reported to the UN Security Council. Such measures would be terminated when the Security Council had taken the necessary steps to restore and maintain international peace and security.

Art. 5. For the purpose of Art. 4, an armed attack on any of the three countries would be deemed to include "an armed attack on the metropolitan territory of any of the parties, or on the island territories under its jurisdiction in the Pacific, or on its armed forces, vessels or aircraft in the Pacific".

Art. 6. The treaty would not affect the rights and obligations of the three countries under the UN Charter, or the responsibility of the United Nations for the maintenance of international peace and security.

Art. 7. The three countries would establish a Council, consisting of their Foreign Ministers or deputies, to consider matters concerning the implementation of the treaty. The Council would be organized so as to be able to meet at any time.

Art. 8. Pending the development of a more comprehensive regional security system in the Pacific, and the development by the United Nations of more effective means to maintain international peace and security, the Council, established under Art. 7, would maintain a consultative relationship with states, regional organizations, associations of states, and other authorities in the Pacific area which were in a position to further the purpose of the treaty and contribute to the security of the area.

Art. 9. The treaty would be ratified by the three countries in accordance with their respective constitutional processes. Instruments of ratification would be deposited with the Australian Government, and the treaty would enter into force as soon as the ratifications of the signatories had been deposited.

Art. 10. The treaty would remain in force indefinitely. Any party to the treaty could cease to be a member of the Council established under Art. 7 one year after notification to the Australian Government.

Art. 11. The treaty, drawn up in the English language, would be deposited in the archives of the Australian Government, which would make copies available to the other signatories.

ORGANIZATION

The Pacific Council. The organ of the ANZUS pact is the Council—known as the Pacific Council—set up under Article 7 of the treaty. It is composed of the Foreign Ministers (or their deputies) of the signatory powers. The Foreign Ministers generally meet once a year, but special Council meetings, attended by the deputies, are held in Washington more frequently. The Council has no permanent staff or funds.

Military Representatives. At the first meeting of the Pacific Council, held in Honolulu on Aug. 4–6, 1952, it was decided to create a military organization. In this organization each of the three signatory countries is represented by a military officer, who attends Council meetings. The military representatives also hold their own meetings from time to time as required by circumstances. Their function is to advise the Council on military co-operation in the Pacific.

PROJECT SPARTA

An agreement signed on March 20, 1966, between Australia, the United Kingdom and the United States on the SPARTA project concerned the firing of certain re-entry vehicles from the Woomera test range (in Australia) and the use of special instrumentation to observe re-entry phenomena.

AUSTRALIAN-NEW ZEALAND CONSULTATIVE COMMITTEE

The establishment of an Australian-New Zealand consultative committee on defence co-operation was officially announced on July 27, 1972, after the Prime Minister of New Zealand had stated on June 20 that the two countries would come to each other's defence if either of them was attacked with or without the ANZUS Pact.

ANZUS DECISION ON AFGHANISTAN, 1980

Following the Soviet Union's military intervention in Afghanistan in December 1979, it was agreed at a meeting of the US Secretary of State and the Foreign Ministers of Australia and New Zealand on Feb. 27–28, 1980, to support "the restoration of a truly non-aligned and neutral government in Afghanistan, responsive to the wishes of the Afghan people". It was also agreed that Australia would deploy an aircraft carrier and a task force in the Indian Ocean; that New Zealand would provide air and naval support; and that the USA would increase maritime surveillance, anti-submarine patrolling and military aid to countries in the region.

US-NEW ZEALAND AGREEMENT, 1982

In a memorandum of understanding between the United States and New Zealand of Feb. 26, 1982, the ANZUS Pact was expanded by provisions for procedures for supplying New Zealand with logistic support in the event of an emergency.

AUSTRALIAN BAN ON NUCLEAR TESTING

On Feb. 1, 1985, the Australian government refused to allow the testing of nuclear devices or nuclear delivery systems on or above Australian territory, but agreed to allow US aircraft monitoring test flights of MX missiles to be stationed in Australia.

On Feb. 4, 1985, the (Labour) government of New Zealand refused a US request for port facilities in New Zealand for a US destroyer with a potential nuclear capability. This refusal was followed by the cancellation of (i) a proposed ANZUS Pact meeting and (ii) New Zealand's participation in joint exercises with US forces.

On Sept. 1, 1985, the New Zealand Prime Minister announced that his government would present a bill to ban nuclear weapons from New Zealand and that port calls by US Navy vessels would not be resumed until such legislation was enacted. The US government, whose policy was not to disclose whether its ships were carrying nuclear weapons or not, insisted that continued naval co-operation with New Zealand required an unrestricted right to use New Zealand ports.

The New Zealand Prime Minister, however, reiterated his government's policy on Sept. 27, 1985, as follows: "We simply do not accept the proposition that the ANZUS alliance requires us to accept nuclear weapons." He added that he would welcome a US review of the treaty, and he also said: "We do not ask the United States to defend New Zealand with nuclear weapons. We do intend to exercise greater self-reliance in our own defence." On Sept. 30 he stated that New Zealand wished to remain in ANZUS and have a good relationship with the United States but would not "surrender our nuclear policy". On Oct. 9 he declared that his government was committed to a conventional defence force and would fulfil its obligations under the ANZUS Pact.

The New Zealand bill, presented on Dec. 10, 1985, established a New Zealand zone free of nuclear arms and biological weapons; ratified various international nuclear and conventional arms control treaties; and implemented the South Pacific Nuclear Free Zone Treaty signed in August 1985 by Australia, New Zealand and the South Pacific nations and renouncing the manufacture, possession or control of nuclear weapons.

In an article published on Jan. 2, 1986, the New Zealand Prime Minister expressed regret at the fact that the United States had curtailed almost all defence co-operation with New Zealand to the point where New Zealand's capacity to develop its own defences was limited.

On Aug. 12, 1986, the United States formally suspended all its security obligations to New Zealand under the ANZUS Pact until New Zealand would restore port and air access to US warships and military aircraft.

The Australian government stated at the same time that the relationship between Australia and the United States under the ANZUS treaty would remain "constant and indivisible" and that Australia, although it "disagreed completely" with New Zealand's nuclear-free zone policy, would maintain its bilateral military ties with New Zealand.

Australia-New Zealand Free Trade Area

An agreement was signed in Wellington on Aug. 31, 1965, by Australia and New Zealand on the establishment of a limited free trade area. The agreement, covering commodities accounting for some 60 per cent of the value of trade between the two countries, and including forestry and dairy products, was to remain in force for a period of 10 years as from Jan. 1, 1966, and it was extended under an agreement of June 30, 1977.

South-East Asia Collective Defence Treaty

A South-East Asia Collective Defence Treaty was signed in Manila on Sept. 8, 1954, and came into force on Feb. 9, 1955. The treaty was concluded by the governments of Australia, France, New Zealand, Pakistan, the Philippines, Thailand, the United Kingdom and the United States, which also agreed on the establishment of a South-East Asia Treaty Organization (SEATO) to be headed by the Council provided for in Art. 5 of the treaty [see below]. This organization was, however, dissolved on June 30, 1977, Pakistan having left it in 1972 and France having withdrawn its financial contribution to it in 1974 after ceasing its participating in the organization's military activities in 1967; moreover, the United States as well as the Philippines and Thailand had improved their relations with the People's Republic of China.

The treaty nevertheless remained in force. It was accompanied by (i) a unilateral US declaration in the form of an "understanding" that the pact was directed against communist aggression; (ii) a protocol on Indo-China; and (iii) the "Pacific Charter", a general statement of principles signed by all the eight contracting parties.

The texts of these documents are given below.

(1) The South-East Asia Collective Defence Treaty

Preamble

"The parties to this treaty: recognizing the sovereign equality of all the parties; retaining their faith in the purposes and principles set forth in the UN Charter, and their desire to live in peace with all peoples and governments; reaffirming that, in accordance with the UN Charter, they uphold the principle of equal rights and self-determination of peoples; declaring that they will earnestly strive by every peaceful means to promote self-government and to secure the independence of all countries whose peoples desire and are able to undertake its responsibilities; intending to declare publicly and formally their sense of unity so that any potential aggressor will appreciate that the parties stand together in the area; and desiring further to co-ordinate their efforts for collective defence for the preservation of peace and security, have agreed as follows:

Articles

"**Art. 1.** The parties undertake, as set forth in the UN Charter, to settle any international disputes in which they may be involved by peaceful means in such a manner that international peace, security and justice are not endangered, and to refrain in their international relations from the threat or use of force in any manner inconsistent with the purpose of the United Nations.

"**Art. 2.** In order more effectively to achieve the objectives of this treaty, the parties, separately and jointly, by means of continuous and effective self-help and mutual aid, will maintain and develop their individual and collective capacity to resist armed attack and to prevent and counter subversive acts from without against their territorial integrity and political stability.

"**Art. 3.** The parties undertake to strengthen their free institutions and to co-operate with one another in the further development of economic measures, including technical assistance, designed both to promote economic progress and social well-being and to further the individual and collective efforts of governments towards these ends.

"**Art. 4.** (1) Each party recognizes that aggression by means of armed attack in the treaty area against any of the parties, or against any state or territory which the parties by unanimous agreement may hereafter designate, would endanger its own peace and safety, and agrees that it will, in that event, act to meet the common danger in accordance with its constitutional processes. Measures taken under this paragraph shall be immediately reported to the UN Security Council.

(2) If, in the opinion of any of the parties, the inviolability or integrity of the territory or the sovereignty or political independence of any party in the treaty area, or of any other state or territory to which the provisions of Paragraph (1) of this article from time to time apply, is threatened in any way other than by armed attack, or is affected or threatened by any fact or situation which might endanger the peace of the area, the parties shall consult immediately in order to agree on the measures which should be taken for the common defence.

(3) It is understood that no action on the territory of any state designated by unanimous agreement under Paragraph (1) of this article, or on any territory so designated, shall be taken except at the invitation or with the consent of the government concerned.

"**Art. 5.** The parties hereby establish a Council, on which each of them shall be represented, to consider matters concerning the implementation of this treaty. The Council shall provide for consultation with regard to military and any other planning as the situation obtaining in the treaty area may from time to time require. The Council shall be organized so as to be able to meet at any time.

"**Art. 6.** This treaty does not affect, and shall not be interpreted as affecting in any way, the rights and obligations of any of the parties under the UN Charter or the responsibility of the United Nations for the maintenance of international peace and security. Each party declares that none of the international engagements now in force between it and any other of the parties, or any third party, is in conflict with the provisions of this treaty, and undertakes not to enter into any international engagement in conflict with the treaty.

"**Art. 7.** Any other state in a position to further the objectives of this treaty and to contribute to the security of the area may, by unanimous agreement of the parties, be invited to accede to this treaty. Any state so invited may become a party to the treaty by depositing its instrument of accession with the Philippine Government.

"**Art. 8.** The treaty area is the general area of South-East Asia, including also the entire territories of the Asian parties, and the general area of the South-West Pacific, not including the Pacific area north of 21 degrees 30 minutes North latitude. The parties may, by unanimous agreement, amend this article to include the territory of any state acceding to this treaty in accordance with Article 7, or otherwise to change the treaty area.

"**Art. 9.** (1) This treaty shall be deposited in the archives of the Philippine Government. Copies thereof shall be transmitted by that Government to the other signatories.

"(2) The treaty shall be ratified and its provisions carried out by the parties in accordance with their respective constitutional processes. Instruments of ratification shall be deposited as soon as possible with the Philippine Government, which shall notify all the other signatories of such deposit.

"(3) The treaty shall enter into force between the states which have ratified it as soon as the instruments of ratification of a majority of signatories shall have been deposited, and shall come into effect with respect to each other state on the date of deposit of its instrument of ratification.

"**Art. 10.** The treaty shall remain in force indefinitely, but any party may cease to be a party one year after notice of denunciation has been given to the Philippine Government, which shall inform the governments of the other parties of each notice of denunciation.

"**Art. 11.** The English text of this treaty is binding on the parties, but when the parties have agreed to the French text thereof and have so notified the Philippine Government, the French text shall be equally authentic and binding."

(2) US 'Understanding'

"The delegation of the United States of America, in signing the present treaty, does so with the understanding that its recognition of the effect of aggression and armed attack, and its agreement with reference thereto in Article 4, Paragraph (1), apply only to communist aggression, but affirms that in the event of other aggression or armed attack it will consult under the provisions of Article 4."

(3) Protocol on Indo-China

"Designations of states and territory as to which the provisions of Articles 3 and 4 are to be applicable—The parties to the South-East Asia Collective Defence Treaty unanimously designate for the purposes of Article 4 of the treaty the States of Cambodia and Laos and the free territory under the jurisdiction of the State of Vietnam.

"The parties further agree that the above-mentioned states and territory shall be eligible in respect of the economic measures contemplated by Article 3. This protocol shall come into force simultaneously with the coming into force of the treaty."

(4) The Pacific Charter

"The delegates, desiring to establish a firm basis for common action to maintain peace and security in South-East Asia and the South-West Pacific, and convinced that common action to this end, in order to be worthy and effective, must be inspired by the highest principles of justice and liberty, to hereby proclaim:

"(1) In accordance with the provisions of the UN Charter, they uphold the principle of equal rights and self-determination of peoples, and will earnestly strive by every peaceful means to promote self-government and to secure the independence of all countries whose peoples desire it and are able to undertake its responsibilities.

"(2) They are each prepared to continue taking effective practical measures to ensure conditions favourable to the orderly achievement of the foregoing purposes in accordance with their constitutional procedures.

"(3) They will continue to co-operate in the economic, social and cultural fields in order to promote higher living standards, economic progress and social well-being in this region.

"(4) As decreed in the South-East Asia Collective Defence Treaty, they are determined to prevent or counter by appropriate means any attempt in the treaty area to subvert freedom or to destroy their sovereignty or territorial integrity."

The Philippine Foreign Minister emphasized on Jan. 24, 1980, that the treaty was "still alive" and that the US President had repeatedly pledged to defend Thailand in case of aggression or invasion under the terms of the treaty.

Bilateral Mutual Defence Treaties of the United States

Basic Content of Treaties

The mutual defence treaties concluded by the USA in the Far East and the Pacific area are all similar in both content and wording. In each, the parties undertake to settle any international dispute in which they may be involved by peaceful means; to consult together at the threat of or in the event of an external armed attack; and to maintain and develop means to deter such an attack. The parties recognize that an armed attack on either would be dangerous to the peace and security of both, and declare their readiness to act to meet the common danger.

USA-Republic of Korea

The USA-Republic of Korea mutual security treaty was initialled in Seoul on Aug. 8, 1953, shortly after the signing of the armistice at the end of the Korean war. The treaty was formally signed in Washington on Oct. 1, 1953, and entered into force on Nov. 17, 1954. Its provisions are given below as an example of the US mutual defence treaties concluded with certain countries of the region.

Preamble

"The parties to this treaty, reaffirming their desire to live in peace with all peoples and governments, and desiring to strengthen the fabric of peace in the Pacific area, to declare publicly and formally their common determination to defend themselves against external armed attack so that no potential aggressor could be under the illusion that either of them stands alone in the Pacific area, and to strengthen their efforts for collective defence for the preservation of peace and security pending the development of a more comprehensive and effective system of regional security in the Pacific area, have agreed as follows:

"**Art. 1.** The parties undertake to settle any international disputes in which they may be involved by peaceful means . . . and to refrain in their international relations from the threat or use of force in any manner inconsistent with the purposes of the United Nations, or the obligations assumed by any party towards the United Nations.

"**Art. 2.** The parties will consult together whenever, in the opinion of either of them, the political independence or security of either of the parties is threatened by external armed attack. Separately and jointly, by self-help and mutual aid, the parties will maintain and develop appropriate means to deter armed attack, and will take suitable measures in consultation and agreement to implement this treaty and further its purposes.

"**Art. 3.** Each party recognizes that an armed attack in the Pacific area on either of the parties in territories now under their respective administrative control, or hereafter recognized by one of the parties as lawfully brought under the administrative control of the other, would be dangerous to its own peace and safety, and declares that it would act to meet the common danger in accordance with its constitutional processes.

"**Art. 4.** The Republic of Korea grants, and the United States accepts, the right to dispose US land, air and sea forces in and about the territory of the Republic of Korea as determined by mutual agreement.

"**Art. 5.** This treaty shall be ratified by the Republic of Korea and the United States in accordance with their respective constitutional processes, and will come into force when instruments of ratification have been exchanged.

"**Art. 6.** The treaty shall remain in force indefinitely. Either party may terminate it one year after notice has been given to the other party."

USA-Philippines

The mutual defence treaty between the USA and the Philippines was signed in Washington on Aug. 30, 1951. The treaty, which was intended to reinforce the Pacific security arrangements embodied in the ANZUS pact [see page 443], entered into force on Aug. 27, 1952.

In this treaty it was stated that an armed attack would be deemed to include "an armed attack on the metropolitan territory of either of the parties, or on the island territories under its jurisdiction in the Pacific, or on its armed forces, public vessels or aircraft in the Pacific".

Agreements on Military Bases. On March 14, 1947, an agreement had been signed in Manila by representatives of the USA and the Philippines, providing for the establishment, for a 99-year period, of 23 American military, naval and air bases in the Philippines. Under the agreement, which came into force on March 26, 1947, certain military bases, established before the Philippines' proclamation of independence in July 1946, would be maintained by the USA, while others would pass to the control of the Philippine Government.

In July 1956 the United States affirmed its recognition of the Philippine Government's sovereignty over all US bases on Philippine territory. The agreement on military bases was revised by a memorandum signed on Oct. 12, 1959. Among the decisions embodied in the memorandum were the shortening of the leases granted to the USA for military bases from 99 years to 25 years from Oct. 12, 1959, and an agreement that the US Government would consult with the Philippine Government on the operational use of the bases, and before setting up long-range missile sites at American bases.

Under a further agreement signed on Jan. 6, 1979, the USA was allowed continued use of the Clark Field air base and the Subic Bay naval base (as well as two associated facilities) for a further five years and was assured "unhampered military operations involving its forces in the Philippines".

At the same time the principle of Philippine sovereignty over the bases was reaffirmed; Filipino commanders were to be appointed to the bases (which was done on Feb. 16, 1979); the land area of the bases was greatly reduced; and the agreement was to be reviewed every five years. Under the agreement the US Government undertook to exert its "best efforts" to obtain congressional approval for US$500,000,000 over the next five years—US$300,000,000 in military assistance and sales credits to the Philippines and US$200,000,000 in "economic support" assistance—and for granting extra development aid of a further US$500,000,000.

A new agreement signed on June 1, 1983, provided for unimpeded US access to the Subic Bay Naval Base and Clark Field air base for another five years with effect from October 1984 and for an increase in US grant aid to US$600,000,000, including US$150,000,000 for the military assistance programme; additional military sales credits amounted to a total of US$300,000,000. A plan for co-ordinated US-Philippine defence of the country in the event of an attack had been signed on May 21, 1983 by the Philippine Armed Forces Chief of Staff and the C.-in-C. of the US Forces in the Pacific.

USA-Japan

A treaty of mutual co-operation and security between the USA and Japan was signed in Washington on Jan. 19, 1960, and entered into force on June 23, 1960. The treaty, which was concluded after some 18 months of negotiations, replaced the US-Japanese defence pact signed in San Francisco on Sept. 8, 1951.

Under the 1951 treaty the United States had the right to dispose land, air and sea forces in and about Japan, and to use those forces, at the request of the Japanese Government, "to put down large-scale internal riots and disturbances in Japan caused through instigation or intervention by an outside power or powers". The treaty also stated that Japan would not grant, without the prior consent of the United States, any bases, or the right of garrison, or transit of forces, to any third power.

Under the new treaty Japan was no longer treated as the weaker partner, but was placed on an equal footing with the United States.

Treaty Provisions. The most important of the provisions peculiar to this treaty are contained in Articles 2, 6 and 10:

Art. 2. The parties will contribute towards the further development of peaceful and friendly international relations by strengthening their free institutions, bringing about a better understanding of the principles upon which these institutions are founded, and promoting conditions of stability and well-being. They will seek to eliminate conflict in their international economic policies and encourage economic collaboration between them.

Art. 6. For the purpose of contributing to the security of Japan and the maintenance of international peace and security in the Far East, the United States of America is granted the use by its land, air and naval forces of facilities and areas in Japan. The use of these facilities and areas, as well as the status of US armed forces in Japan, shall be governed by a separate agreement, replacing the administrative agreement under Article 11 of the Security Treaty between the USA and Japan signed at Tokyo on Feb. 28, 1952, on arrangements for the implementation of the 1951 defence pact.

Art. 10. This treaty shall remain in force until, in the opinion of the Governments of the United States and Japan, there shall have come into force such United Nations arrangements as will satisfactorily provide for the maintenance of international peace and security in the Japan area. However, after the treaty has been in force for ten years, either party may give notice to the other party of its intention to terminate the treaty, in which case the treaty shall terminate one year after such notice has been given.

The treaty was clarified by an exchange of notes. In one of the notes the United States agreed to prior consultation with the Japanese Government over (i) any envisaged increase in its forces in Japan; (ii) any essential change in methods of arming and equipping forces (e.g. nuclear weapons); and (iii) the use of Japanese bases for any action outside the treaty area. The treaty area was defined as the territory under Japanese rule at any time. The parties also agreed to consult together in the event of an armed attack or threat of attack against the islands over which Japan claimed residual sovereignty. The principal islands in question were the Ryukyu Islands, the Bonin Islands, Volcano Island and Marcus Island. (For the return of these islands to Japan in 1972 see page 12.)

Subsequent Developments. On the expiry of the first 10 years of the treaty's currency (on which either party could give notice of its intention to terminate the treaty) Japan explicitly, on June 22, 1970, confirmed its intention of continuing to adhere to the treaty.

On Dec. 21, 1970, it was announced that during 1971 the USA would reduce its armed forces personnel to 28,000 and withdraw almost all its combat aircraft from Japan, and on Nov. 30, 1977, the US military authorities returned to Japan the Tachikawa air base (near Tokyo) held by US forces since September 1945.

President Ford of the USA confirmed on Aug. 6, 1975, that the USA would continue to uphold its treaty commitments in Asia and in particular those under the 1960 treaty with Japan "in the event of an armed attack against Japan, whether by nuclear or by conventional forces".

In 1976 a sub-committee for defence co-operation was established in Japan to study "modalities of US-Japanese co-operation, including its military aspects, for the effective attainment of the purposes of the security treaty".

1973 Vietnam Peace Agreement

An *Agreement on ending the War and restoring Peace in Vietnam* was signed in Paris on Jan. 27, 1973, by the Foreign Ministers of the USA, North and South Vietnam and the South Vietnamese Provisional Revolutionary Government (PRG). The peace agreement consisted of a preamble and 23 articles under nine chapters, and was accompanied by four protocols dealing in detail with specific matters covered by the agreement.

The salient points of the agreement were as follows:

Chap. I. Article 1 stated: "The United States and all other countries respect the independence, sovereignty, unity and territorial integrity of Vietnam as recognized by the 1954 Geneva Agreements on Vietnam." [These agreements ended the war between France and the *Vietminh* in Indo-China.]

Chap. II. Articles 2 and 3 provided for a ceasefire throughout South Vietnam from midnight on Jan. 27, 1973, and the cessation of all United States military activities against North Vietnam at the same time. The ceasefire would be "durable and without limit of time".

Article 4 stated: "The United States will not continue its military involvement or intervene in the internal affairs of South Vietnam."

Articles 5 and 6 provided for the total withdrawal from South Vietnam of troops, military advisers and personnel, armaments, munitions and war material of the USA and other foreign allies within 60 days of the signing of the agreement, and for the dismantlement of all foreign military bases in South Vietnam.

Chap. III. Article 8 dealt with the return of prisoners of war, which, it was stated, should be "carried out simultaneously with and completed not later than the same day as the troop withdrawal". It also provided for co-operation in the passing of information on military personnel and foreign civilians missing in action and for the locating and care of graves of the dead.

Chap. IV. This chapter covered the exercise of the South Vietnamese people's right to self-determination and contained the following articles:

Art. 9. "The Government of the United States of America and the Government of the Democratic Republic of Vietnam undertake to respect the following principles for the exercise of the South Vietnamese people's right to self-determination:

"(a) The South Vietnamese people's right to self-determination is sacred, inalienable, and shall be respected by all countries.

"(b) The South Vietnamese people shall decide themselves the political future of South Vietnam through genuinely free and democratic general elections under international supervision.

"(c) Foreign countries shall not impose any political tendency or personality on the South Vietnamese people.

Art. 10. "The two South Vietnamese parties undertake to respect the ceasefire and maintain peace in South Vietnam, settle all matters of contention through negotiations, and avoid all armed conflict.

Art. 11. "Immediately after the ceasefire, the two South Vietnamese parties will:

"Achieve national reconciliation and concord, end hatred and enmity, prohibit all acts of reprisal and discrimination against individuals or organizations that have collaborated with one side or the other;

"ensure the democratic liberties of the people: personal freedom, freedom of speech, freedom of the press, freedom of meeting, freedom of organization, freedom of belief, freedom of movement, freedom of residence, freedom of work, right to property ownership, and right to free enterprise.

Art. 12. "(a) Immediately after the ceasefire, the two South Vietnamese parties shall hold consultations in a spirit of national reconciliation and concord, mutual respect and mutual non-elimination to set up a National Council of National Reconciliation and Concord of three equal segments.

"The council shall operate on the principle of unanimity. After the National Council of National Reconciliation and Concord has assumed its functions, the two South Vietnamese parties will consult about the formation of councils at lower levels.

"The two South Vietnamese parties shall sign an agreement on the internal matters of South Vietnam as soon as possible and do their utmost to accomplish this within 90 days after the ceasefire comes into effect, in keeping with the South Vietnamese people's aspirations for peace, independence and democracy.

"(b) The National Council of National Reconciliation and Concord shall have the task of promoting the two South Vietnamese parties' implementation of this agreement, achievement of national reconciliation and concord and ensurance of democratic liberties.

"The National Council of National Reconciliation and Concord will organise the free and democratic general elections provided for in Article 9 (b) and decide the procedures and modalities of these general elections.

"The institutions for which the general elections are to be held will be agreed upon through consultations between the two South Vietnamese parties. The National Council of National Reconciliation and Concord will also decide the procedures and modalities of such local elections as the two South Vietnamese parties agree upon.

Art. 13. "The question of Vietnamese armed forces in South Vietnam shall be settled by the two South Vietnamese parties in a spirit of national reconciliation and concord, equality and mutual respect, without foreign interference, in accordance with the post-war situation.

"Among the questions to be discussed by the two South Vietnamese parties are steps to reduce their military effectives and to demobilize the troops being reduced. The two South Vietnamese parties will accomplish this as soon as possible.

Art. 14. "South Vietnam will pursue a foreign policy of peace and independence. It will be prepared to establish relations with all countries irrespective of their political and social systems on the basis of mutual respect for independence and sovereignty, and accept economic and technical aid from any country with no political conditions attached.

"The acceptance of military aid by South Vietnam in the future shall come under the authority of the Government set up after the general elections in South Vietnam provided for in Article 9 (b)."

Chap. V. Article 15, on the reunification of Vietnam, stated: "The reunification of Vietnam shall be carried out step by step through peaceful means on the basis of discussion and agreements between North and South Vietnam, without coercion or annexation by either part, and without foreign interference. The time for reunification will be agreed upon by North and South Vietnam.

"Pending the reunification:

"(a) The military demarcation line between the two zones at the 17th parallel is only provisional and not a political or territorial boundary, as provided for in Paragraph 6 of the final declaration of the 1954 Geneva conference.

"(b) North and South Vietnam shall respect the demilitarized zone on either size of the provisional military demarcation line.

"(c) North and South Vietnam shall promptly start negotiations with a view to re-establishing normal relations in various fields. Among the questions to be negotiated are the modalities of civilian movement across the provisional military demarcation line.

"(d) North and South Vietnam shall not join any military alliance or military bloc and shall not allow foreign powers to maintain military bases, troops, military advisers and military personnel on their respective territories, as stipulated in the 1954 Geneva Agreements on Vietnam."

Chap. VI. Articles 16 and 17 provided for the setting up of a four-party military commission, consisting of representatives of the four signatories of the agreement, and a two-party military commission representing the two South Vietnamese parties. These commissions would implement the provisions of the agreement concerning the ceasefire, the troop withdrawal and dismantlement of bases, and the return of prisoners of war. Under Article 18 an International Commission of Control and Supervision (ICCS) was to be established immediately after signature of the agreement.

Article 19 stated: "The parties agree on the convening of an international conference within 30 days of the signing of this agreement to acknowledge the signed agreements; to guarantee the ending of the war, the maintenance of peace in Vietnam, the respect of the Vietnamese people's fundamental national rights, and the South Vietnamese people's right to self-determination; and to contribute to and guarantee peace in Indo-China.

"The United States and the Democratic Republic of Vietnam, on behalf of the parties participating in the Paris Conference on Vietnam, will propose to the following parties that they participate in this international conference: The People's Republic of China, the Republic of France, the Union of

Soviet Socialist Republics, the United Kingdom, the four countries of the International Commission of Control and Supervision, and the Secretary-General of the United Nations, together with the parties participating in the Paris Conference on Vietnam."

Chap. VII. Article 20, which was concerned with Cambodia and Laos, stated:

"(*a*) The parties participating in the Paris Conference on Vietnam shall strictly respect the 1954 Geneva Agreements on Cambodia and the 1962 Geneva Agreement on Laos [see below], which recognized the Cambodian and the Laos people's fundamental national rights, i.e. the independence, sovereignty, unity and territorial integrity of these countries. The parties shall respect the neutrality of Cambodia and Laos.

"The parties participating in the Paris Conference on Vietnam undertake to refrain from using the territory of Cambodia and the territory of Laos to encroach on the sovereignty and security of one another and of other countries.

"(*b*) Foreign countries shall put an end to all military activities in Cambodia and Laos, totally withdraw from and refrain from reintroducing into these two countries troops, military advisers and military personnel, armaments, munitions and war material.

"(*c*) The internal affairs of Cambodia and Laos shall be settled by the people of each of these countries without foreign interference.

"(*d*) The problems existing between the Indo-Chinese countries shall be settled by the Indo-Chinese parties on the basis of respect for each other's independence, sovereignty and territorial integrity and non-interference in each other's internal affairs."

Chap. VIII. Articles 21 and 22 were concerned with the relationship between the USA and North Vietnam.

Art. 21. "The United States anticipates that this agreement will usher in an era of reconciliation with the Democratic Republic of Vietnam as with all the peoples of Indo-China. In pursuance of its traditional policy, the United States will contribute to healing the wounds of war and to post-war reconstruction of the Democratic Republic of Vietnam and throughout Indo-China.

Art. 22. "The ending of the war, the restoration of peace in Vietnam, and the strict implementation of this agreement will create conditions for establishing a new, equal and mutually beneficial relationship between the United States and the Democratic Republic of Vietnam on the basis of respect for each other's independence and sovereignty, and non-interference in each other's internal affairs. At the same time, this will ensure stable peace in Vietnam and contribute to the preservation of lasting peace in Indo-China and South-East Asia."

Chap. IX. Article 23 provided for the immediate entry into force of the agreement after signature.

The four protocols to the agreement covered the ceasefire, the ICCS, the return of prisoners and the destruction of mines in territorial waters (this last being a bilateral agreement between the USA and North Vietnam).

The treaty's provisions were subsequently implemented only in part. A ceasefire nominally came into force on Jan. 28, 1973, but fighting continued; no agreement was reached in negotiations between the South Vietnamese Government and the PRG; in December 1973 President Nguyen Van Thieu of South Vietnam rejected the holding of elections because the Communists (he said) did "not want to give up their ambition to attack and annex the South"; peace negotiations and the ceasefire machinery broke down in April-June 1974; and in January 1975 North Vietnam and the United States

accused each other of having violated the Paris agreement.

The South Vietnamese forces were finally defeated by Communist forces in April 1975; President Thieu resigned on April 21, saying that the United States had failed to honour a secret commitment to react "violently and immediately" to a North Vietnamese offensive against the South; Communist forces entered the South Vietnamese capital on April 30; and a provisional Revolutionary Government was set up there on May 15, 1975. Following the holding of general elections in the whole of Vietnam on April 25, 1976, the country was proclaimed reunified on July 2, 1976, as the Socialist Republic of Vietnam.

1973 Laos Peace Agreement

A peace agreement between the Government of Laos and the *Pathet Lao* was signed on Feb. 21, 1973. It comprised 12 articles, of which the first laid down the general principles on which the future of Laos should be based.

Art. 1. "(*a*) The desires of the Lao people to safeguard and exercise their cherished fundamental national rights—the independence, sovereignty, unity and territorial integrity of Laos—are inviolable.

"(*b*) The declation on the neutrality of Laos of July 9, 1962, and the 1962 Geneva Agreement on Laos [under which the neutrality of Laos was guaranteed] are the correct bases for the Kingdom of Laos' foreign policies of peace, independence and neutrality. The parties concerned in Laos, the United States, Thailand and other foreign countries must strictly respect and implement this agreement. The internal affairs of Laos must be conducted by the Lao people only, without external interference.

"(*c*) To achieve the supreme objective of restoring peace, consolidating independence, achieving national concord and restoring national unity, and taking into consideration the present reality in Laos, which has two zones separately controlled by the two sides, the internal problems of Laos must be solved in the spirit of national concord and on the basis of equality and mutual respect, free from pressure or annexation by either side.

"(*d*) To safeguard national independence and sovereignty, achieve national concord and restore national unity, the people's democratic freedoms must be scrupulously observed, which compromise individual freedom, freedom of religion, speech, press, assembly, establishment of political organizations and associations, candidacy and elections, movement and residence, free enterprise, and the right to ownership of private property. All laws, regulations and institutions contrary to these freedoms must be abolished."

Articles 2 and 3 provided for a ceasefire throughout Laos from midnight on Feb. 22, 1973, with the cessation of foreign military involvement of any kind. Article 4 dealt with the withdrawal of military personnel and the dissolution of military and paramilitary organizations of foreign countries in Laos within 90 days. Article 5 provided for the return of prisoners of war within the same period.

Articles 6–10 contained provisions for political arrangements.

Art. 6. "Genuinely free and democratic general elections shall be organized to establish the National Assembly and a permanent National Union Government genuinely representing the people of all nationalities in Laos. The procedures and date of the general elections will be discussed and agreed upon by the two sides. Pending the general elections, the two sides shall set up a new Provisional National Union Government and a National Political Consultative Council within 30 days at the latest after the signing of this agreement, to implement the provisions of the agreement and handle state affairs.

Art. 7. "The new Provisional National Union Government will be composed of representatives of the Vientiane Government and of the Patriotic Forces [*Pathet Lao*], in equal numbers, and two intellectuals who stand for peace, independence, neutrality and democracy, who will be chosen by common agreement by the two sides. The future Prime Minister will not be included in the two equal numbers of representatives of the two parties."

Art. 8. The National Political Consultative Council will be an organization of national concord and will be composed of representatives of the Vientiane Government and of the Patriotic Forces in equal numbers, as well as a number of personalities who advocate peace, independence, neutrality and democracy, to be chosen by the two sides by common agreement. It will perform its duties in accordance with the principle of unanimity of the two parties. It has the responsibility to consult with and express views to the Provisional National Union Government on major problems relating to domestic and foreign policies; to support and assist the Provisional National Union Government and the two sides in implementing the agreement in order to achieve national concord; to examine and adopt together the laws and regulations for general elections; and to collaborate with the Provisional National Union Government in holding general elections to establish the National Assembly and the permanent National Union Government."

Article 9 provided for the neutralization of the towns of Luang Prabang and Vientiane, while Article 10 stated:

"(*a*) Pending the establishment of the National Assembly and the permanent National Union Government . . . the two sides will keep the territories under their temporary control, and will endeavour to implement the political programme of the Provisional National Union Government, as agreed upon by both sides.

"(*b*) The two sides will promote the establishment of normal relations between the two zones, and create favourable conditions for the people to move about, make their living, and carry out economic and cultural exchanges with a view to consolidating national concord and bringing about national unification at an early date.

"(*c*) The two parties take note of the declaration of the US Government that it will contribute to healing the wounds of the war and to post-war reconstruction in Indo-China. The Provisional National Union Government will hold discussions with the US Government in connection with such a contribution regarding Laos."

Articles 11 and 12 covered the implementation of the agreement, providing for the setting up by the two sides of a Joint Commission for Implementation of the Agreement and the continued activities of the International Commission for Control and Supervision originally set up under the Geneva Agreements of 1954.

The Laotian Government and the *Pathet Lao* on Sept. 14, 1973, signed an agreement implementing the above peace agreement and aimed at bringing about a coalition Government. The agreement provided for the formation of a provisional national government, headed by Prince Souvanna Phouma and with portfolios equally divided between the two sides, and of a national political consultative council to advise the Government; the neutralization of Vientiane and Luang Prabang and the stationing there of troops and police by both sides; the withdrawal of all foreign troops and advisers within 60 days of the formation of the new Government; and the demarcation of the current ceasefire line with a number of specific points where the armies would particularly avoid confrontation.

After such a coalition Government had been formed in April 1974, however, the *Pathet Lao* gradually extended its influence; in June 1975 elections to a new National Assembly were postponed indefinitely; and in December of that year Laos was proclaimed a People's Democratic Republic under a Government headed by the general secretary of the Lao People's Revolutionary (Communist) Party.

Intergovernmental Organizations and Institutions in the Region

Association of South-East Asian Nations (ASEAN)

Address. P.O.B. 2072, Jakarta, Indonesia.
Officer. Phan Wannamethee (sec. gen.).
Founded. Aug. 8, 1967.
Membership. Brunei, Indonesia, Malaysia, the Philippines, Singapore and Thailand. (An application for membership by Sri Lanka was rejected, on geographical grounds, in June 1982. Brunei became a member on Jan. 7, 1984.)
Establishment. A declaration on the establishment of ASEAN was signed by the Foreign Ministers of Indonesia, Malaysia, the Philippines, Singapore and Thailand.

In the preamble to the declaration, stress was laid on the importance of increased regional co-operation and of raising the standard of living in the contracting states. The declaration defined the objectives of ASEAN as being to accelerate economic growth, social progress and cultural development in the region through joint endeavours; to promote regional peace and stability through abiding respect for justice and the rule of law in the relationship among countries of the region and adherence to the principles of the UN Charter; and to promote active collaboration and mutual assistance in matters of common interest, in particular for the greater utilization of their agriculture and industries, expansion of their trade and improvement of transportation and communications. The declaration also emphasized that all military bases of foreign powers existed only on a temporary basis and with the express consent of the countries concerned and could not be used for direct or indirect interference in the national independence and freedom of the region's states, or in their normal development.

The organs of ASEAN are its ministerial conference, which is composed of the Foreign Ministers of the five member countries and which meets annually; a standing committee, which meets when necessary between ministerial meetings; and a secretariat established in 1976.

DEVELOPMENT OF ASEAN

On April 18, 1975, the five ASEAN member countries jointly recognized the government of Kampuchea (then known as Cambodia) which had assumed power after the fall of Phnom-Penh (Kampuchea's capital) to the (communist) *Khmers Rouges* on the previous day.

At a meeting held on May 13–15, 1975, the ASEAN member countries' Foreign Ministers

451

declared that their countries were ready to enter "into friendly and harmonious relations with each nation in Indo-China" and "to co-operate with these countries in the common task of national development", and that differences in social and political systems should not be an obstacle to the development of constructive and mutually beneficial relations. At this meeting the ministers also decided to expand co-operation with the European Communities, Australia and New Zealand, and they signed an agreement for the facilitation of search for ASEAN member countries' ships in distress and the rescue of survivors of ships' accidents.

On Sept. 4, 1975, it was announced that it had been agreed to set up an ASEAN Council of Petroleum (ASCOPE) for co-operation and mutual assistance in developing oil resources in ASEAN member countries.

At a meeting held at Denpasar, Bali (Indonesia), on Feb. 23–24, 1976, the heads of state and government of the ASEAN member countries signed a *Treaty of Amity and Co-operation in South-East Asia* and a *Declaration of Concord*.

The treaty, consisting of 20 articles grouped in five chapters, laid down binding principles of mutual respect for the independence, sovereignty, equality, territorial integrity and national identity of all nations; the right of every state to lead its national existence free from external interference, subversion or coercion; non-interference in the internal affairs of one another; settlement of differences or disputes by peaceful means (without the threat or use of force); and effective co-operation among the five countries.

Under the heading "Amity" the parties to the treaty undertook to "endeavour to develop and strengthen the traditional, cultural and historical ties of friendship, good-neighbourliness and co-operation which bind them together" and to encourage and facilitate contact among their peoples.

The treaty expressed the determination of the five parties to "promote active co-operation in the economic, social, cultural, technical, scientific and administrative fields as well as in matters of common ideals and aspirations of international peace and stability in the region". To this end the five nations undertook to "maintain regular contacts and consultations . . . on international and regional matters". The treaty further laid down that "no ASEAN nation shall participate in any activity considered a threat to another member's economic and political stability" and that the signatories should "endeavour to strengthen their respective national as well as the regional prosperity and security based on self-reliance, co-operation and solidarity, for a strong and viable community of nations in South-East Asia".

Intra-regional differences were to be settled through direct friendly negotiations, and to facilitate this the five nations would "constitute a High Council comprising a representative at ministerial level" from each nation. This Council would have powers to "recommend or, upon agreement, even itself form a committee of mediation, inquiry or conciliation" to settle disputes which could not be resolved through direct negotiations. (The Council's decisions would, however, require unanimous agreement of the parties in dispute.) Other nations not parties to the dispute might use their good offices for the amicable settlement of differences. The modes of peaceful settlement of disputes contained in Article 33(1) of the UN Charter were, however, not excluded.

The *Declaration of Concord* laid down guidelines for ASEAN in the political, economic, social and cultural fields.

It provided for co-operation in the pursuit of political stability in the region as well as in member states individually; for member states to take active steps, individually and collectively,

towards the early establishment of a Zone of Peace, Freedom and Neutrality; for economic co-operation by helping each other by "according priority to the supply of the individual country's needs in critical circumstances in respect of basic commodities, particularly food and energy", by the establishment of large-scale ASEAN industrial plants, particularly to meet regional requirements of essential commodities, and by giving priority to "projects which utilize the available materials in the member states, contribute to the increase in food production, increase foreign exchange earnings or save foreign exchange and create employment".

The declaration also envisaged "progress towards the establishment of preferential trade arrangements as a long-term objective" and an acceleration of joint efforts to improve access to markets outside ASEAN for member countries' raw materials and finished products "by seeking the elimination of all trade barriers in those markets, developing new usages for those products and adopting common approaches and actions in dealing with regional groups and individual economic powers".

Furthermore, the declaration called for assistance from ASEAN partners in the event of one member being stricken by natural disasters or major calamities. Members would also study the development of judicial co-operation, including the possibility of an ASEAN extradition treaty. Finally the declaration called for "continuation of co-operation on a non-ASEAN basis between member states in security matters in accordance with their mutual needs and interests".

During their meeting in Bali the South-East Asian leaders made it clear that ASEAN was not intended to be a military organization or pact, or to be an association "against any ideology, economic or political".

At a second meeting of heads of state and government of the ASEAN member countries, held in Kuala Lumpur on Aug. 4–5, 1977, it was emphasized that the ASEAN countries desired "to develop peaceful and mutually beneficial relations with all countries in the region, including Cambodia, Laos and Vietnam", and that in their view the economic and social advancement of the member states of ASEAN was "a fundamental element in ensuring the political stability of the ASEAN region". It was noted that an agreement on ASEAN preferential trading arrangements, signed on Feb. 24, 1977, had been ratified by all member countries; that exchange of preferences on a first batch of 71 products had been agreed upon (this agreement actually coming into force on Jan. 1, 1978); and that progress had been made, inter alia, in the development of an ASEAN submarine cable system, studies on the setting up of an ASEAN regional satellite system, the harmonization and modernization of ASEAN national fleets and the promotion of containerization and joint bulk shipments.

(Additional tariff reductions were agreed to at further ministerial meetings, and by March 1979 a total of 1,326 products were included in the preferential trade arrangements, but the amount of trade affected remained limited.)

Following the overthrow of the Pol Pot regime in Cambodia by Vietnamese forces and its replacement by a "People's Revolutionary Council" in January 1979, the ASEAN member countries' Foreign Ministers, meeting in Bangkok on Jan. 12–13, 1979, issued a statement deploring "the armed intervention threatening the independence, sovereignty and territorial integrity of

Cambodia", affirming "the right of the Cambodian people to decide their own future without interference or influence from outside powers", and calling for "the immediate withdrawal of all foreign troops from Cambodian territory".

On the Chinese invasion of Vietnam in February 1979 the ASEAN standing committee, meeting in Bangkok on Feb. 20, 1979, urgently appealed to the conflicting countries to stop all hostile activities against each other and also called for the withdrawal of all foreign troops from areas of conflict in South-East Asia.

An agreement on co-operation in economic development, education, culture and the control of narcotics was signed by ASEAN and the United States on July 2 and Oct. 24, 1979, and entered into force on the latter date.

Continuing to recognize the Pol Pot government of Kampuchea, the ASEAN Foreign Ministers called, at a meeting held on June 17–18, 1981, for the withdrawal of all foreign forces from Kampuchea under the supervision of a UN peacekeeping force. On Aug. 7, 1982, the ministers reaffirmed their call for a total Vietnamese withdrawal from Kampuchea.

After the Japanese government had early in 1983 announced its intention to increase the strength of its armed forces—which had caused concern in ASEAN member countries—the Japanese Prime Minister toured these states between April 30 and May 10, 1983, giving assurances that the proposed reinforcements were of a "purely defensive" nature.

A meeting of ASEAN Foreign Ministers, held in Jakarta on July 9–10, 1984, again strongly condemned Vietnam's "military occupation" of Kampuchea and officially proposed a "national reconciliation" of all groups in Kampuchea, including the Vietnam-backed regime, as a means of achieving a political solution in Kampuchea.

At a meeting of 18 ministers from the ASEAN countries held in Kuala Lumpur on Feb. 7–9, 1985, the Malaysian Prime Minister stated that ASEAN's achievements in the field of economic and trade co-operation were "mediocre or worse" and that an effective and co-ordinated economic system should be enhanced by the sharing of data and the joint production and marketing of commodities.

At a meeting of economic ministers of Japan and the ASEAN member countries held in Tokyo on June 27–28, 1985, the ASEAN ministers urged Japan to increase its imports of manufactured and semi-processed products from ASEAN, to reduce tariff and non-tariff barriers, and to increase the transfer of technology. (On June 28 the Japanese government announced tariff reductions, in principle by 20 per cent, on more than 1,800 processed agricultural and industrial products, probably from April 1, 1986, with other reductions to follow in 1986 or 1987.)

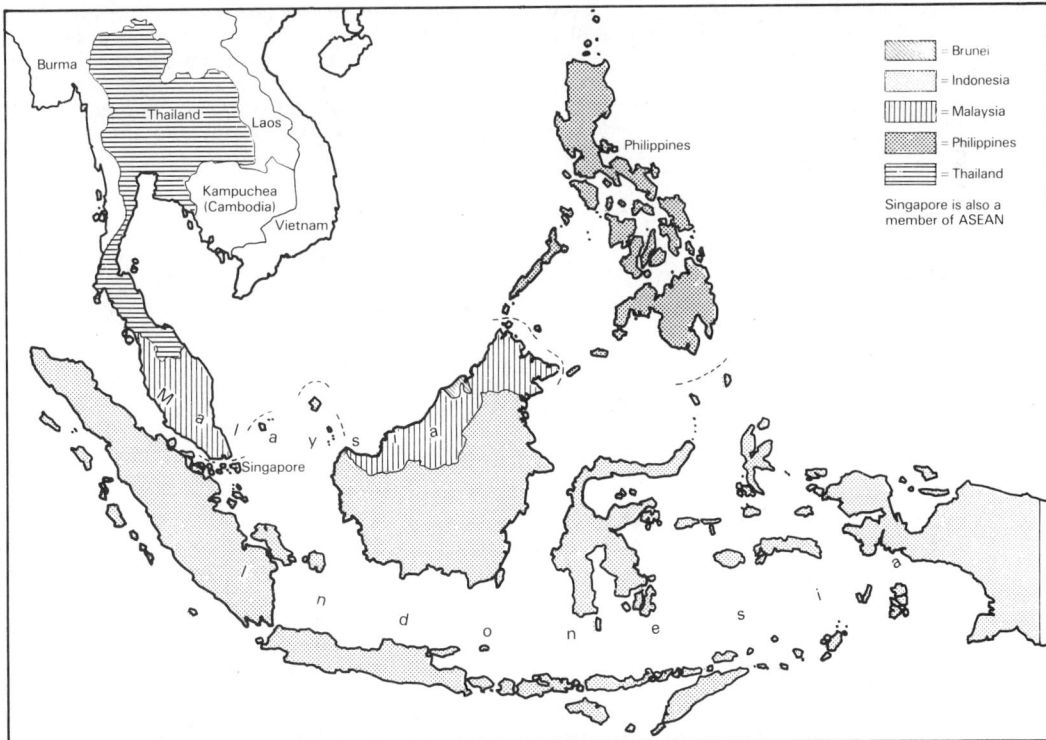

Map 13   Association of South-East Asian Nations (ASEAN)

A Foreign Ministers' meeting in Kuala Lumpur on July 8–9, 1985, called on all concerned to give their support to the convening of an international conference on drug abuse to be held in 1987 under UN auspices and also proposed the strengthening of international drug control, the harmonization of legislation on the punishment of drug traffickers and a programme of crop substitution in drug cultivation regions. The meeting inter alia also called for the early implementation of the main elements of the UNCTAD integrated programme for commodities.

Asian Development Bank

Address. P.O.B. 789, Manila, Philippines 2800.
Officer. Masao Fujioka (ch. of board of directors and pres.).
Founded. Aug. 22, 1966.
Membership. 45, of which 31 are regional countries and 14 non-regional countries, as follows:
Regional Members: Afghanistan, Australia, Bangladesh, Burma, China, Cook Islands, Fiji, Hong Kong, India, Indonesia, Japan, Kampuchea, Kiribati, Republic of Korea, Laos, Malaysia, Maldives, Nepal, New Zealand, Pakistan, Papua New Guinea, Philippines, Singapore, Solomon Islands, Sri Lanka, Taiwan, Thailand, Tonga, Vanuatu, Vietnam, Western Samoa.
Non-regional Members: Austria, Belgium, Canada, Denmark, Finland, France, Federal Republic of Germany, Italy, Netherlands, Norway, Sweden, Switzerland, United Kingdom, United States.
History. On Dec. 4, 1965, 21 countries signed the Charter of the Asian Development Bank, a financial institution set up under the auspices of the United Nations Economic Commission for Asia and the Far East (ECAFE)—since 1974 for Asia and the Pacific (ESCAP).

FUNCTIONS AND ORGANIZATION

The Charter laid down that membership of the Asian Development Bank would be open to members and associate members of ECAFE as well as to other regional countries and non-regional developed countries which were members of the United Nations or any of its specialized agencies.

The bank now has 12 directors, of whom eight represent Asian or Pacific countries. The bank's functions are to further investment in development projects within the region, to contribute to the harmonious economic growth of the whole area, to assist Asian member countries in preparing and co-ordinating their development plans, and to provide technical aid for the preparation, financing and execution of individual development projects.

It was laid down that 90 per cent of the bank's capital could be used for "hard" loans (at 5.5 per cent interest for 25–30 years) and 10 per cent for "soft" loans (low-interest and long-term). Member countries such as Australia, Japan and New Zealand, which, though members of ECAFE, were not underdeveloped countries, would not be entitled to draw any loans. A provision in the Charter authorized the bank to administer trust funds for use as "soft" loan money.

The decision-making organ of the bank is the Board of Governors, on which each member country is represented. The executive organ is the Board of Directors.

The bank was inaugurated on Nov. 24, 1966, and began operations on Dec. 19, 1966. By the end of 1981 its authorized capital was US$8,404,500,000, of which $8,296,800,000 had been subscribed. Paid-in capital was then US$1,609,100,000.

In June 1974 an **Asian Development Fund** was established to provide a systematic mechanism for mobilizing and administering resources for the bank to enable it to grant loans on concessionary terms. By the end of 1981 the total resources of the fund were US$3,184,740,000.

On March 10, 1986, China was admitted as a member of the bank, while Taiwan retained its membership.

Asian Productivity Organization (APO)

Address. 8-4-14 Akasata, Minato-ku, Tokyo 107, Japan.
Officer. Hiroshi Yokota (sec. gen.).
Founded. May 11, 1961.
Membership. 16 countries.
History. The APO was established under a convention signed by India, Japan, the Republic of Korea, Pakistan, the Philippines, Taiwan and Thailand in Manila on April 14, 1961, in order to "increase, by mutual co-operation, productivity in the countries of Asia".

Committee for Co-ordination of Investigations of the Lower Mekong Basin

Address. c/o ESCAP, United Nations Bldg., Rajadamnern Ave., Bangkok 10200, Thailand
Officer. Gala Magdi (exec. agent)
Founded. 1957
Membership. Laos, Thailand, Vietnam and 26 co-operating countries
Objects. To develop the resources of the lower Mekong basin, in particular hydroelectric power, irrigation, navigation, fisheries and food production.
Activities. An agreement on contributions totalling US$22,815,000 for a hydroelectric development project at Nam Ngum (Laos) in the Mekong River area was signed in Washington on May 4, 1966, by Australia, Canada, Denmark, Japan, the Netherlands, New Zealand and the United States. This project was to be completed in 1984.

A further agreement between Thailand and Laos, signed on the same day, provided for cement and power supplies by the former country during construction, and for the repayment by the latter on completion of the dam of funds invested and power consumed.

An agreement providing for the implementation of the Prek Thnot power and irrigation development project on the Lower Mekong River, Cambodia's first multi-purpose river scheme, was signed at the UN headquarters in New York on Nov. 13, 1968, by the 10 co-operating governments—Australia, Canada, West Germany, India, Italy, Japan, the Netherlands, Pakistan, the Philippines and the United Kingdom—and by the Cambodian Government. The 10 governments and the UN Development Programme agreed to contribute US$17,745,000 towards the US$27,000,000 cost.

However, since 1978 an interim committee has supervised work done without co-operation by Kampuchea, which had previously been a member of the committee.

In addition to hundreds of hydrological and meteorological stations, constructed in the area, 13 dams were built on tributaries of the Mekong, and six more were under construction, by 1984. Contributions pledged by the end of 1983 by member countries, co-operating countries and international agencies totalled US$520,500,000.

Committee for Co-ordination of Joint Prospecting for Mineral Resources in Asian Offshore Areas (CCOP/East Asia)

Address. The White Inn, No. 41, Sukhumvit Soi 4, Bangkok, Thailand.

Officer. S. K. Chung (project manager/co-ordinator).

Founded. 1966.

Membership. China, Indonesia, Japan, Kampuchea, the Republic of Korea, Malaysia, Papua New Guinea, the Philippines, Singapore, Thailand and Vietnam.

Objects. To reduce the cost of advanced mineral surveying and prospecting and to work in partnership with developed nations providing technical advisers.

Committee for Co-ordination of Joint Prospecting for Mineral Resources in the South Pacific Area (CCOP/SOPAC)

Address. c/o Mineral Resources Dept., Private Mailbag, GPO, Suva, Fiji.

Officer. Cruz A. Matos (man.).

Founded. 1974.

Membership. The Cook Islands, Fiji, Kiribati, New Zealand, Papua New Guinea, the Solomon Islands, Tonga, the (US) Trust Territory of the Pacific Islands, Tuvalu, Vanuatu and Western Samoa.

Activities. Prospecting for petroleum, manganese and other minerals.

Integrated Rural Development Centre

Founded. March 31, 1979.

Membership. Bangladesh, India, Indonesia, Nepal, Pakistan, Papua New Guinea, the Philippines, Sri Lanka, Thailand and Vietnam.

History. The centre was set up under an agreement signed in Kuala Lumpur on July 29, 1978, at an Asian-Pacific ambassadorial conference with the object of strengthening regional co-operation in agriculture and raising productivity, income and living standards.

South Asian Association for Regional Economic Co-operation (SAARC)

Founded. Dec. 8, 1985

Membership. Bangladesh, Bhutan, India, Maldives, Nepal, Pakistan and Sri Lanka

History. The idea of regional co-operation had first been put forward in 1980 by the then President of Bangladesh and had been developed in 1981–83. A committee for South Asia regional co-operation was formed by the Foreign Ministers of the above seven countries on Aug. 2, 1983, and issued an "integrated programme of action" (IPA) for co-operation in agriculture, rural development, telecommunications, health, population, sports, art and culture. A standing committee was appointed at foreign-secretariat level to implement the programme, identify new areas of co-operation and mobilize regional and external resources, A technical committee was to oversee the progress of regional co-operation. Ministerial meetings were held in July 1984 and May 1985.

At a meeting held in Dhaka (Bangladesh) on Dec. 7–8, 1985, the leaders of the seven countries adopted a Dhaka Declaration setting out their determination to implement regional co-operation in south Asia (containing one-fifth of humanity) to face "the formidable challenges of poverty, underdevelopment, low levels of production, unemployment and pressure of population". They also adopted a charter defining the objectives of the SAARC and also laying down that each member state would have the power of veto, with all decisions requiring unanimity, and that "bilateral and contentious issues" would be excluded from the organization's deliberations.

South Pacific Forum (SPF)

Address. G.P.O. Box 856, Suva, Fiji.

Founded. 1971.

Membership. Australia, the Cook Islands, Fiji, Kiribati, Nauru, New Zealand, Niue, Papua New Guinea, the Solomon Islands, Tonga, Tuvalu, Vanuatu and Western Samoa.

Observer. The Federated States of Micronesia.

Activities. The SPF was formed to provide an opportunity for informal discussions among its members on problems of common interest to them, and its decisions are reached by consensus. It held its first meeting in Wellington (New

Zealand) on Aug. 5–7, 1971, with Fiji, New Zealand, Tonga and Western Samoa being represented by their Prime Ministers, Nauru by its head of state, the Cook Islands by their Premier and Australia by its Minister of External Territories.

At a second meeting, held in Canberra on Feb. 23–25, 1972, it was decided to establish a **South Pacific Bureau for Economic Co-operation** at Suva. Under an agreement reached at the third meeting on April 17, 1973, this bureau was finally set up with a committee as its executive board and a secretariat; in 1975 the bureau became the official secretariat of the SPF. The bureau's activities cover trade, transport, communications, agriculture, industrial development, aid and aid co-ordination, the law of the sea, fisheries and seabed resources, the environment and energy.

The bureau has established the following subsidiary organizations: The Pacific Forum Line (a shipping line); the South Pacific Forum Fisheries Agency, with headquarters at Honiara (Solomon Islands); a South Pacific Trade Commission (in Australia); the Association of South Pacific Airlines; and a South Pacific Regional Disaster Fund. It has also co-ordinated the establishment of a South Pacific Regional Environment Programme.

At a meeting held on March 9, 1976, the SPF endorsed the concept of a nuclear-weapon-free zone in the South Pacific and called for the exclusion from the region of land-based nuclear weapons (in particular with regard to the underground testing of such weapons in French Polynesia) but not for any restriction on the movements of nuclear warships and submarines (especially under the ANZUS defence alliance).

At a meeting held in Kiribati on July 15, 1980, a *South Pacific Regional Trade and Economic Co-operation Agreement* (SPARTECA) was signed by most of the SPF members (but not by Fiji). The agreement removed duty on a wide range of goods (but not on exports from Australia or New Zealand to the islands) with the object of making the SPF member countries less dependent on Australia and New Zealand.

An SPF conference held on Aug. 28–29, 1983, reaffirmed the total opposition of member states to the French underground nuclear testing programme at Mururoa Atoll in French Polynesia but failed to reach a common position in response to a French invitation for Forum members to send scientific observers to inspect the Mururoa site. However, a joint mission from Australia, New Zealand and Papua New Guinea visited the site late in 1983 and reported to an SPF conference held on Aug. 28–29, 1984, that it had no reason to believe that any pollution by radioactive materials had occurred on Mururoa.

The 1983 conference also reiterated a call (first made in August 1982) on the French government to establish a precise timetable for the transition to independence of New Caledonia. The 1984 conference was attended (for the first time) by observers from the New Caledonian independence movement, and the conference agreed on a declaration of support for the movement.

The 1984 conference further extended the range of goods given preferential treatment under the SPARTECA agreement.

South Pacific Nuclear Free Zone Treaty

This treaty, prepared by a working group of the South Pacific Forum, was concluded on Aug. 5, 1985, at Rarotonga (Cook Islands) by Australia, Fiji, Kiribati, New Zealand, Niue, Papua New Guinea, Tuvalu and Western Samoa.

Parties to the treaty undertake to follow established nuclear non-proliferation measures, not to manufacture, acquire or have control of nuclear explosive devices, or to allow the stationing or testing of such devices within their territories, and to prevent the dumping of nuclear wastes. (Principally on the insistence of Australia, the treaty placed no restrictions on access to the region by nuclear-armed or nuclear-powered ships and aircraft.)

There are three protocols to the treaty—(i) providing for parties with dependent territories within the zone to comply with the treaty's relevant provisions, (ii) enabling the five nuclear-weapons powers to undertake not to assist in violations of the treaty and not to use or threaten to use nuclear weapons against parties to the treaty, and (iii) to enable these powers to undertake not to test nuclear weapons within the zone.

The substantive sections of the treaty are given below:

Art. 3. "Each party undertakes: (*a*) not to manufacture or otherwise acquire, possess or have control over any nuclear explosive device by any means anywhere inside or outside the South Pacific Nuclear Free Zone; (*b*) not to seek or receive any assistance in the manufacture or acquisition of any nuclear explosive device; (*c*) not to take any action to assist or encourage the manufacture or acquisition of any nuclear explosive device by any state.

Art. 5. "(i) Each party undertakes to prevent in its territory the stationing of any nuclear explosive device. (ii) Each party in the exercise of its sovereign rights remains free to decide for itself whether to allow visits by foreign ships and aircraft to its ports and airfields, transit of its airspace by foreign aircraft, and navigation by foreign ships in its territorial sea or archipelagic waters in a manner not covered by the rights of innocent passage, archipelagic sea lanes passage or transit passage of straits.

Art. 6. "Each party undertakes: (*a*) to prevent in its territory the testing of any nuclear explosive device; (*b*) not to take any action to assist or encourage the testing of any nuclear explosive device by any state.

Art. 7. "(1) Each party undertakes: (*a*) not to dump radioactive wastes and other radioactive matter at sea anywhere within the South Pacific Nuclear Free Zone; (*b*) to prevent the dumping of radioactive wastes and other radioactive matter by anyone in its territorial sea; (*c*) not to take any action to assist or encourage the dumping by anyone of radioactive wastes and other radioactive matter at sea anywhere within the South Pacific Nuclear Free Zone; (*d*) to support the conclusion as soon as possible of the proposed convention relating to the protection of the natural resources and environment of the South Pacific region and its protocol for the prevention of the pollution of the South Pacific region by dumping, with the aim of precluding dumping at sea of radioactive wastes and other radioactive matter by anyone anywhere in the region.

"(2) Paragraph 1(*a*) and 1(*b*) of this Article shall not apply to areas of the South Pacific Nuclear Free Zone in respect of which such a Convention and Protocol have entered into force."

Requiring at least eight ratifications to enter into force, the treaty had by the end of September 1986 been signed by 11 countries (the initial eight signatories plus Nauru, the Solomon Islands and Tonga), but ratified by only three. None of the treaty's three protocols had been signed by the relevant external powers, although China and the Soviet Union had indicated their willingness to adhere to the second and third protocols.

South Pacific Commission (SPC)

Address. P.O. Box D5, Nouméa, New Caledonia.

Officer. Francis Bugotu (sec. gen.).

Founded. Feb. 6, 1947.

Membership. Australia, the Cook Islands, Fiji, France, Nauru, New Zealand, Niue, Papua New Guinea, the Solomon Islands, Tuvalu, the United Kingdom, the United States and Western Samoa.

Object. To promote the social welfare and economic advancement of the island peoples in the region.

History. The SPC was set up in implementation of the ANZAC agreement (see above).

Activities. The SPC holds an annual South Pacific Conference, at which the following countries and territories are entitled to be represented: American Samoa, the Republic of Belau, the Federated States of Micronesia, French Polynesia, Guam, Kiribati, the Marshall Islands, New Caledonia, the Commonwealth of the Northern Mariana Islands, the Pitcairn Islands, Tokelau, Tonga, Vanuatu and the Wallis and Futuna Islands. The SPC's budget for 1985 was set at US$2,600,000, deriving mainly from grants and contributions from Australia, New Zealand, France, the United Kingdom and the United States, and to be spent chiefly on research, training and consultancy projects in the marine, agricultural, education and health fields.

Other Agreements concluded by South and East Asian and Pacific States

Major Regional Agreements*

Burma and Pakistan. (1) A *treaty of "perpetual peace and friendship"* was signed on June 25, 1952. It provided for mutual co-operation in matters of common concern to both countries, and for periodical meetings of representatives of the two countries.

(2) An *agreement fixing the frontier between Burma and East Pakistan* (now Bangladesh) in the area of the river Naaf was signed on May 9, 1966.

Indonesia and Japan. Under an agreement signed on Aug. 13, 1977, Japan's support for Indonesia was greatly increased (a loan for 1977–78 being equivalent to $185,000,000 and further loans and grants being promised).

Indonesia and the Philippines. Border co-operation and border control agreements were signed between the two countries on March 11, 1975, with the object of preventing the use of border territory, waters and airspace for illegal activities.

Indonesia and Thailand. An agreement defining the seabed boundary between the two countries in the Andaman Sea was concluded in 1975.

Japan and the Republic of Korea. (1) A *Basic Relations Treaty* between Japan and the Republic of Korea was concluded on June 22, 1965. The treaty settled all issues between the two countries after a lapse of 55 years (Korea was a Japanese colony from 1910 until the end of World War II). The treaty, inter alia, provided for the establishment of diplomatic relations; confirmed that "all treaties or agreements concluded between the Empire of Japan and the Empire of Korea on or before Aug. 22, 1910, are null and void"; and confirmed that "the Government of the Republic of Korea is the only lawful Government of Korea".

(2) An *agreement on the joint development of the continental shelf* between Japan and the Republic of Korea was signed in Seoul on Feb. 4, 1974. It provided for the exploration and exploitation of mineral resources, including petroleum and natural gas, in a joint development zone divided into subzones, during specified periods, with the agreement remaining in force for 50 years and further thereafter unless terminated by either party giving three years' advance notice. The agreement was ratified in Korea a few months later but in Japan it was not declared ratified until June 9, 1977. (It was declared null and void on June 13 by the Foreign Ministries of both China and Taiwan, and the Chinese Government declared on June 26, 1978, that it had "inviolable sovereignty" over the continental shelf in the East China Sea and would "never agree" to the Japanese-South Korean agreement.)

(3) An agreement reached on Jan. 12, 1983, provided for Japanese low-interest loans (worth $1,850 million) for Korean industrial projects and export-import loans (worth $2,150 million) at 6 per cent interest and effective over seven years.

Japan and the Philippines. (1) A treaty of friendship, trade and navigation (superseding an earlier such treaty concluded on Dec. 9, 1960) was signed by the two countries on May 10, 1979. It called for an effort by Japan to correct the trade imbalance between the two countries,

* For agreements between Commonwealth countries in the region see pages 319–20.

457

granted Japan most-favoured-nation status and pledged the co-operation of the two sides to "contain, control or minimize the effect" of oil and other pollutants on marine and other resources.

(2) An agreement signed on April 27, 1984, provided for a Japanese loan worth US$188,800,000 for construction projects in the Philippines and Japanese purchases of raw materials from the Philippines.

Nepal and Pakistan. An agreement on economic co-operation was signed on Nov. 29, 1984.

Agreements between Regional and Non-regional Countries*

Burma and the Federal Republic of Germany. A protocol on economic aid was signed on July 12, 1962.

Indonesia and the Federal Republic of Germany. A trade agreement of April 22, 1953, in force from April 1, 1953, was amended on July 12, 1955, with effect from April 4, 1955, and extended (on Nov. 22, 1984) until March 31, 1986.

Agreements on technical co-operation were signed on April 8, 1971, and on April 9, 1984 (effective Feb. 15, 1985).

An agreement on co-operation in peaceful use of nuclear energy signed on June 14, 1976, came into force on Feb. 24, 1977.

An agreement on co-operation in scientific research and technological development signed on March 20, 1979, came into force on Nov. 6, 1979.

Indonesia and Spain. A basic agreement on co-operation in science and technology was signed on Oct. 8, 1982.

Indonesia and Sweden. A trade agreement was signed on July 29, 1954.

Indonesia and Switzerland. A trade agreement was signed on Dec. 30, 1954.

A technical co-operation agreement was signed on Jan. 21, 1971.

Japan and the Federal Republic of Germany. A treaty of commerce and navigation, signed on July 20, 1927, came into force on Aug. 23, 1928, and was, on Dec. 10, 1984, extended until Dec. 31, 1986.

A cultural agreement signed on Feb. 14, 1957, came into force on Oct. 10, 1957.

A trade agreement signed on and in force from July 1, 1960, was, on Sept. 16, 1985, extended until Dec. 31, 1986.

An agreement on co-operation in science and technology was concluded on Oct. 8, 1974.

Japan and South Africa. An agreement on IAEA safeguards for nuclear energy source materials was signed on June 20, 1962.

* For agreements involving Commonwealth countries in the region see pages 321–30.

Japan and Spain. A cultural agreement was signed on March 5, 1982.

Japan and Sweden. A treaty of commerce and navigation was signed on May 19, 1911.

A trade agreement was signed on March 5, 1952.

A ministerial note on co-operation in peaceful uses of nuclear energy was signed on March 27, 1973.

The Republic of Korea and France. An agreement signed on Aug. 2, 1976, provided for French credits for the purchase by the Republic of Korea of two French nuclear power stations.

The Republic of Korea and the Federal Republic of Germany. A trade agreement signed on, and in force from, April 8, 1965, was, on Nov. 22, 1984, extended until April 7, 1986.

A cultural agreement of May 16, 1970, came into force on Aug. 8, 1972.

The Republic of Korea and Spain. A supplementary agreement on co-operation in the development and application of peaceful uses of nuclear energy was signed on Dec. 10, 1976.

A convention on cultural co-operation signed on Feb. 7, 1977, came into force on June 6, 1977.

The Republic of Korea and Sweden. An agreement on technical co-operation in family planning was signed on July 12, 1968.

Nepal and France. A financial protocol worth US$7,400,000 and an agreement on technical and cultural co-operation were signed in May 1983.

Nepal and the Federal Republic of Germany. An agreement on technical co-operation was signed and came into force on May 30, 1974.

Nepal and Spain. A cultural agreement was signed on Sept. 19, 1983.

Nepal and Switzerland. A technical co-operation agreement was signed on Aug. 18, 1972.

Pakistan and Belgium. An atomic energy co-operation agreement was signed on Oct. 9, 1970.

Pakistan and France. An agreement on the purchase by Pakistan of a nuclear reprocessing plant from France (disclosed by the Prime Minister of Pakistan on Feb. 24, 1976) was followed by an agreement between the two states and the International Atomic Energy Agency (IAEA) signed in Vienna on March 18, 1976, under which Pakistan undertook not to use the reprocessing plant or any equipment or material supplied by France for the manufacture of nuclear weapons or any other military purposes.

Under a contract of March 27, 1979, France was to supply Pakistan with 32 Mirage III and Mirage 5 jet fighters.

Pakistan and the Federal Republic of Germany. A provisional trade agreement concluded on March 4, 1950, and in force from May 15, 1953, was, on Dec. 10, 1984, extended until Dec. 31, 1986.

A trade agreement signed on March 9, 1957, and in force from July 1, 1957, was, on Sept. 16, 1985, extended until Dec. 31, 1986.

A cultural agreement signed on Nov. 9, 1961, came into force on Dec. 30, 1962.

An agreement on scientific research and technological development signed on Nov. 30, 1972, came into force on Oct. 15, 1973.

Pakistan and Greece. A cultural co-operation agreement and an agreement on economic and technical co-operation were signed on Dec. 16, 1976.

Pakistan and Italy. A cultural agreement was signed on March 17, 1975, and a scientific and technical co-operation agreement on Aug. 20, 1975.

Pakistan and Spain. Trade agreements were signed on Nov. 11 and 29, 1976.

Pakistan and Switzerland. A technical and scientific co-operation agreement was signed on Nov. 24, 1966.

Papua New Guinea and Switzerland. An extradition treaty was signed on Sept. 22, 1976, and Feb. 25, 1977.

The Philippines and the Federal Republic of Germany. A trade agreement signed on Feb. 28, 1964, was, on Feb. 11, 1985, extended until Aug. 12, 1986.

An agreement on technical co-operation signed on Sept. 7, 1971, came into force on Jan. 25, 1972.

An agreement on cultural co-operation signed on April 13, 1983, came into force on Sept. 20, 1985.

The Philippines and Switzerland. A treaty of friendship was signed on Aug. 30, 1956.

Thailand and the Federal Republic of Germany. An agreement on cultural co-operation was signed on March 24, 1983.

Thailand and Sweden. An agreement on friendship, commerce and navigation signed on Nov. 5, 1937, and abrogated by Thailand on Feb. 27, 1970, was still applied pending conclusion of a new agreement.

Vanuatu and France. An agreement signed on Feb. 10, 1981, provided for the equivalent of US$5,700,000 in French aid to Vanuatu and contained clauses (i) on non-intervention by the two sides in each other's internal affairs and (ii) on guaranteed respect by Vanuatu for the rights of French residents in the country.

Dependent Territories in the Pacific Area and South-East Asia

Australia
External Territories
Christmas Island (in the Indian Ocean), administered by an Official Representative of the Minister for Territories in Canberra.

Cocos (Keeling) Islands (in the Indian Ocean), administered as above,

Norfolk Island.

France
Overseas Territories
New Caledonia.
French Polynesia (which includes Tahiti).
Wallis and Futuna Islands.

New Zealand
Overseas Territories
Cook Islands, an autonomous state in free association with New Zealand since 1965.

Niue, one of the Cook Islands under separate administration.

Tokelau Islands.

Portugal
Special Territory
Macao (consisting of the Macao peninsula and the two adjacent islands of Taipa and Coloane).

The United Kingdom
Colonies
Pitcairn Islands Group, administered by the Governor of Fiji.

Hong Kong (consisting of the island of Hong Kong, Stonecutters Island, the Kowloon Peninsula and the New Territories leased by China to Britain in 1898).

The United States of America
(1) *External Territories*
American Samoa, administered by the US Department of the Interior.

Guam, the largest island of the Marianas group. The island has statutory powers of self-government, and its inhabitants have US citizenship.

(2) *Trust Territory of the Pacific Islands*, administered by the United States under the UN trusteeship system:

The Commonwealth of the Northern Mariana Islands, since Jan. 9, 1978, with the same status as the island of Puerto Rico.

The Federated States of Micronesia (Caroline Islands of Truk, Yap, Ponape and Kosrae);

the Marshall Islands;

Palau (the Republic of Belau from Jan. 1, 1981).

The Federated States of Micronesia have, under their 1978 constitution, full internal self-government and authority and responsibility for foreign affairs, while the United States is responsible for defence and security (for 15 years).

With the Marshall Islands the United States signed a "compact of free association" on May 30, 1982 (retaining responsibility for defence), with US economic support for an initial period of 15 years.

With the Republic of Belau the United States signed a "compact of free association" on Aug. 26, 1982, retaining responsibility for defence and security. A treaty of association concluded on Jan. 10, 1986, contained a clause enabling the United States to establish military bases on Belau as a partial alternative to the US military installations in the Philippines (held under a lease agreement due to expire in 1991), and also to restrict access to Belau of other foreign armed forces. This treaty was subject to ratification by the US Congress and Belau's National Congress and also to approval in a plebiscite to be held in Belau.

18. The "Third World": Attempts at Achieving Cohesion

This section dealing with various moves by third-world countries to achieve greater political cohesion covers in particular (i) the history and development of the non-aligned movement; and (ii) other groupings of developing countries created to achieve greater international effectiveness in various fields.

The Non-Aligned Movement

Membership. 100 countries and two organizations—Afghanistan, Algeria, Angola, Argentina, the Bahamas, Bahrain, Bangladesh, Barbados, Belize, Benin, Bhutan, Bolivia, Botswana, Burkina Faso, Burundi, Cameroon, Cape Verde, the Central African Republic, Chad, Colombia, the Comoros, the Congo, Côte d'Ivoire, Cuba, Cyprus, Djibouti, Dominica, Ecuador, Egypt, Equatorial Guinea, Ethiopia, Gabon, The Gambia, Ghana, Grenada, Guinea, Guinea-Bissau, Guyana, India, Indonesia, Iran, Iraq, Jamaica, Jordan, Kampuchea, Kenya, the People's Democratic Republic of Korea, Kuwait, Laos, Lebanon, Lesotho, Liberia, Libya, Madagascar, Malawi, Malaysia, Maldives, Mali, Malta, Mauritania, Mauritius, Morocco, Mozambique, the South West Africa People's Organization (SWAPO) of Namibia, Nepal, Nicaragua, Niger, Nigeria, Oman, Pakistan, the Palestine Liberation Organization (PLO), Panama, Peru, Qatar, Rwanda, St Lucia, São Tomé and Príncipe, Saudi Arabia, Senegal, Seychelles, Sierra Leone, Singapore, Somalia, Sri Lanka, the Sudan, Suriname, Swaziland, Syria, Tanzania, Togo, Trinidad and Tobago, Tunisia, Uganda, the United Arab Emirates, Vanuatu, Vietnam, the Yemen Arab Republic, the People's Democratic Republic of Yemen, Yugoslavia, Zaïre, Zambia and Zimbabwe.

History. Arising out of the Bandung Conference [see below] a movement of non-aligned countries took shape under the guidance of leading Third World statesmen, the most prominent of whom were Jawaharlal Nehru (the first Prime Minister of India), President Sukarno of Indonesia, Gamal Abdel Nasser (Prime Minister and later President of Egypt) and President Tito of Yugoslavia.

A Co-ordinating Bureau, first set up in Algiers in 1973, was in 1976 enlarged from 17 to 25 members, and to 36 members at the Havana conference in August 1979 [see below]. These 36 seats were distributed as follows: *Africa* 17—Benin, Ethiopia, Ghana, Lesotho, Madagascar, Mauritania, Mozambique, Nigeria, Somalia, Togo, Zambia and six other members to be decided by the African group at the United Nations; *Asia* 12—India, Iraq, Jordan, Democratic People's Republic of Korea, Palestine Liberation Organization, Sri Lanka, People's Democratic Republic of Yemen, and as alternate members Afghanistan/Bangladesh, Indonesia/Singapore, Iran/Bhutan and Vietnam/Laos; *Latin America* five—Cuba, Guyana, Jamaica, Panama and as alternate members Peru/Grenada; *Europe* one—Yugoslavia; and one extra seat shared between *Europe and Africa*—Cyprus as alternate member with Uganda.

Activities and Conferences

Since the mid-1950s, delegations from countries of Asia, Africa and Latin America have met in conference, from time to time, to define their common attitude with relation to international affairs, and to try to bring about closer solidarity in economic, cultural and political fields. These countries, which represent the less privileged parts of the world, are sometimes referred to as the "Third World" or, since most of them form part of neither the Western (capitalist) bloc nor the Eastern (Communist) bloc, as the "non-aligned" or "uncommitted" nations.

THE BANDUNG CONFERENCE

A conference held at Bandung (Indonesia) on April 18–23, 1955, was, as President Sukarno of Indonesia stated in the opening speech, "the first inter-continental conference of the so-called coloured peoples in the history of mankind". It was attended by delegates of the governments of Afghanistan, Burma, Cambodia (Kampuchea), Ceylon (Sri Lanka), the People's Republic of China, Egypt, Ethiopia, the Gold Coast (now

461

Ghana), Indonesia, Iran, Iraq, Japan, Jordan, Laos, Lebanon, Liberia, Libya, Nepal, Pakistan, the Philippines, Saudi Arabia, the Sudan, Syria, Thailand, Turkey, North Vietnam, South Vietnam and Yemen (later the Yemen Arab Republic)—as well as many unofficial observers from other countries.

The decision to hold the conference had been made at a conference of the Prime Ministers of Burma, Ceylon, India, Indonesia and Pakistan, held at Bogor (Indonesia) on Dec. 28–29, 1954. The Prime Ministers agreed that an Afro-Asian conference should be held under their sponsorship, and that its basic purpose would be to make the countries concerned better acquainted with one another's point of view.

Resolutions. The communiqué issued at the end of the Bandung Conference contained resolutions on economic and cultural co-operation; on human rights and self-determination; on problems of dependent peoples; and on world peace and co-operation.

The conference recognized the urgency of promoting economic development in the Asian-African region, and also the desirability of co-operation with countries outside the region. Recommendations were made for, inter alia, the early establishment of a special UN fund for economic development, and the allocation, by the International Bank, of a greater part of its resources to Asian-African countries.

In the cultural field the conference condemned the alleged practice, on the part of colonial powers, of suppressing the national cultures of the peoples of Africa and Asia. This was described as a fundamental denial of the rights of man.

After declaring its full support of the fundamental principles of human rights and of the principle of self-determination of peoples and nations, as set forth in the UN Charter, the conference condemned the policies and practices of racial segregation and discrimination. In a *Declaration on Problems of Dependent Peoples* it was stated that colonialism, in all its manifestations, was an evil which should speedily be brought to an end.

The conference also adopted a *Declaration on World Peace and Co-operation*, in which it agreed that nations should live together in peace with one another as good neighbours, and develop friendly co-operation on the basis of the following principles:

(1) Respect for the fundamental human rights and for the purposes and principles of the UN Charter.

(2) Respect for the sovereignty and territorial integrity of all nations.

(3) Recognition of the equality of all races and nations, large and small.

(4) Abstention from intervention or interference in the internal affairs of other countries.

(5) Respect for the right of each nation to defend itself singly or collectively in conformity with the UN Charter.

(6) Abstention from the use of arrangements of collective defence to serve the particular interests of any of the big powers; and abstention by any country from exerting pressure on other countries.

(7) Refraining from acts or threats of aggression or the use of force against the territorial integrity or political independence of any country.

(8) Settlement of all international disputes by peaceful means such as negotiation, conciliation, arbitration or judicial settlement, as well as other peaceful means of the parties' own choice in conformity with the UN Charter.

(9) Promotion of mutual interest and co-operation.

(10) Respect for justice and international obligations.

The Five Principles. The principles listed above are an extension of the "Five Principles" of peaceful coexistence, or Panch Sila (from the Pali, in which it expresses a Buddhist concept). These principles were first enumerated in an agreement over Tibet—now superseded by China's action in that country—concluded between India and the People's Republic of China in April 1954, where they were given as follows:

(1) Mutual respect for territorial integrity and sovereignty;

(2) mutual non-aggression;

(3) mutual non-interference in each other's internal affairs;

(4) equality and mutual benefit;

(5) peaceful coexistence.

NON-ALIGNED CO-OPERATION IN THE FIELD OF INFORMATION

A pool of non-aligned news agencies, the creation of which had been decided upon at a meeting in New Delhi on July 8–13, 1976, of delegates from 62 non-aligned countries and 45 representatives of news agencies, began operations in that year, with Tanjug (the Yugoslav news agency) collecting and redistributing (through seven regional centres) news reports among non-aligned countries. Statutes and an action programme for the years until 1982 were adopted for the pool at a conference held in Belgrade on Nov. 22–24, 1979.

The statutes committed the pool to the distribution of "objective, factual, clear, precise and fair" information emanating from reliable national sources and reflecting the principles and objectives of the non-aligned movement. The action programme provided inter alia for comprehensive moral, material and technical aid for the least-developed non-aligned news agencies and for national liberation movements in the training of journalists.

Bodies set up with the object of moving towards a "new international information order" and co-ordinating different sectors of information were an Intergovernmental Council for Co-ordination of Co-operation among Non-Aligned Countries in Information; a Co-ordinating Committee of the News Agencies' Pool; a Committee for Co-operation among Broadcasting Organizations; a Committee of Telecommunications Experts; and a Bureau for Co-ordination among Journalists' Associations.

(The non-aligned countries' endeavours in this field had contributed to the adoption of the 1978 UNESCO declaration on the role of the media—see page 32.)

NON-ALIGNED CONFERENCES, 1961–86

1961 Belgrade Conference. A first conference of 25 non-aligned countries took place in Belgrade on Sept. 1–6, 1961. Most of the countries were represented by heads of state or government although, in a few cases, only the Foreign Ministers attended.

The agenda for this conference had been fixed at a preparatory conference held in Cairo on June 5–13, 1961. Items considered included: A general exchange of views on the international situation; the rights of peoples to self-determination; non-interference in the internal affairs of states; the struggle against racial discrimination; general and complete disarmament; peaceful coexistence; and problems of economic development and co-operation.

The Belgrade Conference was attended by delegations from Afghanistan, Algeria, Burma, Cambodia (Kampuchea), Ceylon (Sri Lanka), the Congo (now Zaïre), Cuba, Cyprus, Egypt, Ethiopia, Ghana, Guinea, India, Indonesia, Iraq, Lebanon, Mali, Morocco, Nepal, Saudi Arabia, Somalia, the Sudan, Tunisia, Yemen and Yugoslavia.

At the end of the conference the delegates unanimously adopted a 27-point declaration containing their common views on international problems, and an *Appeal for Peace*, addressed particularly to the USA and the USSR.

The declaration included a demand for all dependent peoples to exercise their right to complete independence, and called for the ending of all armed action and repressive measures against them on the part of colonial powers. It condemned the maintenance of foreign bases in the territories of other countries, and stated that general, complete and internationally-controlled disarmament was "the most urgent task of mankind". It also stated that efforts should be made "to close, through accelerated economic, industrial and agricultural development, the ever widening gap in the standards of living between the few economically advanced countries and the many economically less developed countries".

1964 Cairo Conference. A second international conference of non-aligned countries took place in Cairo on Oct. 5–10, 1964. A total of 47 countries attended as full participants; in addition to the 25 which attended the Belgrade Conference, delegations were sent by Angola (Government-in-exile), Burundi, Cameroon, Chad, the Congo (Brazzaville), Dahomey (now Benin), Jordan, Kenya, Kuwait, Laos, Liberia, Libya, Malawi, Mauritania, Nigeria, Northern Rhodesia (now Zambia), Senegal, Sierra Leone, Syria, Togo, Uganda and the United Republic of Tanganyika and Zanzibar (now Tanzania). Observers were sent by Argentina, Bolivia, Brazil, Chile, Finland, Jamaica, Mexico, Trinidad and Tobago, Uruguay and Venezuela.

The final communiqué of the conference was entitled *Programme for Peace and International Co-operation*. It included statements on the right to self-determination and independence, on peaceful co-existence and on denuclearization. Neo-colonialism and imperialism, in all forms, were condemned, particularly in South Africa.

1970 Lusaka Conference. A third conference of non-aligned countries was held in Lusaka (Zambia) on Sept. 8–10, 1970, and was attended by representatives of 54 countries, i.e. those represented at the Cairo conference (except Angola's Government-in-exile, Burma, Cambodia, Dahomey, Malawi and Saudi Arabia) and also Botswana, the Central African Republic, Equatorial Guinea, Gabon, Guyana, Jamaica, Lesotho, Malaysia, Rwanda, Singapore, South Yemen, Swaziland and Trinidad and Tobago

The conference had been preceded by two preparatory meetings in Belgrade (July 8–11, 1969) and Dar-es-Salaam (April 13–17, 1970), and had been further prepared by visits to African states during February 1970 by President Tito of Yugoslavia, who had proposed a "programme of concrete actions to solve the problems which concern the international community as a whole and world peace, such as the liquidation of the vestiges of colonialism, establishment of democratic relations and co-operation on terms of equality, codification of the principles of coexistence, acceleration of the development of the developing countries, disarmament, strengthening of the United Nations and attainment of its universality".

Documents approved by the conference included the *Lusaka Declaration on Peace, Independence, Co-operation and the Democratization of International Relations*, designed to constitute the *Charter of Non-Alignment*.

This declaration no longer defined non-alignment as "an irreplaceable instrument for the solution of the dangerous contradictions of the contemporary world and the establishment of international relations based upon the principle of active and peaceful coexistence" but rather as "an integral part of the changes in the present structure of the international community in its entirety" and "the product of the anti-colonialist revolution". Instead of "rich" and "poor" countries it distinguished between "oppressors" and "the oppressed", "aggressors" and "victims of aggression". It stated in particular that the immediate danger of a conflict between the super-powers had diminished as the result of their tendency to negotiate, but that this did not contribute to the security of small, medium-sized of developing nations, nor did it prevent the danger of local wars. At the same time the participants in the conference undertook "to continue their efforts to bring about the dissolution of the great military alliances".

1972 Foreign Ministers' Meeting. At a meeting of Foreign Ministers of non-aligned countries in Georgetown (Guyana) on Aug. 8–12, 1972, a *Declaration of Georgetown* was issued, calling for the extension of the process of détente, which had been successfully intensified in Europe, to all regions of the world, so that all military alliances would be dissolved, all foreign military bases evacuated and new areas of peace declared, especially in the Mediterranean and the Indian Ocean. The declaration also reaffirmed the non-aligned countries' support for African liberation movements and for nationalization policies in Latin American countries, and it called for an end to the war in Indo-China on the basis of peace proposals made by the Communist or pro-Communist forces in Vietnam, Laos and Cambodia, and of the withdrawal of all foreign armed forces from these countries.

1973 Algiers Conference. A fourth conference of non-aligned countries was held in Algiers on

Sept. 5–9, 1973, and was attended by 76 full participants, nine observers (i.e. entitled to participate on a consultative basis, but not to vote) and three guests. Also represented at the conference were the United Nations, the Organization of African Unity (OAU), the Arab League, the African, Asian and Latin American Solidarity Organization, and 14 liberation movements recognized by the OAU.

The conference was preceded by meetings of experts on Aug. 27 and of the Ministers of Foreign Affairs on Sept. 1–4, when a definite agenda was decided on and it was agreed to admit to full membership of the non-aligned group Argentina, Bangladesh, Bhutan, Malta (after an undertaking by Malta to evict foreign military bases upon expiry of the current agreements in 1979), Oman, Peru, Qatar, the Provisional Revolutionary Government of (South) Vietnam and the Cambodian Government-in-exile.

During the conference the Algerian Government made strong efforts to give non-alignment a "new meaning", the Algerian Foreign Minister, M. Abdelaziz Bouteflika, defining the objectives of the conference as "the struggle for economic independence", co-operation on the basis of equality, and action on three fronts— (i) "maximum mobilization of our internal resources"; (ii) the "strengthening of co-operation and trade exchanges . . . between developing and non-aligned countries in general"; and (iii) the "democratization of relations between rich and poor countries". The need for a new appraisal of the idea of non-alignment had also been emphasized by other leaders of states in the "Third World".

At its closing session on Sept. 9 the conference approved:

(1) A political declaration, which inter alia demanded "the immediate and unconditional withdrawal of Israel from all occupied territories", and the recognition of the "inalienable right to independence of the non-aligned countries of Latin America still under colonial domination"; reaffirmed their solidarity with the liberation movements in Africa; and called for the holding of an international conference on disarmament;

(2) an economic declaration, which included a number of proposals for a common posture of non-aligned and other developing countries to be adopted in future trade negotiations;

(3) a number of resolutions on specified subjects, which included a call to boycott Israel, and the recognition of the "legitimacy and legality" of the Cambodian Government-in-exile.

It was decided that the next summit conference of the non-aligned countries should be held in Colombo (Sri Lanka) in 1976.

1975 Dakar Conference on Third-World Strategy on Raw Materials and Economic Development. A conference of representatives of some 110 non-aligned developing countries (which did not include Iran and most of the Middle East oil-producing countries, which had only sent observers) took place in Dakar (Senegal) on Feb. 4–8, 1975.

The conference adopted a motion of solidarity between the developing countries and the member countries of the Organization of Petroleum Exporting Countries (OPEC). Inter alia the motion expressed the Third World's solidarity

with all developing countries which decided "to recover their rights by means of nationalizing their natural resources, by taking control of foreign enterprises operating on their territory, or by fixing the prices of the products which they export".

Among other decisions taken by the conference was (i) one to establish a special fund for the building up of stocks and for ensuring the uninterrupted production of raw materials and basic commodities exported by developing countries, with all countries taking part being called upon to contribute to the fund, and (ii) another to establish a special intergovernmental board representing non-aligned and developing countries which would study the methods and detailed arrangements for the operation of the fund.

The conclusions of the conference were summarized in a *Dakar Declaration* which, although it asked the industrialized countries to assist the developing countries by supplying food, technical aid and credits, called upon the developing countries themselves to take joint action which would make them less dependent upon "imperialism", and which expressed the view that the countries of the Third World would "attain economic emancipation only when they succeed in controlling their resources and natural wealth and thereafter achieve economic development".

1975 Lima Conference. The fifth ministerial conference of non-aligned countries, held in Lima (Peru) on Aug. 25–30, 1975, was attended by ministers from 78 full member countries and nine countries with observer status and representatives of 12 liberation movements admitted as observers.

At the conference its total full membership was raised to 82 by the admission of Panama, the Democratic People's Republic of Korea, the Democratic Republic of (North) Vietnam and the Palestine Liberation Organization—but not of the Republic of Korea (whose application for full membership was rejected on the ground of that country's "close links with the United States"). The conference also admitted eight countries as guests but declined to grant observer status to Guatemala and the Philippines. (The Government of Chile had not been invited and was not represented at the conference.)

It became clear at the conference that the non-aligned movement had transferred its chief concern from the struggle for political liberation to the achievement of a "new international economic order", and this was expressed in the two principal resolutions approved—(i) a *Lima Programme of Mutual Solidarity and Aid* setting out the movement's general political and economic aims, and (ii) a declaration outlining an economic strategy for the non-aligned countries.

The first of these documents declared the international situation to be characterized by the existence of an "unjust international order". In a compromise statement on Israel the document said: "By its continued aggression against the Arab countries and its persistent violation of the UN Charter, Israel has excluded itself from the international community. The time has come for the non-aligned countries to examine other measures against Israel." The document also, inter alia, reaffirmed the right of the Palestinian people to return to their homes and to exercise self-determination; expressed support for the independence and territorial integrity of Cyprus and also for the Moroccan position in regard to the Spanish Sahara; and called for declaring the South Pacific a "zone of peace".

In its declaration on an economic strategy the conference called for "rigorous application of the principles of the new international economic order, in particular the principle of permanent sovereignty over natural resources, as well as the adoption of a common strategy for mutual assistance", especially against political or economic pressure or any attempt to use force or aggression against any member of the non-aligned movement.

The conference also decided to set up six funds as follows:

(1) A solidarity fund for the economic and social development of non-aligned countries, with each of the fund's members contributing the equivalent of 500,000 special drawing rights (SDRs), which was expected to produce a basic capital of some SDR 40,000,000;

(2) a special fund for financing buffer stocks of raw materials and primary products by developing countries;

(3) a fund for the development of food production in Third World countries;

(4) another fund for agricultural development;

(5) a special fund for land-locked countries; and

(6) a fund for the post-war reconstruction "of Cambodia, Laos and Vietnam and of the other peoples affected by imperialist aggression".

1976 Colombo Conference. The fifth conference of the heads of state or government of the non-aligned countries was held in Colombo on Aug. 16–19, 1976.

It was preceded by a meeting of Foreign Ministers on Aug. 11–15, which approved the admission of Angola, the Comoros, Maldives and Seychelles as full members of the movement. This meeting was also attended by representatives of 12 countries invited as observers, of seven others as guests (Austria, Finland, the Philippines, Portugal, Romania, Sweden and Switzerland) and of 12 international organizations.

The conference of heads of state or government received goodwill messages from the Soviet Union and China and was addressed by the UN Secretary-General.

Documents approved by consensus were a political declaration, a declaration on economic problems, an action programme for economic co-operation, and various resolutions on economic questions.

In the political declaration the conference reaffirmed the rejection by the non-aligned countries of the idea that world peace could rest in a balance of forces, or that security could be assured by countries associated with blocs and adhering to military alliances with the great powers. Noting that the process of decolonization had reached its "final and decisive phase", the conference called for the withdrawal of France from Mayotte ("an integral part of the Comoros"); reaffirmed the right of self-determination of the people of Puerto Rico, East Timor and Djibouti (then not yet independent); and demanded that sovereignty over Guantánamo (the US base on Cuba), the Panama Canal Zone [see also page 375] and the Malvinas

(Falkland Islands) should be restored to their "rightful owners" (i.e. Cuba, Panama and Argentina respectively). The conference also demanded the withdrawal of all foreign troops from the Republic of Korea, the liquidation of foreign military bases and the termination of the UN Command in that country.

In the declaration on economic problems the conference took the view that the most dangerous source of conflict and tension was the growing disparity between "north" and "south" (the developed and the developing countries), and it demanded "full compensation for the exploitations" of the past, criticized the activities of multinational corporations; and issued a warning against foreign investment which might jeopardize the political and economic sovereignty of the non-aligned countries. It advocated the creation of raw materials cartels on the model of OPEC; called for a fundamental restructuring of world trade; suggested the indexation of commodity prices; expressed itself in favour of "adequate solutions" of the debt problem of the poorest of the developing countries; and demanded a reorganization of the world's monetary system because of its current "chaotic currency fluctuations".

In the action programme for economic co-operation the leaders of the non-aligned countries reaffirmed their belief in the "concept of collective reliance on one's own resources" and called for co-operation between non-aligned and other developing countries in the fields of raw materials, trade, currencies and finance, and in other areas. They called on all member countries to sign and ratify the agreement on the creation of a solidarity fund as decided at the Lima ministerial conference in August 1975 [see above].

1978 Belgrade Conference of Foreign Ministers. A conference of Foreign Ministers of the non-aligned countries was held in Belgrade on July 25–30, 1978.

It was attended by representatives of 85 countries and the Palestine Liberation Organization as full members, of 10 states with observer status and of seven guest states (among them the newly admitted Pakistan and San Marino). Certain liberation movements and international organizations were also represented as observers. (The conference declined to grant full membership to Bolivia and also to admit a delegation from the Comoros, the then Government of which had come to power with the aid of a White mercenary and was therefore not regarded as non-aligned.)

The unity of the non-aligned movement was at that time threatened by disagreement over Cuba's endeavours to commit it to an alliance with the "socialist countries" led by the Soviet Union and over numerous bilateral conflicts between non-aligned countries.

Documents adopted by consensus at the conference included a declaration (with both a political and an economic part) and an action programme for economic co-operation.

In the political part of the declaration it was stated that the non-aligned movement had proved to be "an indispensable factor in resolving fundamental international problems in the conditions of existing contradictions and the world's growing interdependence"; that it was committed to "the struggle against imperialism, expansionism, colonialism, neocolonialism, apartheid, racism, including Zionism, exploitation, power politics and all forms of foreign domination and hegemony, in other words the rejection of any form of subjugation, dependence, interference or pressure, be it economic, political or military"; and that it had "rejected resolutely bloc politics, military alliance, as well as any policy tending to divide the world into spheres of domination and influence".

The declaration also stated: "The ministers point with concern to the more and more overt recourse to interference in the internal affairs of independent, particularly non-aligned countries in order to influence their socio-political development [and] their foreign policies, and to circumscribe their independence. . . . Interference is becoming one of the principal forms of attack against the non-aligned movement and the unity of the non-aligned countries." At the same time they reaffirmed "the legitimate right of peoples under colonial domination and foreign occupation to resort to armed struggle for their national liberation and independence".

For the first time in a document issued by the non-aligned movement the declaration contained a section dealing with human rights, stating inter alia that "the issue of human rights cannot be isolated from its national, economic and social context", that "the freedom of the individual is inseparable from the rights of the people" and that "human rights and the fundamental freedoms of the individual and of the people are inalienable".

In the economic part of the declaration it was noted with concern that "the efforts made to date towards the establishment of the new international economic order and the solution of current economic problems" had "not achieved any significant results", and it was reaffirmed that the movement should "continue to maintain and strengthen its solidarity" with the "Group of 77" [see below] in further negotiations.

1979 Colombo Meeting of Co-ordinating Bureau.

At the end of a meeting of the movement's Co-ordinating Bureau, held in Colombo on June 6–10, 1979, a declaration was issued which inter alia condemned the Egyptian-Israeli peace treaty [see page 415] as a "partial and selective agreement"; criticized "the important role of the United States in aggravating the situation in the Middle East" and Israel's "expansionist, imperialist policy" of "annexing occupied Palestinian territory, including Jerusalem, and establishing paramilitary Zionist settlements"; expressed the belief that the peace treaty violated the decisions and resolutions of the non-aligned movement and the United Nations; and appealed to the non-aligned countries not to extend any recognition to the treaty.

1979 Havana Conference.

The sixth conference of the heads of state or government of the non-aligned countries was held in Havana (Cuba) on Sept. 3–9, 1979.

A meeting of Foreign Ministers held in Havana on Aug. 30–Sept. 1, 1979, approved the admission of seven new full members to the movement (Bolivia, Grenada, Iran, Nicaragua, Pakistan, Suriname and the Zimbabwe Patriotic Front). (The South West Africa People's Organization—SWAPO, regarded as the legitimate representative of the people of Namibia—had been admitted as a full member at a ministerial meeting held in New York on Oct. 2, 1978.) This brought the number of full members of the movement to 95—of which Kampuchea (Cambodia) was excluded from the conference as no consensus could be obtained on the question of its representation, which was claimed by both the *Khmers Rouges* regime of Pol Pot and the Vietnamese-backed People's Revolutionary Council.

The conference of heads of state or government was largely dominated by the threat to its unity arising out of the divergence between Cuba and Yugoslavia over the character of the non-aligned movement.

Cuba, which assumed the presidency of the movement for three years until 1982, had presented the "radical thesis" which identified the socialist bloc led by the Soviet Union as the "natural ally" of the non-aligned countries in the struggle against "imperialism" and for "socialism in the world". Yugoslavia, on the other hand, had (with the support of other member countries of the movement, notably India, Indonesia, Sri Lanka and Tanzania) defended the movement's "anti-bloc" commitment and its opposition to all foreign military intervention, with President Tito stating in his opening address: "The non-aligned movement is an independent, united and autonomous factor in world politics, and such it must remain."

The final declaration of the conference, containing a political and an economic section and adopted by consensus, gave in its political section a redefinition of the principles and objects of the non-aligned movement, as follows:

"*Basic Principles:* National independence, sovereignty and territorial integrity, sovereign equality and the free social development of all countries; independence of non-aligned countries from great-power or bloc rivalries and influences and opposition to participation in military pacts and alliances arising therefrom; the struggle against imperialism, colonialism, neo-colonialism, racism, including Zionism and all forms of expansionism, foreign occupation and domination and hegemony; active peaceful co-existence among all states; indivisibility of peace and security; non-intervention and non-interference in the internal and external affairs of other countries; freedom of all states to determine their political systems and pursue economic, social and cultural development without intimidation, hindrance and pressure; establishment of a new international economic order and development of international co-operation on the basis of equality; the right to self-determination and independence of all peoples under colonial and alien domination and constant support to the struggle of national liberation movements; respect for human rights and fundamental freedoms; opposition to the division of the world into antagonistic military-political alliances and blocs and rejection of outmoded doctrines such as spheres of influence and balance of terror; permanent sovereignty over natural resources; inviolability of legally established international boundaries; non-use of force or threat of use of force and non-recognition of situations brought about by the threat or use of force; and peaceful settlement of disputes.

"*Essential Objectives:* Preservation of the national independence, sovereignty, territorial integrity and security of non-aligned countries; elimination of foreign interference and intervention in the internal and external affairs of states and the use of the threat of force; strengthening of non-alignment as an independent non-bloc factor and the further spread of non-alignment in the world; elimination of colonialism, neo-colonialism and racism including Zionism and support to national liberation movements struggling against colonial and alien domination and foreign occupation; elimination of imperialistic and hegemonistic policies and all other forms of expansionism and foreign domination; safeguarding international peace and security and the universalization of the relaxation of international tensions; promotion of unity, solidarity and co-operation among non-aligned countries with a view to the achievement of the objectives of non-alignment thus preserving its essential character; ending the arms race, particularly the nuclear arms race, and the achievement of general and complete disarmament under effective international control; the early establishment of the new international economic order with a view to accelerating the development of developing countries, eliminating the inequality between developed and developing countries and the eradication of poverty, hunger, sickness and illiteracy in the developing countries; participation on the basis of equality in solving international issues; establishment of a democratic system of international relations based on the equality of states, respect for and preservation of human rights and fundamental freedoms; the strengthening of the United Nations as an effective instrument for promoting international peace and security, resolving international problems, the struggle against colonialism, neo-colonialism, racism, Zionism, racial discrimination and apartheid and as an important factor in the development of international co-operation and the establishment of international co-operation and the establishment of equitable economic relations between states; dissolution of great-power pacts and military alliances and interlocking arrangements arising therefrom; withdrawal of foreign military forces and dismantling of foreign military bases; promotion of economic co-operation among the non-aligned and other developing countries with a view to the achievement of collective self-reliance; establishment of a new international order in the field of information and mass media for the purpose of forging new international relations in general, and revival, preservation and enrichment of the cultural heritage of the peoples of non-aligned countries and promotion of cultural co-operation among them."

The political section also dealt with specific problems.

In regard to Western Sahara the conference deplored Morocco's occupation of the southern part of the territory (previously administered by Mauritania) and expressed the hope that all parties involved would co-operate in implementing the recommendation of the Organization of African Unity calling for a referendum on self-determination for Western Sahara.

The conference also condemned the Egyptian-Israeli peace treaty and any partial settlements or separate treaties relating to the Arab-Israeli conflict, but it deferred a decision on the possible suspension of Egypt from the non-aligned movement. A decision on the question of which regime to recognize in Kampuchea was similarly deferred.

The Government of Burma confirmed, in September 1979, its decision to withdraw from the movement, after its Foreign Minister had criticized "the manoeuvres of countries tending to align themselves" and had unsuccessfully called for the formation of a new, genuinely neutral movement.

1981 New Delhi Meeting of Foreign Ministers. This meeting, held on Feb. 9–13, 1981, and attended by representatives of 93 full members of the movement (including for the first time St Lucia and Zimbabwe) as well as of seven countries with observer status (Brazil, Colombia, Costa Rica, Ecuador, Mexico, the Philippines and Venezuela) and of eight countries with guest status (Austria, Finland, Papua New Guinea, Portugal, Romania, San Marino, Sweden and Switzerland), was marked by deep divisions (over the Soviet intervention in Afghanistan supported by Cuba, over the problem of representation of Kampuchea, and over the Iran-Iraq war). A final declaration, adopted on Feb. 13, called for the withdrawal of foreign forces from Afghanistan

and Kampuchea and announced the establishment of a four-member committee (consisting of the Foreign Ministers of Cuba, India and Zambia and the head of the political department of the PLO) to seek an end to the Iran-Iraq conflict. The committee visited Baghdad and Tehran in April and May 1981 but achieved no reconciliation between the two sides.

1982 Havana Meeting of the Co-ordinating Bureau. This meeting, held on June 2–5, 1982, adopted (for the first time) a declaration on the situation in El Salvador and Guatemala, describing US involvement in these countries as "a threat to peace and security" in Central America. The meeting also approved a resolution sponsored by Cuba (but modified), supporting Argentina's claim to sovereignty over the Falkland (Malvinas) Islands, deploring the British offensive to recapture the islands from Argentina and underlining that the British policy backed by the United States was affecting the whole region.

1983 Managua Meeting of the Co-ordinating Bureau. An extraordinary meeting of the Bureau held in Managua (Nicaragua) on Jan. 10–15, 1983, called for an end to "imperialist intervention" in Latin America and urged the United States to adopt a positive attitude in favour of peace and dialogue with Nicaragua and to contribute to a peaceful solution of the conflict in El Salvador.

1983 New Delhi Conference. The seventh summit conference of the heads of state and government of the non-aligned countries took place in New Delhi on March 7–12, 1983. Of the movement's 101 full members two were not represented (viz. Kampuchea and St Lucia, where a strongly pro-Western government had come to power in May 1982). Countries or organizations attending the conference with observer status were Antigua and Barbuda, Brazil, Costa Rica, Dominica, El Salvador, Mexico, the Philippines, Uruguay, Venezuela (as in 1979) and Papua New Guinea as well as the (South African) African National Congress (ANC) and Pan Africanist Congress, the Organization of African Unity (OAU), the Afro-Asian People's Solidarity Organization, the League of Arab States, the Socialist Party of Puerto Rico and the United Nations. Those attending with guest status were representatives of Austria, Finland, Portugal, Romania, San Marino, Spain, Sweden and Switzerland and also the Dominican Republic, the Vatican and various UN and other international or regional organizations.

The conference adopted a 13-point "New Delhi message", a 54-page political declaration and an equally lengthy economic declaration.

The "message" proposed in particular "the immediate convening of an international conference on money and finance for development, with universal participation, and a comprehensive restructuring of the international monetary and financial system". The political declaration inter alia categorically rejected any "linkage or parallelism being drawn by the US Administration between the independence of Namibia and the withdrawal of Cuban forces from Angola". The declaration also reaffirmed the principles of non-alignment essentially as stated in Havana in 1979. On specific territorial disputes the conference called for a resolution of the conflict in the Western Sahara in line with UN and OAU decisions; affirmed the sovereignty of the Comoros over the island of Mayotte "still under French occupation"; called on France to negotiate with the government of Madagascar over disputed islands; and expressed full support for Mauritian sovereignty over the Chagos Archipelago, including Diego Garcia, where "the establishment and strengthening of the [UK-US] military base" had "endangered the sovereignty, territorial integrity and peaceful development of Mauritius and other states". (The declaration contained no reference to self-determination for East Timor—as called for in 1979). It also demanded the return to Cuba of the "territory illegally occupied by the Guantánamo naval base" of the United States.

The economic declaration adopted a pragmatic approach with emphasis particularly on immediate measures to deal with the global economic crisis. Stating that negotiations for a new international economic order had achieved hardly any progress, the declaration proposed the convening of a UN conference in early 1984 to launch global negotiations. Meanwhile it set out a programme of immediate measures in areas of critical importance to developing countries, covering in particular the level of transfers of official development assistance, indebtedness, the role of the International Monetary Fund and the World Bank, trade and market access and commodity price stabilization, energy, food and agriculture. On debt restructuring the conference sought the establishment of an overall framework for equitable criteria and guidelines for refinancing, and an increase of the overall level of lending by the two international institutions. The conference also proposed the creation of a central council of commodity producers' associations and of research institutions (i) in New Delhi for science and technology and (ii) in Havana to examine the impact of multinational companies on the economies of developing countries.

1984 Jakarta Meeting of Information Ministers. This meeting held on Jan. 26–30, 1984, approved a declaration calling for a new world information and communications order which would "decolonize" the flow of international news, noting "the pervasive hostile propaganda by developed industrial countries against non-aligned countries and the non-aligned movement as a whole" and urging member countries to refrain from permitting the exploitation of their media facilities for such purposes. In a separate "Jakarta appeal" the ministers called on the media not to report any news which was detrimental to the interests of non-aligned countries.

1985 New Delhi Meeting of Foreign Ministers. At this meeting held on April 19–21, 1985, the ministers adopted a 17-point programme on Namibia urging member states and other countries to increase diplomatic, political, material and military aid to the South West Africa People's Organization (SWAPO) and to impose economic, sporting and cultural sanctions against South Africa.

1985 Luanda Meeting of Foreign Ministers. This meeting, held in the Angolan capital on Sept. 4–7, 1985, issued a nine-point final communiqué stressing the need for the international community "to assume its responsibility" on South Africa by the imposition of "comprehensive and mandatory sanctions". The ministers also issued a "Luanda declaration" on the

situation in southern Africa, stating inter alia: "The countdown to the collapse of apartheid has started." The declaration called not only for sanctions against South Africa but also for independence for Namibia and the complete withdrawal of South African troops from Angola. The meeting decided to give the status of invited guests to the Saharan Arab Democratic Republic, the Farabundo Martí Front for National Liberation (FMLN) of El Salvador and Fretilin of East Timor.

1986 Havana Conference on Education and Culture. This conference, held on April 2–4, 1986, and attended by 51 delegations, approved a final document stating that a solution to the educational and cultural problems in the non-aligned and developing countries depended not only on internal structural adjustments but also on the establishment of a new international economic order which would be more just and equitable. It was added in the document that education and culture played "an essential role in the struggle against imperialism, colonialism, neo-colonialism, apartheid and racism—including Zionism and all forms of foreign aggression, occupation, domination, interference and hegemony".

1986 New Delhi Meeting of Foreign Ministers. This meeting was held in New Delhi on April 18–20, 1986, and issued a declaration which sharply criticized the United States for its attack on Libya on April 15, 1986, as well as for its "immoral and illegal act" in funding "subversive" activities in Nicaragua; it also called on Western nations to heed international conventions banning the recruitment, financing, training, transit and drafting of mercenaries; it implicitly criticized these nations for attempting to weaken the role of the United Nations and for using financial power to impair its functioning; and it criticized them expressly for delaying the establishment of a new world economic order.

On the other hand the declaration (for the first time) condemned the growing menace of terrorism, whether perpetrated by individuals, by groups or by states. However, it excluded from the condemnation "the legitimate struggle by people under colonial and racist regimes and other forms of foreign domination and occupation and of their national liberation movements against their oppressors", specifically mentioning South Africa, Namibia and Palestine.

On specific disputes the meeting failed to express a unanimous desire to end the Iran-Iraq war and merely called on India to appeal for peace in the Gulf (as a result of which the Iranian delegation left the meeting as it took the view that Iran and Iraq had been equated, with Iraq not having been condemned for having started the war or for using chemical weapons).

1986 Harare Meeting of Foreign Ministers. This meeting, held in the capital of Zimbabwe on Aug. 28–29, 1986, adopted by acclamation a nine-page special declaration on South Africa calling on third-world nations to take the lead in supporting the threatened economies of the front-line states and demanding a prohibition of the transfer of technology to South Africa, the suspension of any sales or transport to South Africa of oil and related products, a ban on further investments and an end to any promotion or support for trade with South Africa.

1986 Harare Conference. The eighth conference of the heads of state or government of the non-aligned countries was held in Harare (Zimbabwe) on Sept. 1–7, 1986, and was attended by delegations from all members of the movement except the Bahamas (including 45 heads of state or government). The conference adopted a Harare Appeal to the leaders of the United States and the Soviet Union, a special declaration on southern Africa, an economic declaration and a political declaration.

In the Harare Appeal the Soviet Union, the United States and other nuclear powers were urged to continue a dialogue with a view to putting an end to the arms race and reaching real agreements on disarmament, including an agreement on the prevention of the arms race in space, as the choice today was "not between war and peace but between life and death".

In the special declaration on southern Africa sanctions were assessed as the sole peaceful option to compel the South African regime to relinquish its apartheid policy and were elaborated in various fields, including the banning of the transfer of technology, petroleum exports, investments in and credits to South Africa and Namibia, as well as imports from these countries, especially those of strategic raw materials. A call was made on all countries to increase their material and financial aid to the liberation movements of the oppressed people of South Africa with a view to strengthening their struggle against apartheid and for the establishment of a non-racist and representative government in South Africa. In addition to calling for comprehensive defence assistance to the front-line states the non-aligned countries announced their intention to set up a special solidarity fund for the south of Africa and appealed to the international community to contribute to it.

In the economic declaration it was stated that the crisis of the world economic system was not merely a cyclic phenomenon but also a manifestation of deep structural disparities which mostly affected developing countries. Regret was expressed that there had been no significant progress towards the establishment of a new international economic order. The declaration recorded the setting-up of a standing committee for economic co-operation of the developing countries (comprising 22 member countries and three developing countries with

observer status in the movement). In connection with proposed new GATT rules the non-aligned countries demanded full liberalization of trade in agricultural products, a halt to unfair competition due to subsidized exports by developed countries and an end to the developed countries' use of food products as instruments of the policy of pressure on the underdeveloped. The declaration also contained a call for the early finalization of a code of conduct to regulate the activities of transnational corporations.

In the political declaration it was stated inter alia that the particular security perceptions and policies of the major powers and their alliance systems heightened their military and political competition, threatened the security of non-aligned and other states and posed an increasing risk of nuclear war, and that dialogue, especially within the framework of the United Nations, was the key to a solution of the global crisis. The declaration condemned the "notorious system" of colonialism which (it was argued) still obtained in the cases of Namibia, New Caledonia, Puerto Rico, the Malvinas (Falklands), Micronesia and other dependent territories. It also condemned, as a violation of non-aligned principles and the UN Charter, US support for the "contras'" attempt to overthrow the government of Nicaragua, and it supported the efforts of the Contadora Group to secure a negotiated solution of the crisis in Central America. Expressing support for the front-line states as frequent victims of South African aggression, the declaration demanded, "in order to avoid a further escalation of the conflict", the immediate imposition of comprehensive and mandatory sanctions against South Africa. In connection with specific territorial disputes the declaration endorsed a number of recommendations made by the movement's Foreign Ministers.

Among the leaders who addressed the conference Col. Moamer al-Gadaffi, the Libyan leader, struck a discordant note in his address on Sept. 4. He declared that he did not see any usefulness in the non-aligned movement because it contained a number of members who were "not with the cause of freedom" and were "real puppets of imperialism, enemies of the movement and traitors", such as the existing regimes in Cameroon, Côte d'Ivoire, Egypt and Zaïre. He also claimed that the movement had failed to side with Libya after the US attack of April 1986 and had done nothing against the US mining of Nicaraguan ports or the invasion of Grenada. He expressed his "deep belief" in the need for a collective liberation front to face and fight (US) imperialism, and he proposed the creation of "a new international front . . . united in the common struggle against the common enemy". However, his views found no support at the conference.

Other Groupings of Third-World Countries

Afro-Asian Housing Organization (AAHO)

Address. P.O.B. 523, Cairo, Egypt.
Officer. Hassan M. Hassan (sec. gen.).
Founded. 1965.
Objects. To promote co-operation among African and Asian states in housing reconstruction and related matters.

Afro-Asian Rural Reconstruction Organization (AARRO)

Address. C/117–118, Defence Colony, New Delhi 110024, India.

Officers. Dr B. S. Minhas (sec. gen.); M. R. Kaushal (dir.).
Founded. 1962.
Membership. 12 African and 15 Asian countries, and also the Central Union of Agricultural Co-operatives in Japan.
Objects. To restructure the rural economy in Africa and Asia and to co-ordinate efforts to promote welfare and eradicate malnutrition, disease, illiteracy and poverty.
Activities. Research, technical assistance, exchange of information, the holding of international conferences and seminars, and the provision of

training fellowships at five institutes in Egypt, India, Japan and Taiwan.

Asian-African Legal Consultative Committee

Address. 27 Ring Road, Lajput Nagar-VI, New Delhi 110024, India.
Officer. B. Sen (sec. gen.).
Founded. 1956.
Membership. 41 countries—Bangladesh, Botswana, Burma, Cyprus, Egypt, Ethiopia, The Gambia, Ghana, India, Indonesia, Iran, Iraq, Japan, Jordan, Kenya, the Democratic People's Republic of Korea, the Republic of Korea, Kuwait, Libya, Malaysia, Mauritius, Mongolia, Nepal, Nigeria, Oman, Pakistan, the Philippines, Qatar, Saudi Arabia, Senegal, Sierra Leone, Singapore, Somalia, Sri Lanka, Syria, Tanzania, Thailand, Turkey, Uganda, the United Arab Emirates and the Yemen Arab Republic.
History. The committee was founded by the Governments of Burma, Ceylon (Sri Lanka), India, Indonesia, Iraq, Japan and Syria with the object of submitting its views on legal matters to the International Law Commission, considering legal problems referred to it by its member-states and promoting Asian-African co-operation in international law. It was granted observer status at the United Nations General Assembly on Oct. 13, 1980.

The "Group of 77"

This group—set up at the 1964 UN Conference on Trade and Development (UNCTAD) [see page 21] as a pressure group defending the interests of developing countries—had by 1986 reached a membership of 120 developing countries.

At a special ministerial meeting held in Algiers on Feb. 16–19, 1975, the group drafted a "platform" for submission to the UN Industrial Development Organization (UNIDO), proposing that UNIDO should become a UN specialized agency; that UNIDO should eventually assist the needy countries in their efforts to recover their natural resources and in undertaking the processing of these resources in their own territory; that developing countries should have the right to form more raw materials cartels, to nationalize foreign-owned industry and to regulate multinational corporations; that "selected production capacities" should be transferred to the developing countries; that help should be given to "uneconomic and inefficient" domestic industries to phase themselves out, so that the field would be left open to imports from developing countries (e.g. of textiles); and that the generalized system of preferences should be expanded and improved.

In a "position paper" submitted to the UN General Assembly's special session on development and international economic co-operation in September 1975, the group called for adherence to the "indexation" principle by tying the prices of raw material exports to the prices of imports from the developed world so as to provide "insulation from the adverse effects of inflation in developed countries", and for the developed countries to devote a minimum of 0.7 per cent of gross national product to official development assistance (as had been proposed for the UN Second Development Decade in 1970).

At a ministerial meeting held in Manila on Feb. 2–7, 1976, the group issued a *Declaration of Manila* and a programme of action.

The declaration contained 17 objectives for international co-operation, towards the attainment of which the group's member-states expressed "their firm conviction to make full use of the bargaining power of the developing countries through joint and united action". The 17 objectives included action on an integrated programme on commodities designed to guarantee prices; industrial production and trade; the expansion of the developing countries' total export capacity; "substantive results" from the multilateral trade negotiations then being conducted in Geneva [under GATT auspices, on the application of the "Tokyo round"—see page 46]; reforms in the international monetary system; increased financial assistance; debt-relief; technology transfers; controls on multinational corporations; greater economic co-operation among developing countries themselves; expanded trade with the communist world; special measures to aid the least developed countries (LDC—see page 127), land-locked and island countries and those most seriously affected by the the current world economic crisis (MSA—ibid.); greater efforts to improve world food production; and a strengthening of the negotiating function of UNCTAD itself.

An indicative list of 18 commodities to be covered by an integrated programme comprised bananas, bauxite, cocoa, coffee, copper, cotton, hard fibres (e.g. sisal), iron ore, jute, manganese, meat, phosphates, rubber, sugar, tea, timber, tin and vegetable oils.

In the programme of action demands were made for the abolition of customs barriers imposed by developed countries on the entry of manufactured or semi-finished products of the Third World, and an improvement in the generalized system of preferences [see page 178]; an increase in public aid by developed countries (including those of Eastern Europe) to reach by 1980 the target of 0.7 per cent of gross national product, and the introduction of a development tax by these countries; the effective application of measures and methods of indexing prices of basic commodities exported by developing countries to the import prices of articles manufactured in developing countries; a proportion of at least 90 per cent of public development aid to consist of free gifts or interest-free loans not tied to obligatory purchases in the donor country; the cancellation of the public debt of the LDC and MSA countries and the consolidation of other third-world countries' trade debts for 25 years, as well as the creation of "a fund or a bank destined to finance short-term debts of developing countries"; a code of conduct for transfers of technology and the creation of a "multilateral instrument with powers of compulsion"; and a strengthening of the powers of UNCTAD, which should nevertheless retain its links with the UN General Assembly.

At a conference on economic co-operation held in Mexico City on Sept. 13–22, 1976, the group adopted various recommendations, among them one for preparations for studying the possibility of setting up a global system of trade preferences for developing countries only, in order to support their industries, and another for early completion of statutes for a council of raw material producers' associations. (The group agreed on the need to establish its own multinational corporations for

THE "THIRD WORLD": ATTEMPTS AT ACHIEVING COHESION

the marketing of raw materials and to set up commodity exchanges within the group's own territories.)

At a ministerial meeting held at Arusha (Tanzania) on Feb. 12–16, 1979, an Arusha programme for collective self-help and a framework for negotiations were agreed upon.

The Arusha programme inter alia called for a legally binding code for the transfer of technology, changes in the International Monetary Fund, structural reforms in the international trade and monetary system and large-scale resources transfers to the developing countries.

The meeting also agreed to support a proposal for mandatory direct contributions of $1,000,000 towards the capital of the Common Fund for the financing of buffer stocks of raw materials, then being negotiated under UNCTAD auspices.

At a ministerial meeting held in Buenos Aires on March 28–April 9, 1983, the group agreed on a common position for the forthcoming sixth UNCTAD session and it also issued a "Buenos Aires message for dialogue and consensus", stressing the need to accelerate the development of developing countries.

At the UNCTAD session held from June 6 to July 3, 1983, the group sought a declaration stressing the need for extensive reform of the international economic order, but the final resolution adopted by the session constituted a compromise resulting from the developing countries' insistence that the existing system had proved workable. The group's spokesman stated afterwards that the session had had only "meagre results".

Select Bibliography

Under Article 102 of the UN Charter every treaty and every international agreement entered into by any member of the United Nations shall be registered with the UN Secretary-General and be published in the original version with translations in English and French (relevant rules being adopted by the UN General Assembly on Dec. 14, 1946). Publication has since then been effected in the *UN Treaties Series* (UNTS).

Australian Treaty List as at December 31, 1970 (Dept. of Foreign Affairs, Canberra, ACT, Australia), with cumulative supplement as at Aug. 20, 1985

Basic Facts about the United Nations (United Nations, New York 1983)

Bowman, M. J., and Harris, D. J., *Multilateral Treaties—Index and Current Status* (Butterworths, London 1984), with third cumulative supplement to Jan. 1, 1986

Bundesgesetzblatt, Teil II, Fundstellennachweis B, Völkerrechtliche Vereinbarungen und Verträge mit der DDR, abgeschlossen am 31. Dezember 1985 (Bundesminister der Justiz, Bonn, Fed. Rep. of Germany)

Butler, W. E. (ed.), *A Source Book on Socialist International Organizations* (Alphen, USA, 1978)

The Europa Year Book 1986, 2 vols. (London)

Everybody's United Nations, 9th ed. (United Nations, New York, 1979)

Feltham, R. G., *Diplomatic Handbook*, 4th ed. (Longman 1983)

Granville, J. A. S. (ed.), *The Major International Treaties, 1914–1973* (London 1974)

The Law of the Sea—United Nations Convention on the Law of the Sea (United Nations, New York 1983)

McNair, Lord, *The Law of Treaties* (Oxford Univ. Press 1961)

Multilateral Treaties in respect of which the (UN) Secretary-General performs depositary functions, list of signatures, ratifications etc. up to Dec. 31, 1982 (United Nations, New York)

NATO Basic Documents (NATO Information Service, Brussels 1981)

NATO Handbook (NATO Information Service, Brussels 1985)

Nicholas, H. G., *The United Nations as a Political Institution*, 5th ed. (Oxford Univ. Press 1971)

The North Atlantic Treaty Organization—Facts and Figures, 10th ed. (NATO Information Service, Brussels 1984)

Osmańczyk, Edmund J., *The Encyclopedia of the United Nations and International Agreements* (Taylor and Francis, London 1985)

Recueil des lois fédérales et Recueil systématique du droit fédéral (Département fédéral des affaires étrangères, Berne, Switzerland, 1985)

Register över Sveriges överenskommelser med främmende makter Dec. 31, 1984 (Ministry of Foreign Affairs, Stockholm 1985)

Rohn, Peter H., *World Treaty Index,* 5 vols., 2nd ed. (ABC-Clio, USA, 1984)

Satow's Guide to Diplomatic Practice (ed. Lord Gore Booth), 5th ed. (Longman 1979)

Stockholm International Peace Research Institute (SIPRI), *Arms Control: A Survey and Appraisal of Multilateral Agreements* (Taylor & Francis, London 1978)

Treaties in Force: A List of Treaties and Other International Agreements of the United States in Force on January 1, 1985 (US Department of State, Washington, DC 20402, USA 1985)

A Year Book of the Commonwealth (Foreign and Commonwealth Office, London 1986)

Index

Arab Petroleum Services Company, 137

Arab Petroleum Training Institute, 137

Arab Shipbuilding and Repair Company, 137

Argentina
agreements or treaties with
American states, 367, 376, 388–389
states outside the Americas, 264, 316, 321, 322, 390–391, 410
EEC trade agreement, 186
extradition treaties, 322, 386
nuclear co-operation agreements, 45, 164, 384

Arrangement regarding International Trade in Textiles—see Multi-Fibre Arrangement

Ascension Island—see United Kingdom Dependencies

ASEAN—see Association of South East Asian Nations

Asia–Pacific Telecommunity, 86

Asian–African Legal Consultative Committee, 470

Asian and Pacific Coconut Community, 131

Asian Development Bank, 311, 454

Asian Development Fund, 454

Asian–Pacific Postal Union, 86

Asian Productivity Organization, 311, 454

Asistencia Recíproca Petrolera Estatal Latinoamericana—see Mutual Assistance of the Latin American Government Oil Companies

Asociación Latinoamericana de Integración (ALADI)—see Latin American Integration Association

Associated Coffee Producers, 132

Association of African Trade Promotion Organizations (AATPO), 424

Association of Iron-Ore Exporting Countries (AIOEC), 133

Association of Natural Rubber Producing Countries (ANRPC), 138–139

Association of South East Asian Nations (ASEAN), 451–454
EEC, co-operation agreement, 188

Association of Tin Producing Countries, 142

Astronauts—Agreement on the Rescue of Astronauts and the Return of Objects Launched into Outer Space, 89

Astrophysics, convention on co-operation, 85

Atlantic Charter (1941), 14

Australia
agreements or treaties with
Commonwealth member states, 314, 319, 443, 444
states outside the Commonwealth, 260–265, 321–323, 367, 410, 415
extradition treaties, 322–323, 386
nuclear co-operation agreements, 45, 164, 384

Australia–New Zealand free trade area, 445

Austria
agreements and treaties with
communist states, 257, 261, 263
non-communist states, 11, 196, 322, 367, 376, 414
extradition treaties, 318, 322, 386
nuclear co-operation agreements, 45, 384
State Treaty (1955), 13

Autorité du bassin du Niger—see Niger Basin Authority

AWACS—see Airborne early warning and control system

Ayacucho, 1974 Declaration of, 366

Bacteriological Weapons, Convention on Prohibition and Destruction of (1971), 74, 76–82

Bahamas
agreements, 323, 367, 374
extradition treaty, 381

Bahrain
agreements and treaties, 316, 328, 367, 407–408, 410, 414

Baltic Marine Environment Protection Commission (Helsinki Commission), 95

Baltic Sea protection agreements, 96

Bananas, 130

Banco Centroamericano de Integración Económica (BCIE), 364

Bandung Conference, 461–462

Bangladesh
agreements and treaties with
Commonwealth member states, 319–320
states outside the Commonwealth, 323, 376
Communist states, 257, 266
EEC, trade agreement, 187

Bank for International Settlements (BIS), 37, 192

Banque Arabe pour le développement économique en Afrique (BADEA)—see Arab Bank for Economic Development in Africa

Banque de développement des états des grands lacs (BDEGL), 427

Banque des états de l'Afrique Centrale, 334

Banque ouest—africaine de développement (BOAD)—see West African Development Bank

Barbados
agreements, 376
extradition treaty, 386

Barcelona Convention, 96–97

Bauxite—see International Bauxite Association

Beagle Channel dispute, 388

Belau, Republic of, 459–460

Belgium
agreements or treaties with
NATO member states, 196, 197, 222, 223, 367, 376
states outside NATO, 197, 296, 301, 321, 322, 440, 458
extradition treaties, 196, 197, 318, 322, 386
nuclear co-operation agreements, 197, 384, 458

Belgium–Luxembourg Economic Union (BLEU), 154
agreement, 440

Nauru
extradition treaty, 387
NATO—*see* North Atlantic Treaty Organization
NATO agreements, 221 ff.
Nepal
agreements or treaties, 259, 266, 317, 325–326, 381, 458
Netherlands
agreements or treaties with
NATO member states, 157, 197, 199, 200, 220, 222, 223, 317, 372, 381
states outside NATO, 200, 323, 328, 411, 440
extradition treaties, 199, 318, 323, 387
nuclear co-operation agreements, 386
Neutron bomb, 217
New Delhi message (of Non-Aligned Movement), 467–468
New International Economic Order, Declaration on the Establishment of, 117
New World Information and Communications Order, UNESCO resolution, 32
New Zealand
agreements or treaties with
Commonwealth member states, 314, 319, 320, 443–444
states outside the Commonwealth, 329, 372, 381, 444
EEC, butter import agreement, 188
extradition treaty, 387
nuclear co-operation agreement, 386
Nicaragua
agreements or treaties with
American states, 381, 384
non-communist states outside the Americas, 323, 394
Soviet Union, 264
CMEA, co-operation agreement, 244
Niger
agreements, 334, 339, 372, 381–382, 410, 413, 439
Niger Basin Authority, 432
Nigeria
agreements or treaties with
communist states, 254, 261, 264, 265, 266
non-communist states, 329, 382, 436
extradition treaty, 387
Non-Aligned Movement, 461–469
Nordic Co-operation, Treaty of (1962), 153
Nordic Council, 152–153
Nordic Council of Ministers, 153–154
Nordic Institute for Theoretical Atomic Physics (NORDITA), 153
Nordic Investment Bank, 153
North Atlantic Salmon Conservation Organization, 107
North Atlantic Treaty Organization (NATO), 202 ff.
North-East Atlantic Fisheries Commission (NEAFC), 107–108

North Korea—*see* Korea, Democratic People's Republic of
North Pacific Fur Seal Commission, 103
North–South Dialogue, 121 ff.
North-West Atlantic Fisheries Orgnization (NAFO), 108
North Yemen—*see* Yemen Arab Republic
Norway
agreements or treaties with
NATO member states, 199, 223, 317, 324, 372, 382
Nordic states, 154
other states, 323, 327, 328, 330, 439
European Communities, non-adherence to, 170
extradition treaties, 318, 323, 387
nuclear co-operation agreements, 45, 386
Nuclear accident conventions and agreements, 45, 297
Nuclear co-operation agreements, 44–45, 86, 163–164, 197, 198, 201, 252, 259, 287, 301–302, 319 ff., 364–365, 384–386, 411, 458
Nuclear Energy
Inter-American Commission, 347
Nuclear-Free Zones
Latin America, 71
New Zealand policy, 445
South Pacific treaty, 456–457
United Nations resolutions, 75
Nuclear Material, Convention on the Physical Protection of (1980), 75
Nuclear reactors, 44–45, 86
Nuclear Non-Proliferation Treaty, 45, 71–73, 76–82
Nuclear safeguards agreements, 44–45, 163
Nuclear Suppliers' Group, 73–74
Nuclear Test-Ban Treaty (1963), 70–71, 76–82

OAPEC—*see* Organization of Arab Petroleum Exporting Countries
OAS—*see* Organization of American States
OCAS—*see* Organization of Central American States
Ocho Rios Declaration (1982), 312
ODECA—*see* Organization of Central American States
Oder-Neisse frontier agreement, 248
Odra Haff Committee, 96
OECD—*see* Organization for Economic Co-operation and Development
OECD Development Centre, 116
OECD Nuclear Energy Agency, 115–116
Office international de la vigne et du vin (OIV)—*see* International Vine and Wine Office
Okinawa—*see* Ryukyu Islands
OLADE—*see* Latin American Energy Organization
Olive oil, 134
Oman
agreements or treaties with
Arab states, 408, 409, 415